Course	Management
Course Number	**MGT 201**
	Clarissa Cota
	COLLEGE OF SOUTHERN NEVADA
	BUSINESS DIVISION

http://create.mheducation.com

ISBN-10: 1307071783   ISBN-13: 9781307071788

Contents

Online Supplements

Credits

Controlling

Online Supplements

To Joyce Kinicki, the love of my life, best friend, and the wind beneath my wings.

—A.K.

To my wife, Stacey, for her 31 years of steadfast, patient support and for her collaboration and shared adventures; and to my beloved children and their families—Sylvia, Scott, and Atticus and Kirk, Julia, Nicolas, and Lily.

—B.K.W.

Courtesy of Angelo Kinicki

Angelo Kinicki is an emeritus professor of management and held the Weatherup/Overby Chair in Leadership from 2005 to 2015 at the W.P. Carey School of Business at Arizona State University. He joined the faculty in 1982, the year he received his doctorate in business administration from Kent State University. He was inducted into the W.P. Carey Faculty Hall of Fame in 2016.

Angelo is the recipient of six teaching awards from Arizona State University, where he taught in its nationally ranked MBA and PhD programs. He also received several research awards and was selected to serve on the editorial review boards for four scholarly journals. His current research interests focus on the dynamic relationships among leadership, organizational culture, organizational change, and individual, group, and organizational performance. Angelo has published over 95 articles in a variety of academic journals and proceedings and is co-author of 8 textbooks (31 including revisions) that are used by hundreds of universities around the world. Several of his books have been translated into multiple languages, and two of his books were awarded revisions of the year by The McGraw-Hill Company.

Angelo is a busy international consultant and is a principal at Kinicki and Associates, Inc., a management consulting firm that works with top management teams to create organizational change aimed at increasing organizational effectiveness and profitability. He has worked with many Fortune 500 firms as well as numerous entrepreneurial organizations in diverse industries. His expertise includes facilitating strategic/operational planning sessions, diagnosing the causes of organizational and work-unit problems, conducting organizational culture interventions, implementing performance management systems, designing and implementing performance appraisal systems, developing and administering surveys to assess employee attitudes, and leading management/executive education programs. He developed a 360° leadership feedback instrument called the Performance Management Leadership Survey (PMLS), which is used by companies throughout the world.

Angelo and his wife of 35 years, Joyce, have enjoyed living in the beautiful Arizona desert for 34 years. They are both natives of Cleveland, Ohio. They enjoy traveling, hiking, and spending time in the White Mountains with Gracie, their adorable golden retriever. Angelo also has a passion for golfing.

Brian K. Williams has been managing editor for college textbook publisher Harper & Row/Canfield Press in San Francisco; editor-in-chief for nonfiction trade-book publisher J. P. Tarcher in Los Angeles; publications and communications manager for the University of California, Systemwide Administration, in Berkeley; and

Courtesy of Brian Williams

an independent writer and book producer based in the San Francisco and Lake Tahoe areas. He has a BA in English and an MA in communication from Stanford University. Repeatedly praised for his ability to write directly and interestingly to students, he has co-authored 22 books (66, counting revisions). This includes the 2015 *Using Information Technology: A Practical Introduction,* 11th ed., with his wife, Stacey C. Sawyer, for McGraw-Hill Education. In addition, he has written a number of other information technology books, college success books, and health and social science texts. Brian is a native of Palo Alto, California, and San Francisco, but since 1989 he and Stacey, a native of New York City and Bergen County, New Jersey, have lived at or near Lake Tahoe, currently in Genoa (Nevada's oldest town), with views of the Sierra Nevada. In their spare time, they enjoy foreign travel, different cuisine, museum going, music, hiking, contributing to the community (Brian is past chair of his town board), and warm visits with friends and family.

Management: A Practical Introduction *was twice the recipient of McGraw-Hill/Irwin's Revision of the Year Award, for the third and fifth editions.*

new to the eighth edition

We are pleased to share these exciting updates and new additions to the eighth edition!

Teaching Resource Manual (TRM)

We created the resources you need in our newly developed Teaching Resource Manual.

The TRM, created by Angelo Kinicki and subject-matter experts, provides a turn-key solution to creating a discussion-based and experiential learning experience. It is a combination Instructor's Manual, Connect Instructor's Manual and Implementation Guide containing a wide variety of teaching tips, outlines, suggested videos, group exercises, lecture enhancers, supplemental exercises to correspond with cases and pedagogical features of the product as well as answers to all end-of-chapter exercises.

Connect

In our continuing efforts to help students move from comprehension to application, and to ensure they see the personal relevance of management, we have added these new application exercises to our already robust Connect offering:

- **Self-Assessments**—Self-awareness is a fundamental aspect of professional and personal development. Our 90 research-based self-assessments give students frequent opportunities to see how organizational behavioral concepts apply to them personally. New to this edition is structured feedback that explains how students should interpret their scores and what they can do to develop the trait or skill being measured. This feedback is followed immediately by self-reflection quizzes that assess students' understanding of the characteristics being measured and the action steps they may want to take for improvement.

- **iSeeIt Videos**—Brief, contemporary introductions to key course concepts that often perplex students. This series will enhance your student-centered instruction by offering your students dynamic illustrations that guide them through the basics of core principles of management concepts such as motivation, leadership, socialization, and more. The idea behind the series is if a student came to your office and asked you to explain one of these topics to him or her in a few minutes—how might you explain it? Consider using these practical and applicable resources before class as an introduction, during class to launch your lecture, or even after class as a summative assessment.

Chapters

In each chapter we have refreshed examples, research, figures, tables, statistics, and photos, as well as streamlined the design for ease of navigation and improved readability. We have also largely replaced the topics in such popular features as the Manager's Toolbox, Practical Action box, Example boxes, Management in Action, and Legal/Ethical Challenge. While the following list does not encompass *all* the updates and revisions, it does highlight some of the more notable changes.

CHAPTER 1

- Section 1.1—new material in Example box on efficiency versus effectiveness: how airlines deal with "seat densification" and other passenger complaints; updates on financial rewards of being an exceptional manager
- Section 1.3—new Example box on struggle for competitive advantage covers how Airbnb shakes up the hotel business. Re-sequencing of seven challenges to being an exceptional manager. Managing for information technology moved from

#4 to #2 and new material added. Managing for sustainability moved from #6 to #5 and new material added
- Section 1.4—replaced in-text example of nonprofit general manager: now Susan Solomon, CEO of nonprofit New York Stem Cell Foundation
- Section 1.5—principal skills managers need—technical, conceptual, and human—now appear with definitions first. Updates of GM CEO Mary Barra as example of these managerial skills. New Practical Action box added on the soft skills

employers say college graduates lack, including communication and interpersonal skills; critical thinking and problem solving; and ethical judgment, innovation and creativity, and motivation
- Section 1.6—new example of a Mintzberg manager: Paul Orfalea, former CEO of Kinko's
- Section 1.7—outdated example of Homejoy as Example box of hot start-up deleted
- New Management in Action case titled "Yahoo! CEO Marissa Mayer Is under Pressure to Make Big Changes"

CHAPTER 2
- Section 2.1—material added on practical reasons for studying a chapter on theory
- Section 2.3—update with new material of Example box on what behavioral science says about the open-plan office
- Section 2.5—revision of systems discussion to include concept of synergy. New Example box on systems and whether nudges achieve results, with discussion of repaying student loans in closed systems versus open systems.
- Section 2.6—in Practical Action box on evidence-based management, new material on proving and disproving theories, the purpose of research
- New key term for synergy
- New Management in Action case titled "Best Buy Uses Management Theories to Improve Corporate Performance"
- New Legal/Ethical Challenge titled "What Should You Do about an Insubordinate Employee?"

CHAPTER 3
- Section 3.1—material added to introductory discussion of triple bottom line
- Section 3.2—updates to Example box on PG&E and discussion of who are a company's most important stakeholders. Updates to discussion of internal stakeholders: employees, owners, directors
- Section 3.3—update to discussion of external stakeholders, including Example box on Amazon's Bezos and effect of decisions on stakeholders. Revised Example box on local communities as stakeholders and question of financial incentives to sports teams and other businesses. More text details added, including definition of venture capital, FAA and regulation of drones, boycotting of Academy Awards by prominent African Americans, description of GM and recalls, and falling productivity growth in relation to technological innovations. New Example box on how technology disruption changes everything: wider availability of knowledge, engineering of life through gene modification, mobile devices changing human relations. More on effects of sociocultural forces on organizations, with expanded in-text example of sweets and obesity. Expanded details on effects of political–legal forces and international forces
- Section 3.4—expansion of details on manager's ethical responsibilities, including Volkswagen software scandal, accountability of auditors, more on insider trading, Sarbanes–Oxley, cheating by students and corporate employees, whistle-blowing

- Section 3.5—expanded discussion on climate change, including public opinion support and Coca-Cola's goal for replenishing water. Details added on philanthropy and philanthropists, including Apple's Tim Cook. Introduction and discussion of ethical leadership and effect on employee behavior and work performance
- Section 3.6—new discussion of ethics and corporate governance. Updated Example box on late Chesapeake CEO Aubrey McClendon as example of irresponsible corporate governance
- New key terms for ethical leadership, venture capital
- New Management in Action case titled "Blue Bell Is Accused of 'Recall Creep' in Its Handling of Ice Cream Contamination"
- New Legal/Ethical Challenge titled "Should You Apply to Have Your Student Loans Forgiven?"

CHAPTER 4
- Revised Manager's Toolbox, on the benefits of international business travel
- Section 4.1—new details on products made in the U.S., country rankings for competitiveness (Table 4.1) and GDP, and countries considered "most free." New Example box on e-commerce, covering peer-to-peer shopping by smartphone. More material on positive and negative effects of globalization, and new material on worldwide megamergers, such as pharmaceuticals and beer makers. New Example box on the sharing-based economy and starting an Internet enterprise, such as Poshmark and ArtLifting
- Section 4.2—new material introduced on global mind-set, with revised Practical Action box about learning to be a success abroad. Revised material on multinational enterprises. Example box on working overseas revised with new details. New details on classic American brands now foreign owned, such as Jeep, Ben & Jerry's, Gerber, Motel 6
- Section 4.3—new material on involvement of U.S. firms overseas, such as Netflix, Apple, Ford. Discussion of counter trend to offshoring—re-shoring. New details in Practical Action box on jobs lost to outsourcing, including programmers, accountants, lawyers. Revision of Table 4.2 listing top 10 exporting countries.
- Section 4.4—on free trade, updated material on TPP and major competitors the BRICS countries, as well as Brexit. Revised Table 4.3 on top 10 U.S. trading partners. Expanded discussion on embargoes and introduction of concept of sanctions. Update on WTO and Doha Round and overhaul of IMF. Discussion of NAFTA revised, with new details. Discussion of EU includes Brexit controversy along with refugee problems and terrorist attacks in Europe. Discussion of APEC, ASEA, Mercosur, and CAFTA trading blocs collapsed into a table, Table 4.4. New discussion on proposed Trans-Pacific Partnership. Updating of data in Example box on currency exchange rates. Introduction of new discussion of BRICS countries as important international competitors, with definition and new table of comparisons (Table 4.5), plus extended discussion of China, India, and Brazil
- Section 4.5—new in-text examples of the importance of understanding cultural differences and potential cultural

pitfalls. Addition of discussion of Hofstede model of four cultural dimensions. New in-text example of Venezuela and effects of expropriation. New details added about least and most corrupt countries in the world, and addition of details about slave labor

- New key terms for Brexit, BRICS, global mind-set, sanctions, TPP
- New Management in Action case titled "Costco Plans to Grow Its International Markets"
- New Legal/Ethical Challenge titled "How Far Should World Leaders Go in Accommodating Other Leaders?"

CHAPTER 5

- Revisions to Manager's Toolbox, including advantages of having a college degree and importance of writing out goals
- Section 5.1—new chapter lead on planning, and definition of a plan introduced. Revision of Example box on writing a business plan. Redefinition of strategy or strategic plan, with in-text examples. Revision of Figure 5.1 on planning and strategic management to include new elements, including addition of "values" to the first step and addition of "tactical" to third step. New details regarding Starbucks entering China market. Major revision to Example box on developing competitive advantage—who dominates the Internet economy and who's losing, including discussion of big five companies that dominate the Internet economy (Amazon, Apple, Facebook, Google, and Microsoft) and description of the stack fallacy. New subsection introducing concept of VRIO analysis as a way to analyze competitive potential, creation of new Figure 5.2 on VRIO analysis, and explanation of each concept of VRIO (value, rarity, imitability, and organization)
- Section 5.2—new section lead about importance of hope as a basis for having a goal. Discussion that mission and vision should express an organization's values. Revision of Figure 5.2 on making plans, with addition of "values statement" to the mission statement and vision statement. Example box revised on comparison of mission statements of three companies, featuring Hilton and Patagonia and replacing Amazon with Facebook. Example box revised on comparison of vision statements of these three companies. New subsection created about values statement, with definition, and what values firms want to emphasize. New Example box created comparing values statements for Hilton, Facebook, and Patagonia, with explanations. Major rewrite of Example box created about strategic planning by top management, covering problems of conventional quarterly "short-termism" as opposed to the long-term strategy of Amazon
- Section 5.3—distinction introduced between long-term and short-term goals, with definitions. Discussion of means-end chain to show how goals are connected. Redefinition of operating plan and action plan. Major revision of Example box on Southwest Airlines to show long-term and short-term goals
- Section 5.4—section retitled "Promoting Consistencies in Goals: SMART Goals, Management by Objectives, and Goal Cascading." Revised Example box on setting goals, about whether big companies are serious about sustainability and climate change, showing efforts of Walmart. Introduction of

concept of cascading goals in a subsection, making lower-level goals align with top goals, with key term of cascading goals and description of cascading process. Revision of Practical Action box on achieving one's important goals, opening with discussion of problem of noncommitment

- Section 5.5—new Example box on the planning/control cycle, featuring development of the Apple Watch
- New key terms for cascading goals, long-term goals, plan, short-term goals, strategic plan, values statement, VRIO
- New Management in Action box titled "The McCloskeys Plan to Implement Sustainable Dairy Farming While Providing Healthier Products"
- New Legal/Ethical Challenge titled "Do You Think It's Ethical for Companies to Move Their Headquarters to Another Country to Save Taxes?"

CHAPTER 6

- Manager's Toolbox revised to emphasize successful managers have to avoid fads and know their own core values
- Section 6.2—new Example box about when the strategic management process fails, as with Kodak not having an ecosystem, or "wide lens," perspective. Revision of Figure 6.1 showing the strategic management process so first step 1 is "Establish the mission, vision, and values statements"
- Section 6.3—section retitled "Establishing Mission, Vision, and Values Statements." New in-text examples given of mission, vision, and values statements, and characteristics of a good values statement are described. Table 6.1 revised to add characteristics of values statements
- Section 6.4—major revision of Example box on SWOT analysis using example of Toyota. Major revision of Example box on contingency planning to describe problems for insurance companies of rising sea levels and significance of climate change and importance of risk modeling
- Section 6.5—this section on formulating the grand strategy revised to describe four rather than three techniques to help formulate strategy. Concept of innovation strategy introduced, using in-text example of Etsy. Defensive strategy in-text example altered to show pressures on music industry. Figure 6.3 on Porter's four competitive strategies deleted as unnecessary. Focused-differentiation strategy given new in-text examples (Ford GT supercar, elite sections of cruise ships). In-text example added to show change in single-product strategy of Delphi Automotive now supplying self-driving cars, automotive electrification, and safety gear. Under diversification strategy, material deleted on unrelated and related diversification, and concept of vertical integration introduced, with in-text examples of Netflix and Starbucks. New subsection on blue ocean strategy, with discussion of two instances of the strategy—inventing a new industry (as eBay did) or expanding the boundaries of an existing industry (as Home Depot did)
- New key terms for blue ocean strategy, innovation strategy, vertical integration
- New Management in Action case titled "IKEA Focuses on Growth"

CHAPTER 7

- Section 7.1—Example box inserted here and updated on crisis leading to the strategic management process at Starbucks. Example box on making a correct diagnosis updated and revised, changing conclusions as to whether men or women are better investors. Obsolete Example box on faulty implementation of customer service deleted. Example box on evaluation and the Boeing 787 Dreamliner updated and revised. In-text example on satisficing and snap decisions changed from Campbell Soup to Amazon's Echo.
- Section 7.2—new details added on business ethics
- Section 7.3—new details added on evidence-based decision making, including Table 7.3 on Google's rules for building a better manager, and other in-text updates. Example box on analytics in athletics heavily revised to show "Moneyball" takeover of sports. In-text example added on use of drones in same-day delivery. Significant expansion of material on the implications of Big Data and how it is used, with new in-text examples on use in analyzing consumer behavior, improving hiring, tracking movie and music data, exploiting farm data, advancing health and medicine, and aiding public policy. New Example box "Data, Hacking, and Privacy," discussing rise of cyberthieves and possible corruption of automotive software
- Section 7.5—details and updates added, including in-text examples, on how to overcome barriers to decision making, such as confirmation bias, overconfidence bias, framing bias, and escalation of commitment bias
- New Management in Action case titled "How Did Decision Making Contribute to Volkswagen's Emissions Cheating Scandal?"
- New Legal/Ethical Challenge titled "Should Apple Comply with the U.S. Government's Requests to Unlock iPhones?"

CHAPTER 8

- Modifications made to Manager's Toolbox on how to get noticed in a new job
- Section 8.1—new introductory material added to section on aligning strategy, culture, and structure, emphasizing importance of an organization's culture. New figure introduced, Figure 8.1, showing that the right culture and structure are essential in realizing the organizational vision and strategy. In-text examples added on importance of cultural tone in the hiring process. New material added on positive and negative effects of cultures, with examples, including negative cultures of Zenefits, Volkswagen, and Mitsubishi
- Section 8.2—in subsection on four types of organizational culture, competing values framework (CVF) defined and explanation of the organizational effectiveness along horizontal and vertical dimensions detailed. New in-text examples introduced (Acuity insurance for clan culture, Google for adhocracy culture, Uber for market culture, Amazon shipping processes for hierarchy culture). New self-assessment 8.1 introduced, "What Is the Organizational Culture at My Current Employer?" Revision of Example box on cultures representing competing values—the different "personalities"

of Pfizer Pharmaceuticals, with update on shedding U.S. corporate citizenship to lower taxes. Section of three levels of organizational culture moved to earlier in the chapter, and in-text example added of CVS Health ceasing selling of tobacco as example of espoused versus enacted values. In section on how employees learn culture, new subsection added on organizational socialization, with explanation of three phases (anticipatory socialization, encounter, and change and acquisition phases), along with in-text example of Miami Children's Hospital. Revisions to subsection on the importance of culture to various outcomes, including positive work attitudes and better financial performance. Introduction of section on person–organization (PO) fit and how to use it in anticipating a job interview
- Section 8.3—details updated on process of cultural change, such as Zappos experiment in holocracy. New Self-Assessment 8.2 on "Assessing Your Preferred Type of Organizational Culture"
- Section 8.4—revisions added to Practical Action box, "Reading the Culture: Avoiding Pitfalls on Your Way Up"
- Section 8.5—new details added on delegation and in Practical Action box on when to delegate
- Section 8.6—introductory material about Google revising corporate structure into conglomerate called Alphabet to bring more transparency and streamline decision making. Section on virtual organization revised to explain concept of virtual structure, using example of Web-services company Automattic
- New key term for person–organization fit
- New Management in Action case titled "W.L. Gore's Culture Promotes Employee Satisfaction, Innovation, and Retention"
- New Legal/Ethical Challenge titled "Should Socializing outside Work Hours Be Mandatory?"

CHAPTER 9

- Details added to Manager's Toolbox on soft skills and social graces.
- Section 9.1—section lead updated on HR benefits, including some new Google offerings. Under human capital, in-text example added of Scripps Health offering career coaching and tuition reimbursement to develop human capital. Material added on benefits of social capital, as in developing trusting relationships with others. Under job description and job specification, in-text example added of Enterprise Rent-A-Car sorting 50,000 candidates a month
- Section 9.2—new section lead quoting expert that 5% of workforce produces 26% of output. New material added on use of social media and mobile recruiting. New in-text examples of effective ways of finding good job candidates, such as "blind dates" and competency-based selection strategies. New details added on realistic job previews. New Example box created on the changing job market, describing Millennials, the gig economy, and the episodic career. Material added on most common lies found on resumes and additions to Practical Action box about lying on resumes.

Details added to Practical Action box on mistakes to avoid when applying for a job. Practical Action box on interviewing recast from interviewer's to applicant's viewpoint, showing what the employer is looking for. Example box on personality tests at sporting goods chain deleted. New subsection added on how hiring is being changed by robots, talent analytics, algorithms, and the like

- Section 9.3—some details added/updated on compensation and benefits
- Section 9.4—new section lead, introducing onboarding. Under training, discussion added on how high-impact learning programs increase profit growth and aid retention. Under off-the-job training, discussion added on microlearning, with new Example box on technology-enhanced learning, discussing microlearning and e-learning.
- Section 9.5—material and statistics added on performance appraisal. Discussion of 360-degree feedback revised. Discussion of forced ranking heavily revised and expanded
- Section 9.6—introduction of concepts of turnover and attrition, with other details and updates through the section. New material added to Practical Action box on right way to handle a dismissal. Subsection added exit interview and nondisparagement agreement, with discussion
- Section 9.7—discussion and details added on minimum wage, Toxic Substances Control Act, workplace discrimination, gender pay disparity, and bullying
- Section 9.8—update of Table 9.6 snapshot of U.S. union movement and other material, including the two-tier setup. Arbitration discussion broadened, including negatives. Subsection added on new ways to advance employee interests, including easier ways to organize fast-food, construction, contract, and Uber workers
- New key terms for attrition, microlearning, onboarding, turnover
- New Management in Action case titled "Google's Success Builds from Its Progressive Approach toward Human Resource Management"
- New Legal/Ethical Challenge titled "Should Non-compete Agreements Be Legal?"

CHAPTER 10

- Manager's Toolbox revised to stress importance of the agility factor in managing for innovation and change
- Section 10.1—new introductory material about fear as preamble to nature of change. Revision of description of trends happening today, including necessity for faster speed-to-market. New Example box added on radical change, as represented in the decline of Radio Shack. Revision of material on rise of knowledge workers and changes in middle-skill jobs. In-text example on reactive change, discussing U.S. public health authorities dealing with spread of measles in the face of anti-vaccination movement. Example box on Disney World and its MagicBand technology updated. In discussion of forces of change originating outside organization, new material on technological advancements and their significance as the Fourth Industrial Revolution. New Example box on the upending of

transportation, from ride sharing to self-driving cars. Introduction of B corporation under shareholder changes, example of Millennials focusing on app-based shopping options, and influence of Brexit as example of how the global economy influences U.S. business. Under social and political pressures, discussion of sugary sodas and how to use tax to pay for popular programs. Under forces originating inside the organization, new in-text example of human resources concerns using Foxconn's employee suicides. Under managers' behavior, new in-text example of Facebook responding to accusations it suppressed conservative news

- Section 10.2—in-text example introduced of radically innovative change of Amazon's testing new delivery system, Prime Air, involving drones. Kotter's eight steps for leading organizational change deleted as obsolete. New subsection on a systems approach to change introduced, with new Figure 10.4 showing three parts of inputs, target elements of change, and outputs, with extended text discussion. Readiness for change introduced. New Self-Assessment 10.2 introduced, "What Is Your Readiness for Change?" New subsection added on force-field analysis and discussion of which forces facilitate change and which resist it
- Section 10.3—example of "jerks at work" as sources of conflict introduced in discussion of organizational development. In-text example of IBM hiring thousands of designers to challenge conventional thinking. Discussion of feedback loop added to Example box on using OD to make money in the restaurant business
- Section 10.4—under discussion of seeds of innovation, several in-text examples added, such as how GoPro camera was invented, Microsoft's acquiring of LinkedIn, and Adobe Systems using Kickbox as a game to develop ideas. Deletion of section celebrating failure and Example box on 3M, and addition of new subsection on how companies can foster innovation, with seven components explained in the text and in new Table 10.2 on creating an innovation system. Table 10.3 revised of top 2016 organizations whose cultures strongly encourage innovation. New Example box added on achieving success through innovation and collaboration, using example of Tesla's "Culture of Openness," with four tips for "going Tesla"
- Section 10.5—Example box of Collins's five stages of decline deleted for space reasons. Explanations and details added to model of resistance to change, with new in-text examples
- New key terms for force-field analysis, innovation system, readiness for change
- New Management in Action case titled "J.C. Penney Is Effectively Navigating Strategic and Managerial Change"
- New Legal/Ethical Challenge titled "Did L'Oreal Go Too Far in Firing Its Patent Lawyer?"

CHAPTER 11

- Manager's Toolbox on mythical Millennials revised to show generalizations about what they want most Gen Xers and Baby Boomers want as well

- Section 11.1—new details added on personality tests and use in the workplace. Material added on self-esteem and locus of control. Expanded discussion of Emotional Intelligence. Example box revised on EI, considering that empathy works better than self-interest for the impact of compassion on the bottom line
- Section 11.2—section on values and attitudes revised, with in-text example of restaurant chain showing good treatment elevates bottom line. New Practical Action box on methods for reducing cognitive dissonance replaces former Table 11.4 on examples of ways to reduce cognitive dissonance. In-text examples added of ways to create value, including practices by Coca Cola, Disney, Gap
- Section 11.3—four types of distortion of perception expanded to five, with addition of implicit bias, with discussion and in-text examples. Discussion of sex-role, age, and racial/ethnicity stereotypes expanded and of halo effect. Example box deleted on halo effect of good looks. Example box on recency effect expanded, covering performance reviews, student evaluations, and investment decisions. Discussion of self-fulling prophecy, or Pygmalion effect, expanded, but Practical Action box deleted on how managers can harness the effect to lead employees
- Section 11.4—discussion of employee engagement expanded and updated. New Example box introduced on the toxic workplace, describing how incivility saps energy and productivity and increases negative behavior
- Section 11.5—the new diversified workforce updated and in-text examples added. More discussion of women working and statistics and unequal gender pay and discrimination. Expanded discussion of LGBT and sexual orientation, with statistics. Transgender introduced, with expanded discussion of LGBTQ. Coverage of Supreme Court decision on same-sex marriage. Diversity climate and psychological safety introduced, with discussion. Discussion added of hostile work environment for diverse employees. Under coverage of stress, new Example box added on good stress and whether being a worrywart is actually a benefit
- New key terms for diversity climate, implicit bias, psychological safety, transgender
- New Management in Action case titled "Individual Differences, Values, Attitudes, and Diversity at Facebook"
- New Legal/Ethical Challenge titled "Should Airlines Accommodate Oversized People?"

CHAPTER 12

- New Manager's Toolbox, "Managing for Motivation: Scrapping the Traditional 9-to-5 Job?"
- Section 12.1—added inducements described that are offered by some companies as motivators, such as being paid to live near job. In Figure 12.1, integrated model of motivation, two more factors added to personal factors box—values and work attitudes—and two more factors added to contextual factors box—organizational climate and job design. Under extrinsic rewards, in-text examples added

of Air Force offering bonus to drone pilots to extend their service and effect of paying employees to lose weight. Under intrinsic rewards, new in-text example of paid sabbatical offered to employees to work at a charitable organization of their choice. List of why motivation is important incorporated into text, to save space
- Section 12.2—Example box on use of Maslow retitled "The Chief Emotional Officer" and revised with new details. Under acquired needs theory, material expanded on need for achievement. Under self-determination theory, new in-text examples added of ways to motivate employees by Hindustan Unilever, Best Buy, and Apple Store. Under discussion of Herzberg, in-text examples added from the Container Store and Southwest Airlines
- Section 12.3—equity theory retitled equity/justice theory, with expanded discussion of equity theory, involving cognitive dissonance. Former Table 12.1 on ways employees try to reduce inequity deleted to save space. Elements of justice theory—distributive, procedural, and interactional—added and discussed. New subsection added on using equity and justice theories to motivate employees, with five practical lessons. Concept of voice introduced. New material added on some practical results of goal-setting theory, including new in-text examples
- Section 12.4—term *job simplification* deleted in favor of new key term, *scientific management*
- Section 12.5—new key term introduced, *law of effect*. New Example box added about reinforcement, with discussion of tying CEO pay to environmental goals or food safety improvement
- Section 12.6—section reorganized and expanded to cover various forms of compensation, with expanded treatment of gainsharing and stock options. Four types of nonmonetary incentives also discussed: employees' need for work–life balance, balancing work with life, flex-time, vacations and sabbaticals; need to expand their skills, including studying coworkers, receiving tuition reimbursement, and undergoing training; need for a positive work environment, with discussion of well-being and flourishing; and need to matter, with discussion of meaningfulness. Text material converted to new Practical Action box on thoughtfulness, the value of being nice.
- New key terms for distributive justice, flourishing, interactive justice, law of effect, meaningfulness, procedural justice, scientific management, voice, well-being, work–life benefits
- New Management in Action case titled "Acuity Insurance and the Container Store Focus on Employee Motivation"
- New Legal/Ethical Challenge titled "Should College Athletes Be Paid to Perform?"

CHAPTER 13

- Major rewrite of Manager's Toolbox, including new tips for managing virtual teams and a new example of a virtual-team organization
- New examples of effective teams to introduce Section 13.1

- Section 13.1—Updated and revised Example box, including a new example of Panera and storytelling; new material on formal versus informal groups; replaced section titled "Work Teams for Four Purposes: Advice, Production, Project, and Action" with one titled "Types of deleted Table 13.2 on types of teams; new material on work teams, cross-functional teams, self-managed teams, and virtual teams; and new Practical Action box titled "Best Practices for Virtual Teams"
- Section 13.2—new discussion regarding the accuracy of Tuckman's model of group development; new section on punctuated equilibrium model of group development
- Section 13.3—revised all subsections based on new research, which includes new discussion of collaboration, accountability and interdependence, composition, roles, and norms; deleted Tables 13.4 and 13.5; deleted Example box on team size; new table on task and maintenance roles in groups; deleted Example box on team norms; new Practical Action box with examples of Cisco, Pittsburgh Steelers, and GM Volt; deleted material on groupthink.
- Section 13.4—new self-assessment on conflict management styles, new Example box on workplace bullying, new discussion of work–family conflict, new table on negative consequences of work–family conflict, new Practical Action box on work–family balance, new Practical Action box on creativity and conflict
- New key terms for collaboration, punctuated equilibrium, team composition, team member interdependence, virtual teams, work–family conflict
- New Management in Action case titled "Teamwork Is a Driver of Success at Whole Foods Market"

CHAPTER 14

- Manager's Toolbox—updated discussion of how to manage your career
- Section 14.1—restructured the section; new data on corporate spending for leadership development; new research on why leadership matters; section begins with discussing power, including new examples of how power was used at social media company GoFanbase and Ford Motor Co.; new section on influence tactics, which includes a new table and examples of influence tactics, a discussion of hard versus soft tactics, a new self-assessment on influence tactics, and how to match tactics to influence outcomes; deleted tables 14.1 and 14.2; updated discussion on leading versus managing; and new section offering an integrated model of leadership (Figure 14.1)
- Section 14.2—new table of traits and attributes found in leaders (Table 14.2); updated research on gender and leadership; new leadership traits Example box featuring world leaders Justin Trudeau and Angela Merkel, many new examples of leadership traits, new comparison of Blake Mykoskie of TOMS Shoes and Martin Shkreli of Turing Pharmaceuticals; new section on knowledge and skills found in leaders, including Table 14.4 showing four basic skills for leaders; new section on takeaways from trait

theory and research; and new Example box on multicultural leadership
- Section 14.3—new example of the Gates Foundation to illustrate initiating structure; new section on ethical leadership; new Example box of ethical leadership at BuildDirect; new Example box of servant-leadership at Kimpton Hotels and Starbucks
- Section 14.4—new Practical Action box on applying situational theories
- Section 14.5—new examples of Steve Jobs, Pope Francis, and John Mackey (Whole Foods) to illustrate the four types of transformational leadership; updated Example box on Indra Nooyi (Pepsi) as transactional and transformational leader
- Section 14.6—updated research on the LMX model; deleted discussion of e-leadership; new section on leading with humility; a new Practical Action box on leading by being a good follower
- New key terms for ethical leadership, influence tactics, power
- New Management in Action case titled "Mary Barra's Leadership Guides General Motors through a Crisis and Toward Profitability"
- New Legal/Ethical Challenge titled "Jail or a Settlement: Which Is More Appropriate for the Leaders of an Alleged Charity Scam?"

CHAPTER 15

- New Manager's Toolbox regarding the role of communication in landing a job
- Section 15.1—new discussion of research on employers and college students' assessments of students' communication skills; new discussion of jargon as noise; new Example box on secrecy and silence in corporate cultures at Volkswagen and Theranos; updated information about social media as a form of communication media
- Section 15.2—new examples of downward and upward communication; updated and expanded discussion of the grapevine; new section on face-to-face communication, which includes discussion of basic principles to make the most of face-to-face communication; deleted material on management by wandering around; a completely revised Practical Action box on streamlining meetings
- Section 15.3—new discussion of office design as physical barrier or facilitator of communication; new example of Amazon's new headquarters; expanded discussion of listening skills as a barrier and the role of mindlessness; new examples of social media use; new section on generational differences; new section on cross-cultural barriers; updated examples and research on nonverbal communication, including new material on touch; updated discussion and new table of gender differences in communication; new Practical Action box on how men and women can communicate better at work
- Section 15.4—completely rewritten around the title of "Social Media and Management"; new section topics include social

media is changing the fabric of our lives, social media and managerial and organizational effectiveness, downsides of social media, managerial implications of texting, and managerial considerations in creating social media policies. Detailed changes include new Practical Action box on building professional profile online; new discussions of social media's impact on employee and employer productivity; new table of social media benefits for employers; new Example box on controlling social media tools; new discussions of social media and innovation (including crowdsourcing) and social media and sales (including brand recognition); new examples of UnderArmour, TOMS Shoes, and GoPro; new section on social media and reputation; updated discussion of downsides of social media; new table of tips for handling e-mail; new discussion of managerial implications of texting at work; new section on creating a social media policy; new Example box with samples of social media policies at GAP, *Los Angeles Times,* Intel, and others; new self-assessment on social media readiness

- Section 15.5—new data on importance of communication skills; new self-assessment on communication competence; new section on nondefensive communication, including a table on the antecedents of defensive and nondefensive communication; new section on using empathy; new examples of effective listening and new section on listening styles; updated discussion of good writing skills; updated discussion of public speaking skills
- New key terms are crowdsourcing, cyberloafing, empathy, social media policy
- New Management in Action case titled "Nokia Actively Uses Social Media to Communicate"
- New Legal/Ethical Challenge titled "Was the Firing of Curt Schilling for His Social Media Post Fair?"

CHAPTER 16

- Manager's Toolbox—updated with new examples of social media use by the ALS Association, ability diversity hiring at Microsoft, and interview process at Uber
- Section 16.1—new examples of Takata airbag recall and federal safety investigation of Tesla self-driving cars; new examples of Uniqlo, Pepsi, and NASA's Juno mission; revamped and updated Example box on UPS drivers' standards; new section on types of controls, including discussion of feedforward, concurrent, and feedback controls
- Section 16.2—new examples to illustrate the six areas of control; new Example box on Airbnb and HR controls; new section on controlling the supply chain; new supply-chain examples of Hostess Brands, Target, and Amazon; new section on control in service firms
- Section 16.3—new examples to illustrate each of the four categories in a balanced scorecard; new discussion of metrics used to measure performance in each scorecard category; new and expanded discussion of strategy mapping,

including a new figure showing a sample strategy map for Dr Pepper Snapple Group; deleted discussion of measurement management

- Section 16.4—new discussion of gig economy; deleted table showing types of budgets and discussion of ratio analysis; new table to illustrate a profit-and-loss statement for a small company; new discussion of analytics when conducting audits
- Section 16.5—new discussion of 2015 Baldrige Award winner—Midway USA; new example of Toyota's use of TQM; new Example box about Kia Motors; new discussion and Example box about Kaizen, *featuring* Herman Miller, Studio 904, and Wagamama restaurant chain; new examples of Four Seasons Hotels, Ralph Lauren, and Exel Logistics; updated discussion of Six Sigma, Lean Six Sigma, and ISO 9000 and ISO 14000; new section on takeaways from TQM research
- Section 16.6—new example of "Sustainability Accounting Standards"; and new section on micromanagement as a barrier to control
- Section 16.7—new table showing global gross domestic product (GDP); updated discussion of U.S. productivity and the role of information technology and productivity; new section on managing individual productivity
- Epilogue—new examples of all "life lessons"
- New key term *Kaizen*
- New Management in Action case titled "Chipotle's Operational Problems Make People Sick"
- New Legal/Ethical Challenge titled "Is GPS Tracking of Employee Actions an Effective Form of Management Control?"

A BRIDGE TO STUDENT SUCCESS

The study of management is an essential crossing on the road to achievement.

- The cover shows the Margaret Hunt Hill Bridge, which transformed the skyline of Dallas, Texas, when it opened in March 2012. Named for a well-known Dallas heiress and philanthropist, the bridge spans the Trinity River and is distinguished by its striking 40-story-high center-support arch topped with a curved span. The cable-stayed bridge was designed by Spanish/Swiss architect Santiago Calatrava and has a total length of 1,870 feet.
- Some great achievements of history were accomplished by individuals working quietly by themselves, such as scientific discoveries or works of art. But so much more has been achieved by people who were able to leverage their talents and abilities—and those of others—by being managers. None of the great architectural wonders, such as this one, was built single-handedly by one person. Rather, all represent triumphs of management.

PREFACE: Practical skills. Relevant theory. Purposeful application.

Kinicki/Williams, 8e, empowers students to develop the management skills necessary in everyday life through the practical and relevant application of theory. Developed to help students read and learn management with a purpose, K/W, 8e, engages students through current examples, imaginative writing, and resources that work.

The eighth edition of *Management: A Practical Introduction*—a concepts book for the introductory course in management—uses a wealth of instructor feedback to identify which features from prior editions worked best and which should be improved and expanded. By blending Angelo's scholarship, teaching, publishing, and management-consulting experience with Brian's writing and publishing background, we have again tried to create a research-based yet highly readable, practical, and *motivational* text.

Our primary goal is simple to state but hard to execute: to make learning principles of management as easy, effective, and efficient as possible. Accordingly, the book integrates writing, illustration, design, and magazine-like layout in **a program of learning that appeals to the visual sensibilities and respects the time constraints and different learning styles of today's students.** In an approach initially tested in our first edition and fine-tuned in the subsequent editions, **we break topics down into easily grasped portions** and incorporate **frequent use of various kinds of reinforcement techniques.** Our hope, of course, is to make a difference in the lives of our readers: to produce a text that students will enjoy reading and that will provide them with practical benefits.

The text covers the principles that most management instructors have come to expect in an introductory text—planning, organizing, leading, and controlling—plus the issues that today's students need to be aware of to succeed: customer focus, globalism, diversity, ethics, social media, entrepreneurship, work teams, the service economy, and small business.

> Beyond these, our book has four features that make it unique:
>
> 1. **A student-centered approach to learning.**
> 2. **Imaginative writing for readability and reinforcement.**
> 3. **Emphasis on practicality.**
> 4. **Resources that work.**

> " *Kinicki/Williams is an effective principles of management textbook that does an excellent job of conveying the excitement of management and leadership to undergraduates. Engaging and practical, it comes with a comprehensive set of support materials that range from the traditional to exciting new uses of technology that supercharge the teaching of critical concepts. We looked at over ten textbooks before we adopted Kinicki, and we're most certainly glad that we did. Publisher support has been excellent.* "
>
> **—Gary B. Roberts,**
> *Kennesaw State University*

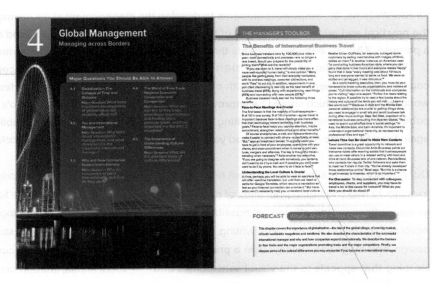

Chapter Openers:

Designed to help students read with purpose

Each chapter begins with four to eight provocative, motivational **Major Questions,** written to appeal to students' concern about "what's in it for me?" and to help them read with purpose.

Instead of opening with the conventional case, as most texts do, we open with **The Manager's Toolbox,** a motivational device offering practical nuts-and-bolts advice pertaining to the chapter content students are about to read—and allowing for class discussion.

Chapter Sections:

Structured into constituent parts for easier learning

Chapters are organized to cover each major question in turn, giving students bite-sized chunks of information. Each section begins with a recap of the **Major Question** and includes **"The Big Picture,"** which presents students with an overview of how the section they are about to read answers the Major Question.

> *This style textbook succeeds in presenting management information with a fresh face. Each chapter is filled with current and useful information for students. The chapters begin by asking major questions of the reader. As the student reads, [he or she is] engaged by these questions and by the information that follows. A totally readable text with great illustrations and end-of-chapter exercises!*

—Catherine Ruggieri,
St. John's University, New York

Imaginative Writing for Readability

Research shows that textbooks written in **an imaginative, people-oriented style significantly improve students' ability to retain information. We employ a number of journalistic devices to make the material as engaging as possible for students.**

We employ a lot of **storytelling** to convey the real "texture of life" in being a manager. This means we **use colorful facts, attention-grabbing quotes, biographical sketches, and lively taglines** to get students' attention as they read.

THE MANAGER'S TOOLBOX

The Benefits of International Business Travel

Since business travelers who fly 100,000-plus miles a year—both domestically and overseas—are no longer a rare breed, should you prepare for the possibility of joining them? What are the rewards?

"If you are open to it, travel will simply make you a more well-rounded human being," is one opinion.[1] Many people like getting away from their everyday workplace, with its endless meetings, coworker distractions, and work "fires" to put out. In addition, respondents in one poll cited discovering a new city as the best benefit of business travel (65%), along with experiencing new things (45%) and connecting with new people (37%).[2]

Business travelers have learned the following three benefits.

Face-to-Face Meetings Are Crucial

The first lesson is that the majority of businesspeople—8 of 10 in one survey, 9 of 10 in another—agree travel is important because face-to-face meetings are more effective than technology toward achieving their business goals.[3] Face-to-face helps you capture attention, inspire commitment, strengthen relationships, and other benefits.[4]

Of course smartphones, e-mail, and videoconferencing make it easier to connect with others—superficially, at least.

Retailer Urban Outfitters, for example, outraged some customers by selling merchandise with images of Hindu deities on them.[8] In another instance, an American used "to conducting business American style, where you can get a deal done in two hours and everyone leaves happy," found that in Asia "every meeting was about 10 hours long and everyone wanted to serve us food. We were so stuffed and jet-lagged, it was ridiculous."[9]

As a world-traveling executive, then, you must do your homework to know cultures, organizations, and holders of power. "Cull information on the individuals and companies you're visiting," says one expert. "Follow the news relating to the region. If possible try to read a few books about the history and culture of the lands you will visit. . . . Learn a few words too."[10] Because in Asia and the Middle East personal relationships are crucial to getting things done, you need to engage in small talk and avoid business talk during after-hours outings. Says Ted Dale, president of international business consulting firm Aperian Global, "You need to spend out-of-office time in social settings." In Asia, the Middle East, and Latin America, it's important to understand organizational hierarchy, as represented by professional titles and age.[11]

E-Commerce: Peer-to-Peer Shopping by Smartphone

EXAMPLE

Perhaps the most well-known story of e-commerce companies is that of Amazon.com, which was started in 1994 by Jeffrey Bezos as an online bookstore, and now offers "new products and services at a rate none of the old-guard companies seem able to match," according to one business writer.[26] (One such company is Gap Inc., whose revenues have fallen at its Banana Republic and Old Navy walk-in stores but have not been made up for in online sales.[27])

The New E-Commerce. Today 68% of U.S. adults have a smartphone and nearly 45% a tablet.[28] Yet most American consumers use their mobile devices for getting directions or listening to music rather than making purchases, according to a survey by Pew Research Center.[29] But in Asia, which is home to the world's two biggest smartphone markets, China and India, things are different. Asian countries account for nearly half of the world's mobile online shopping, worth more than $230 billion annually (in U.S. dollars).[30] A few companies, reports *The Wall Street Journal*, "are starting to change the commercial landscape by offering apps that let individuals buy and sell goods directly from one another more easily than on traditional Web-based sites like eBay."[31] For example, in January 2016, 43% of people in South Korea said they used a smartphone to make a purchase during the past 30 days, the highest proportion in the world.

Our emphasis on practicality and applications extends to the **Example boxes,** "mini-cases" that use snapshots of real-world institutions to explain text concepts. **"Your Call" invites student critical thinking and class discussion at the end of each example.** Suggestions for how to use the Example boxes are found in the Teaching Resource Manual (TRM).

 The Kinicki/Williams text is attractive and well organized. The writing is engaging, and there is much more than my current text in terms of examples, application, summaries, and cases. The graphical quality of the book is much better than the black and white version[s] [of texts]. Overall, I think this book represents an excellent approach to the subject of management from both an instructor and learner perspective.

—**Jeffrey Anderson,**
Ohio University

Emphasis on Practicality

We want this book to be a "keeper" for students, a resource for future courses and for their careers—so we give students a **great deal of practical advice** in addition to covering the fundamental concepts of management. Application points are found not only throughout the text discussion but also in the following specialized features.

Practical Action boxes, appearing one or more times in each chapter, offer students practical and interesting advice on issues they will face in the workplace. Detailed discussions of how to use these Practical Action boxes appear in the Teaching Resource Manual (TRM).

PRACTICAL ACTION

Learning to Be a Success Abroad: Developing a Global Mind-set

Whether you travel abroad on your own or on a work assignment for your company, there are several ways to develop a global mind-set and make your experience enhance your career success.

Be an "I'm-Not-an-Ugly American." Americans "are seen throughout the world as an arrogant people, totally self-absorbed and loud," says Keith Reinhard, former head of advertising conglomerate DDB Worldwide, who had led an effort to reverse that through a nonprofit group called Business for Diplomatic Action (BDA), from which many suggestions here are drawn.[58] (The group publishes *The World Citizens Guide*, which consists of practical advice for Americans traveling abroad.)[59] A survey conducted by DDB in more than 100 countries found that respondents repeatedly mentioned "arrogant," "loud," and "uninterested in the world" when asked their perceptions of Americans.[60] Some sample advice for Americans traveling abroad is: Be patient, be quiet, listen at least as much as you talk, don't use slang, and don't talk about wealth and status.[61]

Be Global in Your Focus, but Think Local. Study up on your host country's local customs and try to meet new people who might help you in the future. For example, Bill Roedy, president of MTV Networks International, spent time hanging out with Arab rappers and meeting the mayor of Mecca before trying to sign a contract that would launch MTV Arabia.[62] His efforts helped seal the deal.

Learn What's Appropriate Behavior. Before you go, spend some time learning about patterns of interpersonal communication. In Japan, for instance, it is considered rude to look directly into the eye for more than a few seconds. In Greece the hand-waving gesture commonly used in America is considered an insult. In Afghanistan, a man does not ask another man about his wife.[63] In China, people generally avoid hugs—at least until recently.[64]

Learn rituals of respect, including exchange of business cards.[65] Understand that shaking hands is always permissible, but social kissing may not be. Dress professionally. For women, this means no heavy makeup, no flashy jewelry, no short skirts

---

Management in Action cases depict how companies students are familiar with respond to situations or issues featured in the text. Discussion questions are included for ease of use in class, as reflection assignments, or over online discussion boards. In addition, follow-up multiple-choice questions contained in Connect measure students' ability to apply what they've learned in the chapter to real life situations managers are facing.

Management in Action

Costco Plans to Grow Its International Markets

Costco Wholesale Corporation is an American membership-only warehouse club selling a large range of products. The company opened its first warehouse in 1983 and currently is the second largest retailer in the U.S.—Walmart is number one. Costco, however, is the largest membership warehouse club chain in the U.S.

Costco operates about 700 warehouses across the U.S. and abroad. As of November 2015, the company had international locations in Canada (89), United Kingdom (26), Australia (8), Mexico (34), Taiwan (10), South Korea (12), Japan (20), and Spain (2).[208] The company's revenue has been growing the last few years, and international expansion is one key contributor. Net sales growth from international operations grew by 45% between 2010 and 2014. This compares to a net sales growth of 21% from Sam's Club, the warehouse outlet run by Walmart, over the same period. "Margins from international operations are also higher, which has benefited the bottom line. That's partly due to little or no competition from other warehouse clubs, as they're a relatively newer concept abroad, and partly due to lower employee costs. Costco earned an operat-

local environment for each market it is operating in. Consider the changes Costco implemented when expanding to Australia.

Costco began by changing its selling practices. Rather than relying on coupons to draw-in customers, the company abandoned their use. Coupons are foreign to Australians and hardly anyone uses them. The company also dropped its use of Costco cards as a form of payment. While Americans like the use of such cards, management thought that Australians would have greater flexibility in payment methods. They were correct in this assessment.

"Also Costco decided not to invest any money in marketing. They played on 'word-of-mouth' marketing. It was smart as in Australia, this is probably the best marketing money can buy. Partially the success of this practice was ensured by the fact that many Australians and Americans travel a lot between the countries. The migration flow is quite strong there. This caused a certain amount of people to have first-hand experience with Costco. This played its role in attracting new customers."[211]

Costco similarly used a customized approach when opening stores in Spain. It opened its first warehouse

---

Legal/Ethical Challenges present cases—often based on real events—that require students to think through how they would handle the situation, helping prepare them for decision making in their careers.

Legal/Ethical Challenge

How Far Should World Leaders Go in Accommodating Other Leaders?

This challenge involves a conflict between national culture and religious beliefs. The context was a state visit from Iran's president, Hassan Rouhani, to Rome and Paris in 2016. This was the first visit for an Iranian president in 17 years.

The Wall Street Journal reported that "The trip succeeded in reviving economic ties that withered after the European Union adopted sanctions over Iran's nuclear program in 2012. The countries cut billions in business deals this week . . ."[213]

The challenge involves how to handle the Iranian leader's request regarding meals during the visits. According to *USA Today*, "Rouhani asked for a halal menu in keeping with his Muslim faith, which meant no wine" during meals.

French President Francois Hollande decided to forgo any meals and instead staged a formal welcome at the Invalides monument. According to Gérard Araud, France's ambassador to the United States, "It is not the halal which was a problem but the wine.

Campidoglio museum to protect the Islamic Republic visitors from gazing at artists' renderings of the human form."

Italian Prime Minister Matteo Renzi's decisions drew strong criticism from others according to *USA Today*. Lawmaker Luca Squeri said, "Respect for other cultures cannot and must not mean negating our own. This isn't respect, it's cancelling out differences and it's kind of surrender." Rome City Councilman Gianluca Peciola started a petition asking Renzi to explain "a disgraceful decision which is a mortification of art and culture as universal values."[214]

SOLVING THE CHALLENGE

What would you have done if you were Hollande or Renzi?

1. These are state dinners involving important matters, and leaders need to be accepting of religious differences. What's the big deal in forgoing some wine with the meal and covering up art? I would hold the dinners, not serve wine, and cover up the offensive

The McGraw-Hill Companies is a proud corporate member of AACSB International. Understanding the importance and value of AACSB accreditation, *Management: A Practical Introduction,* 8th ed., recognizes the curricula guidelines detailed in the AACSB standards for business accreditation by connecting selected questions in the text and/or the test bank to the general knowledge and skill guidelines in the AACSB standards.

The statements contained in *Management: A Practical Introduction,* 8th ed., are provided only as a guide for the users of this textbook. The AACSB leaves content coverage and assessment within the purview of individual schools, the mission of the school, and the faculty. While *Management: A Practical Introduction,* 8th ed., and the teaching package make no claim of any specific AACSB qualification or evaluation, we have within *Management: A Practical Introduction,* 8th ed., labeled selected questions according to the general knowledge and skills areas.

acknowledgments

We could not have completed this product without the help of a great many people. The first edition was signed by Karen Mellon and developed by Glenn and Meg Turner of Burrston House, to all of whom we are very grateful. Sincere thanks and gratitude also go to our former executive editor, John Weimeister, and to our present director, Michael Ablassmeir. Among our first-rate team at McGraw-Hill, we want to acknowledge key contributors: Katie Eddy, product developer; Necco McKinley and Debbie Clare, senior marketing managers; Nicole Young, senior market development manager; Mary E. Powers and Danielle E. Clement, content project managers; designer Jessica Cuevas. We would also like to thank Mindy West and Patrick Soleymani for their work on the *Teaching Resource Manual;* Crystal Fashant for the PowerPoint slides; and Ken Carson, and his affiliation, Grove City College, for his work on the self-assessments for Connect.

Warmest thanks and appreciation go to the individuals who provided valuable input during the developmental stages of this edition, as follows:

Steven W. Abram,
Kirkwood Community College

Laura Alderson,
University of Memphis

Jeffrey Anderson,
Ohio University

Mona Bahl,
Youngstown State University

Valerie Barnet,
Kansas State University

David Allen Brown,
Ferris State University

Jon L. Bryan

Paul Buffa,
Jefferson College, Missouri Baptist University

Mark David Burdsall,
University of Pittsburgh

Melissa M. Cooper,
School of Management, Texas Woman's University

Derek Eugene Crews,
Texas Woman's University

Daniel J. Curtin,
Lakeland Community College

Linda I. De Long,
University of La Verne

Margaret Deck,
Virginia Tech

E. Gordon DeMeritt,
Shepherd University

Anant R. Deshpande,
SUNY Empire State College

John DeSpagna,
Nassau Community College

Ken Dunegan,
Cleveland State University

W. Randy Evans,
University of Tennessee at Chattanooga

Paul A. Fadil,
University of North Florida

Crystal Saric Fashant,
Metropolitan State University

Carla Flores,
Ball State University

Christopher Flynn,
University of North Florida

Charla Fraley,
Columbus State Community College

Dana Frederick,
Missouri State University

Lydia Gilmore,
Columbus State Community College

Ronnie Godshalk,
Penn State University

Constance Golden,
Lakeland Community College

Deborah Cain Good,
University of Pittsburgh

Tita Gray,
San Diego State University

Marie DK. Halvorsen-Ganepola,
University of Notre Dame

Karen H. Hawkins,
Miami Dade College, Kendall Campus

Anne Kelly Hoel,
University of Wisconsin–Stout

David Hollomon,
Victor Valley College

Kathleen Jones,
University of North Dakota

Shaun C. Knight,
The Pennsylvania State University

Leo C. Kotrodimos,
NC Wesleyan College

Chalmer E. Labig Jr.,
Oklahoma State University

Wendy Lam,
Hawaii Pacific University

Robert L. Laud,
William Paterson University

Jessica Lofton,
University of Mount Olive

Gregory Luce,
Bucks County Community College

David R. Matthews,
SUNY Adirondack

Daniel W. McAllister,
UNLV

Lori Merlak,
Kirkwood Community College

Kelly Mollica,
University of Memphis

Jaideep Motwani,
Grand Valley State University

Patrick J. Nedry,
Monroe County Community College, Monroe, Michigan

Joanne Orabone,
Community College of Rhode Island

John Pepper,
The University of Kansas

Clifford R. Perry,
Florida INTL University Miami

Shaun Pichler,
Mihaylo College of Business,
California State University, Fullerton

Tracy H. Porter,
Cleveland State University

Ronald E. Purser,
San Francisco State University

Gregory R. Quinet,
Kennesaw State University

Deborah Reed,
Benedictine College

Sean E. Rogers,
The Cornell Hotel School

Katherine Rosenbusch,
George Mason University

Alex J. Scrimpshire,
Oklahoma State University

Joanna Shaw,
Tarleton State University

Shane Spiller,
Western Kentucky University

George E. Stevens,
Kent State University

Marguerite Teubner,
Nassau Community College

C. Justice Tillman,
Baruch College–City University
of New York

Jody Tolan,
USC Marshall School of Business

Brandi Ulrich,
Anne Arundel Community College

Scot W. Vaver,
University of Wisconsin–Stout

Brian D. Webster,
Ball State University

Eric S. Williams,
University of Alabama–
Tuscaloosa

Joette Wisnieski,
Indiana University of PA

Colette Wolfson,
Ivy Tech Community College

Wendy V. Wysocki,
Monroe County Community
College

Carol Bormann Young,
Metropolitan State University (MN)

Ned D. Young,
Sinclair Community College

Jan T. Zantinga,
The University of Georgia

Mary E. Zellmer-Bruhn,
University of Minnesota

We also extend our gratitude to our *Principles of Management* Board of Advisors, whose insight and feedback greatly enhanced both the print and digital products:

Derek E. Crews,
Texas Woman's University

Crystal Saric Fashant,
Metropolitan State University

Dr. C. Brian Flynn,
University of North Florida

Charla S. Fraley,
Columbus State Community College

Dana Frederick,
Missouri State University

Dr. David Matthews,
SUNY Adirondack

Clifford R. Perry,
Florida International University

Tracy H. Porter,
Cleveland State University

Jan T. Zantinga,
The University of Georgia

We would also like to thank the following colleagues who served as manuscript reviewers during the development of previous editions:

G. Stoney Alder,
Western Illinois University

Phyllis C. Alderdice,
Jefferson Community College

Laura L. Alderson,
University of Memphis

William Scott Anchors,
University of Maine at Orono

Jeffrey L. Anderson,
Ohio University

Darlene Andert,
Florida Gulf Coast University

John Anstey,
University of Nebraska at
Omaha

Maria Aria,
Camden County College

Pamela Ball,
Clark State Community College

James D. Bell,
Texas State University–San Marcos

Jessie Bellflowers,
Fayetteville Technical Institute

Victor Berardi,
Kent State University

Patricia Bernson,
College County of Morris

David Bess,
University of Hawaii

Stephen Betts,
William Paterson University

Danielle Beu,
Louisiana Tech University

Randy Blass,
Florida State University

Larry Bohleber,
University of Southern Indiana

Melanie Bookout,
Greenville Technical College

Robert S. Boothe,
University of Southern
Mississippi

Carol Bormann Young,
Metropolitan State University

Susan M. Bosco,
Roger Williams University

Roger Brown,
Western Illinois University

Marit Brunsell,
Madison Area Technical
College

Jon Bryan,
Bridgewater State College

Becky Bryant,
Texas Woman's University

Neil Burton,
Clemson University

Barbara A. Carlin,
University of Houston

Pamela Carstens,
Coe College

Julie J. Carwile,
John Tyler Community College

Daniel A. Cernas Ortiz,
University of North Texas

Glen Chapuis,
St. Charles Community College

Rod Christian,
Mesa Community College

Mike Cicero,
Highline Community College

Jack Cichy,
Davenport University

Anthony Cioffi,
Lorain County Community
College

Deborah Clark,
Santa Fe Community College

J. Dana Clark,
Appalachian State University

Dean Cleavenger,
University of Central Florida

Sharon Clinebell,
University of Northern
Colorado

Loretta Fergus Cochran,
Arkansas Tech University

Glenda Coleman,
University of South Carolina

Ron Cooley,
South Suburban College

Gary Corona,
Florida Community College

Keith Credo,
McNeese State University

Dan Curtin,
Lakeland Community College

Ajay Das,
Baruch College

Tom Deckelman,
Owens Community College

Kate Demarest,
Caroll Community College

E. Gordon DeMeritt,
Shepherd University

Kathleen DeNisco,
Erie Community College

John DeSpagna,
Nassau Community College

Pamela A. Dobies,
University of Missouri–Kansas City

David Dore,
City College of San Francisco

Lon Doty,
San Jose State University

Ron Dougherty,
Ivy Tech Community College/
Columbus Campus

Scott Droege,
Western Kentucky University

Ken Dunegan,
University of Cincinnati

Steven Dunphy,
University of Akron

Linda Durkin,
Delaware County Community
College

Subhash Durlabhji,
Northwestern State University

Jack Dustman,
Northern Arizona University

Ray Eldridge,
Freed-Hardeman University

Bob Eliason,
James Madison University

Valerie Evans,
Kansas State University

Paul Fadil,
University of North Florida

Jud Faurer,
Metro State College of Denver

Judy Fitch,
Augusta State University

David Foote,
Middle Tennessee State University

Lucy R. Ford,
Saint Joseph's University

Gail E. Fraser,
Kean University

Tony Frontera,
Broome Community College

Dane Galden,
Columbus State Community College

Michael Garcia,
Liberty University

Evgeniy Gentchev,
Northwood University

James Glasgow,
Villanova University

Connie Golden,
Lakeland Community College

Kris Gossett,
Ivy Tech State College

Marie Gould,
Peirce University

Ryan Greenbaum,
Oklahoma State University, Stillwater

Kevin S. Groves,
California State University,
Los Angeles

Joyce Guillory,
Austin Community College

Reggie Hall,
Tarleton State University

Stephen F. Hallam,
The University of Akron

Marie Halvorsen-Ganepola,
University of Notre Dame

Charles T. Harrington,
Pasadena City College

Santhi Harvey,
Central State University

Karen Hawkins,
Miami Dade College

Samuel Hazen,
Tarleton State University

Jack Heinsius,
Modesto Junior College

Duane Helleloid,
University of North Dakota

Evelyn Hendrix,
Lindenwood University

Kim Hester,
Arkansas State University

Anne Kelly Hoel,
University of Wisconsin–Stout

Mary Hogue,
Kent State University

Tammy Hunt,
University of North Carolina,
Wilmington

Aviad Israeli,
Kent State University

Edward Johnson,
University of North Florida

Nancy M. Johnson,
Madison Area Technical College

Kathleen Jones,
University of North Dakota

Rusty Juban,
Southeastern Louisiana University

Dmitriy Kalyagin,
Chabot College

Heesam Kang,
Bacone College

Marvin Karlins,
University of South Florida

Marcella Kelly,
Santa Monica College

Richard Kimbrough,
University of Nebraska–Lincoln

Renee N. King,
Eastern Illinois University

Bobbie Knoblauch,
Wichita State University

Todd Korol,
Monroe Community College

Sal Kukalis,
California State University–Long Beach

Rebecca Legleiter,
Tulsa Community College

David Leonard,
Chabot College

Chris Levan,
University of Tennessee,
Chattanooga

David Levy,
United States Air Force Academy

Chi Lo Lim,
Northwest Missouri State University

Natasha Lindsey,
University of North Alabama

Beverly Little,
Western Carolina University

Guy Lochiatto,
MassBay Community College

Mary Lou Lockerby,
College of DuPage

Michael Dane Loflin,
Limestone College

Paul Londrigan,
Charles Stewart Mott Community
College

Tom Loughman,
Columbus State University

Ivan Lowe,
York Technical College

Margaret Lucero,
Texas A & M–Corpus Christi

James Manicki,
Northwestern College

Christine I. Mark,
University of Southern Mississippi

Marcia A. Marriott,
Monroe Community College

Brenda McAleer,
University of Maine at Augusta

Daniel W. McAllister,
University of Nevada–Las Vegas

David McArthur,
University of Nevada–Las Vegas

Tom McFarland,
Mount San Antonio College

Joe McKenna,
Howard Community College

Zack McNeil,
Longview Community College

Jeanne McNett,
Assumption College

Spencer Mehl,
Coastal Carolina Community
College

Mary Meredith,
University of Louisiana

Lori Merlak,
Kirkwood Community College

Douglas Micklich,
Illinois State University

Christine Miller,
Tennessee Tech University

Val Miskin,
Washington State University

Gregory Moore,
Middle Tennessee State
University

Rob Moorman,
Creighton University

Troy Mumford,
Colorado State University

Robert Myers,
University of Louisville

Christopher P. Neck,
Arizona State University

Francine Newth,
Providence College

Margie Nicholson,
Columbia College, Chicago

Thomas J. Norman,
California State University–
Dominguez Hills

John Orife,
Indiana University of
Pennsylvania

Eren Ozgen,
Troy State University, Dothan

Fernando Pargas,
James Madison University

Jack Partlow,
Northern Virginia Community
College

Don A. Paxton,
Pasadena City College

John Paxton,
Wayne State College

Sheila Petcavage,
Cuyahoga Community College–
Western Campus

Barbara Petzall,
Maryville University

Anthony Plunkett,
Harrison College

Paula Potter,
Western Kentucky University

Cynthia Preston,
University of Northwestern Ohio

George Redmond,
Franklin University

Rosemarie Reynolds,
Embry Riddle Aeronautical
University

H. Lynn Richards,
Johnson County Community College

Leah Ritchie,
Salem State College

Gary B. Roberts,
Kennesaw State University

Barbara Rosenthal,
Miami Dade Community College/
Wolfson Campus

Gary Ross,
Barat College of DePaul University

Catherine Ruggieri,
St. John's University–New York

Storm Russo,
Valencia Community College

Cindy Ruszkowski,
Illinois State University

William Salyer,
Morris College

Diane R. Scott,
Wichita State University

Marianne Sebok,
Community College of Southern
Nevada

Thomas J. Shaughnessy,
Illinois Central College

Randi Sims,
Nova Southeastern University

Frederick J. Slack,
Indiana University of Pennsylvania

Erika E. Small,
Coastal Carolina University

Jim Smas,
Kent State University

Gerald F. Smith,
University of Northern Iowa

Mark Smith,
University of Southwest Louisiana

Shane Spiller,
Western Kentucky University

Jeff Stauffer,
Ventura College

Martin St. John,
Westmoreland County Community College

Raymond Stoudt,
DeSales University

Barb Stuart,
Daniels College of Business

Robert Scott Taylor,
Moberly Area Community College

Virginia Anne Taylor,
William Patterson University

Wynn Teasley,
University of West Florida

Marguerite Teubner,
Nassau Community College

Jerry Thomas,
Arapahoe Community College

Joseph Tomkiewicz,
East Carolina University

Robert Trumble,
Virginia Commonwealth University

Joy Turnheim Smith,
Elizabeth City State University

Isaiah Ugboro,
North Carolina Agricultural & Technical State University

Anthony Uremovic,
Joliet Junior College

Barry Van Hook,
Arizona State University

Susan Verhulst,
Des Moines Area Community College

Annie Viets,
University of Vermont

Tom Voigt Jr.,
Aurora University

Carolyn Waits,
Cincinnati State Technical & Community College

Bruce C. Walker,
University of Louisiana at Monroe

Tekle O. Wanorie,
Northwest Missouri State University

Charles Warren,
Salem State College

Kerry Webb,
Texas Woman's University

Velvet Weems-Landingham,
Kent State University–Geauga

Allen Weimer,
University of Tampa

David A. Wernick,
Florida International University

James Whelan,
Manhattan College

John Whitelock,
Community College of Baltimore/Catonsville Campus

Eric Williams,
University of Alabama, Birmingham

Wendy V. Wysocki,
Monroe County Community College

Mark Zorn,
Butler County Community College

The following professors also participated in an early focus group that helped drive the development of this text. We appreciate their suggestions and participation immensely:

Rusty Brooks,
Houston Baptist University

Kerry Carson,
University of Southwestern Louisiana

Sam Dumbar,
Delgado Community College

Subhash Durlabhji,
Northwestern State University

Robert Mullins,
Delgado Community College

Carl Phillips,
Southeastern Louisiana University

Allayne Pizzolatto,
Nicholls State University

Ellen White,
University of New Orleans

We would also like to thank the following students for participating in a very important focus group to gather feedback from the student reader's point of view:

Marcy Baasch,
Triton College

Diana Broeckel,
Triton College

Lurene Cornejo,
Moraine Valley Community College

Dave Fell,
Elgin Community College

Lydia Hendrix,
Moraine Valley Community College

Kristine Kurpiewski,
Oakton Community College

Michelle Monaco,
Moraine Valley Community College

Shannon Ramey,
Elgin Community College

Arpita Sikand,
Oakton Community College

Finally, we would like to thank our wives, Joyce and Stacey, for being understanding, patient, and encouraging throughout the process of writing this edition. Your love and support helped us endure the trials of completing this text.

We hope you enjoy reading and applying the book. Best wishes for success in your career.

Angelo Kinicki   Brian K. Williams

Introduction

1

The Exceptional Manager

What You Do, How You Do It

A One-Minute Guide to Success in This Class

Got one minute to read this section? It could mean the difference between getting an A instead of a B. Or a B instead of a C.

It is our desire *to make this book as practical as possible for you.* One place we do this is in the Manager's Toolbox, like this one, which appears at the beginning of every chapter and which offers practical advice appropriate to the subject matter you are about to explore. Here we show you how to be a success in this course.

Four Rules for Success

The following four rules will help you be successful in this (or any other) course.

- **Rule 1:** Attend every class. No cutting (skipping) allowed.
- **Rule 2:** Don't postpone studying, then cram the night before a test.
- **Rule 3:** Read or review lectures and readings more than once.
- **Rule 4:** Learn how to use this book.

How to Use This Book Most Effectively

When reading this book, follow the steps below:

- Get an overview of the chapter by reading over the first page, which contains the section headings and Major Questions.

- Read Forecast: What's Ahead in This Chapter.
- Look at the Major Question at the beginning of each section before you read it.
- Read the The Big Picture, which summarizes the section.
- Read the section itself (which is usually only two to six pages), *trying silently to answer the Major Question.* This is important!
- After reading all sections, use the Key Terms, Key Points, and Understanding the Chapter questions at the end of the chapter to see how well you know the concepts. Reread any material you're unsure about.

If you follow these steps consistently, you'll probably absorb the material well enough that you won't have to cram before an exam; you'll need only to lightly review it before the test.

For Discussion Do you sometimes (often?) postpone keeping up with coursework, then pull an "all-nighter" of studying to catch up before an exam? What do you think happens to people in business who do this?

FORECAST What's Ahead in This Chapter

We describe the rewards, benefits, and privileges managers might expect. We also describe the four principal functions of management—planning, organizing, leading, and controlling. We discuss the seven challenges to managers in today's world. We consider levels and areas of management. We describe the three roles managers must play. We describe the three skills required of a manager and the three roles managers play. Finally, we consider the contributions of entrepreneurship.

1.1   Management: What It Is, What Its Benefits Are

What are the rewards of being an exceptional manager?

THE BIG PICTURE

Management is defined as the pursuit of organizational goals efficiently and effectively. Organizations, or people who work together to achieve a specific purpose, value managers because of the multiplier effect: Good managers have an influence on the organization far beyond the results that can be achieved by one person acting alone. Managers are well paid, with the chief executive officers (CEOs) and presidents of even small and midsize businesses earning good salaries and many benefits.

When chief executive officer Mary Barra, 53, took the reins of Detroit-based General Motors in January 2014, she became the first female CEO of an American or any other global automaker. She also became only the 22nd woman at the helm of a Fortune 500 company, one of those 500 largest U.S. companies that appear on the prestigious annual list compiled by *Fortune* magazine. (Other big-time female CEOs: IBM's Virginia "Ginni" Rometty, Hewlett-Packard's Meg Whitman, Xerox's Ursula Burns, PepsiCo's Indra Nooyi, Kraft Foods's Irene Rosenfeld, Sunoco's Lynn Elsenhans.)

What kind of a person is Barra (pronounced *Bahr*-ra), a 30-year GM veteran? "She has a soft-spoken manner that belies her intensity on the job," says one report.[1] "She's the real deal, very down to earth," says another.[2] "Her open, relaxed manner has marked a clear contrast with the far more uptight style of many of the middle-aged men around her in General Motors's management," says a third.[3] Are these qualities—which a lot of people have—enough to propel one to the top of a great organization?

The Rise of the Die Maker's Daughter

The daughter of a die maker with a 39-year career in GM's Pontiac division, Barra grew up in suburban Detroit, joined GM at age 18 on the factory floor as an intern, graduated from General Motors Institute (now Kettering University) with a degree in electrical engineering, and then became a plant engineer at Pontiac. Spotting her talent, GM gave her a scholarship to Stanford University, where she earned a graduate degree in business.

She then began moving up the GM ladder, first as the executive assistant to the CEO, then as the company's head of human resources—formerly often as high as female executives ever got, in autos or many other industries. In 2011, her big break came when she was promoted to lead GM's $15 billion vehicle-development operations, a high-profile role that became the stepping-stone to CEO. In 2016, she was also made chairwoman of the board.[4]

The driving force. One quality that stands out about General Motors CEO Mary Barra is her obvious enthusiasm for cars. She is said to be given to talking excitedly about whatever car she is currently driving and what it demonstrates about GM's product line. Do you think passion about one's work is a necessary quality for managerial success?
© Mark Lennihan/AP Photo

Key to Career Growth: "Doing Things I've Never Done Before"

Did it help that, as one writer put it, Barra "had motor oil running through her veins for most of her life"?[5] No doubt it did. But there is another key to career growth—the ability to take risks. As IBM's Ginni Rometty, another female CEO, has said about herself, she has grown the most in her career because "I learned to always take on things I've never done before."[6] She has found that "you have to be very confident, even though you're so self-critical inside about what it is you may or may not know. . . . And that, to me, leads to taking risks."[7]

The ability to take risks—to embrace change and to keep going forward despite fears and internal criticism—is important to any manager's survival. As Rometty says, "growth and comfort do not coexist."

The Art of Management Defined

Is being an exceptional manager a gift, like a musician having perfect pitch? Not exactly. But in good part it may be an art.[8] Fortunately, it is one that is teachable.

Management, said one pioneer of management ideas, is "the art of getting things done through people."[9]

Getting things done. Through people. Thus, managers are task oriented, achievement oriented, and people oriented. And they operate within an **organization**—a group of people who work together to achieve some specific purpose.

More formally, **management** is defined as (1) the pursuit of organizational goals efficiently and effectively by (2) integrating the work of people through (3) planning, organizing, leading, and controlling the organization's resources.

Note the words *efficiently* and *effectively,* which basically mean "doing things right."

- **Efficiency—the means.** Efficiency is the means of attaining the organization's goals. To be **efficient** means to use resources—people, money, raw materials, and the like—wisely and cost-effectively.

- **Effectiveness—the ends.** Effectiveness regards the organization's ends, the goals. To be **effective** means to achieve results, to make the right decisions, and to successfully carry them out so that they achieve the organization's goals.

Good managers are concerned with trying to achieve both qualities. Often, however, organizations will erroneously strive for efficiency without being effective. Retired U.S. Army general Stanley McChrystal, former commander of all American and coalition forces in Afghanistan, suggests that effectiveness is a more important outcome in today's organizations.[10]

EXAMPLE

Efficiency versus Effectiveness: How Do Airlines Deal with "Seat Densification" and Other Passenger Complaints?

What do airline passengers complain about most? Cancellations, delays, and failed flight connections. Reservations, ticketing problems, and long telephone wait times. Boarding, baggage, and refund hassles.

And that's in addition to complaints about "seat densification," the polite term for the crowded seats in coach class.

How do the airlines handle such complaints? They say they're sorry.

Having representatives routinely say "I'm sorry" for service difficulties may be efficient for the airlines—even when the apologies are accompanied by gift cards, credits, and loyalty points—since it's a lot cheaper than, say, adding more reservation agents, flight crews, baggage handlers, and, of course, airplanes.[11] But it's not effective if it leaves us, the customers, fuming and less inclined to continue doing business.

Bad customer service hurts—in every industry. "Half of the people we surveyed reported leaving a store without making their intended purchase because of poor service," says *Consumer Reports*. "Fifty-seven percent were so steamed that they hung up the phone without a resolution."[12] Asserts one marketing vice president, "80% of CEOs believe they offer a superior customer experience; only 8% of their customers agree."[13]

Effective? Is this irate customer dealing with a company customer support system that is more efficient than effective? © Image Source RF

Efficiency: Saving Company Dollars. A lot of airlines favor efficiency over effectiveness in their customer service—in large part because there are some big events they can't control, such as bad weather. Between 2005 and 2014, there were an average of 335 weather-related disasters each year, up 14%

from the previous decade, and nearly double the level of the decade before that, according to a United Nations report.[14] In the winter of 2014–2015, for instance, relentless snow and ice storms led to the highest number of flight cancellations in 25 years—5.5% of the 1.37 million flights between December 1 and mid-January.

In addition, new government rules went into effect prohibiting airlines from keeping passengers on the tarmac for three hours or more, so airlines canceled blocks of flights rather than risk fines of up to $27,500 per passenger ($4.1 million for a planeload of 150 flyers). The government also implemented a new rule increasing the amount of rest pilots need, making it harder for the companies to operate an irregular schedule, as might follow stormy weather.

Finally, the discount carriers such as Spirit have forced big airlines such as Delta to compete on cheap price/less frills and packing more passengers into planes, particularly in coach. As a result, coach class is now known as "last class."[15] "That's been great for their bottom line," reports the Associated Press, "but has created a nightmare for passengers."[16]

Effectiveness: Retaining Customers and Their Dollars. Apologizing doesn't work when it's a canned response or half-hearted or insincere. "Customers know talk is cheap," says an apology critic.[17] Much better is the method employed by Southwest Airlines, which answered one flyer's complaint about an unpleasant flight by quickly and personally saying it was "truly sorry," addressing each issue he'd brought up, and giving him a credit equal to the value of his one-way fare. "Southwest admitted that there were mistakes, didn't make excuses, and offered sincere and profound apologies," the mollified passenger said.[18]

YOUR CALL

The average telephone wait time to reach a human agent at Southwest Airlines, according to Get2Human.com, was zero minutes and Alaska Air and Jet Blue each one minute.[19] Spirit Air, on the other hand, took 37 minutes and Air Canada 42 minutes.

Get2Human.com (or GetHuman.com) is a website that aims to convince enterprises, whether airlines or other kinds, that "providing high quality customer service and having satisfied customers costs much less than providing low quality customer service and having unsatisfied customers"—in other words, being more effective, not just efficient.

Get2Human also publishes the unpublicized codes for reaching a company's human operators and cut-through-automation tips. What recent unpleasant customer experience would you want to post on this website?

Why Organizations Value Managers: The Multiplier Effect

Some great achievements of history, such as scientific discoveries or works of art, were accomplished by individuals working quietly by themselves. But so much more has been achieved by people who were able to leverage their talents and abilities by being managers. For instance, of the top 10 great architectural wonders of the world named by the American Institute of Architects, none was built by just one person. All were triumphs of management, although some reflected the vision of an individual. (The wonders are the Great Wall of China, the Great Pyramid, Machu Picchu, the Acropolis, the Coliseum, the Taj Mahal, the Eiffel Tower, the Brooklyn Bridge, the Empire State Building, and Frank Lloyd Wright's Falling Water house in Pennsylvania.)

Good managers create value. The reason is that in being a manager you have a *multiplier effect:* Your influence on the organization is multiplied far beyond the results that can be achieved by just one person acting alone. Thus, while a solo operator such as a salesperson might accomplish many things and incidentally make a very good living, his or her boss could accomplish a great deal more—and could well earn two to seven times the income. And the manager will undoubtedly have a lot more influence.

Exceptional managers are in high demand. "The scarcest, most valuable resource in business is no longer financial capital," says a *Fortune* article. "It's talent. If you doubt that, just watch how hard companies are battling for the best people…. Talent of every type is in short supply, but the greatest shortage of all is skilled, effective managers."[20] Even in dismal economic times—maybe *especially* in such times—companies reach out for top talent.

The Financial Rewards of Being an Exceptional Manager

How well compensated are managers? According to the U.S. Bureau of Labor Statistics, the median weekly wage for American workers is $825, or $44,200 a year.[21] Education pays: The median 2015 yearly income for full-time workers with at least a bachelor's degree was $64,740, compared to $35,880 for high-school graduates.[22] People employed full-time in management, professional, and related occupations had the highest median incomes, $73,996 for men and $52,520 for women.

The business press frequently reports on the astronomical earnings of top chief executive officers. The top earner in 2014 was David M. Zaslav, CEO of Discovery Communications, whose total compensation topped $156.1 million.[23] However, this kind of huge payday isn't common. Median compensation for top-ranked CEOs in North America in 2015, based on a survey of 500 bosses of companies listed by Standard & Poor, was $10.8 million.[24] The more usual median wage for CEOs in 2015 was $737,613, according to Salary.com, and for general and operations managers $102,750, according to the Bureau of Labor Statistics.[25]

Managers farther down in the organization usually don't make this much, of course; nevertheless, they do fairly well compared with most workers. At the lower rungs, managers may make between $35,000 and $60,000 a year; in the middle levels, between $45,000 and $120,000. (For examples of managerial salaries, go to *www.bls.gov/ooh/management/home.htm.*[26])

There are also all kinds of fringe benefits and status rewards that go with being a manager, ranging from health insurance to stock options to large offices. And the higher you ascend in the management hierarchy, the more privileges may come your way: personal parking space, better furniture, on up to—for those on the top rung of big companies—company car and driver, corporate jet, company-paid resort-area villa, and even executive sabbaticals (months of paid time off to pursue alternative projects).

Best paid. David M. Zaslav, CEO of Discovery Communications, earned $156.1 million in 2014, making him the highest-paid manager in the United States that year. That's far, far greater than the largest salary paid to any NBA player in that period ($23.5 million to Kobe Bryant of the Los Angeles Lakers). Zaslav's base salary was just $3 million, but he received stock awards of $94.6 million, option awards of $50.5 million, other incentive pay of $6 million, and other compensation and perks of $1.9 million. What do you think your chances are of making even $100 million in your entire lifetime?
© Michael Kovac/Getty Images

What Are the Rewards of Studying and Practicing Management?

Are you studying management but have no plans to be a manager? Or are you trying to learn techniques and concepts that will help you be an exceptional management practitioner? Either way there are considerable rewards.

The Rewards of Studying Management Students sign up for an introductory management course for all kinds of reasons. Many, of course, are planning business careers, but others are taking it to fulfill a requirement or an elective. Some students are in technical or nonprofit fields—computer science, education, health, and the like—and never expect to have to supervise people.

Here are just a few of the payoffs of studying management as a discipline:

- **You will understand how to deal with organizations from the outside.** Since we all are in constant interaction with all kinds of organizations, it helps to understand how they work and how the people in them make decisions. Such knowledge may give you some defensive skills that you can use in dealing with organizations from the outside, as a customer or investor, for example.

- **You will understand how to relate to your supervisors.** Since most of us work in organizations and most of us have bosses, studying management will enable you to understand the pressures managers deal with and how they will best respond to you.

- **You will understand how to interact with coworkers.** The kinds of management policies in place can affect how your coworkers behave. Studying management can give you the understanding of teams and teamwork, cultural differences, conflict and stress, and negotiation and communication skills that will help you get along with fellow employees.

- **You will understand how to manage yourself in the workplace.** Management courses in general, and this book in particular, give you the opportunity to realize insights about yourself—your personality, emotions, values, perceptions, needs, and goals. We help you build your skills in areas such as self-management, listening, handling change, managing stress, avoiding groupthink, and coping with organizational politics.

The Rewards of Practicing Management   Many young people not only want to make money but make a difference.[27] As Swarthmore psychology professor Barry Schwartz, author of *Why We Work,* suggests, "We care about more than money. We want work that is challenging and engaging, that enables us to exercise some discretion and control over what we do, and that provides us with opportunities to learn and grow."[28] Becoming a management practitioner offers many rewards apart from money and status, as follows:

- **You and your employees can experience a sense of accomplishment.** Every successful goal accomplished provides you not only with personal satisfaction but also with the satisfaction of all those employees you directed who helped you accomplish it.

- **You can stretch your abilities and magnify your range.** Every promotion up the hierarchy of an organization stretches your abilities, challenges your talents and skills, and magnifies the range of your accomplishments.

- **You can build a catalog of successful products or services.** Every product or service you provide—the personal Eiffel Tower or Empire State Building you build, as it were—becomes a monument to your accomplishments. Indeed, studying management may well help you in running your own business.

- **You can become a mentor and help others.** According to one survey, 84% of workers who had a **mentor**—an experienced person who provided guidance to someone new to the work world—said the mentor helped them advance their careers.[29] ●

Mentoring. Matthew Wardenaar (right), whose California company produces Tagged, an app that helps users meet new people, gives Mohammed Abdulla assistance (with Google Glass) during a session of the Hidden Genius Project, a mentoring organization that gives underrepresented minorities guidance in moving into technology and science careers. Is helping others one of your life goals? © Ian C. Bates/San Francisco Chronicle/Corbis

1.2 What Managers Do: The Four Principal Functions

MAJOR QUESTION   **What would I actually *do*—that is, what would be my four principal functions—as a manager?**

THE BIG PICTURE

Management has four functions: *planning, organizing, leading,* and *controlling.*

What do you as a manager do to "get things done"—that is, achieve the stated goals of the organization you work for? You perform what is known as the **management process,** also called the **four management functions:** planning, organizing, leading, and controlling. (The abbreviation "POLC" may help you to remember them.)

As the diagram illustrates, all these functions affect one another, are ongoing, and are performed simultaneously. *(See Figure 1.1.)*

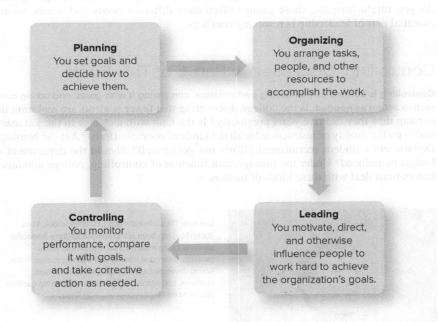

Planning
You set goals and decide how to achieve them.

Organizing
You arrange tasks, people, and other resources to accomplish the work.

Controlling
You monitor performance, compare it with goals, and take corrective action as needed.

Leading
You motivate, direct, and otherwise influence people to work hard to achieve the organization's goals.

FIGURE 1.1

The management process
What you as a manager do to "get things done"—to achieve the stated goals of your organization.

Although the process of management can be quite complex, these four functions represent its essential principles. Indeed, as a glance at our text's table of contents shows, they form four of the part divisions of the book. Let's consider what the four functions are, using the management (or "administration," as it is called in nonprofit organizations) of your college to illustrate them.

Planning: Discussed in Part 3 of This Book

Planning is defined as setting goals and deciding how to achieve them. Your college was established for the purpose of educating students, and its present managers, or administrators, now must decide the best way to accomplish this. Which of several possible degree programs should be offered? Should the college be a residential or a commuter campus? What sort of students should be recruited and admitted? What kind of faculty should be hired? What kind of buildings and equipment are needed?

Organizing: Discussed in Part 4 of This Book

Organizing is defined as arranging tasks, people, and other resources to accomplish the work. College administrators must determine the tasks to be done, by whom, and what the reporting hierarchy is to be. Should the institution be organized into schools with departments, with department chairpersons reporting to deans who in return report to vice presidents? Should the college hire more full-time instructors than part-time instructors? Should English professors teach just English literature or also composition, developmental English, and "first-year experience" courses?

Leading: Discussed in Part 5 of This Book

Leading is defined as motivating, directing, and otherwise influencing people to work hard to achieve the organization's goals. At your college, leadership begins, of course, with the president (who would be the chief executive officer, or CEO, in a for-profit organization). He or she is the one who must inspire faculty, staff, students, alumni, wealthy donors, and residents of the surrounding community to help realize the college's goals. As you might imagine, these groups often have different needs and wants, so an essential part of leadership is resolving conflicts.

Controlling: Discussed in Part 6 of This Book

Controlling is defined as monitoring performance, comparing it with goals, and taking corrective action as needed. Is the college discovering that fewer students are majoring in nursing than they did five years previously? Is the fault with a change in the job market? with the quality of instruction? with the kinds of courses offered? Are the Nursing Department's student recruitment efforts not going well? Should the department's budget be reduced? Under the management function of controlling, college administrators must deal with these kinds of matters. ●

Leading. The co-founder and CEO of Facebook, Mark Zuckerberg has been acknowledged for three leadership qualities: being a hard worker, a pupil who seeks guidance from great leaders, and a strong communicator, having developed a speaking style that is "poised, confident, and articulate."[30] Are these leadership qualities you could develop? © Ben Margot/AP Photo

1.3 Seven Challenges to Being an Exceptional Manager

MAJOR QUESTION

Challenges can make one feel alive. What are seven challenges I could look forward to as a manager?

THE BIG PICTURE

Seven challenges face any manager: You need to manage for competitive advantage—to stay ahead of rivals. You need to manage for the effects of globalization and of information technology. You need to manage for diversity in race, ethnicity, gender, and so on, because the future won't resemble the past. You always need to manage to maintain ethical standards. You need to manage for sustainability—to practice sound environmental policies. Finally, you need to manage for the achievement of your own happiness and life goals.

Would you agree that the ideal state that many people seek is an emotional zone somewhere between boredom and anxiety? That's the view of psychologist Mihaly Csikszentmihalyi (pronounced Me-*high* Chick-sent-me-*high*-ee), founder of the Quality of Life Research Center at Claremont Graduate University.[31]

Boredom, he says, may arise because skills and challenges are mismatched: You are exercising your high level of skill in a job with a low level of challenge, such as licking envelopes. Anxiety arises when one has low levels of skill but a high level of challenge, such as (for many people) suddenly being called upon to give a rousing speech to strangers.

As a manager, could you achieve a balance between these two states—boredom and anxiety, or action and serenity? Certainly managers have enough challenges to keep their lives more than mildly interesting. Let's see what they are.

Challenge #1: Managing for Competitive Advantage—Staying Ahead of Rivals

Competitive advantage is the ability of an organization to produce goods or services more effectively than competitors do, thereby outperforming them. This means an organization must stay ahead in four areas: (1) being responsive to customers, (2) innovation, (3) quality, and (4) efficiency.

The Struggle for Competitive Advantage: Airbnb Shakes Up the Hotel Business

EXAMPLE

In San Francisco in 2007, jobless industrial designers Brian Chesky and Joe Gebbia, wondering how to make the rent, realized that a major design conference was about to be held in the city and that hotel rooms would be scarce. Gebbia had three air mattresses and suggested turning their apartment into an "air bed and breakfast." Within three days they had a quicky website up and had booked three guests, each paying about $70 for several nights.[32]

Thus was born Airbnb, which today appeals to Millennials (those born 1982–2004) and business travelers with $18 shared downtown living rooms but will even serve Beyoncé Knowles, in northern California for a halftime appearance at the 2016 Super Bowl, with a $10,000-a-night estate in the posh Silicon Valley enclave of Los Altos Hills. Offering more than a million rooms in homes, apartments, even treehouses or barns—indeed, even European castles—in 34,000 cities in 190 countries ranging from Cuba to Israel's West Bank, the company is valued at $20 billion.[33]

The Rise of the New Sharing Economy. Airbnb represents an example of the *sharing economy, also known as collaborative* or peer-to-peer marketplaces, a technological variation on past behavior. "Peer-to-peer lodging has been around for quite a while," points out one writer. "For hundreds of years, family-owned boardinghouses were the lodging alternative for frugal travelers; homeowners listed their spare rooms in newspapers; . . . and European families often purchased second homes together."[34]

What is different about today's sharing economy is that ordinary people can now take advantage of the Internet and widespread use of credit cards to effectively turn their homes into hotel rooms. (The sharing economy has also affected other industries, as Uber and Lyft have turned personal cars into taxis, as we discuss in Chapter 10.)[35]

Trouble for the Hotel Industry. Airbnb has had a major impact on the hotel industry, offering more places to sleep than Hilton, Hyatt, or Wyndham combined. In the beginning there were few complaints from traditional hotels, although there is evidence that the greater room supply created by Airbnb helped restrain traditional hotel prices.[36] Some small hotels even started joining the service themselves, such as the Box House Hotel in Brooklyn, New York.

Before long, however, hotels began to feel the upstart's effects and now are fighting back.[37] Large hotel chains have launched new chains (such as Tru by Hilton) aimed at Airbnb's core market of Millennials looking for a lodging experience suited to their tastes and budget. They also started creating "micro-hotels," such as Pod, Yotel, and citizenM, hotels with tiny rooms (think 50 square feet) but big public spaces that appeal to social travelers.

Some hotels now offer "pillow menus," allowing guests to choose from a range of pillow firmnesses and shapes to suit different sleep habits. Some remade their rooms with flexible tables, laptop trays, and abundant electrical outlets to accommodate different work styles. Roughly 40 hotels worldwide joined in creating LobbyFriend, a temporary social network that enables users to get information on nearby events, as well as send messages to other guests.

The hotel industry also funded research that suggests some Airbnb operators are running "illegal" hotels.[38] And they have lobbied for laws that will stop or slow Airbnb's growth by restricting the apartments and homes that can be listed on the service.

YOUR CALL

Airbnb is an example of *disruptive innovation,* a process in which a product or service takes root initially in simple applications at the bottom of the market (as in Chesky and Gebbia providing air mattresses on the floor for temporary guests) and then relentlessly moves up market, eventually displacing established competitors. The notion of "disruptive innovation" by computer technology is a far-reaching development in the ongoing struggle of organizations to stay ahead of rivals by maintaining competitive advantage, and we describe the concept further in Chapter 10.

Which sector, Airbnb or hotels, do you think will prevail in the lodging industry?

Competitive advantage? Do you think traditional hotels will still exist 10 years from now? © Antenna/Getty Images RF

1. Being Responsive to Customers The first law of business is *Take care of the customer.* Without customers—buyers, clients, consumers, shoppers, users, patrons, guests, investors, or whatever they're called—sooner or later there will be no organization. Nonprofit organizations are well advised to be responsive to their "customers," too, whether they're called citizens, members, students, patients, voters, rate-payers, or whatever, since they are the justification for the organizations' existence.

2. Innovation **Finding ways to deliver new or better goods or services is called innovation.** No organization, for-profit or nonprofit, can allow itself to become complacent—especially when rivals are coming up with creative ideas. "Innovate or die" is an important adage for any manager.

We discuss innovation in Chapter 10.

3. Quality If your organization is the only one of its kind, customers may put up with products or services that are less than stellar (as they have with some airlines that have a near monopoly on flights out of certain cities), but only because they have no choice. But if another organization comes along and offers a better-quality travel experience, TV program, cut of meat, computer software, or whatever, you may find your company falling behind. Making improvements in quality has become an important management idea in recent times, as we shall discuss.

4. Efficiency A generation ago, organizations rewarded employees for their length of service. Today, however, the emphasis is on efficiency: Companies strive to produce goods or services as quickly as possible using as few employees (and raw materials) as possible. Although a strategy that downgrades the value of employees might ultimately backfire—resulting in the loss of essential experience and skills and even customers—an organization that is overstaffed may not be able to compete with leaner, meaner rivals. This is the reason why, for instance, today many companies rely so much on temp (temporary) workers.[39]

Challenge #2: Managing for Information Technology—Dealing with the "New Normal"

The challenge of managing for information technology, not to mention other technologies affecting your business, will require your unflagging attention. Most important is the **Internet, the global network of independently operating but interconnected computers, linking hundreds of thousands of smaller networks around the world.**

By 2019, consumers worldwide are projected to spend $3.55 trillion online, double that of 2015.[40]

This kind of **e-commerce, or electronic commerce—the buying and selling of goods or services over computer networks**—has reshaped entire industries and revamped the very notion of what a company is. More important than e-commerce, information technology has led to the growth of **e-business, using the Internet to facilitate every aspect of running a business.** Because the Internet so dramatically lowers the cost of communication, it can radically alter any activity that depends heavily on the flow of information. The result is that disruption has become the "new normal," according to Forrester Research.[41]

Some of the implications of information technology that we will discuss throughout the book are as follows:

- **Far-ranging electronic management: e-communication all the time.** Using mobile devices such as smartphones and tablets, 21st-century managers will need to become masters of electronic communication, able to create powerful messages to create, motivate, and lead teams of specialists all over the world. Their means for doing so will range from **e-mail, electronic-mail messages and documents transmitted over a computer network;** to **texting, quick text messages exchanged among smartphones;** and **social media, Internet-based and mobile technologies such as Facebook and Twitter for generating interactive dialogue with others on a network.** Getting the right balance is important, because many messages may be useful, but many are not. Employees can lose valuable time and productivity when dealing with excessive and unimportant e-mail and text messages, leading to increased conflict and stress.[42]

- **More and more data: challenges to decision making.** The digital universe is growing 40% a year, according to IDC, and by 2020, it will contain nearly as many digital bits as there are stars in the universe.[43] Ninety percent of generated data from now on, says one source, "will be unstructured and this includes tweets, photos, customer purchase history, and even customer service call logs."[44] The Internet, then, not only speeds everything up, it also through **cloud computing—the storing of software and data on gigantic collections of computers located away from a company's principal site** (out there somewhere, "in the cloud")—and huge, interconnected **databases—computerized collections of interrelated files—**can assemble astonishing quantities of information and make them available to us instantaneously. This has led to the phenomenon known as **Big Data, stores of data so vast that conventional database management systems cannot handle them,** and so very sophisticated analysis software and supercomputers are required. The challenge: How do we deal with this massive amount of data to make useful decisions without violating people's right to privacy? We discuss **Big Data** in Chapter 7.

- **The rise of artificial intelligence: more automation in the workforce.** "Software and automation—think self-driving cars, robotic factories, and artificially intelligent reservationists," writes Thomas Friedman, "are not only replacing blue-collar jobs at a faster rate, but now also white-collar skills."[45] **Artificial intelligence (AI) is the discipline concerned with creating computer systems that simulate human reasoning and sensation,** as represented by robots, natural language processing, pattern recognition, and similar technologies. The job losses caused by automation among autoworkers, film processors, travel agents, and the like will probably extend to other fields as robot surgeons, driverless cars, drones (pilotless aircraft), and molecule-sized nanobots (used in medicine) come into use.[46] What will be the implications of these events for you as a manager for staffing and training employees and for your own professional development?

- **Organizational changes: shifts in structure, jobs, goals, and management.** With computers and telecommunications technology, organizations and teams become "virtual"; they are no longer as bound by time zones and locations. Employees, for instance, may **telecommute, or work from home or remote locations using a variety of information technologies.** Telecommuting was found to enhance employee satisfaction and performance.[47] Meetings may be conducted via **videoconferencing, using video and audio links along with computers to let people in different locations see, hear, and talk with one another.** Goal setting and feedback will be conducted via web-based software programs such as eWorkbench, which enables managers to create and track employee goals. Such managers will also rely on **project management software, programs for planning and scheduling the people, costs, and resources to complete a project on time.**

- **Knowledge management and collaborative computing.** The forms of interaction just described will require managers and employees to be more flexible, and there will be an increased emphasis on **knowledge management—the implementing of systems and practices to increase the sharing of knowledge and information throughout an organization.** In addition, **collaborative computing, using state-of-the-art computer software and hardware, will help people work better together.** Many hospitals, for example, now knit various functions together—patient histories, doctors' orders, lab results, prescription information, billing—in a single information system, parts of which patients can access themselves to schedule appointments, question doctors, and request prescription refills.

Challenge #3: Managing for Diversity— The Future Won't Resemble the Past

In 2014, 42 million people in the United States were foreign born, representing 13.3% of the population. In 2020, there will be nearly 48 million foreign born, representing 14.3% of the population, and by 2060 they are projected to be 18.8%.[48]

But greater changes are yet to come. By mid-century, the mix of American racial or ethnic groups will change considerably, with the United States becoming half (54%) racial or ethnic minority. Non-Hispanic whites are projected to decrease from 62% of the population in 2014 to 43% in 2060. African Americans will increase from 13% to 14%, Asians from 5% to 9%, and Hispanics (who may be of any race) from 17% to 29%.[49]

In addition, in the coming years there will be a different mix of women, immigrants, and older people in the general population, as well as in the workforce. For instance, in 2030, nearly one in five U.S. residents is expected to be 65 and older. This age group is projected to increase to 98.1 million in 2060, more than doubling the number in 2014 (40.1 million).[50]

Some scholars think that diversity and variety in staffing produce organizational strength, as we consider elsewhere.[51] Clearly, however, the challenge to the manager of the near future is to maximize the contributions of employees diverse in gender, age, race, ethnicity, and sexual orientation. We discuss this matter in more detail in Chapter 11.

Challenge #4: Managing for Globalization— The Expanding Management Universe

When you ask some Russians "How are you?" the response may not be a simple "Fine" but rather the complete truth as to how they really feel—"a blunt pronouncement of dissatisfaction punctuated by, say, the details of any recent digestive troubles," as one American world traveler explained it.[52] And when you meet Cambodians or Burmese and are asked "Have you eaten yet?" you should not mistake this as an invitation to lunch—all it means is just "Hello."[53]

The point is this: Verbal expressions and gestures don't have the same meaning to everyone throughout the world. Not understanding such differences can affect how well organizations manage globally.

American firms have been going out into the world in a major way, even as the world has been coming to us—leading to what *New York Times* columnist Thomas Friedman has called, in *The World Is Flat,* a phenomenon in which globalization has leveled (made "flat") the competitive playing fields between industrial and emerging-market countries.[54] Managing for globalization will be a complex, ongoing challenge, as we discuss at length in Chapter 4.[55]

Cross-border burger business. American businesspeople operating overseas often face unique problems. The manager of this Johnny Rockets hamburger store, which opened in Lagos, Nigeria, in 2012, found that to achieve an authentic, U.S.-style taste he needed to fly in the toppings—onions, mushrooms, and iceberg lettuce—which meant that he had to start prices at $14 for a single-patty burger. © Sunday Alamba/AP Photo

Challenge #5: Managing for Ethical Standards

With the pressure to meet sales, production, and other targets, managers can find themselves confronting ethical dilemmas. What do you do when, as a manager for a cruise line, say, you learn that an important safety measure will have to be skipped if a 4,200-passenger cruise ship is to sail on time?[56] As a sales manager, how much should you allow your sales reps to criticize the competition? How much leeway do you have in giving gifts to prospective clients in a foreign country to try to land a contract? In an era of climate change, with changing temperatures and rising sea levels, what is your responsibility to "act green"—avoid company policies that are damaging to the environment?

Ethical behavior is not just a nicety; it is a very important part of doing business. This was certainly made clear in December 2008, when financier Bernard Madoff confessed that his investments were all "one big lie"—not investments at all, but rather a $50 billion scheme *(Ponzi scheme),* using cash from newer investors to pay off older ones. A few months later, this perpetrator of the world's biggest fraud, then age 71, was sentenced to 150 years in prison.

Madoff joined a long list of famous business scoundrels of the early 21st century: Tyco International CEO Dennis Kozlowski (now on parole after serving prison time for grand larceny, securities fraud, and tax evasion), WorldCom head Bernard Ebbers (doing 25 years for fraud), Adelphia CEO John Rigas (15 years for conspiracy and bank fraud), former Enron chief Jeffrey Skilling (24 years for similar white-collar crimes), and Galleon Group hedge fund head Raj Rajaratnam and Goldman Sachs director Rajat Gupta (11 years each for insider trading).

Of course, business crime is not perpetrated just by respectable-looking people wearing suits. Hippie entrepreneur Ross Ulbricht, then 29, was arrested in late 2013 for allegedly being the founder of Silk Road, described as an "online illegal-goods bazaar that had been dubbed the eBay of vice," from which he purportedly made nearly half a billion dollars in under three years by selling drugs.[57] He was sentenced to life in prison and ordered to forfeit $183 million. "I wish I could go back and convince myself to take a different path," he said. "I've ruined my life."[58]

We consider ethics in Chapter 3 and elsewhere in the book.

Dread Pirate. Ross Ulbricht, a former Eagle Scout and holder of a master's degree in materials science, was charged by federal prosecutors with being a drug kingpin and attempted murderer named Dread Pirate Roberts. Put on trial as the founder of Silk Road, an online site for selling narcotics, in 2015 at age 31 he was sentenced to life in prison for drug trafficking, computer hacking, money laundering, and running a continuing criminal conspiracy. © Erich Schlegel/Corbis

PRACTICAL ACTION

Preparing Yourself to Behave Right When You're Tempted to Cheat

There are all kinds of things that influence people to cheat. They may cheat more in the afternoon than in the morning, perhaps because mental fatigue sets in as the day wears on.[59] They may cheat more when technology makes it easy. (Access to copy/paste tools was associated with a higher rate of cheating.)[60] They may even cheat because it makes them feel good. (Really! Cheaters in one study reported more positive feelings than subjects who acted honestly.)[61]

Of course, just because somehow you feel okay about cheating doesn't mean it's right, or, from a hard-headed business point of view, even effective—either for you or for the organization you work for.[62] Did you know, for instance, that you can be fired for lying on a job application or resume?

Learning to Be Ethical. Concerned about transgressions in the managerial world, some of the top U.S. researchers in business ethics in January 2014 introduced a new website, EthicalSystems.org (*www.ethicalsystems.org*). One of its purposes is to examine the problem that, as one article describes it, "how we think we're going to act when faced with a moral decision and how we really do act are often vastly different."[63] Originally business ethics grew out of philosophy and was concerned with the right thing to do. Now research is directed toward the underlying reasons people act the way they do, to develop a more psychologically realistic approach and learn what tools will nudge people toward right behavior.

Doing Right versus Being Liked. When people predict how they're going to act in a given situation, "the 'should' self dominates—we should be fair, we should be generous, we should assert our values," says business ethics professor Ann E. Tenbrunsel. "But when the time for action comes, the 'want' self dominates—I don't want to look like a fool, I don't want to be punished."[64] Thus, you may see some wrong occur (such as an act of cheating) and actually mean to do something about it, but can't quite figure how—and then the moment passes and you let it go and tell yourself that what you did was okay.

YOUR CALL

How can you learn to be ethical? First, you need to be aware of when you are apt not to speak up about a matter of wrongdoing—as when it might alienate your friends ("No one will speak to me after this"), when it might cause others to disrespect you ("I'm going to look like an idiot"), or when an authority figure is present ("This will get me fired"). Once you become aware of such thoughts, you need to try to override them, letting the discomfort you're experiencing signal you that you need to be courageous and take action, not just lapse into inaction. Can you tell yourself how you should—and must—behave the next time you're tempted to cheat or see someone cheating?

Challenge #6: Managing for Sustainability— The Business of Green

An apparently changing climate, bringing increased damage from hurricanes, floods, and fires throughout the United States and the world, has brought the issue of "being green" to increased prominence. Following *The World Is Flat*, Friedman wrote *Hot, Flat, and Crowded*, urging a strategy of "Geo-Greenism" in addressing the crises of destabilizing climate change and rising competition for energy.[65] Earlier former U.S. Vice President Al Gore's documentary film *An Inconvenient Truth*, along with his book by the same name, further popularized the concepts of global climate change and the idea of sustainability as a business model.[66]

Our economic system has brought prosperity, but it has also led to unsustainable business practices because it has assumed that natural resources are limitless, which they are not. **Sustainability is defined as economic development that meets the needs of the present without compromising the ability of future generations to meet their own needs.**[67] A number of companies—from PepsiCo to Walmart to UPS—have recognized that corporations have a responsibility to address the causes of climate change.[68] Earlier, the U.S. Chamber of Commerce, which is supposed to represent the views of American business, expressed strong resistance to climate change legislation.[69] However, several companies—Levi Strauss, Apple, Tiffany, Exelon, Pacific Gas & Electric, PNM Resources, and Mohawk Fine Papers—resigned from the Chamber in protest. Perhaps, then, business can begin to take the lead.

Challenge #7: Managing for Happiness and Meaningfulness

Which would you rather have, a happy life or a meaningful life?

One study found that "Happiness was linked to being a taker rather than a giver, whereas meaningfulness went with being a giver rather than a taker," as a study author put it.[70] Happiness is getting what you want, of having your desires fulfilled. Meaningfulness—which may not always make you happy—is achieving a valued sense of one's self and one's purpose within the larger context of life and community. Research clearly shows that a sense of meaningfulness in your life is associated with better health, work and life satisfaction, and performance.[71]

Many people find being a manager doesn't make them happy.[72] They may complain that they have to go to too many meetings, that they can't do enough for their employees, that they are caught in the middle between bosses and subordinates. They may feel, at a time when Dilbert cartoons have created such an unflattering portrayal of managers, that they lack respect. They may decide that, despite the greater income, money doesn't buy happiness.[73]

On the other hand, being a manager can be one of the greatest avenues to a meaningful life, particularly if you are working within a supportive or interesting organizational culture. (We discuss company culture, or style, in Chapter 8.) As Oakland, California, productivity-improvement expert Odette Pollar has stated, being a manager is "an opportunity to counsel, motivate, advise, guide, empower, and influence large groups of people. These important skills can be used in business as well as in personal and volunteer activities." And, we might add, in nonprofit organizations as well. "If you truly like people," she goes on, "and enjoy mentoring and helping others to grow and thrive, management is a great job."[74]

How Strong Is Your Motivation to Be a Manager? The First Self-Assessment

As we stated at the beginning of this chapter, it is our desire to make this book *as practical as possible* for you. As an important means of advancing this goal, we developed 57 **self-assessments**—two to four per chapter—which allow you to gauge how you feel about the material you are reading and how you can make use of it.

Go to the self-assessment website at *connect.mheducation.com*, complete the assessment, then answer the self-assessment questions in the book. (Note: These assessments are only available if your instructor uses Connect and assigns them to you.) Taking them is a valuable way to develop your self-awareness and interpersonal skills. The first one assesses your motivation to lead. Do you desire to hold leadership positions? Find out by taking the self-assessment. ●

⚡ connect SELF-ASSESSMENT 1.1

How Strong Is My Motivation to Lead?

Please be prepared to answer these questions if your instructor has assigned Self-Assessment 1.1 in Connect.

Are you motivated to lead others? Go to connect.mheducation.com and take the self-assessment. When you're done, answer the following questions:

1. Do results match your desire to assume leadership roles at school, work, and home? Explain.

2. Which of the three dimensions do you think is most likely to affect your future success as a leader? Discuss.

3. You can increase your motivation to lead by increasing the scores on the three lowest-rated items in the survey. Identify these items and develop a plan for how you can change your behavior in leadership situations at school and work. Work the plan and get feedback about your effectiveness.

1.4 Pyramid Power: Levels and Areas of Management

MAJOR QUESTION

What are the levels and areas of management I need to know to move up, down, and sideways?

THE BIG PICTURE

Within an organization, there are four levels of managers: *top, middle,* and *first-line managers* as well as *team leaders.* Managers may also be *general managers,* or they may be *functional managers,* responsible for just one organizational activity, such as Research & Development, Marketing, Finance, Production, or Human Resources. Managers may work for for-profit, nonprofit, or mutual-benefit organizations.

The workplace of the future may resemble a symphony orchestra, famed management theorist Peter Drucker said.[75] Employees, especially so-called knowledge workers— those who have a great deal of technical skills—can be compared to concert musicians. Their managers can be seen as conductors.

In Drucker's analogy, musicians are used for some pieces of music—that is, work projects—and not others, and they are divided into different sections (teams) based on their instruments. The conductor's role is not to play each instrument better than the musicians but to lead them all through the most effective performance of a particular work.

This model differs from the traditional pyramid-like organizational model, where one leader sits at the top, with layers of managers beneath, each of whom must report to and justify his or her work to the manager above (what's called *accountability,* as we discuss in Chapter 8). We therefore need to take a look at the traditional arrangement first.

The Traditional Management Pyramid: Levels and Areas

A new Silicon Valley technology start-up company staffed by young people in sandals and shorts may be so small and so loosely organized that only one or two members may be said to be a manager. General Motors or the U.S. Army, in contrast, has thousands of managers doing thousands of different things. Is there a picture we can draw that applies to all the different kinds of organizations and describes them in ways that make sense? Yes: by levels and by areas, as the pyramid shows. *(See Figure 1.2.)*

Four Levels of Management

Not everyone who works in an organization is a manager, of course, but those who are may be classified into four levels—top, middle, and first-line managers and team leaders.

Top Managers: Determining Overall Direction Their offices may be equipped with expensive leather chairs and have lofty views. Or, as with one Internet company, they may have plastic lawn chairs in the CEO's office and beat-up furniture in the lobby. Whatever their decor, an organization's top managers tend to have titles such as "chief executive officer (CEO)," "chief operating officer (COO)," "president," and "senior vice president."

Some may be the stars in their fields, the men and women whose pictures appear on the covers of business magazines, people such as Nike CEO Mark Parker or IBM CEO Virginia Rommety or Lucasfilm president Kathleen Kennedy or Apple CEO Tim Cook, all of whom have appeared on the front of *Fortune.* As we've seen, the median yearly salary for CEOs in 2015 was $737,613 and for general and operations managers $102,750, and can range up to the millions for top executives in large companies.[76]

FIGURE 1.2

The levels and areas of management

Top managers make long-term decisions, middle managers implement those decisions, and first-line managers make short-term decisions. Team leaders facilitate team activities toward achieving a goal.

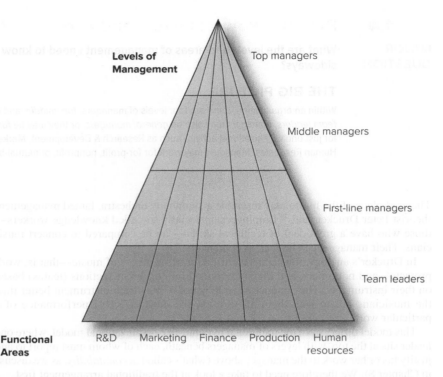

Levels of Management

Top managers

Middle managers

First-line managers

Team leaders

Functional Areas

R&D   Marketing   Finance   Production   Human resources

Successful top manager. India-born Satya Nadella, who joined Microsoft in 1992, became CEO of the technology company in early 2014 and has helped transition it to cloud computing. His net worth in 2016 was $45 million. Do you see yourself joining a company and staying with it for life, as Nadella has (after an earlier job at Sun Microsystems), or is that even possible anymore? © Justin Sullivan/Getty Images

Top managers make long-term decisions about the overall direction of the organization and establish the objectives, policies, and strategies for it. They need to pay a lot of attention to the environment outside the organization, being alert for long-run opportunities and problems and devising strategies for dealing with them. Thus, executives at this level must be future oriented, dealing with uncertain, highly competitive conditions.

These people stand at the summit of the management pyramid. But the nature of a pyramid is that the farther you climb, the less space remains at the top. Thus, most pyramid climbers never get to the apex. However, that doesn't mean that you shouldn't try. Indeed, you might end up atop a much smaller pyramid of some other organization than the one you started out in—and happier with the result.

Middle Managers: Implementing Policies and Plans   **Middle managers** implement the policies and plans of the top managers above them and supervise and coordinate the activities of the first-line managers below them. Titles might include "plant manager," "district manager," and "regional manager," among others. In the nonprofit world, middle managers may have titles such as "clinic director," "dean of student services," and the like. Their salaries may range from under $45,000 up to $120,000 a year.

Middle managers are critical for organizational success because they implement the strategic plans created by CEOs and top managers. (Strategic planning is discussed in Chapter 6.) In other words, these managers have the type of **"high-touch" jobs—dealing with people rather than computer screens or voice-response systems**—that can directly affect employees, customers, and suppliers.[77]

First-Line Managers: Directing Daily Tasks   The job titles at the bottom of the managerial pyramid tend to be on the order of "department head," "foreman" or "forewoman," or "supervisor"—clerical supervisor, production supervisor, research supervisor, and so on. Indeed, *supervisor* is the name often given to first-line managers as a whole. Their salaries may run from $35,000 to $65,000 a year.

Following the plans of middle and top managers, **first-line managers** make short-term operating decisions, directing the daily tasks of nonmanagerial personnel, who are, of course, all those people who work directly at their jobs but don't oversee the work of others.

No doubt the job of first-line manager will be the place where you would start your managerial career. This can be a valuable experience because it will be the training and testing ground for your management ideas.

Team Leaders: Facilitating Team Activities   Not all companies have *teams*—small groups of people with complementary skills who are committed to a common purpose—but teams and teamwork are largely the standard way of operating in today's organizations. (Teams are thoroughly discussed in Chapter 13.)

Members of a team generally report to a first-line manager, who has the authority to hire and fire, controls resources, and is responsible for the team's performance. But one of the members of the team may be charged with being the **team leader, a manager who is responsible for facilitating team activities toward achieving key results.** Team leaders may not have authority over other team members, but they are expected to provide guidance, instruction, and direction to the others; to coordinate team efforts; to resolve conflicts; to represent the team to the first-level manager; and to make decisions in the absence of consensus.

CEO of a no-bosses company. In 1999, at age 24, Tony Hsieh (pronounced *Shay*) sold an advertising network he co-founded for $265 million and then joined Zappos.com, the Nevada online shoe and clothing retailer, where he rose to CEO. In a radical experiment called *holocracy*, Zappos eliminated job titles and its own organization hierarchy. Instead, employees join various impermanent democratic assemblies called "circles," where they propose their own job descriptions, ratify the roles of others, and decide what projects the group should undertake. Would you be happy working in such a seemingly unstructured organization?[78]
© Charley Gallay/Getty Images

Areas of Management: Functional Managers versus General Managers

We can represent the levels of management by slicing the organizational pyramid horizontally. We can also slice the pyramid vertically to represent the organization's departments or functional areas, as we did in Figure 1.2.

In a for-profit technology company, these might be *Research & Development, Marketing, Finance, Production,* and *Human Resources.* In a nonprofit college, these might be *Faculty, Student Support Staff, Finance, Maintenance,* and *Administration.* Whatever the names of the departments, the organization is run by two types of managers—functional and general. (These are line managers, with authority to direct employees. Staff managers mainly assist line managers.)

Functional Managers: Responsible for One Activity   If your title is Vice President of Production, Director of Finance, or Administrator for Human Resources, you are a functional manager. **A functional manager is responsible for just one organizational activity.** Google is particularly noteworthy for its unusual functional management job titles, such as Fitness Program Manager, Green Team Lead, and Vice President of Search Products & User Experience. Yahoo! also has unusual functional titles, such as VP of Talent Acquisition, VP Consumer Platforms, and VP of Research for Europe & LatAm.

General Managers: Responsible for Several Activities   If you are working in a small organization of, say, 100 people and your title is Executive Vice President, you are probably a general manager over several departments, such as Production and Finance and Human Resources. **A general manager is responsible for several organizational activities.**

At the top of the pyramid, general managers are those who seem to be the subject of news stories in magazines such as *Bloomberg Businessweek, Fortune, Forbes,* and *Inc.* Examples are big-company CEOs Denise Morrison of Campbell Soup and Jeff Bezos of Amazon.com, as well as small-company CEOs such as Gayle Martz, who heads New York–based Sherpa's Pet Trading Co., which sells travel carriers for dogs and cats. But not all general managers are in for-profit organizations.

Nonprofit general manager. A general manager is responsible for several organizational activities. As CEO of the nonprofit New York Stem Cell Foundation, Susan L. Solomon does a lot of fundraising, along with directing the activities of the foundation's research scientists, plus keeping up with the latest scientific research. Although her lack of scientific training presented a challenge, Solomon thinks her law background enabled her to see problems with a fresh perspective. "As a lawyer, you learn how to learn about a new field instantly," she says. In addition, she learned how to read quickly—and "I'm really comfortable asking dumb questions." Do you think managerial skills are different for nonprofit and for-profit organizations? © D Dipasupil/Getty Images

Susan L. Solomon is the chief executive officer of the nonprofit New York Stem Cell Foundation. As the parent of a 10-year-old boy diagnosed with Type 1 diabetes, Solomon began reading widely about the disease and came to think that stem cells might transform the understanding and treatment of diabetes, which led her to co-found NYSCF as a research foundation out of her apartment in 2005. As CEO, Solomon has helped to raise $150 million, which makes NYSCF one of the biggest nonprofits dedicated to stem-cell research, employing 45 full-time scientists and funding 75 others around the world. Earlier she started out in law, then went into business and finance, worked for the online auction house Sothebys.com, then formed her own consulting business.[79]

Managers for Three Types of Organizations: For-Profit, Nonprofit, Mutual-Benefit

There are three types of organizations classified according to the three purposes for which they are formed—*for-profit, nonprofit,* and *mutual-benefit.*[80]

1. For-Profit Organizations: For Making Money

For-profit, or business, organizations are formed to make money, or profits, by offering products or services. When most people think of "management," they think of business organizations, ranging from Allstate to Zynga, from Amway to Zagat.

2. Nonprofit Organizations: For Offering Services

Managers in nonprofit organizations are often known as "administrators." Nonprofit organizations may be either in the public sector, such as the University of California, or in the private sector, such as Stanford University. Either way, their purpose is to offer services to some clients, not to make a profit. Examples of such organizations are hospitals, colleges, and social-welfare agencies (the Salvation Army, the Red Cross).

One particular type of nonprofit organization is called the *commonweal organization.* Unlike nonprofit service organizations, which offer services to *some* clients, commonweal organizations offer services to *all* clients within their jurisdictions. Examples are the military services, the U.S. Postal Service, and your local fire and police departments.

3. Mutual-Benefit Organizations: For Aiding Members

Mutual-benefit organizations are voluntary collections of members—political parties, farm cooperatives, labor unions, trade associations, and clubs—whose purpose is to advance members' interests.

Different Organizations, Different Management?

If you became a manager, would you be doing the same types of things regardless of the type of organization? Generally you would be; that is, you would be performing the four management functions—planning, organizing, leading, and controlling—that we described in Section 1.2.

The single biggest difference, however, is that in a for-profit organization, the measure of its success is how much profit (or loss) it generates. In the other two types of organizations, although income and expenditures are very important concerns, the measure of success is usually the effectiveness of the services delivered—how many students were graduated, if you're a college administrator, or how many crimes were prevented or solved, if you're a police chief. ●

1.5   The Skills Exceptional Managers Need

To be a terrific manager, what skills should I cultivate?

THE BIG PICTURE

Good managers need to work on developing three principal skills. The first is *technical*, the ability to perform a specific job. The second is *conceptual*, the ability to think analytically. The third is *human*, the ability to interact well with people.

Lower- and middle-level managers are a varied lot, but what do top managers have in common? A supportive spouse or partner, suggests one study.[81] Regardless of gender, reaching the top demands a person's all-out commitment to work and career, and someone needs to be there to help with children and laundry. Thus, in 2014, 47 of the 51 Fortune 1000 female CEOs were married (but only 80% of those who would disclose their family status had children), and their husbands were apparently willing to defer their ambitions to their wives'—just as so many spouses of men have.

General Motors CEO Mary Barra, who is married and is the mother of two grown children, has been assisted in her rise by her husband, Tony Barra, a technology consultant. Although female managers with supportive partners are becoming more common, society is still struggling with what it means for men and women to be peers and whether one's career should come first or both should be developed simultaneously.

Whether or not they have support at home, aspiring managers also need to have other kinds of the "right stuff." In the mid-1970s, researcher **Robert Katz** (in this book we **boldface** important scholar names to help you remember key contributors to the field of management) found that through education and experience managers acquire three principal skills—*technical, conceptual,* and *human.*[82]

1. Technical Skills—The Ability to Perform a Specific Job

Technical skills consist of the job-specific knowledge needed to perform well in a specialized field. Having the requisite technical skills seems to be most important at the lower levels of management—that is, among employees in their first professional job and first-line managers.

Mary Barra has a bachelor's degree in electrical engineering and a master's in business administration and a well-rounded resume that includes important experience as executive assistant to the CEO, being head of midsize car engineering, managing GM's Detroit-Hamtramck plant, and leading the company's human resources division. Then in 2011 she was made head of GM's huge worldwide product development, where she "brought order to chaos," according to one account, "mostly by flattening its bureaucracy . . . , reducing the number of expensive, global vehicle platforms, and bringing new models to market faster and at lower cost."[83]

Said by her predecessor to be "one of the most gifted executives" he had met in his career, she displays an engineer's enthusiasm for cars, a quality not found among other car-company CEOs promoted from finance operations.[84] Indeed, says one account, "Ms. Barra can often be found on the company's test track putting vehicles through their paces at high speeds."[85]

2. Conceptual Skills—The Ability to Think Analytically

Conceptual skills consist of the ability to think analytically, to visualize an organization as a whole and understand how the parts work together. Conceptual skills are more important as you move up the management ladder, particularly for top managers, who must deal with problems that are ambiguous but that could have far-reaching consequences. Today a top car executive must deal with several radical trends—autonomous (self-driving) cars, electric-powered vehicles, and new business models of start-ups like Uber and Lyft.[86]

Triple threat. Mary Barra unveils the new-model Chevrolet Volt hybrid electric car in Las Vegas in January 2016. Barra seems to have the three skills—technical, conceptual, and human—necessary to be a terrific manager in the complex organization that is General Motors. Which skill do you think you need to work on the most? (Human skills are the most difficult to master.) © Tony Ding/AP Photo

Said a GM executive about Barra, "When you put her in a position that's completely new to her, she does an amazing job of getting grounded, understanding what's important and what's not, and executing very well."[87] Or, as Barra said about her management approach, "Problems don't go away when you ignore them—they get bigger. In my experience, it is much better to get the right people together, to make a plan, and to address every challenge head on."[88]

At every stop along the way in rising through GM, Barra analyzed the situation and simplified things. For example, in her product-development job, she streamlined designs by using the same parts in many different models. She also assigned engineers to work in car dealerships to learn more about what customers want in their vehicles.[89] When promoted to CEO, she stepped into the middle of a safety crisis in which GM had to admit to misleading regulators and consumers about a defective ignition switch and agree to pay a $900 million penalty.[90]

Now she is dealing with bigger issues and trying to make GM a more nimble and forward-thinking company. "We know our industry is being disrupted," Barra says. The century-old company is leading the industry in connected-car technology, new electric and hybrid vehicles, and investing in the ride-share service Lyft to prepare for a future in which city residents use self-driving cars to get around.[91]

3. Human Skills—"Soft Skills," the Ability to Interact Well with People

This may well be the most difficult set of skills to master. **Human skills consist of the ability to work well in cooperation with other people to get things done**—especially with people in teams, an important part of today's organizations (as we discuss in Chapter 13).

Often these are thought of as "soft skills." **Soft skills—the ability to motivate, to inspire trust, to communicate with others**—are necessary for managers of all levels. But because of the range of people, tasks, and problems in an organization, developing your human-interacting skills may turn out to be an ongoing, lifelong effort.[92]

During her more than three decades at GM, Barra has demonstrated exceptionally strong soft skills. She has "an ability with people," says her previous boss, that is critical to GM's team-first approach.[93] "She is known inside GM as a consensus builder who calls her staff together on a moment's notice to brainstorm on pressing issues," says another report.[94] "She's fiercely intelligent yet humble and approachable," says a third account. "She's collaborative but is often the person who takes charge. And she's not afraid to make changes."[95]

Among her most significant changes: hiring people with "diverse views, diverse backgrounds, diverse experiences," she says, to try to reshape the company's notoriously insular corporate culture and to bring GM into the age of Apple and Google.

PRACTICAL ACTION   The Soft Skills Employers Say College Graduates Lack

First you have to learn the right technical skills essential to your area of expertise. Then, hiring managers say, you have to learn the other crucial skills, such as "good judgment, maturity, common sense, problem solving, clear thinking, initiative, and professionalism."[96] When you're finished with college, will you, in fact, have these skills—the ones employers say they are looking for but are hard to find?[97]

The Payoff from College. College is difficult, time consuming, stressful, and expensive. Is it worth it? If you're ever tempted to drop out, think about this: American men with at least four years of college earned *90% more* on average than high school graduates did.[98] The typical worker with a bachelor's degree earns $1.19 million over his or her career.[99] (Results may vary depending on major and college.)[100] Finally, college graduates are more likely than those with high school diplomas to report satisfaction with their careers.[101]

Soft Skills Needed. Still, it's important to emerge from college with the *right skills*, which many grads are lacking. Here are the principal ones:

- **Communication and interpersonal skills:** Sixty percent of employers found that applicants lack "communication and interpersonal skills," according to one survey.[102] Another, by the Association of American Colleges and Universities (AACU), revealed that 85% of employers felt recent college graduates should have "the ability to effectively communicate orally," and 82% said they should also have "the ability to communicate in writing." Eighty-three percent thought that having "teamwork skills in diverse groups"— that is, interpersonal and collaborative skills—were especially desirable.[103]

  Example of faulty skill: "I am an great typist," wrote one job applicant who wasn't hired. "I have a strong ability to communication effectively," said another.[104] We discuss communication skills in Chapter 15, teamwork skills in Chapter 13, and other interpersonal skills throughout the book.

- **Critical thinking and problem solving:** "Critical thinking and analytical reasoning skills" were rated as highly important by 81% of employers in the AACU survey, and "the ability to apply knowledge and skills to real-world settings" was considered necessary by 80%. Employers particularly endorse the idea of learning to solve problems in diverse settings or with people whose views differ from one's own—96% in the AACU survey.

  Example of faulty skill: A tide of "competing ideologies, narratives fighting narratives" currently impedes critical thinking, with people with the most power accused of imposing their version of reality on the rest.[105] On college campuses, debates have raged over free speech versus the right not to be offended.[106] But an open

mind is key to making better predictions, say the authors of *Superforecasting: The Art and Science of Prediction.*[107] "What distinguishes superforecasters," they say, "is their ability to set aside their opinions, at least temporarily, and just focus on accuracy."[108] In other words, to think critically—which is what employers want. We discuss critical thinking and problem solving in Chapter 7 and dealing with people with differing views in Chapters 4 and 11.

- **Ethical judgment, innovation and creativity, and motivation:** Eighty-one percent of employees responding to the AACU survey stressed the desirability of possessing "ethical judgment and decision making," a topic we examine in Chapters 4 and 7. And 65% stressed "the ability to innovate and be creative," which we consider in Chapter 10. The question about ability to motivate others was not asked in this particular survey but has been implied in other research, as we'll describe in Chapter 12. For example, studies of the effect of compassionate practices in the workplace find that providing support for and inspiring one another, avoiding blame and forgiving mistakes, and treating others with respect and trust dramatically improve performance levels.[109]

  Example of faulty skill: Rudeness—from snippy remarks to eye-rolling—is a big problem in the workplace and is contagious, with negative consequences for motivating employees and their work. "If someone is rude to me, it is likely that in my next interaction, I will be rude to whomever I am talking to," says University of Florida researcher Trevor Foulk.[110] Employees are also demotivated by "the jerk at work," people who spread a dispiriting attitude to others.[111]

YOUR CALL

What are the three top soft skills you'd like to improve so as to make yourself more desirable to prospective employers by the time you graduate?

The Most Valued Traits in Managers

Clearly, Barra embodies the qualities sought in star managers, especially top managers. "The style for running a company is different from what it used to be," says a top executive recruiter of CEOs. "Companies don't want dictators, kings, or emperors."[112] Instead of someone who gives orders, they want executives who ask probing questions and force the people beneath them to think and find the right answers.

Among the chief skills companies seek in top managers are the following:

- The ability to motivate and engage others.
- The ability to communicate.
- Work experience outside the United States.
- High energy levels to meet the demands of global travel and a 24/7 world.[113]

Let's see how you can begin to acquire these and other qualities for success. ●

1.6   Roles Managers Must Play Successfully

To be an exceptional manager, what roles must I play successfully?

THE BIG PICTURE

Managers tend to work long hours at an intense pace; their work is characterized by fragmentation, brevity, and variety; and they rely more on verbal than on written communication. According to management scholar Henry Mintzberg, managers play three roles—*interpersonal*, *informational*, and *decisional*. Interpersonal roles include figurehead, leader, and liaison activities. Informational roles are monitor, disseminator, and spokesperson. Decisional roles are entrepreneur, disturbance handler, resource allocator, and negotiator.

Clearly, being a successful manager requires playing several different roles and exercising several different skills. What are they?

The Manager's Roles: Mintzberg's Useful Findings

Maybe, you think, it might be interesting to follow some managers around to see what it is, in fact, they actually do. That's exactly what management scholar **Henry Mintzberg** did when, in the late 1960s, he shadowed five chief executives for a week and recorded their working lives.[114] And what he found is valuable to know, since it applies not only to top managers but also to managers on all levels.

Multitasking. Multiple activities are characteristic of a manager—which is why so many managers use their smartphones to keep track of their schedules. Do you use a mobile electronic device for this purpose?
© Olivier Lantzendörffer/Getty Images RF

Consider this portrait of a manager's workweek: "There was no break in the pace of activity during office hours," reported Mintzberg about his subjects. "The mail (average of 36 pieces per day), telephone calls (average of five per day), and meetings (average of eight) accounted for almost every minute from the moment these executives entered their offices in the morning until they departed in the evening."[115]

Only five phone calls per day? And, of course, this was back in an era before e-mail, texting, and Twitter, which nowadays can shower some executives with 100, even 300, messages a day. Indeed, says Ed Reilly, who heads the American Management Association, all the e-mail, cell-phone calls, text messaging, and so on can lead people to end up "concentrating on the urgent rather than the important."[116]

Obviously, the top manager's life is extraordinarily busy. Here are three of Mintzberg's findings, important for any prospective manager:

1. A Manager Relies More on Verbal Than on Written Communication   Writing letters, memos, and reports takes time. Most managers in Mintzberg's research tended to get and transmit information through telephone conversations and meetings. No doubt this is still true, although the technologies of e-mail, texting, and Twitter now make it possible to communicate almost as rapidly in writing as with the spoken word.

2. A Manager Works Long Hours at an Intense Pace   "A true break seldom occurred," wrote Mintzberg about his subjects. "Coffee was taken during meetings, and lunchtime was almost always devoted to formal or informal meetings."

Long hours at work are standard, he found, with 50 hours being typical and up to 90 hours not unheard of. A 1999 survey by John P. Kotter of the Harvard Business School found that the general managers he studied worked just under 60 hours per week.[117] More recently, decades following the Mintzberg research, another study found that many professionals worked a whopping 72 hours a week, including weekend work.[118]

Prior to the 2007–2009 Great Recession, researchers at Purdue and McGill universities found that more companies were allowing managers to reduce their working hours and spend more time with their families yet still advance their high-powered careers.[119] However, during economic hard times, top managers may be more apt to see subordinates' work–life flexibility as a luxury they can no longer afford.

3. A Manager's Work Is Characterized by Fragmentation, Brevity, and Variety

Only about a 10th of the managerial activities observed by Mintzberg took more than an hour; about half were completed in under 9 minutes. Phone calls averaged 6 minutes, informal meetings 10 minutes, and desk-work sessions 15 minutes. "When free time appeared," wrote Mintzberg, "ever-present subordinates quickly usurped it."

No wonder the executive's work time has been characterized as "the interrupt-driven day" and that many managers—such as GM's Mary Barra—are often in their offices by 6 a.m., so that they will have a quiet period in which to work undisturbed. No wonder that finding balance between work and family lives—"work–life balance," as we consider in Chapter 12—is an ongoing concern.[120] No wonder, in fact, that the division between work and nonwork hours is considered almost obsolete in newer industries such as information technology, where people seem to use their smartphones 24/7 to stay linked to their jobs.[121]

It is clear from Mintzberg's work that *time and task management* are major challenges for every manager. The Practical Action box, "Executive Functioning: How Good Are You at Focusing Your Thoughts, Controlling Your Impulses, and Avoiding Distractions?" examines this challenge further. The box "Getting Control of Your Time: Dealing with the Information Deluge in College and in Your Career" at the end of this chapter also offers some important suggestions.

A Mintzberg manager. Paul Orfalea (pronounced "*Or*-fah-la") was CEO for 30 years of Kinko's, the hugely successful copy store chain, before selling it to UPS. Like other managers, he worked long hours and experienced constant interruptions, but there is one significant difference: Because he grew up with the common language-related learning disabilities of dyslexia and ADHD, he came to rely mostly on verbal rather than on written communication. This learning style actually became a "learning opportunity," Orfalea says, because it forced him to rely on others to help with correspondence, and his restlessness drove him to get outside the office to see what stores in different locations were doing right. What kind of personal adversity have you had to overcome? © E. Charbonneau/WireImage/Getty Images

---

PRACTICAL ACTION

Executive Functioning: How Good Are You at Focusing Your Thoughts, Controlling Your Impulses, and Avoiding Distractions?

Managers are executives, of course, and good managers have what psychologists call good "executive functioning." This is a psychological term, rather than a workplace one, and it involves the ability to manage oneself and one's resources in order to achieve a goal. Specifically, this means the ability to focus your thoughts, control your impulses, and avoid distractions.[122] This is particularly true for managers, who, as one article notes, "must routinely block out distractions and exercise reasoning and problem-solving skills."[123]

Gen Z. The approximately 20 million people born from the mid-90s to the mid-2000s are known as Generation Z, or the Net Generation.[124] These are the folks who were "practically born with a smartphone in their hand," in one description.[125] Indeed, one study found that 92% of college undergraduates are cell-phone or tablet users.[126] How good is their executive functioning?

The typical college student plays with his or her digital device an average of 11 times a day while in class, and more than 80% admit that their use of smartphones, tablets, and laptops can interfere with their learning. More than a fourth say their grades suffer.[127] In addition, students do a lot of multitasking—as in checking out Facebook and listening to music while reading this textbook. You may think you're simultaneously doing three separate tasks, but you're really not. "It's like playing tennis with three balls," says one expert.[128]

The Finite Brain. "Life," says Winifred Gallagher, author of *Rapt,* "is the sum of what you focus on."[129] Another writer says, "You can drive yourself crazy trying to multitask and answer every e-mail message instantly. Or you can recognize your brain's finite capacity for processing information."[130] To be successful not only in school but in the workplace—especially as a manager—you need to learn to *direct your attention.* This is known as *focus* or *mindfulness,* as we explore further later in the book.[131]

YOUR CALL

Do you procrastinate about getting your work done? Most people do—and in fact the problem has worsened over the years: Today about 26% of Americans think of themselves as chronic procrastinators, up from 5% in 1978, and 80%–95% of college students procrastinate on a regular basis. The major reason: too many tempting diversions, especially electronic ones.[132] Is this a problem for you? What can you do to improve your "executive functioning"?

Three Types of Managerial Roles: Interpersonal, Informational, and Decisional

From his observations and other research, Mintzberg concluded that managers play three broad types of roles or "organized sets of behavior": *interpersonal, informational,* and *decisional.*

1. Interpersonal Roles—Figurehead, Leader, and Liaison
In their **interpersonal roles,** managers interact with people inside and outside their work units. The three interpersonal roles include *figurehead, leader,* and *liaison activities.*

2. Informational Roles—Monitor, Disseminator, and Spokesperson
The most important part of a manager's job, Mintzberg believed, is information handling, because accurate information is vital for making intelligent decisions. In their three **informational roles**—as monitor, disseminator, and spokesperson—managers **receive and communicate information** with other people inside and outside the organization.

Mary Barra, for example, wrote an e-mail in early 2014 to all GM employees to discuss how the company was responding to a recall of 1.6 million vehicles. She already had been actively communicating with government officials and a host of senior executives regarding the matter. She noted in her e-mail that "recalls of this size and scope usually take time to play out. Various other parties will naturally be involved, and GM will cooperate fully. You can expect additional developments in the near term."[133]

3. Decisional Roles—Entrepreneur, Disturbance Handler, Resource Allocator, and Negotiator
In their **decisional roles,** managers use information to make decisions to solve problems or take advantage of opportunities. The four decision-making roles are **entrepreneur, disturbance handler, resource allocator, and negotiator.**

These roles are summarized on the next page. *(See Table 1.1.)*

Did anyone say a manager's job is easy? Certainly it's not for people who want to sit on the sidelines of life. Above all else, managers are *doers.* ●

TABLE 1.1   Three Types of Managerial Roles: Interpersonal, Informational, and Decisional

BROAD MANAGERIAL ROLES	TYPES OF ROLES	DESCRIPTION
Interpersonal	Figurehead role	In your *figurehead role,* you show visitors around your company, attend employee birthday parties, and present ethical guidelines to your subordinates. In other words, you perform symbolic tasks that represent your organization.
	Leadership role	In your role of *leader,* you are responsible for the actions of your subordinates, as their successes and failures reflect on you. Your leadership is expressed in your decisions about training, motivating, and disciplining people.
	Liaison role	In your *liaison* role, you must act like a politician, working with other people outside your work unit and organization to develop alliances that will help you achieve your organization's goals.
Informational	Monitor role	As a *monitor,* you should be constantly alert for useful information, whether gathered from newspaper stories about the competition or gathered from snippets of conversation with subordinates you meet in the hallway.
	Disseminator role	Workers complain they never know what's going on? That probably means their supervisor failed in the role of *disseminator.* Managers need to constantly disseminate important information to employees, as via e-mail and meetings.
	Spokesperson role	You are expected, of course, to be a diplomat, to put the best face on the activities of your work unit or organization to people outside it. This is the informational role of *spokesperson.*
Decisional	Entrepreneur role	A good manager is expected to be an *entrepreneur,* to initiate and encourage change and innovation.
	Disturbance handler role	Unforeseen problems—from product defects to international currency crises—require you be a *disturbance handler,* fixing problems.
	Resource allocator role	Because you'll never have enough time, money, and so on, you'll need to be a resource *allocator,* setting priorities about use of resources.
	Negotiator role	To be a manager is to be a continual *negotiator,* working with others inside and outside the organization to accomplish your goals.

1.7   The Link between Entrepreneurship and Management

Do I have what it takes to be an entrepreneur?

THE BIG PICTURE

Entrepreneurship, a necessary attribute of business, means taking risks to create a new enterprise. It is expressed through two kinds of innovators, the *entrepreneur* and the *intrapreneur*.

Most of the popular get-rich stories you hear these days are about technology start-ups, such as Facebook, Yelp, Foursquare, or Uber, a **start-up being defined as a newly created company designed to grow fast.**[134] But there are all kinds of new endeavors constantly being launched, not all of which are about technology and not all of which are intended to quickly become big. Indeed, innovation is an important part of any business, and we consider it in detail in Chapter 10.

Starting Up a Start-up: From Hats to Hamburgers

Big Truck Brands, founded in Truckee, California, in 2010, makes custom-designed trucker hats for Olympic skier Julia Mancuso and actor Zach Efron, as well as average consumers.[135] Brooklyn-based MOD Restoration, launched by a rabbi's daughter, Hanny Lerner, handles furniture reupholstering for clients like Barclays Center and Long Island Hospital; it currently has about 10 employees.[136] Walker & Company, headed by Tristan Walker, aims to revolutionize the skin-care and beauty-products industry for African Americans, with products such as Bevel for coarse and curly hair.[137]

While so far these businesses have remained small, others have experienced rapid growth. Numi, founded in 1999 by brother and sister Ahmed and Reem Rahim in their 750-square-foot Oakland, California, apartment, is now the leading importer of Fair Trade certified teas in the United States.[138] Denver chain Smashburger, founded in 2007 (and acquired by Jollibee), which features a $6 truffle, mushroom, and swiss burger, among other specialties, is up to 380 stores.[139]

Entrepreneurship Defined: Taking Risks in Pursuit of Opportunity

According to the Bureau of Labor Statistics, small companies, defined as having between 1 and 250 employees, created 46.7% of all new jobs in 2013.[140] (Note, however: Because many small firms fail, "new businesses are important to job creation primarily because they get founded," says entrepreneurial studies professor Scott Shane, "not because most of them tend to grow."[141])

Most small businesses originate with entrepreneurs, the people with the idea, the risk takers. The most successful entrepreneurs become wealthy and make the covers of business magazines: Oprah Winfrey (Harpo Productions), Fred Smith (Federal Express), Larry Page and Sergey Brin (Google). Failed entrepreneurs may benefit from the experience to live to fight another day—as did Henry Ford, twice bankrupt before achieving success with Ford Motor Co.

What Entrepreneurship Is   **Entrepreneurship is the process of taking risks to try to create a new enterprise.** There are two types of entrepreneurship:

- An **entrepreneur is someone who sees a new opportunity for a product or service and launches a business to try to realize it.** Most entrepreneurs run small businesses with fewer than 100 employees.

- An **intrapreneur** is someone who works inside an existing organization who sees an opportunity for a product or service and mobilizes the organization's resources to try to realize it. This person might be a researcher or a scientist but could also be a manager who sees an opportunity to create a new venture that could be profitable.

Example of an Intrapreneur: Intel's Anthropologist Genevieve Bell Explores Possible Innovations for Automakers

If being an intrapreneur sounds more attractive than being a manager, consider this: Managers are vital to supporting the intrapreneur's efforts. Microsoft in-house researchers, for instance, have brought forth many truly cutting-edge ideas, often beating out Apple and Google. The problem, says one analysis, is that such intrapreneurs were "not getting the buy-in from management to turn their discoveries into products," a difficulty that its new CEO, Satya Nadella, has been urged to address.[142]

Backing In-House Risk Taking. Richard Branson, CEO of the Virgin Group, who says his 200 companies (including music and airline businesses) were built on the efforts of "a steady stream of intrapreneurs who looked for and developed opportunities," understands the importance of management support. In his view, CEO should stand for "chief enabling officer," to nurture in-house experimentation.[143]

Intel's Dr. Bell. Intel Corporation, most famously known for its computer chips but now anxious to go in other directions, certainly appreciates the infusion of new ideas. Indeed, it has hired anthropologist Genevieve Bell as its "director of user experience research" at Intel Labs, where she heads some 100

social scientists and designers who explore how people use technology in their homes and in public. "The team's findings help inform the company's product development process," says one report, "and are also often shared with the laptop makers, automakers, and other companies that embed Intel processors in their goods."[144]

For example, to find out how people shift back and forth between the built-in technologies in their cars and the personal mobile devices they carry, Bell and a fellow anthropologist have traveled around the world examining, photographing, and describing the contents of people's cars. They learned that, despite the fact that automakers have installed voice-command systems and other technology in their vehicles for the purpose of reducing distracted driving, drivers in traffic—especially when bored—often picked up their handheld personal devices anyway. This has led Intel to join with Jaguar Land Rover to find ways for consumers to better synchronize their personal devices with their cars.

YOUR CALL

Do you think most companies truly support intrapreneurship? Why would they not?

How Do Entrepreneurs and Managers Differ? While the entrepreneur is not necessarily an inventor, he or she "always searches for change, responds to it, and exploits it as an opportunity," Peter Drucker pointed out.[145] Most people are not suited to be entrepreneurs. Let's consider the differences between entrepreneurs and managers.

Being an entrepreneur is what it takes to *start* a business; being a manager is what it takes to *grow or maintain* a business. As an entrepreneur or intrapreneur, you initiate new goods or services; as a manager you coordinate the resources to produce the goods or services—including, as we mentioned, the efforts of the intrapreneurs. Do you think it takes different skills to excel at being a good entrepreneur or manager?

Some of the examples of success we have previously mentioned—Fred Smith (FedEx) and Larry Page (Google)—are actually *both* entrepreneurs and effective managers. Other people, however, find they like the start-up part but hate the management part. For example, Stephen Wozniak, entrepreneurial co-founder with Steve Jobs of Apple Computer, abandoned the computer industry completely and went back to college. Jobs, by contrast, went on to launch another business,

Multiple entrepreneur. South African–born Elon Musk was a co-founder of PayPal, which provides payment processing for online vendors. He went on to shake up the auto business with Tesla Motors, which builds electric cars; developed SpaceX, a space launch vehicle company; and began retooling the energy sector with SolarCity, a residential solar energy provider. He was said to be worth $11.2 billion in 2016. What is your passion that you might turn into a business? © Imaginechina/AP Photo

Pixar, which among other things became the animation factory that made the movies *Toy Story* and *Finding Nemo*.

Entrepreneurial companies have been called "gazelles" for the two attributes that make the African antelope successful: *speed and agility*. "Gazelles have mastered the art of the quick," says Alan Webber, founding editor of *Fast Company* magazine. "They have internal approaches and fast decision-making approaches that let them move with maximum agility in a fast-changing business environment."[146]

Is this the kind of smart, innovative world you'd like to be a part of? Most people prefer the security of a job and a paycheck. Entrepreneurs do seem to have psychological characteristics that are different from managers, as follows:[147]

- **Characteristic of both—high need for achievement.** Both entrepreneurs and managers have a high need for achievement. However, entrepreneurs certainly seem to be motivated to pursue moderately difficult goals through their own efforts in order to realize their ideas and, they hope, financial rewards. Managers, by contrast, are more motivated by promotions and organizational rewards of power and perks.

- **Also characteristic of both—belief in personal control of destiny.** If you believe "I am the captain of my fate, the master of my soul," you have what is known as **internal locus of control, the belief that you control your own destiny,** that external forces will have little influence. (*External locus of control* means the reverse—you believe you don't control your destiny, that external forces do.) Both entrepreneurs and managers like to think they have personal control over their lives.

- **Characteristic of both, but especially of entrepreneurs—high energy level and action orientation.** Rising to the top in an organization probably requires that a manager put in long hours. For entrepreneurs, however, creating a new enterprise may require an extraordinary investment of time and energy. In addition, while some managers may feel a sense of urgency, entrepreneurs are especially apt to be impatient and to want to get things done as quickly as possible, making them particularly action oriented.

IBM CEO Virginia "Ginni" Rometty. The Chicago-area native began her career during the early 1980s, when women began entering corporate America in droves. As the leader of "Big Blue," as IBM is called, Rometty placed No. 1 on *Fortune*'s 2013 list of The 50 Most Powerful Women in the United States (and No. 7 on Forbes 2015 list of the World's Most Powerful Women). Currently she is pushing IBM resources into commercializing Watson, the supercomputer famed for winning on *Jeopardy,* whose ability to learn, Rometty believes, represents new sales opportunities. Are entrepreneurs and managers really two different breeds? © Manu Fernandez/AP Photo

- **Characteristic of both, but especially of entrepreneurs—high tolerance for ambiguity.** Every manager needs to be able to make decisions based on ambiguous—that is, unclear or incomplete—information. However, entrepreneurs must have more tolerance for ambiguity because they are trying to do things they haven't done before.

- **More characteristic of entrepreneurs than managers—self-confidence and tolerance for risk.** Managers must believe in themselves and be willing to make decisions; however, this statement applies even more to entrepreneurs. Precisely because they are willing to take risks in the pursuit of new opportunities—indeed, even risk personal financial failure—entrepreneurs need the confidence to act decisively.

Of course, not all entrepreneurs have this kind of faith in themselves. So-called *necessity* entrepreneurs are people such as laid-off corporate workers, discharged military people, immigrants, and divorced homemakers who suddenly must earn a living and are simply trying to replace lost income and are hoping a job comes along. In the United States, these make up about a quarter of entrepreneurs. However, three-quarters are so-called *opportunity* entrepreneurs—those who start their own business out of a burning desire rather than because they lost a job.[148]

So where do you stand? Do you think you would like to be an entrepreneur? The following self-assessment, was created to provide you with feedback about your entrepreneurial orientation, should your instructor assign it to you. ●

connect SELF-ASSESSMENT 1.2

Please be prepared to answer these questions if your instructor has assigned Self-Assessment 1.2 in Connect.

To What Extent Do You Possess an Entrepreneurial Spirit?

How motivated are you to be an entrepreneur, to start your own company? Do you have the aptitudes and attitudes possessed by entrepreneurs? This self-assessment allows you to compare your motivations, aptitudes, and attitudes with those found in a sample of entrepreneurs from a variety of industries.[149] Go to connect.mheducation.com and take the self-assessment. When you're done, answer the following questions:

1. To what extent are your motives, aptitudes, and attitudes similar to entrepreneurs? Explain.

2. Based on your results, where do you have the biggest gaps with entrepreneurs in terms of the individual motives, aptitudes, and attitudes?

3. What do these gaps suggest about your entrepreneurial spirit? Discuss.

4. Do these results encourage or discourage you from thinking about starting your own business? Explain.

TAKING SOMETHING PRACTICAL AWAY

Getting Control of Your Time: Dealing with the Information Deluge in College and in Your Career

Professionals and managers all have to deal with this central problem: how not to surrender their lives to their jobs. The place to start, however, is in college. If you can learn to manage time while you're still a student, you'll find it will pay off not only in higher grades and more free time but also in more efficient information-handling skills that will serve you well as a manager later on.[150]

Using Your "Prime Study Time"

Each of us has a different energy cycle.[151] The trick is to use it effectively. That way, your hours of best performance will coincide with your heaviest academic demands. For example, if your energy level is high during the mornings, you should plan to do your studying then.

To capitalize on your prime study time, you take the following steps: (1) Make a study schedule for the entire term, and indicate the times each day during which you plan to study. (2) Find some good places to study—places where you can avoid distractions. (3) Avoid time wasters, but give yourself frequent rewards for studying, such as a TV show, a favorite piece of music, or a conversation with a friend.

Improving Your Memory Ability

Memorizing is, of course, one of the principal requirements for succeeding in college. And it's a great help for success in life afterward.

Here are some tips on learning to concentrate:[152]

Choose What to Focus On

"People don't realize that attention is a finite resource, like money," one expert says. "Do you want to invest your cognitive cash on endless Twittering or Net surfing or couch potatoing [watching TV]?" She adds, "Where did the idea come from that anyone who wants to contact you can do so at any time? You need to take charge of what you pay attention to instead of responding to the latest stimuli."[153] For example, to block out noise, you can wear earplugs while reading, to create your own "stimulus shelter."

Devote the First 1½ Hours of Your Day to Your Most Important Task

Studying a hard subject? Make it your first task of the day, and concentrate on it for 90 minutes. After that, your brain will probably need a rest, and you can answer text messages, e-mail, and so on. But until that first break, don't do anything else, because it can take the brain 20 minutes to refocus.

Space Your Studying, Rather Than Cramming

Cramming—making a frantic, last-minute attempt to memorize massive amounts of material—is probably the least effective means of absorbing information. Research shows that it's best to space out your studying of a subject over successive days. A series of study sessions over several days is preferable to trying to do it all during the same number of hours on one day. It is *repetition* that helps move information into your long-term memory bank.

Review Information Repeatedly—Even "Overlearn It"

By repeatedly reviewing information—what is known as "rehearsing"—you can improve both your retention and your understanding of it. Overlearning is continuing to review material even after you appear to have absorbed it.

Use Memorizing Tricks

There are several ways to organize information so that you can retain it better. For example, you can make drawings or diagrams (as of the parts of a computer system). Some methods of establishing associations between items you want to remember are given in the exhibit. *(See Exhibit 1.1.)*

EXHIBIT 1.1
Some Memorizing Tricks

- **Mental and physical imagery:** Use your visual and other senses to construct a personal image of what you want to remember. Indeed, it helps to make the image humorous, action-filled, sexual, bizarre, or outrageous in order to establish a personal connection. Example: To remember the name of the 21st president of the United States, Chester Arthur, you might visualize an author writing the number "21" on a wooden chest. This mental image helps you associate chest (Chester), author (Arthur), and 21 (21st president).

- **Acronyms and acrostics:** An acronym is a word created from the first letters of items in a list. For instance, Roy G. Biv helps you remember the colors of the rainbow in order: red, orange, yellow, green, blue, indigo, violet. An acrostic is a phrase or sentence created from the first letters of items in a list. For example, *Every Good Boy Does Fine* helps you remember that the order of musical notes on the staff is E-G-B-D-F.

- **Location:** Location memory occurs when you associate a concept with a place or imaginary place. For example, you could learn the parts of a computer system by imagining a walk across campus. Each building you pass could be associated with a part of the computer system.

- **Word games:** Jingles and rhymes are devices frequently used by advertisers to get people to remember their products. You may recall the spelling rule "I before E except after C or when sounded like A as in *neighbor* or *weigh*." You can also use narrative methods, such as making up a story.

How to Improve Your Reading Ability: The SQ3R Method

SQ3R stands for "survey, question, read, recite, and review."[154] The strategy behind it is to break down a reading assignment into small segments and master each before moving on. The five steps of the SQ3R method are as follows:

1. *Survey the chapter before you read it:* Get an overview of the chapter or other reading assignment before you begin reading it. If you have a sense of what the material is about before you begin reading it, you can predict where it is going. In this text, we offer on the first page of every chapter a list of the main heads and accompanying key questions. At the end of each chapter we offer a Key Points, which explains what the chapter's terms and concepts mean and why they are important.

2. *Question the segment in the chapter before you read it:* This step is easy to do, and the point, again, is to get you

involved in the material. After surveying the entire chapter, go to the first segment—section, subsection, or even paragraph, depending on the level of difficulty and density of information. Look at the topic heading of that segment. In your mind, restate that heading as a question. In this book, we have done this by following each main section head with a Major Question. As an example, for the first section of this chapter (Management: What It Is, What Its Benefits Are), our restatement question is "What are the rewards of being an exceptional manager?"

After you have formulated the question, go to steps 3 and 4 (read and recite). Then proceed to the next segment and again restate the heading there as a question.

3. *Read the segment about which you asked the question:* Now read the segment you asked the question about. Read with purpose, to answer the question you formulated. Underline or color-mark sentences that you think are important, if they help you answer the question. Read this portion of the text more than once, if necessary, until you can answer the question. In addition, determine whether the segment covers any other significant questions, and formulate answers to these, too. After you have read the segment, proceed to step 4. (Perhaps you can see where this is all leading. If you read in terms of questions and answers, you will be better prepared when you see exam questions about the material later.)

4. *Recite the main points of the segment:* Recite means "say aloud." Thus, you should speak out loud (or softly) the answer to the principal question or questions about the segment and any other main points.

5. *Review the entire chapter by repeating questions:* After you have read the chapter, go back through it and review the main points. Then, without looking at the book, test your memory by repeating the questions.

Clearly the SQ3R method takes longer than simply reading with a rapidly moving color marker or underlining pencil. However, the technique is far more effective because it requires *your involvement and understanding.* This is the key to all effective learning.

Learning from Lectures

Does attending lectures really make a difference? Research shows that students with grades of B or above were more apt to have better class attendance than students with grades of C or below.[155] Some tips for getting the most out of lectures are the following.

Take Effective Notes by Listening Actively

Research shows that good test performance is related to good note taking.[156] And good note taking requires that you listen actively—that is, participate in the lecture process. Here are some ways to take good lecture notes:

- *Read ahead and anticipate the lecturer:* Try to anticipate what the instructor is going to say, based on your previous reading. Having background knowledge makes learning more efficient.

- *Listen for signal words:* Instructors use key phrases such as "The most important point is . . . ," "There are four reasons for . . . ," "The chief reason . . . ," "Of special importance . . . ," "Consequently . . . " When you hear such signal phrases, mark your notes with a ! or *.

- *Take notes in your own words:* Instead of just being a stenographer, try to restate the lecturer's thoughts in your own words, which will make you pay attention more.

- *Ask questions:* By asking questions during the lecture, you necessarily participate in it and increase your understanding.

Review Your Notes Regularly

Make it a point to review your notes regularly—perhaps on the afternoon after the lecture, or once or twice a week. We cannot emphasize enough the importance of this kind of reviewing.

Key Terms Used in This Chapter

Key Points

1.1 Management: What It Is, What Its Benefits Are

- Management is defined as the pursuit of organizational goals *efficiently*, meaning to use resources wisely and cost-effectively, and *effectively* by integrating the work of people through planning, organizing, leading, and controlling the organization's resources.

1.2 What Managers Do: The Four Principal Functions

- The management process, or four management functions, are represented by the abbreviation *POLC*.
- *Planning* is setting goals and deciding how to achieve them.
- *Organizing* is arranging tasks, people, and other resources to accomplish the work.
- *Leading* is motivating, directing, and otherwise influencing people to work hard to achieve the organization's goals.
- *Controlling* is monitoring performance, comparing it with goals, and taking corrective action as needed.

1.3 Seven Challenges to Being an Exceptional Manager

- Managing for competitive advantage, which means an organization must stay ahead in four areas—being responsive to customers, innovating new products or services offering better quality, being more efficient.
- Managing for diversity among different genders, ages, races, and ethnicities.

- Managing for globalization, the expanding universe.
- Managing for computers and telecommunications—information technology.
- Managing for right and wrong, or ethical standards.
- Managing for sustainability.
- Managing for your own happiness and meaningful life goals.

1.4 Pyramid Power: Levels and Areas of Management

- Within an organization, there are managers at four levels.
- *Top managers* make long-term decisions about the overall direction of the organization and establish the objectives, policies, and strategies for it.
- *Middle managers* implement the policies and plans of their superiors and supervise and coordinate the activities of the managers below them.
- *First-line managers* make short-term operating decisions, directing the daily tasks of nonmanagerial personnel.
- *Team leaders* are managers who are responsible for facilitating team activities toward achieving key results.
- There are three types of organizations—for-profit, nonprofit, and mutual benefit.
- *For-profit* organizations are formed to make money by offering products or services.
- *Nonprofit* organizations offer services to some, but not to make a profit.

- *Mutual-benefit* organizations are voluntary collections of members created to advance members' interests.

1.5 The Skills Exceptional Managers Need

- The three skills that exceptional managers cultivate are technical, conceptual, and human.
- *Technical* skills consist of job-specific knowledge needed to perform well in a specialized field.
- *Conceptual* skills consist of the ability to think analytically, to visualize an organization as a whole, and to understand how the parts work together.
- *Human* skills consist of the ability to work well in cooperation with other people in order to get things done.

1.6 Roles Managers Must Play Successfully

- The Mintzberg study shows that, first, a manager relies more on verbal than on written communication; second, managers work long hours at an intense pace; and, third, a manager's work is characterized by fragmentation, brevity, and variety.
- Mintzberg concluded that managers play three broad roles: (1) *interpersonal*—figurehead, leader, and liaison; (2) *informational*—monitor, disseminator, and spokesperson; and (3) *decisional*—entrepreneur, disturbance handler, resource allocator, and negotiator.

1.7 The Link between Entrepreneurship and Management

- Entrepreneurship, a necessary attribute of business, is the process of taking risks to create a new enterprise.
- Two types are the entrepreneur and the intrapreneur.
- The *entrepreneur* sees a new opportunity for a product or service and launches a business to realize it.
- The *intrapreneur* works inside an existing organization and sees an opportunity for a product or service and mobilizes the organization's resources to realize it.
- Entrepreneurs start businesses; managers grow or maintain them. Both (but especially entrepreneurs) have a high need for achievement, high energy level and action orientation, and tolerance for ambiguity. Entrepreneurs are more self-confident and have higher tolerance for risk.

Understanding the Chapter: What Do I Know?

1. What is the difference between being efficient and being effective?
2. What is the formal, three-part definition of management?
3. How would I define the four functions of management?
4. What are the seven challenges of being a manager, and which is the one I will probably most have to worry about during my lifetime?
5. What are the differences among the four levels of managers in the organizational pyramid?
6. How would I distinguish among the three types of organizations?
7. What are the three skills that exceptional managers need to cultivate, and which one do I probably have to work on most?
8. Mintzberg's study in the 1960s came up with three important findings about a manager's routine. What are they, and are they probably still the same today?
9. Mintzberg also found that managers play three important roles. What are they, and what examples can I think of?
10. Which would I rather be—a manager or an entrepreneur/intrapreneur, and why?

Management in Action

Yahoo! CEO Marissa Mayer Is under Pressure to Make Big Changes

Marissa Mayer, former Vice President of Google Product Search, left the company in 2012 to become the CEO of Yahoo!. At that time, the stock sold for $15.74. It sold for $29.77 in January 2016, reaching a high of $52.28 in 2014. Interestingly, investors are not happy with this rate of growth. Some feel that the company's strategies are lacking and that new leadership is needed. Hedge fund investor Starboard Value LP demanded that the board fire Mayer.[157]

Mayer was hired to help turnaround the company's floundering business model. She immediately put in place strategies to grow via acquisitions. For example, Yahoo! paid $1.1 billion for Tumblr, a micro blogging platform and social networking website. This acquisition did not produce the expected growth in revenue. A letter from Canyon Capital Advisors to Yahoo!'s board of directors stated that Yahoo! "has spent more than $3 billion on acquisitions, which, based on the company's stock price, have been getting 'absolutely no (or negative) value' from Wall Street."[158]

One of the poor decisions that has plagued Yahoo!'s financial performance was its reluctance to transition its offerings to mobile devices. Another involved the company's investment in Livetext. This app allows users to chat with friends by sharing video and text, but no sound. One writer described it this way: "You could awkwardly watch, but not talk, as you texted your loved ones and friends."[159]

Several Yahoo! investors are calling for big changes because "Yahoo!'s 15 percent stake in Chinese Web giant Alibaba, valued at $25.7 billion . . . , plus its $8 billion stake in Yahoo! Japan and $5.9 billion in cash, well exceeds Yahoo!'s market cap of $27.5 billion. That implies a negative value for Yahoo!'s core Internet businesses." This has led Canyon Capital to recommend that Yahoo! "prioritize a sale of its core business, a portion of its assets, or the entire company."[160] Yahoo!'s leadership team is against these suggestions.

Yahoo!'s problems have led to layoffs and employee dissatisfaction and turnover. The company has responded by providing a broad set of perks, including iPhones, parties, and free lunches. The firm has a budget of $108,000,000 a year for free food.

"Employees' faith in Ms. Mayer began crumbling in earnest in August 2014, when Yahoo! embarked on a series of stealth layoffs, current and former insiders said. For months, managers called in a handful of employees each week and fired them. No one knew who would be next, and the constant fear paralyzed the company, according to people who watched the process."

It is estimated that 33 percent of the work force left the company in 2015. "Worried about the brain drain, Ms. Mayer has been approving hefty retention packages—in some cases, millions of dollars—to persuade people to reject job offers from other companies. But those bonuses have had the side effects of creating resentment among other Yahoo! employees who have stayed loyal and not sought jobs elsewhere."[161]

Sadly, employee morale does not appear to be improving. Surveys conducted by Glassdoor revealed that "only 34 percent of Yahoo!'s current employees foresee the company's fortunes improving. That compares to 61 percent at tanking, scandal-struck Twitter and 77 percent at Google."[162]

According to one business writer, "Mayer's protracted deliberations over a corporate reorganization last year [2015] that led to the departure of several key lieutenants and broke up the much-ballyhooed mobile team, prompting many mobile engineers to seek other jobs" also contributed to employees' dissatisfaction.[163]

Another potential problem involves Mayer's compensation package. "Executive pay at Yahoo! is essentially based on Alibaba's stock price," which is outside of her control. "Of Mayer's $365 million pay over five years, only 3.3 percent will actually be affected by her performances."[164] This practice is against the common managerial practice of paying people for their performance.

So where does this leave Mayer and Yahoo! as a whole? Some employees, like Jeff Bonforte, Yahoo!'s senior vice president for communications products, love Mayer and the company. Mayer is the best boss he ever had, according to Bonforte.[165] Broadly speaking, however, there are continued threats of more layoffs and calls to sell off parts of the company.

Yahoo! announced in February 2016 that it would layoff about 15% of its workforce. *The Wall Street Journal* further reported that "Yahoo's next step may be to initiate a formal sale process, which entails setting up a virtual data room detailing the company's business metrics, and proactively reaching out to the most likely potential buyers. Or the board could choose to wait until a suitor approaches them with an offer, at which point it would weight that against any counteroffers. . . . A sale process would also likely mark the end of Chief Executive Marissa Mayer's attempt to turn around Yahoo."[166]

To make matters worse, investor "SpringOwl Asset Management called for firing as many as 9,000 of Yahoo!'s workers, who numbered 11,000" in June 2015.[167]

Although key investors are waiting to hear the details of Mayer's turnaround plan, some are very unhappy with the company's strategic direction. They are demanding changes. Jeffrey Smith from Starboard Value L/P, for example, concluded that "dramatically different thinking is required," and that changes are needed "across all aspects of the business starting at the board level, and including executive leadership."[168]

FOR DISCUSSION

1. What are the key problems facing Yahoo!?

2. Which of the four principal management functions seem to be causing the problems faced by Yahoo!? Explain your rationale.

3. Which of the seven managerial challenges discussed in this chapter is Yahoo! facing? How is the company handling these challenges?

4. What is your evaluation of Mayer's ability to effectively execute the three key managerial roles—interpersonal, informational, and decisional? Explain.

5. If you were a consultant to Yahoo!, what advice would you give to senior management about handling the crisis being faced by the company? Discuss.

To Delay or Not to Delay?

You have been hired by a vice president of a national company to create an employee attitude survey, to administer it to all employees, and to interpret the results. You have known this vice president for more than 10 years and have worked for her on several occasions. She trusts and likes you, and you trust and like her. You have completed your work and now are ready to present the findings and your interpretations to the vice president's management team. The vice president has told you that she wants your honest interpretation of the results, because she is planning to make changes based on the results. Based on this discussion, your report clearly identifies several strengths and weaknesses that need to be addressed. For example, employees feel that they are working too hard and that management does not care about providing good customer service. At the meeting you will be presenting the results and your interpretations to a group of 15 managers. You also have known most of these managers for at least 5 years.

You arrive for the presentation armed with slides, handouts, and specific recommendations. Your slides are loaded on the computer, and most of the participants have arrived. They are drinking coffee and telling you how enthused they are about hearing your presentation. You also are excited to share your insights. Ten minutes before the presentation is set to begin, however, the vice president takes you out of the meeting room and says she wants to talk with you about your presentation. The two of you go to another office, and she closes the door. She then tells you that her boss's boss decided to come to the presentation unannounced. She thinks that he is coming to the presentation to look solely for negative information in your report. He does not like the vice president and wants to replace her with one of his friends. If you present your results as planned, it will provide this individual with the information he needs to create serious problems for the vice president. Knowing this, the vice president asks you to find some way to postpone your presentation. You have 10 minutes to decide what to do.

SOLVING THE CHALLENGE

What would you do?

1. Deliver the presentation as planned.

2. Give the presentation but skip over the negative results.

3. Go back to the meeting room and announce that your spouse has had an accident at home and you must leave immediately. You tell the group that you just received this message and that you will contact the vice president to schedule a new meeting.

4. Invent other options. Discuss.

2

Management Theory
Essential Background for the Successful Manager

Major Questions You Should Be Able to Answer

Mind-sets: How Do You Go about Learning?

Learn or die. Isn't that the challenge to us as individuals? Throughout your career, your success will depend on your constantly being a learner, making choices about how to solve various problems—which tools to apply, including the theories we will describe in this chapter. However, one barrier to learning that all of us need to be aware of is our *mind-set*.

The Enemy of Learning

By the time we are grown, the minds of many of us have become set in patterns of thinking, the result of our personal experiences and various environments, that affect how we respond to new ideas. These mind-sets determine what ideas we think are important and what ideas we ignore.

Because we can't pay attention to all the events that occur around us, say the authors of a book on critical analysis, "our minds filter out some observations and facts and let others through to our conscious awareness."[1] Herein lies the danger: "As a result, we see and hear what we subconsciously want to and pay little attention to facts or observations that have already been rejected as unimportant."

Having mind-sets makes life comfortable. However, as the foregoing writers point out, "Familiar relationships and events become so commonplace that we expect them to continue forever. Then we find ourselves completely unprepared to accept changes that are necessary even when they stare us in the face."[2]

What's Your Mind-set? Two Views

What will be your approach to studying management theory (or anything else in this book)? If you can't "get it" right away, will you take that as a reflection on your basic intelligence—that you're somehow deficient, that people will think you're dumb and you'll feel like a loser?

Based on 20 years of research, Stanford psychology professor Carol Dweck suggests that *the view you adopt about yourself profoundly affects the way you lead your life*—including how you learn. In our views of ourselves, she says, most of us have either a *fixed mind-set* or a *growth mind-set*.[3]

- **The fixed mind-set—believing your basic qualities are carved in stone.** People with a fixed mind-set are concerned about how they will be judged, as on intelligence or personal qualities. They believe, "My intelligence is something very basic that can't be changed very much." Or, "I'm a certain kind of person, and there's not much that can be done to change that." They care less about learning than looking bad when failure occurs.

- **The growth mind-set—believing your basic qualities can be changed through your effort.** People with a growth mind-set are concerned with improving. They think, "You can always change your intelligence quite bit." Or, "You can always change basic things about the kind of person you are." Failure for these kinds of people may well feel bad, but instead of hiding their deficiencies from others they try to overcome them. Fortunately, by applying themselves, people of a fixed mind-set can develop a growth mind-set.

For Discussion Your approach to learning won't stop once you leave school. As we discuss at the end of this chapter, most organizations now are "learning organizations," in which employees are continually required to expand their ability to achieve results by obtaining the right knowledge and changing their behavior. Thus, your mind-set matters. Which type are you? What can a person begin to do to move from a fixed mind-set to a growth mind-set?

FORECAST   What's Ahead in This Chapter

This chapter gives you a short overview of the three principal *historical* perspectives or viewpoints on management—*classical, behavioral,* and *quantitative.* It then describes the three principal *contemporary* viewpoints—*systems, contingency,* and *quality-management.* Finally, we consider the concept of *learning organizations.*

2.1 Evolving Viewpoints: How We Got to Today's Management Outlook

MAJOR QUESTION **What's the payoff in studying different management perspectives, both yesterday's and today's?**

THE BIG PICTURE

After studying theory, managers may learn the value of bringing rationality to the decision-making process. This chapter describes two principal theoretical perspectives—the *historical* and the *contemporary*. Studying management theory provides understanding of the present, a guide to action, a source of new ideas, clues to the meaning of your managers' decisions, and clues to the meaning of outside events.

"The best way to predict the future is to create it," Peter Drucker said.

The purpose of this book is, to the extent possible, to *give you the tools to create your own future* in your career and as a manager.

Creating Modern Management: The Handbook of Peter Drucker

Who is **Peter Drucker**? "He was the creator and inventor of modern management," says management guru Tom Peters (author of *In Search of Excellence*). "In the early 1950s, nobody had a tool kit to manage these incredibly complex organizations that had gone out of control. Drucker was the first person to give us a handbook for that."[4]

An Austrian trained in economics and international law, Drucker came to the United States in 1937, where he worked as a correspondent for British newspapers and later became a college professor. In 1954, he published his famous text *The Practice of Management,* in which he proposed the important idea that *management was one of the major social innovations of the 20th century and should be treated as a profession,* like medicine or law.

In this and other books, he introduced several ideas that now underlie the organization and practice of management—namely:

- That workers should be treated as assets.
- That the corporation could be considered a human community.
- That there is "no business without a customer."
- That institutionalized management practices are preferable to charismatic cult leaders.

Many ideas that you will encounter in this book—decentralization, management by objectives, knowledge workers—are directly traceable to Drucker's pen. "Without his analysis," says one writer, "it's almost impossible to imagine the rise of dispersed, globe-spanning corporations."[5] In our time, Drucker's rational approach has culminated in *evidence-based management,* as we describe in Section 2.6 in this chapter.

True learner. In his 70-year career, Peter Drucker published over 35 books and numerous other publications, received the Presidential Medal of Freedom, and achieved near rock-star status for his management ideas, which influenced organizations from General Electric to the Girl Scouts. A true learner who constantly expanded his knowledge, he understood that new experiences are key to nurturing new ideas and new ventures. Do you have this kind of curiosity?
© Steve Smith/Corbis

Six Practical Reasons for Studying This Chapter

"Theory," say business professors Clayton Christensen and Michael Raynor, "often gets a bum rap among managers because it's associated with the word 'theoretical,' which connotes 'impractical.' But it shouldn't."[6] After all, what could be more practical than studying different approaches to see which work best?

Indeed, there are six good reasons for studying theoretical perspectives:

1. **Understanding of the present.** "Sound theories help us interpret the present, to understand what is happening and why," say Christensen and Raynor.[7] Or as scholars Scott Montgomery and Daniel Chirot argue, ideas "do not merely matter, they matter immensely, as they have been the source for decisions and actions that have structured the modern world."[8] Understanding history will help you understand why some practices are still favored, whether for right or wrong reasons.

2. **Guide to action.** Good theories help you make predictions and enable you to develop a set of principles that will guide your actions.

3. **Source of new ideas.** It can also provide new ideas that may be useful to you when you come up against new situations.

4. **Clues to meaning of your managers' decisions.** It can help you understand your firm's focus, where the top managers are "coming from."

5. **Clues to meaning of outside events.** It may allow you to understand events outside the organization that could affect it or you.

6. **Producing positive results.** It can help you understand why certain management practices—such as setting goals that stretch you to the limit (stretch goals), basing compensation and promotion on performance, and monitoring results—have been so successful for many firms.[9]

Pages from a Game Company's Employee Guide: In Flatness Lies Greatness

EXAMPLE

If Management 1.0 is what we're used to now, with its traditional pyramid hierarchy, what would Management 2.0 look like? What if, as management thinker Gary Hamel suggests, Management 2.0 looked a lot like Web 2.0 as represented in Wikipedia, YouTube, and other online communities?[10] Could the traditional hierarchy of boxes with lines actually become a corporate straitjacket?

The Boss-Free System. Bellevue, Washington–based Valve Corp. is an online entertainment and technology company that has created several award-winning games (Half Life, Portal) as well as Steam, an online gaming platform. Its staff consists of (1) all the employees and (2) a founder/president—who is not a manager. In fact, "we don't have any management," says Valve's employee handbook, "and nobody 'reports to' anybody else."[11] One article calls it a "boss-free system."[12]

In other words, Valve is a *flat organization,* defined as one with few or no levels of management (as we discuss further in Chapter 8). Indeed, Valve is the flattest of flat organizations because for an employee, says the handbook, it "removes every organizational barrier between your work and the customer enjoying that work."

Desks with Wheels. Not only do Valve employees have no managers, but they get to select which projects they want to work on, have the power to green-light (approve) new projects, and even ship finished products. Every employee's desk has wheels, serving two purposes. "The first is a symbolic reminder that one should always consider where they could move to be more valuable," says one account. "The other is literal—team members often move their desks close together when working on a project."[13] Instead of managers, Valve relies on rotating team leaders (called "group contributors"), who change according to each project.

YOUR CALL

The basic reason Valve has no formal managers is that it wants to attract the best talent and produce outstanding products year after year. Clearly, the flat structure works very well for Valve—as it does for other organizations, profit and not-for-profit alike, that operate in a rapidly changing environment, depend on innovation to stay on top, and have a shared purpose.[14] Flattened hierarchies even work for some large organizations, such as W.L. Gore, maker of Gore-Tex fabric, which employs 10,000 people. Why do you think, then, that many organizations resist using flat structures? Do you think studying management theory could help you answer this question?

Theory underlies all the achievements of business. Some of the greatest companies in the world are headquartered in these New York City skyscrapers: American Express, Colgate-Palmolive, J.P. Morgan Chase, Time Warner, and Verizon. A number of start-ups are also based here, with names such as DWNLD, Hungryroot, and WayUp. The launch, growth, and profitability of businesses all depend on execution of solid management theory.
© Jupiterimages/Getty Images RF

Two Overarching Perspectives about Management: Historical and Contemporary

In this chapter, we describe two overarching perspectives about management. *(See Figure 2.1.)* They are:

- The **historical perspective** (1911–1950s) includes three viewpoints—*classical, behavioral,* and *quantitative.*

- The **contemporary perspective** (1960s–present) also includes three viewpoints—*systems, contingency,* and *quality-management.* ●

FIGURE 2.1   **The two overarching perspectives—historical and contemporary**

The Historical Perspective (1911–1950s)

**Classical Viewpoint
1911–1947**
Emphasis on ways to manage work more efficiently

**Behavioral Viewpoint
1913–1950s**
Emphasis on importance of understanding human behavior and motivating and encouraging employees toward achievement

**Quantitative Viewpoint
1940s–1950s**
Applies quantitative techniques to management

The Contemporary Perspective (1960s–Present)

The Systems Viewpoint
Regards the organization as systems of interrelated parts that operate together to achieve a common purpose

The Contingency Viewpoint
Emphasizes that a manager's approach should vary according to—i.e., be contingent on—the individual and environmental situation

The Quality-Management Viewpoint
Three approaches

2.2 Classical Viewpoint: Scientific and Administrative Management

MAJOR QUESTION

If the name of the game is to manage work more efficiently, what can the classical viewpoint teach me?

THE BIG PICTURE

The *three historical management viewpoints* we will describe include (1) the classical, described in this section; (2) the behavioral; and (3) the quantitative. The classical viewpoint, which emphasized ways to manage work more efficiently, had two approaches: (a) scientific management and (b) administrative management. *Scientific management,* pioneered by Frederick W. Taylor and Frank and Lillian Gilbreth, emphasized the scientific study of work methods to improve the productivity of individual workers. *Administrative management,* pioneered by Henri Fayol and Max Weber, was concerned with managing the total organization.

Bet you've never heard of a "therblig," although it may describe some physical motions you perform from time to time—as when you have to wash dishes, say. A made-up word you won't find in most dictionaries, *therblig* was coined by Frank Gilbreth and is, in fact, "Gilbreth" spelled backward, with the "t" and the "h" reversed. It refers to 1 of 17 basic motions. By identifying the therbligs in a job, as in the tasks of a brick-layer (which he had once been), Frank and his wife, Lillian, were able to eliminate motions while simultaneously reducing fatigue.

The Gilbreths were a husband-and-wife team of industrial engineers who were pioneers in one of the classical approaches to management, part of the *historical perspective (1911–1950s)*. As we mentioned, there are *three historical management viewpoints* or approaches.[15] *(See Figure 2.2, next page.)* They are

- Classical viewpoint—1911–1947
- Behavioral viewpoint—1913–1950s
- Quantitative viewpoint—1940s–1950s

In this section, we describe the classical perspective of management, which originated during the early 1900s. The **classical viewpoint,** which emphasized finding ways to manage work more efficiently, had two branches—*scientific* and *administrative*—each of which is identified with particular pioneering theorists. In general, classical management assumes that *people are rational.* Let's compare the two approaches.

Scientific Management: Pioneered by Taylor and the Gilbreths

The problem for which scientific management emerged as a solution was this: In the expansive days of the early 20th century, labor was in such short supply that managers were hard-pressed to raise the productivity of workers. **Scientific management** emphasized the scientific study of work methods to improve the productivity of individual workers. Two of its chief proponents were Frederick W. Taylor and the team of Frank and Lillian Gilbreth.

Frederick Taylor and the Four Principles of Scientific Management No doubt there are some days when you haven't studied, or worked, as efficiently as you could. This could be called "underachieving," or "loafing," or what Taylor called it—*soldiering,* deliberately working at less than full capacity. Known as "the father of scientific management," Taylor was an American engineer from Philadelphia who

FIGURE 2.2   The historical perspective: three viewpoints—classical, behavioral, and quantitative

The Historical Perspective (1911–1950s)

Classical Viewpoint 1911–1947	Behavioral Viewpoint 1913–1950s	Quantitative Viewpoint 1940s–1950s
Emphasis on ways to manage work more efficiently	Emphasis on importance of understanding human behavior and motivating and encouraging employees toward achievement	Applies quantitative techniques to management

Scientific management
Emphasized scientific study of work methods to improve productivity of individual workers

Proponents:
Frederick W. Taylor
Frank and Lillian Gilbreth

Early behaviorists

Proponents:
Hugo Munsterberg
Mary Parker Follett
Elton Mayo

Management science
Focuses on using mathematics to aid in problem solving and decision making

Administrative management
Concerned with managing the total organization

Proponents:
Henri Fayol
Max Weber

Human relations movement
Proposed better human relations could increase worker productivity

Proponents:
Abraham Maslow
Douglas McGregor

Operations management
Focuses on managing the production and delivery of an organization's products or services more effectively

Behavioral science approach
Relies on scientific research for developing theory to provide practical management tools

Frederick W. Taylor. Called the father of scientific management, Taylor published *The Principles of Scientific Management* in 1911.
© Bettmann/Corbis

believed that managers could eliminate soldiering by applying four principles of science:

1. Evaluate a task by scientifically studying each part of the task (not use old rule-of-thumb methods).
2. Carefully select workers with the right abilities for the task.
3. Give workers the training and incentives to do the task with the proper work methods.
4. Use scientific principles to plan the work methods and ease the way for workers to do their jobs.

Taylor based his system on *motion studies,* in which he broke down each worker's job—moving pig iron at a steel company, say—into basic physical motions and then trained workers to use the methods of their best-performing coworkers. In addition, he suggested employers institute a *differential rate system,* in which more efficient workers earned higher wages.

Why Taylor Is Important: Although "Taylorism" met considerable resistance from employees fearing that working harder would lead to lost jobs except for the highly productive few, Taylor believed that by raising production both labor and

Lillian and Frank Gilbreth with 11 of their dozen children. As industrial engineers, the Gilbreths pioneered time and motion studies. If you're an athlete, you can appreciate how small changes can make you more efficient. © Bettmann/Corbis

management could increase profits to the point where they no longer would have to quarrel over them. If used correctly, the principles of scientific management can enhance productivity, and such innovations as motion studies and differential pay are still used today.

Frank and Lillian Gilbreth and Industrial Engineering   As mentioned, Frank and Lillian Gilbreth were a husband-and-wife team of industrial engineers who lectured at Purdue University in the early 1900s. Their experiences in raising 12 children—to whom they applied some of their ideas about improving efficiency (such as printing the Morse code on the back of the bathroom door so that family members could learn it while doing other things)—later were popularized in a book, two movies, and a TV sitcom, *Cheaper by the Dozen.* The Gilbreths expanded on Taylor's motion studies— for instance, by using movie cameras to film workers at work in order to isolate the parts of a job.

Lillian Gilbreth, who received a PhD in psychology, was the first woman to be a major contributor to management science.

Administrative Management: Pioneered by Fayol and Weber

Scientific management is concerned with the jobs of individuals. **Administrative management is concerned with managing the total organization.** Among the pioneering theorists were Henri Fayol and Max Weber.

Henri Fayol and the Functions of Management   Fayol was not the first to investigate management behavior, but he was the first to systematize it. A French engineer and industrialist, he became known to American business when his most important work, *General and Industrial Management,* was translated into English in 1930.

Why Fayol Is Important: Fayol was the first to identify the major functions of management—planning, organizing, leading, and controlling, as well as coordinating— the first four of which you'll recognize as the functions providing the framework for this and most other management books.[16]

Max Weber and the Rationality of Bureaucracy   In our time, the word *bureaucracy* has come to have negative associations: impersonality, inflexibility, red tape, a molasses-like response to problems. But to German sociologist Max Weber, a *bureaucracy* was a rational, efficient, ideal organization based on principles of logic. After all, in Weber's Germany in the late 19th century, many people were in positions of authority (particularly in the government) not because of their abilities but because of their social status. The result, Weber wrote, was that they didn't perform effectively.

A better-performing organization, he felt, should have five positive bureaucratic features:

1. A well-defined hierarchy of authority.
2. Formal rules and procedures.
3. A clear division of labor, with parts of a complex job being handled by specialists.
4. Impersonality, without reference or connection to a particular person.
5. Careers based on merit.

Why Weber Is Important: Weber's work was not translated into English until 1947, but it came to have an important influence on the structure of large corporations, such as the Coca-Cola Company.

The Problem with the Classical Viewpoint: Too Mechanistic

A flaw in the classical viewpoint is that it is mechanistic: It tends to view humans as cogs within a machine, not taking into account the importance of human needs. Behavioral theory addressed this problem, as we explain next.

Why the Classical Viewpoint Is Important: The essence of the classical viewpoint was that work activity was amenable to a rational approach, that through the application of scientific methods, time and motion studies, and job specialization it was possible to boost productivity. Indeed, these concepts are still in use today, the results visible to you every time you visit McDonald's or Pizza Hut. The classical viewpoint also led to such innovations as management by objectives and goal setting. ●

Scientific management. Carmakers have broken down automobile manufacturing into its constituent tasks, as shown here for an assembly plant. This reflects the contributions of the school of scientific management. Is there anything wrong with this approach? How could it be improved?
© RainerPlendl/iStock/Getty Images RF

2.3 Behavioral Viewpoint: Behaviorism, Human Relations, and Behavioral Science

MAJOR QUESTION

To understand how people are motivated to achieve, what can I learn from the behavioral viewpoint?

THE BIG PICTURE

The second of the three historical management perspectives was the *behavioral* viewpoint, which emphasized the importance of understanding human behavior and of motivating employees toward achievement. The behavioral viewpoint developed over three phases: (1) *Early behaviorism* was pioneered by Hugo Munsterberg, Mary Parker Follett, and Elton Mayo. (2) The *human relations movement* was pioneered by Abraham Maslow (who proposed a hierarchy of needs) and Douglas McGregor (who proposed a Theory X and Theory Y view to explain managers' attitudes toward workers). (3) The *behavioral science approach* relied on scientific research for developing theories about behavior useful to managers.

The **behavioral viewpoint** emphasized the importance of understanding human behavior and of motivating employees toward achievement. The behavioral viewpoint developed over three phases: (1) early behaviorism, (2) the human relations movement, and (3) behavioral science.

Early Behaviorism: Pioneered by Munsterberg, Follett, and Mayo

The three people who pioneered behavioral theory were Hugo Munsterberg, Mary Parker Follett, and Elton Mayo.

Hugo Munsterberg and the First Application of Psychology to Industry

Called "the father of industrial psychology," German-born Hugo Munsterberg had a PhD in psychology and a medical degree and joined the faculty at Harvard University in 1892. Munsterberg suggested that psychologists could contribute to industry in three ways. They could:

1. Study jobs and determine which people are best suited to specific jobs.

2. Identify the psychological conditions under which employees do their best work.

3. Devise management strategies to influence employees to follow management's interests.

Why Munsterberg Is Important: His ideas led to the field of *industrial psychology,* the study of human behavior in workplaces, which is still taught in colleges today.

Mary Parker Follett and Power Sharing among Employees and Managers

A Massachusetts social worker and social philosopher, Mary Parker Follett was lauded on her death in 1933 as "one of the most important women America has yet produced in the fields of civics and sociology." Instead of following the usual hierarchical arrangement of managers as order givers and employees as order takers, Follett thought organizations should become more democratic, with managers and employees working cooperatively.

The following ideas were among her most important:

1. Organizations should be operated as "communities," with managers and subordinates working together in harmony.

2. Conflicts should be resolved by having managers and workers talk over differences and find solutions that would satisfy both parties—a process she called *integration*.

3. The work process should be under the control of workers with the relevant knowledge, rather than of managers, who should act as facilitators.

Why Follett Is Important: With these and other ideas, Follett anticipated some of today's concepts of "self-managed teams," "worker empowerment," and "interdepartmental teams"—that is, members of different departments working together on joint projects.

Elton Mayo and the Supposed "Hawthorne Effect"

Do you think workers would be more productive if they thought they were receiving special attention? This was the conclusion drawn by a Harvard research group in the late 1920s.

Conducted by Elton Mayo and his associates at Western Electric's Hawthorne (Chicago) plant, what came to be called the *Hawthorne studies* began with an investigation into whether workplace lighting level affected worker productivity. (This was the type of study that Taylor or the Gilbreths might have done.) In later experiments, other variables were altered, such as wage levels, rest periods, and length of workday. Worker performance varied but tended to increase over time, leading Mayo and his colleagues to hypothesize what came to be known as the **Hawthorne effect—namely, that employees worked harder if they received added attention, if they thought that managers cared about their welfare and that supervisors paid special attention to them.**

Elton Mayo. In the 1920s, Elton Mayo (shown with long cigarette holder) and his team conducted studies of Western Electric's Hawthorne plant. Do you think you'd perform better in a robotlike job if you thought your supervisor cared about you and paid more attention to you? © AP Photo

However, later investigators found flaws in the studies, such as variations in ventilation and lighting or inadequate follow-through, that were overlooked by the original researchers. Critics also point out that it's doubtful that workers improved their productivity merely on the basis of receiving more attention rather than because of a particular instructional method or social innovation.[17]

Why the Hawthorne Studies Are Important: Ultimately, the Hawthorne studies were faulted for being poorly designed and not having enough empirical data to support the conclusions. Nevertheless, they succeeded in drawing attention to the importance of "social man" (social beings) and how managers using good human relations could improve worker productivity. This in turn led to the so-called human relations movement in the 1950s and 1960s.

The Human Relations Movement: Pioneered by Maslow and McGregor

The two theorists who contributed most to the **human relations movement—which proposed that better human relations could increase worker productivity—were** Abraham Maslow and Douglas McGregor.

Abraham Maslow and the Hierarchy of Needs

What motivates you to perform: Food? Security? Love? Recognition? Self-fulfillment? Probably all of these, Abraham

Maslow would say, although some needs must be satisfied before others. The chairman of the psychology department at Brandeis University and one of the earliest researchers to study motivation, in 1943 Maslow proposed his famous *hierarchy of human needs:* physiological, safety, love, esteem, and self-actualization.[18] We discuss this hierarchy in detail in Chapter 12, where we explain why Maslow is important.

Douglas McGregor and Theory X versus Theory Y   Having been for a time a college president (at Antioch College in Ohio), Douglas McGregor came to realize that it was not enough for managers to try to be liked; they also needed to be aware of their attitudes toward employees.[19] Basically, McGregor suggested in a 1960 book, these attitudes could be either "X" or "Y."

Theory X represents a pessimistic, negative view of workers. In this view, workers are considered to be irresponsible, to be resistant to change, to lack ambition, to hate work, and to want to be led rather than to lead.

Theory Y represents the outlook of human relations proponents—an optimistic, positive view of workers. In this view, workers are considered to be capable of accepting responsibility, self-direction, and self-control and of being imaginative and creative.

Why Theory X/Theory Y Is Important: The principal contribution offered by the Theory X/Theory Y perspective is that it helps managers understand how their beliefs affect their behavior. For example, Theory X managers are more likely to micromanage, which leads to employee dissatisfaction, because they believe employees are inherently lazy. Managers can be more effective by considering how their behavior is shaped by their expectations about human nature.

Underlying both Maslow's and McGregor's theories is the notion that more job satisfaction leads to greater worker performance—an idea that is somewhat controversial, as we'll discuss in Chapter 11.

What is your basic view of human nature? Your attitude could be key to your career success. To see the general direction of your outlook, try the following self-assessment if your instructor assigns it to you.

connect SELF-ASSESSMENT 2.1

What Is Your Orientation toward Theory X/Theory Y?

This self-assessment is designed to reveal your orientation as a manager—whether it tends toward Theory X or Theory Y.

Please be prepared to answer these questions if your instructor has assigned Self-Assessment 2.1 in Connect.

1. To what extent do you think your results are an accurate reflection of your beliefs about others? Are you surprised by the results?

2. As a leader of a student or work-related project team, how might your results affect your approach toward leading others? Explain.

3. If an employee doesn't seem to show ambition, can that be changed? Discuss.

The Behavioral Science Approach

The human relations movement was a necessary correction to the sterile approach used within scientific management, but its optimism came to be considered too simplistic for practical use. More recently, the human relations view has been superseded by the behavioral science approach to management. **Behavioral science relies on scientific research for developing theories about human behavior that can be used to provide practical tools for managers.** The disciplines of behavioral science include psychology, sociology, anthropology, and economics. •

Application of Behavioral Science Approach: The Open-Plan Office—Productivity Enhancer or Productivity Killer?

Today most office layouts have an open floor plan, mixing managers and workers in completely open offices, often using communal tables.[20] When the concept originated in the 1950s, its purpose was to "facilitate communication and idea flow," according to one report.[21] But does it work?

The Distraction Next to You. On any given day, probably 40%–60% of all your workplace interactions (including face-to-face chats and e-mails) will be with your immediate fellow employees, says a behavioral scientist who studies such things. There is only a 5%–10% chance of your interacting with someone two rows away.[22] And, research shows, face-to-face interruptions constitute one-third more intrusions than do e-mail or phone calls.[23]

Indeed, many behavioral science studies now find that, as one *Bloomberg Businessweek* article puts it, "open-plan offices make employees less productive, less happy, and more likely to get sick."[24] Open arrangements have proven to be cumbersome, noisy, disruptive, and stressful. Instead of feeling closer to their colleagues, workers have become resentful, dissatisfied, more distant—and even sicker.[25]

"This Means I'm Busy!" So how are conscientious workers in open-plan offices to get anything done—to avoid "pesky, productivity-sapping interruptions," in one writer's phrase?[26] Various workers have come up with their own ways of alerting others that they are not to be interrupted. Some wear special bright-colored sashes or vests or hats. Some block off their work spaces with neon-yellow plastic "Do Not Disturb" barricade tape (from CubeGuard). Some retreat to designated closed offices as "no interruption" zones to get necessary work done.

The Right Seating Mix. Another way to reduce disruption is for companies to assign who sits next to whom, rather than using unassigned seating. In open-plan offices, "people literally catch emotions from one another like a virus," says Wharton School management professor Sigal Barsade, who suggests that the people who work best together are those with similar emotional temperaments.[27] For instance, mixing extroverts and introverts can lower the productivity of both, as introverts, who are quiet and like to keep their distance, may resent the intrusions of extroverts, those outgoing coworkers who need interaction and love to talk and talk.[28]

Paul English, co-founder of the travel website Kayak.com, uses new hires as an excuse to alter existing open-office seating arrangements, taking into careful consideration everything from "employees' personalities to their political views to their propensity for arriving at work early—or, more important, their propensity for judging colleagues who arrive late," says one report.[29] "If I put someone next to you that's annoying or there's a total style clash, I'm going to make your job depressing," English says.

YOUR CALL

If about 70% of U.S. employees now work in open offices, yet behavioral science studies largely show they are not a productive or beneficial arrangement, why do you suppose they continue to be so prevalent? What kind of office arrangements do you think would work best and why?

Open-plan seating. What kind of office would you prefer to have for yourself—a private office, a shared private office, a partitioned cubicle, or a desk in an open office scattered with other desks with no partitions? Which would be most comfortable for you personally? Why, theoretically, would the open office best promote superior performance?
© Kelvin Murray/Getty Images

2.4   Quantitative Viewpoints: Management Science and Operations Management

MAJOR QUESTION

If the manager's job is to solve problems, how might the two quantitative approaches help?

THE BIG PICTURE

The third and last category under historical perspectives consists of *quantitative viewpoints*, which emphasize the application to management of quantitative techniques, such as statistics and computer simulations. Two approaches of quantitative management are *management science* and *operations management*.

During the air war known as the Battle of Britain in World War II, a relative few of England's Royal Air Force fighter pilots and planes were able to successfully resist the overwhelming might of the German military machine. How did they do it? Military planners drew on mathematics and statistics to determine how to most effectively allocate use of their limited aircraft.

When the Americans entered the war in 1941, they used the British model to form *operations research (OR)* teams to determine how to deploy troops, submarines, and other military personnel and equipment most effectively. For example, OR techniques were used to establish the optimum pattern that search planes should fly to try to locate enemy ships.

After the war, businesses also began using these techniques. One group of former officers, who came to be called the Whiz Kids, used statistical techniques at Ford Motor Co. to make better management decisions. Later Whiz Kid Robert McNamara, who had become Ford's president, was appointed Secretary of Defense and introduced similar statistical techniques and cost–benefit analyses throughout the Department of Defense. Since then, OR techniques have evolved into **quantitative management, the application to management of quantitative techniques, such as statistics and computer simulations. Two branches of quantitative management are** *management science* **and** *operations management.*

Management Science: Using Mathematics to Solve Management Problems

How would you go about deciding how to assign utility repair crews during a blackout? Or how many package sorters you needed and at which times for an overnight delivery service such as FedEx or UPS? You would probably use the tools of management science.

Management science is not the same as Taylor's scientific management. **Management science focuses on using mathematics to aid in problem solving and decision making.** Sometimes management science is called *operations research*.

Why Management Science Is Important: Management science stresses the use of rational, science-based techniques and mathematical models to improve decision making and strategic planning. Management science is a forerunner to analytics and Big Data, as we will discuss in Chapter 7.

FedEx. What management tools do you use to schedule employees and aircraft to deal with wide variations in package volume—such as December 23 versus December 26? © Zuma Press Inc/Alamy

EXAMPLE   Management Science: "Find Me More Music I Like!"

"Once, all you needed to succeed in the music business were a pair of gold ears and some hustle," says writer Ben Sisario. "Now, it also takes mountains of data."[30]

Four Hundred Unique Musical Qualities. Tim Westergren studied music composition and computer science in college, played in unsuccessful rock bands, and worked as a film-score composer. Then he thought to try to map song musical qualities in what he called the Music Genome Project, which he described as "an enormous collection of songs that have been analyzed, one song at a time, using 400 unique qualities."[31] In 2005 the genome became the basis for Oakland, California–based Pandora Internet Radio, which essentially applies management science (metrics) to music selection.

Recommendations. Pandora is an online music streaming and automated music recommendation service that allows users to type in a favorite song or artist, and then Pandora's software plays other music with the same musical characteristics. In late 2015 the company "that plays only music you like" reported it had 78.1 million monthly active listeners.[32]

YOUR CALL

Today there are many companies that have computer "recommendation engines" to suggest new products keyed to a consumer's individual tastes, such as Spotify, Apple Music, and Warner Music; Amazon for books; and Netflix for films. Do you think there's any room left for experienced human decision makers who don't rely on numbers? Do you think reliance on the automated recommendation process cheats consumers out of "pleasant surprises" and new discoveries?

Operations Management: Being More Effective

Operations management focuses on managing the production and delivery of an organization's products or services more effectively. Operations management is concerned with work scheduling, production planning, facilities location and design, and optimum inventory levels.

Why Operations Management Is Important: Through the rational management of resources and distribution of goods and services, operations management helps ensure that business operations are efficient and effective. ●

EXAMPLE   Operations Management: Using "the Toyota Way" to Benefit Hospital Patients

Over the years, Toyota Motor Corp. has developed a variety of production techniques that drew in part on operations management.[33] Together these methods constitute "the Toyota Way," the company's systematic approach to producing vehicles efficiently, with the ultimate aim of pleasing the customer.

First, the process emphasizes the smoothest possible *flow of work,* by identifying the many steps in a production process and eliminating unnecessary ones (called *value-stream mapping*). It also uses teamwork to examine problems and fix them as soon as they appear *(mistake proofing).* In addition, the carmaker uses the *just-in-time* approach to obtain supplies from vendors only as they are needed in the factory. These efficient techniques, which all come under the term "lean management," has enabled Toyota to sell its cars on the basis of their superior quality.[34]

Adapting Toyota's Philosophy and Practices to Hospitals. A growing number of U.S. hospitals have been forced to compete harder under the federal Affordable Care Act as formerly uninsured patients have begun to understand they do not necessarily have to go to their closest public safety-net hospital but could be a little more choosey. That realization put public hospitals "in the unusual position of having to attract and retain 'paying customers' to survive," writes reporter Victoria Colliver.[35] Accordingly, around 2000, hospital administrators began to apply Toyota's techniques to improving hospital quality, safety, and patient satisfaction.

"A Million Small Changes." The Toyota method is "really focused on the small things," a hospital CEO told Colliver. A team of employees meets for a week-long hands-on session to come up with a plan that makes specific, small changes that can have a major impact. One team, for instance, focused on whittling 10 minutes off the typical 40 minutes of time it took from wheeling a patient into the operating room until the first surgical incision. "Ten minutes may not sound like a lot," observes Colliver, "but those minutes can add up in wasted time and cost when a staff of nurses and doctors has to wait for a piece of equipment or a patient to be ready for them." Another team was able to reduce outpatient wait time from 4–6 hours to 2.5 hours.

YOUR CALL

In Chapter 1, we described the problem of "efficiency versus effectiveness." Which is the focus of lean management?

2.5 Systems Viewpoint

How can the exceptional manager be helped by the systems viewpoint?

THE BIG PICTURE

Three contemporary management perspectives are (1) the *systems,* (2) the *contingency,* and (3) the *quality-management* viewpoints. The *systems viewpoint* sees organizations as a system, either open or closed, with inputs, outputs, transformation processes, and feedback. The systems viewpoint has led to the development of complexity theory, the study of how order and pattern arise from very complicated, apparently chaotic systems. The *contingency viewpoint* emphasizes that a manager's approach should vary according to the individual and environmental situation. It is a forerunner to evidence-based management. The *quality-management viewpoint* has two traditional approaches: *quality control,* the strategy for minimizing errors by managing each stage of production, and *quality assurance,* which focuses on the performance of workers, urging employees to strive for zero defects. A third quality approach is the movement of *total quality management (TQM),* a comprehensive approach dedicated to continuous quality improvement, training, and customer satisfaction.

Being of a presumably practical turn of mind, could you run an organization or a department according to the theories you've just learned? Probably not. The reason: People are complicated. To be an exceptional manager, you need to learn to deal with individual differences in a variety of settings.

Thus, to the historical perspective on management (classical, behavioral, and quantitative viewpoints), let us now add the *contemporary perspective,* which consists of three viewpoints. *(See Figure 2.3.)* These consist of:

- Systems
- Contingency
- Quality-management

In this section, we discuss the systems viewpoint.

FIGURE 2.3   The contemporary perspective: three viewpoints—systems, contingency, and quality-management

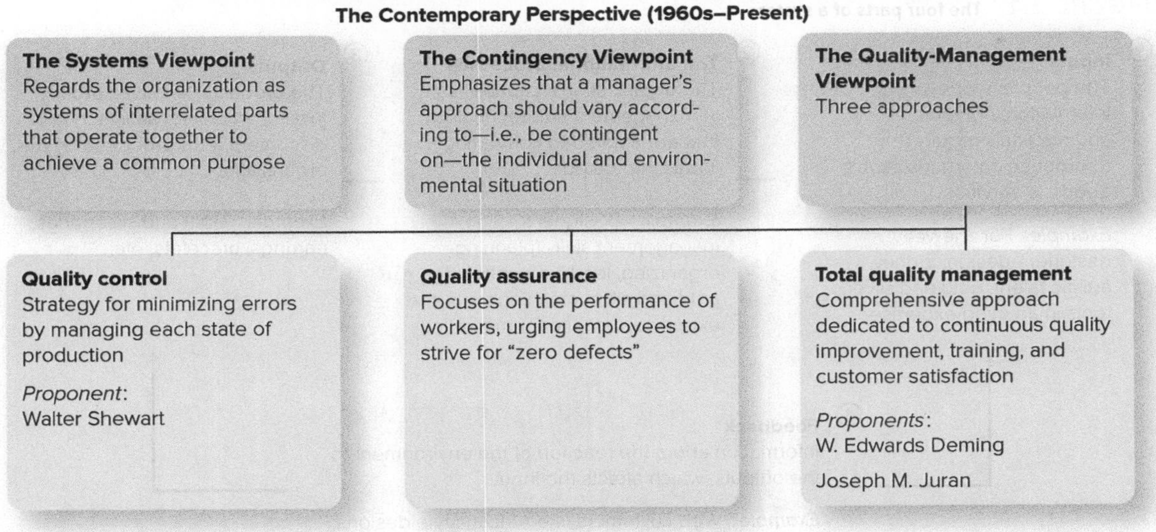

The Contemporary Perspective (1960s–Present)

The Systems Viewpoint
Regards the organization as systems of interrelated parts that operate together to achieve a common purpose

The Contingency Viewpoint
Emphasizes that a manager's approach should vary according to—i.e., be contingent on—the individual and environmental situation

The Quality-Management Viewpoint
Three approaches

Quality control
Strategy for minimizing errors by managing each state of production

Proponent:
Walter Shewart

Quality assurance
Focuses on the performance of workers, urging employees to strive for "zero defects"

Total quality management
Comprehensive approach dedicated to continuous quality improvement, training, and customer satisfaction

Proponents:
W. Edwards Deming

Joseph M. Juran

The Systems Viewpoint

The 27 bones in the hand. The monarchy of Great Britain. A weather storm front. Each of these is a system. **A system is a set of interrelated parts that operate together to achieve a common purpose.** Even though a system may not work very well—as in the inefficient way the Italian government collects taxes, for example—it is nevertheless still a system.

The systems viewpoint regards the organization as a system of interrelated parts. By adopting this point of view, you can look at your organization both as (1) a collection of **subsystems—parts making up the whole system**—and (2) a part of the larger environment. A college, for example, is made up of a collection of academic departments, support staffs, students, and the like. But it also exists as a system within the environment of education, having to be responsive to parents, alumni, legislators, nearby townspeople, and so on.

The Four Parts of a System

The vocabulary of the systems perspective is useful because it gives you a way of understanding many different kinds of organizations. The four parts of a system are defined as follows:

1. **Inputs are the people, money, information, equipment, and materials required to produce an organization's goods or services.** Whatever goes into a system is an input.

2. **Transformational processes are the organization's capabilities in management, internal processes, and technology that are applied to converting inputs into outputs.** The main activity of the organization is to transform inputs into outputs.

3. **Outputs are the products, services, profits, losses, employee satisfaction or discontent, and the like that are produced by the organization.** Whatever comes out of the system is an output.

4. **Feedback is information about the reaction of the environment to the outputs that affects the inputs.** Are the customers buying or not buying the product? That information is feedback.

The four parts of a system are illustrated below. *(See Figure 2.4.)*

FIGURE 2.4   The four parts of a system

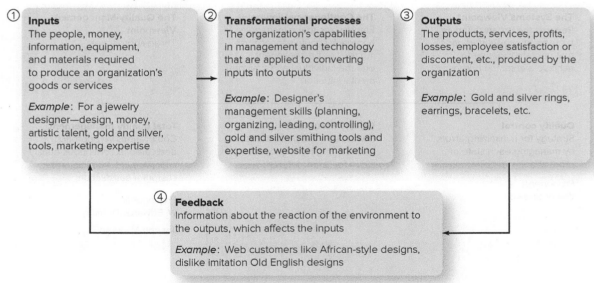

Closed Systems, Open Systems, and the Concept of Synergy

A **closed system** has little interaction with its environment; that is, it receives very little feedback from the outside. The classical management viewpoint often considered an organization a closed system. So does the management science perspective, which simplifies organizations for purposes of analysis. However, any organization that ignores feedback from the environment opens itself up to possibly spectacular failures.

An **open system** continually interacts with its environment. Today nearly all organizations are, at least to some degree, open systems rather than closed. Open systems have the potential of producing synergy. **Synergy** (pronounced "*sin*-ur-jee") is the idea that two or more forces combined create an effect that is greater than the sum of their individual effects, as when a guitarist, drummer, and bassist combine to play a better version of a song than any of them would playing alone. Or a copywriter, art director, and photographer combine to create a magazine ad, each representing various influences from the environment.

Complexity Theory: The Ultimate Open System

The systems viewpoint has led to the development of **complexity theory, the study of how order and pattern arise from very complicated, apparently chaotic systems.** Complexity theory recognizes that all complex systems are networks of many interdependent parts that interact with each other according to certain simple rules. Used in strategic management and organizational studies, the discipline seeks to understand how organizations, considered as relatively simple and partly connected structures, adapt to their environments.

Why the Systems Viewpoint—Particularly the Concept of Open Systems—Is Important: History is full of accounts of products that failed (such as the 1959 Ford Edsel) because they were developed in closed systems and didn't have sufficient feedback. Open systems stress multiple feedback from both inside and outside the organization, resulting in a continuous learning process to try to correct old mistakes and avoid new ones. •

Do Nudges Achieve Results? Using the Systems Viewpoint to Find Out   EXAMPLE

Here's something that social scientists have long known, says economist Justin Wolfers: "Small changes in how choices are presented can lead to big changes in behavior." How can we verify this? "By careful testing of one idea against another," he says. "The idea is to let hard data judge what works."[36]

In 2014 the White House assembled a Social and Behavioral Sciences Team (which came to be known as the "Nudge Unit") to experiment in applying behavioral insights to help government deliver better services and save money. Their small tweaks, described in their 2015 annual report, have yielded impressive results.[37] And, Wolfers suggests, because the cost of the tweaks is so low, even moderate impacts could yield extraordinary benefits.

Repaying Student Loans: Results of a Closed System. If after college you are struggling to repay your student loans, did you know that you can apply to the government to have your monthly payments reduced to a more manageable share of your income? The government mandates that you are obligated to repay your debt, but in this alternate arrangement you are allowed to do so more slowly. However, lots of borrowers who are new to repayment are unaware of this possibility and miss their first payments. This is an example of a closed system.

Repaying Student Loans: Results of an Open System. The problem, observes Wolfers, is that few people are aware of this possibility of making reduced payments over a longer period of time, and so few apply. "That's a shame," says Wolfers, "because the federal government actually knows who is struggling to repay their loans and could help them directly."

How would things be different under an open system? Researchers sent e-mails to student loan borrowers who had missed their first payments reminding them that they had missed a payment and directed them to information about different repayment plans. The result was a four-fold increase in applications for repayment plans.[38]

YOUR CALL

Using "small nudges" like this to create open feedback systems and testing their results to see what works has proven successful in reducing use of printing paper, increasing retirement contributions, spurring health care enrollment, and other matters. Can you think of an idea in which you'd like to try small nudges?

2.6   Contingency Viewpoint

In the end, is there one best way to manage in all situations?

THE BIG PICTURE

The second viewpoint in the contemporary perspective, the contingency viewpoint, emphasizes that a manager's approach should vary according to the individual and environmental situation.

The classical viewpoints advanced by Taylor and Fayol assumed that their approaches had universal applications—that they were "the one best way" to manage organizations. The contingency viewpoint began to develop when managers discovered that under some circumstances better results could be achieved by breaking the one-best-way rule. **The contingency viewpoint emphasizes that a manager's approach should vary according to—that is, be contingent on—the individual and the environmental situation.**

A manager subscribing to the Gilbreth approach might try to get workers to be more productive by simplifying the steps. A manager of the Theory X/Theory Y persuasion might try to use motivational techniques. But the manager following the contingency viewpoint would simply ask, "What method is the best to use under these particular circumstances?"

EXAMPLE   The Contingency Viewpoint: What Are the Best Kinds of Benefits?

Money is not the only motivator for employee productivity. Applying the contingency approach, managers have found there are incentives in offering various kinds of fringe benefits—one recent report listed more than 300 such benefits, from health plans to house down-payment assistance.[39]

Small Incentives. Small businesses may not be able to dangle big raises, but they can offer imaginative benefits that big organizations may find too expensive or impractical.

Examples: Free team lunches every Friday (Hukkster, a sales alert website in New York). "Free Beer Friday" (Universal Information Services, Omaha, Nebraska). "Bring Your Pet to Work"—no messes or barking, please (VoIP Supply, Amherst, New York). Twice-a-week yoga instruction (Litzky Public Relations, Hoboken, New Jersey). Paid week off to volunteer for good causes (teen-counseling company NextStepU.com, Rochester, New York).

Various companies offer other options: at-your-desk meditation, drop-off laundry services, free theme park tickets, even adoption assistance and funeral planning.[40]

Large Incentives. Are little perks all that's required? Netflix has decided that the best way to keep top talent is to hire people who are "fully formed adults" who will put the company first and support a high-performance workplace. Thus, instead

of having a rigid system of vacation days and a formal travel and expense policy, Netflix decided to take the ultimate contingency approach, embodied in the policy "Act in Netflix's best interests." This means salaried employees can take whatever time they feel is appropriate and enforce their own travel and expense policies—in other words, they are trusted to act as fully formed adults.[41]

YOUR CALL

One career analyst suggests that people are motivated most by autonomy, developing their skills, and a sense of higher purpose.[42] This opinion is echoed in a survey that found the top factors in determining people's happiness at work are whether they enjoy the tasks required of them, are able to focus on the things they do best, and are proud of their employer.[43] Another study found that people care, first, about the office environment, positive culture, and compensation; second, a job that makes the world a better place or a company that shares their values; and third, company prestige and rapid promotion.[44]

Considering these findings and applying a contingency approach to stimulating productivity at work, what different kinds of incentives or benefits would you offer for hourly shift workers, salaried middle managers, and work-at-home employees?

Contingency approach. Giving employees more money is not the only way to motivate them to be more productive. Sometimes small rewards, such as allowing pets at work, are equally effective. What incentives would make you stay at a job for which you are not really suited and to do your best while there? © National Geographic Creative/Alamy

Gary Hamel: Management Ideas Are Not Fixed, They're a Process

Discussion of the contingency viewpoint leads us naturally to the thoughts of **Gary Hamel,** co-founder of the Management Innovation Lab and ranked by *The Wall Street Journal* in 2008 as the most influential business thinker.[45] "Over time," he says, "every great invention, management included, travels a road that leads from birth to maturity, and occasionally to senescence."[46] Hamel holds that much of management theory is dated and doesn't fit the current realities of organizational life and that management innovation is essential to future organizational success. Indeed, he suggests, what we need to do is look at management as a *process,* and then make improvements and innovation ongoing and systematic. After all, if managers now innovate by creating new products or new business strategies, why can't they be equally innovative in how they manage their companies?

How do forward-looking managers get the ball rolling in management innovation, particularly in a traditional, conventional company? Hamel believes that the answer can be found by identifying *core beliefs that people have about the organization,* especially those that detract from the pursuit of management innovation. He suggests that these beliefs can be rooted out by repeatedly asking the right questions—namely, the following:

1. **Is this a belief worth challenging?** Is it debilitating? Does it get in the way of an important organizational attribute that we'd like to strengthen?

2. **Is this belief universally valid?** Are there counterexamples? If so, what do we learn from those cases?

3. **How does this belief serve the interests of its adherents?** Are there people who draw reassurance or comfort from this belief?

4. **Have our choices and assumptions conspired to make this belief self-fulfilling?** Is this belief true simply because we have made it true—and, if so, can we imagine alternatives?[47]

Why the Contingency Viewpoint Is Important: The contingency viewpoint would seem to be the most practical of the viewpoints discussed so far because it addresses problems on a case-by-case basis and varies the solution accordingly.

Evidence-Based Management: Facing Hard Facts, Rejecting Nonsense

Evidence-based management is very much in the spirit of the contingency viewpoint's practical approach to management. **Evidence-based management** means translating principles based on best evidence into organizational practice, bringing rationality to the decision-making process.

As its two principal proponents, Stanford business scholars **Jeffrey Pfeffer** and **Robert Sutton,** put it, evidence-based management is based on the belief that "facing the hard facts about what works and what doesn't, understanding the dangerous half-truths that constitute so much conventional wisdom about management, and rejecting the total nonsense that too often passes for sound advice will help organizations perform better."[48]

Learning to make managerial decisions based on evidence is the approach we hope you will learn to take after studying many other approaches—the perspectives we covered in this chapter. We will consider evidence-based management further, along with analytics and Big Data, in Chapter 7. ●

PRACTICAL ACTION   Evidence-Based Management: An Attitude of Wisdom

"These days, there aren't any hot, new trends, just a lot of repackaged ones from the past," writes *Wall Street Journal* columnist Carol Hymowitz.[49] "Executives have been treated to an overdose of management guides that mostly haven't delivered what they promised. Many bosses have adopted them all, regardless of their company's business model, balance sheet, competition, employee bench strength, or any other unique qualities. They have become copycat managers, trying to find a one-stop, fix-it-all answer to their various problems."

How will you know whether the next "fix-it-all" book to hit the business bestseller list is simply a recycling of old ideas? The answer is: You have to have studied history and theory—the subject of this chapter.[50]

Proving and Disproving Theories: The Purpose of Research. "A theory that helps one company succeed can be fatal for another operating under different conditions," write Clayton Christensen and Michael Raynor."[51] By "theory" they don't mean just the sweeping historic ideas we've discussed in this chapter, but also such frequent management considerations as: When should a big company be decentralized into independent "hot businesses"? Should an organization always give priority to its "core competencies," the unique characteristics that provide its competitive advantages? When start-ups are funded by venture capitalists, those professionals who loan money in return for part ownership and profits, does this event make the start-ups more likely to abandon failing initiatives and thus boost their chances of success?

Rather than being selected in a seat-of-the-pants kind of way—which can lead to big mistakes—management theories should be developed and analyzed systematically through research. Theories, Carlson and Raynor suggest, should pinpoint causes, predict possible results, and be fine-tuned when research shows the results aren't as forecast. "Rarely consider positive research findings the final word," they stress. "Progress comes when researchers refine a theory to explain situations in which the theory previously *failed*."

Research should follow the scientific method, a logical process, embodying four steps: (1) You observe events and gather facts. (2) You pose a possible solution or explanation based on those facts. (3) You make a prediction of future events. (4) You test the prediction under systematic conditions.

Following the Evidence. The process of scientific reasoning underlies what is known as evidence-based management. As we stated, *evidence-based management* means translating principles based on best evidence into organizational practice, bringing rationality to the decision-making process.[52] Evidence-based management derives from evidence-based medicine, embracing what Jeffrey Pfeffer and Robert Sutton call *an attitude of wisdom.* This is a mind-set that, first, is willing to set aside belief and conventional wisdom and to act on the facts and, second, has an unrelenting commitment to gathering information necessary to make informed decisions and to keeping pace with new evidence to update practices.[53]

"The way a good doctor or a good manager works," Sutton says, "is to act with knowledge while doubting what you know. So if a patient goes to a doctor, you hope the doctor would do two things: first look at the literature and make the best decision given what's available. Then actually track the progress of the treatment and see what unexpected side effects you're having and what things are working."[54]

Three Truths. Evidence-based management is based on three truths:

- **There are few really new ideas:** Most supposedly new ideas are old, wrong, or both.

- **True is better than new:** Effective organizations and managers are more interested in what is true than in what is new.

- **Doing well usually dominates:** Organizations that do simple, obvious, and even seemingly trivial things well will dominate competitors who search for "silver bullets and instant magic."

YOUR CALL

Do you think managers are often driven by fads, by what they've read in the latest book or heard in the latest management seminar? Have you ever heard of a manager taking an experimental approach, as in trying out a new idea with an open mind to see what happens? How could you profit by taking an evidence-based approach to the ideas we discussed in this chapter?

2.7 Quality-Management Viewpoint

Can the quality-management viewpoint offer guidelines for true managerial success?

THE BIG PICTURE

The quality-management viewpoint, the third category under contemporary perspectives, consists of *quality control, quality assurance,* and especially the movement of *total quality management (TQM),* dedicated to continuous quality improvement, training, and customer satisfaction.

In 1971, in his book *Wheels,* author Arthur Hailey advised Americans not to buy cars that were assembled on Mondays or Fridays—days when cars supposedly suffered from quality problems because they were put together when absenteeism and hangovers were highest among dissatisfied autoworkers. Although cars are not built all in one day (various parts are built at different times) and are not stamped with a "birth date," Hailey's claim reinforced the notion that, despite the efforts of quantitative management, the American cars produced on those days were the most shoddily made of what were coming to look like generally shoddy products.

The energy crisis of the 1970s showed different possibilities, as Americans began to buy more fuel-efficient, better-built cars made in Japan. Today the average American car lasts much longer than it used to, and some U.S. cars are equal or superior to the best foreign competitors—for example, the 2014 Cadillac CTS 3.6 beat the 2014 Mercedes-Benz E350, according to one automotive review.[55]

Although not a "theory" as such, the **quality-management viewpoint,** which includes quality control, quality assurance, and total quality management, deserves to be considered because of its impact on contemporary management perspectives.

Quality Control and Quality Assurance

Quality refers to the total ability of a product or service to meet customer needs. Quality is seen as one of the most important ways of adding value to products and services, thereby distinguishing them from those of competitors. Two traditional strategies for ensuring quality are quality control and quality assurance.

Quality Control **Quality control is defined as the strategy for minimizing errors by managing each stage of production.** Quality control techniques were developed in the 1930s at Bell Telephone Labs by **Walter Shewart,** who used statistical sampling to locate errors by testing just some (rather than all) of the items in a particular production run.

Quality Assurance Developed in the 1960s, **quality assurance focuses on the performance of workers, urging employees to strive for "zero defects."** Quality assurance has been less successful because often employees have no control over the design of the work process.

Total Quality Management: Creating an Organization Dedicated to Continuous Improvement

In the years after World War II, the imprint "Made in Japan" on a product almost guaranteed that it was cheap and flimsy. That began to change with the arrival in Japan of two Americans, **W. Edwards Deming** and **Joseph M. Juran.**

W. Edwards Deming Desperate to rebuild its war-devastated economy, Japan eagerly received mathematician W. Edwards Deming's lectures on "good management." Deming believed that quality stemmed from "constancy of purpose"—steady focus on an organization's mission—along with statistical measurement and reduction of variations in production processes. He also thought that managers should stress teamwork, be helpful rather than simply give orders, and make employees feel comfortable about asking questions.

Joseph M. Juran   Another pioneer with Deming in Japan's quality revolution was Joseph M. Juran, who defined quality as "fitness for use." By this he meant that a product or service should satisfy a customer's real needs. Thus, the best way to focus a company's efforts, Juran suggested, was to concentrate on the real needs of customers.

TQM: What It Is   From the work of Deming and Juran has come the strategic commitment to quality known as total quality management. **Total quality management (TQM) is a comprehensive approach—led by top management and supported throughout the organization—dedicated to continuous quality improvement, training, and customer satisfaction.**

The four components of TQM are as follows:

TQM pioneer. W. Edwards Deming in 1961. Deming proposed his so-called 85–15 rule—namely, when things go wrong, there is an 85% chance that the system is at fault, only a 15% chance that the individual worker is at fault. Most of the time, he thought, managers erroneously blamed individuals rather than the system.
© Bettmann/Corbis

1. **Make continuous improvement a priority.** TQM companies are never satisfied. They make small, incremental improvements an everyday priority in all areas of the organization. By improving everything a little bit of the time all the time, the company can achieve long-term quality, efficiency, and customer satisfaction.

2. **Get every employee involved.** To build teamwork, trust, and mutual respect, TQM companies see that every employee is involved in the continuous improvement process. This requires that workers must be trained and empowered to find and solve problems.

3. **Listen to and learn from customers and employees.** TQM companies pay attention to their customers, the people who use their products or services. In addition, employees within the companies listen and learn from other employees, those outside their own work areas.

4. **Use accurate standards to identify and eliminate problems.** TQM organizations are always alert to how competitors do things better, then try to improve on them—a process known as benchmarking. Using these standards, they apply statistical measurements to their own processes to identify problems.

Why Total Quality Management Is Important: The total quality management viewpoint emphasizes infusing concepts of quality throughout the total organization in a way that will deliver quality products and services to customers. The adoption of TQM helped American companies deal with global competition.

Want to find out how committed to TQM the organizations are that you are most familiar with? Even the most sophisticated organizations, you may be surprised to learn in the following self-assessment, may not measure up very well when it comes to the quality of their products. •

≡ connect SELF-ASSESSMENT 2.2

To What Extent Is Your Organization Committed to Total Quality Management?

This self-assessment is designed to gauge the extent to which the organization you have in mind is committed to total quality management (TQM).

Please be prepared to answer these questions if your instructor has assigned Self-Assessment 2.2 in Connect.

1. Which of the five dimensions is most and least important to the organization? Are you surprised by this conclusion? Explain.

2. Based on the three lowest-rated items in the survey, what advice would you give to senior leaders in the company?

3. Considering all of the questions in the survey, which three do you think are most important in terms of fostering TQM in a company? Why?

2.8 The Learning Organization in an Era of Accelerated Change

MAJOR QUESTION   **Organizations must learn or perish. How do I build a learning organization?**

THE BIG PICTURE

Learning organizations actively create, acquire, and transfer knowledge within themselves and are able to modify their behavior to reflect new knowledge. There are three ways you as a manager can help build a learning organization.

Ultimately, the lesson we need to take from the theories, perspectives, and viewpoints we have described is this: We need to keep on learning. Organizations are the same way: Like people, they must continually learn new things or face obsolescence. A key challenge for managers, therefore, is to establish a culture of shared knowledge and values that will enhance their employees' ability to learn—to build so-called learning organizations.

Learning organizations, says Massachusetts Institute of Technology professor **Peter Senge,** who coined the term, are places "where people continually expand their capacity to create the results they truly desire, where new and expansive patterns of thinking are nurtured, where collective aspiration is set free, and where people are continually learning how to learn together."[56]

The Learning Organization: Handling Knowledge and Modifying Behavior

More formally, a **learning organization** is an organization that actively creates, acquires, and transfers knowledge within itself and is able to modify its behavior to reflect new knowledge.[57] Note the three parts:

1. **Creating and acquiring knowledge.** In learning organizations, managers try to actively infuse their organizations with new ideas and information, which are the prerequisites for learning. They acquire such knowledge by constantly scanning their external environments, by not being afraid to hire new talent and expertise when needed, and by devoting significant resources to training and developing their employees.

2. **Transferring knowledge.** American Express and Apple are not only standouts in their business sectors, says management studies professor Robert Grossman, they "nurture top-to-bottom learning cultures."[58] Managers actively work at transferring knowledge throughout the organization, reducing barriers to sharing information and ideas among employees. Electronic Data Systems (EDS), for instance, practically invented the information-technology services industry, but by 1996 it was slipping behind competitors—missing the onset of the Internet wave, for example. When a new CEO, Dick Brown, took the reins in 1999, he changed the culture from "fix the problem yourself" to sharing information internally.[59]

3. **Modifying behavior.** Learning organizations are nothing if not results oriented. Thus, managers encourage employees to use the new knowledge obtained to change their behavior to help further the organization's goals.[60]

The learning organization. In rigid organizations, employees often keep information to themselves. In learning organizations, workers are encouraged to share information with each other—both inside and outside their department. © Sam Edwards/Getty Images RF

How to Build a Learning Organization: Three Roles Managers Play

To create a learning organization, managers must perform three key functions or roles: (1) *build a commitment to learning,* (2) *work to generate ideas with impact,* and (3) *work to generalize ideas with impact.*[61]

1. **You can build a commitment to learning.** To instill in your employees an intellectual and emotional commitment to the idea of learning, you as a manager need to lead the way by investing in it, publicly promoting it, creating rewards and symbols of it, and performing other similar activities. For example, to encourage employees to overcome fears about losing their jobs and exert some boldness in decision making, Jim Donald, CEO of Extended Stay America, created miniature "Get Out of Jail, Free" cards, which employees could call in whenever they took a big risk on behalf of the company—in effect giving them permission to make and learn from mistakes.[62]

2. **You can work to generate ideas with impact.** As a manager, you need to try to generate ideas with impact—that is, ideas that add value for customers, employees, and shareholders—by increasing employee competence through training, experimenting with new ideas, and engaging in other leadership activities. Xerox, for example, hired researchers called "innovation managers" to hunt for inventions and products from start-ups in India that could be adapted for the North American market. Hewlett-Packard used its research lab in India to see how it could adapt mobile phone web-interface applications in Asia and Africa to markets in developed countries.[63]

3. **You can work to generalize ideas with impact.** Besides generating ideas with impact, you can also generalize them—that is, reduce the barriers to learning among employees and within your organization. You can create a climate that reduces conflict, increases communication, promotes teamwork, rewards risk taking, reduces the fear of failure, and increases cooperation. In other words, you can create a psychologically safe and comforting environment that increases the sharing of successes, failures, and best practices.

Based on the above discussion, do you wonder about the specific behaviors that people exhibit in a learning organization? It would be interesting to determine if you have ever worked for such an organization. The following self-assessment was created to evaluate whether an organization you now work for or formerly worked for could be considered a serious learning organization. The survey items provide a good indication of what it takes to become a learning organization. ●

connect SELF-ASSESSMENT 2.3

Are You Working for a Learning Organization?

This self-assessment provides a measure of the extent to which an organization of your choice is a learning organization. Please be prepared to answer these questions if your instructor has assigned Self-Assessment 2.3 in Connect.

1. What are the strengths and weaknesses of this company in terms of being a learning organization?

2. If you were CEO of this organization, what changes would you make based on your survey results? Explain.

3. What suggestions would you make for how this organization might (1) build a commitment to learning, (2) work to generate ideas with impact, and (3) work to generalize ideas with impact? Discuss.

4. How does the learning score for the organization probably compare with the scores of other organizations you are familiar with?

administrative management 47
behavioral science approach 51
behavioral viewpoint 49
classical viewpoint 45
closed system 57
complexity theory 57
contemporary perspective 44
contingency viewpoint 58
evidence-based management 59
feedback 56
hawthorne effect 50

historical perspective 44
human relations movement 50
inputs 56
learning organization 63
management science 53
open system 57
operations management 54
outputs 56
quality 61
quality assurance 61

quality control 61
quality-management viewpoint 61
quantitative management 52
scientific management 45
subsystems 56
synergy 57
system 56
systems viewpoint 56
total quality management (TQM) 62
transformation processes 56

Key Points

2.1 Evolving Viewpoints: How We Got to Today's Management Outlook

- The two overarching perspectives on management are (1) the historical perspective, which includes three viewpoints—classical, behavioral, and quantitative; and (2) the contemporary perspective, which includes three other viewpoints—systems, contingency, and quality-management.

- Six practical reasons for studying theoretical perspectives are that they provide (1) understanding of the present, (2) a guide to action, (3) a source of new ideas, (4) clues to the meaning of your managers' decisions, (5) clues to the meaning of outside ideas, and (6) understanding as to why certain management practices produce positive outcomes.

2.2 Classical Viewpoint: Scientific and Administrative Management

- The first of the historical perspectives was the classical viewpoint, which emphasized finding ways to manage work more efficiently. It had two branches, scientific management and administrative management.

- Scientific management emphasized the scientific study of work methods to improve productivity by individual workers. It was pioneered by Frederick W. Taylor, who offered four principles of science that could be applied to management, and by Frank and Lillian Gilbreth, who refined motion studies that broke job tasks into physical motions.

- Administrative management was concerned with managing the total organization. Among its pioneers were Henri Fayol, who identified the major functions of management (planning, organizing, leading, controlling), and Max Weber, who identified five positive bureaucratic features in a well-performing organization.

- The classical viewpoint showed that work activity was amenable to a rational approach, but it has been criticized as being too mechanistic, viewing humans as cogs in a machine.

2.3 Behavioral Viewpoint: Behaviorism, Human Relations, and Behavioral Science

- The second of the historical perspectives, the behavioral viewpoint emphasized the importance of understanding human behavior and of motivating employees toward achievement. It developed over three phases: (1) early behaviorism, (2) the human relations movement, and (3) the behavioral science approach.

- Early behaviorism had three pioneers: (a) Hugo Munsterberg suggested that psychologists could contribute to industry by studying jobs, identifying the psychological conditions for employees to do their best work. (b) Mary Parker Follett thought organizations should be democratic, with employees and managers working together. (c) Elton Mayo hypothesized a so-called Hawthorne effect, suggesting that employees worked harder if they received added attention from managers.

- The human relations movement suggested that better human relations could increase worker productivity. Among its pioneers were (a) Abraham Maslow, who proposed a hierarchy of human needs, and (b) Douglas McGregor, who proposed a Theory X (managers have pessimistic view of workers) and Theory Y (managers have positive view of workers).

- The behavioral science approach relied on scientific research for developing theories about human behavior that can be used to provide practical tools for managers.

2.4 Quantitative Viewpoints: Management Science and Operations Management

- The third of the historical perspectives, quantitative viewpoints emphasized the application to management of quantitative techniques.

- Two approaches are (1) management science, which focuses on using mathematics to aid in problem solving and decision making; and (2) operations management, which focuses on managing the

2.5 Systems Viewpoint

- Following the historical perspective, the contemporary perspective includes three viewpoints: (1) systems, (2) contingency, and (3) quality-management.
- The systems viewpoint regards the organization as a system of interrelated parts or collection of subsystems that operate together to achieve a common purpose. A system has four parts: inputs, outputs, transformational processes, and feedback.
- A system can be closed, having little interaction with the environment, or open, continually interacting with it.
- Open systems have the potential of producing synergy, the idea that two or more forces combined create an effect that is greater than the sum of their individual efforts.
- The systems viewpoint has led to the development of complexity theory, the study of how order and pattern arise from very complicated, apparently chaotic systems.

2.6 Contingency Viewpoint

- The second viewpoint in the contemporary perspective, the contingency viewpoint emphasizes that a manager's approach should vary according to the individual and the environmental situation.
- In the spirit of the contingency viewpoint is evidence-based management, which means translating principles based on best evidence into organizational practice, bringing rationality to the decision-making process.

2.7 Quality-Management Viewpoint

- The third category in the contemporary perspective, the quality-management viewpoint is concerned with quality, the total ability of a product or service to meet customer needs.
- Quality management has three aspects: (1) Quality control is the strategy for minimizing errors by managing each stage of production. (2) Quality assurance focuses on the performance of workers, urging employees to strive for "zero defects." (3) Total quality management (TQM) is a comprehensive approach dedicated to continuous quality improvement, training, and customer satisfaction.
- TQM has four components: (a) make continuous improvement a priority; (b) get every employee involved; (c) listen to and learn from customers and employees; and (d) use accurate standards to identify and eliminate problems.

2.8 The Learning Organization in an Era of Accelerated Change

- A learning organization is one that actively creates, acquires, and transfers knowledge within itself and is able to modify its behavior to reflect new knowledge.
- Three roles that managers must perform to build a learning organization are to (1) build a commitment to learning, (2) work to generate ideas with impact, and (3) work to generalize ideas with impact.

Understanding the Chapter: What Do I Know?

1. What are the two overarching perspectives about management, and what are the three viewpoints that each one covers?
2. What are six practical reasons for studying theoretical perspectives?
3. What are the contributions of scientific management?
4. How would I summarize the behavioral viewpoint, and what are its contributions?
5. What is the difference between management science and operations management?
6. What would be an example of the application of the four parts of a system?
7. What would be an example of the application of the contingency viewpoint?
8. Where have I seen an organization employ evidence-based management?
9. Why should I adopt a total quality management viewpoint?
10. What are three roles I could play as a manager in a learning organization?

Management in Action

Best Buy Uses Management Theories to Improve Corporate Performance

The Internet of things affects all of our lives, particularly when it comes to online shopping. This trend in turn has put great pressure on big box retail stores like Best Buy to compete with the likes of Amazon.com. Best Buy has had a hard time competing against Amazon for several reasons.

Amazon had a price advantage because it did not charge sales tax from customers in a number of states. For example, in 2012, Amazon collected sales tax from about 40% of its customers. In 2015, it was 89%. Amazon also has many strategically located distribution centers across the U.S. that permit it to ship its many products in a timely fashion. Amazon also had a deep supply of products to draw from, enabling shoppers to pretty much get what they want, when they want it. All told, the advent of online shopping has put revenue and cost pressure on Best Buy to survive.

In conjunction with these competitive pressures, Best Buy experienced several key leadership challenges. In April 2012, the CEO, Brian Dunn, resigned amid claims that he had an inappropriate relationship with a female employee. While the board of directors investigated this allegation, it learned that Best Buy's founder and chairman, Richard Schulze, knew about the relationship for some time. This led to Schulze's resignation. But he did not go quietly. Schulze responded with an unsolicited bid to take the company private.[64]

According to one business writer, Best Buy had additional problems because "its stores had gotten dingy, populated by a shrinking sales force seemingly interested more in selling customers overpriced extended warranties than in steering them to the most suitable merchandise. The locations seemed destined to serve as 'showrooms' where customers would sample their wares hands-on before going home to order from Amazon."[65]

Enter French-born Hubert Joly as the new CEO in September 2012. Although he had no retail experience, he was motivated to institute change within the company. "This is the most dysfunctional organization I've ever seen," he told the board. "But this is good news because this is self-inflicted, and so this is something we can correct."[66] Joly started his transformation of the company using a strategy labeled "Renew Blue."

The turnaround strategy was based on an extensive diagnosis of the situation.[67] To help in this pursuit, he hired Sharon McCollam as chief financial officer in December 2012. Her experience at retailer Williams-Sonoma helped Joly to diagnose problems and implement solutions. Before accepting the job, for example, she visited 75 stores to help determine the magnitude of changes needed for the company's turnaround. Since being hired, she has "implemented a rigorous budget; overhauled Best Buy's IT, supply chain, and logistics; and even inspected stores with a 'white glove' dust test."[68]

McCollam also uncovered bloating expenses that did not directly improve sales. For example, she dropped the private jets, trips to the World Economic Forum, NASCAR sponsorships, and Super Bowl ads.

She also looked for small ways to cut costs. Corie Barry, chief strategic growth officer, described McCollam's approach as "I don't need you to go find the million-dollar idea—I'd love for you to go find the $10,000 idea."[69]

McCollam also changed Best Buys's no-questions-asked remote-work policy in 2013. This policy allowed employees to work from home as long as they completed their work. McCollam believed that this policy negatively impacted performance. She wanted employees to return to working on-site.

As expected, the company has had significant layoffs since 2012: Peak employment was about 180,000 and currently numbers around 125,000. To offset this loss of employees, Joly implemented employee empowerment at all organizational levels. He believed that this management practice enabled employees to make better and timelier decisions at the point of customer interactions. The improvement in sales results suggest that Joly was accurate.

The strategy of "Renew Blue" included several tactics aimed at overcoming the strengths held by competitors such as Amazon. One amounted to increased investment in the stores. They were redesigned to be roomier, airier, and staffed with well-trained employees. The strategy also included the decision to institute a "price-match" policy. This policy promised to match the prices offered by Amazon and 18 other retailing websites.[70] Another key tactic focused on online shipping, a key competitive advantage held by Amazon. Best Buy committed to increasing its ability to ship products directly from stores to its online customers. This led to more in-store purchases because customers knew that they would not get a better price at Amazon. It also produced more online purchases from Best Buy's website.

Best Buy also used sales performance data to develop methods for improving in-store employee performance. The approach, developed by Chris Schmidt, begins with a spreadsheet that tracks the performance metrics that are important to Best Buy. The data are then used to spot employees who need further training, "perhaps they needed extra training on 'smart' 4K TVs, or tips on conversation openers that wouldn't scare off customers," says Schmidt. Schmidt concluded that "even tiny bits of movement yield massive amounts of return," resulting in increased sales and income for employees.[71]

What is the end result of the changes taking place at Best Buy? Here is what one stock analyst had to say about the company's performance at the start of 2016: "We believe the company has performed better than the industry in several other segments of its business and is on track for improved profitability in the long term, as it continues implementation of its 'Renew Blue' transformation program."[72]

1. To what extent is Best Buy using evidence-based management? Are they overdoing it? Explain.

2. To what extent are the managerial practices being used at Best Buy consistent with principles associated with management science and operations management techniques? Discuss.

3. Use Figure 2.4 to analyze the extent to which Best Buy is using a systems viewpoint.

4. How are the managerial practices being used at Best Buy consistent with a quality-management viewpoint? Explain your rationale.

Legal/Ethical Challenge

What Should You Do about an Insubordinate Employee?

You are a vice president for a company in the insurance industry, and you supervise five managers. These managers in turn supervise a host of employees working in their departments. Your company is having trouble achieving its sales growth goals and your boss, the president of a division, called a meeting with you and your peers to create a plan of action.

The meeting was a bit volatile because layoffs were proposed and it was agreed that all vice presidents had to decrease their budgets. This means that you and your peers were not allowed to hire consultants or send employees to training. You also have to reduce your labor costs by $300,000. This means that you have to lay off employees. You informed the managers that report to you about these decisions and asked them to come up with a list of potential people to lay off. You suggested that performance should be the key criterion for deciding layoffs.

Two weeks later one of your reporting managers walked into your office with a worried look. He told you that Jim, one of your other reporting managers, had just hired a consultant to lead a team building session with his group in another state. Not only did this require significant travel expenses, but the consultant's fees were well outside of your budgeted expenses. Further, your other employees were expressing feelings of unfairness because Jim was taking his team on a team building trip and they were being forced to cut costs. It also was a bit inconsistent to spend money on teambuilding when impending layoffs were just around the corner.

In terms of layoffs, all of your reporting managers submitted a list of potential employees to let go except for Jim. You have no idea why he avoided this task.

Jim's behavior clearly violates the agreement that was made about cost cutting, and you are upset that he has not submitted his list of employees to layoff. You have not yet spoken to him about this insubordination, and now you are wondering what to do.

SOLVING THE CHALLENGE
What would you do?

1. Meet with Jim to review his behavior. Tell him that any more acts of insubordination will result in termination. Don't make a big deal about these events and don't include documentation in his personnel file.

2. Put Jim on the list of people to be laid off. Although the company will have to pay him a severance check, it reduces the chance of any lawsuit.

3. Call your human resource representative and discuss the legality of firing Jim. Jim was insubordinate in hiring a consultant and irresponsible for not submitting his list of potential employees to be laid off. If human resources agrees, I would fire Jim.

4. Reprimand Jim by putting him on Performance Improvement Plan (PIP). This plan outlines specific changes Jim needs to make going forward, and it gives him a chance to make up for his poor decisions.

5. Invent other options. Discuss.

The Environment of Management

3

The Manager's Changing Work Environment and Ethical Responsibilities

Doing the Right Thing

Major Questions You Should Be Able to Answer

3.1 The Triple Bottom Line: People, Planet, and Profit

Major Question: Is profit the only important goal of a business? What are others?

3.2 The Community of Stakeholders inside the Organization

Major Question: Stockholders are only one group of stakeholders. Who are the stakeholders important to me inside the organization?

3.3 The Community of Stakeholders outside the Organization

Major Question: Who are stakeholders important to me outside the organization?

3.4 The Ethical Responsibilities Required of You as a Manager

Major Question: What does the successful manager need to know about ethics and values?

3.5 The Social Responsibilities Required of You as a Manager

Major Question: Is being socially responsible really necessary?

3.6 Corporate Governance

Major Question: How can I trust a company is doing the right thing?

How Do People Excuse Lying and Cheating?

"Students don't just say 'OK I cheated in school, but now I'm in the workplace and it ends here,'" says an Arizona professor of legal and ethical studies. "They are forming bad habits that carry over into the market."[1]

The "Holier-Than-Thou" Effect and Motivated Blindness

Have you ever cheated—had unauthorized help on tests? Or plagiarized—misrepresented others' work as your own? Students know it's wrong, so why do it?

The psychological mechanisms operating here are:

- **The "holier-than-thou" effect.** "People tend to be overly optimistic about their own abilities and fortunes—to overestimate their standing in class, their discipline, their sincerity," suggests science writer Benedict Carey. "But this self-inflating bias may be even stronger when it comes to moral judgment."[2]

- **Motivated blindness.** This is the tendency to overlook information that works against our best interest. "People who have a vested self-interest, even the most honest among us, have difficulty being objective," says one report. "Worse yet, they fail to recognize their lack of objectivity."[3] Motivated blindness enables us to behave unethically while maintaining a positive self-image.[4]

Because of this psychology, cheating and plagiarism have become alarming problems in education, from high school to graduate school.[5] Most students rationalize their behavior by saying "I don't usually do this, but I really have to do it." They would rather cheat, that is, than show their families they got an F.[6]

The Dynamics behind Cheating

Habitual cheating, Carey suggests, "begins with small infractions—illegally downloading a few songs, skimming small amounts from the register, lies of omission on taxes—and grows by increments." As success is rewarded, these "small infractions" can burgeon into an ongoing deliberate strategy of deception or fraud.

How do people rationalize cheating? The justifications are mainly personal and emotional:

- **Cheating provides useful shortcuts.** We constantly make choices "between short- and long-term gains," suggests Carey, "between the more virtuous choice and the less virtuous one." The brain naturally seeks useful shortcuts and so may view low-level cheating as productive.

- **Cheating arises out of resentment.** People often justify lying and cheating because they have resentments about a rule or a boss.[7]

- **Cheating seeks to redress perceived unfairness.** The urge to cheat may arise from a deep sense of unfairness, such as your sense that other people had special advantages.

- **Cheating is to avoid feeling like a chump.** Many people cheat to avoid feeling like a chump—to "not being smart" and "finishing out of the money."

For Discussion How would *you* justify cheating and plagiarism? Is it simply required behavior in order to get through college? ("I'm not going to be a chump.") What do you say to the fact that, as the research shows, students who cheat and thus don't actually do the assigned work are more likely to fail anyway?[8] Do you think you can stop the lying and deception once you're out in the work world?

FORECAST What's Ahead in This Chapter

The triple bottom line of people, planet, and profit represents new standards of success for businesses. This helps define the new world in which managers must operate and their responsibilities, including the community of stakeholders, both internal and external, they must deal with. The chapter also considers a manager's ethical and social responsibilities, as well as the importance of corporate governance.

3.1   The Triple Bottom Line: People, Planet, and Profit

MAJOR QUESTION   **Is profit the only important goal of a business? What are others?**

THE BIG PICTURE

Many businesses, small and large, are beginning to subscribe to a new standard of success—the triple bottom line, representing people, planet, and profit. This outlook has found favor with many young adults (Millennials) who are more concerned with finding meaning than material success.

"Profit is a tool," says Judy Wicks, who founded the White Dog Café in Philadelphia 30 years ago. "The major purpose of business is to serve."[9]

In traditional business accounting, the "bottom line" of a revenue-and-expenses statement is the organization's profit (or loss). But in Wicks's view, making money should be only one goal of business. The others are to foster social and environmental consciousness—the two other elements of what's known as the "triple bottom line." The **triple bottom line**—representing people, planet, and profit (the 3 Ps)—measures an organization's social, environmental, and financial performance. In this view of corporate performance, an organization has a responsibility to its employees and to the wider community (people), is committed to sustainable (green) environmental practices (planet), and includes the costs of pollution, worker displacement, and other factors in its financial calculations (profit), matters high in the minds of many of today's consumers.[10] Success in these areas can be measured through a **social audit**, a systematic assessment of a company's performance in implementing socially responsible programs, often based on predefined goals.

The White Dog Café (now in three locations), for instance, is known for such social and environmental activities as buying wind-powered electricity, organic produce, and humanely raised meat and poultry, as well as sharing ideas with competitors and opening up its premises for educational forums and speakers. But the triple bottom line isn't just to be practiced by small businesses. As a co-author of *Everybody's Business: The Unlikely Story of How Big Business Can Fix the World* observes, "big businesses can . . . be really powerful, positive engines for social change."[11] For instance, Ben & Jerry's ice cream, according to its director of social mission, now has a bigger impact since being taken over by Unilever.[12] The file-storage company Box offers its products free to certain nonprofits.[13] The online bookseller Better World Books donates one book for every book it sells.[14]

The Millennials' Search for Meaning

The notion of the triple bottom line has particular appeal to many of those in the "Millennial" generation, which includes the two parts dubbed Generation Y, born 1977–1989, and Generation Z, born 1990–2000. (The definition of birth years varies.)[15] In Chapter 1, we mentioned that one of the great challenges for a manager is in trying to achieve personal success, whether in striving for a happy life or a meaningful life—or, if possible, both.[16]

"Millennials," write two scholars who have done research in this area, "appear to be more interested in living lives defined by meaning than by what some would call happiness. They report being less focused on financial success than they are on making a difference."[17] In support of this view, various studies have found that the principal factor young adults ages 21–31 wanted in a successful career was a sense of meaning.[18] Another study finds that millennials who came of age during the 2007–2009 Great Recession reported more concern for others and less interest in material goods.[19] They also want work/life balance.[20]

In this chapter, we discuss two factors in achieving a meaningful life:

- Understanding the environment in which a manager operates—the community of stakeholders inside and outside the organization.

- The ethical and social responsibilities of being a manager. ●

3.2   The Community of Stakeholders inside the Organization

Stockholders are only one group of stakeholders. Who are stakeholders important to me inside the organization?

THE BIG PICTURE

Managers operate in two organizational environments—internal and external—both made up of stakeholders, the people whose interests are affected by the organization. The first, or internal, environment consists of employees, owners, and the board of directors.

Is a company principally responsible only to its stockholders and executives? Or are other groups equal in significance?

Perhaps we need a broader term than "stockholders" to indicate all those with a stake in an organization. That term, appropriately, is **stakeholders—the people whose interests are affected by an organization's activities.**

Who Should Be a Company's Most Important Stakeholders?
Natural Gas Utility PG&E Pays a Huge Price

In September 2010, a buried Pacific Gas & Electric natural-gas pipeline in the San Francisco–area suburb of San Bruno blew up in a spectacular pillar of fire, killing 8 people, badly injuring 58 others, and destroying or severely damaging 55 houses.[21]

"The gas-fed flames burned for more than 90 minutes while PG&E scrambled to find a way to shut off the line," reported the *San Francisco Chronicle*.[22]

San Bruno explosion. This 2010 gas explosion and fire in San Bruno, California, which killed eight people, was linked to utility PG&E's low priority given to pipeline safety and high priority to its "focus on financial performance." What group should a company be most responsible to—stockholders, managers, customers, the public? © Dan Honda/Zuma Press/Newscom

To Whom Should a Company Be Responsible? It turned out that PG&E had relied on gas-leak surveys to determine whether transmission pipelines were safe, but the company's incentive system awarded bonuses to supervisors whose crews found fewer leaks and kept repair costs down.[23] Indeed, the company's own internal audit found the incentives actually *encouraged* crews to produce inaccurate surveys.

An independent audit found that over an 11-year period PG&E collected $430 million more from its gas operations than the government had authorized—and it "chose to use the surplus revenues for general corporate purposes" rather than for improved safety, according to an auditor.[24] In fact, in the three years prior to the explosion, the company spent $56 million a year on an incentive plan—stock awards, performance shares, and deferred compensation—for its executives and directors, including millions to the CEO.[25]

The utility was ordered to pay a record $1.6 billion in state penalties and other costs and settled 165 lawsuits with residents' and victims' families for $565 million. It was also indicted on 12 criminal counts, for repeatedly violating the federal Pipeline Safety Act.[26] Later prosecutors decided to seek a criminal obstruction-of-justice case against the company after an investigator complained that PG&E employees were "giggling, laughing and were sarcastic" during interviews he conducted.[27] Subsequent reports found a company history of sloppy maps and inaccurate record keeping, which was blamed for a later gas line explosion in another city.[28]

YOUR CALL

Is a company principally responsible only to its stockholders and executives? Or are other groups equal in significance? Further, is it sufficient that a company simply be legal, as PG&E believes it was?[29] Or, isn't it equally important that it be ethical as well?

Internal and External Stakeholders

Managers operate in two organizational environments, both made up of various stakeholders. *(See Figure 3.1, opposite page.)* As we describe in the rest of this section, the two environments are these:

- Internal stakeholders
- External stakeholders

Internal Stakeholders

Whether small or large, the organization to which you belong has people in it who have an important stake in how it performs. These **internal stakeholders** consist of **employees, owners, and the board of directors, if any.** Let us consider each in turn.

Employees   As a manager, could you run your part of the organization if you and your employees were constantly in conflict? Labor history, of course, is full of accounts of just that. But such conflict may lower the performance of the organization, thereby hurting everyone's stake. In many of today's forward-looking organizations, employees are considered "the talent"—the most important resource.

"My chief assets drive out the gate every day," says Jim Goodnight, CEO of North Carolina–based SAS Institute. "My job is to make sure they come back."[30] SAS is the world's largest privately held software business and was ranked No. 4 on *Fortune*'s 2015 list of "100 Best Companies to Work For."[31] In the recent past, it has been in the magazine's top spot in attracting and holding on to the best talent (it ranked 1, 1, 3, and 2, respectively, in the years 2010–2014), but that prize now belongs to Google.

Even so, SAS treats its employees exceptionally well, resulting in a turnover rate of only 2.6%, compared with a software industry average of 22%.

As we saw in Chapter 1 (manager's challenge #3), the American workforce of the future will consist of employees diverse in gender, age, race, ethnicity, and sexual orientation from what we've been accustomed to. We consider this further in Chapter 11.

FIGURE 3.1   The organization's environment

The two main groups are internal and external stakeholders.

Source: From Diverse Teams at Work by Lee Gardenswartz. Reprinted with permission of the Society for Human Resource Management (www.shrm.org), Alexandria, VA. Copyright © 2003, Society for Human Resource Management.

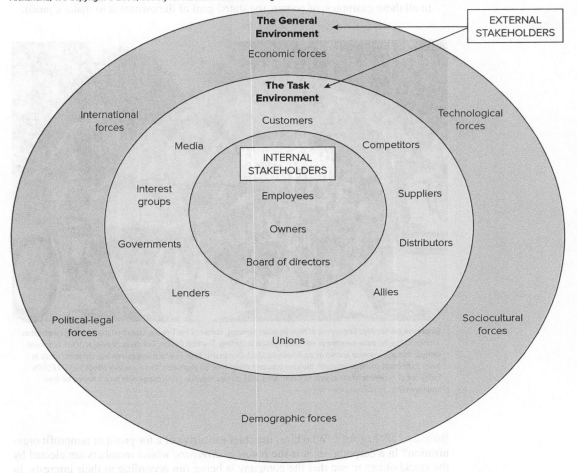

Owners   The **owners of an organization consist of all those who can claim it as their legal property,** such as Walmart's stockholders. There are five principal types of ownership.

- **Sole proprietorship:** In the for-profit world, if you're running a one-person graphic design firm, the owner is just you—you're what is known as a sole proprietorship.

- **Partnership:** If you're in an Internet start-up with your brother-in-law, you're both owners—you're a partnership.

- **Private investors:** If you're a member of a family running a car dealership, you're all owners—you're investors in a privately owned company.

- **Employee owners:** If you work for a company that is more than half owned by its employees (such as W. L. Gore & Associates, maker of Gore-Tex fabric and No. 17 on *Fortune*'s 2015 "Best Companies to Work For" list, or Lakeland, Florida, Publix Super Markets, No. 81), you are one of the joint owners— you're part of an Employee Stock Ownership Plan (ESOP).[32]

- **Stockholders:** And if you've bought a few shares of stock in a company whose shares are listed for sale on the New York Stock Exchange, such as General Motors, you're one of thousands of owners—you're a stockholder.

In all these examples, of course, the stated goal of the owners is to make a profit.

Employee ownership. Employees of New Belgium Brewing, maker of Fat Tire ale, launched the traveling celebration Tour de Fat to increase awareness and participation in cycling. The Fort Collins, Colorado, brewer is 100% employee owned, through a device known as an Employee Stock Ownership Plan, in which employees buy company stock in order to become owners. Although the idea was conceived over 50 years ago, there are only about 10,000 ESOPs today out of hundreds of thousands of businesses. Why do you suppose more companies aren't owned by their employees? © Ed Endicott/Demotix/Corbis

Board of Directors Who hires the chief executive of a for-profit or nonprofit organization? In a corporation, it is the *board of directors,* whose members are elected by the stockholders to see that the company is being run according to their interests. In nonprofit organizations, such as universities or hospitals, the board may be called the *board of trustees* or *board of regents.* Board members are very important in setting the organization's overall strategic goals and in approving the major decisions and salaries of top management.

A large corporation might have eight or so members on its board of directors. Some of these directors (inside directors) may be top executives of the firm. The rest (outside directors) are elected from outside the firm. Sometimes directors follow different strategies with their firm's management. In early 2016, Yahoo!'s directors hired investment bankers to explore selling the company, while CEO Marissa Mayer was courting developers with promises of Yahoo!'s "incredible potential" in mobile devices in the coming years.[33]

We consider directors further in Section 3.6, "Corporate Governance." ●

3.3   The Community of Stakeholders outside the Organization

Who are the stakeholders important to me outside the organization?

THE BIG PICTURE

The external environment of stakeholders consists of the task environment and the general environment. The task environment consists of customers, competitors, suppliers, distributors, strategic allies, employee associations, local communities, financial institutions, government regulators, special-interest groups, and the mass media. The general environment consists of economic, technological, sociocultural, demographic, political–legal, and international forces.

In the first section we described the environment inside the organization. Here let's consider the environment outside it, which consists of **external stakeholders—people or groups in the organization's external environment that are affected by it.** This environment consists of:

- The task environment
- The general environment

The Task Environment

The **task environment consists of 11 groups that present you with daily tasks to handle: customers, competitors, suppliers, distributors, strategic allies, employee organizations, local communities, financial institutions, government regulators, special-interest groups, and mass media.**

1. Customers   The first law of business (and even nonprofits), we've said, is *take care of the customer.* **Customers are those who pay to use an organization's goods or services.** Many customers are generally frustrated by poor customer relations at airlines, banks, cable and satellite service providers, and some big retailers, in part because many of these companies have few competitors and so don't have to worry about making customers happy. Among "America's most hated companies," by one account: Spirit Airlines, Dish Network, Walmart, Sprint, Bank of America, Comcast, and Sears.[34] (Most hated was Volkswagen because it had installed a device on 11 million diesel cars that could deceive emissions tests.)

EXAMPLE

Amazon's Jeff Bezos Obsesses about a Great Customer Experience, but Is It at the Expense of Other Stakeholders' Well-Being?

Since launching Amazon in 1995, founder and CEO Jeff Bezos has been "obsessed," in his words, with what he calls "the customer experience." Customers "care about having the lowest prices, having vast selection, so they have choice, and getting the products . . . fast," Bezos has said. "And the reason I'm so obsessed with these drivers of the customer experience is that I believe that the success we have had over the past . . . years has been driven exclusively by that customer experience."[35]

"Simple Is Not Easy." Amazon has led the "Hall of Fame" of one online national survey of customer satisfaction six years in a row. The reason? "Amazon has always been very good at being simple, and simple is not easy," says a consultant.[36] Because of the company's user-friendly website, low prices, one-click shopping, free-shipping options, no-hassle returns policy, and possibly even the sense of community it fosters, the company served 244 million active users in 2014 who bought 2 billion products.[37] A recent innovation in customer satisfaction is Amazon's anticipatory shipping feature, which is designed to use a customer's order history to predict what he or she will need and then ship the goods to nearby warehouses even before the customer purchases them.[38]

Detractors. Not every stakeholder finds Amazon so congenial. States have objected to its hardball policies on avoiding taxes on Internet sales. (Thirteen states, including Alabama, South Dakota, and Utah, have grown tired of waiting for Congress to let them tax out-of-state retailers, so they are moving to impose taxes themselves.)[39] Suppliers grumble about being squeezed. Walk-in retailers have worried as shoppers have deserted them en masse for Amazon e-commerce. Book publishers and sellers have seethed over loss of readers to online order systems and Kindle e-books. And Amazon's own employees have complained about severe workplace rules in the company's 115 distribution centers.[40] For most customers, however, none of this other stuff matters, and Amazon's famed customer service helped the company grow to $107 billion in revenues in 2015.[41]

YOUR CALL

Does it matter to you how harshly a company treats other stakeholders so long as it handles its customer relations well? To what extent are Amazon's policies consistent with the triple bottom line?

2. Competitors

Is there any line of work you could enter in which there would *not* be **competitors—people or organizations that compete for customers or resources,** such as talented employees or raw materials? We mentioned that some of the most hated companies in America have little competition—but every organization has to be on the lookout for *possible* competitors, even if not yet in sight.

E-commerce companies such as Amazon already represent huge threats to such retailers as Walmart, Sears, Macy's, Kohl's, and Pier 1, for example.[42] In addition, studies seem to show that *experiences,* not objects, bring the most happiness, and, points out one writer, "the Internet is bursting with 'Buy Experiences, Not Things' type of stories that can give retailing executives nightmares."[43]

3. Suppliers

A **supplier,** or vendor, **is a person** or an organization that provides supplies—that is, **raw materials, services, equipment, labor, or energy—to other organizations.** Suppliers in turn have their own suppliers: The printer of this book (in its paper form) buys the paper on which it is printed from a paper merchant, who in turn is supplied by several paper mills, which in turn are supplied wood for wood pulp by logging companies with forests in the United States or Canada.

4. Distributors

A **distributor,** sometimes called a middle man, **is a person or an organization that helps another organization sell its goods and services to customers.** Publishers of magazines, for instance, don't sell directly to newsstands; rather, they go through a distributor, or wholesaler. Tickets to Maroon Five, Phish, or other artists' performances might be sold to you directly by the concert hall, but they are also sold through such distributors as TicketMaster, LiveNation, and StubHub.

Distributors can be quite important because in some industries (such as movie theaters and magazines) there is not a lot of competition, and the distributor has a lot of power over the ultimate price of the product. However, the popularity of the Internet has allowed manufacturers of cell phones, for example, to cut out the "middleman"— the distributor—and to sell to customers directly.

5. Strategic Allies

Companies, and even nonprofit organizations, frequently link up with other organizations (even competing ones) in order to realize strategic advantages. The term **strategic allies describes the relationship of two organizations who join forces to achieve advantages neither can perform as well alone.**

With their worldwide reservation systems and slick marketing, big companies— Hilton, Hyatt, Marriott, Starwood, and so on—dominate the high-end business-center hotels. But in many cities, there are still independents—such as The Rittenhouse in Philadelphia; The Hay-Adams in Washington, DC; and The Adolphus in Dallas—that compete with the chains by promoting their prestigious locations, grand architecture, rich history, and personalized service. In recent years, however, some high-end independents have become affiliated with chains as strategic allies because chains can buy supplies for less and they have more far-reaching sales channels. The 105-year-old U.S. Grant in downtown San Diego, for example, became part of Starwood's Luxury Collection to get better worldwide exposure.

6. Employee Organizations: Unions and Associations   As a rule of thumb, labor unions (such as the United Auto Workers or the Teamsters Union) tend to represent hourly workers; professional associations (such as the National Education Association or The Newspaper Guild) tend to represent salaried workers. Nevertheless, during a labor dispute, salary-earning teachers in the American Federation of Teachers might well act in sympathy with the wage-earning janitors in the Service Employees International Union.

In recent years, the percentage of the labor force represented by unions has steadily declined (from 35% in the 1950s to 11.1% in 2015).[44] Indeed, more than five times as many union members are now public-sector workers compared to private-sector workers, whose unionizing has sharply fallen off, mainly because of job losses in manufacturing and construction. The unionization rates are highest in protective service occupations (36.3%) and in education, training, and library occupations (35.5%).[45] The composition of the membership has also changed, with 45.8% of the unionized workforce now female and 52.4% of union members holding a four-year college degree or more.[46]

7. Local Communities   Local communities are obviously important stakeholders, as becomes evident not only when a big organization arrives but also when it leaves, sending government officials scrambling to find new industry to replace it. Schools and municipal governments rely on the organization for their tax base. Families and merchants depend on its employee payroll for their livelihoods. In addition, everyone from the United Way to the Little League may rely on it for some financial support.

If a community gives a company tax breaks in return for the promise of new jobs and the firm fails to deliver, does the community have the right to institute **clawbacks—rescinding the tax breaks when firms don't deliver promised jobs**? But what is a town to do if a company goes bankrupt, as did Hoku Materials, manufacturer of materials for solar panels, after the struggling town of Pocatello, Idaho, gave it numerous concessions?[47]

Local Communities as Stakeholders: Are Financial Incentives to Sports Teams and Other Business Really Necessary?

EXAMPLE

"The NFL and the owners of its 32 teams are unfamiliar with the concept of reasonableness," editorialized the *San Francisco Chronicle*. "Their audacity is boundless."[48]

The editors were upset because the National Football League had been approached by two cities, St. Louis and San Diego, with plans to apply generous public subsidies to keep their two NFL teams, the Rams and the Chargers, in town. But the NFL turned them down because the owners felt the proposed offers—each expected to exceed $1 billion—weren't good enough. And so the Rams, at least, were being allowed to leave, to move to a $3 billion stadium to be built near

Los Angeles. St. Louis lost its NFL team for the second time in 29 years. (The Chargers, and also the Oakland Raiders, were expected to move later.)[49]

What is the loss to St. Louis taxpayers? Publicly subsidized stadiums are built on the promise that they will generate economic development. But study after study, the *Chronicle* pointed out, show such initiatives provide little if any net gain to the public treasury. The Raiders, for instance, have not provided the economic boost that was predicted when the team relocated back to Oakland from Los Angeles following the 1994 season.[50]

Public Incentives to Private Business. Professional sports teams aren't the only beneficiaries of government incentives, which may come in the form of cash grants and loans, sales tax breaks, income tax credits and exemptions, free services, and property tax abatements. So are film productions, for example. Film companies in California are wooed by tax incentives offered by states such as Georgia, Louisiana, Nevada, New Mexico, New York, Oregon, and Texas, all seeking the supposed economic benefits movie companies bring, such as purchasing supplies from local businesses.[51]

Buffalo, New York, offers $5 million in rewards to retain local entrepreneurs and attract new ones.[52] San Francisco has given tech companies Twitter, Microsoft, Zendesk, Zoosk, and Spotify tax breaks for locating in seedy areas in need of revival. In Arizona, the town of Mesa "offered tax breaks, built power lines, fast-tracked building permits, and got the state to declare a vacant 1.3 million-square-foot plant a foreign trade zone," says one account, to lure Apple Inc. to build a factory employing 700 people.[53] Officials in Massachusetts offered incentives worth up to $145 million to General Electric to lure the conglomerate's headquarters and about 800 jobs from leafy Fairfield, Connecticut, where it had been based since 1974, to the Boston waterfront.[54]

Community stakeholder. Officials in Massachusetts offered incentives worth up to $145 million to General Electric to move from Fairfield, Connecticut (shown here), to the Boston waterfront. Lower corporate taxes and an urban environment attractive to the most promising and talented employees figured in the company's 2016 decision. Several other states (including Connecticut, Georgia, New York, Rhode Island, and Texas) had competed vigorously for GE. In 10 years, do you think this will prove to have been a wise decision for Massachusetts? Or should the $145 million have been given to struggling entrepreneurs or to provide teacher raises? © Bob Child/AP Photo

"Help Us Help You." Such government inducements are extraordinarily commonplace—but often to the financial detriment of the local community. "A portrait arises," *The New York Times* wrote, "of mayors and governors who are desperate to create jobs, outmatched by multinational corporations, and short on tools to fact-check what companies tell them. Many of the officials said they feared that companies would move jobs overseas if they did not get subsidies in the United States."[55] Although most incentive funds are directed toward manufacturing, followed by agriculture, the oil, gas, and mining sectors are in third place, the film business fourth, and technology companies not far behind.

YOUR CALL

How would you advise local public officials to handle the whole matter of tax incentives for business—especially if they are across the table from the shrewd negotiators representing a huge company such as Apple or General Electric? What obligations should a community expect of the companies located there?

8. Financial Institutions   Want to launch a small company? Although normally reluctant to make loans to start-ups, financial institutions—banks, savings and loans, and credit unions—may do so if you have a good credit history or can secure the loan with property such as a house. You might also receive help from venture capitalists. **Venture capital is money provided by investors to start-up firms and small businesses with high risk but perceived long-term growth potential, in return for an ownership stake.**

During the Great Recession, when even good customers found loans hard to get, a new kind of financing emerged called **crowdfunding, raising money for a project or venture by obtaining many small amounts of money from many people ("the crowd"),** using websites such as Kickstarter. We discuss crowdfunding further in Chapter 10.

Established companies also often need loans to tide them over when revenues are down or to finance expansion, but they rely for assistance on lenders such as commercial banks, investment banks, and insurance companies.

9. Government Regulators   The preceding groups are external stakeholders in your organization since they are clearly affected by its activities. But why would **government regulators—regulatory agencies that establish ground rules under which organizations may operate**—be considered stakeholders?

We are talking here about an alphabet soup of agencies, boards, and commissions that have the legal authority to prescribe or proscribe the conditions under which you may conduct business. To these may be added local and state regulators on the one hand and foreign governments and international agencies (such as the World Trade Organization, which oversees international trade and standardization efforts) on the other.

Such government regulators can be said to be stakeholders because not only do they affect the activities of your organization, they are in turn affected by it. The Federal Aviation Agency (FAA), for example, specifies how far planes must stay apart to prevent midair collisions. But when the airlines want to add more flights on certain routes, the FAA may have to add more flight controllers and radar equipment, since those are the agency's responsibility. Recently, the FAA has had to take on the heavy responsibility of regulating the use of drones, which, at 325,000 and counting, now exceed the 320,000 piloted aircraft from Cessnas to Dreamliners.[56]

10. Special-Interest Groups   In recent times, efforts to ban horse-drawn carriages that serve tourists wanting to take in urban sights have spread across the country, from Salt Lake City to Atlanta. In New York City, the 1,200 operators of horse-drawn carriage rides were being pressured by opponents who insisted the horses weren't equipped to handle city noise and traffic, as well as intense summer heat. Spurred by some highly publicized deaths and injuries to horses, many of the complaints came from animal-rights groups, such as People for the Ethical Treatment of Animals (PETA). In New York, however, two-thirds of city voters said they didn't want the bans. Some visitors also said they liked "the clip-clop of the horse's feet."[57]

Special Interests. Fast-food workers demonstrate to demand a $15-an-hour guaranteed wage and the right to union representation. © Paul Weiskel/Demotix/Corbis

Special-interest groups are groups whose members try to influence specific issues, some of which may affect your organization. Examples are People for the Ethical Treatment of Animals, Mothers Against Drunk Driving, the National Organization for Women, and the National Rifle Association.

Special-interest groups may try to exert political influence, as in contributing funds to lawmakers' election campaigns or in launching letter-writing efforts to officials. Or they may organize picketing and *boycotts*—holding back their patronage—of certain companies. In 2016, prominent African Americans, including actors Jada Pinkett Smith and Will Smith, boycotted the Academy Awards over the lack of racial diversity among Oscar nominees.[58] This led host Chris Rock to include a variety of skits and jokes aimed at highlighting a lack of diversity in Academy nominees.[59]

11. Mass Media   No manager can afford to ignore the power of the mass media—print, radio, TV, and the Internet—to rapidly and widely disseminate news both bad and good. Thus, most companies, universities, hospitals, and even government agencies have a public-relations person or department to communicate effectively with the press. In addition, top-level executives often receive special instruction on how to best deal with the media.

EXAMPLE   Managing the Media: What's the Best Practice for Handling Product Recalls?

Every now and then, a company has to issue a product recall for defective products, but recently there has been almost a "recall sprawl."

GM's Cobalt Recall. In 2004 (five years before the company's bankruptcy and government takeover), General Motors received the first reports of engines suddenly shutting down in Chevrolet Cobalts, owing to a defective ignition switch, a condition that ultimately led to 13 fatal crashes. It was not until December 2013, however, when Mary Barra (introduced in Chapter 1) was about to become GM chief, that top management was alerted to the problem, proving the adage that the larger an organization gets, the less likely bad news will travel smoothly up the hierarchy.[60] Although government regulators had been alerted in 2007, they did not open an investigation.[61] Barra herself said she had known nothing about the matter prior to becoming CEO.

Barra Steps Up. In 2014, amid a firestorm of consumer criticism, GM issued recalls, for Cobalts and other vehicles, covering 6.3 million cars and trucks.[62] In a move intended to reassure the public that GM had become more trustworthy and less bureaucratic and arrogant since it emerged from bankruptcy, Barra also testified before a congressional committee, but "her measured, carefully worded responses only seemed to inflame senators," says one report.[63]

On the other hand, Barra has met with families of people killed in Cobalt accidents, something old GM managers would not have done. She also ordered an internal investigation to find out why GM failed to fix a safety defect for more than a decade.[64]

YOUR CALL

For GM, "Mary Barra seems to fully embody the position of the CEO who is sorry," says business ethics professor Amy Sepinwall. "She recognizes that she has to pass on the [corporation's] deepest regrets, and I think she's been pretty convincing on that score."[65] Do you agree? What else should she have done?

The General Environment

Beyond the task environment is the **general environment, or macroenvironment, which includes six forces: economic, technological, sociocultural, demographic, political–legal, and international.**

You may be able to control some forces in the task environment, but you can't control those in the general environment. Nevertheless, they can profoundly affect your organization's task environment without your knowing it, springing nasty surprises on you. Clearly, then, as a manager you need to keep your eye on the far horizon because these forces of the general environment can affect long-term plans and decisions.

1. Economic Forces   Economic forces consist of the general economic conditions and trends—unemployment, inflation, interest rates, economic growth—that may affect an organization's performance. These are forces in your nation and region and even the world over which you and your organization probably have no control, as happened in the Great Recession and its aftermath.

Are banks' interest rates going up in the United States? Then it will cost you more to borrow money to open new stores or build new plants. Is your region's unemployment rate rising? Then maybe you'll have more job applicants to hire from, yet you'll also have fewer customers with money to spend. (A record 45 million Americans are presently considered poor, according to the 2014 census; the poverty rate has fallen only to 14.5% from 19% in two generations.)[66] Are natural resources getting scarce in an important area of supply? Then your company will need to pay more for them or switch to alternative sources.

One indicator that managers often pay attention to is productivity growth. Rising productivity leads to rising profits, lower inflation, and higher stock prices. In recent times, companies have been using information technology to cut costs, resulting in productivity growing at an annual rate of 2.7% from 2001 to 2007. In the recession year 2008, it slumped to 1.2% and then came roaring back to 3.9% in 2010 and 2.8% in 2011. It slipped again to 1.8% in 2012 and 2013 and declined further to 0.7% in 2014 and 0.6% in 2015.[67] Falling productivity affects a company's costs, which in turn, of course, affects its profits.

2. Technological Forces   **Technological forces are new developments in methods for transforming resources into goods or services.** The true age of technological innovation, suggests science writer Michael Hanlon, ran from about 1945 to 1971. "Just about everything that defines the modern world either came about or had its seeds sown during that time," he writes. "The pill. Electronics. Computers and the birth of the Internet. Nuclear power. Television. Antibiotics. Space travel."[68] (Social sciences professor Robert Gordon has his own list: Electricity. The telephone. The combustion engine. Mass production. Indoor plumbing. The conquest of infectious diseases. The computer. Everything else—including the Internet and the smartphone—is simply a variation on these themes, in his view.)[69]

Hanlon thinks we have fewer truly significant technological innovations in the present. "Today, progress is defined almost entirely by consumer-driven, often banal improvements in information technology," he says. "That's not the same as being able to fly across the Atlantic in eight hours or eliminating smallpox."[70] Some, however, might disagree, as suggested by the examples.

EXAMPLE

Technology Changes Everything

The key fact about computer technology is its capacity for *disruption*—disruption of service industries, certainly, such as book selling, music, or air travel, but also disruption in the world's access to knowledge, in health care, in energy sources, and many other matters.

Availability of Knowledge: Boon to Students, Device Geeks, and Everyone Everywhere. By 2020, smartphones will cost less than $50 and inexpensive Internet access will be available by drones, balloons, and microsatellites to another 3 billion of the earth's people, suggests scholar Vivek Wadhwa. "This will be particularly transformative for the developing world," he believes. "Soon everyone, everywhere, will have access to the ocean of knowledge on the Internet."[71]

Computerization is already changing manufacturing, for instance, and assembly lines cranking out standardized products are yielding to customized production. Unquestionably, the shorter product life cycles and frequently changing software packages will require rapid skill updates and continuous learning among workers. However, the availability of low-cost electronics and desktop 3-D printers can also, say experts Mark Muro and Kelly Kline, be a spur to "thousands of hobbyist craftspeople, self-taught designers, students, and device geeks" to develop their manufacturing skills and entrepreneurship.[72]

Engineering of Life: Gene Modification. Wadhwa points out that another truly revolutionary technology that's recently come into the mainstream is CRISPR gene modification. CRISPRs are the elements of a bacterial defense system and can be programmed to edit DNA and allow researchers to permanently modify genes in living cells and organisms. Thus, Wadhwa suggests, CRISPR modification could be used to treat genetic causes of diseases such as cystic fibrosis, sickle-cell anemia, and Alzheimer's, among other applications.[73]

More Awkward Communication? Mobile Devices Changing Human Relations. How confident are you in your communication and social skills? With nearly half of 18- to 29-year-olds saying they use their smartphones to "avoid others around you," according to a 2015 Pew Research Center survey, is an entire generation coming along that can't deal with the awkwardness of face-to-face human relations?[74] Is their avoidance of using their phones to even *talk* to each other an all-out flight from personal contact?[75] "With knowledge of, and access to, the billions of people sharing the planet has come a new loneliness," suggests columnist Roger Cohen.[76]

We consider this subject in more detail in Chapter 15 on communication.

YOUR CALL

Which technological change do you think is apt to affect you personally during the next decade? What kind of strategies for change will managers have to adopt?

3. Sociocultural Forces   **Sociocultural forces** are influences and trends originating in a country's, a society's, or a culture's human relationships and values that may affect an organization or industry. "With more access to social media," says one account, "young people are driving less than they used to and evincing a lack of interest in cars (causing deep worry in the automotive industry)."[77] Piano stores are closing as fewer children take up the instrument, the Associated Press reports; "people are interested in things that don't take much effort," a piano consultant believes.[78] Gambling casinos are "bringing in tattoo studios, mixed martial arts competitions, and other offbeat attractions" to attract Millennial-age patrons, reports another AP story.[79] These are three examples of industries affected by sociocultural forces.

Seismic changes are occurring in Americans' views about sociocultural issues, recent polls show: 87% in approval of interracial marriage in 2013 (versus 48% in 1991), 53% in favor of same-sex marriage in 2013 (versus 27% in 1996), 52% supporting legalization of marijuana in 2014 (versus 12% in 1969), and so on.[80]

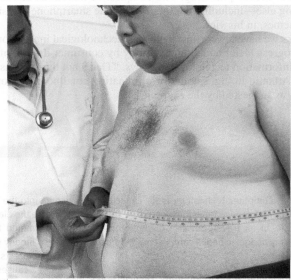

Sociocultural forces. The U.S. obesity rate—68% of Americans are overweight and a full 30% of them are obese—is one of those sociocultural forces capable of altering entire industries. Which do you think would be most affected? © Science Photo Library/Getty Images RF

Entire industries have been rocked when the culture underwent a lifestyle change, most notably changes in approaches to health. Diet sodas, for instance, have gone through a nearly decade-long decline, causing major concerns for Coca-Cola and PepsiCo, because more Americans worry that artificial sweeteners are unhealthy, despite numerous studies that find them safe.[81] Some killer diseases, such as measles, whooping cough, and meningitis, are creeping back because of an anti-vaccine movement based on philosophical and religious exemptions.[82] Recently, with more attention focused on the epidemic of obesity, there has been some turnaround, with Americans consuming fewer calories and cutting back on fast food, cholesterol, and fat.[83] (Obesity can also alter one's personal fortunes. People who are overweight are viewed as being less competent than normal-weight people in a workplace setting, and so it is harder for the overweight to get ahead.)[84]

These trends are affecting the fast-food industry, with a changing customer base calling for more food with ingredients free of additives and antibiotics, that focuses on regional flavors, that is influenced by fine-dining chefs, and that reflects principles of "mindful dining"—sustainability, reduction of food waste, and humane treatment of animals.[85]

4. Demographic Forces

Demographics derives from the ancient Greek word for "people"—*demos*—and deals with statistics relating to human populations. Age, gender, race, sexual orientation, occupation, income, family size, and the like are known as demographic characteristics when they are used to express measurements of certain groups. **Demographic forces are influences on an organization arising from changes in the characteristics of a population, such as age, gender, or ethnic origin.**

We mentioned in Chapter 1 several instances of major shifts to come in racial and ethnic diversity. Among other recent changes: Marriage rates are down, more couples are marrying later, black–white and same-sex marriages are increasing, one-person households are growing, the decline in fertility rates is leveling off, divorce rates are down, secularism (being nonreligious) is up, more households are multigenerational, and the percentage of people living in rural areas is the lowest ever.[86] By 2050, it's predicted, the U.S. population will soar to 401 million (from about 317 million today), and minorities are expected to exceed 50% of the population by around 2043.[87] We consider demographic and diversity matters in more detail in Chapter 9.

5. Political–Legal Forces

Political–legal forces are changes in the way politics shape laws and laws shape the opportunities for and threats to an organization. In the United States, whatever political view tends to be dominant at the moment may be reflected in how the government addresses environmental and sustainability issues, such as those we described in Chapter 1. For instance, should the government permit Shell to drill for oil in the Alaska Arctic?[88] Should coal mining be allowed on public lands?[89] How should public money be spent on dealing with climate change and ocean warming?[90]

As for legal forces, some countries have more fully developed legal systems than others. And some countries have more lawyers per capita. (The United States reportedly has more lawyers per person in its population than any of 29 countries studied except Greece.)[91] American companies may be more willing to use the legal system to advance their interests, as in suing competitors to gain competitive advantage. But they must also watch that others don't do the same to them.

6. International Forces

International forces are changes in the economic, political, legal, and technological global system that may affect an organization.

This category represents a huge grab bag of influences. How does the economic integration of the European Union create threats and opportunities for American companies? U.S. companies that do significant business in Europe are subject to regulation by the European Union. For instance, in one antitrust case, several companies in Europe were able to get Google to change the way it displays its search results, after they complained that, as one consumer rights advocacy group stated, Google could "stack its search results as suits itself."[92] (Google is now blocking certain of these results.)[93] We consider global concerns in Chapter 4.

How well Americans can handle international forces depends a lot on their training. Unfortunately, only 18% of Americans report speaking a language other than English, whereas 53% of Europeans, for example, can converse in a second language.[94] Almost all U.S. high schools offer foreign languages, but less than 1% of American adults are proficient in a foreign language they studied in a U.S. classroom.[95] One writer suggests U.S. companies should hire more key managers whose native language isn't English because "research shows that we behave more rationally when we think in another language"—that is, it reduces biases in decision making.[96] ●

3.4   The Ethical Responsibilities Required of You as a Manager

What does the successful manager need to know about ethics and values?

THE BIG PICTURE

Managers need to be aware of what constitutes ethics, values, the four approaches to ethical dilemmas, and how organizations can promote ethics.

Would you take supplies from the office supply closet on leaving a job? (Twenty-six percent of workers said they would, 74% said they wouldn't, in one survey.)[97] That may be an easy decision. But how would you handle a choice between paying a client money under the table in order to land a big contract, for example, and losing your job? That's a much harder matter.

One of a manager's major challenges, as we stated in Chapter 1, is managing for ethical standards. In business, most ethical conflicts are about choosing between *economic performance* and *social performance*.[98] This is known as an **ethical dilemma, a situation in which you have to decide whether to pursue a course of action that may benefit you or your organization but that is unethical or even illegal.** Volkswagen managers, for instance, allowed software to be installed on diesel-powered cars that would cheat on emissions tests (so that the vehicles seemed more fuel efficient—perceived as an *economic* benefit) and spew more oxides into the air (adding more greenhouse gases and contributing to climate change—working against the intended *social benefit*).[99]

Solving ethical dilemmas is an important skill, according to a recent study. An investigation of 400 senior executives and 455 college students revealed that 62% of the students believed that they were well prepared to deal with ethical judgments whereas only 30% of executives see students as prepared.[100] To help you develop this skill, we ask you to solve an ethical/legal dilemma at the end of each chapter.

Defining Ethics and Values

Seventy-three percent of American employees working full time say they have observed ethical misconduct at work, and 36% have been "distracted" by it.[101] Most of us assume we know what "ethics" and "values" mean, but do we? Let's consider them.

Ethics   **Ethics are the standards of right and wrong that influence behavior.** These standards may vary among countries and among cultures. **Ethical behavior is behavior that is accepted as "right" as opposed to "wrong" according to those standards.**

A tip, a gratuity, a gift, a donation, a commission, a consulting fee, a kickback, a bribe: What are the differences among these?

Regardless of the amount of money involved, each one may be intended to reward the recipient for providing you with better service, either anticipated or performed.

For years, pharmaceutical companies have provided doctors with small gifts—pads with logos, tickets to sports events, free drug samples—to promote their drugs. However, in recent years, points out one editorial, "those trinkets have evolved into big money for doctors to speak to other doctors about new drugs," as in presentations at dinner lectures.[102] What if the drug makers' strategy, as some critics accuse, is to use such methods even to expand the whole concept of high blood pressure or attention deficit disorder so as to increase the pool of people taking medications?[103] Because of such concerns, a Sunshine Act provision was written into the Affordable Care Act, requiring drug companies to report payments to individual doctors.[104]

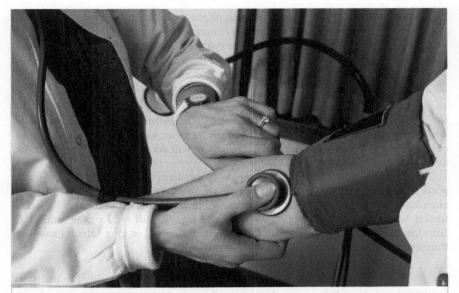

Sunshine on gifts. Some doctors say that medicine changes so rapidly that they rely on drug companies and fellow M.D.'s to keep them up to date, as through presentations at medical society dinners financed by pharmaceutical companies. However, the Physician Payments Sunshine Act now requires that pharmaceutical companies report meals, travel expenses, grants, lecture fees, drug samples, and other gifts to physicians. Do you think such disclosures are necessary? © Jack Star/PhotoLink/Getty Images RF

Values Ethical dilemmas often take place because of an organization's **value system, the pattern of values within an organization. Values are the relatively permanent and deeply held underlying beliefs and attitudes that help determine a person's behavior,** such as the belief that "Fairness means hiring according to ability, not family background." Values and value systems are the underpinnings for ethics and ethical behavior.

Organizations may have two important value systems that can conflict: (1) the value system stressing financial performance versus (2) the value system stressing cohesion and solidarity in employee relationships.[105]

Example: A car dealership may hire an accounting firm to send an accountant to audit its books, and she works alongside employees of the car dealer for several weeks, establishing cohesion and solidarity. But when a task that she estimated would take 10 hours actually takes 15, the dealership's employees might say, "You charged us more hours than you said you would," and so she might report just 10 hours to her superiors at the accounting firm. This action makes the subordinate look good, and keeps the client happy, thereby improving social cohesion. But, of course, the accounting firm unknowingly takes a loss on financial performance.[106] This kind of value system conflict happens all the time.

Four Approaches to Deciding Ethical Dilemmas

How do alternative values guide people's decisions about ethical behavior? Here are four approaches, which may be taken as guidelines:

1. The Utilitarian Approach: For the Greatest Good Ethical behavior in the **utilitarian approach is guided by what will result in the greatest good for the greatest number of people.** Managers often take the utilitarian approach, using financial performance—such as efficiency and profit—as the best definition of what constitutes "the greatest good for the greatest number."[107]

Thus, a utilitarian "cost–benefit" analysis might show that in the short run the firing of thousands of employees may improve a company's bottom line and provide immediate benefits for the stockholders. The drawback of this approach, however, is that it may result in damage to workforce morale and the loss of employees with experience and skills—actions not so readily measurable in dollars.

2. The Individual Approach: For Your Greatest Self-Interest Long-Term, Which Will Help Others

Ethical behavior in the **individual approach** is guided by what will result in the individual's best *long-term* interests, which ultimately are in everyone's self-interest. The assumption here is that you will act ethically in the short run to avoid others harming you in the long run.

The flaw here, however, is that one person's short-term self-gain may *not,* in fact, be good for everyone in the long term. After all, the manager of an agribusiness that puts chemical fertilizers on the crops every year will always benefit, but the fishing industries downstream could ultimately suffer if chemical runoff reduces the number of fish. Indeed, this is one reason why Puget Sound Chinook, or king salmon, has been threatened with extinction in the Pacific Northwest.[108]

3. The Moral-Rights Approach: Respecting Fundamental Rights Shared by Everyone

Ethical behavior in the **moral-rights approach** is guided by respect for the fundamental rights of human beings, such as those expressed in the U.S. Constitution's Bill of Rights. We would all tend to agree that denying people the right to life, liberty, privacy, health and safety, and due process is unethical. Thus, most of us would have no difficulty condemning the situation of immigrants illegally brought into the United States and then effectively enslaved—as when made to work seven days a week as maids.

The difficulty, however, is when rights are in conflict, such as employer and employee rights. Should employees on the job have a guarantee of privacy? Actually, it is legal for employers to listen to business phone calls and monitor all nonspoken personal communications.[109]

4. The Justice Approach: Respecting Impartial Standards of Fairness

Ethical behavior in the **justice approach** is guided by respect for impartial standards of fairness and equity. One consideration here is whether an organization's policies—such as those governing promotions or sexual harassment cases—are administered impartially and fairly regardless of gender, age, sexual orientation, and the like.

Fairness can often be a hot issue. For instance, many employees are loudly resentful when a corporation's CEO is paid a salary and bonuses worth hundreds of times more than what they receive—even when the company performs poorly—and when fired is then given a "golden parachute," or extravagant package of separation pay and benefits.

White-Collar Crime, SarbOx, and Ethical Training

At the beginning of the 21st century, U.S. business erupted in an array of scandals represented in such names as Enron, WorldCom, Tyco, and Adelphia, and their chief executives—Jeffrey Skilling, Bernard Ebbers, Dennis Kozlowski, and John Rigas—went to prison on various fraud convictions. Executives' deceits generated a great deal of public outrage, as a result of which Congress passed the Sarbanes–Oxley Act, as we'll describe. Did that stop the raft of business scandals? Not quite.

Next to hit the headlines were cases of **insider trading, the illegal trading of a company's stock by people using confidential company information.** The federal government launched a six-year crackdown on insider trading on Wall Street that resulted in 87 convictions (14 of which were dismissed or lost on appeal; one trial ended in acquittal).[110] In 2011, for instance, billionaire hedge-fund manager Raj Rajaratnam was sentenced to 11 years in prison for trading on tips from persons at companies who slipped him advance word on inside information.[111] In 2014, Mathew Martoma, a former portfolio manager at SAC Capital Advisors, was sentenced to nine years in federal prison, convicted of insider trading for using confidential information about an experimental Alzheimer's drug.[112] There were even cases in which two San Francisco Bay Area men were accused by federal authorities of doing insider trading because they traded stocks using confidential information gleaned from listening to their wives' phone conversations.[113]

Also there was the shocking news of financier Bernard Madoff, who confessed to a $50 billion **Ponzi scheme, using cash from newer investors to pay off older ones.**[114] He was sentenced to 150 years in prison.[115] Another convicted of creating a Ponzi scheme was Texas financier R. Allen Stanford, who built a flashy offshore $7 billion financial empire; he was sentenced to 110 years in prison in 2012.[116]

The Sarbanes–Oxley Reform Act The **Sarbanes–Oxley Act of 2002,** often shortened to *SarbOx,* or *SOX,* established requirements for proper financial record keeping for public companies and penalties of as much as 25 years in prison for noncompliance.[117] Administered by the Securities and Exchange Commission, SarbOx requires a company's chief executive officer and chief financial officer to personally certify the organization's financial reports, prohibits them from taking personal loans or lines of credit, and makes them reimburse the organization for bonuses and stock options when required by restatement of corporate profits. It also requires the company to have established procedures and guidelines for audit committees.[118] Recently the agribusiness giant Monsanto paid the government $80 million in penalties under SarbOx for misstating earnings associated with a sales program for the herbicide Roundup.[119]

How Do People Learn Ethics? Kohlberg's Theories
American business history is permeated with occasional malfeasance, from railroad tycoons trying to corner the gold market (the 1872 Crédit Mobilier scandal) to 25-year-old bank customer service representatives swindling elderly customers out of their finances. Legislation such as SarbOx can't head off all such behavior. No wonder that now many colleges and universities have required more education in ethics.

"Schools bear some responsibility for the behavior of executives," says Fred J. Evans, dean of the College of Business and Economics at California State University at Northridge. "If you're making systematic errors in the [business] world, you have to go back to the schools and ask, 'What are you teaching?'"[120]

Ponzi schemer. Phony financier R. Allen Stanford on the day of his sentencing to 110 years in prison without parole for masterminding a $7 billion Ponzi scheme involving fraudulent high-interest certificates of deposit at his Caribbean bank. A federal prosecutor said Allen was "utterly without remorse" and "treated all his victims as roadkill." The 28,000 Stanford victims received less than one penny on the dollar in attempting to recover their investments. © Dave Einsel/Getty Images

The good news is that more graduate business schools are changing their curriculums to teach ethics, although there is some question as to their effectiveness.[121] The bad news, however, is that students across educational levels are still cheating. A survey of over 23,000 U.S. high school students revealed that 59% admitted to cheating in the last year.[122] Plagiarism checking service Turnitin.com uncovered 156 million matches between college student papers and previously published material on the Internet.[123]

Cheating extends to corporations. Goldman Sachs fired 20 analysts for cheating on internal training exams, while JPMorgan Chase fired 10 employees for similar lapses in judgment.[124]

Of course, most students' levels of moral development are established by personalities and upbringing long before they get to college, with some being more advanced than others. One psychologist, **Laurence Kohlberg,** has proposed three levels of personal moral development—preconventional, conventional, and postconventional.[125]

- **Level 1, preconventional—follows rules.** People who have achieved this level tend to follow rules and to obey authority to avoid unpleasant consequences. Managers of the Level 1 sort tend to be autocratic or coercive, expecting employees to be obedient for obedience's sake.

- **Level 2, conventional—follows expectations of others.** People whose moral development has reached this level are conformist but not slavish, generally adhering to the expectations of others in their lives. Level 2 managers lead by encouragement and cooperation and are more group and team oriented. Most managers are at this level.

- **Level 3, postconventional—guided by internal values.** The farthest along in moral development, Level 3 managers are independent souls who follow their own values and standards, focusing on the needs of their employees and trying to lead by empowering those working for them. Only about a fifth of American managers are said to reach this level.

What level of development do you think you've reached?

How Organizations Can Promote Ethics

Ethics needs to be an everyday affair, not a one-time thing. This is why many large U.S. companies now have a *chief ethics officer,* whose job is to make ethical conduct a priority issue.

There are several ways an organization may promote high ethical standards on the job, as follows.[126]

1. Creating a Strong Ethical Climate
An **ethical climate represents employees' perceptions about the extent to which work environments support ethical behavior.** It is important for managers to foster ethical climates because they significantly affect the frequency of ethical behavior. Managers can promote ethical climates through the policies, procedures, and practices that are used on a daily basis.

2. Screening Prospective Employees
Companies try to screen out dishonest, irresponsible employees by checking applicants' resumes and references. Some firms, for example, run employee applications through E-Verify, a federal program that allows employers to check for illegal immigrants. Some also use personality tests and integrity testing to identify potentially dishonest people.

3. Instituting Ethics Codes and Training Programs
A **code of ethics consists of a formal written set of ethical standards guiding an organization's actions.** Most codes offer guidance on how to treat customers, suppliers, competitors, and other stakeholders. The purpose is to clearly state top management's expectations for all employees. As you might expect, most codes prohibit bribes, kickbacks, misappropriation of corporate assets, conflicts of interest, and "cooking the books"—making false accounting statements and other records. Other areas frequently covered in ethics codes are political contributions, workforce diversity, and confidentiality of corporate information.

In addition, according to a Society for Human Resource Management Weekly Survey, 32% of human resources professionals indicated that their organizations offered ethics training.[127] The approaches vary, but one way is to use a case approach to present employees with ethical dilemmas. By clarifying expectations, this kind of training may reduce unethical behavior.[128]

4. Rewarding Ethical Behavior: Protecting Whistle-Blowers

It's not enough to simply punish bad behavior; managers must also reward good ethical behavior, as in encouraging (or at least not discouraging) whistle-blowers.

A whistle-blower is an employee, or even an outside consultant, who reports organizational misconduct to the public, such as health and safety matters, waste, corruption, or overcharging of customers.[129] For instance, the law that created the Occupational Safety and Health Administration allows workers to report unsafe conditions, such as "exposure to toxic chemicals; the use of dangerous machines, which can crush fingers; the use of contaminated needles, which expose workers to the AIDS virus; and the strain of repetitive hand motion, whether at a computer keyboard or in a meatpacking plant," according to *The New York Times*.[130] In some cases, whistle-blowers may receive a reward; the IRS, for instance, is authorized to pay tipsters rewards as high as 30% in cases involving large amounts of money.[131]

Whistle-blowing has been on the rise since the Great Recession, and the number of whistle-blower tips received by the Securities and Exchange Commission, for example, is now nearly 4,000 a year.[132] True whistle-blowing involves acts that are against the law. However, the principal kinds of misconduct reported in one study—misuse of company time, abusive behavior, and lying to employees—aren't necessarily illegal, although they may create an offensive work environment, the leading reason people leave their jobs.[133] Retaliation against whistle-blowers is also on the rise, ranging from giving them the cold shoulder to passing them over for promotion.

In exposing unethical behavior, then, it's important to be clear why you're doing it (trying to help the company or just get someone in trouble), not report something for the wrong reason (discuss your concerns with someone who has similar values), and follow proper channels (like addressing the supervisor of the supposed culprit). Don't try to report externally (lashing out on Facebook, for instance) without speaking to those who might resolve the problem.[134]

Some people view ethics in ideal terms, which means that ethical principles or standards apply universally across situations and time. Others, however, take a relativistic view and believe that what is ethical depends on the situation. It will be helpful for you to learn more specifically about your own ethical tendencies. ●

---

connect SELF-ASSESSMENT 3.1

Assessing My Perspective on Ethics

This survey is designed to assess your views about ethics.

Please be prepared to answer these questions if your instructor has assigned Self-Assessment 3.1 in Connect.

1. Are your views more idealistic or more relativistic?

2. What do you think about students cheating on homework assignments in school? What about cheating on exams?

3. Are your answers consistent with your score? Explain.

4. Suppose you're a manager. What does your score imply about the way you would handle the unethical behavior of someone you manage? What about your boss's unethical behavior?

3.5   The Social Responsibilities Required of You as a Manager

Is being socially responsible really necessary?

THE BIG PICTURE

Managers need to be aware of the viewpoints supporting and opposing social responsibility and whether being and doing good pays off financially for the organization.

The slow economic recovery from the Great Recession has had a powerful impact on today's college freshmen, with 86.1% in 2014 declaring that getting "a better job" is the top reason for going to college, the principal goal of freshmen for the past six years. (The second most cited reason, at 82.2%, was "to learn more about things that interest me," which held the top spot for the first half of the past decade.)[135] But is money the be-all and end-all in business? This is the concern behind the triple bottom line discussed earlier.

If ethical responsibility is about being a good individual citizen, social responsibility is about being a good *organizational citizen,* taking on organizational citizenship behaviors that exceed employees' job descriptions—such as altruism, courtesy, sportsmanship, conscientiousness, and civic virtue (as we discuss in Chapter 11).[136] More formally, **social responsibility is a manager's duty to take actions that will benefit the interests of society as well as of the organization.** When generalized beyond the individual to the organization, social responsibility is called **corporate social responsibility (CSR), the notion that corporations are expected to go above and beyond following the law and making a profit.** Areas of CSR include the environment, philanthropy, and ethical labor practices.[137]

Corporate Social Responsibility: The Top of the Pyramid

According to University of Georgia business scholar **Archie B. Carroll,** corporate social responsibility rests at the top of a pyramid of a corporation's obligations, right up there with economic, legal, and ethical obligations. Some people might hold that a company's first and only duty is to make a profit. However, Carroll suggests the responsibilities of an organization in the global economy should take the following priorities, with profit being the most fundamental (base of the pyramid) and corporate citizenship at the top:[138]

- *Be a good global corporate citizen,* as defined by the host country's expectations.
- *Be ethical in its practices,* taking host-country and global standards into consideration.
- *Obey the law* of host countries as well as international law.
- *Make a profit* consistent with expectations for international business.

These priorities are illustrated in the pyramid opposite. *(See Figure 3.2.)*

Is Social Responsibility Worthwhile? Opposing and Supporting Viewpoints

In the old days of cutthroat capitalism, social responsibility was hardly thought of. A company's most important goal was to make money pretty much any way it could, and the consequences be damned. Today for-profit enterprises in the United States and

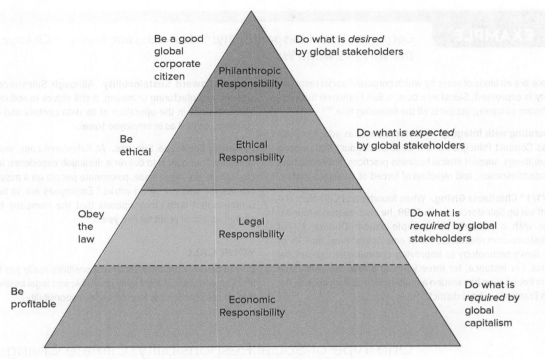

FIGURE 3.2 Carroll's global corporate social responsibility pyramid

Source: Republished with permission of Academy of Management, from A. Carroll, "Managing Ethically and Global Stakeholders: A Present and Future Challenge," Academy of Management Executive, May 2004, p. 116; permission conveyed through Copyright Clearance Center, Inc.

Europe—but increasingly multinational firms from developing nations as well—generally make a point of "putting something back" into society as well as taking something out.[139]

Not everyone, however, agrees with these new priorities. Let's consider the two viewpoints.

Against Social Responsibility   "Few trends could so thoroughly undermine the very foundations of our free society," argued the late free-market economist Milton Friedman, "as the acceptance by corporate officials of social responsibility other than to make as much money for their stockholders as possible."[140]

Friedman represents the view that, as he said, "The social responsibility of business is to make profits." That is, unless a company focuses on maximizing profits, it will become distracted and fail to provide goods and services, benefit the stockholders, create jobs, and expand economic growth—the real social justification for the firm's existence.

This view would presumably support the efforts of companies to set up headquarters in name only in offshore Caribbean tax havens (while keeping their actual headquarters in the United States) in order to minimize their tax burden.

For Social Responsibility   "A large corporation these days not only may engage in social responsibility," said famed economist Paul Samuelson, who passed away in 2009, "it had damned well better to try to do so."[141] That is, a company must be concerned for society's welfare as well as for corporate profits.

Beyond the fact of ethical obligation, the rationale for this view is that since businesses create problems (environmental pollution, for example), they should help solve them. Moreover, they often have the resources to solve problems in ways that the non-profit sector does not. Finally, being socially responsible gives businesses a favorable public image that can help head off government regulation.

Corporate Social Responsibility: Salesforce.com Wants to Change the Way the World Works

There are all kinds of ways by which corporate social responsibility is expressed. Salesforce.com, a San Francisco business software company, supports all the following four.[142]

Operating with Integrity. Salesforce.com has adopted Business Conduct Principles and a Code of Conduct that, among other things, support ethical business practices, anticorruption, antidiscrimination, and rejection of forced or involuntary labor.

"1/1/1" Charitable Giving. When founder and CEO Marc Benioff set up Salesforce.com in 1999, he also created a foundation with a powerful but simple vision: Donate 1% of Salesforce.com resources, 1% of employees' time, and 1% of the firm's technology to improving communities around the world. For instance, for three years in a row, the Salesforce .com Foundation has written a multi-million-dollar check to the San Francisco school district.[143]

Journey toward Sustainability. Although Salesforce.com does no manufacturing or mining, it still strives to reduce carbon emissions in the operation of its data centers and office buildings, as well as in employee travel.

Fostering Employee Success. At Salesforce.com, says the company, "our goal is to deliver a dreamjob experience for our employees. We are intense, passionate people on a mission to change the way the world works." Employees are so heavily compensated with stock options that the company hasn't posted an actual profit for five years.[144]

YOUR CALL

Do you believe corporate social responsibility really has benefits? Can you think of any highly profitable and legal businesses that *do not* practice any kind of social responsibility?

One Type of Social Responsibility: Climate Change, Sustainability, and Natural Capital

Nearly everyone is aware of the growing threat of climate change and global warming, and the vast majority (70%) of Americans in a 2016 poll say they believe climate change is causing extreme weather and a rise in sea level. Twenty-seven percent put most of the blame on human activity and 34% fault both human activity and natural environmental changes; even so, 64% support the U.S. government doing more to reduce the activities that lead to climate change and sea level rise.[145] (Scientists say global warming is "unequivocal" and that it is extremely likely that humans are the primary contributors to it.)[146] **Climate change refers to major changes in temperature, precipitation, wind patterns, and similar matters occurring over several decades. Global warming, one aspect of climate change, refers to the rise in global average temperature near the Earth's surface, caused mostly by increasing concentrations in the atmosphere of greenhouse gases, such as carbon emissions from fossil fuels.**[147] *Sustainability,* as we said in Chapter 1, is economic development that meets the needs of the present without compromising the ability of future generations to meet their own needs. (For more about the social, political, and cultural responses to climate change, including dissenters, see *Why We Disagree about Climate Change* by Mike Hume.)[148]

The Benefits of Being Green   "Coca-Cola has always been more focused on its economic bottom line than on global warming," writes reporter Coral Davenport. But "as global droughts dried up the water needed to produce its soda," its profits took some serious hits. Now the company "has embraced the idea of climate change as an economically disruptive force," she writes, and is focused on water-conservation technologies, along with other sustainability measures.[149] In 2015, the Coca-Cola Company announced it expected to replenish—return to nature—all the water it used to make its beverages by the end of that year, five years ahead of its scheduled goal.[150]

Today going green has entered the business mainstream, where sustainability programs are producing not only environmental benefits but also cost savings, revenue growth, and competitive advantages.[151] Carmaker Subaru of Indiana Automotive, for example, has proved that adopting environmentally friendly processes does not add to the cost of doing business but actually makes it more efficient (reducing water use by

50%, electricity by 14%, and so on).[152] Dow Chemical, collaborating with the Nature Conservancy, an environmental group, is exploring coastal marsh and dune restoration (and paying nearby homeowners to replace lawns with native plants) to shield its Freeport, Texas, chemical complex from storm surges coming off the Gulf of Mexico.[153]

The Value of Earth's Resources: Natural Capital Indeed, planet (of the triple bottom line people, planet, and profit) is now identified by the name *natural capital* (or *natural capital accounting*), which many scholars think should figure seriously in economic decision making. **Natural capital is the value of natural resources, such as topsoil, air, water, and genetic diversity, which humans depend on.** "We're driving natural capital to its lowest levels ever in human history," says Stanford University ecologist Gretchen Daily.[154]

According to this view, we are approaching the planet's limitations, with human activity threatening to exceed the earth's capacity to generate resources and absorb wastes. For example, the mountain of electrical waste disposed of annually worldwide—cell phones, laptops, appliances, anything with a battery or a cord—was forecast in 2013 to grow by a third in four years, with the weight 65.4 million tons, "the weight equivalent of 200 Empire State Buildings or 11 Great Pyramids of Giza."[155] One United Nations report suggests climate change poses a risk to world food supplies, with output dropping perhaps 2% each decade, as rising temperatures make it harder for crops to thrive.[156] The report also warns that waiting to cut carbon emissions could even outstrip technology's ability to preserve the planet.[157] Alarming predictions indeed.

Green power. Many electricity users can run their homes on renewable energy simply by asking their local utility.
© Royalty-Free/Corbis

Another Type of Social Responsibility: Philanthropy, "Not Dying Rich"

"He who dies rich dies thus disgraced," 19th-century steel magnate Andrew Carnegie is supposed to have said, after he turned his interests from making money to **philanthropy, making charitable donations to benefit humankind.** Carnegie became well known as a supporter of free libraries.

When Bill Gates of Microsoft, the current richest person in the world (net worth in 2016: $79.2 billion) stepped down from day-to-day oversight of Microsoft, the company he co-founded, he turned his attention to the Bill and Melinda Gates Foundation, through which he and his wife have pledged to spend billions on health, education, and overcoming poverty.[158] The Gateses have been joined by 136 other billionaires from 14 countries, including Facebook founder Mark Zuckerberg and his wife (the most generous American philanthropists in 2013), oil and gas financier T. Boone Pickens, Berkshire Hathaway chairman Warren Buffett, Chobani yogurt founder Handi Ulukaya, and others—in taking the Giving Pledge, a commitment to dedicate a majority of their wealth to philanthropy.[159]

Not only do wealthy individuals and companies practice philanthropy, so even do ordinary individuals. Mona Purdy, an Illinois hairdresser, noticed while vacationing in Guatemala that many children coated their feet with tar in order to be able to run in a local race. So she went home and established the nonprofit Share Your Soles, which collects shoes and sends them around the world. "I always thought I was too busy to help others," she says. "Then I started this and found myself wondering where I'd been all my life."[160] Apple CEO Tim Cook has also said he will give away most of his fortune.[161] Recently, many donors, large and small, have also been studying the effect of "impact investing"—of finding the best ways to make philanthropy effective.[162]

How Does Being Good Pay Off?

From a hardheaded manager's point of view, does ethical behavior and high social responsibility pay off financially? Here's what some of the research shows.[163]

Effect on Customers According to one survey, 88% of the respondents said they were more apt to buy from companies that are socially responsible than from companies that are not.[164] Nielsen's Global Corporate Citizenship Survey found that 46% of global consumers are willing to pay extra for products and services from companies that have implemented programs to give back to society.[165]

Effect on Employees' Work Attitudes and Intentions to Quit

Employees perceive their work environments as more ethical and fair when managers exhibit ethical leadership.* **Ethical leadership is defined as "leadership that is directed by respect for ethical beliefs and values for the dignity and rights of others.[166]** Research supports the value of ethical leadership. Employees reported higher levels of organizational commitment, job satisfaction, trust in the leader, and motivation when their managers displayed ethical leadership. Ethical leadership also reduced employees' stress and intentions to quit.[167]

Effect on Employees' Behavior and Work Performance

The positive benefits of ethical leadership extend beyond employee attitudes. They include behavior and performance. Employees were more willing to display citizenship behavior and to produce higher task performance when their managers exhibited ethical leadership. Employees also demonstrated less counterproductive behavior when the boss was ethical.[168]

Effect on Sales Growth

The announcement of a company's conviction for illegal activity has been shown to diminish sales growth for several years.[169] One survey found that 80% of people said they decide to buy a firm's goods or services partly on their perception of its ethics.[170]

Effect on Company Efficiency

One study found that 71% of employees who saw honesty applied rarely or never in their organization had seen misconduct in the past year, compared with 52% who saw honesty applied only occasionally and 25% who saw it frequently.[171]

Effect on Company Revenue

Unethical behavior in the form of employee fraud costs the typical organization 5% of its revenues each year, which translates to worldwide fraud loss of $3.7 trillion, according to the Association of Certified Fraud Examiners.[172] The median loss caused by employee frauds was $145,000, but 22% of cases involve losses of at least $1 million.

Effect on Stock Price

One survey found that 74% of people polled said their perception of a firm's honesty directly affected their decision about whether to buy its stock.[173] Other research found that, following fraud or financial restatement (redoing an earlier public financial statement), companies on average lose more than a quarter of their stock value but can nurse the stock price back to health by stepping up charitable giving along with other actions.[174]

Effect on Profits

Studies suggest that profitability is enhanced by a reputation for honesty and corporate citizenship.[175]

Ethical behavior and social responsibility are more than just admirable ways of operating. They give an organization a clear competitive advantage. Where do you stand on these issues? We created the following self-assessment to measure your attitudes toward corporate social responsibility. Taking it will enhance your understanding about your views on social responsibility. ●

connect SELF-ASSESSMENT 3.2

Assessing Your Attitudes toward Corporate Responsibility

Please be prepared to answer these questions if your instructor has assigned Self-Assessment 3.2 in Connect.

1. Where do you stand on corporate social responsibility?

2. What life events have influenced your attitudes toward corporate social responsibility? Discuss.

3. Based on the three lowest-rated items in the survey, how might you foster a more positive attitude toward social responsibility? Explain.

3.6   Corporate Governance

How can I trust a company is doing the right thing?

THE BIG PICTURE

Corporate governance is the system of governing a company so that the interests of corporate owners and other stakeholders are protected. Company directors should be clearly separated in their authority from the CEO by insisting on strong financial reporting systems and more accountability.

What, you might ask, were the company boards of directors doing prior to 2001–2002 when Enron, WorldCom, Tyco, and Adelphia filed for bankruptcy amid allegations their CEOs were committing fraud—for which they later went to prison? Aren't directors elected by the stockholders to see that a company is run according to their interests? Indeed, after the Enron and other scandals there was renewed interest in what is known as **corporate governance, the system of governing a company so that the interests of corporate owners and other stakeholders are protected.**

Ethics and Corporate Governance

Is there any connection between ethics and corporate governance? Certainly, says scholar Henrik Syse. Corporate governance is about such matters as long-term strategies, sustainable finances, accurate reporting, and positive work environment. All are obviously ethical because they are concerned with how a firm relates to stakeholders inside and out.[176]

How can members of the board of directors be chosen to act ethically? As mentioned earlier, inside directors may be members of the firm, but outside directors are supposed to be elected from outside the firm. However, in some companies, the outside directors have been handpicked by the CEO—because they are friends, because they have a business relationship with the firm, or because they supposedly "know the industry." In such instances, how tough do you think the board of directors is going to be on its CEO when he or she asks for leeway to pursue certain policies?

Now, more attention is being paid to strengthening corporate governance so that directors are clearly separated in their authority from the CEO. While, of course, directors are not supposed to get involved with day-to-day management issues, they are now feeling more pressure from stockholders and others to have stronger financial reporting systems and more accountability.[177]

Corporate Governance: Chesapeake Energy's CEO Gets Some Unusual Breaks from His Board of Directors

EXAMPLE

In 2008, CEO Aubrey K. McClendon topped the list of highest-paid chief executives for companies in the Standard & Poor's 500-stock index. His firm, Oklahoma City–based Chesapeake Energy, which he co-founded at age 23, was the second-largest producer of natural gas after ExxonMobil, and his personal fortune was estimated by *Forbes* as exceeding $1.2 billion. One interviewer described him as "without doubt the most admired—and feared—man" in the U.S. petroleum and natural gas industry but "also the most reckless, . . . with an off-the-charts risk tolerance."[178] Another journalist declared "he was on the lunatic fringe in his appetite for risk."

A Little Help from the Company. Because aggressive financing practices combined with plunging oil and gas prices in 2008 lowered the value of Chesapeake stock by 80%, McClendon was forced to sell nearly all of his own shares. Strapped for cash, he turned to his handpicked board of nine directors, which gave him a $100 million pay package plus $75 million over five years to invest for a 2.5% stake in every well the company drilled.[179]

In addition, the company agreed to buy McClendon's personal collection of historical maps of the American Southwest (which decorated the company's headquarters) for $12.1 million.[180]

The $12.1 million, the firm pointed out, was McClendon's cost of acquiring the collection over the preceding six years—an appraisal, it noted, that came from "the dealer who had assisted Mr. McClendon in acquiring this collection."[181]

Shareholders Sue. Besides the above-mentioned perks, the Chesapeake board also voted to give McClendon $600,000 for the private use of the corporate jets, nearly $600,000 for accounting services, and $131,000 for "personal engineering support"—and it agreed to pay $4.6 million to sponsor the NBA's Oklahoma City Thunder, the pro basketball team that is one-fifth owned by McClendon.[182] But when outsiders and stockholders found out about the maps, the story took on a life of its own, prompting several shareholder lawsuits.

Big shareholder groups sued Chesapeake for what they considered an irresponsibly generous 2008 compensation package to McClendon and demanded that the company overhaul its compensation practices. In the resulting settlement, McClendon agreed to buy back the 19th-century maps for $12.1 million plus pay a 2.28% interest for the repurchase. In addition, Chesapeake agreed to some corporate governance reforms: installation of a "more transparent" management pay plan, electing board members by majority vote, and discontinuance of the practice of allowing senior management, such as McClendon, use of their company stock as collateral to buy more company stock, a major cause of the firm's financial strains.[183]

"Worst CEOs" List. Dartmouth College business professor Sydney Finkelstein, who puts out an annual list of the best and

The map collector. Aubrey McClendon, chief of natural gas producer Chesapeake Energy, was the highest-paid of CEOs in 2008. But when plunging gas prices reduced the value of company shares by 80%, he was forced to sell off an antique map collection for $12.1 million. The appraiser: the expert who assembled the collection in the first place. The buyer: Chesapeake Energy. Does this pass the smell test? © Bloomberg/Getty Images.

worst CEOs, ranked McLendon as the second worst CEO of 2012 for being unable to keep his corporate job separate from his personal investments. "He personally borrowed $500 million from a company that is a major investor in Chesapeake," Finkelstein wrote. "He ran a private $200 million hedge fund trading oil and gas even though he is CEO of a company in the same industry. Corporate jets are routinely used for personal purposes." Such actions, Finkelstein felt, demonstrated bad judgment and potential conflicts of interest.[184]

McLendon resigned from Chesapeake Energy in 2013, citing "philosophical differences" with a reconstituted board, after burning through $19.4 billion in 2011 and $21.6 billion in 2012. He started a new energy company, using everything from a fine-wine collection to his stake in the Oklahoma City Thunder to fund his new venture, but in 2015 Chesapeake filed a lawsuit against him accusing him of stealing trade secrets.[185] In early 2016, Chesapeake lost 50% of its value amid rumors that it might be preparing to file bankruptcy.[186] Soon after, its former CEO, Aubrey McClendon, was indicted on charges of bid rigging—of conspiring to rig bids for the purchase of oil and natural gas leases during the time he was running Chesapeake.[187] The day after the indictment he was found dead in his car after a high-speed crash into a concrete wall.[188]

YOUR CALL

If McClendon had stayed on as Chesapeake Energy's CEO, what kinds of corporate reforms would you, as a shareholder, have insisted on so that you could trust what the company told you?

The Need for Trust

In the end, suggests Fordham professor Robert Hurley, "We do not have a crisis of ethics in business today. We have a crisis of trust."[189] Customers or employees may well think that certain people or companies are ethical—that is, moral, honest, and fair—but that does not mean they should trust them. Trust, says Hurley, "comes from delivering every day on what you promise—as a manager, an employee, and a company. It involves constant teamwork, communication, and collaboration."

Trust comes from asking how likely the people you're dealing with are to serve your interests, how much they have demonstrated concern for others, how well they delivered on their promises, how much they try to keep their word—and how effectively they communicate these skills.

Would you agree? ●

Key Terms Used in This Chapter

clawbacks 79

climate change 94

code of ethics 90

competitors 78

corporate governance 97

corporate social responsibility
 (CSR) 92

crowdfunding 80

customers 77

demographic forces 85

distributor 78

economic forces 82

ethical behavior 86

ethical climate 90

ethical dilemma 86

ethical leadership 96

ethics 86

external stakeholders 77

general environment 82

global warming 94

government regulators 81

individual approach 88

insider trading 88

internal stakeholders 74

international forces 85

justice approach 88

macroenvironment 82

moral-rights approach 88

natural capital 95

owners 75

philanthropy 95

political–legal forces 85

Ponzi scheme 89

Sarbanes–Oxley Act of 2002 89

social audit 72

social responsibility 92

sociocultural forces 84

special-interest groups 81

stakeholders 73

strategic allies 78

supplier 78

task environment 77

technological forces 83

triple bottom line 72

utilitarian approach 87

value system 87

values 87

venture capital 80

whistle-blower 91

Key Points

3.1 The Triple Bottom Line: People, Planet, and Profit

- Many businesses subscribe to a new standard of success—the triple bottom line, representing people, planet, and profit. It measures an organization's social, environmental, and financial performance.

- Success in these areas can be measured through a social audit, a systematic assessment of a company's performance in implementing socially responsible programs, often based on predefined goals.

- The triple bottom line has particular appeal to many young adults (Millennials) who are less concerned with finding financial success than with making a difference and achieving a meaningful life.

3.2 The Community of Stakeholders inside the Organization

- Managers operate in two organizational environments—internal and external—both made up of stakeholders, the people whose interests are affected by the organization's activities.

- The first, or internal, environment includes employees, owners, and the board of directors.

3.3 The Community of Stakeholders outside the Organization

- The external environment of stakeholders consists of the task environment and the general environment.

- The task environment consists of 11 groups that present the manager with daily tasks to deal with. (1) Customers pay to use an organization's goods and services. (2) Competitors compete for customers or resources. (3) Suppliers provide supplies—raw materials, services, equipment, labor, or energy—to other organizations. (4) Distributors help another organization sell its goods and services to customers. (5) Strategic allies join forces to achieve advantages neither organization can perform as well alone. (6) Employee organizations are labor unions and employee associations.

- (7) Local communities are residents, companies, governments, and nonprofit entities that depend on the organization's taxes, payroll, and charitable contributions. (8) Financial institutions are commercial banks, investment banks, and insurance companies that deal with the organization. (9) Government regulators are regulatory agencies that establish the ground rules under which the organization operates. (10) Special-interest groups are groups whose members try to influence specific issues that may affect the organization. (11) The mass media are print, radio, TV, and Internet sources that affect the organization's public relations.

- The general environment includes six forces. (1) Economic forces consist of general economic conditions and trends—unemployment, inflation, interest rates, economic growth—that may affect an organization's performance. (2) Technological forces are new developments in methods for transforming resources into goods and services. (3) Sociocultural forces are influences and trends originating in a country, society, or culture's human relationships and values that may affect an organization. (4) Demographic forces are influences on an organization arising from changes in the characteristics of a population, such as age, gender, and ethnic origin. (5) Political–legal forces are changes in the way politics shapes laws and laws shape the opportunities for and threats to an organization. (6) International forces are changes in the economic, political, legal, and technological global system that may affect an organization.

3.4 The Ethical Responsibilities Required of You as a Manager

- Ethics are the standards of right and wrong that influence behavior. Ethical behavior is behavior that is accepted as "right" as opposed to "wrong" according to those standards.
- Ethical dilemmas often take place because of an organization's value system. Values are the relatively permanent and deeply held underlying beliefs and attitudes that help determine a person's behavior.
- Managers should strive for ethical leadership, defined as leadership that is directed by respect for ethical beliefs and values for the dignity and rights of others.
- There are four approaches to deciding ethical dilemmas. (1) Utilitarian—ethical behavior is guided by what will result in the greatest good for the greatest number of people. (2) Individual—ethical behavior is guided by what will result in the individual's best long-term interests, which ultimately is in everyone's self-interest. (3) Moral-rights—ethical behavior is guided by respect for the fundamental rights of human beings, such as those expressed in the U.S. Constitution's Bill of Rights. (4) Justice—ethical behavior is guided by respect for the impartial standards of fairness and equity.
- Public outrage over white-collar crime (Enron, Tyco) led to the creation of the Sarbanes–Oxley Act of 2002 (SarbOx), which established requirements for proper financial record keeping for public companies and penalties for noncompliance.
- Laurence Kohlberg proposed three levels of personal moral development: (1) preconventional level of moral development—people tend to follow rules and to obey authority; (2) conventional level—people are conformist, generally adhering to the expectations of others; and (3) postconventional level—people are guided by internal values.
- There are three ways an organization may foster high ethical standards. (1) Top managers must support a strong ethical climate. (2) The organization may have

a code of ethics, which consists of a formal written set of ethical standards. (3) An organization must reward ethical behavior, as in not discouraging whistle-blowers, employees who report organizational misconduct to the public.

3.5 The Social Responsibilities Required of You as a Manager

- Social responsibility is a manager's duty to take actions that will benefit the interests of society as well as of the organization.
- The idea of social responsibility has opposing and supporting viewpoints. The opposing viewpoint is that the social responsibility of business is to make profits. The supporting viewpoint is that since business creates some problems (such as pollution) it should help solve them.
- One scholar, Archie Carroll, suggests the responsibilities of an organization in the global economy should have the following priorities: (1) Be a good global corporate citizen; (2) be ethical in its practices; (3) obey the law; and (4) make a profit.
- One type of social responsibility is sustainability, "going green," or meeting humanity's needs without harming future generations. A major threat is climate change, which refers to major changes in temperature, precipitation, wind patterns, and similar matters over several decades. Global warming, one aspect of climate change, refers to the rise in global average temperature near the Earth's surface, caused mostly by increasing concentrations in the atmosphere of greenhouse gases, such as carbon emissions from fossil fuels.
- The component of the triple bottom line called planet is now identified by the name *natural capital*, which is the value of natural resources, such as topsoil, air, water, and genetic diversity, which many scholars think should figure seriously in economic decision making.
- Another type of social responsibility is philanthropy, making charitable donations to benefit humankind.
- Positive ethical behavior and social responsibility can pay off in the form of customer goodwill, more efficient and loyal employees, better quality of job applicants and retained employees, enhanced sales growth, less employee misconduct and fraud, better stock price, and enhanced profits.

3.6 Corporate Governance

- Corporate governance is the system of governing a company so that the interests of corporate owners and other stakeholders are protected.
- One way to further corporate governance is to be sure directors are clearly separated in their authority from the CEO by insisting on stronger financial reporting systems and more accountability.

1. How would you explain the difference between internal and external stakeholders?
2. Among external stakeholders, what's the difference between the task environment and the general environment?
3. Of the 11 groups in the task environment, which 5 do you consider most important, and why?
4. Of the six groups in the general environment, which one do you think has the least importance, and why?
5. Distinguish among the four approaches to deciding ethical dilemmas.

6. What's the difference between insider trading and a Ponzi scheme?
7. How would you summarize Kohlberg's levels of personal moral development?
8. What are four ways that organizations can promote ethics?
9. Describe the levels in Carroll's corporate social responsibility pyramid. Where does trying to achieve sustainability fit in?
10. How would you explain the concept of corporate governance?

Management in Action

Blue Bell Is Accused of "Recall Creep" in Its Handling of Ice Cream Contamination

Blue Bell is the nation's third largest ice cream maker, behind Nestlé, which produces Edy's, and Unilever PLC, which makes Ben & Jerry's. Blue Bell started its business in Brenhaman, Texas, in 1911. It grew to having manufacturing operations in Texas, Oklahoma, and Alabama, employing around 3,900 employees. The company's products have been sold in 23 states.

Blue Bell faced a major listeria contamination problem across all of its three major plants in 2015.

The problem gained attention in 2015 when inspectors from South Carolina found *Listeria monocytogenes* in two products that were made in Blue Bell's Brenham plant. The situation got worse once the Centers for Disease Control (CDC) "matched the Blue Bell bug to listeria strains blamed for an unsolved 2014 outbreak at a Wichita hospital: Five patients, already hospitalized with serious illnesses, had been infected; three died. Investigators later confirmed that four drank milkshakes with Blue Bell ice cream. Further testing would link the company to 10 listeriosis cases dating back to 2010."[190]

Blue Bell learned about the South Carolina findings in February 2015. The company responded by retrieving 10 different products produced on the factory line in question. It made no statement to consumers. About one month later the company learned about the Wichita deaths. This led to a decision of stopping production on the tainted production line. Ultimately, the line was shut down permanently.

In March, the listeria problem grew. Listeria was linked to a chocolate ice cream cup made in Oklahoma. The company recalled the ice cream cups. In April, Blue Bell then suspended all operations in Oklahoma after the CDC linked the bacteria in the chocolate cup with five more listeria cases as far back as 2010. The company vowed to find the source of the contamination, and it announced a recall of seven more flavors.

In April, another link was found between listeria in containers of chocolate chip cookie dough ice cream that were produced in Brenham. This led CEO Paul Kruse to publicly apologize and recall all of its products—eight million gallons of ice cream. The company ended up laying off 37% of its 3,900 employees while also furloughing 1,400 more.

Employees interviewed by CBS contend that poor manufacturing practices were potential causes of the problem. Two employees "described antiquated machinery run amuck, oil dripping into the food mix, and melted ice cream left pooling on the factory floor because supervisors didn't want to slow production." Terry Schultz, an employee who worked on the contaminated line in Brenhan, told CBS "A lot of time, I walked in there, and there was just ice cream all over the floor. Sometimes these machines, they would just go haywire, and it would just, the product would just continually run through the conveyor belt, and it would just drop right onto the floor." This was bad because moisture provides a good environment for bacteria to grow.

Schultz said that he complained to a supervisor and was told "Is that all you're going to do is come in here and bitch every afternoon?" He concluded that "Production was probably more important than cleanliness."

The second employee interviewed, Gerald Bland, told CBS that "he was instructed to pour ice cream and fruit juice dripping off the machine throughout the day into barrels of ice cream mix." He also noted that "You'd see oil on top from the fruit feeder leaking that would still go right into the barrel." This practice was discontinued about a year before the plant was shutdown.[191]

Although Blue Bell executives would not respond to CBS's request for an interview, the company told a *Fortune* reporter that "isolated views expressed by two former Blue Bell employees on CBS News do not reflect the experience of the vast majority of our employees . . . Our top priority and commitment is to produce high quality, safe, delicious ice cream for our customers."[192]

Consider this statement in light of an FDA inspection report from 2015. The FDA reported finding bacteria in Blue Bell's Oklahoma plant on 17 occasions beginning in March 2013. In spite of this finding, the FDA noted that Blue Bell did not follow up "'to identify sanitation failures and possible food contamination,' taken proper steps to root out the problem, or informed the agency of its findings."[193]

One reporter concluded that "Blue Bell failed to follow practices recommended by government and industry groups that might have prevented listeria contamination of ice cream at all three of its main plants." In response to this, a company spokesperson said, "We thought our cleaning process took care of any problems, but in hindsight, it was not adequate." He then stated that the company "would immediately clean the surfaces and swab until the tests were negative."[194]

The contamination crisis and its effects on Blue Bell almost led to the company's demise. The company was saved by a loan of up to $125 million from Texas billionaire Sid Bass. The Bass family now owns one-third of the company.

In January 2016, a CNN report indicated that "enhanced testing of its [Blue Bell] facilities has found locations where suspected listeria may be present." This is good news in that the new testing procedures are finding potential problem areas, which then enables the company to clean and sanitize them. The company notes that "We have tested and will continue to test every batch of ice cream produced. No products produced have tested positive (for listeria). No products are shipped to stores until tests confirm they are safe. We will continue to work closely with our regulatory agencies, as we have throughout this process."[195]

As of January 2016, Blue Bell is shipping product to 15 states and plans to use a phased approach for shipping ice cream to its remaining markets.

FOR DISCUSSION

1. How did Blue Bell's response to the contamination at its plants impact the triple bottom line?

2. Which of Blue Bell's internal and external stakeholders were positively and negatively affected by the contamination crisis? Be specific.

3. Which of the six general environmental forces influenced the manner in which Blue Bell responded to this crisis?

4. To what extent did Blue Bell respond ethically to the contamination problem? Explain.

5. To what extent was Blue Bell's approach toward the contamination problem consistent with the four approaches to deciding ethical dilemmas? Explain.

6. Evaluate Blue Bell's approach to solving this crisis against Carroll's model of social responsibility shown in Figure 3.2.

Legal/Ethical Challenge

Should You Apply to Have Your Student Loans Forgiven?

Student loan debt nearly tripled in the last decade thanks to many attending for-profit colleges. For hundreds of thousands buried in student loan debt, a little known 1994 program called "Borrower Defense" or "Defense to Repayment" sponsored by the Education Department offers a lifeline.

The program is available for those students who obtained loans from the government's Direct Loan program. "The law says students are entitled to forgiveness of existing debt—and, possibly, reimbursement of any repaid loans—if they can show their school violated state law in getting them to take out the debt. (An example might be if a school lied in its advertisements about how many of its graduates landed jobs.) However, it's not clear what documentation the borrower needs to prove fraud."[196]

Thousands have applied to have their loans expunged under the program. In the last six months of

2015, for example, 7,500 former students applied to have $164 million in student loans expunged. The U.S. Education Department has already agreed to cancel nearly $28 million in debt and indicated many more will likely get forgiveness.[197]

Assume that you recently graduated from a state university. You took the required courses for your bachelor's degree and excelled in your studies. You made the Dean's List each semester of your last two years and interned for a social services organization in your community. You hoped you'd be able to work in your chosen field of psychology and be able to pay off the debt a few years after graduation.

Like many students, you paid for the majority of your education with student loans. Three years after graduation, your career has not turned out as expected. Instead of working in your chosen field of psychology, you have a low paying job at a retail chain and wait tables on weekends to make ends meet. You weren't aware that psychology positions required a graduate degree. Your student loan debt remains unpaid, and you recently heard about the borrower defense program.

You are considering whether or not to apply for the Borrower Defense program.

SOLVING THE CHALLENGE

What would you do?

1. Apply for loan forgiveness and hope that the broad language of the law will make an exception for your state college education and loan. Besides, what's wrong with asking?

2. Apply for loan forgiveness. After all, you aren't benefitting from your education, someone should have told you that you needed a graduate degree in psychology to get a good job, and there is no clear definition of fraud.

3. Don't apply. You were never promised a job and you made the decision to major in psychology. You could have chosen a field with more job opportunities.

4. Invent other options. Discuss.

4

Global Management
Managing across Borders

Major Questions You Should Be Able to Answer

4.1 Globalization: The Collapse of Time and Distance

Major Question: What three important developments of globalization will probably affect me?

4.2 You and International Management

Major Question: Why learn about international management, and what characterizes the successful international manager?

4.3 Why and How Companies Expand Internationally

Major Question: Why do companies expand internationally, and how do they do it?

4.4 The World of Free Trade: Regional Economic Cooperation and Competition

Major Question: What are barriers to free trade, what major organizations and trading blocs promote trade, and how important are the BRICS countries?

4.5 The Importance of Understanding Cultural Differences

Major Question: What are the principal areas of cultural differences?

The Benefits of International Business Travel

Since business travelers who fly 100,000-plus miles a year—both domestically and overseas—are no longer a rare breed, should you prepare for the possibility of joining them? What are the rewards?

"If you are open to it, travel will simply make you a more well-rounded human being," is one opinion.[1] Many people like getting away from their everyday workplace, with its endless meetings, coworker distractions, and work "fires" to put out. In addition, respondents in one poll cited discovering a new city as the best benefit of business travel (65%), along with experiencing new things (45%) and connecting with new people (37%).[2]

Business travelers have learned the following three benefits.

Face-to-Face Meetings Are Crucial

The first lesson is that the majority of businesspeople—8 of 10 in one survey, 9 of 10 in another—agree travel is important because face-to-face meetings are more effective than technology toward achieving their business goals.[3] Face-to-face helps you capture attention, inspire commitment, strengthen relationships, and other benefits.[4]

Of course smartphones, e-mail, and videoconferencing make it easier to connect with others—superficially, at least. "But," says an investment banker, "in a global world you have to get in front of your employees, spend time with your clients, and show commitment when it comes to joint ventures, mergers, and alliances. The key is thoughtful travel—traveling when necessary."[5] Adds another top executive, "If you are going to disagree with somebody, you certainly don't want to do it by e-mail, and if possible you don't even want to do it by phone. You want to do it face to face."[6]

Understanding the Local Culture Is Crucial

In time, perhaps, you will be able to wear an earpiece that will offer real-time translation, but until then we need to settle for Google Translate, which returns a translation as fast as your Internet connection can provide it.[7] But translation won't necessarily help you understand local culture.

Retailer Urban Outfitters, for example, outraged some customers by selling merchandise with images of Hindu deities on them.[8] In another instance, an American used "to conducting business American style, where you can get a deal done in two hours and everyone leaves happy," found that in Asia "every meeting was about 10 hours long and everyone wanted to serve us food. We were so stuffed and jet-lagged, it was ridiculous."[9]

As a world-traveling executive, then, you must do your homework to know cultures, organizations, and holders of power. "Cull information on the individuals and companies you're visiting," says one expert. "Follow the news relating to the region. If possible try to read a few books about the history and culture of the lands you will visit. . . . Learn a few words too."[10] Because in Asia and the Middle East personal relationships are crucial to getting things done, you need to engage in small talk and avoid business talk during after-hours outings. Says Ted Dale, president of international business consulting firm Aperian Global, "You need to spend out-of-office time in social settings." In Asia, the Middle East, and Latin America, it's important to understand organizational hierarchy, as represented by professional titles and age.[11]

Leisure Time Can Be Used to Make New Contacts

Travel downtime is a great opportunity to network and make new contacts. Columnist Anita Bruzzese points out that some hotels offer evening socials that businesspeople can use to meet others in a relaxed setting with food and drink at hand. Bruzzese tells of one veteran, Patricia Rossi, who contacts her regular Twitter followers and asks them to meet her if she's in their city. "You've already developed those relationships online," Rossi says. "But this is a chance to get kneecap to kneecap, which is so important."[12]

For Discussion To stay connected with colleagues, employees, clients, and suppliers, you may have to travel a lot. Is this cause for concern? What do you think you should do about it?

FORECAST What's Ahead in This Chapter

This chapter covers the importance of globalization—the rise of the global village, of one big market, of both worldwide megafirms and minifirms. We also describe the characteristics of the successful international manager and why and how companies expand internationally. We describe the barriers to free trade and the major organizations promoting trade and the major competitors. Finally, we discuss some of the cultural differences you may encounter if you become an international manager.

4.1   Globalization: The Collapse of Time and Distance

What three important developments of globalization will probably affect me?

THE BIG PICTURE

Globalization, the trend of the world economy toward becoming a more interdependent system, is reflected in three developments: the rise of the "global village" and e-commerce, the trend of the world's becoming one big market, and the rise of both megafirms and Internet-enabled minifirms worldwide.

TABLE 4.1

**Country Rankings for
Competitiveness, 2015–2016**

1. Switzerland

2. Singapore

3. United States

4. Germany

5. Netherlands

6. Japan

7. Hong Kong

8. Finland

9. Sweden

10. United Kingdom

11. Norway

12. Denmark

13. Canada

14. Qatar

15. Chinese Taipei

*Source: World Economic Forum,
The Global Competitiveness
Report 2015-2016, http://
reports.webforum.org/global-
competitiveness-report-2015-2016
(accessed March 5, 2016).*

Is everything for sale in the United States now made outside our borders?

Not quite everything—and Roger Simmermaker, 50, an Orlando, Florida, electronics technician who drives a 1996 Michigan-made Lincoln Town Car, is seriously focused on buying U.S. In fact, Simmermaker has authored a book, *How Consumers Can Buy American,* which lists more than 16,000 U.S.-made products.[13] "It's important to understand that workers in China don't pay taxes to America," he says.[14]

As it happens, the vast majority of goods and services sold in the United States *are* still made in this country, good news for the 78% of U.S. consumers who would rather buy the domestic than the foreign version of a product.[15] The problem is it's hard to tell what's real and what's not. "Some iconic American products, from the Apple iPhone to Cuisinart food processors, have little or no manufacturing presence on these shores, while many foreign makers have invested heavily in manufacturing plants in the U.S.," says *Consumer Reports.*[16] In addition, because of "reshoring," many appliance manufacturers and other companies are moving significant operations back to the United States.

Competition and Globalization: Who Will Be No. 1 Tomorrow?

It goes without saying that the world is a competitive place. Where does the United States stand in it? What's our report card?

Although Americans may like to think "We're No. 1!" on most measures, other nations are in constant pursuit—and in some cases have overtaken us. China, for instance, overtook the United States as the world's largest economy in 2014.[17]

Are we the most competitive? Actually, the World Economic Forum ranks the United States as No. 3, behind Switzerland and Singapore. *(See Table 4.1.)*

Are we the richest? In terms of gross domestic product (total value of all goods and services), by one measure the United States ranks No. 9, behind Qatar, Luxembourg, Singapore, Brunei Darussalam, Kuwait, Norway, United Arab Emirates, and Hong Kong. Canada is No. 20.[18]

How about "most free"? Here Hong Kong, a "special administrative region" of the People's Republic of China, is No. 1. The United States is No. 12, according to criteria embraced by the 2016 Index of Economic Freedom (by *The Wall Street Journal* and the Heritage Foundation). Hong Kong is considered "free" by this standard; both Canada, at No. 6, and the United States are considered "mostly free."[19]

There are many reasons why the winners on these lists achieved their enviable status, but one thing is clear: They didn't do it all by themselves; other countries were involved. We are living in a world being rapidly changed by **globalization—the trend of the world economy toward becoming a more interdependent system.** Time and distance, which have been under assault for 150 years, have now virtually collapsed, as reflected in three important developments we shall discuss.[20]

1. The rise of the "global village" and electronic commerce.

2. The world's becoming one market instead of many national ones.

3. The rise of both megafirms and Internet-enabled minifirms worldwide.

The Rise of the "Global Village" and Electronic Commerce

The hallmark of great civilizations has been their great systems of communications. In the beginning, communication was based on transportation: The Roman Empire had its network of roads, as did other ancient civilizations, such as the Incas. Later the great European powers had their far-flung navies. In the 19th century, the United States and Canada unified North America by building transcontinental railroads. Later the airplane reduced travel time between continents.

From Transportation to Communication   Transportation began to yield to the electronic exchange of information. Beginning in 1844, the telegraph ended the short existence of the Pony Express and, beginning in 1876, found itself in competition with the telephone. The amplifying vacuum tube, invented in 1906, led to commercial radio. Television came into being in England in 1925. During the 1950s and 1960s, as television exploded throughout the world, communications philosopher Marshall McLuhan posed the notion of a "global village," where we all share our hopes, dreams, and fears in a "worldpool" of information. **The global village refers to the "shrinking" of time and space as air travel and the electronic media have made it easier for the people around the globe to communicate with one another.**

Then the world became even faster and smaller. Twenty-five years ago, cell phones, pagers, fax, and voice-mail links barely existed. When AT&T launched the first cellular communications system in 1983, it predicted fewer than a million users by 2000. By the end of 1993, however, there were more than 16 million cellular phone subscribers in the United States.[21] And by 2015, there were nearly 7 billion mobile-cellular subscriptions.[22]

The Net, the Web, and the World   Then came the Internet, the worldwide computer-linked "network of networks." Today, of the 7.4 billion people in the world, 43% are Internet users.[23] The Net might have remained the province of academicians had it not been for the contributions of Tim Berners-Lee, who came up with the coding system, linkages, and addressing scheme that debuted in 1991 as the World Wide Web. "He took a powerful communications system [the Internet] that only the elite could use," says one writer, "and turned it into a mass medium."[24]

The arrival of the web quickly led to **e-commerce, or electronic commerce, the buying and selling of products and services through computer networks.** U.S. retail e-commerce sales were estimated at $341.7 billion for 2015, up 14.7% over the previous year.[25]

E-Commerce: Peer-to-Peer Shopping by Smartphone

EXAMPLE

Perhaps the most well-known story of e-commerce companies is that of Amazon.com, which was started in 1994 by Jeffrey Bezos as an online bookstore, and now offers "new products and services at a rate none of the old-guard companies seem able to match," according to one business writer.[26] (One such company is Gap Inc., whose revenues have fallen at its Banana Republic and Old Navy walk-in stores but have not been made up for in online sales.[27])

The New E-Commerce. Today 68% of U.S. adults have a smartphone and nearly 45% a tablet.[28] Yet most American consumers use their mobile devices for getting directions or listening to music rather than making purchases, according to a survey by Pew Research Center.[29] But in Asia, which is home to the world's two biggest smartphone markets, China and India, things are different. Asian countries account for nearly half of the world's mobile online shopping, worth more than $230 billion annually (in U.S. dollars).[30] A few companies, reports *The Wall Street Journal*, "are starting to change the commercial landscape by offering apps that let individuals buy and sell goods directly from one another more easily than on traditional Web-based sites like eBay."[31] For example, in January 2016, 43% of people in South Korea said they used a smartphone to make a purchase during the past 30 days, the highest proportion in the world.

Consumer-to-Consumer Apps. In the so-called peer-to-peer commerce market, shopping apps like Shopee, from Taiwan, with about 3 million users throughout Asia, makes money by charging small transaction fees or commissions. Consumers can quickly create listings in a minute or two by photographing an item with a smartphone, tapping out a few lines of text, and then finding buyers and sellers through the app's GPS features and built-in payment, chat, and delivery services.

YOUR CALL

Why do you suppose peer-to-peer commerce that is so popular in Asia has not caught on in North America?

One Big World Market: The Global Economy

"We are seeing the results of things started in 1988 and 1989," said Rosabeth Moss Kantor of the Harvard Business School, referring to three historic global changes.[32] The first was in the late 1980s when the Berlin Wall came down, signaling the beginning of the end of communism in Eastern Europe. The second was when Asian countries began to open their economies to foreign investors. The third was the worldwide trend of governments deregulating their economies. These three events set up conditions by which goods, people, and money could move more freely throughout the world—a global economy. **The global economy refers to the increasing tendency of the economies of the world to interact with one another as one market instead of many national markets.**

It's no secret the economies of the world are increasingly tied together, connected by information arriving instantaneously through currency traders' screens, CNN news reports, Twitter feeds, text messages, and other technology. Money, represented by digital blips, changes hands globally in a matter of keystrokes.

Positive Effects   Is a global economy really good for the United States? "Most people see speedy travel, mass communications, and quick dissemination of information through the Internet as benefits of globalization," says University College London

Globalization. Coke and Pepsi already dominate India's beverage market of 1.2 billion people, and now both companies are going after the fruit-juice market among India's increasingly health-conscious consumers. Do you see any negative effects to this? © Taylor Ross/SIPA/Newscom

historian Michael Collins. Other positives are that there is now a worldwide market for companies and consumers who have access to products of different countries, and there is more influx of information between two countries, more cultural intermingling, and often more openness and tolerance toward other people.[33]

In addition, foreign firms are building plants in the United States, revitalizing parts of industrial America. Indeed, almost one-third of the world's new auto plants are under construction in North America, says one report, "with large growth in Mexico but also a resurgence in the United States."[34] In fact, foreign direct investment makes up 16.5% of the country's gross domestic product.[35]

But will worldwide economic growth create "rising prosperity and higher living standards," as some have predicted?[36]

Negative Effects   "There is no question that globalization has been a good thing for many developing countries who now have access to our markets and can export cheap goods," says Collins. It has also benefited multinational corporations and Wall Street, he believes. "But globalization has not been good for working people (blue or white collar)," he asserts, "and has led to the continuing deindustrialization of America."[37]

The biggest problem is the movement, or outsourcing, of formerly well-paying jobs overseas as companies seek cheaper labor costs, particularly in manufacturing. Soaring new U.S. skyscrapers, for example, are more apt to have windows made in China than in Ohio, a glassmaking state.[38] The developers of apps, or software for cell phones and other mobile platforms, are more likely to be overseas, even though more and more people in the United States owe their jobs to the existence of apps.[39] Although global trade has helped lift hundreds of millions of Chinese out of poverty and consumers around the world to benefit from better-priced, better-made goods, U.S. labor markets exposed to Chinese competition lost an estimated 2.4 million jobs from 1999 to 2011.[40] Some economists fear that many jobs lost through the recession and offshoring may simply never come back.[41] (But some are, as we will see.)

Globalization is like being overwhelmed by a snow avalanche," says Collins. "You can't stop it—you can only swim in the snow and hope to stay on top."[42] The alternative is to follow strategies that make the effects of globalization more equitable, such as enforcing trade laws, making the competition play by the same rules, and prohibiting other countries from stealing our technology and other competitive tools.

Cross-Border Business: The Rise of Both Megamergers and Minifirms Worldwide

The global market driven by electronic information "forces things to get bigger and smaller at the same time," suggests technology philosopher Nicholas Negroponte. "There will be an increasing absence of things that aren't either very local or very global."[43]

If Negroponte is correct, this means we will see more and more of two opposite kinds of businesses: mergers of huge companies into even larger companies, and small, fast-moving, start-up companies.

Megamergers Operating Worldwide   Kmart + Sears. Union Pacific + Southern Pacific. Whole Foods + Wild Oats. Bank of America + Merrill Lynch. Roche + Genentech. Ticketmaster + Live Nation. Mattel (maker of Barbie Doll) + Hit Entertainment (Bob the Builder). Jos. A. Bank + Eddie Bauer. Cerberus (Albertsons) + Safeway. Anthem + Cigna. HJ Heinz + Kraft Foods. Dell + EMC. Dow Chemical + DuPont. Charter Communications + Time Warner Cable. Anheuser Busch Inbev + SABMiller.

The last 20 years have seen a surge in mergers.[44] Certain industries—automobiles, airlines, telecommunications, health care, and pharmaceuticals, for instance—aren't

Craft beers. At Costco, craft beers account for 30% of the company's beer sales. What kind of threat do you think the merger of giant breweries Anheuser-Busch InBev (makers of Budweiser, Corona, Beck's) and SABMiller (Miller, Coors) represents to craft breweries?
© David Caudery/Future Publishing/Getty Images

suited to being midsize, let alone small and local, so companies in these industries are trying to become bigger and cross-border. The means for doing so is to merge with other big companies. In pharmaceuticals, for instance, Viagra maker Pfizer targeted Botox maker Allergan, in a move designed to lower its U.S. corporate taxes.[45] Walgreens bid for Rite Aid while CVS took over Target's pharmacies in a battle for the drug business.[46] Other mergers weren't so massive: Yelp purchased food-ordering service Et24.com, and Time Inc. snapped up pop-culture website Hello Giggles for its young female audience.[47]

Not all observers think big mergers are a good idea. "The presence of a few dominant companies in an industry," said one editorial, "makes it harder for entrepreneurs to start new businesses in that sector."[48] For instance, two giant beer makers—Anheuser-Busch InBev (Budweiser, Corona, Beck's) and SABMiller (Miller, Coors)—consolidated distributors as a way of thwarting the advance of craft breweries, which now account for 11% of the beer market.[49]

Minifirms Operating Worldwide   The Internet and the World Wide Web allow almost anyone to be global, with two important results:

1. **Small companies can get started more easily.** Because anyone can put goods or services on a website and sell worldwide, this wipes out the former competitive advantages of distribution and scope that large companies used to have.

2. **Small companies can maneuver faster.** Little companies can change direction faster, which gives them an advantage in terms of time and distance over large companies. ●

EXAMPLE   The Sharing-Based Economy: Starting an Internet Enterprise

Around the world, "consumers are showing a robust appetite for the sharing-based economy," says one analysis.[50] Whether borrowing goods, renting homes, or offering special skills or goods, the Internet, mobile apps, and low barriers to entry have allowed many small firms to start quickly and maneuver faster.

Selling Used Clothing via Apparel App. Founded in 2011 by Manish Chandra, Poshmark of Menlo Park, California, is a mobile marketplace in which women use their smartphones to buy and sell preowned clothes. Savannah Barrozo, after going from a size 2 to size 8 following her pregnancies, used Poshmark (which takes a 20% cut), and now she brings in $80,000 a year. Now Poshmark is maneuvering into a new market—giving fashion brands such as Style Mafia a place to sell in bulk at wholesale prices. "We're giving independent fashion brands a massive new channel to exploit," says Chandra. "They can convert our million sellers to become their sales force."[51]

Helping Homeless Artists. Liz Powers, 27, a Harvard sociology graduate, started organizing a few art shows to promote the work of homeless and disabled artists from Boston-area homeless shelters. She began to think, "How can we help people not just in Boston but across the country? How can we help not just one day a year but every day?" From this thought, in 2013 she and her brother, Spencer, starting with a $4,000 investment, founded ArtLifting, based on the model of the online artisan site Etsy, and now has contracts with more than 70 artists. A principal investor is Blake Mycoskie, founder of TOMS (which gives away a pair of shoes for every pair it sells), who believes that a purpose-driven, profit-oriented business is a better avenue than a nonprofit (which often depends on endless fundraising) for many social causes.[52]

YOUR CALL

Do you have an idea for an uncommon product or skill that might be offered via the sharing-based Internet economy? What would it be?

4.2   You and International Management

Why learn about international management, and what characterizes the successful international manager?

THE BIG PICTURE

Studying international management prepares you to work with foreign customers or suppliers, for a foreign firm in the United States, or for a U.S. firm overseas. Successful international managers aren't ethnocentric or polycentric but geocentric.

Can you see yourself working overseas? It can definitely be an advantage to your career. "There are fewer borders," says Paul McDonald, executive director of recruitment firm Robert Half Management Resources. "Anyone with international experience will have a leg up, higher salary, and be more marketable."[53] The recent brutal U.S. job market has also spurred more Americans to hunt for jobs overseas.[54]

Foreign experience demonstrates independence, resourcefulness, and entrepreneurship, according to management recruiters. "You are interested in that person who can move quickly and is nimble and has an inquiring mind," says one. People who have worked and supported themselves overseas, she says, tend to be adaptive and inquisitive—valuable skills in today's workplace.[55] This outlook represents what is known as a **global mind-set, which combines (1) an openness to and awareness of diversity across cultures and markets with (2) a propensity and ability to see common patterns across countries and markets.**[56] People and organizations with a global mind-set see cultural and geographic diversity as opportunities to exploit and will take good ideas wherever they find them.[57]

PRACTICAL ACTION

Learning to Be a Success Abroad: Developing a Global Mind-set

Whether you travel abroad on your own or on a work assignment for your company, there are several ways to develop a global mind-set and make your experience enhance your career success.

Be an "I'm-Not-an-Ugly American." Americans "are seen throughout the world as an arrogant people, totally self-absorbed and loud," says Keith Reinhard, former head of advertising conglomerate DDB Worldwide, who had led an effort to reverse that through a nonprofit group called Business for Diplomatic Action (BDA), from which many suggestions here are drawn.[58] (The group publishes *The World Citizens Guide,* which consists of practical advice for Americans traveling abroad.)[59] A survey conducted by DDB in more than 100 countries found that respondents repeatedly mentioned "arrogant," "loud," and "uninterested in the world" when asked their perceptions of Americans.[60] Some sample advice for Americans traveling abroad is: Be patient, be quiet, listen at least as much as you talk, don't use slang, and don't talk about wealth and status.[61]

Be Global in Your Focus, but Think Local. Study up on your host country's local customs and try to meet new people who might help you in the future. For example, Bill Roedy, president of MTV Networks International, spent time hanging out with Arab rappers and meeting the mayor of Mecca before trying to sign a contract that would launch MTV Arabia.[62] His efforts helped seal the deal.

Learn What's Appropriate Behavior. Before you go, spend some time learning about patterns of interpersonal communication. In Japan, for instance, it is considered rude to look directly into the eye for more than a few seconds. In Greece the hand-waving gesture commonly used in America is considered an insult. In Afghanistan, a man does not ask another man about his wife.[63] In China, people generally avoid hugs—at least until recently.[64]

Learn rituals of respect, including exchange of business cards.[65] Understand that shaking hands is always permissible, but social kissing may not be. Dress professionally. For women, this means no heavy makeup, no flashy jewelry, no short skirts or sleeveless blouses (particularly in Islamic countries). In some countries, casual dressing is a sign of disrespect. Don't use first names and nicknames with fellow employees overseas, especially in countries with strict social strata.[66]

Know Your Field. If you know your field and behave with courtesy and assurance, you will be well received around the world. Indra Nooyi successfully uses this advice in her role as CEO of PepsiCo. She's cosmopolitan and well educated and is respected by people around the globe.[67]

Become at Least Minimally Skilled in the Language. Whatever foreign country you're in, at the very least you should learn a few key phrases, such as "hello," "please," and "thank you," in your host country's language. Successful international managers have learned there is no adequate substitute for knowing the local language.[68]

YOUR CALL

Have you done much traveling? What tricks have you discovered to make it more satisfying?

Part of the action. If "all of the action in business is international," as one expert says, what role do you think you might play in it? Do you think cultural bias against women in some foreign countries contributes to the low percentage of U.S. female executives working abroad? © Image Source/Getty Images RF

Why Learn about International Management?

International management is management that oversees the conduct of operations in or with organizations in foreign countries, whether it's through a multinational corporation or a multinational organization.

Multinational Corporations   A **multinational corporation**, or multinational enterprise, is a business firm with operations in several countries. Our publisher, McGraw-Hill Education, is owned by Apollo Global Management, one such multinational. In terms of sales revenue, the largest American multinational corporations in 2015 were Wal-Mart Stores, Exxon Mobil, Chevron, Berkshire Hathaway, Apple, McKesson, General Motors, Phillips 66, General Electric, and Ford Motor. The largest foreign firms were the oil companies SinoPec Group, Royal Dutch Shell (Netherlands), PetroChina, Exxon Mobil (USA), and BP (Britain), followed by State Grid (utilities, China), Volkswagen (Germany), and Toyota Motor (Japan).[69]

Multinational Organizations   A **multinational organization** is a nonprofit organization with operations in several countries. Examples are the World Health Organization, the International Red Cross, and the Church of Latter Day Saints.

Even if in the coming years you never travel to the wider world outside North America—an unlikely proposition, we think—the world will assuredly come to you. That, in a nutshell, is why you need to learn about international management.

Working Overseas: Giving Yourself the Extra Edge in the Job Market EXAMPLE

"In the past, Americans took foreign jobs for the adventure or because their career field demanded overseas work," says the wife of a philosophy instructor who found a job in Hong Kong. "Today, these young people are leaving because they can't find jobs in the United States."[70]

Although the U.S. economy has improved a lot since the aftermath of the Great Recession (2007–2009), there are many young people, especially graduates under 34, who say they would move abroad for a job—59% according to one study, 55% according to another (particularly if a higher salary was offered).[71] A growing group of Americans, therefore, are headed overseas for economic opportunity and to learn and grow.[72]

When John Haltiwanger was 23, he took a job as an English teacher in the post-Soviet country of Georgia. "It ended up being one of the best decisions I've ever made," he said.[73] "The key to survival, in any walk of life, is adaptability. Working abroad helps you hone this quality. . . . Indeed, working in a new country requires both the ability to recognize cultural idiosyncrasies and the willingness and capacity to adjust to them."

One possible benefit of working overseas is that—depending on the country and your field—you may have a better chance of taking on high-level positions more quickly. "For example, Mexico and Chile both have cities with interesting tech and startup scenes, but young folks looking for jobs aren't flocking to these cities like they are to San Francisco and New York," points out Chloe Mason Gray, who worked in Mexico City after college. She and the majority of her non-Mexican friends living there "were hired into or quickly advanced to high-level positions in their companies—positions that would have taken them many years to work up to in their home countries."[74]

In addition, working—or even just studying—abroad can give you an edge in the job market when you return to the United States. When Ashley Blackmon, 24, sat down for a job interview in New York City, she didn't talk about her business classes but rather the five months she spent studying and traveling in Spain. "When I left the interview, I felt amazing," she said. By studying in a new culture, "I learned how to be a better businesswoman, critical thinker, and relationship builder."[75]

YOUR CALL

Somewhere between 2.2 million and 6.8 million Americans live abroad.[76] How do you feel about becoming one of them, and which countries would you prefer? How would you prepare yourself to join them?

More specifically, consider yourself in the following situations:

You May Deal with Foreign Customers or Partners While working for a U.S. company you may have to deal with foreign customers. Or you may have to work with a foreign company in some sort of joint venture. The people you're dealing with may be outside the United States or visitors to it.[77] Either way you would hate to blow a deal—and maybe all future deals—because you were ignorant of some cultural aspects you could have known about.

Examples are legion.[78] One American executive inadvertently insulted or embarrassed Thai businessmen by starting gatherings talking about business. "That's a no-no," he says. "I quickly figured out that I was creating problems by talking business before eating lunch and by initiating the talks."[79] People working on multinational teams across the globe need to become aware of some of the reasons information sharing doesn't happen as effectively as it should, as we describe elsewhere.[80]

You May Deal with Foreign Employees or Suppliers While working for an American company you may have to purchase important components, raw materials, or services from a foreign supplier.[81] And you never know where foreign practices may diverge from what you're accustomed to.

Many software developer jobs, for instance, have been moved outside the United States—to places such as India, New Zealand, and Eastern Europe. A lot of U.S. software companies—Microsoft, IBM, Oracle, Motorola, Novell, Hewlett-Packard, and Texas Instruments—have opened offices in India to take advantage of high-quality labor. Many U.S. research scientists have also moved overseas.[82] Even small businesses that lack serious capital regularly ship their development work overseas, with all the risks of miscommunication and dealing with different cultural and technological barriers.[83]

You May Work for a Foreign Firm in the United States   You may sometime take a job with a foreign firm doing business in the United States, such as an electronics, pharmaceutical, or car company. And you'll have to deal with managers above and below you whose outlook is different from yours. For instance, Japanese companies, with their emphasis on correctness and face saving, operate in significantly different ways from American companies.

Working for a foreign firm. If you thought you might work for a foreign firm, either at home or overseas, what should you be doing now to prepare for it? © CKDJ/Corbis/VCG/Getty Images

Sometimes it is even hard to know that an ostensibly U.S. company actually has foreign ownership. For example, among some classic American brands that are now foreign owned are Jeep (made by Fiat Chrysler), Ben & Jerry's Ice Cream (started in Vermont, acquired in 2000 by Anglo-Dutch conglomerate Unilever), Gerber baby food (first made in California, now owned by Nestlé of Switzerland), Motel 6 (also founded in California, acquired by Paris hospitality company Accor), and Vaseline (founded in Brooklyn in 1870, now owned by Unilever), as well as Popsicle (Unilever), Purina (Nestlé), Frigidaire (AB Electrolux, Sweden), and 7-Eleven (Seven & I Holdings, Japan).[84]

You May Work for an American Firm outside the United States—or for a Foreign One   You might easily find yourself working abroad in the foreign operation of a U.S. company. Most big American corporations have overseas subsidiaries or divisions. On the other hand, you might also well work for a foreign firm in a foreign country, such as a big Indian company in Bangalore or Mumbai.

The Successful International Manager: Geocentric, Not Ethnocentric or Polycentric

Maybe you don't really care that you don't have much understanding of the foreign culture you're dealing with. "What's the point?" you may think. The main thing is to get the job done. Certainly there are international firms with managers who have this perspective. They are called *ethnocentric,* one of three primary attitudes among international managers, the other two being *polycentric* and *geocentric.*[85]

Ethnocentric Managers—"We Know Best"

What do foreign executives fluent in English think when they hear Americans using an endless array of baseball, basketball, and football phrases (such as "out of left field" or "Hail Mary pass").[86] **Ethnocentric managers believe that their native country, culture, language, and behavior are superior to all others.** Ethnocentric managers tend to believe that they can export the managers and practices of their home countries to anywhere in the world and that they will be more capable and reliable. Often the ethnocentric viewpoint is less attributable to prejudice than it is to ignorance, since such managers obviously know more about their home environment than the foreign environment. Ethnocentrism might also be called **parochialism—that is, a narrow view in which people see things solely through their own perspective.**

Is ethnocentrism bad for business? It seems so. A survey of 918 companies with home offices in the United States, Japan, and Europe found that ethnocentric policies were linked to such problems as recruiting difficulties, high turnover rates, and lawsuits over personnel policies.[87]

Ethnocentric views also affect our purchasing decisions. Some people believe that we should only purchase products made in our home country. What are your views about being an ethnocentric consumer? You can find out by taking Self-Assessment 4.1.

≣ connect SELF-ASSESSMENT 4.1

Assessing Your Consumer Ethnocentrism

This survey is designed to assess your consumer ethnocentrism. Please be prepared to answer these questions if your instructor has assigned Self-Assessment 4.1 in Connect.

1. Are you surprised by the results? What do they suggest about your purchasing decisions? What are the pros and cons of being an ethnocentric consumer?

2. How do American companies, associations, and unions encourage us to be ethnocentric consumers?

Polycentric Managers—"They Know Best"

Polycentric managers take the view that native managers in the foreign offices best understand native personnel and practices, and so the home office should leave them alone. Thus, the attitude of polycentric managers is nearly the opposite of that of ethnocentric managers.

Geocentric Managers—"What's Best Is What's Effective, Regardless of Origin"

Geocentric managers accept that there are differences and similarities between home and foreign personnel and practices and that they should use whatever techniques are most effective. Clearly, being an ethno- or polycentric manager takes less work. But the payoff for being a geocentric manager can be far greater. The Practical Action Box on page 111, "Learning to Be a Success Abroad: Developing a Global Mind-set," gives some tips on being geocentric. ●

4.3   Why and How Companies Expand Internationally

Why do companies expand internationally, and how do they do it?

THE BIG PICTURE

Multinationals expand to take advantage of availability of supplies, new markets, lower labor costs, access to finance capital, or avoidance of tariffs and import quotas. Five ways they do so are by global outsourcing; importing, exporting, and countertrading; licensing and franchising; joint ventures; and wholly-owned subsidiaries.

Who makes Apple's iPhone? An estimated 90% of the components are manufactured overseas, by workers in Switzerland, Singapore, Korea, and elsewhere. The display screens, for instance, come mostly from Asia, especially South Korea, Taiwan, and Japan; the phone itself is assembled in China.[88] Who makes the furniture sold by Ethan Allen, that most American of names, evoking Ethan Allen and the Green Mountain Boys of the American Revolution? Most of it still is made in the United States, but a lot is made by suppliers in Mexico, China, the Philippines, Indonesia, and Vietnam.[89]

Where is Netflix going for new business as its U.S. growth slows? In early 2016, the Internet streaming video service debuted in 130 countries.[90] There are many reasons why American companies are going global. Let us consider why and how they are expanding beyond U.S. borders.

U.S. export. Popular entertainment is a major U.S. export, as was the 2014 sci-fi film *RoboCop*, which earned only $58.6 million in the U.S. and Canada but an astonishing $184.1 million overseas. It did particularly well in China, where on its opening weekend it grossed $20.5 million. More and more movie studios are profiting from films because of the money they make outside the United States.[91] Are there any negatives to sending American popular culture overseas? © Columbia Pictures/courtesy Everett Collection

Why Companies Expand Internationally

Many a company has made the deliberate decision to restrict selling its product or service to just its own country. Is anything wrong with that?

The answer is: It depends. It would probably have been a serious mistake for NEC, Sony, or Hitachi to have limited their markets solely to Japan during the 1990s, a time when the country was in an economic slump and Japanese consumers weren't consuming. During that same period, however, some American banks might have been better off not making loans abroad, when the U.S. economy was booming but foreign economies were not. Going international or not going international—it can be risky either way.

Why, then, do companies expand internationally? There are at least five reasons, all of which have to do with making or saving money.

1. Availability of Supplies Antique and art dealers, mining companies, banana growers, sellers of hard woods—all have to go where their basic supplies or raw materials are located. For years oil companies, for example, expanded their activities outside the United States in seeking cheaper or more plentiful sources of oil.

2. New Markets Sometimes a company will find, as cigarette makers have, that the demand for their product has declined domestically but that they can still make money overseas. Or sometimes a company will steal a march on its competitors by aggressively expanding into foreign markets, as did Coca-Cola over PepsiCo under the leadership of legendary CEO Robert Goizueta. Apple expanded efforts to sell more iPhones and other products in India, as sales to China slowed.[92] Swedish retailer IKEA did likewise, thinking India's blossoming middle class was a good bet to buy "flat-pack dining tables, cotton dish towels, and Scandinavian-sounding sofas."[93]

3. Lower Labor Costs   The decline in manufacturing jobs in the United States is partly attributable to the fact that American companies have found it cheaper to do their manufacturing outside the States. For example, the rationale for using **maquiladoras— manufacturing plants allowed to operate in Mexico with special privileges in return for employing Mexican citizens**—is that they provide less expensive labor for assembling everything from appliances to cars. When Ford Motor Co.'s attempt to build small cars in the United States, in one description, "hit a pothole" owing to high labor costs, the company decided to move production of its Ford Focus to Mexico, where it was already building the subcompact Fiesta.[94]

Even professional or service kinds of jobs, such as computer programming, may be shipped overseas.

4. Access to Finance Capital   Companies may be enticed into going abroad by the prospects of capital being put up by foreign companies or sudsidies from foreign governments. For example, Woody Allen's 2013 film *Blue Jasmine,* in which Cate Blanchett plays a woman whose husband is revealed to be a Bernie Madoff–like con man, received most of its financing from overseas investors, as do many other American movies.[95]

5. Avoidance of Tariffs and Import Quotas   Countries place tariffs (fees) on imported goods or impose import quotas—limitations on the numbers of products allowed in—for the purpose of protecting their own domestic industries. For example, Japan imposes tariffs on agricultural products, such as rice, imported from the United States. To avoid these penalties, a company might create a subsidiary to produce the product in the foreign country. General Electric and Whirlpool, for example, have foreign subsidiaries to produce appliances overseas.

How Companies Expand Internationally

Most companies don't start out to be multinationals. Generally, they edge their way into international business, at first making minimal investments and taking minimal risks, as shown in the drawing. *(See Figure 4.1.)*

FIGURE 4.1   Five ways of expanding internationally
These range from lowest risk and investment *(left)* to highest risk and investment *(right).*

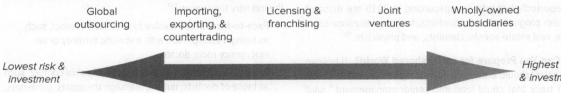

| Global outsourcing | Importing, exporting, & countertrading | Licensing & franchising | Joint ventures | Wholly-owned subsidiaries |

Lowest risk & investment   *Highest risk & investment*

Let's consider the five ways of expanding internationally shown in the figure.

1. Global Outsourcing   A common practice of many companies, **outsourcing is defined as using suppliers outside the company to provide goods and services.** For example, airlines farm out a lot of aircraft maintenance to other companies. Management philosopher Peter Drucker believed that in the near future organizations might be outsourcing all work that is "support"—such as information systems—rather than revenue producing.

Global outsourcing extends this technique outside the United States. **Global outsourcing, or offshoring, is defined as using suppliers outside the United States to provide labor, goods, or services.** The reason may be that the foreign supplier has resources not available in the United States, such as Italian marble. Or the supplier may have special expertise, as do Pakistani weavers. Or—more likely these days—the supplier's labor is cheaper than American labor. As a manager, your first business trip outside the United States might be to inspect the production lines of one of your outsourcing suppliers.

However, a countertrend, called "reshoring" or "nearshoring" or "deglobalization," is that some companies are moving production back home, because long supply chains can be easily affected by the whims of geopolitics and energy prices and the United States remains a manufacturing power for higher-value products.[96]

2. Importing, Exporting, and Countertrading   When **importing, a company buys goods outside the country and resells them domestically.** Nothing might seem to be more American than Caterpillar tractors, but they are made not only in the United States but also in Mexico, from which they are imported and made available for sale in the United States.[97] Many of the products we use are imported, ranging from Heineken beer (Netherlands) to Texaco gasoline (Saudi Arabia) to Honda snowblowers (Japan).

Global Outsourcing: Which Jobs Are Likely to Fall Victim to Offshoring?

Will there be any good jobs left for new college graduates?

Americans are rightly concerned about the changing jobs picture, brought about not only by the dismal aftermath of the 2007–2009 Great Recession but also earlier in part by offshoring of work to low-wage countries such as China, India, and the Philippines. Few of the millions of factory jobs that have been lost during the last 10 years have been replaced, and today just 9% of American workers are employed in manufacturing.[98] This has forced many workers—when they were able to work at all—to accept lower-paying alternatives, such as jobs in retail and health care, which pay far less than manufacturing jobs.[99]

More recently, the same trend—global outsourcing—has been happening with white-collar jobs. Among the top careers that reportedly lost jobs to outsourcing in 2015 are those of computer programmers, accountants, lawyers, insurance sales agents, real estate agents, chemists, and physicists.[100]

How Can You Prepare for an Offshored World? "I believe [companies] should outsource everything for which there is no career track that could lead into senior management," said management philosopher Peter Drucker. An example, he said, is the job of total-quality-control specialist, work that can be done overseas.[101]

"As soon as a job becomes routine enough to describe in a spec sheet, it becomes vulnerable to outsourcing," says another writer. "Jobs like data entry, which are routine by nature, were the first among obvious candidates for outsourcing." But even "design and financial-analysis skills can, with time, become well-enough understood to be spelled out in a contract and signed away."[102] Says Fred Levy, a Massachusetts Institute of Technology economist, "If you can describe a job precisely, or write rules for doing it, it's unlikely to survive. Either we'll program a computer to do it, or we'll teach a foreigner to do it."[103]

Which Jobs Will Remain in the United States? It is difficult to predict which jobs will remain at home, since even the Bureau of Labor Statistics often can't get it right. However, jobs that endure may share certain traits, listed below, regardless of the industry they serve:[104]

- **Face-to-face.** Some involve *face-to-face contact,* such as being a salesperson with a specific territory or an emergency room doctor.

- **Physical contact.** Other jobs involve *physical contact,* such as those of dentists, nurses, massage therapists, gardeners, and nursing-home aides.

- **Making high-end products.** *High-end products* that require intensive research, precision assembly, and complex technology requiring skilled workers are good candidates for the U.S. labor market, says Eric Spiegel, CEO of the Siemens

Corp. Low-end, low-technology products, such as textiles and furniture, will doubtless continue to be offshored.[105]

- **Recognizing complex patterns.** Others involve the human ability to *recognize complex patterns,* which are hard to computerize, such as a physician's ability to diagnose an unusual disease (even if the X-rays are read by a radiologist in India). This also describes such jobs as teaching first grade or selling a mansion to a millionaire or jobs that demand an intimate knowledge of the United States, such as marketing to American teenagers or lobbying Congress.

Survival Rules. For you, as a prospective manager, there are perhaps three ideas to take away from all this:

- **Teamwork and creativity.** "Jobs that persist are dynamic and creative and require the ability to team with others," says Jim Spohrer of the IBM Almaden Research Center in San Jose, California, which studies the business operations of IBM's corporate clients. "At its heart, a company is simply a group of teams that come together to create" products and services.[106]

- **Flexibility.** "Jobs used to change very little or not at all over the course of several generations," says Spohrer.

"Now, they might change three or four times in a single lifetime."[107] Flexibility—as in being willing to undergo retraining—thus becomes important. Fortunately, as Drucker pointed out, the United States is "the only country that has a very significant continuing education system. This doesn't exist anywhere else."[108] The United States is also the only country, he said, in which it is easy for younger people to move from one area at work to another.[109]

- **Education.** The more education one has, the more one is apt to prevail during times of economic change. Men and women with four years of college, for instance, earned 98% more an hour on average in 2013 than people without a degree.[110] *For young adults ages 25–34 in that year, those with a bachelor's degree earned more than twice as much as those without a high school credential ($48,500 versus $23,900).*[111]

YOUR CALL

What kind of job or jobs are you interested in that would seem to provide you with some hopes of prevailing in a fast-changing world?

When **exporting**, a company produces goods domestically and sells them outside the country. The U.S. was ranked the number 1 exporter in the world in 2015, up from number 3 two years earlier. *(See Table 4.2.)* One of the greatest U.S. exports is American pop culture, in the form of movies, music, and fashion. The United States is also a leader in exporting computers and other information technology.

Sometimes other countries may wish to import American goods but lack the currency to pay for them. In that case, the exporting U.S. company may resort to **countertrading**—that is, bartering goods for goods. When the Russian ruble plunged in value in 1998, some goods became a better medium of exchange than currency.

3. Licensing and Franchising

Licensing and franchising are two aspects of the same thing, although licensing is used by manufacturing companies and franchising is used more frequently by service companies.

In **licensing,** a company allows a foreign company to pay it a fee to make or distribute the first company's product or service. For example, the Du Pont chemical company might license a company in Brazil to make Teflon, the nonstick substance that is found on some frying pans. Thus, Du Pont, the licensor, can make money without having to invest large sums to conduct business directly in a foreign company. Moreover, the Brazilian firm, the licensee, knows the local market better than Du Pont probably would.

Franchising is a form of licensing in which a company allows a foreign company to pay it a fee and a share of the profit in return for using the first company's brand name and a package of materials and services. For example, Burger King, Hertz, and Hilton Hotels,

TABLE 4.2   Top 10 Exporting Countries, 1999 and 2015

RANK IN 1999	RANK IN 2015
1. U.S.	U.S.
2. Germany	China
3. Japan	Japan
4. France	Germany
5. Britain	France
6. Canada	South Korea
7. Italy	Netherlands
8. Netherlands	Italy
9. China	Russia
10. Belgium	United Kingdom

Source: "Top Ten Highest Exporting Countries in the the World," Wevio, March 6, 2015, www.wevio.com/general/top-10-highest-exporting-countries-in-the-world (accessed March 10, 2016).

which are all well-known brands, might provide the use of their names plus their operating know-how (facility design, equipment, recipes, management systems) to companies in the Philippines in return for an up-front fee plus a percentage of the profits.

By now Americans traveling throughout the world have become accustomed to seeing so-called U.S. stores everywhere. Some recently active companies: Toys R Us opened a store in Poland and then an e-commerce site there. Gap opened an Old Navy store in Japan, a Banana Republic store in Paris, and a Gap store in Delhi. Tiffany's opened a jewelry store in Russia and another one in Bangkok. Starbucks opened a store in Colombia and then its first store in Milan, Italy.[112]

Volvo. Who owns what car brand these days? Formerly British brands Jaguar and Land Rover now belong to Tata of India. Volkswagen owns the formerly British Bentley and Italian Lamborghini. Volvo, whose cars and trucks are still made in Sweden, is owned by Chinese automaker Geely. Do you think the American companies General Motors and Ford could ever wind up under foreign ownership, as Chrysler has (owned by Fiat)? © Gerlach Delissen/Corbis/Getty Images

4. Joint Ventures   *Strategic allies* (described in Chapter 3) are two organizations that have joined forces to realize strategic advantages that neither would have if operating alone. A U.S. firm may form a **joint venture,** also known as a *strategic alliance,* **with a foreign company to share the risks and rewards of starting a new enterprise together in a foreign country.** For instance, General Motors operates a joint venture with Shanghai Automotive Industry Group to build Buicks in China (which are now being imported into the United States).[113] Ford also has a joint venture in China with Changan Ford.[114]

Sometimes a joint venture is the only way an American company can have a presence in a certain country, whose laws may forbid foreigners from ownership. Indeed, in China, this is the only way foreign cars may be sold in that country.

5. Wholly-Owned Subsidiaries   **A wholly-owned subsidiary is a foreign subsidiary that is totally owned and controlled by an organization.** The foreign subsidiary may be an existing company that is purchased outright. **A greenfield venture is a foreign subsidiary that the owning organization has built from scratch.**

General Motors owns majority stakes in Adam Opel AG in Germany and Vauxhall Motor Cars Ltd. in the United Kingdom. ●

4.4   The World of Free Trade: Regional Economic Cooperation and Competition

MAJOR QUESTION

What are barriers to free trade, and what major organizations and trading blocs promote trade, and how important are the "BRICS" countries?

THE BIG PICTURE

Barriers to free trade are tariffs, import quotas, and embargoes. Organizations promoting international trade are the World Trade Organization, the World Bank, and the International Monetary Fund. We discuss two major trading blocs, NAFTA and the EU, as well as the still to-be-approved Trans-Pacific Partnership. Major competitors with the United States are the "BRICS" countries—Brazil, Russia, India, China, and South Africa.

If you live in the United States, you see foreign products on a daily basis—cars, appliances, clothes, foods, beers, wines, and so on. Based on what you see every day, which countries would you think are our most important trading partners? China? Japan? Germany? United Kingdom? South Korea?

These five countries do indeed appear among the top leading U.S. trading partners. Interestingly, however, our foremost trading partners are our immediate neighbors—Canada and Mexico—whose products may not be quite so visible. *(See Table 4.3.)*

Let's begin to consider **free trade,** the movement of goods and services among nations without political or economic obstruction.

TABLE 4.3   **Top 10 U.S. Trading Partners in Goods, January 2016**

TOP 10 NATIONS THE U.S. EXPORTS TO	TOP 10 NATIONS THE U.S. IMPORTS FROM
1. Canada	China
2. Mexico	Mexico
3. China	Canada
4. Japan	Japan
5. United Kingdom	Germany
6. Germany	South Korea
7. South Korea	India
8. Hong Kong	United Kingdom
9. Netherlands	France
10. Belgium	Taiwan

Source: U.S. Census Bureau, "Top Trading Partners—January 2016," December 12, 2015, https://www.census.gov/foreign-trade/statistics /highlights/toppartners.html (accessed March 11, 2016).

Barriers to International Trade

Countries often use **trade protectionism—the use of government regulations to limit the import of goods and services—** to protect their domestic industries against foreign competition. The justification they often use is that this saves jobs. Actually, protectionism is not considered beneficial, mainly because of what it does to the overall trading atmosphere.

The devices by which countries try to exert protectionism consist of *tariffs, import quotas,* and *trade embargoes* and *sanctions.*

1. Tariffs   A tariff is a trade barrier in the form of a customs duty, or tax, levied mainly on imports. At one time, for instance, to protect the American shoe industry, the United States imposed a tariff on Italian shoes. Actually, there are two types of tariffs: One, called a *revenue tariff,* is designed simply to raise money for the government, such as a tax on all oil imported into the United States. The other, which concerns us more, is a *protective tariff,* which is intended to raise the price of imported goods to make the prices of domestic products more competitive.

Beginning in late 2011, in a dispute that was still ongoing five years later, seven U.S. makers of solar panels sought trade tariffs from the U.S. Commerce Department of more than 100% on solar panels made in China, on the grounds that it used billions of dollars in government subsidies to help gain sales in the American market.[115]

Playing by the rules? Four of the five top solar cell producers are based in China, where the government has subsidized the development of this technology, to the detriment of American and European solar industries. What do you think the United States should do to equalize the situation? Impose tariffs (special taxes) on some Chinese imports? Subsidize our own solar industry? © Imaginechina/Corbis

A couple of months later, four U.S. makers of steel towers for wind turbines also filed a trade complaint against China and Vietnam seeking tariffs of 60% for the same reasons.[116] For its part, China raised tariffs on foreign auto brands, presumably to protect its own domestic car industry.[117] (A fully loaded Mini Cooper costing $52,500 in the United States might well go for around $85,000 in China, which has a 25% import tax plus a 17% value-added and consumption tax. A Ferrari costing $230,000 in the U.S. might set you back $724,000 in China.)[118]

2. Import Quotas   An **import quota is a trade barrier in the form of a limit on the numbers of a product that can be imported.** Its intent is to protect domestic industry by restricting the availability of foreign products.

As a condition of being allowed into the World Trade Organization, China agreed, starting in 2005, to cancel car import quotas, which it had used to protect its domestic car manufacturing industry against imported vehicles from the United States, Japan, and Germany.[119] However, it has not done the same with export quotas, where it has been found to have broken international trade law by imposing quotas on the export from China of rare earth elements (17 minerals with names like indium, gallium, and tellurium), which are crucial to making high-technology products, including mobile phones, hybrid cars, and 3-D TV screens.[120]

Quotas are designed to prevent **dumping, the practice of a foreign company's exporting products abroad at a lower price than the price in the home market—or even below the costs of production—in order to drive down the price of the domestic product.** In 2009, the U.S. International Trade Commission imposed antidumping duties of 10%–16% more on Chinese government–subsidized steel imported into the United States that damaged the American steel industry.[121]

3. Embargoes and Sanctions   In December 2014, President Barack Obama ordered the restoration of full diplomatic relations with Cuba, and in March 2016 he paid a visit to the island nation, the first U.S. president to do so in nearly 90 years.[122] Both events signaled the beginning of the end for the trade embargo imposed in 1960 by President Dwight D. Eisenhower at the height of the Cold War. For 54-plus years the embargo had prohibited anyone from importing Cuban cigars and sugar into the United States or for an American firm to do business in Cuba.

An **embargo is a complete ban or prohibition of trade of one country with another,** so that no goods or services can be imported or exported from or to the embargoed nation. The key word here is *complete,* as in "complete ban." Shortly after the Obama announcement, the departments of Commerce and Treasury weakened the embargo by publishing new rules that made it easier for Americans to trade with and travel to Cuba.[123]

An embargo is different from a sanction. **A sanction is the trade prohibition on certain types of products, services, or technology to another country for specific reasons,** including nuclear nonproliferation and humanitarian purposes. The key words here are *certain types.* Sanctions may be considered "partial embargoes," since they restrict trade in certain areas. For instance, the United States has trade sanctions with North Korea that prohibit the export of any material that would help North Korea in its nuclear program.[124] Chinese smartphone maker ZTE violated American sanctions against Iran by selling United States–made goods (such as U.S. chips in its phones) to that country, and as a result in 2016 was blocked from buying any technology from American companies unless it first obtained a special license.[125]

Organizations Promoting International Trade

In the 1920s, the institution of tariff barriers did not so much protect jobs as depress the demand for goods and services, thereby leading to the loss of jobs anyway—and the massive unemployment of the Great Depression of the 1930s.[126] As a result of this lesson, after World War II the advanced nations of the world began to realize that if all countries could freely exchange the products that each could produce most efficiently, this would lead to lower prices all around. Thus began the removal of barriers to free trade.

The three principal organizations designed to facilitate international trade are the *World Trade Organization,* the *World Bank,* and the *International Monetary Fund.*

1. The World Trade Organization (WTO)   Consisting of 164 member countries, the **World Trade Organization (WTO) is designed to monitor and enforce trade agreements.** The agreements are based on the *General Agreement on Tariffs and Trade (GATT),* an international accord first signed by 23 nations in 1947, which helped to reduce world-wide tariffs and other barriers. Out of GATT came a series of "rounds," or negotiations, that resulted in the lowering of barriers; for instance, the Uruguay Round, implemented in 1996, cut tariffs by one-third. The last round of negotiations, the Doha Round, which began in Doha, Qatar, in 2001, aimed at helping the world's poor by, among other things, reducing trade barriers, including improving customs rules and procedures. However, after 14 years of talks, the Doha Round was effectively ended—unsuccessfully, because of trade ministers' inability to agree on how to lower trade barriers, contribute to development in poor nations, and other issues. Now world leaders will have to rethink global trade pacts that encourage development and sustainable economic growth.[127]

Founded in 1995 and headquartered in Geneva, Switzerland, WTO succeeded GATT as the world forum for trade negotiations and has the formal legal structure for deciding trade disputes. WTO also encompasses areas not previously covered by GATT, such as services and intellectual property rights. A particularly interesting area of responsibility covers telecommunications—cell phones, pagers, data transmission, satellite communications, and the like—with half of the WTO's members agreeing to open their markets to foreign telecommunications companies.[128]

2. The World Bank   The World Bank was founded after World War II to help European countries rebuild. Today the purpose of the **World Bank is to provide low-interest loans to developing nations for improving transportation, education, health, and telecommunications.** The bank has 188 member nations, with most contributions coming from Britain, the United States, Japan, and Germany.

In recent times, protesters have complained the World Bank has financed projects that could damage the ecosystem, such as the Three Gorges Dam on China's Yangtze River, or supported countries that permit low-paying sweatshops or that suppress religious freedom. Others think it has dragged its feet on getting affordable AIDS drugs to less-developed countries in Africa and lent millions to a palm oil company in Honduras accused of links to assassinations and forced evictions.[129] In 2014 the World Bank underwent a sweeping reorganization to encourage better collaboration and a quicker response.[130] It also announced it was nearly doubling its potential lending to developing countries such as China, India, and Brazil.[131]

3. The International Monetary Fund   Founded in 1945 and now affiliated with the United Nations, the International Monetary Fund is the second pillar supporting the international financial community. Consisting of 188 member nations, the **International Monetary Fund (IMF) is designed to assist in smoothing the flow of money between nations.**

The IMF operates as a last-resort lender that makes short-term loans to countries suffering from unfavorable balance of payments (roughly the difference between money coming into a country and money leaving the country, because of imports, exports, and other matters). In recent times, the IMF has become more high profile because of its role in trying to shore up some weaker European economies, including making loans to Greece, Portugal, and Ireland and considering how to assist Italy and Spain.[132] Lately it has been more concerned with addressing income inequality, which has worsened in most countries in the past three decades.[133] The IMF was overhauled in late 2015 to increase its capital and give countries such as China and India a greater say in the organization.[134]

Major Trading Blocs: NAFTA and the EU

A trading bloc, also known as an *economic community,* is a group of nations within a geographical region that have agreed to remove trade barriers with one another. The two major trading blocs we will consider are the *NAFTA nations* and the *European Union.*

1. NAFTA—The Three Countries of the North American Free Trade Agreement

Formed in 1994, the **North American Free Trade Agreement (NAFTA) is a trading bloc consisting of the United States, Canada, and Mexico, encompassing 444 million people.** The agreement is supposed to eliminate 99% of the tariffs and quotas among these countries, allowing for freer flow of goods, services, and capital in North America. Trade with Canada and Mexico in 2014 accounted for 34% of the U.S. total, up from one-quarter in 1989, and trade among the three nations has gone from $290 billion in 1993 to $1 trillion in 2011, according to government data.[135] Still, as one reporter points out, "the treaty never met many of its sweeping promises to close Mexico's wage gap with the United States, boost job growth, fight poverty, and protect the environment."[136]

Is NAFTA a job killer, as some have complained? In the United States, around 845,000 jobs have been lost because of increased imports from Canada and Mexico and the relocation of factories in the past two decades, according to government watchdog group Public Citizen.[137] However, some experts suggest that many jobs lost to Mexico during this period would probably have gone to China or elsewhere.[138] Between 1993 (before NAFTA took effect) and 2013, the U.S. trade deficit with Mexico and Canada increased from $17 billion to $177.2 billion, displacing more than 850,000 U.S. jobs.[139] However, supporters insist NAFTA ultimately will result in more jobs and a higher standard of living among all trading partners. For instance, Howard Dean, former Vermont governor and Democratic presidential aspirant, says he he supported NAFTA because he believed "that it would raise the family incomes of Mexicans and emancipate Mexican women. And there's a fair amount of that actually happened. Mexico is now the 20th strongest economy in the world. It's a good thing for America to have two strong economies on either side of it."[140]

2. The EU—The 28 Countries of the European Union

Formed in 1957, the **European Union (EU) consists of 28 trading partners in Europe, covering** nearly 500 million consumers.

Nearly all internal trade barriers have been eliminated (including movement of labor between countries), making the EU a union of borderless neighbors and the world's largest free market, with a gross domestic product of $18.12 trillion in 2014, exceeding that of the United States ($17.35 trillion).[141]

By 2002, such national symbols as the franc, the mark, the lira, the peseta, and the guilder had been replaced with the EU currency, the euro, which is presently used by 23 European countries (plus Vatican City). There was even speculation that someday the euro could replace the U.S. dollar as the dominant world currency.[142] However, in 2010 and 2011, the shaky finances and massive government debts of Portugal, Ireland, Italy, Greece, and Spain (so-called PIIGS) revealed an inherent weakness of the union—that both weak and strong economies were expected to coexist.

Recently, the influx of thousands of refugees pouring out of war-torn and poverty-stricken nations in the Middle East and Africa, including many middle-class Syrians, has put more pressure on the European Union, including calls to either reduce or severely limit free movement across Europe's borders. Several members had reintroduced passport checks and beefed up police presence at their borders in response to the migration crisis, as well as the terrorist attacks in Paris in November 2015.[143]

In addition, on June 23, 2016, the majority of voters in the United Kingdom supported a referendum dubbed "Brexit," short for "Britain exit," to leave the European Union (Scotland and Northern Ireland voted to remain), a process that is expected to take several years but whose effects have already had a severely negative economic impact on the UK.

Four other trading blocs—APEC, ASEAN, Mercosur, and CAFTA—are described below. (See Table 4.4.)

TABLE 4.4   Four Other Important Trading Blocs

Source: Brian Williams.

TRADING BLOC	COUNTRIES	PURPOSES
Asia-Pacific Economic Cooperation (APEC)	21 Pacific Rim countries, most with a Pacific coastline, including the U.S., Canada, and China	To improve economic and political ties and to reduce tariffs and other trade barriers across the Asia-Pacific region
Association of Southeast Asian Nations (ASEAN)	10 countries in Asia, comprising a market of 610 million people: Brunei, Cambodia, Indonesia, Laos, Malaysia, Myanmar (Burma), the Philippines, Singapore, Thailand, and Vietnam	To reduce trade barriers among member countries. A China-ASEAN Free Trade Area was established in 2010, the largest free trade area in the world in terms of population.
Mercosur	Largest trade bloc in Latin America, with 5 core members—Argentina, Brazil, Paraguay, Uruguay, and Venezuela—and 7 associate members: Bolivia, Chile, Colombia, Ecuador, Guyana, Peru, and Suriname	To reduce tariffs by 75% and achieve full economic integration. The alliance is also negotiating trade agreements with NAFTA, the EU, and Japan.
Central America Free Trade Agreement (CAFTA-DR)	Costa Rica, the Dominican Republic, El Salvador, Guatemala, Honduras, Nicaragua, and the U.S.	To reduce tariffs and other barriers to free trade

The Trans-Pacific Partnership—12 Pacific Rim Countries   Negotiated over seven years, the **Trans-Pacific Partnership (TPP)** is a trade agreement among 12 Pacific Rim countries. It was signed on February 4, 2016, but can't take effect "without the approval from a deeply divided U.S. Congress and other parliaments in the bloc," in the words of one reporter.[144] Besides the United States, the pact includes Australia, Brunei, Canada, Chile, Japan, Malaysia, Mexico, New Zealand, Peru, Singapore, and Vietnam.

Although the United States already has free-trade agreements with six of the 11 countries, the TPP removes over time several further barriers to trade, including most tariffs, and sets commercial rules for everything from labor and environmental standards to drug patents. A World Bank study found that Japan, Vietnam, and Malaysia would get a big economic boost (from increasing their exports) from the TPP, while the three North American countries would see much smaller gains.[145]

Most Favored Nation Trading Status

Besides joining together in trade blocs, countries will also extend special, "most favored nation" trading privileges to one another. **Most favored nation trading status describes a condition in which a country grants other countries favorable trading treatment such as the reduction of import duties.** The purpose is to promote stronger and more stable ties between companies in the two countries.

Exchange Rates

The exchange rate is the rate at which the currency of one area or country can be exchanged for the currency of another's. Americans deal in dollars with each other, but beyond the U.S. border we have to deal with pounds in England, euros in Europe, pesos in Mexico, and yuan in China. Because of changing economic conditions, the values of currencies fluctuate in relation to each other, so that sometimes a U.S. dollar, for example, will buy more goods and sometimes it will buy less.

EXAMPLE

An American in London Dealing with Currency Exchange— How Much *Are* Those Jeans, Really?

Let's pretend $1 trades equal to 1 British pound, symbolized by £1. Thus, an item that costs 3 pounds (£3) can be bought for $3. If the exchange rate changes so that $1 buys £1½, then an item that costs £3 can be bought for $2 (the dollar is said to be "stronger" against the pound). If the rate changes so that $1 buys only ½ a pound (£0.5), an item that costs £6 can be purchased for $9 (the dollar is "weaker").[146] In mid 2016, the dollar was stronger, buying .77 of a pound, whereas back in 2014, it was weaker, averaging .59 of a pound. (Stated another way, £1 bought $1.56 in 2010 and $1.68 in April 2014 and $1.29 in August 2016.)

How the Exchange Rate Matters. As this is written, the dollar is strong and the pound is weak, so that $1 will buy .77 of a pound. Thus, staying in London became less expensive for Americans. A hotel room that rents for £100 cost an American $168 in 2014, but cost only $129 in 2016. Indeed, if during those years, 2014 to 2016, you were an American living in England working for a U.S. company and paid in dollars, your standard of living went up.

The Varying Cost of Living for Different Cities. Prices also vary among countries and cities throughout the world, with the standard of living of London, say, being 22% more than that of Chicago. To give you a sense of what an American's purchasing power is worth in London when $1 equals .77 British pound (or

£1 equals $1.29)—the exchange rate in April 2016—consider these prices for various goods in Chicago versus London (estimated in U.S. dollars, computed on *www.expatistan.com*):

	CHICAGO	LONDON
2-liter Coke	$1.87	$2.56 (£5.80)
Big Mac meal	$7	$8 (£2.34)
Month's rent, furnished studio	$951	$1,432 (£1,101)
Levi's 501 jeans	$54	$87 (£67)
Nike sports shoes	$86	$89 (£69)
Volkswagen Golf 2.0 TDI	$24,352	$24,318 (£18,696)

With this example you can see why it's important to understand how exchange rates work and what value your U.S. dollars actually have.

Of course, if you're a Londoner looking at this kind of currency exchange rate and price differentials, you may decide it's a terrific time to visit Chicago for food, lodging, and clothes.[147]

YOUR CALL

Planning to visit Mexico, Canada, or one of those European countries (Germany, France) that uses the euro? Go online to *www.x-rates.com* and figure out the exchange rate of the U.S. dollar and that country's currency. Then go to *www.expatistan .com* and figure out what things cost in that country's principal city versus a U.S. city near you. Could you afford to go?

Get out much? Over one-third of Americans (110 million) have passports, more than double the number of U.S. passports (48 million) in circulation in 2000 and 15 times those in 1989 (7 million). At the same time, more visitors from foreign countries are coming to the United States, with four countries expected to account for 59% of the projected growth in the near future: Canada (23%), China (18%), Mexico (11%), and Brazil (7%). How does the travel boom figure in your career plans? © U. Baumgarten/Getty Images

The BRICS Countries: Important International Competitors Coined by a financial analyst who saw the countries as promising markets for finance capital in the 21st century, the term *BRICS* stands for the five major emerging economies of Brazil, Russia, India, China, and South Africa.[148] *(See Table 4.5.)*

TABLE 4.5

BRICS Countries, 2015

Sources: Internet World Stats, www.internetworldstats.com /stats8.htm; Knoema, and IMF World Economic Outlook, October 15, 2015, http://knoema.com /nwnfkne/world-gdp-ranking- 2015-data-and-charts; Statistics Times, and IMF World Economic Outlook, April 18, 2015, http:// statisticstimes.com/economy /countries-by-projected-gdp-capita. php (all accessed March 12, 2016).

COUNTRY	POPULATION	ECONOMY (GDP) (IN U.S. $)	GDP PER CAPITA (IN U.S. $)	GROWTH RATE
China	1.36 billion	$19,510 billion	$8,154	6.8%
India	1.25 billion	$8,027 billion	$1,808	7.3%
Brazil	204 million	$3,208 billion	$9,312	–3.0%
Russia	146 million	$3,474 billion	$8,184	–3.8%
South Africa	50 million	$724 billion	$5,902	1.4%
For comparison U.S.A.	321 million	$17,968 billion	$56,421	2.6%

Though not a trading bloc as such, the BRICS are important because they make up 40% of the world's population, represent about 20% of the world's economic activity, and have established their own $100 billion reserve fund to rival the International Monetary Fund.[149] By 2050, economists predict, they will join the United States in the exclusive club of the five largest economies in the world.[150] Let's consider the largest of these countries in the order of their population size: China, India, and Brazil.

China   For 20 years, China sustained double-digit growth, benefiting from its manufacturing expertise, low income levels, huge labor market, and a willingness to embrace Western investment.[151] For North American and European capitalists, however, doing business in the "middle kingdom," as China has been called, can be difficult.[152] China, says one observer, "often frustrates with bewildering bureaucracy, entrenched corruption, and a byzantine legal system."[153]

In recent times, operating in China became even harder, as economic growth slowed—from a 12% annual rate down to 6.8% in 2015, although many economists think the number should be far lower.[154] Bad loans that Chinese bankers had made around the world were estimated to exceed $5 trillion.[155] Reports of decline in manufacturing caused stocks to plunge on the Shanghai stock exchange, spooking investors around the world and spreading losses to European and U.S. stock markets.[156] As financial troubles threatened to undermine confidence in the Communist Party, according to one account, the leadership in Beijing began "tightening the flow of economic information, and even criminalizing commentary that officials believe could hurt stocks or the currency."[157]

The challenges don't end there. By 2034, points out another writer, China's population will be falling, not rising, with 87 million fewer people of working age and 149 million more dependents. "In the meantime," he says, "the existing cheap labor pool and the high-capital-investment, low-technology model of economic development is becoming exhausted."[158]

India   If China is well known for its manufacturing advantages, India's have been its large English-speaking population, its technological and scientific expertise, and its reputation in services, such as "back office" accounting systems and software engineering. India's Ministry of Urban Development announced an ambitious program to build 100 smart cities, "to give a decent quality of life to its citizens, a clean and sustainable environment, and application of 'smart' solutions," such as use of apps for parents to keep track of their children.[159] Already India has the second-largest Internet user base in the world, fueled by a boom in smartphone ownership.[160]

U.S. intelligence predicts that by 2030 India could be the ascending economic power in the world. "India's rate of economic growth is likely to rise while China's slows," said a report by the National Intelligence Council.[161] Whereas China's working-age population began a steep decline in 2015, India's working-age population was predicted not to peak until about 2050.

Brazil   With the seventh-largest economy in the world, benefiting from agriculture, mining, manufacturing, and services, Brazil experienced a decade of economic and social progress from 2003 to 2013, lifting 26 million people out of poverty.[162] In 2016, however, the country suffered a recession, the worst economic slump in 25 years, brought about by worldwide declines in commodity prices, a domestic political crisis, and rising inflation.[163] ●

4.5   The Importance of Understanding Cultural Differences

MAJOR QUESTION **What are the principal areas of cultural differences?**

THE BIG PICTURE

Managers trying to understand other cultures need to understand the importance of national culture and cultural dimensions and basic cultural perceptions embodied in language, interpersonal space, communication, time orientation, religion, and law and political stability.

There you are, an American manager in Brazil, nearing the head of a long line for a downtown cash machine, when suddenly a gray-haired elderly man cuts in front of you. "I'm next," he says, and feeds his ATM card into the machine. What do you do? Vigorously protest his line crashing? Start a fight?

Maybe you didn't know that Brazil requires all private businesses and government facilities to give people aged 60 and over "immediate" and "differentiated" attention—and if they don't, they can be fined the equivalent of $750 for each infraction. Such preferential treatment for seniors (and pregnant women and mothers with young children) "is a prized perk in Brazil, and other parts of Latin America, where long lines and spotty service are all too common," says one report.[164]

There are a lot of cultural differences American managers are going to have to get used to and a lot of potential cultural pitfalls in doing business in other countries. "Whether a multinational or a startup business out of a garage, everybody is global these days," says international consultant Dean Foster. "In today's economy, there is no room for failure. Companies have to understand the culture they are working in from Day 1."[165]

Tipping point. The culture of tipping in restaurants varies from country to country. Some restaurants in the U.S. and Canada are eliminating tipping or adding an 18% "auto-gratuity" to the bill, but in most places the customer is expected to add 15%–20% to the total bill as a standard tip (10% is considered insulting). However, in Japan and China, tips are not expected and are even considered inappropriate. In Hong Kong and Singapore, it's up to the diner's discretion (a 10% service charge is already added to the bill). In Europe, hotels and restaurants add a 10% charge and tipping is expected only for exceptional service. In Latin America, a tip of 10% is customary in most restaurants, and you're expected to hand it to the person directly, not just leave it on the table. All clear?

© Aagamia/The Image Bank/Getty Images

In China you should know that people draw different lines between personal and work spaces, so that, for example, it is permissible for office colleagues to inquire about the size of your apartment and your salary and to give assessments of your wardrobe and your muscle tone, matters considered personal in the United States. In South Korea, if you want to give a gift that's considered classy and glamorous, you might present a can or two of Spam—yes, Spam, viewed as a thrifty tinned-meat staple in the United States but in Korea still thought of as a symbol of luxury descending from a time of deprivation during the Korean war when only Americans had the product.[166] In the Arab world, which has historically been segregated by sex, men spend a lot of time together, and so holding hands, kissing cheeks, and long handshakes are meant to express devotion and equality in status.

The Importance of National Culture

A nation's **culture** is the shared set of beliefs, values, knowledge, and patterns of behavior common to a group of people. We begin learning our culture starting at an early age through everyday interaction with people around us. This is why, from the outside looking in, a nation's culture can seem so intangible and perplexing. As cultural anthropologist Edward T. Hall puts it, "Since much of culture operates outside our awareness, frequently we don't even know what we know. . . . We unconsciously learn what to notice and what not to notice, how to divide time and space, how to walk and talk and use our bodies, how to behave as men or women, how to relate to other people, how to handle responsibility. . . ."[167] Indeed, says Hall, what we think of as "mind" is really internalized culture.

And because a culture is made up of so many nuances, this is why visitors to another culture may experience *culture shock*—the feelings of discomfort and disorientation associated with being in an unfamiliar culture. According to anthropologists, culture shock involves anxiety and doubt caused by an overload of unfamiliar expectations and social cues.[168]

Cultural Dimensions: The Hofstede and GLOBE Project Models

Misunderstandings and miscommunications often arise in international business relationships because people don't understand the expectations of the other side. A person from North America, Great Britain, Scandinavia, Germany, or Switzerland, for example, comes from a **low-context culture, in which shared meanings are primarily derived from written and spoken words.** Someone from China, Korea, Japan, Vietnam, Mexico, or many Arab cultures, on the other hand, comes from a **high-context culture, in which people rely heavily on situational cues for meaning when communicating with others,** relying on nonverbal cues as to another person's official position, status, or family connections.

One way to avoid cultural collisions is to have an understanding of various cultural dimensions, as expressed in the Hofstede model and the GLOBE project.

Hofstede's Model of Four Cultural Dimensions   Thirty years ago Dutch researcher and IBM psychologist **Geert Hofstede** collected data from 116,000 IBM employees in 53 countries and proposed his **Hofstede model of four cultural dimensions, which identified four dimensions along which national cultures can be placed: (1) individualism/ collectivism, (2) power distance, (3) uncertainty avoidance, and (4) masculinity/femininity.**[169]

Individualism/collectivism indicates how much people prefer a loosely knit social framework in which people are expected to take care of themselves (as in the United States and Canada) or a tightly knit social framework in which people and organizations are expected to look after each other (as in Mexico and China). *Power distance* refers to the degree to which people accept inequality in social situations (high in Mexico and India, low in Sweden and Australia). *Uncertainty avoidance* expresses people's intolerance for uncertainty and risk (high in Japan, low in the United States). *Masculinity/femininity* expresses how much people value performance-oriented traits (masculinity: high in Mexico) or how much they embrace relationship-oriented traits (femininity: high in Norway). In general, the United States ranked very high on individualism, relatively low on power distance, low on uncertainty avoidance, and moderately high on masculinity.

The GLOBE Project's Nine Cultural Dimensions   Started in 1993 by University of Pennsylvania professor **Robert J. House,** the **GLOBE project is a massive and ongoing cross-cultural investigation of nine cultural dimensions involved in leadership and organizational processes.**[170] (GLOBE stands for Global Leadership and Organizational Behavior Effectiveness.) GLOBE extends Hofstede's theory and results and evolved into a network of more than 150 scholars from 62 societies. Most of these researchers are native to the particular cultures being studied. The nine cultural dimensions are as follows:

- **Power distance—how much unequal distribution of power should there be in organizations and society?** *Power distance* expresses the degree to which a society's members expect power to be unequally shared.

- **Uncertainty avoidance—how much should people rely on social norms and rules to avoid uncertainty?** *Uncertainty avoidance* expresses the extent to which a society relies on social norms and procedures to alleviate the unpredictability of future events.

- **Institutional collectivism—how much should leaders encourage and reward loyalty to the social unit?** *Institutional collectivism* expresses the extent to which individuals are encouraged and rewarded for loyalty to the group as opposed to pursuing individual goals.

- **In-group collectivism—how much pride and loyalty should people have for their family or organization?** In contrast to individualism, *in-group collectivism* expresses the extent to which people should take pride in being members of their family, circle of close friends, and their work organization.[171]

- **Gender egalitarianism—how much should society maximize gender role differences?** *Gender egalitarianism* expresses the extent to which a society should minimize gender discrimination and role inequalities.

- **Assertiveness—how confrontational and dominant should individuals be in social relationships?** *Assertiveness* represents the extent to which a society expects people to be confrontational and competitive as opposed to tender and modest.

- **Future orientation—how much should people delay gratification by planning and saving for the future?** *Future orientation* expresses the extent to which a society encourages investment in the future, as by planning and saving.

- **Performance orientation—how much should individuals be rewarded for improvement and excellence?** *Performance orientation* expresses the extent to which society encourages and rewards its members for performance improvement and excellence.

- **Humane orientation—how much should society encourage and reward people for being kind, fair, friendly, and generous?** *Humane orientation* represents the degree to which individuals are encouraged to be altruistic, caring, kind, generous, and fair.

Data from 18,000 managers yielded the country profiles shown below. *(See Table 4.6.)*

TABLE 4.6

Countries Ranking Highest and Lowest on the GLOBE Cultural Dimensions

Source: "How Cultures Collide," Psychology Today, July 1976, p. 69.

DIMENSION	HIGHEST	LOWEST
Power distance	Morocco, Argentina, Thailand, Spain, Russia	Denmark, Netherlands, South Africa (black sample), Israel, Costa Rica
Uncertainty avoidance	Switzerland, Sweden, Germany (former West), Denmark, Austria	Russia, Hungary, Bolivia, Greece, Venezuela
Institutional collectivism	Sweden, South Korea, Japan, Singapore, Denmark	Greece, Hungary, Germany (former East), Argentina, Italy
In-group collectivism	Iran, India, Morocco, China, Egypt	Denmark, Sweden, New Zealand, Netherlands, Finland
Gender egalitarianism	Hungary, Poland, Slovenia, Denmark, Sweden	South Korea, Egypt, Morocco, India, China
Assertiveness	Germany (former East), Austria, Greece, United States, Spain	Sweden, New Zealand, Switzerland, Japan, Kuwait
Future orientation	Singapore, Switzerland, Netherlands, Canada (English speaking), Denmark	Russia, Argentina, Poland, Italy, Kuwait
Performance orientation	Singapore, Hong Kong, New Zealand, Taiwan, United States	Russia, Argentina, Greece, Venezuela, Italy
Humane orientation	Philippines, Ireland, Malaysia, Egypt, Indonesia	Germany (former West), Spain, France, Singapore, Brazil

Have you thought about how you stand in relation to various norms—in both your society and others? Would your views affect your success in taking an international job? The following self-assessment was created to provide feedback regarding these questions and to aid your awareness about your views of the GLOBE dimensions.

≡ connect SELF-ASSESSMENT 4.2

Assessing Your Standing on the GLOBE Dimensions

This survey is designed to assess your values in terms of the GLOBE dimensions. Please be prepared to answer these questions if your instructor has assigned Self-Assessment 4.2 in Connect.

1. What are your three highest and lowest rated dimensions? How might these beliefs affect your ability to work with people from Europe, Asia, and South America?

2. How do your dimensional scores compare to the norms for Americans shown in Table 4.6?

Recognizing Cultural Tendencies to Gain Competitive Advantage   The GLOBE dimensions show a great deal of cultural diversity around the world, but they also show how cultural patterns vary. For example, the U.S. managerial sample scored high on assertiveness and performance orientation—which is why Americans are widely perceived as being pushy and hardworking. Switzerland's high scores on uncertainty avoidance and future orientation help explain its centuries of political neutrality and world-renowned banking industry. Singapore is known as a great place to do business because it is clean and safe and its people are well educated and hardworking—no surprise, considering the country's high scores on social collectivism, future orientation, and performance orientation. By contrast, Russia's low scores on future orientation and performance orientation could foreshadow a slower-than-hoped-for transition from a centrally planned economy to free-enterprise capitalism. The practical lesson to draw from all this: *Knowing the cultural tendencies of foreign business partners and competitors can give you a strategic competitive advantage.*[172]

GLOBE researchers also set out to find which, if any, attributes of leadership were universally liked or disliked. Throughout the world, visionary and inspirational leaders who are good team builders generally do the best; self-centered leaders who are seen as loners or face-savers receive a poor reception.[173]

Other Cultural Variations: Language, Interpersonal Space, Communication, Time Orientation, Religion, and Law and Political Stability

How do you go about bridging cross-cultural gaps? It begins with understanding. Let's consider variations in six basic culture areas: (1) *language,* (2) *interpersonal space,* (3) *communication,* (4) *time orientation,* (5) *religion,* and (6) *law and political stability.*

Note, however, that such cultural differences are to be viewed as *tendencies* rather than absolutes. We all need to be aware that the *individuals* we are dealing with may be exceptions to the cultural rules. After all, there *are* talkative and aggressive Japanese, just as there are quiet and deferential Americans, stereotypes notwithstanding.[174]

1. Language   More than 3,000 different languages are spoken throughout the world, and it's indeed true that global business speaks English.[175] However, even if you are operating in English, there are nuances between cultures that can lead to misperceptions. For instance, in Asia, a "yes" answer to a question "simply means the question is understood," says one well-traveled writer. "It's the beginning of negotiations."[176] (Using "huh?" to indicate a lack of understanding is common to 31 different languages.)[177]

In communicating across cultures you have four options: (a) You can speak your own language. (The average American believes that about half the world can speak English, when actually it's close to 18%.)[178] (b) You can use a translator. (Try to get one who will be loyal to you rather than to your overseas host.) (c) You can try using a translation app, such as Google Translate, that turns a smartphone into an interpreter, although this can be cumbersome.[179] (d) You can learn the local language—by far the best option. Gallup pollsters surveyed 2,007 U.S. citizens and 250 opinion leaders and asked them, "If you were given a chance to learn a new foreign language, which language would you rather learn?" Spanish led the way (58%), followed by Chinese (15%), Arabic (11%), and Japanese (10%).[180]

2. Interpersonal Space   Men holding hands may raise eyebrows among most Americans, but it is common in the Middle East and does not carry any sexual connotation. "Holding hands is the warmest expression of affection between men," says one Lebanese sociologist. "It's a sign of solidarity and friendship."[181]

People of different cultures have different ideas about what is acceptable interpersonal space—that is, how close or far away one should be when communicating with another person. For instance, the people of North America and northern Europe tend to conduct business conversations at a range of 3–4 feet. For people in Latin American and Asian cultures, the range is about 1 foot. For Arabs, it is even closer.

This can lead to cross-cultural misunderstandings. "Arabs tend to get very close and breathe on you," says anthropologist Hall. "The American on the receiving end can't identify all the sources of his discomfort but feels that the Arab is pushy. The Arab comes close, the American backs up. The Arab follows, because he can only interact at certain distances."[182] However, once the American understands that Arabs handle interpersonal space differently and that "breathing on people is a form of communication," says Hall, the situation can sometimes be redefined so that the American feels more comfortable.

3. Communication

For small companies doing business abroad, "the important thing to remember is that you don't know what you don't know," says the head of a U.S. firm that advises clients on cross-cultural matters.[183] For instance, an American who had lived in Brazil and was fluent in Portuguese was angling to make a deal in São Paulo and thought his pitch was going well. "It was picture-perfect until my client suggested I stay for the weekend to go to a soccer game" and enjoy the local food with him, but the American diplomatically declined the invitation.

The next day he found the prospective clients not as receptive, saying they liked the program but would need more time to decide. On the plane home, he analyzed what had gone wrong and realized he had given them a "task" reason instead of a "relationship" reason for declining the invitation. "It's a relationship culture, and I could just as easily and more successfully [have said], 'There are people back home who are expecting me to be with them.'" But the reason he gave "sent the message that I was not as Brazilian as they initially thought—and it came out of my profit."[184]

If you, like a growing number of young Americans, head to China for employment, you need to recall that you were brought up in a commercial environment, but younger Chinese were raised at a time when China was evolving from a government-regulated economy to a more free-market system, and so they may have less understanding of business concepts and client services. "In the West, there is such a premium on getting things done quickly," says an American manager, "but when you come to work in China, you need to work on listening and being more patient and understanding of local ways of doing business."[185] In particular, Americans have to be careful about giving criticism directly, which the Chinese consider rude and inconsiderate.

We consider communication matters in more detail in Chapter 15.

4. Time Orientation

Time orientation is different in many cultures. For example, Americans are accustomed to calling ahead for appointments, but South Koreans believe in spontaneity. Thus, when Seoul erupted in protests over tainted American beef, Korean legislators simply hopped on a plane to the United States, saying they would negotiate with the U.S. government. "But since they failed to inform the Americans ahead of time," says one report, "they were unable to meet with anyone of importance."[186]

Anthropologist Hall makes a useful distinction between *monochronic* time and *polychronic* time:

- **Monochronic time.** This kind of time is standard American business practice—at least until recently. That is, **monochronic time is a preference for doing one thing at a time.** In this perception, time is viewed as being limited, precisely segmented, and schedule driven. This perception of time prevails, for example, when you schedule a meeting with someone and then give the visitor your undivided attention during the allotted time.[187]

  Indeed, you probably practice monochronic time when you're in a job interview. You work hard at listening to what the interviewer says. You may well take careful notes. You certainly don't answer your cell phone or gaze repeatedly out the window.

- **Polychronic time.** This outlook on time is the kind that prevails in Mediterranean, Latin American, and especially Arab cultures. **Polychronic time is a preference for doing more than one thing at a time.** Here time is viewed as being flexible and multidimensional.

  This perception of time prevails when you visit a Latin American client, find yourself sitting in the waiting room for 45 minutes, and then learn in the meeting that the client is dealing with three other people at the same time.

EXAMPLE

Dinner at 10? Spain's Cultural Differences in Time

Spaniard Miguel Carbayo, 26, who once interned in the Netherlands, where work started at 8 and ended at 5, with a half hour for lunch, is appalled at the notion of Spain doing away with its customary two- or three-hour midday meal. "Reduce lunchtime?" he said. "No, I'm completely against that. It is one thing to eat. It is another thing to nourish oneself."[188]

Out of Whack. Spain operates on its own clock and rhythms, different from the rest of Europe. But the country's apportionment of time, say critics, is out of whack, "dictating notoriously late hours that sap the country of efficiency and make it hard for anyone with a regular job to have time for much else," says one report.[189]

Spaniards generally start work at 9, pause for a late-morning snack (which cuts into work productivity), then quit for lunch around 2 or 2:30 to take a siesta break—although fewer and fewer people actually take naps. They then return to work around 4 or so and work well into the evening. Most workplaces close at 9.

Thus, at a time when people in other countries are getting ready for bed, that is the point in the day when Spaniards are sitting down to dinner. Prime-time television shows start at 10 p.m. and don't end until after 1 a.m. Night life goes on into the wee hours.

Longer on the Job and Sleepier. What's the effect of this? "Everything is late in Spain, and this has a detrimental effect on

everyone," says a business school professor. "We live in a permanent jet lag."[190] She points out that, compared to other Europeans, Spaniards sleep nearly an hour less per night and frequently doze in school and at work. Spanish workers are also on the job longer than German workers but complete only 59% of their daily tasks, says the president of the Association for the Rationalization of Spanish Working Hours, which advocates revising the country's business hours.[191] Finally, for 70 years, the entire country has been one hour out of step with the countries around it.

Varying Tempos. Every culture has its own "tempo," or sense of time, points out psychologist Robert Levine, with different definitions of "what constitutes early and late, waiting and rushing, the past, the present, and the future."[192] Cultures that work on "clock time" (such as the United States and most of Europe), where a timepiece governs the start and end of activities, tend to value punctuality. In cultures that work on "event time" (such as Mexico, Brazil, and Indonesia), schedules are spontaneous and events happen when participants "feel" the time is right.[193]

YOUR CALL

Where does Spain fit in here in terms of tempo? If you were starting a business in Spain that depended on close interaction with nearby European countries observing different business times, how would you ask your Spanish staff to adjust?

5. Religion   Trying to get wealthy Muslim investors in Dubai to buy some of your bank's financial products? Then you need to know that any investment vehicle needs to "conform to the spirit of the Koran, which forbids any investments that pay interest," as one writer puts it. "No mortgages. No bonds."[194] Are you a Protestant doing business in a predominantly Catholic country? Or a Muslim in a Buddhist country? What are the most popular world religions, and how does religion influence the work-related values of the people we're dealing with? *(See Table 4.7.)*

A study of 484 international students at a midwestern university uncovered wide variations in the work-related values for different religious affiliations.[195] For example, among Catholics, the primary work-related value was found to be consideration. For Protestants, it was employer effectiveness; for Buddhists, social responsibility; for Muslims, continuity. There was, in fact, virtually *no agreement* among religions as to what is the most important work-related value. This led the researchers to conclude: "Employers might be wise to consider the impact that religious differences (and more broadly, cultural factors) appear to have on the values of employee groups."

6. Law and Political Stability   Every firm contemplating establishing itself abroad must deal with other countries' laws and business practices, which frequently involves making calculations about political risk that might cause loss of a company's assets or impair its foreign operations. Among the risks an organization

TABLE 4.7   Current Followers of the Major World Religions

All population counts are estimated. Adherents.com actually puts "Secular/nonreligious/agnostic/atheist" in third place, with a population of 1.1 billion. Judaism is estimated to have 14 million followers.

RELIGION	NUMBER OF ADHERENTS
Christianity	2.1 billion
Islam	1.5 billion
Hinduism	900 million
Buddhism	376 million
Chinese traditional religions	394 million
Primal-indigenous	300 million
African traditional & diasporic	100 million

Source: Adapted from Adherents.com, "Major Religions of the World Ranked by Major Adherents," last modified August, 9, 2007, www.adherents.com/Religions_By_Adherents.html (accessed March 14, 2016).

Prayer. The term "Muslim culture" covers many diverse groups—Middle Eastern, African, Asian Muslim, and European and American Muslims—each with its own customs. Muslims are required to pray five times a day, prostrating themselves on a prayer mat. Some American Muslims keep a prayer mat in their cars. © Purestock/Getty Images RF

might anticipate abroad are *instability, expropriation, corruption,* and *labor abuses.*

- **Instability.** Even in a developed country a company may be victimized by political instability, such as riots or civil disorders, as happened in 2014 among Russian-speaking populations in Ukraine. In some developed nations, their very existence is threatened by separatist movements, with large sections clamoring to split off and become independent states—Quebec from Canada, Scotland from the United Kingdom, and Catalonia from Spain, for example—which could result in changes to the currency in use.

- **Expropriation. Expropriation is defined as a government's seizure of a domestic or foreign company's assets.** After socialist Hugo Chavez became president of Venezuela, his government (and his successor's) stepped up a campaign to seize land and businesses, such as a rice plant owned by Cargill, one of the United States's largest privately owned companies. Results have not been good: In 2015, the country had the world's highest inflation, and prices for food and beverages rose by 315%, clothing by 146%, and health care by 110.6%.[196]

- **Corruption.** Whether it's called *mordida* (Mexico), *huilu* (China), or *vzyatka* (Russia), it means the same thing: a bribe. Although the United States is relatively free of such corruption, it is an acceptable practice in other countries. In African, Latin American, and newly independent states, frequent bribe paying is the norm; in Asia and the Pacific and southeast Europe, it is moderate; and in North America and the European Union, bribes are seldom paid for services.[197]

American businesspeople are prevented from participating in overseas bribes under the 1978 **Foreign Corrupt Practices Act, which makes it illegal for employees of U.S. companies to make "questionable" or "dubious" contributions to political decision makers in foreign nations.** While this creates a competitive disadvantage for Americans working in foreign countries in which government bribery may be the only way to obtain business, the United Nations Global Compact is attempting to level the playing field by promoting anticorruption standards for business.

- **Labor abuses.** Overseas suppliers may offer low prices, but working conditions can be harsh, as has been the case with garment makers in Bangladesh, Cambodia, the Dominican Republic, Haiti, Mexico, Pakistan, and Vietnam. Among the problems: "padlocked fire exits, buildings at risk of collapse, falsified wage records, and repeated hand punctures from sewing needles when workers were pushed to hurry up," according to one report.[198] Some suppliers have been accused of using underage workers, and some (such as Apple iPhone suppliers) of pushing their workers to the point of suicide.[199] Among the worst incidents are those involving slave labor, such as the slave labor supposedly working in Thailand that produced shrimp that Costco has been accused of selling.[200] At least 20 million people across the world are said to be forced to work with no pay.[201]

U.S. Managers on Foreign Assignments: Why Do They Fail?

Somewhere between 2.2 million and 6.8 million Americans live outside American borders, in at least 100 countries—a class of people known as **expatriates—people living or working in a foreign country.**[202] Many of them, perhaps 300,000, are managers, and supporting them and their families overseas is not cheap. A partner at one human resources consulting firm estimates that it costs twice an executive's $300,000 salary to send him or her from the United States to Shanghai for a year.[203] Are the employers getting their money's worth? Probably not.

One study of about 750 companies (U.S., European, and Japanese) asked expatriates and their managers to evaluate their experiences. They found that 10%–20% of all U.S. managers sent abroad returned early because of job dissatisfaction or adjustment difficulties. Of those who stayed for the length of their assignments, about one-third did not perform to their superiors' expectations and one-fourth left the company, often to join a competitor—a turnover rate double that of managers who did not go abroad.[204]

Unfortunately, problems continue when expatriates return home. "Studies suggest between 8% to 25% of managers may leave a company after returning to the U.S.," says one report.[205] Another study indicated that 25% of repatriated employees quit their jobs within one year. Organizations can help reduce this turnover by communicating with employees throughout the international assignment and by providing at least six months' notice of when employees will return home.[206]

If you were to go abroad as a manager, what are the survival skills or outlook you would need? Perhaps the bottom line is revealed in a study of 72 human resource managers who were asked to identify the most important success factors in a foreign assignment. Nearly 35% said the secret was *cultural adaptability:* patience, flexibility, and tolerance for others' beliefs.[207]

Do you think you have what it takes to be an effective global manager? The following self-assessment can provide input to answering this question. It assesses your potential to be a successful global manager. ●

connect SELF-ASSESSMENT 4.3

Assessing Your Global Manager Potential

This survey is designed to assess how well suited you are to becoming a global manager. Please be prepared to answer these questions if your instructor has assigned Self-Assessment 4.3 in Connect.

1. What is your reaction to the results?
2. Based on considering your five lowest-rated survey items, what can you do to improve your global manager potential?

countertrading 119
culture 130
dumping 122
e-commerce 107
embargo 122
ethnocentric managers 115
European Union (EU) 124
exchange rate 126
expatriates 137
exporting 119
expropriation 136
Foreign Corrupt Practices Act 136
franchising 119
free trade 121
geocentric managers 115
global economy 108
global mind-set 111
global outsourcing 118

global village 107
globalization 106
GLOBE project 131
greenfield venture 120
high-context culture 130
Hofstede model of four cultural
    dimensions 130
import quota 122
importing 118
International Monetary Fund
    (IMF) 123
joint venture 120
licensing 119
low-context culture 130
maquiladoras 117
monochronic time 134
most favored nation 126
multinational corporation 112

multinational organization 112
North American Free Trade
    Agreement (NAFTA) 124
offshoring 118
outsourcing 117
parochialism 115
polycentric managers 115
polychronic time 134
sanction 122
tariff 121
trade protectionism 121
trading bloc 124
Trans-Pacific Partnership (TPP) 125
wholly-owned subsidiary 120
World Bank 123
World Trade Organization
    (WTO) 123

Key Points

4.1 Globalization: The Collapse of Time and Distance

- Globalization is the trend of the world economy toward becoming more interdependent. Globalization is reflected in three developments: (1) the rise of the global village and e-commerce; (2) the trend of the world's becoming one big market; and (3) the rise of both megafirms and Internet-enabled minifirms.

- The rise of the "global village" refers to the "shrinking" of time and space as air travel and the electronic media have made global communication easier. The Internet and the web have led to e-commerce, the buying and selling of products through computer networks.

- The global economy is the increasing tendency of the economies of nations to interact with one another as one market.

- The rise of cross-border business has led to megamergers, as giant firms have joined forces, and minifirms, small companies in which managers can use the Internet and other technologies to get enterprises started more easily and to maneuver faster.

4.2 You and International Management

- Studying international management prepares you to work with foreign customers or partners, with foreign suppliers, for a foreign firm in the United States, or for a U.S. firm overseas. International management is management that oversees the conduct of operations in or with organizations in foreign countries.

- The successful international manager is not ethnocentric or polycentric but geocentric. Ethnocentric managers believe that their native country, culture, language, and behavior are superior to all others. Polycentric managers take the view that native managers in the foreign offices best understand native personnel and practices. Geocentric managers accept that there are differences and similarities between home and foreign personnel and practices, and they should use whatever techniques are most effective.

4.3 Why and How Companies Expand Internationally

- Companies expand internationally for at least five reasons. They seek (1) cheaper or more plentiful supplies, (2) new markets, (3) lower labor costs, (4) access to finance capital, and (5) avoidance of tariffs on imported goods or import quotas.

- There are five ways in which companies expand internationally. (1) They engage in global outsourcing, using suppliers outside the company and the United States to provide goods and services. (2) They engage in importing, exporting, and countertrading (bartering for goods). (3) They engage in licensing (allow a foreign company to pay a fee to make or distribute the company's product) and franchising (allow a foreign company to pay a fee and a share of the profit in return for using the first company's brand name). (4) They engage in joint ventures, a strategic alliance to share the risks and rewards of starting a new enterprise together in a foreign country. (5) They become wholly-owned subsidiaries, or foreign subsidiaries that are totally owned and controlled by an organization.

4.4 The World of Free Trade: Regional Economic Cooperation

- Free trade is the movement of goods and services among nations without political or economic obstructions.
- Countries often use trade protectionism—the use of government regulations to limit the import of goods and services—to protect their domestic industries against foreign competition. Three barriers to free trade are tariffs, import quotas, and embargoes and sanctions. (1) A tariff is a trade barrier in the form of a customs duty, or tax, levied mainly on imports. (2) An import quota is a trade barrier in the form of a limit on the numbers of a product that can be imported. (3) An embargo is a complete ban on the import or export of certain products. A sanction is the trade prohibition on certain types of products, services, or technology to another country for specific reasons, including nuclear nonproliferation and humanitarian purposes.
- Three principal organizations exist that are designed to facilitate international trade. (1) The World Trade Organization is designed to monitor and enforce trade agreements. (2) The World Bank is designed to provide low-interest loans to developing nations for improving transportation, education, health, and telecommunications. (3) The International Monetary Fund is designed to assist in smoothing the flow of money between nations.
- A trading bloc is a group of nations within a geographical region that have agreed to remove trade barriers. We considered two major trading blocs: (1) the North American Free Trade Agreement (NAFTA: U.S., Canada, and Mexico), and (2) the European Union (EU: 28 trading partners in Europe). Others are the Association of Southeast Asian Nations, Asia-Pacific Economic Cooperation, Mercosur, and the Central America Free Trade Agreement. Negotiated over seven years, the Trans-Pacific Partnership (TPP) is a proposed trade agreement among 12 Pacific Rim countries that can't take effect until it is approved by the U.S. Congress and other parliaments in the bloc. Besides joining together in trade blocs, countries also extend special, "most favored nation" trading privileges—that is, grant other countries favorable trading treatment such as the reduction of import duties.
- When doing overseas trading, managers must consider exchange rates, the rate at which the currency of one area or country can be exchanged for the currency of another's, such as American dollars in relation to Mexican pesos or European euros.
- The term BRICS stands for the five major emerging economies of Brazil, Russia, India, China, and South Africa—five countries that make up 40% of the world's population, represent about 20% of the world's economic activity, and have established their own $100 billion reserve fund. The largest of these countries in the order of their population size are China, India, and Brazil.

4.5 The Importance of Understanding Cultural Differences

- Misunderstandings and miscommunications often arise because one person doesn't understand the expectations of a person from another culture. In low-context cultures, shared meanings are primarily derived from written and spoken words. In high-context cultures, people rely heavily on situational cues for meaning when communicating with others.
- Geert Hofstede proposed the Hofstede model of four cultural dimensions, which identified four dimensions along which national cultures can be placed: (1) individualism/collectivism, (2) power distance, (3) uncertainty avoidance, and (4) masculinity/femininity.
- Robert House and others created the GLOBE (for Global Leadership and Organizational Behavior Effectiveness) Project, a massive and ongoing cross-cultural investigation of nine cultural dimensions involved in leadership and organizational processes: (1) power distance, (2) uncertainty avoidance, (3) institutional collectivism, (4) in-group collectivism, (5) gender egalitarianism, (6) assertiveness, (7) future orientation, (8) performance orientation, and (9) humane orientation.
- A nation's culture is the shared set of beliefs, values, knowledge, and patterns of behavior common to a group of people. Visitors to another culture may experience culture shock—feelings of discomfort and disorientation. Managers trying to understand other cultures need to understand six basic cultural perceptions embodied in (1) language, (2) interpersonal space, (3) communication, (4) time orientation, (5) religion, and (6) law and political stability.
- Regarding language, when you are trying to communicate across cultures you have three options: Speak your own language (if others can understand you), use a translator, or learn the local language.
- Interpersonal space involves how close or far away one should be when communicating with another person, with Americans being comfortable at 3–4 feet but people in other countries often wanting to be closer.
- Communication involves not only differences in understanding about words and sounds and their meanings but also in expectations about relationships and business concepts.
- Time orientation of a culture may be either monochronic (preference for doing one thing at a time) or polychronic (preference for doing more than one thing at a time).
- Managers need to consider the effect of religious differences. In order of size (population), the major world religions are Christianity, Islam, Hinduism, Buddhism, Chinese traditional religions, primal-indigenous, and African traditional and diasporic religions.
- Every company must deal with other countries' laws and business practices, which means weighing the risks of political instability; expropriation, or government seizure of a domestic or foreign company's assets; political corruption, including bribery; and labor abuses.

1. What are three important developments in globalization?

2. What are some positives and negatives of globalization?

3. What are the principal reasons for learning about international management?

4. How do ethnocentric, polycentric, and geocentric managers differ?

5. What are five reasons companies expand internationally, and what are five ways they go about doing this expansion?

6. What are some barriers to international trade?

7. Name the three principal organizations designed to facilitate international trade and describe what they do.

8. What are the principal major trading blocs, and what are the BRICS countries?

9. Define what's meant by "culture" and describe some of the cultural dimensions studied by the Hofstede model and the GLOBE project.

10. Describe the six important cultural areas that international managers have to deal with in doing cross-border business.

Management in Action

Costco Plans to Grow Its International Markets

Costco Wholesale Corporation is an American membership-only warehouse club selling a large range of products. The company opened its first warehouse in 1983 and currently is the second largest retailer in the U.S.—Walmart is number one. Costco, however, is the largest membership warehouse club chain in the U.S.

Costco operates about 700 warehouses across the U.S. and abroad. As of November 2015, the company had international locations in Canada (89), United Kingdom (26), Australia (8), Mexico (34), Taiwan (10), South Korea (12), Japan (20), and Spain (2).[208]

The company's revenue has been growing the last few years, and international expansion is one key contributor. Net sales from international operations grew by 45% between 2010 and 2014. This compares to a net sales growth of 21% from Sam's Club, the warehouse outlet run by Walmart, over the same period. "Margins from international operations are also higher, which has benefited the bottom line. That's partly due to little or no competition from other warehouse clubs, as they're a relatively newer concept abroad, and partly due to lower employee costs. Costco earned an operating margin of 4.1% from international sales in fiscal 2015 compared to 2.7% from domestic sales."[209]

One investment analyst noted that Costco's international strategy was very carefully devised. He concluded that the "retailer appears to be very selective in choosing the locations for expansion as a new store requires significant capital. Before opening an outlet, Costco looks to make sure that customer response will be good. For instance, the warehouse retailer has started its operations in China through an e-commerce partnership with Alibaba and has seen tremendous success so far."[210]

Experts say that Costco's international success is mostly based on the company's ability to adapt to the local environment for each market it is operating in. Consider the changes Costco implemented when expanding to Australia.

Costco began by changing its selling practices. Rather than relying on coupons to draw-in customers, the company abandoned their use. Coupons are foreign to Australians and hardly anyone uses them. The company also dropped its use of Costco cards as a form of payment. While Americans like the use of such cards, management thought that Australians would like greater flexibility in payment methods. They were correct in this assessment.

"Also Costco decided not to invest any money in marketing. They played on 'word-of-mouth' marketing. It was smart as in Australia, this is probably the best marketing money can buy. Partially the success of this practice was ensured by the fact that many Australians and Americans travel a lot between the countries. The migration flow is quite strong there. This caused a certain amount of people to have first-hand experience with Costco. This played its role in attracting new customers."[211]

Costco similarly used a customized approach when opening stores in Spain. It opened its first warehouse in Seville, Spain's fourth-largest city, in 2014. Jim Murphy, Costco's head of international operations, selected Seville because it has a population of about 1.3 million within a 30-minute drive of the store.

There are several challenges that Costco must overcome to effectively expand into Spain. For one, bulk purchasing is not popular because people have smaller families. The fertility rate is 1.3 children per woman, which is below 1.9 for the U.S. Retail prices are also depressed due to economic conditions, and people tend to buy small quantities in small shops that are close to their homes. Third, many people live in small apartments and houses, limiting the shelf space that can be used to store the larger packaged goods sold at Costco. Finally, there are challenges in getting suppliers to change their packaging to fit Costco requirements. These changes are costly for suppliers.

Costco tried to overcome these challenges by implementing a variety of customized solutions. First, it is sending employees to small businesses to discuss how they can save money by becoming members. Costco also is asking big employers to allow it to send representatives to talk with their employees in staff break rooms. Costco is also using local employees to run the operations. To meet local needs and tastes, Costco typically sells two-thirds of the products that originate in that country. "At the Seville Costco, the meat section will have Spanish specialties such as octopus, rabbit and piglet, depending on the season. The store will carry Spanish olives, tuna made by the locally famous brand Ortiz, and rows of hanging *jamón ibérico,* Spain's answer to prosciutto."[212]

Costco is planning to continue its international expansion through 2017.

FOR DISCUSSION

1. What are the biggest challenges Costco will experience in trying to expand globally?

2. How did Costco attempt to avoid, ethnocentric, polycentric, or geocentric attitudes? Provide examples to support your conclusions.

3. Use Table 4.6 to identify cultural differences that are likely to arise between Costco's U.S. employees and local employees working in Australia, Spain, and China. How might these differences affect interpersonal interactions, and what can the company do to reduce any unintended consequences from these differences?

4. What are the most important lessons to be learned about global management from this case? Discuss.

Legal/Ethical Challenge

How Far Should World Leaders Go in Accommodating Other Leaders?

This challenge involves a conflict between national culture and religious beliefs. The context was a state visit from Iran's president, Hassan Rouhani, to Rome and Paris in 2016. This was the first visit for an Iranian president in 17 years.

The Wall Street Journal reported that "The trip succeeded in reviving economic ties that withered when the European Union adopted sanctions over Iran's nuclear program in 2012. The countries cut billions in business deals this week . . ."[213]

The challenge involves how to handle the Iranian leader's request regarding meals during the visits. According to *USA Today,* "Rouhani asked for a halal menu in keeping with his Muslim faith, which meant no wine" during meals.

French President Francois Hollande decided to forgo any meals and instead staged a formal welcome at the Invalides monument. According to Gérard Araud, France's ambassador to the United States, "It is not the halal which was a problem but the wine. Nobody should constrain anybody to drink or not to drink." It is important to remember that wine is an important aspect of the culinary experience in France.

"In Italy, where wine is as much a part of the culinary routine as in France, officials submitted to the Iranian leader's demands and did not serve wine at Monday's state dinner. Italian officials also covered up several nude statues with large boxes at Rome's

Campidoglio museum to protect the Islamic Republic visitors from gazing at artists' renderings of the human form."

Italian Prime Minister Matteo Renzi's decisions drew strong criticism from others according to *USA Today.* Lawmaker Luca Squeri said, "Respect for other cultures cannot and must not mean negating our own. This isn't respect, it's cancelling out differences and it's kind of surrender." Rome City Councilman Gianluca Peciola started a petition asking Renzi to explain "a disgraceful decision which is a mortification of art and culture as universal values."[214]

SOLVING THE CHALLENGE

What would you have done if you were Hollande or Renzi?

1. These are state dinners involving important matters, and leaders need to be accepting of religious differences. What's the big deal in forgoing some wine with the meal and covering up art? I would hold the dinners, not serve wine, and cover up the offensive art. Renzi got it right.

2. I would forgo wine at the meals, but covering up the art goes too far. Renzi's decisions were partially correct.

3. I agree with France's president. Tolerance goes two ways. Rouhani should be served the halal menu and he can pass on the wine. Holland got it right.

4. Invent other options.

Planning

5

Planning
The Foundation of Successful Management

Major Questions You Should Be Able to Answer

5.1 Planning and Strategy

Major Question: What are planning, strategy, and strategic management; why are they important to me as a manager; and how does VRIO work?

5.2 Fundamentals of Planning

Major Question: What are mission, vision, and value statements, and what are three types of planning?

5.3 Goals and Plans

Major Question: What are the two types of goals, and what are different kinds of plans?

5.4 Promoting Consistencies in Goals: SMART Goals, Management by Objectives, and Goal Cascading

Major Question: What are SMART goals and how can they be implemented through management by objectives and goal cascading?

5.5 The Planning/Control Cycle

Major Question: How does the planning/control cycle help keep a manager's plans headed in the right direction?

Setting Big Goals: Is This the Road to Success?

What's a big goal? A four-year college degree.

Is it worth it? Not getting a degree has been estimated at about half a million dollars in lost income over your lifetime![1] College graduates enjoy higher pay and lower unemployment than noncollege graduates.[2] They are more apt to say their job is a path to a career.[3] They enjoy longer and healthier lives.[4] They are happier.[5] Good enough reasons?

Big Goals, Hard Goals

Getting a college degree is not only a big goal, it's a hard goal—difficult, stressful, expensive, time consuming. Still, do you perform better when you set difficult goals? If goals are made harder, people may achieve them less often, but they nevertheless perform at a higher level.[6]

If you have outsize ambitions, you might set yourself a *really hard* goal ("Increase study time 50%")—what's known as a *stretch goal,* "stretching yourself beyond what your mind might think is safe," in one definition.[7] Richard Branson, founder of Virgin Atlantic airlines, Virgin records, and many other enterprises, has done a lot of incredible things, in part because of setting stretch goals: "My interest in life," he says, "comes from setting myself huge, apparently unachievable challenges and trying to rise above them."[8] However, in organizations, stretch goals may spur extraordinary efforts but may also lead to excessive risk taking, cheating, and interpersonal strife.[9]

Writing Out Your Goals

You are more likely to achieve your goals if they are "SMART"—specific, measurable, attainable, results-oriented, and have target dates. Achievement is also increased if you make a plan for attaining your goals.[10] Writing about two paragraphs outlining your goals will help you create this plan.[11]

Some tips for helping you think through this process are as follows:

- Make a concrete plan—which embeds your intentions firmly in your memory.
- Break your goals into manageable bites—and set out clear steps that you can use to record and track your progress.
- Put something of value on the line—such as money that will be forfeited if you're unsuccessful. (You can deposit the money at *stickK.com.*)
- Bundle your temptations or rewards to your efforts—such as tying your reading of pleasurable trashy novels to when you do gym workouts.
- Seek social support—pursue your goal with the help of a mentor or fellow strivers.

If you fail, don't give up entirely. Realize that you may have other opportunities to make a fresh start.

For Discussion One writer advises setting one somewhat "crazy" personal goal from time to time. This is a stretch goal, he suggests, "that if accomplished would create a new, different, and exciting future state, the kind of goal that if you can only get halfway there, you will still feel good about the progress you have made and will be better for the effort."[12] What would that goal be for you?

FORECAST   What's Ahead in This Chapter

We describe planning and its link to strategy. We define planning, strategy, and strategic management and state why they are important. We discuss VRIO for analyzing competitive potential. We deal with the fundamentals of planning, including the mission, vision, and value statements, and the three types of planning—strategic, tactical, and operational. We consider goals, operating plans, and action plans; SMART goals, management by objectives, and cascading goals; and finally the planning/control cycle.

5.1   Planning and Strategy

What are planning, strategy, and strategic management; why are they important to me as a manager; and how does VRIO work?

THE BIG PICTURE

The first of four functions in the management process is planning, which involves setting goals and deciding how to achieve them and which is linked to strategy. We define planning, strategy, and strategic management. We then describe three reasons why strategic management and strategic planning are important. We discuss how VRIO analysis can be used to determine if a business idea is competitive.

The *management process,* as you'll recall (from Chapter 1), involves the four management functions of *planning, organizing, leading,* and *controlling,* which form four of the part divisions of this book. In this and the next two chapters we discuss *planning* and *strategy.*

Planning, Strategy, and Strategic Management

"Move fast and break things."

Is that a plan or strategy? No, it's a slogan. In fact, it used to be Facebook's mantra to its software developers, suggesting that "moving quickly is so important that we were even willing to tolerate a few bugs in order to do it," as Facebook CEO Mark Zuckerberg explained.[13] (Then, he says, the company realized "that it wasn't helping us to move faster because we had to slow down to fix these bugs.")

Planning, which we discuss in this chapter, is used in conjunction with *strategy* and *strategic management,* as we describe in Chapter 6. Let's consider some definitions.

Planning: Coping with Uncertainty   As we've said (Chapter 1), **planning is defined as setting goals and deciding how to achieve them.** Another definition: **planning is coping with uncertainty by formulating future courses of action to achieve specified results.**[14] A **plan is a document that outlines how goals are going to be met.** When you make a plan, you make a blueprint for action that describes what you need to do to realize your goals.

Example: One important type of plan is a **business plan, a document that outlines a proposed firm's goals, the strategy for achieving them, and the standards for measuring success.** Here you would describe the basic idea behind your business—the **business model, which outlines the need the firm will fill, the operations of the business, its components and functions, as well as the expected revenues and expenses.** It also describes the industry you're entering, how your product will be different, how you'll market to customers, how you're qualified to run the business, and how you will finance your business.

EXAMPLE   Write a Business Plan? Why Bother?

"My business plan was to wing it," says Lucinda Cross, who started a virtual marketing assistance business in New York City and planned to make it big. "I really thought I had it all under control."[15]

Two years after the launch, the lights were turned off, her cars repossessed, and Cross had to move in with her mother. "It was a huge mistake," she says. "A six-figure mistake."

Why Plan? Almost everyone starting a new business is advised to write a business plan. The reasons: Creating such a plan helps you think through important details. ("Don't rush things; it's best to get the strategy right.") It also helps you get financing. ("If you want us to invest our money, show us your plan.") Finally, it better guarantees your firm will succeed. (A study of 396 entrepreneurs in Sweden found that a greater number of firms that failed never had a formal business plan.[16] Another survey found that a business plan doubles your chances of success.[17])

Start-ups without a Plan. However, like Lucinda Cross, many entrepreneurs never write a business plan. Three possible reasons, suggests Case Western Reserve professor Scott A. Shane: (1) They are ignorant and haven't yet learned the lessons more experienced businesspeople have. (2) They are eager to Just Do It, to get into action—set up shop, hire employees, and so on. (3) They worry their ideas might have weaknesses a business plan could expose, but they're afraid to find them out.[18]

In the End, Do You Really Need a Business Plan? A study by Babson College professor William Bygrave and others found that entrepreneurs who began with formal plans had no greater success than those who started without them.[19] Unless the entrepreneurs needed to raise a lot of start-up capital, the researchers concluded, "there is no compelling reason to write a detailed business plan before opening a new business."[20] Still, Bygrave says, "Every business has to start with a plan," even if it's only jottings on the back of an envelope or a mental construction never committed to paper.[21]

It's important to know, however, that *business plans evolve.* One scholar found that "93% of all successful companies had to abandon their original business plan—because the original plan proved not to be viable."[22] The same is true with a company's business model; it, too, must evolve.[23] All in all, though, *you have to start somewhere*—with some sort of plan.

YOUR CALL

Got an idea for a business? Don't write a formal business plan, one writer suggests; instead, write a blog. "Unlike a business plan," he believes, "*a few* people will actually read your blog."[24] A blog will not only give you useful feedback ("from places other than the voices inside your head") but also will serve both as a vehicle for crystallizing your thinking and as a tool for marketing. Of course, if you do put your plan in the form of a blog, realize that you may be giving away your unique insights or strategic advantage to anyone who happens onto your message. What's a better idea for roughing out your plan?

Strategy: Setting Long-Term Direction

A strategy, or strategic plan, sets the long-term goals and direction for an organization. It represents an "educated guess" about what long-term goals or direction to pursue for the survival or prosperity of the organization. We hear the word expressed in terms like "Apple's ultimate strategy . . ." or "Visa's overseas strategy . . ." or financial strategy, marketing strategy, and human resource strategy.

An example of a strategy is "Grow the business organically," which means "Increase revenue from existing and new customers rather than from acquiring other companies." However, strategy is not something that can be decided on just once. It generally is reconsidered every year because of ever-changing business conditions.

Strategic Management: Involving All Managers in Strategy

In the late 1940s, most large U.S. companies were organized around a single idea or product line. By the 1970s, Fortune 500 companies were operating in more than one industry and had expanded overseas. It became apparent that to stay focused and efficient, companies had to begin taking a strategic-management approach.

Strategic management is a process that involves managers from all parts of the organization in the formulation and the implementation of strategies and strategic goals. This definition doesn't mean that managers at the top dictate ideas to be followed by people lower down. Indeed, precisely because middle managers in particular are the ones who will be asked to understand and implement the strategies, they should also help to formulate them.

As we will see, strategic management is a process that involves managers from all parts of the organization—top managers, middle managers, and first-line managers—in the formulation, implementation, and execution of strategies and strategic goals to advance the purposes of the organization. Thus, planning covers not only strategic planning (done by top managers) but also tactical planning (done by middle managers) and operational planning (done by first-line managers).

Planning and strategic management derive from an organization's mission and vision about itself, as we describe in the next section. *(See Figure 5.1.)*

FIGURE 5.1   Planning and strategic management
The details of planning and strategic management are explained in Chapters 5 and 6.

1. Establish the mission and vision and values → 2. Assess the current reality → 3. Formulate the grand strategy & strategic, tactical, & operational plans → 4. Implement the strategy → 5. Maintain strategic control

Why Planning and Strategic Management Are Important

An organization should adopt planning and strategic management for three reasons: They can (1) *provide direction and momentum,* (2) *encourage new ideas,* and above all (3) *develop a sustainable competitive advantage.*[25] Let's consider these three matters.

1. Providing Direction and Momentum   Some executives are unable even to articulate what their strategy is.[26] Others are so preoccupied with day-to-day pressures that their organizations can lose momentum. But planning and strategic management can help people focus on the most critical problems, choices, and opportunities.

If a broad group of employees is involved in the process, that can foster teamwork, promote learning, and build commitment across the organization. Indeed, as we describe in Chapter 8, strategy can determine the very structure of the organization—for example, a top-down hierarchy with lots of management levels, as might be appropriate for an electricity-and-gas power utility, versus a flat-organization with few management levels and flexible roles, as might suit a fast-moving social media start-up.

Unless a plan is in place, managers may well focus on just whatever is in front of them, putting out fires—until they get an unpleasant jolt when a competitor moves out in front because it has been able to take a long-range view of things and act more quickly. In recent times, this surprise has been happening over and over as companies have been confronted by some digital or Internet trend that emerged as a threat—as Amazon.com was to Borders bookstores; as Uber has been to taxi cabs; as Google News, blogs, and citizen media were to newspapers.[27]

But there are many other instances in which a big company didn't take competitors seriously (as Sears didn't Walmart, as IBM didn't Microsoft, and as GM didn't Toyota). "We were five years late in recognizing that [microbreweries] were going to take as much market as they did," says August Busch III, CEO of massive brewer Anheuser-Busch, "and five years late in recognizing we should have joined them."[28]

Of course, a poor plan can send an organization in the wrong direction. Bad planning usually results from faulty assumptions about the future, poor assessment of an organization's capabilities, ineffective group dynamics, and information overload.[29] And it needs to be said that while a detailed plan may be comforting, it's not necessarily a strategy.[30]

2. Encouraging New Ideas Some people object that planning can foster rigidity, that it creates blinders that block out peripheral vision and reduces creative thinking and action. "Setting oneself on a predetermined course in unknown waters," says one critic, "is the perfect way to sail straight into an iceberg."[31]

Actually, far from being a straitjacket for new ideas, strategic planning can help encourage them by stressing the importance of innovation in achieving long-range success. Management scholar Gary Hamel says that companies such as Apple have been successful because they have been able to unleash the spirit of "strategy innovation." Strategy innovation, he says, is the ability to reinvent the basis of competition within existing industries—"bold new business models that put incumbents on the defensive."[32]

Some successful innovators are companies creating new wealth in the food and restaurant industries, where Starbucks Coffee, Trader Joe's, ConAgra, and Walmart, for example, developed entirely new grocery product categories and retailing concepts. Starbucks, when entering the Chinese market, decided not to threaten China's tea-drinking culture and instead introduced drinks with green tea along with a chic restaurant interior that made young Chinese feel "cool and trendy."[33] GrubHub Seamless, an online takeout and delivery company, serves customers armed with cell phones and delivery apps, delivering pizzas and other foods anywhere they want—at the gym, in the park, on the playground.[34] Vending machines are now serving everything from salads to smoothies to caviar, and supermarkets are experimenting with personalized pricing, using complex shopping data to ascertain the unique needs of individual customers.[35]

3. Developing a Sustainable Competitive Advantage Strategic management provides a sustainable *competitive advantage,* which, you'll recall (from Chapter 1), is the ability of an organization to produce goods or services more effectively than its competitors do, thereby outperforming them. Sustainable competitive advantage occurs when an organization is able to get and stay ahead in four areas: (1) in being responsive to customers, (2) in innovating, (3) in quality, and (4) in effectiveness. Today technology has made achieving a sustainable competitive advantage nearly impossible in many industries, so the advantage may well be fleeting.[36]

Developing Competitive Advantage: Who Dominates the Internet Economy and Who's Losing?

Who are now the lords of tech? Which giant companies control our digital life?

It's generally agreed that the "frightful five" companies that dominate the Internet economy are Amazon, Apple, Facebook, Google, and Microsoft.[37] These are the companies that power the virtual technology infrastructure that delivers "online search, messaging, advertising, applications, computing, and storage on demand," says one report. "They own the digital equivalent of railroad lines just as the Web enters a new phase of growth," rapidly expanding in cloud computing, mobile devices, social networks, and other services.[38]

The Big Five Platforms: Competitive Advantages. The basic building blocks dominated by these five companies on which every other business depends are called *platforms,* points out technology writer Farhad Manjoo.[39] Each platform also represents a company's competitive advantage. Amazon has cloud computing, on which many start-ups run, as well as a shopping and shipping infrastructure.[40] Apple controls one form of mobile phone operating system and the apps that run on it; Google controls another. Google (now part of parent company Alphabet) also rules web search and has its own cloud infrastructure. Google and Facebook dominate the Internet advertising business, and Facebook "keeps amassing greater power in that most fundamental of platforms: human social relationships," Manjoo writes. Microsoft still has Windows, the king of desktop operating systems, and has moved aggressively into cloud computing.

Who's Up, Who's Down? In the struggle for competitive advantage, the state of play is constantly shifting. "Not long ago people thought IBM, Cisco Systems, Intel, and Oracle were unbeatable in tech," Manjoo observes. "They're all still large companies, but they're far less influential than they were once."[41] Meanwhile, Yahoo!, once a huge success story, may be running out of time, its ad revenues slipping far behind those of its rivals, its decline hastened by the rise of mobile devices and social media.[42]

The Stack Fallacy. Why do some companies lose their competitive advantage? Venture capitalist Anshu Sharma suggests one possibility. Although a company may have the resources and brainpower to build "the next big thing," it may subscribe to the *stack fallacy*—"the mistaken belief that it is trivial to build the layer above yours" in the stack that is the layer cake of technology.[43] The reason, argues Sharma: the companies don't have firsthand understanding for what customers of the product one level above theirs in the stack actually want. Thus, Oracle, which is a database company, can't seem to beat Salesforce in building database management software for customer relations because Oracle doesn't truly understand how this kind of customer relations works.

YOUR CALL

If you can visualize a "frightful 5" Internet company losing its competitive advantage, how do you think it would come about?

Using VRIO as a Way to Analyze Competitive Potential: Value, Rarity, Imitability, and Organization

Say you have an idea for a product or service, such as "Let's develop a ride service for kids, similar to that of Uber and Lyft for adults." Actually, several such endeavors have been launched, one of the more recent ones being Shuddle in San Francisco.[44] How do you determine if this idea might work?

VRIO (pronounced by its letters, "V-R-I-O") is a framework for analyzing a resource or capability to determine its competitive strategic potential by answering four questions about its Value, Rarity, Imitability, and Organization.[45] The questions are shown on the page opposite. *(See Figure 5.2.)*

VRIO is a way to analyze a firm's competitive potential by asking four questions about Value, Rarity, Imitability, and Organization. A "Yes" answer to each question means the resource or capability—that is, the business idea—has a competitive advantage.

Value: Is the Resource or Capability Valuable?

Valuable means "Does the resource or capability allow your firm to exploit an opportunity or neutralize a threat?" If the answer is yes, the resource puts you in a competitive position. If no, then you're at a competitive disadvantage.

Example: The idea of an on-demand ride service for unaccompanied children provided by drivers in their personal cars exploits an opportunity—because some parents say they really need such a service.

Rarity: Is the Resource or Capability Currently Controlled by Only a Few Firms or No Other Firms?

If the answer is yes, that status gives your firm at least some temporary competitive advantage. If the answer is no (several competing firms exist), you're at least at equal competitive advantage, because you're no worse than the competition.

Example: No other firms in your area are yet offering on-demand children's ride services, so this is a competitive advantage.

Imitability: Is the Resource or Capability Costly for Other Firms to Imitate?

If the answer is yes, that gives you a definite competitive advantage. If no—because other firms can get into the market without much expense—that gives you only a temporary competitive advantage.

Example: Offering a children's ride service with drivers using their own personal cars is probably not so costly that other firms might not try to imitate you. Here you have a competitive advantage, but it may be temporary.

Organization: Is the Firm Organized to Exploit the Resource or Capability?

If the answer is yes—that is, the firm has the necessary structure, culture, control systems, employee policies, and particularly financing—then, assuming yes answers on Value, Rarity, and Imitability, it would seem the firm has the competitive potential to go forward. If no, it may only have a temporary competitive advantage.

Example: San Francisco's Shuddle began in fall 2014 with 350 independent-contractor drivers and rose to about 2,600 customers booking 7,000 rides a month. But the rides were more expensive than Uber and Lyft (owing to higher expenses for more-extensive background checks and additional insurance for Shuddle drivers), with trips averaging $24 each. Unfortunately, Shuddle suffered from needing not only more riders but also more drivers in order to better balance supply and demand. It also was unable to raise additional venture capital money. Clearly, then, it did not have everything needed to answer yes to the question of Organization. The pioneering ride service went out of business in April 2016. ●

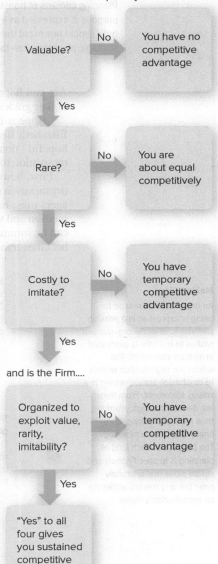

FIGURE 5.2   **Is the resource or capability . . .**

Source: Adapted from F. T. Rothaermel, Strategic Management: Concepts and Cases (New York: McGraw-Hill Education, 2012), p. 91.

5.2   Fundamentals of Planning

What are mission, vision, and values statements, and what are three types of planning?

THE BIG PICTURE

Planning consists of translating an organization's mission and vision into objectives. The organization's purpose is expressed as a mission statement, and what it becomes is expressed as a vision statement; both should represent the organization's values, expressed in a values statement. From these are derived strategic planning, then tactical planning, then operational planning.

Are you hopeful? That's a good thing. Students who have more hope reportedly have higher grades and are more apt to finish college.

"Hope is the belief that the future will be better than the present," says columnist Elizabeth Bernstein, "and that you have some power to make it so." People who are hopeful "don't just have a goal or a wish, they have a strategy to achieve it and the motivation to implement their plan."[46]

First, however, you must determine your "goal or wish"—that is, your purpose. An organization must determine its purpose, too—what's known as its *mission*. And managers must have an idea of where they want the organization to go—the *vision*. Both mission and vision should express the organization's *values*. The approach to planning can be summarized in the diagram below, which shows how an organization's mission becomes translated into action plans. *(See Figure 5.3.)*

FIGURE 5.3

Making plans

An organization's reason for being is expressed in a *mission statement*. What the organization wishes to become is expressed in a *vision statement*. The values the organization wishes to emphasize are expressed in a *values statement*. From these are derived *strategic planning*, then *tactical planning*, and finally *operational planning*. The purpose of each kind of planning is to specify *goals* and *action plans* that ultimately pave the way toward achieving an organization's vision.

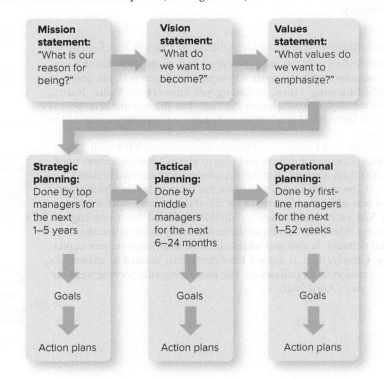

Mission statement: "What is our reason for being?"

Vision statement: "What do we want to become?"

Values statement: "What values do we want to emphasize?"

Strategic planning: Done by top managers for the next 1–5 years

Tactical planning: Done by middle managers for the next 6–24 months

Operational planning: Done by first-line managers for the next 1–52 weeks

Goals

Goals

Goals

Action plans

Action plans

Action plans

Mission, Vision, and Values Statements

The planning process begins with three attributes: a mission statement (which answers the question "What is our reason for being?"), a vision statement (which answers the question "What do we want to become?"), and a values statement (which answers the question "What values do we want to emphasize?").

The Mission Statement—"What Is Our Reason for Being?" An organization's **mission** is its purpose or reason for being. Determining the mission is the responsibility of top management and the board of directors. It is up to them to formulate a **mission statement, which expresses the purpose of the organization.**

"Only a clear definition of the mission and purpose of the organization makes possible clear and realistic . . . objectives," said Peter Drucker.[47] Whether the organization is for-profit or nonprofit, the mission statement identifies the goods or services the organization provides and will provide. Sometimes it also gives the reasons for providing them (to make a profit or to achieve humanitarian goals, for example).

The Vision Statement—"What Do We Want to Become?" A **vision** is a long-term goal describing "what" an organization wants to become. It is a clear sense of the future and the actions needed to get there. "[A] vision should describe what's happening to the world you compete in and what you want to do about it," says one *Fortune* article. "It should guide decisions."[48]

After formulating a mission statement, top managers need to develop a **vision statement, which expresses what the organization should become, where it wants to go strategically.**[49]

The concept of a vision statement also is important for individuals. Harvard professor Clayton Christensen believes that creating a personal life vision statement is akin to developing a strategy for your life. He finds that people are happier and lead more meaningful lives when they are directed by personal vision statements.[50] Do you have a vision for your future career? Is it vague or specific? The following self-assessment was created to help you evaluate the quality of your career vision and plan.

Assessing Career Behaviors and Future Career Identity

This self-assessment is designed to help you reflect on the vision of your career identity. Please be prepared to answer these questions if your instructor has assigned Self-Assessment 5.1 in Connect.

1. What did you learn about your future career identity? Are you surprised by the results?

2. Write a personal mission and vision statement using ideas discussed in this section. Share it with a friend for feedback.

3. What is the value of creating a personal mission and vision statement? Explain.

The Values Statement—"What Values Do We Want to Emphasize?" *Values,* we said in Chapter 3, are the relatively permanent and deeply held underlying beliefs and attitudes that help determine a person's behavior: integrity, dedication, teamwork, excellence, compassion, or whatever. Values reflect the qualities that represent an organization's deeply held beliefs, highest priorities, and core guiding principles.

After formulating a vision statement, then, top managers need to develop a **values statement,** also called a *core values statement,* which expresses what the company stands for, its core priorities, the values its employees embody, and what its products contribute to the world.[51] Values statements "become the deeply ingrained principle and fabric that guide employee behavior and company decisions and actions—the behaviors the company and employees expect of themselves," says former executive Eric Jacobsen. "Without a statement, the company will lack soul."[52]

EXAMPLE　　Values Statements for Three Different Companies: Hilton, Facebook, and Patagonia

Values statements answer the question "What values do we want to emphasize?"

Here is Hilton Hotels's statement of its values (whose initial letters spell H-I-L-T-O-N):[53]

- *Hospitality*—We're passionate about delivering exceptional guest experiences.
- *Integrity*—We do the right thing, all the time.
- *Leadership*—We're leaders in our industry and in our communities.
- *Teamwork*—We're team players in everything we do.
- *Ownership*—We're the owners of our actions and decisions.
- *Now*—We operate with a sense of urgency and discipline.

Facebook's values statement is as follows:[54]

- *Focus on Impact*—If we want to have the biggest impact, the best way to do this is to make sure we always focus on solving the most important problems. It sounds simple, but we think most companies do this poorly and waste a lot of time. We expect everyone at Facebook to be good at finding the biggest problems to work on.
- *Move Fast*—Moving fast enables us to build more things and learn faster. However, as most companies grow, they

slow down too much because they're more afraid of making mistakes than they are of losing opportunities by moving too slowly. . . .

- *Be Bold*—Building great things means taking risks. This can be scary and prevents most companies from doing the bold things they should. However, in a world that's changing so quickly, you're guaranteed to fail if you don't take any risks. We have another saying: "The riskiest thing is to take no risks." We encourage everyone to make bold decisions, even if that means being wrong some of the time.

- *Be Open*—We believe that a more open world is a better world because people with more information can make better decisions and have a greater impact. That goes for running our company as well. We work hard to make sure everyone at Facebook has access to as much information as possible about every part of the company so they can make the best decisions and have the greatest impact.

- *Build Social Value*—Once again, Facebook exists to make the world more open and connected, and not just to build a company. We expect everyone at Facebook to focus every day on how to build real value for the world in everything they do.

Patagonia's values statement:[55]

- *Quality*—The pursuit of ever greater quality in everything we do.
- *Integrity*—Relationships built on integrity and respect.
- *Environmentalism*—Serve as a catalyst for personal and corporate action.

- *Not Bound by Convention*—Our success—and much of the fun—lies in developing innovative ways of doing things.

YOUR CALL

What do you think of these values statements? Are they explicit enough to "guide employee behavior and company decisions and actions—the behaviors the company and employees expect of themselves"?

Three Types of Planning for Three Levels of Management: Strategic, Tactical, and Operational

Inspiring, clearly stated mission statements and vision statements provide the focal point of the entire planning process. Then three things happen:

- **Strategic planning by top management.** Using their mission and vision statements, top managers do **strategic planning**—they determine what the organization's long-term goals should be for the next one to five years with the resources they expect to have available. "Strategic planning requires visionary and directional thinking," says one authority.[56] It should communicate not only general goals about growth and profits but also ways to achieve them. Today, because of the frequency with which world competition and information technology alter marketplace conditions, a company's strategic planning may have to be done closer to every one or two years than every five. Still, at a big company like Boeing or Ford or Amazon, top executives cannot lose sight of long-range, multiyear planning.

Strategic Planning by Top Management: Is "Quarterly Earnings Hysteria" Contrary to Effective Long-Term Strategy?   EXAMPLE

With most publicly owned companies, shareholders constantly pressure management to produce profits that will boost the stock every quarter (that is, every three months). But Laurence D. Fink, CEO of BlackRock, the world's largest investor, thinks that's bad for long-term strategy. "Today's culture of quarterly earnings hysteria is totally contrary to the long-term approach we need," Fink wrote 500 chief executives.[57]

The Problems with "Short-Termism." Fink wants to eliminate the tyranny of what are known as *earnings calls,* where company executives discuss quarterly results with investors, analysts, and the media, which tends to focus everyone's attention on short-term (that is, quarterly) results.

What is the effect of this short-termism? One study found "that short-term companies attracted short-term investors (bringing with them a whole new set of performance pressures on executives) and that the financial and strategic performance of these companies were more volatile—and riskier—than that of the long termers."[58]

Fink wants to not only reduce the importance of the quarterly earnings call but also to encourage CEOs and directors to provide "a strategic framework for long-term value creation" that could extend for multiple years.

Companies with short-term outlooks included Chevron, Cisco, and Goldman Sachs, and short-term-oriented industries tended to be banking, electronic equipment, business services, and wholesale.

Talking Long-Term. Despite the intense concentration on quarterly results, there *are* industries that tend to be long-term-focused, including beverages, medical goods, retail, and pharmaceuticals. Companies with this outlook include Coca-Cola, Ford, Nordstrom, and Apple. ("We don't live in 90-day quarters, and we don't invest in 90-day quarters," Apple CEO Tim Cook says.)[59] The most notable long-termer is Amazon.

Amazon founder and CEO Jeff Bezos continually "preaches customer focus and long-term thinking," says a *Fortune* article.[60] Bezos, whose 18% of Amazon's stock is worth $46 billion, has an unconventional opinion about profitability.[61] Back in 1997, Bezos warned stockholders that "it's all about the long term. We may make decisions and weigh trade-offs differently than some companies."[62]

Most top managers, with their attention constantly focused on the next upcoming earnings call, do strategic planning on a one- to three-year time line. Says Bezos, "If everything you do needs to work on a three-year time horizon, then you're competing against a lot of people. But if you're willing to invest on a seven-year horizon, you're now competing against a fraction of those people, because very few people are willing to do that." Actually, Bezos is *very* long-term, operating on a 10- to 20-year time line.

Profits? "Profits will come down the road," says business writer James Stewart, "when Kindle [and Fire] users buy content through Amazon."[63] Says Bezos, "We're willing to plant seeds, let them grow—and we're very stubborn."[64]

Ambitions for the Future. The large time window and freedom from having to deliver immediate profits allow Amazon to pursue the powerful long-range strategy it has planned.[65] It continues to cut prices on its merchandise, which is undercutting retail competitors.[66] It is realizing Walmart-like economies of scale, achieving enormous savings from buying supplies in huge quantities. Amazon Prime, its subscription delivery service, has become such a hit that one analyst predicts in five years 50% of American households will have joined the service.[67] Now it is on a tear to dominate cloud computing.[68]

YOUR CALL

After 20 years of thin or no profits, in January 2016 Amazon delivered the largest quarterly profit in its history. Yet the stock price went *down,* because investors apparently were thirsty for more.[69] If Amazon's strategy hurts short-run profits, should your parents or grandparents invest in Amazon? Should you? What if Amazon's strategic plan is wrong?

- ■ *Tactical planning by middle management.* The strategic priorities and policies are then passed down to middle managers, who must do **tactical planning— that is, they determine what contributions their departments or similar work units can make with their given resources during the next 6–24 months.**

- ■ *Operational planning by first-line management.* Middle managers then pass these plans along to first-line managers to do **operational planning—that is, they determine how to accomplish specific tasks with available resources within the next 1–52 weeks.**

The three kinds of managers are described further in the figure below. *(See Figure 5.4.)* ●

FIGURE 5.4   Three levels of management, three types of planning
Each type of planning has different time horizons, although the times overlap because the plans are somewhat elastic.

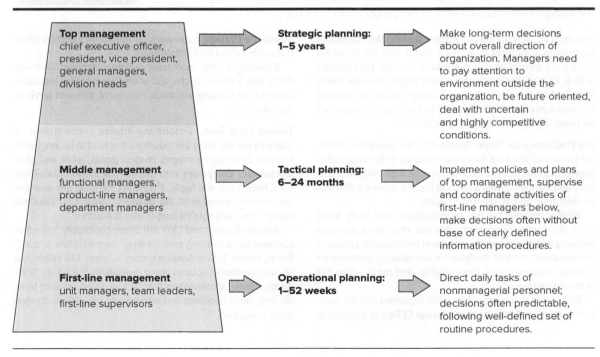

| **Top management** chief executive officer, president, vice president, general managers, division heads | → | **Strategic planning: 1–5 years** | → | Make long-term decisions about overall direction of organization. Managers need to pay attention to environment outside the organization, be future oriented, deal with uncertain and highly competitive conditions. |

| **Middle management** functional managers, product-line managers, department managers | → | **Tactical planning: 6–24 months** | → | Implement policies and plans of top management, supervise and coordinate activities of first-line managers below, make decisions often without base of clearly defined information procedures. |

| **First-line management** unit managers, team leaders, first-line supervisors | → | **Operational planning: 1–52 weeks** | → | Direct daily tasks of nonmanagerial personnel; decisions often predictable, following well-defined set of routine procedures. |

5.3 Goals and Plans

MAJOR QUESTION

What are the two types of goals, and what are different kinds of plans?

THE BIG PICTURE

The purpose of planning is to set a goal and then an action plan. There are two types of goals, short-term and long-term, and they are connected by a means-end chain. Types of plans include standing and single-use plans.

Whatever its type—long-term or short-term—the purpose of planning is to set a *goal* and then to formulate an *action plan*.

Long-Term and Short-Term Goals

A goal, also known as an objective, is a specific commitment to achieve a measurable result within a stated period of time. Goals may be long-term or short-term.

Long-term goals are generally referred to as **strategic goals. They tend to span 1 to 5 years and focus on achieving the strategies identified in a company's strategic plan.** An example is to increase revenue from new customers by 10% over the next 12 months.

Short-term goals are sometimes referred to as *tactical* or *operational goals*, or just plain *goals*. **They generally span 12 months and are connected to strategic goals in a hierarchy known as a means-end chain.**

A means-end chain shows how goals are connected or linked across an organization. For example, a low-level goal such as responding to customer inquiries in less than 24 hours is the means to accomplishing a higher-level goal of achieving 90% customer satisfaction.

As we will see later in Section 5.4, goals should be SMART—specific, measurable, attainable, results-oriented, and with target dates.

The Operating Plan and Action Plan

Larry Bossidy, former CEO of both Honeywell International and Allied Signal, and global consultant Ram Charan define an **operating plan** as a plan that "breaks long-term output into short-term targets" or goals.[70] In other words, operating plans turn strategic plans into actionable short-term goals and action plans.

An **action plan defines the course of action needed to achieve a stated goal.** Whether the goal is long-term or short-term, action plans outline the tactics that will be used to achieve a goal. Each tactic also contains a projected date for completing the desired activities. Consider the following example of a means-ends chain to illustrate these concepts:

- *Strategic goal.* Increase revenue from new customers by 10% over the next 12 months.
- *Operational goal.* Introduce (roll out) two new product offerings over the next 12 months.
- *Action plan.* (1) Product development team to propose two new products by March 31. (2) Products to be produced and pilot-tested in selected markets by May 1. (3) Products to be modified as needed and a marketing plan prepared to support their introduction (rollout) by May 31. (4) Sales force to be trained to sell products and execution of marketing plan begun by June 30. (5) Sales managers to meet with sales force to discuss progress and receive comments on marketing plan: ongoing.

EXAMPLE   Long-Term and Short-Term Goals at Southwest Airlines

Ranking No. 7 on *Fortune*'s 2016 Most Admired Companies list, Dallas-based Southwest Airlines has inspired a host of low-fare imitators—big ones like Alaska and JetBlue and small ones like Allegiant, Frontier, Spirit, Sun Country, and Virgin America—which have grown rapidly in recent years compared to mainline or "legacy" carriers American, Delta, and United Continental. It has continually achieved its strategic goals and as of 2016 had been profitable for 43 consecutive years.[71]

Long-Term Strategic Goals. Employee engagement, customer satisfaction, and profitability have been key strategic goals for Southwest since its inception. Employee engagement is created through the company's corporate culture, which focuses on employee satisfaction and well-being. Southwest CEO Gary Kelly highlighted this theme by noting that "our people are our single greatest strength and our most enduring long-term competitive advantage."[72]

The goal of Southwest's top managers is to ensure that the airline is highly profitable, and for years it has followed the general strategy of (a) keeping costs and fares down, to appeal to budget rather than business travelers; (b) offering a superior on-time arrival record and squeezing more flights per day from every plane; and (c) keeping passengers happy with its cheerful cabin crew and staff.

One of the most important strategic decisions Southwest made was to fly just one type of airplane—Boeing 737s, 692 of them—to hold down training, maintenance, and operating expenses.[73] Another was to create a strong corporate culture that, according to one former CEO, allows employees to "feel like they're using their brains, they're using their creativity, they're allowed to be themselves and have a sense of humor, and they understand what the mission of the company is."[74]

In the last 10 years, however, Southwest began to dramatically change its strategy. Traditionally it had not served major cities (Atlanta, Denver) and had served only the secondary airports of metropolises such as New York and San Francisco. Now it has decided to go head to head with legacy carriers by flying to key airports of major cities—and even to develop international routes, principally to Latin America. The reason: to go after business travelers and their higher per-seat fares.[75]

Southwest has always had a strategic focus on keeping passengers happy, which it does via its vaunted customer service. "What I like best is the attitude of the flight attendants," says one traveler, a public-relations firm co-founder. "I've taken 1,100 flights on Southwest and maybe met two or three flight attendants who were unpleasant. On other airlines you hear them complaining all the time."[76] The same enthusiasm is seen in the behavior of ground crews charging toward the airplane even before it has come to rest—unlike their counterparts at other airlines, who don't move until the airplane has turned off its engines.[77]

Part of Southwest's customer service strategy revolves around offering two freebies that other airlines do not: (1) no charge for checked-in luggage up to two pieces (which might cost a business traveler $200 on other airlines), and (2) no extra charge for changing a ticket (a money saver for business travelers, who make lots of last-minute changes).

Short-Term Goals. Cutting costs and keeping fares low have traditionally been key operational goals for Southwest. For example, until recently the airline flew only short-haul flights to midsize cities to save time and money by avoiding traffic. There was just one class of seating, doing away with the distinction between coach and first class. Passengers are not served in-flight meals, mostly just peanuts. The airline saves on maintenance by doing more work on a plane when it's in for a check instead of bringing it in three different times.

How does the airline achieve a superior on-time arrival record? To achieve this second operational goal, the company did away with guaranteed seat reservations before ticketing, so that no-shows wouldn't complicate (and therefore delay) the boarding process. In its new campaign to go after business travelers, Southwest changed the reservations policy slightly to ensure that passengers paying extra for "business select" fares would be placed at the front of the line.

In addition, the airline has tried to turn planes around in exactly 20 minutes, so that on-time departures are more apt to produce on-time arrivals. Although the airline is about 83% unionized, turnaround was helped by looser work rules, so that workers could pitch in to do tasks outside their normal jobs. "If you saw something that needed to be done," said one former employee, "and you thought you could do it, you did."[78]

Unfortunately, in 2013, in an attempt to offer more convenient flight schedules, the airline instituted a new system to reduce times it allowed for flights and compressed its turnaround times even further—the result of which sent its on-time performance reeling to last place among U.S. carriers.[79] In 2015, however, Southwest's on-time arrival rate climbed back to third place among major carriers (behind Alaska and Delta), and it was second lowest (after Alaska) in customer complaints.[80]

The New Southwest. In January 2014, as part of its new strategy to go after business travelers, Southwest began ven-

Lookalikes. One key to the success of Southwest Airlines is that all the planes in its fleet have been the same type, Boeing 737s, which saves on maintenance and training costs. © Charles Rex Arbogast/AP Photo

turing into the international market, beginning with flights to Latin America.[81] With this significant shift, some operations, such as fast turnaround times, may be difficult to implement because of departure restrictions.[82] Southwest also faces costly upgrades to its computer systems and an antiquated phone system, and its traditionally low fares are not so low anymore.[83] Most important is the question whether the airline can compete with the upscale perks that Delta, American, and United Continental offer businesspeople—assigned seats, first-class cabins, and luxurious club lounges to wait in—and not alienate the traditional Southwest customer.

YOUR CALL

Do you think recent changes will allow the company to continue to achieve its strategic goals?

Types of Plans: Standing Plans and Single-Use Plans

Plans are of two types—*standing plans* and *single-use plans. (See Table 5.1.)*

PLAN	DESCRIPTION
Standing plan	For activities that occur repeatedly over a period of time
• Policy	Outlines general response to a designated problem or situation
• Procedure	Outlines response to particular problems or circumstances
• Rule	Designates specific required action
Single-use plan	For activities not likely to be repeated in the future
• Program	Encompasses a range of projects or activities
• Project	Has less scope and complexity than a program

TABLE 5.1

Standing Plans and Single-Use Plans

There are three types of standing plans and two types of single-use plans.

Standing Plans: Policies, Procedures, and Rules **Standing plans** are plans developed for activities that occur repeatedly over a period of time. Standing plans consist of policies, procedures, and rules.

- **A policy** is a standing plan that outlines the general response to a designated problem or situation. Example: "This workplace does not condone swearing." This policy is a broad statement that gives managers a general idea about what is allowable for employees who use bad language, but gives no specifics.
- **A procedure** (or *standard operating procedure*) is a standing plan that outlines the response to particular problems or circumstances. Example: McDonald's specifies exactly how a hamburger should be dressed, including the order in which the mustard, ketchup, and pickles are applied.
- **A rule** is a standing plan that designates specific required action. Example: "No smoking is allowed anywhere in the building." This allows no room for interpretation.

Single-Use Plans: Programs and Projects **Single-use plans** are plans developed for activities that are not likely to be repeated in the future. Such plans can be programs or projects.

- **A program** is a single-use plan encompassing a range of projects or activities. Example: The U.S. government space program has had several projects, including the *Challenger* project, the Hubble Telescope project, and the space shuttle project.
- **A project** is a single-use plan of less scope and complexity than a program. Example: The space shuttle project, one of several projects in the government's space program, consisted of three shuttles: *Discovery, Endeavour,* and *Atlantis.* ●

5.4   Promoting Consistencies in Goals: SMART Goals, Management by Objectives, and Goal Cascading

MAJOR QUESTION   **What are SMART goals and how can they be implemented through management by objectives and goal cascading?**

THE BIG PICTURE

This section discusses SMART goals—goals that are Specific, Measurable, Attainable, Results-oriented, and have Target dates. It also briefly discusses a technique for setting goals, management by objectives (MBO), a four-step process for motivating employees. Finally, it introduces the concept of goal cascading, which attempts to ensure that higher-level goals are communicated and aligned with the goals at the next levels down in the organizational hierarchy.

Anyone can define goals. But as we mentioned earlier, the five characteristics of a good goal are represented by the acronym SMART.

SMART Goals

A **SMART goal** is one that is *Specific, Measurable, Attainable, Results-oriented, and has Target dates.*

Specific   Goals should be stated in *specific* rather than vague terms. The goal "As many planes as possible should arrive on time" is too general. The goal that "Ninety percent of planes should arrive within 15 minutes of the scheduled arrival time" is specific.

Measurable   Whenever possible, goals should be *measurable,* or quantifiable (as in "90% of planes should arrive within 15 minutes"). That is, there should be some way to measure the degree to which a goal has been reached.

Of course, some goals—such as those concerned with improving quality—are not precisely quantifiable. In that case, something on the order of "Improve the quality of customer relations by instituting 10 follow-up telephone calls every week" will do. You can certainly quantify how many follow-up phone calls were made.

Attainable   Goals should be challenging, of course, but above all they should be realistic and *attainable.* It may be best to set goals that are quite ambitious so as to challenge people to meet high standards. Always, however, the goals should be achievable within the scope of the time, equipment, and financial support available. *(See Figure 5.5.)*

If too easy (as in "half the flights should arrive on time"), goals won't impel people to make much effort. If impossible ("all flights must arrive on time, regardless of weather"), employees won't even bother trying. Or they will try and continually fail, which will end up hurting morale. Or they will cheat. (An example was the unrealistic goal of cutting wait times for appointments by more than half at Veterans Affairs hospitals, as revealed in ongoing scandals in which VA administrators were found to have falsified figures.)[84]

FIGURE 5.5   Relationship between goal difficulty and performance

Source: Adapted from E. A. Locke and G. P. Latham, A Theory of Goal Setting and Task Performance (Englewood Cliffs, NJ: Prentice Hall, 1990).

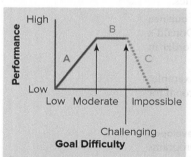

Performance
A Committed individuals with adequate ability
B Committed individuals who are working at capacity
C Individuals who lack commitment to high goals

Results-Oriented   Only a few goals should be chosen—say, five for any work unit. And they should be *results-oriented*—they should support the organization's vision.

In writing out the goals, start with the word "To" and follow it with action-oriented verbs—"complete," "acquire," "increase" ("to decrease by 10% the time to get passengers settled in their seats before departure").

Some verbs should not be used in your goal statement because they imply activities— the ways used to accomplish goals (such as having baggage handlers waiting). For example, you should not use "to develop," "to conduct," "to implement."

Target Dates   Goals should specify the *target dates* or deadline dates when they are to be attained. For example, it's unrealistic to expect an airline to improve its on-time arrivals by 10% overnight. However, you could set a target date—three to six months away, say—by which this goal is to be achieved. That allows enough time for lower-level managers and employees to revamp their systems and work habits and gives them a clear time frame in which they know what they are expected to do.

EXAMPLE

Setting Goals: Are Big Companies Serious about Sustainability and Climate Change? How Will We Know?

In 2015, Apple, Bank of America, Coca-Cola, Google, Microsoft, and other Fortune 500 companies signed a pledge to take measures to curb greenhouse gas emissions and invest in clean energy.[85] Others, such as Nike and Procter & Gamble, announced plans to switch to sourcing 100% renewable energy.[86] How do we know how serious these companies are? Can we measure the results?

The Walmart Experience.   Earlier, in 2006 Walmart, partnering with the Environmental Defense Fund, began to seriously stress its devotion to sustainability by stating three goals it wanted to achieve over 10 years: (1) Be supplied by 100% renewable energy. (2) Create zero waste. (3) Sell products that sustain people and the environment.[87]

Two years later, its CEO announced to a meeting of 7,000 store managers that Walmart was determinedly pursuing energy efficiency, had sold over 145 million energy-saving fluorescent bulbs, and intended to make power-hungry appliances (TVs, air conditioners) 25% more energy-efficient over the next three years.[88] Later, the retail giant pledged to eliminate 20 million tons of carbon emissions from its global supply chain by 2015.[89]

In 2013, it added two more goals for avoiding greenhouse gas, to be achieved by 2020: (1) a 600% increase (over 2010 levels) in power purchases of renewable energy globally every year, and (2) a reduction by 20% globally (compared to 2010) in kilowatts required to power Walmart buildings. Such efficiencies are to be achieved by adding solar power to buildings and buying wind, hydro, and geothermal sources of energy, as well as increasing LED lighting in and around stores.[90]

Endgame.   By 2014, Walmart had shot from 15th to 6th place in Environmental Protection Agency (EPA) rankings of

Better environmental objectives. In 2015, over a dozen Fortune 500 companies pledged to curb greenhouse gas emissions and invest in clean energy. How should these goals be structured and measured?
© Jeff Michell/Corbis

the country's top purchasers of green power—electricity produced by wind, solar, and similar means.[91] However, critics asserted all the good things Walmart was doing were offset by the fact that that "the company is adding more stores and selling more stuff."[92] Some produced studies showing Walmart's greenhouse gas emissions had actually grown 14% because the company's calculations had failed to account for major sources of pollution from international shipping, new store construction, and product manufacturing.[93] One of the strongest criticisms was that the company had failed to set *science-based targets* for its climate emissions.[94] (For more on science-based targets, see *sciencebasedtargets.org*.)

In any case, despite the lofty goals, by 2016 the company had slipped to 17th place overall in EPA green-power purchasers' ratings (which was led by Intel, Microsoft, Kohl's, Cisco, and Apple). Even so, among the top 30 retailers, Walmart ranked third (behind Kohl's and Starbucks) in green power usage.[95] Not bad for the massive energy turnaround effort required of the largest company in the world.

YOUR CALL

Even if Walmart has not included all the sources of emissions in its calculation, as critics assert, how do the objectives outlined above reflect the criteria for SMART goals?

Management by Objectives: The Four-Step Process for Motivating Employees

First suggested by **Peter Drucker** in 1954, *management by objectives* has spread largely because of the appeal of its emphasis on converting general objectives into specific ones for all members of an organization.[96]

Management by objectives (MBO) is a four-step process in which (1) managers and employees jointly set objectives for the employee, (2) managers develop action plans, (3) managers and employees periodically review the employee's performance, and (4) the manager makes a performance appraisal and rewards the employee according to results. The purpose of MBO is to *motivate* rather than to control subordinates.

Before we begin discussing these four steps, you may want to consider the quality of the goal-setting process in a current or former employer. Management by objectives and goal cascading will not work without an effective goal setting process. The following self-assessment was developed to provide insight into the quality of goal setting within an organization.

connect SELF-ASSESSMENT 5.2

What Is the Quality of Goal Setting within a Current or Past Employer?

This self-assessment is designed to assess the quality of goal setting in a company. Please be prepared to answer these questions if your instructor has assigned Self-Assessment 5.2 in Connect.

1. What are the strengths and weaknesses of goal setting in the company you selected?

2. Based on your results, what recommendations would you provide to senior management about improving the goal-setting process in this company? Explain.

3. What actions could you take to improve the goal-setting process in this company? Be specific.

1. Jointly Set Objectives   You sit down with your manager and the two of you jointly set objectives for you to attain. Later you do the same with each of your own subordinates. Joint manager/subordinate participation is important to the program. It's probably best if the objectives aren't simply imposed from above (don't say, "Here are the objectives I want you to meet"). Managers also should not simply approve the employee's objectives ("Whatever you aim for is okay with me"). It's necessary to have back-and-forth negotiation to make the objectives practicable.[97]

Jointly setting objectives. An important part of MBO is joint manager/subordinate participation in setting objectives. Have you ever held a job that featured this kind of process? © Chris Ryan/agefotostock RF

One result of joint participation, research shows, is that it impels people to set more difficult goals—to raise the level of their aspirations—which may have a positive effect on their performance.[98] The objectives should be expressed in writing and should be SMART. There are three types of objectives, shown in the following table. *(See Table 5.2.)*

TABLE 5.2

Three Types of Objectives Used in MBO: improvement, personal development, and maintenance

Improvement Objectives
Purpose Express performance to be accomplished in a specific way for a specific area   **Examples** "Increase sport utility sales by 10%." "Reduce food spoilage by 15%."

Personal Development Objectives
Purpose Express personal goals to be realized   **Examples** "Attend five days of leadership training." "Learn basics of Microsoft Office software by June 1."

Maintenance Objectives
Purpose Express the intention to maintain performance at previously established levels   **Examples** "Continue to meet the increased sales goals specified last quarter." "Produce another 60,000 cases of wine this month."

2. Develop Action Plan   Once objectives are set, managers at each level should prepare an action plan for attaining them. Action plans may be prepared for both individuals and work units, such as departments.

3. Periodically Review Performance   You and your manager should meet reasonably often—either informally as needed or formally every three months—to review progress, as should you and your subordinates. Indeed, frequent communication is necessary so that everyone will know how well he or she is doing in meeting the objectives.

During each meeting, managers should give employees feedback, and objectives should be updated or revised as necessary to reflect new realities. If you were managing a painting or landscaping business, for example, changes in the weather, loss of key employees, or a financial downturn affecting customer spending could force you to reconsider your objectives.

4. Give Performance Appraisal and Rewards, If Any   At the end of 6 or 12 months, you and your subordinate should meet to discuss results, comparing performance with initial objectives. *Deal with results,* not personalities, emotional issues, or excuses.

Because the purpose of MBO is to *motivate* employees, performance that meets the objectives should be rewarded—with compliments, raises, bonuses, promotions, or other suitable benefits. Failure can be addressed by redefining the objectives for the next 6- or 12-month period, or even by taking stronger measures, such as demotion. Basically, however, MBO is viewed as being a learning process. After step 4, the MBO cycle begins anew.[99]

Cascading Goals: Making Lower-Level Goals Align with Top Goals

For goal setting to be successful, the following three things have to happen.

1. Top Management Must Be Committed   "When top-management commitment [to MBO] was high," said one review, "the average gain in productivity was 56%. When commitment was low, the average gain in productivity was only 6%."[100]

2. The Goals Must Be Applied Organizationwide   The goal-setting program has to be put in place throughout the entire organization. That is, it cannot be applied in just some divisions and departments; it has to be done in all of them.

3. Goals Must "Cascade"—Be Linked Consistently Down through the Organization   Cascading goals is the process of ensuring that the strategic goals set at the top level align, or "cascade," downward with more specific short-term goals at lower levels within an organization, including employees' objectives and activities. Top managers set *strategic goals,* which are translated into *divisional goals,* which are translated into *departmental goals,* which are translated into *individual goals.* The cascading process ends when all individuals have a set of goals that support the overall strategic goals. This process helps employees understand how their work contributes to overall corporate success.

Example: The Vice President of the Claims Division of an automobile insurance company, which pays off requests, or claims, by customers seeking insurance payments to repair damage to their cars, may set the major goal (and SMART goal) of "Increase customer satisfaction in Claims Division by 10%." In the cascading goals process, the same goal would be embraced by the Assistant Vice President of Claims and the Recovery Director beneath him or her. Further down the hierarchy, the Recovery Unit Manager would reword the goal to be more specific: "Decrease the number of customer complaints about claims by 10% over last year's average." For the individual Recovery Analyst at the lowest level, the goal could become: "Return all customer phone calls about claims within 24 hours."[101] Thus, all the subgoals in the organization are in alignment with the major goal of top management.

The Importance of Deadlines

There's no question that college is a pressure cooker for many students. The reason, of course, is the seemingly never-ending deadlines. But consider: Would you do all the course work you're doing—and realize the education you're getting—if you *didn't* have deadlines?

As we saw under the "T" (for "has Target dates") in SMART goals, deadlines are as essential to goal setting in business as they are to your college career. Because the whole purpose of planning and goals is to deliver to a client specified results within a specified period of time, deadlines become a great motivator, both for you and for the people working for you.

It's possible, of course, to let deadlines mislead you into focusing too much on immediate results and thereby ignore overall planning—just as students will focus too much on preparing for a test in one course while neglecting others. In general, however, deadlines can help you keep your eye on the "big picture" while simultaneously paying attention to the details that will help you realize the big picture. Deadlines can help concentrate the mind, so that you make quick decisions rather than put them off. Deadlines help you ignore extraneous matters (such as cleaning up a messy desk) in favor of focusing on what's important—realizing the goals on time and on budget. Deadlines provide a mechanism for giving ourselves feedback. ●

PRACTICAL ACTION

How to Achieve Your Important Goals: Forget the Endless Possibilities

"I talk to so many people who say they don't know what they should do next," says Penelope Trunk, who has founded four start-ups (the most recent is Quistic, a career-building online learning site). "But actually they just don't have the guts to close off options."[102]

We all know people like this. "They wait years before declaring a major," says another writer, "date someone for years before getting married, favor stores with a guaranteed return policy," and so on.[103] But noncommitment actually leads to *lower* levels of satisfaction, more anxiety, and poorer performance.

"We have a limited amount of willpower," Trunk adds, "and if all our options are open, we have to use our willpower constantly. *We are much better off removing choices and creating routines* that preserve our willpower."

Where's the Money? The natural reluctance to close any door is pointed out by Dan Ariely, a behavioral economist at the Massachusetts Institute of Technology and author of *Predictably Irrational: The Hidden Forces That Shape Our Decisions.*[104] In that book, he describes experiments involving hundreds of MIT students who showed that they could not bear to let go of their options—even though it was bad strategy. The experiments involved playing a computer game in which students had 100 mouse clicks to look for money behind three

doors on the screen and were paid real cash each time they found it. To earn the most money, a student would quickly find out that the best strategy was to check out the three doors and settle on the one with the highest rewards. But when students stayed out of a room, the door would start shrinking and eventually disappear. Researchers found that most students would waste clicks by rushing back to reopen doors, even though they lost money by doing so—and they continued to frantically keep all their doors open even when they were fined for switching.

Fear of Loss? Were the students just trying to "keep their options open"? Ariely doesn't think so. The real motivation, he suggests, is fear of loss. "Closing a door on an option is experienced as a loss, and people are willing to pay a price to avoid the emotion of loss," he says.[105]

YOUR CALL

Obviously, this lesson has some practical payoffs for all of us who are overscheduled and overworked and need all the help we can get to stay focused on our important goals. Are you presently considering adding a class, switching majors, or pursuing another career? Are you wondering whether to continue a personal relationship that no longer benefits you? What would be the advantages of—just saying no?

5.5 The Planning/Control Cycle

How does the planning/control cycle help keep a manager's plans headed in the right direction?

THE BIG PICTURE

The four-step planning/control cycle helps you keep in control, to make sure you're headed in the right direction.

Once you've made plans, how do you stay in control to make sure you're headed in the right direction? Actually, there is a continuous feedback loop known as the planning/control cycle. (The "organizing" and "leading" steps within the Planning—Organizing—Leading—Controlling sequence are implied here.) **The planning/control cycle has two planning steps (1 and 2) and two control steps (3 and 4), as follows: (1) Make the plan. (2) Carry out the plan. (3) Control the direction by comparing results with the plan. (4) Control the direction by taking corrective action in two ways—namely (a) by correcting deviations in the plan being carried out or (b) by improving future plans.** *(See Figure 5.6.)* (We will see this model echoed later in Chapter 16 in the discussion of the Plan-Do-Check-Act cycle.)

FIGURE 5.6

The planning/control cycle

This describes a constant feedback loop designed to ensure plans stay headed in the right direction.

Source: From Robert Kreitner, Management, 8th edition, copyright © 2001 South-Western, a part of Cengage Learning, Inc. Reproduced with permission. www.cengage.com/permissions.

The Two Planning Steps

The Two Control Steps

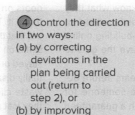

① Make the plan → ② Carry out the plan

④ Control the direction in two ways:
(a) by correcting deviations in the plan being carried out (return to step 2), or
(b) by improving future plans (go to step 1 to start over)

③ Control the direction by comparing the results with the plan

The planning/control cycle loop exists for each level of planning—strategic, tactical, and operational. The corrective action in step 4 of the cycle (a) can get a project back on track before it's too late or (b) if it's too late, can provide data for improving future plans. ●

EXAMPLE

The Planning/Control Cycle: Developing the Apple Watch

Apple Inc., maker of the iPhone, iPod, and iPad, has been *Fortune's* No. 1 Most Admired Company nine years in a row, 2008–2016. In 2008, it was also ranked No. 1 among Fortune 500 companies for total return to shareholders over the preceding 10 years. In 2015, consulting company Interbrand ranked Apple as the world's most valuable brand (followed by Google, Coca-Cola, and Microsoft).[106] The company got there by upending three categories of consumer electronics by transforming them from ordinary appliances to instruments of popular culture: MP3 players (before the iPod), smartphones (before the iPhone), and tablets (before the iPad). For its next act, it chose a watch.[107]

An important part of Apple's strategy is the idea of the "ecosystem," or suite of products. "The bet is that once you get users on one part of the ecosystem, they will be friendly to the remainder of the Apple ecosystem," explains Wharton management professor David Hsu.[108] The Apple Watch was developed as part of this strategy. Let's see how the planning/control cycle figures in how well the plan worked.

Step 1: The Plan. Apple's core product lines, which appear in multiyear cycles, are iPhones and iPads. The Apple Watch was planned for the "Other Products" category (which includes the Apple TV and iPod) to "provide much-needed organic growth for Apple until its next massive revenue opportunity," according to one financial analyst.[109] Other companies (FitBit, Xiaomi, Garmin, Samsung) had already been producing wrist-wearable watches and fitness trackers, but Apple's strategy was to tie the Apple Watch to the Apple ecosystem—namely, the user's iPhone, which would be used for processing and communications.[110] But unlike the invasive phone, the watch would serve up only important information. It would be designed to solve, by technology, the very problem created by technology—namely, overwhelming the user with distracting texts, e-mails, and other alerts.

Step 2: Carrying Out the Plan. In developing the watch, the development team looked at what problems it might solve, what new ways people might interact with the device. As a result, everything that worked on a smartphone was completely rethought and re-engineered, from software to display to messages to voice control to sounds and taps to the 5 to 10 seconds allowed for interaction time—with "maniacal attention to detail," according to *Wired* magazine writer David Pierce.[111]

Finally, the Apple team also decided to offer the Watch in three options: the $349 Sport, the $599 Watch, and—as a significant fashion statement—the gold-encased $17,000 Edition. "Options were central to the plan from the beginning," says Pierce, with "two sizes, three tiers, easily interchangeable straps, and tons of watch faces and . . . digital add-ons that show relevant information like the weather and your activity level to make your Watch uniquely yours."

Step 3: Comparing Results. The Watch began shipping on April 24, 2015. Apple's marketing challenge was to convince users overwhelmed by a flood of gadgets that the device was worth bringing into their lives—that it could help solve the problems of technology constantly diverting our attention from family and friends by sorting the inessential from the essential.

New York Times reporter Michael D. Shear, for one, loved the device. After wearing it for eight months, he said that the Apple Watch felt like the future and that it had changed the way he communicated via e-mail and text messages. "I direct all the most important messages to my watch, which alerts me with a subtle tap on my wrist or a soft ding. I ignore most after a quick glance. . . . Many get a quick 'O.K.' or 'Sounds good.' I pull out my phone only for the ones I need to respond to at length."[112]

He also used the Watch to screen phone calls, handle personal scheduling, check the weather, monitor deliveries and restaurant reservations, and use the Apple Pay feature to wave the watch next to the cash register in many restaurants and retail stores. "I'm convinced," he said, "that people will eventually view a smartwatch as an essential purchase."

As for sales, Apple shipped 11.6 million Watches in the nine months it was available in 2015, according to research firm IDC, making Apple the third-largest wearable maker that year (after Fitbit and Xiaomi).[113]

Apple Watch. New product in the Apple ecosystem. © Lars Hagberg/Alamy

Step 4: Taking Corrective Action. The Apple Watch will probably never produce the kind of high revenues that the iPhone does. Even so, the Watch claimed over *half* the 2015 smartwatch market in 2015—in less than a year of sales.[114] So what kind of corrective action should the company take?

In March 2016, Apple dropped the price of the Sports model from $349 to $299—"smart business if you make money off selling an interconnected ecosystem of devices and accessories, as indeed Apple does," says one analyst. For instance, it opens up "a whole new spectrum of accessories—Watch bands—that the company can charge premium prices for."[115] Indeed, Apple has already shown signs that it wants to use the Watch to enter into the market for luxury goods.[116] The next version of the Watch could also be thinner and faster, include standalone wireless capability, and feature health and medical research apps that can be used with the iPhone to help users actively manage their own medical conditions such as Parkinson's disease.[117]

YOUR CALL

What other kinds of products do you think Apple should get involved with? (What about an Apple Car? Actually, it's planning one.) What kind of planning/control cycle issues would it raise?

action plan 155

business model 144

business plan 144

cascading goals 162

goal 155

long-term goals 155

management by objectives (MBO) 160

means-end chain 155

mission 151

mission statement 151

objective 153

operating plan 155

operational goals 155

operational planning 154

plan 144

planning 144

planning/control cycle 164

policy 157

procedure 157

program 157

project 157

rule 157

short-term goals 155

single-use plans 157

SMART goal 158

standing plans 157

strategic goals 155

strategic management 145

strategic planning 153

strategy 144

tactical goals 155

tactical planning 154

values statement 152

vision 151

vision statement 151

VRIO 148

Key Points

5.1 Planning and Strategy

- Planning is defined as setting goals and deciding how to achieve them. It is also defined as coping with uncertainty by formulating future courses of action to achieve specified results.

- A plan is a document that outlines how goals are going to be met. One important type of plan is a business plan, a document that outlines a proposed firm's goals, the strategy for achieving them, and the standards for measuring success. The business plan describes the business model, which outlines the need the firm will fill, the operations of the business, its components and functions, as well as the expected revenues and expenses.

- A strategy, or strategic plant, sets the long-term goals and direction for an organization.

- Strategic management is a process that involves managers from all parts of the organization in the formulation and implementation of strategies and strategic goals.

- An organization should adopt planning and strategic management for three reasons: They can (1) provide direction and momentum, (2) encourage new ideas, and above all (3) develop a sustainable competitive advantage.

- VRIO is a framework for analyzing a resource or capability to determine its competitive strategic potential by answering four questions about its Value, Rarity, Imitability, and Organization.

5.2 Fundamentals of Planning

- An organization's reason for being is expressed in a mission statement.

- A vision is a long-term goal describing "what" an organization wants to become. It is a clear sense of the future and the actions needed to get there.

- A vision statement expresses what the organization should become, where it wants to go strategically.

- Both mission and vision should express the organization's values. A values statement, or core values statement, expresses what the company stands for, its core priorities, the values its employees embody, and what its products contribute to the world.

- From these are derived strategic planning, then tactical planning, then operational planning. In strategic planning, managers determine what the organization's long-term goals should be for the next 1–5 years with the resources they expect to have available. In tactical planning, managers determine what contributions their work units can make with their given resources during the next 6–24 months. In operational planning, they determine how to accomplish specific tasks with available resources within the next 1–52 weeks.

5.3 Goals and Plans

- Whatever its type, the purpose of planning is to set a goal and then formulate an action plan.

- Goals are of two types: long-term and short-term.

- Long-term goals are generally referred to as strategic goals. They tend to span one to five years and focus on achieving the strategies identified in a company's strategic plan.

- Short-term goals are sometimes referred to as tactical goals, operational goals, or just plain goals. They generally span 12 months and are connected to strategic goals in a hierarchy known as a means-end chain.

- A means-end chain shows how goals are connected or linked across an organization. The accomplishment of low-level goals is the means leading to the accomplishment of high-level goals or ends.

- Strategic goals are set by and for top management and focus on objectives for the organization as a whole. Tactical goals are set by and for middle managers and focus on the actions needed to achieve strategic goals. Operational goals are set by and for first-line managers and are concerned with short-term matters associated with realizing tactical goals.
- An operating plan is a plan that breaks long-term output into short-term targets or goals. Operational plans turn strategic plans into actionable short-term goals and action plans.
- An action plan defines the course of action needed to achieve the stated goal. Whether the goal is long-term or short-term, action plans outline the tactics that will be used to achieve the goal. Each tactic also contains a projected date for completing the desired activities.
- The goal should be followed by an action plan, which defines the course of action needed to achieve the stated goal. The operating plan, which is typically designed for a one-year period, defines how you will conduct your business based on the action plan; it identifies clear targets such as revenues, cash flow, and market share.
- Plans may be either standing plans, developed for activities that occur repeatedly over a period of time, or single-use plans, developed for activities that are not likely to be repeated in the future.
- There are three types of standing plans: (1) A policy is a standing plan that outlines the general response to a designated problem or situation. (2) A procedure outlines the response to particular problems or circumstances. (3) A rule designates specific required action.
- There are two types of single-use plans: (1) A program encompasses a range of projects or activities. (2) A project is a single-use plan of less scope and complexity.

5.4 Promoting Consistencies in Goals: SMART Goals, Management by Objectives, and Goal Cascading

- The five characteristics of a good goal are represented by the acronym SMART. A SMART goal is one that is Specific, Measurable, Attainable, Results oriented, and has Target dates.
- Management by objectives (MBO) is a four-step process in which (1) managers and employees jointly set objectives for the employee, (2) managers develop action plans, (3) managers and employees periodically review the employee's performance, and (4) the manager makes a performance appraisal and rewards the employee according to results. The purpose of MBO is to motivate rather than to control subordinates.
- For MBO to be successful three things have to happen. (1) The commitment of top management is essential. (2) The goals must be applied organizationwide. (3) Goals must cascade—be linked consistently down through the organization. Cascading goals is the process of ensuring that the strategic goals set at the top level align, or "cascade," downward with more specific short-term goals at lower levels within an organization, including employees' objectives and activities.
- Deadlines are essential to planning because they become great motivators both for the manager and for subordinates.

5.5 The Planning/Control Cycle

- Once plans are made, managers must stay in control using the planning/control cycle, which has two planning steps (1 and 2) and two control steps (3 and 4), as follows: (1) Make the plan. (2) Carry out the plan. (3) Control the direction by comparing results with the plan. (4) Control the direction by taking corrective action in two ways—namely, (a) by correcting deviations in the plan being carried out or (b) by improving future plans.

Understanding the Chapter: What Do I Know?

1. What are planning, strategy, and strategic management?
2. Why are they important?
3. What is the difference between a mission and a vision, a mission statement and a vision statement?
4. What are three types of planning?
5. What are two types of goals?
6. What are different kinds of plans?
7. What are SMART goals?
8. What is management by objectives?
9. What three things have to happen for MBO to be successful?
10. Explain the planning/control cycle.

The McCloskeys' Plan to Implement Sustainable Dairy Farming While Providing Healthier Products

Dr. Mike McCloskey and his wife, Sue, grew a successful veterinarian office in San Diego during the 1980s. However, they had bigger dreams. Mike wanted to implement some of the ideas he learned in school to improve farming practices in the U.S. So the couple and a partner started a farm with 250 cows. This led to a move in 1990 to New Mexico to pursue full-time dairy farming.

Dissatisfied with the co-op that was selling their milk, the McCloskeys' entrepreneurial spirit drove them to start their own co-op, Select Milk Products. Mike was the CEO. Select is composed of 92 dairies, now the sixth-largest dairy co-op in the U.S., and produces "6 billion pounds of raw milk a year and reaping nearly $2 billion in annual revenue."

The initial success of Select Milk resulted in the McCloskeys' move to Indiana and the birth of Fair Oaks Farms.

Fair Oaks consists of 12 family-run dairies and 36,000 cows. This is a very large dairy farm—only 1% of U.S. dairy farms have more than 2,500 cows. Big farms like this can foster negative stereotypes due to their impact on the environment. According to a *Fortune* reporter, "Agriculture is a major contributor to climate change, accounting for about 9% of U.S. greenhouse gas emissions, and the farming sector hasn't succeeded in reducing its output as much as the transportation and energy industries have. . . . In the production and consumption of a gallon of milk, the equivalent of 17.6 pounds of carbon dioxide is emitted."[118] The McCloskeys wanted to operate a farm that improved on these results.

Fair Oaks started with Mike's mission. He articulated it like this: "We are committed to educating the public about modern farming efforts, but also to protecting the environment, caring for our animals and ensuring the highest quality products possible."[119] Of course he wanted to do this while making a profit.

In terms of protecting the environment, Mike has a vision "to have a zero-carbon-footprint dairy," and he believes that Fair Oaks can get there. Others think it's impossible. Undeterred, Mike, Sue, and his partners created a detailed plan to enact this vision.

The plan began with a consideration of how the farm could convert 430,000 gallons of daily manure into a sustainable asset. It first had to be collected, which required special accommodations for the animals. The bedding areas were designed so that cows would "defecate and urinate only in alleyways on either side of their bedding. The setup keeps the cows' beds (and their udders) clean and makes it easier for workers to gather the manure three times a day while the cows are milked. The manure is separated from sand and dirt and deposited into the farms' anaerobic digesters." A 21-day process then is used to break down the manure into "compost-like material while releasing biogas, which is captured in pipes." Fifty percent of this gas, which is 60% methane, is used to generate the electricity used to run the farm.[120]

The next part of the plan focused on what to do with the remaining gas generated from the process of manure decomposition. Fair Oaks could not sell it to the power grid because it was too expensive. The company then decided to turn the gas into 99% methane and sell it as fuel. This worked until the price of natural-gas began to fall in 2008.

After considering other alternatives, the company to decide to use the gas in their own operations. The McCloskeys then set out to find milk trucks that would run on compressed natural gas (CNG). The initial set of trucks did not work very well because they only had 9-liter engines. Fortunately, Cummins developed a 12-liter engine that could handle the load. Today, the company possesses a fleet of 42 trucks that operate 24/7 on its CNG fuel. The trucks average about 270,000 miles a year.

This process was not easy or cheap. Fair Oaks spent over $30 million over a period of 10 years to arrive at its current level of performance. Today, there are about 200 dairy farms using the technology developed by the McCloskeys. Still, Mike wants to find a way to offer a scaled down version of the technology that will be affordable to smaller farms.

Another aspect of Mike's mission involved improving the image of big farming to the public. To accomplish this, Fair Oaks opened its operations to the public. The company allows facility tours to the public, which gives people a chance to reconnect with nature and to learn how milk originates. Because Mike wants total transparency, the tour shows "visitors everything from the cow pens designed to encourage the cows to relax, to the innovative rotating milking parlor that also promotes cow sociability, and the Fair Oaks–developed processes that turn manure into fuel for their milk-hauling trucks."

The McCloskeys have other goals in mind for the future. Mike wants to "add a hotel, convention center, inflatable sports dome, fruit picking, beehives, eggs, goats and sheep to the 35,000-acre cow and pig farm. In addition, shoppers seeking farm-fresh milk and a variety of cheeses soon may be able to purchase them at Fair Oaks Farms retail locations throughout Northwest Indiana."[121]

A final aspect of Fair Oaks's mission involved the production of high-quality products. While the company has been doing this since its inception, the McCloskeys decided to form a new company to expand this focus. As such, Select Milk recently partnered with Coca-Cola to form Fairlife LLC. The company developed "a lactose-free mild drink with less sugar, more protein and more calcium." The product is called fairlife ultra-filtered milk. "The milk is created through a method called ultra-filtration—a process invented by Indiana's own Mike and Sue McCloskey, owners of Fair Oaks."[122] The product will be distributed via Coca-Cola's Minute Maid division.

FOR DISCUSSION

1. Which of the fundamentals of planning did the McCloskeys effectively execute? Explain your rationale.

2. Does Fair Oaks focus more on long or short-term goals? Explain your rationale.

3. State two SMART goals that the McCloskeys might establish for Fair Oaks or Fairlife.

4. Using Figure 5.6, describe what executives at Fairlife can do to increase the chances of fairlife ultra-filtered milk being a successful product?

5. What did you learn about planning based on this case? Explain.

Legal/Ethical Challenge

Do You Think It's Ethical for Companies to Move Their Headquarters to Another Country to Save Taxes?

Tax planning is an important aspect of a firm's planning process. As you might expect, companies would prefer to reduce their tax payments. This is a big issue in the U.S. because our corporate income tax rate is 35%. This is the highest rate in the developed world.

To reduce taxes, "51 U.S. companies have reincorporated in low-tax countries since 1982." These moves or mergers, such as the recent one between John Controls and Tyco, are called inversions. "A lot of drug companies are doing it, and low-tax Ireland is a popular home." Johnson Controls, for example, will move its headquarters from Milwaukee to Cork, Ireland.

Although the U.S. government has tried to stop inversions, they continue to occur. "Most companies achieve inversion by acquiring a foreign company at least 25 percent their size." This is how Minneapolis-based Medtronic became an Irish company and Burger King became Canadian.[123]

The inversion between Johnson Controls and Tyco will save the combined entity $150 million, according to *The New York Times*. Alex Molinaroli, chairman and CEO of Johnson Controls, told the *Times* that "the real impetus of the deal was the ability to better serve customers and share technological advances."

Tyco is not new to the tax avoidance game. The company did an inversion in 1997 when it acquired ADT Ltd. and moved its headquarters to Bermuda. From there the company moved to Switzerland, and then finally to Cork, Ireland.[124]

SOLVING THE CHALLENGE

If you were a member of Congress, what would you do about the issue of inversions?

1. I would put a stop to them. These companies are clearly trying to avoid paying taxes and this is not right. Corporations operating in the U.S. should pay U.S. taxes.

2. What's wrong with saving taxes? I applaud companies that take advantage of this tax loophole.

3. Rather than trying to directly outlaw inversions, change the tax code so that companies are penalized for engaging in them.

4. Invent other options.

6

Strategic Management
How Exceptional Managers Realize a Grand Design

Being a Successful Manager: Avoid Fads, Know Your Own Core Values

"How can we build organizations that are as nimble as change itself—not only operationally, but strategically?" asks famed management professor Gary Hamel.[1]

One way is to learn which management tools work and which don't. Every year since 1993, business consulting firm Bain & Company surveys the use of and satisfaction with the most popular management tools. The 2015 survey, which polled 13,000 respondents from more than 70 countries, found that one of the most widely used management tools was one that has been around for years—namely, strategic planning, thought to be effective by about 50% of the North American senior managers surveyed. Strategic planning is concerned with developing a comprehensive program for long-term success. Mission and vision statements, discussed in Chapter 5, also continued to be popular, favored by about 45%.[2] Mission statements describe the organization's purpose and vision statements its intended long-term goal. All of these should reflect the organization's *core values,* as we'll describe.

Are there lessons that can apply to you personally and that can help you be more successful in your career? Consider the following.

Lesson 1—Learn to Avoid Management Fads

Unfortunately, the way many people deal with the uncertainty of change is by succumbing to fads, or short-lived enthusiasms, suggests University of Delaware sociologist Joel Best, author of *Flavor of the Month: Why Smart People Fall for Fads.*[3] A fad, he says, "is seen as the way of the future, a genuine innovation that will help solve a big problem. . . . A lot of the attraction of a fad is that if you embrace it early, then you feel that you're ahead of other people, that you're hipper and maybe

smarter than they are."[4] (Two of the world's worst management fads, in the opinion of one *Inc.* magazine writer, are "management by consensus" and "business process reengineering"—you can look these up.)[5]

Lesson 2—Define Your Own Core Values

One way to know how to avoid faddish ideas is to understand your own core values, and this knowledge will help you create or accept the core values of your company. To understand your own values, says entrepreneur and author Keven Daum, you need, first, to articulate them clearly in writing and, second, to test them through daily decision making.[6] Grab a notebook, find a quiet space, and take an hour to do the following, suggests Daum: (1) Write down your three greatest accomplishments and your three greatest moments of efficiency; then see if you can identify common rules or themes. (2) Then write down the opposite—your three greatest failures, three greatest moments of inefficiency, and any common rules or themes. (3) Based on these rules/themes, write four brief pieces of advice to yourself. (4) Sharpen this advice into a brief few words—your core values. (5) Test the values by thinking of a situation where a value hurts rather than helps you.

For Discussion Earlier we described the importance of practicing *evidence-based management*, with managers "seeing the truth as a moving target, always facing the hard facts, avoiding falling prey to half-truths, and being willing to admit when they're wrong and change their ways."[7] Do you think you would have this mind-set when thinking about the overall direction of your organization or work unit?

FORECAST What's Ahead in This Chapter

We describe strategic positioning and the principles underlying it and then consider the five steps in the strategic-management process: (1) establishing mission, vision, and values statements, (2) assessing the current reality, (3) formulating the grand strategy, (4) implementing the strategy, and (5) maintaining strategy control. In assessing current reality, we describe competitive intelligence and the tools of SWOT analysis, forecasting, benchmarking, and Porter's model for industry analysis. In formulating the grand strategy, we describe Porter's four competitive strategies, single-product versus diversification strategies, blue ocean strategy, and the BCG matrix. Under implementation and strategic control, we discuss the importance of execution.

6.1   What Is Effective Strategy?

What is strategic positioning, and what are the three principles underlying it?

THE BIG PICTURE

Strategic positioning attempts to achieve sustainable competitive advantage by preserving what is distinctive about a company. It is based on the principles that strategy is the creation of a unique and valuable position, requires trade-offs in competing, and involves creating a "fit" among activities.

Strategy guru. Harvard Business School professor Michael Porter suggests that every company is subject to five forces: its current competitors, possible new competitors, the threat of substitutes for its products or services, the bargaining power of its suppliers, and the bargaining power of its customers. Operating within that five-forces framework, a company must choose the right strategy—or be beaten by competitors. Do you think there are other forces that are equally important in forming strategy? © Bloomberg/Getty Images

Harvard Business School professor **Michael Porter** "is the single most important strategist working today, and maybe of all time," raved Kevin Coyne of consulting firm McKinsey & Co.[8] He is "the most famous and influential business professor who has ever lived," says *Fortune* writer Geoffrey Colvin. "He is widely and rightly regarded as the all-time greatest strategy guru."[9]

Is this high praise deserved? Certainly Porter's status as a leading authority on competitive strategy is unchallenged. The Strategic Management Society, for instance, voted Porter the most influential living strategist. We refer to him repeatedly in this chapter.

Strategic Positioning and Its Principles

According to Porter, **strategic positioning** attempts to achieve sustainable competitive advantage by preserving what is distinctive about a company. "It means," he says, "performing *different* activities from rivals, or performing *similar* activities in different ways."[10]

Three key principles underlie strategic positioning.[11]

1. Strategy Is the Creation of a Unique and Valuable Position   Strategic position emerges from three sources:

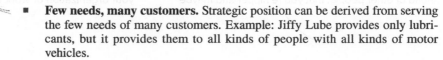

- **Few needs, many customers.** Strategic position can be derived from serving the few needs of many customers. Example: Jiffy Lube provides only lubricants, but it provides them to all kinds of people with all kinds of motor vehicles.

- **Broad needs, few customers.** A strategic position may be based on serving the broad needs of just a few customers. Example: Wealth management and investment advisory firm Bessemer Trust focuses exclusively on high–net worth clients.

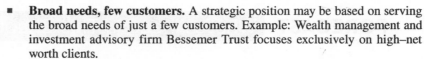

- **Broad needs, many customers.** Strategy may be oriented toward serving the broad needs of many customers. Example: National movie theater operator Carmike Cinemas operates only in cities with populations of fewer than 200,000 people.

2. Strategy Requires Trade-offs in Competing   As a glance at the preceding choices shows, some strategies are incompatible. Thus, a company has to choose not only what strategy to follow but what strategy *not* to follow. Example: Neutrogena soap, points out Porter, is positioned more as a medicinal product than as a cleansing agent. In achieving this narrow positioning, the company gives up sales based on deodorizing, gives up large volume, and accordingly gives up some manufacturing efficiencies.

3. Strategy Involves Creating a "Fit" among Activities

"Fit" has to do with the ways a company's activities interact and reinforce one another. Example: A mutual fund such as Vanguard Group follows a low-cost strategy and aligns all its activities accordingly, distributing funds directly to consumers and minimizing portfolio turnover. However, when the short-lived (1993–1995) Continental Lite airline tried to match some but not all of Southwest Airlines's activities, it was not successful because it didn't apply Southwest's entire interlocking system.

Does Strategic Management Work for Small as Well as Large Firms?

You would expect that a large organization would benefit from strategic management and planning, but what about smaller companies? One analysis found companies with fewer than 100 employees could benefit as well, if only slightly. Even so, the researchers concluded, "it may be that the small improvement in performance is not worth the effort involved in strategic planning unless a firm is in a very competitive industry where small differences in performance may affect the firm's survival potential."[12] •

EXAMPLE

Comparing Strategies: Big-Company "Make the Consumer a Captive" versus Small-Firm "Offer Personal Connections"

Big companies—especially big-tech companies such as Amazon, Google, or Apple—"are no longer content simply to enhance part of your life," says one report. "The new strategy is to build a device, sell it to consumers, and then sell them the content to play on it. And maybe some ads too."[13]

Big-Company Ways. That is, the idea is to get consumers tied not just to a brand or device or platform but to make them captive of the company's system of products and services, and to get them connected "as tightly as possible so they and their content are locked into one system," says analyst Michael Gartenberg.[14] Thus, Amazon, for example, sells the Kindle e-book readers at a low price so that it can then sell e-books. "Amazon is in a race to embed itself into the fabric of world-wide commerce in a way that would make it indispensable to everyone's shopping habits," says one columnist, "and to do so before its rivals wise up."[15] Amazon's strategy of "free shipping" for its products (actually consumers pay $99 a year for two-day shipping, but then many of them begin to think of it as "free") is another giant competitive advantage big online companies have over small retailers.[16]

Small-Company Ways. "I don't feel they behave in a way that I want to support with my consumer dollars," says Chicago professor Harold Pollack about big Internet retailers like Amazon.[17] So instead, Pollack started buying from small online retailers. Their prices are often higher, but he says he now has a clear conscience.

Whereas the strategy of big e-commerce companies is to try to tightly connect consumers with discounted prices, free shipping, and easy-to-use apps, the strategy of small retailers—like Hello Hello Books in Maine—is to discourage price comparisons (as in creating "buy it where you try it" campaigns or refusing to carry popular items carried by big retailers), offer freebies, and attempt to establish a personal or emotional connection with customers. They also try to exploit the sympathies of shoppers to "support the little guy," as Pollack is doing.

YOUR CALL

Considering the proliferation of price comparison sites (Pricegrabber.com, Bizrate.com, FreePriceAlerts.com) that will usually direct consumers to big e-commerce retailers, do you think low prices will always win in the end? Is there any strategy a small retailer can take to maintain an advantage?

6.2   The Strategic-Management Process

What's the five-step recipe for the strategic-management process?

THE BIG PICTURE

The strategic-management process has five steps: Establish the mission, vision and values statements. Assess the current reality. Formulate the grand strategy. Implement the strategy. Maintain strategic control. All the steps may be affected by feedback that enables the taking of constructive action.

When is a good time to begin the strategic-management process? Often it's touched off by some crisis.

As we'll see later in the chapter, in 2009 and 2010 Toyota Motor encountered severe quality problems involving what seemed to be uncontrollable acceleration in its automobiles. President Akio Toyoda concluded that these problems were partly due to the company's "excessive focus on market share and profits," requiring that the company reorient its strategy toward quality and innovation.[18] For Edward Lampert, who in 2005 merged Kmart and Sears into megaretailer Sears Holdings, the pressure was felt in years of underperforming returns despite cost cutting and store closures.[19]

EXAMPLE   When the Strategic-Management Process Fails: Not Having an Ecosystem, or "Wide-Lens" Perspective

Most Fortune 500 companies averaged profit margins of around 5% the past 60 years. Imagine a company whose profit margin was an awesome 80%—for years and years.

No, we're not talking about Apple, whose profit margin in 2015 was a spectacular 39.7%. We are referring to one of the biggest brands ever . . . Kodak.

The Curse of Being Profitable. Founded in 1888, the once-great film company filed for bankruptcy in early 2012, supposedly blindsided by the digital revolution and foreign competition.[20] Before then, however, it dominated the world of film and popular photography, with film in particular driving the company's expansion. "It is very hard," said Kodak's director of research in those heady days, "to find anything [with profit margins] like color photography that is legal."[21]

For a long time, many observers believed that film's profitability contributed to Kodak's doom—that managers feared introducing digital technologies would disrupt the company's film-related earnings.[22] Indeed, in 1975, the company invented the digital camera—and then supposedly stuck it in a safe lest it destroy its lucrative film business. "By the time Kodak was ready to unleash its digital prowess," says one report, "everyone from Canon to Sony was selling their own digital cameras."[23]

The conventional story is that myopic managers continued to push forward with Kodak's existing business model—selling film—rather than look at what the market wanted. But the reality is not so simple.

The Real Story: Kodak Goes Digital, but Still Loses Out. "Although Kodak had a slow start," says Dartmouth strategy professor Ron Adner, "it did, in fact, manage a miraculous, successful digital transformation," churning out some critical innovations.[24] Indeed, by 2005 it ranked No. 1 in U.S. digital-camera sales, and by 2010 it was No. 4 in the inkjet-printer market. So why did it fail?

"Kodak was so focused on its own technology transition," says Adner, "that it missed the fact that the improvements in the very same components that gave rise to digital printing would, with further progress, undermine its very basis." Adner is referring to three components critical to digital-imaging systems: charge-coupled devices, or CCDs (which determine resolution in digital cameras); flash memory (which determines how many photos can be stored on a flash card); and LCD screens (which govern the quality of image previews).

For a while these technologies helped to accelerate the sales of both digital cameras and home photo printers. But other companies installed CCDs in mobile phones for taking pictures, undercutting the market for digital cameras. As flash-memory capacity improved so that thousands of pictures could be stored and as LCD screen resolution improved, the effect was to cause consumers to want to view most photos on their phones, tablets, and computers—circumventing Kodak's goal of getting users to buy digital printers, photo paper, and printer inks to print photos on paper.

An Ecosystem Viewpoint. Central to Kodak's failure is the concept of *business ecosystem*—the economic community of interacting organizations and individuals—including suppliers, lead producers, and other stakeholders—over which Kodak presided in its digital-camera development. The blind spot in Kodak's strategy, Adner believes, was that the company was so focused on trying to develop a new way of printing photos on paper that it failed to see how progress by other companies "in the *other* components of its ecosystem would eliminate the value of the end goal."

Today, he concludes, it's necessary to take an ecosystem, or wide-lens, viewpoint in which you are able to distinguish between two situations: those in which value in a product is created by your own ability and those in which value is affected by the efforts of other firms and technologies.

YOUR CALL

Do you think automobile companies ought to stick with what they know and focus principally on building better cars for transporting people? What do you think of GM, Ford, and others setting up shop in Silicon Valley, the technology capital of California? What are their concerns?

The Five Steps of the Strategic-Management Process

The strategic-management process has five steps, plus a feedback loop, as shown below. *(See Figure 6.1.)* Let's consider these five steps.

FIGURE 6.1   The strategic-management process
The process has five steps.

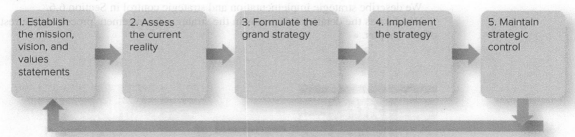

Feedback: Revise actions, if necessary, based on feedback

Step 1: Establish the Mission, Vision, and Values Statements   We discussed mission, vision, and values statements in Chapter 5 and explain them further in the next section. The *mission statement,* you'll recall, expresses the organization's purpose or reason for being. The *vision statement* states what the organization wants to become, where it wants to go strategically. The *values statement* describes what the organization stands for, its core priorities, the values its employees embody, and what its products contribute to the world.

Step 2: Assess the Current Reality   The second step is to do a **current reality assessment,** or *organizational assessment,* to look at where the organization stands and see what is working and what could be different so as to maximize efficiency and effectiveness in achieving the organization's mission. Among the tools for assessing the current reality are SWOT analysis, forecasting, benchmarking, and Porter's model for industry analysis, all of which we discuss in Section 6.4.

Step 3: Formulate the Grand Strategy   The next step is to translate the broad mission and vision statements into a **grand strategy,** which, after the assessment of the current reality, explains how the organization's mission is to be accomplished. Three common grand strategies are growth, stability, and defensive, as we'll describe.

Strategy formulation is the process of choosing among different strategies and altering them to best fit the organization's needs. Formulating strategy is a time-consuming process both because it is important and because the strategy must be translated into more specific *strategic plans,* which determine what the organization's long-term goals should be for the next one to five years.

In Section 6.5, we consider the three common grand strategies (growth, stability, and defensive), Porter's four competitive strategies, single-product strategy versus diversification strategy, blue ocean strategy, and the BCG matrix.

Step 4: Implement the Strategy

Putting strategic plans into effect is strategy implementation. Strategic planning isn't effective, of course, unless it can be translated into lower-level plans. This means that top managers need to check on possible roadblocks within the organization's structure and culture and see if the right people and control systems are available to execute the plans.[25] We describe strategic control in Section 6.6.

Step 5: Maintain Strategic Control: The Feedback Loop

Strategic control consists of monitoring the execution of strategy and making adjustments, if necessary. To keep strategic plans on track, managers need control systems to monitor progress and take corrective action—early and rapidly—when things start to go awry. Corrective action constitutes a feedback loop in which a problem requires that managers return to an earlier step to rethink policies, redo budgets, or revise personnel arrangements.

We describe strategic implementation and strategic control in Section 6.6.

We discuss the details of the steps in the strategic-management process in the rest of this chapter. ●

A public library's new strategy. As Americans spend more time online, public libraries are having to find new strategies for remaining relevant. After the Skokie Public Library near Chicago put its reference collection online, it turned the newly freed-up space into a "fully functioning, Wi-Fi equipped office suite, capable of accommodating more than 50 people," according to one report. "Users who can't afford their own office space reserve it by the hour."[26] Can you think of other public or nonprofit institutions that need to reinvent themselves because information technology has altered their original purpose? © Hill Street Studios/Getty Images RF

6.3 Establishing the Mission, Vision, and Values Statements

MAJOR QUESTION | **What are the characteristics of good mission, vision, and values statements?**

THE BIG PICTURE

A mission statement should express the organization's purpose or reason for being. A vision statement should be positive and inspiring, and it should stretch the organization and its employees to achieve a desired future state that appears beyond its reach. A values statement should describe what the organization stands for, its core priorities, the values its employees embody, and what its products contribute to the world.

Why am I here? What am I trying to do? What do I want to become?

These are bedrock questions that you should ask about your education. They are also the kind that top managers should ask about their organizations, whether profit or not-for-profit, as expressed in the mission, vision, and values statements.

If you were called on to write these statements, how would you go about it?

Characteristics of a Good Mission Statement

The *mission,* we said, is the organization's purpose or reason for being; it is expressed in a *mission statement.* For example, the mission statement of McGraw-Hill Education, publisher of this book, is as follows:

> To accelerate learning through intuitive, engaging, efficient, and effective experiences—grounded in research.

Characteristics of a Good Vision Statement

An organization's *vision,* its long-term goal of what it wants to become, is expressed in a *vision statement,* which describes its long-term direction and strategic intent. For example, Walt Disney's original vision for Disneyland went in part like this:

> Disneyland will be something of a fair, an exhibition, a playground, a community center, a museum of living facts, and a showplace of beauty and magic. It will be filled with the accomplishments, the joys and hopes of the world we live in. And it will remind us and show us how to make those wonders part of our own lives.[27]

Although a vision statement can be short, it should be positive and inspiring, and it should stretch the organization and its employees to achieve a desired future state that appears beyond its reach. Google's vision, for example, is "to provide access to the world's information in one click."[28] For the nonprofit Smithsonian Institution (19 museums, nine research centers, and a zoo), it is "Shaping the future by preserving our heritage, discovering new knowledge, and sharing our resources with the world."[29]

Characteristics of a Good Values Statement

An organization's values are expressed in a *values statement,* which should describe what the organization stands for, its core priorities, the values its employees embody, and what its products contribute to the world. It's important, says

Family business. Do small, family-owned businesses need a vision statement? If no, why not? How many small business owners with firms of, say, five employees or fewer would you guess have taken the time to compose such a vision? © Ariel Skelley/Blend Images RF

management book writer Patrick Lenioni, that values statements not be *hollow* statements—bland, toothless, dishonest—which can create cynicism among employees and customers. They must be ingrained, inherent, and sacrosanct; "they can never be compromised." "If you're not willing to accept the pain real values incur," he adds, "don't bother going to the trouble of formulating a values statement."[30]

Here is the core values statement ("HEART Principles") of Bright Horizons Family Solutions, which runs more than 900 child care centers: "Honesty. Excellence. Accountability. Respect. Teamwork."[31] Whole Foods Market has a so-called Higher Purpose statement—namely, "With great courage, integrity and love—we embrace our responsibility to co-create a world where each of us, our communities, and our planet can flourish. All the while, celebrating the sheer love and joy of food."[32]

Guidelines for constructing powerful mission, vision, and values statements are shown below. *(See Table 6.1.)* "Visions that have these properties challenge and inspire people in the organization and help align their energies in a common direction," says Burt Nanus of the University of Southern California's School of Business Administration. "They prevent people from being overwhelmed by immediate problems because they help distinguish what is truly important from what is merely interesting."[33] As for values, they "serve as the foundation on which tough company decisions are made," says Chris Moody, vice-president of data strategy at Twitter.[34] •

TABLE 6.1   Mission, Vision, and Values Statements

MISSION STATEMENTS: DOES YOUR COMPANY'S MISSION STATEMENT ANSWER THESE QUESTIONS?

1. Who are our customers?
2. What are our major products or services?
3. In what geographical areas do we compete?
4. What is our basic technology?
5. What is our commitment to economic objectives?
6. What are our basic beliefs, values, aspirations, and philosophical priorities?
7. What are our major strengths and competitive advantages?
8. What are our public responsibilities, and what image do we wish to project?
9. What is our attitude toward our employees?

VISION STATEMENTS: DOES YOUR COMPANY'S VISION STATEMENT ANSWER "YES" TO THESE QUESTIONS?

1. Is it appropriate for the organization and for the times?
2. Does it set standards of excellence and reflect high ideals?
3. Does it clarify purpose and direction?
4. Does it inspire enthusiasm and encourage commitment?
5. Is it well articulated and easily understood?
6. Does it reflect the uniqueness of the organization, its distinctive competence, what it stands for, what it's able to achieve?
7. Is it ambitious?

VALUES STATEMENTS: DOES YOUR COMPANY'S VALUES STATEMENT ANSWER "YES" TO THESE QUESTIONS?

1. Does it express the company's distinctiveness, its view of the world?
2. Is it intended to guide all the organization's actions, including how you treat employees, customers, etc.?
3. Is it tough, serving as the foundation on which difficult company decisions can be made?
4. Will it be unchanging, as valid 100 years from now as it is today?
5. Does it reflect the beliefs of those who truly care about the organization—the founders, CEO, and top executives—rather than represent a consensus of all employees?
6. Are the values expressed in the statement limited (five or so) and easy to remember, so that employees will have them top-of-mind when making decisions?
7. Would you want the organization to continue to hold these values, even if at some point they become a competitive disadvantage?

Sources: F. R. David, "How Companies Define Their Mission," Long Range Planning, February 1989, pp. 90–97; and B. Nanus, Visionary Leadership: Creating a Compelling Sense of Direction for Your Organization (San Francisco: Jossey-Bass, 1992), pp. 28–29; Jim Collins, "Aligning Action and Values," The Forum, June 2000, www.jimcollins.com/article_topics/articles/aligning-action.html (accessed April 23, 2016); P. M. Lencioni, "Make Your Values Mean Something," Harvard Business Review, July 2002, pp. 113–117; and C. Moody, "Startup Culture: Values vs. Vibe," Chrismoody.com, February 15, 2011, http://chrismoody.com/startup-culture (accessed April 23, 2016).

6.4   Assessing the Current Reality

MAJOR QUESTION

What tools can help me describe where the organization stands from a competitive point of view?

THE BIG PICTURE

To develop a grand strategy, you need to gather data and make projections, using the tools of competitive intelligence, SWOT analysis, forecasting, benchmarking, and Porter's model for industry analysis.

The second step in the strategic-management process, *assess the current reality,* looks at where the organization stands internally and externally—to determine what's working and what's not, to see what can be changed so as to increase efficiency and effectiveness in achieving the organization's vision. An assessment helps to create an objective view of everything the organization does: its sources of revenue or funding, its work-flow processes, its organizational structure, client satisfaction, employee turnover, and other matters.[35]

Among the tools for assessing the current reality are *competitive intelligence, SWOT analysis, forecasting, benchmarking,* and *Porter's model for industry analysis.*

Competitive Intelligence

Practicing **competitive intelligence** means gaining information about one's competitors' activities so that you can anticipate their moves and react appropriately. If you are a manager, one of your worst nightmares is that a competitor will surprise you with a service or product—as boutique beers did major brewers and mountain bikes did major bicycle makers—that will revolutionize the market and force you to try to play catch-up. Successful companies make it a point to conduct competitive intelligence.

Competitive intelligence venue. Since 1967, the International Consumer Electronics Show (CES) in Las Vegas has traditionally been a place where blockbuster products were introduced. Recently, however, the hottest gadgets from Apple, Amazon, and Microsoft have been unveiled in other, more exclusive venues. Still, CES remains the world's largest consumer technology convention. © Alex Wong/ Getty Images

Gaining competitive intelligence isn't always easy, but there are several avenues—and, surprisingly, most of them are public sources—including the following:

- **The public prints and advertising.** A product may be worked on in secret for several years, but at some point it becomes subject to announcement—through a press release, advertising piece, news leak, or the like. Much of this is available free through the Internet or by subscription to certain specialized databases, such as Nexus, which contains hundreds of thousands of news stories.

- **Investor information.** Information about new products and services may also be available through the reports filed with the Securities and Exchange Commission and through corporate annual reports.

- **Informal sources.** Want to know the latest in consumer electronics? You would probably go to the annual International Consumer Electronics Show, a major trade show in Las Vegas, when companies roll out their new products.[36] What about cars? New cars are rolled out at the North American International Auto Show in Detroit. Trying to find out what's cutting edge with drones? Go to InterDrone, the International Drone Conference and Exposition, also in Las Vegas, or perhaps to TED, the Technology, Education, Design conference in Vancouver, Canada. At all such events, people also engage in industry-gossip conversation to find out about future directions. Finally, salespeople and marketers, who are out calling on corporate clients, may return with tidbits of information about what competitors are doing.

SWOT Analysis

After competitive intelligence, the next point in establishing a grand strategy is **environmental scanning,** careful monitoring of an organization's internal and external environments to detect early signs of opportunities and threats that may influence the firm's plans. The process for doing such scanning is **SWOT analysis**—also known as a situational analysis—which is a search for the Strengths, Weaknesses, Opportunities, and Threats affecting the organization. A SWOT analysis should provide you with a realistic understanding of your organization in relation to its internal and external environments so you can better formulate strategy in pursuit of its mission. *(See Figure 6.2.)*

FIGURE 6.2   SWOT analysis
SWOT stands for Strengths, Weaknesses, Opportunities, Threats.

INSIDE MATTERS—Analysis of Internal Strengths & Weaknesses

S—Strengths: inside matters
Strengths could be work processes, organization, culture, staff, product quality, production capacity, image, financial resources & requirements, service levels, other internal matters.

W—Weaknesses: inside matters
Weaknesses could be in the same categories as stated for Strengths: work processes, organization, culture, etc.

O—Opportunities: outside matters
Opportunities could be market segment analysis, industry & competition analysis, impact of technology on organization, product analysis, governmental impacts, other external matters.

T—Threats: outside matters
Threats could be in the same categories as stated for Opportunities: market segment analysis, etc.

OUTSIDE MATTERS—Analysis of External Opportunities & Threats

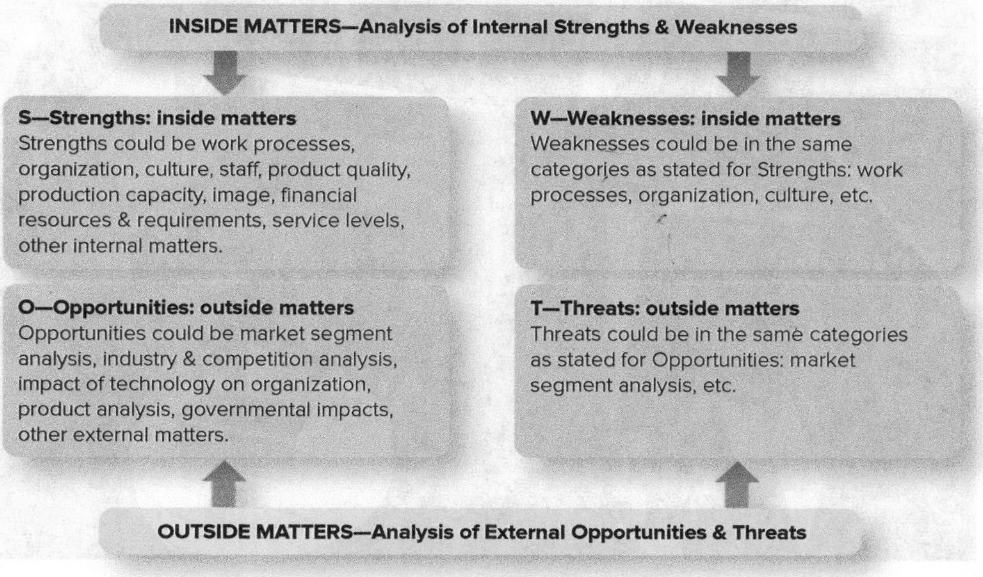

The SWOT analysis is divided into two parts: inside matters and outside matters—that is, an analysis of *internal strengths and weaknesses* and an analysis of *external opportunities and threats*. The following table gives examples of SWOT characteristics that might apply to a college. *(See Table 6.2.)*

TABLE 6.2   SWOT Characteristics That Might Apply to a College

S—STRENGTHS (INTERNAL STRENGTHS)	W—WEAKNESSES (INTERNAL WEAKNESSES)
• Faculty teaching and research abilities • High-ability students • Loyal alumni • Strong interdisciplinary programs	• Limited programs in business • High teaching loads • Insufficient racial diversity • Lack of high-technology infrastructure
O—OPPORTUNITIES (EXTERNAL OPPORTUNITIES)	**T—THREATS (EXTERNAL THREATS)**
• Growth in many local skilled jobs • Many firms give equipment to college • Local minority population increasing • High school students take college classes	• Depressed state and national economy • High school enrollments in decline • Increased competition from other colleges • Funding from all sources at risk

Inside Matters: Analysis of Internal Strengths and Weaknesses   Does your organization have a skilled workforce? a superior reputation? strong financing? These are examples of **organizational strengths**—the skills and capabilities that give the organization special competencies and competitive advantages in executing strategies in pursuit of its vision.

Or does your organization have obsolete technology? outdated facilities? a shaky marketing operation? These are examples of **organizational weaknesses**—the drawbacks that hinder an organization in executing strategies in pursuit of its vision.

Outside Matters: Analysis of External Opportunities and Threats   Is your organization fortunate to have weak rivals? emerging markets? a booming economy? These are instances of **organizational opportunities**—environmental factors that the organization may exploit for competitive advantage.

Alternatively, is your organization having to deal with new regulations? a shortage of resources? substitute products? These are some possible **organizational threats**—environmental factors that hinder an organization's achieving a competitive advantage.

SWOT Analysis: How Would You Analyze Toyota?   **EXAMPLE**

"I fear the pace at which we have grown may have been too quick," said Akio Toyoda, the grandson of Toyota Motor's founder, in 2010 testimony before a U.S. congressional committee looking into sudden acceleration problems. "Priorities became confused, and we were not able to stop, think, and make improvements as much as we were able to before."[37]

Toyota's U.S. sales fell 9% that month because of safety-related recalls of millions of vehicles, and by late 2010 journalists were writing that the company had lost its edge.[38] By the end of 2011, Toyota Motor, formerly the world's largest automaker,

had slipped to third place in production behind General Motors and Volkswagen.

Toyota's new young president, Akio Toyoda, whose motto is "be fast, be flexible," energetically took on the automaker's problems, traveling to the United States to fire up dealers, personally taking charge of the sagging Lexus brand, and redesigning the firm's reporting system and flattening the management hierarchy.[39] In late 2013, profits were up 70%, close to their previous record high, and the company had displaced General Motors as the world's largest automaker; by the following year, net profit was up more than fivefold.[40] In 2015, it sold more than 10 million vehicles worldwide, edging out Volkswagen and GM, and its profit rose 4.7%.[41]

Still, the challenges have kept on coming. If you were a top Toyota manager, what would be the kinds of things you would identify in a SWOT analysis?

The Internal Strengths. Originally the "Toyota Way," as practiced from assembly line to boardroom, stressed the values of continuous improvement ("kaizen") and eliminating waste ("muda"). The Toyota Way, says one report, "mandates planning for the long term; highlighting problems instead of hiding them; encouraging teamwork with colleagues and suppliers; and, perhaps most important, instilling a self-critical culture that fosters continuous and unrelenting improvement."[42] Developed in the 1950s, these precepts later became the basis for such concepts as lean manufacturing and just-in-time inventory management (discussed in Chapter 2).

"At their core," says one analysis, "was an attention to detail and a noble frugality that shunned waste of every kind."[43] Said its top engineer, "Basically, Toyota's growth has been underpinned by QDR [quality, dependability, reliability] that was very high compared with competitors'."[44] QDR has gone a long way to enhance Toyota's image as a strong brand. As of 2016, Toyota continues to lead most other car companies in quality rankings: Its brands appeared in the top 10 J.D. Power 2016 rankings for dependability, with Lexus ranked No. 1 for the fifth consecutive year and Toyota Prius ranked No. 4. Surprisingly, however, the Toyota Scion ranked toward the bottom—clearly a weakness.[45] Still, along with a global supply chain and a strong ability to innovate, Toyota Motor has considerable internal strengths indeed.

Toyota How fast, how flexible? © Hitoshi Yamada/NurPhoto/Getty Images

The Internal Weaknesses. In the 1990s, Toyota launched an effort to become the world's largest automaker, embarking on aggressive overseas expansion and doubling its plants in North America, Asia, and Europe. During this time, the focus on cost reduction intensified to the point that the virtue became a vice. Suppliers were continually pushed to design parts that were 10% cheaper and 10% lighter. Common parts were used in most Toyota models, acquired from outside companies instead of trusted traditional suppliers.[46] Toyota also began to treat its cars like "transportation appliances," causing it to fall behind in design leadership, making buyers feel less of an emotional connection with Toyota products. The company was said to have succumbed to "big-company disease," becoming ponderous and bureaucratic, with every

decision tightly controlled in Japan, to the detriment of its managers in the United States.[47]

Then came the recall years. Suddenly, from 2000 to 2010, driver complaints to the National Highway Traffic and Safety Administration (NHTSA) about "vehicle speed control" issues soared, with 11.7% of faulty vehicle components identified as Toyota's.[48] Next came widely publicized problems with sticking accelerators, prompting two huge recalls of 10 million vehicles and suspension of the sales and production of eight models in the American market.[49] Later it developed that the "unintended acceleration" was probably caused by sticky pedals or floor mats rather than Toyota electronics (although some critics thought it traced to driver error).[50] In 2014, the company agreed to a $1.2 billion penalty to end a U.S. criminal probe into the sudden-acceleration problems.[51] It also admitted it misled American consumers by concealing and making deceptive statements about the acceleration safety issues.[52]

No sooner had it done so, however, than the company's reputation for integrity, reliability, and assembly-line mastery took another massive hit, when Toyota was forced to recall 6.4 million vehicles for five potential hazards, including faulty power-window switches, possibly unstable steering column brackets, and potential hindrances to deployment of driver's-side air bags.[53] In 2015 Toyota recalled an additional 1.4 million cars, trucks, and SUV's after the NHTSA declared many air bags defective (the air bags were made by Takata, a major supplier); that brought the number of Toyota vehicles recalled in the United States to 2.9 million.[54] In 2016, another 320 Toyotas were recalled for air bag issues, then another 17,000.[55]

All the recalls inflicted severe damage to Toyota's vaunted reputation for quality. "When your whole deal was quality, every mistake is a big deal," said a manufacturing expert.[56]

The External Opportunities. Today, under the new president's direction, the 1950s-style traditional organization has been modernized, with layers of management removed and with Akio meeting weekly with five top advisors to make on-the-spot decisions. The company has also reorganized its vehicle-development system to speed decision making, cut costs, and generate more worldwide appeal.[57]

In addition, Toyota moved to give its cars more exciting designs, taking initiatives to "improve upon the emotion of cars" with better styling and high-quality interiors.[58] It joined forces with Ford to develop a gas-electric hybrid fuel system for trucks and sport utility vehicles and has continued to push green technology, as with the plug-in Prius and a new concept car powered by hydrogen fuel cells.[59] It launched the sporty $375,000 Lexus LFA, a carbon fiber supercar. Along with Stanford and M.I.T., it is engaging in $50 million robotics and artificial intelligence research to develop "intelligent" cars—cars that make humans better drivers (a different concept from self-driving cars).[60] To take advantage of growing markets in developing countries and the increased demand for fuel-efficient vehicles, Toyota's affiliate, Daihatsu Motor, is building and selling small cars in India.[61]

Toyota has been lucky in that competitors have had their own problems to deal with. Because Takata air bags appeared in many different makes of cars, 14 automakers were forced to recall 24 million cars to fix air bag mechanisms.[62] Volkswagen's emissions cheating scandal with its diesel engines caused a drop in VW's new-car sales and may well cloud the prospects for diesel for years.[63] General Motors's fatal ignition switch mistakes, which led to 124 deaths and the recall of 2.6 million vehicles, was described by GM's CEO Mary Barra as representing "a pattern of incompetence and neglect"—and this was only part of the total of GM recalls, which, for this and other reasons, rose to a record 30.4 million cars and trucks.[64] Perhaps these setbacks present Toyota with an unprecedented opportunity to grab its rivals' customers.

The External Threats. Toyota was able to work past its accelerator-sticking troubles of 2009–2010, which presented its American and European rivals with a chance to cut into the Japanese automaker's market share.[65] Like other car companies, Toyota has also faced the worldwide Great Recession, which damaged auto spending. In addition, Toyota had to face setbacks brought about by the 2011 deadly earthquake and tsunami, which devastated plants in the north of Japan and disrupted the supply of over 500 parts, and by flooding in Thailand, which led to new supply difficulties.[66] In 2016, it had to shut down 26 car assembly lines in Japan because of disruptions at a parts supplier caused by earthquakes in the southern part of the country.[67] In recent years, the company has had to deal with currency problems of a strong yen against a weak U.S. dollar, which further reduced revenues.[68] Finally, Toyota competitors have began to close the quality gap, with the Ford Fusion, Hyundai Sonata, Volkswagen Passat, and other midsize vehicles severely impacting sales of the Toyota Camry.[69]

By 2011, Toyota's market share in the United States had fallen all the way from 18.3% to 12.9%. It bounced back to 13.3% in early 2016, putting it in third place behind General Motors at 16.7% and Ford at 15.7%.[70]

YOUR CALL

"Comfortably preoccupied with rooting out internal weakness," said one writer in 2010, "the Toyota Way is lost when it comes to contending with outside threats. . . . If a flaw does get through, the company as a whole is loath to admit that the system broke down."[71] Do you agree? How well do you think its president, Akio Toyoda, is doing in dealing with Toyota's threats and opportunities, both internal and external?

Forecasting: Predicting the Future

Once they've analyzed their organization's Strengths, Weaknesses, Opportunities, and Threats, planners need to do forecasting for making long-term strategy. **A forecast is a vision or projection of the future.**

Lots of people make predictions, of course—and often they are wrong.[72] In the 1950s, the head of IBM, Thomas J. Watson, estimated that the demand for computers would never exceed more than five for the entire world. In the late 1990s, many computer experts predicted power outages, water problems, transportation disruptions, bank shutdowns, and far worse because of computer glitches (the "Y2K bug") associated with the change from year 1999 to 2000.

Of course, the farther into the future one makes a prediction, the more difficult it is to be accurate, especially in matters of technology. Yet forecasting is a necessary part of planning.

Two types of forecasting are *trend analysis* and *contingency planning*.

Trend Analysis   **A trend analysis is a hypothetical extension of a past series of events into the future.** The basic assumption is that the picture of the present can be projected into the future. This is not a bad assumption, if you have enough historical data, but it is always subject to surprises. And if your data are unreliable, they will produce erroneous trend projections.

An example of trend analysis is a time-series forecast, which predicts future data based on patterns of historical data. Time-series forecasts are used to predict long-term trends, cyclic patterns (as in the up-and-down nature of the business cycle), and seasonal variations (as in Christmas sales versus summer sales).

Contingency Planning: Predicting Alternative Futures **Contingency planning—** also known *as scenario planning* and **scenario analysis**—is the creation of alternative hypothetical but equally likely future conditions. For example, scenarios may be created with spreadsheet software such as Microsoft Excel to present alternative combinations of different factors—different economic pictures, different strategies by competitors, different budgets, and so on.

EXAMPLE

Contingency Planning for Insurance Companies: Dealing with Rising Sea Levels

Some recent headlines from *Insurance Journal,* which covers news important to the insurance industry:

SEA LEVEL RISE WILL BE WORSE AND COME SOONER

THE NATURE CONSERVANCY LOOKS TO ADDRESS SOUTH FLORIDA CLIMATE, CATASTROPHE RISKS

STUDY: FLOOD RISK ON RISE FOR NEW YORK CITY, NEW JERSEY COAST

RESEARCH SAYS WASHINGTON, D.C. IS SLOWLY SINKING INTO THE OCEAN

IN CONNECTICUT, SEA LEVEL PREDICTIONS PROMPT NEW AWARENESS IN COMMUNITIES

"From Hurricane Sandy's devastating blow to the Northeast to the protracted drought that hit the Midwest Corn Belt," pointed out economics writer Eduardo Porter, "natural catastrophes pounded insurers [in 2012], generating $35 billion in privately insured property damage, $11 billion more than the average over the last decade."[73] Indeed, in terms of insured losses, 8 of the 10 costliest hurricanes in U.S. history and 9 of the costliest floods have occurred since 2000.[74] Now insurers have to prepare for even worse news.

"As each decade passes," writes William Gail, founder of the Global Weather Corporation, "knowledge of Earth's past becomes progressively less effective as a guide to the future. . . . Cycles that have been largely unwavering during modern human history are disrupted by substantial changes in temperature and precipitation."[75] How can predictions be made if, as the Earth warms, nature's patterns will no longer be reliable?

Warming Seas, Rising Seas. China Ocean Shipping Co. actually sees opportunities in rising ocean temperatures: It has introduced regular Asia-to-Europe sailings through the Arctic in the summer through fall, shaving travel time by two weeks compared to going through the Suez Canal, because melting ice has made the route more viable.[76] But recent studies find that global temperature rise is increasing with each passing decade, and the corresponding sea rise is the fastest in 28

centuries, producing floods along many coasts and threatening many coastal cities by 2100.[77] Several government agencies, such as the U.S. Navy, have launched contingency planning to prepare for the effects of rising seas, and some governments of coastal cities are trying to make plans to anticipate the effect of rising oceans on their infrastructures.[78] Miami Beach, Florida, for instance, has already spent something like a hundred million dollars to cope with recurrent flooding and plans to spend several hundred million more.[79]

The Effect on Insurance Companies. A 2013 report by Ceres, a Boston-based nonprofit promoting eco-minded business practices, said most U.S. insurance companies, large and small, had not adopted comprehensive strategies to cope with climate change.[80] "Of 184 companies surveyed," said one account, "only 23 had such strategies, and 13 of those were foreign-owned."[81] However, research by a scientist at the federally funded Lawrence Berkeley National Laboratory, which studied large global insurers, said the industry was stepping up to the challenge, having made 1,148 efforts to adapt and mitigate climate change.[82] In particular, the insurance industry has enthusiastically embraced risk modeling, allowing flooding and other phenomena linked to global warming to be examined in greater detail. "Risk modeling has become more comprehensive and refined," said an executive with a German insurance company. "With each extreme weather event, we gather additional data and test how well the models perform."[83] Contingency planning in action.

YOUR CALL

Based on contingency planning for climate variability and volatility in every part of the globe, what is the responsibility of insurance companies? Just try to avoid catastrophic losses by raising premiums, adding exclusions, and refusing to cover high-risk communities? Or try to educate consumers about building more resilient structures in less risky areas, particularly those exposed to rising oceans?

The effect of climate change? *Left:* AT&T Park, home to baseball's San Francisco Giants, usually looks like this. *Right:* If the sea level were to rise 25 feet, the ball park and the surrounding city could look like this. What kind of contingency planning should insurance companies be doing with regard to climate change?
(Both): Photo illustration by Nickolay Lamm; data courtesy of Climate Central

Because the scenarios try to peer far into the future—perhaps five or more years—they are necessarily written in rather general terms. Nevertheless, the great value of contingency planning is that it not only equips an organization to prepare for emergencies and uncertainty, it also gets managers thinking strategically.

Benchmarking: Comparing with the Best

Benchmarking is a process by which a company compares its performance with that of high-performing organizations.[84] Professional sports teams do this all the time, but so do other kinds of organizations, including nonprofit ones. Example: Airlines use such benchmarks as average turnaround time, on-time arrivals, cost per seat per passenger mile, fuel cost, numbers of lost bags, and so on. At Xerox Corp., generally thought to be the first American company to use benchmarking, it is defined as, in one description, "the continuous process of measuring products, services, and practices against the toughest competitors or those companies recognized as industry leaders."[85]

Porter's Five Competitive Forces

What determines competitiveness within a particular industry? After studying several kinds of businesses, strategic-management expert Michael Porter suggested in his **Porter's model for industry analysis** that business-level strategies originate in five primary competitive forces in the firm's environment: **(1) threats of new entrants, (2) bargaining power of suppliers, (3) bargaining power of buyers, (4) threats of substitute products or services, and (5) rivalry among competitors.**[86]

1. Threats of New Entrants New competitors can affect an industry almost overnight, taking away customers from existing organizations. Example: Kraft Macaroni & Cheese is a venerable, well-known brand but is threatened from the low end by store brands, such as Walmart's brand, and from the high end by Annie's Organic & Natural Mac and Cheese.

2. Bargaining Power of Suppliers Some companies are readily able to switch suppliers in order to get components or services, but others are not. Example: Clark Foam of Laguna Niguel, California, supplied nearly 90% of the foam cores used domestically to make custom surfboards. When it suddenly closed shop in late 2005, blaming government agencies for trying to shut it down, many independent board shapers and small retailers found they couldn't afford to get foam from outside the country. On the other hand, Surftech in Santa Cruz, California, was one of the few board manufacturers to use resin instead of foam, and so it saw a spike in sales.[87]

3. Bargaining Power of Buyers Customers who buy a lot of products or services from an organization have more bargaining power than those who don't. Customers who use the Internet to shop around are also better able to negotiate a better price. Example: Buying a car used to be pretty much a local activity, but now potential car buyers can use the Internet to scout a range of offerings within a 100-mile or larger radius, giving them the power to force down the asking price of any one particular seller.

4. Threats of Substitute Products or Services Again, particularly because of the Internet, an organization is in a better position to switch to other products or services when circumstances threaten their usual channels. Example: Oil companies worried when Brazil achieved energy self-sufficiency in 2006, able to meet its growing demand for vehicle fuel by substituting ethanol derived from sugar cane for petroleum—until 2007, when population and economic growth forced the country to start importing oil again.[88]

5. Rivalry among Competitors The preceding four forces influence the fifth force, rivalry among competitors. Think of the wild competition among makers and sellers of portable electronics, ranging from smartphones to tablets to videogame systems. Once again, the Internet has intensified rivalries among all kinds of organizations.

An organization should do a good SWOT analysis that examines these five competitive forces, Porter felt. Then it was in a position to formulate effective strategy, using what he identified as four competitive strategies, as we discuss in the next section.

To what extent do you think that a current or past employer was good at strategic thinking? Based on past research, firms that are better at strategic thinking should outperform those that are not. •

---

connect SELF-ASSESSMENT 6.1

Assessing Strategic Thinking

This survey is designed to assess an organization's level of strategic thinking. Please be prepared to answer these questions if your instructor has assigned Self-Assessment 6.1 in Connect.

1. What is the level of strategic thinking? Are you surprised by the results?

2. If you were meeting with an executive from the company you evaluated, what advice would you provide based on the survey results and what you learned about assessing current reality?

6.5   Formulating the Grand Strategy

MAJOR QUESTION

How can four techniques—Porter's four competitive strategies, diversification strategy, blue ocean strategy, and the BCG matrix—help me formulate strategy?

THE BIG PICTURE

Strategies may be growth, stability, or defensive strategies. Strategy formulation makes use of several concepts, including Porter's four competitive strategies; diversification, including vertical integration; blue ocean strategy; and the BCG matrix.

After assessing the current reality (Step 2 in the strategic-management process), it's time to turn to strategy formulation—developing a grand strategy (Step 3). Examples of techniques that can be used to formulate strategy are *Porter's four competitive strategies, diversification, blue ocean strategy,* and *the BCG matrix.*

The grand strategy must then be translated into more specific *strategic plans,* which determine what the organization's long-term goals should be for the next one to five years. These should communicate not only the organization's general goals about growth and profits but also information about how these goals will be achieved. Moreover, like all goals, they should be SMART—Specific, Measurable, Attainable, Results-oriented, and specifying Target dates (Chapter 5).

Three Common Grand Strategies

The three common grand strategies are *growth, stability,* and *defensive.*

1. The Growth Strategy   A **growth strategy** is a grand strategy that involves expansion—as in sales revenues, market share, number of employees, or number of customers or (for nonprofits) clients served.

Often a growth strategy takes the form of an **innovation strategy,** growing market share or profits by innovating improvements in products or services (as in using an e-business approach in calculatedly disseminating information). We consider innovation further in Chapter 10.

Example: Etsy is a Brooklyn, New York, company that runs an online marketplace for handmade and vintage goods—jewelry, housewares, T-shirts—for which it charges fees to sellers for use of its platform. The firm showed strong growth in 2015, when revenues in the fourth quarter rose 35% to $87.9 million.[89] What's behind the surge? In part it was the creation of a separate online enterprise called Etsy Manufacturing, which departs from the firm's artisanal roots (which prohibited sellers from outsourcing their production, saying all goods had to be handmade) by offering a service that matches sellers with small manufacturers, many of which had been devastated by the shift of U.S. production generally to low-wage countries.[90] The innovation allowed Molly Goodall, for instance, to evolve from sewing her quirky animal coats one at a time at her dining room table to using small manufacturers near her Texas home.

2. The Stability Strategy   A **stability strategy** is a grand strategy that involves little or no significant change. Example: Without much changing their product, the makers of Timex watches decided to stress the theme of authenticity ("Wear it well") over durability (the old slogan was "It takes a licking and keeps on ticking"). In an age of smartphones and other gadgets, when people don't need a watch to tell the time, the new theme of authenticity makes sense, according to *The New York Times,* "as consumers watching what they spend seek out products with longevity whose ability to stand the test of time implies they are worth buying."[91]

3. The Defensive Strategy   A defensive strategy, or a *retrenchment strategy,* is a grand strategy that involves reduction in the organization's efforts. Example: The "big sales numbers that have sustained the recorded music business for years are way down, and it is hard to see how they could ever return to where they were even a decade ago," says one analysis. "The result is that the music industry finds itself fighting over pennies while waving goodbye to dollars."[92] Principal sources of revenue are now largely the result of a 45% increase in streaming revenue, rather than from sales of CDs. There is also a growing but still specialized market for vinyl records.[93]

Variations of the three strategies are shown below. *(See Table 6.3.)*

TABLE 6.3

How a Company Can Implement a Grand Strategy

GROWTH STRATEGY
- It can improve an existing product or service to attract more buyers.
- It can increase its promotion and marketing efforts to try to expand its market share.
- It can expand its operations, as in taking over distribution or manufacturing previously handled by someone else.
- It can expand into new products or services.
- It can acquire similar or complementary businesses.
- It can merge with another company to form a larger company.

STABILITY STRATEGY
- It can go for a no-change strategy (if, for example, it has found that too-fast growth leads to foul-ups with orders and customer complaints).
- It can go for a little-change strategy (if, for example, the company has been growing at breakneck speed and feels it needs a period of consolidation).

DEFENSIVE STRATEGY
- It can reduce costs, as by freezing hiring or tightening expenses.
- It can sell off (liquidate) assets—land, buildings, inventories, and the like.
- It can gradually phase out product lines or services.
- It can divest part of its business, as in selling off entire divisions or subsidiaries.
- It can declare bankruptcy.
- It can attempt a turnaround—do some retrenching, with a view toward restoring profitability.

Porter's Four Competitive Strategies

Porter's four competitive strategies (also called *four generic strategies*) are (1) cost-leadership, (2) differentiation, (3) cost-focus, and (4) focused-differentiation. The first two strategies focus on *wide* markets, the last two on *narrow* markets. Time Warner, which produces lots of media and publications, serves wide markets around the world. Your neighborhood video store (if one still exists) serves a narrow market of just local customers.

Let's look at these four strategies.

1. Cost-Leadership Strategy: Keeping Costs and Prices Low for a Wide Market   The **cost-leadership strategy** is to keep the costs, and hence prices, of a product or service below those of competitors and to target a wide market.

This puts the pressure on R&D managers to develop products or services that can be created cheaply, production managers to reduce production costs, and marketing managers to reach a wide variety of customers as inexpensively as possible.

Firms implementing the cost-leadership strategy include Timex, computer maker Acer, hardware retailer Home Depot, and pen maker Bic.

2. Differentiation Strategy: Offering Unique and Superior Value for a Wide Market   The **differentiation strategy** is to offer products or services that are of unique and superior value compared with those of competitors but to target a wide market.

Because products are expensive, managers may have to spend more on R&D, marketing, and customer service. This is the strategy followed by Ritz-Carlton hotels and the makers of Lexus automobiles.

The strategy is also pursued by companies trying to create *brands* to differentiate themselves from competitors. Although Coca-Cola may cost only cents more than a supermarket's own house brand of cola, Coke spends millions on ads.

3. Cost-Focus Strategy: Keeping Costs and Prices Low for a Narrow Market
The **cost-focus strategy** is to keep the costs, and hence prices, of a product or service below those of competitors and to target a narrow market.

This is a strategy you often see executed with low-end products sold in discount stores, such as low-cost beer or cigarettes, or with regional gas stations, such as the Terrible Herbst, Rotten Robbie, and Maverik chains in parts of the West.

Needless to say, the pressure on managers to keep costs down is even more intense than it is with those in cost-leadership companies.

4. Focused-Differentiation Strategy: Offering Unique and Superior Value for a Narrow Market
The **focused-differentiation strategy** is to offer products or services that are of unique and superior value compared to those of competitors and to target a narrow market.

Ford Motor Co., for instance, is building only 250 vehicles a year of its new GT supercar, which costs roughly $450,000 each—and prospective buyers must submit applications convincing the company they are ready to drive it.[94] Norwegian Cruise Line offers on its cruise ship *Norwegian Escape* a special section called the Haven for 275 elite passengers, who enjoy 24-hour butler service as well as a private pool, sun deck, and restaurant.[95] Other companies following the strategy are jeweler Cartier and shirtmaker Turnbull & Asser. Yet focused-differentiation products need not be expensive. The publisher Chelsea Green has found success with niche books, such as *The Straw Bale House.*

Focused differentiation. Ford Motor Co. is building 250 high-performance GT supercars a year costing $450,000 each. The cars are so exclusive that buyers have to convince the company, through writing and supporting videos and social media posts, of their enthusiasm for driving it. "We really want to find those customers who will use this car and drive this car and be true ambassadors for Ford," says Henry Ford II, great-great grandson of the founder. The company clearly does not want the GT to become an object of the super wealthy to be stored away. © Stephen Smith/ Sipa USA/Newscom

Single-Product Strategy versus Diversification Strategy

A company also needs to think about whether to have a *single-product strategy* or a *diversification strategy.* After all, if you have only one product to sell, what do you do if that product fails?

The Single-Product Strategy: Focused but Vulnerable   In a **single-product strategy**, a company makes and sells only one product within its market. This is the kind of strategy you see all the time as you drive past the small retail businesses in a small town: There may be one shop that sells only flowers, one that sells only security systems, and so on.

The single-product strategy has both positives and negatives:

- **The benefit—focus.** Making just one product allows you to focus your manufacturing and marketing efforts just on that product. This means that your company can become savvy about repairing defects, upgrading production lines, scouting the competition, and doing highly focused advertising and sales.

A small-business example: Green Toys of Mill Valley, California, makes all its toddler tea sets, toy trucks, and building blocks out of plastic recycled from milk jugs and, in a strategy called "reverse globalization," carries out all its operations in California, a push back against offshoring and outsourcing.[96] Another example: Delphi Automotive used to be a sprawling conglomerate making all kinds of motor vehicle components, but after going through bankruptcy it has narrowed its focus and now is considered among the leading suppliers of parts for autonomous vehicles (self-driving cars), automotive electrification, and safety gear.[97]

- **The risk—vulnerability.** The risk, of course, is that if you do *not* focus on all aspects of the business, if a rival gets the jump on you, or if an act of God intervenes (for a florist, roses suffer a blight right before Mother's Day), your entire business may go under.

Example: Indian Motorcycle Company, once a worthy rival to Harley-Davidson, sold only motorcycles. It went bankrupt twice, the second time because of quality problems, notably an overheating engine. (Purchased by Polaris Industries in 2011, it is presently being manufactured in Spirit Lake, Iowa.)[98]

The Diversification Strategy: Operating Different Businesses to Spread the Risk   The obvious answer to the risks of a single-product strategy is **diversification, operating several businesses in order to spread the risk.** You see this at the small retailer level when you drive past a store that sells gas *and* food *and* souvenirs *and* rents DVD movies.

One kind of diversification strategy is **vertical integration, in which a firm expands into businesses that provide the supplies it needs to make its products or that distribute and sell its products.** For many years, Hollywood movie studios followed this model, not only producing movies but also distributing them and even owning their own theaters.[99] Today Netflix follows the same path by producing and distributing its own entertainment programming. Starbucks has long followed a plan of vertical integration by buying and roasting all its own coffee and then selling it through Starbucks coffee stores.[100]

The Blue Ocean Strategy

In their book *Blue Ocean Strategy,* **W. Chan Kim** and **Renee Mauborgne** define a "blue ocean" as a completely new market, in contrast to a "red ocean," in which industry boundaries are defined and accepted and the competitive rules of the game are known.[101] More formally, **blue ocean strategy refers to a company's creating a new, uncontested market space that makes competitors irrelevant, creates new consumer value, and decreases costs.** "Competing in overcrowded industries is no way to sustain high performance," the authors write. "The real opportunity is to create blue oceans of uncontested market space."

Examples: There are two ways to create a blue ocean. One is to invent a completely new industry, as eBay did when it created the online auction industry and as Cirque du Soleil did when it reinvented the circus by blending opera, dance, and athletic skill and eliminating star performers and animals. The second way is to create a blue ocean within a red ocean, as when a company expands the boundaries of an existing industry, as Home Depot did in offering the prices and ranges of a lumberyard along with do-it-yourself classes for customers.

The BCG Matrix

Developed by the Boston Consulting Group, the **BCG matrix is a means of evaluating strategic business units on the basis of (1) their business growth rates and (2) their share of the market.** Business growth rate is concerned with how fast the entire industry is increasing. Market share is concerned with the business unit's share of the market in relation to competitors.

In general, the BCG matrix suggests that an organization will do better in fast-growing markets in which it has a high market share rather than in slow-growing markets in which it has a low market share. These concepts are illustrated below. *(See Figure 6.3.)*

FIGURE 6.3   **The BCG matrix**

Market growth is divided into two categories, low and high. Market share is also divided into low and high. Thus, in this matrix, "Stars" are business units that are highly desirable (high growth, high market share), compared to "Dogs," which are not so desirable (low growth, low market share).

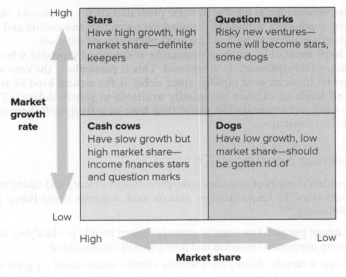

Now that you have learned about the tools companies use to create their grand strategies, what type of skills do you think managers need to use these tools? Do you think you possess those skills? ●

Core Skills Required for Strategic Planning

This survey is designed to assess the skills needed in strategic planning. Please be prepared to answer these questions if your instructor has assigned Self-Assessment 6.2 in Connect.

1. Do you have what it takes? Are you surprised by the results?

2. Based on the results, what are your top two strengths and deficiencies when it comes to strategic planning?

3. Assuming you wanted to do strategic planning at some point in your career, what can you do to improve your skills associated with strategic planning? Be specific.

6.6 Implementing and Controlling Strategy: Execution

MAJOR QUESTION

How does effective execution help managers during the strategic-management process?

THE BIG PICTURE

Strategic implementation is closely aligned with strategic control. Execution is a process that helps align these two phases of the strategic-management process.

Stage 1 of the strategic-management process was establishing the mission and the vision. Stage 2 was assessing the current reality. Stage 3 was formulating the grand strategy. Now we come to the last two stages—4, strategic implementation, and 5, strategic control.

Implementing the Strategy

Strategy implementation is putting strategic plans into effect. As we said, this means dealing with roadblocks within the organization's structure and culture and seeing if the right people and control systems are available to execute the plans.

Often implementation means overcoming resistance by people who feel the plans threaten their influence or livelihood. This is particularly the case when the plans must be implemented rapidly, since delay is the easiest kind of resistance there is (all kinds of excuses are usually available to justify delays). Thus, top managers can't just announce the plans; they have to actively sell them to middle and supervisory managers.

Maintaining Strategic Control

Strategic control consists of monitoring the execution of strategy and taking corrective action, if necessary. To keep a strategic plan on track, suggests Bryan Barry, you need to do the following:[102]

- **Engage people.** You need to actively engage people in clarifying what your group hopes to accomplish and how you will accomplish it.
- **Keep it simple.** Keep your planning simple, unless there's a good reason to make it more complex.
- **Stay focused.** Stay focused on the important things.
- **Keep moving.** Keep moving toward your vision of the future, adjusting your plans as you learn what works.

Execution. Occupying a sprawling campus in Cary, North Carolina, software maker SAS has always been ranked in the top positions on *Fortune*'s lists of "100 Best Companies to Work For" (No. 1 in 2010 and 2011, No. 2 in 2013 and 2014, No. 3 in 2012, and No. 4 in 2015). Its ability to execute effectively has also made it highly profitable and the world's largest privately owned software company.
Courtesy of SAS

Execution: Getting Things Done

In implementing strategy and maintaining strategic control, what we are talking about is effective *execution*. **Larry Bossidy,** former CEO of AlliedSignal (later Honeywell), and **Ram Charan,** a business adviser to senior executives, are authors of *Execution: The Discipline of Getting Things Done.*[103] **Execution,** they say, is not simply tactics; it is a central part of any company's strategy. It consists of using questioning, analysis, and follow-through to mesh strategy with reality, align people with goals, and achieve results promised.

How important is execution to organizational success in today's global economy? A survey of 769 global CEOs from 40 countries revealed that "excellence in execution" was their most important concern—more important than "profit growth," "customer loyalty," "stimulating innovation," and "finding qualified employees."[104]

Bossidy and Charan outline how organizations and managers can improve the ability to execute. Effective execution requires managers to build a foundation for execution within three core processes found in any business: people, strategy, and operations.[105]

The Three Core Processes of Business: People, Strategy, and Operations

A company's overall ability to execute is a function of effectively executing according to three processes: *people, strategy,* and *operations.* Because all work ultimately entails some human interaction, effort, or involvement, Bossidy and Charan believe that the *people* process is the most important.

The First Core Process—People: "You Need to Consider Who Will Benefit You in the Future"

"If you don't get the people process right," say Bossidy and Charan, "you will never fulfill the potential of your business." But today most organizations focus on evaluating the jobs people are doing at present, rather than considering which individuals can handle the jobs of the future. An effective leader tries to evaluate talent by linking people to particular strategic milestones, developing future leaders, dealing with nonperformers, and transforming the mission and operations of the human resource department.

The Second Core Process—Strategy: "You Need to Consider How Success Will Be Accomplished"

In most organizations, the strategies developed fail to consider the "how" of execution. According to the authors, a good strategic plan addresses nine questions. *(See Table 6.4.)* In considering whether the organization can execute the strategy, a leader must take a realistic and critical view of its capabilities and competencies. If it does not have the talent in finance, sales, and manufacturing to accomplish the vision, the chances of success are drastically reduced.

The Third Core Process—Operations: "You Need to Consider What Path Will Be Followed"

The strategy process defines where an organization wants to go, and the people process defines who's going to get it done. The third core process, operations, or the operating plan, provides the path for people to follow. The operating plan, as we described in Chapter 5, should address all the major activities in which the company will engage—marketing, production, sales, revenue, and so on—and then define short-term objectives for these activities, to provide targets for people to aim at. We also discuss operations management in Chapter 16.

How Execution Helps Implement and Control Strategy

Many executives appear to have an aversion to execution, which they associate with boring tactics—with the tedium of doing, as opposed to the excitement of visioning—and which they hand off to subordinates. Further, there are many

TABLE 6.4   Necessary Answers: What Questions Should a Strong Strategic Plan Address?

1. What is the assessment of the external environment?

2. How well do you understand the existing customers and markets?

3. What is the best way to grow the business profitably, and what are the obstacles to growth?

4. Who is the competition?

5. Can the business execute the strategy?

6. Are the short term and long term balanced?

7. What are the important milestones for executing the plan?

8. What are the critical issues facing the business?

9. How will the business make money on a sustainable basis?

Source: From Execution by Larry Bossidy and Ram Charan, Crown Business, a division of Random House, Inc., 2002.

organizational obstacles to effective execution, and many of these are associated with organizational culture. Organizational culture is a system of shared beliefs and values within an organization that guides the behavior of its members. In this context, effective execution will not occur unless the culture supports an emphasis on getting quality work done in a timely manner. Chapter 8 presents 11 ways managers can attempt to create an execution-oriented culture.[106]

PRACTICAL ACTION   Building a Foundation of Execution

The foundation of execution is based on leadership (as we discuss in Chapter 14) and organizational culture (discussed in Chapter 8). Bossidy and Charan suggest that there are seven essential types of leader behaviors that are needed to fuel the engine of execution. Managers are advised to engage in seven kinds of behaviors, as follows.

Know Your People and Your Business: "Engage Intensely with Your Employees." In companies that don't execute, leaders are usually out of touch with the day-to-day realities. Bossidy and Charan insist leaders must engage intensely and personally with their organization's people and its businesses. They cannot rely on secondhand knowledge through other people's observations, assessments, and recommendations.

Insist on Realism: "Don't Let Others Avoid Reality." Many people want to avoid or shade reality, hiding mistakes or avoiding confrontations. Making realism a priority begins with the leaders being realistic themselves, and making sure realism is the goal of all dialogues in the organization.

Set Clear Priorities: "Focus on a Few Rather Than Many Goals." Leaders who execute focus on a very few clear priorities that everyone can grasp.

Follow Through: "Establish Accountability and Check on Results." Failing to follow through is a major cause of poor execution. "How many meetings have you attended where people left without firm conclusions about who would do what and when?" Bossidy and Charan ask. Accountability and follow-up are important.

Reward the Doers: "Show Top Performers That They Matter." If people are to produce specific results, they must be rewarded accordingly, making sure that top performers are rewarded far better than ordinary performers.

Expand People's Capabilities: "Develop the Talent." Coaching is an important part of the executive's job, providing useful and specific feedback that can improve performance.

Know Yourself: "Do the Hard Work of Understanding Who You Are." Leaders must develop "emotional fortitude" based on honest self-assessments. Four core qualities are authenticity, self-awareness, self-mastery, and humility.

YOUR CALL

Which behavior is probably the most difficult for you to adopt personally?

Do you think your current or a past employer is or was good at execution? What obstacles may have impaired the company's ability to execute?

connect SELF-ASSESSMENT 6.3

Assessing the Obstacles to Strategic Execution

This survey is designed to assess the obstacles to strategic execution that may be impacting an organization's ability to execute. Please be prepared to answer these questions if your instructor has assigned Self-Assessment 6.3 in Connect.

1. How does the company stand with respect to execution?
2. Based on the results, what are the company's strengths and weaknesses when it comes to execution?
3. What advice would you give to senior management about improving the company's ability to execute based on the results? Be specific.

In conclusion, by linking people, strategy, and operating plans, execution allows executives to direct and control the three core processes that will advance their strategic vision. ●

Key Terms Used in This Chapter

Key Points

6.1 What Is Effective Strategy?

- Strategic positioning attempts to achieve sustainable competitive advantage by preserving what is distinctive about a company.
- Strategic positioning is based on the principles that strategy is the creation of a unique and valuable position, requires trade-offs in competing, and involves creating a "fit" among activities, so that they interact and reinforce each other.
- Strategic management works best for large firms but can also be effective for small firms.
- Every organization needs to have a "big picture" about where it's going and how to get there, which involves strategy, strategic management, and strategic planning. A strategy is a large-scale action plan that sets the direction for an organization. Strategic management involves managers from all parts of the organization in the formulation and implementation of strategies and strategic goals. Strategic planning determines the organization's long-term goals and ways to achieve them.
- Three reasons an organization should adopt strategic management and strategic planning: They can (1) provide direction and momentum, (2) encourage new ideas, and (3) develop a sustainable competitive advantage. Sustainable competitive advantage occurs when an organization is able to get and stay ahead in four areas: (1) in being responsive to customers, (2) in innovating, (3) in quality, and (4) in effectiveness.

6.2 The Strategic-Management Process

- The strategic-management process has five steps plus a feedback loop.
- Step 1 is to establish the mission, vision, and values statements. The mission statement expresses the

organization's purpose or reason for being. The vision statement states what the organization wants to become, where it wants to go strategically. The values statement describes what the organization stands for, its core priorities, the values its employees embody, and what its products contribute to the world.
- Step 2 is to do a current reality assessment, to look at where the organization stands and see what is working and what could be different so as to maximize efficiency and effectiveness in achieving the organization's mission. Among the tools for assessing the current reality are SWOT analysis, forecasting, benchmarking, and Porter's model for industry analysis (described below).
- Step 3 is strategy formulation, to translate the broad mission and vision statements into a grand strategy that explains how the organization's mission is to be accomplished. Strategy formulation is the translation of the grand strategy into more specific strategic plans, choosing among different strategies and altering them to best fit the organization's needs.
- Step 4 is strategy implementation—putting strategic plans into effect.
- Step 5 is strategic control, monitoring the execution of strategy and making adjustments.
- Corrective action constitutes a feedback loop in which a problem requires that managers return to an earlier step to rethink policies, budgets, or personnel arrangements.

6.3 Establishing the Mission, Vision, and Values Statements

- A mission statement should express the organization's purpose or reason for being.
- A vision statement should be positive and inspiring, and it should stretch the organization and its

employees to achieve a desired future state that appears beyond its reach.

- A values statement should describe what the organization stands for, its core priorities, the values its employees embody, and what its products contribute to the world. Values statements must not be hollow; they must be ingrained, inherent, and sacrosanct and can never be compromised.

6.4 Assessing the Current Reality

- Step 2 in the strategic-management process, assess the current reality, looks at where the organization stands internally and externally—to determine what's working and what's not, to see what can be changed so as to increase efficiency and effectiveness in achieving the organization's vision.
- An assessment helps to create an objective view of everything the organization does: its sources of revenue or funding, its work-flow processes, its organizational structure, client satisfaction, employee turnover, and other matters.
- Among the tools for assessing the current reality are *competitive intelligence, SWOT analysis, forecasting, benchmarking,* and *Porter's model for industry analysis.*
- Practicing competitive intelligence means gaining information about one's competitors' activities, through public news sources, investor information, and informal sources, so that you can anticipate their moves and react appropriately.
- The next point in establishing a grand strategy is environmental scanning, careful monitoring of an organization's internal and external environments to detect early signs of opportunities and threats that may influence the firm's plans. The process for doing such scanning is called SWOT analysis, a search for the Strengths, Weaknesses, Opportunities, and Threats affecting the organization.
- Organizational strengths are the skills and capabilities that give the organization special competencies and competitive advantages. Organizational weaknesses are the drawbacks that hinder an organization in executing strategies. Organizational opportunities are environmental factors that the organization may exploit for competitive advantage. Organizational threats are environmental factors that hinder an organization's achieving a competitive advantage.
- Another tool for developing a grand strategy is forecasting—creating a vision or projection of the future. Two types of forecasting are (1) trend analysis, a hypothetical extension of a past series of events into the future; and (2) contingency planning, the creation of alternative hypothetical but equally likely future conditions.
- Benchmarking is a process by which a company compares its performance with that of high-performing organizations.
- Porter's model for industry analysis suggests that business-level strategies originate in five primary competitive forces in the firm's environment: (1) threats of

new entrants, (2) bargaining power of suppliers, (3) bargaining power of buyers, (4) threats of substitute products or services, and (5) rivalry among competitors.

6.5 Formulating the Grand Strategy

- Three common grand strategies are the following: (1) a growth strategy involving expansion—as in sales revenues or market share; one form of growth strategy is an innovation strategy, growing market share or profits by innovating improvements in products or services; (2) a stability strategy, which involves little or no significant change; and (3) a defensive strategy, which involves reduction in the organization's efforts.
- Strategy formulation (Step 3 in the strategic-management process) makes use of several concepts, including (1) Porter's four competitive strategies, (2) diversification strategy, (3) blue ocean strategy, and (4) the BCG matrix.
- Porter's four competitive strategies are as follows: (1) The cost-leadership strategy is to keep the costs, and hence the prices, of a product or service below those of competitors and to target a wide market. (2) The differentiation strategy is to offer products or services that are of unique and superior value compared with those of competitors but to target a wide market. (3) The cost-focus strategy is to keep the costs and hence prices of a product or service below those of competitors and to target a narrow market. (4) The focused-differentiation strategy is to offer products or services that are of unique and superior value compared with those of competitors and to target a narrow market.
- Companies need to choose whether to have a single-product strategy, making and selling only one product within their market, or a diversification strategy, operating several businesses to spread the risk.
- One kind of diversification strategy is vertical integration, in which a firm expands into businesses that provide the supplies it needs to makes products or that distribute and sell its products.
- Blue ocean strategy refers to a company's creating a new, uncontested market space that makes competitors irrelevant, creates new consumer values, and decreases costs.
- The BCG matrix is a means of evaluating strategic business units on the basis of (1) their business growth rates and (2) their share of the market. In general, organizations do better in fast-growing markets in which they have a high market share rather than slow-growing markets in which they have low market shares.

6.6 Implementing and Controlling Strategy: Execution

- The last two steps of the strategic-management process are strategy implementation and strategic control.
- Strategy implementation is putting strategic plans into effect, dealing with roadblocks within the organization's structure and culture, and seeing if

the right people and control systems are available to execute the plans.

- Strategic control consists of monitoring the execution of strategy and taking corrective action, if necessary. To keep a strategic plan on track, you should engage people, keep your planning simple, stay focused, and keep moving.

- Implementing strategy and maintaining strategic control require effective execution. Execution is not simply tactics; it is a central part of any company's strategy; it consists of using questioning, analysis, and follow-through to mesh strategy with reality, align people with goals, and achieve results promised.

- Three core processes of execution are people, strategy, and operations. (1) You have to evaluate

talent by linking people to particular strategic milestones, developing future leaders, dealing with nonperformers, and transforming the mission and operations of the human resource department. (2) In considering whether the organization can execute the strategy, a leader must take a realistic and critical view of its capabilities and competencies. (3) The third core process, operations, or the operating plan, provides the path for people to follow. The operating plan should address all the major activities in which the company will engage and then define short-term objectives for these activities, to provide targets for people to aim at. By linking people, strategy, and operating plans, execution allows executives to direct and control the three core processes that will advance their strategic vision.

Understanding the Chapter: What Do I Know?

1. What is strategic positioning, and what are the three principles that underlie it?
2. What are the five steps in the strategic management process?
3. Name some characteristics of good mission, vision, and values statements.
4. What is competitive intelligence?
5. What are the tools that can help you assess the current reality?

6. Explain what SWOT is.
7. Describe four techniques that can help you formulate a grand strategy.
8. What are three common grand strategies?
9. Explain Porter's four competitive strategies.
10. In execution, what are the three core processes of business?

Management in Action

IKEA Focuses on Growth

IKEA, the global Swedish home furnishing company, has been on a growth spurt. Revenue grew 28% from 2010 to 2015, resulting in total revenue of 9.2 billion Euros ($10.3 billion) in 2015. The company is more profitable than Target and Lowe's.

IKEA operates a total of 328 stores in 28 countries. It has 20,500 employees and sells 9,500 products from 978 suppliers.

The company's vision is "To create a better everyday life for the many people." The mission is "to offer a wide range of well-designed, functional home furnishing products at prices so low that as many people as possible will be able to afford them." To accomplish this vision, the company strives to "achieve quality at affordable prices . . . through optimizing our entire value chain, by building long-term supplier relationships, investing

in highly automated production and producing large volumes."[107]

The company's growth strategy is based on the goal of achieving €50 billion in sales by 2020. This requires successfully opening stores in emerging markets like China and India. The good news is that IKEA has a proven traffic record of global expansion. One expert noted that IKEA is "ferocious about not expanding too rapidly." Mikael Palmquist, IKEA's regional manager for retail in Asia Pacific, said, "The more global, the more complex it gets." He also believes that IKEA is very careful in how it plans such expansions.

To make his point, Palmquist told a reporter from *Fortune* that it took about six years to plan and open IKEA's inaugural store in Gwangmyeong, South Korea. This 624,000-square-foot store is the company's largest and is on track to be a top performer.[108]

Strategic Management Insight, an online resource that focuses on strategic management, conducted a SWOT analysis of IKEA. Results uncovered the following conclusions:

- **Strengths:** customer and market knowledge; low cost provider, and an integrated supply chain
- **Weaknesses:** public criticism of its treatment of employees, questionable advertising, and decreases in quality associated with continually trying to lower costs
- **Opportunities:** global expansion, online sales, and expansion into selling groceries
- **Threats:** growing competition from companies like Walmart and Tesco and increasing average consumer income.[109]

IKEA's product development process is based on extensive market research. For example, the company did a study of over 8,000 people to investigate their morning routines. The idea was to understand how people's routines could be enhanced by designing products that met their needs. This led to creating the Knapper, a freestanding mirror that contains a rack on the back side for hanging clothes. Additional research revealed that more people are moving into cities, creating the need for multifunctional products. IKEA thus developed lamps and bedside tables that contained built-in wireless charging for mobile devices.[110]

IKEA's strategic mantra is volume at low costs. This requires a continuous focus on cost containment and efficiency. The company does things like "skip an extra coating of lacquer on the underside of a table" because people don't see it. They also reduce labor costs by pushing assembly tasks to the consumer. The use of flat-packed furniture also saves costs. It reduces the expense of stocking and delivery.

Allan Dickner, deputy manager of packaging, has a goal of reducing "air space" in the packaging. *Fortune* noted that "The magic of flat packing allows goods to be jammed into shipping containers without wasting any space." Space is money, according to Dickner. He said, "I hate air." To find creative ideas to reduce the spacing in packaging, the company implemented an

"air hunt competition." The winner received a two-week vacation in Thailand.

To ensure that flat packing does not put too much burden on the assembly of its products, IKEA uses an instruction-manual team. The team writes about 1,400 sets of assembly instructions every year. The goal of these instructions is to reduce the time it takes for people who are not "handy" to assemble products.[111]

A reporter for the *Business Insider* concluded that there are four key strategic issues that continue to guide IKEA's success. They are

- *Solving the worst part of buying.* IKEA has designed products that many shoppers desire. They are attractive, yet not overly durable. They are designed to be used until they wear out, or until the buyer wants to purchase higher-quality furnishings.
- *Hitting the right demographic.* The company has targeted younger shoppers, particularly Millennials. Products are designed to meet their tastes and values.
- *Not expensive, but not cheap.* The price point is in the sweet spot between deep discounters like Aldi and higher-end outlets like Bed, Bath & Beyond.
- *Stores are a destination.* People still like to visit IKEA stores due to their showrooms and cafeterias.[112]

FOR DISCUSSION

1. Based on Michael Porter's discussion of the characteristics of an effective strategy, does IKEA have a good strategy for growth? Explain.

2. To what extent is IKEA following the five steps of the strategic-management process?

3. What are your thoughts about IKEA's vision and mission statements?

4. Which of Michael Porter's four competitive strategies is IKEA trying to follow? Discuss.

5. To what extent does the SWOT analysis support IKEA's strategies? Explain your rationale.

6. What is the greatest takeaway from this case in terms of strategic management?

Legal/Ethical Challenge

Should Companies Be Pressured to Recruit Females for Boards of Directors?

A company's board of directors plays a role in the strategic-management process. Not only can a board provide input into the planning process, but it ultimately

signs off on the intended strategies. Interestingly, a 2014 study by MSCI, a global firm that provides research-based indices and analytics, revealed a significant relationship between the gender composition of boards and a firm's financial performance.

Firms with strong female leadership had an average return on equity of 10.1% compared to 7.4% for companies with no women at senior levels. "MSCI defines strong female leadership as those companies that have three or more women on the board, or a female CEO and at least one other female board member." Firms were also less likely to have corporate scandals when women were members of the board.[113] This challenge pertains to whether it is appropriate for outside groups to pressure a company to include women on its board of directors.

Small percentages of female board members may be caused by many factors, such as a lack of specific experience (e.g., finance), limited social networks, and negative stereotypes. Regardless of the cause, external groups are sprouting up around the United States that are focused on putting pressure on companies to recruit female directors. One example is a group that calls itself "2020 Women on Boards." This nonprofit group has a goal of mobilizing stakeholders to encourage companies to increase female representation on boards of directors. The group plans to publish a list of the Fortune 1000 companies that have no female directors. Some believe that efforts like this will promote good corporate governance, while others see it as an intrusion into the internal functioning of an organization.[114]

SOLVING THE CHALLENGE

Where do you stand on this issue?

1. It is a great idea to pressure companies to include more females on boards of directors. After all, the MSCI study showed that female representation was associated with higher financial performance.

2. Companies should be allowed to select people for boards based on their experience, networks, and performance. Gender should not be considered as a relevant criterion for selecting board members. I am not in favor of this type of social pressure because it does not ensure that the most qualified people are placed on boards of directors.

3. I'm middle of the road on this issue. Part of me feels that organizations should be left alone to put whomever they want on a board. At the same time, sometimes organizational leaders need to be nudged to do the right thing, such as putting females on the board. I thus think that social pressure from groups like "2020 Women on Boards" is okay, but organizations should not feel forced to do anything they do not want to do.

4. Invent other options. Discuss.

7

Individual and Group Decision Making

How Managers Make Things Happen

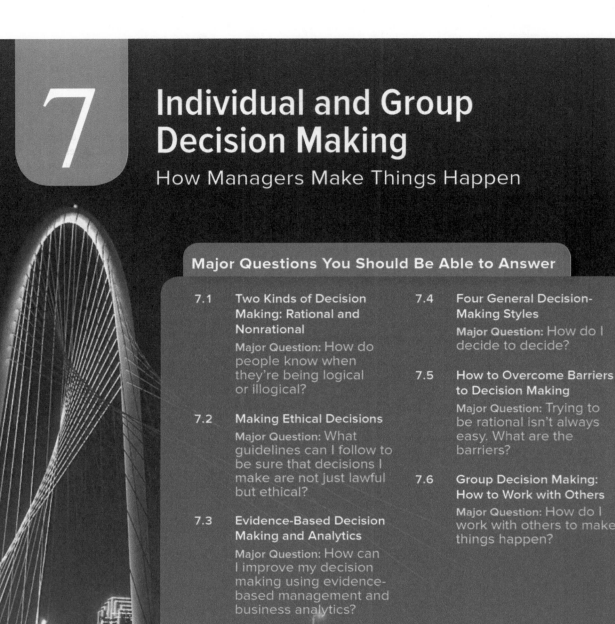

Major Questions You Should Be Able to Answer

7.1 Two Kinds of Decision Making: Rational and Nonrational

Major Question: How do people know when they're being logical or illogical?

7.2 Making Ethical Decisions

Major Question: What guidelines can I follow to be sure that decisions I make are not just lawful but ethical?

7.3 Evidence-Based Decision Making and Analytics

Major Question: How can I improve my decision making using evidence-based management and business analytics?

7.4 Four General Decision-Making Styles

Major Question: How do I decide to decide?

7.5 How to Overcome Barriers to Decision Making

Major Question: Trying to be rational isn't always easy. What are the barriers?

7.6 Group Decision Making: How to Work with Others

Major Question: How do I work with others to make things happen?

How Exceptional Managers Check to See If Their Decisions Might Be Biased

The biggest part of a manager's job is making decisions—and quite often they are wrong. Some questions you might ask next time you're poised to make a decision:

"Am I Too Cocky?" The Overconfidence Bias

If you're making a decision in an area in which you have considerable experience or expertise, you're less likely to be overconfident. Interestingly, however, you're more apt to be overconfident when dealing with questions on subjects you're unfamiliar with or questions with moderate to extreme difficulty.[1]

Recommendation: When dealing with unfamiliar or difficult matters, think how your impending decision might go wrong. Afterward pay close attention to the consequences of your decision.

"Am I Considering the Actual Evidence, or Am I Wedded to My Prior Beliefs?" The Prior-Hypothesis Bias

Do you tend to have strong beliefs? When confronted with a choice, decision makers with strong prior beliefs tend to make their decision based on their beliefs— even if evidence shows those beliefs are wrong. This is known as the *prior-hypothesis bias.*[2]

Recommendation: Although it's more comforting to look for evidence to support your prior beliefs, you need to be tough-minded and weigh the evidence.

"Are Events Really Connected, or Are They Just Chance?" The Ignoring-Randomness Bias

Is a rise in sales in athletic shoes because of your company's advertising campaign or because it's the start of

the school year? Many managers don't understand the laws of randomness.

Recommendation: Don't attribute trends or connections to a single, random event.

"Is There Enough Data on Which to Make a Decision?" The Unrepresentative Sample Bias

If all the secretaries in your office say they prefer dairy creamer to real cream in their coffee, is that enough data on which to launch an ad campaign trumpeting the superiority of dairy creamer? It might if you polled 3,000 secretaries, but 3 or even 30 is too small a sample.

Recommendation: You need to be attuned to the importance of sample size.

"Looking Back, Did I (or Others) Really Know Enough Then to Have Made a Better Decision?" The 20-20 Hindsight Bias

Once managers know what the consequences of a decision are, they may begin to think they could have predicted it. They may remember the facts as being a lot clearer than they actually were.[3]

Recommendation: Try to keep in mind that hindsight does not equal foresight.

For Discussion Facing the hard facts about what works and what doesn't, how able do you think you are to make the tough decisions that effective managers have to make? Can you describe an instance in which you were badly wrong about something or someone?

FORECAST   What's Ahead in This Chapter

We begin by distinguishing between rational and nonrational decision making, and we describe two nonrational models. We next discuss ethical decision making. We then consider evidence-based decision making and the use of analytics. Next we describe general decision-making styles. We follow by considering how individuals respond to decision situations and nine common decision-making biases. We conclude with a discussion of group decision making, including group problem-solving techniques.

7.1 Two Kinds of Decision Making: Rational and Nonrational

MAJOR QUESTION

?

How do people know when they're being logical or illogical?

THE BIG PICTURE

Decision making, the process of identifying and choosing alternative courses of action, may be rational, but often it is nonrational. Four steps in making a rational decision are (1) identify the problem or opportunity, (2) think up alternative solutions, (3) evaluate alternatives and select a solution, and (4) implement and evaluate the solution chosen. Two examples of nonrational models of decision making are (1) satisficing and (2) intuition.

The subject of decisions and decision making is a fascinating subject that is at the heart of what managers do.

A decision is a choice made from among available alternatives. **Decision making** is the process of identifying and choosing alternative courses of action.

If your company's product is first place in its market and is making tons of money, is that a sign of great decision making? Consider the decisions that framed success at Starbucks.

EXAMPLE

Crisis Leading to the Strategic-Management Process: Starbucks Reclaims Its Soul

Among the many things that Starbucks has going for it is this: it survived a near-death experience.[4]

Today's CEO, Howard Schultz, joined the Seattle-based company as marketing director in 1982, when it was only a small chain selling coffee equipment. Over nearly two decades, he gained control and, inspired by the coffee houses of Europe, transformed the company into a comfortable "third place" between home and work, a place with a neighborhood feel selling fresh-brewed by-the-cup lattes and cappuccinos. By 2000, Starbucks (named for the first mate of the whaling ship in Herman Melville's *Moby Dick*) had become the world's largest specialty coffee retailer, with 3,501 stores, 78% of them in the United States.[5]

"Starbucks became, for many of us, what we talk about when we talk about coffee," wrote one reporter. "It changed how we drink it (on a sofa, with Wi-Fi, or on the subway), how we order it ('for here, grande, two-pump vanilla, skinny extra hot latte'), and what we are willing to pay for it," such as $4.99 for a Frappuccino.[6]

Shultz Steps Down. Schultz stepped down as CEO in 2000 (remaining as chairman), and for a while the business continued to thrive. Then two things happened that provoked a crisis. First, the company "lost a certain soul," says Schultz, as the management became more concerned with profits than store atmosphere and company values and extended existing product lines rather than creating new ones. Second, as the Great Recession took hold in 2007, tight-fisted consumers abandoned specialty coffees, causing the stock price to nosedive. In January 2008, after an eight-year absence, Schultz returned as CEO.

The Reinvention Begins. "I didn't come back to save the company—I hate that description," Schultz told an interviewer. "I came back to rekindle the emotion that built it."[7]

Among the risks he took to restore the company's luster, he closed 800 U.S. stores, laid off 4,000 employees, and let go most top executives. As a morale booster, he flew 10,000 store managers to New Orleans, recently destroyed by hurricane Katrina. Along with attending strategy sessions, they bonded in community-service activities, contributing thousands of volunteer hours to helping to restore parts of the city. "We wanted to give back to that community post-Katrina," says Schultz, "and

Starbucks in India The world's biggest coffee chain launched its first Indian outlet in October 2012 in an upscale part of Mumbai. © Punit Paranjpe/AFP/Getty Images

remind and rekindle the organization with the values and guiding principles of our company before we did a stitch of business." Later he closed all U.S. stores for half a day so baristas could be retrained in how to make espresso.

The Payoff. After a couple of years, the company turned around, the result of better operations, modernized technology, a reinvigorated staff, and several innovations: It offered Via premium instant coffee, offered more coffee from a single origin rather than blends, switched to a cold-brew process for iced coffee instead of simply brewing hot coffee and then chilling it, acquired (and then later closed) the La Boulange bakery chain, opened (and then closed) Teavana "tea bars," enabled customers to pay for coffee via a mobile-payment app, and even launched alcohol sales.[8] By early 2016, it had 23,921 stores in 64 countries, it had surpassed Subway to become the No. 2 restaurant chain in U.S. sales (second only to McDonald's),

and its revenues had risen 146% in the last decade, while earnings grew more than five-fold.[9]

Schultz feels strongly that "there's an opportunity for businesses to demonstrate a role in society that's beyond profitability," providing health insurance even for temps, creating tuition reimbursement, helping to raise loans for small businesses, building better opportunities for minority youth.[10]

YOUR CALL

Some critics feel Starbucks is the symbol of "affordable luxury." If we can't afford a McMansion or a Lexus, says one observer, we may be "willing to make that $5 splurge at Starbucks simply because it makes us feel a bit better about ourselves."[11] Thus, despite the innovation in products, attempts to rekindle the cozy neighborhood café, and emphasis on positive social values, do you think another economic downturn could alter Starbucks's fortunes?

Decision Making in the Real World

Sometimes we are able to make thoughtful decisions, making rational choices among well-defined alternatives. But that is not always the way it works in the real world.

Two Systems of Decision Making   In *Thinking, Fast and Slow,* psychologist Daniel Kahneman, winner of the 2002 Nobel Prize in economics, describes two kinds of thinking, which he labels System 1 and System 2:[12]

- **System 1—intuitive and largely unconscious:** System 1 operates automatically and quickly; it is our fast, automatic, intuitive, and largely unconscious mode, as when we detect hostility in a voice or detect that one object is more distant than another.

- **System 2—analytical and conscious:** System 2 is our slow, deliberate, analytical, and consciously effortful mode of reasoning, which swings into action when we have to fill out a tax form or park a car in a narrow space.

"System 1 uses association and metaphor to produce a quick and dirty draft of reality," says one explanation, "which System 2 draws on to arrive at explicit beliefs and reasoned choices."[13]

Why don't we use the more deliberate and rational System 2 more often? Because it's lazy and tires easily, so instead of slowing things down and analyzing them, it is content to accept the easy but unreliable story that System 1 feeds it.

The "Curse of Knowledge"   Why do some engineers design electronic products (such as DVD remote controls) with so many buttons, devices ultimately useful only to other engineers? Why are some professional investors and bankers prone to taking excess risks?[14] Why are some employees so reluctant to adopt new processes? The answer may be what's known as *the curse of knowledge.* As one writer put it about engineers, for example, "People who design products are experts cursed by their knowledge, and they can't imagine what it's like to be as ignorant as the rest of us."[15] Specialization improves efficiency, suggests another writer, but it also leads to tunnel vision and blind spots.[16] In other words, as our knowledge and expertise grow, we may be less and less able to see things from an outsider's perspective—hence, we are often apt to make irrational decisions.

Let us look at the two approaches managers may take to making decisions: They may follow a *rational model* or various kinds of *nonrational models.*

Rational Decision Making: Managers Should Make Logical and Optimal Decisions

The **rational model of decision making**, also called the *classical model*, explains how managers *should* make decisions; it assumes managers will make logical decisions that will be the optimum in furthering the organization's best interests.

Typically there are four stages associated with rational decision making. *(See Figure 7.1.)*

FIGURE 7.1　The four steps in rational decision making

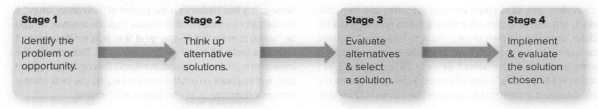

Stage 1	Stage 2	Stage 3	Stage 4
Identify the problem or opportunity.	Think up alternative solutions.	Evaluate alternatives & select a solution.	Implement & evaluate the solution chosen.

Stage 1: Identify the Problem or Opportunity—Determining the Actual versus the Desirable

As a manager, you'll probably find no shortage of **problems, or difficulties that inhibit the achievement of goals:** customer complaints, supplier breakdowns, staff turnover, sales shortfalls, competitor innovations.

However, you'll also often find **opportunities—situations that present possibilities for exceeding existing goals.** It's the farsighted manager, however, who can look past the steady stream of daily problems and seize the moment to actually do *better* than the goals he or she is expected to achieve. When a competitor's top salesperson unexpectedly quits, that creates an opportunity for your company to hire that person away to promote your product more vigorously in that sales territory.

Whether you're confronted with a problem or an opportunity, the decision you're called on to make is how to make *improvements*—how to change conditions from the present to the desirable. This is a matter of **diagnosis—analyzing the underlying causes.**

EXAMPLE　　**Making a Correct Diagnosis: Does Billionaire Warren Buffet, the World's Third Richest Man, Invest Like a Girl?**

Warren Buffett is the renowned billionaire investor (the third richest person in the world, worth $60.8 billion in early 2016) known as the "Oracle of Omaha" who heads the financial juggernaut Berkshire Hathaway.[17] His investment decisions are so successful that $1,000 invested with him in 1957 reportedly was worth upwards of $30 million in 2014.[18] "In the 50 years since Buffett took over Berkshire, its stock has appreciated by 1,826,163%," says one reporter. "That is an astounding number."[19]

Buffett is said to "invest like a girl," taking the same cautious approach that many women supposedly do.[20] He uses basic arithmetic to analyze several file-cabinet drawers of annual reports and other readily available company financial documents and to look for a record of "high returns on equity capital, low debt, and a consistent, predictable business with

sustainable advantages—like Coca-Cola's soft-drink franchise."[21] In other words, Buffett takes pains to make a correct diagnosis before making a decision.[22]

The Better Investors. When men and women are asked to self-assess their financial knowledge, according to a study of eight countries, men tend to give themselves high scores and women give themselves lower scores—even when that is not warranted by their actual knowledge.[23] "Women are aware of their lack of knowledge," speculates a study author, while "men are less willing to admit what they don't know."[24] Unfortunately, women are also falling behind men in financial literacy, according to more recent research. The worse news is that "men apparently don't know much about the topic in the first place."[25]

So which sex is the better class of investors? A seven-year study of single (unmarried) investors found females outperformed males by 2.3%, female investment groups outperformed male groups by 4.6%, and women overall outperformed men by 1.4%.[26] The basic reason, suggests one account: "Women trade much less often than men, do a lot more research, and tend to base their investment decisions on considerations other than just numbers."[27] Men, offers another report, "tend to trade more, and the more you trade, typically the more you lose—not to mention running up transaction costs."[28]

Are the Sexes Really That Different? But wait, are men really so bad at investing compared to women? Some research shows that when "everything is low-key and manageable, men and women make decisions about risk in similar ways," says cognitive psychologist Therese Huston.[29] However, when

stress is added to the situation, men are apparently more prone to taking risky bets with little payoff, according to some neuroscientists.[30] Another paper, by economist Julie Nelson, suggests that as individuals men and women aren't all that different with regard to risk taking—but when men make decisions as *part of a group,* they adopt more risky strategies.[31] "Men in groups tend to show off. They egg one another on to display . . . the 'cultural norm of male daring.'"

YOUR CALL

When preparing to make important decisions—especially financial decisions—do you spend a lot of time trying to make a correct diagnosis, doing deep research, or do you chase "hot" tips and make snap judgments? How well do you do when you're under stress or participating in a group?

Stage 2: Think Up Alternative Solutions—Both the Obvious and the Creative

Employees burning with bright ideas are an employer's greatest competitive resource. "Creativity precedes innovation, which is its physical expression," says *Fortune* magazine writer Alan Farnham. "It's the source of all intellectual property."[32]

After you've identified the problem or opportunity and diagnosed its causes, you need to come up with alternative solutions.

Stage 3: Evaluate Alternatives and Select a Solution—Ethics, Feasibility, and Effectiveness

In this stage, you need to evaluate each alternative not only according to cost and quality but also according to the following questions: (1) Is it *ethical*? (If it isn't, don't give it a second look.) (2) Is it *feasible*? (If time is short, costs are high, technology unavailable, or customers resistant, for example, it is not.) (3) Is it ultimately *effective*? (If the decision is merely "good enough" but not optimal in the long run, you might reconsider.)

Stage 4: Implement and Evaluate the Solution Chosen

With some decisions, implementation is usually straightforward (though not necessarily easy—firing employees who steal may be an obvious decision, but it can still be emotionally draining). With other decisions, implementation can be quite difficult; when one company acquires another, for instance, it may take months to consolidate the departments, accounting systems, inventories, and so on.

Successful Implementation　For implementation to be successful, you need to do two things:

- **Plan carefully.** Especially if reversing an action will be difficult, you need to make careful plans for implementation. Some decisions may require written plans.
- **Be sensitive to those affected.** You need to consider how the people affected may feel about the change—inconvenienced, insecure, even fearful, all of which can trigger resistance. This is why it helps to give employees and customers latitude during a changeover in business practices or working arrangements.

Now that you understand the four stages of the rational model, to what extent do you think you use them when making decisions? Would you like to improve your problem-solving skills? If yes, then you will find the following self-assessment valuable. It assesses your problem-solving skills.

≡ connect SELF-ASSESSMENT 7.1

Assessing Your Problem-Solving Potential

This survey is designed to assess your approach to problem solving. Please be prepared to answer these questions if your instructor has assigned Self-Assessment 7.1 in Connect.

1. What is the status of your problem-solving skills? Are you surprised by the results?

2. Based on identifying the four lowest scored items on the assessment, what can you do to improve your problem-solving skills? Explain.

3. Reflect on a recent decision you made that did not turn out to your satisfaction. Now, consider what you learned about the rational model and your problem-solving skills and think through the decision for a second time. What would you do differently based on these considerations?

Evaluation   One "law" in economics is the Law of Unintended Consequences—things happen that weren't foreseen. For this reason, you need to follow up and evaluate the results of the decision.

What should you do if the action is not working? Some possibilities:

- **Give it more time.** You need to make sure employees, customers, and so on have had enough time to get used to the new action.

- **Change it slightly.** Maybe the action was correct, but it just needs "tweaking"—a small change of some sort.

- **Try another alternative.** If Plan A doesn't seem to be working, maybe you want to scrap it for another alternative.

- **Start over.** If no alternative seems workable, you need to go back to the drawing board—to Stage 1 of the decision-making process.

EXAMPLE   Evaluation: The Boeing 787 Dreamliner, a Bet-the-Company Decision

In 2002, a time when Boeing Co., the Chicago-headquartered aerospace giant, was losing business to its European rival Airbus and rising fuel costs were dramatically impacting the commercial airline industry, Boeing management made a bold decision: It would build a new medium-sized commercial jet, the 787 Dreamliner, its first new aircraft in 10 years, designed to fly faster than the competition and to consume 20% less fuel than similar-sized planes.

To achieve this, the 787 would feature more fuel-efficient engines and the fuselage would be built from plastic composite materials instead of aluminum. This would cut down on structural fatigue and corrosion, thereby reducing the number of inspections necessary and increasing the number of flights possible. "A light, strong plane is the big payoff for the huge technical risk Boeing is taking in crafting parts out of composites," said one aerospace reporter.[33]

A Bumpy Ride.   First planned for a summer 2007 launch, the date was revised for 2008. Then, in mid-2006, the company began encountering the first of many stories of bad news. The fuselage section had failed in testing, and engineers had discovered worrisome bubbles in its skin. The carbon-fiber wing

was too heavy, adding to the plane's overall weight. To hold costs down, Boeing had outsourced about 70% of the production to major suppliers acting as risk-sharing partners and playing a greater role in design and manufacturing. In return for investing more up front and taking on a share of the development costs, suppliers were given major sections of the airplane to build.[34]

Dream on. Boeing's 787 Dreamliner. © Bloomberg/Getty Images

By late 2007, however, it was apparent that suppliers were struggling to meet the exacting technological demands and deadlines, and their software programs were having trouble communicating with each other. In October, Boeing announced it would no longer meet its May 2008 target date and was postponing its first delivery to late fall of that year.[35]

Changing Dates. In early 2008, the company said the poor quality of outsourced work and the unprecedented amount of coordination among suppliers caused Boeing to shift much of the work back to its Everett, Washington, assembly plant, adding to delays. It said it was working to try to begin deliveries to customers not in late 2008 but in the first quarter of 2009, which then became the third quarter.[36] Then in 2009, stress testing revealed new flaws around bolts inside the wings.[37]

Finally, after six delays and nearly 10 years of anticipation, the Dreamliner had its first flight, on December 15, 2009.[38] Then, on October 28, 2011, after months of testing and three years behind schedule, the 787 was put into service for the first time, carrying 264 passengers for All Nippon Airways from Tokyo to Hong Kong.[39]

After More Problems, Finally Success. Then in January 2013, two Japanese-owned 787 Dreamliners experienced mysterious battery fires, resulting in the entire fleet of jetliners being grounded worldwide for 3½ months.[40] In March 2014, Boeing and a key supplier discovered hairline cracks while inspecting the wings of 42 yet-to-be-delivered Dreamliners, which forced changes to the manufacturing process.[41] In 2016, the company was ordered to fix General Electric engines on some Dreamliners after an icing problem caused them to shut down in mid-flight.[42] Even so, the Federal Aviation Administration declared the plane's design, including its revolutionary use of composite materials and increased reliance on electronic systems, to be "fundamentally sound."[43] The company also learned from its earlier mishaps by bringing more of the Dreamliner's manufacturing process back in-house after outsourcing it, to avoid the design and production missteps that plagued them earlier.

Through it all, as Boeing dealt with the additional setbacks, it continued to pick up orders as the airlines' financial health improved in the wake of the Great Recession and as high fuel prices continued to drive demand for more efficient aircraft like the Dreamliner.[44] Passengers loved the travel experience, praising the plane's bigger windows, higher ceilings, electronic window shades, big overhead bins, better cabin speakers, lavatories with motion-activated taps and flush, better cabin pressurization, "gust proof suppression system" for a smoother ride, and great looks.[45] (The Dreamliner "is just a gorgeous craft," said one reviewer, "with its sweptback wings and sleek lines.")[46]

From 2011 to 2014, Boeing made its profit expectations, although it missed them in 2015.[47] Still, because the 787 had been put into service three years late and cost twice the original estimate of $5 billion, it has not yet recovered its costs.[48] Will it do so?

The New 787s. The original Dreamliner was called the 787-8, which carries about 210 people and costs $224.6 million; this version accounted for nearly 80% of the Dreamliners delivered up until the end of 2015.[49] As of 2016, Boeing was making two additional versions of the plane: the 787-9, carrying 270 people and costing $264.6 million, and the 787-10, carrying 300 people and costing $306.1 million. To offset the billions of dollars in losses in building the first few hundred 787s, Boeing will need to sell more of the larger and more profitable models, particularly the 787-10. As of March 2016, Boeing needed another 150 orders on the various 787s in order to reach a target of 1,300 planes (at an average profit of $35 million per plane), and it cannot suffer any cancellations.[50]

YOUR CALL

How would you evaluate Boeing's decisions? Do you think despite all the effort on the 787-8 that the company will be able to apply what it learned regarding the use of carbon fiber composite materials and global experiments with different vendors to the newer Dreamliner versions (787-9, 787-10)? Was this a risky bet-the-company decision?

What's Wrong with the Rational Model?

The rational model is *prescriptive,* describing how managers ought to make decisions. It doesn't describe how managers *actually* make decisions. Indeed, the rational model makes some highly desirable assumptions—that managers have complete information, are able to make an unemotional analysis, and are able to make the best decision for the organization. *(See Table 7.1.)* We all know that these assumptions are unrealistic.

- **Complete information, no uncertainty:** You should obtain complete, error-free information about all alternative courses of action and the consequences that would follow from each choice.

- **Logical, unemotional analysis:** Having no prejudices or emotional blind spots, you are able to logically evaluate the alternatives, ranking them from best to worst according to your personal preferences.

- **Best decision for the organization:** Confident of the best future course of action, you coolly choose the alternative that you believe will most benefit the organization.

TABLE 7.1

Assumptions of the Rational Model

Nonrational Decision Making: Managers Find It Difficult to Make Optimal Decisions

Nonrational models of decision making explain how managers make decisions; they assume that decision making is nearly always uncertain and risky, making it difficult for managers to make optimal decisions. The nonrational models are *descriptive* rather than prescriptive: They describe how managers *actually* make decisions rather than how they should. Two nonrational models are (1) *satisficing* and (2) *intuition*.

1. Bounded Rationality and the Satisficing Model: "Satisfactory Is Good Enough"

During the 1950s, economist **Herbert Simon**—who later received the Nobel Prize—began to study how managers actually make decisions. From his research he proposed that managers could not act truly logically because their rationality was bounded by so many restrictions.[51] Called **bounded rationality**, the concept suggests that the ability of decision makers to be rational is limited by numerous constraints, such as complexity, time and money, and their cognitive capacity, values, skills, habits, and unconscious reflexes. *(See Figure 7.2.)*

FIGURE 7.2   Some hindrances to perfectly rational decision making

Complexity: The problems that need solving are often exceedingly complex, beyond understanding.	**Different cognitive capacity, values, skills, habits, and unconscious reflexes:** Managers aren't all built the same way, of course, and all have personal limitations and biases that affect their judgment.	**Information overload:** There is too much information for one person to process.
Time and money constraints: There is not enough time or money to gather all relevant information.	**Imperfect information:** Managers have imperfect, fragmentary information about the alternatives and their consequences.	**Different priorities:** Some data are considered more important, so certain facts are ignored. **Conflicting goals:** Other managers, including colleagues, have conflicting goals.

Because of such constraints, managers don't make an exhaustive search for the best alternative. Instead, they follow what Simon calls the **satisficing model**—that is, managers seek alternatives until they find one that is satisfactory, not optimal. While "satisficing" might seem to be a weakness, it may well outweigh any advantages gained from delaying making a decision until all information is in and all alternatives weighed.

However, making snap decisions can also backfire. Example: In the fall of 2014, Amazon.com was about to release its new voice-controlled smart speaker (what came to be called the Echo), but there was one lingering uncertainty: the choice of "wake word" that, when spoken, would cue the device to take voice commands. (Because of technical limitations, a wake word cannot be just any sound.) One possibility was "Echo." Another was "Alexa." Amazon CEO Jeff Bezos thought the best word was "Amazon." However, the difficulty with Bezos's choice, according to Amazon's engineers, as reported in *Bloomberg Businessweek,* was that "the speakers would wake upon hearing Amazon ads on television and, because it connects to a Wi-Fi network, could start buying stuff from the Internet."[53] In the end Bezos agreed with his engineers that the wake word would be "Alexa"—a satisfactory, if not optimal, solution for Bezos.

Nonrational decision making? When gasoline prices fall, Americans do two things: They buy more gas but they also buy higher-octane gas. Thus, instead of saving money by buying their previous gallons and grades, they opt to go fancy on their fill-ups.[52] Why do you suppose this is? How do you deal with this kind of nonrational decision?
© NithidPhoto/Getty Images RF

2. The Intuition Model: "It Just Feels Right" Small entrepreneurs often can't afford in-depth marketing research and so they make decisions based on hunches—their subconscious, visceral feelings. For instance, Ben Hugh, 32, decided to buy *I Can Has Cheezburger?*—a blog devoted to silly cat pictures paired with viewer-submitted quirky captions—when it linked to his own pet blog and caused it to crash from a wave of new visitors. Putting up $10,000 of his own money and acquiring additional investor financing, he bought the site for $2 million from the Hawaiian bloggers who started it. "It was a white-knuckle decision," he said later. But he expanded the Cheezburger blog into an empire that now includes 53 sites.[54]

"Going with your gut," or **intuition, is making a choice without the use of conscious thought or logical inference.**[55] Intuition that stems from *expertise*—a person's explicit and tacit knowledge about a person, a situation, an object, or a decision opportunity— is known as a *holistic hunch*. Intuition based on feelings—the involuntary emotional response to those same matters—is known as *automated experience*. It is important to try to develop your intuitive skills because they are as important as rational analysis in many decisions.[56] Some suggestions appear in the following Practical Action box.

Tips for Improving Your Intuition
PRACTICAL ACTION

1. **Trust your intuitive judgments.** Your feelings count. Trust them and rely on your "gut" when it feels right.

2. **Seek feedback.** Confirm your intuitive judgments by asking trusted others for feedback.

3. **Test your intuitive success rate.** Think back over the last year and assess how many times you relied on your intuition. What was your success rate? If your intuition was wrong, assess why and try to use this knowledge in the future.

4. **Try visualizing solutions.** Visualizing solutions will help engage the System 1 thinking needed to activate your intuition.

5. **Challenge your intuition.** Rather than automatically accepting your intuitive thoughts, challenge them. Test your intuition by thinking of counterarguments. Then challenge those counterarguments.[57]

YOUR CALL

Which of the five tips might be most helpful in improving your intuition? Outline a brief action plan for using this tip.

As a model for making decisions, intuition has at least two benefits. (1) It can speed up decision making, useful when deadlines are tight.[58] (2) It can be helpful to managers when resources are limited. A drawback, however, is that it can be difficult to convince others that your hunch makes sense. In addition, intuition is subject to the same biases as those that affect rational decision making, as we discuss in Section 7.5.[59] Finally, says one senior executive, intuition is fine for start-ups but "often deceives CEOs as their businesses become more complex."[60] Still, we believe that intuition and rationality are complementary and that managers should develop the courage to use intuition when making decisions.[61]

To what extent do you use intuition when making decisions? Are you curious about how you can improve your level of intuition? ●

---

connect SELF-ASSESSMENT 7.2

Assessing Your Level of Intuition

This survey is designed to assess the extent you use intuition in your current job. Please be prepared to answer these questions if your instructor has assigned Self-Assessment 7.2 in Connect.

1. Are you intuitive at work? Did the results surprise you?

2. What can you do to increase the amount of intuition you use at work? Describe.

3. What factors are inhibiting your use of intuition? What, if anything, can be done to eliminate these hindrances?

7.2   Making Ethical Decisions

MAJOR QUESTION   **What guidelines can I follow to be sure that decisions I make are not just lawful but ethical?**

THE BIG PICTURE

A graph known as a decision tree can help one make ethical decisions.

The ethical behavior of businesspeople, as we discussed at length in Chapter 3, has become of increasing concern in recent years, brought about by a number of events.

The Dismal Record of Business Ethics

First were the business scandals of the early 2000s, from Enron to WorldCom, producing photos of handcuffed executives. "The supposedly 'independent' auditors, directors, accountants, and stock market advisers and accountants were all tarnished," wrote Mortimer Zuckerman, editor-in-chief of *U.S. News & World Report*. "The engine of the people's involvement, the mutual fund industry, was shown to be permeated by rip-off artists rigging the system for the benefit of insiders and the rich."[62] Then, as the Iraq war wore on, reports came back of sweetheart deals and gross abuses by civilian contractors working in Iraq war zones.

In 2007, it became apparent that banks and others in the financial industry had forsaken sound business judgment—including ethical judgments—by making mortgage loans (subprime loans) to essentially unqualified buyers, which led to a wave of housing foreclosures and helped push the country into a recession. Since then, the media have presented us with a display of Ponzi schemes (Bernard Madoff, Allen Stanford), insider trading (Sam Waksal, Raj Rajaratnam), corporate sleaziness (work-stressed suicides at Apple's China supplier Foxconn, a fatality at a Kentucky coal mine evading safety regulations), excessive profiteering (as when a pharmaceutical company raised the price of one medication from $13.50 a pill to an astonishing $750 a pill), and similar matters.[63]

Through it all, voices were being raised that American capitalism was not doing enough to help the poorer nations in the world. Companies in wealthier countries, Microsoft's Bill Gates has urged, should focus on "a twin mission: making profits and also improving lives for those who don't fully benefit from market forces."[64]

All these concerns have forced the subject of right-minded decision making to the top of the agenda in many organizations. Indeed, many companies now have an **ethics officer, someone trained about matters of ethics in the workplace, particularly about resolving ethical dilemmas.** More and more companies are also creating values statements to guide employees as to what constitutes desirable business behavior.[65] As a result of this raised consciousness, managers now must try to make sure their decisions are not just lawful but also ethical.[66]

Buy a pair, give a pair. Warby Parker (named after two characters in a journal by 1950s Beat Generation writer Jack Kerouac) was established in 2010 by four former Wharton School students. The company operates on two premises: (a) Designer glasses can be sold at a fraction of the price of the hugely marked-up luxury alternatives. (b) For every pair of glasses sold, a pair could be distributed among the hundreds of thousands of people in need. "Glasses are one of the most effective poverty-alleviation tools in the world," says one of the founders. "They increase one's income by 20%, which is equivalent to adding a full extra day of work a week."[67] Are you more inclined to buy from companies like Warby Parker or shoe seller TOMS (which gives away a pair of shoes to a needy person for every pair sold) that tie sales of their products to helping impoverished people around the world? © Astrid Stawiarz/WireImage/Getty Images

Road Map to Ethical Decision Making: A Decision Tree

Undoubtedly the greatest pressure on top executives is to maximize shareholder value, to deliver the greatest return on investment to the owners of their company. But is a decision that is beneficial to shareholders yet harmful to employees—such as forcing them to contribute more to their health benefits, as IBM has done—unethical? Harvard Business School professor Constance Bagley suggests that what is needed is a decision tree to help with ethical decisions.[68] **A decision tree is a graph of decisions and their possible consequences; it is used to create a plan to reach a goal. Decision trees are used to aid in making decisions.** Bagley's ethical decision tree is shown opposite. *(See Figure 7.3.)*

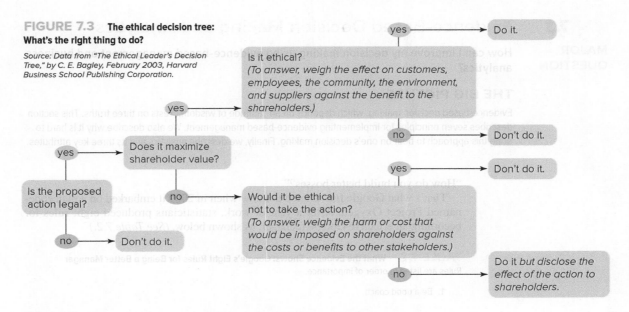

FIGURE 7.3 **The ethical decision tree: What's the right thing to do?**

Source: Data from "The Ethical Leader's Decision Tree," by C. E. Bagley, February 2003, Harvard Business School Publishing Corporation.

When confronted with any proposed action for which a decision is required, a manager should ask the following questions.

1. Is the Proposed Action Legal? This may seem an obvious question. But, Bagley observes, "corporate shenanigans suggest that some managers need to be reminded: If the action isn't legal, don't do it."

2. If "Yes," Does the Proposed Action Maximize Shareholder Value? If the action is legal, one must next ask whether it will profit the shareholders. If the answer is "yes," should you do it? Not necessarily.

3. If "Yes," Is the Proposed Action Ethical? As Bagley points out, though directors and top managers may believe they are bound by corporate law to always maximize shareholder value, the courts and many state legislatures have held they are not. Rather, their main obligation is to manage "for the best interests of the corporation," which includes the interests of the larger community.

Thus, says Bagley, building a profitable-but-polluting plant in a country overseas may benefit the shareholders but be bad for that country—and for the corporation's relations with that nation. Ethically, then, managers should add pollution-control equipment.

4. If "No," Would It Be Ethical *Not* to Take the Proposed Action? If the action would not directly benefit shareholders, might it still be ethical to go ahead with it?

Not building the overseas plant might be harmful to other stakeholders, such as employees or customers. Thus, the ethical conclusion might be to build the plant with pollution-control equipment but to disclose the effects of the decision to shareholders.

As a basic guideline to making good ethical decisions on behalf of a corporation, Bagley suggests that directors, managers, and employees need to follow their own individual ideas about right and wrong.[69] There is a lesson, she suggests, in the response of the pension fund manager who, when asked whether she would invest in a company doing business in a country that permits slavery, responded, "Do you mean me, personally, or as a fund manager?" When people feel entitled or compelled to compromise their own personal ethics to advance the interests of a business, "it is an invitation to mischief."[70]

To learn more about your own ethics, morality, and/or values (while contributing to scientific research), go to *www.yourmorals.org.*[71] ●

7.3 Evidence-Based Decision Making and Analytics

How can I improve my decision making using evidence-based management and business analytics?

THE BIG PICTURE

Evidence-based decision making, which depends on an "attitude of wisdom," rests on three truths. This section describes seven principles for implementing evidence-based management. We also describe why it is hard to bring this approach to bear on one's decision making. Finally, we describe analytics and its three key attributes.

"How do you build better bosses?"

That's what Google Inc. wanted to know when in 2009 it embarked on a plan code-named Project Oxygen. After a year of work, statisticians produced eight rules for becoming an effective Google manager, as shown below. *(See Table 7.2.)*

TABLE 7.2   What the Evidence Shows: Google's Eight Rules for Being a Better Manager
Rules are listed in order of importance.

1. Be a good coach.

2. Empower your team, don't micromanage.

3. Express interest in team members' success and personal well-being.

4. Don't be a "sissy": Be productive and results oriented.

5. Be a good communicator and listen to your team.

6. Help your employees with career development.

7. Have a clear vision and strategy for the team.

8. Have key technical skills so you can help advise the team.

Source: J.-C. Spender and B. A. Strong, Strategic Conversations: Creating and Directing the Entrepreneurial Workforce (Cambridge, MA: Cambridge University Press, 2014), p. 141.

Some of these may seem obvious, even silly: "Have a clear vision and strategy for the team." "Don't be a 'sissy': Be productive and results oriented." Really?

What's important here, however, is how Google arrived at what would seem to be commonsensical advice: by analyzing performance reviews, employee surveys, nominations for top-manager awards, and other sources. "The result was more than 10,000 observations of manager behaviors," says one report. "The research team complimented the quantitative data with qualitative information from interviews."[72] In other words, Google looked at the *evidence*.

Evidence-Based Decision Making

"Too many companies and too many leaders are more interested in just copying others, doing what they've always done, and making decisions based on beliefs in what ought to work rather than what actually works," say Stanford professors **Jeffrey Pfeffer** and **Robert Sutton.** "They fail to face the hard facts and use the best evidence to help navigate the competitive environment."[73] Companies that use *evidence-based management—* the translation of principles based on best evidence into organizational practice, bringing rationality to the decision-making process, as we defined it in Chapter 2—routinely trump the competition, Pfeffer and Sutton suggest.[74]

Seven Implementation Principles Pfeffer and Sutton identify seven implementation principles to help companies that are committed to doing what it takes to profit from evidence-based management:[75]

- **Treat your organization as an unfinished prototype.** Leaders need to think and act as if their organization were an unfinished prototype that won't be ruined by dangerous new ideas or impossible to change because of employee or management resistance. Example: Some Internet start-ups that find their original plan not working have learned to master "the art of the pivot," to fail gracefully by cutting their losses and choosing a new direction—as did the founders of Fabulus, a review site and social network that attracted no users, and so they launched a high-end e-commerce site called Fab.com.[76] (Unfortunately, Fab CEO Jason Goldberg was inclined to pivot the business rather than solve basic problems. "You can change a business once or twice," says one former employee, "but after that you're drowning."[77] After creating and losing 500 jobs and creating and losing $850 million, Fab ended and was bought for a fraction of its value by another company.)

- **No brag, just facts.** This slogan is an antidote for over-the-top assertions about forthcoming products, such as "the deafening levels of managed hype across much of Silicon Valley," as one reporter characterized it.[78] Other companies, such as DaVita, which operates dialysis centers, take pains to evaluate data before making decisions. So does SAS Institute, the privately owned software company, No. 8 on *Fortune*'s 2016 "Best Places to Work For" list. As we've seen, Google has used data to find out what makes a better boss.[79]

- **See yourself and your organization as outsiders do.** Most managers are afflicted with "rampant optimism," with inflated views of their own talents and prospects for success, which causes them to downplay risks and continue on a path despite evidence that things are not working. "Having a blunt friend, mentor, or counselor," Pfeffer and Sutton suggest, "can help you see and act on better evidence."

- **Evidence-based management is not just for senior executives.** The best organizations are those in which everyone, not just the top managers, is guided by the responsibility to gather and act on quantitative and qualitative data and share results with others.

- **Like everything else, you still need to sell it.** "Unfortunately, new and exciting ideas grab attention even when they are vastly inferior to old ideas," the Stanford authors say. "Vivid, juicy stories and case studies sell better than detailed, rigorous, and admittedly dull data—no matter how wrong the stories or how right the data." To sell an evidence-based approach, you may have to identify a preferred practice based on solid if unexciting evidence, then use vivid stories to grab management attention.

Evidence-based decisions. Google used evidence-based analysis to find out what makes a better boss. They found that what employees value most are even-keeled bosses who take an interest in employees' lives and careers, who make time for one-on-one meetings, and who help people work through problems by asking questions instead of dictating answers. Would you expect a "just-the-facts" approach to be normal in high-tech businesses or unusual?
© Cole Burston/Bloomberg/Getty Images

- **If all else fails, slow the spread of bad practice.** Because many managers and employees face pressures to do things that are known to be ineffective, it may be necessary for you to practice "evidence-based misbehavior"—that is, ignore orders you know to be wrong or delay their implementation.

- **The best diagnostic question: What happens when people fail?** "Failure hurts, it is embarrassing, and we would rather live without it," the authors write. "Yet there is no learning without failure. . . . If you look at how the most effective systems in the world are managed, a hallmark is that when something goes wrong, people face the hard facts, learn what happened and why, and keep using those facts to make the system better."[80] From the U.S. civil aviation system, which rigorously examines airplane accidents, near misses, and equipment problems, to mall owners replacing vacant department stores (Macy's, Sears) with new kinds of anchor tenants (Dick's Sporting Goods, Wegmans Food Markets) as the backbone of shopping centers, evidence-based management makes the point that failure is a great teacher.[81] This means, however, that the organization must "forgive and remember" people who make mistakes, not be trapped by preconceived notions, and confront the best evidence and hard facts.

What Makes It Hard to Be Evidence Based   Despite your best intentions, it's hard to bring the best evidence to bear on your decisions. Among the reasons:[82] (1) There's too much evidence. (2) There's not enough *good* evidence. (3) The evidence doesn't quite apply. (4) People are trying to mislead you. (5) *You* are trying to mislead you. (6) The side effects outweigh the cure. (Example: Despite the belief that social promotion in school is a bad idea—that is, that schools shouldn't advance children to the next grade when they haven't mastered the material—the side effect is skyrocketing costs because it crowds schools with older students, and angrier students, demanding more resources.) (7) Stories are more persuasive, anyway.

EXAMPLE   Evidence-Based Decision Making: "If People Are Your Most Important Assets, Why Would You Get Rid of Them?"

It's an axiom of many managers that it's often necessary to cut back on workers during economic downturns—or even in good times—because it helps to increase profitability or drive the company's stock price higher. But Stanford professor Jeffrey Pfeffer, advocate for evidence-based management, takes issue with this assumption. "There is a growing body of academic research suggesting that firms incur big costs when they cut workers," he writes.[83]

What Are the Costs of Layoffs? While agreeing that there are circumstances in which layoffs are necessary for a firm to survive (as when an industry is shrinking or competitors are resorting to cheaper overseas labor), Pfeffer suggests companies incur big costs when they cut their labor forces. He cites the direct and indirect costs of layoffs listed by University of Colorado professor Wayne Cascio in his book *Responsible Restructuring:* "severance pay; paying out accrued vacation and sick pay; outplacement costs; higher unemployment-insurance taxes; the cost of rehiring employees when business improves; low morale and risk-averse survivors; potential lawsuits, sabotage, or even workplace violence from aggrieved employees or former employees; loss of institutional memory and knowledge; diminished trust in management; and reduced productivity."

Looking at the evidence, Pfeffer finds that firms that announce layoffs actually *do not* enjoy higher stock prices than their peers, either immediately or over time. Layoffs also don't increase individual company productivity and, in fact, don't even reliably cut costs (because companies often lose the best people first; there is lower morale among survivors, resulting in reduced customer service, innovation, and productivity; and remaining employees are spurred to look for other jobs once things improve).

The Most Successful Airline. Following the 9/11 tragedy in 2001, which coincided with the start of a recession, all U.S. airlines except one announced tens of thousands of layoffs. The exception was Southwest, which has never had an involuntary layoff in its 47-year history and which most Americans voted the most desirable brand in 2012.[84] (It still ranked high as a brand, at number 7, in 2015 and 2016 among *Fortune*'s World's Most Admired Companies.)[85] "If people are your most important assets," Pfeffer quotes a former head of the airline's human resources department, "why would you get rid of them?"

YOUR CALL

Can you think of any instances of people being laid off unnecessarily? What is your evidence that it was not necessary?

In Praise of Analytics

Perhaps the purest application of evidence-based management is the use of **analytics,** or *business analytics*, the term used for sophisticated forms of business data analysis. One example of analytics is portfolio analysis, in which an investment adviser evaluates the risks of various stocks. Another example is the time-series forecast, which predicts future data based on patterns of historical data.

Some leaders and firms have become exceptional practitioners of analytics. Gary Loveman, CEO of the Harrah's gambling empire, wrote a famous paper, "Diamonds in the Data Mine," in which he explained how data-mining software was used to analyze vast amounts of casino customer data to target profitable patrons.[86] Marriott International, through its Total Hotel Optimization program, has used quantitative data to establish the optimal price for hotel rooms, evaluate use of conference facilities and catering, and develop systems to optimize offerings to frequent customers.[87] To aid in recruitment, Microsoft studies correlations between its successful workers and the schools and companies they arrived from.[88]

Analytics in Athletics: The Personal "Moneyball" Takeover of Sports   EXAMPLE

After her first set during the 2015 Bank of the West Classic at Stanford, California, pro tennis player Angelique Kerber called her coach over for a 90-second conference (recently allowed under experimental World Tennis Association rules). Referring to his data-laden iPad, as well as his courtside observations, the coach told Kerber that her opponent was serving to her backhand nearly every time. With this knowledge Kerber went on to defeat her competitor, and then her subsequent contender, to win the tournament, for her fourth title of the year.[89]

Better Indicators of Player Success. The obsession with analytics in professional tennis—a latecomer, after baseball, football, basketball, and hockey, to the use of sophisticated data analysis in pro sports—is the logical result of the whole *Moneyball* phenomenon. The film of that name, which starred Brad Pitt and supporting actor Jonah Hill and which received six 2012 Academy Award nominations, was adapted from a book by Michael Lewis, *Moneyball: The Art of Winning an Unfair Game.* The book described how the Oakland Athletics, one of the poorest teams in Major League Baseball (2002 payroll $41 million, versus the New York Yankees's $126 million), managed to go to the playoffs five times in seven years against better-financed contenders. They accomplished this by avoiding the use of traditional baseball statistics and finding better indicators of player success in on-base percentage, slugging percentage, and the like. For a time, this creative use of analytics enabled managers of the California club to concentrate their limited payroll resources on draft picks who were primarily talented college players rather than veteran professionals.[90]

Analytics in Pro Sports. Since then, analytic measures, such as WAR (wins above replacement) and PER (player efficiency rating), have been used to find better ways to value players and strategies in all major sports.[91] For instance, Major League Baseball's Kansas City Royals, operating without the huge budgets of the Yankees and Los Angeles Dodgers, has used analytics to replace its bigger-name stars with "under-the-radar veteran alternatives in search of a World Series ring," says one report.[92]

In basketball, the application of data and analytics reached its zenith with the Golden State Warriors, the National Basketball Association's defending champion. In 2010, a group of data-loving Silicon Valley investors bought the floundering team for $450 million (it's now worth $2 billion) and proceeded to fix it by trying to answer the question "What would happen if you built a basketball team by ignoring every orthodoxy of building a basketball team?" One unusual idea: Focus less on recruiting big men who could stuff the basket and more on players who could make 3-point shots.[93]

Delving into the statistics, the executives began to rebuild the team around star 3-point shooters Stephen Curry and Klay Thompson and other players, which helped the Warriors make a higher percentage of 3-pointers than any other team in the league. The team also applied emerging technology (wearable Catapult GPS devices, SportVU cameras) during practices to learn whether players were performing to baseline standards and which might be candidates for forced rest. The Warriors became the healthiest team in the NBA, according to an ESPN study.[94]

"We're lightyears ahead of probably every other team in structure, in planning, in how we're going to go about things," says Golden State majority owner Joe Lacob. "We're going to be a handful for the rest of the NBA to deal with for a long time."[95] The Warriors won the NBA championship in 2015 and nearly did so again in 2016, ultimately losing to Cleveland.

YOUR CALL

Executives and personnel people in other lines of work are often like the old sports traditionalists, relying on resume, degree, years of experience, and even looks in evaluating job applicants. What other, more quantifiable measures might be used instead when hiring new college graduates?

Thomas H. Davenport and others at Babson College's Working Knowledge Research Center studied 32 organizations that made a commitment to quantitative, fact-based analysis and found three key attributes among analytics competitors: *use of modeling, multiple applications,* and *support from top management.*[96]

1. Use of Modeling: Going beyond Simple Descriptive Statistics

Companies such as Capital One look well beyond basic statistics, using data mining and predictive modeling to identify potential and most profitable customers. **Predictive modeling is a data-mining technique used to predict future behavior and anticipate the consequences of change.** Thus, Capital One conducts more than 30,000 experiments a year, with different interest rates, incentives, direct-mail packaging, and other variables to evaluate which customers are most apt to sign up for credit cards and will pay back their debt.

2. Multiple Applications, Not Just One

UPS (formerly United Parcel Service) applies analytics not only to tracking the movement of packages but also to examining usage patterns to try to identify potential customer defections so that salespeople can make contact and solve problems. More recently, as e-commerce has required UPS to make lots of single-package deliveries throughout neighborhoods, it has invested in a same-day delivery startup called Deliv Inc., hoping to prevail in the so-called last-mile delivery, considered the priciest part of an order's journey.[97] The company is also exploring the use of drones to deliver life-saving medicines.[98] Analytics competitors "don't gain advantage from one killer app [application], but rather from multiple applications supporting many parts of the business," says Davenport.

3. Support from the Top

"A companywide embrace of analytics impels changes in culture, processes, behavior, and skills for many employees," says Davenport. "And so, like any major transition, it requires leadership from executives at the very top who have a passion for the quantitative approach."[99]

"Big Data": What It Is, How It's Used

A recent study says the world's information will reach 40 zettabytes by 2020, a 50% growth over 2010 and equal to 57 times the number of grains of sand on all the beaches of the world.[100] (Just 1 zettabyte is equal to the contents of 20 million four-drawer file cabinets—multiplied by a million.)[101] This has led to a concept known as *Big Data,* stores of data so vast that conventional database management systems cannot handle them and so very sophisticated analysis software and supercomputing-level hardware are required.[102] **Big Data includes not only data in corporate databases but also web-browsing data trails, social network communications, sensor data, and surveillance data.**[103]

"One of the most extraordinary features of Big Data is that it signals the end of the reign of statistics," suggests technology writer Michael Malone. "For 400 years, we've been forced to sample complex systems and extrapolate. Now, with Big Data, *it is possible to measure everything,* from the movement of billions of stars to every beat of the human heart [our emphasis added]."[104] Attracting a lot of attention in science, business, medicine, and technology, the concept of Big Data has been dubbed "the next frontier for innovation, competition, and productivity."[105] Today 62.5% of Fortune 1000 firms in one survey reported they are using Big Data, twice what the rate was in 2013, and 69.9% view Big Data as very important or critical to their business success.[106] **Big Data analytics is the process of** examining large amounts of data of a variety of types to uncover hidden patterns, unknown correlations, and other useful information. Among some of the uses of Big Data analytics are the following:[107]

- **Analyzing consumer behavior and spurring sales:** Online behavior can be analyzed "to create ads, products, or experiences that are most appealing to consumers—and thus most lucrative to companies," says one technology journalist. "There's also great potential to more accurately predict market fluctuations or react faster to shifts in consumer sentiment or supply chain issues."[108] Specialists in what's known as financial planning and analysis (FP&A) at Dunkin Brands have mined customer loyalty data to encourage customers to buy more coffee and doughnuts.[109] Salesforce .com offers tools that draw on staff e-mails, calendars, and databases to offer tips to salespeople on how to interact with specific customers.[110] Real estate analytics firm RealtyTrac looks at the impact of Trader Joe's and Whole Foods groceries on the price of homes near the stores' neighborhoods.[111]

- **Improving hiring and personnel management:** JetBlue applies people analytics to hiring for all the airline's positions, which helps the company sort through the 125,000 job applications it receives each year.[112] Google uses data to figure out how to put together optimal-sized teams for projects and to figure out what characteristics make for effective leaders.[113] Some firms are using Big Data to figure out which employees might get sick, based on "the prescription drugs workers use, how they shop, and even whether they vote," in an effort to contain health costs, according to one description.[114]

- **Tracking movie, music, TV, and reading data:** HP Labs researchers have used Twitter data to accurately predict box-office revenues of Hollywood movies.[115] Record collectors and the music industry use Discogs.com to keep track of records and their various releases and to identify sources of royalties where copyrighted songs are played.[116] Television networks use new ways of pinpointing audience data to pitch live programs to advertisers.[117] Jellybooks, a reading analytics company based in London, hopes to use data about people's reading habits to reshape how publishers acquire, edit, and market books.[118]

- **Exploiting farm data:** Farmers can use data-collection devices to gather information about crops and soil conditions to sell to seed, pesticide, and equipment makers looking into how and when farmers use machinery and supplies.[119] Similar data can be used "to come up with trillions of scenarios for insurance coverage," says Michael Malone.[120]

- **Advancing health and medicine:** New internal and external monitoring devices are helping medical researchers gather enormous quantities of health data, helping us to understand, for instance, the effects of external influences on autism, what changes in lifestyle (social media usage, diminishing movement) can produce depression, or what procedures are more apt to lead to malpractice claims.[121]

- **Aiding public policy:** On the wall of his office, Boston mayor Marty Walsh has a so-called dashboard with dozens of different charts and graphs that use data to indicate whether the city is fulfilling its goals, such as quicker ambulance response times. Analytics can tackle large-scale public sector problems such as traffic congestion, train passenger commute patterns, and handling of federal funds in child welfare.[122] Social scientists are using Big Data to fight poverty, finding out which policies actually work.[123] They are doing the same thing with crime-fighting strategies.[124]

Down on the farm. This server farm, or data center, contains thousands of computers storing terabytes of information on everyone and everything—"Big Data" that can be subjected to data analytics to work on large-scale projects. With data centers like this, you can see why everything you enter online, whether via e-mail, Facebook, texting, or twittering, no matter how innocuous, can be stored and used later to try to sell you things. Are you okay with this? © Bloomberg/Getty Images

EXAMPLE   Data, Hacking, and Privacy: Who's Driving My Car?!

Big Data and analytics clearly have enormous benefits. But half the people in a Pew Research Center survey said they felt they had little or no control over their personal data. Indeed, two-thirds of adults said they were not confident that online video sites, search engine providers such as Google, or social media sites such as Facebook protected their information.[125] Are they right to be concerned?

Rise of the Cyberthieves. Hacking—gaining illegal access to computer systems—has become a major concern when, for example, an intruder is able to gain access to information on thousands of employees at the U.S. Justice Department and the Department of Homeland Security, as happened in 2016 (although there was no indication information had been stolen).[126] Hackers—so-called cyberthieves—have broken into hospital systems, such as that at Hollywood Presbyterian Hospital, demanding a ransom of roughly $17,000 to return control of the network.[127] Data thieves have successfully infiltrated Target's computers, stealing customer names and credit card numbers of as many as 40 million accounts.[128] Cyberthieves have also scammed $3 million from Mattel Inc., maker of Barbie dolls.[129]

Auto Corrupt. Even some cars can be hacked, as two security researchers proved in 2015 with a Jeep. "From the Internet," says one report, "they were able to track cars down by their location, see how fast they were going, turn their blinkers and lights on and off, mess with their windshield wipers, radios, navigation, and, in some cases, control their brakes and steering."[130] Scary stuff.

With all this, no wonder each case of unauthorized computer access by hackers trying to steal information or disrupt a firm's operations on average costs a U.S. company $3.5 million.[131] No wonder that companies are adding cybersecurity experts to their boards of directors.[132]

YOUR CALL

As companies begin to monitor their employees' health and habits, with a view toward reducing health costs, are you concerned how that information might be used? For instance, if an employer picks up symptoms of diabetes in you after you've used a retina scanner to enter secure facilities, should you be informed of that fact, or is that an invasion of privacy? How would you feel if devices were used to track your presence at, say, union meetings or meetings with other companies who might recruit you?[133]

7.4   Four General Decision-Making Styles

MAJOR QUESTION

How do I decide to decide?

THE BIG PICTURE

Your decision-making style reflects how you perceive and respond to information. It could be directive, analytical, conceptual, or behavioral.

A **decision-making style** reflects the combination of how an individual perceives and responds to information. A team of researchers developed a model of decision-making styles based on the idea that styles vary along two different dimensions: value orientation and tolerance for ambiguity.[134]

Value Orientation and Tolerance for Ambiguity

Value orientation reflects the extent to which a person focuses on either task and technical concerns or people and social concerns when making decisions. Some people, for instance, are very task focused at work and do not pay much attention to people issues, whereas others are just the opposite.

The second dimension pertains to a person's *tolerance for ambiguity*. This individual difference indicates the extent to which a person has a high need for structure or control in his or her life. Some people desire a lot of structure in their lives (a low tolerance for ambiguity) and find ambiguous situations stressful and psychologically uncomfortable. In contrast, others do not have a high need for structure and can thrive in uncertain situations (a high tolerance for ambiguity). Ambiguous situations can energize people with a high tolerance for ambiguity.

When the dimensions of value orientation and tolerance for ambiguity are combined, they form four styles of decision making: *directive, analytical, conceptual,* and *behavioral. (See Figure 7.4.)*

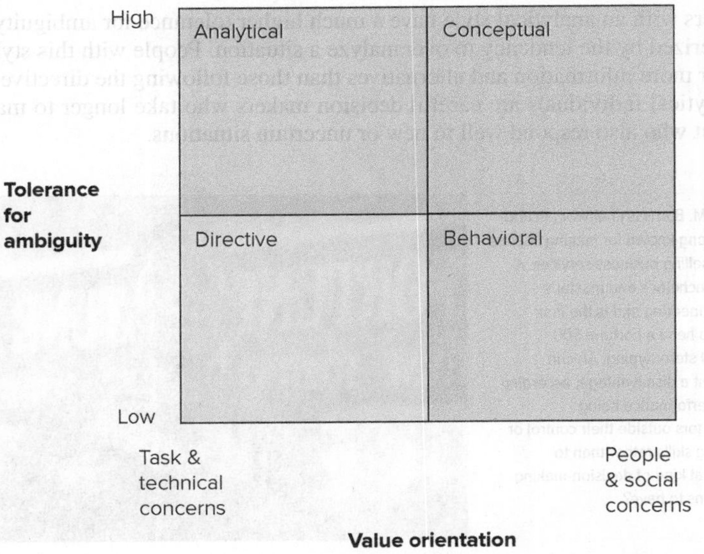

FIGURE 7.4

Decision-making styles

Success. Peyton Manning, quarterback for the Denver Broncos, led his team to victory 24–10 over the Carolina Panthers in the 2016 Super Bowl. As the leader of his team, a quarterback must make many decisions about what is the right way to success. If you were a quarterback, which of the four general decision-making styles do you think you would embody? © Zuma Press Inc/Alamy

1. The Directive Style: Action-Oriented Decision Makers Who Focus on Facts

People with a directive style have a low tolerance for ambiguity and are oriented toward task and technical concerns in making decisions. They are efficient, logical, practical, and systematic in their approach to solving problems.

People with this style are action oriented and decisive and like to focus on facts. In their pursuit of speed and results, however, these individuals tend to be autocratic, to exercise power and control, and to focus on the short run.

2. The Analytical Style: Careful Decision Makers Who Like Lots of Information and Alternative Choices

Managers with an analytical style have a much higher tolerance for ambiguity and are characterized by the tendency to overanalyze a situation. People with this style like to consider more information and alternatives than those following the directive style.

Analytical individuals are careful decision makers who take longer to make decisions but who also respond well to new or uncertain situations.

Fortune 500 CEO. Ursula M. Burns is chairwoman and CEO of Xerox, a company long known for making copiers and printers but now also selling business services. A bright student, she holds bachelor's and master's degrees in mechanical engineering and is the first African American woman to head a Fortune 500 company. Because of racial stereotyping, African American leaders operate at a disadvantage, according to one study, with strong performance being misattributed to market factors outside their control or to humor or public speaking skills rather than to intellectual prowess.[135] What kind of decision-making style would you expect Burns to have? © Paul Morigi/Getty Images

3. The Conceptual Style: Decision Makers Who Rely on Intuition and Have a Long-Term Perspective

People with a conceptual style have a high tolerance for ambiguity and tend to focus on the people or social aspects of a work situation. They take a broad perspective to problem solving and like to consider many options and future possibilities.

Conceptual types adopt a long-term perspective and rely on intuition and discussions with others to acquire information. They also are willing to take risks and are good at finding creative solutions to problems. However, a conceptual style can foster an indecisive approach to decision making.

4. The Behavioral Style: The Most People-Oriented Decision Makers

The behavioral style is the most people oriented of the four styles. People with this style work well with others and enjoy social interactions in which opinions are openly exchanged. Behavioral types are supportive, are receptive to suggestions, show warmth, and prefer verbal to written information.

Although they like to hold meetings, people with this style have a tendency to avoid conflict and to be concerned about others. This can lead behavioral types to adopt a wishy-washy approach to decision making and to have a hard time saying no.

Which Style Do You Have?

Research shows that very few people have only one dominant decision-making style. Rather, most managers have characteristics that fall into two or three styles. Studies also show that decision-making styles vary across occupations, job levels, and countries.[136] There is not a best decision-making style that applies to all situations.

You can use knowledge of decision-making styles in the following three ways.

Know Thyself   Knowledge of styles helps you to understand yourself. Awareness of your style assists you in identifying your strengths and weaknesses as a decision maker and facilitates the potential for self-improvement.

Influence Others   You can increase your ability to influence others by being aware of styles. For example, if you are dealing with an analytical person, you should provide as much information as possible to support your ideas.

Deal with Conflict   Knowledge of styles gives you an awareness of how people can take the same information yet arrive at different decisions by using a variety of decision-making strategies. Different decision-making styles are one likely source of interpersonal conflict at work.

What style of decision making do you prefer? Would you like to learn how to use all of the styles more effectively? The following self-assessment can help. ●

---

connect SELF-ASSESSMENT 7.3

What Is Your Decision-Making Style?

This survey is designed to assess your decision-making style. Please be prepared to answer these questions if your instructor has assigned Self-Assessment 7.3 in Connect.

1. What is your dominant decision-making style?

2. What are the pros and cons of your style?

3. Based on your results, what are some things you can do to incorporate aspects of your less dominant styles into your decision making? Explain.

7.5 How to Overcome Barriers to Decision Making

Trying to be rational isn't always easy. What are the barriers?

THE BIG PICTURE

Responses to a decision situation may take the form of four ineffective reactions or three effective reactions. Managers should be aware of nine common decision-making biases.

Do your moods influence your decisions? Do you, for instance, spend more when you're sad and self-absorbed? That's what one experiment found: When researchers exposed student participants to a sadness-inducing video clip about the death of a boy's mentor, the students were inclined to offer more money for a product (a sporty-looking water bottle) than were other subjects who had watched a neutral clip.[137]

Decision Making and Expectations about Happiness

Not just moods themselves perhaps can influence your decisions, but also so can your expectations about how happy or unhappy you think future outcomes will make you. It seems that people expect certain life events to have a much greater emotional effect than, in fact, they do, according to Harvard University psychologist Daniel Gilbert, who has studied individual emotional barometers in decision making. College professors, for example, expect to be quite happy if they are given tenure and quite unhappy if they aren't. However, Gilbert found those who received tenure were happy but not as happy as they themselves had predicted, whereas those denied tenure did not become very unhappy.

The expectation about the level of euphoria or disappointment was also found to be true of big-jackpot lottery winners and of people being tested for HIV infection. That is, people are often right when they describe what outcome will make them feel good or bad, but they are often wrong when asked to predict how strongly they will feel that way and how long the feeling will last. Even severe life events have a negative impact on people's sense of well-being and satisfaction for no more than three months, after which their feelings at least go back to normal.[138]

Perhaps knowing that you have this "immune system" of the mind, which blunts bad feelings and smoothes out euphoric ones, can help make it easier for you to make difficult decisions.

How Do Individuals Respond to a Decision Situation? Ineffective and Effective Responses

What is your typical response when you're suddenly confronted with a challenge in the form of a problem or an opportunity? There are perhaps four ineffective reactions and three effective ones.[139]

Four Ineffective Reactions There are four defective problem-recognition and problem-solving approaches that act as barriers when you must make an important decision in a situation of conflict.

1. Relaxed Avoidance—"There's No Point in Doing Anything; Nothing Bad's Going to Happen" In **relaxed avoidance,** a manager decides to take no action in the belief that there will be no great negative consequences. This condition, then, is a form of complacency: You either don't see or you disregard the signs of danger (or of opportunity).

Example: Relaxed avoidance was vividly demonstrated in the months before the subprime mortgage meltdown that began in 2007, when banks made cheap housing loans to a lot of unqualified buyers, precipitating a huge financial crisis and drying up of credit. During that time, a lot of smart people in denial said not to worry, that the mortgage mess would be "contained." They included many bank presidents and even Ben Bernanke, chairman of the Federal Reserve.[140] One nationwide online survey has also found that investors' forecasts of future returns go up after the stock market has risen and go down after it has fallen—complacency indeed.[141]

2. Relaxed Change—"Why Not Just Take the Easiest Way Out?" In **relaxed change,** a manager realizes that complete inaction will have negative consequences but opts for the first available alternative that involves low risk. This is, of course, a form of "satisficing"; the manager avoids exploring a variety of alternatives in order to make the best decision.

Example: Perhaps people really don't like a lot of choices. In one experiment, 40% of customers stopped by a large assortment of jam jars (24) and only 30% by a small assortment (6)—but only 3% made a purchase in the first case versus 30% in the second.[142]

3. Defensive Avoidance—"There's No Reason for Me to Explore Other Solution Alternatives" In **defensive avoidance,** a manager can't find a good solution and follows by (a) procrastinating, (b) passing the buck, or (c) denying the risk of any negative consequences. This is a posture of resignation and a denial of responsibility for taking action.

By procrastinating, you put off making a decision ("I'll get to this later").[143] In passing the buck, you let someone else take the consequences of making the decision ("Let George do it"). In denying the risk that there will be any negative consequences, you are engaging in rationalizing ("How bad could it be?"). As one article states, deliberating on the matter of why no one at Penn State did more to pursue allegations that an assistant football coach was abusing young boys, "companies overlook internal problems that at best impede performance and at worst could bring down the entire organization."[144]

Example: Defensive avoidance often occurs in firms with high turnover. Although some executives try to stop high performers from exiting by offering raises or promotions, others react defensively, telling themselves that the person leaving is not a big loss. "It's psychologically threatening to those who are staying to acknowledge there's a reason some people are leaving," says the CEO of a corporate-psychology consulting company, "so executives often dismiss them as untalented or even deny that an exodus is occurring."[145] He mentions one financial-services company whose executives insisted turnover was low, when in fact 50% of hundreds of new employees quit within years.

4. Panic—"This Is So Stressful, I've Got to Do Something—Anything—to Get Rid of the Problem" This reaction is especially apt to occur in crisis situations. In **panic,** a manager is so frantic to get rid of the problem that he or she can't deal with the situation realistically. This is the kind of situation in which the manager has completely forgotten the idea of behaving with "grace under pressure," of staying cool and calm. Troubled by anxiety, irritability, sleeplessness, and even physical illness, if you're experiencing this reaction, your judgment may be so clouded that you won't be able to accept help in dealing with the problem or to realistically evaluate the alternatives.

Example: "The day we left," writes Kevin Thornton about the panicky May 2016 flight of 88,000 people from the enormous (four times the size of New York City) Fort McMurray wildfire in Alberta, Canada, "some of our friends were dousing their cedar-shingled roofs with their garden hoses. It was futile, and they knew it, but the brain seizes under pressure. One neighbor packed his lawn mower, surely not an essential wherever he was heading."[146]

Three Effective Reactions: Deciding to Decide In **deciding to decide,** a manager agrees that he or she must decide what to do about a problem or opportunity and take effective decision-making steps. Three ways to help you decide whether to decide are to evaluate the following.[147]

1. Importance—"How High Priority Is This Situation?"   You need to determine how much priority to give the decision situation. If it's a threat, how extensive might prospective losses or damage be? If it's an opportunity, how beneficial might the possible gains be?

2. Credibility—"How Believable Is the Information about the Situation?"   You need to evaluate how much is known about the possible threat or opportunity. Is the source of the information trustworthy? Is there credible evidence?

3. Urgency—"How Quickly Must I Act on the Information about the Situation?"   Is the threat immediate? Will the window of opportunity stay open long? Can actions to address the situation be done gradually?

EXAMPLE   Deciding to Decide: How Should a Paper Maker Reinvent Itself?

"Failure isn't fatal, but failure to change might be," legendary UCLA basketball coach John Wooden once said.[148]

At the beginning of the 21st century, the paper industry was at its height, with 94 million tons of paper and paper-based packaging being produced. Then the computer revolution and the vogue phrase "the paperless office" really began to be felt, and the demand for paper plummeted. Paper companies such as 83-year-old family-owned Mohawk Fine Papers, located in a Civil War–era ax handle factory in Cohoes, New York, saw failure looming as companies cut back on paper for brochures, reports, and marketing materials. President Thomas D. O'Connor Jr. faced the dilemma of rescuing the firm founded by his grandfather.

Is This High-Priority? The first decision about how to handle the response—*Should this be considered a high-priority matter?*—was certainly much in evidence, as revenues slipped and operations at Mohawk's 350,000-square-foot mill shrank from seven days a week to five and then to four. Clearly, this was a high-priority concern.

Are the Data Believable? The second decision—*How believable is the information?*—was reinforced in depressing numbers throughout the paper industry, with the decline in orders for newsprint and writing paper, which accounted for about 85% of the decrease in paper sales. The copy-machine paper business also shrank. Meanwhile, the U.S. government stepped up its campaign to "go paperless," creating more government websites and permitting taxpayers to file income tax returns online.

How Fast Do We Need to Act? The answer to the final decision—*How quickly should this information be acted on?*—was evident in the speed of the preceding events. "For the first time in hundreds of years," O'Connor said, "paper had to justify itself."[149] As the digital revolution appeared ready to wipe out Mohawk and every other paper company, in 2004, reports *The Wall Street Journal*, O'Connor made an extraordinary bet: His company decided to expand into the fine stationery business, borrowing millions of dollars to do so.[150] It decided to take advantage of paper's transformation from commodity to keepsake, supplying high-quality, highly profitable paper for personalized holiday cards, photo books, and announcements from Shutterfly, Minted.com, and others. In 2015, Mohawk solidified its position by forming a strategic alliance with Arjowiggins Creative Papers, maker of creative and technical papers, to share manufacturing capabilities, technologies, and sales and marketing resources.[151]

YOUR CALL

Today Mohawk's sales, which first began declining in 1996, are way up. "We couldn't just downsize and hope to survive," O'Connor said later. "We knew we had to change our product completely." With this knowledge in hindsight, how would you have handled O'Connor's initial decisions about finding a new direction for the company?

Nine Common Decision-Making Biases: Rules of Thumb, or "Heuristics"

If someone asked you to explain the basis on which you make decisions, could you even say? Perhaps, after some thought, you might come up with some "rules of thumb." Scholars call them **heuristics** (pronounced "hyur-*ris*-tiks")—**strategies that simplify the process of making decisions.**

Despite the fact that people use such rules of thumb all the time, that doesn't mean they're reliable. Indeed, some are real barriers to high-quality decision making (as we saw in the Manager's Toolbox at the start of this chapter). Among those that tend to bias how decision makers process information are (1) *availability,* (2) *representativeness,* (3) *confirmation,* (4) *sunk cost,* (5) *anchoring and adjustment,* (6) *overconfidence,* (7) *hindsight,* (8) *framing,* and (9) *escalation of commitment.*[152]

1. The Availability Bias: Using Only the Information Available If you had a perfect on-time work attendance record for nine months but then were late for work four days during the last two months because of traffic, shouldn't your boss take into account your entire attendance history when considering you for a raise? Yet managers tend to give more weight to more recent behavior. This is because of the **availability bias—managers use information readily available from memory to make judgments.**

The bias, of course, is that readily available information may not present a complete picture of a situation. The availability bias may be stoked by the news media, which tend to favor news that is unusual or dramatic. Thus, for example, because of the efforts of interest groups or celebrities, more news coverage may be given to AIDS or to breast cancer than to heart disease, leading people to think the former are the bigger killers, when in fact the latter is.

2. The Representativeness Bias: Faulty Generalizing from a Small Sample or a Single Event As a form of financial planning, playing state lotteries leaves something to be desired. When, for instance, in 2016 the U.S. Powerball jackpot reached $1.6 billion, the largest in world history, the odds of winning it were put at 1 in 292.2 million.[153] (A person would have a far greater chance of being struck by lightning, 1 in 700,000.) Nevertheless, millions of people buy lottery tickets because they read or hear about a handful of fellow citizens who have been the fortunate recipients of enormous winnings. This is an example of the **representativeness bias, the tendency to generalize from a small sample or a single event.**

The bias here is that just because something happens once, that doesn't mean it is representative—that it will happen again or will happen to you. For example, just because you hired an extraordinary sales representative from a particular university, that doesn't mean that the same university will provide an equally qualified candidate next time. Yet managers make this kind of hiring decision all the time.

3. The Confirmation Bias: Seeking Information to Support One's Point of View The **confirmation bias** is when people seek information to support their point of view and discount data that do not. Though this bias would seem obvious, we practice it all the time, listening to the information we want to hear and ignoring the rest. "We typically focus on anything that agrees with the outcome we want," suggests economist Noreena Hertz. "We need to be aware of our natural born optimism. . . . We need to acknowledge our tendency to incorrectly process challenging news and actively push ourselves to hear the bad as well as the good."[154]

4. The Sunk-Cost Bias: Money Already Spent Seems to Justify Continuing The **sunk-cost bias,** or *sunk-cost fallacy*, **is when managers add up all the money already spent on a project and conclude it is too costly to simply abandon it.**

Most people have an aversion to "wasting" money. Especially if large sums have already been spent, they may continue to push on with an iffy-looking project to justify the money already sunk into it. The sunk-cost bias is sometimes called the "Concorde" effect, referring to the fact that the French and British governments continued to invest in the Concorde supersonic jetliner even when it was evident there was no economic justification for the aircraft.

5. The Anchoring and Adjustment Bias: Being Influenced by an Initial Figure Managers will often give their employees a standard percentage raise in salary, basing the decision on whatever the workers made the preceding year. They may do this even though the raise may be completely out of alignment with what other companies are paying for the same skills. This is an instance of the **anchoring and adjustment bias, the tendency to make decisions based on an initial figure.**

The bias is that the initial figure may be irrelevant to market realities. This phenomenon is sometimes seen in real estate sales. Before the 2008 crash in real estate markets, many homeowners might have been inclined at first to list their houses at an extremely high (but perhaps randomly chosen) selling price. These sellers were then unwilling later to come down substantially to match the kind of buying offers that reflected what the marketplace thought the house was really worth.

6. The Overconfidence Bias: Blind to One's Own Blindness

The **overconfidence bias is the bias in which people's subjective confidence in their decision making is greater than their objective accuracy.** Overconfidence, it's suggested, may be behind the reasons for the BP Deepwater Horizon drilling rig explosion and disaster in 2010 that flooded the Gulf of Mexico with 200 million gallons of oil. Because technology often works flawlessly, BP ignored warning signs such as a dead battery, a leaky cement job, and loose hydraulic fittings.[155]

"Overconfidence arises because people are often blind to their own blindness," says behavioral psychologist Daniel Kahneman. For instance, with experienced investment advisors whose financial outcomes simply depended on luck, he found "the illusion of skill is not only an individual aberration; it is deeply ingrained in the culture of the industry."[156] In general, he advises, we should not take assertive and confident people at their own evaluation unless we have independent reasons to believe they know what they're talking about.

7. The Hindsight Bias: The I-Knew-It-All-Along Effect

The **hindsight bias is the tendency of people to view events as being more predictable than they really are,** as when at the end of watching a game we decide the outcome was obvious and predictable, even though in fact it was not. Sometimes called the "I-knew-it-all-along" effect, this occurs when we look back on a decision and try to reconstruct why we decided to do something.

8. The Framing Bias: Shaping How a Problem Is Presented

The **framing bias is the tendency of decision makers to be influenced by the way a situation or problem is presented to them.** For instance, customers have been found to prefer meat that is framed as "85% lean meat" instead of "15% fat," although they are the same thing.[157] In general, people view choices more favorably when they are framed in terms of gains rather than losses.[158] You would be more likely to invest in a product that had a 60% chance of success rather than a 40% chance of failure. Try framing your decision questions in alternate ways to avoid this bias.

9. The Escalation of Commitment Bias: Feeling Overly Invested in a Decision

If you really hate to admit you're wrong, you need to be aware of the **escalation of commitment bias, whereby decision makers increase their commitment to a project despite negative information about it.**

Would you invest more money in an old or broken car? The Drug Enforcement Administration and the Pentagon continued to spend on a spy plane for use in Afghanistan that was supposed to be completed in 2012 at a cost of $22 million, even though the project had missed every projected delivery date. In March 2016, it had not yet left the ground, and total payouts had reached $86 million.[159]

To reduce the escalation of commitment, researchers recommend that decision makers set minimum targets for performance and then compare their performance results with their targets. Managers should also be rotated in key positions during a project, and decision makers should be encouraged to become less ego involved with the work. Finally, decision makers should be made aware of the costs of persistence.[160] ●

7.6   Group Decision Making: How to Work with Others

MAJOR QUESTION   **How do I work with others to make things happen?**

THE BIG PICTURE

Group decision making has five potential advantages and four potential disadvantages. The disadvantage of groupthink merits focus because it leads to terrible decisions. There also are a number of characteristics of groups that a manager should be aware of as group problem-solving techniques.

The movies celebrate the lone heroes who, like Bruce Willis or Mark Wahlberg, make their own moves, call their own shots. Most managers, however, work with groups and teams (as we discuss in Chapter 13). Although groups don't make as high-quality decisions as the best individual acting alone, research suggests that groups make better decisions than *most* individuals acting alone.[161] Thus, to be an effective manager, you need to learn about decision making in groups.

Advantages and Disadvantages of Group Decision Making

Because you may often have a choice as to whether to make a decision by yourself or to consult with others, you need to understand the advantages and disadvantages of group-aided decision making.

Advantages   Using a group to make a decision offers five possible advantages.[162] For these benefits to happen, however, the group must be made up of diverse participants, not just people who all think the same way.

- **Greater pool of knowledge.** When several people are making the decision, there is a greater pool of information from which to draw. If one person doesn't have the pertinent knowledge and experience, someone else might.

- **Different perspectives.** Because different people have different perspectives—marketing, production, legal, and so on—they see the problem from different angles.

- **Intellectual stimulation.** A group of people can brainstorm or otherwise bring greater intellectual stimulation and creativity to the decision-making process than is usually possible with one person acting alone.

- **Better understanding of decision rationale.** If you participate in making a decision, you are more apt to understand the reasoning behind the decision, including the pros and cons leading up to the final step.

- **Deeper commitment to the decision.** If you've been part of the group that has bought into the final decision, you're more apt to be committed to seeing that the course of action is successfully implemented.

Disadvantages   The disadvantages of group-aided decision making spring from problems in how members interact.[163]

- **A few people dominate or intimidate.** Sometimes a handful of people will talk the longest and the loudest, and the rest of the group will simply give in. Or one individual, such as a strong leader, will exert disproportionate influence, sometimes by intimidation. This cuts down on the variety of ideas.

- **Groupthink.** Groupthink occurs when group members strive to agree for the sake of unanimity and thus avoid accurately assessing the decision situation.

Different perspectives or groupthink? A diversified team can offer differing points of view, as well as a greater pool of knowledge and intellectual stimulation. Or it can offer groupthink and satisficing. What has been your experience as to the value of decision making in the groups you've been in?
© Sam Edwards/agefotostock RF

Here the positive team spirit of the group actually works against sound judgment.[164] See more about groupthink below.

- **Satisficing.** Because most people would just as soon cut short a meeting, the tendency is to seek a decision that is "good enough" rather than to push on in pursuit of other possible solutions. Satisficing can occur because groups have limited time, lack the right kind of information, or are unable to handle large amounts of information.[165]

- **Goal displacement.** Although the primary task of the meeting may be to solve a particular problem, other considerations may rise to the fore, such as rivals trying to win an argument. **Goal displacement occurs when the primary goal is subsumed by a secondary goal.**

Groupthink

Cohesiveness isn't always good. When it results in groupthink, group or team members are friendly and tight-knit but unable to think "outside the box." Their "strivings for unanimity override their motivation to realistically appraise alternative courses of action," says Irwin Janis, author of *Groupthink*.[166]

The results of groupthink can include failure to consider new information and a loss of new ideas. For instance, some blame the 2015 ouster of Ellen Kullman, DuPont's high-performing CEO, who had 27 years with the company, on a case of groupthink by the firm's insulated board of directors, who never asked Kullman to meet with them to defend her actions.[167] Investors in Silicon Valley also often show a herd mentality in their desire to be part of "the next big thing," according to one writer.[168]

Symptoms of Groupthink   How do you know that you're in a group or team that is suffering from groupthink? Some symptoms include the following:[169]

- **Sense of invulnerability.** Group members have the illusion that nothing can go wrong, breeding excessive optimism and risk taking. They may also be so assured of the rightness of their actions that they ignore the ethical implications.

- **Rationalization.** Rationalizing protects the pet assumptions underlying the group's decisions from critical questions.

- **Illusion of unanimity and peer pressure.** The illusion of unanimity is another way of saying that a member's silence is interpreted as consent. If people do disagree, peer pressure leads other members to question the dissenters' loyalty.

- **"The wisdom of crowds."** Groupthink's pressure to conform often leads members with different ideas to censor themselves—the opposite of collective wisdom, says James Surowiecki, in which "each person in the group is offering his or her best independent forecast. It's not at all about compromise or consensus."[170]

No doubt you've felt yourself pulled into a "groupthink opinion" at some point. Probably we all have. Self-Assessment 7.4 provides you with a way to evaluate the extent to which groupthink is affecting a team. Results provide insight into reducing this counterproductive group dynamic.

connect SELF-ASSESSMENT 7.4

Assessing Groupthink

The following survey was designed to assess groupthink. Please be prepared to answer these questions if your instructor has assigned Self-Assessment 7.4 in Connect.

1. Where does the team stand on the three aspects of groupthink?

2. Based on your survey scores, what would you do differently to reduce groupthink in the group you evaluated? Be specific.

Preventing Groupthink: Making Criticism and Other Perspectives Permissible

Janis believes it is easier to prevent groupthink than to cure it. As preventive measures, he and other writers suggest the following:[171]

- **Allow criticism.** Each member of a team or group should be told to be a critical evaluator, able to actively voice objections and doubts. Subgroups within the group should be allowed to discuss and debate ideas. Once a consensus has been reached, everyone should be encouraged to rethink his or her position to check for flaws. It is sometimes helpful for the group leader to withhold his or her opinion at first, to encourage others to speak up.

- **Allow other perspectives.** Outside experts should be used to introduce fresh perspectives. Different groups with different leaders should explore the same policy questions. Top-level executives should not use policy committees to rubber-stamp decisions that have already been made. When major alternatives are discussed, someone should be made devil's advocate to try to uncover all negative factors.

What Managers Need to Know about Groups and Decision Making

If you're a manager deliberating whether to call a meeting for group input, there are four characteristics of groups to be aware of.

1. They Are Less Efficient Groups take longer to make decisions. Thus, if time is of the essence, you may want to make the decision by yourself. Faced with time pressures or the serious effect of a decision, groups use less information and fewer communication channels, which increases the probability of a bad decision.[172]

2. Their Size Affects Decision Quality The larger the group, the lower the quality of the decision.[173] Some research says that seven people is the optimal size.[174] Others suggest five is best.[175] (An odd number is also considered best, when the group uses majority rules.)

3. They May Be Too Confident Groups are more confident about their judgments and choices than individuals are. This, of course, can be a liability because it can lead to groupthink.

4. Knowledge Counts Decision-making accuracy is higher when group members know a good deal about the relevant issues. It is also higher when a group leader has the ability to weight members' opinions.[176] Depending on whether group members know or don't know one another, the kind of knowledge also counts. For example, people who are familiar with one another tend to make better decisions when members have a lot of unique information. However, people who aren't familiar with one another tend to make better decisions when the members have common knowledge.[177]

Remember that individual decisions are not *necessarily* better than group decisions. As we said, although groups don't make as high-quality decisions as the *best* individual acting alone, groups generally make better decisions than *most* individuals acting alone. Some guidelines to using groups are presented on the next page. (*See Table 7.3.*)

In general, group decision making is more effective when members feel that they can freely and safely disagree with each other. This belief is referred to as **minority dissent, dissent that occurs when a minority in a group publicly opposes the beliefs, attitudes, ideas, procedures, or policies assumed by the majority of the group.**[178] Minority

Toward consensus. Working to achieve cooperation in a group can tell you a lot about yourself. How well do you handle the negotiation process? What do you do when you're disappointed in a result achieved by consensus?
© Xavier Arnau/Getty Images RF

TABLE 7.3

When a Group Can Help in Decision Making: Three Practical Guidelines

These guidelines may help you as a manager decide whether to include people in a decision-making process and, if so, which people.

1. **When it can increase quality:** If additional information would increase the quality of the decision, managers should involve those people who can provide the needed information. Thus, if a type of decision occurs frequently, such as deciding on promotions or who qualifies for a loan, groups should be used because they tend to produce more consistent decisions than individuals do.

2. **When it can increase acceptance:** If acceptance within the organization is important, managers need to involve those individuals whose acceptance and commitment are important.

3. **When it can increase development:** If people can be developed through their participation, managers may want to involve those whose development is most important.

Source: Derived from George P. Huber, Managerial Decision Making (Glenview, IL: Scott, Foresman, 1980), p. 149.

dissent is associated with increased innovation within groups.[179] Do your teams at school or work allow minority dissent? If not, what can be done to increase its existence? Self-Assessment 7.5 can help answer these questions.

≡ connect SELF-ASSESSMENT 7.5

Assessing Participation in Group Decision Making

The following survey measures minority dissent, participation in group decision making, and satisfaction with a group. Please be prepared to answer these questions if your instructor has assigned Self-Assessment 7.5 in Connect.

1. What is the level of minority dissent in the group, and to what extent are you satisfied with being a member of this group?

2. Use the three lowest items that measure minority dissent to answer the following question: What can you do to increase the level of minority dissent in this group? Be specific.

3. Why do you think many groups muzzle the level of minority dissent?

Group Problem-Solving Techniques: Reaching for Consensus

Using groups to make decisions generally requires that they reach a **consensus, which occurs when members are able to express their opinions and reach agreement to support the final decision.** More specifically, consensus is reached "when all members can say they either agree with the decision or have had their 'day in court' and were unable to convince the others of their viewpoint," says one expert in decision making. "In the final analysis, everyone agrees to support the outcome."[180] This does not mean, however, that group members agree with the decision, only that they are willing to work toward its success.

One management expert offers the following dos and don'ts for achieving consensus.[181]

- **Dos:** Use active listening skills. Involve as many members as possible. Seek out the reasons behind arguments. Dig for the facts.

- **Don'ts:** Avoid log rolling and horse trading ("I'll support your pet project if you'll support mine"). Avoid making an agreement simply to keep relations amicable and not rock the boat. Finally, don't try to achieve consensus by putting questions to a vote; this will only split the group into winners and losers, perhaps creating bad feelings among the latter.

More Group Problem-Solving Techniques

Decision-making experts have developed several group problem-solving techniques to aid in problem solving. Three we will discuss here are (1) *brainstorming*, (2) the *Delphi technique*, and (3) *computer-aided decision making*.

1. Brainstorming: For Increasing Creativity

Brainstorming is a technique used to help groups generate multiple ideas and alternatives for solving problems.[182] Developed by advertising executive A. F. Osborn, the technique consists of having members of a group meet and review a problem to be solved. Individual members are then asked to silently generate ideas or solutions, which are then collected (preferably without identifying their contributors) and written on a board or flip chart. A second session is then used to critique and evaluate the alternatives. (Incidentally, taking a brief stroll, even around the office, can significantly increase creativity.)[183]

A modern-day variation is **electronic brainstorming, sometimes called** *brainwriting,* **in which members of a group come together over a computer network to generate ideas and alternatives.**[184] Technology has also turned the smartphone into a device that uses various apps to spur the thinking process and unblock creative juices.[185]

Some rules for brainstorming suggested by IDEO, a product design company, are shown below. *(See Table 7.4.)*

TABLE 7.4

Six Rules for Brainstorming

1. **Defer judgment.** Don't criticize during the initial stage of idea generation. Phrases such as "we've never done it that way," "it won't work," "it's too expensive," and "our manager will never agree" should not be used.

2. **Build on the ideas of others.** Encourage participants to extend others' ideas by avoiding "buts" and using "ands."

3. **Encourage wild ideas.** Encourage out-of-the-box thinking. The wilder and more outrageous the ideas, the better.

4. **Go for quantity over quality.** Participants should try to generate and write down as many new ideas as possible. Focusing on quantity encourages people to think beyond their favorite ideas.

5. **Be visual.** Use different-colored pens (for example, red, purple, blue) to write on big sheets of flip-chart paper, whiteboards, or poster boards that are put on the wall.

6. **One conversation at a time.** The ground rules are that no one interrupts another person, no dismissing of someone's ideas, no disrespect, and no rudeness.

Source: These recommendations and descriptions were derived from B. Nussbaum, "The Power of Design,"
BusinessWeek, *May 17, 2004, pp. 86–94.*

The benefit of brainstorming is that it is an effective technique for encouraging the expression of as many useful new ideas or alternatives as possible. That said, brainstorming also can waste time generating a lot of unproductive ideas, and it is not appropriate for evaluating alternatives or selecting solutions.[186]

2. The Delphi Technique: For Consensus of Experts

The Delphi technique was originally designed for technological forecasting but now is used as a multipurpose planning tool. The **Delphi technique is a group process that uses physically dispersed experts who fill out questionnaires to anonymously generate ideas; the judgments are combined and in effect averaged to achieve a consensus of expert opinion.**

The Delphi technique is useful when face-to-face discussions are impractical. It's also practical when disagreement and conflicts are likely to impair communication, when certain individuals might try to dominate group discussions, and when there is a high risk of groupthink.[187]

3. Computer-Aided Decision Making

As in nearly every other aspect of business life, computers have entered the area of decision making, where they are useful not only in collecting information more quickly but also in reducing roadblocks to group consensus.

A decision support system, for instance, is a computer-based information system that provides a flexible tool for analysis and helps managers focus on the future. This kind of computer-based system aims to produce collected information known as *business*

Traditional group work. This photo shows the kind of traditional arrangement we expect of groups—colleagues are seated close together in clusters to better focus on their particular projects. Do you think you'd rather work in this type of arrangement than in one that is more individually based? Why or why not?
© Rawpixel.com/Shutterstock RF

intelligence, gathering data from a wide range of sources in a way that can be interpreted by humans and used to support better business decision making. Example: American Airlines developed a decision support system called the yield management system that helps managers decide how much to overbook and how to set prices for each seat so that a plane is filled and profits are maximized.[188] ●

PRACTICAL ACTION   How Exceptional Managers Make Decisions

"Failure is a great teacher." That was one of the life lessons expressed by one CEO who has had to make thousands of decisions during his career.[189] Failure is always a possibility, but that possibility can't stop one from making decisions. And you can probably always learn from the result.

"When Should I Make a Decision and When Should I Delay?" Often you want to stay open-minded before making a decision. But sometimes that can just be a cover for procrastination. (After all, *not* making a decision is in itself a kind of decision.) How do you know when you're keeping an open mind or are procrastinating? Here are some questions to consider:[190]

Understanding: "Do I have a reasonable grasp of the problem?"

Comfort level about outcome: "Would I be satisfied if I chose one of the existing alternatives?"

Future possible alternatives: "Would it be unlikely that I could come up with a better alternative if I had more time?"

Seizing the opportunity: "Could the best alternatives disappear if I waited?"

If you can answer yes to those questions, you almost certainly should decide now, not wait.

"Are There Guidelines for Making Tough Choices?" "On a daily and weekly basis we can be faced with making hundreds of decisions," says management consultant Odette Pollar. "Most of them are small, but the larger ones where more is at

stake can be truly painful." Here are some ways she suggests making decision making easier:[191]

Decide in a timely fashion: "Rarely does waiting significantly improve the quality of the decision," says Pollar. In fact, delay can result in greater unpleasantness in loss of money, time, and peace of mind.

Don't agonize over minor decisions: Postponing decisions about small problems can mean that they simply turn into large ones later.

Separate outcome from process: Does a bad outcome mean you made a bad decision? Not necessarily. The main thing is to go through a well-reasoned process of choosing among alternatives, which increases the chances of success. But even then you can't be sure there will always be a positive outcome.

Learn when to stop gathering facts: "Gather enough information to make a sound decision," suggests Pollar, "but not all the possible information." Taking extra time may mean you'll miss a window of opportunity.

When overwhelmed, narrow your choices: Sometimes there are many good alternatives, and you need to simplify decision making by eliminating some options.

YOUR CALL

Some experts suggest that to help make good decisions you should "be visual," using more pictures and diagrams, and "walk and point" to stimulate areas of the brain that control memory, emotion, and problem solving.[192] What have you found aids you in making decisions?

Key Points

7.1 Two Kinds of Decision Making: Rational and Nonrational

- A decision is a choice made from among available alternatives. Decision making is the process of identifying and choosing alternative courses of action. Two models managers follow in making decisions are rational and nonrational.

- In the rational model, there are four steps in making a decision: Stage 1 is identifying the problem or opportunity. A problem is a difficulty that inhibits the achievement of goals. An opportunity is a situation that presents possibilities for exceeding existing goals. This is a matter of diagnosis—analyzing the underlying causes. Stage 2 is thinking up alternative solutions. Stage 3 is evaluating the alternatives and selecting a solution. Alternatives should be evaluated according to cost, quality, ethics, feasibility, and effectiveness. Stage 4 is implementing and evaluating the solution chosen. The rational model of decision making assumes managers will make logical decisions that will be the optimum in furthering the organization's best interests. The rational model is prescriptive, describing how managers ought to make decisions.

- Nonrational models of decision making assume that decision making is nearly always uncertain and risky, making it difficult for managers to make optimum decisions. Two nonrational models are satisficing and intuition. (1) Satisficing falls under the concept of bounded rationality—that is, that the ability of decision makers to be rational is limited by enormous constraints, such as time and money. These

constraints force managers to make decisions according to the satisficing model—that is, managers seek alternatives until they find one that is satisfactory, not optimal. (2) Intuition is making choices without the use of conscious thought or logical inference. The sources of intuition are expertise and feelings.

7.2 Making Ethical Decisions

- Corporate corruption has made ethics in decision making once again important. Many companies have an ethics officer to resolve ethical dilemmas, and more companies are creating values statements to guide employees as to desirable business behavior.

- To help make ethical decisions, a decision tree—a graph of decisions and their possible consequences—may be helpful. Managers should ask whether a proposed action is legal and, if it is intended to maximize shareholder value, whether it is ethical—and whether it would be ethical *not* to take the proposed action.

7.3 Evidence-Based Decision Making and Analytics

- Evidence-based management means translating principles based on best evidence into organizational practice. It is intended to bring rationality to the decision-making process.

- Scholars Jeffrey Pfeffer and Robert Sutton identify seven implementation principles to help companies that are committed to doing what it takes to profit from evidence-based management: (1) treat your organization as an unfinished prototype; (2) "no brag, just facts"; (3) see yourself and your organization as outsiders do; (4) have everyone, not just top executives, be guided by the responsibility to gather and act on quantitative and qualitative data; (5) you may need to use vivid stories to sell unexciting evidence to others in the company; (6) at the very least, you should slow the spread of bad practices; and (7) you should learn from failure by using the facts to make things better.

- Applying the best evidence to your decisions is difficult, for seven reasons: (1) There's too much evidence. (2) There's not enough *good* evidence. (3) The evidence doesn't quite apply. (4) People are trying to mislead you. (5) *You* are trying to mislead you. (6) The side effects outweigh the cure. (7) Stories are more persuasive, anyway.

- Perhaps the purest application of evidence-based management is the use of analytics, or business analytics, sophisticated forms of business data analysis. Analytics competitors have three key attributes: (1) They go beyond simple descriptive statistics and use data mining and predictive modeling to identify potential and most profitable customers. (2) They don't have just one principal application but rather use analytics in multiple applications. (3) The use of analytics is supported by top executives.

- A new concept is that of Big Data, which requires handling by very sophisticated analysis software and supercomputing-level hardware. Big Data includes not only data in corporate databases but also web-browsing data trails, social network communications, sensor data, and surveillance data.

- Big Data analytics is the process of examining large amounts of data of a variety of types to uncover hidden patterns, unknown correlations, and other useful information.

7.4 Four General Decision-Making Styles

- A decision-making style reflects the combination of how an individual perceives and responds to information.

- Decision-making styles may tend to have a value orientation, which reflects the extent to which a person focuses on either task or technical concerns versus people and social concerns when making decisions.

- Decision-making styles may also reflect a person's tolerance for ambiguity, the extent to which a person has a high or low need for structure or control in his or her life.

- When the dimensions of value orientation and tolerance for ambiguity are combined, they form four styles of decision making: directive (action-oriented decision makers who focus on facts), analytical (careful decision makers who like lots of information and alternative choices), conceptual (decision makers who rely on intuition and have a long-term perspective), and behavioral (the most people-oriented decision makers).

7.5 How to Overcome Barriers to Decision Making

- When confronted with a challenge in the form of a problem or an opportunity, individuals may respond in perhaps four ineffective ways and three effective ones.

- The ineffective reactions are as follows: (1) In relaxed avoidance, a manager decides to take no action in the belief that there will be no great negative consequences. (2) In relaxed change, a manager realizes that complete inaction will have negative consequences but opts for the first available alternative that involves low risk. (3) In defensive avoidance, a manager can't find a good solution and follows by procrastinating, passing the buck, or denying the risk of any negative consequences. (4) In panic, a manager is so frantic to get rid of the problem that he or she can't deal with the situation realistically.

- The effective reactions consist of deciding to decide—that is, a manager agrees that he or she must decide what to do about a problem or opportunity and take effective decision-making steps. Three ways to help a manager decide whether to decide are to evaluate (1) importance—how high priority the situation is; (2) credibility—how believable the information about the situation is; and (3) urgency—how quickly the manager must act on the information about the situation.

- Heuristics are rules of thumb or strategies that simplify the process of making decisions. Some heuristics or barriers that tend to bias how decision makers process information are availability, confirmation, representativeness, sunk-cost, anchoring and adjustment, and escalation of commitment.

- (1) The availability bias means that managers use information readily available from memory to make judgments. (2) The confirmation bias means people seek information to support their own point of view and discount data that do not. (3) The representativeness bias is the tendency to generalize from a small sample or a single event. (4) The sunk-cost bias is when managers add up all the money already spent on a project and conclude that it is too costly to simply abandon it. (5) The anchoring and adjustment bias is the tendency to make decisions based on an initial figure or number. (6) The escalation of commitment bias describes when decision makers increase their commitment to a project despite negative information about it. An example is the prospect theory, which suggests that decision makers find the notion of an actual loss more painful than giving up the possibility of a gain.

7.6 Group Decision Making: How to Work with Others

- Groups make better decisions than most individuals acting alone, though not as good as the best individual acting alone.

- Using a group to make a decision offers five possible advantages: (1) a greater pool of knowledge; (2) different perspectives; (3) intellectual stimulation; (4) better understanding of the reasoning behind the decision; and (5) deeper commitment to the decision.
- It also has four disadvantages: (1) a few people may dominate or intimidate; (2) it will produce groupthink, when group members strive for agreement among themselves for the sake of unanimity and so avoid accurately assessing the decision situation; (3) satisficing; and (4) goal displacement, when the primary goal is subsumed to a secondary goal.
- Some characteristics of groups to be aware of are (1) groups are less efficient, (2) their size affects decision quality, (3) they may be too confident, and (4) knowledge counts—decision-making accuracy is higher when group members know a lot about the issues.
- Using groups to make decisions generally requires that they reach a consensus, which occurs when members are able to express their opinions and reach agreement to support the final decision. Minority dissent should be allowed, so members can safely disagree with each other.
- Three problem-solving techniques aid in problem solving. (1) Brainstorming is a technique used to help groups generate multiple ideas and alternatives for solving problems. A variant is electronic brainstorming, in which group members use a computer network to generate ideas. (2) The Delphi technique is a group process that uses physically dispersed experts who fill out questionnaires to anonymously generate ideas; the judgments are combined and in effect averaged to achieve a consensus of expert opinion. (3) In computer-aided decision making, decision support systems provide flexible tools for analysis and help managers focus on the future. This kind of computer-based system aims to produce collected information known as business intelligence, gathering data from a wide range of sources in a way that can be interpreted by humans and used to support better business decision making.

Understanding the Chapter: What Do I Know?

1. What are the steps in rational decision making?
2. What are two models of nonrational decision making?
3. What are four ethical questions a manager should ask when evaluating a proposed action to make a decision?
4. Competitors using analytics have what three key attributes?
5. What is Big Data?
6. Describe the four general decision-making styles.
7. Discuss the four ineffective and three effective ways that individuals can respond to a decision situation.
8. Can you name the nine common decision-making biases?
9. What are the advantages and disadvantages of group decision making?
10. What are three group problem-solving techniques?

Management in Action

How Did Decision Making Contribute to Volkswagen's Emissions Cheating Scandal?

The top three global automobile manufacturers in 2015 were Toyota (10.23 million units), Volkswagen (10.14 million units), and General Motors (9.92 million units).[193] Interestingly, all three have been involved in recent automotive scandals involving 2.6 million cars (GM's ignition switch defect), 8.1 million cars (Toyota's unintended acceleration), and 11.0 million cars (Volkswagen's diesel emissions cheating).[194]

Preliminary investigations suggest that a purposeful effort to deceive was the root cause of the Volkswagen scandal. Let's explore the case in more detail to determine the role of decision making, beginning with the details of the cheating.

THE PROCESS OF CHEATING

"Volkswagen installed emissions software on more than a half-million diesel cars in the U.S. . . . that allows them to sense the unique parameters of an emission drive cycle set by the Environmental Protection Agency." These "so-called 'defeat devices' detect steering, throttle, and other inputs used in the test to switch between two distinct operating modes."

"In the test mode, the cars are fully compliant with all federal emissions levels. But when driving normally, the computer switches to a separate model— significantly changing the fuel pressure, injection timing, exhaust-gas recirculation, and in models with AdBlue, the amount of urea fluid [cat pee] sprayed into the exhaust. While this mode likely delivers higher mileage and power, it also permits heavier nitrogen-oxide emissions (NOx)—a smog-forming pollutant linked to lung cancer—that are up to 40 times higher than the federal limit."[195]

It appears that Volkswagen used defeat devices because it could not satisfy the tough U.S. emission standards while trying to grow market share in the U.S. According to *The Wall Street Journal,* the origins of the "cheat" go back to 2012, when "EPA officials and California regulators were in touch with European counterparts about high emissions in diesel vehicles. California regulators tested Volkswagen cars and continually found them to pollute more on the road than in the lab." Volkswagen was informed about these irregularities at the time and executives concluded that they were the result of "technical glitches."

Three years later, then CEO Winterkorn "acknowledged 'misconduct' on Volkswagen's part while pledging 'Everything will be put on the table at this time, as quickly, thoroughly and transparently as possible.'"[196]

THE ROLE OF VISION, STRATEGY, AND GOALS

Volkswagen has pursued a goal of being the largest automobile manufacturer by 2018, selling 800,000 vehicles in the U.S. alone. To achieve this goal, VW made a strategic decision to dominate the diesel market. Diesels were a niche market in the U.S. in the mid 2000s, but they represented more than 50% of new car registrations in the European Union. The company thought diesel was the way to grow revenue because "They were cheaper than hybrids and packed more muscle under the hood yet still often got more than 40 miles to the gallon."[197]

To grow the diesel market, VW needed to invent a way to deal with the sooty exhaust produced by diesel engines. The company knew it had to meet tougher emission standards in the U.S. than in Europe.

The company hired Wolfgang Bernhard to solve this problem, and his team came up with a solution that appeared very promising. Bernhard found a system created by Daimler called BlueTec. "It sprayed urea [cat pee] into the exhaust stream to neutralize harmful nitrogen oxides. . . . To make it work, cars need to be fitted with an extra pump and a tank of what is essentially cat pee." Unfortunately, Bernhard had a falling out with CEO Winterkorn and was fired. Wolfgang Hatz took over and quickly dropped BlueTec because of the classic case of "not-invented here," according to *Bloomberg Businessweek*. He replaced BlueTec with a system that was supposed to trap harmful emissions in the tailpipe. We now know that Hatz's decisions were ineffective at satisfying U.S. emission standards.[198]

Given the scandal, Volkswagen has changed its overall goal to achieve "qualitative growth" over sheer volume. Current CEO Matthias Müller said that "many people outside of Volkswagen, but also some of us, did not understand that our Strategy 2018 is about much more than production numbers. A lot of things were subordinated to the desire to be 'Faster, Higher, Larger,' especially return on sales."[199]

Some VW employees agreed with Müller's conclusions. They believe that the "cheat" occurred because former CEO Martin Winterkorn established goals that were too difficult to achieve. German newspaper *Bild am Sonntag* reported that "several engineers said that they had overinflated tyres and mixed motor oil with diesel to make the company's cars use less fuel in tests, a deception that began in 2013 and carried on until the spring of this year [2015]."[200]

OTHER CONTRIBUTORS TO THE PROBLEM

VW is seeking employees' input to determine the causes of the "cheat." A memo was sent by Herbert Diess, head of VW's brand division, to all employees, asking them to come forward with any information related to the emissions scandal. According to the memo, "Employees have until Nov 30 [2015] to provide 'complete and truthful' information about events as part of the internal investigation. . . . Those who come forward before the deadline 'have nothing to fear from the company in the way of repercussions on the job such as being fired or held liable for damages.'"[201] This only applies to people covered by collective bargaining contracts.

For all others, VW is reserving "the right to transfer employees or change their responsibilities if they incriminate themselves. The company also warned that it has no influence over a decision by German prosecutors to seek criminal charges against any employees who confess to being part of the deception."[202]

The organizational culture and structure are also seen as contributing to the problem. CEO Müller believes that decision making is too centralized at the top, where a triumvirate of forces—"heirs to original Beetle designer Ferdinand Porsche, the German state of Lower Saxony, where most of Volkswagen's German factories are located, and labor representatives that control half the seats on the company's supervisory board"—have too much power. He also perceives that "the top-down power structure under Mr. Winterkorn had begun to slow down the business, most noticeably in the U. S. . . . Müller pressed for far-reaching decentralization of the company and the greatest possible autonomy for the brands."[203]

WHAT'S BEEN HAPPENING SINCE THE SCANDAL CAME TO LIGHT?

VW has hired Deloitte to conduct an investigation into the causes of the "cheat." It's a large investigation that involves over 450 experts. As of December 2015 the experts had conducted "87 interviews, told 2,000 employees not to destroy documents and emails, seized 1,500 devices such as smartphones and laptops, and secured enough data to fill 50 million books."[204]

Volkswagen executives think that the problem was caused by a chain of errors that dates back to the promotion of diesel vehicles in the U.S. in 2005. CEO Müller "has said a company investigation so far points to a small circle of employees as being involved in the scheme." VW's former U.S. chief, Michael Horn, similarly concluded, "This was a couple of software engineers who put this in for whatever reasons."[205] Horn resigned in 2016 as he came under increased fire for the scandal.[206] Other experts doubt that senior managers were unaware of what was going on because they tend to be engineers who understand the complexity of meeting global emission standards.[207]

A fix has been found for diesel engines used in Europe. Repairs started in 2016.[208] In contrast, VW's proposed fix in the U.S. has been deemed "unacceptable because they lacked detail and inadequately addressed concerns about vehicle performance, emissions, and safety."[209]

Volkswagen has set aside $6.5 billion to deal with costs associated with the scandal but this may not be enough. The lawsuits are starting to pile up. The U.S. Justice Department filed a lawsuit in 2016 that could cost the company $45 billion. The U.S. Federal Trade Commission also filed a lawsuit in March 2016 accusing VW of "deceiving U.S. consumers into buying emission-spewing diesel vehicles, seeking more than

$15 billion in damages in what could be the largest false-advertising case in U.S. history," according to *The Wall Street Journal*. Making matters worse, the South Korean Ministry of Environment filed a complaint in 2016 against the company. According to *The Wall Street Journal*, VW "had submitted a proposal to recall and fix some 125,000 of its vehicles in South Korea on Jan 6 [2016]. But the ministry said the proposal failed to explain why the problem occurred and how it would be fixed."[210]

FOR DISCUSSION

1. What are the major causes of Volkswagon's emissions cheating scandal?

2. Do you think the causes of the "cheat" were more intuitive and unconscious or analytical and conscious? Explain.

3. Do you think it is ethical for VW to offer amnesty only for employees covered by a collective bargaining agreement? What about the other employees? How will this decision affect employees coming forward?

4. Do you see any evidence that the decision-making styles of Winterkorn, Müller, or Horn contributed to the scandal?

5. What type of decision-making style would be most effective at helping to resolve the scandal? Provide your rationale.

6. Which of the common decision-making biases played a role in how this case unfolded?

7. What is your biggest takeaway from reading this case?

Legal/Ethical Challenge

Should Apple Comply with the U.S. Government's Requests to Unlock iPhones?

This case involves the long-term implications of Apple's decision to deny the U.S. Justice Department's request to unlock an iPhone. It all started with the terrorist attack perpetrated by Syed Rizwan Farook and his wife. They killed 14 people in San Bernardino, California, in 2016.

The FBI wanted to see the contents of Farook's phone in order to gain information about others who may have been involved with the terrorist attack. It wanted Apple to "create a special version of the iPhone's software that only works on the recovered device. Apple has to sign it with its secret keys in order to install it on the subject's iPhone. This custom version will 'bypass or disable the auto-erase function' so it will not wipe the phone after a number of failed passcode guesses."[211]

Although Apple had already provided the government "what it has that fits the usual kind of document demands, including information the terrorists had stored in Apple's cloud service," it was not enough. The terrorists quit backing up their phone, leading the FBI to find a way to bypass Apple's security features. Apple had no way of doing this.[212]

Apple refused to comply with the request, which led to a court order demanding that Apple create the software needed to bypass the phone's security features.

In an interview with ABC, Apple CEO Tim Cook said "the government shouldn't be able to force Apple to compromise the privacy of hundreds of millions of iPhone users in order to unlock a terrorist's iPhone." He added that it would "force Apple to create 'the software equivalent of cancer.'" The company further contends that "coding a 'back door' in the iPhone would compromise the security of hundreds of millions of its customers."[213]

When pressed about the fact that Apple's cooperation might prevent other terrorist attacks, Cook replied, "Some things are hard, and some things are right, and some things are both. This is one of those things." CEOs Mark Zuckerberg of Facebook and Sundar Pichai of Google supported Cook's decision.[214]

As a court showdown mounted in early 2016, the FBI sought the help of hackers to break into the device. Companies in both the U.S. and Israel participated in the effort and one of them came up with a solution.[215] The government then dropped its legal case against Apple.

Although the immediate case involving Farook's phone is over, there are still long-term implications about encryption-protected technology. According to U.S. Justice Department spokesperson Melanie Newman, "It remains a priority for the government to ensure that law enforcement can obtain crucial digital information to protect national security and public safety, either with cooperation from relevant parties, or through the court system when cooperation fails." In response, "Apple believes deeply that people in the United States and around the world deserve data protection, security and privacy. Sacrificing one for the other only puts people and countries at greater risk."[216]

The government's interest in this issue is unlikely to go away because "state and local authorities are confronted with more than 1,000 locked smartphones and other devices, blocking access to potential evidence."[217] A case in point involves the Justice Department's decision to seek a court order in April 2016 that would force Apple to unlock an iPhone taken during a drug investigation in Brooklyn. According to *The Wall Street Journal,* "The technical issues in the Brooklyn case are somewhat different than in San Bernardino because they involve different iPhone hardware and software. Apple has a technique for pulling data from the Brooklyn phone but is resisting applying it, saying compelling it to do so would amount to government overreach and an invasion of customers' privacy."[218] Tim Cook is adamant in his resolve. He said, "We will not shrink from this responsibility. . . . We need to decide as a nation how much power the government should have over our data and over our privacy."[219]

Where do you stand on this issue?

SOLVING THE CHALLENGE

1. I think national security is more important than privacy. After all, we are talking about unlocking the phones of criminals. Technology firms need to be forced to comply with government officials' requests to unblock encrypted devices.

2. Although our data and privacy need to be protected, I think Apple and other technology companies should be forced to comply only when the case involves terrorism. Encrypted devices should not be unlocked for other criminal activities.

3. The privacy of our data and phone contents needs to be protected. I am not in favor of forcing Apple or any technology firm to unblock encrypted devices.

4. Invent other options.

Organizing

8

Organizational Culture, Structure, and Design
Building Blocks of the Organization

Major Questions You Should Be Able to Answer

How to Get Noticed in a New Job: Fitting into an Organization's Culture in the First 60 Days

"Once you are in the real world—and it doesn't make any difference if you are 22 or 62, starting your first job or your fifth," say former business columnists Jack and Suzy Welch, "the way to look great and get ahead is to overdeliver."[1]

Overdelivering means doing more than what is asked of you—not just doing the report your boss requests, for example, but doing the extra research to provide him or her with something truly impressive. "You must continue to 'sell yourself' after you are hired," says one human resources director. "Keep your boss informed of things you are working on, including projects others ask you to assist with."[2]

Among things you should do in the first 60 days are the following.[3]

Be Aware of the Power of First Impressions

Within three minutes of meeting someone new, people form an opinion about where the future of the relationship is headed, according to one study.[4] "When meeting someone for the first time, concentrate on one thing: your energy level," urges one former CEO, who thinks that seven seconds is all the time people need to start making up their minds about you. Amp it up, he advises. "If you don't demonstrate energetic attitude on your first day, you're already screwing up."[5]

See How People Behave by Arriving Early and Staying Late

"Many aspects of a company's culture can be subtle and easy to overlook," writes one expert. "Instead, observe everything." Thus, try coming in 30 minutes early and staying a little late just to observe how people operate—where they take their meals, for example.

Network with People and Find Out How the Organization Works

"You've got to realize that networking inside a company is just as important as when you were networking on the outside trying to get in," says a business consultant.[6] During the first two weeks, get to know a few people and try to have lunch with them. Find out how the organization works, how people interact with the boss, what the corporate culture encourages and discourages. Walk the halls and get to know receptionists, mail room clerks, and office managers, who can help you learn the ropes. Your role here is to listen, rather than to slather on the charm. Realize that you have a lot to learn.[7]

Ask for Advice

Be aware that those who seek advice are perceived as being more competent than those who do not.[8]

Ask your boss, coworkers, and subordinates to give you feedback about how you're doing. Be prepared to take unpleasant news gracefully.[9] At the end of 30 days, have a "How am I doing?" meeting with your boss.

Overdeliver

Because performance reviews for new hires generally take place at 60 to 90 days, you need to have accomplished enough—and preferably something big—to show your boss your potential. In other words, do as the Welches suggest: overdeliver.

For Discussion How does the foregoing advice square with your past experiences in starting a new job? Are there things you wish you could have done differently?

FORECAST | What's Ahead in This Chapter

We consider organizational cultures and organizational structures, and how they should be aligned to help coordinate employees in the pursuit of the organization's strategic goals. We then consider the three types of organizations and seven basic characteristics of an organization. We next discuss seven types of organizational structures. Finally, we look at five factors that should be considered when one is designing the structure of an organization.

8.1 Aligning Strategy, Culture, and Structure

MAJOR QUESTION **Why is it important for managers to align a company's vision and strategies with its organizational culture and structure?**

THE BIG PICTURE

The study of organizing, the second of the four functions in the management process, begins with the study of organizational culture and structure, which managers must determine so as to implement a particular strategy. Organizational culture consists of the set of shared, taken-for-granted implicit assumptions that a group holds in the workplace. Organizational structure describes who reports to whom and who does what.

How important is *culture,* the "social glue" that binds together organizations?

"Culture and people are everything," says Brett Wilson, CEO of TubeMogul, a video advertising software company. "Nothing else matters, and our ability to stay ahead is a function of having the best people and moving faster than our competitors. . . . Creating an exceptional culture is the only way to build a sustainable competitive advantage."[10]

How an Organization's Culture and Structure Are Used to Implement Strategy

"A leader's job is to help inspire every employee to help execute strategy," says one report. "This requires consistently and constantly demonstrating, celebrating, and modeling the cultural traits that reinforce strategy."[11] Or, for better performance, perhaps the leader's style should even be *different* from the organization's culture (as we'll discuss later).[12]

Strategy, as we saw in Chapter 6, consists of the large-scale action plans that reflect the organization's vision and are used to set the direction for the organization. To implement a particular strategy, managers must determine the right kind of (1) *organizational culture* and (2) *organizational structure,* which mutually influence each other. (*See Figure 8.1.*)

FIGURE 8.1   **Drivers and flow of organizational culture**

Drivers of culture → Organizational culture → Organizational structure & internal processes → Group & social processes → Work attitudes & behaviors → Overall performance

Realizing the Organizational Vision and Strategy: Get the Right Culture and the Right Structure   Let's consider these two concepts—organizational culture and organizational structure.

Organizational Culture: The Shared Assumptions That Affect How Work Gets Done   We described the concept of *culture* in Chapter 4 on global management as "the shared set of beliefs, values, knowledge, and patterns of behavior common to a group of people." Here we are talking about a specific kind of culture called an *organizational culture.*

According to scholar **Edgar Schein, organizational culture, sometimes called corporate culture,** is defined as the set of shared, taken-for-granted implicit assumptions that a group holds and that determines how it perceives, thinks about, and reacts to its various environments.[13] These are the beliefs and values shared among a group of people in the workplace that are passed on to new employees by way of socialization and mentoring, which significantly affect work outcomes at all levels.[14] As we said, culture is the "social glue" that binds members of the organization together. Just as a human being has a personality—fun-loving, warm, uptight, competitive, or whatever—so an organization has a "personality," too, and that is its culture. The culture helps employees understand why the organization does what it does and how it intends to accomplish its long-term goals.

The cultural tone is often set in the hiring process. "The ultimate filter we use is that we only hire nice people," says Peter Miller, CEO of Optinose, a pharmaceutical company.[15] MuleSoft, a software company, looks for people with "high integrity, being a great team player, and they want to win as a company first, team second, individually third," says CEO Greg Schott.[16]

TubeMogul CEO Brett Wilson, mentioned earlier, also prefers nice people. "I . . . really value people who are kind to one another," he says. "That makes the workplace better, and they end up having a deeper sense of empathy with our clients." In addition, "we want a culture where people aren't afraid to make mistakes. . . . Our ability to win is a function of how innovative we are. So making mistakes is encouraged." Finally, he says, "it's a culture where we value the people who do what they say—they have a high 'do-to-say' ratio."[17]

Culture can vary considerably, with different organizations having differing emphases on risk taking, treatment of employees, teamwork, rules and regulations, conflict and criticism, and rewards.

As such, culture can have both positive and negative effects on employees and overall corporate performance. Zenefits, a San Francisco health-insurance brokerage start-up, for example, is being sued for actions associated with a *negative culture*. Its director of real estate and workplace services had to send employees a note asking them to cut out using the headquarters stairwells for smoking, drinking, eating, and sex.[19]

Some other organizations, believing that the office has become "too nice," have embraced a culture known as "radical candor" or "front-stabbing," in which workers are encouraged "to drop the polite workplace veneer and speak frankly to each other no matter what," according to one report.[20] Still other companies go beyond candor to fraudulent behavior: The serious blow the auto industry took to its reputation when Volkswagen admitted in 2015 that its culture had led to cheating on emissions tests was followed by another one when Mitsubishi admitted to 25 years of company engineers' intentionally manipulating fuel-economy tests.[21]

In addition, the elements that drive an organization's culture also vary. They may represent the values of the founder, the industry and business environment, the national culture, the organization's vision and strategies, and the behavior of leaders. *(See Table 8.1.)*

We thoroughly discuss organizational culture in Sections 8.2 and 8.3.

Organizational Structure: Who Reports to Whom and Who Does What **Organizational structure** is a formal system of task and reporting relationships that coordinates and motivates an organization's members so that they can work together to achieve the organization's goals. As we describe in Sections 8.4–8.6, organizational structure is concerned with who reports to whom and who specializes in what work.

Whether an organization is for-profit or nonprofit, the challenge for top managers is to align the organization's vision and strategies with its organizational culture and organizational structure, as shown in the two gold boxes in the drawing opposite. *(See Figure 8.1.)*

Figure 8.1 shows that the consistency among these elements in turn impacts (see the three green boxes) group and social processes (discussed in Chapters 13–15), individual work attitudes and behaviors (discussed in Chapters 11–12), and the organization's overall performance. As you can see from the diagram, consistency across strategy, culture, and structure leads to higher performance. ●

TABLE 8.1

What Drives an Organizational Culture?

- Founder's values
- Industry & business environment
- National culture
- Organization's vision & strategies
- Behavior of leaders

Freewheeling culture. Mic, a New York City news website created by and for Millennials, which has 106 mostly Millennial employees, is described as having a "playful vibe."[18] Here CEO Chris Altchek *(right)* talks with an employee. At Mic, oversharing, acting entitled, and second-guessing the boss are the norm. Dogs wander between desks, some employees use a megaphone for impromptu announcements, others ride hoverboards into the kitchen for free snacks. Could the Mic culture work in, say, the labs of Pfizer Inc., the global pharmaceutical company, where drug discovery is a high-risk, costly endeavor?
© Jennifer S. Altman/The New York/Redux Pictures

How Strategy Affects Culture and Culture Affects Structure: EndoStim, a Medical Device Start-up, Operates Virtually

Nowadays a firm can be completely international. An example is the medical device start-up EndoStim, nominally based in St. Louis but operating everywhere.

The company, reports *New York Times* columnist Thomas Friedman, came together as a result of some chance encounters:[22] Cuban immigrant Raul Perez, a physician, came to St. Louis, where he met Dan Burkhardt, a local investor, with whom he began making medical investments. Perez also suffered from acid reflux (abnormal heartburn caused by stomach acid rising in the esophagus) and went to Arizona for treatment by an Indian American physician, V. K. Sharma. During the visit, Sharma proposed an idea for a pacemaker-like device to control the muscle that would choke off acid reflux.

The Strategy: Creating a New Medical Device. Perez, Burkhardt, and Sharma all agreed they wanted to build such an electrical-stimulation device. They joined forces with South Africa–born Bevil Hogg, a founder of Trek Bicycle Corporation, who became the CEO of the company they named EndoStim and who helped to raise initial development funds. (Hogg was succeeded later by Rohan Hoare, PhD, of The Netherlands, educated in Australia and at Harvard.)[23] This strategy then began to dictate whom they had to work with, which in turn influenced the company's culture and structure.

The Culture: An International "Adhocracy." To advance their strategy of building the device, the four principals recruited two Israelis, a medical engineer and a gastroenterologist. The Israelis collaborated with a Seattle engineering team to develop the design. A company in Uruguay specializing in pacemakers was lined up to build the EndoStim prototype. It was arranged for the clinical trials to be conducted in India and Chile. How much more international can you get?

Thus, the culture of the company could be called an *adhocracy,* which (as we'll describe a little later in the chapter) is a risk-taking culture that values flexibility and creativity and that is focused on developing innovative products.

The Structure: A Virtual, Boundaryless Company. As a very lean start-up operating all over the world, with the principals rarely in the same office at the same time, EndoStim is clearly very different from, say, the usual top-down organization operating in one locality. To access the best expertise and high-quality materials and obtain low-cost manufacturing anywhere around the globe, EndoStim thus was forced to take advantage of all the technological tools—teleconferencing, e-mail, the Internet, and faxes—to maintain communications.

This EndoStim structure, then, is that of a *virtual, boundaryless* organization—*virtual* because its members are operating geographically apart, connected by electronic means, and *boundaryless* because the members (whether coworkers or suppliers) come together in fluid, flexible ways on an as-needed basis. We describe these structures further in another few pages.

YOUR CALL

Are you comfortable enough to work in a virtual, boundaryless organization? Many people like the social interaction that comes with working in a physical office with other people. Others, however, are turned off by the office game playing and time-wasting activities that seem to be a necessary concomitant. They welcome the opportunity to do task-oriented work in a makeshift home office, occasionally having to cope with loneliness and restlessness. Which would you favor?

8.2 What Kind of Organizational Culture Will You Be Operating In?

MAJOR QUESTION

How do I find out about an organization's "social glue," its normal way of doing business?

THE BIG PICTURE

Organizational culture appears as three layers: observable artifacts, espoused values, and basic assumptions. Cultures can be classified into four types: clan, adhocracy, market, and hierarchy. Culture is transmitted to employees through symbols, stories, heroes, rites and rituals, and organizational socialization.

Want to get ahead in the workplace but hate the idea of "office politics"?

Probably you can't achieve the first without mastering the second. Although hard work and talent can take you a long way, "there is a point in everyone's career where politics becomes more important," says management professor Kathleen Kelley Reardon. You have to know the political climate of the company you work for, says Reardon, who is author of *The Secret Handshake* and *It's All Politics*.[24] "Don't be the last person to understand how people get promoted, how they get noticed, how certain projects come to attention. Don't be quick to trust. If you don't understand the political machinations, you're going to fail much more often."[25]

A great part of learning to negotiate the politics—that is, the different behavioral and psychological characteristics—of a particular workplace means learning to understand the organization's *culture*. The culture consists not only of the slightly quirky personalities you encounter but also all of an organization's normal way of doing business, as we'll explain.

The Three Levels of Organizational Culture

Organizational culture appears as three layers: (1) *observable artifacts,* (2) *espoused values,* and (3) *basic assumptions.*[26] Each level varies in terms of outward visibility and resistance to change, and each level influences another level.

Level 1: Observable Artifacts—Physical Manifestations of Culture   At the most visible level, organizational culture is expressed in *observable artifacts*—physical manifestations such as manner of dress, awards, myths and stories about the company, rituals and ceremonies, and decorations, as well as visible behavior exhibited by managers and employees.

Example: In a conference room reserved for sensitive discussions, online travel company Kayak has a 2-foot-high stuffed elephant named Annabelle—the "elephant in the room"—that is an artifact believed to bring forth more honest and constructive communications among employees.[27] (The expression "elephant in the room" is used in business and politics to mean an obvious truth that is either being ignored or going unaddressed.)

Level 2: Espoused Values—Explicitly Stated Values and Norms   **Espoused values** are the explicitly stated values and norms preferred by an organization, as may be put forth by the firm's founder or top managers.

Example: The founders of technology company Hewlett-Packard stressed the "HP Way," a collegial, egalitarian culture that gave as much authority and job security to employees as possible. Although managers may hope the values they espouse will directly influence employee behavior, employees don't always "walk the talk," frequently being more influenced by **enacted values, which represent the values and norms actually exhibited in the organization.**[28]

Another example: Leaders at retailer and health care company CVS Health recognized the gap between espoused values ("We sell health products") and enacted values ("We also sell tobacco products") and made a key strategic change to create alignment. A transformative moment came in early 2014 when CEO Larry Merlo announced that CVS would cease selling tobacco products by October 1st of that year. "The decision meant sacrificing about $2 billion in sales," says one report. "Led by Merlo, CVS's executive team decided that continuing to sell cigarettes had become untenable for a company that was simultaneously trying to sell itself as a health care giant."[29]

Level 3: Basic Assumptions—Core Values of the Organization *Basic assumptions,* which are not observable, represent the core values of an organization's culture—those that are taken for granted and, as a result, are difficult to change.

Example: At insurance giant AIG, people worked so hard that the joke around the offices was "Thank heavens it's Friday, because that means there are only two more working days until Monday."[30]

Another example: Many founders of start-ups hate rules and red tape. College Hunks Hauling Junk, for instance, was co-founded by Nick Friedman with no formal policies about dress code, vacation, sick days, and other things because he envisioned "a real-life Never Never Land where work is always fun, and the culture is always stress-free."[31] However, when the enterprise grew from a single cargo van to over 50 franchises, the freewheeling spirit made employees lose focus, and client-service ratings, employee morale, and profitability all declined. The firm had to come up with rules and procedures while at the same time trying to "maintain a healthy balance of fun company culture with an accountable organization and team," Friedman said.

Four Types of Organizational Culture: Clan, Adhocracy, Market, and Hierarchy

The competing values framework (CVF) provides a practical way for managers to understand, measure, and change organizational culture. The CVF, which has been validated by extensive research involving 1,100 companies, classifies organizational cultures into four types: (1) clan, (2) adhocracy, (3) market, and (4) hierarchy, as we'll explain.[32] *(See Figure 8.2.)*

FIGURE 8.2

Competing values framework

Adapted from K.S. Cameron, R.E. Quinn, J. Degraff, and A.V. Thakor, Competing Values Leadership (Northampton, MA: Edward Elgar, 2006), p. 32.

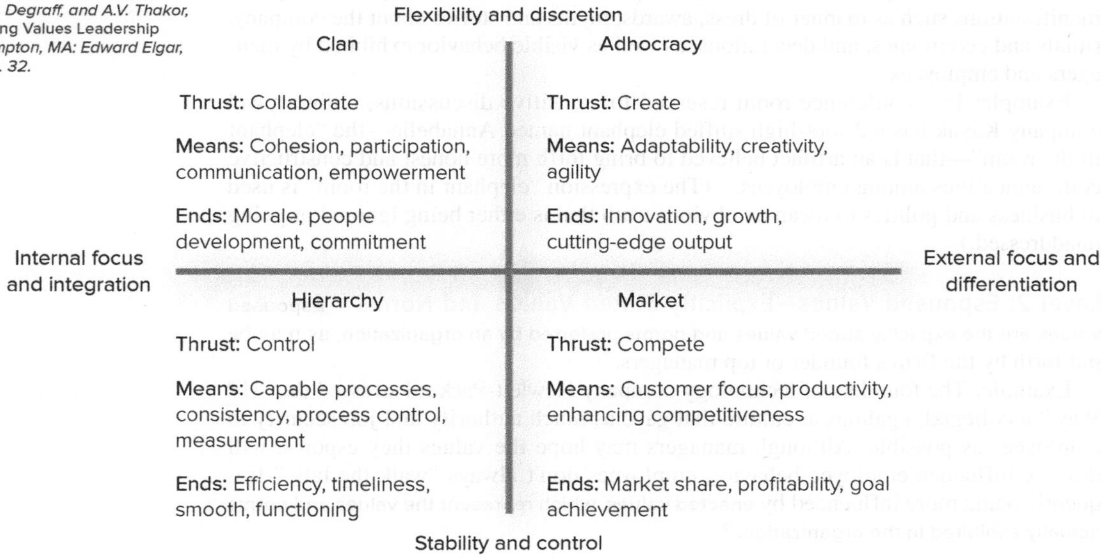

Flexibility and discretion

Clan — Adhocracy

Thrust: Collaborate

Means: Cohesion, participation, communication, empowerment

Ends: Morale, people development, commitment

Thrust: Create

Means: Adaptability, creativity, agility

Ends: Innovation, growth, cutting-edge output

Internal focus and integration — External focus and differentiation

Hierarchy — Market

Thrust: Control

Means: Capable processes, consistency, process control, measurement

Ends: Efficiency, timeliness, smooth, functioning

Thrust: Compete

Means: Customer focus, productivity, enhancing competitiveness

Ends: Market share, profitability, goal achievement

Stability and control

Research leading to the development of the CVF found that organizational effectiveness varied along two dimensions:

- **The horizontal dimension—inward or outward focus?** This dimension expresses the extent to which an organization focuses its attention and efforts inward on internal dynamics and employees ("internal focus and integration") versus outward toward its external environment and its customers and shareholders ("external focus and differentiation").

- **The vertical dimension—flexibility or stability?** This dimension expresses the extent to which an organization prefers flexibility and discretion versus stability and control. Combining these two dimensions creates the four types of organizational culture based on different core values—namely, clan, adhocracy, market, and hierarchy.

Each culture type has different characteristics, and while one type tends to dominate in any given organization, it is the mix of types that creates competitive advantage. We begin our discussion of culture types in the upper-left-hand quadrant of the CVF.

1. Clan Culture: An Employee-Focused Culture Valuing Flexibility, Not Stability

A **clan culture** has an internal focus and values flexibility rather than stability and control. Like a family-type organization, it encourages collaboration among employees, striving to encourage cohesion through consensus and job satisfaction and to increase commitment through employee involvement. Clan organizations devote considerable resources to hiring and developing their employees, and they view customers as partners.

Example: Property and casualty insurance company Acuity, *Fortune*'s No. 2 Best Company to Work For in 2016, strongly endorses a clan culture. CEO Ben Salzmann believes "that if employees are given a fun, rewarding place to work where they can express their creativity, in return the firm will get innovation, diehard loyalty, and world-class customer service."[33] Employees have generous perks and are empowered to participate in the way the company is run. The end results are profitability and an enviably low 2% turnover rate.

2. Adhocracy Culture: A Risk-Taking Culture Valuing Flexibility

An **adhocracy culture** has an external focus and values flexibility. Creation of new products and services is the strategic thrust of this culture, as we saw with EndoStim in the Example box, p. 244. This type of culture attempts to create innovative products by being adaptable, creative, and quick to respond to changes in the marketplace. Employees are encouraged to take risks and experiment with new ways of getting things done. Adhocracy cultures are well suited for start-up companies, those in industries undergoing constant change, and those in mature industries that are in need of innovation to enhance growth.

Example: Google, now under parent company Alphabet, is an example of a company with an adhocracy culture. "Though well past its start-up days," says one account, "Google is not afraid of massive, embarrassing failures. This is, after all, a company that [teamed up with another company] to invest $1 billion in commercial space startup SpaceX days after it crashed a rocket."[34] As one headline about the technology sector expresses it, "A Fearless Culture Fuels Tech."[35]

Chick-fil-A culture. Among the quick-service restaurant's ways of engaging employees are hiring only nice people (harder than it sounds); hiring managers with people skills, not just functional skills; and closing stores on Sundays so employees can have family time. What kind of culture is that? © Zuma Press Inc/Alamy

3. Market Culture: A Competitive Culture Valuing Profits over Employee Satisfaction

A **market culture** has a strong external focus and values stability and control. Because market cultures are focused on the external environment and driven by competition and a strong desire to deliver results, customers, productivity, and profits take precedence over employee development and satisfaction. Employees are expected to work hard, react fast, and deliver quality work on time; those who deliver results are rewarded.

Example: Uber, the ride-hailing company, is described by its CEO as having a "champions mind-set." "It's about putting everything you have on the field. . . . And if you get knocked down, overcoming adversity."[36] The company uses an approach called "principled competition" to establish itself in new markets, developing a base of enthusiastic new riders and drivers and using that grass-roots support to fend off opposition.[37] "Uber doesn't play nice," says one writer. "It plays to win—and that strategy appears to be working."[38]

4. Hierarchy Culture: A Structured Culture Valuing Stability and Effectiveness A

hierarchy culture has an internal focus and values stability and control over flexibility. Companies with this kind of culture are apt to have a formalized, structured work environment aimed at achieving effectiveness through a variety of control mechanisms that measure efficiency, timeliness, and reliability in the creation and delivery of products.

Example: Amazon relies on the benefits of a hierarchical culture to effectively manage its vast shipping processes. A *Fortune* reporter commented that the company has achieved success by "sticking steadfastly—even boringly—to a few key principles. . . . Instead of focusing on competitors or technology shifts [a market culture orientation], they continually invest in getting a little bit better. In their core retail business, they grind out incremental improvements in delivery speed and product offerings while chipping away at prices."[39]

Are you curious about the type of culture that exists in a current or past employer? Do you wonder whether this culture is best suited to help the company achieve its strategic goals? The following self-assessment allows you to consider these questions.

≡ connect SELF-ASSESSMENT 8.1

What Is the Organizational Culture at My Current Employer?

Please be prepared to answer these questions if your instructor has assigned Self-Assessment 8.1 in Connect.

1. How would you describe the organizational culture?
2. Do you think this type of culture is best suited to help the company achieve its strategic goals? Explain.

EXAMPLE   Cultures Representing Competing Values: The Different "Personalities" of Pfizer Pharmaceuticals

"What makes culture so important is that it's unique; it's something that no one can copy," says Ian C. Read, chairman and CEO of Connecticut-based Pfizer Pharmaceuticals. "Culture can become your competitive advantage. Get it wrong and you'll pay dearly for it . . . for years to come."[40]

Read became head of Pfizer in December 2010, after mismanagement ("micro micro" management, or indecisiveness) by the previous CEO failed to lift the company's fortunes.[41] Read has instituted a commitment to "our OWNIT! culture. I challenged Pfizer's leaders to recognize that they can only own the *future* if they own *change* and can make change work *for* us, not *against* us."

Pfizer employees, he asserts, "understand that our ownership culture can differentiate us within our industry. They also understand it requires a willingness to take prudent risks, be accountable for their decisions and results, and understand how their work contributes to the company's performance." The success of the culture especially depends on the efforts of first- and second-line managers, who create a climate of trust that is "essential to providing the space employees need to work, take considered risks, and own the results," he says.

Organizational cultures are nearly as varied as human personalities, and conflicting cultures can exist within the same organization. Sometimes they interfere with each other, but sometimes competing cultures may be strong contributors to an organization's success. Consider the different cultures associated with Pfizer, both before Read took over and during his tenure. Do you recognize the different types?

$2.3 Billion in Fines. In 2009, Pfizer was fined $2.3 billion for improperly marketing drugs to doctors. "The whole culture of Pfizer is driven by sales," said a former sales representative whose complaint helped the government's case, "and if you didn't sell drugs illegally, you were not seen as a team player."[42] Almost every major drug company has in recent years been accused of giving kickbacks to doctors or short-changing federal programs.

Free Prescription Drugs to Unemployed. But also in that year, as unemployment hovered around 10% in the United States, Pfizer launched a program in which it offered to supply 70 of its name-brand drugs, such as Lipitor and Viagra, free of charge for up to a year to customers who had lost their jobs and lacked prescription coverage. "We did it because it was the right thing to do," said Pfizer's then CEO. "But it was motivational for our employees and got a great response from customers. In the long run, it will help our business."[43]

Ongoing Experimentation. At Pfizer, drug discovery is a high-risk, costly endeavor in which hundreds of scientists screen thousands of chemicals against specific disease targets, but 96% of these compounds are ultimately found to be unworkable. The culture, then, is one of managing failure

and disappointment, of helping drug researchers live for the small victories. Thus, says one account, "when a researcher publishes a paper, or when a lab gets some positive results on a new therapy, it's trumpeted throughout the organization."[44] Another example of experimentation, aimed at helping remaining employees to be productive after heavy job cuts, is PfizerWorks, in which 4,000 employees pass off tedious and time-consuming parts of their jobs, such as creating PowerPoint slides and riffling through spreadsheets, to outsiders in India.[45]

Shedding U.S. Corporate Citizenship to Lower Taxes. In 2015, Read informed federal officials that Pfizer, which was founded in Brooklyn in 1849, proposed to merge with Dublin-based Allergan, maker of Botox, and to move the company's headquarters to Ireland, a lower-tax country, thereby significantly cutting Pfizer's U.S. tax bill.[46] He defended the move, which is called an "inversion," by saying it could result in more cash that could be invested in the United States and ultimately add jobs. Critics decried it as a gift to an industry "that's blessed with lengthy drug patents that stave off competition, keep prices high, and protect earnings for years."[47] Calling the plan "one of the most insidious tax loopholes out there," the Obama administration tightened tax rules, removing the planned inversion's benefits. Pfizer and Allergan called off the merger.[48]

YOUR CALL

What cultural types are illustrated in these examples? Does it make more sense that a company would have one dominant cultural type or an equal mixture of clan, adhocracy, market, and hierarchy? Explain your rationale.

How Employees Learn Culture: Symbols, Stories, Heroes, Rites and Rituals, and Organizational Socialization

Culture is transmitted to employees in several ways, most often through such means as (1) *symbols*, (2) *stories*, (3) *heroes*, (4) *rites and rituals*, and (5) *organizational socialization*.[49]

1. Symbols A **symbol** is an object, an act, a quality, or an event that conveys meaning to others. In an organization, symbols convey its most important values.

Example: One of the most iconic products of IKEA, maker of inexpensive home furnishings, whose vision is "to create a better life for the many," is the LACK table, a 22-inch by 22-inch side table that sells for only $9.99.[50]

2. Stories A **story** is a narrative based on true events, which is repeated—and sometimes embellished upon—to emphasize a particular value. Stories are oral histories that are told and retold by members about incidents in the organization's history.

Example: Marc Benioff is founder of cloud computing business Salesforce.com, a San Francisco company known for its great sense of social responsibility and generosity (and rated No. 23 on *Fortune's* 2016 Best Companies to Work For list).[51] Its spirit of philanthropy is embodied in a story called the 1-1-1 rule. "When we started the company," Benioff says, "we took 1% of our equity [stock value] and 1% of our profit and 1% of all our employees' time, and we put it into a . . . public charity. At the time, it was very easy because we had no profit, we had no time, we had no equity. But then, it turned out that our company is worth, you know, tens of billions of dollars."[52] Salesforce.com also runs 10,000 nonprofits for free, doesn't charge universities for its services, and, says Benioff, delivers "hundreds of thousands of hours of community service."

3. Heroes   A **hero** is a person whose accomplishments embody the values of the organization. IKEA employees are expected to work hard, inspired by an anecdote from their Swedish founder, Invar Kamprad, in his 1976 "A Furniture Dealer's Testament." In that essay he recounts how he was berated by his father for failing repeatedly to get out of bed to milk the cows on his family's farm. Then one day he got an alarm clock. "'Now by jiminy, I'm going to start a new life,' he determined, setting the alarm for twenty to six and removing the 'off button.'"[53]

4. Rites and Rituals   **Rites and rituals** are the activities and ceremonies, planned and unplanned, that celebrate important occasions and accomplishments in the organization's life. Military units and sports teams have long known the value of ceremonies handing out decorations and awards, but many companies have rites and rituals as well.

Example: Employees of New Belgium Brewery in Fort Collins, Colorado, which makes Fat Tire Ale, are given a cruiser bicycle during their first year. After five years, they get a free brewery-hopping trip to Belgium. Ten years of employment is acknowledged with a tree planted in their name in the campus orchard. (The company boasts a 97% employment retention rate.)[54]

5. Organizational Socialization   **Organizational socialization** is defined as the process by which people learn the values, norms, and required behaviors that permit them to participate as members of an organization.[55] Converting from outsider into organizational insider may take weeks or even years and occurs in three phases, researcher Daniel Feldman suggests—before one is hired, when one is first taken on, and when one has been employed a while and is adjusting to the job.[56]

The first phase *(anticipatory socialization phase)* occurs before one joins the organization, when a person learns—from career advisors, from web sources, from current employees—what the organization's job needs and values are and how one's own needs, values, and skills might fit in. The second phase *(encounter phase)* takes place when a person is first hired and comes to learn what the organization is really like and how to adjust his or her expectations. The company may help to advance this socialization process through various familiarization programs (known as "onboarding" programs). The third phase *(change and acquisition phase)* comes about once the employee understands his or her work role and now must master the necessary skills and tasks and learn to adjust to the work group's values and norms. The company may advance this phase of socialization through goal setting, incentives, employee feedback, continued support, and ceremonies ("graduation") that celebrate completion of the process.

Example: Organizational socialization at Miami Children's Hospital in Florida is helped along by assigning new employees a "buddy" trained in coaching and mentoring;

supporting new recruits with direct supervision, lunch meetings, and frequent use of online surveys and employee feedback; having monthly reviews by management; and at 90 days rewarding successful employees with a two-day culture-shaping retreat and graduation ceremony.[57]

The Importance of Culture

Many people believe culture powerfully shapes an organization's long-term success by enhancing its competitive advantage. A team of researchers tested this hypothesis with a meta-analysis (a statistical procedure combining data from multiple studies) of more than 38,000 organizational units—either organizations as a whole or departments in different organizations—and 616,000 individuals.[58] The results are shown below. *(See Figure 8.3.)*

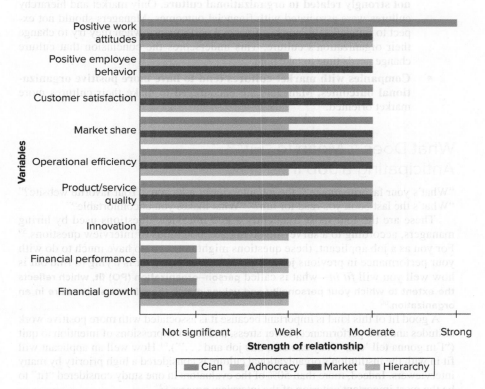

FIGURE 8.3 **What organizational benefits are associated with what organizational cultures?**

Source: A. Y. Ou, C. Hartnell, A. Kinicki, E. Karam, and D. Choi, "Culture in Context: A Meta-Analysis of the Nomological Network of Organizational Culture." Presentation as part of symposium Connecting Culture and Context: Insights from Organizational Culture Theory and Research at the 2016 National Academy of Management meeting in Anaheim, California.

Results revealed that culture is positively associated with a variety of outcomes. Most relationships were of moderate strength, meaning they are important to today's managers. Closer examination of Figure 8.3 leads to the following six conclusions:

- **An organization's culture matters.** The type of organizational culture can be a source of competitive advantage.

- **Employees have more positive work attitudes when working in organizations with clan cultures.** Employees clearly prefer to work in organizations that value flexibility over stability and control, as well as those that are more concerned with satisfying the needs of employees than those of shareholders or customers.

- **Clan and market cultures are more likely to deliver higher customer satisfaction and market share.** We suspect this result holds because the positive employee attitudes associated with clan cultures motivate employees to provide better customer service.

- **Operational outcomes, quality, and innovation are more strongly related to clan, adhocracy, and market cultures than to hierarchical ones.** Managers should avoid the use of too many rules and procedures—hierarchical characteristics—when trying to improve these outcomes.

- **An organization's financial performance (profit and revenue growth) is not strongly related to organizational culture.** Only market and hierarchy cultures were associated with financial outcomes. Managers should not expect to immediately increase financial performance when they try to change their organization's culture. This underscores the conclusion that culture change needs time to take hold.

- **Companies with market cultures tend to have more positive organizational outcomes.** Managers are encouraged to make their cultures more market oriented.

What Does It Mean to "Fit"?
Anticipating a Job Interview

"What's your favorite movie?" the job interviewer asks you. "Your favorite website?" "What's the last book you read for fun?" "What makes you uncomfortable?"

These are the four most frequently asked interview questions used by hiring managers, according to a survey involving 285,000 kinds of interview questions.[59] For you as a job applicant, these questions might not seem to have much to do with your performance in previous jobs. But what the interviewer is trying to find out is how well you will *fit in*—what is called **person–organization (PO) fit, which reflects the extent to which your personality and values match the climate and culture in an organization.**[60]

A good fit of this kind is important because it is associated with more positive work attitudes and task performance, lower stress, and fewer expressions of intention to quit ("I'm gonna tell 'em, 'They can take this job and . . .'").[61] How well an applicant will fit in with the institution's organizational culture is considered a high priority by many interviewers. Indeed, more than 50% of the evaluators in one study considered "fit" to be the most important criterion of the interview process.[62]

How can you determine how well you might fit in before you go into a job interview? You should write down your strengths, weaknesses, and values—and then do the same for the organization you're interviewing with, by researching it online and talking with current employees. You can then prepare questions to ask the interviewer about how well you might fit.[63]

Example: If being recognized for hard work is important to you, ask the interviewer how the company rewards performance. If the answer doesn't show a strong link between performance and rewards ("Well, we don't really have a policy on that"), you'll probably have a low person–organization fit and won't be happy working there. Incidentally, a positive corporate culture that engages and motivates employees will help a company's bottom line, according to a study of car dealerships, but the reverse is not true—a company's success isn't enough to ensure a positive culture.[64] ●

8.3 The Process of Culture Change

What can be done to an organization's culture to increase its economic performance?

THE BIG PICTURE

There are 12 ways a culture becomes established in an organization.

A particular culture can become embedded in an organization in many ways, 12 of which are described here. *(See Table 8.2.)*

Changing organizational culture is essentially a teaching process—that is, a process in which members instruct each other about the organization's preferred values, beliefs, expectations, and behaviors. The process is accomplished by using one or more of the following 12 mechanisms.[65]

1. Formal Statements

The first way to embed preferred culture is through the use of formal statements of organizational philosophy, mission, vision, and values, as well as materials used for recruiting, selecting, and socializing employees.

Example: At fashion website Polyvore, CEO Jess Lee wrote down three statements she thought represented the company's distinct culture: (1) "delight the user," (2) "do a few things well," and (3) "make an impact."[66] Walmart founder Sam Walton stated that three basic values represented the core of the retailer's culture: (1) respect for the individual, (2) service to customers, and (3) striving for excellence.[67]

2. Slogans and Sayings

The desirable corporate culture can be expressed in language, slogans, sayings, and acronyms.

Example: David Cote, chairman and CEO of global technology company Honeywell, has adopted the principle "Your job as a leader is to be right at the end of the meeting, not at the beginning of the meeting." That is, a leader's job is to flush out all the facts and opinions so at the end he or she can make a good decision.[68]

3. Rites and Rituals

As we mentioned earlier, rites and rituals represent the planned and unplanned activities and ceremonies that are used to celebrate important events or achievements.

Example: After a day's meetings with clients, employees at Boston advertising agency Arnold Worldwide like to meet at a beer-vending machine in the office (nicknamed "Arnie"), where they sip bottles of home-brewed beer, chitchat, and exchange ideas.[69] (Of course, employers need to be cautious about encouraging drinking alcohol at work, for both health and liability reasons.)

4. Stories, Legends, and Myths

A story is a narrative about an actual event that happened within the organization and that helps to symbolize its vision and values to employees.

TABLE 8.2

A Dozen Ways to Change Organizational Culture

1. Formal statements
2. Slogans & sayings
3. Rites & rituals
4. Stories, legends, & myths
5. Leader reactions to crises
6. Role modeling, training, & coaching
7. Physical design
8. Rewards, titles, promotions, & bonuses
9. Organizational goals & performance criteria
10. Measurable & controllable activities
11. Organizational structure
12. Organizational systems & procedures

Example: Until a decade ago, major drug companies treated countries in the developing world as not worth the trouble of marketing to. But Andrew Witty, who in 2008 at age 43 became the youngest CEO of GlaxoSmithKline, the world's second-largest pharmaceutical company, is making a name for himself by doing more for the poor people of the world than any other big drug company leader. While working in poor countries, Witty found "just unbelievable energy to self-improve, to lift themselves up." He has promised to keep prices of drugs sold in poor countries to no more than 25% of what is charged in rich ones and to donate one-fifth of all profits made in such countries toward building their health systems. Now for four years running Glaxo has been ranked No. 1 on the Access to Medicine index, which rates pharmaceutical companies on their stances toward the poor.[70]

5. Leader Reactions to Crises

How top managers respond to critical incidents and organizational crises sends a clear cultural message.

Example: Cory Booker (now a U.S. senator from New Jersey) was the mayor of financially struggling Newark in 2010 when a serious snowstorm hit the city. "Throughout the storm," reports *The Wall Street Journal,* "those in distress hit up Mr. Booker on Twitter, one of the mayor's preferred methods of keeping in touch with residents. After they cried out for plows, ambulances, and diapers, he responded, electronically and sometimes by driving to the location, shovel in hand. . . . He ordered his driver to pull over several times to help shovel out or push cars."[71] His on-the-ground efforts were an answer to critics who accused him of being out of touch.

6. Role Modeling, Training, and Coaching

Many companies provide structured training to provide an in-depth introduction to their organizational values.

Example: Triage Consulting Group, a health care financial consulting firm in California, places a high value on superior performance at achieving measurable goals. New employees are immediately prepared for this culture with a four-day orientation in Triage's culture and methods, followed by 15 training modules scheduled in six-week intervals. After less than a year, the best performers are ready to begin managing their own projects, furthering their career development. Performance evaluations take place four times a year, further reinforcing the drive for results.[72]

7. Physical Design

There is constant experimenting going on as to the best office layout that will encourage employee productivity and send a strong message about the culture.

Example: After power producer Dynegy emerged from bankruptcy, the new CEO abandoned his private office and moved into a 64-square-foot cubicle—identical to the ones used by the 235 other employees—signaling his aim "to transform a business previously focused on day-to-day survival into an agile operator poised for growth," according to one report.[73]

Another example: Pharmaceutical company GlaxoSmithKline has embraced an open-space philosophy that abandons individual desks in favor of "hoteling," where everyone is assigned to "neighborhoods," or areas of workers engaged in related tasks (you store your personal belongings in a small locker), on the theory that chance encounters among employees will spark conversations and collaboration.[74]

8. Rewards, Titles, Promotions, and Bonuses

Rewards and status symbols are among the strongest ways to embed organizational culture.

Example: At Triage Consulting Group, employees at the same level of their career earn the same pay, but employees are eligible for merit bonuses, again reinforcing the culture of achievement. The awarding of merit bonuses is partly based on co-workers' votes for who contributed most to the company's success, and the employees who receive the most votes are recognized each year at the company's "State of Triage" meeting.[75]

9. Organizational Goals and Performance Criteria

Many organizations establish organizational goals and criteria for recruiting, selecting, developing, promoting, dismissing, and retiring people, all of which reinforce the desired organizational culture.

Example: Las Vegas–based Zappos, the online shoe retailer, spends a great deal of time analyzing applicants to see if they will fit into its clan-based culture. "We spend seven to 10 hours [with potential recruits] over four occasions at happy hours, team building events, or other things outside the office," says the company's human resources director. "We can see them, and they can us."[76] Until recently, this careful selection process along with paying full employee benefits and emphasizing having fun at work (the "wow factor") resulted in a low turnover rate of only 20% in 2009, a remarkable statistic for call centers. That figure changed when Zappos instituted a new form of organization, as we'll describe.

The wow culture. The "wow" factor that encourages Zappos's clan-based culture is partly created by encouraging employees to have fun at work. Is this a place you could stick with? © Jared McMillen/Aurora Photos

10. Measurable and Controllable Activities

An organization's leaders can pay attention to, measure, and control a number of activities, processes, or outcomes that can foster a certain culture.

Example: Adam Nash, the CEO of Wealthfront, an online financial management firm, believes that how you keep score on employee progress is important. "If you don't give people metrics [methods of measurement]," he says, "smart people will make up their own," and "you'll get incessant fighting and arguments."[77]

11. Organizational Structure

The hierarchical structure found in most traditional organizations is more likely to reinforce a culture oriented toward control and authority compared with the flatter organization that eliminates management layers in favor of giving employees more power.

Example: The hierarchical structure of a railroad provides a much different culture from that of the "spaghetti organization" formerly employed by Danish hearing-aid maker Oticon, in which employees worked at mobile desks on wheels and were always subject to reorganization. Zappos has gone further by instituting a radical experiment called *holocracy,* which is supposed to encourage collaboration by eliminating workplace hierarchy—no titles and no bosses. Unfortunately, employees weren't sure how to get things done anymore, which resulted in such confusion that the company's 2015 turnover rate went from 20% to 30%.[78]

12. Organizational Systems and Procedures

Companies are increasingly using electronic networks to increase collaboration among employees, to increase innovation, quality, and efficiency.

Example: Molson Coors CEO Peter Swinburn, in knitting together employees of several former companies, made sure they had better tools to interact with each other. One technology he introduced was Yammer, a website for short messages similar to Twitter, on which some 2,000 employees now provide updates and collaborate on projects.[79]

Don't Forget about Person–Organization Fit

Now that we have described the four key types of organizational culture and the mechanisms managers can use to change culture, it's time to reflect on your person–organization (PO) fit. Recall that PO fit reflects the extent to which your personality and values match the climate and culture in an organization. Your PO fit matters because it links to your work attitudes and performance.[80]

We have two activities for you to complete to measure your level of fit and see what you can do about it. The first is Self-Assessment 8.2, which measures your preference for the four types of culture in the CVF. The second is to answer the discussion questions associated with this assessment. You will be asked to conduct a gap analysis between the culture for a current or past employer and your preferred culture type. You can use this gap to make a plan of action for improving your PO fit. ●

---

connect SELF-ASSESSMENT 8.2

Assessing Your Preferred Type of Organizational Culture

This survey is designed to assess your preferred type of organizational culture. Please be prepared to answer these questions if your instructor has assigned Self-Assessment 8.2 in Connect.

1. In rank order, what are your preferred culture types? Are you surprised by the results?

2. Compute the gap between your preferred and actual culture types by subtracting your actual culture type score (Self-Assessment 8.1) from your preferred type score (Self-Assessment 8.2). Where are the largest gaps?

3. Make a plan to improve your person–organization fit. Focusing on your two largest culture types, identify what is causing the gaps. You will find it helpful to look at the survey items that measure these types.

4. Now use the 12 embedding mechanisms just discussed and suggest at least two things you can do to improve your level of fit.

8.4   Organizational Structure

MAJOR QUESTION   **How are for-profit, nonprofit, and mutual-benefit organizations structured?**

THE BIG PICTURE

The organizational structure of the three types of organizations—for-profit, nonprofit, and mutual-benefit—may be expressed vertically or horizontally on an organization chart.

Once an organization's vision and strategy have been determined, as we stated at the beginning of this chapter, the challenge for top managers is, first, to create a culture that will motivate its members to work together and, second, a structure that will coordinate their actions to achieve the organization's strategic goals. Here let us begin to consider the second part—an organization's structure.

In Chapter 1, we defined an organization as a group of people who work together to achieve some specific purpose. According to **Chester I. Barnard's** classic definition, **an organization is a system of consciously coordinated activities or forces of two or more people.**[81] By this wording, a crew of two coordinating their activities to operate a commercial tuna fishing boat is just as much an organization as tuna companies Bumble Bee and StarKist with their thousands of employees.

The Organization: Three Types

As we stated in Chapter 1, there are three types of organizations classified according to the three different purposes for which they are formed:[82]

- **For-profit organizations.** These are formed to make money, or profits, by offering products or services.

- **Nonprofit organizations.** These are formed to offer services to some clients, not to make a profit (examples: hospitals, colleges).

- **Mutual-benefit organizations.** These are voluntary collectives whose purpose is to advance members' interests (examples: unions, trade associations).

Who sells the electricity? About 80% of U.S. drivers drive 40 miles or less a day—and the Ford Focus Electric can drive nearly twice that far, 76 miles, on a single electric charge. The Focus is made by Ford Motor Company, a for-profit organization. What kind of organizations might sell the electricity and the charging stations—for-profit, nonprofit, or mutual-benefit? © Lucas Jackson/Reuters/Alamy

Clearly, you might have an occupation (such as auditor or police officer) that is equally employable in any one of these three sectors. As a manager, however, you would be principally required to focus on different goals—making profits, delivering public services, or satisfying member needs—depending on the type of organization.

The Organization Chart

Whatever the size or type of organization, it can be represented in an organization chart. **An organization chart is a box-and-lines illustration showing the formal lines of authority and the organization's official positions or work specializations.** This is the family-tree-like pattern of boxes and lines posted on workplace walls and given to new hires, such as the following for a hospital. *(See Figure 8.4.)*

FIGURE 8.4

Organization chart

Example for a hospital.

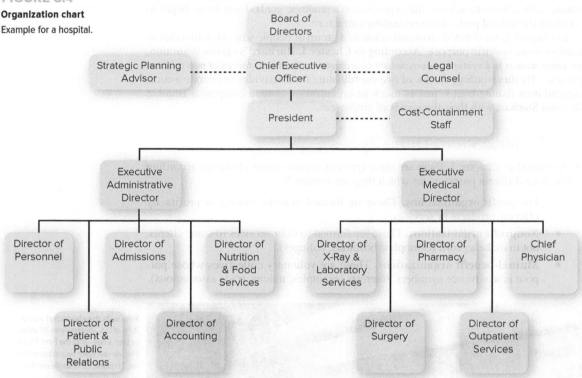

Two kinds of information that organization charts reveal about organizational structure are (1) the *vertical hierarchy of authority,* who reports to whom, and (2) the *horizontal specialization,* who specializes in what work.

The Vertical Hierarchy of Authority: Who Reports to Whom A glance up and down an organization chart shows the *vertical hierarchy,* the chain of command. A formal vertical hierarchy also shows the official communication network—who talks to whom. In a simple two-person organization, the owner might communicate with just a secretary or an assistant. In a complex organization, the president talks principally to the vice presidents, who in turn talk to the assistant vice presidents, and so on.

The Horizontal Specialization: Who Specializes in What Work A glance to the left and right on the line of an organization chart shows the *horizontal specialization,* the different jobs or work specialization. The husband-and-wife partners in a two-person desktop-publishing firm might agree that one is the "outside person," handling sales, client relations, and finances and the other is the "inside person," handling production and research. A large firm might have vice presidents for each task—marketing, finance, and so on. ●

Reading the Culture: Avoiding Pitfalls on Your Way Up   PRACTICAL ACTION

Although corporations and managements may make noises about training and support, newly promoted managers may not see any of this and may simply be expected to know what to do. And as managers move up the ladder, they may encounter other problems that they have not anticipated. How can you avoid some pitfalls as you make your ascent? In general, says one business professor, it begins by understanding "the culture you're in and what your organization's key values are."[83] You have to learn how to read the culture, and you have to learn how to build strong relationships.

Some suggestions follow.[84]

Have Realistic Expectations and Think about the Kind of Manager You Want to Be. New managers often focus on the rights and privileges of their new jobs and underestimate the duties and obligations. Make a list of all your previous bosses and their good and bad attributes. This may produce a list of dos and don'ts that can serve you well.

Don't Forget to Manage Upward and Sideways as Well as Downward. You need to manage not only your subordinates but also the perceptions of your peers and your own managers above you. In addition, you need to have good relationships with managers in other departments—and be perceptive about their needs and priorities—since they have resources you need to get your job done. One expert on building relationship networks suggests you ask four key questions: (1) Whose cooperation do I need? (2) Whose compliance do I need? (3) Whose opposition would keep me from accomplishing my work? (4) Who needs my cooperation and compliance?[85] Work on identifying what you have in common with the other person, and invest time in nurturing and maintaining the relationship.

Get Guidance from Other Managers. You may not get advice on how to manage from your own manager, who may have promoted you to help reduce his or her workload, not add to it by expecting some coaching. If this is the case, don't be shy about consulting other managers as well as people in professional organizations. "Keep listening to and for advice," says one former Major League Baseball commissioner. "Never complain; never explain. No one listens. Take the blame if something goes wrong."[86]

Resist Isolation. If you're promoted beyond supervisor of a small team and you have to manage hundreds rather than dozens, or thousands rather than hundreds, you may find the biggest surprise is isolation. The way to stay in touch is to talk daily with your senior managers, perhaps have "town meetings" with staffers several times a year, and use "management by wandering around"—bringing teams together to talk.

YOUR CALL

How would you try to manage the perceptions not only of subordinates but of your peers?

Managing. Being a manager requires a lot of interaction with others—as in "town meetings" with staffers. Do you think you'll need to resist a tendency toward isolation?
© Thomas Barwick/Getty Images

8.5 The Major Elements of an Organization

MAJOR
QUESTION

When I join an organization, what seven elements should I look for?

THE BIG PICTURE
Seven basic elements or features of an organization are described in this section.

Whether for-profit, nonprofit, or mutual-benefit, organizations have a number of elements in common. We discuss four proposed by an organizational psychologist, and then describe three others that most authorities agree on.

Common Elements of Organizations: Four Proposed by Edgar Schein

Organizational psychologist **Edgar Schein** proposed the four common elements of (1) *common purpose,* (2) *coordinated effort,* (3) *division of labor,* and (4) *hierarchy of authority.*[87] Let's consider these.

1. Common Purpose: The Means for Unifying Members
An organization without purpose soon begins to drift and become disorganized. The **common purpose** unifies employees or members and gives everyone an understanding of the organization's reason for being.

2. Coordinated Effort: Working Together for Common Purpose
The common purpose is realized through **coordinated effort, the coordination of individual efforts into a group or organizationwide effort.** Although it's true that individuals can make a difference, they cannot do everything by themselves.

3. Division of Labor: Work Specialization for Greater Efficiency
Division of labor, also known as *work specialization,* is the arrangement of having discrete parts of a task done by different people. Even a two-person crew operating a fishing boat probably has some work specialization—one steers the boat and the other works the nets. With division of labor, an organization can parcel out the entire complex work effort to be performed by specialists, resulting in greater efficiency.

4. Hierarchy of Authority: The Chain of Command
The hierarchy of authority, or *chain of command,* is a control mechanism for making sure the right people do the right things at the right time. If coordinated effort is to be achieved, some people—namely, managers—need to have more authority, or the right to direct the work of others. Even in member-owned organizations, some people have more authority than others, although their peers may have granted it to them.

In addition, authority is most effective when arranged in a hierarchy. Without tiers or ranks of authority, a lone manager would have to confer with everyone in his or her domain, making it difficult to get things done. Even in newer organizations that flatten the hierarchy, there still exists more than one level of management.[88] **A flat organization is defined as one with an organizational structure with few or no levels of middle management between top managers and those reporting to them.**

Finally, a principle stressed by early management scholars was that of **unity of command, in which an employee should report to no more than one manager in order to avoid** conflicting priorities and demands. Today, however, with advances in computer technology and networks, there are circumstances in which it makes sense for a person to communicate with more than one manager (as is true, for instance, with the organizational structure known as the matrix structure, as we'll describe).

Common Elements of Organizations: Three More That Most Authorities Agree On

To Schein's four common elements we may add three others that most authorities agree on: (5) *span of control*, (6) *authority, responsibility, and delegation*, and (7) *centralization versus decentralization of authority*.

5. Span of Control: Narrow (or Tall) versus Wide (or Flat)
The **span of control**, or *span of management*, refers to the number of people reporting directly to a given manager.[89] There are two kinds of spans of control, narrow (or tall) and wide (or flat).

Narrow Span of Control   This means a manager has a limited number of people reporting—three vice presidents reporting to a president, for example, instead of nine vice presidents. An organization is said to be *tall* when there are many levels with narrow spans of control.

Wide Span of Control   This means a manager has several people reporting—a first-line supervisor may have 40 or more subordinates, if little hands-on supervision is required, as is the case in some assembly-line workplaces. An organization is said to be *flat* when there are only a few levels with wide spans of control.

Historically, spans of about 7 to 10 subordinates were considered best, but there is no consensus as to what is ideal. In general, when managers must be closely involved with their subordinates, as when the management duties are complex, they are advised to have a narrow span of control. This is why presidents tend to have only a handful of vice presidents reporting to them. By contrast, first-line supervisors directing subordinates with similar work tasks may have a wide span of control.

Today's emphasis on lean management staffs and more efficiency means that spans of control need to be as wide as possible while still providing adequate supervision. Wider spans also fit in with the trend toward allowing workers greater autonomy in decision making. Research suggests that, when aided by technology to communicate and monitor, a manager can oversee 30 employees or more.[90]

6. Authority, Responsibility, and Delegation: Line versus Staff Positions
Male sea lions have to battle other males to attain authority over the herd. In human organizations, however, authority is related to the management authority in the organization; it has nothing to do with the manager's fighting ability or personal characteristics. With authority goes *accountability, responsibility,* and the ability to *delegate* one's authority.

Accountability   **Authority** refers to the rights inherent in a managerial position to make decisions, give orders, and utilize resources. (Authority is distinguished from *power*, which, as we discuss in Chapter 14, is the extent to which a person is able to influence others so they respond to orders.) In the military, of course, orders are given with the expectation that they will be obeyed, disobedience making one liable to a dishonorable discharge or imprisonment. In civilian organizations, disobeying orders may lead to less dire consequences (demotion or firing), but subordinates are still expected to accept that a higher-level manager has a legitimate right to issue orders.

Authority means **accountability**—managers must report and justify work results to the managers above them. Being accountable means you have the responsibility for performing assigned tasks.

Responsibility   With more authority comes more responsibility. **Responsibility is the obligation you have to perform the tasks assigned to you.** A car assembly-line worker has little authority but also little responsibility: just install those windshields over and over. A manager, however, has greater responsibilities.

It is a sign of faulty job design when managers are given too much authority and not enough responsibility, in which case they may become abusive to subordinates and capricious in exerting authority.[91] Conversely, managers may not be given enough authority, so the job becomes difficult.

Delegation   **Delegation is the process of assigning managerial authority and responsibility to managers and employees lower in the hierarchy.** To be more efficient, most managers are expected to delegate as much of their work as possible. However, many bosses get hung up on perfection, failing to realize that delegation is a necessary part of managing.

A smart rule is the "70% Rule": If the person you would like to perform the task is able to do it at least 70% as well as you can, you should delegate it. "Is it frustrating that the task won't be done with the same degree of perfection or perceived perfection that [you] could achieve?" asks one writer. "Sure! But let go of perfection."[92]

PRACTICAL ACTION   When Should You Delegate and When Not? How Managers Get More Done

All managers must learn how to delegate—to assign management authority and responsibilities to people lower in the company hierarchy. When it comes to a choice between micromanaging and delegating tasks, "err on the side of delegation," former GE head Jack Welch has recommended. "It makes your employees love being at the company and helps them flourish. And it gives managers a feel for who needs more attention."[93]

Delegation also helps you avoid exhaustion from overwork. "To do more in a day, you must do less—not do everything faster," says Oakland, California, productivity expert Odette Pollar.[94] If as a manager you find yourself often behind, always taking work home, doing your subordinates' work for them, and constantly having employees seeking your approval before they can act, you're clearly not delegating well.

How do you decide when to delegate and when not to? Here are some guidelines:[95]

Delegate Routine and Technical Matters. Always try to delegate routine tasks and routine paperwork. When there are technical matters, let the experts handle them.

Delegate Tasks That Help Your Subordinates Grow. Let your employees solve their own problems whenever possible. Let them try new things so they will grow in their jobs.

Don't Delegate Confidential and Personnel Matters. Any tasks that are confidential or that involve the evaluation, discipline, or counseling of subordinates should never be handed off to someone else.

Don't Delegate Emergencies. By definition, an emergency is a crisis for which there is little time for solution, and you should handle this yourself.

Don't Delegate Special Tasks That Your Boss Asked You to Do—Unless You Have His or Her Permission. If your supervisor entrusts you with a special assignment, such as attending a particular meeting, don't delegate it unless you have permission to do so.

Match the Tasks Delegated to Your Subordinates' Skills and Abilities. While recognizing that delegation involves some risk, make your assignments appropriate to the training, talent, skills, and motivation of your employees.

YOUR CALL

Managers fail to delegate for many reasons.[96] An excessive need for perfection. A belief that only they should handle "special," "difficult," or "unusual" problems or clients. A wish to keep the parts of a job that are fun. A fear that others will think them lazy. A reluctance to let employees lower down in the hierarchy take risks. A worry that subordinates won't deliver. A concern that the subordinates will do a better job and show them up. Are any of these why you might not be very good at delegating? What are some others?

Regarding authority and responsibility, the organization chart distinguishes between two positions, line and staff. *(See Figure 8.5.)*

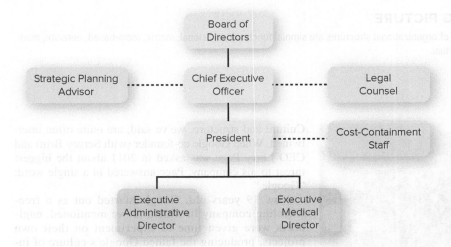

FIGURE 8.5

Line and staff

Line responsibilities are indicated by solid lines, staff responsibilities by dotted lines.

Line Position **Line managers** have authority to make decisions and usually have people reporting to them. Examples are the president, the vice presidents, the director of personnel, and the head of accounting. Line positions are indicated on the organization chart by a *solid line* (usually a vertical line).

Staff Position **Staff personnel** have authority functions; they provide advice, recommendations, and research to line managers (examples: specialists such as legal counsels and special advisers for mergers and acquisitions or strategic planning). Staff positions are indicated on the organization chart by a *dotted line* (usually a horizontal line).

7. Centralization versus Decentralization of Authority Who makes the important decisions in an organization? That is what the question of centralization versus decentralization of authority is concerned with.

Centralized Authority With **centralized authority,** important decisions are made by higher-level managers. Very small companies tend to be the most centralized, although nearly all organizations have at least some authority concentrated at the top of the hierarchy. Kmart and McDonald's are examples of companies using this kind of authority.

An advantage in using centralized authority is that there is less duplication of work, because fewer employees perform the same task; rather, the task is often performed by a department of specialists. Another advantage of centralization is that procedures are uniform and thus easier to control; all purchasing, for example, may have to be put out to competitive bids.

Decentralized Authority With **decentralized authority,** important decisions are made by middle-level and supervisory-level managers. Here, obviously, power has been delegated throughout the organization. Among the companies using decentralized authority are General Motors and Harley-Davidson.

An advantage in having decentralized authority is that managers are encouraged to solve their own problems rather than to buck the decision to a higher level. In addition, decisions are made more quickly, which increases the organization's flexibility and efficiency. ●

8.6   Basic Types of Organizational Structures

How would one describe the eight organizational structures?

THE BIG PICTURE

Eight types of organizational structures are simple, functional, divisional, matrix, team-based, network, modular, and virtual.

Small firm. What type of organizational structure is best suited to a local bicycle shop? Should the number of employees influence the decision? © Matthew Simmons/WireImage/Getty Images

Culture and structure, we've said, are quite often intertwined. When Google co-founder (with Sergey Brin) and CEO Larry Page was asked in 2011 about the biggest threat to his company, Page answered in a single word: "Google."

Now 19 years old, Google started out as a freewheeling company in which, as we mentioned, engineers were given time to experiment on their own projects, producing the famed Google's culture of innovation. The problem, however, was that the company grew so quickly (it's now over 61,000 people) that decision making had become molasses-like. For instance, the two co-founders, who had been trained as engineers, had hired a professional manager, Eric Schmidt, to be CEO, but the three of them "had to agree before anything could be done," says one report. "The unwieldy management and glacial pace of decision making were particularly noticeable in [Silicon Valley], where start-ups overtake behemoths in months."[97]

In 2015 Google revamped its corporate structure into a conglomerate called Alphabet Inc., with individual operations headed by separate chief executives. The word *conglomerate* (defined as a large company that is doing business in different, quite unrelated areas—General Electric and Berkshire Hathaway are two examples) is unpopular with most companies today because critics think it spreads top management focus too widely.[98] However, for the Google founders, the purpose of Alphabet was not only to streamline the company's structure and decision-making processes but also to bring more transparency into the company's operations to satisfy investors who, as one editorial explained it, "admired its cash-rich search businesses but complained that its other sidelines are hard to measure."[99] The reorganization separated the collection of traditional businesses most associated with Google—such as Search, Android, YouTube, and Google Maps—from more speculative "moonshot" ventures such as Calico (life extension), Google X (self-driving cars), Nest (smart-home devices), and Sidewalk (city infrastructure).[100]

Organizational design is concerned with designing the optimal structures of accountability and responsibility that an organization uses to execute its strategies. We can categorize organizational designs as three types: (1) traditional designs, (2) horizontal designs, and (3) designs that open boundaries between organizations.[101]

1. Traditional Designs: Simple, Functional, Divisional, and Matrix Structures

Traditional organizational designs tend to favor structures that rely on a vertical management hierarchy, with clear departmental boundaries and reporting arrangements, as follows.

The Simple Structure: For the Small Firm The first organizational form is the simple structure. This is the form often found in a firm's very early, entrepreneurial stages, when the organization is apt to reflect the desires and personality of the owner or founder. **An organization with a simple structure has authority centralized in a single person, a flat hierarchy, few rules, and low work specialization.** *(See Figure 8.6, right.)*

Hundreds of thousands of organizations are arranged according to a simple structure—for instance, small mom-and-pop firms running landscaping, construction, insurance sales, and similar businesses. Examples: Both Hewlett-Packard and Apple Computer began as two-man garage start-ups that later became large.

The Functional Structure: Grouping by Similar Work Specialties The second organizational form is the functional structure. **In a functional structure, people with similar occupational specialties are put together in formal groups.** This is a quite commonplace structure, seen in all kinds of organizations, for-profit and nonprofit. *(See Figure 8.7.)*

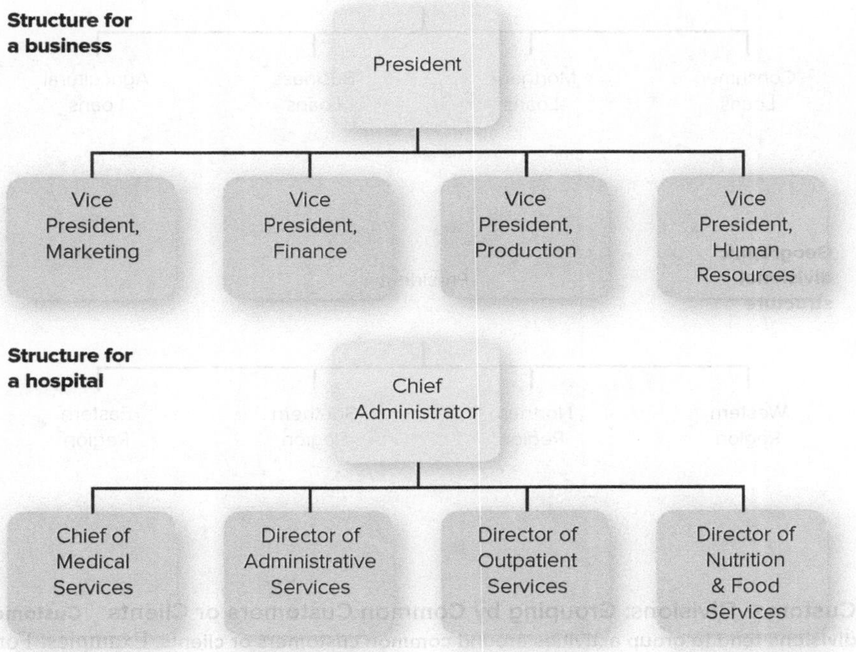

FIGURE 8.6

Simple structure: An example

There is only one hierarchical level of management beneath the owner.

FIGURE 8.7

Functional structure: Two examples

This shows the functional structure for a business and for a hospital.

Structure for a business

President

- Vice President, Marketing
- Vice President, Finance
- Vice President, Production
- Vice President, Human Resources

Structure for a hospital

Chief Administrator

- Chief of Medical Services
- Director of Administrative Services
- Director of Outpatient Services
- Director of Nutrition & Food Services

Examples: A manufacturing firm will often group people with similar work skills in a Marketing Department, others in a Production Department, others in Finance, and so on. A nonprofit educational institution might group employees according to work specialty under Faculty, Admissions, Maintenance, and so forth.

The Divisional Structure: Grouping by Similarity of Purpose The third organizational form is the divisional structure. **In a divisional structure, people with diverse occupational specialties are put together in formal groups by similar products or services, customers or clients, or geographic regions.** *(See Figure 8.8, next page.)*

Product Divisions: Grouping by Similar Products or Services **Product divisions** group activities around similar products or services. Examples: The media giant Time Warner has different divisions for magazines, movies, recordings, cable television, and so on. The Warner Bros. part of the empire alone has divisions spanning movies and television, a broadcast network, retail stores, theaters, amusement parks, and music.

Divisional structure: Three examples

This shows product, customer, and geographic divisions.

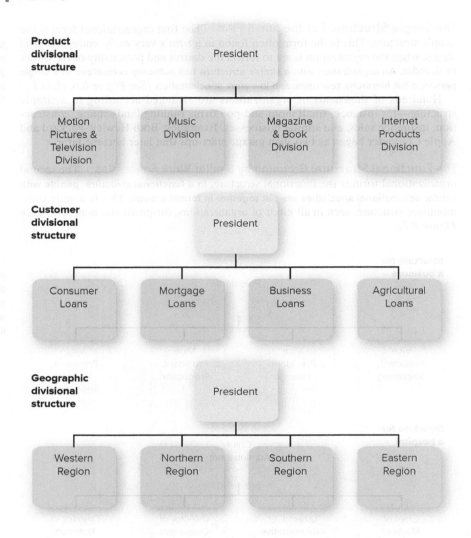

Product divisional structure

President

- Motion Pictures & Television Division
- Music Division
- Magazine & Book Division
- Internet Products Division

Customer divisional structure

President

- Consumer Loans
- Mortgage Loans
- Business Loans
- Agricultural Loans

Geographic divisional structure

President

- Western Region
- Northern Region
- Southern Region
- Eastern Region

Customer Divisions: Grouping by Common Customers or Clients **Customer divisions** tend to group activities around common customers or clients. Examples: Ford Motor Co. has separate divisions for passenger-car dealers, for large trucking customers, and for farm products customers. A savings and loan might be structured with divisions for making consumer loans, mortgage loans, business loans, and agricultural loans.

Geographic Divisions: Grouping by Regional Location **Geographic divisions** group activities around defined regional locations. Example: This arrangement is frequently used by government agencies. The Federal Reserve Bank, for instance, has 12 separate districts around the United States. The Internal Revenue Service also has several districts.

The Matrix Structure: A Grid of Functional and Divisional for Two Chains of Command The fourth organizational form is the matrix structure. In a **matrix structure,** an organization combines functional and divisional chains of command in a grid so that there are two command structures—vertical and horizontal. The functional structure usually doesn't change—it is the organization's normal departments or divisions, such as Finance, Marketing, Production, and Research & Development. The divisional structure may vary—as by product, brand, customer, or geographic region. *(See Figure 8.9.)*

FIGURE 8.9 **Matrix structure**

An example of an arrangement that Ford might use.

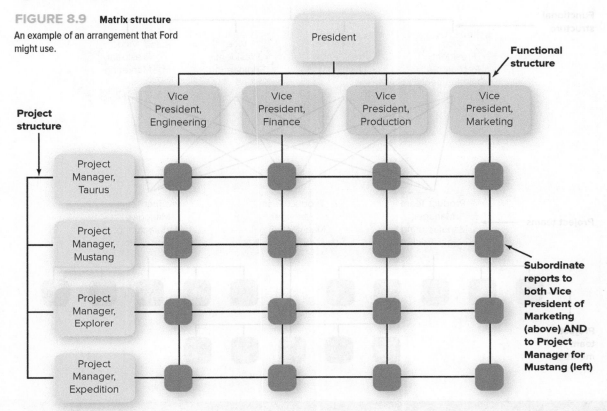

A hypothetical example, using Ford Motor Co.: The functional structure might be the departments of Engineering, Finance, Production, and Marketing, each headed by a vice president. Thus, the reporting arrangement is vertical. The divisional structure might be by product (the new models of Taurus, Mustang, Explorer, and Expedition, for example), each headed by a project manager. This reporting arrangement is horizontal. Thus, a marketing person, say, would report to *both* the Vice President of Marketing *and* the project manager for the Ford Mustang. Indeed, Ford Motor Co. used the matrix approach to create the Taurus and a newer version of the Mustang.

2. The Horizontal Design: Eliminating Functional Barriers to Solve Problems

The second organizational design is the horizontal design. **In a horizontal design, also called a team-based design, teams or workgroups, either temporary or permanent, are used to improve collaboration and work on shared tasks by breaking down internal boundaries.** For instance, when managers from different functional divisions are brought together in teams—known as cross-functional teams—to solve particular problems, the barriers between the divisions break down. The focus on narrow divisional interests yields to a common interest in solving the problems that brought them together. Yet team members still have their full-time functional work responsibilities and often still formally report to their own managers above them in the functional-division hierarchy. *(See Figure 8.10, next page.)*

FIGURE 8.10　Horizontal design

This shows a mix of functional (vertical) and project-team (horizontal) arrangements.

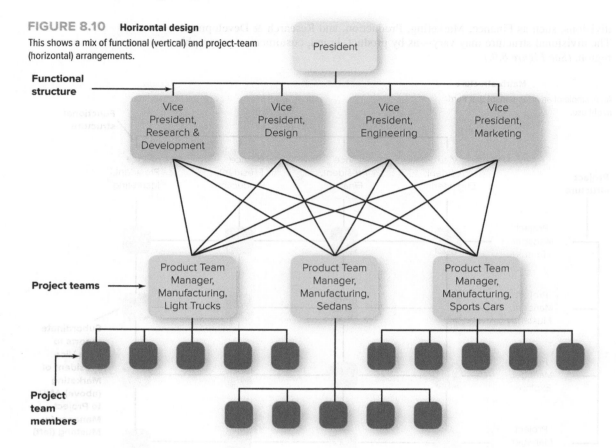

EXAMPLE　　Use of a Horizontal Design: Whole Foods Market

Upscale natural and organic-food grocery Whole Foods Market started out in 1980 as one store in Austin, Texas, and today has revenues of $15.3 billion and 447 stores in North America and the United Kingdom.[102] It was rated No. 24 in 2016 on *Fortune* magazine's annual "World's Most Admired Companies" list.[103] It has also been chosen as one of *Fortune*'s "100 Best Companies to Work For" every year for 17 years (No. 75 in 2016).[104] But as one writer observed, if its values are "soft-hearted," emphasizing Whole Food, Whole People, Whole Planet, "its competitive logic is hard-headed."[105] That's because its management strategy is based not on hierarchy but on autonomous profit centers of self-managed teams.

"Radical Decentralizing": Empowering Small Teams. One of Whole Foods's core operating principles is that all work is teamwork. Thus, each store is organized into roughly eight self-managed teams, each with a designated team leader. The leaders in each store also operate as a team, as do the store leaders in each region. Additionally, the directors of the company's 11 regions operate as a team.

At most retail companies, employees are hired by supervisors (not fellow employees), decisions about what products to order are made by someone high up at central headquarters, and the amounts of people's paychecks are kept secret. Whole Foods, however, believes in "radical decentralizing," in the words of influential management professor Gary Hamel.[106]

At the individual-store level, compensation is tied to team rather than individual performance, and performance measurements and individual pay schedules are open to all. Each team has the mission of improving the food for which it is responsible; is given wide flexibility in how it manages its responsibilities, hires and fires its members, and stocks its shelves; and is given a lot of power in how it responds to the changing tastes of local consumers.

A Steady Diet of Growth. Whole Foods employees are given both the freedom to do the right thing for customers and the incentive to do the right thing for profits. The financial results of this business model are that Whole Foods is the most profitable food retailer in the United Sates, when measured by profit per square foot. Although its stock price was down somewhat in 2014, it still was up 12-fold since its 2008 recession-era low.[107]

YOUR CALL

In designing new products, such as cell phones, the horizontal design team approach, known as *concurrent engineering* or *integrated product development,* has been found to speed up design because all the specialists meet at once, instead of separately doing their own thing, then handing off the result to the next group of specialists. Why do you think a horizontal design would be better in a retail business such as groceries?

---

3. Designs That Open Boundaries between Organizations: Hollow, Modular, and Virtual Structures

The opposite of a bureaucracy, with its numerous barriers and divisions, a **boundaryless organization** is a fluid, highly adaptive organization whose members, linked by information technology, come together to collaborate on common tasks. The collaborators may include not only coworkers but also suppliers, customers, and even competitors. This means that the form of the business is ever-changing, and business relationships are informal.[108]

Three types of structures in this class of organizational design are *hollow, modular,* and *virtual* structures.

The Hollow Structure: Operating with a Central Core and Outsourcing Functions to Outside Vendors   In the **hollow structure**, often called the network structure, the organization has a central core of key functions and outsources other functions to vendors who can do them cheaper or faster. *(See Figure 8.11.)* A company with a hollow structure might retain such important core processes as design or marketing and outsource most other processes, such as human resources, warehousing, or distribution, thereby seeming to "hollow out" the organization.[109]

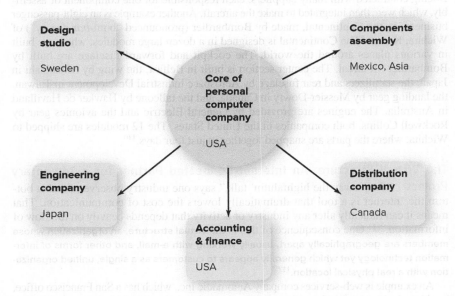

FIGURE 8.11

Hollow structure

This is an example of a personal computer company that outsources noncore processes to vendors.

A firm with a hollow structure might operate with extensive, even worldwide operations, yet its basic core could remain small, thus keeping payrolls and overhead down. The glue that holds everything together is information technology, along with strategic alliances and contractual arrangements with supplier companies. An example of a hollow structure is EndoStim, the medical device start-up we described earlier.

Modular structure. The center section of Bombardier's eight-passenger Continental business jet is built in Ireland and is shipped to Wichita, Kansas, where it is assembled with 12 other major components in just four days.
© epa european pressphoto agency b.v./Alamy

The Modular Structure: Outsourcing Pieces of a Product to Outside Firms

The modular structure differs from the hollow structure in that it is oriented around outsourcing certain *pieces of a product* rather than outsourcing certain *processes* (such as human resources or warehousing) of an organization. In a **modular structure, a firm assembles product chunks, or modules, provided by outside contractors.** One article compares this form of organization to "a collection of Lego bricks that can snap together."

An example of the modular structure is the massive 787 Dreamliner project, in which Boeing contracted with many suppliers, each responsible for one component or assembly, which were then integrated to make the aircraft. Another example is an eight-passenger business jet, the Continental, made by Bombardier (pronounced "bom-*bar*-dee-ay") of Wichita, Kansas. The Continental is designed in a dozen large modules, which are built in various places around the world. The cockpit and forward fuselage are built by Bombardier Montreal. The center section is built in Belfast, the wing by Mitsubishi in Japan, the stabilizers and rear fuselage by Aerospace Industrial Development in Taiwan, the landing gear by Messier-Dowty in Canada, and the tailcone by Hawker de Havilland in Australia. The engines are provided by General Electric and the avionics gear by Rockwell Collins, both companies in the United States. The 12 modules are shipped to Wichita, where the parts are snapped together in just four days.[110]

The Virtual Structure: An Internet-Connected Partner for a Temporary Project

"Strip away the highfalutin' talk," says one industry observer, "and at bottom the Internet is a tool that dramatically lowers the cost of communication. That means it can radically alter any industry or activity that depends heavily on the flow of information."[111] One consequence of this is the **virtual structure, an organization whose members are geographically apart, usually working with e-mail, and other forms of information technology yet which generally appears to customers as a single, unified organization with a real physical location.**[112]

An example is web-services company Automattic Inc., which has a San Francisco office, but it's only for occasional use. Its real offices are the homes of its 123 employees working in 26 countries, 94 cities, and 28 U.S. states. Although occasionally employees hop on a plane and meet face to face, they mainly transmit messages via text-based internal blogs or, when misunderstandings occur, talk on the phone. With a virtual structure, companies can "tap into a wider talent pool not limited by geography," says one report. "Firms can also save money on real estate, though sizable travel budgets may partly offset that."[113] ●

8.7 Contingency Design: Factors in Creating the Best Structure

MAJOR QUESTION

?

What factors affect the design of an organization's structure?

THE BIG PICTURE

Three factors that should be considered when determining the best organizational culture involve whether an organization's environment is mechanistic or organic, whether its environment stresses differentiation or integration, and how its strategy can affect its structure.

What is the optimal size for an organization? How big is too big?

Medical records company gloStream, which sells software to doctors' offices, was founded in 2005 as a virtual structure, and for four years the approach worked well, with costs kept low and salespeople having no choice but to be out in the field. But in 2009, CEO Mike Sappington decided it was time to "take the company physical." "We've gotten too big to be a virtual company," he told *Inc.* magazine. By the following year, gloStream planned to have 100 employees in the United States and another 100 in India. "Setting up a conference call or arranging everyone's schedules for a meeting," he said, "started to take an enormous amount of time."[114]

Three Factors to Be Considered in Designing an Organization's Structure

When managers are considering what organizational arrangements to choose from, such factors as stage of development are among the factors, or *contingencies,* they must consider. Recall from Chapter 2 that the *contingency approach* to management emphasizes that a manager's approach should vary according to—that is, be contingent on—the individual and environmental situation. Thus, the manager following the contingency approach simply asks, "What method is the best to use under these particular circumstances?" **The process of fitting the organization to its environment is called contingency design.**

Managers taking a contingency approach must consider the following factors in designing the best kind of structure for their particular organization at that particular time:

1. *Environment—mechanistic versus organic*
2. *Environment—differentiation versus integration*
3. *Link between strategy, culture, and structure*

1. The Environment: Mechanistic versus Organic Organizations—the Burns and Stalker Model

Making beds—how hard could it be?

Actually, a hotel housecleaner may be expected to whip not just beds but entire rooms, 16–30 of them, into spick-and-span shape during an eight-hour shift. Here every job is broken down into the smallest of steps, with vacuuming, dusting, mopping, making beds, and so on expected to take about 20–24 minutes per room, according to time-motion studies. Making a neatly tucked bed should take no more than 3 minutes.[115] Marriott allows 30 minutes for tidying up a room and has developed a 66-step manual with very specific directions ("Wipe the nightstand's glass top with a blue rag, using the blue bottle. Wipe the phone and clock").[116]

Could anyone do this? Hotel housekeepers, following the model of a mechanistic organization, are supposed to be able to make beds in no more than 3 minutes and ready an entire room within 24 minutes. The tasks are physically demanding, and the staff must be taught how to bend properly to make the work easier on the body. If you had this job, what would you do to vary the routine to avoid monotony—or would that sacrifice speed? © Simon Dawson/Bloomberg/Getty Images

Much of this kind of mundane hotel work exemplifies what British behavioral scientists **Tom Burns** and **G. M. Stalker** call a *mechanistic organization,* as opposed to an *organic organization.*[117] *(See Table 8.3.)*

MECHANISTIC ORGANIZATIONS	ORGANIC ORGANIZATIONS
Centralized hierarchy of authority	Decentralized hierarchy of authority
Many rules and procedures	Few rules and procedures
Specialized tasks	Shared tasks
Formalized communication	Informal communication
Few teams or task forces	Many teams or task forces
Narrow span of control, taller structures	Wider span of control, flatter structures

Mechanistic Organizations: When Rigidity and Uniformity Work Best

In a **mechanistic organization,** authority is centralized, tasks and rules are clearly specified, and employees are closely supervised. Mechanistic organizations, then, are bureaucratic, with rigid rules and top-down communication. This kind of structure is effective in certain aspects of hotel work because the market demands uniform product quality and cleanliness.

In general, mechanistic design works best when an organization is operating in a stable environment. Yet new companies that have gone through a rough-and-tumble start-up period may decide to change their structures so that they are more mechanistic, with clear lines of authority.

Organic Organizations: When Looseness and Flexibility Work Best

In an **organic organization,** authority is decentralized, there are fewer rules and procedures, and networks of employees are encouraged to cooperate and respond quickly to unexpected tasks. Tom Peters and Robert Waterman called this kind of organization a "loose" structure.[118]

Organic organizations are sometimes termed "adhocracies" because they operate on an ad hoc basis, improvising as they go along. As you might expect, information-technology companies favor the organic arrangement because they constantly have to adjust to technological change. New York–based Dark Arts Consulting, a technology consulting firm, has used the practice of co-working—sharing office space with other businesses—to expand into territories in New Jersey and Pennsylvania, enabling it to hire salespeople and engineers without having the added expense of an underutilized office.[119] Companies that need to respond to fast-changing consumer tastes also favor organic arrangements.

No doubt you would be more comfortable in some organizational structures than others. If you value autonomy and the chance to make decisions, you probably prefer a hollow or virtual structure as opposed to one that is more structured. What type of structure do you think would bring out the best in you?

connect SELF-ASSESSMENT 8.3

Assessing Your Organizational Structure Preference

This survey is designed to assess your preferred type of organizational structure. Please be prepared to answer these questions if your instructor has assigned Self-Assessment 8.3 in Connect.

1. Do you prefer a more mechanistic or organic structure? What do you think is the cause for this preference?

2. If you were interviewing for a job, what questions might you ask to determine if the company is more mechanistic or organic?

2. The Environment: Differentiation versus Integration— the Lawrence and Lorsch Model

Burns and Stalker's ideas were extended in the United States by Harvard University researchers **Paul R. Lawrence** and **Jay W. Lorsch**.[120] Instead of a *mechanistic–organic dimension,* however, they proposed a *differentiation–integration* dimension— forces that impelled the parts of an organization to move apart or to come together. The stability of the environment confronting the parts of the organization, according to Lawrence and Lorsch, determines the degree of differentiation or integration that is appropriate.

Differentiation: When Forces Push the Organization Apart   **Differentiation is the tendency of the parts of an organization to disperse and fragment.** The more subunits into which an organization breaks down, the more highly differentiated it is.

This impulse toward dispersal arises because of technical specialization and division of labor. As a result, specialists behave in specific, delimited ways, without coordinating with other parts of the organization. For example, a company producing dental floss, deodorants, and other personal-care products might have different product divisions, each with its own production facility and sales staff—a quite differentiated organization.

Integration: When Forces Pull the Organization Together   **Integration is the tendency of the parts of an organization to draw together to achieve a common purpose.** In a highly integrated organization, the specialists work together to achieve a common goal. The means for achieving this are a formal chain of command, standardization of rules and procedures, and use of cross-functional teams and computer networks so that there is frequent communication and coordination of the parts.

3. Linking Strategy, Culture, and Structure

We began this chapter by discussing why it makes sense that a company's organizational culture and organizational structure should be aligned with its vision and strategies. Thus, if the managers of an organization change its strategy, as gloStream did when it decided to add lots more people and put them under one roof instead of in a virtual network, they need to change the organization's culture and structure to support that strategy. Indeed, companies often begin by offering a single product or product line that requires only a simple structure, but as they grow and their strategies become more ambitious and elaborate, the culture and structure need to change to support those strategies.[121]

All the organizational cultures and structures described in this chapter are used today because all of them have advantages that make them appropriate for some cases and disadvantages that make them not useful for others. For example, the clear roles and strict hierarchy of an extremely mechanistic organization are clearly suitable in a system valuing careful routines and checks and balances, such as a nuclear power plant. A fast-moving start-up drawing on sources of expertise throughout the world may benefit from a more flexible culture and organic structure that lowers boundaries between functions and organizations. ●

Key Points

8.1 Aligning Strategy, Culture, and Structure

- Person–organization fit reflects the extent to which your personality and values match the climate and culture in an organization. A good fit is associated with more positive work attitudes and task performance, lower stress, and fewer intentions to quit.

- The challenge for top managers is to align the organization's vision and strategies with its organizational culture and organizational structure.

- Organizational culture is defined as the set of shared, taken-for-granted implicit assumptions that a group holds and that determines how it perceives, thinks about, and reacts to its various environments. The culture helps employees understand why the organization does what it does and how it intends to accomplish its long-term goals.

- Organizational structure is a formal system of task and reporting relationships that coordinates and motivates an organization's members so that they can work together to achieve the organization's goals.

8.2 What Kind of Organizational Culture Will You Be Operating In?

- Organizational culture appears as three layers. Level 1 is observable artifacts, the physical manifestations of culture. Level 2 is espoused values, explicitly stated values and norms preferred by an organization, although employees are frequently influenced by enacted values, which represent the values and norms actually exhibited in the organization. Level 3 consists of basic assumptions, the core values of the organization.

- According to one common methodology known as the *competing values framework,* organizational cultures can be classified into four types: (1) clan, which has an internal focus and values flexibility; (2) adhocracy, which has an external focus and values flexibility; (3) market,

which has a strong external focus and values stability and control; and (4) hierarchy, which has an internal focus and values stability and control.

- Culture is transmitted to employees in symbols, stories, heroes, rites and rituals, and organizational socialization. A symbol is an object, an act, a quality, or an event that conveys meaning to others. A story is a narrative based on true events, which is repeated—and sometimes embellished on—to emphasize a particular value. A hero is a person whose accomplishments embody the values of the organization. Rites and rituals are the activities and ceremonies, planned and unplanned, that celebrate important occasions and accomplishments in the organization's life. Organizational socialization is defined as the process by which people learn the values, norms, and required behaviors that permit them to participate as members of an organization.

8.3 The Process of Culture Change

- Among the 12 mechanisms managers use to embed a culture in an organization are (1) formal statements; (2) slogans and sayings; (3) rites and rituals; (4) stories, legends, and myths; (5) leader reactions to crises; (6) role modeling, training, and coaching; (7) physical design; (8) rewards, titles, promotions, and bonuses; (9) organizational goals and performance criteria; (10) measurable and controllable activities; (11) organizational structure; and (12) organizational systems and procedures.

8.4 Organizational Structure

- An organization is a system of consciously coordinated activities or forces of two or more people.

- There are three types of organizations classified according to the three different purposes for which they are formed: for-profit, nonprofit, and mutual-benefit.

- Whatever the size of an organization, it can be represented in an organization chart, a boxes-and-lines illustration showing the formal lines of authority and the organization's official positions or division of labor.
- Two kinds of information that organizations reveal about organizational structure are (1) the vertical hierarchy of authority, who reports to whom, and (2) the horizontal specialization, who specializes in what work.

8.5 The Major Elements of an Organization

- Organizations have seven elements. Four proposed by Edgar Schein are (1) common purpose, which unifies employees or members and gives everyone an understanding of the organization's reason for being; (2) coordinated effort, the coordination of individual efforts into a group or organizationwide effort; (3) division of labor, having discrete parts of a task done by different people; and (4) hierarchy of authority, a control mechanism for making sure the right people do the right things at the right time.
- Two other common elements are (5) span of control, which refers to the number of people reporting directly to a given manager, and (6) authority and accountability, responsibility, and delegation.
- *Authority* refers to the rights inherent in a managerial position to make decisions, give orders, and utilize resources. Accountability means that managers must report and justify work results to the managers above them. Responsibility is the obligation you have to perform the tasks assigned to you. Delegation is the process of assigning managerial authority and responsibility to managers and employees lower in the hierarchy.
- Regarding authority and responsibility, the organization chart distinguishes between two positions, line and staff. Line managers have authority to make decisions and usually have people reporting to them. Staff personnel have advisory functions; they provide advice, recommendations, and research to line managers.
- The final common element of organizations is (7) centralization versus decentralization of authority. With centralized authority, important decisions are made by higher-level managers. With decentralized authority, important decisions are made by middle-level and supervisory-level managers.

8.6 Basic Types of Organizational Structures

- Organizations may be arranged into seven types of structures. (1) In a simple structure, authority is centralized in a single person; this structure has a flat hierarchy, few rules, and low work specialization. (2) In a functional structure, people with similar occupational specialties are put together in formal groups. (3) In a divisional structure, people with diverse occupational specialties are put together in formal groups by similar products or services, customers or clients, or

geographic regions. (4) In a matrix structure, an organization combines functional and divisional chains of command in grids so that there are two command structures—vertical and horizontal.
- (5) In a horizontal design or team-based design, teams or workgroups are used to improve horizontal relations and solve problems throughout the organization. (6) A boundaryless organization is a fluid, highly adaptive organization whose members, linked by information technology, come together to collaborate on common tasks. Three designs that open boundaries between organizations are hollow, modular, and virtual structures. In the hollow structure, often called the network structure, the organization has a central core of key functions and outsources other functions to vendors who can do them cheaper or faster. In a modular structure, a firm assembles product chunks, or modules, provided by outside contractors. The virtual structure is an organization whose members are geographically apart, usually working with e-mail and other forms of information technology, yet which generally appears to customers as a single, unified organization with a real physical location.

8.7 Contingency Design: Factors in Creating the Best Structure

- The process of fitting the organization to its environment is called contingency design. Managers taking a contingency approach must consider at least three factors in designing the best kind of structure for their organization at that particular time.
- The first is that an organization may be either mechanistic or organic. In a mechanistic organization, authority is centralized, tasks and rules are clearly specified, and employees are closely supervised. In an organic organization, authority is decentralized, there are fewer rules and procedures, and networks of employees are encouraged to cooperate and respond quickly to unexpected tasks.
- The second is that an organization may also be characterized by differentiation or integration. Differentiation is the tendency of the parts of an organization to disperse and fragment. Integration is the tendency of the parts of an organization to draw together to achieve a common purpose.
- The third is the link between strategy, culture, and structure. If the managers of an organization change its strategy, they need to change the organization's culture and structure to support that strategy. Indeed, companies often begin by offering a single product or product line that requires only a simple structure, but as they grow and their strategies become more ambitious and elaborate, so the culture and structure need to change to support those strategies.

Understanding the Chapter: What Do I Know?

1. To implement an organization's strategy, what are the two kinds of important areas that managers must determine?

2. How would you describe the four kinds of organizational cultures, according to the competing values framework?

3. Describe and explain the three levels of organizational culture.
4. What are five ways in which culture is transmitted to employees?
5. Name 12 mechanisms by which an organization's members teach each other preferred values, beliefs, expectations, and behaviors.
6. What are seven common elements of organizations?

7. Describe the four types of traditional organizational designs.
8. Explain what is meant by horizontal organizational designs.
9. What are three designs that open boundaries between organizations?
10. What are three factors to consider in designing an organization's structure?

Management in Action

W.L. Gore's Culture Promotes Employee Satisfaction, Innovation, and Retention

W.L. Gore & Associates was founded in 1958 by Wilbert (Bill) and Genevieve (Vieve) Gore. The company started in the basement of their home. Success transformed the business from the basement to its first manufacturing plant in 1960. Today, Gore has over $3 billion in revenue and 10,000 employees working in offices across 25 countries. It is one of the 200 largest privately held companies in the U.S.[122]

The company is best known for its Gore-Tex water and windproof fabrics that are used in a variety of outdoor apparel. But the company has expanded its products to include vacuum filters, microwave cable assemblies, guitar strings, dental floss, acoustic vents for cell phones, and medical devices.[123]

The company has been profitable every year since its foundation and has been ranked on *Fortune*'s "100 Best Companies to Work For" list every year since 1998. Its best ranking was as No. 2 in 2005, and it was No. 12 in 2016. Not surprisingly, employees tend to remain at Gore once hired. The annual turnover rate is about 3%.[124]

Structure, Culture, and Values Leadership Conviction

Bill Gore wanted to start a company that was free from bureaucracy and a command and control style of leadership. He felt that this was the best way to foster creativity, engagement, and innovation. He was a strong believer in autonomy and creating an environment in which people flourished. To support this philosophy, the company established a unique organizational structure and cultural values.

Gore's organizational structure is referred to as a team-based "lattice" organization. "There are no traditional organizational charts, no chains of command, nor predetermined channels of communication." Employees, who are all called associates, are accountable to the member of their multi-disciplined teams. Teams form in an ad hoc fashion around perceived "opportunities," and leaders emerge.[125]

"Leadership opportunities at Gore are based on how much of a 'followership' someone has among co-workers. Gore also uses peer assessments to determine compensation," according to *Fortune*.[126]

Associates are "responsible for managing their own workload" and for independently making commitments that support team goals. Goals are not dictated from the top down. Rather, associates establish their own commitments, and these percolate upward to form corporate forecasts.

High-quality relationships "with each other, with customers, with vendors and suppliers, and with our surrounding communities" are essential at Gore. Associates are encouraged to "build and maintain long-term relationships by communicating directly." Face-to-face meetings and phone calls are preferred over less rich media, like e-mail and texting.[127]

The company established a set of fundamental beliefs to help embed its desired culture:

- *Belief in the individual:* If you trust individuals and believe in them, they will be motivated to do what's right for the company.
- *Power of small teams:* Our lattice organization harnesses the fast decision-making, diverse perspectives, and collaboration of small teams.
- *All in the same boat:* All Gore associates are part owners of the company through the associate stock plan.
- *Long-term view:* Our investment decisions are based on long-term payoff, and our fundamental beliefs are not sacrificed for short-term gain.[128]

How Does it All Work?

Associates are not hired for specific jobs. Rather, they are "hired for general work areas. With the guidance of their sponsors [everyone has a sponsor, whose goal is to help people succeed] and a growing understanding of opportunities and team objectives, associates commit to projects that match their skills. . . . Sponsors help associates chart a course in the organization that will offer personal fulfillment while maximizing their contribution to the enterprise."[129] They do this by actively providing feedback on performance and personal development and by helping associates network with others.

Bill Gore also believed in keeping operational facilities small due to his focus on high-quality interpersonal relationships. He observed that it was hard to know everyone once the number of employees at a facility exceeded 150–200 people. The company thus splits up people at a facility once it reaches this size by creating a new location.

The final piece of the cultural puzzle involves a set of guiding principles that Bill Gore called freedom, fairness, commitment, and waterline:

- Associates have the freedom to encourage, help, and allow other associates to grow in knowledge, skill, and scope of responsibility.
- Associates should demonstrate fairness to each other and everyone with whom they come in contact.
- Associates are provided the ability to make one's own commitments and are expected to keep them.
- A waterline situation involves consultation with other associates before undertaking actions that could impact the reputation or profitability of the company and otherwise "sink the ship."[130]

Associates are expected to live by these principles, and the company spends considerable effort trying to hire people who fit into its culture. It is also important to note that the company does not believe in showering associates with lavish perks as do many of the other companies listed on *Fortune*'s list of best companies. The "headquarters doesn't have foosball tables or napping pods," according to *Fortune*. One employee described the culture this way: "It's authentic. It's not a façade or marketing strategy."[131]

FOR DISCUSSION

1. Using the competing values framework as a point of reference, how would you describe the current organizational culture at Gore? Provide examples to support your conclusions.
2. Which of the 12 ways to embed organizational culture has Gore used to create its current culture? Provide examples to support your conclusions.
3. Which of the three types of organizational design discussed in the chapter is most similar to Gore's lattice structure? Explain your rationale.
4. Is Gore's structure more organic or mechanistic? Explain.
5. What is the most important lesson from this case? Discuss.

Legal/Ethical Challenge

Should Socializing outside Work Hours Be Mandatory?

Person–organization fit reflects the extent to which someone's personality and values match, or fit, an organization's culture and climate. Good fit is important for both employees and organizations. This challenge involves the cultural considerations of asking employees to socialize outside work hours. If socializing outside work is an expectation of new hires, then it becomes something to consider when applying for jobs.

Why would companies ask employees to socialize outside of work hours? There are a number of good reasons: (1) fostering comfort and relaxation among employees, (2) helping people de-stress after a hard day, (3) learning more about one's colleagues, and (4) building teamwork and unity.[132] All of these benefits should improve interpersonal relationships and potentially boost productivity and customer service.

If such requests are voluntary, however, then it is likely that fewer people will show up, thereby reducing the benefits. People who show up are more likely to be like-minded and share a common race and gender, as well as hobbies, and tastes. Voluntary requests can thus serve as a subtle way of promoting homogeneity rather than diversity.

Moreover, voluntary requests potentially set up a situation in which people develop unequal social networks. This can have unfair career advantages for those who attend because people discuss work-related issues at such gatherings. It thus makes some sense to make it mandatory to socialize outside of work.

Some companies accept this conclusion. Zappos did in the past, and other companies continue the practice today.

One woman told a reporter that there was an unwritten requirement at her employer that "employees were expected to spend extra money and time on group lunches and twice-weekly drinks. This kind of socializing was necessary in order to get ahead." She was not told about the requirement during the hiring process, and she now feels a lack of fit. Her problem with the expectation is that she has two children to pick up from school and she tries to save money by taking her lunch to work. In a recent performance appraisal, she was told "I needed to be more of a team player." Her feedback was partly based on her lack of socializing outside of work.[133]

SOLVING THE CHALLENGE

What are your thoughts about making it mandatory to socialize outside of work hours?

1. I think it's a good idea. The benefits exceed the costs and I don't agree that it fails to appreciate diversity. The socializing activities can be varied to fit the values and needs of diverse employees, thereby supporting diversity.
2. I don't like it. What employees do after work hours is their business and companies should not infringe on them. Socializing outside work hours should be voluntary.
3. I believe that employers have no business interfering with how employees spend time outside of work. This means that I don't want either voluntary or mandatory requests about socializing outside of work hours. If people want to socialize outside work, let them arrange it on their own.
4. Invent other options.

9

Human Resource Management
Getting the Right People for Managerial Success

Soft Skills and Social Graces: Boosting Your Advantage in the Hiring World

Didn't get hired? Maybe you're lacking in the right *soft skills:* appearance, manners, punctuality, ability to communicate well—in other words, *professional behavior.* As discussed in Chapter 1, it's what employers complain they can't find in many job applicants, especially among Millennials.[1]

Dress for Success

If you dress casually on campus, rethink your wardrobe before showing up for a job interview (or a career fair). No sandals or flip-flops, torn jeans, tank tops, short skirts, or revealing dresses. Wear simple earrings (men not at all), cover tattoos, and don't try to look sexy. Employers are "looking for people who can assume the role of a business professional," says one recruitment manager.[2] For men, this could mean wearing a suit and tie and leather shoes with dress socks. For women, it could be a blazer and a blouse with a skirt or slacks, along with low heels and hosiery. Do the same the first day at work on a new job.[3] Wearing formal clothes, research suggests, can boost your confidence and abstract thinking ability, as well as raise others' perception about how successful you are.[4]

Going Forward with Fork and Knife

If you're asked to lunch, be aware that observing applicants' dining etiquette has become an informal part of the selection process. (To sharpen their competitive advantage, Chinese executives are now trained in Western table manners and social graces before trips abroad.)[5] Keep your fingers clean (don't order greasy sandwiches, pasta, or sushi), so you can deal with any paperwork and shake hands when you leave. Break bread or rolls into bite-size pieces, butter them, and eat them one at a time. Scoop the spoon away from (not toward) you when consuming soup. Don't chew the ice cubes from your drink. Put your napkin on your chair (not the table) if you have to leave the table in mid-meal. Above all, chew with your mouth closed. And don't talk until you've swallowed your food.[6]

Avoiding Bad Tech Habits

Sixty percent of U.S. smartphone users in one survey said they couldn't go an hour without looking at their devices.[7] In research involving human resource managers, 76% of respondents said breaches of tech etiquette hurt work life.[8] The most annoying smartphone behaviors at work: having loud private conversations (65%), not silencing the phone (59%), checking the phone during conversation (52%), and checking the phone in a meeting (38%).[9] We hope you're not one of those who doesn't participate in meal conversations (or meetings) because you're texting or gaming or Facebooking. Or who sets the ringtone at full volume. Or who talks or texts in public restrooms.[10]

Watching What You Do on Social Media—Today

Having good manners starts even before you meet any company recruiters. If you tweet obscenities, show a lack of spelling skills on Facebook, post sexy photos or even selfies, or talk about alcohol and marijuana, you may already have blown a good job opportunity, since human resource departments regularly check applicants out on social media.[11]

For Discussion Which of the activities described above do you need to work on? How will you go about doing it?

FORECAST What's Ahead in This Chapter

This chapter considers human resource (HR) management—planning for, attracting, developing, and retaining an effective workforce. We consider how this subject fits in with the overall company strategy, how to evaluate current and future employee needs, and how to recruit and select qualified people. We describe orientation, training, and development and how to assess employee performance and give feedback. We discuss how to manage compensation and benefits, promotions and discipline, and workplace performance problems. We go over basic legal requirements. Finally, we consider the role of labor unions.

9.1   Strategic Human Resource Management

How do effective managers view the role of people in their organization's success?

THE BIG PICTURE

Human resource management consists of the activities managers perform to plan for, attract, develop, and retain an effective workforce. Planning the human resources needed consists of understanding current employee needs and predicting future employee needs.

How do you get hired by one of the companies on *Fortune* magazine's annual "100 Best Companies to Work For" list—companies such as Google, SAS Institute, Boston Consulting Group, Edward Jones, and Genentech, which are on the 2016 list?[12]

You try to get to know someone in the company, suggests one guide.[13] You play up volunteer work on your resume. You get ready to interview and interview and interview. And you do extensive research on the company—far more than just online research, as by talking to customers.

And what kinds of things does an employee of a *Fortune* "Best" company get? At Google (now part of Alphabet), the Mountain View, California, search engine company (ranked No. 1 Best Company seven times in the last 10 years), you're entitled to eat in 1 of 11 free gourmet cafeterias, take your dog to work, get haircuts on-site, work out at the gym, study Mandarin or other languages, have your laundry done free, and get virtual doctor visits. You may also be a candidate for millions of dollars in compensation incentives, special bonuses, and founders' awards.[14]

The reason for this exceptional treatment? "Happy people are more productive," says Eric Schmidt, former Google CEO, now executive chairman of Alphabet.[15] That productivity has made the company an earnings powerhouse; for 2015, for example, it reported a 14% growth in revenue and 38% growth in profits for its core Internet businesses.[16] Google has discovered, in other words, that its biggest competitive advantage lies in its human resources—its people.

Human Resource Management: Managing an Organization's Most Important Resource

Human resource (HR) management consists of the activities managers perform to plan for, attract, develop, and retain an effective workforce. Whether it's McKenzie looking for entry-level business consultants, the U.S. Navy trying to fill its ranks, or churches trying to recruit priests and ministers, all organizations must deal with staffing.

The fact that the old personnel department is now called the human resources department is not just a cosmetic change. It is intended to suggest the importance of staffing to a company's success. Although talking about people as "resources" might seem to downgrade them to the same level as financial resources and material resources, in fact, people are an organization's most important resource.

Indeed, companies ranked No.1 on *Fortune* magazine's Best Companies list in the past—which, besides Google, include SAS, NetApp, Genentech, Wegmans Food Markets, J. M. Smucker, Edward Jones, and The Container Store—have discovered that putting employees first has been the foundation for their success. "If you're not thinking all the time about making every person valuable, you don't have a chance," says former General Electric head Jack Welch. "What's the alternative? Wasted minds? Uninvolved people? A labor force that's angry or bored? That doesn't make sense!"[17]

Clearly, companies listed among the best places to work become famous by offering progressive and valued programs, policies, and procedures.[18] Are you curious to see if a current or past employer is one of these progressive companies? You can find out by taking Self-Assessment 9.1.

≣ connect SELF-ASSESSMENT 9.1

Assessing the Quality of HR Practices

This survey is designed to assess the quality of HR practices at your current place of employment. If you are not currently working, consider a previous job when completing the survey. Please be prepared to answer these questions if your instructor has assigned Self-Assessment 9.1 in Connect.

1. How did you rate the quality of the company's HR practices?

2. Based on your responses, what advice would you give the senior HR leader about how to improve its HR practices? Be specific. What are the consequences of having poor-quality HR practices? Explain.

FIGURE 9.1

The strategic human resource management process

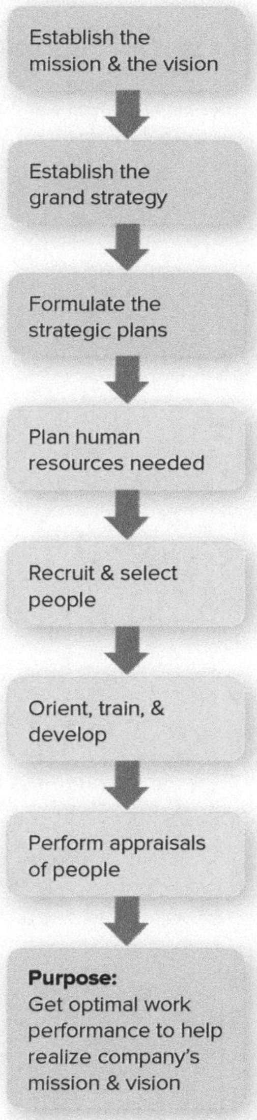

Human Resources as Part of Strategic Planning

Some companies—those with flat management structures, for instance—have done away with HR departments entirely, letting the regular line managers handle these tasks. But most workers say they feel the absence of an in-house HR staff, especially when it comes to resolving pay problems and mediating employee disputes.[19] So what should organizations do in regard to investing in human resources? Based on research findings, we come down on the side that people are an organization's most important asset and it's important to invest in human resources. All told, studies show that companies have higher levels of employee satisfaction, financial performance, and service performance when the company has high-quality human resource practices and programs.[20] At many companies, human resources has become part of the strategic planning process. Thus, HR departments deal not only with employee paperwork and legal accountability—a very important area, as we describe in Section 9.7—but also with helping to support the organization's overall strategy.

Example: Is it important, as Wegmans's owners think, to have loyal, innovative, smart, passionate employees who will give their best to promote customer satisfaction (the grocery chain's mission)? Who, then, should be recruited? How should they be trained? What's the best way to evaluate and reward their performance? The answers to these questions should be consistent with the firm's strategic mission.

The purpose of the strategic human resource process, then—shown in the gold shaded boxes at right—is to get the optimal work performance that will help the company's mission and goals.[21] *(See Figure 9.1.)*

Three concepts important in this view of human resource management are *human capital, knowledge workers,* and *social capital.*

Human Capital: Potential of Employee Knowledge and Actions

"We are living in a time," says one team of human resource management authors, "when a new economic paradigm—characterized by speed, innovation, short cycle times, quality, and customer satisfaction—is highlighting the importance of intangible assets, such as brand recognition, knowledge, innovation, and most particularly human capital."[22] **Human capital is the economic or productive potential of employee knowledge, experience, and actions.**[23]

Scripps Health, a nonprofit health care system in San Diego and 42nd on *Fortune*'s 2016 list of "Best Places to Work For," helps employees develop human capital by providing career coaching and up to $7,300 per year in tuition reimbursement and scholarships. The company also offers a wide variety of internal courses that focus on employee development.[24]

It's also important to take responsibility for your own human capital. You may find this surprising, but a recent study showed that lack of sleep depletes your human capital and lowers performance.[25] To perform at their best, people need their full ration of sleep.

Establish the mission & the vision

Establish the grand strategy

Formulate the strategic plans

Plan human resources needed

Recruit & select people

Orient, train, & develop

Perform appraisals of people

Purpose:
Get optimal work performance to help realize company's mission & vision

Knowledge Workers: Potential of Brain Workers   A knowledge worker is someone whose occupation is principally concerned with generating or interpreting information, as opposed to manual labor. Knowledge workers add value to the organization by using their brains rather than their muscle and sweat, and as such they are the most common type of worker in 21st-century organizations.[26] Over the past three decades, automation has threatened a lot of routine jobs, but the rise of knowledge workers has been accelerating.

Social Capital: Potential of Strong and Cooperative Relationships   Social capital is the economic or productive potential of strong, trusting, and cooperative relationships. It can help you land a job. For example, a national survey of recruiters revealed that 74% had found the highest-quality job applicants came through employee referrals. Employees hired through referrals also tend to stay longer at their jobs, a result of better person–organization fit.[27]

Social capital is also beneficial beyond the early stages of your career, particularly when you are developing trusting relationships with others. Trusting relationships lead to more job and business opportunities, faster advancement, greater capacity to innovate, and more status and authority.[28] All told, it pays to have a rich network of good relationships, and social capital helps makes this possible.

Planning the Human Resources Needed

When a building contractor, looking to hire someone for a few hours to dig ditches, drives by a group of idle day laborers standing on a street corner, is that a form of HR planning? Certainly it shows the contractor's awareness that a pool of laborers usually can be found in that spot. But what if the builder needs a lot of people with specialized training—to give him or her the competitive advantage that the strategic planning process demands?

Here we are concerned with something more than simply hiring people on an "as needed" basis. Strategic human resource planning consists of developing a systematic, comprehensive strategy for (a) understanding current employee needs and (b) predicting future employee needs. Let's consider these two parts.

Understanding Current Employee Needs   To plan for the future, you must understand the present—what today's staffing picture looks like. This requires that you (or a trained specialist) first do a *job analysis* and from that write a *job description* and a *job specification.*[29]

- **Job analysis.** The purpose of job analysis is to determine, by observation and analysis, the basic elements of a job. Specialists who do this interview job occupants about what they do, observe the flow of work, and learn how results are accomplished. For example, UPS has specialists who ride with the couriers and time how long it takes to deliver a load of packages and note what problems are encountered (traffic jams, vicious dogs, recipients not home, and so on).

- **Job description and job specification.** Once the fundamentals of a job are understood, then you can write a job description, which summarizes what the holder of the job does and how and why he or she does it. Next you can write a job specification, which describes the minimum qualifications a person must have to perform the job successfully.

This process can produce some surprises. Jobs that might seem to require a college degree, for example, might not after all. Thus, the process of writing job analyses, descriptions, and specifications can help you avoid hiring people who are overqualified (and presumably more expensive) or underqualified (and thus not as productive) for a particular job.

In addition, by entering a job description and specification with their attendant characteristics into a database, an organization can do computer searching for candidates by matching keywords (nouns) on their resumes with the keywords describing the job.

Enterprise Rent-A-Car, for example, sorts through 50,000 candidates a month to identify those with a bachelor's degree, good driving record, and customer-service or leadership experience who might qualify for the company's management training program.[30]

Predicting Future Employee Needs Job descriptions change, of course: Auto mechanics, for instance, now have to know how computer chips work in cars. (Current 7-Series BMWs and S-class Mercedes have about 100 processors apiece.) And new jobs are created: Who could have visualized the position of "e-commerce accountant" 10 years ago, for example?

As you might expect, predicting future employee needs means you have to become knowledgeable about the *staffing the organization might need* and the *likely sources for that staffing:*

- **The staffing the organization might need.** You could assume your organization won't change much. In that case, you can fairly easily predict that jobs will periodically become unoccupied (because of retirement, resignations, and so on) and that you'll need to pay the same salaries and meet the same criteria about minority hiring to fill them.

     Better, however, to assume the organization will change. Thus, you need to understand the organization's vision and strategic plan so that the proper people can be hired to meet the future strategies and work. We discussed strategic plans in Chapter 6.

- **The likely sources for staffing.** You can recruit employees from either inside or outside the organization. In looking at those inside, you need to consider which employees are motivated, trainable, and promotable and what kind of training your organization might have to do. A device for organizing this kind of information is a **human resource inventory,** a report listing your organization's employees by name, education, training, languages, and other important information. In looking outside, you need to consider the availability of talent in your industry's and geographical area's labor pool, the training of people graduating from various schools, and such factors as what kinds of people are moving into your area. The U.S. Bureau of Labor Statistics and the U.S. Census Bureau issue reports on such matters. ●

9.2 Recruitment and Selection: Putting the Right People into the Right Jobs

How can I reduce mistakes in hiring and find great people who might work for me?

THE BIG PICTURE

Qualified applicants for jobs may be recruited from inside or outside the organization. The task of choosing the best person is enhanced by such tools as reviewing candidates' application forms, resumes, and references; doing interviews, either structured or unstructured; and screening with ability, personality, performance, and other kinds of employment tests.

"We know that 5% of your workforce produces 26% of your output, so you need to focus on hiring people who really make the difference," says San Francisco State University professor John Sullivan, an expert in human resources strategy. Hiring has become a science, Sullivan states, but most people doing the recruiting think it is still an art. "Most people in HR have no clue. We don't measure failed hires. There's no feedback loop."[31]

However difficult it may be, then, it's important to try to get hiring right. "We're essentially in an innovation economy where good people come up with really good ideas," says one CEO. "Companies want to hit home runs with the next greatest product, and the imperative is making sure you have great people to do that."[32]

Recruitment: How to Attract Qualified Applicants

At some time nearly every organization has to think about how to find the right kind of people. **Recruiting is the process of locating and attracting qualified applicants for jobs open in the organization.** The word *qualified* is important: You want to find people whose skills, abilities, and characteristics are best suited to your organization. Recruiting is of two types: *internal* and *external*.

1. Internal Recruiting: Hiring from the Inside
Internal recruiting means making people already employed by the organization aware of job openings. Indeed, most vacant positions in organizations are filled through internal recruitment, mainly through **job posting, placing information about job vacancies and qualifications on bulletin boards, in newsletters, and on the organization's intranet.** Companies looking to make strategic changes do better hiring CEOs from within the ranks rather than from outside, according to a recent study.[33] In one twist on recruiting from within, more firms are now *rehiring* former workers who had left (a tactic once frowned upon), because so many employers are having difficulty finding qualified people.[34]

2. External Recruiting: Hiring from the Outside
External recruiting means attracting job applicants from outside the organization. In years past, notices of job vacancies were placed through newspapers, employment agencies, executive recruiting firms, union hiring halls, college job-placement offices, and word of mouth. Today more and more companies are also using social media to recruit.[35] For example, experts estimate that 89% of U.S. organizations use social networks to find new employees. Recent research suggests, therefore, that it's practically mandatory for job seekers to have a presence online.[36]

In one survey of 3,500 U.S. college students, 80% said they use smartphones for job hunting or see themselves doing so in the future.[37] LinkedIn, a social network with more than 1.23 billion active users, accounts for 94% of the people hired via social media, followed by Facebook and Twitter.[38] LinkedIn Students, a mobile app, helps graduating collegians find what companies might be a good fit and suggests occupations they might not have previously considered.[39] Mobile recruiting, incidentally, is reportedly poised to become a primary global recruiting strategy.[40]

Both internal and external methods have advantages and disadvantages.[41] *(See Table 9.1, below.)*

INTERNAL RECRUITING	
ADVANTAGES	**DISADVANTAGES**
1. Employees tend to be inspired to greater effort and loyalty. Morale is enhanced because they realize that working hard and staying put can result in more opportunities.	1. Internal recruitment restricts the competition for positions and limits the pool of fresh talent and fresh viewpoints.
2. The whole process of advertising, interviewing, and so on is cheaper.	2. It may encourage employees to assume that longevity and seniority will automatically result in promotion.
3. There are fewer risks. Internal candidates are already known and are familiar with the organization.	3. Whenever a job is filled, it creates a vacancy elsewhere in the organization.

EXTERNAL RECRUITING	
ADVANTAGES	**DISADVANTAGES**
1. Applicants may have specialized knowledge and experience.	1. The recruitment process is more expensive and takes longer.
2. Applicants may have fresh viewpoints.	2. The risks are higher because the persons hired are less well known.

Which External Recruiting Methods Work Best?   In general, the most effective sources are employee referrals, say human resource professionals, because, to protect their own reputations, employees are fairly careful about whom they recommend, and they know the qualifications of both the job and the prospective employee.[42] HR expert John Sullivan, mentioned above, states that this method is preferred by the better companies, which ask their own top-performing employees, "Who do you learn from? Who's better than you? Who mentors you?"[43]

Other effective ways of finding good job candidates are e-recruitment tools, such as "dot-jobs" websites; membership directories for associations and trade groups; social networking sites; and industry-specific blogs, forums, and newsgroups.[44]

Among some newer ideas: San Francisco–based BlueCrew is a tech-enabled employment agency focused on hiring for warehouse workers, forklift operators, and other blue-collar temporary employees.[45] Barclays, the international bank, uses a free mobile videogame called Stockfuse, a stock-trading game, to attract and evaluate job applicants.[46] A cloud-storage firm named Compose and an employment firm named Woo, both in northern California, arrange "blind dates" between job seekers and employers, using resumes that feature only a person's work, no names.[47] Devereux Cleo Wallace, a Colorado health care organization, also avoids relying on people's credentials, pursuing instead "competency-based selection" strategies that measure whether job applicants have the competencies—such as the soft skills of empathy and listening ability—to fill specific roles in psychiatric facilities.[48] Netflix specializes in recruiting for trustworthiness, making a point of "hiring, rewarding, and tolerating only fully formed adults"—people who will put the company's interests first.[49]

How do you feel about the job you are in now, if you have one, or the last job you had? Do you feel like you are a "good fit" for the job? That is, do you like the work and does the work match your skills? Research shows that we are happier and more productive when our needs and skills fit the job requirements. If you would like to see whether or not you fit with your current (or last) job, complete Self-Assessment 9.2. You may find the results very interesting.

connect SELF-ASSESSMENT 9.2

Assessing Your Person–Job Fit

This survey is designed to assess your job fit. If you are not currently working, consider a previous job when completing the survey. Please be prepared to answer these questions if your instructor has assigned Self-Assessment 9.2 in Connect.

1. What is your level of fit?
2. Whether you have high or low fit, what are the main causes for your level of fit? Explain.
3. What questions might you ask a future recruiter to ensure a higher level of person–job fit? Be specific.

Realistic Job Previews **A realistic job preview (RJP)** gives a candidate a picture of both positive and negative features of the job and the organization before he or she is hired. This recruiting technique is very effective at reducing turnover within 30–90 days of employment.[50] For instance, hiring managers at the Hilton Baltimore demonstrate to housekeeping job applicants how to make a bed, then ask the applicants to do it themselves. With this realistic job preview, says Tishuana Hodge, regional director of HR, says, "We can see who is genuinely interested and physically up to the challenge."[51]

EXAMPLE   The Changing Job Market: Millennials, the Gig Economy, and the Episodic Career

Young adults (Millennials and Gen Z—those born between 1981 and the mid-2000s) are said to be less focused on finding jobs that nourish the wallet than those that nourish the soul, less concerned with finding financial success than on making a difference, as we said at the start of Chapter 3. But will the economy and the job market cooperate?

"A lot of people are despairing about the future of America in different ways or about their ability to earn a good steady living," says New York University professor and journalist Farai Chideya. "It's a time of mixed opportunity."[52]

The Gig Economy. Most of the job growth among American workers during the past decade has been not in traditional jobs but rather among those who work as independent contractors, through temporary services or on-call, which rose 15.8% from 2005 to 2015, according to one study.[53] In this so-called *gig economy*, organizations contract with independent workers—usually through their smartphones—for short-term engagements, and the burden of providing workers' compensation, health insurance, and the like falls on the workers themselves rather than on the employer.[54]

More than 5% of adults younger than 35 earned some income from an online platform between October 2014 and September 2015, according to some research.[55] Regardless of age, low-earning gig workers tend to provide direct labor, such as being on-demand drivers for Uber or furniture movers for TaskRabbit. Top-income gig earners make money mostly from their assets, as by renting their vacation homes through VRBO or selling craft merchandise through Etsy.

Although the gig economy employs only 0.5% of the workforce at present, Intuit predicts that by 2020 contingent workers will exceed 40% of American workers, and traditional full-time, full-benefit jobs will be harder to find.[56]

The Episodic Career. Chideya, mentioned above, is the author of *The Episodic Career: How to Thrive at Work in the Age of Disruption*.[57] Because of decades of wage stagnation, the effects of the Great Recession, and "an incredible sense that perhaps the future will not be better than the past," she says, we have entered into the era of "the episodic career."[58] Surviving this challenge will require three qualities, she suggests:

- *Emotional resilience:* "The reality is that we're living in a time where there's more and more disruption in the workplace and you absolutely have to roll with the punches," she says.

- *Understanding the job market:* If the industry you're contemplating entering or are in is starting to go downhill, you should know it. You may have to "reboot" several times.

- *Self-knowledge:* You need to make a list of all the skills you have, including those you don't use for work. "You're not just the job you have now or the job you had five years ago," says Chideya, "you're a compilation of skills and assets, which can be used in many contexts."

YOUR CALL

What kind of good skills inventory could you bring to the job market? What networks are you keeping alive, including "the weaker ties and links in your network, . . . people on the fringes of your circle who live in completely different worlds," who can be the most important in a job search?

Selection: How to Choose the Best Person for the Job

Whether the recruitment process turns up a handful of job applicants or thousands, now you turn to the **selection process, the screening of job applicants to hire the best candidate.** Essentially, this becomes an exercise in *prediction:* How well will the candidate perform the job and how long will he or she stay?

Three types of selection tools are *background information, interviewing,* and *employment tests.*

1. Background Information: Application Forms, Resumes, and Reference Checks

Application forms and resumes provide basic background information about job applicants, such as citizenship, education, work history, and certifications.

Unfortunately, a lot of resume information consists of mild puffery and even outrageous fairy tales—as many as 35% of resumes, by one estimate.[59] It is risky to lie about your background information because it can be used later as a reason for terminating your employment. Nevertheless, lots of people try it. A 2015 survey of 2,500 hiring professionals reported that the most common lies found on resumes are about skill sets (62%), responsibilities (54%), employment dates (39%), job titles (31%), and academic degrees (28%).[60] No wonder the business of background checks is booming.[61]

PRACTICAL ACTION

Would You Lie Like This on Your Resume?

What kind of lies do people put on their resumes? Consider the following examples.

Lying about Education. Lying about education may be the most prevalent distortion (such as pretending to hold a degree or an advanced degree).[62] A few years ago, RadioShack CEO David Edmondson achieved some notoriety and had to resign after a newspaper discovered he had falsely claimed on his resume to hold degrees in psychology and theology.[63] In 2012, Yahoo CEO Scott Thompson was revealed to not have earned a college degree in computer science, as claimed on his resume and on the company's website.[64] Automatic Data Processing of Roseland, New Jersey, which has studied employee background verification, reported that 41% of education records showed a difference between the information provided by an applicant and that provided by the educational institution.[65]

Lying about Employment Histories, Ages, Salaries, and Job Titles. Another common fabrication includes creative attempts to cover gaps in employment history (although there are straightforward ways an applicant can deal with this, such as highlighting length of service instead of employment dates).[66] Some people try to cover up taking years off from work to do child care, but it is better to explain than to hide these dates.[67] People also lie about

their ages for fear of seeming to be too experienced (hence expensive) or too old.[68] As you might expect, people also embellish their salary histories, job titles, and achievements on projects.

Lying about Criminal Background or Immigration Status. In 2007, it came out that the foundation that runs online encyclopedia Wikipedia had neglected to do a basic background check before hiring Carolyn Doran as its chief operating officer; she had been convicted of drunken driving and fleeing the scene of a car accident.[69] Now, more and more job seekers are seeking to legally clear their criminal records—to have their arrests or convictions expunged, when possible.[70] Public efforts are also being made to remove hiring hurdles faced by felons trying to restart their lives, such as the National Reentry Resource Center.[71]

In addition, as the number of illegal (undocumented) workers has risen, it has become incumbent on human resource officers to verify U.S. citizenship.[72] Use of E-Verify, the federal program that allows employers to quickly check the legal status of potential employees, has taken a big jump.[73] Still, perhaps half of illegal workers slip by the system.[74]

YOUR CALL

What past events are you most worried potential employers will find out about you? What can you do to put them in a better light?

Many companies are finding conventional resumes not all that useful (because they don't quantify an applicant's accomplishments or are too full of fluff descriptors such as "outstanding" or "energetic") and are increasingly relying on social networks such as LinkedIn, video profiles, or online quizzes to assess candidates.[75] The federal government, for instance, now scans security-clearance applicants' posts on social media.[76] Other firms are so inundated with resumes that they now have to use resume-filtering software, causing applicants to learn to game the system by loading their resumes with keywords from the job description.[77] Some applicants try "stunt resumes," such as those delivered by a stuffed carrier pigeon.[78] College students often assemble e-portfolios, giant Web-based dossiers that showcase writing samples, class presentations, and other evidence of skills attractive to employers; unfortunately, says *The Wall Street Journal*, "few employers are actually looking at them."[79]

References are also a problem. Many employers don't give honest assessments of former employees, for two reasons: (1) They fear that if they say anything negative, they can be sued by the former employee. (2) They fear if they say anything positive, and the job candidate doesn't pan out, they can be sued by the new employer.[80] Despite liability worries, HR recruiters know that if they get a former supervisor on the phone, they can find out a lot—such as the way he or she answers the question "Can you enthusiastically recommend this person?" or "What were this person's strengths and weaknesses?"[81]

Many employers also like to check applicants' credit references, although there is no evidence that people with weak credit scores are apt to be unqualified or dishonest employees.[82] (Note: Prospective employers need to get written consent to run credit checks on job applicants.)[83]

PRACTICAL ACTION   Applying for a Job? Here Are Some Mistakes to Avoid

There are several mistakes that job candidates often make in initial interviews. Here are some tips.[84]

Be Prepared—Very Prepared. Can you pronounce the name of the company with whom you're interviewing? Of the person or people interviewing you? Do you understand the company and the position you're interviewing for? Do you know the company's competition? What new products or services are being offered? How about your reasons for leaving your present employer (or why you're now unemployed)? What are your greatest strengths? Your weaknesses? What do you need to improve on to move ahead? Where do you want to be in five years, careerwise?

Go online and read the company's website. Search for any news articles written about the firm. Call the company and ask about pronunciation. Determine how your strengths fit directly into the context of what the prospective employer does. Also, when asked about your weaknesses, state how you recognized a weakness, overcame a dilemma, and were improved by it. Take time to practice questions and answers, so you'll sound confident.[85]

Dress Right and Pay Attention to Your Attitude. Is the company dress code "business casual"? That doesn't mean you should dress that way (or the way you dress on campus) for the interview.

Dress professionally for the interview. Be aware of your attitude as soon as you enter the building. Be on time. (Time your commute by doing a test run a day or so before the interview, and make sure you know the exact location of the interview.) If unforeseeable circumstances arise and cause you to be late, call to inform your interviewer. Be polite to the receptionist, and greet everyone who greets you. Turn off your cell-phone ringer.

Don't Get Too Personal with the Interviewer. Don't be over-friendly and share too much, especially in the initial interview. Although the interviewer will try to make you feel comfortable, you should focus on the position. Rehearse questions to ask

the interviewer, such as the challenges for the position in the future. Don't make negative comments about your old company or boss. Rather, figure out the positives and convey what you learned and gained from your experience. If asked an inappropriate question (about age, marital status, whether you have children or plan to), politely state you don't believe the question is relevant to your qualifications. Be enthusiastic; enthusiasm is contagious. Incidentally, be sure to mention any organizational citizenship behavior, which scores well with interviewers.[86] After the interview, within 24 hours, send an e-mail (with no misspellings or faulty grammar) thanking the interviewer. If you think you messed up part of the interview, use the e-mail to smooth over your mistakes.[87]

Be Aware That Your Background and Social Networks Will Be Checked. Because it seems to be getting harder to distinguish honest job applicants from dishonest ones, companies now routinely check resumes or hire companies that do so.[88] Most employers conduct background checks—in fact, two-thirds conduct criminal background checks, according to one study.[89] Some may also ask for your SAT scores.[90] Some have been known to scrutinize checking accounts.[91]

As mentioned earlier, if you are a Facebook, YouTube, or Twitter user, be aware that employers now frequently use search engines to do continuous and stealthy background checks on prospective employees to see if they've posted any racy content. "Many job hunters," says one report, "are . . . continuing to overlook the dangers of posting provocative photos and other dubious content on social-media sites."[92] Checking your Facebook page is also a way employers can make an end run around discrimination laws.[93] Indeed, you may be asked in the interview for your Facebook user name and password so the interviewer can access your private settings—a practice whose legality is questionable but nevertheless being done by more companies.[94]

(More and more people are getting savvy about privacy and pruning their friend lists and removing unwanted comments on their social networks.)[95] Some companies are slashing the time it takes to get new workers, as by skipping reference checks (which can lead to costly mistakes).[96] Most of the time, however, the process of getting hired seems to be taking longer than ever—the average is about 23 days, though it can be as long as 6–12 months—but while you're waiting for the company's decision you should avoid the temptation of telephoning and demanding to know your status.[97]

YOUR CALL

What kind of advice do you see here that you wish you'd followed in the past?

2. Interviewing: Unstructured, Situational, and Behavioral-Description

The interview, which is the most commonly used employee-selection technique, may take place face to face, by videoconference, or—as is increasingly the case—via the Internet. (In-depth phone interviews of an hour or more are also frequently used.[98] However, face-to-face interviews have been perceived as being more fair and leading to higher job acceptance intentions than videoconferencing and telephone interviews.)[99] To help eliminate bias, interviews can be designed, conducted, and evaluated by a committee of three or more people.

The most commonly used employee-selection technique, interviewing, takes three forms: *unstructured interviews* and *two types of structured interviews*.[100]

Unstructured Interview

Like an ordinary conversation, an **unstructured interview involves asking probing questions to find out what the applicant is like.** There is no fixed set of questions asked of all applicants and no systematic scoring procedure. As a result, the unstructured interview has been criticized as being overly subjective and apt to be influenced by the biases of the interviewer. Equally important, it is susceptible to legal attack because some questions may infringe on non-job-related matters such as privacy, diversity, or disability.[101] However, compared with the structured interview method, the unstructured interview has been found to provide a more accurate assessment of an applicant's job-related personality traits.[102]

Structured Interview Type 1: The Situational Interview

The **structured interview involves asking each applicant the same questions and comparing their responses to a standardized set of answers.**

In one type of structured interview, the **situational interview,** the interviewer focuses on hypothetical situations. Example: "What would you do if you saw two of your people arguing loudly in the work area?" The idea here is to find out if the applicant can handle difficult situations that may arise on the job.

Structured Interview Type 2: The Behavioral-Description Interview

In the second type of structured interview, the **behavioral-description interview,** the interviewer explores what applicants have actually done in the past. Example: "What was the best idea you ever sold to a supervisor, teacher, peer, or subordinate?" This question (the U.S. Army asked it of college students applying for its officer training program) is designed to assess the applicants' ability to influence others.

The Right Way to Handle an Interview: What the Employer Is looking For

PRACTICAL ACTION

Because hiring people who later have to be let go is such an expensive proposition, companies are now putting a great deal of emphasis on effective interviewing. The previous Practical Action box provided a few tips for job applicants, but here let us explain how the interview process is being conducted from the interviewer's point of view.[103]

Before the Interview: employers define their needs and review applicants' resumes. It's been said that looking to hire somebody is like going to the supermarket; the employer needs to have a list and know what he or she needs. Thus, the HR department will write out (or be told) what skills, traits, and qualities the job requires that the company is trying to fill. The interviewer will also look at the applicant's resume or application form to determine relevant experience, gaps, and discrepancies.

The interviewer prepares the questions to be asked. The interviewer should use a structured approach that asks all candidates the same set of questions, so that their answers can be compared. (This helps keep the company out of legal trouble, too, as in being accused of racial or gender bias.) In general, the questions should be designed to elicit the following types of information.

- **What drawbacks does the applicant's previous work experience show?** Examples: "Why are you leaving your current job, or why are you currently unemployed?"

- **Does the applicant have the knowledge to do the job?** Examples: "Give an example where you came up with a creative solution." "How would you distinguish our product from competitors'?"

- **Can the applicant handle difficult situations?** Examples: "What is your greatest weakness?" "Tell me about a time when you dealt with an irate customer. How did you handle the situation and what was the outcome?"

- **Is the applicant willing to cope with the job's demands?** Examples: "How do you feel about making unpopular decisions?" "Are you willing to travel 30% of the time?"

- **Will the applicant fit in with the organization's culture?** Examples: "Where do you see yourself in five years?" "How would your last supervisor describe you?" "How much leeway did they give you in your previous job in charging travel expenses?"

Interviewers Often Follow a Three-Scene Interview Scenario. The interview itself may follow a three-scene script.

- **Scene 1: The first three minutes—small talk and "compatibility" test.** The first scene is really a "compatibility test." It takes about three minutes and consists of exchanging small talk, giving the interviewer a chance to establish rapport and judge how well the candidate makes a first impression. Note: As many as four out of five hiring decisions are made within the first 10 minutes of an interview, according to some research. Thus, be aware that if you, the job applicant, have immediately impressed the interviewer, he or she may spend more time talking than listening—perhaps even trying to sell you on the job rather than screen your qualifications.[104]

- **Scene 2: The next 15–60 minutes—asking questions and listening to the applicant's "story."** In the next scene, the interviewer will ask you the questions he or she previously wrote out (and answer those that you have). A good interviewer will allow you, the interviewee, to do 70%–80% of the talking, and he or she will take notes to remember important points. Be aware that the interviewer's intuition can play a strong role in the hiring decision.

- **Scene 3: The final two minutes—closing the interview and setting up the next steps.** In the final minutes, the interviewer will listen to determine whether the candidate expresses interest in taking the job.

After the Interview. After you have left, the interviewer will probably write a short report making some sort of quantitative score of your qualifications and indicating reasons for the decision. If he or she decides to invite you back for a second interview (or pass you along to another interviewer), your references will also be checked.

YOUR CALL

What additional questions would you like to be asked that would showcase you as the best candidate? How would you work what you want to say into the interview?

3. Employment Tests: Ability, Personality, Performance, Integrity, and Others   Employment selection tests used to consist of paper-and-pencil, performance, and physical-ability tests. Now, however, **employment tests are legally considered to consist of any procedure used in the employment selection decision process, even application forms, interviews, and educational requirements.**[105] Indeed, today applicants should expect just about anything, such as spending hours on simulated work tasks, performing role-playing exercises, or tackling a business case study.[106]

Probably the most common employment tests are the following.

Ability Tests   *Ability tests* measure physical abilities, strength and stamina, mechanical ability, mental abilities, and clerical abilities. Telephone operators, for instance, need to be tested for hearing, and assembly-line workers for manual dexterity. Intelligence tests are also catching on as ways to predict future executive performance.[107] The military tests for physical qualifications, along with behavioral and educational abilities (71% of 17- to 24-year-olds don't qualify for military service, a surprisingly high figure).[108] Corporate-event company Windy City Fieldhouse uses a test that measures attention to detail, asking takers to do such things as "do a count of the letter 'l' in a three-sentence paragraph to measure how carefully a respondent works," according to one account.[109]

Performance Tests *Performance tests,* or *skills tests,* measure performance on actual job tasks—so-called job tryouts—as when computer programmers take a test on a particular programming language such as C++ or middle managers work on a small project.[110] Some companies have an **assessment center, in which management candidates participate in activities for a few days while being assessed by evaluators.**[111]

Personality Tests *Personality tests* measure such personality traits as adjustment, energy, sociability, independence, and need for achievement. Career-assessment tests that help workers identify suitable jobs tend to be of this type.[112] One of the most famous personality tests, in existence for 65-plus years, is the 93-question Myers–Briggs Type Indicator, with about 2.5 million tests given each year throughout the world. Myers–Briggs endures, observers say, "because it does a good job of pointing up differences between people, offers individuals a revealing glimpse of themselves, and is a valuable asset in team-building, improving communication, and resolving personality-conflict."[113] However, this and other personality tests need to be interpreted with caution because of the difficulty of measuring personality characteristics and of making a legal defense if the results are challenged.[114]

EXAMPLE

Personality Tests: How a Sporting-Goods Chain Screens Job Applicants Online

More than 80% of midsize and large companies use personality and ability assessments for entry- and mid-level jobs, according to one executive at a global human resources consulting firm.[115]

Southwest Airlines, for instance, has found the Myers–Briggs test helps build trust in developing teams.[116] Hewlett-Packard uses a personality test to see if employees are temperamentally suited to working alone at home—that is, telecommuting—and can handle limited supervision.[117] At Children's Healthcare of Atlanta, personality tests are used to find employees who will be "nice people"—those with "the qualities of being nurturing, kind, and warm-hearted," in the words of a human resources vice president.[118]

Online Personality Tests. At Finish Line, a nationwide chain of sporting-goods stores, store managers use the results of web-based personality tests developed by Unicru, of Beaverton, Oregon, to screen applicants for jobs as retail sales clerks. Candidates may apply through Unicru's kiosks or computer phones, which are installed in the stores. One Finish Line store in Chicago screens as many as 70 applicants a week during the store's preholiday season.

Unicru's computer scores test takers according to how strongly they agree or disagree (on a four-point scale) with statements such as "You do not fake being polite" and "You love to listen to people talk about themselves." High scores on attributes such as sociability and initiative reward applicants with a "green" rating that allows them to move on to an interview with a human manager. Scores in the middle earn a "yellow," and a lesser chance of landing a job; low-scoring "reds" are not considered.

Measurable Results. "The kinds of people who do well," says Unicru psychologist David Scarborough, "obviously have to have good self-control. They have to be patient. They have to enjoy helping people. All those characteristics are quite measurable."[119] Finish Line says that Unicru's system has reduced turnover by 24%.

YOUR CALL

There are, by some estimates, around 2,500 cognitive and personality employment tests on the market, and it's important that employers match the right test for the right purpose.[120] Moreover, tests aren't supposed to have a disparate impact on a protected class of people, such as certain racial or ethnic groups.[121] What questions would you want to ask about a personality test before you submitted yourself to it? (Note: Don't try to psych the test. You might wind up being miserable in a job that doesn't suit you.)

Integrity Tests   *Integrity tests* assess attitudes and experiences related to a person's honesty, dependability, trustworthiness, reliability, and prosocial behavior.[122] The tests are designed to identify people likely to engage in inappropriate, antisocial, or dishonest workplace behavior. Typically, integrity tests ask direct questions about past experiences related to ethics and integrity. You might be asked, for example, "What is the most you have ever stolen? (a) $0; (b) $1–$200; (c) $201–$500; (d) more than $500." Or interviewers may ask questions about preferences and interests from which inferences may be drawn about future behavior—so-called covert tests, where the answers give a sense of the person's conscientiousness, emotional maturity, and so on.[123]

Other Tests   The list of employment testing techniques has grown to include—in appropriate cases—drug testing, polygraph (lie detectors), genetic screening, and even (a questionable technique) handwriting analysis.[124] Human resource professionals need to be aware, incidentally, that there are a variety of products available on the Internet to help employees beat many kinds of drug tests.[125] Recently, however, the hair test (of hair follicles) has begun to find favor, since it's said to be able to detect a pattern of repetitive drug use over a period of up to 90 days.[126] Even so, failure to pass illicit drug tests has been edging up (from 4.3% in 2013 to 4.7% in 2014), according to one compiler of employer-testing data.[127]

Reliability and Validity: Are the Tests Worth It?   With any kind of test, an important legal consideration is the test's **reliability—the degree to which a test measures the same thing consistently**—so that an individual's score remains about the same over time, assuming the characteristics being measured also remain the same.

Another legal consideration is the test's **validity—the test measures what it purports to measure and is free of bias.** If a test is supposed to predict performance, then the individual's actual performance should reflect his or her score on the test. Using an invalid test to hire people can lead to poor selection decisions. It can also create legal problems if the test is ever challenged in a court of law.

Geeks, Robots, and People Analytics: How Hiring Is Being Changed   "Recruitment decision making is rife with behavioral biases," says Kate Glazebrook, a principal advisor to the London-based company Behavioral Insights Team, "but most organizations haven't embedded any of that knowledge of best practice into what they do."[128]

That is now changing with the rise of "talent analytics" or "people analytics," as engineers, statisticians, and computer scientists ("geeks," in a word) begin applying analytics and robotics to HR.[129] For instance, some companies use automated recruiters to canvass the Web for ideal employees, based on an algorithm (computerized step-by-step operations) that applies the same job-fit criteria to applicants that managers use to rate their best employees.[130] As mentioned earlier, other companies have robots scanning resumes, looking for the right keywords—and with great success. For instance, a study of 300,000 hires for low-skill service-sector jobs (data entry, phone answering) found that workers picked by an algorithm tended to stay in the job 8% longer and were more productive than those picked by a hiring manager.[131] We suspect that the use of talent analytics and Big Data will continue to grow throughout many aspects of HR management. ●

No drugs. Many jobs, such as those in warehousing and trucking, require that job applicants take a drug test to see if they test positive for marijuana, heroin, and other opioid drugs. However, many potential applicants simply skip tests they think they cannot pass. Would this be a concern for you? © Cultura/Getty Images RF

9.3   Managing an Effective Workforce: Compensation and Benefits

MAJOR QUESTION

What are the various forms of compensation?

THE BIG PICTURE

Managers must manage for compensation—which includes wages or salaries, incentives, and benefits.

Do we work only for a paycheck? Many people do, of course. But money is only one form of compensation.

Compensation has three parts: (1) wages or salaries, (2) incentives, and (3) benefits. In different organizations one part may take on more importance than another. For instance, in some nonprofit organizations (education, government), salaries may not be large, but health and retirement benefits may outweigh that fact. In a high-technology start-up, the salary and benefits may actually be somewhat humble, but the promise of a large payoff in incentives, such as stock options or bonuses, may be quite attractive. Let's consider these three parts briefly. (We expand on them in Chapter 12, when we discuss ways to motivate employees.)

Wages or Salaries

Base pay consists of the basic wage or salary paid employees in exchange for doing their jobs. The basic compensation is determined by all kinds of economic factors: the prevailing pay levels in a particular industry and location, what competitors are paying, whether the jobs are unionized, if the jobs are hazardous, what the individual's level is in the organization, and how much experience he or she has.

Incentives

To attract high-performing employees and to induce those already employed to be more productive, many organizations offer incentives, such as commissions, bonuses, profit-sharing plans, and stock options. We discuss these in detail in Chapter 12.

Stock options. Companies like to offer favored employees stock options rather than higher salaries as benefits. Not only do employees place a high value on options, but companies can issue as many as they want without hurting corporate profits because, under present accounting rules, they don't have to count the options' value as an expense. However, some critics believe that making stock options a big part of CEO compensation does not spur better performance. When the stock is up, the CEO benefits. When the stock is down, he or she doesn't really lose money but rather just makes less money. © Comstock Images RF

Why Rewards May Fail to Motivate

Incentive compensation plans, ranging from cash awards and gifts to profit sharing and stock ownership, are intended to recruit top performers and to spur their best efforts once they are hired. Despite the huge investments of time and money, such incentives do not achieve their desired results. Here are eight possible reasons:[132]

- **"I don't work just for the money."** Sometimes there is too much emphasis on monetary rewards.

- **"They don't care what I do."** There may be the absence of an "appreciation effect."

- **"It's no more than what I deserve."** The benefits may be extensive, but employees feel they are entitled to them just as part of the job.

- **"Let's see how little work we can get away with."** The rewards may have the unintended consequence of producing nonproductive, even counterproductive, work behavior. (Example: Albuquerque, New Mexico, city officials decided to pay trash truck crews for eight hours regardless of time spent, so as to encourage quick completion of the work and lower overtime costs. However, the policy only led crews to work fast and cut corners, missing pickups, speeding and causing accidents, and generating extra dump fees for overloading vehicles.)[133]

- **"Why bother? It takes forever to get paid."** There is too long a delay between performance and rewards.

- **"Another $25 gift card? Who needs it?"** There are too many one-size-fits-all rewards.

- **"A half day off on Friday—so what."** Managers use one-shot rewards with a short-lived motivational impact.

- **"There they go again. . . ."** Management continues to use demotivating practices such as layoffs, across-the-board pay cuts, and excessive compensation for executives but not workers.[134]

Five keys to a successful incentive-pay plan are the following:[135]

1. **Simplicity.** Does the plan pass the simplicity test? Can you explain it on an elevator ride?

2. **Clear goals.** Are the goals clear? Are the goals fully supported by management?

3. **Realistic goals.** Are the goals realistic—that is, neither too difficult nor too easy to achieve?

4. **Consistency with present goals.** Is the plan in line with the organization's present goals? Company goals change. Few organizations have the same business objective for more than five to seven years.

5. **Regular communication.** Do managers regularly communicate with employees about the plan? People want a scorecard.

Benefits

Benefits, or *fringe benefits*, **are additional nonmonetary forms of compensation** designed to enrich the lives of all employees in the organization, which are paid all or in part by the organization. We discuss benefits in more detail in Chapter 12, but examples are many: health insurance, dental insurance, life insurance, disability protection, retirement plans, holidays off, accumulated sick days and vacation days, recreation options, country club or health club memberships, family leave, discounts on company merchandise, counseling, credit unions, legal advice, and education reimbursement. For top executives, there may be "golden parachutes," generous severance pay for those who might be let go in the event the company is taken over by another company.

Benefits are no small part of an organization's costs. In December 2015, private industry spent an average of $31.70 per hour worked in employment compensation, of which wages and salaries accounted for 68.7% and benefits for the remaining 31.3%.[136] ●

Communication is everything. Human resource managers need to keep these questions in mind: What good does it do a company to have attractive incentive plans if employees don't understand them? Will an employee exert the extra effort in pursuit of rewards if he or she doesn't know what the rewards are? © ColorBlind Images/Blend Images RF

9.4   Orientation, Training, and Development

MAJOR QUESTION

Once people are hired, what's the best way to see that they do what they're supposed to do?

THE BIG PICTURE

Three ways newcomers are helped to perform their jobs are through *orientation,* to fit them into the job and organization; *training,* to upgrade the skills of technical and operational employees; and *development,* to upgrade the skills of professionals and managers.

On your first day of work at a new job, you will probably have to fill out a bunch of forms. (Don't forget to take your documentation—driver's license, Social Security card, perhaps passport—so you'll get the paperwork right and be paid on time.) After that, the process of orientation begins.

Today when a hire is made, companies often perform what is known as **onboarding, programs that help employees to integrate and transition to new jobs by making them familiar with corporate policies, procedures, cultures, and politics by clarifying work-role expectations and responsibilities.**[137] Thus, a company may roll out a welcome by assigning "buddies," providing detailed orientations, even sending goody baskets, to bring rookies up to speed quickly and give them a fast introduction to company culture.[138]

This is because, as we said, the emphasis is on "human capital." Only a third to half of most companies' stock-market value is accounted for by hard assets such as property, plant, and equipment, according to a Brookings Institution report. Most of a firm's value is in such attributes as patents, processes, and—important to this discussion—employee or customer satisfaction.[139] The means for helping employees perform their jobs are *orientation, training,* and *development.*

> **Group training.** In large companies, orientation and ongoing training are often conducted in group sessions led by a presenter while the employees follow along. Do you see any problems with this approach? © Rawpixel.com/ Shutterstock RF

Orientation: Helping Newcomers Learn the Ropes

The finalist candidate is offered the job, has accepted it, and has started work. Now he or she must begin, in that old sailor's phrase, to "learn the ropes." This is the start of **orientation, helping the newcomer fit smoothly into the job and the organization.**

Helping New Employees Get Comfortable: The First Six Months

"How well will I get along with other employees?" "What if I screw up on a project?" Going into a new job can produce a lot of uncertainty and anxiety. In part this is because, depending on the job, it may take 2–24 months for an average employee to be fully productive.[140]

The first six months on a job can be critical to how one performs over the long haul, because that's when the psychological patterns are established. Thus, employers have discovered that it's far better to give newcomers a helping hand than to let them learn possibly inappropriate behavior that will be hard to undo later.[141]

The Desirable Characteristics of Orientation

Like orientation week for new college students, the initial socialization period is designed to give new employees the information they need to be effective. In a large organization, orientation may be a formal, established process. In a small organization, it may be so informal that employees find themselves having to make most of the effort themselves.

Following orientation, the employee should emerge with information about three matters (much of which he or she may have acquired during the job-application process):

- **The job routine.** At minimum, the new employee needs to have learned what is required in the job for which he or she was hired, how the work will be evaluated, and who the immediate coworkers and managers are. This is basic.

- **The organization's mission and operations.** Certainly all managers need to know what the organization is about—its purpose, products or services, operations, and history. And it's now understood that low-level employees perform better if they, too, have this knowledge.

- **The organization's work rules and employee benefits.** A public utility's HR department may have a brochure explaining formalized work rules, overtime requirements, grievance procedures, and elaborate employee benefits. A technology start-up may be so fluid that many of these matters will not have been established yet. Even so, there are matters of law (such as those pertaining to sexual harassment) affecting work operations that every employee should be made aware of.

Training and Development: Helping People Perform Better

Companies with high-impact learning programs delivered profit growth *three times greater* than competing firms during a recent four-year period, according to one business learning analyst. "Why is this?" he asks. "Simply put—if you can keep your employees current and skilled, you can evolve and perform better than your competitors."[142] In addition, because 70% of employees say they are dissatisfied with career growth opportunities at their companies, training programs can keep people engaged with their work—and not looking for jobs elsewhere.[143] Unfortunately, this message hasn't caught up with a lot of employers: A 2015 manpower shortage survey found only 20% of businesses offer training to their employees.[144]

Of course, in hiring, an employer always tries to get people whose qualifications match the requirements of the job. Quite often, however, there are gaps in what new employees need to know. These gaps are filled by training. The training process involves five steps, as shown below. *(See Figure 9.2.)*

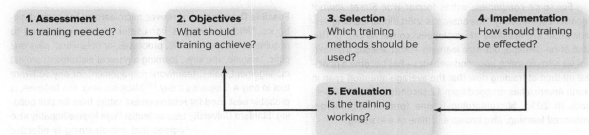

FIGURE 9.2   Five steps in the training process

HR professionals distinguish between *training* and *development*.

- **Training—upgrading skills of technical and operational employees.** Electronics technicians, data processors, computer network administrators, and X-ray technicians, among many others, need to be schooled in new knowledge as the requirements of their fields change. **Training, then, refers to educating technical and operational employees in how to better do their current jobs.**

- **Development—upgrading skills of professionals and managers.** Accountants, nurses, lawyers, and managers of all levels need to be continually educated in how to do their jobs better not just today but also tomorrow. **Development is educating professionals and managers in the skills they need to do their jobs in the future.**

Typical areas for which employee training and development are given are customer service, safety, leadership, computer skills, quality initiatives, communications, human relations, ethics, diversity, and sexual harassment.

The Different Types of Training or Development   There are all kinds of training and development methods, and their effectiveness depends on whether facts or skills are being taught. If people are to learn *facts*—such as work rules or legal matters—lectures, videotapes, and workbooks are effective. If people are to learn *skills*—such as improving interpersonal relations or the use of new tools—then techniques such as discussion, role-playing, and practice work better.

Another way to categorize training methods is to distinguish on-the-job from off-the-job methods.

- **On-the-job training.** This training takes place in the work setting while employees are performing job-related tasks. Four major training methods are coaching, training positions, job rotation, and planned work activities.

- **Off-the-job training.** This training consists of classroom programs, workbooks, videos, and games and simulations. Today, of course, lots of off-the-job training consists of technology-enhanced learning—online learning, or e-learning (for electronic learning).[145] A relatively new approach is **microlearning,** or *bite-size learning*, which segments learning into bite-size content, enabling a student to master one piece of learning before advancing to anything else. Most microlearning mixes video and interactive lessons that take under five minutes to complete and include a quiz.[146]

EXAMPLE   Technology-Enhanced Learning: Getting Ahead through Microlearning

How do you train workers who are constantly distracted by smartphones, social media, and on-demand entertainment?

For some companies, writes former *Wall Street Journal* reporter Lora Kolodny, "the answer is short digital learning sessions that are available at employees' convenience."[147] This kind of on-demand, bite-size learning—short lessons transmitted via microlearning apps and websites—has become a principal method of training now that the average attention span in North America has dropped from 12 seconds in 2000 to 8 seconds in 2015. Microlearning is one form of technology-enhanced learning, also known as online or e-learning.

The Surge in E-Learning. E-learning has also become a well-established fact in company training. According to a 2015 survey, although instructor-led classrooms were still the dominant training method, at about 46% of total student hours, 26.5% of training was delivered by online or computer-based technologies, 1.8% by mobile devices, and 31.9% by blended techniques.[148] The benefits of e-learning in general and microlearning in particular are that no transportation is

Off-the-job training. How does receiving feedback from an instructor affect your retention of knowledge? © stevecoleimages/Getty Images RF

needed and you can follow a flexible schedule and often work at your own pace.

Possible Drawbacks. However, microlearning has some drawbacks. "Micro-learning is *not* useful when people need to acquire/learn complex skills, processes, or behaviors," says one critic. Imagine, she says, learning a musical instrument, project management, sales, teamwork management, or any software tool in only 4.5 minutes a day.[149] Microlearning, she believes, is probably best used for reinforcement rather than for skill building. Stanford University neuroscientist Priya Rajasethupathy also agrees that microlearning is effective but limited, with bite-size lessons not likely to carry emotional weight—an important component of learning—for students compared to practicing something learned in a workshop or classroom.[150]

YOUR CALL

Neuroscientists are finding out that the human brain is a "social animal" that needs interaction with others.[151] How do you think this fact relates to e-learning? Do you think you learn better in a classroom rather than online?

What If No One Shows Up? Many employers offer employee training, whether internal or external, or funding to attend seminars. But research has shown that a surprisingly high percentage of employees simply don't know about it. For instance, while 92% of employers in one survey offered funding to attend seminars and trade shows, only 28% of employees were aware the funding existed.[152] Clearly, then, employers need to find out whether the training offered fits with the majority of employee development goals.

You now have learned about the different HR programs and practices, such as recruiting, training, and compensation. Do careers in these fields interest you? Not everyone is suited for HR work, but it is very rewarding for some. The following self-assessment will help you decide whether or not a career in HR fits for you. ●

connect SELF-ASSESSMENT 9.3

Is a Career in HR Right for You?

This survey is designed to assess your skills and interests and determine if a career in human resources is right for you. Please be prepared to answer these questions if your instructor has assigned Self-Assessment 9.3 in Connect.

1. Are you suited for a career in human resources? Which specific aspect of human resources do you prefer?

2. Look at the top two areas of HR for which you tested as being best suited. Look over the descriptions of these fields and then identify what skills you need to have to be successful.

3. Even if you do not pursue a career in HR, which skills do you feel you should continue to develop? Explain.

9.5 Performance Appraisal

MAJOR QUESTION

How can I assess employees' performance more accurately and give more effective feedback?

THE BIG PICTURE

Performance appraisal, assessing employee performance and providing them feedback, may be objective or subjective. Appraisals may be by peers, subordinates, customers, or oneself. Feedback may be formal or informal.

Want to know how well your managers think you're doing at work? Be prepared to be disappointed: 60% of employees say they don't get adequate feedback, according to a 2015 study, and 43% say they don't get enough feedback to improve performance.[153] Feedback about how you're doing in your job is part of performance management.

Performance Management in Human Resources

No doubt you've had the experience at some point of having a sit-down with a superior, a boss or a teacher, who told you how well or poorly you were doing—a *performance appraisal*. A performance appraisal is a single event, as we discuss later in this section. Performance management, by contrast, is a powerful ongoing activity that has produced such spectacular results as 48% higher profitability, 22% higher productivity, 30% higher employee engagement scores, and 19% lower turnover.[154]

Performance management is defined as a set of processes and managerial behaviors that involve defining, monitoring, measuring, evaluating, and providing consequences for performance expectations.[155] It consists of four steps: (1) define performance, (2) monitor and evaluate performance, (3) review performance, and (4) provide consequences. *(See Figure 9.3.)*

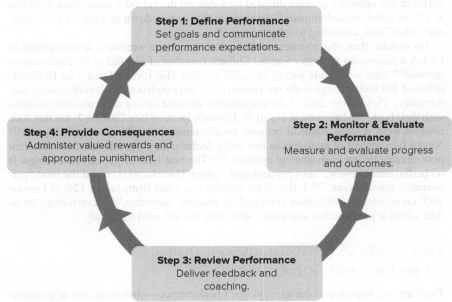

Step 1: Define Performance
Set goals and communicate performance expectations.

Step 2: Monitor & Evaluate Performance
Measure and evaluate progress and outcomes.

Step 3: Review Performance
Deliver feedback and coaching.

Step 4: Provide Consequences
Administer valued rewards and appropriate punishment.

FIGURE 9.3

Performance management: four steps

Source: Adapted from A. J. Kinicki, K. J. L. Jacobson, S. J. Peterson, and G. E. Prussia, "Development and Validation of the Performance Management Behavior Questionnaire," Personnel Psychology, Vol. 66 (2013), pp. 1–45.

Performance management, which is often exerted through an organization's managers and human resources policies and practices, is a powerful means for improving individual, group, and organizational effectiveness.[157]

EXAMPLE   Performance Management: How Domino's Pizza Built a Billion-Dollar Business

The founder of Domino's Pizza, Tom Monaghan, grew the business, which he later sold for $1 billion, by using performance management, as follows:[156]

1. **Define Performance.** In order to meet Domino's promise of delivering customers a pizza within 30 minutes or no payment required, Monaghan made clear to his employees in his performance expectations the importance of speed, even showing employees how to run out the door.

2. **Monitor and Evaluate Performance.** Domino's employees filled out a form showing they understood what was expected of them; then every one of them met with their manager and listed goals for the month and action plans for achieving them. Employees also described what the manager was supposed to do for them to support their efforts.

3. **Review Performance.** Employees met with their managers every three months to review their performance, and

managers met with their own superiors once a month to do the same.

4. **Provide Consequences.** Monaghan is a big believer in rewarding performance and retaining talent. Thus, Domino's store managers received not only salaries but also 30% of profits. To retain talent, Monaghan rewarded franchisees (individual store owners who had purchased the right to use the Domino's trademark and business model) by encouraging them to develop their managers into store owners themselves, for which the original franchisees were rewarded with a percentage of the earnings from the new store.

YOUR CALL

In your current job—being a student—how effective do you think the Domino's approach to performance management could be in helping you excel at college? Whom would you designate as your "manager," how often would you meet, and what kind of goals and action plans would you set?

Performance Appraisals: Are They Worthwhile?

A performance appraisal, or *performance review*, consists of (1) assessing an employee's performance and (2) providing him or her with feedback. Unlike performance management, which is an ongoing, interactive process between managers and employees, a performance appraisal is often dictated by a date on the calendar rather than need and is a "one-sided, boss-dominated" assessment that comes down to whether your superior "likes" you, according to some critics.[158]

No wonder, then, that so many performance reviews are worthless, in the opinion of UCLA management professor Samuel Culbert, coauthor of *Get Rid of the Performance Review!*[159] One worldwide survey of 1,300 workers also revealed that 7 in 10 people believed that their managers did not remain calm and constructive when discussing performance. This is why 20% of the respondents dreaded having difficult conversations with their boss.[160] Management expert W. Edwards Deming (see Chapter 2) felt that such reviews were actually harmful because people remember only the negative parts.[161] Ninety-five percent of managers in one study declared they were dissatisfied with their performance review/management systems.[162] "The best kind of performance review is no performance review," says psychologist Aubrey Daniels, who coined the term "performance management."[163] It thus is no surprise that some firms (about 12% of Fortune 1000 companies in 2014) have scrapped the practice altogether.[164] Nevertheless, let us take a look at performance appraisals, since they are still used frequently.

Two Kinds of Performance Appraisal: Objective and Subjective

There are two ways to evaluate an employee's performance—objectively and subjectively.

1. Objective Appraisals   **Objective appraisals, also called** *results appraisals,* **are based on facts and are often numerical.** In these kinds of appraisals, you would keep track of such matters as the numbers of products the employee sold in a month, customer complaints filed against an employee, miles of freight hauled, and the like.

There are two good reasons for having objective appraisals:

- **They measure results.** It doesn't matter if two appliance salespeople have completely different personal traits (one is formal, reserved, and patient; the other is informal, gregarious, and impatient) if each sells the same number of washers and dryers. Human resource professionals point out that, just as in business we measure sales, profits, shareholder value, and other so-called metrics, it is likewise important to measure employee performance, benefit costs, and the like as an aid to strategy.[165]

- **They are harder to challenge legally.** Not being as subject to personal bias, objective appraisals are harder for employees to challenge on legal grounds, such as for age, gender, or racial discrimination.

We discussed an objective approach in Chapter 5 under *management by objectives (MBO)*, which can encourage employees to feel empowered to adopt behavior that will produce specific results. MBO, you'll recall, is a four-step process in which (1) managers and employees jointly set objectives for the employee, (2) managers develop action plans, (3) managers and employees periodically review the employee's performance, and (4) the manager makes a performance appraisal and rewards the employee according to results. For example, an objective for a copier service technician might be to increase the number of service calls 15% during the next three months.

2. Subjective Appraisals   Few employees can be adequately measured just by objective appraisals—hence the need for **subjective appraisals, which are based on a manager's perceptions of an employee's (1) traits or (2) behaviors.**

"Here's the deal . . ." One of the most important tasks of being a manager is giving employees accurate information about their work performance. Which would you be more comfortable giving—objective appraisals or subjective appraisals? © Asia Images Group/ Getty Images RF

- **Trait appraisals.** *Trait appraisals* are ratings of such subjective attributes as "attitude," "initiative," and "leadership." Trait evaluations may be easy to create and use, but their validity is questionable because the evaluator's personal bias can affect the ratings.

- **Behavioral appraisals.** Behavioral appraisals measure specific, observable aspects of performance—being on time for work, for instance—although making the evaluation is still somewhat subjective. An example is the **behaviorally anchored rating scale (BARS), which rates employee gradations in performance according to scales of specific behaviors.** For example, a five-point BARS rating scale about attendance might go from "Always early for work and has equipment ready to fully assume duties" to "Frequently late and often does not have equipment ready for going to work," with gradations in between.

Who Should Make Performance Appraisals?

If one of your employees was putting on a good show of solving problems that, it turned out, she had actually *created* herself so that she could be an "office hero" and look good, how would you know about it? (This phenomenon has been dubbed "Munchausen—pronounced *mun-chow-zen*—at work" because it resembles the rare psychological disorder in which sufferers seek attention by making up an illness.)[166] Most performance appraisals are done by managers; however, to add different perspectives, sometimes appraisal information is provided by other people knowledgeable about particular employees.

Peers, Subordinates, Customers, and Self   Among additional sources of information are coworkers and subordinates, customers and clients, and the employees themselves.

- **Peers and subordinates.** Coworkers, colleagues, and subordinates may well see different aspects of your performance. Such information can be useful for development, although it probably shouldn't be used for evaluation. (Many managers will resist soliciting such information about themselves, of course, fearing negative appraisals.)

- **Customers and clients.** Some organizations, such as restaurants and hotels, ask customers and clients for their appraisals of employees. Publishers ask authors to judge how well they are doing in handling the editing, production, and marketing of their books. Automobile dealerships may send follow-up questionnaires to car buyers.

- **Self-appraisals.** How would you rate your own performance in a job, knowing that it would go into your personnel file? Probably the bias would be toward the favorable. Nevertheless, *self-appraisals* help employees become involved in the whole evaluation process and may make them more receptive to feedback about areas needing improvement.

360-Degree Assessment: Appraisal by Everybody   We said that performance appraisals may be done by peers, subordinates, customers, and oneself. Sometimes all these may be used in a technique called 360-degree assessment.

In a "theater in the round," the actors in a dramatic play are watched by an audience on all sides of them—360 degrees. Similarly, as a worker, you have many people watching you from all sides. Thus has arisen the idea of the **360-degree assessment,** or *360-degree feedback appraisal,* **in which employees are appraised not only by their managerial superiors but also by peers, subordinates, and sometimes clients,** thus providing several perspectives.

Typically, an employee chooses evaluators from 6 to 12 other people to make evaluations, who then fill out anonymous forms, the results of which are tabulated by computer. Or using a Facebook-style program such as Performance Multiplier or Twitter-like software called Rypple, employees can solicit evaluations through social networking–style systems.[167] The employee then goes over the results with his or her manager and together they put into place a long-term plan for performance goals.

All told, collecting performance information from multiple sources helps the person being evaluated get a broad view of his or her performance, and it highlights any biases and perceptual errors that are occurring. Finally, using multiple raters also makes it much more difficult for managers to unfairly favor or punish particular employees.

Forced Ranking: Grading on a Curve   To increase performance, an estimated 60% of Fortune 500 companies (such as General Electric, Ford, Cisco, and Intel) have some variant of performance review systems known as forced ranking (or "rank and yank") systems.[168] In **forced ranking performance review systems, all employees within a business unit are ranked against one another and grades are distributed along some sort of bell curve**—just like students being graded in a college course. Top performers (such as the top 20%) are rewarded with bonuses and promotions; the worst performers (such as the bottom 20%) are given warnings or dismissed.

This type of performance review system is rapidly losing favor, with presently about 27% (down from 44% in 2013) of Fortune 1000 companies measuring the performance of some part of their workforce using a forced ranking (also known as "stacked ranking," "rank and yank," or "rack and whack") system.[169] Another survey found that 200 mostly mid- to large-size companies still use the system.[170]

Proponents of forced ranking say it encourages managers to identify and remove poor performers and structures a predetermined compensation curve, which enables them to reward top performers. However, opponents contend that the system eventually gets rid of talented as well as untalented people.[171] There may also be legal ramifications, as when employees file class-action lawsuits alleging that the forced ranking methods had a disparate effect on particular groups of employees.[172] In addition, numeric ratings, rankings, and formal evaluations without positive feedback may produce the opposite of their intended results—namely, create a culture of *reduced* performance, according to recent neurological and psychological research.[173]

Finally, forced ranking systems—originally conceived at the turn of the 20th century to measure the performance of manual laborers and factory workers—seem inappropriate today, when over 70% of workers are employed in service or knowledge-intensive jobs in which skills, attitudes, and abilities are hard to evaluate along a bell curve. Forced ranking is particularly damaging at talent-intensive companies, in the opinion of Lisa Barry of Deloitte Touche Tohmatsu. "Regardless of whether they work for banks or software companies, technology professionals are expected to innovate, work effectively in teams, and adapt to an ever-accelerating rate of change," she points out. "They need incentives to collaborate and be creative, yet forced ranking typically produces the opposite behavior."[174] Even General Electric, famously known for "rank and yank" performance reviews under former CEO Jack Welch, has replaced its five-category ratings system (from "role model" to "unsatisfactory") with a mobile app to help employees share feedback.[175]

Effective Performance Feedback

The whole point of performance appraisal, of course, is to stimulate better job performance. But, says Lawrence Bossidy, former CEO of AlliedSignal, the typical appraisal is often three pages long and filled with vague, uncommunicative language and is useless to ensure that improvement happens.[176] Bossidy recommends an appraisal take up half a page and cover just three topics: what the boss likes about your performance, what you can improve, and how you and your boss are going to make sure that improvement happens.

Bossidy's suggestions are much in the spirit of recent thinking, in which more companies are choosing a qualitative approach to employee appraisals.[177] Now managers are trained on how to coach and regularly check in with employees, giving them continuous, real-time feedback and solutions, the cornerstone of performance management. To help increase employee performance, a manager can use two kinds of appraisals—formal and informal.

1. Formal Appraisals
Formal appraisals are conducted at specific times throughout the year and are based on performance measures that have been established in advance. An emergency medical technician might be evaluated twice a year by his or her manager, using objective performance measures such as work attendance time sheets and more subjective measures such as a behaviorally anchored rating scales (BARS) to indicate the employee's willingness to follow emergency procedures and doctors' and nurses' orders.

As part of the appraisal, the manager should give the employee feedback, describing how he or she is performing well and not so well and giving examples. Managers are sometimes advised to keep diaries about specific incidents so they won't have to rely on their memories (and so that their evaluations will be more lawsuit-resistant). Facts should always be used rather than impressions.

2. Informal Appraisals
Formal appraisals are the equivalent of a student receiving a grade on a midterm test and a grade on a final test—weeks may go by during which you are unaware of how well you're doing in the course. Informal appraisals are the equivalent of occasional unscheduled pop quizzes and short papers or drop-in visits to the professor's office to talk about your work—you have more frequent feedback about your performance. **Informal appraisals** are conducted on an unscheduled basis and consist of less rigorous indications of employee performance.

As a manager, you may not feel comfortable about critiquing your employees' performance, especially when you have to convey criticism rather than praise. Nevertheless, giving performance feedback is one of the most important parts of the manager's job. Some suggestions for improvement appear in the table. *(See Table 9.2.)* ●

TABLE 9.2

How to Give Performance Feedback to Employees

Think of yourself as a coach, as though you were managing a team of athletes.

- *Take a problem-solving approach, avoid criticism, and treat employees with respect.* Recall the worst boss for whom you ever worked. How did you react to his or her method of giving feedback? Avoid criticism that might be taken personally.
  Example: Don't say, "You're picking up that bag of cement wrong" (which criticizes by using the word *wrong*). Say, "Instead of bending at the waist, a good way to pick up something heavy is to bend your knees. That'll help save your back."

- *Be specific in describing the employee's present performance and in the improvement you desire.* Describe your subordinate's current performance in specific terms and concentrate on outcomes that are within his or her ability to improve.
  Example: Don't say, "You're always late turning in your sales reports." Say, "Instead of making calls on Thursday afternoon, why don't you take some of the time to do your sales reports so they'll be ready on Friday along with those of the other sales reps."

- *Get the employee's input.* In determining causes for a problem, listen to the employee and get his or her help in crafting a solution.
  Example: Don't say, "You've got to learn to get here by 9:00 a.m. every day." Say, "What changes do you think could be made so that your station is covered when people start calling at 9:00?"

9.6 Managing Promotions, Transfers, Disciplining, and Dismissals

What are some guidelines for handling promotions, transfers, disciplining, and dismissals?

THE BIG PICTURE

As a manager, you'll have to manage employee replacement actions, as by promoting, transferring, demoting, laying off, or firing.

"The unemployment rate is an abstraction, an aggregation of bodiless data," writes journalist/novelist Walter Kirn, "but losing a job is a lived experience, written on the nerves. . . . Some blame themselves and some blame everybody. Still others, not knowing whom to blame, explode."[178]

Among the major—and most difficult—decisions you will make as a manager are those about employee movement within an organization: Whom should you let go? promote? transfer? discipline? All these matters go under the heading of *employee replacement*. And, incidentally, any time you need to deal with replacing an employee in a job, that's a time to reconsider the job description to see how it might be made more effective for the next person to occupy it.

As regards replacement, HR specialists distinguish between *turnover* (employee is replaced) and *attrition* (employee is not replaced), both of which occur when an employee leaves the company. *Turnover* occurs when an employee abandons, resigns, retires, or is terminated from a job, and the employer seeks to replace him or her. Attrition occurs when an employee retires or when the company eliminates his or her job, and the employer leaves the vacancy unfilled.[179] You'll have to deal with replacement whenever an employee quits, retires, becomes seriously ill, or dies. Or you may initiate the replacement action by promoting, transferring, demoting, laying off, or firing.[180]

Promotion: Moving Upward

Promotion—moving an employee to a higher-level position—is the most obvious way to recognize that person's superior performance (apart from giving raises and bonuses). Three concerns are the following.

Fairness It's important that promotion be *fair*. The step upward must be deserved. It shouldn't be for reasons of nepotism, cronyism, or other kind of favoritism.

Nondiscrimination The promotion cannot discriminate on the basis of race, ethnicity, gender, age, or physical ability.

Others' Resentments If someone is promoted, someone else may be resentful about being passed over. As a manager, you may need to counsel the people left behind about their performance and their opportunities in the future. In fact, if you are passed over yourself, it is important not to let your anger build. Instead, you should gather your thoughts, then go in and talk to your boss and find out what qualities were lacking, suggests one report. You should also create a career action plan and look for ways to improve your knowledge, skills, and abilities.[181]

Transfer: Moving Sideways

Transfer is movement of an employee to a different job with *similar responsibility*. It may or may not mean a change in geographical location (which might be part of a promotion as well).

Employees might be transferred for four principal reasons: (1) to solve organizational problems by using their skills at another location; (2) to broaden their experience in being assigned to a different position; (3) to retain their interest and motivation by being presented with a new challenge; or (4) to solve some employee problems, such as personal differences with their bosses. In 2015, top Volkswagen managers considered implementing a mandatory rotation of key executives to new positions in order to disrupt what they perceived was "a culture of tolerance for breaking rules [that was] at the heart of its emissions crisis," according to *The Wall Street Journal*.[182]

Disciplining and Demotion: The Threat of Moving Downward

Poorly performing employees may be given a warning or a reprimand and then disciplined. That is, they may be temporarily removed from their jobs, as when a police officer is placed on suspension or administrative leave—removed from his or her regular job in the field and perhaps given a paperwork job or told to stay away from work.

Alternatively, an employee may be demoted—that is, have his or her current responsibilities, pay, and perquisites taken away, as when a middle manager is demoted to a first-line manager. (Sometimes this may occur when a company is downsized, resulting in fewer higher-level management positions.)

Dismissal: Moving Out of the Organization

Dismissals are of three sorts: layoffs, downsizings, and firings. We will also describe exit interviews and nondisparagement agreements, which often go along with dismissals.

Layoffs The phrase being *laid off* tends to suggest that a person has been dismissed *temporarily*—as when a carmaker doesn't have enough orders to justify keeping its production employees—and may be recalled later when economic conditions improve. Layoffs are cited by many companies (recently Nordstrom, Sprint, and American Express) as needed to improve profitability, although research suggests they do not, in fact, improve profits.[183]

Downsizings A *downsizing* is a *permanent* dismissal; there is no rehiring later. An automaker discontinuing a line of cars or on the path to bankruptcy might permanently let go of its production employees.

Firings The phrase being *fired,* with all its euphemisms and synonyms—being "terminated," "separated," "let go," "sacked," "axed," "canned"—tends to mean that a person was dismissed *permanently "for cause"*: absenteeism, sloppy work habits, failure to perform satisfactorily, breaking the law, and the like. (A CEO "never gets fired," comments one writer dryly; rather, he or she leaves "to pursue other opportunities" or "spend more time with the family.")[184]

It used to be that managers could use their discretion about dismissals. Today, however, because of the changed legal climate, steps must be taken to avoid employees suing for "wrongful termination." That is, an employer has to carefully *document* the reasons for dismissals. You also need to take into account the fact that survivors in the company can suffer just as much as, if not more than, their colleagues who were let go.[185]

Incidentally, in terms of your own career, be aware that dismissals rarely come as a surprise. Most bosses are conflict-averse, and you may see the handwriting on the wall when your own manager begins to interact with you less.[186]

In some industries, such as those in information technology, "treating workers as if they are widgets to be used up and discarded is a central part of the revised relationship between employers and employees," in the view of one former employee of a Cambridge, Massachusetts, "digital sweatshop."[187] Start-ups are also quick to fire if new hires don't measure up quickly.[188]

The Practical Action box below offers some suggestions for handling dismissals.

Fired. Being fired can be one of the most stressful events of one's life— more than the death of a close friend, separation from one's spouse over marital problems, or an injury requiring hospitalization. Some people who have been let go from their jobs suffer major health consequences. If you as a manager ever had to fire someone, what would you do to try to soften the blow? © Vgstockstudio/Shutterstock RF

PRACTICAL ACTION   The Right Way to Handle a Dismissal

"Employment at will" is the governing principle of employment in the great majority of states, which means that anyone can be dismissed at any time for any reason at all—or for no reason. Exceptions are whistle-blowers and people with employment contracts. Civil-rights laws also prohibit organizations' dismissing people for their gender, skin color, or physical or mental disability.[189]

Four suggestions for handling a dismissal follow.

Give the Employee a Chance First. If you're dealing with someone who has a problem with absenteeism, alcohol/drug dependency, or the like, articulate to that employee what's wrong with his or her performance; then set up a plan for improvement (which might include counseling). Or if you're dealing with an employee who has a bad cultural or personality fit

with the company—a buttoned-down, by-the-book style, say, that's at odds with your flexible, fast-moving organization— have a conversation and give the employee time to find a job elsewhere.[190]

Don't Delay the Dismissal, and Make Sure It's Completely Defensible. If improvements aren't forthcoming, don't carry the employee along because you feel sorry for him or her. Your first duty is to the performance of the organization. Make sure, however, that you've *documented* all the steps taken in advance of the dismissal. Also be sure that the steps taken follow the law and all important organizational policies.[191]

Be Aware How Devastating a Dismissal Can Be—Both to the Individual and to Those Remaining. To the person being let go, the event can be as much of a blow as a divorce or a death in the family. Dismissals can also adversely affect those remaining with the company. This is what psychiatrist Manfred Kets de Vries calls *layoff survivor sickness,* which is characterized by anger, depression, fear, guilt, risk aversion, distrust, vulnerability, powerlessness, and loss of motivation. Indeed, a five-year study by Cigna and the American Management Association found an enormous increase in medical claims, particularly for stress-related illnesses, not only among those dismissed but among continuing employees as well.[192]

Offer Assistance in Finding Another Job. Dismissing a long-standing employee with only a few weeks of severance pay hurts not only the person let go but also the organization itself, as word gets back to the employees who remain, as well as to outsiders who might be prospective employees. Knowledgeable employers offer assistance in finding another job.

"The best demonstration that a company's values are real," says management scholar Rosabeth Moss Kanter, "is to act on them today even for people who will not be around tomorrow. A company, like a society, can be judged by how it treats its most vulnerable. . . . Bad treatment of departing employees can destroy the commitment of those who stay."[193]

On this score, current thinking is that the best day to lay people off is not Friday (the traditional day, when often managers didn't want to deal with other employees' reactions) and not Monday (when leaders may not have time to prepare for the aftermath) but rather the middle of the week, which gives former employees a chance to look for work before the week is over.[194]

Getting Yourself Back Together after a Job Loss. "Losing a job can be a blow to your confidence and pride," says writer Debra Auerbach. But you can put yourself back on your feet more quickly, she suggests, if you take the following steps: Take time to grieve, as in taking a week to process what happened—but don't take much longer than that. Assess your finances, accept any assistance or outplacement counseling from your previous employer, set a daily schedule that keeps you from feeling adrift, start networking by getting referrals from former clients or vendors, add to your skills, and find a support group that will "cheer you through each [new job] possibility and lament each dead end."[195]

Exit Interview and Nondisparagement Agreement An **exit interview** is a formal conversation between a manager and a departing employee to find out why he or she is leaving and to learn about potential problems in the organization. For example, one company looked at the exit interviews of four employees and learned they all told the same story: their manager "lacked critical leadership skills, such as showing appreciation, engendering commitment, and communicating vision and strategy," according to one article. Moreover, "the organization was promoting managers on the basis of technical rather than managerial skill."[196]

A departing employee may want to pound the desk during an exit interview and shout about all that went wrong, but that's not a good idea. "The last impression is the one people remember," suggests a *Wall Street Journal* article. "A graceful exit can burnish an employee's reputation and shore up valuable relationships. A bad one can do serious damage to both."[197]

A **nondisparagement agreement** is a contract between two parties that prohibits one party from criticizing the other; it is often used in severance agreements to prohibit former employees from criticizing their former employers. Employees who are laid off or whose jobs have been eliminated are often obliged to sign nondisparagement agreements in return for receiving severance pay—pay an employer may give a worker who leaves, such as the equivalent of two weeks of salary for each year he or she was employed. A nondisparagement clause at Abbott Laboratories in Libertyville, Illinois, reads "You agree to make every effort to maintain and protect the reputation of Abbott and its products and agents." However, some former Abbott employees say the provision "stopped them from speaking openly with elected officials or appearing at congressional hearings" about what they say was the misuse of temporary work visas (H-1B visas) to replace American workers with foreign-born workers, according to one account.[198] •

9.7 The Legal Requirements of Human Resource Management

MAJOR QUESTION

To avoid exposure to legal liabilities, what areas of the law do I need to be aware of?

THE BIG PICTURE

Four areas of human resource law any manager needs to be aware of are labor relations, compensation and benefits, health and safety, and equal employment opportunity.

Laws underlie all aspects of the human resource process discussed so far. Whatever your organization's human resource strategy, in the United States (and in U.S. divisions overseas) it has to operate within the environment of the American legal system. Four areas you need to be aware of are as follows. Some important laws are summarized in the table opposite. *(See Table 9.3.)*

1. Labor Relations

The earliest laws affecting employee welfare had to do with unions, and they can still have important effects. Legislation passed in 1935 (the Wagner Act) resulted in the **National Labor Relations Board (NLRB),** which enforces procedures whereby employees may vote to have a union and for collective bargaining. **Collective bargaining** consists of negotiations between management and employees about disputes over compensation, benefits, working conditions, and job security.

A 1947 law (the Taft-Hartley Act) allows the president of the United States to prevent or end a strike that threatens national security. (We discuss labor-management issues further in Section 9.8.)

2. Compensation and Benefits

The Social Security Act in 1935 established the U.S. retirement system. The passage of the **Fair Labor Standards Act** of 1938 established minimum living standards for workers engaged in interstate commerce, including provision of a federal minimum wage (currently $7.25 an hour; 29 states have higher minimums, 5 states do not have minimums) and a maximum workweek (now 40 hours, after which overtime must be paid), along with banning products from child labor. Salaried executive, administrative, and professional employees are exempt from overtime rules.

Proponents of a $15 minimum wage say it would help people pay their bills, because existing minimum wages have not kept up with inflation, and it would create a fairer working environment, since different states now pay wildly different minimums. Detractors say that higher wages would produce job losses, hurt low-skilled workers, have little effect on reducing poverty, and result in higher prices to consumers.[199]

3. Health and Safety

From miners risking tunnel cave-ins to cotton mill workers breathing lint, industry has always had dirty, dangerous jobs. Beginning with the Occupational Safety and Health Act (OSHA) of 1970, a body of law has grown that requires organizations to provide employees with nonhazardous working conditions (most recently augmented by an update to the Toxic Substances Control Act of 1976).[200] Later laws extended health coverage, including 2010 health care reform legislation, which requires employees with more than 50 employees to provide health insurance.[201] (More than 60% of working-age Americans who signed up for Medicaid or a private health plan through the Affordable Care Act get health care they previously couldn't get.)[202]

TABLE 9.3

Some Important Recent U.S. Federal Laws and Regulations Protecting Employees

YEAR	LAW OR REGULATION	PROVISIONS
Labor Relations		
1974	Privacy Act	Gives employees legal right to examine letters of reference concerning them
1986	Immigration Reform & Control Act	Requires employers to verify the eligibility for employment of all their new hires (including U.S. citizens)
2003	Sarbanes-Oxley Act	Prohibits employers from demoting or firing employees who raise accusations of fraud to a federal agency
Compensation and Benefits		
1974	Employee Retirement Income Security Act (ERISA)	Sets rules for managing pension plans; provides federal insurance to cover bankrupt plans
1993	Family & Medical Leave Act	Requires employers to provide 12 weeks of unpaid leave for medical and family reasons, including for childbirth, adoption, or family emergency
1996	Health Insurance Portability & Accountability Act (HIPPA)	Allows employees to switch health insurance plans when changing jobs and receive new coverage regardless of preexisting health conditions; prohibits group plans from dropping ill employees
2007	Fair Minimum Wage Act	Increased federal minimum wage to $7.25 per hour on July 24, 2009
Health and Safety		
1970	Occupational Safety & Health Act (OSHA)	Establishes minimum health and safety standards in organizations
1985	Consolidated Omnibus Budget Reconciliation Act (COBRA)	Requires an extension of health insurance benefits after termination
2010	Patient Protection & Affordable Care Act	Employers with more than 50 employees must provide health insurance
Equal Employment Opportunity		
1963	Equal Pay Act	Requires men and women be paid equally for performing equal work
1964, amended 1972	Civil Rights Act, Title VII	Prohibits discrimination on basis of race, color, religion, national origin, or sex
1967, amended 1978 and 1986	Age Discrimination in Employment Act (ADEA)	Prohibits discrimination in employees over 40 years old; restricts mandatory retirement
1990	Americans with Disabilities Act (ADA)	Prohibits discrimination against essentially qualified employees with physical or mental disabilities or chronic illness; requires "reasonable accommodation" be provided so they can perform duties
1991	Civil Rights Act	Amends and clarifies Title VII, ADA, and other laws; permits suits against employers for punitive damages in cases of intentional discrimination

4. Equal Employment Opportunity

The effort to reduce discrimination in employment based on racial, ethnic, and religious bigotry and gender stereotypes began with Title VII of the Civil Rights Act of 1964. This established the **Equal Employment Opportunity (EEO) Commission, whose job is to enforce antidiscrimination and other employment-related laws.** Title VII applies to all organizations or their agents engaged in an industry affecting interstate commerce that employs 15 or more employees. Contractors who wish to do business with the U.S. government (such as most colleges and universities, which receive federal funds) must be in compliance with various executive orders issued by the president covering antidiscrimination. Later laws prevented discrimination against older workers and people with physical and mental disabilities.[203]

Workplace Discrimination, Affirmative Action, Sexual Harassment, and Bullying

Three important concepts covered by EEO laws are *workplace discrimination, affirmative action,* and *sexual harassment,* which we discuss in this section. We also consider *bullying,* which is *not* covered by EEO laws.

Workplace Discrimination　A large gap exists in perceptions between the sexes as to whether men or women have more opportunities for advancement. In a survey of 1,834 business professionals worldwide, 66% of men said opportunities to move to top management were gender neutral, compared with 30% of women who stated that.[204] (In actuality, only 4.2% of CEOs at S&P 500 companies were women.[205] Just 21 CEOs of the Fortune 500 companies were women in 2016, down from 24 in 2014.)[206]

Workplace discrimination occurs when people are hired or promoted—or denied hiring or promotion—for reasons not relevant to the job, such as skin color or eye shape, gender, religion, national origin, and the like. Two fine points to be made here are that (1) although the law prohibits discrimination in all aspects of employment, it does not require an employer to extend *preferential treatment* because of race, color, religion, and so on and (2) employment decisions must be made on the basis of job-related criteria.

There are two types of workplace discrimination:

- *Adverse impact:* **Adverse impact occurs when an organization uses an employment practice or procedure that results in unfavorable outcomes to a protected class (such as Hispanics) over another group of people (such as non-Hispanic whites).** For example, requiring workers to have a college degree can inadvertently create adverse impact against Hispanics because fewer Hispanics graduate from college than whites. This example would not be a problem, however, if a college degree was required to perform the job.

- *Disparate treatment:* **Disparate treatment results when employees from protected groups (such as disabled individuals) are intentionally treated differently.** An example would be making a decision to give all international assignments to people with no disabilities because of the assumption that they won't need any special accommodations related to travel.

When an organization is found to have been practicing discrimination, the people discriminated against may sue for back pay and punitive damages. In 2015, among complaints to the Equal Employment Opportunity Commission (EEOC), the most frequently cited basis for charges of discrimination was retaliation (44.5%), followed by race discrimination (34.7%); sex discrimination, including sexual harassment and pregnancy discrimination (29.5%); and discrimination based on disability (30.2%).[207]

In recent years, pay discrepancies between women and men improved slightly, but as of 2014 women overall still earned only 79 cents to every $1 for a man, according to a *Wall Street Journal* analysis, or 83 cents, according to the U.S. Census Bureau.[208] In some occupations, such as financial managers, women earn as little as 67 cents to a man's dollar, but among dental hygienists, travel agents, and lodging managers, the pay is equal between men and women. In other words, the gap widens in higher-paying occupations such as business, medicine, and law. American women in elite jobs earn well below men, with doctors, compensation managers, and personal financial advisors showing the greatest earnings differences.[209]

Women are more likely to suffer from depression and anxiety compared to men, and one study suggests an important reason: American women make significantly less money than their male counterparts, besides having to assume greater responsibility in child care and housework.[210]

Gender Discrimination: Silicon Valley and the "Brogrammer" Culture   EXAMPLE

Since 1997, women have started 608 new businesses every day, making up 30% of all U.S. businesses and providing one out of seven jobs among privately owned firms.[211] Moreover, venture capital firms that invested in women-led companies during the decade 2000–2010 outperformed those that didn't.[212] Women-led venture-backed companies earn 12% more revenue than male-led companies.[213]

Women in Tech. Despite such achievements, women are significantly underrepresented among the tech companies of Silicon Valley, long a male stronghold. Google's global staff is only 30% female, Facebook's 31%, and Yahoo's 38%.[214] In part, suggests one writer, women may not be going into tech to begin with because so many are brought up to assume that girls are not good at science or math and so do not see themselves as computer scientists.[215]

Frat-Boy Behavior. Lack of gender diversity doesn't *necessarily* result in a culture of sexism and sexual harassment. But sometimes it is exceedingly so. Sexist attitudes start in computer science classes, women say, and are reinforced by the tech industry's "brogrammer" ("bro" + "programmer") fraternity-house attitudes and behavior of some male software engineers and executives.[216] "Bro culture" also is said to lock many minorities out.[217]

YOUR CALL

Recently, regulators, venture capitalists, tech companies, and women themselves have been making serious efforts to achieve more diversity in the tech sector.[218] Still, do you see sexist and demeaning behavior in the culture of your campus, which you worry you might encounter later in a future workplace?

Affirmative Action   **Affirmative action** focuses on achieving equality of opportunity within an organization. It tries to make up for past discrimination in employment by actively finding, hiring, and developing the talents of people from groups traditionally discriminated against. Steps include active recruitment, elimination of prejudicial questions in interviews, and establishment of minority hiring goals. It's important to note that EEO laws *do not* allow the use of hiring quotas.[219]

Affirmative action has created tremendous opportunities for women and minorities, but it has been resisted more by some white males who see it as working against their interests.[220] Affirmative action plans are more successful when employees view them as being fair and equitable and when whites are not prejudiced against people of color.[221] In addition, research shows that women and minorities hired on the basis of affirmative action felt stigmatized as unqualified and incompetent.[222]

Sexual Harassment   **Sexual harassment** consists of unwanted sexual attention that creates an adverse work environment. This means obscene gestures, sex-stereotyped jokes, sexually oriented posters and graffiti, suggestive remarks, unwanted dating pressure, physical nonsexual

Sexual harassment. If this woman is unaware of the man ogling her legs, does that make his behavior acceptable? Or does it still contribute to an offensive work environment? © Phanie/Superstock

contact, unwanted touching, sexual propositions, threatening punishment unless sexual favors are given, obscene phone calls, and similar verbal or physical actions of a sexual nature.[223] The harassment may be by a member of the opposite sex or a member of the same sex, by a manager, by a coworker, or by an outsider.[224] If the harasser is a manager or an agent of the organization, the organization itself can be sued, even if it had no knowledge of the situation.[225]

Two Types of Sexual Harassment   There are two types of sexual harassment, both of which violate Title VII of the 1964 Civil Rights Act.

In the *quid pro quo harassment* type, the person to whom the unwanted sexual attention is directed is put in the position of jeopardizing being hired for a job or obtaining job benefits or opportunities unless he or she implicitly or explicitly acquiesces.

More typical is the *hostile environment* type, in which the person being sexually harassed doesn't risk economic harm but experiences an offensive or intimidating work environment. According to one survey, 38% of women said they had heard sexual innuendos, wisecracks, or taunts at the office.[226] Anti-female remarks are particularly prevalent on social media.[227]

The table below presents some guidelines for preventing sexual harassment. *(See Table 9.4.)*

TABLE 9.4

Preventing Sexual Harassment

- Don't suggest sexual favors for rewards related to work or promotion.

- Don't do uninvited touching, patting, or hugging of others' bodies—especially if they wince, frown, or pull away.

- Don't make sexually suggestive jokes, demeaning remarks, slurs, or obscene gestures or sounds.

- Don't display sexual pictures in your workplace or write notes of a sexual nature.

- Don't laugh at others' sexually harassing words or behaviors.

What Managers Can Do   To help prevent harassment from occurring, managers can make sure their companies have an effective sexual harassment policy in place. The policy should be shown to all current and new employees, who should be made to understand that sexual harassment will not be tolerated under any circumstances. A formal complaint procedure should be established, which should explain how charges will be investigated and resolved. Supervisors should be trained in Title VII requirements and the proper procedures to follow when charges occur. If charges occur, they should be investigated promptly and objectively, and if substantiated, the offender should be disciplined at once—no matter what his or her rank in the company.

Bullying   If college professors can be bullied, can't anyone?

For years, mathematics professor Bill Lepowsky experienced abusive behavior at the San Francisco Bay Area community college where he taught. It began with a group of managers spreading rumors and false accusations that threatened his job—for instance, saying he was holding class in the wrong classroom and was skipping important meetings (meetings he actually wasn't supposed to attend). It was emotionally draining—like "being a soldier in a foxhole with shells exploding," he said—and took time and focus away from his job. It didn't end until his tormentors left the college.[228]

The Meaning of Mean   **Bullying** is repeated mistreatment of one or more persons by one or more perpetrators; it is abusive physical, psychological, verbal, or nonverbal behavior that is threatening, humiliating, or intimidating. "People have only thought about bullying related to children," says one expert, "but the fact is that right now adult bullying is rampant."[229]

Indeed, bullying on the job has been experienced by 27% of employees, according to one survey; 37%, according to another; and 51%, according to yet another.[230] Bullying by supervisors that takes the form of forcing long hours on workers or yelling and behaving in a threatening way is more apt to occur in small businesses (50 or fewer employees), where the education level of bosses is often less high than in larger firms and where one person's bad behavior may have greater influence.[231]

Bullies can be male or female, although the majority (about 60%) are men and most are bosses. Women tend to be bullied more than men. Bullying can occur between colleagues, managers, and employees. Bullying on the job may be physically aggressive, such as pushing, pinching, or cornering someone. However, it is more apt to be verbal, including shouting, swearing, and name calling. Or it may be relational, including malicious gossip, rumors, and lies that may cause someone to feel isolated or cut off. Bullying through technology (cyberbullying), such as Facebook, Twitter, or e-mail, accounts for about one in five incidents.[232]

Bullying. A surprisingly common activity, bullying is apt to be verbal, involving shouting and name calling, or relational, including spreading malicious rumors and lies. In some cases, however, it can be physically aggressive, involving pinching or pushing. Perhaps as many as half of all employees have experienced some sort of bullying on the job. Have you? What did you do about it? © Jetta Productions/The Image Bank/Getty Images

The Effects of Bullying Unfortunately, many workplace bullies are quite charming and manipulative and so receive positive evaluations from their supervisors and achieve high levels of career success, according to one dispiriting study.[233] "If people are politically skilled, they can do bad things really well," says one of the study authors.[234] Of course, that doesn't make this behavior right. Indeed, bullying can devastate a workplace.[235]

Bullying, says Gary Namie, director of the Workplace Bullying Institute, can be especially damaging in work sites where the bullied may be trapped in close proximity to their bully.[236] Bullied employees are less satisfied at work, more likely to spend time gossiping and not putting in their full effort, and more likely to quit.[237] Victims also tend to experience stress-related health problems, such as anxiety, panic attacks, depression, even suicide.[238]

The table below presents some guidelines for combating bullying. *(See Table 9.5.)* ●

• Recognize **the mistreatment as bullying:** Don't blame yourself.
• Get **others on your side:** Don't become socially isolated.
• Don't **strike back:** It might get you fired. Ask to be treated with fairness and respect.
• Stay **calm and confident:** Don't feed the bully's sense of power by showing fear.
• Avoid **being alone with the bully:** Make sure someone can hear your interactions. Or record them on your smartphone.
• Document **the events—and be truthful:** When reporting bullying to supervisors, give them the FACTS, not just the emotional effects. Save examples of online bullying, notes, and other physical evidence. Remember, the bully will probably deny your accusations.

TABLE 9.5

Beating Back the Bully

Sources: A. Bruzzese, "Workplace Becomes New Schoolyard for Bullies," USA Today, August 24, 2011, http://usatoday30.usatoday.com/money/jobcenter/workplace/bruzzese/2011-08-24-bully-bosses-overtake-workplace_n.htm (accessed June 6, 2016); K. V. Brown, "Far beyond School Playground, Bullying Common in Workplace," San Francisco Chronicle, November 6, 2011, pp. A1, A10; and Robert Half International, "6 Tips for Dealing with the Office Bully," The Arizona Republic, November 29, 2015, p. 4E.

9.8 Labor-Management Issues

What are the principal processes and issues involved in organizing labor unions?

THE BIG PICTURE

We describe the process by which workers get a labor union to represent them and how unions and management negotiate a contract. This section also discusses the types of union and nonunion workplaces and right-to-work laws. It covers issues unions and management negotiate, such as compensation, cost-of-living adjustments, two-tier wage systems, and givebacks. It concludes by describing mediation and arbitration.

Starting in 1943, James Smith worked his way up from washing dishes in the galley of a passenger train's dining car to waiter, earning tips on top of his wages of 36 cents an hour. The union job with the Brotherhood of Sleeping Car Porters, the first African American union, enabled him to go to college, and when he left the railroad he was hired as a civil engineer for the city of Los Angeles. "His story," says one report, "is emblematic of the role the railroads and a railroad union played in building a foundation for America's black middle class."[239] Unions also helped to grow the American (and European) middle classes in general, bringing benefits to all, organized or not.

Labor unions are organizations of employees formed to protect and advance their members' interests by bargaining with management over job-related issues. The union movement is far less the powerhouse that it was in the 1950s—indeed, its present membership is the lowest since 1916—but it is still a force in many sectors of the economy. *(See Table 9.6, left.)* Nearly half (48%) of Americans hold a favorable view of unions, while 39% hold an unfavorable view.[240]

TABLE 9.6

Snapshot of Today's U.S. Union Movement

Who's in a union (2015)?

- 11.1% of full-time U.S. workers—down from 35.5% in 1945

- 6.7% of private-sector workers (7.6 million)

- 35.2% of public-sector workers (7.2 million)

- Most members, public sector: local government (41.3%), including teachers, police officers, and firefighters

- Most members, private sector: utilities (21.4%), transportation and warehousing (18.9%), educational services (13.7%), telecommunications (13.3%), construction (13.2%)

Source: Bureau of Labor Statistics, "Union Members Summary," Economic News Release, January 28, 2016; www .bls.gov/news. release/union2.nr0 .htm (accessed June 6, 2016).

How Workers Organize

When workers in a particular organization decide to form a union, they first must get each worker to sign an *authorization card,* which designates a certain union as the workers' bargaining agent. When at least 30% of workers have signed cards, the union may ask the employer for official recognition.

Usually the employer refuses, at which point the union can petition the National Labor Relations Board (NLRB) to decide which union should become the *bargaining unit* that represents the workers, such as the Teamsters Union, United Auto Workers, American Federation of Teachers, or Service Employees International Union, as appropriate. (Some workers, however, are represented by unions you would never guess: Zookeepers, for instance, are represented by the Teamsters, which mainly organizes transportation workers. University of California, Berkeley, graduate student instructors are represented by the United Auto Workers.) An election is then held by the NLRB, and if 50% or more of the votes cast agree to unionization, the NLRB *certifies* the union as the workers' exclusive representative.

How Unions and Management Negotiate a Contract

Once a union is recognized as an official bargaining unit, its representatives can then meet with management's representatives to do collective bargaining—to negotiate pay and benefits and other work terms.

When agreement is reached with management, the union representatives take the collective bargaining results back to the members for *ratification*—they vote to accept or reject the contract negotiated by their leaders. If they vote yes, the union and management representatives sign a *negotiated labor-management contract,* which sets the general tone and terms under which labor and management agree to work together during the contract period.

The Issues Unions and Management Negotiate About

The key issues that labor and management negotiate are compensation, employee benefits, job security, work rules, hours, and safety matters. However, the first issue is usually union security and management rights.

Union Security and Types of Workplaces

A key issue is, Who controls hiring policies and work assignments—labor or management? This involves the following matters:

- **The union security clause.** The basic underpinning of union security is the **union security clause,** the part of the labor-management agreement that states that employees who receive union benefits must join the union, or at least pay dues to it. In times past, a union would try to solidify the union security clause by getting management to agree to a *closed shop agreement*—which is illegal today—in which a company agreed it would hire only current union members for a given job.

- **Types of unionized and nonunionized workplaces.** The four basic kinds of workplaces are *closed shop, union shop, agency shop,* and *open shop. (See Table 9.7.)*

WORKPLACE	DEFINITION	STATUS
Closed shop	Employer may hire only workers for a job who are already in the union.	Illegal
Union shop	Workers aren't required to be union members when hired for a job but must join the union within a specified time.	Not allowed in 22 states (right-to-work states)
Agency shop	Workers must pay equivalent of union dues but aren't required to join the union.	Applies to public-sector teachers in some states, prohibited in others
Open shop	Workers may choose to join or not join a union.	Applies in 22 states (right-to-work states)

TABLE 9.7

Four Kinds of Workplace Labor Agreements

- **Right-to-work laws.** Individual states are allowed (under the 1947 Taft-Hartley Act) to pass legislation outlawing union and agency shops. As a result, 22 states have passed **right-to-work laws,** statutes that prohibit employees from being required to join a union as a condition of employment.

Business interests supporting such laws argue that forcing workers to join a union violates their rights and makes a state less attractive to businesses considering moving there. Union supporters say that states with such laws have overall lower wages and that all workers benefit from union gains, so everyone should be compelled to join.

The 22 work-to-right states are shown in the map on the next page. *(See Figure 9.4.)*

Compensation: Wage Rates, COLA Clauses, and Givebacks

Unions strive to negotiate the highest wage rates possible, or to trade off higher wages for something else, such as better fringe benefits. Some issues involved with compensation are as follows:

- **Wage rates—same pay or different rates?** Wage rates subject to negotiation include overtime pay, different wages for different shifts, and bonuses. In the past, unions tried to negotiate similar wage rates for unionized employees working in similar jobs for similar companies or similar industries. However, the pressure of competition abroad and deregulation at home has forced many unions to negotiate **two-tier wage contracts, in which new employees are paid less or receive lesser benefits than veteran employees have.**

  Example: In 2011, when automakers began to create new jobs, new union hires were offered about half the pay ($14 an hour) that autoworkers were

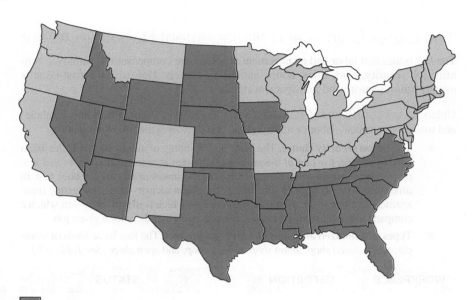

- Right-to-work states
- Non–right-to-work states

getting before ($28). Such two-tier wage systems can be attractive to employers, who are able to hire new workers at reduced wages, but it also benefits veteran union members, who experience no wage reduction. However, among auto-workers, at least, such contracts may be on the way out.[241] One study found that the two-tier setup wasn't, in fact, any more profitable for companies.[242]

- **Cost-of-living adjustment.** Because the cost of living is always going up (at least so far), unions often try to negotiate a **cost-of-living adjustment (COLA) clause, which during the period of the contract ties future wage increases to increases in the cost of living,** as measured by the U.S. Bureau of Labor Statistics's consumer price index (CPI). (An alternative is the *wage reopener clause,* which allows wage rates to be renegotiated at certain stated times during the life of the contract. Thus, a 10-year contract might be subject to renegotiation every 2 years.)

- **Givebacks.** During tough economic times, when a company (or, in the case of public employee unions, a municipality) is fighting for its very survival, management and labor may negotiate **givebacks, in which the union agrees to give up previous wage or benefit gains in return for something else.** Usually the union seeks job security, as in a no-layoff policy.

Settling Labor-Management Disputes

Even when a collective-bargaining agreement and contract have been accepted by both sides, there may likely be ongoing differences that must be resolved. Sometimes differences lead to walkouts and strikes, or management may lock out employees. However, conflicts can be resolved through *grievance procedures* and *mediation* or *arbitration.*

Grievance Procedures **A grievance is a complaint by an employee that management has violated the terms of the labor-management agreement.** Example: An employee may feel he or she is being asked to work too much overtime, is not getting his or her fair share of overtime, or is being unfairly passed over for promotion.

Grievance procedures are often handled initially by the union's *shop steward,* an official elected by the union membership who works at the company and represents the interests of unionized employees on a daily basis to the employees' immediate supervisors. If this process is not successful, the grievance may be carried to the union's chief shop steward and then to the union's grievance committee, who deal with their counterparts higher up in management.

If the grievance procedure is not successful, the two sides may decide to try to resolve their differences by one of two ways—*mediation* or *arbitration.*

Mediation　**Mediation is the process in which a neutral third party, a *mediator,* listens to both sides in a dispute, makes suggestions, and encourages them to agree on a solution.** Mediators may be lawyers or retired judges or specialists in various fields, such as conflict resolution or labor matters.

Arbitration　**Arbitration is the process in which a neutral third party, an *arbitrator,* listens to both parties in a dispute and makes a decision that the parties have agreed will be binding on them.** Arbitrators are often retired judges. Many corporations, including recently tech start-ups, have vigorously embraced arbitration as a business tool with consumers and employees, and some for-profit colleges have even required it of their students, forbidding them from resolving their complaints through class-action suits (when a large number of plaintiffs with similar complaints band together to sue a company).[243] Critics, however, contend that forcing consumers to sign agreements that require arbitration and prevent lawsuits has the effect of biasing resolutions in favor of business and constitutes a "privatization of the justice system."[244]

Leo Kanne, head of Local 440 for the United Food & Commercial Workers International Union in Denison, Iowa, home of a Smithfield meat-processing plant, says plant workers earn enough to take their children to Pizza Ranch or maybe Dairy Queen every week and go on vacation once a year. "That's all these people want," he says. "Nobody is getting rich working in these plants." Word that a Chinese company had acquired Smithfield had everyone worried. Would they cut costs and not honor past labor agreements?[245] Considering these kinds of concerns, what is your feeling about labor unions? Self-Assessment 9.4 enables you to answer this question by assessing your general attitudes toward unions. ●

connect SELF-ASSESSMENT 9.4

Assessing Your Attitudes toward Unions

This survey is designed to assess your attitude toward unions. Please be prepared to answer these questions if your instructor has assigned Self-Assessment 9.4 in Connect.

1. Where do you stand on your attitude toward unions—positive, neutral, or negative?

2. What experiences or events in your life have led to your attitude toward unions? Describe. What do you think lies in the future for labor unions?

3. Why has there been growing dislike for unions in the United States?

New Ways to Advance Employee Interests　From time to time, labor organizations take on new permutations. For instance, fast-food, construction, and contract workers are now able to more easily unionize, following a National Labor Relations Board decision that recognizes that the modern U.S. economy increasingly relies on shift work and temporary employees.[246] In 2015, carwash workers in Santa Fe, New Mexico, formed a workers committee (not a union), which is protected under the National Labor Relations Act from employer retaliation when employees are engaged in "concerted" activity to improve wages and conditions.[247] In 2016, Uber started a guild for its drivers in New York, which would provide limited benefits and protections, but would stop short of unionization and would not allow drivers to turn to the National Labor Relations Board to intervene on issues.[248] Finally, many employers are trying to advance workplace democracy by giving employees the chance to vote (as through digital survey tools such as TinyPulse and Know Your Company) "on issues from hiring to holiday parties," which, according to one report, "helps spark loyalty to the company."[249]

Key Terms Used in This Chapter

Key Points

9.1 Strategic Human Resource Management

- Human resource (HR) management consists of the activities managers perform to plan for, attract, develop, and retain an effective workforce. The purpose of the strategic human resource management process is to get the optimal work performance that will help realize the company's mission and vision.

- Three concepts important to human resource management are (1) human capital, the economic or productive potential of employee knowledge; (2) knowledge workers, people whose occupations are principally concerned with generating or interpreting information, as opposed to manual labor; and (3) social capital, the economic or productive potential of strong, trusting, and cooperative relationships.

- Strategic human resource planning consists of developing a systematic, comprehensive strategy for (a) understanding current employee needs and (b) predicting future employee needs.

- Understanding current employee needs requires first doing a job analysis to determine, by observation and analysis, the basic elements of a job. Then a job description can be written, which summarizes what the holder of the job does and how and why he or she does it. Next comes the job specification, which

describes the minimum qualifications a person must have to perform the job successfully.

- Predicting employee needs means a manager must become knowledgeable about the staffing an organization might need and the likely sources of staffing, perhaps using a human resource inventory to organize this information.

9.2 Recruitment and Selection: Putting the Right People into the Right Jobs

- Recruiting is the process of locating and attracting qualified applicants for jobs open in the organization. Recruiting is of two types: internal and external.

- Internal recruiting means making people already employed by the organization aware of job openings, as through job postings.

- External recruiting means attracting job applicants from outside the organization. A useful approach is the realistic job preview, which gives a candidate a picture of both positive and negative features of the job and organization before he or she is hired.

- The selection process is the screening of job applicants to hire the best candidates. Three types of selection tools are background information, interviewing, and employment tests.

- Background information is ascertained through application forms, resumes, and reference checks.
- Interviewing takes three forms. (a) The unstructured interview involves asking probing questions to find out what the applicant is like. (b) The structured interview involves asking each applicant the same questions and comparing his or her responses to a standardized set of answers. The first type of structured interview is the situational interview, in which the interview focuses on hypothetical situations. (c) The second type of structured interview is the behavioral-description interview, in which the interviewer explores what applicants have actually done in the past.
- Employment tests are legally considered to consist of any procedure used in the employment selection decision process, but the most common tests are ability tests, personality tests, performance tests, and integrity tests. Some companies have assessment centers, in which management candidates participate in activities for a few days while being assessed in performance tests by evaluators.
- Other tests include drug testing, polygraphs, and genetic screening. With any kind of test, an important legal consideration is the test's reliability, the degree to which a test measures the same thing consistently, and validity, whether the test measures what it purports to measure and is free of bias.

9.3 Managing an Effective Workforce: Compensation and Benefits

- Compensation has three parts: wages or salaries, incentives, and benefits.
- In the category of wages or salaries, the concept of base pay consists of the basic wage or salary paid employees in exchange for doing their jobs.
- Incentives include commissions, bonuses, profit-sharing plans, and stock options.
- Benefits are additional nonmonetary forms of compensation, such as health insurance, retirement plans, and family leave.

9.4 Orientation, Training, and Development

- Companies often perform what is known as onboarding, programs that help employees to integrate and transition to new jobs by making them familiar with corporate policies, procedures, cultures, and politics by clarifying work-role expectations and responsibilities.
- Three ways in which newcomers are helped to perform their jobs are through orientation, training, and development.
- Orientation consists of helping the newcomer fit smoothly into the job and organization. Following orientation, the employee should emerge with information about the job routine, the organization's mission and operations, and the organization's work rules and employee benefits.
- Training must be distinguished from development. *Training* refers to educating technical and operational employees in how to do their current jobs better.

- *Development* is the term describing educating professionals and managers in the skills they need to do their jobs in the future. Both training and development may be effected through on-the-job training methods and off-the-job training methods.

9.5 Performance Appraisal

- Performance management is defined as a set of processes and managerial behaviors that involve defining, monitoring, measuring, evaluating, and providing consequences for performance expectations. It consists of four steps: (1) define performance, (2) monitor and evaluate performance, (3) review performance, and (4) provide consequences.
- Performance appraisal consists of assessing an employee's performance and providing him or her with feedback. Appraisals are of two general types—objective and subjective.
- Two good reasons for having objective appraisals are that they measure results and they are harder to challenge legally. Objective appraisals are based on facts and are often numerical. An example is management by objectives.
- Subjective appraisals are based on a manager's perceptions of an employee's traits or behaviors. Trait appraisals are ratings of subjective attributes such as attitude and leadership. Behavioral appraisals measure specific, observable aspects of performance. Most performance appraisals are made by managers, but they may also be made by coworkers and subordinates, customers and clients, and employees themselves (self-appraisals). Sometimes all of these may be used, in a technique called the 360-degree assessment, in which employees are appraised not only by their managerial superiors but also by their peers, subordinates, and sometimes clients.
- In another evaluation technique, forced ranking performance review systems, all employees within a business unit are ranked against one another, and grades are distributed along some sort of bell curve.
- Performance feedback can be effected in two ways: (1) Formal appraisals are conducted at specific times throughout the year and are based on performance measures that have been established in advance. (2) Informal appraisals are conducted on an unscheduled basis and consist of less rigorous indications of employee performance.

9.6 Managing Promotions, Transfers, Disciplining, and Dismissals

- Managers must manage promotions, transfers, disciplining, and dismissals, which often involve replacing an employee with a new employee.
- As regards replacement, turnover must be distinguished from attrition. Turnover occurs when an employee abandons, resigns, retires, or is terminated from a job, and the employer seeks to replace him or her. Attrition occurs when an employee retires or when the company eliminates his or her job, and the employer leaves the vacancy unfilled.

- In considering promotions, managers must be concerned about fairness, nondiscrimination, and other employees' resentment.
- Transfers, or moving employees to a different job with similar responsibility, may take place in order to solve organizational problems, broaden managers' experience, retain managers' interest and motivation, and solve some employee problems.
- Poor-performing employees may need to be disciplined or demoted.
- Dismissals may consist of layoffs, downsizings, or firings.
- An exit interview is a formal conversation between a manager and a departing employee to find out why he or she is leaving and to learn about potential problems in the organization. A nondisparagement agreement is a contract between two parties that prohibits one party from criticizing the other; it is often used in severance agreements to prohibit former employees from criticizing their former employers.

9.7 The Legal Requirements of Human Resource Management

- Four areas of human resource law that any manager needs to be aware of are labor relations, compensation and benefits, health and safety, and equal employment opportunity.
- Labor relations are dictated in part by the National Labor Relations Board, which enforces procedures whereby employees may vote to have a union and for collective bargaining. Collective bargaining consists of negotiations between management and employees about disputes over compensation, benefits, working conditions, and job security.
- Compensation and benefits are covered by the Social Security Act of 1935 and the Fair Labor Standards Act, which established minimum wage and overtime pay regulations.
- Health and safety are covered by the Occupational Safety and Health Act of 1970, among other laws.
- Equal employment opportunity is covered by the Equal Employment Opportunity (EEO) Commission, whose job it is to enforce antidiscrimination and other employment-related laws.
- Three important concepts covered by EEO are (a) discrimination, which occurs when people are hired or promoted—or denied hiring or promotion—

for reasons not relevant to the job, such as skin color or national origin; (b) affirmative action, which focuses on achieving equality of opportunity within an organization; and (c) sexual harassment, which consists of unwanted sexual attention that creates an adverse work environment and which may be of two types—the quid pro quo type, which may cause direct economic injury, and the hostile environment type, in which the person being harassed experiences an offensive work environment.
- Another area of concern, though not covered by EEO laws, is bullying, repeated mistreatment by one or more perpetrators. Bullying is abusive physical, psychological, verbal, or nonverbal behavior that is threatening, humiliating, or intimidating.

9.8 Labor-Management Issues

- Labor unions are organizations of employees formed to protect and advance their members' interests by bargaining with management over job-related issues.
- Workers organize by signing authorization cards designating a certain union as their bargaining agent, and if enough cards are signed, the National Labor Relations Board will recognize the union as the bargaining unit. If 50% of workers agree, the NLRB certifies the union as the workers' exclusive representative. In negotiating a contract in collective bargaining, workers in the union must ratify the contract, after which union and management sign a negotiated labor-management contract.
- Among the issues unions negotiate are the union security clause, which states that workers must join the union or at least pay benefits to it.
- The four types of workplaces are closed shop (now illegal), union shop, agency shop, and open shop. Twenty-two states have right-to-work laws that prohibit employees from being required to join a union as a condition of employment.
- Unions also negotiate wage rates, including two-tier wage contracts, with newer employees being paid less, and cost-of-living (COLA) adjustments giving wages that increase with the cost of living. Sometimes unions must negotiate givebacks, in which employees give up previous wage or benefit gains in return for something else.
- To avoid strikes, labor-management disputes may be resolved through grievance procedures or through mediation or arbitration.

Understanding the Chapter: What Do I Know?

1. What is human resource management and its purpose, and what are the three concepts important to it?
2. What is performance management, and what are the four steps in it?
3. Explain the two steps in strategic human resource planning.
4. What are the two types of recruiting, and how do the three types of selection tools work?
5. Differentiate among the three types of compensation.

6. Describe orientation, training, and development.

7. Explain the difference between objective and subjective performance appraisals, and describe 360-degree assessment, forced ranking, and formal versus informal performance feedback.

8. What are the four areas of human resource law a manager needs to be aware of?

9. Explain the concepts of discrimination, affirmative action, sexual harassment, and bullying.

10. What are the principal labor-management issues?

Management in Action

Google's Success Builds from Its Progressive Approach toward Human Resource Management

Google, which is owned by Alphabet Inc., was rated as the number one place to work by *Fortune* seven times between 2006 and 2016. The company employs over 61,000 people in over 70 offices in more than 40 countries, and it generated $75 billion in revenue in 2015, with $23 billion in operating profit.[250]

Google's success is partly a function of its progressive approach to human resource management. *People Operations,* or POPS, is the name of Google's HR department. The department is headed by Laszlo Bock, and it relies on people analytics to determine many of its HR programs, policies, and procedures. Prasad Setty, the leader of the POPS "people analytics group" said that "what we try to do is bring the same level of rigor to people decisions that we do to engineering decisions. Our mission is to have all people decisions be informed by data."[251] Consider how POPS responded to a high turnover rate among women.

Bock sent his team to study the causes of female turnover. The research revealed that the problem pertained to new mothers, not women in general. Women having babies were quitting at twice Google's average rate of turnover. One potential reason for this was the company's maternity leave policy, which allowed 12 weeks of paid time off. Google decided to see what would happen if it changed this policy. New mothers were given five months off at full pay, and they can use it in any way they wish. The change was a success. The quit rate for new mothers dropped 50% and equaled the average for the remainder of the company. Results from Googlegeist—the company's annual employee survey—further showed that employees' happiness had increased as well.[252]

Let's consider some of the other human resources practices used by Google.

Hiring

Historically, Google's interview process was known for being one of the most difficult in the high-technology industry. Candidates frequently were asked "notoriously impossible brainteaser interview questions." Examples are "Model raindrops falling on a sidewalk (sidewalk is 1 meter and raindrops are 1 cm). How could we know when the sidewalk is completely wet?" and "If ads were removed from YouTube, how would you monetize it?"[253]

POPS did research on the hiring process partly because it was taking too long to hire people. The average time to hire was three or more months in 2005, with some people waiting six months to receive an offer. The average is now down to about five to six weeks, and clear hires are selected within three weeks.[254]

Two of the big changes in the hiring process pertained to the number of interviews applicants went through and the structure of interviews. In the past, recruits met with 12 or more people. Research by POPS demonstrated that there were diminishing returns after four interviews, which is the current standard.

The structure of the selection process also was revised to match what is known from HR research. Laszlo Bock described the selection process as "combining behavioral and situational structured interviews with assessments of cognitive ability, conscientiousness, and leadership. To help interviewers, we've developed an internal tool called qDroid, where an interviewer picks the job they are screening for, checks the attributes they want to test, and is emailed an interview guide with questions designed to predict performance for that job. This makes it easy for interviewers to find and ask great interview questions."[255]

Training

Google does not follow tradition when it comes to training. For one, about 55% of the company's official training classes are taught by Googlers. These classes are called "Googler to Googler." The company believes that employees learn more when they are taught by fellow employees. One manager noted that "telling your employees that you want them to learn is different than asking them to promote that culture themselves. Giving employees teaching roles . . . makes learning part of the way employees work together rather than something HR is making them do."[256]

The company does not rely on traditional classroom-style teaching. It replaces this with approaches that are suited for the needs of Google employees. One example is the weekly program called "Product

Spotlight." It is a dial-in conference call that is run like a talk show. "A moderator interviews a product manager about a particular new feature, as sales agents across the country, and around the world, listen in. Sometimes there are also slides or video to follow along with online, and the agents get to ask questions via chat."[257]

Google also offers quarterly classes that dig deeper into various topics. One example is Sales Pro, "which takes a deep dive into one particular strategic issue, like display advertising or the mobile business. The soup-to-nuts program takes about six hours, but rather than delivering it all in one fell swoop, or even through a series of hour-long, do-it-yourself modules, Google breaks the information into bite-sized chunks lasting no more than seven minutes each."[258] This enables employees to download the modules when and where they want.

To make training stick, the company follows classes with online games to help employees master this knowledge. "Leaderboards foster friendly competition. And quizzes following each training make sure the agents are absorbing the new information."[259]

Performance Management

The performance management process begins with setting objectives and key results, known as OKRs. OKRs consist of a goal, which is established by the employee, and an associated set of key results that guide the employee in achieving the goal. Managers rate an employee's performance on a five-point scale anchored from "needs improvement" to "superb."

Employees and their managers also select a group of peers to conduct semi-annual evaluations. Peers are asked to "list one thing the person they're reviewing should do more of and one thing the employee could do differently to have a greater impact on the company." Once this feedback is received, groups of managers come together to review the peer ratings. The goal of these meetings is to reduce rater bias and provide more accurate evaluations.

The final stage of the cycle entails making pay decisions. These decisions are made about a month after the annual performance reviews are conducted. Employees, of course, receive feedback at every stage of the process.[260]

FOR DISCUSSION

1. What is it about Google's human resource practices and procedures that make it an attractive company to work for? Explain.

2. To what extent are Google's hiring procedures consistent with recommendations proposed in this chapter? Discuss your logic.

3. How would you describe Google's approach toward training its employees?

4. To what extent does Google follow the performance management process depicted in Figure 9.3?

5. Do you see any downside to the performance management approach used at Google? Explain your rationale.

6. What is your key takeaway from this case?

Legal/Ethical Challenge

Should Noncompete Agreements Be Legal?

This challenge involves the human resource policy of asking new hires to sign a noncompete agreement. Noncompete agreements specify "in contract law under which one party (usually an employee) agrees not to enter into or start a similar profession or trade in competition against another party (usually the employer)." In other words, the agreement prohibits the person signing it from working with another company that could be viewed as a competitor. The concept was born from the idea that an "employee might begin working for a competitor or starting a business, and gain competitive advantage by exploiting confidential information about their former employer's operations or trade secrets, or sensitive information such as customer/client lists, business practices, upcoming products, and marketing plans."[261]

Arthur Valdez was sued by Amazon.com Inc. for violating a noncompete agreement. Valdez was a supply-chain and logistics executive for Amazon who was hired by Target. Target clearly competes against Amazon, and Valdez's agreement required an 18-month lag before taking a position with similar responsibilities. According to *The Wall Street Journal*, Amazon claims that "Mr. Valdez's new post will necessarily involve 'the disclosure and use of Amazon's confidential and proprietary information to Amazon's detriment and Target's advantage.'" Target denies that it wants confidential information about Amazon and says "this suit is without merit."[262] This same issue has snagged quite a few new college graduates.

Stephanie Russell-Kraft signed a noncompete agreement at her first full-time job in journalism. She worked for Law360, a legal newswire. She told *The*

Wall Street Journal that she was given the document, along with tax and benefit forms, on the first day of work. She was not given a copy and did not really understand the impact of signing the form. She forgot about it and "didn't hear a single word about it over the course of the next two years, during which time many colleagues left to cover the same beat at competing news outlets without any issue," she said.[263]

After leaving Law360, Russell-Kraft took a better job at Thomson Reuters. Her excitement with the new job was dashed a few weeks later when the company asked her to leave because of the noncompete agreement with Law360. Law360 contacted Reuters and informed the company about the details in the noncompete agreement. Reuters let her go because she had checked a box on her application indicating that she was not subject to a noncompete agreement. Russell-Kraft told *The Wall Street Journal* that "she has since disclosed the agreement to prospective employers, who have said they wouldn't hire her because of it."[264] She is now looking for work in a different industry.

The use of noncompete agreements has extended to lower-level jobs. Sandwich chain Jimmy John's, for example, requires employees to sign an agreement that prohibits them from working at other sandwich shops for two years.[265]

The use of noncompete agreements is increasing, and their legality varies by state. About 12% of American workers have signed such agreements.

SOLVING THE CHALLENGE

Should companies be allowed to force employees to sign noncompete agreements?

1. Of course. Every company needs to protect its proprietary and confidential information.

2. With moderation. I agree that it makes sense to protect proprietary information like formulas, equations, trade secrets, and intellectual property for certain occupations or industries. But this should not apply to all jobs, such as working in a sandwich shop.

3. No. They should be against the law because they prohibit people from finding employment.

4. Invent other options. Explain.

10

Organizational Change and Innovation

Lifelong Challenges for the Exceptional Manager

Managing for Innovation and Change: How Important Is the Agility Factor?

Business writer Tom Peters's bottom-line hypothesis is that "nobody has a sweet clue what they're doing." Therefore, says the author of *In Search of Excellence*, "you better be trying stuff at an insanely rapid pace." Living in today's Discontinous Times, or "a brawl with no rules," means that we must be relentless in our experimentation—"it's do or die."[1]

Dealing with change is an ongoing challenge for every manager. "A leader's job is less about getting through the current storm," says Martin McGuinn, past CEO of Mellon Financial Corp., "and more about enabling people to navigate the ongoing series of storms."[2]

Managing for innovation and change takes a careful hand, because many organizations are stymied by fear of failure and by internal politics.[3] "Even when their jobs depend on adopting and inventing new maneuvers," says columnist Carol Hymowitz, "most workers hold fast to old ones. The majority either are overwhelmed when asked to do things differently or become entrenched, clinging harder to the past."[4]

Some ways to deal with change and innovation include the following.[5]

Allow Room for Failure

"The more ideas you create," says Adam Grant, author of *Originals,* "the more variety you have. Some of those ideas are going to be blind alleys or random walks in bad directions."[6] At Intuit, the software company famous for TurboTax and QuickBooks, if somebody has an idea, people are not allowed to stomp on it. "It's more important to get the stupidest idea out there and build on it than not to have it in the first place," says an Intuit psychologist.[7]

Give One Consistent Explanation for the Change

When a company is undergoing change, myriad rumors will fly and employees will be uneasy; you and the managers who report to you need to give one consistent explanation. In McGuinn's case, the explanation for overhauling Mellon Bank's retail division was "We want to be the best retailer in financial services."

Look for Opportunities in Unconventional Ways

Most "new" products and services are really knockoffs or marginal variations of the things already on the market and hence are doomed to failure, says Robert Cooper, professor of marketing at Ontario's McMaster University. This doesn't mean, of course, that there isn't room for leveraging existing products with utterly unoriginal ideas. But most people are blinded by the limits of conventional wisdom and their own experience and fail to see huge potential markets in unconventional concepts. Try this advice from a Yale entrepreneurship instructor: Write down every hassle you encounter during the day. "At the end of the month, you will have 20 business ideas," he says, "and some of them will work."[8]

Have the Courage to Follow Your Ideas

This may be the hardest job of all—trying to convince others that your ideas for change are feasible, especially if the ideas are radical. This may mean working to gain allies within the organization, standing up to intimidating competitors inside and out, and perhaps being prepared to follow a lonely course for a long time.

The Agility Factor

A few large companies consistently outperform their peers over long periods of time, even in the face of significant business changes. What do they have in common? Agility. "They adapt to business change more quickly and reliably than their competitors," says a Booz & Company study.[9] "They have found a way to turn as quickly as speedboats when necessary." Can you take lessons from this?

For Discussion What do you think agility requires? If you were going to instill a culture of innovation in a company you worked for, what kinds of things would you do?

FORECAST   What's Ahead in This Chapter

In this chapter, we consider the nature of change in organizations, including the two types of change—reactive and proactive—and the forces for change originating outside and inside the organization. Next we explore types and models of change. We then describe organizational development, a set of techniques for implementing planned change. We then discuss how you can manage employee fear and resistance. Finally, we discuss how to promote innovation within an organization.

10.1 The Nature of Change in Organizations

Since change is always with us, what should I understand about it?

THE BIG PICTURE

Two types of change are reactive and proactive. Forces for change may consist of forces outside the organization—demographic characteristics; technological advancements; shareholder, customer, and market changes; and social and political pressures. Or they may be forces inside the organization—human resources concerns and managers' behavior.

"Every journey starts with fear. . . . Do you know what fear stands for? False Evidence Appearing Real."[10]

Of course, not every fear rests on false evidence—often the evidence is very real indeed. But in an age of discontinuous change, we are all having to make our own new journeys. "There is a need to retool yourself," says the CEO of AT&T, "and you should not expect to stop."[11]

Fundamental Change: What Will You Be Called On to Deal With?

"It is hard to predict, especially the future," physicist Niels Bohr is supposed to have quipped.

But it is possible to identify and prepare for the future that has already happened, in the words of management theorist Peter Drucker.[12]Among the trends: Today's digitally savvy kids will grow up and continue to be early adopters of new technology. Women will be a dominant force in the global marketplace. More people will move from rural to urban areas. Social networks will replace traditional institutions in driving change. Consumers will grow more informed, changing the power balance in the marketplace. A rising developing-world middle class will fuel global consumer spending. Spending on health and wellness will soar. Starting a new business will become easier. Niche markets will flourish. Cloud computing will do away with the brick-and-mortar office. Data will be critical for competitive advantage. Smart machines will get smarter.[13]

There are also some supertrends specifically shaping the future of business: (1) The marketplace is becoming more segmented; (2) competitors offering specialized solutions require we get our products to market faster; (3) some companies are unable to survive disruptive innovation; (4) offshore suppliers are changing the way we work; and (5) knowledge, not information, is becoming the new competitive advantage.[14]

1. The Marketplace Is Becoming More Segmented and Moving toward More Niche Products In the recent past, managers could think in terms of mass markets—mass communication, mass behavior, and mass values. Now we have "demassification," with customer groups becoming segmented into smaller and more specialized groups responding to more narrowly targeted commercial messages.

"Our culture and economy are increasingly shifting away from a focus on a relatively small number of hits (mainstream products and markets) . . . and moving toward a huge number of niches," says Chris Anderson of *Wired* magazine. "In an era without the constraints of physical shelf space and other bottlenecks of distribution, narrowly targeted goods and services can be as economically attractive as mainstream fare."[15] Thus, he says, "the future of business is selling less of more."

Example: In the Internet Age, retailers like Amazon and Apple are not constrained by physical shelf space and can offer consumers a much wider variety of products, yet small sales, one or two rather than millions of items at a time, can produce big profits.

2. More Competitors Are Offering Targeted Products, Requiring Faster Speed-to-Market Companies that take too long to commercialize their products may fail to capitalize on a narrow window of opportunity before competitors swoop in and pass them by," points out a *Forbes* writer.[16] Some of these competitors may be in and out of a market in a matter of days or months—like pop-up stores, "here today, gone tomorrow" retailers, such as those selling Halloween products.

Example: Virgin Group Ltd., headed by Sir Richard Branson, is known mainly for its music and airline businesses, but it has entered around 400 new businesses, one after the other—mobile phones, credit cards, hotels, games, trains, and most recently foot races and cruise ships—and very quickly. Virgin Comics, started in 2006, aimed at India's multibillion-dollar comics market, went from idea to public announcement in less than 11 months. In mid-2008, it restructured and changed its name to Liquid Comics.

Virgin train. A brainchild of British multiple entrepreneur Richard Branson, Virgin Trains was launched in 1997 to provide long-distance passenger services in the United Kingdom. Among Branson's many companies, perhaps 400 derivatives in all: Virgin Records, Virgin Mobile, Virgin Cola, Virgin Vodka, Virgin Car, and Virgin Galactic (for space tourism). Branson is quick to enter a new industry but also quick to get out if it isn't profitable. Branson's entrepreneurial approach: "Think, what's the most amazing way to do it?" ©Alvey & Towers Picture Library/Alamy

3. Some Traditional Companies May Not Survive Radical Change In *The Innovator's Dilemma: When New Technologies Cause Great Firms to Fail,* **Clayton M. Christensen,** a Harvard Business School professor, argues that when successful companies are confronted with a giant technological leap that transforms their markets, all choices are bad ones.

Indeed, he thinks, it's very difficult for an existing successful company to take full advantage of a technological breakthrough such as digitalization—what he calls **disruptive innovation, a process by which a product or service takes root initially in simple applications at the bottom of a market and then relentlessly moves up market, eventually displacing established competitors.**[17] Some companies that have the resources to survive disruption—to build "the next big thing"—often fail to do so.[18]

Lower-level managers are rarely rewarded for telling powerful senior executives that a competitive advantage is fading away, adds Columbia Business School professor Rita Gunther McGrath. "Better to shore up an existing advantage for as long as possible, until the pain becomes so obvious there is no choice. That's what happened at . . . Nokia, Kodak, and a host of other firms that got themselves into terrible trouble."[19]

Radical Change: The Decline of Radioshack   EXAMPLE

Electronics retailer RadioShack, which once sold electronic parts, including the first mass-produced personal computer (the TRS-80), in the 1980s failed to spot up-and-coming competition from Amazon, as well as undertook confused marketing strategies and a poor mix of inventory.[20] The chain's demise also coincided with the decline of free time that once had allowed electronic hobbyists to flourish (a loss of 181 hours a year between 1979 and 2007).

From Computers to Cell Phones and E-Commerce. Told that computers weren't a money maker, RadioShack stopped making them in 1993 and turned to cell phones. Unfortunately, signing up phone customers took about 45 minutes each, tying up store employees. In the late 1990s, the chain's website didn't allow consumers to shop, at the same time Best Buy and Walmart were running e-commerce sites.

Weird Marketing, Small Inventory, Missing the Maker Movement. For a time the company tried a marketing campaign, widely ridiculed, in which it tried to seem cool by referring to

itself as "The Shack." In addition, its stores, never the size of big box competitors, were limited by store space, which restricted their inventory. Finally, while it was trying to sell mobile phones and remote-controlled cars, the chain missed stocking the kind of inventory that would appeal to the burgeoning Maker movement—the do-it-yourselfers wanting to build homemade robots and other tech projects.

YOUR CALL

In March 2015, RadioShack filed for bankruptcy. "I wouldn't even call this failure. I'd call it an assisted suicide," said one marketing professor.[21] It's always easy in retrospect to find the faults of a failed enterprise, although RadioShack's demise is "like tracing the steps and doings of a drunk person," says one former employee.[22] As you consider the disruptive effects of technology on a host of other industries, what kind of strategy do you think they should embrace? How, for instance, would you advise the owner of an automobile body shop whose business in the next few years might be imperiled by the accident-free driving of self-driving cars?[23]

4. China, India, and Other Offshore Suppliers Are Changing the Way We Work As we said in Chapter 2, globalization and outsourcing are transforming whole industries and changing the way we work. China, India, Mexico, the Philippines, and other countries possess workers and even professionals willing to work twice as hard for half the pay, giving American businesses substantial labor savings. While unquestionably some American jobs are lost, others become more productive, with some engineers and salespeople, for example, being liberated from routine tasks so that they can spend more time innovating and dealing with customers.

Example: Querétaro is not a place students would probably go for spring break, but it has become known for something not normally associated with Mexico: aircraft construction. American aircraft makers from Bombardier to Cessna Aircraft to Hawker Beechcraft have various kinds of subassembly work there, where wages are lower but skill levels are not.[24]

But if some manufacturing jobs have moved cross-border, dozens of foreign manufacturers in aerospace, chemicals, and other industries are bringing jobs *to* the United States. British-based Rolls-Royce, for instance, makes engine parts in Virginia. Siemens, a German company, makes power-plant turbines in North Carolina.[25] In addition, in 2015, the United States added roughly as many jobs due to foreign investment and American companies returning from offshore as it lost to offshoring.[26]

Overseas firms also now look to the United States for talented workers in technology, finance, and research.[27]

5. Knowledge, Not Information, Is Becoming the New Competitive Advantage "Information is rapidly becoming a profitless commodity, and knowledge is becoming the new competitive advantage," says San Diego management consultant Karl Albrecht.[28]

That is, as information technology does more of the work formerly done by humans, even in high-tech areas (such as sorting data for relevance), many low-level employees previously thought of as knowledge workers are now being recognized as "data workers," who contribute very little added value to the processing of information. Unlike routine information handling, knowledge work is analytic and involves problem solving and abstract reasoning—exactly the kind of thing required of skillful managers, professionals, salespeople, and financial analysts. The rise of knowledge workers is accelerating despite the threat of automation, and indeed the number of people in knowledge-work jobs—nonroutine cognitive occupations—has more than doubled in the last 30 years, and shows no sign of slowing down.[29]

Example: Middle-skill jobs like bookkeeping, clerical work, and repetitive assembly-line work are being rapidly taken over by automation, according to MIT economist David Autor. But higher-paying knowledge-work jobs, which require creativity and problem solving—often aided by computers—have grown rapidly, as have lower-skilled jobs that are resistant to automation.[30]

Two Types of Change: Reactive versus Proactive

Most CEOs, general managers, and senior public-sector leaders agree that incremental changes are no longer sufficient in a world that is operating in fundamentally different ways. Life in general, they say, is becoming more complex, and the firms that are able to manage that complexity are the ones that will survive in the long term.[31] Clearly, we are all in for an interesting ride.

As a manager, you will typically have to deal with two types of change: *reactive* and *proactive*.

1. Reactive Change: Responding to Unanticipated Problems and Opportunities

When managers talk about "putting out fires," they are talking about **reactive change, making changes in response to problems or opportunities as they arise.**

U.S. public health authorities went to reactive-change high alert when measles, declared eliminated in 2000 because of widespread vaccination, came back with a vengeance in 2015 after being initiated by an infected international visitor to Disneyland in southern California.[32] The virus rapidly spread among American adults and children who had refused to be vaccinated ("anti-vaxxers"), a growing population concerned about a famous British medical study that claimed to link the measles vaccine with autism (complex disorders of brain development).[33] "The study was not only spectacularly wrong," writes pediatrics professor and vaccine expert Paul Offit, "but also fraudulent."[34] Nevertheless, misinformed U.S. parents opted out of vaccinations at a rate of 6% a year between 1991 and 2006, some swayed by passionate celebrities such as former *Playboy* model Jenny McCarthy.[35]

Reactive Change: The BP Gulf of Mexico Blowout

EXAMPLE

Crises can happen quickly and without warning, and many companies have shown they don't deal with them well, as happened with Toyota's and GM's slow reactions in recalling defective vehicles. But for oil giant BP (formerly British Petroleum), the crisis was catastrophic—both for itself and most certainly for the United States.[36]

Crisis in the Gulf of Mexico. In April 2010, an explosion on the BP drilling platform Deepwater Horizon in the Gulf of Mexico led to sinking of the rig, the loss of 11 lives, and the largest oil spill ever to happen in U.S. waters. Oil wells have emergency shutoff valves called blowout preventers, which can be triggered from the rig. The Deepwater Horizon, which floated 5,000 feet above the ocean floor, was equipped with this device, which nearly always works when wells surge out of control. However, it failed to operate on the day of the Gulf accident.

And what the rig did not have was a *backup* shutoff switch, a remote-control device that carries an acoustic signal through the water that can be activated as a last resort. Such acoustic backup triggers, which cost about $500,000, are not mandated by U.S. regulators, but they also haven't been tested under real-world conditions, because major offshore oil-well blowouts are so rare. (Even so, Norway and Brazil require

them, and some major oil companies, such as Royal Dutch Shell, carry them even when not mandated.)

BP Reacts. As 2.5 million gallons of oil a day leaked from the open wellhead, the question was asked: Why wasn't BP prepared for such an accident? Eventually they capped the leak, but in the aftermath BP pled guilty to federal felony charges and environmental-law violations and was forced to sell almost $40 billion in assets to meet its liabilities, a move that cut its number of wells and platforms in half.[37] In the six years following, BP tried to settle with thousands of Gulf victims, from shrimpers to hotel owners—and deal with many dubious claims of businesses hundreds of miles from the Gulf, including a Florida escort service.[38] In 2016, a federal judge approved a $20 billion settlement to end the years of litigation. BP has reportedly set aside nearly $54 billion to cover the costs associated with the disaster.[39]

YOUR CALL

The BP blowout happened 21 years after the tanker Exxon *Valdez*'s catastrophic 1989 oil spill in the Gulf of Alaska, the effects of which are still being felt. Wasn't that enough time for oil companies to plan for major accidents? What should BP have done?

---

2. Proactive Change: Managing Anticipated Problems and Opportunities

In contrast to reactive change, **proactive change, or planned change, involves making carefully thought-out changes in anticipation of possible or expected problems or opportunities.**[40]

EXAMPLE   Proactive Change: Disney World Gets Out Front with Its MagicBand

Even big companies in the constantly changing landscape of California's Silicon Valley are nervous. "Everyone is trying to position themselves for the new style of information technology," says Hewlett-Packard CEO Meg Whitman. "The fittest will survive."[41]

The Game Changer. Across the country in Orlando, Florida, however, the Walt Disney Company has been taking a giant proactive stride: investing $1 billion into a wearable technology designed to revolutionize the way visitors spend money at Walt Disney World. It begins with the MyMagic+ vacation-planning system, which features a website ("My Disney Experience") and data-collecting wristbands ("MagicBands") that interact with scanners throughout the 40-square-mile theme park. The electronic band can digitally carry everything a guest might need—"park tickets, photos, coupons, even money," says one description.[42]

"Because it is a reservation system, it is a game changer," says a professor who teaches theme-park management. "Now you can plan your vacation and your ride sequence well ahead of your trip."[43] For instance, you can "prebook front-of-the-line access to three rides, parades, or [Disney cartoon] character meet-and-greets," says writer Brooks Barnes. To buy food and merchandise, you just stand at the register and

swipe your wristband. The MagicBand also functions as a hotel room key, parking claim, and VIP access (so that Disney employees will greet you by name). Says Barnes, "Disney thinks people will spend more money and time at the [park] if they find it easier to navigate."[44]

Onward to Phones. During testing of the system, Disney found it could accommodate 3,000 additional daily guests and that use of the FastPass reservation system had increased 40%, freeing people from standing in line and increasing their number of experiences. Today, however, much of what the bracelets do can be done with cell phones, and indeed it was decided when the Shanghai Disney Resort opened in June 2016 it would not use the bands.[45]

YOUR CALL

Disney plans for the technology will give people the flexibility to visit multiple Disney parks in a single day and keep them from going to competing central Florida parks, such as Universal Orlando Resort.

Do you think Disney is onto something? Could the technology be applied to zoos, Las Vegas resorts, and other venues, as the company hopes? How? What about Disney cruise ships?

As we've stated, change can be hard, and the tools for survival are flexibility and adaptability. We also know that organizations like to hire people who are flexible and willing to accept change. How well do you think you fare in this regard? You can find out by taking Self-Assessment 10.1.

connect SELF-ASSESSMENT 10.1

Assessing Your Attitudes toward Change at Work

The following survey was designed to assess your attitudes toward change at work. Please be prepared to answer these questions if your instructor has assigned Self-Assessment 10.1 in Connect.

1. Where do you stand when it comes to your attitude toward change? Are you surprised by the results?

2. Based on your three lowest scoring survey items, how might you foster a more positive attitude toward change? Be specific.

3. What types of questions might a recruiter ask you during an interview to assess your attitude toward change? What would be your response to these questions?

The Forces for Change outside and inside the Organization

How do managers know when their organizations need to change? The answers aren't clear-cut, but you can get clues by monitoring the forces for change—both outside and inside the organization. (*See Figure 10.1, opposite page.*)

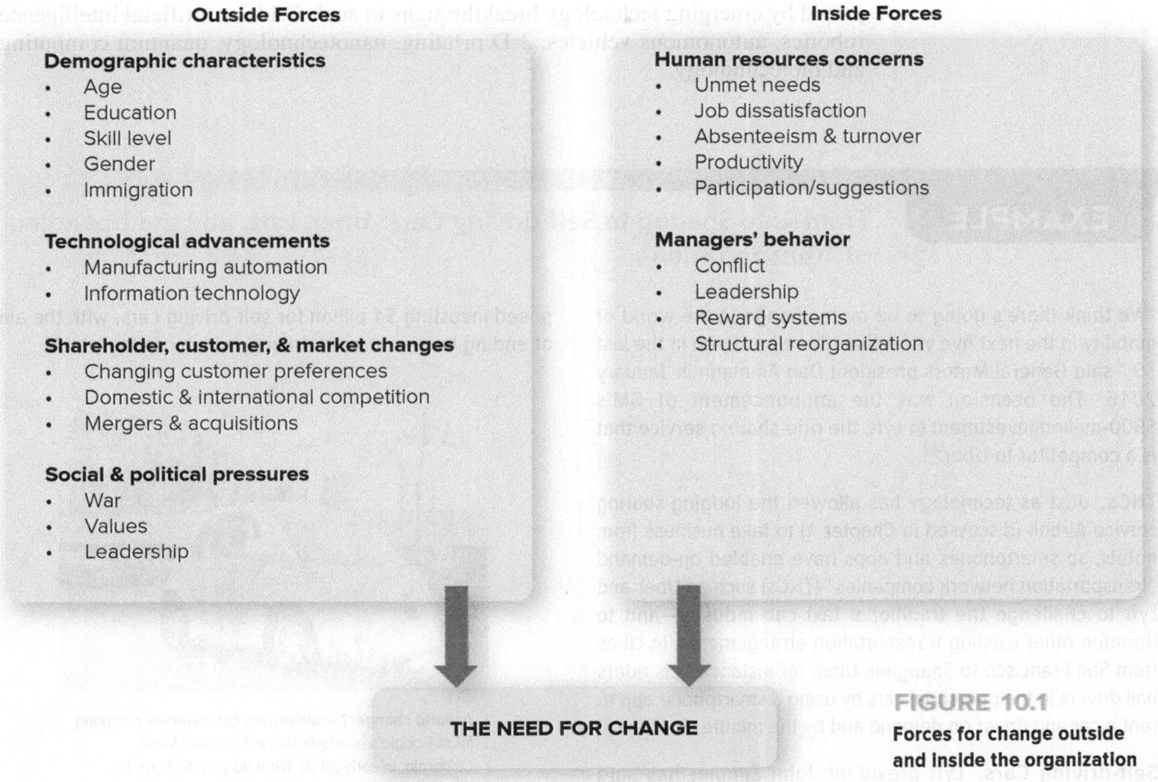

Outside Forces

Demographic characteristics
- Age
- Education
- Skill level
- Gender
- Immigration

Technological advancements
- Manufacturing automation
- Information technology

Shareholder, customer, & market changes
- Changing customer preferences
- Domestic & international competition
- Mergers & acquisitions

Social & political pressures
- War
- Values
- Leadership

Inside Forces

Human resources concerns
- Unmet needs
- Job dissatisfaction
- Absenteeism & turnover
- Productivity
- Participation/suggestions

Managers' behavior
- Conflict
- Leadership
- Reward systems
- Structural reorganization

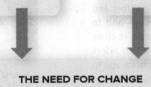

THE NEED FOR CHANGE

FIGURE 10.1

Forces for change outside and inside the organization

Forces Originating outside the Organization   External forces consist of four types, as follows.

1. Demographic Characteristics   Earlier we discussed the demographic changes occurring among U.S. workers, with the labor force becoming more diverse. Example: For the first time since 1880, Americans ages 18 to 34 (Millennials) are more likely to be living with their parent(s) than in a household shared with a spouse or partner.[46] How might this affect their spending habits?

2. Technological Advancements   Technology is not just computer technology; it is any machine or process that enables an organization to gain a competitive advantage in changing materials used to produce a finished product.

"We stand on the brink of a technological revolution that will fundamentally alter the way we live, work, and relate to one another," writes Klaus Schwab, executive chairman of the World Economic Forum. "In its scale, scope, and complexity, the transformation will be unlike anything humankind has experienced before."[47] This is the Fourth Industrial Revolution, characterized by "a fusion of technologies that is blurring the lines between the physical, digital, and biological spheres."

Example: The First Industrial Revolution (1784) used water and steam to mechanize production, the Second (1870) used electric power to create mass production, and the Third (1969) used electronics and information technology to automate production. The Fourth, which is now ongoing and is disrupting nearly every industry in every country, is characterized by billions of people connected by mobile devices with unprecedented processing power, storage capacity, and access to knowledge—

joined by emerging technology breakthroughs in such fields as artificial intelligence, robotics, autonomous vehicles, 3-D printing, nanotechnology, quantum computing, and biotechnology.

EXAMPLE   From Ride Sharing to Self-driving Cars: Uber, Lyft, and the Upending of Transportation

"We think there's going to be more change in the world of mobility in the next five years than there has been in the last 50," said General Motors president Dan Ammann in January 2016. The occasion was the announcement of GM's $500-million investment in Lyft, the ride-sharing service that is a competitor to Uber.[48]

TNCs. Just as technology has allowed the lodging-sharing service Airbnb (discussed in Chapter 1) to take business from hotels, so smartphones and apps have enabled on-demand "transportation network companies" (TNCs) such as Uber and Lyft to challenge the traditional taxi cab industry—and to threaten other existing transportation arrangements. In cities from San Francisco to Shanghai, Uber, for instance, lets riders hail drivers in their personal cars by using a smartphone app to rent a car and driver on demand and by the minute.

Self-driving Cars. Lyft president John Zimmer has said that he believes that individual car ownership will fade in favor of autonomous vehicles—self-driving cars or robot cars—that are run through a network, and clearly GM agrees. GM and Lyft will begin co-developing an on-demand network of self-driving cars as well as other car-sharing services. These are areas in which there has also been recent enormous interest—and investment—from competitors ranging from Tesla to Toyota, Ford to Fiat, and Google to Apple.[49] Initial efforts will probably be in self-driving taxis, buses, and big-rig trucks.[50] The U.S. government has pro-

posed investing $4 billion for self-driving cars, with the aim of ending human error in driving, which can be fatal.[51]

A world changer? A self-driving car traverses a parking lot at Google's headquarters in Mountain View, California, in early 2016. What do you think are the chances for self-driving cars realizing the high hopes predicted for them? ©Noah Berger/AFP/Getty Images

YOUR CALL

Clearly transportation is coming in for severe technological disruption in the coming years. But how safe do you think self-driving cars have to be before they can be deployed on the highway? How will self-driving cars affect the insurance industry? Will your costs for car insurance go up or down?

---

3. Shareholder, Customer, and Market Changes   Shareholders have begun to be more active in pressing for organizational change. Example: Some shareholders may form a **B corporation,** or *benefit corporation,* in which the company is legally required to adhere to socially beneficial practices, such as helping consumers, employees, or the environment. The largest B corp is Brazilian cosmetics manufacturer Natura, with $3 billion U.S. in annual revenues.[52]

Customers are also becoming more demanding, being more inclined to take their business elsewhere if they do not get what they want from a given company.

Example: Millennials have been found to be more focused on app-based shopping options, like those offered by Starbucks, where many customers can preorder their beverages through their phones before picking them up. Millennials also prefer specialty stores to department stores, so stores like Macy's have been trying out "stores within a store."[53]

The global economy continues to influence the way U.S. companies have to do business.[54] Perhaps the most momentous recent example occurred in June 2016, when voters in the United Kingdom voted for a British exit ("Brexit") from the European Union, setting off shockwaves around the world and causing stock markets to fall off a cliff. Among the possible long-term results were trade restrictions harmful to Britain, a deep recession, the separation of Scotland and Northern Ireland from the U.K., and other countries trying to leave the EU.[55]

Another example: Recently, Apple Inc. received 25% of its revenue from China. Imagine the shock to the company, then, when the major city of Beijing banned sales of Apple's iPhones 6 and 6 Plus, on the grounds that their design might have been lifted from that of a local Chinese-made phone. Earlier, Apple's online book and movie sales were shut down by Chinese censors.[56]

4. Social and Political Pressures Social events can create great pressures.

Example: Poor diet choices, such as reliance on sugary sodas, have led to nearly 70% of U.S. adults being overweight or obese, which in turn has produced an epidemic of type 2 diabetes. Soda tax proposals have failed in more than 30 cities and states in recent years, mainly because they are promoted for health reasons, and "Americans generally reject other people telling them what's healthy for them," as one report notes.[57] In 2016, the Philadelphia city council passed such an ordinance—despite a multimillion-dollar campaign against it by the beverage industry—because backers argued that the tax money would be used not to discourage sugar consumption but to pay for popular programs such as universal pre-kindergarten and improvements to parks and libraries.

Forces Originating inside the Organization Internal forces affecting organizations may be subtle, such as low job satisfaction, or more dramatic, such as constant labor-management conflict. Internal forces may be of the two following types: *human resources concerns* and *managers' behavior.*

1. Human Resources Concerns Is there a gap between the employees' needs and desires and the organization's needs and desires? Job dissatisfaction—as expressed through high absenteeism and turnover—can be a major signal of the need for change. Organizations may respond by addressing job design, reducing employees' role conflicts, and dealing with work overload, to mention a few matters.

Example: After Foxconn's Chinese facilities had problems with employee suicides, other Chinese companies like Pegatron implemented HR policies and practices to reduce employee work hours and overtime. Pegatron, which operates an iPhone assembly facility outside Shanghai, requires employees to scan ID cards, use face scanners, and walk through turnstiles in order to monitor compliance with new overtime regulations.[58]

2. Managers' Behavior Excessive conflict between managers and employees or between a company and its customers is another indicator that change is needed. Perhaps there is a personality conflict, so that an employee transfer may be needed. Or perhaps some interpersonal training is required.

Example: Facebook's leadership decided to respond to tech blog Gizmodo's conclusion that "curators of Facebook's 'trending topics' feature suppressed news about conservative events and from conservative sources," according to *The Wall Street Journal*. The company is now training employees "to identify and check their political leanings."[59] ●

10.2 Types and Models of Change

MAJOR
QUESTION

What are three types of change, and how is Lewin's approach designed to handle change?

THE BIG PICTURE

This section discusses the three types of change, from least threatening to most threatening: adaptive, innovative, and radically innovative. It also describes Lewin's three-stage change model: unfreezing, changing, and refreezing. Finally, it describes the systems approach to change: inputs, target elements of change, and outputs.

As we mentioned in Section 10.1, change may be forced upon an organization—*reactive change,* requiring you to make adjustments in response to problems or opportunities as they arise. Or an organization may try to get out in front of changes—*proactive change,* or *planned change,* which involves making carefully thought-out changes in anticipation of possible problems or opportunities.

As a manager, particularly one working for an American organization, you may be pressured to provide short-term, quick-fix solutions. But when applied to organizational problems, this approach usually doesn't work: Quick-fix solutions have little staying power.

What, then, do we need to understand in order to effectively manage organizational change? In this section, we discuss the following:

- Three kinds of change.
- Lewin's change model.
- The systems approach to change.

Three Kinds of Change: From Least Threatening to Most Threatening

Whether organizational change is administrative or technological, it can be *adaptive, innovative,* or *radically innovative,* depending on (1) the degree of complexity, cost, and uncertainty and (2) its potential for generating employee resistance.[60]

Least Threatening: Adaptive Change—"We've Seen Stuff Like This Before"

Adaptive change is reintroduction of a familiar practice—the implementation of a kind of change that has already been experienced within the same organization. This form of change is lowest in complexity, cost, and uncertainty. Because it is familiar, it is the least threatening to employees and thus will create the least resistance.

For example, during the annual Labor Day sale, a department store may ask its sales employees to work 12 hours a day instead of the usual 8. During tax-preparation time, the store's accounting department may imitate this same change in work hours. Although accounting employees are in a different department from sales employees, it's expected they wouldn't be terribly upset by the temporary change in hours, since they've seen it in effect elsewhere in the store.

Somewhat Threatening: Innovative Change—"This Is Something New for This Company"

Innovative change is the introduction of a practice that is new to the organization. This form of change involves moderate complexity, cost, and uncertainty. It is therefore apt to trigger some fear and resistance among employees.

For example, should a department store decide to adopt a new practice of competitors by staying open 24 hours a day, requiring employees to work flexible schedules, it may be felt as moderately threatening.

Very Threatening: Radically Innovative Change—"This Is a Brand-New Thing in Our Industry" **Radically innovative change** involves introducing a practice that is new to the industry. Because it is the most complex, costly, and uncertain, it will be felt as extremely threatening to managers' confidence and employees' job security and may well tear at the fabric of the organization.[61]

For example, Amazon is currently testing a new delivery system called Prime Air in Canada, the United Kingdom, and the Netherlands. The program uses drones to carry packages up to 5 pounds in 30 minutes or less. The goal is to safely operate the drones for a distance of 10 miles or more beyond the line of sight.[62]

Imagine the implications of companies using drones to distribute products.

Lewin's Change Model: Unfreezing, Changing, and Refreezing

Most theories of organizational change originated with the landmark work of social psychologist **Kurt Lewin.** Lewin developed a model with three stages—*unfreezing, changing,* and *refreezing*—to explain how to initiate, manage, and stabilize planned change.[63] *(See Figure 10.2.)*

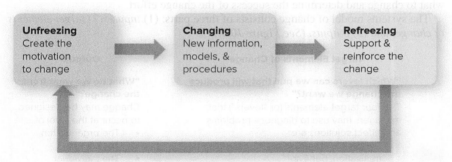

Unfreezing
Create the motivation to change

Changing
New information, models, & procedures

Refreezing
Support & reinforce the change

FIGURE 10.2
Lewin's model of change

1. "Unfreezing": Creating the Motivation to Change In the *unfreezing stage,* managers try to instill in employees the motivation to change, encouraging them to let go of attitudes and behaviors that are resistant to innovation. For this "unfreezing" to take place, employees need to become dissatisfied with the old way of doing things. Managers also need to reduce the barriers to change during this stage.

Example: Wireless handheld computers—personal digital assistants (PDAs)—are becoming established tools for health professionals, who use them to access patient records in hospital information systems. How well have they been accepted? Studies exploring nurses' perceptions about using PDAs in their daily patient practice found initial resistance, with some nurses concerned about the cost and short technological life cycle of these devices—the *unfreezing* stage.[64]

2. "Changing": Learning New Ways of Doing Things In the *changing stage,* employees need to be given the tools for change: new information, new perspectives, new models of behavior. Managers can help here by providing benchmarking results, role models, mentors, experts, and training. It's advisable, experts say, to convey the idea that change is a continuous learning process, not just a one-time event.[65]

Example: In the *changing* stage, nurses learning PDAs were allowed to continue their manual patient-charting systems while learning the PDA-accessible versions, but only for a limited time to avoid adding to their already heavy workloads. They were assisted with educational programs to help them learn and implement the new technology, programs that also stressed the need to protect confidential patient records.

3. "Refreezing": Making the New Ways Normal   In the *refreezing stage,* employees need to be helped to integrate the changed attitudes and behavior into their normal ways of doing things. Managers can assist by encouraging employees to exhibit the new change and then, through additional coaching and modeling, by reinforcing the employees in the desired change, as we'll discuss in Section 10.5.

Example: In the *refreezing* stage, as hospitals eliminated barriers that precluded the use of wireless networks, nurses learned to appreciate the usefulness of having a widely pervasive and portable technology, with its easier access to drug and diagnostic/laboratory reference applications and improved communications.

A Systems Approach to Change

Change creates additional change—that's the lesson of systems theory. Promoting someone from one group to another, for instance, may change the employee interactions in both (as from cordial to argumentative, or the reverse). Adopting a team-based structure may require changing the compensation system to pay bonuses based on team rather individual performance. A *systems approach* to change presupposes that any change, no matter how small, has a rippling effect throughout an organization.

A *system,* you'll recall from Chapter 2, is a set of interrelated parts that operate together to achieve a common purpose. The systems approach can be used to diagnose what to change and determine the success of the change effort.

The systems model of change consists of three parts: (1) *inputs,* (2) *target elements of change,* and (3) *outputs. (See Figure 10.3.)*

FIGURE 10.3

Systems model of change

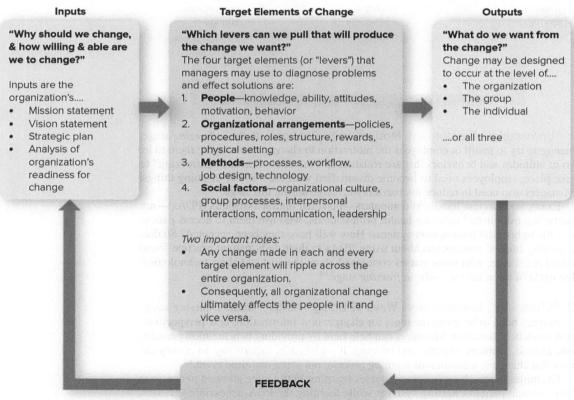

Inputs

"Why should we change, & how willing & able are we to change?"

Inputs are the organization's....
- Mission statement
- Vision statement
- Strategic plan
- Analysis of organization's readiness for change

Target Elements of Change

"Which levers can we pull that will produce the change we want?"
The four target elements (or "levers") that managers may use to diagnose problems and effect solutions are:
1. **People**—knowledge, ability, attitudes, motivation, behavior
2. **Organizational arrangements**—policies, procedures, roles, structure, rewards, physical setting
3. **Methods**—processes, workflow, job design, technology
4. **Social factors**—organizational culture, group processes, interpersonal interactions, communication, leadership

Two important notes:
- Any change made in each and every target element will ripple across the entire organization.
- Consequently, all organizational change ultimately affects the people in it and vice versa.

Outputs

"What do we want from the change?"
Change may be designed to occur at the level of....
- The organization
- The group
- The individual

....or all three

FEEDBACK

Source: Based on A. Kinicki and M. Fugate, Organizational Behavior: A Practical, Problem-Solving Approach *(New York: McGraw-Hill Education, 2016), Figure 16.4, p. 567, which was adapted from D. R. Fuqua and D. J. Kurpius, "Conceptual Models in Organizational Consultation,"* Journal of Counseling and Development, *July-August 1993, pp. 602–618; and D. A. Nadler and M. L. Tushman, "Organizational Frame Bending: Principles for Managing Reorientation,"* Academy of Management Executive, *August 1989, pp. 194–203.*

Inputs: "Why Should We Change, and How Willing and Able Are We to Change?" "Why change?" A systems approach always begins with the question of why change is needed at all—what the problem is that needs to be solved. (Example: "Why change? Because our designers are giving us terrible products that we can't sell.")

Whatever the answer, the systems approach must make sure the desired changes align with the organization's *mission statement, vision statement,* and *strategic plan—* subjects we discussed in Chapter 5:[66]

- **Mission statement:** This expresses the organization's reason for being (Southwest Airlines: "To give people the freedom to fly").

- **Vision statement:** This expresses what the organization wishes to become (Amazon: "To be earth's most customer-centric company, to build a place where people can come to find and discover anything they might want to buy online").

- **Strategic plan:** This sets the long-term goals and direction for an organization, based on the mission and vision statements (Example: "To increase revenue from existing and new customers rather than from acquiring other companies; thus, we intend to increase product quality and customer satisfaction so customers are more attracted to our merchandise"). A good plan, you'll recall from Chapter 6, reflects an analysis of the company's strengths, weakness, opportunities, and threats (SWOT).

A second question is "How willing and able are management and employees to make the necessary change?" **Readiness for change is defined as the beliefs, attitudes, and intentions of the organization's staff regarding the extent of the changes needed and how willing and able they are to implement them.**[67] Readiness has four components: (1) how strongly the company needs the proposed change, (2) how much the top managers support the change, (3) how capable employees are of handling it, and (4) how pessimistic or optimistic employees are about the consequences of the result.

Self-Assessment 10.2 will help you gauge your readiness for change. You can also use it to measure the readiness of an organization to which you belong.

≡ connect SELF-ASSESSMENT 10.2

What Is Your Readiness for Change?

If your instructor has assigned Self-Assessment 10.2 in Connect, think of a change at school, work, or another area of your life. Take Self-Assessment 10.2 to learn the extent of your readiness for change, or that of the organization in which the change needs to occur.

1. Of the four components, which is the lowest?

2. How do you think this result will affect the success of the particular change? Be specific.

3. Who seems to be most ready, you (components 1 and 2) or the organization (components 3 and 4)?

4. Given what the readiness measure tells you, what do you recommend to improve your and your organization's readiness?

Target Elements of Change: "Which Levers Can We Pull That Will Produce the Change We Want?" The target elements of change represent four levers that managers may use to diagnose problems (such as "Our designers are too inbred and don't look outside the company for ideas") and identify solutions (such as "We need new managers and new blood in the Design Group").

As Figure 10.3 shows, the four target elements of change (the four levers) are

1. People—their knowledge, ability, attitudes, motivation, and behavior.
2. Organizational arrangements—such as policies and procedures, roles, structure, rewards, and physical setting.
3. Methods—processes, work flow, job design, and technology.
4. Social factors—culture, group processes, interpersonal interactions, communication, and leadership.

Two things are important to realize:

- **Any change made in each and every target element will ripple across the entire organization.** For example, if a manager changes a system of *rewards* (part of the organizational arrangements) to reinforce team rather than individual performance, that change is apt to affect *organizational culture* (one of the social factors).

- **All organizational change ultimately affects the people in it and vice versa.** Thus, organizational change is more likely to succeed when managers carefully consider the prospective impact of a proposed change on the employees.

Outputs: "What Results Do We Want from the Change?"   Outputs represent the desired goals of a change, which should be consistent with the organization's strategic plan. Results may occur at the organizational, group, or individual level (or all three) but will be most difficult to effect at the organizational level, since changes will mostly likely affect a wide variety of target elements.

Feedback: "How Is the Change Working and What Alterations Need to Be Made?"   Not all changes work out well, of course, and organizations need to monitor their success. This is done by comparing the status of an output such as employee or customer satisfaction before the change to the same measurable output sometime after the change has been implemented.

Force-Field Analysis: "Which Forces Facilitate Change and Which Resist It?"   In most change situations being considered, there are forces acting for and against the change. **Force-field analysis is a technique to determine which forces could facilitate a proposed change and which forces could act against it.** The first step is to identify the positive forces (called *thrusters*) and the negative forces (called *counter-thrusters*). The second step is to remove the negative forces and then, if necessary, increase the positive forces. Although this may sound simple, it can be tricky to identify the forces at work.

Example: In late 2015, Procter & Gamble (P&G), maker of such household staples as Tide, Crest, and Gillette, reported that sales abroad were shrinking. Among the negative forces were the following: In countries overseas, the company had too many unprofitable products; smaller, nimbler rivals were taking away business; and currency fluctuations had made pricing difficult. Among the positive forces were these: P&G had extensive market data about customer needs, a strong enough financial position that it could forgo revenue in the short term, and an experienced management team that was ready to change. By exiting nearly 100 brands, narrowing its focus to 65 core brands, and forgoing sales in the short run, P&G could improve its profitability later. Thus, for example, in Mexico, the company shifted from selling cheap tissues to higher-priced variations, a move that cut sales but made the business more profitable.[68] ●

10.3 Organizational Development: What It Is, What It Can Do

MAJOR
QUESTION

What are the uses of OD, and how effective is it?

THE BIG PICTURE

Organizational development (OD) is a set of techniques for implementing change, such as managing conflict, revitalizing organizations, and adapting to mergers. OD has three steps: diagnosis, intervention, and evaluation. Four factors have been found to make OD programs effective.

Organizational development (OD) is a set of techniques for implementing planned change to make people and organizations more effective. Note the inclusion of people in this definition. OD focuses specifically on people in the change process. (Some scholars apply the term "organizational development" to techniques designed to improve *organizational* effectiveness and the term "change management" to techniques designed to improve *people* effectiveness—techniques that will help them, in one definition, to adopt "new mindsets, policies, practices, and behaviors to deliver organizational results.")[69]

Often OD is put into practice by a person known as a **change agent,** a consultant with a background in behavioral sciences who can be a catalyst in helping organizations deal with old problems in new ways.

What Can OD Be Used For?

OD can be used to address the following three matters.

1. Managing Conflict   Conflict is inherent in most organizations. Sometimes an OD expert, perhaps in the guise of an executive coach, can help advise on how to improve relationships within the organization.

Example: Difficult coworkers—"jerks at work"—can damage others' job performance and hurt a company's bottom line. Such "de-energizers" spread a dark cloud over everyone and leave you feeling deflated and depleted, says business professor Gretchen Spreitzer, who has done research in this area.[70] An organizational behavior specialist might be brought in to help buffer workers from the de-energizers by showing them how to limit interactions, make sure their own work is meaningful, and increase the time they spend with people who make them feel good, among other activities.

2. Revitalizing Organizations   Information technology is wreaking such change that nearly all organizations these days are placed in the position of having to adopt new behaviors in order to resist decline. OD can help by opening communication, fostering innovation, and dealing with stress.

Example: For IBM, confronting the relentless advance of digital technology means confronting the question "Can you grow in the new businesses faster than your older, lucrative businesses decline?" The company is responding by hiring thousands of designers to challenge IBM's conventional thinking (such as coming up with a product idea and trying to sell to the customers) with new thinking (such as identifying users' needs as a starting point).[71]

3. Adapting to Mergers   Mergers and acquisitions are associated with increased anxiety, stress, absenteeism, turnover, and decreased productivity.[72] What is the organizational fit between two disparate organizations, such as American Airlines and U.S. Airways, which merged in 2014? OD experts are often called upon in such situations to help integrate two firms with varying cultures, products, and procedures.

How OD Works

Like physicians, OD managers and consultants follow a medical-like model. (Or to use our more current formulation, they follow the rules of evidence-based management.) They approach the organization as if it were a sick patient, using *diagnosis, intervention,* and *evaluation*—"diagnosing" its ills, "prescribing" treatment or intervention, and "monitoring" or evaluating progress. If the evaluation shows that the procedure is not working effectively, the conclusions drawn are then applied (via a feedback loop) to refining the diagnosis, and the process starts again. *(See Figure 10.4.)*

FIGURE 10.4

The OD process

Sources: Adapted from W.L. French and C.H. Bell Jr., Organization Development: Behavioral Interventions for Organizational Improvement (Englewood Cliffs, NJ: Prentice Hall. 1978); and E. G Huse and T. G. Cummings, Organizational Development and Change, 3rd ed. (St. Paul: West, 1985).

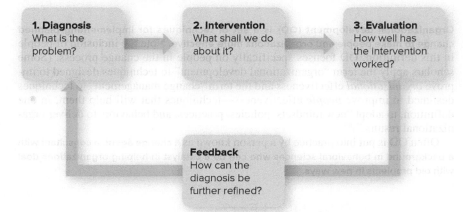

1. Diagnosis
What is the problem?

2. Intervention
What shall we do about it?

3. Evaluation
How well has the intervention worked?

Feedback
How can the diagnosis be further refined?

1. Diagnosis: What Is the Problem? To carry out the diagnosis, OD consultants or managers use some combination of questionnaires, surveys, interviews, meetings, records, and direct observation to ascertain people's attitudes and to identify problem areas.

2. Intervention: What Shall We Do about It? "Treatment," or **intervention, is the attempt to correct the diagnosed problems.** Often this is done using the services of an OD consultant who works in conjunction with management teams. Some OD activities for implementing planned change are communicating survey results to employees to engage them in constructive problem solving, observing employee communication patterns and teaching them skills to improve them, helping group members learn to function as a team, stimulating better cohesiveness among several work groups, and improving work technology or organizational design.

3. Evaluation: How Well Has the Intervention Worked? An OD program needs objective evaluation to see if it has done any good. Answers may lie in hard data about absenteeism, turnover, grievances, and profitability, which should be compared with earlier statistics. The change agent can use questionnaires, surveys, interviews, and the like to assess changes in employee attitudes.

4. Feedback: How Can the Diagnosis and Intervention Be Further Refined? If evaluation shows that the diagnosis was wrong or the intervention was not effective, the OD consultant or managers need to return to the beginning to rethink these two steps.

EXAMPLE

Organizational Development: Using OD to Make Money in the Restaurant Business

"Restaurants are so focused on the day-to-day business," says Eli Chait, "that they don't have time to grow the business."[73]

If you own or manage a restaurant, how can you improve your chances? You could hire a change agent such as Chait, now 28, who co-founded San Francisco–based Copilot Labs, a restaurant marketing analytics company, not long after graduating from the University of California, Berkeley.

Diagnosis: "What Is the Problem?" Organizational development is often focused on "big wins" (such as merging two companies), but it can also be used in a small business like a restaurant where small or incremental wins are important. Thus, an owner might want to know "Which is more effective—promoting our happy hours or promoting our daily deals?" (A "happy hour" is a period, such as 5 to 7 p.m., when drinks are served at reduced prices or with free snacks. "Daily deals" are meals served at discounted prices, such as two meals for the price of one for a particular menu item; such deals are frequently promoted by Groupon and similar marketing services.)

Intervention: "What Shall We Do about It?" Analyzing sales data over 19 months for one restaurant, Copilot found that, in Chait's words, "happy hour contributes specifically to the hours of the day that are otherwise the slowest, driving critical off-peak [customer] traffic that is so important to restaurants. The deal traffic, however, is distributed across several periods of time, many of which are already busy," making it less effective.[74]

Evaluation: "How Well Has the Intervention Worked?" The outcome would seem to be foreshadowed by Copilot's research, but it would be up to the change agent to evaluate an activity's success when put into practice. There are all kinds of factors, after all, that can affect restaurant traffic. For instance, more data don't always translate into better customer service.[75] Some days are busier than others (Valentine's Day—busy; Super Bowl Sunday—not busy; Mother's Day—depends on the restaurant), when a promotion wouldn't be effective.[76]

Feedback: "How Can the Diagnosis and Intervention Be Further Refined?" Depending on the results of evaluation—namely, the profitability of the process according to the kind of promotions—the change agent might feel the diagnosis and intervention deserve a revisit. And the process would start over.

YOUR CALL

One of the latest trends in business is "hyperlocal marketing"—building a large, dedicated, loyal base of local customers.[77] Do you think an organizational development approach can be helpful to this effort?

The Effectiveness of OD

Among organizations that have practiced organizational development are American Airlines, B.F. Goodrich, General Electric, Honeywell, ITT, Procter & Gamble, Prudential, Texas Instruments, and Westinghouse Canada—companies covering a variety of industries.

Research has found that OD is most apt to be successful under the following circumstances.

1. Multiple Interventions OD success stories tend to use multiple interventions. Goal setting, feedback, recognition and rewards, training, participation, and challenging job design have had good results in improving performance and satisfaction.[78] Combined interventions have been found to work better than single interventions.[79]

2. Management Support OD is more likely to succeed when top managers give the OD program their support and are truly committed to the change process and the desired goals of the change program.[80] Using employee feedback during the change process is one way to demonstrate this support.[81]

3. Goals Geared to Both Short- and Long-Term Results Change programs are more successful when they are oriented toward achieving both short-term and long-term results. Managers should not engage in organizational change for the sake of change. Change efforts should produce positive results.[82]

4. OD Is Affected by Culture OD effectiveness is affected by cross-cultural considerations. Thus, an OD intervention that worked in one country should not be blindly applied to a similar situation in another country.[83] ●

Team building. One technique for implementing change is team building. Teams are often diverse in gender, age, ethnicity, and educational background and experience. Would you prefer to work with a highly diverse team of people?
©BananaStock/PictureQuest/Getty Images RF

10.4   Promoting Innovation within the Organization

What do I need to know to encourage innovation?

THE BIG PICTURE

Innovation may be a product innovation or a process innovation, a core (incremental) innovation or a transformational (radical) innovation. Two myths about innovation are that it happens in a "Eureka!" moment and that it can be systematized. Ways to encourage innovation are by providing the organizational culture, the people, the resources, and the reward system. To make innovation happen, you need to recognize problems and opportunities, gain allies, overcome employee resistance, and execute well.

If **invention** is creating or making up something new and **creativity** is the act of developing new and imaginative ideas into reality, innovation is something else. *Innovation,* as we've said earlier in the book, is the activity of creating new ideas and converting them into *useful applications*—specifically, new goods and services.

"You need creativity and invention," says Procter & Gamble's former CEO A. G. Lafley, "but until you can connect the creativity to the customer in the form of a product or service that meaningfully changes their lives, I would argue you don't have innovation."[84] The spirit of innovation is essential to keeping an organization vital and maintaining a competitive advantage. Otherwise, the innovation will come from your competitors, forcing you to scramble to catch up—if you can.

Innovation is more likely to occur when organizations have the proper culture, resources, and reward systems to support it. We now take a closer look into innovation and how it can be encouraged within organizations.

How Does Failure Impede Innovation?

"You learn more from failure than you do from success," says Lafley, "but the key is to fail early, fail cheaply, and don't make the same mistake twice."[85] Lafley, who doubled sales and quadrupled profits for P&G, admits to having had "my fair share of failure. But you have to get past the disappointment and blame and really understand what happened and why it happened."[86]

Lafley is comfortable with the idea of learning from failure, but many people are not. They're reluctant to experiment, they blame others, and they refuse to recognize that not all failures are of equal seriousness. All of these can detract from an organization's ability to learn from its mistakes, as the table below indicates. *(See Table 10.1.)*

TABLE 10.1

Factors That Reduce an Organization's Ability to Learn from Failure

EMPLOYEES . . .
1. Play the "blame game," blaming an individual when failures are due to internal or external matters
2. Suffer "self-serving bias"
3. Don't recognize failures are not created equal; some may be preventable, some uncontrollable
4. Are afraid to discuss failures and take risks; the company isn't a learning organization
5. Are reluctant to experiment

Source: Adapted from A. C. Edmondson, "Strategies for Learning from Failure," Harvard Business Review, April 2011, pp. 151–176.

Two Myths about Innovation

Two myths about innovation that need to be dispelled are the following.

Myth No. 1: Innovation Happens in a "Eureka!" Moment   Many people think that innovation often happens like a bolt from the blue. In this view, innovation happens as a "Eureka!" or "Aha!" moment of discovery, like the instant revelation about the law of gravity supposedly experienced by Sir Isaac Newton under a tree when an apple fell on his head. Most of the time, however, innovation is the product of hard work and dedication, "forged by a mixed bag of coworkers from up, down, and across an organization, sitting and wrangling it out in the trenches," in the words of Jack and Suzy Welch.[87]

Myth No. 2: Innovation Can Be Systematized   Lots of people also believe that innovation can be systematized—made a codified and standardized process that can be designed to always yield fruitful results. Obviously, if this could be done, many companies would be doing it. The problem with innovation, however, is that there are too many challenges associated with it, which makes success unpredictable, although it's possible to establish cultural and other conditions (as discussed next) that increase the likelihood of a payoff.

The Seeds of Innovation: Starting Point for Experimentation and Inventiveness

Former Microsoft employee Scott Berkun, author of *The Myths of Innovation,* has identified six **seeds of innovation, the starting point for organizational innovation.** They are as follows:[88]

1. **Hard work in a specific direction.** Most innovations come from dedicated people diligently working to solve a well-defined problem, hard work that can span many years.
   Example: This was certainly the case with Boeing's long endeavor to build and fly the Dreamliner.

2. **Hard work with direction change.** Innovations frequently occur when people change their approach to solving a problem. In other words, hard work closes some doors and opens others.
   Example: Supergerms have developed that resist traditional antibacterial treatments. But researchers exploring whether garments might be developed that clean themselves are also testing whether minute flecks of silver and copper embedded in cotton fabric might not only repel dirt but also degrade superbugs.[89]

3. **Curiosity.** Innovations can begin when people are curious about something of interest to them, which leads to experimentation and inventiveness.
   Example: The GoPro camera was invented by a surfer, Nick Woodman, who wondered if there was a way to capture video of his amazing rides. His wearable camera captured new angles never before recorded on film.[90]

4. **Wealth and money.** Innovations frequently occur because an organization or an individual simply wants to make money. Being near bankruptcy, for instance, drove Fiat, the Italian auto company, to look for innovative ways to cut costs and grow its market share in the United States. This is why Fiat took a stake in Chrysler in return for imparting its knowledge of small-car technology.[91]
   Example: Because its old Windows software licensing business model is fading, Microsoft has been trying to move into other businesses, such as cloud

and mobile computing. As a result, in 2016 it acquired the professional social network LinkedIn Corp. in a deal that, as one writer says, "attempts to put itself at the center of people's business lives." Microsoft "largely missed out on the consumer Web boom dominated by the likes of Google and Facebook," and with this new deal it hopes to pull ahead in the social tools race—in this case, with social tools for professionals.[92]

5. **Necessity.** Many innovations grow from the desire to achieve something or to complete a task that is needed to accomplish a broader goal.

Example: Microsoft took an employee-driven grassroots idea called the "Microsoft Garage," which draws on engineers, marketers, testers, or employees in other disciplines, and "we all can come together with ideas, make things and fail, learn and try again," says senior quality manager Todd Rawlings.[93] The ideas "come from people's passions or start from problems." The purpose of The Garage is to make sure Microsoft stays on the cutting edge in innovation, certainly a necessity for a technology company.

6. **Combination of seeds.** Many innovations occur as a result of multiple factors.
Example: "Innovation these days is in dire need of some innovations," says business reporter Thomas Lee. Companies seeking breakthroughs "use the same mind-numbing mush of clichés to encourage creativity: hackathons, innovation centers, white boards, prizes, etc."[94] San Jose software maker Adobe Systems (maker of PhotoShop) is trying something else: Called Kickbox, the approach "is something of a game that allows any of its employees to develop an idea—whether or not the idea is related to the employee's expertise or regular work responsibility," Lee says. Employees who enter Kickbox get a prepaid $1,000 debit card to spend to validate the idea, and they do not need to get managers to okay the project before proceeding. In addition, they can try the idea out with actual customers.

Types of Innovation: Product or Process, Core or Transformational

Innovations may be of the following two types.

Product versus Process Innovations   As a manager, you may need to improve your organization's product or service itself; this is generally a technological innovation. Or you may need to improve the process by which the product or service is created, manufactured, or distributed; this is generally a managerial innovation.

More formally, a **product innovation is a change in the appearance or the performance of a product or a service or the creation of a new one. A process innovation is a change in the way a product or service is conceived, manufactured, or disseminated.**

Today, innovation is about much more than new products. It is about reinventing business processes and building entirely new markets that meet untapped customer needs.

Core versus Transformational Innovations   An innovation may be small or large, incremental or radical. The difference is in modifying versus replacing existing products or services. That is, you might have **core innovations—the optimizing of products or services for existing customers,** as when Procter & Gamble modified a liquid detergent to make it available as a concentrated powder in a pouch. Or you might have **transformational innovations—the invention of breakthrough products or services that don't exist yet and that are aimed at creating brand new markets and customers.** Example: Alphabet, Google's parent, is experimenting with sending off high-altitude balloons, such as one launched into Sri Lankan airspace, in an ambitious plan to beam high-speed Internet to remote areas.[95]

What Makes a Successful Start-up?

According to the Ewing Marion Kauffman Foundation, which works to further understanding of entrepreneurship, the vast majority of entrepreneurs (called *replicative entrepreneurs*) are those with small businesses that replicate, or duplicate, products and services already in existence, such as restaurants and dry cleaners. Less common are those entrepreneurs *(innovative entrepreneurs)* who pioneer never-seen-before products and services or production methods, such as eBay.[96]

Entrepreneurship: Exploiting Niche Opportunities. Some replicative entrepreneurs, however, simply do things better and faster. One economist, Amar V. Bhidé (pronounced *"Beh-dee"*), suggests that many successful entrepreneurs start out not by having radical ideas but by making a small modification in what somebody else is doing.[97] Indian drugmakers, for instance, are now targeting niche markets by developing new treatments for ailments that were ignored by big American and European pharmaceutical companies.[98]

That is, replicative entrepreneurs see a niche opportunity—one in which the company they are working for is already involved, or a supplier or customer is involved. "And the person jumps [into a new business] with very little preparation and analysis," says Bhidé, "but with direct firsthand knowledge of the profitability of that opportunity—and pretty much does what somebody else is already doing, but does it better and faster."

And "better and faster" seems to be the main difference. Usually, such entrepreneurs don't have anything in the way of technology or concept that differentiates them from other businesses. "They just work harder, hustle for customers, and know that the opportunity may not last for more than six or eight months," says Bhidé. "But they expect to make a reasonable return on those six to eight months. And along the way they'll figure out something else that will keep the business going."

Tolerance for Ambiguity. Another quality of entrepreneurs is "a tolerance for ambiguity," Bhidé says. They are willing to jump into things when it's hard to even imagine what the possible outcomes will be, going ahead in the absence of information, very much capital, or even a very novel idea.

An example of a start-up that fits these criteria is Build-a-Bear Workshop, which offers mall customers a make-your-own stuffed animal experience, choosing from models of teddy bears, bunnies, dogs, and the like, then adding "a unique personality" from hundreds of teddy bear–sized outfits and accessories.

The idea came to Maxine Clark, a former department store executive, in 1997, when she was shopping with a friend who collected Ty Beanie Babies. When they couldn't find anything new, the friend said, "We could make one." Says Clark, "Her words gave me the idea to create a company that would allow people to create their own customized stuffed animals. . . . Build-a-Bear Workshop would be like a theme park factory in a mall."

There were no formal focus groups, but from the beginning she relied on children for advice. "Kids have insights and offer inspiration by looking at the world differently," says Clark.[99]

The Illusions of Entrepreneurship. Think you'd like to create a start-up yourself and make yourself rich? "One-third of new ventures close within two years, half within five years," says a *Bloomberg Businessweek* writer. "Only one in four is still around 15 years after opening day."[100] The biggest myth, says Case Western professor Scott Shane, is that entrepreneurs believe "the growth and performance of their start-ups depends more on their entrepreneurial talent than on the businesses they choose."[101]

Over a 20-year period, he found, about 4% of all the start-ups in the computer and office equipment industry made *Inc.* magazine's Inc. 500 list of America's fastest-growing companies. But only about 0.005% of start-ups in the hotel and motel industries made that list, and 0.007% of start-ups in eating and drinking establishments. "So that means the odds that you make the *Inc.* 500," Shane says, "are 840 times higher if you start a computer company than if you start a hotel or motel."[102]

YOUR CALL

Suppose you want to be your own boss. What "better and faster" niche opportunity do you see? Assuming it's not a computer company that you're starting, what do you think your chances are of being successful?

How Companies Can Foster Innovation: Seven Components

If you're going to not just survive but prevail as a manager, you need to know how to make innovation happen within an organization. Here we offer an **innovation system,** which is defined as "a coherent set of interdependent processes and structures that dictates how the company searches for novel problems and solutions, synthesizes ideas into a business concept and product designs, and selects which projects get funded."[103] The components of the innovation system are shown on next page.[104] *(See Table 10.2.)*

TABLE 10.2

Creating an Innovation System: Seven Parts

1. Create an innovation strategy.

2. Get commitment from top managers.

3. Foster an innovation culture and climate.

4. Establish the required structure and processes.

5. Obtain the necessary human capital.

6. Institute the necessary human resource policies, practices, and procedures.

7. Obtain the appropriate resources.

1. Create an Innovation Strategy A successful innovation effort requires an *innovation strategy* by which a company integrates its innovation activities into its business strategies. This effort will encourage top managers to invest resources in innovation and employees to commit to it.[105]

Example: Corning makes everything from glassware to specialized components for electronic displays, life sciences instruments, and telecommunications systems. The company's business strategy is to sell key components that will improve the performance of its customers' complex system products. To execute this strategy, Corning has launched innovation efforts by investing heavily in long-term research to put itself at the leading edge of glass and materials science.[106]

TABLE 10.3

Top Organizations in 2016 Whose Cultures Strongly Encouraged Innovation

Buzzfeed (news)

Facebook

CVS Health

Uber

Netflix

Amazon

Apple

Alphabet

Black Lives Matter (race)

Taco Bell

Robinhood (stock trading)

Universal Studios

Huawei (smartphones)

Cyanogen (free Android)

inMobi (mobile ads)

Source: Data from "The World's Most Innovative Companies 2016," Fast Company, February 16, 2016.

2. Get Commitment from Top Managers Strategic goals are unlikely to be achieved without the commitment of top managers.

Example: PepsiCo CEO Indra Nooyi is driving innovation by prioritizing design, as expressed in her hiring of the company's first-ever chief design officer, Mauro Pircini, formerly of 3M. Nooyi gave Pircini what he asked for—"resources, a design studio, and a seat at the [top decision makers'] table." Now, she says, "our teams are pushing design through the entire system, from product creation, to packaging and labeling, to how a product looks on the shelf, to how consumers interact with it."[107]

3. Foster an Innovative Culture and Climate Innovation requires a corporate culture and climate that permit experimentation, risk taking, and tolerance for failure.[108] An organizational culture, as we said in Chapter 8, is defined as the set of shared, taken-for-granted, implicit assumptions that a group holds and that determines how it perceives, thinks about, and reacts to its various environments. An organizational culture that doesn't just allow but *celebrates* failure is vital in fostering innovation. Most new ideas will fail. Only a few will be successful. But as Pixar president Ed Catmull says, "Mistakes aren't a necessary evil. They aren't evil at all. They are an inevitable consequence of doing something new . . . and should be seen as valuable."[109]

Example: After Extended Stay America went through bankruptcy, employees suffered from job insecurity and were loath to make decisions that might cost the company money. New CEO Jim Donald told them they needed to take calculated risks and generate daring ideas to improve customer service and profitability. To encourage them to let go of fear of failure, Donald distributed Monopoly-style "Get Out of Jail Free" cards to the 9,000 employees, which they could turn in "when they took a big risk on behalf of the company—no questions asked." A few results: A California hotel manager used her "Get Out of Jail" card to justify grabbing 20 guest business cards from a fishbowl in the lobby of a rival hotel as a way of finding prospective customers. A New Jersey manager used it to try cold-calling a movie-production company filming in the area, leading to the crew's booking $250,000 in accommodations at her hotel.[110]

If an organization doesn't encourage this kind of risk taking, that organization won't become a superstar in innovation. The top 15 superstars for 2016 designated by *Fast Company* magazine are shown in the table at left. *(See Table 10.3.)*

4. Establish the Required Structure and Processes   Organizational structure and internal processes can promote innovation if they foster collaboration, cross-functional communication, and agility. In particular, organic structures (described in Chapter 8) are often better suited than mechanistic ones for innovation.

Example: Juniper Networks, a leader in computer network integration, concluded that its formal organizational structure didn't lead to the kinds of rich interactions and conversations that made innovation thrive. "We were not integrating diverse expertise and experience across engineering, infrastructure, and sales teams the way we could when we were a small company," says Vince Molinaro, executive vice president of worldwide sales. Accordingly, Juniper changed its structure.[111]

5. Obtain the Necessary Human Capital   Human capital, we said (see Chapter 9), is the economic or productive potential of employee knowledge, experience, and actions. Some employee characteristics that help organizations innovate are creativity, creative-thinking skills, intrinsic motivation, and international work experience, as well as the quality of the relationship between managers and employees.[112] Research also shows that work teams are more creative when team members have different sets of knowledge and experience.[113]

Example: General Electric has hired hundreds of software engineers to develop its analytic and Big Data capabilities, with the strategic goal of becoming a top-10 software company by 2020.[114]

6. Institute Necessary Human Resource Policies, Practices, and Procedures   Companies that are able to make human resource policies, practices, and procedures consistent with, and reinforcing of, the other five components we just described are more likely to be innovative and to have higher financial performance.[115]

Example: Bringing people together from different disciplines to train and to brainstorm ideas can foster the collaboration needed for innovation. For instance, the University of Michigan's Biointerfaces Institute tries to locate materials scientists, chemical engineers, biomechanical engineers, and medical researchers near each other. The resulting collaborations produced a blood test that is able to both capture and culture cancer cells for faster cancer diagnoses.[116]

7. Obtain the Appropriate Resources   If top managers want innovation, they must dedicate resources to its development, whether people, dollars, time, energy, knowledge, focus, or all of these.

Example: To help employees be innovative, Heineken spent $2 million on training employees in beer basics.[117]

Achieving Success through Innovation and Collaboration: Tesla's Culture of Openness

EXAMPLE

Who are the greatest innovators? For three years, it was Apple, Google, and Amazon atop Booz & Co.'s annual 1,000 global "Most Innovative Companies" list. Then in 2015, Amazon dropped from third to fifth place, and electric carmaker Tesla Motors of Palo Alto, California, rose to claim the new third spot.[118]

Most of the top five companies on the "Most Innovative" list are information technology and electronics companies (Apple, Google, Samsung, and Amazon). And they are the biggest spenders on research and development. (Google, for instance, spent $9.8 billion in 2015; Samsung spent $14.1 billion.) Tesla spent a mere half a billion dollars on R&D, yet it not only became No. 3 on the Booz & Co. list, it was also named to No. 1 on *Forbes*

magazine's 2015 "World's Most Innovative Companies" list and No. 4 on *MIT Technology Review*'s "50 Smartest Companies 2016" list, and the Tesla Model S luxury electric car was named No. 1 on *Consumer Reports*'s list of best cars for 2015.[119]

Disrupting Mobility. Tesla was founded in 2003 by South Africa–born Elon Musk, currently "the most well-known innovative business leader in America," according to one technology observer.[120] Earlier, in 1998, Musk disrupted e-commerce by creating PayPal, the widely deployed and secure payment system. In 2002, he developed SpaceX for launching rockets and spacecraft, with the idea of enabling people to live on other planets. (Musk himself wants to "die on Mars.") He has also outlined a high-speed transit system called Hyperloop, designed to go the 400 miles from Los Angeles to San Francisco in 35 minutes. With Tesla, says one report, "Musk is focused on disrupting mobility."[121]

A Tech Company That Makes Cars. Tesla is closer to being a technology company than a traditional automobile company, or "a tech company that happens to make cars."[122] By being born into the San Francisco–to–San Jose corridor of tech innovation known as Silicon Valley, it learned to design and build its vision of mobility by drawing on ideas and employees from leading technology companies of the area. For instance, at a time when traditional car builders took four years to complete a model change, Tesla was able to have an immediate competitive advantage by deploying over-the-air software updates to upgrade features or address recall problems in short order. And because Tesla sells cars directly to customers, rather than through third-party dealers, the changes could be made immediately.[123] (Some of the automatic updates may enable Teslas to become self-driving at some point.)[124]

By avoiding the path of the traditional automotive industry, Tesla also avoided being constrained by its traditional thought processes—as shown by the fact that a Tesla automobile has a "frunk"—a trunk in the front—with the battery located underneath the seats, whereas other electric cars reflected the design of combustion-engine vehicles.[125] In addition, Tesla avoided the customary path of new carmakers of going after the low-end, price-sensitive customers with cheaper technology; instead, it targeted the high-end buyers capable of spending thousands of dollars on a car that was a sexy status symbol and fun to drive. "While Toyota was busy making something affordable that competed with other vehicles in its class," pointed out one report, "Tesla Motors claimed the elite niche of luxury sports cars and

catapulted ahead with an entirely new game."[126] And all this with *no* marketing department.

Innovation and Collaboration. The culture of Tesla has been described by writer Jacqueline Zhou as being "innovative and collaborative."[127] Four tips she offers for "going Tesla" and creating an open culture to support innovation are the following.

1. **Share information.** In many companies, employees often withhold information, even between teams in the same department. Tesla has removed all such "knowledge silos." "The more you share," says Zhou, "the more others will share with you. This increases efficiency by reducing redundancies in work between teams."

2. **Don't immediately dismiss new ideas.** "By avoiding immediately dismissing ideas, you are showing those in your community that ideas are valued and considered even if they cannot be immediately implemented," says Zhou. "Others will be more willing to share ideas if they know that their ideas matter."

3. **Help others without expecting anything back.** "When someone comes to you for help, you should always say yes, if you can. In the end people will be more willing to help you."

4. **Credit others.** "We rarely accomplish things on our own, and if we can show appreciation for the help that we've been given, it shows that we value the collaboration."

YOUR CALL

Tesla's innovative, collaborative culture even extends to making its patents available to the rest of the industry, in hopes that other companies will join the expansion of electric vehicles. What other components of an innovation system have been used by Tesla?

Executing Well   What finally will make or break an organization's attempts at bringing new products and services to market is *execution*—the process, as we stated back in Chapter 6, of discussing hows and whats and of using questioning, analysis, and follow-through to achieve the results promised and ensure accountability.[128] Execution requires organizations to effectively manage people, groups, and organizational processes and systems in the pursuit of innovation.

In the end, then, the innovation process must be *managed*. This is what is precisely what is done at Apple, Google, and other top innovative companies.

Research tells us that companies are unlikely to innovate unless the culture and climate support it. How would you know if a potential employer had an innovative climate? You can find out by completing Self-Assessment 10.3. ●

☰ connect SELF-ASSESSMENT 10.3

How Innovative Is the Organizational Climate?

The following survey was designed to assess the innovation climate of your organization. Please be prepared to answer these questions if your instructor has assigned Self-Assessment 10.3 in Connect.

1. To what extent does the company have an innovative climate?

2. Based on your survey scores, what advice would you give to management if they wanted to increase innovation? Be specific.

10.5 The Threat of Change: Managing Employee Fear and Resistance

MAJOR QUESTION

How are employees threatened by change, and how can I help them adjust?

THE BIG PICTURE

This section discusses the causes of resistance to change and the reasons employees fear change.

As we mentioned in Section 10.1, change may be forced upon an organization—*reactive* change, requiring you to make changes in response to problems or opportunities as they arise. Or an organization may try to get out in front of changes—*proactive* change, or planned change, which involves making carefully thought-out changes in anticipation of possible problems or opportunities.

What, then, are effective ways to manage organizational change and employees' fear and resistance to it? In this section, we discuss the following:

- The causes of resistance to change.
- Why employees resist change.

The Causes of Resistance to Change

Resistance to change is an emotional/behavioral response to real or imagined threats to an established work routine. Resistance can be as subtle as passive resignation and as overt as deliberate sabotage. As you will learn, change experts believe that resistance does not primarily reside within the individual but instead is a result of the context in which change occurs.[129]

Resistance can be considered to be the interaction of three causes. *(See Figure 10.5.)* They are

1. Employee characteristics
2. Change agent characteristics
3. The change agent–employee relationship.

For example, an employee's resistance is partly based on his or her perception of change, which is influenced by the attitudes and behaviors exhibited by the change agent and the level of trust between the change agent and the employee.

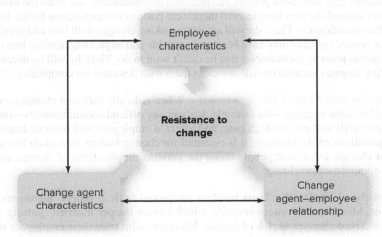

FIGURE 10.5

A model of resistance to change

Source: Adapted from R. Kreitner and A. Kinicki. Organizational Behavior, 9th ed. (Burr Ridge, IL: McGraw-Hill/Irwin, 2010), p. 549.

Let us consider these three sources.

1. Employee Characteristics   The characteristics of a given employee consist of his or her individual differences (discussed in Chapter 11), actions and inactions, and perceptions of change. The next section discusses a variety of employee characteristics related to resistance to change. One of them involves a person's level of adaptability or flexibility.[130] How adaptable are you? You can find out by taking Self-Assessment 10.4.

---

connect SELF-ASSESSMENT 10.4

How Adaptable Are You?

The following survey was designed to assess your level of adaptability. Please be prepared to answer these questions if your instructor has assigned Self-Assessment 10.4 in Connect.

1. What is your level of adaptability? Are you surprised by the results?
2. Based on your scores, identify three things you can do to increase your level of adaptability. Explain.
3. Why would recruiters prefer to hire adaptable people?

---

2. Change Agent Characteristics   The characteristics of the change agent—the individual who is a catalyst in helping organizations change—also consist of his or her individual differences, experiences, actions and inactions, and perceptions of change. Such characteristics that might contribute to employee resistance to change include leadership style, personality, tactfulness, sense of timing, awareness of cultural traditions or group relationships, and ability to empathize with the employee's perspective.[131]

3. Change Agent–Employee Relationship   As you might expect, resistance to change is reduced when change agents and employees have a trusting relationship—faith in each other's intentions. Mistrust, on the other hand, encourages secrecy, which begets deeper mistrust, and can doom an otherwise well-conceived change.[132]

Ten Reasons Employees Resist Change

Whether changes are adaptive, innovative, or radically innovative, employees may resist change for all kinds of reasons. Ten of the leading reasons for not accepting change are as follows.[133]

1. Individuals' Predisposition toward Change   How people react to change depends a lot on how they learned to handle change and ambiguity as children. One person's parents may have been patient, flexible, and understanding, and from the time the child was weaned she may have learned there were positive compensations for the loss of immediate gratification. Thus, she will associate making changes with love and approval. Another person's parents may have been unreasonable and unyielding, forcing him to do things (piano lessons, for example) that he didn't want to do. Thus, he will be distrustful of making changes because he will associate them with demands for compliance.[134]

2. Surprise and Fear of the Unknown   When radically different changes are introduced without warning—for example, without any official announcements—the office rumor mill will go into high gear, and affected employees will become fearful of the implications of the changes. It is essential for change leaders to explain the rationale for change, to educate people about the personal implications of change, and to garner commitment to change.[135]

3. Climate of Mistrust   Trust involves reciprocal faith in others' intentions and behavior. Mistrust encourages secrecy, which causes deeper mistrust, putting even well-conceived changes at risk of failure. Managers who trust their employees make the change process an open, honest, and participative affair. All told, employees who feel fairly treated by managers during change are less likely to resist.[136]

4. Fear of Failure   Intimidating changes on the job can cause employees to doubt their capabilities. Self-doubt erodes self-confidence and cripples personal growth and development.

5. Loss of Status or Job Security   Administrative and technological changes that threaten to alter power bases or eliminate jobs—as often happens during corporate restructurings that threaten middle-management jobs—generally trigger strong resistance.

6. Peer Pressure   Even people who are not themselves directly affected by impending changes may actively resist in order to protect the interests of their friends and coworkers.

7. Disruption of Cultural Traditions or Group Relationships   Whenever individuals are transferred, promoted, or reassigned, it can disrupt existing cultural and group relationships.

Example: Traditionally, Sony Corp. promoted insiders to new positions. When an outsider, Howard Stringer, was named as the next chairman and CEO and six corporate officers were asked to resign, creating a majority board of foreigners, the former CEO, Nobuyuki Idei, worried the moves might engender strong employee resistance.[137]

8. Personality Conflicts   Just as a friend can get away with telling us something we would resent hearing from an adversary, the personalities of change agents can breed resistance.

9. Lack of Tact or Poor Timing   Introducing changes in an insensitive manner or at an awkward time can create employee resistance. Employees are more apt to accept changes when managers effectively explain their value, as, for example, in demonstrating their strategic purpose to the organization.

10. Nonreinforcing Reward Systems   Employees are likely to resist when they can't see any positive rewards from proposed changes, as, for example, when one is asked to work longer hours without additional compensation.

Where do you stand on change? Do you tend to accept and embrace change, or do you have tendencies to resist it? The following self-assessment will provide feedback on your attitudes toward change. If your scores indicate resistance, you should consider what can be done to move your attitudes in a more positive direction. •

Change is hard. Lots of people don't like change. Among the reasons are one's individual predisposition toward change, surprise and fear of the unknown, mistrust, loss of status or job security, and poor timing. Do some of these reasons seem particularly to apply to you? When was the last time you had to wrestle with momentous changes? ©Lev Dolgachov/Alamy RF

▤ connect SELF-ASSESSMENT 10.5

Assessing Your Resistance to Change

The following survey was designed to assess your resistance to change. Please be prepared to answer these questions if your instructor has assigned Self-Assessment 10.5 in Connect.

1.   Are you more or less willing to accept change? Discuss.

2.   Based on your scores, identify three things you can do to lower your resistance to change. These changes may involve new thoughts or beliefs or the display of new behaviors.

3.   What questions might a recruiter ask during an interview to determine whether or not you tend to resist change? What would be your answers?

Key Points

10.1 The Nature of Change in Organizations

- Among supertrends shaping the future of business: (1) The marketplace is becoming more segmented and moving toward more niche products. (2) More competitors are offering targeted products, requiring faster speed-to-market. (3) Some traditional companies may not survive radical change. (4) China, India, and other offshore suppliers are changing the way we work. (5) Knowledge, not information, is becoming the new competitive advantage.

- Two types of change are reactive and proactive. Reactive change is making changes in response to problems or opportunities as they arise. Proactive change involves making carefully thought-out changes in anticipation of possible or expected problems or opportunities.

- Forces for change may consist of forces outside the organization or inside it. (1) External forces consist of four types: demographic characteristics; technological advancements; shareholder, customer, and market changes; and social and political pressures. (2) Internal forces may be of two types: human resources concerns and managers' behavior.

10.2 Types and Models of Change

- Whether organizational change is administrative or technological, it can be adaptive, innovative, or radically innovative, depending on (1) the degree of complexity, cost, and uncertainty and (2) its potential for generating employee resistance.

- Adaptive change, the least threatening, is reintroduction of a familiar practice. Innovative change is the introduction of a practice that is new to the organization. Radically innovative change, the most threatening, involves introducing a practice that is new to the industry.

- Kurt Lewin's change model has three stages—unfreezing, changing, and refreezing—to explain how to initiate, manage, and stabilize planned change. (1) In the unfreezing stage, managers try to instill in employees the motivation to change. (2) In the changing stage, employees need to be given the tools for change, such as new information. (3) In the refreezing stage, employees need to be helped to integrate the changed attitudes and behavior into their normal behavior.

- A systems approach to change consists of three parts: inputs, target elements of change, and outputs, plus a feedback loop. (1) Inputs answer two questions: Why should we change? How willing and able are we to change? To answer the first question requires the organization's mission statement, vision statement, and strategic plan. To answer the second question requires knowing an organization's readiness for change—the staff's beliefs, attitudes, and intentions as to the extent of the changes needed and how willing and able they are to implement them. (2) Target elements of change represent the four levers that managers need to use to diagnose problems—people, organizational arrangements, methods, and social factors. (3) Outputs represent the desired goals of change, which should be consistent with the organization's strategic plan. (4) There is a feedback loop to determine how the change is working and what alterations need to be made.

- Force-field analysis is a technique to determine which forces could facilitate a proposed change and which forces could act against it.

10.3 Organizational Development: What It Is, What It Can Do

- Organizational development (OD) is a set of techniques for implementing planned change to make people and organizations more effective. Often OD is put into practice by a change agent, a consultant with a background in behavioral sciences who can be a catalyst in helping organizations deal with old problems in new ways. OD can be used to manage conflict, revitalize organizations, and adapt to mergers.

- The OD process follows a three-step process: (1) Diagnosis attempts to ascertain the problem. (2) Intervention is the attempt to correct the diagnosed problems. (3) Evaluation attempts to find out how well the intervention worked.
- Four factors that make OD work successfully are (1) multiple interventions are used; (2) top managers give the OD program their support; (3) goals are geared to both short- and long-term results; and (4) OD is affected by culture.

10.4 Promoting Innovation within the Organization

- Invention is creating or making up something new. Creativity is the act of developing new or imaginative ideas into reality. Innovation, by contrast, is the activity of creating new ideas and converting them into useful applications—specifically, new goods and services.
- Two myths about innovation are (1) innovation happens in a "Eureka!" moment and (2) innovation can be systematized.
- The starting point for organizational innovation involves the six seeds of innovation: (1) Innovation comes from dedicated people working to solve a well-defined problem; (2) innovations often occur when people change their approach to solving a problem; (3) innovations can begin when people are curious about something of interest to them; (4) innovation happens because an organization wants to make money; (5) many innovations grow from the desire to achieve something or complete a task that is needed to accomplish a broader goal; and (6) many innovations occur as a result of multiple factors.
- Innovations may be a product innovation or a process innovation. A product innovation is a change in the appearance or performance of a product or service or the creation of a new one. A process innovation is a change in the way a product or service is conceived, manufactured, or disseminated.
- Innovations may also be core innovations, the optimizing of products or services for existing customers, or transformational innovations, the invention of breakthrough products or services that don't exist yet and that are aimed at creating

brand new markets and customers. Innovation doesn't happen as a matter of course.
- Companies can foster innovation through an innovation system, a coherent set of interdependent processes and structures that dictates how the company searches for novel problems and solutions, synthesizes ideas into a business concept and product designs, and selects which projects get funded. Seven components for creating an innovation system are (1) create an innovation strategy; (2) get commitment from top managers; (3) foster an innovative culture and climate; (4) establish the required structure and processes; (5) obtain the necessary human capital; (5) institute necessary human resource policies, practices, and procedures; and (7) obtain the appropriate resources.
- What finally will make or break an organization's attempts at bringing new products and services to market is execution—discussing hows and whats, of using questioning, analysis, and follow-through to achieve the results promised and ensure accountability. Execution requires organizations to effectively manage people, groups, and organizational processes and systems in the pursuit of innovation.

10.5 The Threat of Change: Managing Employee Fear and Resistance

- Resistance to change is an emotional/behavioral response to real or imagined threats to an established work routine. Resistance can be considered to be the interaction of three causes: (1) employee characteristics, (2) change-agent characteristics, and (3) the change agent–employee relationship.
- Ten reasons employees resist change are as follows: (1) individuals' predisposition toward change; (2) surprise and fear of the unknown; (3) climate of mistrust; (4) fear of failure; (5) loss of status or job security; (6) peer pressure; (7) disruption of cultural traditions or group relationships; (8) personality conflicts; (9) lack of tact or poor timing; and (10) nonreinforcing reward systems.

Understanding the Chapter: What Do I Know?

1. What are the two principal types of change?
2. Describe the four kinds of external forces of change and two kinds of internal forces of change.
3. Organizational change ranges along a continuum of what three levels of threat?
4. How does Kurt Lewin's model of change work?
5. What is the organizational development process?

6. What's the difference between a product innovation and a process innovation?
7. Explain four ways to encourage innovation to happen.
8. What are four steps for fostering innovation?
9. Employee resistance can be considered to be the interaction of what three causes?
10. There are 10 reasons employees resist change. What are some of them?

Management in Action

J.C. Penney Is Effectively Navigating Strategic and Managerial Change

J.C. Penney was founded in 1902. It began as a Wyoming dry goods store and grew to be one of the largest department stores and catalogue retailers. Given the growth of Internet shopping, Penney's sales, along with those of other big retailers, began to fall in the 2000s. The company hired former Apple retail store executive Ron Johnson as CEO in 2011 to turn things around.

Johnson's vision was to make Penney hipper, and he changed long-held strategies and management practices that defined the company's culture and identity. One of his first actions was to fire 600 employees at corporate headquarters. He continued to cut costs over the next two years by firing 19,000 store employees. This created a toxic environment in which people feared for their jobs, and morale plunged.[138]

Johnson replaced most of the company's top executives with people from Apple, who brought with them a culture that clashed with that of Penney. These executives decided to eliminate Penney's long-standing strategies regarding discounting and promotional pricing. He then converted stores toward a boutique shop image and dropped many private label brands driving Penney's past sales.[139] Existing employees did not completely buy in to these top down strategies, creating resistance to change.

According to *Fortune*, "The makeover bombed, sales plummeted, and some 40,000 jobs were eliminated" during Johnson's tenure as CEO. Further, "the chain's inventory management and e-commerce operations were in chaos, and Penney ended up with some $5 billion in long-term debt."[140] Johnson was fired in 2013, and the company hired former CEO, Myron Ullman, as interim CEO.

New Leadership

Ullman immediately brought back Penney's promotional pricing strategy and the private label brands. Cost cutting, however, continued as the company was near bankruptcy.

J.C. Penney hired Marvin Ellison as the new CEO in November 2014. He had 12 years of senior management experience at Home Depot and was responsible for Home Depot's very successful omnichannel strategy. Omnichannel strategies integrate different methods of shopping (e.g., online, in-store, catalogues, phone) into a consolidated sales approach. Penney has adopted an omnichannel growth strategy to fuel sales.[141]

One condition of Ellison's hiring was that he would spend a year as president under Ullman. Penney wanted Ellison to learn the business and understand the company's culture. The two men conducted more than 60 employee town hall meetings and visited 100 stores. They also traveled the world, visiting vendors and partners, so that Ellison could learn more about apparel factories, sourcing, and merchandising.

These face-to-face interactions were instrumental to Ellison as he was looking for disconnects between corporate strategy and store operations. One example involved seeing senior management in stores wearing designer clothes that store employees or customers could not afford. Ellison created a policy requiring executives to wear J.C. Penney clothes when visiting stores, along with the same name tags worn by store employees.[142]

New Strategies and Goals

Ellison and his management team established a goal of $1.2 billion in Ebitda, which stands for "earnings before interest, taxes, depreciation, and amortization," for 2017. This goal is double what the company earned in 2015. To accomplish this goal, Ellison established several strategies and action plans:

- Hiring experienced senior executives to lead efforts in e-commerce, supply chain, information technology, and marketing.
- Creating internal promotion opportunities for employees and involving them with implementation decisions.
- Opening 60 more Sephora cosmetic shops inside the stores.
- Redesigning the center court areas of the stores, where the stores experience high traffic volume and sell high-margin products like jewelry, sunglasses, and accessories.
- Investing in technology—the company committed 29% of its capital expense budget to technology.
- Expanding the number of private label clothing brands.
- Reducing the number of out-of-stock items by improving inventory management.
- Using data analytics and Big Data to determine products desired by customers.
- Reducing the company's dependence on weather-sensitive categories such as apparel and experimenting with selling appliances—this is a new product line—in 22 stores.
- Implement a program that ensures customers can buy online and pick up in the store on the same day.[143]

Are the Changes Working?

Gross margins have increased and general administrative expenses have gone down 10% in each of the last two years. Sales increased more than 3% in both 2014 and 2015, but the company is still not making a profit.[144] The company also paid off a half billion dollars of debt in 2015, with plans to do the same in 2016.[145]

A reporter from CNBC asked Ellison if he was worried about the generic decrease in mall traffic. He said, "Mall traffic is down. Our conversion and our point of sale transactions are up. So we're becoming a destination in the malls we're in. Although traffic is down, our traffic is up relative to the mall and our point of sale conversion, which is the most important measurement, is actually up versus last year."[146]

FOR DISCUSSION

1. Which forces for change are driving the changes at J.C. Penney? Explain.
2. Describe how Marvin Ellison is using Lewin's change model. Be specific.
3. To what extent is J.C. Penney following the four steps for fostering innovation? Explain.
4. Use the model of resistance to change (*Figure 10.5*) to explain why employees resisted Ron Johnson's strategic changes.
5. Do you think that the company's strategies will help it achieve the 2017 Ebitda goal? Discuss your rationale.

Legal/Ethical Challenge

Did L'Oreal Go Too Far in Firing Its Patent Lawyer?

Patents give companies competitive advantage. They create legal protection for products and can be used for marketing purposes. They are most frequently pursued by innovative firms, particularly in the high-technology industry. For example, IBM, Samsung, and Canon received the top three number of patents in the United States in 2015, 2014, and 2013.[147] There were 300,678 patents issued by the United States Patent and Trademark Office in 2014.[148]

This challenge deals with L'Oreal's firing of Steven Trzaska. Trzaska was a patent lawyer in charge of a team that examined L'Oreal researchers' work to determine if it contained patentable work product. The team submitted patent applications when appropriate.

The company spends about $1 billion a year on research and development while employing 4,000 people in research labs around the world. L'Oreal is clearly committed to innovating its product offerings.

Trzaska filed a lawsuit against the company, claiming that he was let go for "refusing to make filings for dubious inventions just so the company could fill an annual quota." He said that L'Oreal "ordered him to apply for at least 40 patents last year to help fill a companywide global quota of 500 applications. The company sought to post on its cosmetics packaging that the contents were 'patent pending,' thus increasing their allure to consumers, according to the lawsuit."[149] The company denies the charges and plans to vigorously fight them.

The U.S. patent office is trying to enhance the evaluation process because it feels many applications cover vague ideas that are not real inventions. Trzaska said the company was interested in improving the quality of its applications, but "a review by an outside organization

had found 'the vast majority of its inventions were of low or poor quality,'" according to the lawsuit. This in turn led L'Oreal researchers to submit fewer ideas for potential application, and an increase in the number rejected by Trzaska's team. All told, this led to a reduction in submitted applications and a reduced chance to achieve the company's global patent goals.

The lawsuit claims that Trzaska was fired "for his refusal to draft and file patent applications for proposed inventions which were not patentable" and for his failure to allow his team members to file such applications.[150]

SOLVING THE CHALLENGE

How would you rule if you were a judge evaluating this case?

1. I would side with the company. It's not Trzaska's job to be a gatekeeper. Let the U.S. patent office make these decisions. His role is to help the company acquire patents for its products, and he was jeopardizing future sales by taking an unduly hard stance about patentable work product. Further, the company's goal pertained to submitting 500 applications, not to the number of submissions that were accepted.

2. I would side with Trzaska. He demonstrates a quality stance on the submission of patent applications. The company should focus on the quality of ideas submitted by researchers rather than the work of Trzaska's team. What is Trzaska supposed to do when people submit poor ideas?

3. I'm not sure who is right or wrong, but I don't like the idea of setting firm goals for innovation such as the number of patent applications submitted.

4. Invent other options.

Leading

11

Managing Individual Differences and Behavior

Supervising People as People

Major Questions You Should Be Able to Answer

The Mythical Millennials: Are They Really Different from Gen Xers and Baby Boomers?

Are the 75 million so-called Millennials, now the largest demographic group, born between 1981 and 1997, really so different from earlier generations (the Baby Boomers, born 1946–1964, and Gen Xers, 1965–1980)? Do they need to be managed in different ways?

"The word Millennial right now is sexy," says talent development consultant Jessica Kriegel, "and it gets clicks, and that's why people use it."[1] But no generation is a monolithic block. "Pigeonholing workers into categories is nothing new," says *New York Times* columnist Farhad Manjoo, "and it's rarely helpful in running a workplace."[2]

You see all kinds of generalizations made about Millennials. Some examples follow.

Tech-Savvy, Entitled, . . . and Swayed by Free Food?

Tech-savvy. Entitled. Innovative. These are three connotations of the word *Millennial*, says Kriegel—and they aren't necessarily true.[3] Another three attributes, according to one self-described Millennial expert: "First, they expect work to be meaningful. Second, they crave frequent feedback. Third, they despise voicemail."[4] Strip out numbers from internal presentations, advises consultant Lisa McLeod, because Millennials find stories more compelling than figures.[5] Other advice: Make full use of their skills. Respect their desire for work–life balance. Let them work flexible or fewer hours. And, of course, it never hurts to provide free food at work.[6] But these aren't generation specific. Wouldn't the Boomers and Gen Xers want all these as well?[7]

It is *not* true, as a report from the IBM Institute for Business Values points out, that Millennials' career goals are different from those of older generations, that they want acclaim and think everyone should get a trophy, that they do everything online, that they can't make a decision without inviting everyone to weigh in, and that they are likely to leave if a job doesn't fulfill their passions.[8]

How to Manage Millennials

Of course, there *are* some differences among the generations. For instance, Millennials are more racially and ethnically diverse. Many are burdened by financial hardships. A great many are forced to live with their parents for financial reasons and are unable, because of student-loan debt, to buy their own homes.[9]

Do these factors bear on the following advice about how to manage Millennials in the workplace?

- **Allow them independent decision making and expression.** Millennials are impatient, skeptical, blunt, and expressive, it's said, but they are used to adapting and making decisions. Show appreciation for their individuality and let them participate in decision making.

- **Train them and mentor them.** Millennials are reputedly strongly attracted to education and training, the best kind not being classroom training but forms of independent learning. At the same time, they should be given the chance to create long-term bonds with mentors.

- **Give them constant feedback and recognition.** Millennials need to know they are making an impact and need to be recognized for their workplace contributions. Thus, supervisors should show them how their work contributes to the bottom line.

- **Provide them with access to technology.** To attract and retain Millennial employees, companies need to provide the newest and best technology.

- **Create customized career paths.** Millennials would most like to be self-employed, but few are able to do it because of high start-up costs. Employers can reinforce these employees' sense of control by providing them with a realistic account of their progress and their future within the organization.

For Discussion As a worker, you might hope to be led by someone who would follow the preceding suggestions. Do you think this advice applies only to Millennials or would it work for all employees?

FORECAST What's Ahead in This Chapter

This first of five chapters on leadership discusses how to manage for individual differences and behaviors. We describe personality and individual behavior; values, attitudes, and behavior; and specific work-related attitudes and behaviors managers need to be aware of. We next discuss distortions in perception, which can affect managerial judgment. Finally, we consider what stress does to individuals.

11.1   Personality and Individual Behavior

In the hiring process, do employers care about one's personality and individual traits?

THE BIG PICTURE

Personality consists of stable psychological and behavioral attributes that give you your identity. We describe five personality dimensions and five personality traits that managers need to be aware of to understand workplace behavior.

In this and the next four chapters we discuss the third management function (after planning and organizing)—namely, leading. *Leading,* as we said in Chapter 1, is defined as *motivating, directing, and otherwise influencing people to work hard to achieve the organization's goals.*

How would you describe yourself? Are you outgoing? aggressive? sociable? tense? passive? lazy? quiet? Whatever the combination of traits, which result from the interaction of your genes and your environment, they constitute your personality. More formally, **personality** consists of the stable psychological traits and behavioral attributes that give a person his or her identity.[10] As a manager, you need to understand personality attributes because they affect how people perceive and act within the organization.[11]

The Big Five Personality Dimensions

In recent years, the many personality dimensions have been distilled into a list of factors known as the Big Five.[12] The **Big Five personality dimensions** are (1) extroversion, (2) agreeableness, (3) conscientiousness, (4) emotional stability, and (5) openness to experience.

- **Extroversion.** How outgoing, talkative, sociable, and assertive a person is.
- **Agreeableness.** How trusting, good-natured, cooperative, and soft-hearted one is.
- **Conscientiousness.** How dependable, responsible, achievement-oriented, and persistent one is.
- **Emotional stability.** How relaxed, secure, and unworried one is.
- **Openness to experience.** How intellectual, imaginative, curious, and broad-minded one is.

Sociable and assertive. Does it take a certain kind of personality to be a good salesperson? Have you ever known people who were quiet, unassuming, even shy but who were nevertheless very persistent and persuasive—that is, good salespeople?
© Blend Images/Alamy RF

Current estimates are that approximately 76% of organizations with more than 100 employees now use some sort of pre- or post-hiring assessment, including personality tests,[13] spending more than $500 million annually on such services.[14] Companies use these tests, believing that hiring decisions will be more accurate and predictive of high performers. But are they? We'll discuss this shortly. Dimensions in the Big Five have been associated with performance, leadership behavior, turnover, creativity, and workplace safety.[15] Do you wonder if your personality has affected your behavior at work?

Where do you think you stand in terms of the Big Five? You can find out by completing Self-Assessment 11.1.

Where Do You Stand on the Big Five Dimensions of Personality?

This survey is designed to assess your personality, using the Big Five index. Please be prepared to answer these questions if your instructor has assigned Self-Assessment 11.1 in Connect.

1. What is your personality profile, according to the Big Five?

2. Which of the Big Five is most likely going to help you achieve good grades in your classes and gain employment after graduation?

The Proactive Personality   A person who scores well on the Big Five dimension of conscientiousness is probably a good worker. He or she may also be a **proactive personality, someone who is more apt to take initiative and persevere to influence the environment.** Research reveals that proactive people tend to be more satisfied with their job and committed to their employer, as well as produce more work, than nonproactive individuals.[16]

Do Personality Tests Work for the Workplace?   Personality tests are more commonly used to hire managers than entry-level employees (80% and 59% of the time, respectively).[17] Nevertheless, many experts conclude personality tests are not a valid predictor of job performance.[18] One explanation for this finding is that test takers don't describe themselves accurately, instead guessing answers that might make them look better. Another is that companies use "off-the-shelf" tests possessing limited validity. You should avoid administering such tests. To overcome these limitations, companies like Pymetrics and Knack use games to assess cognitive ability and decision making. Other companies are looking toward genetic testing.[19]

The table below will help managers avoid abuses and discrimination lawsuits when using personality and psychological testing for employment decisions.[20] *(See Table 11.1.)*

TABLE 11.1

Cautions about Using Personality Tests in the Workplace

- *Use professionals.* Rely on reputable, licensed psychologists for selecting and overseeing the administration, scoring, and interpretation of personality and psychological tests. This is particularly important, since not every psychologist is expert at these kinds of tests.

- *Don't hire on the basis of personality test results alone.* Supplement any personality test data with information from reference checks, personal interviews, ability tests, and job performance records. Also avoid hiring people on the basis of specified personality profiles. As a case in point, there is no distinct "managerial personality."

- *Be alert for gender, racial, and ethnic bias.* Regularly assess any possible adverse impact of personality tests on the hiring of women and minorities. This is truly a matter of great importance, since you don't want to find your company (or yourself) embroiled in a lawsuit at some point downstream.

- *Graphology tests don't work, but integrity tests do.* Personality traits and aptitudes cannot be inferred from samples of people's penmanship, as proponents of graphology tests claim. However, dishonest job applicants can often be screened by integrity tests, since dishonest people are reportedly unable to fake conscientiousness, even on a paper-and-pencil test.

Core Self-Evaluations

A core self-evaluation represents a broad personality trait comprising four positive individual traits: (1) *self-efficacy,* **(2)** *self-esteem,* **(3)** *locus of control,* **and (4)** *emotional stability.* Managers need to be aware of these personality traits so as to understand workplace behavior.

1. Self-Efficacy: "I Can/Can't Do This Task"   **Self-efficacy is the belief in one's personal ability to do a task.** This is about your personal belief that you have what it takes to successfully complete a specified task.

Have you noticed that those who are confident about their ability tend to succeed, whereas those preoccupied with failure tend not to? Indeed, high expectations of self-efficacy have been linked with all kinds of positives: not only success in varied physical and mental tasks but also reduced anxiety and increased tolerance for pain.[21] One study found that the sales performance of life-insurance agents was much better among those with high self-efficacy.[22] A meta-analysis involving 21,616 people also found significant positive correlation between self-efficacy and job performance.[23] Low self-efficacy is associated with **learned helplessness, the debilitating lack of faith in one's ability to control one's environment.**[24]

Self-efficacy. Former Marine Corps Staff Sgt. Charlie Linville, 30, shown here (left) with his climbing partner, Tim Medvetz. Linville reached the 29,029-foot summit of Mt. Everest in May 2016, becoming the first combat-wounded veteran to do so. He had already conquered some of the highest peaks in the world on one leg. He was injured while defusing bombs in Afghanistan in 2011, when an explosive device detonated, leading to the amputation of his right leg below the knee. Do you have a personal belief that you can succeed at great things? © Niranjan Shrestha/AP Photo

Among the implications for managers are the following:

- **Assign jobs accordingly.** Complex, challenging, and autonomous jobs tend to enhance people's perceptions of their self-efficacy. Boring, tedious jobs generally do the opposite.

- **Develop self-efficacy.** Self-efficacy is a quality that can be nurtured. Employees with low self-efficacy need lots of constructive pointers and positive feedback.[25] Goal difficulty needs to match individuals' perceived self-efficacy, but goals can be made more challenging as performance improves.[26] Small successes need to be rewarded. Employees' expectations can be improved through guided experiences, mentoring, and role modeling.[27]

2. Self-Esteem: "I Like/Dislike Myself"   How worthwhile, capable, and acceptable do you think you are? The answer to this question is an indicator of your **self-esteem, the extent to which people like or dislike themselves, their overall self-evaluation.**[28]

Research offers some interesting insights about how high or low self-esteem can affect people and organizations.

- **People with high self-esteem.** Compared with people with low self-esteem, people with high self-esteem are more apt to handle failure better, to emphasize the positive, to take more risks, and to choose more unconventional jobs.[29] However, when faced with pressure situations, high-self-esteem people have been found to become egotistical and boastful.[30] Some have even been associated with aggressive and violent behavior.

- **People with low self-esteem.** Conversely, low-self-esteem people confronted with failure have been found to have focused on their weaknesses and to have had primarily negative thoughts.[31] Moreover, they are more dependent on others and are more apt to be influenced by them and to be less likely to take independent positions.

Self-esteem varies around the world. A survey of 13,000 students from 31 countries showed that self-esteem and life satisfaction were moderately related. The relationship was stronger in individualistic countries (United States, Canada, New Zealand) than collectivist cultures (Korea and Japan).[32]

Can self-esteem be improved? According to one study, "low self-esteem can be raised more by having the person think of *desirable* characteristics *possessed* rather than of undesirable characteristics from which he or she is free."[33] Some ways in which managers can build employee self-esteem are shown below. *(See Table 11.2.)*

- Reinforce employees' positive attributes and skills.

- Provide positive feedback whenever possible.

- Break larger projects into smaller tasks and projects.

- Express confidence in employees' abilities to complete their tasks.

- Provide coaching whenever employees are seen to be struggling to complete tasks.

TABLE 11.2

Some Ways That Managers Can Boost Employee Self-Esteem

3. Locus of Control: "I Am/Am Not the Captain of My Fate"

As we discussed briefly in Chapter 1, **locus of control** indicates how much people believe they control their fate through their own efforts. If you have an *internal locus of control,* you believe you control your own destiny. If you have an *external locus of control,* you believe external forces control you.

Research shows internals and externals have important workplace differences. Internals exhibit less anxiety, greater work motivation, and stronger expectations that effort leads to performance. They also obtain higher salaries.[34] Most importantly, one's internal locus of control can be improved by providing more job autonomy.[35]

These findings have two important implications for managers:

- **Expect different degrees of structure and compliance for each type.** Employees with internal locus of control will probably resist close managerial supervision. Hence, they should probably be placed in jobs requiring high initiative and lower compliance. By contrast, employees with external locus of control might do better in highly structured jobs requiring greater compliance.

- **Employ different reward systems for each type.** Since internals seem to have a greater belief that their actions have a direct effect on the consequences of that action, internals likely would prefer and respond more productively to incentives such as merit pay or sales commissions. (We discuss incentive compensation systems in Chapter 12.)

4. Emotional Stability: "I'm Fairly Secure/Insecure When Working under Pressure"

Emotional stability is the extent to which people feel secure and unworried and how likely they are to experience negative emotions under pressure. People with low levels of emotional stability are prone to anxiety and tend to view the world negatively, whereas people with high levels tend to show better job performance.

Emotional Intelligence: Understanding Your Emotions and the Emotions of Others

Emotional intelligence (EI or EQ) has been defined as "the ability to carry out accurate reasoning about emotions and the ability to use emotions and emotional knowledge to enhance thought."[36] Said another way, **emotional intelligence is the ability to monitor your and others' feelings and to use this information to guide your thinking and actions.** The trait of emotional intelligence was first introduced in 1909. Since that time some claim it to be the secret elixir to happiness and higher performance. Are you curious if research supports such lofty conclusions?

What Do We Know about EI?   Recent research underscores the importance of developing higher EI, but it does not confirm its lofty expectations. EI was moderately associated with (1) better social relations, well-being, and satisfaction across all ages and contexts, (2) higher creativity, (3) better emotional control, (4) conscientiousness and self-efficacy, and (5) self-rated performance. Interestingly, EI was not found to be a driver of supervisory ratings of performance.[37] **Daniel Goleman,** a psychologist who popularized the trait of EI, concluded that EI is composed of four key components: self-awareness, self-management, social awareness, and relationship management.[38] *(See Table 11.3.)*

TABLE 11.3

The Traits of Emotional Intelligence

1. *Self-awareness.* The most essential trait. This is the ability to read your own emotions and gauge your moods accurately, so you know how you're affecting others.
2. *Self-management.* This is the ability to control your emotions and act with honesty and integrity in reliable and adaptable ways. You can leave occasional bad moods outside the office.
3. *Social awareness.* This includes empathy, allowing you to show others that you care, and organizational intuition, so you keenly understand how your emotions and actions affect others.
4. *Relationship management.* This is the ability to communicate clearly and convincingly, disarm conflicts, and build strong personal bonds.

Sources: For a current review, see D. Joseph, J. Jin, D. Newman, and E. O'Boyle, "Why Does Self-Reported Emotional Intelligence Predict Job Performance? A Meta-Analytic Investigation of Mixed EI," Journal of Applied Psychology, March 2015, pp. 298–342. See the box titled "Get Happy Carefully" in D. Goleman, R. Boyatzis, and A. McKee, "Primal Leadership: The Hidden Driver of Great Performance," Harvard Business Review, Special Issue: Breakthrough Leadership, December 2001, p. 49.

Can You Raise Your EI?   Is there any way to raise your own emotional intelligence, to sharpen your social skills? Although parts of EI represent stable traits that are not readily changed, other aspects, such as using empathy, can be developed.[39] Two suggestions for improvement are as follows:

- **Develop awareness of your EI level.** Becoming aware of your level of emotional intelligence is the first step. The self-assessment on following page can be used for this purpose. (Some companies use the Personal Profile Analysis during the hiring process to provide insights into a person's EI.)[40]

■ **Learn about areas needing improvement.** The next step is to learn more about those EI aspects in which improvement is needed. For example, to improve your skills at using empathy, find articles on the topic and try to implement their recommendations. One such article suggests that empathy in communications is enhanced by trying to (1) understand how others feel about what they are communicating and (2) gaining appreciation of what people want from an exchange.[41]

Emotional Intelligence: Does Empathy Work Better Than Self-interest?   EXAMPLE

When JetBlue identifies candidates for flight attendants, it not only uses psychological assessments, structured interviews, and the like, it also looks for the nicest people—and then something else: Using customer data analysis, it found that "being helpful trumps being nice," as two JetBlue executives observed. Indeed, "being helpful even balances out the effect of somebody who is *not* so nice."[42] As a result of policies developed out of these insights—both reflections of emotional intelligence—customer feedback became more positive.

Is Compassion Good for the Bottom Line? A man named Drake, described as a "happy, generous, and other-focused person, . . . always interested in helping others whenever he can," joined banker Bear Stearns, whose managers treated junior staff abusively, furthering an atmosphere of cut-throat

competition. Drake was determined to follow his own values and as a senior staffer treated junior bankers with compassion and respect, as well as giving them more opportunities. As a result of one deal in which he gave a junior analyst much responsibility, she pitched a deal that turned out to be the most profitable of the year—catching the eye of senior management.[43]

YOUR CALL

Providing support for one another, including offering kindness and compassion when others are struggling. Inspiring one another at work. Avoiding blame and forgiving mistakes. Have you observed these expressions of EQ in a business situation? Do you think they pay off in a happier and even productive workplace?[44]

Both research and our experience suggest that your emotional intelligence can help or hurt your career. Would you like to know where you stand and what you might do to improve your level of emotional intelligence? ●

---

connect SELF-ASSESSMENT 11.2

What Is Your Level of Emotional Intelligence?

The following survey is designed to assess your emotional intelligence. Please be prepared to answer these questions if your instructor has assigned Self-Assessment 11.2 in Connect.

1. How do you stand on the five dimensions of emotional intelligence?

2. Use the scores from the items to identify your strengths and liabilities.

3. Identify two things you might focus on to enhance your emotional intelligence.

11.2 Values, Attitudes, and Behavior

How do the hidden aspects of individuals—their values and attitudes—affect employee behavior?

THE BIG PICTURE

Organizational behavior (OB) considers how to better understand and manage people at work. In this section, we discuss individual values and attitudes and how they affect people's actions and judgments.

FIGURE 11.1 Formal and informal aspects of an organization

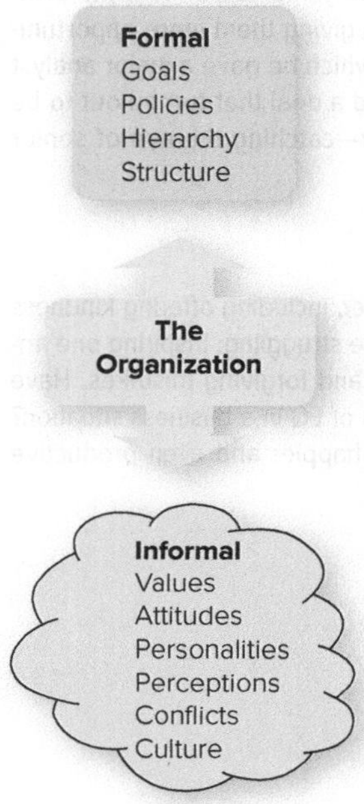

Formal
Goals
Policies
Hierarchy
Structure

The Organization

Informal
Values
Attitudes
Personalities
Perceptions
Conflicts
Culture

If you look at a company's annual report or at a brochure from its corporate communications department, you are apt to be given a picture of its *formal aspects:* Goals. Policies. Hierarchy. Structure.

Could you exert effective leadership if the formal aspects were all you knew about the company? What about the *informal aspects*? Values. Attitudes. Personalities. Perceptions. Conflicts. Culture. Clearly, you need to know about these hidden, "messy" characteristics as well. *(See Figure 11.1, left.)*

Organizational Behavior: Trying to Explain and Predict Workplace Behavior

The informal aspects are the focus of the interdisciplinary field known as **organizational behavior (OB)**, which is dedicated to better understanding and managing people at work. In particular, OB tries to help managers not only *explain* workplace behavior but also *predict* it, so that they can better lead and motivate their employees to perform productively. OB looks at two areas:

- **Individual behavior.** This is the subject of this chapter. We discuss such individual attributes as values, attitudes, personality, perception, and learning.

- **Group behavior.** This is the subject of later chapters, particularly Chapter 13, where we discuss norms, roles, and teams.

Let's begin by considering individual values, attitudes, and behavior.

Values: What Are Your Consistent Beliefs and Feelings about *All* Things?

Values are abstract ideals that guide one's thinking and behavior across all situations.[45] Lifelong behavior patterns are dictated by values that are fairly well set by the time people are in their early teens. After that, however, one's values can be reshaped by significant life-altering events, such as having a child, undergoing a business failure, or surviving the death of a loved one, a war, or a serious health threat.

From a manager's point of view, it's helpful to know that values represent the ideals that underlie how we behave at work. Ideals such as concern for others, self-enhancement, independence, and security are common values in the workplace.[46] Managers who understand an employee's values are better suited to assign them to meaningful projects and to help avoid conflicts between work activities and personal values.[47]

Attitudes: What Are Your Consistent Beliefs and Feelings about *Specific* Things?

Values are abstract ideals—global beliefs and feelings—that are directed toward all objects, people, or events. Values tend to be consistent both over time and over related situations.

By contrast, attitudes are beliefs and feelings that are directed toward *specific* objects, people, or events. More formally, an **attitude is defined as a learned predisposition toward a given object.**[48] It is important for you to understand the components of attitudes because attitudes directly influence our behavior.[49]

Example: Job satisfaction is moderately associated with performance and strongly related to turnover.[50] Unhappy workers are less likely to demonstrate high performance, while happy workers are less likely to quit. This is why it is important for managers to track employees' attitudes and to understand their causes. For example, Earls, a Canadian chain of 65 restaurants with as many as 8,000 employees, has truly adopted this recommendation. The company sends short surveys measuring workplace attitudes to employees' mobile devices every three months. According to *The Wall Street Journal,* Earls does this because management has concluded that "the components of engagement—employee happiness and commitment to the business—are exactly what drives sales, and therefore the bottom line."[51]

The Three Components of Attitudes: Affective, Cognitive, and Behavioral

Attitudes have three components—*affective, cognitive,* and *behavioral.*[52]

- **The affective component—"I feel."** The **affective component of an attitude consists of the feelings or emotions one has about a situation.** How do you *feel* about people who talk loudly on cell-phones in restaurants? If you feel annoyed or angry, you're expressing negative emotions, or affect. (If you're indifferent, your attitude is neutral.)

- **The cognitive component—"I believe."** The **cognitive component of an attitude consists of the beliefs and knowledge one has about a situation.** What do you *think* about people in restaurants talking on cell-phones? Is what they're doing inconsiderate, acceptable, even admirable (because it shows they're productive)? Your answer reflects your beliefs or ideas about the situation.

- **The behavioral component—"I intend."** The **behavioral component of an attitude, also known as the intentional component, is how one intends or expects to behave toward a situation.** What would you *intend to do* if a person talked loudly on a cell-phone at the table next to you? Your action may reflect your negative or positive feelings (affective), your negative or positive beliefs (cognitive), and your intention or lack of intention to do anything (behavioral).

All three components are often manifested at any given time. For example, if you call a corporation and get one of those telephone-tree menus ("For customer service, press 1 . . .") that never seem to connect you to a human being, you might be so irritated that you would say

- "I hate being given the runaround." [*affective component—your feelings*]
- "That company doesn't know how to take care of customers." [*cognitive component—your perceptions*]
- "I'll never call them again." [*behavioral component—your intentions*]

When Attitudes and Reality Collide: Consistency and Cognitive Dissonance One of the last things you want, probably, is to be accused of hypocrisy—to be criticized for saying one thing and doing another. Like most people, you no doubt want to maintain consistency between your attitudes and your behavior.

But what if a strongly held attitude bumps up against a harsh reality that contradicts it? Suppose you're extremely concerned about getting AIDS, which you believe you might get from contact with body fluids, including blood. Then you're in a life-threatening auto accident in a third-world country and require surgery and blood transfusions—including transfusions of blood from (possibly AIDS-infected) strangers in a blood bank. Do you reject the blood to remain consistent with your beliefs about getting AIDS?

In 1957, social psychologist **Leon Festinger** proposed the term **cognitive dissonance to describe the psychological discomfort a person experiences between his or her**

Leon Festinger. In 1957, the psychologist and his associates penetrated a cult whose members predicted that most people on earth would perish in a cataclysmic event, except for a handful who would be rescued by aliens in a flying saucer. Festinger found himself standing with cult members on a hilltop, awaiting the event, which, of course, did not happen. Later he proposed the term *cognitive dissonance* to explain how they rationalized the failure of their prophecy. Have you observed people employing this mechanism when the surefire thing they predicted did not occur? © New School for Social Research/AP Photo

cognitive attitude and incompatible behavior.[53] Because people are uncomfortable with inconsistency, Festinger theorized, they will seek to reduce the "dissonance," or tension, of the inconsistency. How they deal with the discomfort, he suggested, depends on three factors:

- **Importance.** How important are the elements creating the dissonance? Most people can put up with some ambiguities in life. For example, many drivers don't think obeying speed limits is very important, even though they profess to be law-abiding citizens. People eat greasy foods, even though they know that ultimately those foods may contribute to heart disease.

- **Control.** How much control does one have over the matters that create dissonance? A juror may not like the idea of voting the death penalty but believe that he or she has no choice but to follow the law in the case. A taxpayer may object to his taxes being spent on, say, special-interest corporate welfare for a particular company but not feel that he can withhold taxes.

- **Rewards.** What rewards are at stake in the dissonance? You're apt to cling to old ideas in the face of new evidence if you have a lot invested emotionally or financially in those ideas. If you're a police officer who worked 20 years to prove a particular suspect guilty of murder, you're not apt to be very accepting of contradictory evidence after all that time.

The Practical Action box below provides an example of three key methods Festinger suggested to reduce cognitive dissonance.

PRACTICAL ACTION　Methods for Reducing Cognitive Dissonance

Suppose Juanita has a positive attitude about helping others. One day her boss asks her to work on a special project for an important new client—and it must get done in two months. The project represents significant revenue, and her boss even promises a bonus for successfully completing it on time. Juanita would like to use the bonus to purchase a new car. The rub is that two of her peers have also come to her, seeking help on *their* project. Juanita believes she is well suited to help them, given her past experience, but she feels it would take time away from completing her special project. Should she make time to help her peers or focus solely on the special project?

Festinger suggested three key ways Juanita can reduce the cognitive dissonance associated with her current situation:

- **Change your attitude or behavior or both.** Juanita could either (a) tell herself that she can't help her peers because

the special project is too important for the company or (b) schedule extra time each day or week to help her peers.

- **Belittle the importance of the inconsistent behavior.** Juanita could belittle (in the sense of "make small") the belief that she needs to help peers every time they ask for assistance.

- **Find consonant elements that outweigh dissonant ones.** Juanita could tell herself that she can't help because the company needs the revenue and she needs the bonus.

YOUR CALL

Have you found yourself in a similar dilemma? Which solution seemed to work best—or would work best—in your case?

Behavior: How Values and Attitudes Affect People's Actions and Judgments

Values (global) and attitudes (specific) are generally in harmony, but not always. For example, a manager may put a positive *value* on helpful behavior (global) yet may have a negative *attitude* toward helping an unethical coworker (specific). Together, however, values and attitudes influence people's workplace **behavior—their actions and judgments.** ●

How Values and Attitudes Affect Behavior: Thinking beyond Profit to Create Value for Society

As a manager, would you think most employees would agree that innovation is beneficial—that the original Silicon Valley firms prospered because they were constantly creating new products and services? Employees may have the *value,* then, that innovation is good—that it leads to productivity and profitability.

However, what if employees think that a company's purpose is to be solely a money-making machine? They might have the *attitude* that social innovation is unnecessary, even discouraged.

The Thinking behind Great Companies. Great companies, suggests Rosabeth Moss Kanter of Harvard Business School, have broader values—and attitudes. Firms such as IBM, PepsiCo, and Procter & Gamble, she says, "work to make money, of course, but in their choices of how to do so, they think about building enduring institutions. . . . Society and people are not afterthoughts or inputs to be used and discarded but are core to their purpose."[54] Balancing public interest with financial interest means that CEOs must expand their investments beyond profit-maximizing activities such as marketing and research and development and include employee empowerment, emotional engagement, values-based leadership, and related social contributions.

Ways of Creating Value. "Affirming purpose and values through service is a regular part of how great companies express their identities," Kanter believes. Thus, JPMorgan Chase has The Fellowship Initiative, a program to help young American men of color achieve academic and professional success. Coca-Cola invests in small African mango plantations to help farmers in Africa gain livelihoods. Microsoft partners with nonprofit NETHope to create apprenticeships in information technology in Kenya. Gap Inc. has a program for teaching health awareness and literacy to women garment workers in Cambodia and India. The Disney Company provides conservation grants to protect wildlife.[55] In West Africa, Procter & Gamble set up Pampers mobile clinics to reduce infant mortality by having health care professionals teach postnatal care, examine babies, and hand out Pampers diapers. "The emotional tugs for P&G employees are strong," says Kanter; "they feel inspired by the fact that their product is at the center of a mission to save lives."

YOUR CALL

Where do you think the inspiration for giving a firm a motivating purpose and values beyond making money should come from? Does it have to come from a company's leaders? Do you think it could begin as voluntary activity, as with employees finding each other through company chat rooms and sharing ideas in their free time?

Creating value. The Nature Conservancy Disney Wilderness Preserve, consisting of 11,500 acres near Orlando, Florida, was created by the Disney Company to protect more than 1,000 species of plants and animals. It's considered the "secret Disney park," because few people know about it.
© Ian Dagnall/Alamy

11.3 Perception and Individual Behavior

What are the distortions in perception that can cloud one's judgment?

THE BIG PICTURE

Perception, a four-step process, can be skewed by five types of distortion: stereotyping, implicit bias, the halo effect, the recency effect, and causal attribution. We also consider the self-fulfilling prophecy, which can affect our judgment as well.

If you were a smoker, which warning on a cigarette pack would make you think more about quitting? "Smoking seriously harms you and others around you"? A blunt "Smoking kills"? Or a stark graphic image showing decaying teeth?

This is the kind of decision public health authorities in various countries are wrestling with. (One study found that highly graphic images about the negative effects of smoking had the greatest impact on smokers' intentions to quit.)[56] These officials, in other words, are trying to decide how *perception* might influence behavior.

The Four Steps in the Perceptual Process

Perception is the process of interpreting and understanding one's environment. The process of perception is complex, but it can be boiled down to four steps.[57] *(See Figure 11.2.)*

FIGURE 11.2   The four steps in the perceptual process

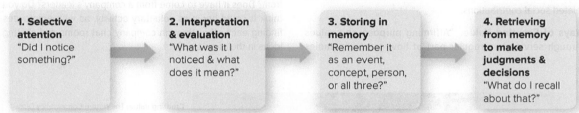

1. Selective attention "Did I notice something?" → **2. Interpretation & evaluation** "What was it I noticed & what does it mean?" → **3. Storing in memory** "Remember it as an event, concept, person, or all three?" → **4. Retrieving from memory to make judgments & decisions** "What do I recall about that?"

In this book, we are less concerned about the theoretical steps in perception than in how perception is distorted, since this has considerable bearing on the manager's judgment and job. In any one of the four stages of the perception process, misunderstandings or errors in judgment can occur. Perceptual errors can lead to mistakes that can be damaging to yourself, other people, and your organization.

Five Distortions in Perception

Although there are other types of distortion in perception, we will describe the following: (1) *stereotyping,* (2) *implicit bias,* (3) the *halo effect,* (4) the *recency effect,* and (5) *causal attribution.*

1. Stereotyping: "Those Sorts of People Are Pretty Much the Same"   If you're a tall African American man, do people make remarks about basketball players? If you're of Irish descent, do people believe you drink a lot? If you're Jewish, do people think you're money-oriented? If you're a woman, do people think you're automatically nurturing? All these are stereotypes. **Stereotyping** is the tendency to attribute to an individual the characteristics one believes are typical of the group to which that individual belongs.[58]

Principal areas of stereotyping that should be of concern to you as a manager are (1) *sex-role stereotypes,* (2) *age stereotypes,* and (3) *race/ethnicity stereotypes.* (People with disabilities, discussed in Section 11.5, are also apt to be stereotyped.)

Sex-Role Stereotypes   A *sex-role stereotype* is the belief that differing traits and abilities make males and females particularly well suited to different roles. Thus, for example, people tend to prefer male bosses (33%) to female bosses (20%) in a new job, according to a recent Gallup poll, even though the public generally views women as being every bit as capable as men at being leaders, according to Pew Research.[59] (Reverse bias can occur when managers fighting bias against women overdo it and discriminate against men.)[60]

A summary of research revealed that

- Men were preferred for male-dominated jobs (such as firefighter), but there was no preference for either gender in female-dominated jobs (such as nurse).
- Women have a harder time than men in being perceived as effective leaders. (The exception: Women were seen as more effective when the organization faced a crisis and needed a turnaround.)
- Women of color are more negatively affected by sex-role stereotypes than are white women or men in general.[61]

Age Stereotypes   Another example of an inaccurate stereotype is the belief that older workers are less motivated, more resistant to change, less trusting, less healthy, and more likely to have problems with work–life balance. A recent study refuted all these negative beliefs about age.[62] Unfortunately, these stereotypes likely fuel bias against older employees. A 2013 survey of 1,500 older workers, for example, showed that 92% considered bias against them "very" or "somewhat" commonplace.[63]

Race/Ethnicity Stereotypes   Studies of race-based stereotypes have demonstrated that people of color experienced more perceived discrimination and less psychological support than whites.[64] Perceived racial discrimination was also associated with more negative work attitudes, physical health, psychological health, and organizational citizenship behavior.[65]

2. Implicit Bias: "I Really Don't Think I'm Biased, but I Just Have a Feeling about Some People"   More than 85% of Americans consider themselves to be unprejudiced, but researchers conclude that most hold some degree of implicit racial bias.[66]

Explicit bias reflects attitudes or beliefs endorsed at a conscious level—for example, "I don't let any teenage black men wearing hoodies come into my store; they might hold me up." **Implicit bias is the attitudes or beliefs that affect our understanding, actions, and decisions in an unconscious manner**—for example, from several New York City police officers, "We had to shoot him, he seemed to be reaching for a gun." (This was the 1999 shooting of Guinean immigrant Amadou Diallo, who was killed when police fired 41 rounds as he pulled out his wallet.)[67]

Implicit bias has come more into the forefront of public discussion with the rise in the number of deaths of African Americans at the hands of the police in Ferguson, Missouri; in Cleveland; and on Staten Island in New York, among other places (as well as the 2016 shooting of several white police officers by an African American male in Dallas).[68] But implicit bias also operates on more subtle levels: In one famous study, social scientists sent thousands of resumes with identical content to employers with job openings and measured which received callbacks for interviews. On some resumes, some stereotypically African American names were used (such as "Jamal") and on others stereotypically white names were used (like "Brendan"). The same resume was roughly 50% more likely to result in callback for an interview if it had a "white" name.[69]

If changing explicit bias is difficult, taking steps to root out implicit bias is even harder. Nevertheless, police departments, in particular, are taking great steps forward, requiring intergroup contact, positive feedback, clear norms of behavior, and similar matters.[70]

3. The Halo Effect: "One Trait Tells Me All I Need to Know"

We often use faces as markers for gender, race, and age, but face and body characteristics can lead us to fall back on cultural stereotypes. For example, height has been associated with perceptions of prosperity—high income—and occupational success. Excess weight can be stereotypically associated with negative traits such as laziness, incompetence, and lack of discipline.[71] These examples illustrate the **halo effect, in which we form an impression of an individual based on a single trait.** (The phenomenon is also called the *horn-and-halo effect,* because not only can a single positive trait be generalized into an array of positive traits but the reverse is also true.)

As if we needed additional proof that life is unfair, it has been shown that attractive people generally are treated better than unattractive people. Attractive members of Congress get more TV coverage, and attractive political candidates win more often.[72] Attractive students have higher expectations by teachers in terms of academic achievement.[73] Attractive employees are generally paid higher salaries than unattractive ones are, and attractive CEOs are paid more than less appealing CEOs.[74] (Male CEOs also tend to be taller—6 feet compared to an average man's 5-feet-10.5 inches, in one Swedish study.)[75] Clearly, however, if a manager fails to look at *all* of an individual's traits, he or she has no right to complain if that employee doesn't work out.

EXAMPLE   The Halo Effect: Do Good Looks Make People Richer and Happier?

Are attractive employees paid more than ordinary (or unattractive) people for the same work? Are they happier? That would seem to be the case, according to a study involving more than 25,000 people worldwide.[76]

$250,000 More. Five large surveys conducted from 1971 to 2009 in the United States, Britain, and Germany found that beautiful people earn an extra $250,000 during their careers than the least attractive people. In addition, says University of Texas economist Daniel Hamermesh, leader of the study, the best-looking people are more likely to remain employed, get promoted, find a higher-earning (and better-looking) spouse, and even get better deals on home loans.[77] Hamermesh is also author of *Beauty Pays: Why Attractive People Are More Successful.*[78] "In economic terms, beauty is scarce. People distinguish themselves and pay attention to beauty," he says. "Companies realize that hiring better-looking people helps in various ways. In every market, whether it's jobs or marriage, beauty matters."[79] The result of all this is that beautiful people are generally happier people than ordinary folks. "The majority of beauty's effect on happiness works through its impact on economic outcomes," says Hamermesh.[80]

Do Good Looks Produce Confident Communicators? Another study produces additional insights:[81]

- Although beautiful people are no better than ordinary people at solving puzzles such as mazes, they are more

self-confident about their abilities. "Being good looking," says one article about the study, "seems to be strongly associated with self-confidence, a trait that is apparently attractive to employers."[82]

- When study subjects pretending to be employers looked only at resumes, physical appearance had no effect on their judgments, as you might expect. When photos, in-person interviews, and even phone interviews were involved, employers showed higher estimates for beautiful people's productivity—especially when they had face-to-face interviews but even with telephone-only interviews, the result, apparently, of the effect of self-confidence that came across on the phone.

- Good-looking people are good communicators, which also contributes to employers' positive perceptions.

The Halo Misperception. In sum, "Employers (wrongly) expect good-looking workers to perform better than their less-attractive counterparts under both visual and oral interaction," said the researchers, "even after controlling for individual worker characteristics and worker confidence."[83]

YOUR CALL

Are you influenced in your judgment of people by how attractive they are? Do you think as a manager you could look beyond people's physical appearance to be a good judge of their competence? Why?

Handsomely compensated. Attractive employees are generally paid better than unattractive ones are. Why do you think that is? Do you think it's inevitable? © Monkey Business Images/Shutterstock RF

4. The Recency Effect: "The Most Recent Impressions Are the Ones That Count"

The **recency effect** is the tendency to remember recent information better than earlier information, perhaps because when you activate your recall, the later recollections are still present in working memory.[84] You see this misperception often operating among investors (even professionals), who are more likely to buy a stock if they see something about it in the news or if it has a high one-day return.[85]

The Recency Effect: Performance Reviews, Student Evaluations, and Investment Decisions

Not just a few employees have had the experience of making some mistake happen recently, and then it ends up being "the entire topic of your performance review even if you've done a great job the rest of the year," as one writer points out.[86] This is just one example of the recency effect in action.

Another is when students do their own "performance reviews"—do student course evaluations of their professors. Here, too, their ratings may be affected by course activities that are closer to the time of the formal appraisal.[87]

The recency effect appears quite frequently among stock market investors. "People extrapolate what just happened into more of the same," says one wealth fund manager.[88] That is,

people leap into holdings that are doing well and cash out investments that are doing poorly, forgetting that at some point the trends will be reversed.

YOUR CALL

Why does the recency effect occur? Like other habits, it makes things easier, says one financial planner. "Because it's easier, we're inclined to use our recent experience as the baseline for what will happen in the future."[89] What decision(s) would you admit to making in which you were influenced by the recency effect?

---

5. Causal Attributions

Causal attribution is the activity of inferring causes for observed behavior. Rightly or wrongly, we constantly formulate cause-and-effect explanations for our own and others' behavior. Attributional statements such as the following are common: "Joe drinks too much because he has no willpower, but I need a few drinks after work because I'm under a lot of pressure."

Even though our causal attributions tend to be self-serving and are often invalid, it's important to understand how people formulate attributions because they profoundly affect organizational behavior. For example, a supervisor who attributes an employee's poor performance to a lack of effort might reprimand that person. However, training might be deemed necessary if the supervisor attributes the poor performance to a lack of ability.

As a manager, you need to be alert to two attributional tendencies that can distort one's interpretation of observed behavior—the *fundamental attribution bias* and the *self-serving bias.*

- **Fundamental attribution bias.** In the **fundamental attribution bias,** people attribute another person's behavior to his or her personal characteristics rather than to situational factors.

  Example: A study of manufacturing employees found that top managers attributed the cause of industrial back pain to individuals, whereas workers attributed it to the environment.[90]

- **Self-serving bias.** In the **self-serving bias,** people tend to take more personal responsibility for success than for failure.

  Example: Europeans blamed Wall Street for the 2010 economic collapse in Greece. However, a *Wall Street Journal* article points out that a close look at Greece's finances "over the nearly 10 years since it adopted the euro shows not only that Greece was the principal author of its debt problems, but also that fellow European governments repeatedly turned a blind eye to its flouting of rules."[91]

The Self-Fulfilling Prophecy, or Pygmalion Effect

The **self-fulfilling prophecy,** also known as the *Pygmalion* ("pig-*mail*-yun") *effect,* describes the phenomenon in which people's expectations of themselves or others lead them to behave in ways that make those expectations come true.

Expectations are important. An example is a waiter who expects some poorly dressed customers to be stingy tippers, who therefore gives them poor service and so gets the result he or she expected—a much lower tip than usual. Research has shown that by raising managers' expectations for individuals performing a wide variety of tasks, higher levels of achievement and productivity can be achieved.[92]

The lesson for you as a manager is that when you expect employees to perform badly, they probably will, and when you expect them to perform well, they probably will. (In the G. B. Shaw play *Pygmalion,* a speech coach bets he can get a lower-class girl to change her accent and her demeanor so that she can pass herself off as a duchess. In six months, she successfully "passes" in high society, having assumed the attributes of a woman of sensitivity and taste.)

Research in a variety of industries and occupations shows that the effect of the self-fulfilling prophecy can be quite strong.[93] That is, managerial expectations powerfully influence employee behavior and performance. Among the things managers can do to create positive performance expectations: Recognize that everyone has the potential to increase his or her performance. Introduce new employees as if they have outstanding potential. Encourage employees to visualize the successful execution of tasks. Help them master key skills.[94] ●

11.4 Work-Related Attitudes and Behaviors Managers Need to Deal With

MAJOR QUESTION

Is it important for managers to pay attention to employee attitudes?

THE BIG PICTURE

Attitudes are important because they affect behavior. Managers need to be alert to the key work-related attitudes having to do with engagement, job satisfaction, and organizational commitment. Among the types of employee behavior they should attend to are their on-the-job performance and productivity, absenteeism and turnover, organizational citizenship behaviors, and counterproductive work behaviors.

"Keep the employees happy," we often hear. It's true that attitudes are important, the reason being that *attitudes affect behavior.* But is keeping employees happy all that managers need to know to get results? We discuss motivation for performance in the next chapter. Here, let us consider what managers need to know about key work-related attitudes and behaviors.

Three types of attitudes managers are particularly interested in are (1) *employee engagement,* (2) *job satisfaction,* and (3) *organizational commitment.*

1. Employee Engagement: How Connected Are You to Your Work?

Research on job involvement has evolved into the study of an individual difference called **employee engagement, defined as an individual's involvement, satisfaction, and enthusiasm for work.**[95] Engaged employees are expected to have feelings of urgency, intensity, and enthusiasm, as well as focus, which make them more committed to their employer and to put more effort into their jobs.[96] In other words, such employees "give their all" at work.

The U.S. workforce displays above-average global levels of engagement, according to consulting firm Aon Hewitt. The firm's 15-year study of engagement shows worldwide levels at 62% in comparison to a North American rate of 66%. This bodes well for the U.S. workforce because highly engaged employees can achieve 12% higher customer satisfaction/loyalty, 18% more productivity, and 12% greater profitability.[97] Other recent academic studies similarly showed a positive relationship between employee engagement, performance, and physical and psychological well-being and corporate-level financial performance and customer satisfaction.[98] Engaged employees tend to be positive or optimistic, proactive, and conscientious and to possess high levels of human and social capital.

Employees are also more likely to become engaged when an organization has the kind of culture that promotes employee development, recognition, and trust between management and employees.[99] Job security and feelings of psychological safety (when employees feel free of fear in trying new ideas) also propel job engagement.[100]

Do you want to achieve higher grades in your classes? If yes, you will find that being engaged in your studies will help. You can determine your level of engagement with your studies by completing Self-Assessment 11.3. Results can be used to develop an engagement improvement plan.

---

connect SELF-ASSESSMENT 11.3

To What Extent Are You Engaged in Your Studies?

The following survey was designed to assess your level of engagement in your studies. Please be prepared to answer these questions if your instructor has assigned Self-Assessment 11.3 in Connect.

1. What is your level of engagement?

2. Find your three lowest-rated items. Based on the content of these items, what can you do to improve your level of engagement? Hint: Doing this requires you to identify the cause of the low ratings for each item.

2. Job Satisfaction: How Much Do You Like or Dislike Your Job?

Job satisfaction is the extent to which you feel positive or negative about various aspects of your work. Most people don't like everything about their jobs. Their overall satisfaction depends on how they feel about several components, such as *work, pay, promotions, coworkers,* and *supervision.*[101] Among the key correlates of job satisfaction are stronger motivation, job involvement, organizational commitment, and life satisfaction and less absenteeism, tardiness, turnover, and perceived stress.[102]

Reportedly only 48.3% of U.S. workers were satisfied with their jobs in 2015, down from 61.1% in 1987, according to a study of 5,000 households.[103] But another survey found that employee job satisfaction in 2015 was 88%, up from a low of 77% in 2002.[104] Job satisfaction today is much better, of course, than in the aftermath of the Great Recession. Then Americans were forced to work longer hours and often for the same or less pay, and many struck back by suing employers for violating wage-and-hour laws, as by forcing them to work off the clock or without overtime pay.[105]

But what is the relationship between job satisfaction and job performance—does more satisfaction cause better performance or does better performance cause more satisfaction? This is a subject of much debate among management scholars.[106] One comprehensive study found that (1) job satisfaction and performance are moderately related, meaning that employee job satisfaction is a key work attitude managers should consider when trying to increase performance; but (2) the relationship between satisfaction and performance is complex and it seems that both variables influence each other through a host of individual differences and work-environment characteristics.[107]

How satisfied are you with the job you are in now, if you have one, or the last job you had?

---

connect SELF-ASSESSMENT 11.4

How Satisfied Are You with Your Present Job?

The following survey was designed to assess how satisfied you are with your current job, or a previous job, if you're not presently working. Please be prepared to answer these questions if your instructor has assigned Self-Assessment 11.4 in Connect.

1. What is your level of satisfaction with recognition, compensation, and supervision?

2. If you have low to medium satisfaction with any aspect of the job, identify what can be done to increase your job satisfaction. Be sure to consider what you can do, what your boss might do, or what the organization might do. Be specific.

---

3. Organizational Commitment: How Much Do You Identify with Your Organization?

Organizational commitment reflects the extent to which an employee identifies with an organization and is committed to its goals. For instance, some managers question whether mothers with children can be fully committed to their jobs, although one survey found that only 4% of more than 2,612 women said that their bosses think that they are not as committed to their jobs because they have children.[108] Research shows a significant positive relationship between organizational commitment and job satisfaction, performance, turnover, and organizational citizenship behavior—discussed in the next section.[109] Thus, if managers are able to increase job satisfaction, employees may show higher levels of commitment, which in turn can elicit higher performance and lower employee turnover.[110]

Important Workplace Behaviors

Why, as a manager, do you need to learn how to manage individual differences? The answer, as you might expect, is so that you can influence employees to do their best work. Among the types of behavior are (1) *performance and productivity,* (2) *absenteeism and turnover,* (3) *organizational citizenship behaviors,* and (4) *counterproductive work behaviors.*

1. Evaluating Behavior When Employees Are Working: Performance and Productivity

Every job has certain expectations, but in some jobs performance and productivity are easier to define than in others. How many contacts should a telemarketing sales rep make in a day? How many sales should he or she close? Often a job of this nature will have a history of accomplishments (from what previous job holders have attained), so that it is possible to quantify performance behavior.

However, an advertising agency account executive handling major clients such as a carmaker or a beverage manufacturer may go months before landing this kind of big account. Or a researcher in a pharmaceutical company may take years to develop a promising new prescription drug.

In short, the method of evaluating performance must match the job being done.

2. Evaluating Behavior When Employees Are Not Working: Absenteeism and Turnover

Should you be suspicious of every instance of absenteeism? Of course, some absences—illness, death in the family, or jury duty, for example—are legitimate. However, a lot of no-show behavior is related to job dissatisfaction.[111] One study of 700 managers found that 20% called in sick simply because they didn't feel like going to work that day. The top three reasons for employees taking bogus sick days are for doing personal errands, catching up on sleep, and relaxing.[112]

Thriving employees. Zingerman's, an Ann Arbor, Michigan, community of food-related businesses, encourages employees to thrive through such devices as sharing information and experimenting with ways to solve problems on their own. Employees with high job satisfaction can help organizations grow. Courtesy of Zingerman's Community of Businesses

Absenteeism may be a precursor to turnover, which, as we saw in Chapter 9, is when an employee abandons, resigns, retires, or is terminated from a job. Every organization experiences some turnover, as employees leave for reasons of family, better job prospects, or retirement. However, except in low-skill industries, a continual revolving door of new employees is usually not a good sign, since replacement and training are expensive.[113] For a high-turnover, low-paying job (under $30,000 a year), the Center for American Progress estimates that the costs to replace an employee is 16% of salary; for a mid-range position ($30,000–$50,000 a year), it is 20%; and for a highly educated executive position (such as $100,000 a year), it is 213%.[114]

Experience demonstrates five practical ways to reduce turnover: (1) Base hiring decisions on the extent to which an applicant's values fit the organization's values. (2) Provide post-hiring support, which is referred to as onboarding. As we mentioned in Chapter 9, onboarding programs help employees to integrate and transition to new jobs by making them familiar with corporate policies, procedures, culture, and politics by clarifying work-role expectations and responsibilities.[115] (3) Focus on enhancing employee engagement. (4) Incorporate realistic job previews (RJPs, discussed in Chapter 9) into the hiring process. (5) Offer employees benefits, such as flexible work hours (discussed in Chapter 12), that meet their needs and values.[116]

3. Evaluating Behavior That Exceeds Work Roles: Organizational Citizenship Behaviors

Organizational citizenship behaviors are those employee behaviors that are not directly part of employees' job descriptions—that exceed their work-role requirements. Examples, according to one description, include "such gestures as constructive statements about the department, expression of personal interest in the work of others, suggestions for improvement, training new people, respect for the spirit as well as the letter of housekeeping rules, care for organizational property, and punctuality and attendance well beyond standard or enforceable levels."[117] Research demonstrates a significant and moderately positive correlation between organizational citizenship behaviors and job satisfaction, productivity, efficiency, and customer satisfaction.[118]

4. Evaluating Behavior That Harms the Organization: Counterproductive Work Behaviors   The flip side of organizational citizenship behaviors would seem to be what are called **counterproductive work behaviors (CWB), types of behavior that harm employees and the organization as a whole.** Such behaviors may include absenteeism and tardiness, drug and alcohol abuse, and disciplinary problems but also extend beyond them to more serious acts such as accidents, sabotage, sexual harassment, violence, theft, and white-collar crime.[119] Some 96% of workers say they have experienced uncivil behavior, and 98% have witnessed it.[120]

Clearly, if an employee engages in some kind of CWB, the organization needs to respond quickly and appropriately, defining the specific behaviors that are unacceptable and the requirements for acceptable behavior.[121] It is more desirable, however, to take preventive measures. One way is to screen for CWB during the hiring process. For instance, it's been found that applicants scoring higher on cognitive ability (intelligence) tests are less likely to be involved in violence and property damage after they are hired.[122] Employees are also less likely to engage in CWB if they have satisfying jobs that offer autonomy or that don't require them to supervise too many people.[123] ●

EXAMPLE   The Toxic Workplace: "Rudeness Is Like the Common Cold"

Incivility. Rudeness. Jerks at work. They're all forms of CWB, and they're the bane of the office.

"Nothing is more costly to an organization's culture than a toxic employee," says management professor Christine Porath, a researcher in this area. "Rudeness is like the common cold—it's contagious, spreads quickly, and anyone can be a carrier."[124] Researcher Trevor Foulk concurs. "If someone is rude to me" he says, "it is likely that in my next interaction I will be rude to whomever I am talking to. You respond to their rudeness with your own rudeness."[125]

Sapping Energy and Productivity. Difficult coworkers are "de-energizers" who spread their dispiriting attitude to others, says Gretchen Spreitzer, also a management professor (and Porath's co-author). "They leave you feeling depleted, fatigued, and exhausted."[126] The more one has to interact with a de-energizer, the lower one's own performance.[127]

The incivility may be expressed by fellow employees' snippy remarks, eye-rolling, or chastising of another employee for being late. Toxic bosses may demoralize employees by such actions as "walking away from a conversation because they lose interest; answering calls in the middle of meetings without leaving the room; openly mocking people by pointing out their flaws or personality quirks in front of others," and similar incivilities, says Porath.[128]

The Price of Incivility. People who engage in negative and harmful behavior can hurt an organization's bottom line, say the authors of the study "Toxic Workers."[129] In fact, "avoiding a toxic employee can save a company more than twice as much as bringing on a star performer—specifically, avoiding a toxic worker was worth about $12,500 in turnover costs," says one writer reporting on the study.[130]

A paper by Porath and Christine Pearson says the costs of incivility are diminishing creativity, deteriorating performance and team spirit, and fleeing customers. "Employees are less creative when they feel disrespected, and many get fed up and leave," they write. "About half deliberately decrease their effort or lower the quality of their work. And incivility damages customer relationships."[131]

Spotting the Toxic Office. You'll know you're working in a toxic office when you see employees "congregate in hush-hush circles around cubicles after meetings to put a negative spin on what just transpired," says one report. Or when managers withhold information or employees feel it's not safe to offer their ideas, creativity, or inputs. And you'll know it's really time to update your resume when people around you start breaking down and experiencing health issues.[132]

YOUR CALL

If you were working in a toxic workplace and had to stay there for a while, what would you do to try to make things better?

11.5 The New Diversified Workforce

MAJOR QUESTION

What trends in workplace diversity should managers be aware of?

THE BIG PICTURE

One of today's most important management challenges is working with stakeholders of all sorts who vary widely in diversity—in age, gender, race, religion, ethnicity, sexual orientation, capabilities, and socioeconomic background. Managers should also be aware of the differences between internal and external dimensions of diversity and barriers to diversity.

Might you hold a few preconceptions that are worth examining? Here's a reality check:

■ **Assumption: Illegal immigrants dramatically impact the U.S. economy.** No, says the Pew Research Center. Undocumented immigrants represent only about 5.1% of the civilian workforce.[133]

■ **Assumption: Customer bias favoring white men has just about disappeared.** Unfortunately not, suggests a study of college students, which found that people give higher ratings for customer satisfaction to white men than to women and members of minorities.[134]

■ **Assumption: Young workers earn less than they used to.** Yes, evidently. The wages for young college graduates dropped an average of 2.5% between 2000 and 2015.[135]

The United States is becoming more diverse in its ethnic, racial, gender, and age makeup—more nonwhite, more single, more working parents, and so on—and the consequences are not always what you would expect.

In the view of Scott E. Page, professor of complex systems, political science, and economics at the University of Michigan, diversity and variety in staffing produce organizational strength.[136] "Diverse groups of people bring to organizations more and different ways of seeing a problem," he told an interviewer, "and, thus, faster/better ways of solving it. . . . There's certainly a lot of evidence that people's identity groups—ethnic, racial, sexual, age—matter when it comes to diversity in thinking."[137]

Diversity may have its benefits, but it can also be an important management challenge. Let's consider this.

How to Think about Diversity: Which Differences Are Important?

Diversity represents all the ways people are unlike and alike—the differences and similarities in age, gender, race, religion, ethnicity, sexual orientation, capabilities, and socioeconomic background. Note here that diversity is not synonymous with differences. Rather, it encompasses both differences and similarities. This means that as a manager you need to manage both simultaneously.

To help distinguish the important ways in which people differ, diversity experts Lee Gardenswartz and Anita Rowe have identified a "diversity wheel" consisting of four layers of diversity: (1) *personality*, (2) *internal dimensions*, (3) *external dimensions*, and (4) *organizational dimensions. (See Figure 11.3, next page.)*

Let's consider these four layers:

Personality   At the center of the diversity wheel is personality. It is at the center because, as we said in Section 11.1, *personality* is defined as the stable physical and mental characteristics responsible for a person's identity.

Internal Dimensions   **Internal dimensions of diversity** are those human differences that exert a powerful, sustained effect throughout every stage of our lives: gender, age,

FIGURE 11.3   The diversity wheel
Four layers of diversity

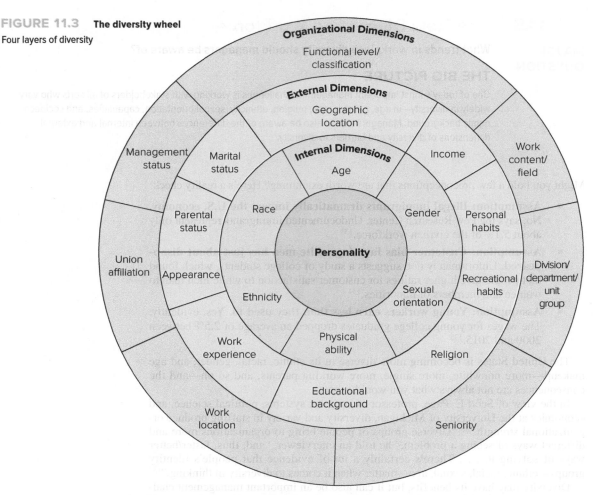

Source: From Diverse Teams at Work *by Lee Gardenswartz and Anita Rowe. Copyright 2003, Society for Human Resource Management, Alexandria, VA.*

ethnicity, race, sexual orientation, and physical abilities.[138] These are referred to as the *primary* dimensions of diversity because they are not within our control, for the most part. Yet they strongly influence our attitudes, expectations, and assumptions about other people, which in turn influence our own behavior.

What characterizes internal dimensions of diversity is that they are visible and salient in people. And precisely because these characteristics are so visible, they may be associated with certain stereotypes—for instance, that black people work in menial jobs.

Example: In a 2014 television interview, President Barack Obama recalled how, while waiting outside a restaurant after dinner, he had been handed car keys to fetch a vehicle from valet parking. Michelle Obama recounted while, as First Lady and on a trip to a Target store, she was asked by another shopper to help get something off a high shelf. (She added, "These incidents in the black community, this is the regular course of life.")[139]

External Dimensions   **External dimensions of diversity** include an element of choice; they consist of the personal characteristics that people acquire, discard, or modify throughout their lives: educational background, marital status, parental status, religion, income, geographic location, work experience, recreational habits, appearance, and personal habits. They are referred to as the *secondary* dimensions of diversity because we have a greater ability to influence or control them than we do internal dimensions.

These external dimensions also exert a significant influence on our perceptions, behavior, and attitudes. If you are not a believer in the Muslim religion, for example, you may not perceive the importance of some of its practices—as did Abercrombie and Fitch subsidiary Hollister, which told college student Hani Khan that she had to remove her hijab (Islamic headscarf) to work at its San Mateo, California, store, then fired her when she refused. The Equal Employment Opportunity Commission sued the company in 2011 on Khan's behalf, on the grounds that a headscarf did not affect her job performance.[140]

Organizational Dimensions   Organizational dimensions include management status, union affiliation, work location, seniority, work content, and division or department.

Trends in Workforce Diversity

How is the U.S. workforce apt to become more diverse in the 21st century? Let's examine five categories on the internal dimension—*age, gender, race/ethnicity, sexual orientation,* and *physical/mental abilities*—and one category on the external dimension, *educational level.*

Age: More Older People in the Workforce   The most significant demographic event, the late Peter Drucker suggested, "is that in the developed countries the number and proportion of younger people is rapidly shrinking. . . . Those shrinking numbers of younger people will have to both drive their economies and help support much larger numbers of older people."[141] Particularly in Europe and Northeast Asia, and to a lesser extent in the United States, an aging population is "a looming economic and social burden," says a recent Pew Research Center report.[142]

Because the median age of Americans is currently 37.8 years—the oldest in our history—it seems clear that managers will probably be dealing with an older workforce (indeed, 38% of employees now are older than their boss).[143] Many such employees, whether by choice or by necessity, will continue working.[144] At 95 years old, Harriett Clopper, for instance, was still driving herself to work to her job as a greeter at a McDonald's in Hagerstown, Maryland—something she'd been doing for 20 years.[145]

In the United States, workers 55 and older are expected to make up a full *one-quarter* of the labor force in 2024 (up from 21.7% in 2014). Young workers, those ages 16–24, are projected to decline to 11.3% of the labor force in 2024 (down from 13.7% in 2014). The in-betweeners, those ages 25–54, will probably account for about two-thirds (64%) of the workforce in 2024.[146]

Diversity enriches. A diverse population in a company can provide ideas, experience, and points of view that strengthen the business culture. What has been your experience, if any, with a diverse workplace?
© The Businessman/Alamy RF

Do you have much experience being around older people? How do you feel about the idea of working with them? To find out, try Self-Assessment 11.5.

connect SELF-ASSESSMENT 11.5

What Are Your Attitudes about Working with Older Employees?

The following survey was designed to assess your attitudes about working with older employees. Please be prepared to answer these questions if your instructor has assigned Self-Assessment 11.5 in Connect.

1. What is the quality of your relationships with older employees? How about your satisfaction with working with older people?

2. How might the quality of relationships with older employees affect your performance and promotability?

3. To what extent might your satisfaction with working with older people impact your performance and promotability?

Gender: More Women Working   Since the 1960s, women have been flooding into the workplace in great numbers, making up 46.8% of the labor force in 2014 and expected to increase to 47.2% in 2024, whereas men are expected to decline from 53.2% to 52.8% in the same period.[147] In addition, more and more businesses are now owned by women—between 2007 and 2016, the number of women-owned firms increased by 45%, compared to just a 9% increase among all businesses.[148] Finally, women are gaining some ground in the top rungs of business. In 2016, women held 21 (4.2%) of CEO positions at S&P 500 companies, and the same number (21, or 4.2%) of Fortune 500 companies (up from 15 in 2009, but down from 24 women CEOs in 2014).[149]

But if pay discrepancies between women and men have improved slightly, as of 2014 (as we noted in Chapter 9) women overall still earned only 79 cents to every $1 for a man, according to a *Wall Street Journal* analysis, or 83 cents, according to the U.S. Census Bureau.[150] Traditionally, women have earned roughly the same pay as men only in jobs paying $25,000–$30,000 a year, but the farther up the pay scale and the higher the education level, the wider the earnings gap. For every dollar a man earns, a woman earns the following: cashier—92 cents; registered nurse—91 cents; administrative assistant—87 cents. For professionals, however, a woman earns proportionately less: psychologist—77 cents; lawyer or judge—75 cents; physician or surgeon—68 cents.[151]

The obstacles to women's progress are known as the **glass ceiling**—the metaphor for an invisible barrier preventing women and minorities from being promoted to top executive jobs. For instance, in one recent survey of Fortune 500 companies, females accounted for only 14.6% of executive-officer positions.[152]

What factors are holding women back? Three that are mentioned are negative stereotypes, lack of mentors, and limited experience in line or general management.[153] Among the strategies suggested for fighting gender discrimination: getting more women on boards, increasing the diversity of the applicant pool, evaluating work assignments to ensure they are fairly distributed, making everyone's salary public, and helping with work/life management.[154]

Interestingly, however, peers, managers, direct reports, and judges/trained observers rated women executives as more effective than men. Men also rated themselves as more effective than women evaluated themselves.[155] Indeed, one study, by Catalyst, an advocacy group for women in business, found that companies with more women executives have better financial performance.[156] In Chapter 9 we mentioned that venture capital firms that invested in women-led companies during the decade 2000–2010 outperformed those that didn't.[157] We discuss women in leadership further in Chapter 14 and women and communication in Chapter 15.

Race and Ethnicity: More People of Color in the Workforce   The non-Hispanic white population is projected to peak in 2024, then to slowly decrease. Whites are projected to change from 77.5% in 2014 to 68.5% in 2060, African Americans from 13.2% to 14.3%, Asians from 5.4% to 9.3%, Hispanics or Latinos from 17.4% to 28.6%, and American Indian/Alaskan Native from 1.2% to 1.5%.[158] We already mentioned that people of color have hit the glass ceiling, with whites holding more of the managerial and professional jobs. In addition, there are two other trends that show that American businesses need to do a lot better by minority populations.

First, minorities tend to earn less than whites. Median household income in 2014 was $35,398 for African Americans and $42,491 for Hispanics. It was $60,256 for non-Hispanic whites. (Asians had the highest median income, at $75,297.)[159]

Second, a number of studies have shown that minorities experienced more perceived discrimination, racism-related stress, and less psychological support than whites did.[160]

Sexual Orientation: LGBT People Become More Visible   A May 2015 Gallup survey found that the American public thinks that, on average, 23% of Americans are gay or lesbian—wildly off the mark from the 3.8% of the adult population who self-identified as lesbian, gay, bisexual, or transgender (LGBT) in another Gallup poll four months earlier.[161] Regardless, Americans have become far more tolerant of gay and lesbian behavior, with 63% in 2015 saying they found LGBT relations "morally acceptable" (up from 38% in 2002) and 60% favoring legalized same-sex marriage (up from 35% in 1999).[162]

Despite the changing social and legal landscape, however, over half (53%) of LGBT workers nationwide said they hide who they are at work, according to a 2014 report.[163] LGBT workers report higher levels of stress compared with other workers, stress that can be alleviated with LGBT-supportive workplace policies.[164] Finally, gay and bisexual male workers were found to earn 10%–32% less than equally qualified heterosexual counterparts.[165]

By now the vocabulary surrounding LGBT issues has changed considerably. For instance, **transgender is an umbrella term for people whose sense of their gender differs from what is expected based on the sex characteristics with which they are born.**[166] That is, these are the estimated 0.03% of Americans who feel their bodies and genders do not match, that the gender label they received at birth does not fit.[167] These are people who don't feel distinctly male or female and who use labels that describe a sense of gender that's neither "man" nor "woman"—labels such as *gender fluid* and *nonbinary*.

Indeed, with such distinctions, "LGBT" isn't considered inclusive enough to suit many people today, and the rubric has been expanded to LGBTQ, or even LGBTQQIAP, in which the different letters stand for different things. "Q," for instance, can stand for "Queer," but it can also stand for "Questioning." "I" stands for "Intersex." "A" can stand for "Ally," but it can also stand for "Asexual," characterized by the absence of sexual attraction.[168] "P" stands for "Pansexual." These are not just academic issues, as one can see in the way authorities are having to rethink how men's and women's bathrooms and locker rooms should accommodate transgender people.[169]

How important is the issue of sexual orientation? Once again, if managers are concerned about hiring and keeping workplace talent, they shouldn't ignore the motivation and productivity of 3.8% of the workforce. Many employers are recognizing this: 88% of Fortune 500 companies include sexual orientation in their nondiscrimination policies, and more than 60% offer domestic partner health benefits for same-sex couples, according to the Human Rights Campaign.[170]

No doubt things will change further, since the U.S. Supreme Court made it clear in June 2015 that marriage is no longer *solely* a legal union between a man and a woman. "The right to marry is a fundamental right inherent in the liberty of the person," Justice Anthony Kennedy wrote (in *Obergefell* v. *Hodges*) in support of the majority ruling that states may not refuse to marry same-sex couples. "Under the Due Process and Equal Protection Clauses of the Fourteenth Amendment couples of the same sex may not be deprived of that right and that liberty."[171]

People with Differing Physical and Mental Abilities   About 20% of civilian, noninstitutionalized Americans have a physical or mental disability, according to the U.S. Census Bureau.[172] Since 1992 we have had the **Americans with Disabilities Act (ADA),** which prohibits discrimination against the disabled and requires organizations to reasonably accommodate an individual's disabilities.[173]

Even so, disabled people have difficulty finding work. The Census Bureau found less than half (41.1%) of disabled people ages 21–64 were employed, compared to 79.1% of abled people.[174] Here, too, is a talent pool that managers will no doubt find themselves tapping into in the coming years. (Disability studies, incidentally, has become a hot subject on college campuses.)[175]

Disability. Everyone recognizes the wheelchair as signifying that a person is disabled, but other disabilities are not easily identified—and may not invite understanding. Do you think that mental disabilities, for example, should be accommodated in employment? If you were subject to mood swings, would you think that would prevent you from doing your job effectively?
© Scott T. Baxter/Getty Images RF

Educational Levels: Mismatches between Education and Workforce Needs Two important mismatches between education and workplace are these:

- **College graduates may be in jobs for which they are overqualified.** Almost half a million college graduates are working minimum-wage jobs—260,000 with bachelor's degrees, 200,000 with associates degrees.[176] In other words, a great many college graduates are **underemployed—working at jobs that require less education than they have**—for example, in 2014, 16.3% of all workers who worked in restaurants and bars in the United States had a bachelor's degree or higher, compared to 14.2% in 2000.[177]

- **High-school dropouts and others may not have the literacy skills needed for many jobs.** A recent study found that 7% of all people in the United States between the ages of 16 and 24 had dropped out of high school in 2014.[178] Men make up 55% of such dropouts. If, as has been alleged, more than two-thirds of the American workforce reads below ninth-grade level, that is a problem for employers, because about 70% of the on-the-job reading materials are written at or above that level.[179]

Barriers to Diversity

Some barriers are erected by diverse people themselves. In the main, however, most barriers are put in their paths by organizations.[180] When we speak of "the organization's barriers," we are, of course, referring to the *people* in the organization—especially those who may have been there for a while—who are resistant to making it more diverse.

Resistance to change in general is an attitude that all managers come up against from time to time, and resistance to diversity is simply one variation. It may be expressed in the following six ways.

1. Stereotypes and Prejudices   **Ethnocentrism is the belief that one's native country, culture, language, abilities, or behavior is superior to those of another culture.** (An example was the "Linsanity," or surprised enthusiasm, expressed by sports fans in 2012 over pro basketball player Jeremy Lin, a Harvard-educated economics graduate of Chinese descent, who defied racial stereotypes by scoring at least 23 points—in one case, 38 points—in his first four games with the New York Knicks. Before Lin, many people assumed that blacks and whites were better basketball players than Asian Americans.)[181] When differences are viewed as being weaknesses—which is what many stereotypes and prejudices ultimately come down to—this may be expressed as a concern that diversity hiring will lead to a sacrifice in competence and quality.

2. Fear of Discrimination against Majority Group Members   Some employees are afraid that attempts to achieve greater diversity in their organization will result in bias against the majority group—that more black or Asian employees will be promoted to fire captain or police lieutenant, for example, over the heads of supposedly more qualified whites.

3. Resistance to Diversity Program Priorities   Some companies, such as PepsiCo, IBM, and Deloitte & Touche, have taken aggressive diversity approaches, such as offering special classes teaching tolerance for diversity and seminars in how to get along.[182] Some employees may see diversity programs as distracting them from the organization's "real work." In addition, they may be resentful of diversity-promoting policies that are reinforced through special criteria in the organization's performance appraisals and reward systems.

4. A Negative Diversity Climate   **Diversity climate is a subcomponent of an organization's overall climate and is defined as the employees' aggregate "perceptions about the**

Woman manager. On the job she might be a high-powered manager of scores of people, but at home she may still be expected to be the principal manager of an important few—the children. © Liam Norris/Getty Images RF

organization's diversity-related formal structure characteristics and informal values."[183] Diversity climate is positive when employees view the organization as being fair to all types of employees, which promotes employee loyalty and overall firm performance.[184] It also enhances psychological safety. **Psychological safety reflects the extent to which people feel free to express their ideas and beliefs without fear of negative consequences.**[185]

5. Lack of Support for Family Demands

In 2015, there were over 34.3 million married couples with children under 18 in the United States. In 60.6% of such families, both parents worked; in 20.8%, only the father worked; and in 5.3%, only the mother worked.[186] But more and more women are moving back and forth between being at-home mothers and in the workforce, as economic circumstances dictate.[187] Yet in a great many households, it is still women who primarily take care of children, as well as other domestic chores. When organizations aren't supportive in offering flexibility in hours and job responsibilities, these women may find it difficult to work evenings and weekends or to take overnight business trips.

6. A Hostile Work Environment for Diverse Employees

Hostile work environments are characterized by sexual, racial, and age harassment and can be in violation of Equal Employment Opportunity law, such as Title VII of the Civil Rights Act.[188] Whether perpetrated against women, men, older individuals, or LGBTQ people, hostile environments are demeaning, unethical, and appropriately called "work environment pollution." A recent example involved former Fox anchor Gretchen Carlson. She filed a complaint saying she was fired because she refused to sleep with Fox News CEO Roger Ailes. Data from the U.S. Equal Employment Opportunity Commission revealed that almost half of its 30,000 harassment complaints received in 2015 involved sex.[189] You certainly won't get employees' best work if they believe the work environment is hostile toward them. ●

11.6   Understanding Stress and Individual Behavior

What causes workplace stress, and how can it be reduced?

THE BIG PICTURE

Stress is what people feel when enduring extraordinary demands or opportunities and are not sure how to handle them. There are six sources of stress: individual differences, individual task, individual role, group, organizational, and nonwork demands. We describe some consequences of stress and three ways to reduce it in the organization.

Stress is the tension people feel when they are facing or enduring extraordinary demands, constraints, or opportunities and are uncertain about their ability to handle them effectively.[190] Stress is the feeling of tension and pressure; the source of stress is called a **stressor.**

A 2015 study by the American Psychological Association found that parents, younger generations, and those living in households making less than $50,000 per year report higher levels of stress than Americans overall, especially when it comes to money. Those who have particularly high stress about money are more likely to say they engage in unhealthy behaviors to manage their stress.[191]

There's no question that work is stressful. The 2015 study found that the top two sources of stress are money (67%) and work (65%). More adults are also reporting "extreme stress," with 24% saying they were highly stressed in 2015 compared to 18% a year earlier. Commonly cited causes of work stress include low salaries (54%), lack of opportunities for growth or advancement (53%), lack of recognition (53%), and dissatisfaction with their employer's work–life balance practices (43%).[192]

The Toll of Workplace Stress

The American Institute of Stress estimates that workplace stress costs the U.S. economy over $300 billion a year in health care, missed work, and stress-reduction treatment.[193] Stress can cause conflicts at work, make you fatigued all the time, and generate problems like insomnia, backaches, headaches, and chest pain.[194]

Work stress can also, as you might guess, put managers at risk. Men who suppress anger at work are two to five times more likely to suffer heart attacks or die from heart disease as those who express their "desk rage."[195] Losing one's job is, as you might imagine, a very stressful event, being associated with decreased psychological and physical well-being.[196] A Yale study found that layoffs more than doubled the risk of heart attack and stroke among older workers.[197]

Workplace stress diminishes positive emotions, job satisfaction, organizational commitment, and job performance and increases alcohol and illicit drug use, sleeplessness, overeating, and job turnover.[198] Indeed, historically researchers have generally believed that there is an *inverted U-shaped relationship* between stress and performance. That is, low levels of stress lead to low performance (because people are not "charged up" to perform), but high levels of stress also lead to an energy-sapping fight-or-flight response that produces low performance. Optimal performance, according to this hypothesis, results when people are subjected to moderate levels of stress.

How Does Stress Work?

Stress has both physical and emotional components. Physically, according to Canadian researcher Hans Selye, considered the father of the modern concept of stress, stress is "the nonspecific response of the body to any demand made upon it."[199] Emotionally, stress has been defined as the feeling of being overwhelmed, "the perception that events or circumstances have challenged, or exceeded, a person's ability to cope."[200]

Stressors can be *hassles,* or simple irritants, such as misplacing or losing things, having concerns about one's physical appearance, and having too many things to do. Or they can be *crises,* such as sudden occasions of overwhelming terror—a horrible auto accident, an incident of childhood abuse. Or they can be *strong stressors,* which can dramatically strain a person's ability to adapt—extreme physical discomfort, such as chronic severe back pain.

Stressors can be both *negative* and *positive.* That is, one can understand that being fired or being divorced can be a great source of stress, but so can being promoted or getting married. As Selye writes, "It is immaterial whether the agent or the situation we face is pleasant or unpleasant; all that counts is the intensity of the demand for adjustment and adaptation."[201] In addition, Selye distinguished between bad stress (what he called "distress"), in which the result of the stressor can be anxiety and illness, and good stress ("eustress," pronounced *yu stress*), which can stimulate a person to better coping and adaptation, such as performing well on a test.[202] In this discussion, however, we are mainly concerned with how stress negatively affects people and their performance.

EXAMPLE

Good Stress: Is Being a Worrywart a Benefit?

Worrying about possible upcoming bad news, such as maybe a dismal grade in a course? That's stressful, of course. But such worrying can also be beneficial—depending on how you handle it.

Awaiting Important News. A study of law school graduates waiting to hear of high-stakes results ("Did I pass the California bar exam?") found those who tried coping techniques (exercise, work, binge-watching TV, talking with friends) failed "miserably at suppressing distress," says a report of the study. But for those who actively worried, when the news arrived, "the worriers were more elated than their relaxed peers, if it was good; if bad, the worriers were better prepared."[203] Of three strategies of waiting—distracting oneself and trying not to freak out, looking for a silver lining to failure, and anticipating the possibility of failure—the third one, called "defensive pessimism," worked best.[204]

Does Worrying Lead to Better Performance? "Constructive worry enables you to develop an adversity plan, in the sense that you're worrying about all the things that could go wrong and how you're going to fix them," says psychologist Gregg Steinberg. "This can prepare you very well for whatever might come"—tough questions in a job interview, for instance, or criticism of your work by your boss.[205] It's important, however, that you not ruminate over things you can't control.

YOUR CALL

Some jobs are better than others for worrywarts—particularly if they also have a "realistic, detail-focused mindset," according to one report—among them engineering, computer science, and accounting.[206] An actuarial accountant looking for negligence by clients, for instance, will be better motivated by worrying to pay more attention to the evidence—and thus do a better job. How about you? Do you sweat the small stuff? Maybe you should.

The Sources of Job-Related Stress

There are six sources of stress on the job: (1) *demands created by individual differences,* (2) *individual task demands,* (3) *individual role demands,* (4) *group demands,* (5) *organizational demands,* and (6) *nonwork demands.*

1. Demands Created by Individual Differences: The Stress Created by Genetic or Personality Characteristics Some people are born worriers, those with a gene mutation (known as BDNF) that Yale researchers identify with people who chronically obsess over negative thoughts.[207] Others are impatient, hurried, deadline-ridden, competitive types with the personality characteristic known as **Type A behavior pattern,** meaning they are involved in a chronic, determined struggle to accomplish more in less time.[208] Type A behavior has been associated with increased performance in the work of professors, students, and life insurance brokers.[209] However, it also has been associated with greater cardiovascular activity and higher blood pressure, as well as to heart disease, especially for individuals who showed strong feelings of anger, hostility, and aggression.[210]

2. Individual Task Demands: The Stress Created by the Job Itself

Some occupations are more stressful than others.[211] Being a retail store manager, for instance, can be quite stressful for some people.[212] But being a home-based blogger, paid on a piecework basis to generate news and comment, may mean working long hours to the point of exhaustion.[213] Jobs that require "emotional labor"—pretending to be cheerful or smiling all the time, no matter how you feel—can be particularly demanding.[214]

Low-level jobs can be more stressful than high-level jobs because employees often have less control over their lives and thus have less work satisfaction. Being a barista, day care teacher, hotel concierge, or purchasing agent, which don't usually pay very well, can be quite stressful.[215]

3. Individual Role Demands: The Stress Created by Others' Expectations of You

Roles are sets of behaviors that people expect of occupants of a position. Stress may come about because of *role overload, role conflict,* and *role ambiguity.*

- **Role overload.** Role overload occurs when others' expectations exceed one's ability. Example: If you as a student are carrying a full course load plus working two-thirds time plus trying to have a social life, you know what role overload is—and what stress is. Similar things happen to managers and workers.

- **Role conflict.** Role conflict occurs when one feels torn by the different expectations of important people in one's life. Example: Your supervisor says the company needs you to stay late to meet an important deadline, but your family expects you to be present for your child's birthday party.

- **Role ambiguity.** Role ambiguity occurs when others' expectations are unknown. Example: You find your job description and the criteria for promotion vague, a complaint often voiced by newcomers to an organization.

4. Group Demands: The Stress Created by Coworkers and Managers

Even if you don't particularly care for the work you do but like the people you work with, that can be a great source of satisfaction and prevent stress. When people don't get along, that can be a great stressor. Alternatively, even if you have stress under control, a coworker's stress might bother you, diminishing productivity.[216]

In addition, managers can create stress for employees. People who have bad managers are five times more likely to have stress-induced headaches, upset stomachs, and loss of sleep.[217]

5. Organizational Demands: The Stress Created by the Environment and Culture

The physical environments of some jobs are great sources of stress: poultry processing, asbestos removal, coal mining, fire fighting, police work, ambulance driving, and so on. Even white-collar work can take place in a stressful environment, with poor lighting, too much noise, improper placement of furniture, and no privacy.[218]

An organizational culture that promotes high-pressure work demands on employees will fuel the stress response.[219] The pace of information technology certainly adds to the stress. "For example," says Michael Patsalos-Fox, chairman of the Americas region for consulting firm McKinsey & Company, "you used to have media companies and you used to have telecom [telecommunications] companies, right? . . . The problem is that they are encroaching on each other. The onset of a lot of technologies is blurring the boundary between industries that were quite separate, creating opportunities for industries to attack each other."[220] Such rapidly changing technologies and financial pressures are what keep top executives awake at night.

Stressful No. 7. Many jobs are stressful, some because people's lives are at stake (military personnel, firefighters, police officers), some because they are highly deadline-driven (event coordinators, public relations executives). Senior corporate executives ranked No. 7 on CareerCast's 2014 list of 10 most stressful jobs. If you hate stress, what kind of job should you have? © Comstock/PunchStock RF

6. Nonwork Demands: The Stresses Created by Forces outside the Organization   As anyone knows who has had to cope with money problems, divorce, support of elderly relatives, or other serious nonwork concerns, the stresses outside one's work life can have a significant effect on work. Even people with ordinary lives can find the stress of coping with family life rugged going.

The Consequences of Stress

Positive stress is constructive and can energize you, increasing your effort, creativity, and performance. Negative stress is destructive, resulting in poorer-quality work, dissatisfaction, errors, absenteeism, and turnover.

Symptoms of Stress   Negative stress reveals itself in three kinds of symptoms:

De-stressing. Experts say that exercise can be a tremendous stress reliever. Many companies maintain physical-fitness centers not only as an employee perk but also because they realize that exercise helps to improve stamina and endurance while reducing tension.
© Ariel Skelley/Blend Images RF

- **Physiological signs.** Lesser physiological signs are sweaty palms, restlessness, backaches, headaches, upset stomach, and nausea. More serious signs are hypertension and heart attacks.

- **Psychological signs.** Psychological symptoms include forgetfulness, boredom, irritability, nervousness, anger, anxiety, hostility, and depression.[221]

- **Behavioral signs.** Behavioral symptoms include sleeplessness, changes in eating habits, and increased smoking/alcohol/drug abuse. Stress may be revealed through reduced performance and job satisfaction.

Burnout   "When you keep investing more energy and the return remains low, that's when you burn out," suggests Michael Staver, founder of an executive training company.[222]

Burnout is a state of emotional, mental, and even physical exhaustion, expressed as listlessness, indifference, or frustration. The Maslach Burnout Inventory lists 22 elements, including emotional exhaustion, cynicism or depersonalization, and reduced personal efficacy.[223] Clearly, the greatest consequence of negative stress for the organization is reduced productivity. Overstressed employees are apt to call in sick, miss deadlines, take longer lunch breaks, and show indifference to performance. However, some may put in great numbers of hours at work without getting as much accomplished as previously.[224]

Alcohol and Other Drug Abuse   Have an employee who's often late? Who frequently calls in sick on Mondays? Who is somewhat sloppy? Whose memory is slipping?[225] Maybe he or she is afflicted with *alcoholism,* a chronic, progressive, and potentially fatal disease characterized by a growing compulsion to drink. Alcoholics come from every occupation and social class, from students to college professors to priests to airline pilots. Alcoholism may not interfere with a person's job in an obvious way until it shows up in absenteeism, accidents, slipshod work, or significant use of a company's medical benefits.

As is well known, there is an epidemic of drug abuse and drug overdose deaths across America.[226] Alcohol is the most common drug of abuse, but the misuse of others may also affect a person's productivity—legal drugs, such as tranquilizers or opioids, or illegal drugs such as marijuana, methamphetamine, cocaine, or heroin.

If you as a manager think you might be dealing with an employee with a substance-abuse problem, it's suggested you not try to make accusations but firmly point out that productivity is suffering and that it's up to the subordinate to do something about it. While not doing any counseling yourself, you can try steering the employee to the human resources department, which may have an employee assistance program to help employees overcome personal problems affecting their job performance.

Incidentally, although many people swear by 12-step programs, such as that offered by Alcoholics Anonymous, an examination of several studies found that such programs were no more and no less successful than any other interventions in reducing alcohol dependence and alcohol-related problems.[227]

Reducing Stressors in the Organization

There are all kinds of **buffers, or administrative changes, that managers can make to reduce the stressors that lead to employee burnout.**[228] Examples: Extra staff or equipment at peak periods. Increased freedom to make decisions. Recognition for accomplishments. Time off for rest or personal development. Assignment to a new position. Three-to five-day employee retreats at off-site locations for relaxation and team-building activities. Sabbatical leave programs to replenish employees' energy and desire to work.

Some general organizational strategies for reducing unhealthy stressors are the following:[229]

- **Roll out employee assistance programs. Employee assistance programs (EAPs) include a host of programs aimed at helping employees to cope with stress, burnout, substance abuse, health-related problems, family and marital issues, and any general problem that negatively influences job performance.**[230]

- **Recommend a holistic wellness approach. A holistic wellness program focuses on self-responsibility, nutritional awareness, relaxation techniques, physical fitness, and environmental awareness.** This approach goes beyond stress reduction by encouraging employees to try to balance physical, mental, and social well-being by accepting personal responsibility for developing and adhering to a health promotion program. For instance, if you're too stressed to exercise, you might try some meditation.[231] (In India, well-off urban professionals relieve stress by chanting Buddhist mantras.)[232]

- **Create a supportive environment.** Job stress often results because employees work under poor supervision and lack freedom. Wherever possible, it's better to keep the organizational environment less formal, more personal, and more supportive of employees. Mentors can also help reduce stress.[233]

- **Make jobs interesting.** Stress also results when jobs are routinized and boring. It's better to try to structure jobs so that they allow employees some freedom.

- **Make career counseling available.** Companies such as IBM make career planning available, which reduces the stress that comes when employees don't know what their career options are and where they're headed. ●

Good times—for now. Office stress can certainly lead to "a few drinks after work" becoming a regular pastime—and then almost a necessity, for some people. More than 30% of American adults have abused alcohol or suffered from alcoholism at some point in their lives. Those who get treatment first receive it, on average, at about age 30—eight years after they develop their dependency on drinking. Only 24% of alcoholics, however, receive any treatment at all. Do you find alcohol helps relieve your stress? Are you concerned about it?
© Image Source/Getty Images RF

affective component of an attitude 365

Americans with Disabilities Act (ADA) 381

attitude 365

behavior 366

behavioral component of an attitude 365

Big Five personality dimensions 358

buffers 388

burnout 387

causal attribution 371

cognitive component of an attitude 365

cognitive dissonance 365

core self-evaluation 359

counterproductive work behaviors (CWB) 376

diversity 377

diversity climate 382

emotional intelligence 362

emotional stability 362

employee assistance programs (EAPs) 388

employee engagement 373

ethnocentrism 382

external dimensions of diversity 378

fundamental attribution bias 372

glass ceiling 380

halo effect 370

holistic wellness program 388

implicit bias 369

internal dimensions of diversity 377

job satisfaction 374

learned helplessness 360

locus of control 361

organizational behavior (OB) 364

organizational citizenship behaviors 375

organizational commitment 374

perception 368

personality 358

proactive personality 359

psychological safety 383

recency effect 371

roles 386

self-efficacy 360

self-esteem 360

self-fulfilling prophecy 372

self-serving bias 372

stereotyping 368

stress 384

stressor 384

transgender 381

Type A behavior pattern 385

underemployed 382

values 364

Key Points

11.1 Personality and Individual Behavior

- Personality consists of the stable psychological traits and behavioral attributes that give a person his or her identity. There are five personality dimensions and five personality traits that managers need to be aware of to understand workplace behavior.
- The Big Five personality dimensions are extroversion, agreeableness, conscientiousness, emotional stability, and openness to experience. Extroversion, an outgoing personality, is associated with success for managers and salespeople. Conscientiousness, or a dependable personality, is correlated with successful job performance. A person who scores well on conscientiousness may be a proactive personality, someone who is more apt to take initiative and persevere to influence the environment.
- A core self-evaluation represents a broad personality trait comprising four positive individual traits: (1) Self-efficacy is the belief in one's personal ability to do a task. Low self-efficacy is associated with learned helplessness, the debilitating lack of faith in one's ability to control one's environment. (2) Self-esteem is the extent to which people like or dislike themselves. (3) Locus of control indicates how much people believe they control their fate through their own efforts. (4) Emotional stability is the extent to which people feel secure and unworried and how likely they are to experience negative emotions under pressure.

- Emotional intelligence is defined as the ability to monitor your and others' feelings and use this information to guide your thinking and actions.

11.2 Values, Attitudes, and Behavior

- Organizational behavior (OB) is dedicated to better understanding and managing people at work. OB looks at two areas: individual behavior (discussed in this chapter) and group behavior (discussed in later chapters).
- Values must be distinguished from attitudes and from behavior. Values are abstract ideals that guide one's thinking and behavior across all situations.
- Attitudes are defined as learned predispositions toward a given object. Attitudes have three components. The affective component consists of the feelings or emotions one has about a situation. The cognitive component consists of the beliefs and knowledge one has about a situation. The behavioral component is how one intends or expects to behave toward a situation.
- When attitudes and reality collide, the result may be cognitive dissonance, the psychological discomfort a person experiences between his or her cognitive attitude and incompatible behavior. Cognitive dissonance depends on three factors: importance, control, and rewards. The ways to reduce cognitive dissonance are to change your attitude and/or your behavior, belittle the importance of the inconsistent behavior, or find consonant elements that outweigh the dissonant ones.

- Together, values and attitudes influence people's workplace behavior—their actions and judgments.

11.3 Perception and Individual Behavior

- Perception is the process of interpreting and understanding one's environment. Four types of distortion in perception are (1) stereotyping, the tendency to attribute to an individual the characteristics one believes are typical of the group to which that individual belongs; (2) implicit bias, which refers to the attitudes or beliefs that affect our understanding, actions, and decisions in an unconscious manner; (3) the halo effect, the forming of an impression of an individual based on a single trait; (4) the recency effect, the tendency to remember recent information better than earlier information; and (5) causal attribution, the activity of inferring causes for observed behavior. Two attributional tendencies that can distort one's interpretation of observed behavior are the fundamental attribution bias, in which people attribute another person's behavior to his or her personal characteristics rather than to situational factors, and the self-serving bias, in which people tend to take more personal responsibility for success than for failure.
- The self-fulfilling prophecy (Pygmalion effect) describes the phenomenon in which people's expectations of themselves or others lead them to behave in ways that make those expectations come true.

11.4 Work-Related Attitudes and Behaviors Managers Need to Deal With

- Managers need to be alert to work-related attitudes having to do with (1) employee engagement, an individual's involvement, satisfaction, and enthusiasm for work; (2) job satisfaction, the extent to which you feel positive or negative about various aspects of your work; and (3) organizational commitment, reflecting the extent to which an employee identifies with an organization and is committed to its goals.
- Among the types of behavior that managers need to influence are (1) performance and productivity; (2) absenteeism, when an employee doesn't show up for work, and turnover, when employees leave their jobs; (3) organizational citizenship behaviors, those employee behaviors that are not directly part of employees' job descriptions—that exceed their work-role requirements; and (4) counterproductive work behaviors, behaviors that harm employees and the organization as a whole.

11.5 The New Diversified Workforce

- Diversity represents all the ways people are alike and unlike—the differences and similarities in age, gender, race, religion, ethnicity, sexual orientation, capabilities, and socioeconomic background.
- There are two dimensions of diversity: (1) Internal dimensions of diversity are those human differences that exert a powerful, sustained effect throughout every stage of our lives: gender, ethnicity, race, physical abilities, age, and sexual orientation. (2) External dimensions of diversity

consist of the personal characteristics that people acquire, discard, or modify throughout their lives: personal habits, educational background, religion, income, marital status, and the like.
- By now the vocabulary surrounding LGBT issues has changed considerably. *Transgender* is an umbrella term for people whose sense of their gender differs from what is expected based on the sex characteristics with which they are born. LGBT isn't considered inclusive enough to suit many people today, and the rubric has been expanded to LGBTQ, in which "Q" can stand for "Queer" or for "Questioning."
- There are five categories in the internal dimension and one category in the external dimension in which the U.S. workforce is becoming more diverse: (1) age, (2) gender, (3) race and ethnicity, (4) sexual orientation, (5) physical/mental abilities, and, on the external dimension, (6) educational level.
- There are six ways in which employees and managers may express resistance to diversity: (1) Some express stereotypes and prejudices based on ethnocentrism, the belief that one's native country, culture, language, abilities, or behavior is superior to that of another country. (2) Some employees are afraid of discrimination against majority group members. (3) Some employees see diversity programs as distracting them from the organization's supposed "real work." (4) There may be a negative diversity climate, defined as the employees' aggregate perceptions about the organization's diversity-related formal structure characteristics and informal values and their feelings of psychological safety, the extent to which they feel free to express ideas without negative consequences. (5) Organizations may not be supportive of flexible hours and other matters that can help employees cope with family demands. (6) Organizations may show lack of support for career-building steps for diverse employees.

11.6 Understanding Stress and Individual Behavior

- Stress is the tension people feel when they are facing or enduring extraordinary demands, constraints, or opportunities and are uncertain about their ability to handle them effectively. Stress is the feeling of tension and pressure; the source of stress is called a stressor.
- There are six sources of stress on the job: (1) Demands created by individual differences may arise from a Type A behavior pattern, meaning people have the personality characteristic that involves them in a chronic, determined struggle to accomplish more in less time. (2) Individual task demands are the stresses created by the job itself. (3) Individual role demands are the stresses created by other people's expectations of you. Roles are sets of behaviors that people expect of occupants of a position. Stress may come about because of role overload, role conflict, or role ambiguity. (4) Group demands are the stresses created by coworkers and managers. (5) Organizational demands

are the stresses created by the environment and culture of the organization. (6) Nonwork demands are the stresses created by forces outside the organization, such as money problems or divorce.

- Positive stress can be constructive. Negative stress can result in poor-quality work; such stress is revealed through physiological, psychological, or behavioral signs. One sign is burnout, a state of emotional, mental, and even physical exhaustion. Stress can lead to alcohol and other drug abuse.

- There are buffers, or administrative changes, that managers can make to reduce the stressors that lead to employee burnout, such as adding extra staff or giving employees more power to make decisions. Some general organizational strategies for reducing unhealthy stressors are to roll out employee assistance programs, recommend a holistic wellness approach, create a supportive environment, make jobs interesting, and make career counseling available.

Understanding the Chapter: What Do I Know?

1. What are the Big Five personality dimensions?
2. What are four personality traits managers need to be aware of to understand workplace behavior?
3. How is emotional intelligence defined?
4. How do you distinguish values from attitudes and behavior?
5. What is the process of perception?
6. What are five types of distortion in perception, and what is the Pygmalion effect?
7. What are three work-related attitudes managers need to be conscious of?
8. What are four types of behavior that managers need to influence?
9. Explain the two dimensions of diversity.
10. What are six sources of stress on the job?

Management in Action

Individual Differences, Values, Attitudes, and Diversity at Facebook

Mark Zuckerberg, co-founder and creator of Facebook, is now its CEO. He was born in 1984 to well-educated parents: His mom was a psychiatrist and dad a dentist. He went to an exclusive preparatory school and was captain of the fencing team. He liked the classics and writing. He also had passion and skill for working with computers at a very young age.

Zuckerberg created his first messaging program using Atari BASIC around age 12. His family used it to communicate, and his dad used it in his dental office. He entered Harvard in 2002 and quickly became known as a skilled software developer. Zuckerberg developed computer skills at Harvard working on projects like CourseMatch, Facemash, and Harvard Connection. The Harvard Connection experience resulted in the famous lawsuit between the founders of Harvard Connection and Zuckerberg: Zuckerberg settled for around $65 million. He started the core of Facebook from his dorm room and left Harvard in 2004 to work full-time on Facebook.[234]

In 2016, there were more than 1.65 billion active Facebook users. This represents a 15% increase year over year. The most common demographic of users is age 25–34 (29.7%). There are over 300 million photos posted daily and over 4.5 million daily likes. The company's revenue grew from $7.8 billion in 2013 to over $17 billion in 2015. Facebook is clearly the largest, and potentially most influential, social media site on the planet.[235]

Zuckerberg's Personal Characteristics

Zuckerberg, or Zuck, as known to most of his acquaintances, is pale, medium build, and about five feet eight. He stands erect and generally dresses in T-shirts, jeans, and sneakers. "His affect can be distant and disorienting, a strange mixture of shy and cocky," according to a *New Yorker* writer. "When he's not interested in what someone is talking about, he'll just look away and say, 'Yeah, yeah.'" He's known to come across as flip and condescending, but "face to face he is often charming," says the writer.[236]

Zuckerberg does not prefer speaking to the press or participating in public appearances. He is highly motivated and turned down offers to sell Facebook for billions in the early 2000s because he wanted to keep running and growing the company. Founding and growing the company demonstrates intelligence and risk taking. It certainly took courage to drop out of Harvard to pursue a dream.[237]

He's generous and believes in equality, world peace, and happiness. In 2013, "he donated $100 million to the failing Newark Public School system in New Jersey" and "signed the 'Giving Pledge,' promising to donate at least 50 percent of his wealth to charity over the course of his lifetime."[238]

Zuckerberg is driven to achieve and has high expectations of others. He stated, "Move fast and break things. Unless you are breaking stuff, you are not moving fast enough." He also cares about building something that improves the lives of others. "And if you can make something that makes people's life better, then that's something that's really good," he said.[239]

Facebook's Mission, Values, and Culture

Zuckerberg did not start Facebook to make money. Rather, he was pursuing a social mission "to make the world more open and connected." In Facebook's IPO letter, Zuckerberg wrote, "Facebook aspires to build the services that give people the power to share and help them once again transform many of our core institutions and industries. . . . We don't build services to make money; we make money to build better services."[240]

Facebook's five core values include the following: focus on impact, move fast, be bold, be open, and build social value.[241] These values compose the core of Facebook's culture, which Zuckerberg refers to as the "Hacker Way."

Zuckerberg described the hacker way as "an approach to building that involves continuous improvement and iteration. Hackers believe that something can always be better, and that nothing is ever complete. . . . Hacker culture is also extremely open and meritocratic. Hackers believe that the best idea and implementation should always win—not the person who is lobbying for an idea or the person who manages the most people."[242]

The company encourages this culture by conducting hackathons every few months. People build and share prototypes at these sessions. At the end, the best ideas are selected for further development.

Employees are happy with Facebook's culture and work environment, according to a survey conducted by jobs site Payscale. Ninety-six percent of employees reported high satisfaction, and 44% had high stress. These results are better than those from peer companies like Google, Apple, Amazon, and Tesla.[243]

Facebook Lacks Diversity

Managing diversity is a hot topic among technology companies. This is an outgrowth of the demographic composition of people working in this industry. Rather than hide from this profile, companies have started to display transparency by publishing their diversity profiles.

Facebook's diversity report showed 68% male and 32% female. Ethnicity data for its U.S. workforce revealed 55% white, 36% Asian, 4% Hispanic, 3% two or more races, and 2% black. This pattern is similar to those of Google and Apple. Google's diversity report showed 70% male and U.S. workforce diversity of 61% white, 30% Asian, 4% two or more races, 3% Hispanic, and 2% black. Apple's U.S. demographics found 30% female and 55% white, 15% Asian, 11% Hispanic, 7% black, 2% two or more races, 1% other, and 9% undeclared.[244]

Facebook executives acknowledge that the workforce is not overly diverse and committed to improving its demographic profile. Maxine Williams, global director of diversity, commented that "diversity is central to Facebook's mission of creating a more open and connected world: it's good for our products and for our business. Cognitive diversity, or diversity of thought, matters because we are building a platform that currently serves 1.4 billion people around the world. It's vital for us to have a broad range of perspectives, including people of different genders, races, ages, sexual orientations, characteristics and points of view."[245]

Facebook has initiated a number of programs aimed at improving its demographic profile. They include the following:

1. **Diverse slate approach.** This pilot program ensures that every job opening considers at least one candidate from an underrepresented group.

2. **Facebook University.** This program invites college freshmen with exceptional talent from underrepresented groups to work on summer projects with Facebook mentors.

3. **Managing Bias training course.** This course educates employees about stereotypes and implicit biases.

4. **Computer Science & Engineering Lean In Circles.** This program partners with LeanIn.org, LinkedIn, and The Anita Borg Institute to create a community of support for women and some men as they pursue technology and engineering careers.[246]

FOR DISCUSSION

1. How would you evaluate Zuckerberg in terms of the Big Five personality dimensions?

2. How would you evaluate Zuckerberg in terms of core self-evaluations and emotional intelligence? Explain.

3. How will Facebook's mission, values, and culture affect the three components of employees' attitudes and workplace behavior?

4. What are your thoughts about Facebook's diversity statistics? Explain.

5. Are you concerned that 44% of Facebook's employees are experiencing high stress? Explain.

Should Airlines Accommodate Oversized People?

Traveling on an airplane can be extra difficult for overweight and tall people. Boeing's 757 standard seat width is 17 inches, while Airbus's 319s is 17.2 inches wide.[247] Given individual differences in hip width, this can be a problem, particularly for women. This issue was investigated by the Civilian American and European Surface Anthropometry Resource Project (Caesar). The project was funded by a consortium of companies.

The Caesar project measured over 4,000 people from the United States and Europe and uncovered the following: "The hip breadth of men in the 95th percentile of the population, i.e., on the very big side, measures 17.6 inches." This means that 95% of all men can fit into a standard Airbus seat. In contrast, females face a different situation. According to Caesar's report, "the hip breadth of women in the 90th percentile is 19.2 inches, and those in the 95th percentile have hips measuring 22.4 inches."[248] The core skeletal system is the reason for the difference between men and women. Females simply have a larger pelvis than men.

Do you think airlines should accommodate people with larger hips? Although there are not any regulations in the United States to accommodate people, New York senator Charles Schumer wants the Federal Aviation Administration (FAA) to establish minimum seat size standards. Some people believe that forcing airlines to establish bigger, standard seat sizes ultimately increases fares. Industry group Airlines for America opposes the idea. "The group notes that the FAA should regulate seat size for safety, but should not substitute its judgments for market forces on what people are willing to pay."[249]

Seat pitch, the distance between seat backs, also is decreasing. This makes for less leg room for all people. The typical seat pitch in Economy class is 29–32 inches, with a range of 29–36.[250]

The trends are clear. In general, airlines are adding seats while decreasing seat width and pitch. These changes clearly impact taller, wider, and heavier individuals. Somoa Air is resolving this issue by charging fees based on passengers' weight. Does this seem ethical?

The question to consider is whether seat width and pitch should be regulated or determined by market forces.

SOLVING THE CHALLENGE

1. I recommend creating a national standard for seat width based on the average hip size of men and women. I would also standardize seat pitch so that it accommodates the average height of men and women. Once this is done, I would charge passengers a special fee for more space.

2. Let market forces determine the design of airplanes and fares. The government should stay out of this issue. For example, Bombardier's CS100 expanded seat width to 18.5 inches and included 19 inches for the middle seat. The airline maker did this to compete with smaller seats offered in planes made by Airbus and Boeing.[251]

3. Because women on average have larger hip breadth than men, it is not fair to base fees on the size of a seat. This would disadvantage women. I would standardize seat width based on the average size of women. People can pay extra fees if they want additional seat width or pitch.

4. Invent other options.

12 Motivating Employees
Achieving Superior Performance in the Workplace

Managing for Motivation: Scrapping the Traditional 9-to-5 Job?

Punch in at 9:00, punch out at 5:00—does it have to be that way?

Perhaps not. Companies are becoming more open to hiring freelancers, independent contractors, and others in "the gig economy" who (with freedom to choose affordable health insurance plans) are able to designate their own hours.[1] Indeed, a great deal of the job growth in the past decade has been among temporary and contract workers.[2]

Prizing Flexibility

In addition, employers have become attuned to the idea of a *flexible workplace,* in which employees— especially Millennials, who prize flexibility, convenience, and more options in their lives—are encouraged to set their own schedules, work remotely, and be judged by their performance.[3]

The top benefits organizations saw in their work flex programs, according to a 2015 study, were improved employee satisfaction (87%), increased productivity (71%), and retention of current talent (65%).[4] Several studies have found that employees with flexible work arrangements are healthier, happier, more productive, more positive about their work, and less likely to change jobs.[5]

Among the types of alternative work schedules available are the following:

- **Part-time work—less than 40 hours.** Part-time work has spread beyond clerical help and programmers to market researchers, lawyers, and even part-time top executives.[6]
- **Flextime hours—flexible working hours.** Flextime workers may start and finish an hour earlier or an hour later, but they usually make themselves available at core hours for meetings and consultations. (Men, unfortunately, have been more likely than women to be granted a flexible schedule.)[7]
- **"4/10" workweek—four 10-hour days per week.** Allows employees three consecutive days off, providing more leisure and less commuting time. (But meetings and consultations may remain a problem.)
- **Job sharing—two people split the same job.** Each person may work half the same day or work alternate days or weeks. Absences may create communication problems with coworkers or customers. (Today only 18% of employers in one survey allowed two workers to job share, down from 29% in 2008.)[8]
- **Telecommuting—working at home all or part time.** Employees keep in touch with employers and coworkers by email, text, and phone. The advantages to employers are increased productivity because telecommuters experience less distraction at home and can work flexible hours.[9] (Today 37% of U.S. workers say they have telecommuted, four times greater than the 9% found in 1995.)[10] Working from home can make you happier, but face time at the office has value as well.[11]

For Discussion For what you're doing at this point in your life, which of these possibilities would suit you best, and why? Would it be workable for your employer if all your coworkers did it as well?

FORECAST · What's Ahead in This Chapter

This chapter discusses motivation from four perspectives: content (theories by Maslow, McClelland, Deci and Ryan, and Herzberg); process (equity, expectancy, and goal-setting theories); job design; and reinforcement. We then consider rewards for motivating performance.

12.1 Motivating for Performance

What's the motivation for studying motivation?

THE BIG PICTURE

Motivation is defined as the psychological processes that arouse and direct people's goal-directed behavior. The model of how it works is that people have certain needs that motivate them to perform specific behaviors for which they receive rewards, both extrinsic and intrinsic, that feed back and satisfy the original need. The four major perspectives on motivation are content, process, job-design, and reinforcement.

What would make you rise a half hour earlier than usual to ensure you got to work on time—and to perform your best once there?

Among the possible inducements (such as those offered by SAS, Google, and Salesforce): free snacks and free meals, on-site laundry, Friday afternoons off, child care assistance, freedom to paint your walls, tuition reimbursement, career counseling, and having your dog at work. How about repayment of your student loan—there's a big one! (But only 3% of companies offer it.)[12] How about getting paid to live near your job? (Housing subsidies are sometimes offered to attract new hires to high-rent areas like Silicon Valley.)[13]

Whether employment rates are high or low, there are always companies, industries, and occupations in which employers feel they need to bend over backward to retain their human capital.

Motivation: What It Is, Why It's Important

Why do people do the things they do? The answer is this: They are mainly motivated to fulfill their wants and needs.

What Is Motivation and How Does It Work?   **Motivation** may be defined as the psychological processes that arouse and direct goal-directed behavior.[14] Motivation is difficult to understand because you can't actually see it or know it in another person; it must be *inferred* from one's behavior. Nevertheless, it's imperative that you as a manager understand the process of motivation if you are to guide employees in accomplishing your organization's objectives.

The way motivation works actually is complex, the result of multiple *personal and contextual factors. (See Figure 12.1.)*

FIGURE 12.1

An integrated model of motivation

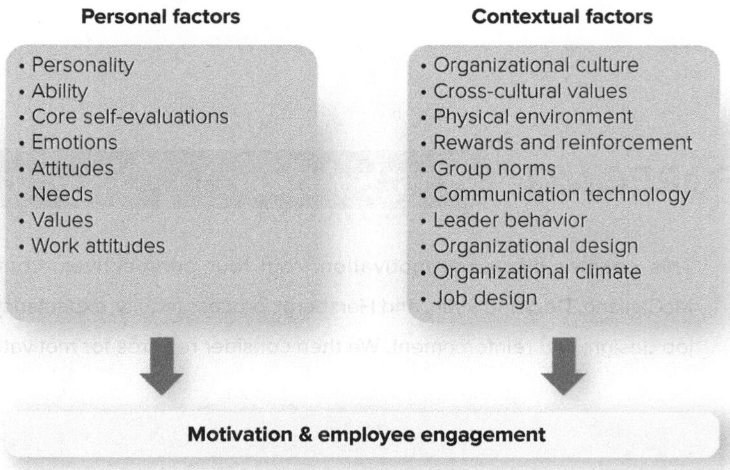

Personal factors	Contextual factors
• Personality • Ability • Core self-evaluations • Emotions • Attitudes • Needs • Values • Work attitudes	• Organizational culture • Cross-cultural values • Physical environment • Rewards and reinforcement • Group norms • Communication technology • Leader behavior • Organizational design • Organizational climate • Job design

Motivation & employee engagement

The individual personal factors that employees bring to the workplace range from personality to attitudes, many of which we described in Chapter 11. The contextual factors include organizational culture, cross-cultural values, the physical environment, and other matters we discuss in this chapter and the next. Both categories of factors influence an employee's level of motivation and engagement at work.

However, motivation can also be expressed in a simple model—namely, that people have certain *needs* that *motivate* them to perform specific *behaviors* for which they receive *rewards* that *feed back* and satisfy the original need. *(See Figure 12.2, below.)*

FIGURE 12.2 **A simple model of motivation**

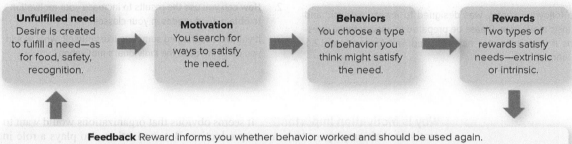

Feedback Reward informs you whether behavior worked and should be used again.

For example, as an hourly worker you desire more money (need), which impels you (motivates you) to work more hours (behavior), which provides you with more money (reward) and informs you (feedback loop) that working more hours will fulfill your need for more money in the future.

Rewards (as well as motivation itself) are of two types—*extrinsic* and *intrinsic*.[15] Managers can use both to encourage better work performance.

- **Extrinsic rewards—satisfaction in the payoff from others.** An extrinsic reward is the payoff, such as money, a person receives from others for performing a particular task. An extrinsic reward is an external reward; the payoff comes from pleasing others.

    Example: The Air Force is offering a bonus to drone pilots if they extend their commitment to remain in the military. These pilots can earn $15,000 a year by extending for either five or nine years, and they have the option to receive half the total bonus up front. The Air Force is doing this because the demand for drone pilots exceeds the supply.[16]

    Another example: Companies are trying to reduce health care costs by paying employees to lose weight.[17] (Some firms are asking their employees to pay higher insurance premiums to spur them to take off pounds, but that has not been found to be a strong enough motivation. "Financial incentives can work well—if they are separated from insurance premiums," suggests one team of researchers.)[18]

- **Intrinsic rewards—satisfaction in performing the task itself.** An intrinsic reward is the satisfaction, such as a feeling of accomplishment, a person receives from performing the particular task itself. An intrinsic reward is an internal reward; the payoff comes from pleasing yourself.

    Example: When Debbie Feit, a senior copywriter at MARS, a Southfield, Michigan–based marketing agency, was given a month-long paid sabbatical at a charitable organization of her choice, she chose to donate her time writing marketing materials and completing grant applications for children's mental health organizations. "MARS could have just sent money to the organization," Feit says, "but instead they also devoted my time to something I felt passionate about. I was very touched by the experience."[19]

We all are motivated by a combination of extrinsic and intrinsic rewards. Which type of reward is more valuable to you? Answering this question can help you generate self-motivation and higher performance.

connect SELF-ASSESSMENT 12.1

Are You More Interested in Extrinsic or Intrinsic Rewards?

The following survey was designed to assess extrinsic and intrinsic motivation. Please be prepared to answer these questions if your instructor has assigned Self-Assessment 12.1 in Connect.

1. What is more important to you, extrinsic or intrinsic rewards? Are you surprised by the results?

2. How can you use the results to increase your motivation to obtain good grades in your classes?

3. If you were managing someone like yourself, what would you do to increase the individual's motivation?

Why Is Motivation Important?   It seems obvious that organizations would want to motivate their employees to be more productive. But motivation also plays a role in influencing a host of outcomes, including employee engagement, organizational citizenship, absenteeism, and service quality.[20] In order of importance, you as a manager want to motivate people to:

1. **Join your organization.** You need to instill in talented prospective workers the desire to come to work for you.

2. **Stay with your organization.** Whether you are in good economic times or bad, you always want to be able to retain good people.

3. **Show up for work at your organization.** In many organizations, absenteeism and lateness are tremendous problems.

4. **Be engaged while at your organization.** Engaged employees produce higher-quality work and better customer service.

5. **Do extra for your organization.** You hope your employees will perform extra tasks above and beyond the call of duty (be organizational "good citizens").

The Four Major Perspectives on Motivation: Overview

There is no theory accepted by everyone as to what motivates people. In this chapter, therefore, we present the four principal perspectives. From these, you may be able to select what ideas seem most workable to you. The four perspectives on motivation are (1) *content,* (2) *process,* (3) *job design,* and (4) *reinforcement,* as described in the following four main sections. ●

12.2 Content Perspectives on Employee Motivation

What kinds of needs motivate employees?

THE BIG PICTURE

Content perspectives are theories emphasizing the needs that motivate people. Needs are defined as physiological or psychological deficiencies that arouse behavior. The content perspective includes four theories: Maslow's hierarchy of needs, McClelland's acquired needs theory, Deci and Ryan's self-determination theory, and Herzberg's two-factor theory.

Content perspectives, also known as *need-based perspectives,* are theories that emphasize the needs that motivate people. Content theorists ask, "What kind of needs motivate employees in the workplace?" **Needs** are defined as physiological or psychological deficiencies that arouse behavior. They can be strong or weak, and, because they are influenced by environmental factors, they can vary over time and from place to place.

In addition to McGregor's Theory X/Theory Y (see Chapter 2), content perspectives include four theories:

- Maslow's hierarchy of needs theory.
- McClelland's acquired needs theory.
- Deci and Ryan's self-determination theory.
- Herzberg's two-factor theory.

Maslow's Hierarchy of Needs Theory: Five Levels

In 1943, one of the first researchers to study motivation, Brandeis University psychology professor **Abraham Maslow** (mentioned previously in Chapter 2), put forth his **hierarchy of needs theory,** which proposes that people are motivated by five levels of needs: (1) physiological, (2) safety, (3) love, (4) esteem, and (5) self-actualization.[21] *(See Figure 12.3.)*

FIGURE 12.3

Maslow's hierarchy of needs

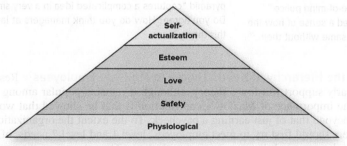

1. **Physiological need—the most basic human physical need:** Need for food, clothing, shelter, comfort, self-preservation. *Workplace example: these are covered by wages.*

2. **Safety need:** Need for physical safety, emotional security, avoidance of violence. *Workplace examples: health insurance, job security, work safety rules, pension plans satisfy this need.*

3. **Love need:** Need for love, friendship, affection. *Workplace examples: office parties, company softball teams, management retreats.*

4. **Esteem need:** Need for self-respect, status, reputation, recognition, self-confidence. *Workplace examples: bonuses, promotions, awards.*

5. **Self-actualization need—the highest level need:** Need for self-fulfillment: increasing competence, using abilities to the fullest. *Workplace example: sabbatical leave to further personal growth.*

The Five Levels of Needs   In proposing this hierarchy of five needs, ranging from basic to highest level, Maslow suggested that needs are never completely satisfied. That is, our actions are aimed at fulfilling the "deprived" needs, the needs that remain unsatisfied at any point in time. Thus, for example, once you have achieved safety (security), which is the second most basic need, you will then seek to fulfill the third most basic need—love (belongingness).

EXAMPLE   The "Chief Emotion Officer": A Hotel CEO Applies Maslow's Hierarchy to Employees, Customers, and Investors

Chip Conley is CEO and founder of boutique hotel company Joie de Vivre (JDV), whose mission statement is "creating opportunities to celebrate the joy of life." In *Peak: How Great Companies Get Their Mojo from Maslow,* he describes how JDV used Maslow's theory to motivate the business's three key stakeholders—employees, customers, and investors—by tapping into the power of self-actualization to create peak performance.[22]

Leaders act as CEOs—"Chief Emotion Officers"—says Conley.[23] Drawing on the notion that emotions are just as contagious as the flu virus, Conley believes that you can spread positive emotions in the same way. Thus, for example, every senior management meeting ends with a leader describing someone in the organization who has done outstanding work, and then an executive is dispatched to thank that person.[24]

Motivating Employees. Applying the Maslow pyramid to employees, says Conley, "the basic need that a job satisfies is money. Toward the middle are needs like recognition for a job well done, and at the top are needs like meaning and creative expression."[25]

Thus, housekeepers, who represent half of a hotel's workers, would be gathered in small groups and asked what the hotels would look like if they weren't there each day. Following their answers (unvacuumed carpets, piled-up trash, bathrooms filled with wet towels), they were then asked to come up with alternative names for housekeeping. Some responses: "serenity keepers," "clutter busters," "the peace-of-mind police."

From this exercise, workers developed a sense of how the customer experience would not be the same without them.[26]

And that, says Conley, "gets to a sense of meaning in your work that satisfies that high-level human motivation." Addressing the highest-level need gives employees "a sense that the job helps them become the best people they can be."[27]

Motivating Customers. Many hotels offer clean, safe accommodations. JDV designs each of its 30 hotels to "flatter and vindicate a different category of customers' distinct self-image," says Conley. Thus, in San Francisco, the Hotel Rex's tweedy décor and Jack London touches appeal to urbane literary types. The corridors feature quotes by novelists John Steinbeck and Dashiell Hammett, the bar is called the Vicious Circle (a reference to the famed New York Algonquin literary hangout), and the lobby is stuffed with books and 1920s art.[28] The Vitale's fitness-conscious services and minimalist design target "the kind of bourgeois bohemian who might like *Dwell Magazine.*"[29]

Motivating Investors. Although most investors focus on a "returns-driven relationship" (bottom of the pyramid), some have higher motivations. They are driven not by the deal "but rather [by] an interesting, worthwhile deal," which JDV attempts to provide.[30]

YOUR CALL

Part of the appeal of Maslow's hierarchy, says social psychologist Douglas Kenrick of Arizona State University, is that the pyramid "captures a complicated idea in a very simple way."[31] Do you agree? How do you think managers at large can use this theory?

Using the Hierarchy of Needs Theory to Motivate Employees   Research does not clearly support Maslow's theory, although it remains popular among managers. Still, the importance of Maslow's contribution is that he showed that workers have needs beyond that of just earning a paycheck. To the extent the organization permits, managers should first try to meet employees' level 1 and level 2 needs, of course, so that employees won't be preoccupied with them. Then, however, they need to give employees a chance to fulfill their higher-level needs in ways that also advance the goals of the organization.[32]

McClelland's Acquired Needs Theory: Achievement, Affiliation, and Power

David McClelland, a well-known psychologist, investigated the needs for affiliation and power and as a consequence proposed the **acquired needs theory,** which states that three needs—achievement, affiliation, and power—are major motives determining people's behavior in the workplace.[33] McClelland believes that we are not born with our needs; rather, we learn them from the culture—from our life experiences.

The Three Needs Managers are encouraged to recognize three needs in themselves and others and to attempt to create work environments that are responsive to them. The three needs, one of which tends to be dominant in each of us, are as follows. *(See Figure 12.4, right.)*

- **Need for achievement—"I need to excel at tasks."** This is the desire to excel, to do something better or more efficiently, to solve problems, to achieve excellence in challenging tasks.

- **Need for affiliation—"I need close relationships."** This is the desire for friendly and warm relations with other people.

- **Need for power—"I need to control others."** This is the desire to be responsible for other people, to influence their behavior or to control them.[34]

McClelland identifies two forms of the need for power—personal and institutional.

The negative kind is the need for *personal power,* as expressed in the desire to dominate others, and involves manipulating people for one's own gratification.

The positive kind, characteristic of top managers and leaders, is the desire for *institutional power,* as expressed in the need to solve problems that further organizational goals.

Research tells us that your performance will vary along the lines of the three acquired needs. Where do you think you stand in terms of being motivated by these three needs? You can find out by completing Self-Assessment 12.2.

FIGURE 12.4
McClelland's three needs

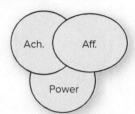

A "well-balanced" individual: achievement, affiliation, and power are of equal size.

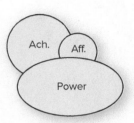

A "control freak" individual: achievement is normal, but affiliation is small and power is large.

≡connect SELF-ASSESSMENT 12.2

Assessing Your Acquired Needs

The following survey was designed to assess your motivation in terms of acquired needs. Please be prepared to answer these questions if your instructor has assigned Self-Assessment 12.2 in Connect.

1. What is the order of your most important needs? Are you surprised by this result?

2. Given that achievement and power needs are associated with career advancement, how might you increase these two need states?

Using Acquired Needs Theory to Motivate Employees You can apply acquired needs theory by appealing to the preferences associated with each need when you (1) set goals, (2) provide feedback, (3) assign tasks, and (4) design the job.[35] Let's consider how you can apply this theory.[36]

Need for Achievement People motivated by the *need for achievement* prefer working on challenging, but not impossible, tasks or projects. They like situations in which good performance relies on effort and ability rather than luck, and they like to be rewarded for their efforts. High achievers also want to receive a fair and balanced amount of positive and negative feedback. This enables them to improve their performance.

Need for Power If you, like most effective managers, have a *high need for power,* that means you enjoy being in control of people and events and being recognized for this responsibility. Accordingly, your preference would probably be for work that allows you to control or have an effect on people and be publicly recognized for your accomplishments.

Need for Affiliation   If you tend to seek social approval and satisfying personal relationships, you may have a *high need for affiliation*. In that case, you may not be the most efficient manager because at times you will have to make decisions that will make people resent you. Instead, you will tend to prefer work, such as sales, that provides for personal relationships and social approval.

Deci and Ryan's Self-Determination Theory: Competence, Autonomy, and Relatedness

Developed by **Edward Deci** (pronounced "*Dee*-see") and **Richard Ryan,** psychologists at the University of Rochester, **self-determination theory assumes that people are driven to try to grow and attain fulfillment, with their behavior and well-being influenced by three innate needs: competence, autonomy, and relatedness.**[37]

Focus on Intrinsic Motivation   Self-determination theory focuses primarily on intrinsic motivation and rewards (such as feeling independent) rather than on extrinsic motivation and rewards (such as money or fame). Intrinsic motivation is longer lasting than extrinsic motivation and has a more positive impact on task performance.[38]

The Three Innate Needs   To achieve psychological growth, according to the theory, people need to satisfy the three innate (that is, inborn) needs of competence, autonomy, and relatedness:

1. **Competence—"I want to feel a sense of mastery."** People need to feel qualified, knowledgeable, and capable of completing a goal or task and to learn different skills.

2. **Autonomy—"I want to feel independent and able to influence my environment."** People need to feel they have freedom and the discretion to determine what they want to do and how they want to do it.

3. **Relatedness—"I want to feel connected to other people."** People need to feel a sense of belonging, of attachment to others.

Using Self-Determination Theory to Motivate Employees   Managers can apply this theory by engaging in leader behavior that fosters the experience of competence, autonomy, and relatedness.[39] Following are some specific suggestions:

- **Competence.** Managers can provide tangible resources, time, contacts, and coaching to improve employee competence, making sure that employees have the knowledge and information they need to perform their jobs. Example: At Hindustan Unilever, senior managers are expected to spend 30% to 40% of their time in grooming people below them. Executives also change roles every two or three years, so they are always learning different aspects of the business.[40]

- **Autonomy.** To enhance feelings of autonomy, managers can develop trust with their employees and empower them by delegating meaningful tasks to them. Example: Best Buy's corporate employees work in a "Results Only Work Environment" (ROWE), which means that no one in the company cares where, when, or how you work, only what you accomplish.[41]

- **Relatedness.** Many companies, such as Sacramento-based Nugget Market, use camaraderie to foster relatedness. Example: Reporter Jeremy McCarthy reported being at an Apple Store "when every employee in the store broke into a standing ovation for ten minutes to celebrate the transfer of one of their colleagues to a new store." He goes on: "For her the 'relatedness' score must have been through the roof as they all lined up to give her a hug and cheer her on for her next role."[42]

Are you feeling motivated in this course? To what extent does the instructor for this course satisfy your needs for competence, autonomy, and relatedness? You can find out by taking Self-Assessment 12.3.

connect SELF-ASSESSMENT 12.3

Assessing Your Needs for Self-Determination

The following survey was designed to assess the extent to which an instructor is satisfying your needs for self-determination. Please be prepared to answer these questions if your instructor has assigned Self-Assessment 12.3 in Connect.

1. Are your needs being met? Do the results make sense in terms of your level of motivation in this course?

2. Based on the results, identify two things you might do to increase your motivation.

3. Based on the results, identify two things your instructor might do to increase your motivation.

Herzberg's Two-Factor Theory: From Dissatisfying Factors to Satisfying Factors

Frederick Herzberg arrived at his needs-based theory as a result of a landmark study of 203 accountants and engineers who were interviewed to determine the factors responsible for job satisfaction and dissatisfaction.[43] Job satisfaction was more frequently associated with achievement, recognition, characteristics of the work, responsibility, and advancement. Job dissatisfaction was more often associated with working conditions, pay and security, company policies, supervisors, and interpersonal relationships. The result was Herzberg's **two-factor theory, which proposed that work satisfaction and dissatisfaction arise from two different factors—work satisfaction from** *motivating factors* **and work dissatisfaction from** *hygiene factors.*

Hygiene Factors versus Motivating Factors   In Herzberg's theory, the hygiene factors are the lower-level needs, and the motivating factors are the higher-level needs. The two areas are separated by a zone in which employees are neither satisfied nor dissatisfied. *(See Figure 12.5, next page.)*

How much do you want? Would a big desk in a big office with a view represent the tangible realization of managerial success for you? Would this be a motivation that would make you feel satisfied? © Baris Simsek/Getty Images RF

FIGURE 12.5

Herzberg's two-factor theory: satisfaction versus dissatisfaction

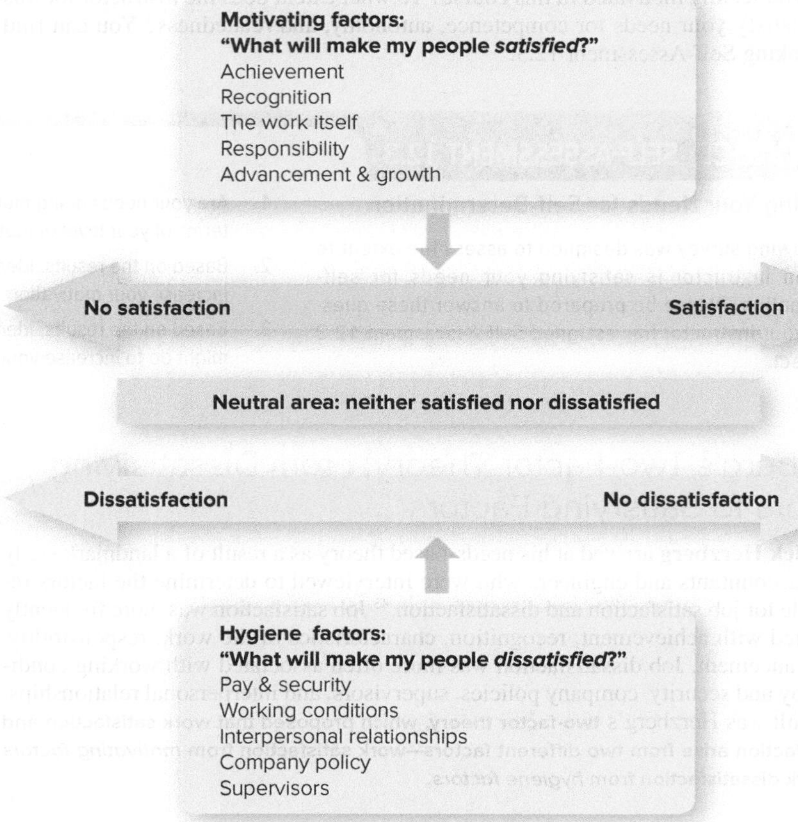

Motivating factors:
"What will make my people *satisfied*?"
Achievement
Recognition
The work itself
Responsibility
Advancement & growth

No satisfaction   Satisfaction

Neutral area: neither satisfied nor dissatisfied

Dissatisfaction   No dissatisfaction

Hygiene factors:
"What will make my people *dissatisfied*?"
Pay & security
Working conditions
Interpersonal relationships
Company policy
Supervisors

■ **Hygiene factors—"Why are my people dissatisfied?"** The lower-level needs, **hygiene factors,** are factors associated with job dissatisfaction—such as salary, working conditions, interpersonal relationships, and company policy—all of which affect the job context in which people work.

We believe you can satisfy and motivate people by providing good hygiene factors. The Container Store, regularly rated as one of the top companies to work for by *Fortune* (No. 27 in 2016), is a good example. The company pays retail hourly salespeople roughly *double* the industry average, approximately $50,000 a year in 2014.[44] Its rate of employee turnover, about 5.7%, is overwhelmingly lower than the industry average of 74.9%.[45]

■ **Motivating factors—"What will make my people satisfied?"** The higher-level needs, **motivating factors,** or simply *motivators*, are factors associated with job *satisfaction*—such as achievement, recognition, responsibility, and advancement—all of which affect the job content or the rewards of work performance. Motivating factors—challenges, opportunities, recognition—must be instituted, Herzberg believed, to spur superior work performance.

An example of a motivating factor would be to give workers more control over their work. When Southwest Airlines decided not to charge passengers for shipping their luggage (though many competitors had long done so), one reason was to avoid turning flight attendants into baggage handlers, as passengers tried to stuff more and more carry-on luggage into overhead bins—which would have made the flight attendants unhappy and in turn made passengers unhappy. "We want our employees to feel that their job [is] a calling," said Southwest CEO Garry Kelly. "And the people who most have to feel that way are the ones closest to the customer."[46]

Using Two-Factor Theory to Motivate Employees   During the Great Recession, with fewer jobs available, many people felt they were stuck in jobs they disliked—only 39% said they were happy with their positions in 2009, according to a survey by the Conference Board.[47] In 2015, the survey found better results—49.63% of American workers said they were satisfied with their jobs.[48] Another study, however, finds that 88% of U.S. employees report overall satisfaction with their current job, with the important parts being compensation/pay (by 60%), job security (59%), and opportunities to use skills/abilities (also 59%).[49]

There will always be some employees who dislike their jobs, but the basic lesson of Herzberg's research is that you should first eliminate dissatisfaction (hygiene factors), making sure that working conditions, pay levels, and company policies are reasonable. You should then concentrate on spurring motivation by providing opportunities for achievement, recognition, responsibility, and personal growth (motivating factors).

Positive hygiene factors include allowing pets at work; offering video game arcades, fitness classes, and intramural sports (volleyball, soccer); and providing a library of free movies, books, and magazines.[50] If you work at Google, you could also have a college reimbursement plan, legal aid, and travel assistance—and if you die, the company will pay your family half your salary for a decade.[51]

The four needs theories are compared below. *(See Figure 12.6.)* Note how acquired needs theory (McClelland) and self-determination theory (Deci and Ryan) focus only on higher-level needs. ●

FIGURE 12.6   A comparison of needs and satisfaction theories: Maslow hierarchy of needs, McClelland acquired needs, Deci and Ryan self-determination, and Herzberg two-factor

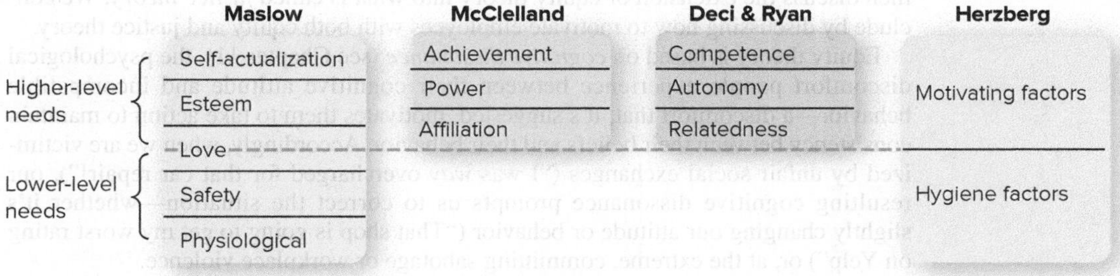

Maslow	McClelland	Deci & Ryan	Herzberg
Higher-level needs: Self-actualization, Esteem	Achievement, Power, Affiliation	Competence, Autonomy, Relatedness	Motivating factors
Lower-level needs: Love, Safety, Physiological			Hygiene factors

12.3 Process Perspectives on Employee Motivation

Is a good reward good enough? How do other factors affect motivation?

THE BIG PICTURE

Process perspectives, which are concerned with the thought processes by which people decide how to act, have three viewpoints: equity/justice theory, expectancy theory, and goal-setting theory.

Process perspectives are concerned with the thought processes by which people decide how to act—how employees choose behavior to meet their needs. Whereas need-based perspectives simply try to understand employee needs, process perspectives go further and try to understand why employees have different needs, what behaviors they select to satisfy them, and how they decide if their choices were successful.

In this section we discuss three process perspectives on motivation:

- Equity/justice theory
- Expectancy theory
- Goal-setting theory

Equity/Justice Theory: How Fairly Do You Think You're Being Treated in Relation to Others?

Fairness—or, perhaps equally important, the *perception* of fairness—can be a big issue in organizations. For example, if, as a salesperson for Target, you received a 10% bonus for doubling your sales, would that be enough? What if other Target salespeople received 15%?

Equity theory is a model of motivation that explains how people strive for *fairness* and *justice* in social exchanges or give-and-take relationships. Pioneered by psychologist **J. Stacey Adams,** equity theory is based on the idea that employees are motivated to see fairness in the rewards they expect for task performance and are motivated to resolve feelings of injustice.[52] We will discuss Adams's ideas and their application, then discuss the extension of equity theory into what is called *justice theory.* We conclude by discussing how to motivate employees with both equity and justice theory.

Equity theory is based on *cognitive dissonance* (see Chapter 11), the psychological discomfort people experience between their cognitive attitude and incompatible behavior—a discomfort that, it's suggested, motivates them to take action to maintain consistency between their beliefs and their behavior. Accordingly, when we are victimized by unfair social exchanges ("I was *way* overcharged for that car repair!"), our resulting cognitive dissonance prompts us to correct the situation—whether it's slightly changing our attitude or behavior ("That shop is going to get my worst rating on Yelp") or, at the extreme, committing sabotage or workplace violence.

Example: The typical American believes a CEO earns $1 million in annual pay, whereas the actual median compensation is about $10.3 million. Regardless, most Americans (74%) believe that CEOs are paid too much relative to the average worker.[53] How, then, might employees respond to knowing that the average pay for CEOs in 2015 was about 210 times the average worker's pay, up from 181 times in 2009?[54] Some experts suggest that such imbalances are partly responsible for the $600 billion that is stolen annually in U.S. workplaces, or roughly $4,500 per employee.[55]

The Elements of Equity Theory: Comparing Your Inputs and Outputs with Those of Others The key elements in equity theory are *inputs, outputs (rewards),* and *comparisons. (See Figure 12.7, opposite page.)*

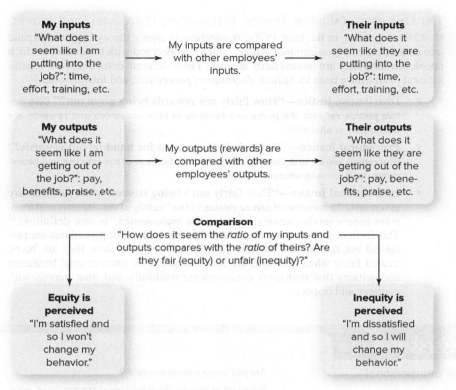

FIGURE 12.7

Equity theory

How people perceive they are being fairly or unfairly rewarded.

- **Inputs—"What do you think you're putting into the job?"** The inputs that people perceive they give to an organization are their time, effort, training, experience, intelligence, creativity, seniority, status, and so on.

- **Outputs or rewards—"What do you think you're getting out of the job?"** The outputs are the rewards that people receive from an organization: pay, benefits, praise, recognition, bonuses, promotions, status perquisites (corner office with a view, say, or private parking space), and so on.

- **Comparison—"How do you think your ratio of inputs and rewards compares with those of others?"** Equity theory suggests that people compare the *ratio* of their own outcomes to inputs against the *ratio* of someone else's outcomes to inputs. When employees compare the ratio of their inputs and outputs (rewards) with those of others—whether coworkers within the organization or even other people in similar jobs outside it—they then make a judgment about fairness. Either they perceive there is *equity*, and so they are satisfied with the ratio and don't change their behavior, or they perceive there is *inequity*, and so they feel resentful and act to change the inequity.[56]

Using Equity Theory to Motivate Employees   Adams suggests that employees who feel they are being underrewarded will respond to the perceived inequity in one or more negative ways, as by reducing their inputs ("I'm just going to do the minimum required"), trying to change the outputs or rewards they receive ("If they won't give me a raise, I'll just take stuff"), distorting the inequity ("They've never paid me what I'm worth"), changing the object of comparison ("They think I don't work as hard as Bob? He's a slacker compared to Sid"), or leaving the situation ("I'm outta here!"). By contrast, employees who think they are treated fairly are more likely to support organizational change, more apt to cooperate in group settings, and less apt to turn to arbitration and the courts to remedy real or imagined wrongs.

The Elements of Justice Theory: Distributive, Procedural, and Interactional   Beginning in the later 1970s, researchers in equity theory began to expand into an area called *organizational justice,* which is concerned with the extent to which people perceive they are treated fairly at work. Three different components of organizational justice have been identified: *distributive, procedural*, and *interactional.*[57]

- **Distributive justice—"How fairly are rewards being given out?"** **Distributive justice** reflects the perceived fairness of how resources and rewards are distributed or allocated.

- **Procedural justice—"How fair is the process for handing out rewards?"** **Procedural justice** is defined as the perceived fairness of the process and procedures used to make allocation decisions.

- **Interactional justice—"How fairly am I being treated when rewards are given out?"** **Interactional justice** relates to the "quality of the interpersonal treatment people receive when procedures are implemented," in one definition.[58] This form of justice is not about how decision making or procedures are perceived but rather with whether people themselves believe they are being treated fairly when decisions are implemented. Fair interpersonal treatment necessitates that managers communicate truthfully and treat people with courtesy and respect.

connect SELF-ASSESSMENT 12.4

Measuring Perceived Fair Interpersonal Treatment

The following survey was designed to assess the extent to which you are experiencing fair interpersonal treatment at work. Please be prepared to answer these questions if your instructor has assigned Self-Assessment 12.4 in Connect.

1. Are you being treated equitably?
2. Based on examining the three lowest scoring items, what could your manager do to improve your perceptions of equity?
3. What can you do to increase your perceptions of fair interpersonal treatment?

Using Equity and Justice Theories to Motivate Employees   Employees often may feel quite strongly about what they perceive to be an inequitable or unjust work situation. Often the source of their frustration is pay; one Gallup poll revealed that 51% of Americans felt they were underpaid.[59]

Your knowledge of equity and justice theories will allow you to hear out and better understand employee concerns. As an employee yourself, you can motivate other workers by clearly understanding and communicating their opportunities to improve their situations. You can communicate reasonable expectations and make sure objective measures for rewards are well understood.

Five practical lessons can be drawn from equity and justice theories, as follows.

1. Employee Perceptions Are What Count   No matter how fair management thinks the organization's policies, procedures, and reward system are, each employee's perception of the equity of those factors is what counts.

Example: Financial services corporation Morgan Stanley decided to pay 2012 bonuses in four equal installments, starting in May 2013 and going through January 2016. "Employees who quit or are laid off before the payments," reported *The Wall Street Journal,* "stand to lose their deferred compensation unless they negotiate a separate deal with the company."[60] Executives at the company think that this is a good way to reduce risky behavior. Employees, however, think it is unfair. What do you think?

2. Employees Want a Voice in Decisions That Affect Them   Managers benefit by allowing employees to participate in making decisions about important work outcomes. In general, employees' perceptions of procedural justice are enhanced when they have a voice in the decision-making process. **Voice is defined as "employees' upward expression of challenging but constructive opinions, concerns, or ideas on work-related issues to their managers."**[61]

Managers are encouraged to seek employee input on organizational changes that are likely to affect the workforce, but many managers are reluctant to follow this recommendation, according to a recent study. Moreover, employees were evaluated more negatively when they engaged in challenging forms of voice. Managers also were less likely to use these employees' ideas.[62] The lesson here: Be careful when you challenge your boss's decisions.

3. Employees Should Be Given an Appeals Process   Employees who are given the opportunity to appeal decisions that affect their welfare enhance the perceptions of distributive and procedural justice.

4. Leader Behavior Matters   Employees' perceptions of justice are strongly influenced by the leadership behavior exhibited by their managers (leadership is discussed in Chapter 14). Thus, it is important for managers to consider the justice-related implications of their decisions, actions, and public communications.

Example: Employees at Honeywell, a multinational conglomerate, felt better about being asked to take furloughs—unpaid leave, while remaining employed—when they learned that their CEO and chairman, David Cole, did not take his $4 million bonus during the time employees were furloughed.[63]

5. A Climate for Justice Makes a Difference   Managers need to pay attention to the organization's climate for justice. For example, an aggregation of 38 research studies demonstrated that an organization's climate for justice was significantly related to team performance.[64] Researchers also believe a climate of justice can significantly influence the type of customer service provided by employees. In turn, this level of service is likely to influence customers' perceptions of "fair service" and their subsequent loyalty and satisfaction.

The discussion of equity/justice theory has important implications for your own career. For example, you could work to resolve negative inequity by asking for a raise or a promotion (raising your outputs) or by working fewer hours or exerting less effort (reducing inputs). You could also resolve the inequity cognitively, by adjusting your perceptions as to the value of your salary or other benefits (outcomes) or the value of the actual work done by you or your coworkers (inputs).

Expectancy Theory: How Much Do You Want and How Likely Are You to Get It?

Introduced by **Victor Vroom, expectancy theory suggests that people are motivated by two things: (1) how much they want something and (2) how likely they think they are to get it.**[65] In other words, assuming they have choices, people will make the choice that promises them the greatest reward if they think they can get it.

The Three Elements: Expectancy, Instrumentality, and Valence   What determines how willing you (or an employee) are to work hard at tasks important to the success of the organization? The answer, says Vroom, is that you will do what you *can* do when you *want* to.

Your motivation, according to expectancy theory, involves the relationship between your *effort,* your *performance,* and the desirability of the *outcomes* (such as pay or recognition) of your performance. These relationships, which are shown in the following drawing, are affected by the three elements of *expectancy, instrumentality,* and *valence. (See Figure 12.8.)*

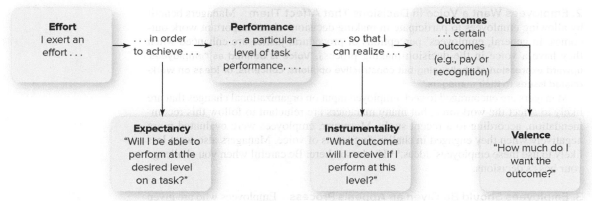

FIGURE 12.8

Expectancy theory: the major elements

1. Expectancy—"Will I Be Able to Perform at the Desired Level on a Task?" **Expectancy** is the belief that a particular level of effort will lead to a particular level of performance. This is called the *effort-to-performance expectancy*.

Example: If you believe that putting in more hours working at Target selling clothes will result in higher sales, then you have high effort-to-performance expectancy. That is, you believe that your efforts will matter. You think you have the ability, the product knowledge, and so on so that putting in extra hours of selling can probably raise your sales of clothes.

2. Instrumentality—"What Outcome Will I Receive If I Perform at This Level?" **Instrumentality** is the expectation that successful performance of the task will lead to the outcome desired. This is called the *performance-to-reward expectancy*.

Example: If you believe that making higher sales will cause Target to give you a bonus, then you have high performance-to-reward expectancy. You believe that, *if* you can achieve your goals, the outcome will be worthwhile. This element is independent of the previous one—you might decide you don't have the ability to make the extra sales, but if you did, you'd be rewarded. (For instance, lately, because of the public's concern about the quality of the educational system in the United States, school boards and politicians are implementing programs that tie teachers' pay to student performance.)[66]

3. Valence—"How Much Do I Want the Outcome?" **Valence** is value, the importance a worker assigns to the possible outcome or reward.

Example: If you assign a lot of importance or a high value to Target's prospective bonus or pay raise, then your valence is said to be high.

For your motivation to be high, you must be high on all three elements—expectancy, instrumentality, and valence. If any element is low, your motivation goes down. Your effort-to-performance expectancy might be low, for instance, because you doubt making an effort will make a difference (because retail clothing selling has too much competition). Or your performance-to-reward expectancy might be low because you don't think Target is going to give you a bonus for being a star at selling. Or your valence might be low because you don't think the bonus or raise is going to be high enough to justify working evenings and weekends.

Using Expectancy Theory to Motivate Employees The principal problem with expectancy theory is that it is complex. Even so, the underlying logic is understandable, and research seems to show that many managers are not following its principles.[67]

When attempting to motivate employees, managers should ask the following questions:

- **What rewards do your employees value?** As a manager, you need to get to know your employees and determine what rewards (outcomes) they value, such as pay raises or recognition.

- **What are the job objectives and the performance level you desire?** You need to clearly define the performance objectives and determine what performance level or behavior you want so that you can tell your employees what they need to do to attain the rewards.

- **Are the rewards linked to performance?** You want to reward high performance, of course. Thus, employees must be aware that *X* level of performance within *Y* period of time will result in *Z* kinds of rewards. In a team context, however, research shows that it is best to use a combination of individual and team-based rewards.[68]

- **Do employees believe you will deliver the right rewards for the right performance?** Your credibility is on the line here. Your employees must believe that you have the power, the ability, and the will to give them the rewards you promise for the performance you are requesting.

Reducing the F's: Applying Expectancy Theory to Failing Students   EXAMPLE

"A highly skilled CEO is hard to find," observes a business writer. "Highly paid CEOs, however, are everywhere you look."[69]

Indeed, the mass media are full of stories about top managers who don't produce results but are still rewarded (such as the Staples executives who didn't make their 2013 goals but received a special bonus anyway—"for effort").[70] Where's the inducement to deliver superior performance when you're going to be rewarded anyway?[71]

Maybe we can learn from high school.

Fewer F's. As a principal in Arizona high schools, Dr. Tim Richard has used a motivational program called Celebration/Remediation to improve the grades of students. For instance, at 3,000-student Westwood High School in Mesa, which had 1,200 failing pupils, the number of students with F grades dropped to 900 within the first few months. At Poston Butte High School, the number of students with one or more F's was reduced from 555 to 262 in nine weeks. "Once we changed the culture by bringing on Celebration/Remediation . . . ," Richard said, "the kids have completely embraced it."[72] (Poston Butte also rewards students who pass all their classes with an early release from school.)

Celebration or Remediation? At Westwood, the program works like this: "Students are allowed to go outside and have fun with their friends for 28 minutes on four mornings a week," Richard told *The Arizona Republic*. "But those who have even one F must stay inside for 'remediation'—28 minutes of extra study, help from peer tutors, or meetings with teachers."[73]

Richard believes the key to motivating students is to link a highly valued reward—socializing with friends outside—with grades. Socializing includes not only hanging out but also eating snacks, playing organized games, and listening and dancing to music. "You really appreciate celebration after you have been in remediation," said Ivana Baltazar, a 17-year-old senior who raised her grade in economics from an F to a B after receiving help through the program.

YOUR CALL

The tricky part, observes Westwood student tutor Joseph Leung, is addressing expectancy—"getting people out of the mindset that they can't succeed. . . . A lot of times they just haven't done their homework. I try to help them understand that the difference between a person passing and failing is their work ethic." For top executives in business, expectancy doesn't seem to be a problem; rather, it's instrumentality and valence. How could you apply Richard's program to reward performance in business?

Goal-Setting Theory: Objectives Should Be Specific and Challenging but Achievable

We have been considering the importance of goal setting since first introducing the topic in Chapter 5. **Goal-setting theory suggests that employees can be motivated by goals that are specific and challenging but achievable.** According to psychologists **Edwin Locke** and **Gary Latham,** who developed the theory, it is natural for people to set and strive for goals; however, the goal-setting process is useful only if people *understand* and *accept* the goals.

The Four Motivational Mechanisms of Goal-Setting Theory   Goal setting helps motivate you by doing the following:

1. It Directs Your Attention   Goal setting directs your attention toward goal-relevant tasks and away from irrelevant ones.

2. It Regulates the Effort Expended   The effort you expend is generally proportional to the goal's difficulty.

3. It Increases Your Persistence   Goal setting makes obstacles become challenges to be overcome, not reasons to fail.

4. It Fosters Use of Strategies and Action Plans   The use of strategies and action plans make it more likely that you will realize success.

Some Practical Results of Goal-Setting Theory   A *goal* is defined as an objective that a person is trying to accomplish through his or her efforts. Goal-setting experts Locke and Latham proposed the following recommendations when implementing a goal-setting program.[74] To result in high motivation and performance, according to recent research, goals must have a number of characteristics, as follows.

1. Goals Should Be Specific   Goals that are specific and difficult lead to higher performance than general goals like "Do your best" or "Improve performance." This is why it is essential to set specific, challenging goals. Goals such as "Sell as many cars as you can" or "Be nicer to customers" are too vague. Instead, goals need to be specific—usually meaning *quantitative,* as in "Boost your revenues 25%" and "Cut absenteeism by 10%."[75]

2. Certain Conditions Are Necessary for Goal Setting to Work   People must have the ability and resources needed to achieve the goal, and they need to be committed to the goal.

3. Goals Should Be Linked to Action Plans   An action plan outlines the activities or tasks that need to be accomplished in order to obtain a goal and reminds us of what we should be working on. Both individuals (such as college students) and organizations are more likely to achieve their goals when they develop detailed action plans.[76]

Example: Teams of employees at Tornier, a medical device manufacturer in Amsterdam, meet every 45, 60, or 90 days to create action plans for completing their goals. Implementation of the plans can take between 6 and 18 months, depending on the complexity of the goal.[77]

4. Performance Feedback and Participation in Deciding How to Achieve Goals Are Necessary but Not Sufficient for Goal Setting to Work   Feedback and participation enhance performance only when they lead employees to set and commit to a specific, difficult goal.

Example: Take Jim's Formal Wear, a tuxedo wholesaler in Illinois. "Once a week," says one report, "employees meet with their teams to discuss their efforts and what changes should be made the next week. Employees frequently suggest ways to improve efficiency or save money, such as reusing shipping boxes and hangers."[78] Goals lead to higher performance when you use feedback and participation to stay focused and committed to a specific goal. Some of the preceding recommendations are embodied in the advice we presented in Chapter 5—namely, that goals should be SMART: Specific, Measurable, Attainable, Results-oriented, and having Target dates. ●

12.4   Job Design Perspectives on Motivation

What's the best way to design jobs—adapt people to work or work to people?

THE BIG PICTURE

Job design, the division of an organization's work among employees, applies motivational theories to jobs to increase performance and satisfaction. The traditional approach to job design is to fit people to the jobs; the modern way is to fit the jobs to the people, using job enrichment and approaches that are based on Herzberg's landmark two-factor theory, discussed earlier in this chapter. The job characteristics model offers five job attributes for better work outcomes.

About half of workers reported in a recent year that their current job was stagnant.[79] Is there anything that can be done about this?

Job design is (1) the division of an organization's work among its employees and (2) the application of motivational theories to jobs to increase satisfaction and performance. There are two different approaches to job design—one traditional, one modern—that can be taken in deciding how to design jobs. The traditional way is *fitting people to jobs;* the modern way is *fitting jobs to people.*[80]

Fitting People to Jobs

Fitting people to jobs is based on the assumption that people will gradually adapt to any work situation. Even so, jobs must still be tailored so that nearly anyone can do them. This is the approach often taken with assembly-line jobs and jobs involving routine tasks. For managers the main challenge becomes "How can we make the worker most compatible with the work?"

One technique is **scientific management, the process of reducing the number of tasks a worker performs.** When a job is stripped down to its simplest elements, it enables a worker to focus on doing more of the same task, thus increasing employee efficiency and productivity. This may be especially useful, for instance, in designing jobs for mentally disadvantaged workers, such as those jobs run by Goodwill Industries. However, research shows that simplified, repetitive jobs lead to job dissatisfaction, poor mental health, and a low sense of accomplishment and personal growth.[81]

Fitting Jobs to People

Fitting jobs to people is based on the assumption that people are underutilized at work and that they want more variety, challenges, and responsibility. This philosophy, an outgrowth of Herzberg's theory, is one of the reasons for the popularity of work teams in the United States. The main challenge for managers is "How can we make the work most compatible with the worker so as to produce both high performance and high job satisfaction?"

Two techniques for this type of job design are (1) *job enlargement* and (2) *job enrichment.*

Job Enlargement: Putting More Variety into a Job   The opposite of scientific management, **job enlargement consists of increasing the number of tasks in a job to increase variety and motivation.** For instance, the job of installing flat screens in television sets could be enlarged to include installation of the circuit boards as well.

Although proponents claim job enlargement can improve employee satisfaction, motivation, and quality of production, research suggests job enlargement by itself won't have a significant and lasting positive effect on job performance. After all, working at two boring tasks instead of one doesn't add up to a challenging job. Instead, job enlargement is just one tool of many that should be considered in job design.[82]

Job Enrichment: Putting More Responsibility and Other Motivating Factors into a Job   Job enrichment is the practical application of Frederick Herzberg's two-factor motivator-hygiene theory of job satisfaction.[83] Specifically, **job enrichment consists of building into a job such motivating factors as responsibility, achievement, recognition, stimulating work, and advancement.**

However, instead of the job-enlargement technique of simply giving employees additional tasks of similar difficulty (known as *horizontal loading*), with job enrichment employees are given more responsibility (known as *vertical loading*).

Intuit, for example, encourages employees "to spend 10% of their working time on projects and ideas of their own, even if they are not related to their assignments." The company has found that this practice has led to the creation of several successful new products.[84]

The Job Characteristics Model: Five Job Attributes for Better Work Outcomes

Developed by researchers **J. Richard Hackman** and **Greg Oldham,** the job characteristics model of design is an outgrowth of job enrichment.[85] The **job characteristics model consists of (a) five core job characteristics that affect (b) three critical psychological states of an employee that in turn affect (c) work outcomes—the employee's motivation, performance, and satisfaction.** The model is illustrated below. *(See Figure 12.9.)*

FIGURE 12.9   The Job characteristics model

Source: From J. Richard Hackman and Greg R. Oldham, Work Redesign, 1e ©1980. Reproduced by permission of Pearson Education, Inc., Upper Saddle River, New Jersey.

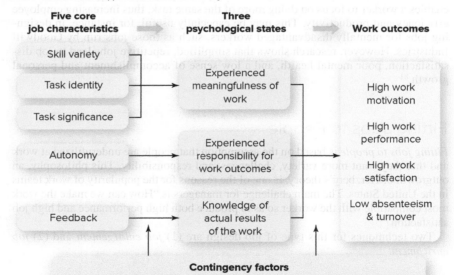

Five Job Characteristics   The five core job characteristics are *skill variety, task identity, task significance, autonomy,* and *feedback,* as follows.

1. Skill Variety—"How Many Different Skills Does Your Job Require?"   *Skill variety* describes the extent to which a job requires a person to use a wide range of different skills and abilities.

Example: The skill variety required by an executive chef is higher than that for a coffeehouse barista.

Skill variety. Being a symphony conductor—or an airline pilot, a building contractor, a physician, or a watch maker—requires a greater number of skills than, say, driving a truck. Do highly skilled employees typically make good managers? What skills do airline pilots have that would make them effective managers in other kinds of work?
© Alenavlad/Shutterstock RF

2. Task Identity—"How Many Different Tasks Are Required to Complete the Work?"   *Task identity* describes the extent to which a job requires a worker to perform all the tasks needed to complete the job from beginning to end.

Example: The task identity for a craftsperson who goes through all the steps to build a stained-glass church window is higher than it is for an assembly-line worker who installs just the windshields on cars.

3. Task Significance—"How Many Other People Are Affected by Your Job?"   *Task significance* describes the extent to which a job affects the lives of other people, whether inside or outside the organization.

Example: A technician who is responsible for keeping a hospital's electronic equipment in working order has higher task significance than a person wiping down cars in a carwash.

4. Autonomy—"How Much Discretion Does Your Job Give You?"   *Autonomy* describes the extent to which a job allows an employee to make choices about scheduling different tasks and deciding how to perform them.

Example: College-textbook salespeople have lots of leeway in planning which campuses and professors to call on. Thus, they have higher autonomy than do toll-takers on a bridge, whose actions are determined by the flow of vehicles.

5. Feedback—"How Much Do You Find Out How Well You're Doing?"   *Feedback* describes the extent to which workers receive clear, direct information about how well they are performing the job.

Example: Professional basketball players receive immediate feedback on how many of their shots are going into the basket. Engineers working on new weapons systems may go years before learning how effective their performance has been.

How the Model Works   According to the job characteristics model, these five core characteristics affect a worker's motivation because they affect three critical psychological states: *meaningfulness of work, responsibility for results,* and *knowledge of results.* (Refer to Figure 12.9 again.) In turn, these positive psychological states fuel *high motivation, high performance, high satisfaction,* and *low absenteeism and turnover.*

One other element—shown at the bottom of Figure 12.9—needs to be discussed: *contingency factors.* This refers to the degree to which a person wants personal and psychological development. Job design works when employees are motivated; to be so, they must have three attributes: (1) necessary knowledge and skill, (2) desire for personal growth, and (3) context satisfactions—that is, the right physical working conditions, pay, and supervision.

Job design works. But keep in mind that it is not for everyone. It is more likely to work when people have the required knowledge and skills, when they want to develop, and when they are satisfied with their jobs.

Applying the Job Characteristics Model   There are three major steps to follow when applying the model.

- **Diagnose the work environment to see whether a problem exists.** Hackman and Oldham developed a self-report instrument for managers to use called the *job diagnostic survey.* This will indicate whether an individual's so-called motivating potential score (MPS)—the amount of internal work motivation associated with a specific job—is high or low.

- **Determine whether job redesign is appropriate.** If a person's MPS is low, an attempt should be made to determine which of the core job characteristics is causing the problem. You should next decide whether job redesign is appropriate for a given group of employees. Job design is most likely to work in a participative environment in which employees have the necessary knowledge and skills.

- **Consider how to redesign the job.** Here you try to increase those core job characteristics that are lower than national norms.

Example: Employers want to save on health costs by helping employees with diabetes, heart disease, and similar chronic conditions avoid emergency room visits and hospital admissions.[86] However, since primary care doctors, who could help patients manage their conditions (as by reminding diabetics to monitor their blood-glucose levels daily), are paid less than physicians in other specialties, the system has turned such doctors "into little chipmunks on a wheel, pumping out patients every five minutes," as one observer described it.[87]

The proposed solution? Redesign the job by rewarding primary care doctors for spending more time with patients.[88] (Some perils to avoid: complex compensation designs, poor alignment of goals, and lack of defined, actionable measures, all of which can lead to unintended consequences and failure.)[89] ●

12.5 Reinforcement Perspectives on Motivation

MAJOR
QUESTION
?

What are the types of incentives I might use to influence employee behavior?

THE BIG PICTURE

Reinforcement theory suggests behavior will be repeated if it has positive consequences and won't be if it has negative consequences. There are four types of reinforcement: positive reinforcement, negative reinforcement, extinction, and punishment. This section also describes how to use some reinforcement techniques to modify employee behavior.

Reinforcement evades the issue of people's needs and thinking processes in relation to motivation, as we described under the need-based and process perspectives. Instead, the reinforcement perspective, which was pioneered by **Edward L. Thorndike** and **B. F. Skinner,** is concerned with how the consequences of a certain behavior affect that behavior in the future.[90]

Skinner was the father of *operant conditioning,* the process of controlling behavior by manipulating its consequences. Operant conditioning rests on Thorndike's **law of effect, which says behavior with favorable consequences tends to be repeated, while behavior with unfavorable consequences tends to disappear.**[91]

From these underpinnings has come **reinforcement theory, which attempts to explain behavior change by suggesting that behavior with positive consequences tends to be repeated, whereas behavior with negative consequences tends not to be repeated.** The use of reinforcement theory to change human behavior is called *behavior modification.*

The Four Types of Reinforcement: Positive, Negative, Extinction, and Punishment

Reinforcement is anything that causes a given behavior to be repeated or inhibited, whether praising a child for cleaning his or her room or scolding a child for leaving a tricycle in the driveway.

There are four types of reinforcement: (1) *positive reinforcement,* (2) *negative reinforcement,* (3) *extinction,* and (4) *punishment. (See Figure 12.10, next page.)*

Positive Reinforcement: Strengthens Behavior **Positive reinforcement is the use of positive consequences to strengthen a particular behavior.**

Example: A supervisor who has asked an insurance salesperson to sell more policies might reward successful performance by saying, "It's great that you exceeded your sales quota, and you'll get a bonus for it. Maybe next time you'll sell even more and will become a member of the Circle of 100 Top Sellers and win a trip to Paris as well." Note the rewards: praise, more money, recognition, awards. Presumably this will *strengthen* the behavior and the sales rep will work even harder in the coming months.

Negative Reinforcement: Also Strengthens Behavior **Negative reinforcement is the process of strengthening a behavior by withdrawing something negative.**

Example: A supervisor who has been nagging a salesperson might say, "Well, so you exceeded your quota" and stop the nagging. Note the neutral statement; there is no praise but also no longer any negative statements. This could cause the sales rep to *maintain* his or her existing behavior.

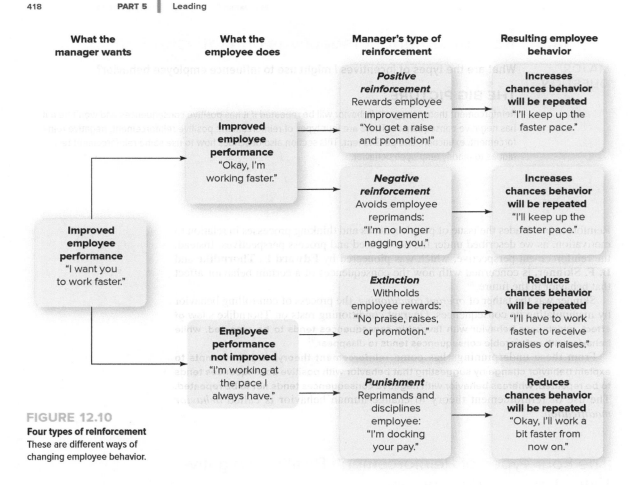

What the manager wants	What the employee does	Manager's type of reinforcement	Resulting employee behavior

Improved employee performance
"I want you to work faster."

Improved employee performance
"Okay, I'm working faster."

Employee performance not improved
"I'm working at the pace I always have."

Positive reinforcement
Rewards employee improvement:
"You get a raise and promotion!"

Negative reinforcement
Avoids employee reprimands:
"I'm no longer nagging you."

Extinction
Withholds employee rewards:
"No praise, raises, or promotion."

Punishment
Reprimands and disciplines employee:
"I'm docking your pay."

Increases chances behavior will be repeated
"I'll keep up the faster pace."

Increases chances behavior will be repeated
"I'll keep up the faster pace."

Reduces chances behavior will be repeated
"I'll have to work faster to receive praises or raises."

Reduces chances behavior will be repeated
"Okay, I'll work a bit faster from now on."

FIGURE 12.10

Four types of reinforcement
These are different ways of changing employee behavior.

Extinction: Weakens Behavior   **Extinction** is the weakening of behavior by ignoring it or making sure it is not reinforced.

Example: A supervisor might tell a successful salesperson, "I know you exceeded your sales-goal quota, but now that our company has been taken over by another firm, we're not giving out bonuses anymore." Presumably this will *weaken* the salesperson's efforts to perform better in the future.

Punishment: Also Weakens Behavior   **Punishment** is the process of weakening behavior by presenting something negative or withdrawing something positive.

Example: The U.S. Department of Transportation now fines airlines up to $27,500 per passenger for planes left on the tarmac for more than three hours. This policy reduced reported cases from 535 to 12 in the first year it was implemented.[92]

EXAMPLE   Reinforcement: How Do You Tie CEO Pay to Performance?

Earlier we mentioned the problem of CEOs who don't produce results but are still rewarded with special bonuses anyway. However, some boards of directors are now trying to tie CEO compensation to actual performance. Consider the following.

Better Food Safety? In 2016, Chipotle Mexican Grill, which had suffered from a series of illness outbreaks thought to originate in its restaurants' food-safety practices, decided to tie the future compensation of its executives directly to the company's share price performance.[93]

However, some critics question whether this is a fair arrangement, saying that it might be better to base compensation on improvements in food safety rather than on stock price alone.[94]

Realizing Environmental Goals? At Intel and other companies, executive compensation is being tied to corporate sustainability goals, including reduction in energy costs and consumption. "Sustainability has slowly moved into the realm of finance and corporate oversight," says a *Forbes* writer, "as energy, carbon emissions, water, and waste have become financial assets in terms of reduced cost, risk mitigation, and new lines of revenue."[95] However, not everyone is convinced tying CEO pay to sustainability is a slam dunk. For publicly traded companies that live and die by their quarterly earnings, this kind of long-term plan "is a tough nut to crack," says one experienced observer.[96]

YOUR CALL

You can understand how increasing executive compensation can easily be based on performance—if the only indicator of performance is the company's higher stock price. But what if what is *really* wanted is something other than money, such as food safety or better environmental practices? One study, in fact, found a link between lavish stock option grants to executives and serious product recalls.[97] What's missing, in your opinion? (To get some clarity, read on.)

Using Reinforcement to Motivate Employees

The following are some guidelines for using two types of reinforcement—positive reinforcement and punishment.

Positive Reinforcement   There are several aspects of positive reinforcement, which should definitely be part of your toolkit of managerial skills:

- **Reward only desirable behavior.** You should give rewards to your employees only when they show *desirable* behavior. Thus, for example, you should give praise to employees not for showing up for work on time (an expected part of any job) but for showing up early.
- **Give rewards as soon as possible.** You should give a reward as soon as possible after the desirable behavior appears. Thus, you should give praise to an early-arriving employee as soon as he or she arrives, not later in the week.
- **Be clear about what behavior is desired.** Clear communication is everything. You should tell employees exactly what kinds of work behaviors are desirable, and you should tell everyone exactly what he or she must do to earn rewards.
- **Have different rewards and recognize individual differences.** Recognizing that different people respond to different kinds of rewards, you should have different rewards available. Thus, you might give a word of praise verbally to one person, text or e-mail a line or two to another person, or send a hand-scrawled note to another.

Punishment   Unquestionably there will be times when you'll need to threaten or administer an unpleasant consequence to stop an employee's undesirable behavior. Sometimes it's best to address a problem by combining punishment with positive reinforcement. Some suggestions for using punishment are as follows.

- **Punish only undesirable behavior.** You should give punishment only when employees show frequent *undesirable* behavior. Otherwise, employees may come to view you negatively, as a tyrannical boss. Thus, for example, you should reprimand employees who show up, say, a half hour late for work but not 5 or 10 minutes late.

Punishment. What do you feel if you see a police car with lights and siren coming up behind you? Would getting a $260 speeding ticket change your behavior? What if it happened several times? Yet consider also other, presumably stronger forms of governmental punishment that are supposed to act as deterrents to bad behavior. Does the possibility of the death penalty really deter homicides? Why or why not? © Brand X Pictures RF

- **Give reprimands or disciplinary actions as soon as possible.** You should mete out punishment as soon as possible after the undesirable behavior occurs. Thus, you should give a reprimand to a late-arriving employee as soon as he or she arrives.

- **Be clear about what behavior is undesirable.** Tell employees exactly what kinds of work behaviors are undesirable and make any disciplinary action or reprimand match the behavior. A manager should not, for example, dock an hourly employee's pay if he or she is only 5 or 10 minutes late for work.

- **Administer punishment in private.** You would hate to have your boss chew you out in front of your subordinates, and the people who report to you also shouldn't be reprimanded in public, which would lead only to resentments that may have nothing to do with an employee's infractions.

- **Combine punishment and positive reinforcement.** If you're reprimanding an employee, be sure to also say what he or she is doing right and state what rewards the employee might be eligible for. For example, while reprimanding someone for being late, say that a perfect attendance record over the next few months will put that employee in line for a raise or promotion. ●

12.6 Using Compensation, Nonmonetary Incentives, and Other Rewards to Motivate: In Search of the Positive Work Environment

MAJOR QUESTION

How can I use compensation and other rewards to motivate people?

THE BIG PICTURE

Compensation, the main motivator of performance, includes pay for performance, bonuses, profit sharing, gainsharing, stock options, and pay for knowledge. Other, nonmonetary incentives address needs that aren't being met, such as work–life balance, growth in skills, positive work environment, and meaning in work.

Here let us consider the principal tools found in the modern workplace to motivate employees to perform—and to perform at the height of their abilities. We begin with various forms of compensation. We then address nonmonetary incentives: employees' (1) *need for work–life balance,* (2) *need to expand their skills,* (3) *need for a positive work environment,* and (4) *need to matter—to find meaning in their work.*

Would you, as a young professional, be willing to take a $7,600 pay cut for a better quality of work life?

That's what most Millennial professionals said, in a recent study by Fidelity Investments.[98] Most said they wouldn't mind taking a hefty pay cut "if it meant improved work–life balance, career development, company culture, and purposeful work," according to one report.[99]

Is Money the Best Motivator?

Whatever happened to good old money as a motivator?

Most workers rate having a caring boss higher than they value monetary benefits, according to several surveys.[100] For 30 years, the Great Place to Work Institute has determined that the bedrock features of a great workplace consist of three things: "pride, camaraderie, and trust in leaders"—that is, pride in the company, camaraderie with colleagues, and trust in management.[101] Clearly, then, motivating doesn't just involve dollars.

Motivation and Compensation

Most people are paid an hourly wage or a weekly or monthly salary. Both of these are easy for organizations to administer, of course. But by itself a wage or a salary gives an employee little incentive to work hard. Incentive compensation plans try to do so, although no single plan will boost the performance of all employees. (Indeed, a *Wall Street Journal* analysis found that none of 2015's highest-paid CEOs ran one of the 10 best-performing companies. Only three of those executives headed a firm ranked among the top 10% in total shareholder return.)[102]

Characteristics of the Best Incentive Compensation Plans In accordance with most of the theories of motivation we described earlier, for incentive plans to work, certain criteria are advisable, as follows. (1) Rewards must be linked to performance and be measurable. (2) The rewards must satisfy individual needs. (3) The rewards must be agreed on by manager and employees. (4) The rewards must be believable and achievable by employees.

Popular Incentive Compensation Plans In what way would you like to be rewarded for your efforts? Some of the most well-known incentive compensation plans are *pay for performance, bonuses, profit sharing, gainsharing, stock options,* and *pay for knowledge.*

- **Pay for performance.** Also known as *merit pay,* pay for performance bases pay on one's results. Thus, different salaried employees might get different pay raises and other rewards (such as promotions) depending on their overall job performance.[103]

  Examples: One standard pay-for-performance plan is payment according to a piece rate, in which employees are paid according to how much output they produce, as is often used with farm workers picking fruits or vegetables. Another is the sales commission, in which sales representatives are paid a percentage of the earnings the company made from their sales, so that the more they sell, the more they are paid.[104]

- **Bonuses.** Bonuses are cash awards given to employees who achieve specific performance objectives.

  Example: The department store Nieman Marcus pays its salespeople a percentage of the earnings from the goods they sell.

  Unfortunately, the documents that most companies file (proxy documents to the Securities and Exchange Commission) to explain what specific targets executives had to meet to earn their bonuses are not very clear, being couched mainly in legalese.[105]

- **Profit sharing.** Profit sharing is the distribution to employees of a percentage of the company's profits.

  Example: In one T-shirt and sweatshirt manufacturing company, 10% of pretax profits are distributed to employees every month, and more is given out at the end of the year. Distributions are apportioned according to such criteria as performance, attendance, and lateness for individual employees.

- **Gainsharing.** Gainsharing is the distribution of savings or "gains" to groups of employees who reduced costs and increased measurable productivity. Gainsharing has been applied in a variety of industries, from manufacturing to nonprofit, and is said to be used in more than a quarter of Fortune 1,000 companies, as well as many small to mid-size businesses.[106] In one version (the so-called *Scanlon plan*), a portion of any cost savings, usually 75%, is distributed to employees.

  Example: In a recent year, Indianapolis-based Mike's Carwash paid out $569,000 in gainsharing to 437 employees in 37 locations who had been challenged to beat targets set at the corporate level. Employees averaged $1.25 extra per hour.[107] Gainsharing has also been used to get truck drivers to ease off the accelerator in order to achieve fleet sustainability goals to increase fuel economy and decrease greenhouse gas emissions.[108]

- **Stock options.** With stock options, certain employees are given the right to buy stock at a future date for a discounted price. About 20% of the U.S. workforce outside the government participate in some sort of employee stock ownership program.[109] The motivator here is that employees holding stock options will supposedly work hard to make the company's stock rise so that they can obtain it at a cheaper price. Along with its other benefits, by giving stock options to all employees who work 20 or more hours a week, Starbucks Corp. has been able to hold its employee turnover rate to about 65% per year (25% for managers) compared to 150%–400% for employees at chain retailers (50% for managers).[110]

- **Pay for knowledge.** Also known as *skill-based pay,* pay for knowledge ties employee pay to the number of job-relevant skills or academic degrees they earn.[111]

  Example: The teaching profession is a time-honored instance of this incentive, in which elementary and secondary teachers are encouraged to increase their salaries by earning further college credit. However, firms such as FedEx also have pay-for-knowledge plans.

Motivation as a small business owner. Pizza chef Tony Gemignani demonstrates the proper technique for making pizza. Gemignani, who worked in and studied many U.S. pizza parlors, was inspired by a 2000 visit to Italy to learn how to make award-winning char-spotted, soft-centered Neapolitan pizza, a learning process that took seven years and involved grinding his own sausage and pulling his own mozarella. Opening his own restaurant in 2009 showed that he had read the market correctly for American public taste and love of choices. Coupling good food with a flair for the dramatic (restaurant decor featuring metal sculptures resembling tribal tattoos, for instance), Gemignani and his partners opened Pizza Rock, which now has several California and Nevada stores.[112] For some people, like Gemignani, the only way to merge motivation and compensation is to own and manage their own business. What factors or incentives motivate you to work hard?
© Eric Risberg/AP Photo

Nonmonetary Ways of Motivating Employees

Employees who can behave autonomously, solve problems, and take the initiative are apt to be the very ones who will leave if they find their own needs aren't being met—namely, (1) the need for work–life balance, (2) the need to expand their skills, (3) the need for a positive work environment, and (4) the need to matter—to find meaning in their work.

The Need for Work–Life Balance   For more than half of men and women in a 2013 Accenture survey, work–life balance was the key determinant of career success—ahead of money, recognition, autonomy, or making a difference.[113] In another survey, 46% of employees said work–life balance was the thing they valued most when looking for a new job (second only to salary, cited by 57%). According to Pew Research, Millennials in particular are apt to say the most important things in life are "being a good parent" (52%) and "having a successful marriage" (30%), rather than "having a high-paying career" (15%).[114]

As mentioned, most Millennial professionals said they wouldn't mind taking a big pay cut if it meant improved work–life balance, career development, and purposeful work.[115] A Gallup poll finds they want good jobs, with regular paychecks from employers, and they want to be engaged in those jobs, but they want to be able to talk to their managers about non-work-related issues.[116]

Among the employer offerings designed to cater to the desire for work–life balance (at least for some employees) are *work–life benefits, flex-time,* and *vacation/sabbatical time*:

- **Work–life benefits.** Work–life benefits are employer-sponsored benefit programs or initiatives designed to help all employees balance work life with home life.[117] The purpose of such benefits is to remove barriers that make it hard for people to strike a balance between their work and personal lives, such as allowing parents time off to take care of sick children. The worst obstacles to work–life balance, according to one survey, are *bad bosses*—defined as "demanding, overbearing, and mean." Constant work beyond standard business hours and inflexible scheduling tied for second. Third were incompetent colleagues and long commutes.[118]

  Work–life benefits include helping employees with day care costs or even establishing on-site centers; offering domestic-partner benefits; giving job-protected leave for new parents; and providing technology such as mobile phones and laptops to enable parents to work at home.[119] (Unfortunately, the workplace culture often tends to discourage paid leave for parents, particularly fathers.)[120]

  How good are U.S. employers at making work–life benefits available? The United States actually ranks fairly low on this feature—29 out of 36 on a list of countries with the best work–life balance.[121] And although two-thirds (67%) of HR professionals *think* their employees have a balanced work life, according to one survey, among employees themselves nearly half (45%) still crave more time each week for personal activities.[122]

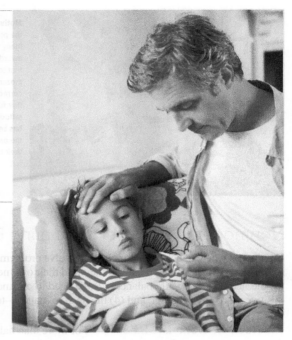

Balancing work with life. Work factors don't always allow for life factors—sick children, school appointments, family emergencies, problems with aging parents, medical appointments, and other personal matters. People around the world are urging employees to ease the single-minded focus on jobs by introducing more flexibility and balance into their lives—work–life balance. What are the top three nonwork concerns that you might have to deal with that you hope your employer might accommodate for you?

© Paul Bradbury/Getty Images RF

- **Flex-time.** By *flex-time,* we do not mean the so-called *on-call schedules* once practiced by Abercrombie & Fitch, Williams-Sonoma, and other stores that required workers to be on call for shifts that could be canceled with little notice—schedules that demoralized employees and hurt children's well-being.[123] Rather, we are talking about the flexible workplace—including part-time work, flex-time, a compressed workweek, job sharing, and telecommuting—discussed in the Manager's Toolbox at the start of this chapter.

  In one flex-time experiment, in which employees were told they could work wherever and whenever they chose as long as projects were completed on time and goals were met, such employees not only met their goals (as well as did a control group) but were sleeping better, less stressed, and less interested in leaving the organization a year later.[124]

- **Vacations and sabbaticals.** It used to be a badge of honor for Citigroup's junior bankers to put in 100-hour work weeks. Now, says CEO Michael Corbat, "I want people to have family lives, personal lives." Recently, the bank unveiled a program that lets young employees take a long sabbatical—an extended vacation—during which the Citigroup volunteers are paid 60% of their salary, and take a year off to do charitable work helping, say, businesses develop growth plans in Kenya.[125]

  Tech companies like Apple and Genentech certainly understand that in a climate of 80-hour work weeks people need to recharge themselves. But even The Cheesecake Factory offers employees with at least five years of service sabbaticals of up to three weeks, with additional ones every five years thereafter. (One employee planned to hike the 220-mile John Muir Trail in California from Yosemite to Mt. Whitney.)[126]

  About 4% of American corporations, most of them technology firms, offer *unlimited* paid time off.[127] Whatever the arrangement, the aim, of course, is to enable employees to reenergize themselves but also, it is hoped, to cement their loyalty to the organization.[128] (Ironically, however, most employees with unlimited time off are unlikely to use much of it—and if they quit or get fired, they will not get a payout for unused vacation days.)

The Need to Expand Skills   As mentioned in Chapter 9, 70% of employees say they are dissatisfied with career growth opportunities at their companies, and training programs can keep them engaged with their work.[129] Young workers in particular, having watched their parents undergo downsizing, are apt to view a job as a way of gaining skills that will enable them to earn a decent living in the future. Employers have another point of view: They see it as developing *human capital,* which, as we saw in Chapter 9, is the economic or protective potential of employee knowledge, experience, and actions.

Learning opportunities can take three forms:

- **Studying coworkers.** Managers can see that workers are matched with coworkers from whom they can learn, allowing them, for instance, to "shadow" (watch and imitate) workers in other jobs or be in interdepartmental task forces.

- **Tuition reimbursement.** There can also be tuition reimbursement for part-time study at a college or university.[130]

- **Training.** About 30% of small companies, 41% of midsize companies, and 29% of large companies offer some sort of training, according to a 2015 training industry report.[131] Although instructor-led classrooms are still the dominant training method, we pointed out earlier that at about 46% of total student hours, 26.5% of training was delivered by online or computer-based technologies, 1.8% by mobile devices, and 31.9% by blended techniques.[132]

The Need for a Positive Work Environment   Wanting to work in a positive environment begins with the idea of well-being. **Well-being is the combined impact of five elements—positive emotions, engagement, relationships, meaning, and achievement (PERMA),** according to renowned psychologist Martin Seligman.[133] There is one essential consideration to remember about these elements: We must pursue them for their own sake, not as a means to obtain another outcome. In other words, well-being comes about by freely pursuing one or more of the five elements in PERMA.

Flourishing represents the extent to which our lives contain PERMA. When we flourish, our lives result in "goodness . . . growth, and resilience."[134] We should all strive to flourish because of its association with other positive outcomes, like lower cardiovascular risk, lower levels of inflammation, longer life, better sleep, and positive mental health.[135] Unfortunately, many people are not flourishing. For example, a recent survey of 160,000 people around the world revealed that 33% reported above-average stress.[136] U.S. data further showed that a majority of people lose sleep because of work-related stress and many people are abusing painkillers to combat it. Painkiller abuse costs employers about $25.5 billion a year in absenteeism and lost productivity.[137]

By contrast, positive emotions *broaden* your perspective about how to overcome challenges in your life—joy, for instance, is more likely to lead you to envision creative ideas during a brainstorming session. Positive emotions also *build* on themselves, resulting in a spreading of positive emotions within yourself and those around you.[138]

What is it that employers can do to create a positive work environment? Elsewhere in the book we have touched on such matters as employee engagement, social support, and recognition for achievement. Here let us discuss just two other factors: (1) *surroundings* and (2) *an understanding boss.*

- **Surroundings.** The cubicle, according to new research, is stifling the creativity and morale of many workers, and the bias of modern-day office designers for open spaces and neutral colors is leading to employee complaints that their workplaces are too noisy or too bland. Some businesses, such as advertising giant Grey Group in New York, have even moved beyond cubicles to completely open offices, which at Grey required a business psychologist to hold "space therapy" sessions to ease employee concerns.[139]

"The key to successful workspaces is to empower individuals by giving them choices that allow control over their work environment," says a *Harvard Business Review* article.[140] That's especially key when it comes to keeping employees happy.

EXAMPLE   Successful Workspaces

As we said, the traditional private office has yielded to cubicles and more recently to open-plan offices with few or no walls. (Indeed, Facebook hired a world-famous architect to design an office that is a single room stretching 10 acres and accommodating several thousand engineers.)[141]

Distractions or Performance? Although crowding people together can promote cooperative behavior, it also, of course, leads to lack of privacy and increased distractions, which can stifle creativity, dampen morale, and lead to diminished individual and organizational performance.[142]

"There is no such thing as something that works for everybody," says Alan Hedge, a professor of environmental analysis at Cornell University.[143] An 8-foot-by-8-foot cubicle may not be a good visual trigger for human brains, and com-

panies wanting to improve creativity and productivity may need to think about giving office employees better things to look at.[144]

YOUR CALL

Although 70% of today's organizations have open-plan offices, other designs are now being tried that go beyond the "open" and "closed" models and can balance people's wishes for privacy against the competing desire for collaboration.[145] "The emerging trend is the hybrid approach," says one workplace strategist, "which includes about a 15% to 30% closed plan with a variety of other work areas to supplement just sitting at a desk."[146] What kind of office surroundings would work best for you?

- **Thoughtful bosses.** It's said that "people don't leave jobs, they leave managers," points out a *Forbes* writer, citing evidence of a survey from the United Kingdom in which 42% of 1,374 employees left a job because of a bad boss and almost a third felt their present boss was a bad manager.[147] A Gallup study also found that about 50% of the 7,200 adults surveyed left a job "to get away from their manager."[148] Some of these employees were well paid, but is this enough?

PRACTICAL ACTION   Thoughtfulness: The Value of Being Nice

"Feeling cared for by one's supervisor has a more significant impact on people's sense of trust than any other behavior by a leader," says one article summarizing the results of a global workforce study. "Employees who say they have more supportive supervisors are 1.3 times as likely to stay with the organization and are 67% more engaged."[149]

A study by McKinsey & Company, a global management consulting firm, found that nonfinancial incentives such as praise and commendation from one's immediate management (which 67% of those surveyed thought extremely or very effective) and attention from leaders (by 63%) were better motivators than three financial incentives: performance-based cash bonuses (60%), increase in base pay (52%), and stock or stock options (35%).[150]

What the Managers Should Do

The co-founder of one start-up, James Lintern of software maker RotaCloud, suggests you need to learn to look for disgruntled employees (those who moan a lot, feign ignorance or innocence, or simply stay quiet and stop working) and then speak with them privately but professionally and provide support, if necessary.[151]

Giving Praise

"Being nice" to employees means, for example, giving personal and frequent praise, writing celebratory emails to supervisors (and copying the employee), giving public recognition, and writing handwritten thank-you notes. You might even imitate that former KFC president who recognized valued employees by giving away floppy rubber chickens and $100.[152]

It's important, of course, that praise be *effective.* One business writer points out that managers often undermine the power of recognition by (1) withholding it altogether (so as not to accidentally favor or ignore anyone), (2) spreading praise 100% evenly across a team, and (3) mindlessly crediting groups at the expense of individuals.[153]

YOUR CALL

What are the top three things you'd like to see in a thoughtful boss? Would you rather work for someone who is "nice" but lacking in other qualities (decisiveness, leadership)? Or would you prefer to report to someone who seems to be indifferent to your feelings and never listens to you but is running a successful operation that's giving you a good paycheck?

The Need to Matter—Finding Meaning in Work   Workers now want to be with an organization that allows them to feel they matter. They want to commit to their profession or fellow team members rather than have to profess a blind loyalty to the corporation.[154] In particular, employees of small firms (under 1,000 people) "want to feel their ideas and efforts materially contribute to the success of their employers," according to one survey.[155]

World War II concentration camp survivor Viktor Frankl, author of *Man's Search for Meaning,* strongly believed that "striving to find a meaning in one's life is the primary motivational force" for people.[156] In other words, it is the drive to find meaning in our lives that instills in us a sense of purpose and motivation to pursue goals.

Meaningfulness, then, is the sense of "belonging to and serving something that you believe is bigger than the self."[157] What follows are three suggestions for building meaning into your life.

1. **Identify activities you love doing.** Try to do more of these activities or find ways to build them into your work role.

    Example: Employees at St. Jude Children's Research Hospital in Memphis embody this suggestion. They truly enjoy participating in the St. Jude Marathon weekend because it raises money for the children being treated at the hospital. One employee, a cancer survivor, commented, "Each year it provides me with another opportunity to give back so that we can help countless other children have anniversaries of their own."[158]

2. **Find a way to build your natural strengths into your personal and work life.** Want to be more engaged with your school, work, and leisure activities? Take the time to list your highest strengths, your weaknesses, which strengths you use on a daily basis—and find what you can do to incorporate your strengths into your school, work, and leisure activities.

3. **Go out and help someone.** Research shows that people derive a sense of meaningfulness from helping others, that it creates an upward spiral of positivity.[159]

    Example: Salesforce.com encourages this result by giving employees six paid days a year to volunteer. All told, company employees logged over 1 million volunteer hours in 2015.[160] ●

Key Points

12.1 Motivating for Performance

- Motivation is defined as the psychological processes that arouse and direct goal-directed behavior.

- In a simple model of motivation, people have certain needs that motivate them to perform specific behaviors for which they receive rewards that feed back and satisfy the original need.

- Rewards are of two types: (1) An extrinsic reward is the payoff, such as money, a person receives from others for performing a particular task. (2) An intrinsic reward is the satisfaction, such as a feeling of accomplishment, that a person receives from performing the particular task itself.

- As a manager, you want to motivate people to do things that will benefit your organization—join it, stay with it, show up for work at it, perform better for it, and do extra for it.

- Four major perspectives on motivation are (1) content, (2) process, (3) job design, and (4) reinforcement.

12.2 Content Perspectives on Employee Motivation

- Content perspectives or need-based perspectives emphasize the needs that motivate people. Needs are defined as

physiological or psychological deficiencies that arouse behavior.

- Besides the McGregor Theory X/Theory Y (Chapter 2), need-based perspectives include (1) the hierarchy of needs theory, (2) the acquired needs theory, (3) the self-determination theory, and (4) the two-factor theory.

- The hierarchy of needs theory proposes that people are motivated by five levels of need: physiological, safety, love, esteem, and self-actualization needs.

- The acquired needs theory states that three needs—achievement, affiliation, and power—are major motives determining people's behavior in the workplace.

- The self-determination theory assumes that people are driven to try to grow and attain fulfillment, with their behavior and well-being influenced by three innate needs: competence, autonomy, and relatedness.

- The two-factor theory proposes that work satisfaction and dissatisfaction arise from two different factors: work satisfaction from so-called motivating factors, and work dissatisfaction from so-called hygiene factors.

- Hygiene factors, the lower-level needs, are factors associated with job dissatisfaction—such as salary and working conditions—which affect the environment in which people work. Motivating factors, the higher-level needs, are factors associated with job satisfaction—such as achievement and advancement—which affect the rewards of work performance.

12.3 Process Perspectives on Employee Motivation

- Process perspectives are concerned with the thought processes by which people decide how to act. Three process perspectives on motivation are (1) equity theory, (2) expectancy theory, and (3) goal-setting theory.
- Equity theory focuses on employee perceptions as to how fairly they think they are being treated compared with others.
- The key elements in equity theory are inputs, outputs (rewards), and comparisons. (1) With inputs, employees consider what they are putting into the job in time, effort, and so on. (2) With outputs or rewards, employees consider what they think they're getting out of the job in terms of pay, praise, and so on. (3) With comparison, employees compare the ratio of their own outcomes to inputs against the ratio of someone else's outcomes to inputs.
- Equity theory has expanded into an area called organizational justice, which is concerned with the extent to which people perceive they are treated fairly at work. Three different components of organizational justice have been identified. Distributive justice reflects the perceived fairness of how resources and rewards are distributed or allocated. Procedural justice is defines as the perceived fairness of the process and procedures used to make allocation decisions. Interactional justice relates to the quality of the interpersonal treatment people receive when procedures are implemented.
- Five practical lessons of equity and justice theories are that employee perceptions are what count, employee participation helps, having an appeal process helps, leader behavior matters, and a climate for justice makes a difference.
- Expectancy theory suggests that people are motivated by how much they want something and how likely they think they are to get it. The three elements affecting motivation are expectancy, instrumentality, and valence. (1) Expectancy is the belief that a particular level of effort will lead to a particular level of performance. (2) Instrumentality is the expectation that successful performance of the task will lead to the outcome desired. (3) Valence is the value, the importance a worker assigns to the possible outcome or reward.

- When attempting to motivate employees, according to the logic of expectancy theory, managers should ascertain what rewards employees value, what job objectives and performance level they desire, whether there are rewards linked to performance, and whether employees believe managers will deliver the right rewards for the right performance.
- Goal-setting theory suggests that employees can be motivated by goals that are specific and challenging but achievable and linked to action plans.
- In addition, the theory suggests that goals should be set jointly with the employee, be measurable, and have a target date for accomplishment and that employees should receive feedback and rewards.

12.4 Job Design Perspectives on Motivation

- Job design is, first, the division of an organization's work among its employees and, second, the application of motivational theories to jobs to increase satisfaction and performance.
- Two approaches to job design are fitting people to jobs (the traditional approach) and fitting jobs to people.
- Fitting jobs to people assumes people are underutilized and want more variety. Two techniques for this type of job design include (1) job enlargement, increasing the number of tasks in a job to increase variety and motivation, and (2) job enrichment, building into a job such motivating factors as responsibility, achievement, recognition, stimulating work, and advancement.
- An outgrowth of job enrichment is the job characteristics model, which consists of (a) five core job characteristics that affect (b) three critical psychological states of an employee that in turn affect (c) work outcomes—the employee's motivation, performance, and satisfaction.
- The five core job characteristics are (1) skill variety—how many different skills a job requires; (2) task identity—how many different tasks are required to complete the work; (3) task significance—how many other people are affected by the job; (4) autonomy—how much discretion the job allows the worker; and (5) feedback—how much employees find out how well they're doing.
- These five characteristics affect three critical psychological states: meaningfulness of work, responsibility for results, and knowledge of results.
- Three major steps to follow when applying the job characteristics model are (1) diagnose the work

environment to see if a problem exists, (2) determine whether job redesign is appropriate, and (3) consider how to redesign the job.

12.5 Reinforcement Perspectives on Motivation

- Reinforcement theory attempts to explain behavior change by suggesting that behavior with positive consequences tends to be repeated whereas behavior with negative consequences tends not to be repeated. Reinforcement is anything that causes a given behavior to be repeated or inhibited. The theory rests on Thorndike's law of effect, which says behavior with favorable consequences tends to be repeated, while behavior with unfavorable consequences tends to disappear. The use of reinforcement theory to change human behavior is called behavior modification.

- There are four types of reinforcement. (1) Positive reinforcement is the use of positive consequences to strengthen a particular behavior. (2) Negative reinforcement is the process of strengthening a behavior by withdrawing something negative. (3) Extinction is the weakening of behavior by ignoring it or making sure it is not reinforced. (4) Punishment is the process of weakening behavior by presenting something negative or withdrawing something positive.

- In using positive reinforcement to motivate employees, managers should reward only desirable behavior, give rewards as soon as possible, be clear about what behavior is desired, and have different rewards and recognize individual differences.

- In using punishment, managers should punish only undesirable behavior, give reprimands or disciplinary actions as soon as possible, be clear about what behavior is undesirable, administer punishment in private, and combine punishment and positive reinforcement.

12.6 Using Compensation and Other Rewards to Motivate

- Compensation is only one form of motivator. For incentive compensation plans for work, rewards must be linked to performance and be measurable; they must satisfy individual needs; they must be agreed on by manager and employee; and they must be perceived as being equitable, believable, and achievable by employees.

- Popular incentive compensation plans are the following. (1) Pay for performance bases pay on one's results. One kind is payment according to piece rate, in which employees are paid according to how much output they produce. Another is the sales commission, in which sales representatives are paid a percentage of the earnings the company made from their sales. (2) Bonuses are cash awards given to employees who achieve specific performance objectives. (3) Profit sharing is the distribution to employees of a percentage of the company's profits. (4) Gainsharing is the distribution of savings or "gains" to groups of employees who reduced costs and increased measurable productivity. (5) Stock options allow certain employees to buy stock at a future date for a discounted price. (6) Pay for knowledge ties employee pay to the number of job-relevant skills or academic degrees they earn.

- There are also nonmonetary ways of compensating employees. Some employees will leave because they feel the need for work–life balance, the need to expand their skills, and the need to matter. To retain such employees, nonmonetary incentives have been introduced, such as the flexible workplace.

- Other incentives that keep employees from leaving are thoughtfulness by employees' managers, work–life benefits such as day care, attractive surroundings, skill-building and educational opportunities, and work sabbaticals.

Understanding the Chapter: What Do I Know?

1. What is motivation, and how does it work?
2. What are the two principal types of rewards?
3. What are the four major perspectives on motivation?
4. Briefly describe the four content perspectives discussed in this chapter: hierarchy of needs theory, acquired needs theory, self-determination theory, and two-factor theory.
5. What are the principal elements of the three process perspectives: equity theory, expectancy theory, and goal-setting theory?

6. What is the definition of job design, and what are two techniques of job design?
7. Describe the five job attributes of the job characteristics model.
8. What are the four types of reinforcement?
9. What are six incentive compensation plans?
10. Discuss some nonmonetary ways of motivating employees.

Acuity Insurance and the Container Store Focus on Employee Motivation

Acuity Insurance and the Container Store were ranked as the 2nd and 14th Best Place to Work by *Fortune* in 2016. Both companies put a premium on attracting, retaining, and developing great workers, resulting in an engaged and motivated workforce.

Acuity Insurance

Acuity is a property and casualty insurer headquartered in Sheboygan, Wisconsin. The company generated over $2 billion in revenue in 2015 through 1,000 independent agencies in 24 states. There are 1,110 employees in the U.S.[161]

About 98% of employees reported to *Fortune* in 2016 that the company has unique benefits, effectively contributes to its local communities, and celebrates special events with employees. These employees in turn noted that facilities contributed to a good working environment.

Acuity employs a variety of programs to motivate employees. They include the following:[162]

- **The Magic Happens Gossip Line:** The company recognizes 20 to 30 employees each month through the Magic Happens program. The program begins by posting any positive feedback from customers, agents, or colleagues outside the local cafeteria. Next, one employee is drawn from this list and the positive feedback is shared over voice mail to all employees throughout the company. This employee also receives a $100 cash gift card.

- **Lunch with an Officer:** This program is used to foster open communication. Groups of 10 to 15 employees are invited to have lunch with an officer of the executive team every few months. Employees are asked to provide feedback or suggestions for improving any aspect of the company. Employees also spend time getting to know each other.

- **Wellness programs:** The company built a 9,800-square-foot fitness center that offers classes at no cost to employees. The facility is open 24/7 and includes massage therapists on-site three days per week. In addition to providing opportunities to participate in local races or athletic events, Acuity hosts a Weight Watchers at Work program. The company reimburses 25% of the cost when an employee attends 50% of the meetings.

- **5 Year Club:** "All employees who have been with ACUITY for fewer than five years are invited to special social events that range from happy hours and kayaking trips to bean bag tournaments, NCAA March Madness competitions, and other events that encourage our employees to get out and explore the community of Sheboygan."[163]

- **Generous benefits:** In addition to perks like free snacks during the day, subsidized daily lunches, dry cleaning service, free beverages during the day, on-site package/mailing service, and banking services, Acuity pays 85% of health coverage for employees and their dependents. The company's 401(k) "program features an 8% contribution to all employee accounts, regardless of their personal contributions. Employees benefit from a profit-sharing bonus as well. . . . Employees have received a 10% total contribution to their 401 (k) on behalf of the company."[164]

The Container Store

The Container store, founded in 1978, strives to provide "a differentiated shopping experience offering customers innovative, time and space saving solutions coupled with astonishing customer service from happy, well trained, well paid salespeople." The company has 4,281 employees working at 73 U.S. sites. Worldwide revenues were $781.88 million in 2015.[165]

Kip Tindell, founder and former CEO, told *The Wall Street Journal* that the company was grown around the core principle that "one great person can easily do the business productivity of three good people." This belief has led the company to pay employees 50%–100% above industry average. For example, the average salesperson at The Container Store makes $48,000 per year. In contrast the Bureau of Labor Statistics reports that the average earnings for retail sales people in the U.S. in 2013 was $31,096. He also said that "We give big annual increases each year because we believe in keeping people mildly tickled about their rate of increase. We really and truly believe in paying according to contribution."[166] Annual raises range from 0$ to 8%.

Annual raises are given after an employee and manager follow a two-step process. The first step entails having the focal manager and employee complete a formal written review using the same form. The two then meet for a few hours to review their evaluations and arrive at a final consensus. Managers ultimately rank their employees in terms of contribution and pay. The idea is to ensure that someone's contribution matches his or her pay in a work unit. For example, if an employee is ranked third in contribution, then the goal is to provide raises that result in the person being number three in pay. This can take a few years to catch up.[167]

The company also tries to increase employees' competence and performance by providing over 260 hours of training in the first year of employment. Employees then receive an additional 170 hours of training per year.[168]

Part-time workers, who represent about 70% of the workforce, also get health benefits. The company matches employees' contributions to a 401(k) account up to 4% of pay. There have not been any company-wide layoffs.

Over 90% of employees reported to *Fortune* in 2016 that the company has great atmosphere, rewards, communication, and bosses. Ninety-five percent also noted people care about each other there and they are proud to tell others about working at the company.[169] These positive attitudes help explain the low annual turnover rate of 10%: The retail industry averages 100% per year.[170]

FOR DISCUSSION

1. To what extent are Acuity's and The Container Store's approaches toward motivation consistent with need theories of motivation? Discuss.

2. To what extent is The Container Store's pay and reward system consistent with equity theory? Explain.

3. To what extent is The Container Store's approach toward rewards consistent with expectancy theory? Explain.

4. How do Acuity and The Container Store use principles associated with the Job Characteristics Model to motivate employees? Specifically describe.

5. What are the key lessons learned from this case?

Legal/Ethical Challenge

Should College Athletes Be Paid to Perform?

Do you think a college athlete's motivation to perform is a function of pay? College athletes cannot be paid because of rules established by the National Collegiate Athletic Association (NCAA). This governing body believes that college athletes are amateurs and created rules barring them from being paid. The NCAA believes that athletes should not receive any direct compensation because they receive benefits such as athletic scholarships, medical care, academic support services, and first-class training. If we assume that these benefits constitute the pay received for playing college sports, then players are certainly motivated by something other than money. But is this fair or ethical?

Consider that the NCAA also refused to pay college athletes for the use of their likeness in licensing agreements. This led to a lawsuit in 2009 by Ed O'Bannon, a former University of California at Los Angeles basketball player. His image was used in video games, yet he received nothing from the profits. He filed an antitrust suit against the NCAA, and a federal judge ruled in his favor in August 2014. The judge concluded that basketball and football players can earn "a limited share of the revenues generated from the use of their names, images, and likeness in addition to a full grant-in-aid."[171]

Some people believe that universities and the NCAA are unfairly benefiting from the talent and dedication of college athletes. As one *New York Times* reporter stated, "the N.C.A.A. and the college sports establishment exploit the players who generate billions that the grown-ups pocket."[172] Consider the revenue generated by the 64 schools in the major five conferences (the ACC, Big 10, Big 12, Pac 12, and SEC) during the 2103–2014 academic year. They earned a combined $2.8 billion.[173]

The NCAA claims that its member institutions cannot afford to pay athletes because most universities do not make a profit from their athletic programs. The *Huffington Post* investigated this finding with the help of five sports economists. The economists noted that universities spend revenue from college sports as soon as they get it, and this is why they are not making a profit. They proposed that prudent budgetary management would change the profitability of athletic programs. They also concluded that universities could pay athletes by simply reallocating sports revenue from one category such as coaches salaries to students.[174]

SOLVING THE CHALLENGE

Is it fair that college athletes don't get paid for performing a sport?

1. Yes. I agree with the NCAA. Athletes receive plenty of benefits such as scholarships, medical coverage, and world-class training.

2. No. The athletes risk personal injury and they spend lots of time practicing instead of studying, which can impact their nonathletic marketability upon graduation. Athletes deserve to be paid.

3. No, but doing so would create havoc with college sports. It would mean that players in every sport would need to be paid. This would likely lead to the cancellation of low revenue sports like volleyball, swimming, golf, and gymnastics. I would pay athletes for the use of their likenesses in games and marketing, but no direct compensation for playing the sport.

4. Invent another option.

13

Groups and Teams
Increasing Cooperation, Reducing Conflict

Major Questions You Should Be Able to Answer

13.1 **Groups versus Teams**
Major Question: How is one collection of workers different from any other?

13.2 **Stages of Group and Team Development**
Major Question: How does a group evolve into a team?

13.3 **Building Effective Teams**
Major Question: How can I as a manager build an effective team?

13.4 **Managing Conflict**
Major Question: Since conflict is a part of life, what should a manager know about it in order to deal successfully with it?

Reaching across Time and Space: The Challenge of Managing Virtual Teams

Josh Steimle is the founder of MWI, a digital marketing firm based in Salt Lake City, Utah. With team members in Washington, Texas, Utah, Illinois, Arizona, and now Hong Kong, Steimle recently abandoned the idea of maintaining a central office space, and MWI now operates as a virtual-team organization.[1] Virtual teams are groups of people who collaborate seamlessly across time and space with the help of a wide array of communication technologies.

Not every firm has gone as far as MWI in relying on virtual workers, but many managers agree with Steimle that a big advantage of using virtual teams is that it's now possible to hire the best people no matter where they live. Here are some tips for managing virtual employees, from those who are doing it successfully.[2]

1. Hire selectively, choosing people with proven work experience and personal maturity. You want to feel comfortable that they can handle their work without the constant in-person contact that comes with working in the office.

2. Check in regularly—some managers recommend very brief daily meetings—but resist the urge to micromanage. "Have a regular video call to assess how they're doing—it's important to have face-to-face connection,"[3] says Leah Mason, director of operations at Four Kitchens.

3. Set clear objectives that focus on results. "Let people work when they're most productive and judge them on output not hours,"[4] says Alex Turnbull, CEO and co-founder of Groove.

4. Take advantage of appropriate communication and work-sharing technology. You can use intranets, scheduling software, Skype, chatrooms, online agendas, wikis, Google Docs, Dropbox, and WorldTimeBuddy.

5. Set up small teams to help people develop coworker relationships and get the work done. Says Ben Welch-Bolen, CEO and co-owner of World Wide Web Hosting, "We've found that a small team structure works best—where they all get to know each other and can't disappear into a group."[5]

6. Share the praise and attention. Make an effort to pay attention to all employees, particularly those working virtually. You want distributed workers to feel like they belong to an entire work unit.

For Discussion What do you feel might be the greatest difficulties of always working online with numerous people you never see? How would you try to avoid or solve these difficulties?

FORECAST — What's Ahead in This Chapter

In this chapter, we consider groups versus teams and discuss different kinds of teams. We describe how groups evolve into teams and discuss how managers can build effective teams. We also consider the nature of conflict, both good and bad.

13.1 Groups versus Teams

How is one collection of workers different from any other?

THE BIG PICTURE

Teamwork promises to be a cornerstone of future management. A team is different from a group. A group typically is management-directed, a team self-directed. Groups may be formal, created to do productive work, or informal, created for friendship. Work teams engage in collective work requiring coordinated effort. Other types of teams are project teams, cross-functional teams, self-managed teams, and virtual teams.

Over a quarter century ago, management philosopher Peter Drucker predicted that future organizations would not only be flatter and information-based but also organized around teamwork—and that has certainly come to pass.[6]

In fact, your ability to work well as a team member can affect your job opportunities and success, as well as influencing the kind of employers that might appeal to you. Jenny Gottstein is director of games at The Go Game, a company that builds interactive games to promote team-building in large organizations including Facebook, Google, and American Express. "We're seeing companies use their strong corporate culture as a bargaining chip to recruit the best and brightest talent. When applying for jobs, millennial employees are not only assessing their salary and benefits, but also whether or not they relate to the working environment, and enjoy rolling up their sleeves next to their peers. As a result of this culture shift, team-building is being used as a marketing and recruitment tool."[7]

When you take a job in an organization, the chances are you won't be working alone. You'll be working with others in situations requiring teamwork.

The argument for promoting diversity suggested by scholar Scott E. Page (see Chapter 3)—namely, that different kinds of people "bring to organizations more and different ways of seeing a problem and, thus, faster/better ways of solving it"—is also a principal strength of teams.[8] However, teamwork is now the cornerstone of progressive management for many other reasons, as the table below shows. *(See Table 13.1.)*

TABLE 13.1   Why Teamwork Is Important

THE IMPROVEMENTS	EXAMPLE
Increased productivity	At one GE factory, teamwork resulted in a workforce that was 20% more productive than comparable GE workforces elsewhere.
Increased speed	Guidant Corp., maker of lifesaving medical devices, halved the time it took to get products to market.
Reduced costs	Boeing used teamwork to develop the 777 at costs far less than normal.
Improved quality	Westinghouse used teamwork to improve quality performance in its truck and trailer division and within its electronic components division.
Reduced destructive internal competition	Men's Wearhouse fired a salesman who wasn't sharing walk-in customer traffic, and total clothing sales volume among all salespeople increased significantly.
Improved workplace cohesiveness	Cisco Systems told executives they would gain or lose 30% of their bonuses based on how well they worked with peers and in three years had record profits.

Groups and Teams: How Do They Differ?

Aren't a group of people and a team of people the same thing? By and large, no. One is a collection of people, the other a powerful unit of collective performance. One is typically management-directed, the other self-directed.

Consider the differences, as follows.

What a Group Is: A Collection of People Performing as Individuals

A group is defined as (1) two or more freely interacting individuals who (2) share norms, (3) share goals, and (4) have a common identity.[9] A group is different from a crowd, a transitory collection of people who don't interact with one another, such as a crowd gathering on a sidewalk to watch a fire. And it is different from an organization, such as a labor union, which is so large that members also don't interact.

An example of a work group would be a collection of 10 employees meeting to exchange information about various companies' policies on wages and hours.

What a Team Is: A Collection of People with Common Commitment

McKinsey & Company management consultants Jon R. Katzenbach and Douglas K. Smith say it is a mistake to use the terms *group* and *team* interchangeably. Successful teams, they say, tend to take on a life of their own. Thus, a **team is defined as a small group of people with complementary skills who are committed to a common purpose, performance goals, and approach for which they hold themselves mutually accountable.**[10] "The essence of a team is common commitment," say Katzenbach and Smith. "Without it, groups perform as individuals; with it, they become a powerful unit of collective performance."[11]

An example of a team is a collection of 2–10 employees who are studying industry pay scales, with the goal of making recommendations for adjusting pay grades within their own company.

Xero, an award-winning maker of accounting software for small businesses, relies on motivation to help its employee teams keep sight of their common commitment in the midst of the company's rapid global growth. "Clearly defining your purpose, communicating it effectively, and empowering your employees is one of the purest ways to motivate a team," says CEO Rod Drury.[12]

How do you feel about working in teams? To find out, try Self-Assessment 13.1.

≡ connect SELF-ASSESSMENT 13.1

Attitudes toward Teamwork

The following survey was designed to assess your attitude toward teamwork. Please be prepared to answer these questions if your instructor has assigned Self-Assessment 13.1 in Connect.

1. What is your attitude toward teamwork?

2. If you do not have a positive teamwork attitude, consider the reason and identify what you might do to foster a more positive attitude.

3. Develop three potential questions that a recruiter might ask to determine if you are positively disposed to teamwork. Now answer the questions.

Formal versus Informal Groups

Groups can be either formal or informal.[13]

- Formal groups—created to accomplish specific goals. **A formal group is a group assigned by organizations or its managers to accomplish specific goals.** A formal group may be a division, a department, a work group, or a committee. It may be permanent or temporary. In general, people are assigned to them according to their skills and the organization's requirements.

- Informal groups—created for friendship. **An informal group is a group formed by people whose overriding purpose is getting together for friendship or a common interest.** An informal group may be simply a collection of friends who hang out with one another, such as those who take coffee breaks together, or it may be as organized as a prayer breakfast, a bowling team, a service club, a company "alumni group" (for example, former Apple employees), or other voluntary organization.

What's important for you as a manager to know is that informal groups can advance or undercut the plans of formal groups. The formal organization may make efforts, say, to speed up the plant assembly line or to institute workplace reforms. But these attempts may be sabotaged through the informal networks of workers who meet and gossip over lunch pails and after-work beers.[14]

However, interestingly, informal groups can also be highly productive—even more so than formal groups.

EXAMPLE

Informal Groups and Informal Learning: Sharing Knowledge in the Lunchroom and on Social Media

As a manager, what would you think if you saw employees making brief conversation near the lunchroom coffeepot? "The assumption was made that this was chitchat, talking about their golf game," said a training director at the Siemens Power Transmission and Distribution plant in Wendell, North Carolina, where managers worried about workers gathering so often in the cafeteria. "But there was a whole lot of work activity."[15]

Workplace Learning: Mostly Informal. And indeed research has found that *70% of workplace learning is informal.*[16] With this knowledge, Siemens managers alerted supervisors about the informal meetings and even placed overhead projectors and empty pads of paper in the lunchroom to facilitate the exchange of information. Employees at Ed Doherty's Panera Bread restaurants learn about customer service and company culture from storytelling. In one often recounted incident, a customer drove to a store during a blizzard to place an order. He inadvertently left his food there by mistake and called the store to inform the manager. "The store was about to close as the snow piled up, so the manager decided to deliver the order to the customer's house."[17]

Talking it out. Ever worked in a job in which you got a lot of informal training through conversations over coffee? Could this be done with social networking?
© BananaStock/JupiterImages RF

The Peer-to-Peer Web. What about when employees are in far-flung places? "Sales reps are out in the field and they're kind of on islands," pointed out an Indianapolis software-firm executive. "It's a challenge to keep everyone connected."[18] So when the 75 reps started overwhelming the sales-support staff with questions about product details and client information, the company created a website on which the reps could post and answer questions in an informal peer-to-peer learning setting. (Incidentally, to do parts of their jobs, 47% of business technology users at North American and European companies use websites that are not sanctioned by their corporate information technology department, according to one study.)[19]

YOUR CALL

Can games (such as the online multiplayer game Second Life) or other social media (Facebook, Twitter) be used to foster informal workplace collaboration? How about allowing employees to BYOD— "bring your own device" to work, such as their own smartphone or tablet?[20]

Types of Teams

Different types of teams have different characteristics. We can differentiate some typical teams according to their

1. Purpose.
2. Duration.
3. Level of member commitment.

Work Teams   A company's audit team and a professional sports team have several things in common. Like all work teams, they have a clear purpose that all members share. These teams are usually permanent, and members must give their complete commitment to the team's purpose in order for the team to succeed.

Project Teams   If you have ever completed a team project for a class, you have been part of a project team. Project teams at work are assembled to solve a particular problem or complete a specific task, such as brainstorming new marketing ideas for one of the company's products. Members can meet just once or work together for many years, depending on the nature of the assignment, and they may meet virtually or face to face. They can come from the same or different departments or functional areas, and while serving on the project team, they continue to fulfill their primary responsibilities.

Cross-Functional Teams   **Cross-functional teams are designed to include members from different areas within an organization, such as finance, operations, and sales.** Cross-functional teams can serve any purpose, they can be work teams or project teams, and their assignment can be long- or short-term. Brian Walker, CEO of furniture maker Herman Miller, described how his company uses cross-functional teams to work on new-product design:

> "We're big believers in putting teams together. . . . We're very willing to move folks around between departments. In our design process, for example, we deliberately create tension by putting together a cross-functional team that includes people from manufacturing, finance, research, ergonomics, marketing and sales. The manufacturing guys want something they know they can make easily and fits their processes. The salespeople want what their customers have been asking for. The tension comes from finding the right balance, being willing to follow those creative leaps to the new place, and convincing the organization it's worth the risk."[21]

Self-Managed Teams   **Self-managed teams are defined as groups of workers who are given administrative oversight for their task domains.** Experts estimate about 80% of Fortune 1,000 and 81% of manufacturing firms use self-managed teams.[22] They are expected to foster increased productivity and employee quality of work life because employees are delegated greater authority and granted increased autonomy.[23]

The most common chores of today's self-managed teams are work scheduling and customer interaction, and the least common are hiring and firing. Most self-managed

Working as a team. This group of employees seems to be acting like a team. We see everyone actively focused on the task at hand. Have you experienced the difference in working for a group verse a team? How would you describe the key differences?
© Gregory Kramer/Getty Images RF

teams are also found at the shop-floor level in factory settings, although some experts predict growth of the practice in service operations and even management ranks. Self-managed teams have been found to have a positive effect on productivity and attitudes of self-responsibility and control, although there is no significant effect on job satisfaction and organizational commitment.[24]

Research also shows self-managed teams are most effective when some guidance is provided by a leader and when the team has supportive technology.[25] Although these conclusions don't qualify as a sweeping endorsement of self-managed teams, experts expect a trend toward such teams in North America because of a strong cultural bias in favor of direct participation.

Virtual Teams   **Virtual teams work together over time and distance via electronic media to combine effort and achieve common goals.** Given technological advances, they are growing in popularity. A recent survey revealed 66% of multinational companies rely on them.[26]

Advocates say virtual teams are very flexible and efficient because they are driven by information and skills, not by time and location. People with needed information and/or skills can be team members, regardless of where or when they actually do their work.[27] Nevertheless, virtual teams have pros and cons like every other type of team.

Virtual teams and distributed workers present many potential benefits: reduced real estate costs (limited or no office space); ability to leverage diverse knowledge, skills, and experience across geography and time (you don't have to have an SAP expert in every office); ability to share knowledge of diverse markets; and reduced commuting and travel expenses. The flexibility often afforded by virtual teams also can reduce work–life conflicts for employees, which some employers contend makes it easier for them to attract and retain talent.[28]

Virtual teams have challenges, too. It is more difficult for them than for face-to-face teams to establish team cohesion, work satisfaction, trust, cooperative behavior, and commitment to team goals.[29] Thus, virtual teams should be used with caution. It should be no surprise that building team relationships is more difficult when members are geographically distributed. This hurdle and time zone differences are challenges reported by nearly 50% of companies using virtual teams. Members of virtual teams also reported being unable to observe the nonverbal cues of other members and a lack of collegiality.[30] These challenges apply to virtual teams more generally, as does the difficulty of leading such teams.[31] When virtual teams cross country borders, cultural differences, holidays, and local laws and customs also can cause problems.

Working virtually. Technology not only allows people to communicate where, when, and with whom they wish, but it also allows many people and organizations to work without offices. What are the advantages and disadvantages for you personally of telecommuting and virtual work? © Image Source/ Getty Images RF

Best Practices for Virtual Teams

We put together a collection of best practices to help focus your efforts and accelerate your success as a member or leader of a virtual team.[32]

1. **Adapt your communications.** Learn how the various remote workers function, including their preferences for e-mail, texts, and phone calls. It often is advisable to have regularly scheduled calls (via Skype). Be strategic and talk to the right people at the right times about the right topics. Don't just blanket everybody via e-mail—focus your message. Accommodate the different time zones in a fair and consistent manner.

2. **Share the love.** Use your company's intranet or other technology to keep distributed workers in the loop. Acknowledging birthdays and recognizing accomplishments are especially important for those who are not regularly in the office. Newsletters also can help and serve as a touch point and vehicle for communicating best practices and success stories.

3. **Develop productive relationships with key people on the team.** This may require extra attention, communication, and travel, but do what it takes. Key people are the ones you can lean on and the ones who will make or break the team assignment.

4. **Be a good partner.** Often members of virtual teams are not direct employees of your employer but are independent contractors. Nevertheless, your success and that of

your team depend on them. *Treat them like true partners and not hired help.* You need them and presumably they need you.

5. **Be available.** Managers and remote workers all need to know when people can be reached, where, and how. Let people know and make yourself available.

6. **Document the work.** Because of different time zones, some projects can receive attention around the clock, as they are handed off from one zone to the next. Doing this effectively requires that both senders and receivers clearly specify what they have completed and what they need in each transfer.

7. **Provide updates.** Even if you are not the boss, or your boss doesn't ask for them, be sure to provide regular updates on your progress to the necessary team members.[33]

8. **Select the right people.** "The best virtual workers tend to be those who thrive in interdependent work relationships . . . [and] are self-reliant and self-motivated. . . . Virtual work requires independent thought and willingness to take initiative. Those who tend to struggle in virtual team situations are people who wait for instructions and want to be told what to do."[34]

9. **Use your communication skills.** Because so much communication is written, virtual team members must have excellent communication skills and write well in-easy-to-understand and to-the-point language.

Researchers and consultants agree about one aspect of virtual teams—*there is no substitute for face-to-face contact.* Meeting in person is especially beneficial early in virtual team development, and team leaders are encouraged to meet even more frequently with key members.[35] Face-to-face interactions can be as simple as lunch, water-cooler conversations, social events, or periodic meetings. Whatever the case, such interactions enable people to get familiar with each other and build credibility, trust, and understanding. This reduces misunderstandings and makes subsequent virtual interactions more efficient and effective, and it increases job performance and reduces conflict and intentions to quit.[36]

Face-to-face interactions enable people to get real-time feedback, forge meaningful and real connections, and get a better sense of what others actually think and feel.[37] Moreover, virtual teams cannot succeed without some additional and old-fashioned factors, such as effective decision making, good communication, training, a clear mission and specific objectives, effective leadership, schedules, and deadlines.[38] Underlying many of these is one of the truly essential elements to effective teams of all types—trust. ●

13.2 Stages of Group and Team Development

How does a group evolve into a team?

THE BIG PICTURE

Groups can evolve into teams by going through five stages of development: forming, storming, norming, performing, and adjourning. They can also develop if they are forced to change in response to a crisis. We'll look at both these processes.

FIGURE 13.1

Five stages of group and team development

Forming
Getting oriented & getting acquainted

Storming
Individual personalities & roles emerge

Norming
Conflicts resolved, relationships develop, unity emerges

Performing
Solving problems & completing the assigned task

Adjourning
Preparing for disbandment

Tuckman's Five-Stage Model

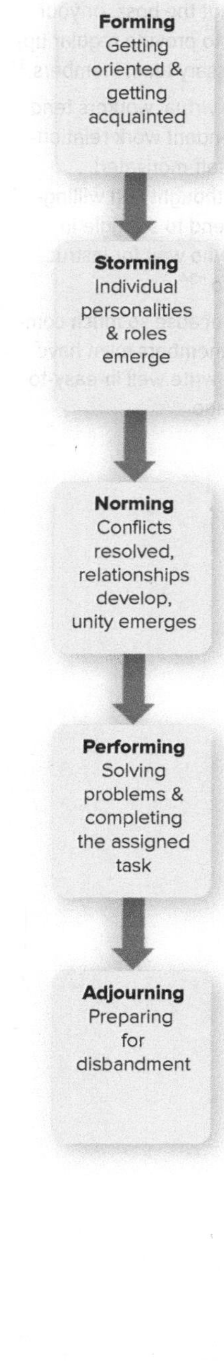

Managers often talk of products and organizations going through stages of development, from birth to maturity to decline. Groups and teams go through the same thing. One theory proposes five stages of development: *forming, storming, norming, performing, adjourning.*[39] *(See Figure 13.1.)*

Let us consider these stages in which groups may evolve into teams—bearing in mind that the stages often aren't of the same duration or intensity or even necessarily always in this sequence.

Stage 1: Forming—"Why Are We Here?"   The first stage, **forming, is the process of getting oriented and getting acquainted.** This stage is characterized by a high degree of uncertainty as members try to break the ice and figure out who is in charge and what the group's goals are. For example, if you were to become part of a team that is to work on a class project, the question for you as an individual would be "How do I fit in here?" For the group, the question is "Why are we here?"[40]

At this point, mutual trust is low, and there is a good deal of holding back to see who takes charge and how. Conflict at this stage may actually be beneficial, leading to increased creativity.[41] At this juncture, if the formal leader (such as the class instructor or a supervisor) does not assert his or her authority, an emergent leader will eventually step in to fill the group's need for leadership and direction. During this stage, leaders should allow time for people to become acquainted and to socialize.

Stage 2: Storming—"Why Are We Fighting over Who's in Charge and Who Does What?"   The second stage, **storming, is characterized by the emergence of individual personalities and roles and conflicts within the group.** For you as an individual, the question is "What's my role here?" For the group, the issue is "Why are we fighting over who's in charge and who does what?" This stage may be of short duration or painfully long, depending on the goal clarity and the commitment and maturity of the members.

This is a time of testing. Individuals test the leader's policies and assumptions as they try to determine how they fit into the power structure. Subgroups take shape, and subtle forms of rebellion, such as procrastination, occur. Many groups stall in stage 2 because power politics may erupt into open rebellion.

In this stage, the leader should encourage members to suggest ideas, voice disagreements, and work through their conflicts about tasks and goals.

Stage 3: Norming—"Can We Agree on Roles and Work as a Team?"   In the third stage, **norming, conflicts are resolved, close relationships develop, and unity and harmony emerge.** For individuals, the main issue is "What do the others expect me to do?" For the group, the issue is "Can we agree on roles and work as a team?" Note, then, that the *group* may now evolve into a *team.*

Teams set guidelines related to what members will do together and how they will do it. The teams consider such matters as attendance at meetings, being late, and missing assignments as well as how members treat one another.

Groups that make it through stage 2 generally do so because a respected member other than the leader challenges the group to resolve its power struggles so something can be accomplished. Questions about authority are resolved through unemotional, matter-of-fact group discussion. A feeling of team spirit is experienced because members believe they have found their proper roles. **Group cohesiveness, a "we feeling" binding group members together,** is the principal by-product of stage 3.[42] (We discuss cohesiveness next, in Section 13.3.)

This stage generally does not last long. Here the leader should emphasize unity and help identify team goals and values.

Stage 4: Performing—"Can We Do the Job Properly?" In **performing, members concentrate on solving problems and completing the assigned task.** For individuals, the question here is "How can I best perform my role?" For the group/team, the issue is "Can we do the job properly?" During this stage, the leader should allow members the empowerment they need to work on tasks.

Turning teamwork into action. This group of students is participating in a science fair in Athens, Greece. The group clearly is in the performing stage of group development. Does it appear that all participants are equally engaged in dealing with the task at hand? If you were a member of this group, what would you do to motivate all members to actively participate in completing the task?
© Melanie Stetson Freeman/AP Photo

Stage 5: Adjourning—"Can We Help Members Transition Out?" In the final stage, **adjourning, members prepare for disbandment.** Having worked so hard to get along and get something done, many members feel a compelling sense of loss. For the individual, the question now is "What's next?" For the team, the issue is "Can we help members transition out?"

The leader can help ease the transition by rituals celebrating "the end" and "new beginnings." Parties, award ceremonies, graduations, or mock funerals can provide the needed punctuation at the end of a significant teamwork project. The leader can emphasize valuable lessons learned in group dynamics to prepare everyone for future group and team efforts.

Is Tuckman's Model Accurate? Although research does not support the notion that groups can't perform until the performing stage, both academics and practitioners agree that groups have a life cycle.[43] Research also tells us that high-performing teams successfully navigating the process of group or team development tend to display productive energy toward getting things done.[44] Do your current teams at work or school display this productive energy? You can find out by completing Self-Assessment 13.2.

Punctuated Equilibrium

Groups don't always follow the distinct stages of Tuckman's model. In another type of group development, called **punctuated equilibrium, they establish periods of stable functioning until an event causes a dramatic change in norms, roles, and/or objectives. The group then establishes and maintains new norms of functioning, returning to equilibrium.** *(See Figure 13.2.)* Punctuated equilibrium often occurs in the wake of unexpected change. When in June 2016 a slim majority of voters in the UK voted in favor of leaving the European Union, for example, the remaining 27 member countries faced major changes in the economic and political stability of the 23-year-old economic and trade group. Alterations in the way they trade, share resources, and maintain peaceful borders are expected to develop over many years as the EU remakes itself following the loss of one of Europe's largest economies. In the world of retailing, Walmart's low-price approach was a change that revolutionized an industry. Companies and teams that can adapt will realize tremendous new opportunities, but those that don't often find themselves obsolete. Punctuated equilibrium can drive significant change, development, and opportunity. ●

FIGURE 13.2

Punctuated equilibrium

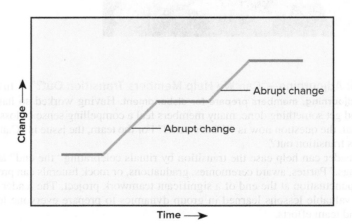

13.3 Building Effective Teams

MAJOR QUESTION

How can I as a manager build an effective team?

THE BIG PICTURE

To build a group into a high-performance team, managers must consider matters of collaboration, trust, performance goals and feedback, motivation through mutual accountability and interdependence, team composition, roles, and norms.

"What is a high-performance team?" Current research and practice suggest seven attributes: shared leadership, shared accountability, sense of common purpose, trust and open communication, clear role expectations, early conflict resolution, and collaboration.[45] Thus, as a future manager, the first thing you have to realize is that building a high-performance team is going to require some work. But the payoff will be a stronger, better-performing work unit.[46]

The most essential considerations in building a group into an effective team are (1) *collaboration,* (2) *trust,* (3) *performance goals and feedback,* (4) *motivation through mutual accountability and interdependency,* (5) *composition,* (6) *roles,* and (7) *norms.*

1. Collaboration—the Foundation of Teamwork

Human collaboration has a long history, with some hunter-gatherers in Tanzania—who live much as humans did about 10,000 years ago—linked in social networks very much like ours (without the cell phones and other connections, of course). Indeed, unlike other animals, such as chimpanzees and monkeys, humans are able to build bigger and better tools by sharing knowledge and learning from one another—in short, by collaborating.

Collaboration is the act of sharing information and coordinating efforts to achieve a collective outcome. As you might expect, teams are more effective when members collaborate.[47] Collaboration is the secret sauce enabling teams to produce more than the sum of their parts.[48] Many factors can influence collaboration, including how teams are rewarded.[49] For example, Whole Foods reinforces teamwork in its team-based structure by focusing rewards on team rather than individual performance.[50]

A recent and exhaustive survey by Google was aimed at discovering what made the best of its hundreds of work teams successful. The researchers found that the company's highest-performing teams shared two characteristic behaviors: (1) Everyone on the team spoke in about equal proportion, meaning that no one hogged the floor or held comments back, and (2) members were very good at interpreting other members' feelings based on their tone of voice and nonverbal cues. These characteristics led to unusually high levels of collaboration and success.[51]

2. Trust: "We Need to Have Reciprocal Faith in Each Other"

Trust is defined as reciprocal faith in others' intentions and behaviors.[52] The word *reciprocal* emphasizes the give-and-take aspect of trust—that is, we tend to give what we get: Trust begets trust, distrust begets distrust. Trust is based on *credibility*—how believable you are based on your past acts of integrity and follow-through on your promises.

The importance of trust. David A. Ferucci (center), with two IBM colleagues, led a team of artificial intelligence researchers that programmed a computing system named Watson to compete on the game show *Jeopardy,* whose host, Alex Trebeck, is shown in 2011 talking about the upcoming event. Watson beat the previous (human) grand champions. All successful teams operate within a climate of trust. (left): © Suzanne DeChillo/The New York Times/ Redux Pictures; (right): © Seth Wenig/AP Photo

As you might expect, research supports a positive relationship between team members' trust and team performance.[53]

"The best way to engage employees is to build a culture of trust," says Jenny Gottstein of The Go Game. "A team that trusts each other and respects everyone's contribution can make significant cognitive leaps when innovating or problem-solving."[54]

3. Performance Goals and Feedback

As an individual, you no doubt prefer to have measurable goals and to have feedback about your performance. The same is true with teams. Teams are not just collections of individuals. They are individuals organized for a collective purpose. That purpose needs to be defined in terms of specific, measurable performance goals with continual feedback to tell team members how well they are doing.[55]

Cooperation and collaboration. A crew swarms over a car driven by A. J. Allmendinger during a pit stop in the NASCAR 2014 Sprint Cup All-Star Race at Watkins Glen, New York. Cereal maker General Mills was able to cut the time workers changed a production line for a Betty Crocker product from 4.5 hours to just 12 minutes by adapting ideas in efficiency and high performance from a NASCAR pit crew working at blinding speed. © Bob Jordan/ AP Photo

An obvious example is the teams you see on television at Indianapolis or Daytona Beach during automobile racing. When the driver guides the race car off the track to make a pit stop, a team of people quickly jack up the car to change tires, refuel the tank, and clean the windshield—all in a matter of seconds. The performance goal is to have the car back on the track as quickly as possible. The number of seconds of elapsed time—and the driver's place among competitors once back in the race—tells the team how well they are doing.

4. Motivation through Mutual Accountability and Interdependence

Do you work harder when you're alone or when you're in a group? When clear performance goals exist, when the work is considered meaningful, when members believe their efforts matter, and when they don't feel they are being exploited by others—this kind of culture supports teamwork.[56] Being mutually accountable to other members of the team rather than to a supervisor makes members feel mutual trust and commitment—a key part in motivating members for team effort. Mutual accountability is fostered by having team "members share accountability for the work, authority over how goals are met, discretion over resource use, and ownership of information and knowledge related to the work."[57]

Do you like it when your performance is contingent on someone else's efforts? Your answer reflects your experience with team member interdependence. **Team member interdependence** reveals the extent to which team members rely on common task-related team inputs, such as resources, information, goals, and rewards, and the amount of interpersonal interactions needed to complete the work.[58] A recent study of over 7,000 teams showed that interdependence affects team functioning, which in turn influences team performance.[59] The key takeaway from this study is reinforcement of the need for team leaders to monitor the quality of team member interdependence.

5. Team Composition

Team composition reflects the collection of jobs, personalities, values, knowledge, experience, and skills of team members. The concept is related to our discussion of workforce diversity in Chapter 11. You learned that diversity is good for business and that it must be effectively managed. The same is true for team composition.[60]

For example, a recent study examining the characteristics of effective teams at Cisco found that one of the top three such qualities was members' conviction that their values were shared.[61] This is a feeling you've probably experienced as a member of a team or club built around common interests.

The most important idea to remember is that team member composition should fit the responsibilities of the team. Fit enhances effectiveness and misfit impedes it.[62] Let's consider a few examples.

Teams perform better when members have a high tolerance for uncertainty (a personality trait) during the early stages of team development (forming and storming). This same finding applies to self-managed and virtual teams, due to their relative lack of imposed direction and face-to-face communication.[63] Team research also shows that teams with members who possess high levels of openness or emotional stability deal with task conflict better than those without these composition characteristics.[64] Finally, in the university context, top management teams (presidents, vice presidents, and chancellors) who were more diverse in terms of educational and disciplinary backgrounds generated more funding for research and improved school reputations.[65]

6. Roles: How Team Members Are Expected to Behave

Roles are socially determined expectations of how individuals should behave in a specific position. As a team member, your role is to play a part in helping the team reach its goals. Members develop their roles based on the expectations of the team, of the organization, and of themselves, and they may do different things. You, for instance, might be a team leader. Others might do some of the work tasks. Still others might communicate with other teams.[66]

Two types of team roles are task and maintenance. *(See Table 13.2.)*

TABLE 13.2

Task and Maintenance Roles

TASK ROLES	DESCRIPTION
Initiator	Suggests new goals or ideas
Information seeker/giver	Clarifies key issues
Opinion seeker/giver	Clarifies pertinent values
Elaborator	Promotes greater understanding through examples or exploration of implications
Coordinator	Pulls together ideas and suggestions
Orienter	Keeps group headed toward its stated goal(s)
Evaluator	Tests group's accomplishments with various criteria such as logic and practicality
Energizer	Prods group to move along or to accomplish more
Procedural technician	Performs routine duties (handing out materials or rearranging seats)
Recorder	Performs a "group memory" function by documenting discussion and outcomes

MAINTENANCE ROLES	DESCRIPTION
Encourager	Fosters group solidarity by accepting and praising various points of view
Harmonizer	Mediates conflict through reconciliation or humor
Compromiser	Helps resolve conflict by meeting others halfway
Gatekeeper	Encourages all group members to participate
Standard setter	Evaluates the quality of group processes
Commentator	Records and comments on group processes/dynamics
Follower	Serves as a passive audience

Adapted from discussion in K. D. Benne and P. Sheats, "Functional Roles of Group Members," Journal of Social Issues, Spring 1948, 41–49.

Task Roles: Getting the Work Done
A task role, or *task-oriented role,* consists of behavior that concentrates on getting the team's tasks done. Task roles keep the team on track and get the work done. If you stand up in a team meeting and say, "What is the real issue here? We don't seem to be getting anywhere," you are performing a task role.

Examples: Coordinators, who pull together ideas and suggestions; orienters, who keep teams headed toward their stated goals; initiators, who suggest new goals or ideas; and energizers, who prod people to move along or accomplish more are all playing task roles.

Maintenance Roles: Keeping the Team Together
A maintenance role, or relationship-oriented role, consists of behavior that fosters constructive relationships among team members. Maintenance roles focus on keeping team members. If someone at a team meeting says, "Let's hear from those who oppose this plan," he or she is playing a maintenance role.

Examples are encouragers, who foster group solidarity by praising various viewpoints; standard setters, who evaluate the quality of group processes; harmonizers, who mediate conflict through reconciliation or humor; and compromisers, who help resolve conflict by meeting others "halfway."

7. Norms: Unwritten Rules for Team Members

Norms are more encompassing than roles. **Norms are general guidelines or rules of behavior that most group or team members follow.** Norms point out the boundaries between acceptable and unacceptable behavior.[67] Although some norms can be made explicit, typically they are unwritten and seldom discussed openly; nevertheless, they have a powerful influence on group and organizational behavior.

Why Norms Are Enforced: Four Reasons
Norms tend to be enforced by group or team members for four reasons:[68]

- **To help the group survive—"Don't do anything that will hurt us."** Norms are enforced to help the group, team, or organization survive.

  Example: The manager of your team or group might compliment you because you've made sure it has the right emergency equipment.

- **To clarify role expectations—"You have to go along to get along."** Norms are also enforced to help clarify or simplify role expectations.

  Example: At one time, new members of Congress wanting to buck the system by which important committee appointments were given to those with the most seniority were advised to "go along to get along"—go along with the rules in order to get along in their congressional careers.

- **To help individuals avoid embarrassing situations—"Don't call attention to yourself."** Norms are enforced to help group or team members avoid embarrassing themselves.

  Examples: You might be ridiculed by fellow team members for dominating the discussion during a report to top management ("Be a team player, not a show-off"). Or you might be told not to discuss religion or politics with customers, whose views might differ from yours.

- **To emphasize the group's important values and identity—"We're known for being special."** Finally, norms are enforced to emphasize the group's, team's, or organization's central values or to enhance its unique identity.

  Examples: Nordstrom's department store chain emphasizes the great lengths to which it goes in customer service. Some colleges give an annual award to the instructor whom students vote best teacher.

PRACTICAL ACTION   How to Build a High-Performing Team

High-Performing Teams at Cisco. Francine Katsoudas is the senior vice president and chief people officer at Cisco. Her top suggestions for building a high-performing team, based on a recent survey by the company, are the following:[69]

- Focus on team members' individual strengths.
- Let every member know his or her values are shared.
- Building on the first two suggestions, ensure a psychologically safe work environment characterized by trust.

Practicing Camaraderie. Mike Tomlin, head coach of the Pittsburgh Steelers, advises letting team members periodically spend time together having fun. Each year the Steelers spend a day together, playing arcade games at Dave and Buster's and acting like kids to build camaraderie.[70]

Taking Risks and Coming Together. Finally, the team that put together the Volt, GM's new electric car, says team success comes from the ability to take risks. With low production numbers, the team faced only moderate expectations and was able to work with fewer supplies, manage just one production plant, bend a few rules, and develop fast and nimble strategies for getting the job done. Exceeding their original mileage goal for the car, says chief engineer Andrew Farah, was "less about authority and more about cooperating and figuring out how to take on risk."[71]

YOUR CALL

How well do you think an organization could incorporate all the suggestions listed here for creating high-performance teams? What other strategies do you think contribute to outstanding team results?

Putting It All Together

Thus far in this chapter we have considered the things that make groups and teams both effective and ineffective. We hope you understand creating and leading a high performance team takes planning and skill. The first step in improving a team's performance, however, involves an assessment of its effectiveness.

So how can you determine whether a team is effective? A group's output surely is one indicator, but there are others that are more "process-oriented." You can get an idea of these process-oriented indicators by taking Self-Assessment 13.3. ●

connect SELF-ASSESSMENT 13.3

Assessing Team Effectiveness

The following survey was designed to assess the overall effectiveness of a team's internal processes. Please be prepared to answer these questions if your instructor has assigned Self-Assessment 13.3 in Connect.

1. How effective is the team?

2. What aspects of the team's internal processes are most in need of positive development?

3. Based on your survey scores, what are three recommendations for improving the team's internal processes? Be specific.

13.4 Managing Conflict

Since conflict is a part of life, what should a manager know about it in order to deal successfully with it?

THE BIG PICTURE

Conflict, an enduring feature of the workplace, is a process in which one party perceives that its interests are being opposed or negatively affected by another party. Conflict can be negative (bad) or functional (good). Indeed, either too much or too little conflict can affect performance. This section identifies four sources of conflict in organizations and describes four ways to stimulate constructive conflict.

Mistakes, pressure-cooker deadlines, increased workloads, demands for higher productivity, and other kinds of stress—all contribute to on-the-job conflict.[72] Most people envision *conflict* as meaning shouting and fighting, but as a manager you will encounter more subtle, nonviolent forms: opposition, criticism, arguments. Thus, a definition of conflict seems fairly mild: **Conflict is a process in which one party perceives that its interests are being opposed or negatively affected by another party.**[73]

Conflict is a natural aspect of life. A place to begin our discussion of conflict is for you to learn about your tendencies for conflicts with others. Do you see yourself as easy to get along with and relatively conflict free, which may be true? Let's consider your self-perceptions by completing Self-Assessment 13.4.

---

connect SELF-ASSESSMENT 13.4

Interpersonal Conflict Tendencies

If your instructor has assigned Self-Assessment 13.4 in Connect, you will learn how well you get along with others at work and/or school.

1. Does your score match your perception of yourself?

2. The assessment measures how well you get along with others and how they treat you; both are sources of conflict. If you were to improve the measure, what other factors do you think should be included?

The Nature of Conflict: Disagreement Is Normal

Conflict is simply disagreement, a perfectly normal state of affairs. Conflicts may take many forms: between individuals, between an individual and a group, between groups, within a group, and between an organization and its environment.

Although all of us might wish to live lives free of conflict, it is now recognized that certain kinds of conflict can actually be beneficial. Let us therefore distinguish between *dysfunctional conflict* (bad) and *functional conflict* (good).

- **Dysfunctional conflict—bad for organizations.** From the standpoint of the organization, **dysfunctional conflict** is conflict that hinders the organization's performance or threatens its interests. As a manager, you need to do what you can to remove dysfunctional conflict, sometimes called negative conflict.

- **Functional conflict—good for organizations.** The good kind of conflict is **functional conflict**, which benefits the main purposes of the organization and serves its interests.[74] There are some situations in which this kind of conflict—also called *constructive conflict* or *cooperative conflict*—is considered advantageous.

EXAMPLE   Dysfunctional and Functional Conflict: Do Nasty Bosses Get Better Performance?

A recent study by Career Builder found that 45% of workplace bullies are bosses, and an additional 25% are higher executives (the rest are peers). Their behavior ranges from threats, humiliation, and intimidation to taking credit for other people's work and even committing acts of workplace sabotage.[75]

Unfortunately, this kind of tyranny is very common. Research conducted by the Workplace Bullying Institute estimates that 27% of the U.S. workforce has been bullied. Another 21% has witnessed bullying. All told, then, nearly half the U.S. workforce has been exposed to bullying. Interestingly, the majority of bullies are men (about 60%), and women are bullied more than men.[76]

Abuse Flows Downhill. Does such negative conflict get results? Surprisingly, often it does. One study of 373 randomly chosen employees found that, although some reacted to abusive bosses by doing little or nothing, others performed better—in part, it's speculated, to make themselves look good and others look worse.[77]

Yet other research shows that abuse flows downhill, and when supervisors feel they have been unjustly treated, they may vent their resentment by abusing those who report to them. Subordinates generally cope either through avoidance or, less commonly, through confrontation and are in any case

less inclined to feel committed to their organizations, to speak unfavorably about their companies to outsiders, and to seek jobs elsewhere.[78]

The "No-Jerk Rule." When Stanford organizational psychologist Robert Sutton published a short essay in which he urged more civility in organizations by steady application of what he calls "the no-jerk rule" (although he used a far stronger word than "jerk"), he elicited more e-mails than he had received on any other subject, showing the topic had touched a nerve.[79]

Options for dealing with a bullying boss include documenting the incidents to be sure there is a pattern of abusive behavior, investigating your organization's policy on bullying and any consequences for the bully, and reporting offensive behavior to a higher-level executive. You can try not to react in the moment, to avoid giving the bully the satisfaction he or she seeks, or you can speak out as calmly and rationally as you can.[80]

YOUR CALL

Have you ever worked for jerks (otherwise known, as Sutton puts it, as "tyrants, bullies, boors, destructive narcissists, and psychologically abusive people")? How did you respond to them?

The Jerk. Ever worked for an angry boss? How did you deal with the situation? Have there been circumstances in which people working for you might have called *you* a jerk (or worse)? What should you have done differently?
© John Lund/Nevada Wier/Blend Images/Corbis RF

Can Too Little or Too Much Conflict Affect Performance?

It's tempting to think that a conflict-free work group is a happy work group, as indeed it may be. But is it a productive group? In the 1970s, social scientists specializing in organizational behavior introduced the revolutionary idea that organizations could suffer from *too little* or *too much* conflict. Neither scenario is good.

- **Too little conflict—indolence.** Work groups, departments, or organizations that experience too little conflict tend to be plagued by apathy, lack of creativity, indecision, and missed deadlines. The result is that organizational performance suffers.

- **Too much conflict—warfare.** Excessive conflict, on the other hand, can erode organizational performance because of political infighting, dissatisfaction, lack of teamwork, and turnover. Workplace aggression and violence are manifestations of excessive conflict.[81]

Thus, it seems that a moderate level of conflict can induce creativity and initiative,[82] thereby raising performance, as shown in the diagram below. *(See Figure 13.3.)*[83] As you might expect, however, what constitutes "moderate" will vary among managers.

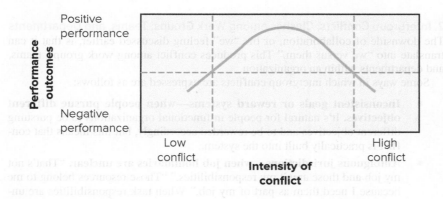

FIGURE 13.3

The relationship between intensity of conflict and performance outcomes
Too little conflict or too much conflict causes performance to suffer.

Source: Derived from L. D. Brown, Managing Conflict at Organizational Interfaces (Englewood Cliffs, NJ: Prentice-Hall, 1983).

Four Kinds of Conflict: Personality, Intergroup, Cross-Cultural, and Work–Family

There are a variety of sources of conflict—so-called *conflict triggers*. Four of the principal ones are (1) *between personalities,* (2) *between groups,* (3) *between cultures,* and (4) *between work and family responsibilities.* By understanding these, you'll be better able to take charge and manage the conflicts rather than letting the conflicts take you by surprise and manage you.

1. Personality Conflicts: Clashes Because of Personal Dislikes or Disagreements   We've all had confrontations, weak or strong, with people because we disagreed with them or disliked their personalities, such as their opinions, their behavior, their looks, whatever. **Personality conflict is defined as interpersonal opposition based on personal dislike or disagreement.** Such conflicts often begin with instances of *workplace incivility,* or employees' lack of regard for each other, which, if not curtailed, can diminish job satisfaction and team work engagement.[84] Unfortunately, personality conflicts are quite common. Recent research reports that 98% of employees reported experiencing some form of incivility, and 50% said they had been treated rudely at least once a week!

> **EXAMPLE** "What We've Got Here Is a Failure to Communicate":
> The Plight of the Tongue-Tied
>
> Miscommunication happens for all kinds of reasons—sometimes because there is no communication at all.
>
> **Clamming Up in Small Groups.** Some people simply clam up in small-group settings, often because they think others are smarter or of higher status. Becoming tongue-tied this way seems to be more common in women and in people with higher IQs, according to a Virginia Tech study.[85] The researchers speculate they are "more attuned to group social dynamics, subconsciously worrying about their performance and evaluating themselves in relation to others," says one report.[86]
>
> **Ways to Cope.** If speaking up is hard for you to do in small groups, you can take comfort that the people who froze the most in the study were actually the smartest. Otherwise, you can cope by preparing before the meeting (practice your delivery and bring notes), telling the person running the meeting beforehand that you have some points and would like the opportunity to be called upon, or joining with a more outgoing or higher-status member in the group who can bring up your points and then toss you an opening.[87]
>
> **YOUR CALL**
>
> Do you tend to go silent during some small-group settings or social situations? Perhaps it's not that you're shy but rather an introvert and want to collect your thoughts before speaking—hard to do in the company of extroverts who "think out loud." Could any of this advice work for you?

TABLE 13.3

Ways to Build Cross-Cultural Relationships

1. Be a good listener.

2. Be sensitive to others' needs.

3. Be cooperative, not overly competitive.

4. Advocate inclusive (participative) leadership.

5. Compromise rather than dominate.

6. Build rapport through conversations.

7. Be compassionate and understanding.

8. Avoid conflict by emphasizing harmony.

9. Nurture others (develop and mentor).

Source: Adapted from R. L. Tung, "American Expatriates Abroad: From Neophytes to Cosmopolitans," Journal of World Business, Summer 1998, table 6, p. 136.

2. Intergroup Conflicts: Clashes among Work Groups, Teams, and Departments

The downside of collaboration, or the "we" feeling discussed earlier, is that it can translate into "we versus them." This produces conflict among work groups, teams, and departments within an organization.

Some ways in which intergroup conflicts are expressed are as follows:

- **Inconsistent goals or reward systems—when people pursue different objectives.** It's natural for people in functional organizations to be pursuing different objectives and to be rewarded accordingly, but this means that conflict is practically built into the system.

- **Ambiguous jurisdictions—when job boundaries are unclear.** "That's not my job and those aren't my responsibilities." "Those resources belong to me because I need them as part of my job." When task responsibilities are unclear, that can often lead to conflict.

- **Status differences—when there are inconsistencies in power and influence.** It can happen that people who are lower in status according to the organization chart actually have disproportionate power over those theoretically above them, which can lead to conflicts.

3. Multicultural Conflicts: Clashes between Cultures

With cross-border mergers, joint ventures, and international alliances common features of the global economy, there are frequent opportunities for clashes between cultures. Often success or failure, when business is being conducted across cultures, arises from dealing with differing assumptions about how to think and act.

One study of 409 expatriates (14% of them female) working for U.S. and Canadian multinational firms in 51 countries identified nine specific ways to facilitate interaction with host-country nationals, the results of which are shown at left. *(See Table 13.3.)* Note that "Be a good listener" tops the list—the very thing lacking in so many U.S. managers, who are criticized for being blunt to the point of insensitivity.[88]

4. Work–Family Conflicts

Work–family conflict occurs when the demands or pressures from work and family domains are mutually incompatible.[89] Work and family can conflict in two ways: Work responsibilities can interfere with family life, and family demands can interfere with work responsibilities.[90]

For instance, an employee who is caring for an aging mother skips a department meeting to take his mother to a doctor's appointment (family interferes with work). Perhaps another day he works late to finish a report on time and has to reschedule his mother's follow-up appointment (work interferes with family).

Both these types of conflicts matter, because their effects spill over both at home and at work, as Table 13.4 shows. Research also tells us that work interferes with family far more often than family does with work and is the more serious problem of the two.[91]

TABLE 13.4

Negative Consequences of Conflicts among Work, Family, and Other Life Domains

WORK INTERFERES WITH FAMILY	FAMILY INTERFERES WITH WORK	OUTCOMES LINKED TO LIFE MORE GENERALLY
Job satisfaction	Marital satisfaction	Life satisfaction
Intentions to quit	Family satisfaction	Health problems
Absenteeism	Family-related strain	Depression
Job performance	Family-related performance	Substance use/abuse

Source: Adapted from F. T. Amstad, L. L. Meier, U. Fasel, A. Elfering, and N. K. Semmer, "A Meta-Analysis of Work-Family Conflict and Various Outcomes with a Special Emphasis on Cross-Domain versus Matching Domain Relations," Journal of Occupational Health Psychology, 2011, Vol. 16, No. 2, 151–169.

Identifying Companies with Good Work–Family Balance   PRACTICAL ACTION

What do you want in a job? A recent report by consulting firm Deloitte shows that Millennials value their personal lives more highly than they do organizational goals or corporate reputations. It's not surprising, then, that good work–life balance was the quality Millennials wanted most in a job; flexible hours and a sense of meaning were close behind.[92]

The job search site Indeed.com recently compiled a list of the top 25 companies for good work–life balance.[93] Among them were Colgate-Palmolive, Wegmans supermarket chain, the brokerage Coldwell Banker, H&R Block, Google, Nokia, Philips Electronics, Johnson & Johnson, Disney, Prudential Financial, and the YWCA. A study of the worst employers to work for, in which poor work–life balance featured heavily, was based on data from Glassdoor, the employer rating site.[94] Leading this list were companies including CVS, Dollar General, DISH Network, Sears, Xerox, Forever 21, and Kmart.

If you are more interested in scoping out a particular career's potential for work–life balance than an individual employer's, a study by GOBankingRates[95] found that the professions where work–life balance is most respected include data scientists, graphic designer, elementary school teacher,

social media manager, hair stylist, and dietitian. However, some experts say working long hours indicates people really love their jobs. In that light, consider these careers in which work–life balance takes a back seat: surgeon, lawyer, massage therapist, nurse, general manager, firefighter, airline pilot, and journalist.

If you're wondering how to find out where a company stands on work–life balance before you take the job, here's a tip: Schedule your job interview early in the morning or late in the day and observe how many people are at their desks outside normal working hours.[96]

YOUR CALL

Some companies say it's the employee's responsibility to keep his or her work and life in an appropriate balance, and some employees who don't have children feel workplace policies meant to offer flexibility to parents of young children are unfair, since everyone can't take advantage of them. Do you think such policies are fair? Are they necessary? If you agree that employees should take charge of their own work–life balance, how should they do so?

How to Stimulate Constructive Conflict

As a manager you are being paid not just to manage conflict but even to create some, where it's constructive and appropriate, in order to stimulate performance. Constructive conflict, if carefully monitored, can be very productive under a number of circumstances: when your work group seems afflicted with inertia and apathy, resulting in low performance; when there's a lack of new ideas and resistance to change; when there seem to be a lot of yes-men and yes-women (expressing groupthink) in the work unit; when there's high employee turnover; or when managers seem unduly concerned with peace, cooperation, compromise, consensus, and their own popularity rather than in achieving work objectives.

The following four strategies are used to stimulate constructive conflict.

1. Spur Competition among Employees   Competition is, of course, a form of conflict, but competition is often healthy in spurring people to produce higher results. Thus, a company will often put its salespeople in competition with one another by offering bonuses and awards for achievement—a trip to a Caribbean resort, say, for the top performer of the year.

2. Change the Organization's Culture and Procedures   Competition may also be established by making deliberate and highly publicized moves to change the corporate culture—by announcing to employees that the organization is now going to be more innovative and reward original thinking and unorthodox ideas. Procedures, such as paperwork sign-off processes, can also be revamped. Results can be reinforced in visible ways through announcements of bonuses, raises, and promotions.

3. Bring In Outsiders for New Perspectives   Without "new blood," organizations can become inbred and resistant to change. This is why managers often bring in outsiders—people from a different unit of the organization, new hires from competing companies, or consultants. With their different backgrounds, attitudes, or management styles, these outsiders can bring a new perspective and can shake things up.

4. Use Programmed Conflict: Devil's Advocacy and the Dialectic Method
Programmed conflict is designed to elicit different opinions without inciting people's personal feelings. Sometimes decision-making groups become so bogged down in details and procedures that nothing of substance gets done. The idea here is to get people, through role-playing, to defend or criticize ideas based on relevant facts rather than on personal feelings and preferences.

Top employee. Companies frequently stimulate constructive competition among employees to produce better performance. Top salespeople, for instance, may be rewarded with a trip to a resort. Do you think you would do well in a company that makes you compete with others to produce higher results? © Tony Tallec/Alamy RF

The method for getting people to engage in this debate of ideas is to do disciplined role-playing, for which two proven methods are available: *devil's advocacy* and the *dialectic method*. These two methods work as follows:

- Devil's advocacy—role-playing criticism to test whether a proposal is workable. **Devil's advocacy is the process of assigning someone to play the role of critic** to voice possible objections to a proposal and thereby generate critical thinking and reality testing.

  Periodically role-playing devil's advocate has a beneficial side effect in that it is great training for developing analytical and communicative skills. However, it's a good idea to rotate the job so no one person develops a negative reputation.

- The dialectic method—role-playing two sides of a proposal to test whether it is workable. Requiring a bit more skill training than devil's advocacy does, the **dialectic method is the process of having two people or groups play opposing roles in a debate in order to better understand a proposal.** After the structured debate, managers are more equipped to make an intelligent decision.[97]

Five Basic Behaviors to Help You Better Handle Conflict

Whatever kind of organization you work for, you'll always benefit from knowing how to manage conflict. There are five basic behaviors that enable you to work on disagreements and keep them from flaring into out-of-control personality conflicts: *openness, equality, empathy, supportiveness,* and *positiveness.*[98]

1. Openness   State your views openly and honesty, not trying to disguise the real object of your disagreement. Look at the conflict as a way to better understand the situation and find a solution. Concentrate on identifying the problem and taking a problem-solving approach.

2. Equality   Treat the other's status and ideas as equal to yours, allowing that person time to completely express his or her opinions. Evaluate all ideas fairly and logically, without regard to ownership.

3. Empathy   Try to experience the other person's feelings and point of view, showing you are truly listening by using such expressions as "I appreciate how you feel. . . ."

4. Supportiveness   Let the other person know you want to find a resolution that will benefit you both. Describe the specifics you have difficulty understanding, without evaluating or judging them. Support the other person's position when it makes sense to do so.

5. Positiveness   Be positive about the other person and your relationship. Express your willingness to work toward a resolution that will be feasible for everyone.

Before beginning to try to adopt these behaviors preparatory to dealing with a dispute, you should also try to be aware of your customary conflict-handling style.

Dealing with Disagreements: Five Conflict-Handling Styles

Even if you're at the top of your game as a manager, working with groups and teams of people will now and then put you in the middle of disagreements, sometimes even destructive conflict. How can you deal with it?

There are five conflict-handling styles, or techniques, a manager can use for handling disagreements with individuals: *avoiding, accommodating, forcing, compromising,* and *problem solving.*[99]

Avoiding—"Maybe the Problem Will Go Away"

Avoiding is ignoring or suppressing a conflict. Avoidance is appropriate for trivial issues, when emotions are high and a cooling-off period is needed, or when the cost of confrontation outweighs the benefits of resolving the conflict. It is not appropriate for difficult or worsening problems.

The benefit of this approach is that it buys time in unfolding and ambiguous situations. The weakness is that it provides only a temporary fix and sidesteps the underlying problem.

Accommodating—"Let's Do It Your Way"

An accommodating manager is also known as a "smoothing" or "obliging" manager. *Accommodating* is allowing the desires of the other party to prevail. As one writer describes it, "An obliging [accommodating] person neglects his or her own concern to satisfy the concern of the other party."[100] Accommodating may be an appropriate conflict-handling strategy when it's possible to eventually get something in return or when the issue isn't important to you. It's not appropriate for complex or worsening problems.

The advantage of accommodating is that it encourages cooperation. The weakness is that once again it's only a temporary fix that fails to confront the underlying problem.

Forcing—"We Have to Do It My Way"

Also known as "dominating," *forcing* is simply ordering an outcome, when a manager relies on his or her formal authority and power to resolve a conflict, but the needs of the other party are largely ignored. Forcing is appropriate when an unpopular solution must be implemented and when it's not important that others be committed to your viewpoint.

The advantage of forcing is speed: It can get results quickly. The disadvantage is that in the end it doesn't resolve personal conflict—if anything, it aggravates it by breeding hurt feelings and resentment.

Compromising—"Let's Split the Difference"

In *compromising,* both parties give up something in order to gain something. Compromise is appropriate when both sides have opposite goals or possess equal power. But compromise isn't workable when it is used so often that it doesn't achieve results—for example, continual failure to meet production deadlines. Compromise, says one writer, sometimes represents "the mistaken idea that any agreement is better than no agreement."[101]

The benefit of compromise is that it is a democratic process that seems to have no losers. However, since so many people approach compromise situations with a win–lose attitude, they may be disappointed and feel cheated.

Collaborating—"Let's Cooperate to Reach a Win–Win Solution That Benefits Both of Us"

Problem solving, or integrating, is about collaboration. In this style, the manager strives to confront the issue and cooperatively identify the problem, generating and weighing alternatives and selecting a solution. Problem solving is appropriate for complex issues plagued by misunderstanding. It is inappropriate for resolving conflicts rooted in opposing value systems.

The strength of problem solving is its longer-lasting impact because it deals with the underlying problem, not just its symptoms. Its weakness is that it's very time-consuming. Nevertheless, problem solving is usually the best approach for dealing with groups and teams of people.

Wringing Creativity from Conflict

What if your group is experiencing workplace conflict and is stuck for creative solutions to a problem? Can conflict help you find your way out? Some experts say conflict can indeed drive creativity. Here are some suggestions for doing just that.[102]

Ask the Right Questions about the Problem. Sometimes conflict distorts what the group's real task is. Test your assumptions and make sure you've correctly framed the issue before the group.

Actively Draw Input from All Members. If someone hasn't spoken up yet, or someone's ideas are often disregarded because they are a little off the wall, make sure those members have a chance to speak. When they get a hearing, others will chime in, too.

Work with the Resources You Have. The great American conductor and composer Leonard Bernstein once said, "To achieve great things, two things are needed: a plan, and not quite enough time."[103]

Keep a Dialogue Going, Not a Debate. A debate has only two sides; you want to hear as many sides and ideas as possible. To avoid polarizing a discussion and forcing group members to face off, check your emotions.

Reward Nonconformity. The unusual, the offbeat, the "we never tried *that* before" ideas can lead you to creative solutions. Sir Ken Robinson, an expert on creativity, says, "If you're not prepared to be wrong, you'll never come up with anything original."[104]

Don't Try Too Hard to Smooth the Way between Group Members. When group members have to work out their own interpersonal differences, they often come up with more genuine ways of doing so that can fire up their creativity in other areas.

connect SELF-ASSESSMENT 13.5

What Is Your Conflict-Management Style?

The following exercise is designed to determine your conflict-handling style. Please be prepared to answer these questions if your instructor has assigned Self-Assessment 13.5 in Connect.

1. Were you surprised by the results? Why or why not? Explain.

2. Were the scores for your primary and backup conflict-handling styles relatively similar, or was there a large gap? What does this imply? Discuss.

3. Is your conflict-handling style one that can be used in many different conflict scenarios? Explain.

4. What are some skills you can work on to become more effective at handling conflict?

Key Points

13.1 Groups versus Teams

- Groups and teams are different—a group is typically management-directed, a team self-directed. A group is defined as two or more freely interacting individuals who share collective norms, share collective goals, and have a common identity. A team is defined as a small group of people with complementary skills who are committed to a common purpose, performance goals, and approach for which they hold themselves mutually accountable.

- Groups may be either formal, established to do something productive for the organization and headed by a leader, or informal, formed by people seeking friendship with no officially appointed leader.

- Teams are of various types, but one of the most important is the work team, which engages in collective work requiring coordinated effort. A project team may also be a cross-functional team, staffed with specialists pursuing a common objective.

- Three other types of teams are continuous improvement teams, consisting of small groups of volunteers or workers and supervisors who meet intermittently to discuss workplace and quality-related problems; self-managed teams, defined as groups of workers given administrative oversight for their task domains; and virtual teams, which work together over time and distance via electronic media to combine effort and achieve common goals.

13.2 Stages of Group and Team Development

- A group may evolve into a team through five stages. (1) Forming is the process of getting oriented and getting acquainted. (2) Storming is characterized by the emergence of individual personalities and roles and conflicts within the group. (3) In norming, conflicts are resolved, close relationships develop, and unity and harmony emerge. (4) In performing, members concentrate on solving problems and

completing the assigned task. (5) In adjourning, members prepare for disbandment.

- A group can also develop by means of punctuated equilibrium, in which it establishes periods of stable functioning until an event causes a dramatic change in norms, roles, and/or objectives. The group then establishes and maintains new norms of functioning, returning to equilibrium.

13.3 Building Effective Teams

- There are seven considerations managers must take into account in building a group into an effective team. (1) They must ensure individuals are collaborating, or systematically integrating their efforts to achieve a collective objective. (2) They must establish a climate of trust, or reciprocal faith in others' intentions and behaviors. (3) They must establish measurable performance goals and have feedback about members' performance.

- (4) They must motivate members by making them mutually accountable to one another. (5) They must consider team composition. Diversity is good for business and must be effectively managed. The most important idea to remember is that team member composition should fit the responsibilities of the team.

- (6) They must consider the role each team member must play. A role is defined as the socially determined expectation of how an individual should behave in a specific position. Two types of team roles are task and maintenance. A task role consists of behavior that concentrates on getting the team's tasks done. A maintenance role consists of behavior that fosters constructive relationships among team members.

- (7) They must consider team norms, the general guidelines or rules of behavior that most group or team members follow. Norms tend to be enforced by group or team members for four reasons: to help the group survive, to clarify role expectations, to help individuals avoid embarrassing situations, and to emphasize the group's important values and identity.

13.4 Managing Conflict

- Conflict is a process in which one party perceives that its interests are being opposed or negatively affected by another party. Conflict can be dysfunctional, or negative. However, constructive, or functional, conflict benefits the main purposes of the organization and serves its interests. Too little conflict can lead to indolence; too much conflict can lead to warfare.
- Four devices for stimulating constructive conflict are (1) spurring competition among employees, (2) changing the organization's culture and

procedures, (3) bringing in outsiders for new perspectives, and (4) using programmed conflict to elicit different opinions without inciting people's personal feelings.

- Two methods used in programmed conflict are (1) devil's advocacy, in which someone is assigned to play the role of critic to voice possible objections to a proposal, and (2) the dialectic method, in which two people or groups play opposing roles in a debate in order to better understand a proposal. There are five basic behaviors that enable you to work on disagreements and keep them from flaring into out-of-control personality conflicts: openness, equality, empathy, supportiveness, and positiveness.

Understanding the Chapter: What Do I Know?

1. How do groups and teams differ?
2. What's the difference between formal groups and informal groups?
3. Describe four types of work teams.
4. What are the stages of group and team development?
5. Explain the nine most essential considerations in building a group into an effective team.
6. How do functional and dysfunctional conflict differ?
7. What are four types of conflict?
8. How would you go about stimulating constructive conflict?
9. What are devil's advocacy and the dialectic method?
10. What are five basic behaviors to help you better handle conflict?

Management in Action

Teamwork Is a Driver of Success at Whole Foods Market

Whole Foods Market was established in 1980. In 2015 it had grown to 413 store locations and 91,000 employees in the United States, Canada, and the United Kingdom. The company is the first certified organic grocer in the U.S. Whole Foods "only sells products that meet its self-created quality standards for being 'natural', which the store defines as: minimally processed foods that are free of hydrogenated fats as well as artificial flavors, colors, sweeteners, preservatives, and many others as listed on their online 'Unacceptable Food Ingredients' list."[105]

Whole Foods was rated as the 75th best place to work in 2016 by *Fortune*. This rating is partly a function of the company's commitment to teams and an egalitarian culture. For example, the company has a policy capping executive salaries at no more than 19 times the average worker.[106]

Organizational Culture

Whole Foods creates competitive advantage through its quality products, service, and organizational culture. An organization's culture is driven by its mission and values. Whole Foods is clearly a mission-driven company. Its managerial practices and procedures are guided by its purpose statement and core values. The company's purpose statement is "With great courage, integrity, and love—we embrace our responsibility to co-create a world where each of us, our communities and our planet can flourish. All the while, celebrating the sheer love and joy of food."[107] You can see the theme of collaboration and teamwork in this purpose statement.

The theme of collaboration and teamwork also shows up when considering Whole Foods's core values. They include the following: sell the highest quality natural and organic products available; satisfy, delight, and nourish our customers; support team member excellence and happiness; create wealth through profits and growth; serve and support our local and global communities; practice and advance environmental stewardship; create ongoing win–win partnerships with our suppliers; and promote the health of our stakeholders through healthy eating education.[108]

The culture at Whole Foods focuses on team-based activities and transparency. All employees are encouraged to participate in monthly team and store meetings, as well as hiring decisions. According to one business writer, the company "integrates the principle of transparency. The company aims to keep stakeholders informed. Whole Foods Market provides financial reports not just to investors but also to employees. Employees use this information to understand the firm's situation."[109] The company also makes its annual individual compensation report available for all to see.

Structure, Hiring, and Rewards

Each store is structured around 8 to 10 semiautonomous teams. Each teach represents a department or section of the store such as produce, meat, prepared foods, and checkout. The teams are given autonomy and empowerment. Tom Neal, the store team leader in Glastonbury, England, commented that "workers are empowered and encouraged to learn about the products, resolve problems and take part in the company's growth." As examples, he noted that "if there's a new kind of cheese, everyone gets information on it and they all try it. We're always trying to bring in new kinds of produce. When the first crop of peaches comes in from Georgia, we all try it so that when the customer comes by you can say, 'I'd give 'em a week,' or 'They're comin' in nice this year.'"[110]

Teamwork extends behind the stores. Regional presidents are considered a team, and founder John Mackey is co-CEO.

The hiring process revolves around team input. "New associates undergo a 60-day process that involves a variety of interviews, including phone interviews, one-to-one interviews with store leaders, and panel interviews with teams built from recruiters, managers, and select employees." Once hired, store managers provisionally assign the employee to a team, but only on a trial basis. "After the trial period, the existing team votes on whether to fully vest the new associate. It takes a two-thirds majority vote from the team to become an employee. The voting step is required, but the method is left up to the team. New associates who don't get voted in are off the team and must either find a new team—repeating the trial period—or leave the company."[111] This process is used for all employees.

Teams are also the basic unit of measurement for performance and rewards. All teams are given "their profit per labor-hour every four weeks, as well as their historical performance, the performance of other teams in their store, and the performance of similar teams in other stores."[112] Teams ultimately compete against other teams and themselves as one method to improve performance. Bonuses also are based on team data. The greater the increase in a team's performance gains, the more team members receive in bonus pay.[113]

FOR DISCUSSION

1. Are the department teams at Whole Foods more of a group or a team? Explain your rationale.

2. What does Whole Foods do to promote collaboration and cohesiveness among their teams?

3. What are the pros and cons to the company's hiring and rewards process? Discuss.

4. The text discussed seven considerations for building a group into an effective team. To what extent has Whole Foods effectively implemented these considerations?

5. What is your biggest takeaway about teams based on this case?

Legal/Ethical Challenge

When Employees Smoke Marijuana Socially: A Manager's Quandary

This challenge involves conflict that may occur among coworkers as a result of ethical considerations.

You work in a state where it is illegal to smoke marijuana, and your employer has a zero-tolerance policy regarding the use of drugs. You also are a supervisor at a telephone call center and have very

positive relationships with members of your work team and your manager. A friend of yours, Christina, is also a supervisor, and her younger brother, Blake, is a member of your work team.

Christina invites you to her birthday party at her home, and you happily agree to attend. During the party, you walk out to the backyard to get some fresh air and notice that Blake and several other employees of your company are smoking marijuana: None of these individuals have prescriptions for medical marijuana. You have been told on several occasions by members of your own work team that these same individuals have used marijuana at other social events.

Although Blake is a member of your work team, his friends are not. You don't really feel any need to tell management about these people smoking pot because you have never noticed their being impaired at work. At the same time, you feel conflicted because your employer takes a hard stand against the use of any drugs. If the company found out that you knew about their smoking, it would adversely affect your career. The company expects managers to act with honesty and integrity and to be forthright with senior management.

You are experiencing even more conflict between your values and those of your employer because Blake applied for a promotion to a supervisory position. Although he is a good worker, you wonder if his smoking marijuana might affect his judgment. More importantly, the vice president of human resources just requested a recommendation from you regarding Blake's promotion.

SOLVING THE DILEMMA

As a supervisor, what would you do?

1. I would not tell the vice president of human resources about Blake's drug use. He's doing a good job and I have not seen any impairment.

2. I would tell the vice president of human resources about the incident in which I observed Blake smoking marijuana. I need to honor the company's directives about a zero-tolerance policy on drug use.

3. I would talk to Blake. I would explain my predicament and then ask him about the frequency of his drug use. If Blake promised to stop smoking marijuana, I would not tell the vice president of human resources about the incident.

4. Invent other options. Discuss.

14

Power, Influence, and Leadership

From Becoming a Manager to Becoming a Leader

Advancing Your Career: Staying Ahead in the Workplace of Tomorrow

Someday maybe you can afford to have a *personal career coach*—the kind long used by sports and entertainment figures and now adopted in the upper ranks of business. Until then, you can consider more widely available advice about networking strategies, image management, and career growth. Women in particular tend to overlook career planning in favor of getting immediate tasks done. Here are a few suggestions for avoiding that trap.[1]

Take Charge of Your Own Career

Because you, not others, are in charge of your career, and because it's an ongoing process, you should develop a career plan and base your choices on that plan. As Yogi Berra once said, "If you don't know where you're going, you'll end up somewhere else." When considering a new job or industry, find out how that world *really* works. Research the companies you want to work for; find out their corporate "style" or culture by talking to their employees.

Anticipate and Embrace Change

Learn to analyze, anticipate, and adapt to new circumstances in the world and in your own life. For instance, as technology changes the rules, *embrace* the new rules rather than clinging to the old. Those who are able to adapt nimbly to new environments and circumstances—and who can lead others along new paths—are increasingly valuable to employers.

Keep Learning

Try taking a brief course in a new work-related area. It might be enough to qualify you to ask for a role in a new or special project with high visibility, and if you enjoy your new knowledge you can pursue it further. Employers continue to value people with both specialized and generalized skills. Don't underestimate the value of picking up other talents as well, such as fluency in a second or third language.

Develop Your People and Problem-Solving Skills

"People rise in organizations because of their hard skills and fall due to a dearth of soft skills."[2] This explains why many organizations weigh soft skills so heavily when hiring for top positions. The most sought-after skills for business school graduates are problem solving, leadership, and communication.[3] These skills also are the most difficult to find.

Know Your Own Value

Be sure you can articulate what you contribute to your organization. What makes your input unique? What does this suggest about your future with your current industry or employer? Says executive coach Bonnie Marcus, "The first step to developing your own authentic leadership style is to recognize the value you bring to an organization and be confident that your talent and experience benefits the company."

For Discussion Which of these five rules do you think is most important—and why?

FORECAST What's Ahead in This Chapter

How do leaders use their power and influence to get results? This chapter considers this question. We discuss the sources of a leader's power and how leaders use persuasion to influence people. We then consider the following approaches to leadership: trait, behavioral, situational, transformational, and three additional perspectives.

14.1 The Nature of Leadership: The Role of Power and Influence

MAJOR
QUESTION

How do effective leaders use power and influence?

THE BIG PICTURE

Leadership skills are needed to create and communicate a company's vision, strategies, and goals as well as to execute on these plans and goals. This section highlights the way successful managers use power and influence to achieve these ends and describes five sources of power and nine influence tactics they use to lead others. Leaders use the power of persuasion to get others to follow them. Five approaches to leadership are described in the next five sections.

Leadership. What is it? Is it a skill anyone can develop? How important is it to organizational success?

Leadership is the ability to influence employees to voluntarily pursue organizational goals.[4] Although not everyone is suited to being a good leader, evidence shows that people can be trained to be more effective leaders. In response, more companies are using management development programs to build a pipeline of leadership talent. Total U.S. spending by organizations for leadership training was $61.8 billion in 2014 and $70.6 billion in 2015.[5]

Effective leadership matters! A recent study spanning 60 years and more than 18,000 firm-years showed that CEO behavior significantly impacted organizational performance.[6] Don't take this study to mean effective leadership only matters at the top. Other research reinforces the value of fostering effective leadership at all organizational levels.

Let's begin our study of leadership by considering the role of power and influence skills and the difference between leading and managing.

Five Sources of Power

Power is the ability to marshal human, informational, and other resources to get something done. Defined this way, power is all about influencing others. The more influence you have, the more powerful you are, and vice versa.

Global leaders. Leadership impacts the security, sustainability, and well-being of our planet. These leaders of the Group of 20 major economies clearly impact our lives in many ways. The purpose of the meeting taking place here was to determine how advanced and emerging economies can create mutually beneficial growth strategies. © Kyodo News/Getty Images

To really understand leadership, we need to understand the concept of power and authority. *Authority* is the right to perform or command; it comes with the job. In contrast, *power* is the extent to which a person is able to influence others so they respond to orders.

People who pursue **personalized power**—power directed at helping oneself—as a way of enhancing their own selfish ends may give the word *power* a bad name. However, there is another kind of power, **socialized power**—power directed at helping others. This is the kind of power you hear in expressions such as "My goal is to have a powerful impact on my community."[7]

Within organizations there are typically five sources of power leaders may draw on: *legitimate, reward, coercive, expert,* and *referent.*

1. Legitimate Power: Influencing Behavior Because of One's Formal Position

Legitimate power, which all managers have, is power that results from managers' formal positions within the organization. All managers have legitimate power over their employees, deriving from their position, whether it's a construction boss, ad account supervisor, sales manager, or CEO. This power may be exerted both positively or negatively—as praise or as criticism, for example.

2. Reward Power: Influencing Behavior by Promising or Giving Rewards

Reward power, which all managers have, is power that results from managers' authority to reward their subordinates. Rewards can range from praise to pay raises, from recognition to promotions.

Example: GoFanbase, a company that helps other firms manage social media, offers employees a $20 "idea bounty" if they present ideas in meetings that their peers agree are worthwhile and the founder approves. Unlimited vacation time and paid time off for volunteering are other, increasingly popular incentives.[8]

3. Coercive Power: Influencing Behavior by Threatening or Giving Punishment

Coercive power, which all managers have, results from managers' authority to punish their subordinates. Punishment can range from verbal or written reprimands to demotions to terminations. In some lines of work, fines and suspensions may be used. Coercive power has to be used judiciously, of course, since a manager who is seen as being constantly negative will produce a lot of resentment among employees. Before Alan Mulally took over at Ford Motor Co., for instance, the expectation fostered by a culture of blame at the firm was that any manager who had bad news to report would be fired. Mulally's corrective action was to say a manager *had* a problem, not that he or she *was* the problem.[9]

4. Expert Power: Influencing Behavior Because of One's Expertise

Expert power is power resulting from one's specialized information or expertise. Expertise, or special knowledge, can be mundane, such as knowing the work schedules and assignments of the people who report to you. Or it can be sophisticated, such as having computer or medical knowledge. Secretaries may have expert power because, for example, they have been in a job a long time and know all the necessary contacts. CEOs may have expert power because they have strategic knowledge not shared by many others.

5. Referent Power: Influencing Behavior Because of One's Personal Attraction

Referent power is power deriving from one's personal attraction. As we will see later in this chapter (under the discussion of transformational leadership, Section 14.5), this kind of power characterizes strong, visionary leaders who are able to persuade their followers by dint of their personality, attitudes, or background. Referent power may be associated with managers, but it is more likely to be characteristic of leaders.

Now that you've learned about the five bases of power, complete Self-Assessment 14.1 to identify which bases you prefer to use. Answering the associated questions will help you understand how the various forms of power can both help and hurt you when trying to influence others.

connect SELF-ASSESSMENT 14.1

What Kind of Power Do I Prefer?

If your instructor has assigned Self-Assessment 14.1 in Connect, you will learn which bases of power you prefer to use.

1. Which of the five bases of power do you prefer to use?

2. Describe how this form of power helps you at school, at work, and in social situations.

3. Which of the five bases is your least preferred? What are the implications for you at school, at work, and in social situations?

4. What two specific things can you do to increase your expert power? Two things to increase your referent power?

Common Influence Tactics

Influence tactics are conscious efforts to affect and change behaviors in others. The nine most common ways people try to get their bosses, coworkers, and subordinates to do what they want are listed in Table 14.1, beginning with the most frequently used.

These are considered *generic* influence tactics because they characterize social influence as we use it in all directions. Research has also shown this ranking to be fairly consistent regardless of whether the direction of influence is downward, upward, or lateral.

Hard versus Soft Tactics
Some refer to the first five influence tactics—rational persuasion, inspirational appeals, consultation, ingratiation, and personal appeals—as *"soft"* tactics because they are friendlier than, and not as coercive as, the last four tactics—exchange, coalition, pressure, and legitimating tactics, which are *"hard"* tactics because they exert more overt pressure.

Influence tactics. In mid-2015 Taylor Swift asserted her immense power and influence and successfully changed one of Apple's policies. Before the launch of Apple Music, the company said it intended not to compensate musicians for their music used during the free trial of its new subscription service. Swift, who often speaks on behalf of other musicians, threatened to withhold her new album from Apple, now the largest single retailer of music. She said, "We don't ask for free iPhones. Please don't ask us to provide you with our music for no compensation." Apple quickly changed its policy and compensated musicians for the use of their work during the free trial and since. Which tactics (and bases of power) did Swift use to influence Apple? © Mike Coppola/Getty Images

TABLE 14.1 Nine Common Influence Tactics

INFLUENCE TACTIC	DESCRIPTION	EXAMPLE
1. Rational persuasion	Trying to convince someone with reason, logic, or facts	As CEO, Allan Mullally reversed the negative meeting culture at Ford Motor Co.—and its financial fortunes—by encouraging open and honest discussion and collaboration focused on finding solutions rather than placing blame.[10]
2. Inspirational appeals	Trying to build enthusiasm by appealing to others' emotions, ideals, or values	The late Steve Jobs's understanding that people want to fulfill their dreams, not just purchase products, continues to inform every design and marketing decision at Apple, the company he founded.[11]
3. Consultation	Getting others to participate in planning, decision making, and changes	"I end up asking a lot of questions," says Nike's CEO, Mark Parker. Known for encouraging and seeking ideas from even junior members of management, Parker deliberately avoids a micro managing style.[12]
4. Ingratiation	Getting someone in a good mood prior to making a request	This is being friendly and helpful and using praise, flattery, or humor. A particular form of ingratiation is "brown nosing."[13]
5. Personal appeals	Referring to friendship and loyalty when making a request, asking a friend to do a favor	Employees who volunteer might make a personal appeal to colleagues to donate time, clothing, or money to a cause.[14]
6. Exchange	Making explicit or implied promises and trading favors	Leaders must be careful not to allow favoritism and coercion to evolve, however.[15]
7. Coalition tactics	Getting others to support your efforts to persuade someone	Cory Booker, U.S. Senator from New Jersey, credits coalition leadership with the economic revival of Newark during his past job as mayor: "None of these accomplishments happened because of one individual's effort. They happened because, in Newark, we brought together new coalitions of grassroots neighborhood groups and elected leaders, nonprofits and business groups, labor unions and leaders in the capital markets, developers and philanthropists. I am proud of the unity that was forged in Newark—it's proof, to me, that people will rally around bold goals and, in turn, achieve significant progress."[16]
8. Pressure	Demanding compliance or using intimidation or threats	Chinese philosopher Lao-Tzu wrote, "The highest type of ruler is one of whose existence the people are barely aware. Next comes one whom they love and praise. Next comes one whom they fear. Next comes one whom they despise and defy."[17]
9. Legitimating tactics	Basing a request on authority or right, organizational rules or policies, or explicit/implied support from superiors	The assertive style of Jeb Bush, former governor of Florida and a one-time contender for the Republican presidential nomination, was based on his deep understanding of the use of executive authority.[18]

See D. Kipnis, S. Schmidt, and I. Wilkinson, "Intraorganizational Influence Tactics: Exploration in Getting One's Way," Journal of Applied Psychology, August 1980, pp. 440–452; and Table 1 in G. Yukl, C. M. Falbe, and J. Y. Youn, "Patterns of Influence Behavior for Managers, Group & Organization Management, March 1993, pp. 5–28.

Which Influence Tactics Do You Prefer?   When you read the list of tactics, each probably meant something to you. Which do you most commonly use? Knowing the answer can help you better choose the appropriate tactic for any given situation and thus increase the chance of achieving your desired outcome. The next step to realizing these benefits is to complete Self-Assessment 14.2.

Which Influence Tactics Do I Use?

If your instructor has assigned Self-Assessment 14.2 in Connect, you will learn which of the nine influence tactics you use and in what order of frequency.

1. Is your rational persuasion score the highest? Regardless, give some specific examples of ways you use this tactic.

2. Which tactic is your least preferred (lowest score)? Provide examples of situations when and how you may use this tactic.

Match Tactics to Influence Outcomes

Research and practice provide some useful lessons about the relative effectiveness of influence tactics.

- **Rely on the core.** *Core influence tactics*—rational persuasion, consultation, collaboration, and inspirational appeals—are most effective at building commitment.

- **Be authentic.** Don't try to be someone else. Be authentic to your values and beliefs.

- **Consult rather than legitimate.** Some employees are more apt to accept change when managers rely on a consultative strategy and are more likely to resist change when managers use a legitimating tactic.

- **"Glad handing" is not a good long-term strategy.** Ingratiation improved short-term sales goal achievement but reduced it in the long term in a study of salespeople. Glad handing may help today's sales but not tomorrow's.

- **Be subtle.** Subtle flattery and agreement with the other person's opinion (both forms of ingratiation) were shown to increase the likelihood that executives would win recommendation to sit on boards of directors.

- **Learn to influence.** Research with corporate managers of a supermarket chain showed that influence tactics can be taught and learned. Managers who received 360-degree feedback on two occasions regarding their influence tactics showed an increased use of core influence tactics.

You'll need to understand *and* effectively apply a range of influence tactics to be effective. But you can learn and improve influence tactics to move resisters to compliance and move those who are compliant to commitment.

What Is the Difference between Leading and Managing?

Bernard Bass, a leadership expert, concluded that "leaders manage and managers lead, but the two activities are not synonymous."[19] Broadly speaking, managers typically perform functions associated with planning, investigating, organizing, and control, and leaders focus on influencing others. Leaders inspire others, provide emotional support, and try to get employees to rally around a common goal. Leaders also play a key role in *creating* a vision and strategic plan for an organization. Managers, in turn, are charged with *implementing* the vision and plan. We can draw several conclusions from this division of labor.

First, good leaders are not necessarily good managers, and good managers are not necessarily good leaders. Second, effective leadership requires effective managerial skills at some level. For example, United's former CEO, Jeff Smisek, resigned due to managerial deficiencies that produced labor problems, poor customer service, and poor financial results.[20] In contrast, both Tim Cook, CEO of Apple, and Mary Dillon,

CEO of Ulta Beauty, are recognized for their use of good managerial skills when implementing corporate strategies.[21]

Do you want to lead others or understand what makes a leader tick? Then take the following self-assessment. It provides feedback on your readiness to assume a leadership role and can help you consider how to prepare for a formal leadership position.

▤ connect SELF-ASSESSMENT 14.3

Assessing Your Readiness to Assume the Leadership Role

The following survey was designed to assess your readiness to assume the leadership role. Please be prepared to answer these questions if your instructor has assigned Self-Assessment 14.3 in Connect.

1. What is your level of readiness? Are you surprised by the results?

2. Looking at the three highest- and lowest-rated items in the survey, what can you do to increase your readiness to lead? Think of specific actions you take right now.

3. Do you think your readiness to lead will change over time? Explain your rationale.

An Integrated Model of Leadership

Figure 14.1 provides an overview of what you will learn in this chapter. It presents an integrated model of leadership. Starting at the far right of the model, you see that leadership effectiveness is the outcome we want to explain. The center of the model shows this outcome is influenced by four types of leadership behavior: *task-oriented, relationship-oriented, passive,* and *transformational.* In turn, our ability to effectively engage in these leader behaviors is affected by traits, gender, and leadership skills (the left side of the model).

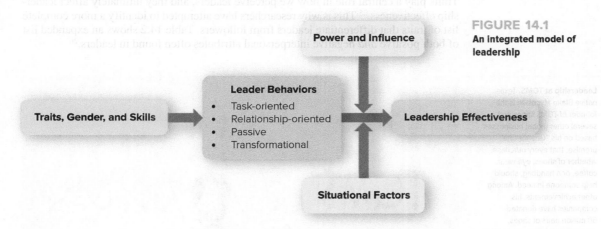

FIGURE 14.1

An integrated model of leadership

Moreover, Figure 14.1 shows that the relationship between leader behavior and leadership effectiveness is affected by two other considerations: power and influence and situational factors. For example, people with more power and strong influence skills are better suited to execute the four types of leader behavior in a more effective manner. Similarly, you will be more effective if you exhibit the four leader behaviors at the right time. Different situations call for different leader behaviors. This chapter helps you understand when to change your leadership style and behavior. ●

14.2 Trait Approaches: Do Leaders Have Distinctive Traits and Personal Characteristics?

MAJOR QUESTION What does it take to be a successful leader?

THE BIG PICTURE

Trait approaches attempt to identify distinctive characteristics that account for the effectiveness of leaders. We describe (1) positive task-oriented traits and positive/negative interpersonal attributes (narcissism, Machiavellianism, psychopathy) and (2) some results of gender studies.

Consider a leader dubbed "CEO of the Decade" in 2009 by *Fortune* magazine for 10 years of achievements in the fields of music, movies, and mobile phones, not to mention computing. "Remaking any one business is a career-defining achievement," wrote *Fortune* editor Adam Lashinsky; "four is unheard of."[22]

That leader was, of course, the late Steve Jobs of Apple. Did he have distinctive personality traits that might teach us something about leadership? Perhaps he did. He seemed to embody the traits of (1) dominance, (2) intelligence, (3) self-confidence, (4) high energy, and (5) task-relevant knowledge.

These are the five traits that researcher **Ralph Stogdill** in 1948 concluded were typical of successful leaders.[23] Stogdill is one of many contributors to **trait approaches to leadership**, which attempt to identify distinctive characteristics that account for the effectiveness of leaders.[24]

Positive Task-Oriented Traits and Positive/Negative Interpersonal Attributes

Traits play a central role in how we perceive leaders, and they ultimately affect leadership effectiveness.[25] This is why researchers have attempted to identify a more complete list of traits that differentiate leaders from followers. Table 14.2 shows an expanded list of both positive *and* negative interpersonal attributes often found in leaders.[26]

Leadership at TOMS. Texas native Blake Mycoskie is the founder of TOMS shoes and several other global businesses based on his "One for one"® premise: that every purchase, whether of shoes, eye wear, coffee, or a handbag, should help someone in need. Among other achievements, his companies have donated 60 million pairs of shoes, restored eyesight to almost half a million people, and provided safe water and childbirth services to thousands.[31] What positive leadership traits do you think Mycoskie possesses?
© Zuma Press, Inc/Alamy.

POSITIVE TASK-ORIENTED TRAITS	POSITIVE/NEGATIVE INTERPERSONAL ATTRIBUTES
• Intelligence	• Extraversion (+)
• Conscientiousness	• Agreeableness (+)
• Open to experience	• Emotional intelligence (+)
• Emotional stability	• Narcissism (−)
• Positive affect	• Machiavellianism (−)
	• Psychopathy (−)

TABLE 14.2

Key Task-Oriented Traits and Interpersonal Attributes

We have discussed most positive interpersonal attributes elsewhere, but we need to describe the negative, or "dark side," traits of some leaders: narcissism, Machiavellianism, and psychopathy.[27]

■ **Narcissism** is defined as having "a self-centered perspective, feelings of superiority, and a drive for personal power and glory."[28] Narcissists have inflated views of themselves, seek to attract the admiration of others, and fantasize about being in control of everything. Although passionate and charismatic, narcissistic leaders may provoke counterproductive work behaviors in others, such as strong resentments and resistance.[29]

■ **Machiavellianism.** Inspired by the pessimistic beliefs of Niccolò Machiavelli, a philosopher and writer (*The Prince*) in the Italian Renaissance, **Machiavellianism** (pronounced "mah-kyah-*vel*-yahn-izm") displays a cynical view of human nature and condones opportunistic and unethical ways of manipulating people, putting results over principles. This view is manifested in such expressions as "All people lie to get what they want" and "You have to cheat to get ahead." Like narcissism, Machiavellianism is also associated with counterproductive work behaviors, especially as people begin to understand that they are being coldly manipulated.

■ **Psychopathy. Psychopathy** ("sigh-*kop*-a-thee") is characterized by lack of concern for others, impulsive behavior, and a dearth of remorse when the psychopath's actions harm others. Not surprisingly, a person with a psychopathic personality can be a truly toxic influence in the workplace.

If you have a propensity for any of these, you need to know that the expression of "dark side" traits tends to result in career derailment—being demoted or fired.[30]

Do Women and Men Display Similar Leadership Traits?

The increase in the number of of women in the workforce has generated much interest in understanding the similarities and differences between female and male leaders. Research reveals the following four conclusions:

1. Men were observed to display more task leadership and women more relationship leadership.[33]

Leadership at Turing Pharmaceuticals. Martin Shkreli (seated, center), founder and former CEO of Turing Pharmaceuticals, tried to build a business strategy of purchasing the rights to inexpensive but life-saving prescription drugs and raising their prices to dizzying heights. Public response was swift and devastatingly negative; meanwhile, Shkreli has pleaded not guilty to fraud charges associated with other firms he managed.[32] Do you think he possesses any dark-side traits?
© Tom Williams/CQ Roll Call/Newscom

Sheryl Sandberg. Named in 2014 the ninth most powerful woman in the world by *Forbes* and the 10th most powerful woman in business by *Fortune,* Sandberg is the chief operating officer (COO) and business face of Facebook. She's also a passionate advocate for women achieving more top corporate leadership jobs. As she told a Barnard College graduating class, "A world where men ran half our homes and women ran half our institutions would be just a much greater world." © Bloomberg/ Getty Images

2. Women used a more democratic or participative style than men, and men used a more autocratic and directive style.[34]

3. Female leadership was associated with more cohesion, cooperative learning, and participative communication among team members.[35]

4. Peers, managers, direct reports, and judges/trained observers rated women executives as more effective than men. Men also rated themselves as more effective than women evaluated themselves.[36]

EXAMPLE   Great Leaders Worldwide

Canada's Justin Trudeau. Although he is the son of an earlier and long-time prime minister, Canada's popular new leader Justin Trudeau came to politics by an unusual route. He has been a teacher, a bouncer, the leader of a nonprofit organization, and even an occasional actor. As prime minister he has won praise for championing the rights of women and Canada's indigenous population (his cabinet is 50% women and includes an openly gay politician, a member who is blind, Sikhs, and Aboriginals), for highlighting his role as a husband and father, and for leading the country with grace and skill. His humility, optimism, and willingness to admit mistakes and open dialogues with those who disagree with him reflect a high degree of emotional intelligence. As one Canadian observer says of Trudeau, "The very skills the prime minister honed as a teacher and third-sector leader are key to his ability to motivate and react with agility—not just his caucus but Canadians and other global leaders. The successful teacher and senior leader has an ability to parse diverse threads, read situations, motivations, and personali-

ties, and respond in real time. An increasingly in-demand skill amidst huge change."[37]

Germany's Angela Merkel. Angela Merkel, long-time chancellor of Germany, grew up in the Communist-controlled sector of a divided country struggling to overcome the horrors of World War II and its disastrous defeat. A chemist by training who also served as environmental minister, she is now the longest-term leader in Europe and one of the most powerful women on the planet. Her generally cautious and low-key approach has helped her lead her re-unified country through globalization, enormous economic and technological change, and a worldwide financial crisis. More recently this disciplined realist has also taken the lead in offering shelter to more than 1 million Muslim and other refugees who have crossed Germany's border.

Though some are critical of her humane and generous stance and even suggest it could lead to her political downfall, Merkel herself says, "In many regions war and terror prevail.

States disintegrate. For many years we have read about this. We have heard about it. We have seen it on TV. But we had not yet sufficiently understood that what happens in Aleppo and Mosul can affect Essen or Stuttgart. We have to face that now."[38]

Justin Trudeau. Prime Minister of Canada Justin Trudeau (in green) participates in a Pride Parade in Vancouver, Canada. © Sergei Bachlakov/ Shutterstock RF

YOUR CALL

What leadership traits do you think Justin Trudeau exhibits? What leadership traits does Angela Merkel seem to have? Which do they share, and how do they differ? What might account for any differences?

Angela Merkel. Federal Chancellor of Germany Angela Merkel. © Thomas Frey/imageBROKER/Alamy

Are Knowledge and Skills Important?

Knowledge and skills are extremely important! A team of researchers identified four basic skills leaders need. *(See Table 14.3.)*

WHAT LEADERS NEED	AND WHY
Cognitive abilities to identify problems and their causes in rapidly changing situations	Leaders must sometimes devise effective solutions in short time spans with limited information. One situation requiring quick action that many managers will likely face is a data breach. Says Ralph de la Vega, president & CEO, AT&T Mobile & Business Solutions, "There are only two kinds of companies today . . . those that have experienced a data breach and those that will be breached."[39]
Interpersonal skills to influence and persuade others	Leaders need to work well with diverse people. Alan Colberg, president and CEO of Assurant, says civility is one of a handful of key interpersonal skills in every career. The others he cites are the abilities to build relationships, conscientiousness, and integrity.[40]
Business skills to maximize the use of organizational assets	Leaders increasingly need business skills as they advance up through an organization. Three valuable but often-overlooked skills that most people can develop with a little effort are mindfulness, curiosity, and optimism.[41]
Strategic skills to draft an organization's mission, vision, strategies, and implementation plans	Strategic skills matter most for individuals in the top ranks in an organization. Entrepreneurs may have their strategic skills tested on a regular basis. Sara Blakely's father regularly asked her, "What have you failed at this week?" After repeated setbacks, she eventually came up with the line of slimming intimate wear she called Spanx.[42]

TABLE 14.3

Four Basic Skills for Leaders

Source: Adapted from T. V. Mumford, M. A. Campion, and F. P. Morgeson, "Leadership Skills Strataplex: Leadership Skill Requirements across Organizational Levels," Leadership Quarterly, 2007, 154–166.

So What Do We Know about Leadership Traits?

Trait theory offers us four conclusions.

1. **We cannot ignore the implications of leadership traits.** Traits play a central role in the way we perceive leaders, and they do ultimately affect leadership effectiveness. For instance, focus, confidence, transparency, and integrity were among the top traits listed in a survey of current business leaders, along with patience, openness, and generosity.[43]

   More specifically, many companies attempt to define leadership traits important for their context. The Cardiac Rhythm Disease Management Group within Medtronic Inc., for example, identified nine types of traits and skills necessary for leaders (such as giving clear performance feedback and being courageous). The company then designed a leadership development program to help its employees learn and apply these traits.[44]

2. **The positive and "dark triad" traits suggest the qualities you should cultivate and avoid if you want to assume a leadership role in the future.** Elon Musk, founder of electric car manufacturer Tesla, is widely admired for his vision and daring but admits to being a micro manager to an extreme degree. Limiting employees' freedom in this way is generally viewed as a negative quality in a leader.[45] Personality tests and other trait assessments can help evaluate your strengths and weaknesses on these traits. The website for this book contains a host of tests you can take for this purpose.

3. **Organizations may want to include personality and trait assessments in their selection and evaluation processes.** For example, Cisco's UK leader, Vice President Eleanor Cavanagh-Lomas, uses "data analytics," an algorithm designed to assess her management team's individual strengths based on a brief multiple-choice self-assessment test. The app suggests how each person works best and how to motivate him or her.[46]

4. **A global mind-set is an increasingly valued task-oriented trait.** As more companies expand their international operations and hire more culturally diverse people for domestic operations in the United States, they want to enhance employees' global mind-set.[47] **A global mind-set is your belief in your ability to influence dissimilar others in a global context.** For an illustration, see the Example box. •

EXAMPLE   Multicultural Leadership

When she was in her early 20s, Ava Brown struggled to start a teaching career in the UK and soon returned to her native Jamaica, where she continued working while enrolled in a distance-learning MBA program. Now in her 30s, she is back in the UK, as a global business development manager for IHS Global in London. Of the differences between leadership styles in Jamaica and the UK, Brown says, "The thing about England is that it's very multicultural. You're dealing with people from different cultures and you've got to think about a lot of other factors when you're managing them. I find the management style here in the UK is a bit more consultative. There's more staff involvement. It's certainly very different from when I was managing people in Jamaica. . . . My advice on leadership is deal with people from different cultures as individuals. Respect

people and also understand that at the end of the day we're humans first. I think that's what counts. If you can do that then that takes care of it all."[48]

Experts agree with Brown that respect for individuals truly matters in developing a global mind-set. Building trust, empathizing, and fostering openness and team identity by making time for regular face-to-face communication all pave the way for cross-cultural understanding.[49]

YOUR CALL

What positive leadership traits and attributes do you think Ava Brown possesses? How do you think they contribute to her ability to manage people in cultures as different as Jamaica's and the United Kingdom's?

14.3 Behavioral Approaches: Do Leaders Show Distinctive Patterns of Behavior?

MAJOR QUESTION

Do effective leaders behave in similar ways?

THE BIG PICTURE

Behavioral leadership approaches try to determine unique behaviors displayed by effective leaders. These approaches can be divided into four categories, the first three of which are discussed in this section: (1) task-oriented behavior, (2) relationship-oriented behavior, (3) passive behavior, and (4) transformational behavior (discussed in Section 14.5).

Maybe what's important to know about leaders is not their *personality traits* but rather their *patterns of behavior*. This is the line of thought pursued by those interested in **behavioral leadership approaches,** which attempt to determine the unique behaviors displayed by effective leaders. These approaches can be divided into four categories:

- Task-oriented behavior.
- Relationship-oriented behavior.
- Passive behavior.
- Transformational behavior (discussed in Section 14.5).

Task-Oriented Leader Behaviors: Initiating-Structure Leadership and Transactional Leadership

The primary purpose of **task-oriented leadership behaviors** is to ensure that people, equipment, and other resources are used in an efficient way to accomplish the mission of a group or organization.[50] Examples of task-oriented behaviors are planning, clarifying, monitoring, and problem solving. However, two kinds are particularly important: (1) *initiating-structure leadership* and (2) *transactional leadership*.[51]

Men of steel. What kind of leadership behavior is appropriate for directing these kinds of workers—the kind that directs them how to complete the task or the kind that develops good worker–boss relationships? © Steve Dunwell/Getty Images

Initiating-Structure Leadership: "Here's What We Do to Get the Job Done"

Initiating-structure leadership is leader behavior that organizes and defines—that is, "initiates the structure for"—what employees should be doing to maximize output. Clearly, this is a very task-oriented approach.

Example: The Seattle-based Bill and Melinda Gates Foundation is the largest philanthropic foundation in the world, dedicated to relieving poverty and enhancing health care and educational opportunities with an annual endowment of nearly $40 billion. The organization holds regular "failure fests," at which employees, relieved of the fear of failure, are free to discuss missteps and uncover ways to learn from them. Each future initiative can then benefit from lessons learned on what to do and what not to do.[52]

Transactional Leadership: "Here's What We Do to Get the Job Done, and Here Are the Rewards"

As a manager, your power stems from your ability to provide rewards (and threaten reprimands) in exchange for your subordinates' doing the work. When you do this, you are performing **transactional leadership, focusing on clarifying employees' roles and task requirements and providing rewards and punishments contingent on performance.** As with initiating-structure leadership, transactional leadership also encompasses setting goals and monitoring progress.[53]

Example: Chicago-based ThoughtWorks, a software developer, employs 40 sales representatives. When the company was founded in 1993, CEO Craig Gorsline determined that the sales reps' roles and task requirements were to explain software pricing and policies, as well as close sales and do customer hand holding. The rewards paid to reps consisted of commissions on the revenue they generated, a common method of compensation in sales.

Recently, ThoughtWorks executives decided this transactional model had to be changed. Customers now use the Internet to compare pricing and policies. Moreover, paying sales commissions ran the risk of such negative behaviors as, according to *The New York Times,* "focusing on an individual's profit over the company's, emphasizing short-term outcomes, and encouraging competition among sales representatives."[54] The new world demanded reps who could do what was right for the customer rather than themselves. Accordingly, ThoughtWorks abolished commissions in favor of paying reps a straight salary—a move many favored because it guaranteed them a steady paycheck.

Initiating-structure leadership has a moderately strong positive relationship with leadership effectiveness, according to research.[55] Transaction leadership also has a positive association with leader effectiveness and group performance.[56]

Relationship-Oriented Leader Behavior: Consideration, Empowerment, Ethical Leadership, and Servant Leadership

Relationship-oriented leadership is primarily concerned with the leader's interactions with his or her people. The emphasis is on enhancing employees' skills and creating positive work relationships among coworkers and between the leader and the led. Such leaders often act as mentors, providing career advice, giving employees assignments that will broaden their skills, and empowering them to make their own decisions.[57]

There are four kinds of relationship-oriented behaviors:

- Consideration
- Empowering leadership
- Ethical leadership
- Servant leadership

Consideration: "The Concerns and Needs of My Employees Are Highly Important" **Consideration** is leader behavior that is concerned with group members' needs and desires and that is directed at creating mutual respect or trust. This is an important type of behavior to use in addition to task leadership because it promotes social interactions and identification with the team and leader. Considerate leader behavior has a moderately strong positive relationship with measures of leadership effectiveness.[58]

The most effective leaders use different blends of task behavior and consideration when interacting with others. To what extent do you think you do this when interacting with school or work colleagues? You can answer this question by taking Self-Assessment 14.4.

≡ connect SELF-ASSESSMENT 14.4

Assessing Your Task- and Relationship-Oriented Leader Behavior

The following survey was designed to evaluate your own leader behavior. Please be prepared to answer these questions if your instructor has assigned Self-Assessment 14.4 in Connect.

1. Do you prefer to use task or relationship leadership? Why do you think this is the case?

2. Look at the items for the two lowest scored items for initiating structure and consideration and then identify how you can increase the extent to which you display both types of leadership.

3. When would it be most important to display initiating structure and consideration? Explain your rationale.

Empowering Leadership: "I Want My Employees to Feel They Have Control over Their Work" **Empowering leadership** represents the extent to which a leader creates perceptions of psychological empowerment in others. **Psychological empowerment** is employees' belief that they have control over their work. Such psychological empowerment is expected to drive intrinsic motivation, creativity, and performance.[59] Let's see how this process works.

Increasing employee psychological empowerment requires four kinds of behaviors—leading for (1) meaningfulness, (2) self-determination, (3) competence, and (4) progress.

- **Leading for meaningfulness: inspiring and modeling desirable behaviors.** Managers lead for meaningfulness by *inspiring* their employees and *modeling* desired behaviors. Example: Employees may be helped to identify their passions at work by the leader's creating an exciting organizational vision that employees can connect with emotionally. Employees at drug maker Millennium, for example, are inspired by the company's vision to cure cancer.[60]

- **Leading for self-determination: delegating meaningful tasks.** Managers can lead for employee self-determination by *delegating* meaningful tasks to them. "Delegating is essential," says Gail Evans, an executive vice president at Atlanta-based CNN. "If you refuse to let your staff handle their own projects, you're jeopardizing their advancement—because they aren't learning new skills and adding successes to their resume."[61]

- **Leading for competence: supporting and coaching employees.** It goes without saying that employees need to have the necessary knowledge to perform their jobs. Accomplishing this goal involves managers' *supporting* and *coaching* their employees. Assigning a challenging task will help to fuel workers' intrinsic motivation and self-efficacy.[62]

- **Leading for progress: monitoring and rewarding employees.** Managers lead for progress by *monitoring* and *rewarding* others. We discussed how to do this in Chapter 12.

Ethical Leadership: "I Am Ready to Do the Right Thing"   **Ethical leadership represents normatively appropriate behavior that focuses on being a moral role model.** This includes communicating ethical values to others, rewarding ethical behavior, and treating followers with care and concern.[63]

Ethical leadership is clearly driven by personal factors related to our beliefs and values. It also has a reciprocal relationship with an organization's culture and climate. In other words, an ethical culture and climate promote ethical leadership, and ethical leadership in turn promotes an ethical culture and climate. Such leadership is positively related to employee job satisfaction, organizational commitment, organizational citizenship behavior, motivation, and task performance.[64] It also is negatively associated with job stress, counterproductive work behavior, and intentions to quit.[65] It appears that ethical leadership has many positive benefits.

EXAMPLE   An Empowering and Ethical Leader

Jeff Booth is the co-founder of a Canadian company that helps customers buy home-improvement products online. BuildDirect currently has 315 employees and over $150 million in revenue; both figures have been growing fast. The company has twice won awards based on employee engagement, a quality Booth encourages with his explicit focus on empowering his teams. Employees lead and participate in regular "fireside chats," social committees, charitable giving, and decisions about the company's future.

Booth's leadership advice is as follows:

1. **Lead by example.** "To be a successful leader," he says, "I believe your actions must align with who you are. If you believe and trust in who you are, your employees will too. Then leading becomes easy. What's more, you'll attract the people that will comfortably follow your authentic example."

2. **Stick with your message.** "Believe in your decisions, give people the time to adjust and process the change, and then help them find ways to adapt."

3. **Hear what people aren't saying.** "Active investigation" of what's going on below the surface will allow leaders to uncover and resolve the real issues.

4. **See things from employees' perspectives.** "A strong leader is empathetic. You must walk in another's shoes to truly understand her perspective. Only then can you begin to address challenges and move towards helping that person grow and achieve great things."

5. **Prioritize the success of others.** "A great leader works for his team. Empowering people means genuinely committing to their success, not your own."[66]

YOUR CALL

How are Booth's guidelines both ethical and empowering? Which of his leadership actions allow employees to feel they have control over their work, which demonstrate an ethical belief system, and how do they interconnect to make his company successful?

Servant-Leadership: "I Want to Serve My Subordinates and the Organization, Not Myself"   The term *servant-leadership,* coined by Robert Greenleaf in 1970, reflects not only his onetime background as a management researcher for AT&T but also his views as a lifelong philosopher and devout Quaker.[67] **Servant-leadership focuses on providing increased service to others—meeting the goals of both followers and the organization—rather than to oneself.**

Servant-leadership is not a quick-fix approach to leadership. Rather, it is a long-term approach to life and work. Ten characteristics of the servant leader are shown opposite. *(See Table 14.4.)* One can hardly go wrong by trying to adopt these characteristics.

1. Focus on listening

2. Ability to empathize with others' feelings

3. Focus on healing suffering

4. Self-awareness of strengths and weaknesses

5. Use of persuasion rather than positional authority to influence others

6. Broad-based conceptual thinking

7. Ability to foresee future outcomes

8. Believe they are stewards of their employees and resources

9. Commitment to the growth of people

10. Drive to build community within and outside the organization

TABLE 14.4

Ten Characteristics of the Servant Leader

Source: From L. C. Spears, "Introduction: Servant-Leadership and the Greenleaf Legacy," in L. C. Spears, ed., Reflections on Leadership: How Robert K. Greenleaf's Theory of Servant-Leadership Influenced Today's Top Management (New York: John Wiley & Sons, 1995), pp. 1–14.

Servant-Leadership: Leaders Who Work for the Led

EXAMPLE

Who are some successful servant leaders?

A Listener First. Mike DeFrino defines servant-leadership as "the ability to both serve and lead and to do so without expecting anything back." DeFrino is the CEO of Kimpton Hotels & Restaurants, and because he believes that "most of the intelligence in the organization is much closer to the ground than the corner office," around his employees he is a dedicated listener rather than a talker.[68]

An Advocate for the Public Good. Starbucks CEO Howard Schultz is not running for president, but he is not afraid to say the United States deserves a servant leader and that publicly owned companies, too, should "use our scale for good."[69] Part of his effort to promote that "good" is to provide generous employee benefits, even for part-timers, including full health care coverage, stock options, and fully paid community college degrees for all. Schultz has also promised to provide 100,000 jobs and internships for young people and to hire 10,000 military veterans.[70]

YOUR CALL

Understandably, servant-leadership is popular with employees. Can you think of situations in which this kind of leadership role would *not* be appropriate?

Employees whose manager displays the characteristics shown in Table 14.4 are likely to be happier, more productive, more creative, and more willing to go above and beyond their customary duties.[71] The following self-assessment measures the extent to which you possess a serving orientation. Results from the assessment will enhance your understanding of what it takes to really be a servant leader.

---

connect SELF-ASSESSMENT 14.5

Assessing Your Servant Orientation

The following survey is designed to assess the extent to which you possess a servant orientation. Please be prepared to answer these questions if your instructor has assigned Self-Assessment 14.5 in Connect.

1. To what extent do you possess a servant orientation? Are you surprised by the results?

2. How might you demonstrate more servant-leadership in your teams at work or school? Be specific.

Passive Leadership: The Lack of Leadership Skills

Passive leadership is a form of leadership behavior characterized by a lack of leadership skills. For example, in the type of passive leadership called the *management-by-exception* style, managers do not intervene until problems are brought to their attention or until the problems become serious enough to demand action.[72]

Another passive type is **laissez-faire leadership, a form of "leadership" characterized by a general failure to take responsibility for leading.** Not taking responsibility can hardly be considered leadership (although it often seems to be manifested by CEOs whose companies get in trouble, as when they say, "I had no idea about the criminal behavior of my subordinates"). Interestingly, laissez-faire ("*lay*-zay fair") leadership is seen more in men than women.[73]

Examples of laissez-faire leadership are seen in various kinds of failure—failing to deal with conflict, to coach employees on difficult assignments, to help set performance goals, to give performance feedback, to deal with bullying, and so on. This passive leadership has a huge negative impact on employee perceptions of leaders— outweighing their *positive* perceptions of contributions by initiating structure, transactional, and consideration forms of leadership.[74]

Passive leadership. Do you really hate to get involved in conflict, like the man looking out the window? Passive leadership like this does not lead to positive outcomes. Have you ever been managed by a passive leader? Where you happy in this situation?
© Digital Vision RF

Some Practical Implications of the Behavioral Approaches

Two key conclusions we may take away from the behavioral approaches are the following:

1. **A leader's behavior is more important than his or her traits.** It is important to train managers on the various forms of task and relationship leadership.
2. **There is no one best style of leadership.** How effective a particular leadership behavior is depends on the situation at hand. ●

14.4 Situational Approaches: Does Leadership Vary with the Situation?

MAJOR QUESTION How might effective leadership vary according to the situation at hand?

THE BIG PICTURE

Effective leadership behavior depends on the situation at hand, say believers in two contingency approaches: Fiedler's contingency leadership model and House's path–goal leadership model.

Perhaps leadership is not characterized by universally important traits or behaviors. There is no one best style that will work in all situations. This is the point of view of proponents of the **situational approach** (or *contingency approach*) to leadership, who believe that effective leadership behavior depends on the situation at hand. That is, as situations change, different styles become appropriate.

Let's consider two situational approaches: (1) the *contingency leadership model* by Fiedler and (2) the *path–goal leadership model* by House.

1. The Contingency Leadership Model: Fiedler's Approach

The oldest model of the contingency approach to leadership was developed by **Fred Fiedler** and his associates in 1951.[75] The **contingency leadership model** determines if a leader's style is (1) task-oriented or (2) relationship-oriented and if that style is effective for the situation at hand. Fiedler's work was based on 80 studies conducted over 30 years.

Contingency leadership. What type of leadership would be most effective for this employee working at a small, owner-operated grocery store? Do you think she needs more or less task leadership? Why? © Jeff Greenberg 4 of 6/Alamy

Two Leadership Orientations: Tasks versus Relationships Are you task-oriented or relationship-oriented? That is, are you more concerned with task accomplishment or with people?

To find out, you or your employees would fill out a questionnaire (known as the least preferred coworker, or LPC, scale), in which you think of the coworker you least enjoyed working with and rate him or her according to an eight-point scale of 16 pairs of opposite characteristics (such as friendly/unfriendly, tense/relaxed, efficient/inefficient). The higher the score, the more the relationship-oriented the respondent; the lower the score, the more task-oriented.

The Three Dimensions of Situational Control Once the leadership orientation is known, then you determine *situational control*—how much control and influence a leader has in the immediate work environment.

There are three dimensions of situational control: *leader-member relations, task structure,* and *position power.*

- **Leader-member relations—"Do my subordinates accept me as a leader?"** This dimension, the most important component of situational control, reflects the extent to which a leader has or doesn't have the support, loyalty, and trust of the work group.

- **Task structure—"Do my subordinates perform unambiguous, easily understood tasks?"** This dimension refers to the extent to which tasks are routine, unambiguous, and easily understood. The more structured the jobs, the more influence a leader has.
- **Position power—"Do I have power to reward and punish?"** This dimension refers to how much power a leader has to make work assignments and reward and punish. More power equals more control and influence.

For each dimension, the amount of control can be *high*—the leader's decisions will produce predictable results because he or she has the ability to influence work outcomes. Or it can be *low*—he or she doesn't have that kind of predictability or influence. By combining the three different dimensions with different high/low ratings, we have eight different leadership situations. These are represented in the diagram below. (*See Figure 14.2.*)

FIGURE 14.2 **Representation of Fiedler's contingency model**

Situational Control	High-Control Situations			Moderate-Control Situations				Low-Control Situations
Leader-member relations	Good	Good	Good	Good	Poor	Poor	Poor	Poor
Task structure	High	High	Low	Low	High	High	Low	Low
Position power	Strong	Weak	Strong	Weak	Strong	Weak	Strong	Weak
Situation	1	11	111	1V	V	V1	V11	V111
Optimal Leadership Style		Task-Motivated Leadership			Relationship-Motivated Leadership			Task-Motivated Leadership

Source: Adapted from F. E. Fiedler, "Situational Control and a Dynamic Theory of Leadership," in Managerial Control and Organizational Democracy, ed. B. King, S. Streufert, and F. E. Fiedler (New York: John Wiley & Sons, 1978), p. 114.

Which Style Is Most Effective?   Neither leadership style is effective all the time, Fiedler's research concludes, although each is right in certain situations.

- **When task-oriented style is best.** The task-oriented style works best in either *high-control* or *low-control* situations.

  Example of a *high-control* situation (leader decisions produce predictable results because he or she can influence work outcomes): Suppose you were supervising parking-control officers ticketing cars parked illegally in expired meter zones, bus zones, and the like. You have (1) high leader-member relations because your subordinates are highly supportive of you and (2) high task structure because their jobs are clearly defined. (3) You have high position control because you have complete authority to evaluate their performance and dole out punishment and rewards. Thus, a task-oriented style would be best.

  Example of a *low-control* situation (leader decisions can't produce predictable results because he or she can't really influence outcomes): Suppose you were a high school principal trying to clean up graffiti on your private-school campus, helped only by students you can find after school. You might have

(1) low leader-member relations because many people might not see the need for the goal. (2) The task structure might also be low because people might see many different ways to achieve the goal. And (3) your position power would be low because the committee is voluntary and people are free to leave. In this low-control situation, a task-oriented style would also be best.

- **When relationship-oriented style is best.** The relationship-oriented style works best in situations of *moderate control.*

  Example: Suppose you were working in a government job supervising a group of firefighters fighting wildfires. You might have (1) low leader-member relations if you are promoted over others in the group but (2) high task structure, because the job is fairly well defined. (3) You might have low position power, because the rigidity of the civil-service job prohibits you from doing much in the way of rewarding and punishing. Thus, in this moderate-control situation, relationship-oriented leadership would be most effective.

What do you do if your leadership orientation does not match the situation? Then, says Fiedler, it's better to try to move leaders into suitable situations rather than try to alter their personalities to fit the situations.[76]

2. The Path–Goal Leadership Model: House's Approach

A second situational approach, advanced by **Robert House** in the 1970s and revised by him in 1996, is the **path–goal leadership model,** which holds that the effective leader makes available to followers desirable rewards in the workplace and increases their motivation by clarifying the *paths,* or behavior, that will help them achieve those *goals* and providing them with support. A successful leader thus helps followers by tying meaningful rewards to goal accomplishment, reducing barriers, and providing support, so as to increase "the number and kinds of personal payoffs to subordinates for work-goal attainment."[77]

Numerous studies testing various predictions from House's original path–goal theory provided mixed results.[78] As a consequence, he proposed a new model, a graphical version of which is shown below. *(See Figure 14.3.)*

FIGURE 14.3

General representation of House's revised path–goal theory

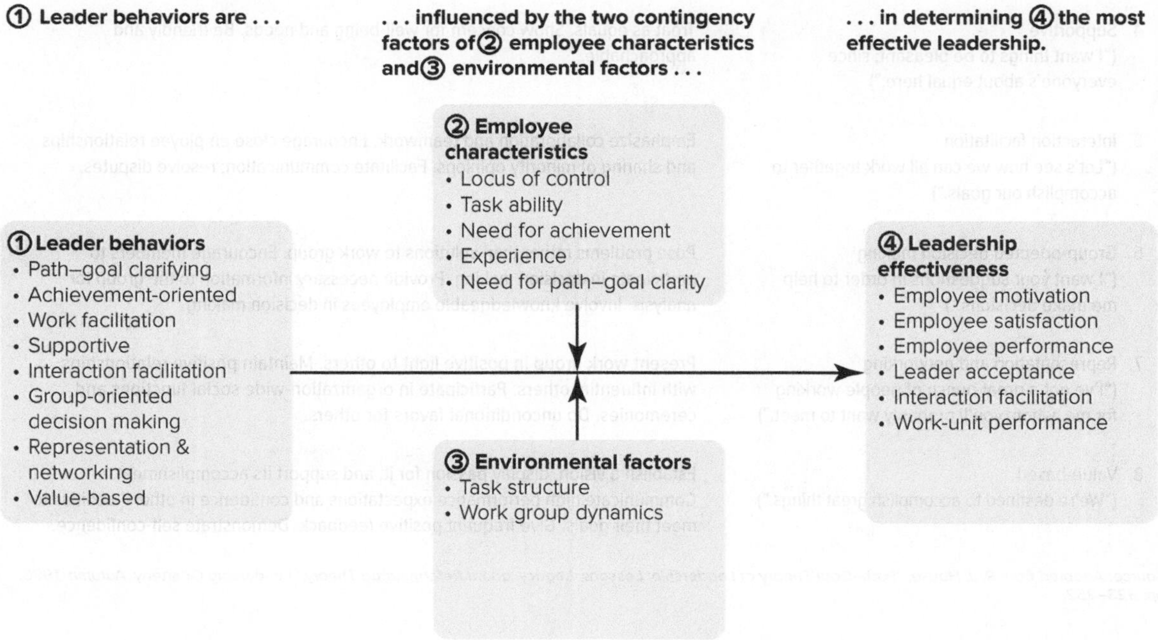

① Leader behaviors are . . .   . . . influenced by the two contingency factors of ② employee characteristics and ③ environmental factors . . .   . . . in determining ④ the most effective leadership.

① Leader behaviors
- Path–goal clarifying
- Achievement-oriented
- Work facilitation
- Supportive
- Interaction facilitation
- Group-oriented decision making
- Representation & networking
- Value-based

② Employee characteristics
- Locus of control
- Task ability
- Need for achievement
- Experience
- Need for path–goal clarity

③ Environmental factors
- Task structure
- Work group dynamics

④ Leadership effectiveness
- Employee motivation
- Employee satisfaction
- Employee performance
- Leader acceptance
- Interaction facilitation
- Work-unit performance

What Determines Leadership Effectiveness: Employee Characteristics and Environmental Factors Affect Leader Behavior   Two contingency factors, or variables—*employee characteristics* and *environmental factors*—cause some *leadership behaviors* to be more effective than others.

- **Employee characteristics.** Five employee characteristics are locus of control (described in Chapter 11), task ability, need for achievement, experience, and need for path–goal clarity.

- **Environmental factors.** Two environmental factors are task structure (independent versus interdependent tasks) and work group dynamics.

- **Leader behaviors.** Originally, House proposed that there were four leader behaviors, or leadership styles—*directive* ("Here's what's expected of you and here's how to do it"), *supportive* ("I want things to be pleasant, since everyone's about equal here"), *participative* ("I want your suggestions in order to help me make decisions"), and *achievement-oriented* ("I'm confident you can accomplish the following great things"). The revised theory expands the number of leader behaviors from four to eight. *(See Table 14.5, below.)*

TABLE 14.5   Eight Leadership Styles of the Revised Path–Goal Theory

STYLE OF LEADER BEHAVIORS	DESCRIPTION OF BEHAVIOR TOWARD EMPLOYEES
1. Path–goal clarifying ("Here's what's expected of you and here's how to do it.")	Clarify performance goals. Provide guidance on how employees can complete tasks. Clarify performance standards and expectations. Use positive and negative rewards contingent on performance.
2. Achievement-oriented ("I'm confident you can accomplish the following great things.")	Set challenging goals. Emphasize excellence. Demonstrate confidence in employee abilities.
3. Work facilitation ("Here's the goal, and here's what I can do to help you achieve it.")	Plan, schedule, organize, and coordinate work. Provide mentoring, coaching, counseling, and feedback to assist employees in developing their skills. Eliminate roadblocks. Provide resources. Empower employees to take actions and make decisions.
4. Supportive ("I want things to be pleasant, since everyone's about equal here.")	Treat as equals. Show concern for well-being and needs. Be friendly and approachable.
5. Interaction facilitation ("Let's see how we can all work together to accomplish our goals.")	Emphasize collaboration and teamwork. Encourage close employee relationships and sharing of minority opinions. Facilitate communication; resolve disputes.
6. Group-oriented decision making ("I want your suggestions in order to help me make decisions.")	Pose problems rather than solutions to work group. Encourage members to participate in decision making. Provide necessary information to the group for analysis. Involve knowledgeable employees in decision making.
7. Representation and networking ("I've got a great bunch of people working for me, whom you'll probably want to meet.")	Present work group in positive light to others. Maintain positive relationships with influential others. Participate in organization-wide social functions and ceremonies. Do unconditional favors for others.
8. Value-based ("We're destined to accomplish great things.")	Establish a vision, display passion for it, and support its accomplishment. Communicate high performance expectations and confidence in others' abilities to meet their goals. Give frequent positive feedback. Demonstrate self-confidence.

Source: Adapted from R. J. House, "Path–Goal Theory of Leadership: Lessons, Legacy, and a Reformulated Theory," Leadership Quarterly, Autumn 1996, pp. 323–352.

Co-leaders. David Byttow (left) and Chrys Bader are co-founders of San Francisco–based Secret, an app that allows people to share messages anonymously with their friends. Which of the eight path-goal leadership styles would you expect to find dominating this organization? © David Paul Morris/Bloomberg/Getty Images

Thus, for example, employees with an internal locus of control are more likely to prefer achievement-oriented leadership or group-oriented decision making (formerly participative) leadership because they believe they have control over the work environment. The same is true for employees with high task ability and experience.

Employees with an external locus of control, however, tend to view the environment as uncontrollable, so they prefer the structure provided by supportive or path–goal clarifying (formerly directive) leadership. The same is probably true of inexperienced employees.

Besides expanding the styles of leader behavior from four to eight, House's revision of his theory also puts more emphasis on the need for leaders to foster intrinsic motivation through empowerment. Finally, his revised theory stresses the concept of shared leadership, the idea that employees do not have to be supervisors or managers to engage in leader behavior but rather may share leadership among all employees of the organization.

Does the Revised Path–Goal Theory Work? There have not been enough direct tests of House's revised path–goal theory using appropriate research methods and statistical procedures to draw overall conclusions. Research on transformational leadership, however, which is discussed in Section 14.5, is supportive of the revised model.[79]

Although further research is needed on the new model, it offers three important implications for managers:[80]

- **Use more than one leadership style.** Effective leaders possess and use more than one style of leadership. Thus, you are encouraged to study the eight styles offered in path–goal theory so that you can try new leader behaviors when a situation calls for them.

- **Help employees achieve their goals.** Leaders should guide and coach employees in achieving their goals by clarifying the path and removing obstacles to accomplishing them.

- **Modify leadership style to fit employee and task characteristics.** A small set of employee characteristics (ability, experience, and need for independence) and environmental factors (task characteristics of autonomy, variety, and significance) are relevant contingency factors, and managers should modify their leadership style to fit them. ●

PRACTICAL ACTION   Applying Situational Theories

How can you make situational theories work for you? A team of researchers proposed a general strategy managers can use across a variety of situations. It has five steps.[81] We explain how to implement the steps by using the examples of a head coach of a sports team and sales manager.

- **Step 1: Identify important outcomes.** Managers must first identify the goals they want to achieve. For example, the head coach may have games to win or wish to avoid injury to key players, whereas a sales manager's goal might be to increase sales by 10 percent or reduce customers' complaints by half.

- **Step 2: Identify relevant leadership behaviors.** Next managers need to identify the specific types of behaviors that may be appropriate for the situation at hand. The list in Table 14.5 is a good starting point. A head coach in a championship game, for instance, might focus on achievement-oriented and work-facilitation behaviors. In contrast, a sales manager might find path-goal–clarifying, work-facilitation, and supportive behaviors more relevant for the sales team. Don't try to use all available leadership behaviors. Rather, select the one or two that appear most helpful.

- **Step 3: Identify situational conditions.** Fiedler and House both identify a set of potential contingency factors to consider, but there may be other practical considerations. For example, a star quarterback on a football team may be injured, which might require the team to adopt a different strategy for winning the game. Similarly, the need to manage a virtual sales team with members from around the world will affect the types of leadership most effective in this context.

- **Step 4: Match leadership to the conditions at hand.** There are too many possible situational conditions for us to provide specific advice. This means you should use your knowledge about organizational behavior to find the best match between your leadership styles and behaviors and the situation at hand. The coach whose star quarterback is injured might use supportive and values-based behaviors to instill confidence that the team can win with a different quarterback. Our sales manager also might find it useful to use the empowering leadership associated with work-facilitation behaviors and avoid directive leadership.

- **Step 5: Decide how to make the match.** Managers can use guidelines from either contingency theory or path-goal theory: change the person in the leadership role or change his or her behavior. It is not possible to change the head coach in a championship game. This means the head coach needs to change his or her style or behavior to meet the specific challenge. In contrast, the organization employing the sales manager might move him or her to another position because the individual is too directive and does not like to empower others. Or the sales manager could change his or her behavior, if possible.

14.5   The Uses of Transformational Leadership

What does it take to truly inspire people to perform beyond their normal levels?

THE BIG PICTURE

Four key behaviors of transformational leaders in affecting employees are they inspire motivation, inspire trust, encourage excellence, and stimulate them intellectually.

We have considered the major traditional approaches to understanding leadership—the trait, behavioral, and situational approaches. But newer approaches seem to offer something more by trying to determine what factors inspire and motivate people to perform beyond their normal levels.

One recent approach proposed by **Bernard Bass and Bruce Avolio,** known as **full-range leadership,** suggests that leadership behavior varies along a full range of leadership styles, from passive (*laissez-faire*) "leadership" at one extreme, through transactional leadership, to transformational leadership at the other extreme.[82] As we stated, passive leadership is not leadership, but transactional and transformational leadership behaviors are both positive aspects of being a good leader.[83] We considered transactional leadership in Section 14.3. Here let's consider transformational leadership.

Transformational Leaders

Transformational leadership transforms employees to pursue organizational goals over self-interests. Transformational leaders, in one description, "engender trust, seek to develop leadership in others, exhibit self-sacrifice, and serve as moral agents, focusing themselves and followers on objectives that transcend the more immediate needs of the work group."[84] Whereas transactional leaders try to get people to do *ordinary* things, transformational leaders encourage their people to do *exceptional* things—significantly higher levels of intrinsic motivation, trust, commitment, and loyalty—that can produce significant organizational change and results.

Transformational leaders are influenced by two factors:

- **Individual characteristics.** The personalities of such leaders tend to be more extroverted, agreeable, proactive, and open to change than nontransformational leaders. (Female leaders tend to use transformational leadership more than male leaders do.)[85]

- **Organizational culture.** Adaptive, flexible organizational cultures are more likely than are rigid, bureaucratic cultures to foster transformational leadership.

The Best Leaders Are Both Transactional and Transformational

It's important to note that transactional leadership is an essential *prerequisite* to effective leadership, and the best leaders learn to display both transactional and transformational styles of leadership to some degree. Indeed, research suggests that transformational leadership leads to superior performance when it "augments," or adds to, transactional leadership.[86]

Four Key Behaviors of Transformational Leaders

Whereas transactional leaders are dispassionate, transformational leaders excite passion, inspiring and empowering people to look beyond their own interests to the interests of the organization. They appeal to their followers' self-concepts—their values and personal identity—to create changes in their goals, values, needs, beliefs, and aspirations.

Transformational leaders have four key kinds of behavior that affect followers.[87]

1. Inspirational Motivation: "Let Me Share a Vision That Transcends Us All"

Transformational leaders have **charisma** ("kar-*riz*-muh"), a form of interpersonal attraction that inspires acceptance and support. At one time, **charismatic leadership**—which was assumed to be an individual inspirational and motivational characteristic of particular leaders, much like other trait-theory characteristics—was viewed as a category of its own, but now it is considered part of transformational leadership.[88] Someone with charisma, then, is presumed to be more able to persuade and influence people than someone without charisma.

A transformational leader inspires motivation by offering an agenda, a grand design, an ultimate goal—in short, a *vision,* "a realistic, credible, attractive future" for the organization, as leadership expert Burt Nanus calls it.[89] This form of transformational leadership is more effective when leaders communicate their visions in abstract, far-reaching, and timeless messages, and when they establish specific, challenging goals to accompany the vision.[90]

Examples: Civil rights leader Martin Luther King Jr. had a vision—a "dream," as he put it—of racial equality. Candy Lightner, founder of Mothers Against Drunk Driving, had a vision of getting rid of alcohol-related car crashes. Apple Computer's Steve Jobs had a vision of developing an "insanely great" desktop computer. To recruit John Scully, who was CEO of Pepsi at the time, Jobs asked, "Do you want to sell sugared water the rest of your life, or do you want a chance to change the world?"[91]

2. Idealized Influence: "We Are Here to Do the Right Thing"

Transformational leaders are able to inspire trust in their followers because they express their integrity by being consistent, single-minded, and persistent in pursuit of their goal. Not

Martin Luther King Jr. Civil rights leader Martin Luther King was an inspiration to millions of people. Here he is addressing people during the March on Washington at the Lincoln Memorial. This is where he gave his famous "I Have a Dream" speech. Do you think charismatic business leaders like King are able to be more successful than more conventional and conservative managers? © Agence France Presse/Central Press/Getty Images

only do they display high ethical standards and act as models of desirable values, but they are also able to make sacrifices for the good of the group.

Example: Pope Francis, current leader of the Roman Catholic Church, challenges believers of all faiths to question old assumptions and to open their minds and hearts to those who are different from them. His mission is clear, and he expresses it powerfully.[92]

3. Individualized Consideration: "You Have the Opportunity Here to Grow and Excel"

Transformational leaders don't just express concern for subordinates' well-being. They actively encourage them to grow and to excel by giving them challenging work, more responsibility, empowerment, and one-on-one mentoring.

Example: Google discovered that one of the most essential characteristics of good leaders is the ability to get out of their subordinates' way. Simply by being consistent, even predictable, in their own behavior, such managers empower their people with enormous freedom to be creative and excel.[93]

4. Intellectual Stimulation: "Let Me Describe the Great Challenges We Can Conquer Together"

These leaders are gifted at communicating the organization's strengths, weaknesses, opportunities, and threats so that subordinates develop a new sense of purpose. Employees become less apt to view problems as insurmountable or "that's not my department." Instead they learn to view them as personal challenges that they are responsible for overcoming, to question the status quo, and to seek creative solutions.

Example: John Mackey, CEO and co-founder of Whole Foods, feels the organic food industry hasn't gone far enough to address social issues like responsible use of water and energy and fair labor standards for migrant workers. So he instituted a rating system to measure such practices, believing Whole Foods should play a role in pointing out and correcting gaps. Organic farmers protested the new system, calling it expensive and burdensome, but Mackey made only a few changes to it. "I am absolutely a contrarian," he said of his decision. "You need dissonance, and you need someone who is challenging things. Otherwise you get stuck."[94]

EXAMPLE

The Superior Performance of Both a Transactional and Transformational Leader: PepsiCo's CEO, Indra Nooyi

PepsiCo's Indra Nooyi, the company's first female CEO, ranks in the top 15 of *Forbes*'s list of the 100 most powerful women in the United States.[95]

An Early Lesson in Task Performance. As a young girl growing up in India, Nooyi competed against her sister every day as their mother asked them each to imagine herself a different world leader, deliver a campaign speech, and then wait to see which had won her mother's "vote." This "incredibly formative experience" taught Nooyi that she could become anything she wanted to be.[96]

Long Term: Healthier Food. Nooyi, says Howard Schultz, CEO of Starbucks, which has a joint-venture partnership with PepsiCo, was "way ahead of her competitors in moving the company toward healthier products. She pushed for PepsiCo to buy Quaker Oats and Tropicana, and . . . PepsiCo removed trans fats from its products well before most other companies did."[97]

Short Term: Stay Profitable. However, in remaking PepsiCo over the long term so that it sells less fat and sugar, Nooyi has also run up against the other goal for a public company—short-term results, or "maximizing shareholder value." Although profits are up overall, earnings in some of the company's overseas markets are down because of continued economic instability, higher input costs, and inflation.[98]

YOUR CALL

Which of the four key transformational leader behaviors did Nooyi display? What other types of leader behavior are evident in this example?

Have you worked for a transformational leader? The following self-assessment measures the extent to which a current or former manager used transformational leadership. Taking the assessment provides a good idea about the specific behaviors you need to exhibit if you want to lead in a transformational manner.

Assessing Your Boss's Transformational Leadership

Please be prepared to answer these questions if your instructor has assigned Self-Assessment 14.6 in Connect.

1. What could your manager have done to be more transformational?

2. What three behaviors can you exhibit to increase your application of transformational leadership?

Implications of Transformational Leadership for Managers

The research shows that transformational leadership yields many positive outcomes. For example, it is positively associated with (1) measures of organizational effectiveness;[99] (2) measures of leadership effectiveness and employee job satisfaction;[100] (3) more employee identification with their leaders and with their immediate work groups;[101] (4) commitment to organizational change;[102] and (5) higher levels of intrinsic motivation, group cohesion, work engagement, setting of goals consistent with those of the leader, and proactive behavior.[103] Emloyees also are less likely to quit when their manager displays transformational leadership.[104]

Besides the fact that, as we mentioned, the best leaders are *both* transactional and transformational, there are three important implications of transformational leadership for managers, as follows.

1. It Can Improve Results for Both Individuals and Groups   You can use the four types of transformational behavior just described to improve results for individuals—such as job satisfaction, organizational commitment, and performance. You can also use them to improve outcomes for groups—an important matter in today's organization, where people tend not to work in isolation but in collaboration with others.

2. It Can Be Used to Train Employees at Any Level   Not just top managers but employees at any level can be trained to be more transactional and transformational.[105] This kind of leadership training among employees should be based on an overall corporate philosophy that constitutes the foundation of leadership development.

3. It Requires Ethical Leaders   While ethical transformational leaders enable employees to enhance their self-concepts, unethical ones select or produce obedient, dependent, and compliant followers.

To better ensure positive results from transformational leadership, top managers should follow the practices shown below. *(See Table 14.6.)* ●

TABLE 14.6

The Ethical Things Top Managers Should Do to Be Effective Transformational Leaders

• **Employ a code of ethics.** The company should create and enforce a clearly stated code of ethics.
• **Choose the right people.** Recruit, select, and promote people who display ethical behavior.
• **Make performance expectations reflect employee treatment.** Develop performance expectations around the treatment of employees; these expectations can be assessed in the performance-appraisal process.
• **Emphasize value of diversity.** Train employees to value diversity.
• **Reward high moral conduct.** Identify, reward, and publicly praise employees who exemplify high moral conduct.

Source: These recommendations were derived from J. M. Howell and B. J. Avolio, "The Ethics of Charismatic Leadership: Submission or Liberation?" The Executive, May 1992, pp. 43–54.

14.6 Three Additional Perspectives

MAJOR QUESTION | **If there are many ways to be a leader, which one would describe me best?**

THE BIG PICTURE

Two other kinds of leadership are the *leader–member exchange model,* which emphasizes that leaders have different sorts of relationships with different subordinates, and *leading with humility,* grounded in the belief that something exists that is greater than ourselves. A third perspective is the role of followers in the leadership process.

Two additional kinds of leadership deserve discussion: (1) the *leader–member exchange (LMX) model of leadership* and (2) *leading with humility.*

Leader–Member Exchange (LMX) Leadership: Having Different Relationships with Different Subordinates

Proposed by **George Graen** and **Fred Dansereau,** the **leader–member exchange (LMX) model of leadership** emphasizes that leaders have different sorts of relationships with different subordinates.[106] Unlike other models we've described, which focus on the behaviors or traits of leaders or followers, the LMX model looks at the quality of relationships between managers and subordinates. Also, unlike other models, which presuppose stable relationships between leaders and followers, the LMX model assumes each manager–subordinate relationship is unique.

In-Group Exchange versus Out-Group Exchange   The unique relationship, which supposedly results from the leader's attempt to delegate and assign work roles, can produce two types of leader–member exchange interactions.[107]

- **In-group exchange: trust and respect.** In the *in-group exchange,* the relationship between leader and follower becomes a partnership characterized by mutual trust, respect and liking, and a sense of common fates. Subordinates may receive special assignments and special privileges.

- **Out-group exchange: lack of trust and respect.** In the *out-group exchange,* leaders are characterized as overseers who fail to create a sense of mutual trust, respect, or common fate. Subordinates receive less of the manager's time and attention than those in in-group exchange relationships.

What type of exchange do you have with your manager? The quality of the relationship between you and your boss matters. Not only does it predict your job satisfaction and happiness, but it also is related to turnover. You can assess the quality of the relationship with a current or former boss by completing Self-Assessment 14.7.

≡ connect SELF-ASSESSMENT 14.7

Assessing Your Leader–Member Exchange

The following survey was designed to assess the quality of your leader–member exchange. Please be prepared to answer these questions if your instructor has assigned Self-Assessment 14.7 in Connect.

1. Where do you stand on the different dimensions underlying leader–member exchange? Are you surprised by the results?

2. Do you think the quality of your leader–member exchange is impacting your job satisfaction or performance? Explain.

3. Based on your survey scores, how might you improve the quality of your relationship with your boss? Be specific.

Is the LMX Model Useful?   Yes! Consider that a high LMX is associated with individual-level behavioral outcomes like task performance, turnover, organizational citizenship, counterproductive behavior, and attitudinal outcomes such as organizational commitment, job satisfaction, and justice.[108] Differential treatment of team members (due to LMXs of different quality) also leads to negative outcomes.[109] For example, a team of researchers found that differential treatment among members of soccer, hockey, and basketball teams led to negative team atmospheres, which in turn promoted poor perceptions of team performance.[110]

The Power of Humility

Humility is a relatively stable trait grounded in the belief that "something greater than the self exists."[111] Although some think it is a sign of weakness or low self-esteem, nothing could be further from the truth.

Lazlo Bock. Google's former senior vice president of People Operations, Lazlo Bock, is a strong believer in the power of humility. He was instrumental in getting Google to consider humility as a trait to be assessed during the recruiting process. ChrisGoodney/ Bloomberg/Getty Images

Humble leaders tend to display five key qualities valued by employees: high self-awareness, openness to feedback, appreciation of others, low self-focus, and appreciation of the greater good.[112] Lazlo Bock, Google's former senior vice president of People Operations, said humility is one of the traits he's looking for in new hires. He concluded that "it is not just humility in creating space for others to contribute, 'it's intellectual humility. Without humility, you are unable to learn."[113]

Although the scientific study of humility is relatively new, it has shown proven benefits for this trait. A Catalyst study of 1,500 workers in Australia, China, Germany, India, Mexico, and the United States revealed that employees felt included in their work teams when the boss was humble.[114] Another study conducted in China demonstrated cascading positive effects of CEO humility across two organizational levels. CEO humility positively influenced employee engagement, commitment, and performance.[115]

What can we conclude about humility in the context of managing others? First, try to be more humble by changing the focus of your accomplishment from "me" to "we." Share credit with others, but by all means be authentic. Don't try to fake humility.[116] Second, a humble style is better than an arrogant or complacent one.[117] Third, an organization's culture can promote humility. Employee-owned construction company TDIndustries does so with its agreed-upon set of cultural norms: "No rank in the room, everyone participates—no one dominates, and listen as an ally." Employees also strive to be on a first-name basis with everyone.[118]

Followers: What Do They Want, How Can They Help?

Is the quality of leadership dependent on the qualities of the followers being led? So it seems. Leaders and followers need each other, and the quality of the relationship determines how we behave as followers.[119]

What Do Followers Want in Their Leaders? Research shows that followers seek and admire leaders who create feelings of

- **Significance.** Such leaders make followers feel that what they do at work is important and meaningful.

- **Community.** These leaders create a sense of unity that encourages followers to treat others with respect and to work together in pursuit of organizational goals.

- **Excitement.** The leaders make people feel energetic and engaged at work.[120]

What Do Leaders Want in Their Followers? Followers vary, of course, in their level of compliance with a leader, with *helpers* (most compliant) showing deference to their leaders, *independents* (less compliant) distancing themselves, and *rebels* (least compliant) showing divergence.[121]

Leaders clearly benefit from having helpers (and, to some extent, independents). They want followers who are productive, reliable, honest, cooperative, proactive, and flexible. They do not want followers who are reluctant to take the lead on projects, fail to generate ideas, are unwilling to collaborate, withhold information, provide inaccurate feedback, or hide the truth.[122]

We give some suggestions on how to be a better follower—and enhance your own career prospects—in the Practical Action box below. ●

How to Be a Good Leader by Being a Good Follower | PRACTICAL ACTION

Changing business culture and the increasing power of technology have shifted the relationship between leaders and followers. Good followers today don't simply follow. They are empowered to let leaders know when things are going in the wrong direction.

Here's how you can become an intelligent follower. These same skills can make you a good leader, too.[123]

1. **Understand what motivates people.** Learn about what coworkers, customers, and bosses want, and what drives them to do their best work (or to prevent others from working well). It sounds obvious, but don't overlook the value of asking your boss how you can best communicate with each other and how often.

2. **Choose your battles.** You can't win at everything, but you can choose where to invest your time and energy. Learn how to get along with coworkers, subordinates, and bosses who are similar to you as well as with those who are different.

3. **Be brave.** Don't be afraid to tell your boss—diplomatically— when you think he or she may be wrong, and to offer

intelligent alternatives. Helpful feedback is always valuable, and remember to be supportive when things are going well.

4. **Work collaboratively.** Being a good team player, meeting your goals, and letting the team take credit when appropriate can go a long way toward bringing out the best in others, including your boss when you are in a follower role. Also keep your boss informed; no one likes being caught by surprise.

5. **Think critically.** Develop your ability to ask the right questions, raise intelligent challenges, and maintain your own competence and motivation.

YOUR CALL

Although it's always in your and the leader's best interest if you become a good follower, sometimes the two of you may differ so completely in habits, dislikes, and so on that you may simply have to look for opportunities outside your present work situation. Do you think you've been a good follower in past jobs?

Key Terms Used in This Chapter

Key Points

14.1 The Nature of Leadership: The Role of Power and Influence

- Leadership is the ability to influence employees to voluntarily pursue organizational goals. Power is the ability to marshal human, informational, and other resources to get something done.

- To understand leadership, we must understand authority and power. Authority is the right to perform or command; it comes with the manager's job. People may pursue personalized power, power directed at helping oneself, or, better, they may pursue socialized power, power directed at helping others.

- Within an organization there are typically five sources of power leaders may draw on; all managers have the first three. (1) Legitimate power is power that results from managers' formal positions within the organization. (2) Reward power is power that results from managers' authority to reward their subordinates. (3) Coercive power results from managers' authority to punish their subordinates. (4) Expert power is power resulting from one's specialized information or expertise. (5) Referent power is power deriving from one's personal attraction.

- There are nine influence tactics for trying to get others to do something you want, ranging from most used to least used tactics as follows: rational persuasion, inspirational appeals, consultation, ingratiating tactics, personal appeals, exchange tactics, coalition tactics, pressure tactics, and legitimating tactics.

- Four principal approaches or perspectives on leadership, as discussed in the rest of the chapter, are (1) trait, (2) behavioral, (3) situational, and (4) transformational.

14.2 Trait Approaches: Do Leaders Have Distinctive Traits and Personal Characteristics?

- Trait approaches to leadership attempt to identify distinctive characteristics that account for the effectiveness of leaders. We describe (1) positive task-oriented traits and positive/negative interpersonal attributes (narcissism, Machiavellianism, and psychopathy) and (2) some results of gender studies.

- Four positive task-oriented traits are (1) intelligence, (2) consciousness, (3) openness to experience, and (4) emotional stability. These traits in turn can be expanded into a list of both positive and negative interpersonal attributes often found in leaders. Among the positive attributes are extraversion, agreeableness, and communication skills. Among the negative attributes are narcissism, Machiavellianism, and psychopathy.

- Men were observed to display more task leadership and women more relationship leadership. Women used a more democratic or participative style than men, and female leadership was associated with more cohesion, cooperative learning, and participative communication among team members. Peers, managers, direct reports, and judges/trained observers rated women executives as more effective than men.

14.3 Behavioral Approaches: Do Leaders Show Distinctive Patterns of Behavior?

- Behavioral leadership approaches try to determine the unique behaviors displayed by effective leaders. Four categories are task-oriented behavior, relationship-oriented behavior, passive behavior, and transformational behavior (discussed in Section 14.5).

- Task-oriented behaviors are those that ensure that people, equipment, and other resources are used in an efficient way to accomplish the mission of a group or organization. Two types of task-oriented behaviors are (1) initiating-structure leadership, leader behavior that organizes and defines what employers should be doing to maximize output, and (2) transactional leadership, which focuses on clarifying employees' roles and task requirements and providing rewards and punishments contingent on performance.
- Relationship-oriented leadership is primarily concerned with the leader's interaction with his or her people. There are four kinds of relationship-oriented behaviors: (1) consideration, (2) empowering leadership, (3) ethical leadership, and (4) servant leadership.
- Consideration is leader behavior that is concerned with group members' needs and desires and that is directed at creating mutual respect or trust.
- Empowering leadership represents the extent to which a leader creates perceptions of psychological empowerment in others. Psychological empowerment is employees' belief that they have control over their work. Increasing employee psychological empowerment requires four kinds of behaviors—leading for (a) meaningfulness, (b) self-determination, (c) competence, and (d) progress. Leading for meaningfulness is inspiring and modeling desirable behaviors. Leading for self-determination is delegating meaningful tasks. Leading for competence is supporting and coaching employees. Leading for progress is monitoring and rewarding employees. One technique used to empower employees is participative management (PM), the process of involving employees in setting goals, making decisions, solving problems, and making changes in the organization.
- Ethical leadership represents normatively appropriate behavior that focuses on being a moral role model. This includes communicating ethical values to others, rewarding ethical behavior, and treating followers with care and concern.
- Servant-leadership focuses on providing increased service to others—meeting the goals of both followers and the organization—rather than to oneself.
- Passive leadership is a form of leadership behavior characterized by a lack of leadership skills. One type of passive leadership is laissez-faire leadership, a form of "leadership" characterized by a general failure to take responsibility for leading.
- Two conclusions that may be drawn from behavioral approaches are that (1) a leader's behavior is more important than his or her traits and (2) there is no one best style of leadership.

14.4 Situational Approaches: Does Leadership Vary with the Situation?

- Proponents of the situational approach (or contingency approach) to leadership believe that effective leadership behavior depends on the situation at hand—that as situations change, different styles become effective. Two contingency approaches are described: the Fiedler contingency leadership model and the path–goal leadership model.
- The Fiedler contingency leadership model determines if a leader's style is task-oriented or relationship-oriented and if that style is effective for the situation at hand. Once it is determined whether a leader is more oriented toward tasks or toward people, then it's necessary to determine how much control and influence a leader has in the immediate work environment.
- The three dimensions of situational control are leader-member relations, which reflect the extent to which a leader has the support of the work group; the task structure, which reflects the extent to which tasks are routine and easily understood; and position power, which reflects how much power a leader has to reward and punish and make work assignments.
- For each dimension, the leader's control may be high or low. A task-oriented style has been found to work best in either high-control or low-control situations; the relationship-oriented style is best in situations of moderate control.
- The House path–goal leadership model, in its revised form, holds that the effective leader clarifies paths through which subordinates can achieve goals and provides them with support. Two variables, employee characteristics and environmental factors, cause one or more leadership behaviors—which House expanded to eight from his original four—to be more effective than others.

14.5 The Uses of Transformational Leadership

- Full-range leadership describes leadership along a range of styles (from passive to transactional to transformational), with the most effective being transactional/transformational leaders.
- Transformational leadership transforms employees to pursue goals over self-interests. Transformational leaders are influenced by two factors: (1) Their personalities tend to be more extroverted, agreeable, and proactive. (2) Organizational cultures are more apt to be adaptive and flexible.
- The best leaders are both transactional and transformational. Four key behaviors of transformational leaders in affecting employees are they inspire motivation, inspire trust, encourage excellence, and stimulate them intellectually.
- Transformational leadership has three implications. (1) It can improve results for both individuals and groups. (2) It can be used to train employees at any level. (3) It can be used by both ethical or unethical leaders.

14.6 Three Additional Perspectives

- Two additional kinds of leadership are (1) the leader–member exchange model and (2) leading with humility, grounded in the belief that something exists that is greater than ourselves. A third perspective is the role of followers in the leadership process.

- The leader–member exchange (LMX) model of leadership emphasizes that leaders have different sorts of relationships with different subordinates.
- Humble leaders tend to display five key qualities valued by employees: high self-awareness, openness to feedback, appreciation of others, low self-focus, and appreciation of the greater good.

- Whatever their type, leaders need followers who vary in compliance from helpers to independents to rebels. Leaders want followers who are productive, reliable, honest, cooperative, proactive, and flexible. They do not want followers who are reluctant to take the lead on projects, fail to generate ideas, are unwilling to collaborate, withhold information, provide inaccurate feedback, or hide the truth.

Understanding the Chapter: What Do I Know?

1. What is the difference between being a manager and being a leader?
2. What are five sources of power?
3. In brief, what are five approaches to leadership described in this chapter?
4. What are some positive task-oriented traits and positive/negative interpersonal attributes?
5. Explain the two types of task-oriented behavior.

6. Describe the three types of relationship-oriented behaviors.
7. Briefly discuss the two types of situational leadership approaches.
8. What are key constituents of transformational leadership?
9. Explain how the leader–member exchange (LMX) model works.

Management in Action

Mary Barra's Leadership Guides General Motors through a Crisis and toward Profitability

Mary Barra became the first female CEO of General Motors (GM) in December 2013. Her predecessor, Dan Akerson, commented that "Mary was not picked because of her gender. Mary is one of the most gifted executives I've met in my career. She was picked for her talent."[124] Barra's effective leadership since that time resulted in her being promoted to chairperson of the board in 2016. The company's net income grew from $5,346 million in 2013 to $9,687 million in 2015.[125]

Barra started her career at General Motors at 18. She earned an engineering degree from the General Motors Institute and then an MBA from Stanford. She also developed a wide breadth of experience and skills by working in a variety of positions at GM: "Plant Manager, Detroit Hamtramck Assembly; Executive Vice President of Global Product Development, Purchasing and Supply Chain; Vice President of Global Manufacturing Engineering; Executive Director of Competitive Operations Engineering; and Vice President of Global Human Resources."[126]

Barra's Early Time as CEO: The Ignition Switch Crisis

GM was focusing on overcoming its 2009 bankruptcy and around $18 billion in losses when Barra became CEO. Then in February 2014 the company started a recall of 30 million cars containing defective ignition switches that had led to 275 injuries and 124 deaths. Although the causes of the defects occurred long before Barra was appointed CEO, it fell to her to deal with the aftermath.

Barra was called before four congressional hearings and had to set up a $400-million victim-compensation fund. An internal report by U.S. Attorney Anton Valukas revealed that GM "knew about the switch problem since 2001, but because of silence and blame games, led to no action to rectify the problem," according to *Fortune*. The company settled with the U.S. Justice Department for $900 million.[127]

Fortune magazine called Barra the crisis manager of the year in 2014 for her handling of this crisis. *Fortune* reporter Ben Geier stated, "Somehow, though, even as GM has seen its reputation raked over the coals, Barra has come out more admired and more likely to be emulated than ever." Geier concluded Barra created this image by "a simple combination of honesty, humbleness, and a seemingly sincere desire to fundamentally change the errors that led to the problems she faced."[128] Barra told employees at a town hall meeting, "I never want to put this behind us. . . . I want to put this painful experience permanently in our collective memories." She also "apologized publicly and profusely, visited the families of victims, and set up a compensation fund for them before any legal liability had been established."[129]

History tells us that Barra displayed two essential leader behaviors while handling this crisis. First, she was honest. She stated publicly, "The mistakes that led to the ignition-switch recall should never have happened,"[130] and "I will not rest until these problems are resolved."[131] Second, she committed to making organizational change. She fired 15 people who were deeply involved with the original cause of the problem and created the "Speaking for Safety" program, which encouraged employees to act as whistle-blowers. Barra also attempted to institute culture change.[132]

The change focused on getting leaders and employees to demonstrate four key behaviors: ownership, candidness, accountability, and improvement. Barra started by telling the top 17 people who run the company to demonstrate these behaviors. She believes change gains momentum when people observe senior leaders modeling the desired behaviors. For example, she plans to model accountability by being more impatient when others do not hit their goals and plans. She feels this is needed because she was too "nice" in the past.[133] She modeled improvement by establishing a global product development organization responsible for ensuring that technical issues are handled quickly. Barra noted, "This new way of developing vehicles will provide the highest levels of safety, quality, and customer service."[134]

Barra Displays a Variety of Leader Behaviors

Barra is described as humble, collaborative, and inclusive. She prefers an environment in which employees feel safe to voice their opinions. An *Industry Week* reporter noted that "once she receives diverse input she gauges the efficacy of all ideas and provides feedback. Co-workers and mentors have praised Barra's listening skills and her approachability."[135]

Barra likes giving others credit rather than stealing the limelight, and she is passionate about cars. She actively seeks feedback from the board of directors and her team. Although she is inclusive, people note that she is not afraid to make hard decisions. Barra told a reporter from the *Los Angeles Times,* "At the end of the day, the decision has to be made. If we don't have complete unanimity, I have no qualms about making it. I want tension in a constructive way to make sure we evaluate things from every angle."[136]

Barra is organized and task-oriented. For example, "GM's product development process was in disarray when Barra took over as product chief in 2011. There were 30 different platforms, and inefficiency and poor quality ran rampant. Barra immediately set to work, rationalizing the product line, improving quality and efficiency, and better aligning the product with customer needs."[137]

Barra told an audience at the Catalyst Awards that one of her main leadership objectives is to create a happy and productive workforce. She is trying to do this by modeling work–life balance. "General Motors—or any company—will take from you 24/7 and not feel bad," Barra said. "It's a company. There's always something new. There's always a priority." Barra and her leadership team strive to respect employees' activities and responsibilities outside work. Her feeling is "We need to find the opportunity not to do everything, but to do the important things."[138]

One Piece of Advice

Barra was asked to provide one piece of leadership advice at a conference. She said, "Do something you're passionate about, do something you love. Life's too short."[139]

FOR DISCUSSION

1. What sources of power and influence tactics were displayed by Mary Barra? Provide examples.

2. Use Table 14.1 to evaluate the extent to which Barra displays the key positive and negative attributes found in leaders. Explain your rationale.

3. Which task- and relationship-oriented behaviors were exhibited by Barra? Cite examples.

4. Which of the four types of transformational leadership behavior were displayed by Barra? Provide examples.

5. Did Barra demonstrate any of the five qualities associated with humble leadership? Explain.

6. What did you learn about leadership from this case?

Jail or a Settlement: Which Is More Appropriate for the Leaders of an Alleged Charity Scam?

This challenge seeks your view of the consequences the courts or federal agencies should level against leaders who orchestrated an alleged charity scam. It all began when James T. Reynolds Sr. started the Cancer Fund of America in 1987.

Reynolds expanded the organization into four separate groups—the other three were Cancer Support Services, Children's Cancer Fund of America, and the Breast Cancer Society. These organizations were run by Reynolds, members of his family, and people from his church congregation in Knoxville, Tennessee.

The charities raised about $200 million, and a federal lawsuit alleges they scammed consumers of some portion of $187 million.[140]

The New York Times reported the charities' claim of spending "100 percent of proceeds on services like hospice care, transporting patients to and from chemotherapy sessions and buying pain medications for children." The lawsuit states, "These were lies," and that the charities spent about only 3% on cancer patients.

Where did the money go? NBC News noted that "85 percent of the more than $187 million the four groups raised went to professional fundraisers. Operators used much of the remaining donations to cover their salaries and personal expenses, including trips to Disney World, concert tickets and date site memberships."[141] The *Times* reported that other expenditures included meals at Hooters, products from Victoria's Secret, jet ski joy rides, and cruises to the Caribbean.[142]

The Federal Trade Commission, along with attorneys general in all 50 states, filed a lawsuit against the four charities, claiming they had violated federal and state laws. To date, Children's Cancer Fund of America and the Breast Cancer Society have arrived at a settlement and have been dissolved. Three of the organization's top executives—Rose Perkins, James Reynolds II, and Kyle Effler—settled charges against them. "They will be banned from fundraising, charity management and oversight of charitable assets. Judgments against the groups and their executives total $137 million" and will be redistributed to cancer patients.[143] The FTC doubts that the full amount of fraudulently spent funds is collectible, because defendants' bank accounts have insufficient money to cover it.

A lawsuit is continuing against James Reynolds Sr. and Cancer Funds of America Inc. and Cancer Support Services Inc.

Rather than admitting any wrongdoing, James T. Reynolds II sent a letter to supporters stating that neither the organization nor any of its officers and directors were found guilty of any allegations. He goes on to say that "it does not help those who we seek to serve, and those who remain in need, for us to engage in a highly publicized, expensive and distracting legal battle around our fundraising practices."[144]

SOLVING THE CHALLENGE

Do you think James T. Reynolds II and his friends got off easy? What is your feeling about James Reynolds Sr.?

1. I don't think the three executives who settled with the government are being punished to the full extent. They won't be able to pay back the fraud because they spent the money, and they are not going to jail. I think these people need to go to jail.

2. The settlements are a done deal. However, James Reynolds Sr. is the senior leader of this alleged fraud and he needs to go jail.

3. In general, I am fine with making settlements like this. It could be that the government has a weak case and a settlement is better than nothing.

4. Invent another option.

15

Interpersonal and Organizational Communication

Mastering the Exchange of Information

Major Questions You Should Be Able to Answer

15.1 The Communication Process: What It Is, How It Works

Major Question: What do I need to know about the communication process to be an effective communicator?

15.2 How Managers Fit into the Communication Process

Major Question: How can I use the different channels and patterns of communication to my advantage?

15.3 Barriers to Communication

Major Question: What are the important barriers I need to be aware of, so I can improve my communication skills?

15.4 Social Media and Management

Major Question: How do contemporary managers use social media to communicate more effectively?

15.5 Improving Communication Effectiveness

Major Question: How can I be a better listener, writer, and speaker?

Communication Counts in Landing a Job

As a job seeker, you are responsible for proving you're the best candidate for the job. Here are some tips for communicating that message effectively.

- *Be an active participant.* Don't wait to be asked questions. You can use small talk to get things started, but be brief. You can also use your key selling points to guide the conversation, and even state them upfront, saying, "I'd like to cover A, B, and C."
- *Pick your selling points.* Focus on only your top two or three selling points. If you have little work experience, focus on personal qualities. If you have experience, highlight significant achievements.
- *Substantiate.* Provide evidence (such as stories or data) to illustrate your selling points. Use action words to describe your achievements, like "created" and "organized."
- *Describe what's in it for them.* Explain why you're a good match for the job and what you can contribute to the company or the team.
- *Be sure you've done your homework.* Thoroughly research the company and people so you can ask intelligent and interested questions about its current and future goals.
- *Anticipate challenging questions.* Expect to be asked what your weaknesses are. The best way to answer is to briefly describe a challenge, the way you overcame it, and how it helped you grow.

Remember that the *way* you communicate your strengths in a job interview can be just as important as the things you say.

- *Smile.* It's one of the easiest ways to win people over.
- *Express your interest physically and behaviorally.* Sit erect in your chair and lean forward at times to convey interest. State your willingness to tackle all parts of the job; don't assume that will be taken for granted just because you applied for the job.
- *Slow down.* Making an effort to adopt a normal speed when you speak will both calm you down and make you seem more relaxed.
- *Make eye contact.* Don't stare into the other person's eyes, but don't avoid them, either. In a group interview, make eye contact with all participants.
- *Close with a handshake.* End the interview with a "thank you" and a firm handshake.
- *Follow up.* At the end of the interview, ask when the interviewer would like you to follow up. Then drop him or her a note of thanks.[1]

For Discussion How good are you at preparing for and rehearsing for a job interview? How good are you at listening? How do you think you appear to other people in an important interaction?

FORECAST What's Ahead in This Chapter

This chapter describes the process of transferring information and understanding from one person to another. It also describes several communication barriers—physical, personal, cross-cultural, nonverbal, and gender differences. It shows how you can use different channels and patterns of communication, both formal and informal, to your advantage. It discusses how star managers use information technology to communicate more effectively. Finally, we talk about how to be a better listener, writer, and speaker.

15.1 The Communication Process: What It Is, How It Works

What do I need to know about the communication process to be an effective communicator?

THE BIG PICTURE

Communication is the transfer of information and understanding from one person to another. The process involves sender, message, and receiver; encoding and decoding; the medium; feedback; and "noise," or interference. Managers need to tailor their communication to the appropriate medium (rich or lean) for the appropriate situation.

Everything's clicking. Today some people can work almost anywhere, even more so as laptops, tablets, and cell phones have become such versatile instruments, permitting Internet and e-mail access, text messaging, and access to huge databases. Do you think our ability to work outside traditional offices because of today's technology will negatively affect the communication process and employee camaraderie? © Erik Isakson/Tetra Images/Alamy RF

How good a communicator do you think you are? A survey of 400 U.S. employers and 613 college students revealed that more than 80% of employers and 75% of students believe oral and written communication skills are important for workplace success. However, while more than 60% of students reported they were skilled in oral and written communication, only 27% of employers endorsed this conclusion.[2]

Communication Defined: The Transfer of Information and Understanding

Researchers have begun to examine communication as a form of social information processing, in which receivers interpret messages by cognitively processing them. This work has led to development of a perceptual model of communication that depicts it as a process in which receivers create meaning in their own minds.[3]

Communication—the transfer of information and understanding from one person to another—is an activity that you as a manager will have to do a lot of. The fact that managers do a lot of communicating doesn't mean they're necessarily good at it—that is, that they are efficient or effective. You are an *efficient communicator* when you can transmit your message accurately in the least time. You are an *effective communicator* when your intended message is accurately understood by the other person. Thus, you may well be efficient in sending a group of people a reprimand by e-mail. But it may not be effective if it makes them angry so that they can't absorb its meaning.

How the Communication Process Works

Communication has been said to be a process consisting of "a sender transmitting a message through media to a receiver who responds."[4] A diagram of this communication process is shown on next page. *(See Figure 15.1.)* Let's take a look at its different parts.

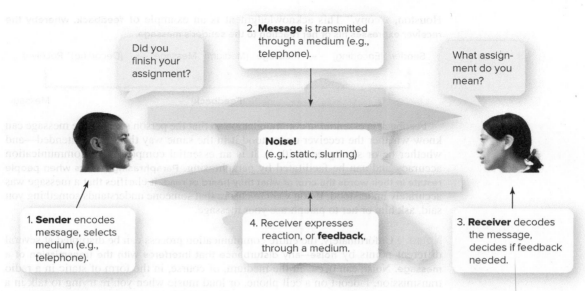

FIGURE 15.1 **The communication process**

"Noise" is not just noise or loud background sounds but any disturbance that interferes with transmission—static, fadeout, distracting facial expressions, an uncomfortable meeting site, competing voices, and so on.

(left): © Fuse/Getty Images RF; (right): © Image Source/Getty Images RF

Sender, Message, and Receiver **The sender is the person wanting to share information—called a message—and the receiver is the person for whom the message is intended,** as follows.

Sender → Message → Receiver

Encoding and Decoding Of course, the process isn't as simple as just sender/message/receiver. If you were an old-fashioned telegraph operator using Morse code to send a message over a telegraph line, you would first have to encode the message, and the receiver would have to decode it. But the same is true when you are sending the message by voice to another person in the same room and have to decide what language to speak in and what terms to use, and when you are texting a friend and can choose your words, your abbreviations and even an emoji or two.

Encoding is translating a message into understandable symbols or language. Decoding is interpreting and trying to make sense of the message. Thus, the communication process is now

Sender **[Encoding]** → Message → **[Decoding]** Receiver

The Medium The means by which you as a communicator send a message is important, whether it is typing a text or an e-mail, hand-scrawling a note, or communicating by voice in person or by phone or videoconference. This means is the **medium, the pathway by which a message travels:**

Sender [Encoding] → Message **[Medium]** Message → [Decoding] Receiver

Feedback "Flight 123, do you copy?" In the movies, that's what you hear the flight controller say when radioing the pilot of a troubled aircraft to see whether he or she received ("copied") the previous message. And the pilot may radio back, "Roger,

Houston, I copy." This acknowledgment is an example of **feedback, whereby the receiver expresses his or her reaction to the sender's message.**

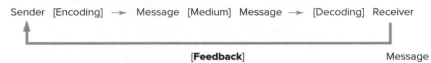

Sender [Encoding] → Message [Medium] Message → [Decoding] Receiver

[**Feedback**]   Message

Feedback is essential in communication so that the person sending the message can know whether the receiver understood it in the same way the sender intended—and whether he or she agrees with it. It is an essential component of communication accuracy and can be facilitated by paraphrasing. **Paraphrasing occurs when people restate in their words the crux of what they heard or read.** It clarifies that a message was accurately understood. If you want to ensure that someone understands something you said, ask him or her to paraphrase your message.

Noise   Unfortunately, the entire communication process can be disrupted at several different points by **noise—any disturbance that interferes with the transmission of a message.** Noise can occur in the medium, of course, in the form of static in a radio transmission, fadeout on a cell phone, or loud music when you're trying to talk in a restaurant. Or it can occur in the encoding or decoding, as when people from different cultures stumble over each other's languages. One of your authors—Angelo Kinicki—was consulting in Asia and found, for instance, that his suggestion that Asian managers "touch base" with their colleagues drew blank looks. We discuss cross-cultural barriers to communication later in the chapter.

Even within the same culture, we can encounter semantic problems (problems that revolve around the meaning of words). When a supervisor tells you, "We need to get this done right away," what does it mean? Does "We" mean just you? You and your coworkers? Or you, your coworkers, and the boss? Does "right away" mean today, tomorrow, or next week?

Another language barrier is jargon. **Jargon is terminology specific to a particular profession or group.** (Example: "The HR VP wants the RFP to go out ASAP." Translation: "The vice president of human resources wants the request for proposal to go out as soon as possible.") *Buzzwords* are designed to impress rather than inform. (Example: "Could our teams interface on the ad campaign that went viral, and then circle back with the boss?")[5] Noise also occurs in *nonverbal communication* (discussed later in this chapter), when our physical movements and our words send different messages.

EXAMPLE   **Secrecy and Silence**

The recent revelation that about 11 million Jettas, Beetles, Golfs, and other Volkswagen cars were equipped at the factory with the means to cheat a federal emissions test has dragged down the high-flying company's fortunes. CEO Martin Winterkorn resigned, and Mattias Mueller has taken his place. Mueller blames the company's insular character and what some have called a "culture of silence" for preventing employees at many levels from speaking out about a clear violation of the law that went on for about 10 years.

Volkswagen is conducting its own internal investigation of the cheating scandal, but it seems clear that several high-ranking executives knew employees had decided to install the emissions software, to cover up the fact that they could not

meet standards set by the Environmental Protection Agency. Prosecutors in Germany, where the company is headquartered, say Winterkorn received a memo about "irregularities" in the cars' emissions at least a year before a U.S. nonprofit group discovered what was going on. Whether he read it has not been made clear.[6]

Secrecy was an operational mandate at Theranos, Inc., a biomedical testing company founded by CEO Elizabeth Holmes. Different departments had separate key cards for entry, and the company's chemists and engineers were discouraged from discussing their work, even with one another. The resulting "silo" effect prevented staff from collaborating to solve problems with the company's blood-testing products,

Martin Winterkorn. Dr. Martin Winterkorn resigned as Volkswagen's CEO in September 2015 after the Environmental Protection Agency began investigating emission test issues. © Bernhard Classen/Alamy

Elizabeth Holmes. Elizabeth Holmes, CEO of Theranos, speaking to Fortune's Most Powerful Women Conference. The company received sanctions from the Centers for Medicare & Medicaid Services, leading the company to close its laboratory operations. The company is now focusing on selling miniature medical testing machines. © Krista Kennell/Shutterstock RF

which failed to live up to Holmes's public claims that they would be innovative.

As multiple investigations into the company began, Holmes continued to deny problems with Theranos products, keeping up the positive spin that had earned the company early praise. She falsely claimed that a 2015 product recall ordered by the FDA was voluntary and even gave allegedly inaccurate presentations to employees, failing to say that many Theranos products were only in the research stage. Employees didn't learn the extent of the company's troubles until investigators' reports were released to the press. Their confidence in Holmes waned, and the government's Centers for Medicare and Medicaid Research recently shut the company's flagship laboratory and banned Holmes from owning or running a lab for two years. Federal and SEC investigations and civil suits are ongoing.[7]

YOUR CALL

In terms of the communications process modeled in Figure 15.1, do you think a "culture of silence" can constitute a form of noise? What about the "silo" effect? At what other point or points in the communication model do you think silence and secrecy can interfere with communication? Where do they seem to have operated at Volkswagen and Theranos?

Selecting the Right Medium for Effective Communication

All kinds of communications tools are available to managers, ranging from one-to-one face-to-face conversation all the way to use of the mass media. However, managers need to know how to use the right tool for the right condition—when to use e-mail or when to meet face-to-face, for example. Should you congratulate a team for exceeding its goals by addressing the group in person, sending an e-mail, posting an announcement near the office coffee machine—or all three? What medium would you select for delivering a reprimand?

All media have their own advantages and disadvantages, and there are a few different criteria to consider when choosing the right medium.[8] For instance, texts and tweets require the writer to be brief and precise, and like e-mails (which should also be brief), they provide a record of the communication that in-person and phone communication don't. They can also be sent almost without regard to time-zone differences. But unlike voice, video call, and in-person messages, written communications often fail to convey nuances of meaning through tone of voice and body language, and thus they can more easily be misinterpreted. Many a manager has discovered that a simple phone call can cut through layers of misinterpreted e-mails.

We can generally categorize differences between communication media in terms of whether a given medium is *rich* or *lean*. What does this mean?

Is a Medium Rich or Lean in Information?

Media richness indicates how well a particular medium conveys information and promotes learning. That is, the "richer" a medium is, the better it is at conveying information.[9] The term *media richness* was proposed by respected organizational theorists Richard Daft and Robert Lengel as part of their contingency model for media selection.[10]

Types of media can be positioned along a continuum ranging from high to low media richness, as follows:

High media richness
(Best for nonroutine, ambiguous situations)

Low media richness
(Best for routine, clear situations)

| Face-to-face presence | Video-conferencing | Telephone | Personal written media (e-mail, text messages, memos, letters) | Impersonal written media (newsletters, fliers, general reports) |

Face-to-face communication, also the most personal form of communication, is the richest. It allows the receiver of the message to observe multiple cues, such as body language and tone of voice. It allows the sender to get immediate feedback, to see how well the receiver comprehended the message. At the other end of the media richness scale, impersonal written media are just the reverse—only one cue and no feedback—making them low in richness.

As you might expect, people have preferences for the type of medium they like to use. For example, males and people with extroverted and agreeable personality characteristics tend to use media high in richness. Contrary to stereotypes, age has no impact on media richness preference.[11] What are your preferences?

Matching the Appropriate Medium to the Appropriate Situation

In general, use the following guidelines.[12]

Rich Medium: Best for Nonroutine Situations and to Avoid Oversimplification A *rich* medium is more effective with nonroutine situations. Examples: In what way would you like your boss to inform you of a nonroutine change, like the introduction of a new employee benefit you can take advantage of? Via a memo tacked on the bulletin board (a lean medium)? Or via a face-to-face meeting or phone call (a rich medium)?

The danger of using a rich medium for routine matters (such as monthly sales reports) is that it results in information *overloading*—the delivery of more information than necessary.

Lean Medium: Best for Routine Situations and to Avoid Overloading A *lean* medium is more effective in routine situations. Examples: In what manner would you as a sales manager like to get routine monthly sales reports from your 50 sales reps? Via time-consuming phone calls (a somewhat rich medium)? Or via e-mails or text messages (a somewhat lean medium)? The danger of using a lean medium for nonroutine matters (such as an announcement of a company reorganization) is that it results in information *oversimplification*—it doesn't provide enough of the information the receiver needs and wants.

E-mail and Facebook and Twitter messages (social media, discussed in Section 15.4) vary in media richness, being leaner if they impersonally blanket a large audience and richer if they mix personal textual and video information that prompts quick conversational feedback.[13] ●

15.2 How Managers Fit into the Communication Process

How can I use the different channels and patterns of communication to my advantage?

THE BIG PICTURE

Formal communication channels follow the chain of command, which is of three types—vertical, horizontal, and external. Informal communication channels develop outside the organization's formal structure. One type is the grapevine. Another, face-to-face communication, builds trust and depends heavily on managers' effective listening skills.

If you've ever had a low-level job in nearly any kind of organization, you know that there is generally a hierarchy of management between you and the organization's president, director, or CEO. If you had a suggestion that you wanted him or her to hear, you doubtless had to go up through management channels. That's formal communication. However, you may have run into that top manager in the elevator. Or in the restroom. Or in a line at the bank. You could have voiced your suggestion casually then. That's informal communication.

Formal Communication Channels: Up, Down, Sideways, and Outward

Formal communication channels follow the chain of command and are recognized as official. The organization chart we described in Chapter 8 indicates how official communications—memos, letters, reports, announcements—are supposed to be routed.

Formal communication is of three types: (1) *vertical*—meaning upward and downward, (2) *horizontal*—meaning laterally (sideways), and (3) *external*—meaning outside the organization.

1. Vertical Communication: Up and Down the Chain of Command Vertical communication is the flow of messages up and down the hierarchy within the organization: bosses communicating with subordinates, subordinates communicating with bosses. As you might expect, the more management levels through which a message passes, the more it is prone to some distortion.

Upward bound. How do you communicate with a manager two or three levels above you in the organization's hierarchy? You can send a memo through channels. Or you can watch for informal opportunities like this when a manager heads for a cup of coffee.
© Jacobs Stock Photography/Getty Images RF

- **Downward communication—from top to bottom. Downward communication flows from a higher level to a lower level (or levels).** In small organizations, top-down communication may be delivered face-to-face. In larger organizations, it's delivered via meetings, e-mail, official memos, and company publications.
- **Upward communication—from bottom to top. Upward communication flows from a lower level to a higher level(s).** Often this type of communication is from a subordinate to his or her immediate manager, who in turn will relay it up to the next level, if necessary. Effective upward communication depends on an atmosphere of trust. No subordinate is going to want to be the bearer of bad news to a manager who is always negative and bad-tempered.

Types of downward and upward communication are shown below. *(See Table 15.1.)*

TABLE 15.1   **Types of Downward and Upward Communication**

Downward Communication

Most downward communication involves one of the following kinds of information:

- Instructions related to particular job tasks. Example (supervisor to subordinate): "The store will close Monday for inventory. All employees are expected to participate."
- Explanations about the relationship between two or more tasks. Example: "While taking inventory, employees need to see what things are missing. Most of that might be attributable to shoplifting."
- Explanations of the organization's policies, practices, and procedures. Example: "The human resources department sends an e-mail blast about new benefits or procedures for taking vacations."
- A manager's feedback about a subordinate's performance. Example: "You missed the project deadline by two days. What caused you to be late?"
- Attempts to encourage a sense of mission and dedication to the organization's goals. Example: "Manager calls team meeting to discuss how the team is contributing to company's strategic goals."

Upward Communication

Most upward communication involves the following kinds of information:

- Reports of progress on current projects. Example: "We are three hours behind in taking inventory. What can we do to catch up?"
- Reports of unsolved problems requiring help from people higher up. Example: "We can't make our merchandise count jibe with the stock reports."
- New developments affecting the work unit. Example: "Two employees want to take vacation the same week. How would you like to handle this?"
- Suggestions for improvements. Example: "I don't have the software needed to create the customer survey."
- Reports on employee attitudes and efficiency. Example: "Our customer satisfaction scores have gone down over the last year. Let's schedule a department meeting to create a plan of action."

Sources: Adapted from D. Katz and R. Kahn, The Social Psychology of Organizations *(New York: Wiley, 1966); and E. Planty and W. Machaver, "Upward Communications: A Project in Executive Development,"* Personnel *Vol. 28 (1952), pp. 304–318.*

2. Horizontal Communication: Within and between Work Units   Horizontal communication flows within and between work units; its main purpose is coordination. As a manager, you will spend perhaps as much as a third of your time in this form of communication—consulting with colleagues and coworkers at the same level as you within the organization. In this kind of sideways communication, you will be sharing information, coordinating tasks, solving problems, resolving conflicts, and getting the support of your peers. Horizontal communication is encouraged through the use of meetings, committees, task forces, and matrix structures.

Horizontal communication can be impeded in three ways: (1) by specialization that makes people focus on only their jobs; (2) by rivalry between workers or work units, which prevents sharing of information; and (3) by lack of encouragement from management.

3. External Communication: Outside the Organization **External communication** flows between people inside and outside the organization. This form of communication is increasingly important because organizations desire to communicate with other stakeholders—customers, suppliers, shareholders, or other owners—in pursuit of their strategic goals. Small business owners particularly rely on external communication to help grow their businesses. A recent study, for example, revealed that small business owners tended to seek input or counsel from two sources: peers in the same community or online from a peer they had never met.[14]

Informal Communication Channels

Informal communication channels develop outside the formal structure and do not follow the chain of command—they are more spontaneous, can skip management levels, and can cut across lines of authority.

Two types of informal channels are (1) the *grapevine* and (2) *face-to-face communication.*

The Grapevine **The grapevine is the unofficial communication system of the informal organization,** a network of in-person and online gossip and rumor. It is never silent and is not always accurate. But research shows that the grapevine delivers as much as 70% of all organizational communication, although only a little more than half of executives understand that the rumor mill is more active when official communication is lacking. In a recent series of interviews with 1,100 employees in a range of industries, almost half said that when official and unofficial communications conflict, they are more likely to believe the grapevine. Written or online company communications, such as e-mails and newsletters, edged out the grapevine, but only slightly; 51% of those interviewed said they trusted a newsletter more than rumor.[15]

As public speaker and communications coach Carol Kinsey Goman says, "Social media has put the grapevine on steroids. You can't outrun [the] rumor mill and you can't kill it. The challenge is to understand how the grapevine works within your organization—and how you can most effectively influence it."[16]

Face-to-Face Communication Despite the entrenched use of quick and efficient electronic communication in our lives, face-to-face conversation is still justifiably a major part of most people's work day. Employees value authentic human contact with the boss and welcome the implication that their manager cares about them. Face time builds relationships and trust, shows respect for employees as individuals, and thus is highly motivating. Netflix CEO Reed Hastings doesn't have an office at all. "I just had no need for it," he says. "It is better for me to be meeting people all around the building."[17] And as one writer noted, while Millennials may spend a lot of time texting, a major reason is that they're making plans to get together in person.[18]

Some basic principles apply to making the most of face-to-face communication in the work environment.[19]

1. **Make time for face-to-face.** Rather than hoping to catch people at random, schedule time with individual employees, and make sure you'll both be free of distractions (including cell phones) for the few minutes your interaction will take. This is not the moment to multi-task.

2. **Listen more and talk less.** Listen not just to the words the other person is saying but also to the emotional content behind the words. Make eye contact and observe body language. This will help you be empathetic, a topic discussed in the last section of this chapter. When it's your turn to speak, be brief. If your message is specific or factual, prepare your facts and outline your thoughts ahead of time. Expect questions and be prepared with answers.

3. **Deliver good news up front; lead in to bad.** Happy tidings don't require a long build-up. Bad news and controversial decisions, however, may go over better if you build up to them by explaining the situation, identifying factors

A town hall meeting. U.S. President Barack Obama (left) and Facebook CEO Mark Zuckerberg (right) talk to Facebook employees at a town hall meeting at corporate headquarters in Palo Alto, California. Why would a president of the U.S. want to participate in such events? © Justin Sullivan/Getty Images

you can't control, and giving the other side of the argument its due.

4. **Hold employee town hall meetings.** For in-person meetings with groups of employees, "town hall" meetings, often held monthly or quarterly, usually consist of a presentation by managers and an open question-and-answer session. Be available for informal conversations with individuals afterwards. Town hall meetings are a great way for politicians to communicate with their constituents.[20]

5. **Use webcasts when you can't be there.** You can still achieve face time even if your employees work remotely. Use webcasts, video conferencing, or a social video portal to keep communications direct and personal. If possible, try to make sure everyone has the same communication experience. That is, try to avoid having meetings that mix in-person and remote attendees. ●

PRACTICAL ACTION   How to Streamline Meetings

Managers spend a great deal of time in meetings—too much time, according to most. In fact, mid-level managers average more than 20 meetings a week,[21] and workers reportedly judge nearly 50% of their meetings to be a waste of time.[22] Productive meetings are short, held in convenient locations away from distraction, and attended by only the people who will be most directly affected by decisions made or who can contribute most usefully to problem solutions. Here are some other ways to make sure the meetings you run or attend, whether virtually or in person, are as brief and effective as possible.[23]

What to Do as a Meeting Leader

1. **Set a clear goal and communicate it beforehand.** Before you call a meeting, ask yourself what specific task or tasks you want the meeting to accomplish. Write these down in the form of an agenda with time limits for each point, leaving brief time slots for attendees' input and discussion. At least a day beforehand, share the agenda with everyone invited to attend.

2. **Start and end on time.** Respect other people's time commitments. Be the first in the meeting room and start when you said you would. Stick to the time limits you've allowed for each agenda item, and keep your eye on the clock. Learn how to gently but firmly cut off unproductive discussion. ("Thanks for your contribution, Jay. Let's quickly hear from one more person before we move on to the next point.")

3. **Consider frequent, short meetings rather than infrequent, long ones.** People focus better during meetings of an hour or less and feel more energized afterwards to accomplish the goals they've been assigned. They also

find it easier to make time for short meetings than to give up an entire morning or afternoon.

4. **Follow up.** Within 24 hours of the meeting, clarify results and expectations by sending attendees a summary of decisions made, tasks to be performed, and who is to perform them and when.

What to Do as a Meeting Participant

1. **Prepare.** Respond promptly to the meeting invitation. Read the agenda (ask for one if you don't receive it ahead of time), and be prepared with any facts or data you may be called upon to present. Turn off your cell phone or leave it behind.

2. **Be on time.** Showing up late is disrespectful and disruptive. It can also make the meeting run over time if the leader decides to wait for you.

3. **Participate intelligently.** Expect to contribute to the meeting, but make sure your contributions are brief, professional, and on point. Don't start distracting side conversations with other participants; support the leader by focusing your attention on him or her so the meeting can end on time.

4. **Follow up.** If you came away from the meeting with a to-do list, be sure you act on it in a timely way so the goals of the meeting can be achieved. You may even be able to avoid having to attend another meeting to go over the same agenda all over again.

YOUR CALL

What can you add to these suggestions to make meetings run better? For more about running meetings, go to EffectiveMeetings.com (**www.effectivemeetings.com**).

15.3 Barriers to Communication

MAJOR QUESTION   **What are the important barriers I need to be aware of, so I can improve my communication skills?**

THE BIG PICTURE

We describe several barriers to communication. Physical barriers include sound, time, and space. Personal barriers include variations in communication skills, processing and interpreting information, trustworthiness and credibility, ego strength, listening skills, judging others, and generational considerations. Cross-cultural barriers are a greater challenge as more jobs include interactions with others around the globe. Nonverbal communication can present a barrier if it conflicts with the spoken message. Finally, gender differences can present barriers but can be overcome.

If you have ever been served the wrong drink because the server couldn't hear you in a noisy bar, clicked on a broken web link, missed your boarding call because the airport's public address system was full of static, or taken offense at a text you later found you misinterpreted, you've experienced a barrier to communication. Some barriers occur within the communication process itself, as shown below. (*See Table 15.2.*) We'll look at several types—physical, personal, cross-cultural, nonverbal, and gender differences.

TABLE 15.2   Some Barriers That Happen within the Communication Process

All it takes is one blocked step in the communication process for communication to fail. Consider the following.

- **Sender barrier—no message gets sent.** Example: If a manager has an idea but is afraid to voice it because he or she fears criticism, then obviously no message gets sent.

- **Encoding barrier—the message is not expressed correctly.** Example: If your vocabulary is lacking or English is not your first language, you may have difficulty expressing to a supervisor, coworker, or subordinate what it is you mean to say.

- **Medium barrier—the communication channel is blocked.** Example: When someone's phone always has a busy signal or a computer network is down, these are instances of the communication medium being blocked.

- **Decoding barrier—the recipient doesn't understand the message.** Example: You pulled an all-nighter traveling back from spring break and today your brain is fuzzy and unfocused during class lectures.

- **Receiver barrier—no message gets received.** Example: Because you were texting during a class lecture, you weren't listening when the professor announced a new assignment due to tomorrow.

- **Feedback barrier—the recipient doesn't respond enough.** Example: You give some people street directions, but since they only nod their heads and don't repeat the directions back to you, you don't really know whether you were understood.

1. Physical Barriers: Sound, Time, Space

Try shouting at someone over the roar of earth-moving machinery on a construction site and you know what physical communication barriers are. Other such barriers are time-zone differences, telephone-line static, and crashed computers. Office design can be a physical barrier, too, if it isolates people in cubicles or surrounds them with noisy open space that makes conversation difficult.

Amazon hopes its new headquarters in downtown Seattle will be an enabler of communication. The ambitious complex will consist of a collection of buildings centered around three high-tech greenhouses filled with 3,000 species of plants, many of which are endangered or even extinct in the wild. The greenhouse "spheres" will bring the outdoors in and offer treehouse-style meeting rooms, suspension bridges, walls made of vines, and an indoor creek. "The whole idea," says the project's lead architect, "was to get people to think more creatively."[24]

2. Personal Barriers: Individual Attributes That Hinder Communication

"Is it them or is it me?" How often have you wondered, when someone has shown a surprising response to something you said, how the miscommunication happened? Let's examine seven personal barriers that contribute to miscommunication.

Variable Skills in Communicating Effectively   Some people are simply better communicators than others. They have the vocabulary, the writing ability, the speaking skills, the facial expressions, the eye contact, the dramatic ability, the "gift of gab," the social skills to express themselves in a superior way. But better communication skills can be learned.[25] The final section in this chapter discusses a variety of ways you can improve your communication effectiveness.

Variations in the Way We Process and Interpret Information   Are you from a working-class or a privileged background? Are you from a particular ethnic group? Because communication is a perceptual process in which people use different frames of reference and experiences to interpret the world around them, they are selective about what things have meaning to them and what don't. These differences affect what we say and what we think we hear.

What differentiates effective communicators, according to communications expert Zamira Jones, is their understanding that ensuring the receiver's correct interpretation of the intended message is up to the sender. "Effective communication is defined by the receiver. If your receiver fails to understand your message, it is your fault, not theirs."[26]

Variations in Trustworthiness and Credibility   Without trust between you and the other person, communication is apt to be flawed. Instead of communicating, both of you will be concentrating on defensive tactics, not the meaning of the message being exchanged. In the end, low trust damages communication, which in turn reduces outcomes like job satisfaction, creativity, collaboration, and performance.[27]

The solution, says writer Martin Zwilling, is to work on relationships first. "When people are listening to someone with confidence and trust, there is a predisposition to hear the message and agree."[28]

Oversized Egos   Our egos—our pride, our self-esteem, even arrogance—are a fourth barrier. Egos can cause political battles, turf wars, and the passionate pursuit of power, credit, and resources. They influence the way we treat each other and how receptive we are to being influenced by others.

Too much ego—the trait of narcissism—is a handicap, but so is too little. Some successful leaders and communicators are what one expert calls "productive narcissists," such as Bill Gates and Steve Jobs.[29] But for most of us, a little perspective on our ego is in order. Most of the time, it's not about us, and that's a good thing.[30]

Faulty Listening Skills   Do you find your mind wandering over the course of a day? Do you forget people's names shortly after meeting them? These are signs of mindlessness. **Mindlessness** **is a state of reduced attention. It is expressed in behavior that is rigid, or thoughtless.**[31] Life's dynamics put all of us into occasional states of mindlessness. Our brains simply can't keep up with all the stimuli we receive, according to noted psychiatrist Edward Hallowell. "Never in history has the human brain been asked to track so many data points," Hallowell says. He believes overloading of our brains is a primary cause of poor listening and poor performance at school and work. "We're simply expecting more of our brains than they have the energy to handle."[32]

Another barrier to listening, ironically, is cell phones. If we're looking at our screens all the time, how can we really be listening to those who are right before us?[33]

Tendency to Judge Others' Messages Some people assume the phrase "Black Lives Matter" is meant to imply that only black lives matter, while others believe the rejoinder "All Lives Matter" is intended to negate the value of black lives. In fact, neither belief is true. The point is that we all have a natural tendency, according to psychologist Carl Rogers, to judge others' statements from our own point of view (especially if we have strong feelings about the issue).[34]

Generational Differences If you've tried to teach an older relative how to text or use Facebook, you may have some appreciation for how difficult it can be for older generations to adapt to new technologies. On the other hand, Senator Bernie Sanders, 74, maintains an active Twitter feed with 2.2 million followers.[35]

Younger people themselves differ in their use of and preferences for different forms of communication. For example, Patty Baxter, publisher at Metro Guide Publishing in Halifax, Nova Scotia, urged her sales reps, all under 35, to use the phone rather than e-mail to reach potential clients. As you might expect, the reps preferred the convenience of e-mail, but sales were down without the personal touch of a phone call.

In contrast, Kevin Castle, 32-year-old chief technology officer at Technossus in Irvine, California, keeps his office phone in a cabinet, unplugged, believing that being respectful of others' needs means e-mailing first before making a potentially intrusive phone call.[36]

And for Brit Morin, CEO and founder of Brit + Co., a media and e-commerce platform based in San Francisco, e-mail is outdated. Morin says, "Half my team doesn't use email anymore. . . . The Gen X and older generations—they're not adopting Slack [an internal communications platform] and they're missing out on a lot of community and information that might be useful in their jobs."[37]

3. Cross-Cultural Barriers

Culture **"encompasses the ideas, values, practices, and material objects that allow a group of people, even an entire society, to carry out their collective lives in relative order and harmony."**[38]

Because the norms and beliefs of our culture are so deeply ingrained in our thoughts and behaviors, culture naturally affects the way we communicate, both with those who share that culture and especially with those from other cultures. One obvious reason is that language differences often exist. For example, jokes and humor are very much linked to culture.[39] One of your authors found that good American jokes don't necessarily get laughs in Europe, Asia, and Scandanavia. Even the United States and Great Britain, whose cultures share many elements, are often said to be "two countries divided by a common language" (an ironic observation often attributed to the British playwright George Bernard Shaw).

Other causes of cultural differences that can impede communication are nonverbal signs and symbols (such as crossed fingers or thumbs-up, which mean very different things around the world), prejudice and bias, religious and other beliefs, and the tendency to value our own culture above all others, called ethnocentrism.[40]

This barrier has been partially overcome via cross-cultural communication training.[41] In Brooklyn, New York, for example, where the population of Chinese immigrants has increased 50% since 2000, Midwood Ambulance, a private ambulance company run by an Italian-American family, recently began hiring Chinese-speaking health care workers to staff three ambulances with lettering in Chinese and English on their sides. The response was so positive that three more ambulances have been ordered. "The fact that I can speak their language was a tremendous help," said Jason Lau, a medical technician who helped deliver a Chinese couple's baby on the way to the hospital.[42] Help with training is available from the American Ambulance Association, which just published its first handbook for cross-cultural communication. The handbook cites barriers to communication, key communication tips for EMTs and paramedics, and cultural norms to be aware of.[43]

Cross-cultural training is particularly important for expatriates, or employees working abroad. Success in such assignments can hinge on the employee's adaptability and cultural awareness. Preparation is the key. Says Scott T. Sullivan, executive vice president of Brookfield Global Relocation Services, "Our research indicates that one of the top 5 causes of assignment failure is the inability to adapt, which can be substantially prevented with cultural training."[44]

4. Nonverbal Communication: How Unwritten and Unspoken Messages May Mislead

Nonverbal communication consists of messages sent outside of the written or spoken word. We primarily express nonverbal communication through (1) *eye contact,* (2) *facial expressions,* (3) *body movements and gestures,* and (4) *touch.*[45] Some research suggests that about 55% of what we communicate is transmitted nonverbally.[46]

1. Eye Contact   Westerners use eye contact to signal the beginning and end of a conversation, to reflect interest and attention, and to convey both honesty and respect. Most people from Western cultures tend to avoid eye contact when conveying bad news or negative feedback. Asians, however, lower their eyes to show respect, while members of Latin cultures do so to show remorse.[47] Interpreting these nonverbal communications as evasive behavior will lead to misunderstanding.[48]

2. Facial Expressions   You're probably used to thinking that smiling represents warmth, happiness, or friendship, whereas frowning represents dissatisfaction or anger. But people in some cultures are less openly demonstrative than people in the United States.[49] The Japanese, for example, feel those in the United States smile too much and too broadly. They themselves may smile, slightly, when angry or embarrassed, as well as when happy. Before the 2008 Beijing Olympics, to accommodate Western visitors, both Chinese and Russian officials at the Games were trained to smile more than they are accustomed to do.[50]

Bored or tired? People's behavior doesn't always reflect what's going on around them. It may reflect what's going on *inside* of them. Perhaps this man on the right was up late the night before with a sick child or working to meet a project deadline. Even so, when speaking, you need to watch your audience for their reactions.
© mediaphotos/Getty Images RF

3. Body Movements and Gestures Open body positions, such as leaning slightly backward, express openness, warmth, closeness, and availability for communication. Closed body positions, such as folded arms or crossed legs, represent defensiveness. Angling your body away from the other person generally makes you look disinterested.[51] You can use these conclusions to improve relationships with others.

A recent experimental study demonstrated the power of using positive, defensive, or no hand gestures when communicating. Participants were shown a video of a leader giving a speech while displaying either positive (community hands—palms facing up, humility—hands clasped at waist level, and steepling—hands form a steeple with fingertips touching), defensive (hands in pockets, crossed arms, hands clasped behind the back), or no hand gestures (keeping hands at one's side). They then rated the extent to which they liked the leader and their positive emotions toward the person. Results showed that people had more positive reactions and emotions toward leaders employing positive hand gestures.[52]

But keep in mind that interpretations of body language can depend on context and culture. For instance, waving your hand with your palm facing away from you means "good-bye" in the United States but "come here" in Korea.[53]

4. Touch Norms for touching vary significantly around the world. For example, kissing on the cheek, patting on the shoulder, and embracing may be appropriate in the U.S., but many people in Asia find these actions offensive.[54]

Western women tend to use touching of other women to show friendship or sympathy, whereas men are less likely to touch other men and more likely to associate being touched with sexual behavior.[55] Other cultures are often more conservative about the use of touch between men and women.

The table below gives some suggestions for better nonverbal communication skills. (See Table 15.3.)

DO . . .	DON'T . . .
Maintain eye contact	Look away from the speaker
Lean toward the speaker	Turn away from the speaker
Speak at a moderate rate	Speak too quickly or slowly
Speak in a quiet, reassuring tone	Speak in an unpleasant tone
Smile and show animation	Yawn excessively
Occasionally nod your head in agreement	Close your eyes
Be aware of your facial expressions	Lick your lips, bite your nails, play with your hair

Source: Adapted from P. Preston, "Nonverbal Communication: Do You Really Say What You Mean?" Journal of Healthcare Management, March–April 2005, pp. 83–86.

TABLE 15.3

Toward Better Nonverbal Communication Skills

You can practice these skills by watching TV with the sound off and interpreting people's emotions and interactions.

5. Gender Differences

Women and men process language in different parts of the brain, so perhaps it's not surprising that gender differences in communication exist.[56] A recent series of more than 100,000 interviews with male and female executives revealed some of these

Exchange of views? Men and women have different communication styles. How effective do you think you are at communicating with the opposite sex? © Brand X Pictures/ PunchStock RF

differences. For instance, women view questioning as their best contribution and use questions to spark ideas, build consensus, and show concern for others. Men think women ask too many questions. They tend to interpret them as barriers to progress or signs of overly controlling behavior.[57]

Many women often feel excluded during meetings and discussions, while about 90% of men feel women have equal opportunities to contribute. Both have a point; women prefer to be asked to participate, while men assume someone who doesn't voluntarily speak up simply has nothing to say.[58]

Because stress heightens different hormones in men and in women, men tend to withdraw and isolate themselves when problem solving, whereas women seek out others for support and can interpret men's withdrawing as lack of caring.[59]

Some possible general differences in communication between genders are summarized below. (See Table 15.4.) Note, however, that these don't apply in all cases, which would constitute stereotyping.

TABLE 15.4   Gender and Communication Differences: How Do Men and Women Differ?

COMMUNICATION CHARACTERISTIC	MEN	WOMEN
Taking credit	Greater use of "I" statements (e.g., "I did this" and "I did that"); more likely to boast about their achievements	Greater use of "We" statements, (e.g., "We did this" and "We did that"); less likely to boast about their achievements
Displaying confidence	Less likely to indicate that they are uncertain about an issue	Mostly likely to indicate a lack of certainty about an issue
Being polite	More likely to appear certain and definitive	Greater use of qualifiers and hedging
Focus of messaging	Focused on self and more likely to mention "Me" or "I"	Focused on other person and more likely to mention "We" or "You"
Talking patterns	More apt to interrupt women and talk over others	Less apt to interrupt men and talk over others
Listening	More likely to take in words and content, less likely to use positive overlaps such as "Yea" or "I see" to demonstrate listening	More likely to hear words and the emotions behind them, more likely to use positive overlaps such as "I agree" or "That's right" to demonstrate listening
Nonverbal patterns	Less expressive (e.g., smile less) and focus more on words than nonverbal cues, less likely to touch	More expressive (e.g., smile more) and skilled at deciphering nonverbal cues, more likely to touch
Answering questions	Quick and to the point	Tend to provide more information than needed
Using emoticons	Use emoticons more often to express sarcasm and banter	Use smiling and laughing emoticons more than men

Source: Derived from A. Nelson and C.D. Brown, The Gender Communication Handbook *(San Francisco, CA: Pfeiffer, 2012); and D. Tannen,* You Just Don't Understand: Women and Men in Conversation *(New York: Ballantine Books, 1990).*

Deborah Tannen recommends that everyone become aware of how differing linguistic styles affect our perceptions and judgments. A **linguistic style is a person's characteristic speaking patterns**—pacing, pausing, directness, word choice, and use of questions, jokes, stories, apologies, and similar devices. For example, in a meeting, regardless of gender, "those who are comfortable speaking up in groups, who need little or no silence before raising their hands, or who speak out easily without waiting to be recognized are more apt to be heard," she says. "Those who refrain from talking until it's clear that the previous speaker is finished, who wait to be recognized, and who are inclined to link their comments to those of others will do fine at a meeting where everyone else is following the same rules but will have a hard time getting heard in a meeting with people whose styles are more like the first pattern."[60] ●

How Can Men and Women Communicate Better at Work?

EXAMPLE

Are the communication differences between men and women an unbridgeable gap? Few experts think so. Here are some suggestions for both men and women to become more aware of gender differences and try closing the gap.[61]

1. **Recognize hidden bias.** Everyone has biases where gender is concerned, including the notion that there are only two genders. Examining unacknowledged prejudices is the first step in overcoming them.

2. **Allow for different communication styles.** There is no one "best" way for anyone to communicate. Men may focus on "I" statements, while women may qualify their contributions, but these differences should not influence the group's assessment of the value of the messages. Men can acknowledge that women are motivated to be inclusive, for instance, while women can recognize that it's sometimes more important to men to just get the job done. It's not usually personal.

3. **Remember that everyone wants to feel that his or her contribution matters.** Listening is the most important communication skill. Being open-minded and attentive and avoiding snap judgments when others speak are good rules for all to follow. Really listening means you are not planning and rehearsing your response while the other person is still speaking.

4. **Step out of your comfort zone.** Women can try being more assertive in groups and meetings, while men can be more willing to listen and interrupt less. Women can try taking an ad hoc approach to problem solving, while men can look for more overt ways to include others in the process while asking questions along the way.

YOUR CALL

Do you think it is possible to adapt our preferred communication styles? Why or why not? How would this kind of adaptation improve communication at work?

The 2016 Presidential debates underscored communication differences between men and women. In this town hall debate at Washington University, Donald Trump regularly stood behind Hillary Clinton in this manner. What message was he sending by behaving in this regard? Trump clearly exhibited several of the male communication characteristics shown in Table 15.4 such as taking credit, displaying confidence, being less polite, talking patterns, and answering questions. Clinton similarly used the female characteristics pertaining to taking credit, focus of messaging, listening, and nonverbal patterns.
© Pool/Getty Images

15.4 Social Media and Management

How do contemporary managers use social media to communicate more effectively?

THE BIG PICTURE

We discuss social media and their use by employees and managers. We look at the impact of social media on managers' and organizations' effectiveness, including applications to recruiting, productivity, sales, innovation, and reputation management. We also consider the costs of social media use, such as the effects of cyberloafing and the need to manage e-mail, as well as growing concerns about security and privacy. We look at the use of texting in organizations, and finally at the implications for managers of setting social media policy.

Social media, which use web-based and mobile technologies to generate interactive dialogue with members of a network, are woven into every aspect of our lives. We begin our exploration of these technologies by documenting their general use. We then examine the effects of social media on managerial and organizational effectiveness, review the downside of social media, discuss the key impacts of texting on management and organizational behavior, and discuss the need for organizations to develop social media policies.

Social Media Is Changing the Fabric of Our Lives

The widespread use of social media is changing our personal lives and the very nature of how businesses operate and the principles of management. A recent survey of 9,200 travelers across 31 countries, for example, provides insight into the impact of social media in our lives. Eighty-one percent reported that they would rather travel with their mobile devices than with a loved one.[62] From a business perspective, Facebook's new live streaming feature may not yet rival its main social media site in popularity, but it has already attracted small business users who compare its features and benefits with that of Periscope, a similar application from Twitter. Despite some differences, both channels allow business managers to reach and interact with customers in new ways.[63] Researchers suggest that application of such tools can increase a company's brand awareness and sales.[64]

Besides the business application of social media, it is affecting our lives in countless other ways. Consider, for example, when Republican representatives cut off the live television feed in the House at the end of a legislative session in June 2016. The Democrats who had been pressing for a vote on gun control legislation refused to leave the chamber and used Periscope to stream their impromptu sit-in via cell phone. They held their ground for about 36 hours as C-Span picked up the feed and the legislators' protest went viral.[65] And, with undoubtedly profound implications for law enforcement, gun control, and race relations in the United States, Diamond Reynolds stunned the world in 2016 when she live-streamed on Facebook the fatal shooting by police of her boyfriend, Philandro Castile, who had been pulled over for a broken tail light and died in the emergency room. Within a few days the video had been viewed 3.2 million times on Reynolds's page alone.[66]

What does data suggest about the use of social media? Figure 15.2 shows the usage of various social networks across all age groups. Although some differences across age cohorts exist, it appears all age groups use these tools, underscoring the need for managers to use social media tools with employees of all ages.

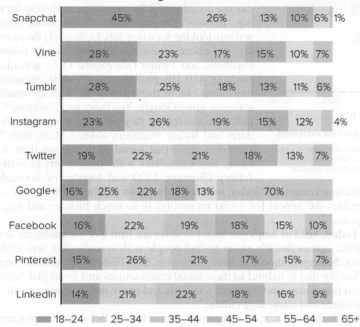

US Data - Users Aged 18 and over - December 2014

Legend: ■ 18–24 ■ 25–34 ■ 35–44 ■ 45–54 ■ 55–64 ■ 65+

Network	18–24	25–34	35–44	45–54	55–64	65+
Snapchat	45%	26%	13%	10%	6%	1%
Vine	28%	23%	17%	15%	10%	7%
Tumblr	28%	25%	18%	13%	11%	6%
Instagram	23%	26%	19%	15%	12%	4%
Twitter	19%	22%	21%	18%	13%	7%
Google+	16%	25%	22%	18%	13%	70%
Facebook	16%	22%	19%	18%	15%	10%
Pinterest	15%	26%	21%	17%	15%	7%
LinkedIn	14%	21%	22%	18%	16%	9%

FIGURE 15.2

Age distribution at the top social networks

Source: M. Hoelzel, Business Insider Australia, June 3, 2015, "Social Network Demographics: Here's who's on Facebook, Snapchat, Instagram, and Other Top Social Networks Now," http://www.businessinsider.com.au/update-a-breakdown-of-the-demographics-for-each-of-the-different-social-networks-2015-6?r=US&IR=T.

A recent survey of more than 3,500 professionals in France, Germany, Japan, Spain, the UK, and the United States documented their use of mobile devices at work. Results showed

- 60% check or send personal e-mail at least once a day.
- 57% send personal text messages at least once a day.
- 53% make personal voice calls at least once a day.
- 50% check or use social media at least once a day.[67]

It's no wonder, then, that the communications capabilities of social media continue to grow and expand, and that managers need to keep up with their increasing potential.

Moreover, those whose businesses are global, for instance, are using social medial platforms to reach audiences in developing countries around the world. And it's not just a matter of mastering Facebook or Twitter; in fact, some overseas governments actively block their citizens' access to Western media channels. Instead, adapting to local conditions also means knowing, for instance, that "the largest social network in China is QQ, Orkut is widely used in India and Brazil, Kontakte is strong in Russia, Hi5 is the leading network in Peru, and Maktoob is the choice throughout the Arab world."[68]

Social Media and Managerial and Organizational Effectiveness

With their ease of use, speed, and potentially huge audiences, social media have increasing application for managers' and organizations' effectiveness. We will look at social media use in employment recruiting, employee and employer productivity, sales, innovation, and corporate reputation.

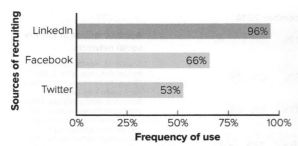

FIGURE 15.3   **Social media sources used for recruiting**

Source: R. Maurer, "Survey: Employers Using Social Media to Find Passive Candidates," https://www.shrm.org/ResourcesAndTools/hr-topics/talent -acquisition/Pages/Using-Social-Media-Find-Passive-Candidates.aspx, accessed July 2016.

Employment Recruiting   About 82% of companies today use social media for recruiting, especially for recruiting "passive" job candidates, that is, those who aren't actively looking for a new job. LinkedIn is the most popular (and effective) for this purpose, closely followed by Facebook and Twitter (see Figure 15.3), according to a study of 410 HR professionals.[69] Most companies use more than one of these platforms, with far smaller percentages using Google, YouTube, and Pinterest.[70] Nearly half of recruiters say they use texting to reach job candidates and hiring managers alike.[71] More than 70% of recruiters agree that social media allows them to more easily find candidates with specific sets of skills. Says Jeffery Giesener, CEO and founder of SourceMob, a social recruiting company, "Today, with social being on mobile and with over 4 billion global profiles the appeal [of social recruiting] is so much broader and reaches all demographics."[72]

Craig Fisher, head of employer brand at software firm CA Technologies and CEO of TalentNet, agrees that it's easier to find people with specific skill sets with social media tools. Managers should be savvy, however. Says Fisher, they should "keep good content flowing that is helpful to their social communities and avoid just 'asking' all the time, so that when candidates see these ads and check out the company, they see a helpful resource and interesting culture."[73]

As you probably know, most company websites have a "Jobs" or "Employment" tab where interested job seekers can search and apply for open positions. Beyond this fairly simple interaction, job seekers can also customize their searches on job posting sites like Monster and Indeed.com and apply directly to the hiring firm, attaching resumes, writing samples, links to blogs and videos, and other pertinent information. Companies can also post jobs on industry-specific hosting and social networking platforms, like GitHub (software developers), Dribble (web designers),[74] and Mediabistro (media professionals). More than 60,000 jobs are tweeted on Monster every day.[75] And according to Career Builder's website, 52% of companies check out potential hires' social media pages, including their sometimes unguarded profiles on Facebook and LinkedIn.[76]

PRACTICAL ACTION   Building Your Professional Profile Online

Employers increasingly value the "full circle view" of job candidates they can get by recruiting them online,[77] and more than half check their social media profiles.[78] Apparently, few are forgiving if they don't like what they see, however.[79] How can you ensure that the view of yourself you're projecting is an attractive and positive one? Here are some tips for managing your online image.

1. **Regularly update your profile at LinkedIn and industry-specific networking sites.** Make sure you list up-to-the-minute and accurate information about your current and recent jobs, and that your increasing level of experience or broadening set of skills is clear from your descriptions. Key words important to recruiters in your industry are as valuable here as they are on your resume.

2. **Follow the companies you hope will hire you.** Use the Internet to research a small group of companies you want to work for, and then use social media and networking sites to follow them and find or ask for connections to people who work there. Adding these connections to your network demonstrates your interest in the firm.[80] Effective networking takes time, so be patient.

3. **Participate in industry-related chat rooms and discussion groups.** If you are experienced and knowledgeable in a field and have something to offer, you can contribute positively to ongoing conversations that will raise your profile and introduce your name to new connections. If you're still learning the ropes, asking intelligent questions can still help your networking efforts. If you're really an expert in a relevant field, consider starting an industry-specific blog.

4. **Edit your general online social presence.** While you can and should sensibly limit those who can see your personal information and candid photos online, your overall presence on Facebook, Instagram, LinkedIn, and other

sites should still reflect a reasonably mature and responsible individual and include nothing you'd be afraid to see in the newspaper. Think before you post anything, anywhere.[81] After all, someday you may "friend" your colleagues at your new job.

YOUR CALL

In which industry or industries would you look for 8 or 10 companies you'd like to work for? What kind of online profile do you think recruiters at those companies would be looking for?

Social media can also lead to hiring discrimination (by revealing applicants' religious affiliation, age, family composition, or sexual orientation). Says Craig Fisher of TalentNet, "anything that is public information is fair game in researching prospective candidates. When those candidates become applicants, the rules change a bit." At the same time, "you just can't use that information in consideration of employment if it is a protected characteristic."[82]

Online or not, recruiting still requires a human touch. Instead of sending rejected applicants away unhappy, Virgin Media hopes to create $7 million in new business by converting them into customers. How? By using lessons learned in customer service to "story board" a memorable recruiting experience.[83]

Employee Productivity   While overuse of and even addiction to social media exist and can cause serious problems,[84] there seems little doubt that social media tools at work, used appropriately, can make communication by and among employees more productive. In fact, productivity is a driving force behind the use of all forms of technology at work, including social media. The key for employees, managers, and employers is to harness the speed and reach of social media to enhance individual performance.

Results like reduced turnover, higher performance, increased job satisfaction, and greater creativity and collaboration are common findings in research about the effects of social media.[85] Employees who work remotely are particular beneficiaries of social media's communications capabilities. Customized scheduling, organizing, networking, document sharing, messaging, and other digital communication options help relieve them of the need to commute, attend routine meetings, and be distracted by colleagues.[86] Digital productivity tools that control e-mail, organize links and contacts, prioritize tasks, and even edit prose can help remote workers stay focused and organized so they can meet deadlines and enjoy work–life balance.[87]

Work–life balance. Like this family, vacations are good for everyone. Research shows that everyone needs some down time. It also helps to give our electronic devices a break as well. © David Buffington/Blend Images LLC RF

At the same time, managers need to remember that employees don't have to be in touch all the time, no matter how easy it is. There is plenty of evidence that everyone should unplug from e-mail and social media on a regular basis, if not during every evening, weekend, and vacation.[88] Concerned that productivity was actually suffering, health care consulting firm Vynamic began discouraging employees from sending e-mails between 11 p.m. and 7 a.m. Monday through Friday and all day on weekends. Job satisfaction is up since the change took place.[89]

How often do you use social media while at work? Do you think it is helping or hindering your performance? You can find out by completing Self-Assessment 15.1.

To What Extent Are You Effectively Using Online Social Networking at Work?

The following survey was designed to assess how well you are using social networking in your job. Please be prepared to answer these questions if your instructor has assigned Self-Assessment 15.1 in Connect.

1. To what extent are social media helping or hurting your performance at work?

2. Based on your survey scores, what can you do to more effectively use social media at work? Be specific.

3. What policies might companies install to ensure that social media are used in a productive manner? Explain.

Employer Productivity   Companies of all sizes and industries believe in the benefits of social media. Procter and Gamble (P&G) spends more than any other U.S. company on advertising, and it now devotes more than a third of its US marketing budget to digital media. Marc Pritchard, Global Brand Officer, says, "Digital technology . . . is enabling P&G to expand creativity with an unprecedented delivery machine that is constantly evolving. . . . This is why P&G is quickly shifting to a digital-first approach to building brands."[90] If used effectively, social media allow companies to reap many of the benefits listed in Table 15.5.

TABLE 15.5

Social Media Benefits for Employers

BENEFIT	DESCRIPTION
Connect in real time over distance	Employees, customers, communities, suppliers, prospective talent, and many others can communicate as needed and while work is being completed.
Collaborate within and outside organization	Linking sources of knowledge is a means for realizing the potential of employee diversity and enhancing productivity. Social media are by definition a way of connecting people virtually, so their effective implementation benefits virtual teamwork.
Expand boundaries	Social networks can become critical means for organizational innovation and effectiveness, allowing them to utilize knowledge, skills, and experience of people outside (not employed by) the organization.

Adapted from L. McFarland and R. Ployhart, "Social Media: A Contextual Framework to Guide Research and Practice," Journal of Applied Psychology, 2015, 1653–1677.

The essence of social media is *connectivity*. If deployed effectively, social media enable businesses to do the following:

- **Connect with key stakeholders.** The use of social media allows you to connect in real time and over distances with many customers, suppliers, employees, potential talent, and other key stakeholders.

- **Connect with varied sources of expertise inside the organization.** We've seen such connectivity demonstrated in virtual teams, redefining conventional organizational boundaries and drawing on different sources of talent, knowledge, and experience throughout the organization.

- **Connect with varied sources of expertise outside the organization.** Social media can cross organizational boundaries and connect with outsiders to help in problem solving. An example is *crowdsourcing*, as we'll see below. A variant is *crowdfunding,* raising money via online sources.

On the other hand, if not managed effectively, social media can create many legal, financial, and human resource risks.[91] For instance, each employee who plays fantasy football loses about one hour a week of work time.[92] The price tag for productivity lost to fantasy football was $16 billion in 2015. That's $1 billion a week during the football season.[93]

Controlling Social Media Tools

EXAMPLE

Slack is a real-time communications and collaboration tool for groups or communities, launched in 2013, that includes chat rooms, public and private messaging, and private groups. All its content is shareable and searchable. Slack has been adopted by many companies (and private groups) and now has more than 15 million active users every day. It's cloud-based and helps companies consolidate their internal communications in one place, relieving some of their reliance on e-mail.[94]

At LUSH, for example, a global producer of handmade soaps and cosmetics, reliance on e-mail for internal messages has dropped 75% since Slack was introduced. Given LUSH's rapid growth, "it's a struggle at times to maintain consistent communication internally and with our global network—Slack has filled that hole," says Maddie Saunders, global planner for the firm. "It has improved communication between groups greatly."[95]

Some business users find, however, that as with any communication channel, they need to set limits on its use to keep employees from being overwhelmed. One writer advises enforcing a policy for creating consistent user names, dedicating certain channels to messages about specific tasks or projects, giving some users "guest" status with limited access (to protect others' privacy or fine-tune employees' focus), and setting up "do not disturb" hours to accommodate users in different time zones. Closed discussions can also be archived to reduce "clutter."[96]

YOUR CALL

Are you familiar with Slack? Do you think the suggestions here would improve its effectiveness (or that of any other internal network) in an organizational environment? What other tips would you suggest?

Social Media and Innovation: Crowdsourcing If you are looking for an innovative solution to a problem, you might conclude that the more people you have thinking about the problem, the more potential ideas will be generated. That's the idea behind **crowdsourcing, using the Internet and social media to enlist a group outside the organization for help solving a problem.** The strategy has drawn a lot of attention, especially for its use in fundraising (crowdfunding) on such sites as Kickstarter,[97] but it has a mixed record of success.

Some crowdsourcing efforts are organized as competitions, with teams volunteering to solve a problem by a certain deadline and win a cash prize. Netflix, for example, offered $1 million to the team that could come up with an algorithm that would do a better job of recommending movies to customers than what the company was using at the time. A multinational team won with minutes to spare (but the company never implemented its solution).[98] Some companies recruit temporary or contingent workers through crowdsourcing and pay them for their time and efforts whether or not they succeed.[99] Critics say, however, that large groups of people working on a problem have been shown to produce only average results; they advise hiring real experts to get the job done.[100]

Because more and more companies are exploring the use of social media to enhance the product development process, researchers are starting to quantitatively study its benefits. Although it is too soon to make a definitive conclusion, results from a global study of the product development process in over 660 companies is enlightening. The researchers concluded "despite the promise, the expected positive results are frequently not realized in practice. . . . We believe that social media provides a game-changing opportunity for companies that learn how to exploit it. But taking advantage of the opportunity requires more than having a Facebook presence with a loyal base of 'friends' who say they 'like' you. In order to use social media for innovation, organizations need clear strategies and objectives."[101]

Social Media and Sales and Brand Recognition   Is it logical to expect that an "effective" social media presence generates customers and brand recognition? Yes, for the following reasons:

1. Social media can increase product/service awareness and generate customer inquiries.
2. Social media can enhance relationships with customers.
3. Social media can increase the ability to reach customers on a global scale.
4. For small or local businesses, social media can foster co-promotion of local businesses and the image of small businesses in the area.[102]
5. Social media can foster consumers' conversations about brands.[103]

Promoting green. This 2009 Volkswagen AG Jetta TDI was named Green Car of the Year by the *Green Car Journal* in 2008. Do you think this designation helped promote sales of the vehicle? Would your answer change based on the emissions scandal confronting the company in 2015–2016? © Armando Arorizo/Bloomberg/Getty Images

   Don't assume that the mere use of social media automatically results in more sales and brand recognition. Recent research suggests that social media won't create positive outcomes unless two conditions are present.[104] First, the company must possess both competence in social media skills and technology and commitment in the form of dedicated resources. Second, a successful social media strategy requires consumers or customers with social media skills. If a company is selling a product or service to a segment of the market without such skills, the benefits will not be achieved.[105]

   UnderArmour scored a big success with its "I Will What I Want" videos of female athletes on YouTube, for example. These brief films were intended to "[empower] women of all shapes and sizes to get moving and not let anyone hold them back," One notable entry in the series, drawing more than 7.5 million views, featured rising ballet star Misty Copeland, the first African American dancer to be promoted to principal dancer at American Ballet Theater.[106] TOMS Shoes was another social media winner, with an Instagram campaign in which the socially conscious company promised to donate one pair of shoes for every photo someone posted of their own bare feet. Almost 300,000 pairs were donated as a result of the drive.[107] Also popular on Instagram is GoPro's regular showcasing of user-generated content. Action-camera enthusiasts are invited to post their own photos for the company's popular Photo of the Day opportunity.[108]

Misty Copeland. Misty Copeland performing "Giselle" at the Metropolitan Opera House.
© Hiroyuki Ito/Getty Images

Social Media and Reputation   Some companies have been very successful at using social media to build and protect their reputations online. The benefits are real.[109] Research with KLM Royal Dutch Airline showed that customers who engaged with the company online had more positive perceptions about its reputation.[110]

One of the biggest dangers managers face is negative comments about the organization posted by disgruntled customers or even employees. Some tips for defusing these and limiting the harm they can do are:[111]

1. **Create and enforce a social media policy for employees.** We'll discuss social media policies in more detail. At a minimum your policy should limit what employees can say on the organization's web pages and ensure that all posted content meets the highest ethical standards.

2. **Appoint experienced managers to monitor your social media presence and respond quickly and appropriately to negative posts.** Vitamin Water waited 24 hours before responding to customers voicing anger on Facebook about its new flavor.[112] A Mississippi woman received an insensitive e-mail from her state representative about her problems getting medical supplies for her diabetic child. She posted the legislator's crass response on Facebook, where it went viral.[113] A great deal of damage can occur online in a short time, and all of it in the public eye.

3. **Acknowledge there is a problem.** Gracefully accepting that someone has a genuine issue with the organization, its product or service, or its posts—even if the problem is a misunderstanding on his or her part—can go a long way toward defusing bad feelings. If the organization is in error, the appropriate manager should say so and apologize.

4. **Take the conversation offline if necessary.** If a customer refuses to be satisfied, take the conversation to a private sphere such as phone or e-mail. Not only will this keep it out of the public eye and prevent further damage to the brand but the individualized attention may also reduce the customer's ire.

A company's reputation is affected by posts made by current and former employees. Sites like Glassdoor.com, for instance, allow people to publicly (and anonymously) rate their employers on criteria like salary, benefits, work–life balance, career advancement possibilities, and even the quality of the employment interview. Firms that are confident they have happy employees can encourage them to spread the buzz about office parties, outings, and incentives and rewards on corporate websites, social media, and blogs, building the company's image as a good place to work.[114]

Downsides of Social Media

It's fair to say the digital age and rise of social media have introduced almost as many difficulties as efficiencies into people's lives. Some of these problems relate to cyberloafing, security breaches, privacy concerns, and the volume of e-mail.

Cyberloafing   Lost productivity due to **cyberloafing—using the Internet at work for personal use**—is a primary concern for employers in their adoption of social media. Some studies put the cost at $85 billion per year and report that employees spend 60%–80% of their time at work pretending to do actual or legitimate work.[115] How do employees waste time on social media?

- Fifty percent are talking on a cell phone or texting.
- Thirty-nine percent are surfing the Internet.
- Thirty-eight percent are on social media.
- Twenty-three percent are sending personal e-mail.[116]

Then there is shopping online while at work. A survey by CareerBuilder found that on average 47% of workers planned to shop online.[117]

Software tools can reduce cyberloafing. One program developed by researchers at Arizona State University restricts the websites employees are allowed to access from work, the length of time they are permitted to spend there, or both. The program "significantly" reduced cyberloafing at the company where it was installed. The lead researcher advises that managers engage employees in decisions about how to use such tools, however, both to make sure rules are fair and to make employees feel like "part of the conversation."[118]

Another consideration for managers is that most employees can and do bring their own devices to work and so are perfectly capable of bypassing controls installed on office computers. And, say some observers who think reports of cyberloafing's extent are exaggerated, taking an online break from work might not be such a bad thing. It can reduce stress and improve concentration. The key, again, is fairness in setting and upholding policies about social media use, which we discuss below.[119]

Security: Guarding against Cyberthreats   **Security is defined as a system of safeguards for protecting information technology against disasters, system failures, and unauthorized access that result in damage or loss.** Security is a continuing challenge, with computer and cell-phone users constantly having to deal with threats ranging from malicious software (malware) that tries to trick people into yielding passwords and personal information to viruses that can destroy or corrupt data.[120] According to the Norton *Cyber Crime Report for 2013,* the cost per cybercrime victim shot up to $298, a 50% increase over 2012, with the total cost of those crimes amounting to $113 billion.[121]

Biggest hack. Gary McKinnon arrives at the High Courts in London to appeal his extradition to the U.S. He is a Scottish systems administrator and was accused of conducting the biggest U.S. military hack of all time. The British government blocked his extradition order to the U.S. Do you think governments around the world should prosecute hackers like McKinnon to the fullest extent?
© John Stillwell/PA Images/Alamy

Hacking and human error by careless or improperly trained employees are part of the problem and will likely continue to be.[122] A recent poll by the Organization of American States surveyed 575 respondents in North and South America and found that 40% had experienced efforts to shut down their networks.[123] And in a demonstration of just how critical to an organization effective managers really are, internal attacks by disgruntled employees are one of the biggest security threats a business can face.[124]

The key to protecting digital communication systems against fraud, hackers, identity theft, and other threats is prevention. The table below presents some ways to protect yourself. *(See Table 15.6.)* The federal government also offers valuable advice at the FCC's website.[125]

TABLE 15.6

Protecting against Security and Privacy Breaches on the Internet

- **Don't use passwords that can be easily guessed.** Use weird combinations of letters, numbers, and punctuation, and mix uppercase and lowercase, along with special characters such as !, #, and %.

- **Don't use the same password for multiple sites.** Avoid using the same password at different sites, since if hackers or scammers obtain one account, they potentially have your entire online life.

- **Don't reveal sensitive information on social networking sites.** Even people who set their profiles to Facebook's strictest privacy settings may find sensitive information leaked all over the web.

- **Be careful about free and illegal downloads.** File-sharing programs often contain spyware, as do sites containing free and illegal songs, movies, and TV shows.

- **Be mindful of liability issues.** Employers routinely monitor employee e-mail for offensive messages or risky material that may expose them to lawsuits.

- **Keep antivirus software updated.** The antivirus software on your computer won't protect you forever. Visit the antivirus software maker's website and enable the automatic update features.

Source: Derived from B. K. Williams and S. C. Sawyer, Using Information Technology: A Practical Introduction, 11th ed. (New York: McGraw-Hill Education, 2015), pp. 94, 100, 101, 357, 478.

Privacy: Keeping Things to Yourself

Privacy is the right of people not to reveal information about themselves. Threats to privacy can range from name migration, as when a company sells its customer list to another company, to online snooping, to government prying and spying. A potentially devastating violation of privacy is **identity theft, in which thieves hijack your name and identity and use your good credit rating to get cash or buy things.** Many of the cautions in Table 15.6 apply here, too.

The most important thing to know about online and social media privacy is that nothing posted is ever truly private.[126] In some cases, Internet users are their own worst enemies, posting compromising images and information about themselves on social networking sites that may be available to, say, potential employers. Others, like the Mississippi representative mentioned previously whose unhelpful response to a constituent in need went viral, disastrously fail to think before they post. It has been said that if you wouldn't want to see something on the front page of the newspaper, don't post it.

As for privacy at work, monitoring of electronic communications is widespread. In most circumstances employers are permitted to monitor—that is, read—their employees' e-mail and track their Internet use, and two-thirds of those in a recent survey said they did so.[127] More than a quarter of all employers in the survey also said they had fired someone for "email misuse," and more than 7 in 10 have disciplined employees for social media gaffes.[128] And your privacy rights may be limited when you are using your employer's computer and other equipment.[129] Monitoring can become a source of bias, however, and determined employees can often get around monitoring tools and devices, sometimes weakening the organization's security protocols in the process.[130]

The Need to Manage E-mail

Employees tend to have a love–hate relationship with e-mail. We love that we can send and receive e-mail 24/7 from anywhere. But we hate the fact that the average worker can receive hundreds of e-mails a day, and the fact that most of us can handle no more than a few dozen in that time. While texting, social networking, and other forms of electronic and digital communication have begun to reduce the dominance of e-mail, it's predicted that the number of e-mail users worldwide will continue to grow, reaching nearly 3 billion people (or one-third of the world's population) by 2019. One reason is that so many other communications applications, as well as online shopping sites, require a valid e-mail address for access.[131]

The table below provides some practical tips for handling e-mail. *(See Table 15.7.)*

TABLE 15.7

Tips for Better E-mail Handling

- **Turn off all noncritical notifications and unsubscribe from newsletters.** An important first step is to reduce the amount of unnecessary e-mail you get.

- **Set aside one or two 15-minute periods each day to review e-mail.** Don't check it compulsively, and try not to read or send e-mails before or after work hours. About 40% of Gen X and Gen Y employees say they do so, but intrusions into off-work hours can disrupt work–life balance.

- **Treat all e-mail as confidential.** See the discussion of privacy above. Also think twice about including other people in your message who may not need to read it.

- **Be brief and professional, and proofread (twice).** Keep your message as short as possible and avoid spelling, grammatical, and other errors, especially in people's names and titles. Save emojis for personal messages.

- **Remember that not every topic belongs on e-mail.** Complicated or controversial topics may be better discussed on the phone or in person to avoid misunderstandings.

Source: Money (Contributor), Forbes, April 7, 2015, "Why Checking Email After Work Is Bad for Your Career—and Health," http://fortune.com/2015/04/07/why-checking-email-after-work-is-bad-for-your-career-and-health-2/, accessed July 2016; A. Samuel "How I Tamed the Email Beast at Work," Wall Street Journal, March 14, 2016, http://www.wsj.com/articles/how-i-tamed-the-email-beast-at-work-1457921533, accessed July 2016; A. Fridman, "How to Stop Email Distractions at Work," Inc. June 23, 2016, http://www.inc.com/adam-fridman/how-to-stop-email -distractions-at-work.html, accessed July 2016; D. Ecker, "15 Clever Tips for Managing Email Overload at Work," Redbooth, July 15, 2015 https://redbooth.com/blog/managing-email-overload, accessed July 2016.

Managerial Implications of Texting

Common sense says that a colleague or customer standing in front of you or talking to you by phone or videoconference deserves your full and immediate attention, while the person texting you about your plans for the evening can wait. But texting does have some legitimate workplace applications. How can managers best make use of its capabilities?

Many feel that those who deal directly with customers should not be texting at work. A cashier, a crossing guard, a customer service rep, and a salesperson—not to mention a cab or bus driver—are good examples of employees whose phones should be tucked in a bag or a drawer at all times.[132] At the same time, some very limited use of texting for personal reasons at work, in the right time and place, can be a big help in increasing work–life balance and relieving stress.[133]

If texting is an integral part of your workplace communications—not least because it can reduce costs and eliminate the time phone customers spend waiting on hold[134]— ideally it should be covered under the organization's social media policy (discussed below). Who participates in or initiates group messages, for instance? How quickly are people expected to reply to texts? For what purposes can texts be sent, and to whom?

Here are a few tips for making the most of texting for work purposes:[135]

1. **As with all social media tools, strictly limit your use for personal reasons during the work day.** It helps to let your friends and family know you will not respond while at work.

2. **Text only important messages.** Avoid using texting for routine information, and make it clear in your message why it is urgent. As always, be brief. If you must deliver bad news, be courteous and do it over the phone or in person.

3. **Avoid texting during meetings.** Not only is it rude to text during a meeting; it's likely the people you might need to text will be in the meeting with you, so there should be no problem leaving your phone behind.

4. **Don't use abbreviations or emojis.** Abbreviations like "omw" and "btw" look unprofessional in a business message and can confuse some readers. Save emojis for texts with family and friends.

5. **As always, proofread.** Read every message before sending, and be especially alert for potential miscommunication instigated by auto-correct features.

Managerial Considerations in Creating Social Media Policies

The purpose of a social media policy at work is not to completely close off employees' access to personal e-mails and texts or even to shopping websites. Many employees already feel guilty if they need to deal with personal messages at work but say they would quit their job if their ability to do at least some personal tasks during the work day were restricted.[136] And while as much as half of social media use during work hours may be taking place for non-work reasons, many employees do use social media for constructive work purposes, such as making and nurturing professional connections and seeking solutions to problems from those both inside and outside the organization.[137]

Social Media Policy A **social media policy** describes the who, how, when, and for what purposes of social media use, and the consequences for noncompliance. Such a policy can not only clarify expectations and relieve guilt but also prevent impulsive or abusive posts and messages that can damage an organization's or an individual's reputation. The elements of an effective social media policy are outlined in Table 15.8.

TABLE 15.8   **Seven Elements of an Effective Social Media Policy**

ELEMENT	DESCRIPTION
Create safe channels for employees to air their concerns before going online.	The key words here are *safe* and *before*. Conflicts happen, but managers and organizations should provide means by which employees' concerns are reported and handled without retaliation so they don't feel the need to take them to the Internet.
Clarify what is confidential.	Clearly explain what information employees can and cannot share online. Providing an approval process for the release of information may help, too.
Outline consequences for violations.	Make it known that employees can be held responsible for what they post (such as videos of undesirable behavior on the job or in company uniform), and list the consequences.
Discuss appropriate ways to engage others online.	It is typically a poor idea to have any and all employees responding to others' comments about the company online. Instruct them to be polite and nonconfrontational, and then to notify the designated person to respond.
Explain what is considered illegal.	It is illegal to divulge proprietary information and to violate trademarks and copyrights. The organization is responsible for educating employees on these matters.
Align social media policy with the organization's culture.	Your company's social media policy is a great place to reaffirm what you want your company culture to be while conveying your stance on this serious topic.
Educate employees.	It's not enough to have a social media policy; it is necessary to educate and train people about it and to embed it in social media practices. (One of the authors, for instance, could not locate a social media policy, or a person responsible for it, at his university.)

Adapted from A. Akitunde, "Employees Gone Wild: Eight Reasons You Need a Social Media Policy TODAY," Open Forum, August 15, 2013, http://www .openforum.com/articles/employee-social-media-policy/, accessed September 9, 2013.

The Example box below describes selected elements of several companies' current social media policies.

EXAMPLE   A Sampling of Social Media Policies

Here are selected provisions from some prominent companies' social media policies.[138]

At Adidas, employees may say in their posts that they work for the company but must label their personal posts as such. They are not permitted to post any sensitive information, such as about new products or pending legal actions.

Best Buy employees are prohibited from posting racial, ethnic, sexual, religious, and physical disability slurs.

Hewlett-Packard "reserves the right to edit or amend any misleading or inaccurate content depicted in blog posts" and to "delete blog posts violating the code of conduct."

GAP encourages caution when discussing topics like politics and religion online and recommends fixing any goofs immediately. The company's social media team is available to help in case of serious problems with a post.

Reporters at the *Los Angeles Times* are advised to observe "principles of integrity, professionalism, privacy and impartiality"[139] in their posts and to verify any factually questionable content before posting.

Intel asks employees to stick to what they know and to specify that their posts "don't necessarily represent Intel's positions, strategies, or opinions." It also requires them to disclose their "former employee" status on their social media profiles once they have left the company.

YOUR CALL

One writer says that since employees today are unable to fully separate their personal posts from the reputation of their organization, each one is, in effect, "a mouthpiece, a critic, a supporter, a case in point, an endorsement, a walking billboard."[140]

Do you agree or disagree? Do you think having a social media policy can effectively mitigate the dangers of allowing employees to fill these roles?

Assessing an Organization's Social Media Readiness   Consider the social media readiness of an organization to which you belong. Self-Assessment 15.2 helps you assess leadership's attitude toward social media, such as

- How supportive management is of creating communities.
- How well the culture fosters collaboration and knowledge sharing.
- How widely social media is used to collaborate.

With this knowledge you can determine how well your own attitudes fit with those of the organization, and it may even unveil opportunities for you to improve the organization's readiness. ●

---

connect SELF-ASSESSMENT 15.2

Assessing Social Media Readiness

Please be prepared to answer these questions if your instructor has assigned Self-Assessment 15.2 in Connect.

1. To what extent is the organization ready for capitalizing on social media?

2. Based on the results, what recommendations would you make to management about improving the value of social media within the company? Be specific.

15.5 Improving Communication Effectiveness

MAJOR QUESTION

How can I be a better listener, writer, and speaker?

THE BIG PICTURE

We describe how you can be a more effective listener, as in learning to concentrate on the content of a message, communicating nondefensively, and employing empathy. We offer four tips for becoming a more effective writer. Finally, we discuss how to be an effective speaker, through three steps.

Given that research suggests managers spend more than 75% of their time communicating, and that poor communication is estimated to cost organizations more than $9.3 billion annually,[141] it's no surprise that written and verbal communications skills are among the top five qualities employers look for most in college graduates. (Leadership, teamwork, and problem-solving skills are the other three.)[142]

How would you assess your communication skills? Do you think you are better than most? You can find out by completing the following self-assessment. If your score is lower than you prefer, find ideas for improving your interpersonal skills.

---

connect SELF-ASSESSMENT 15.3

Assessing My Communication Competence

This scale measures your communication competence. Please be prepared to answer these questions if your instructor has assigned Self-Assessment 15.3 in Connect.

1. Are you surprised by the results? Explain.

2. Based on your scores, what are your top three strengths and your three biggest weaknesses?

3. How might you use your strengths more effectively in your role as a student?

4. How might you improve on your weaknesses?

Let's see how you can be more effective at the essential communication skills.

Nondefensive Communication

Using evaluative or judgmental comments such as "Your work is terrible" or "You're always late for meetings" spurs defensiveness, which can lead to **defensive communication—either aggressive, attacking, angry communication or passive, withdrawing communication.** The better alternative is **nondefensive communication—communication that is assertive, direct, and powerful.**

You may be surprised to learn that defensiveness is often triggered by nothing more than a poor choice of words or nonverbal posture during interactions. In the language of behavior modification, these triggers are *antecedents* of defensiveness. For example, using absolutes like "always" or "never" is very likely to create a defensive response. Try to avoid using absolutes because they are rarely true. You can instead increase your communication competence by avoiding the defensive antecedents and employing the positive antecedents of nondefensive communication shown in Table 15.9.

TABLE 15.9   Antecedents of Defensive and Nondefensive Communication

TOWARD DEFENSIVENESS		TOWARD NONDEFENSIVENESS	
STYLE	**EXAMPLE**	**STYLE**	**EXAMPLE**
Evaluative	"Your work is sloppy."	Descriptive	"Your work was two days late."
Controlling	"You need to . . ."	Problem solving	*"What do you think are the causes of the missed deadline?"*
Strategizing	*"I'd like you to agree with me during the meeting so that we can overcome any challenges."*	Straightforward	*"Vote your conscious at the meeting. You can agree or disagree with my proposal."*
Neutral	*"Don't worry about missing the deadline. It's no big deal."*	Empathetic	*"I sense you are disappointed about missing the deadline. Let's figure out how we can get back on schedule."*
Superior	*"Listen to me, I've worked here 20 years."*	Equal	*"Let's figure out the causes of the missed deadline together."*
Certain	*"We tried this idea in the past. It just doesn't work."*	Honest and open	*Using I-messages:* "I am angry about the way you spoke to the customer because our department looked unresponsive."

Based on J. R. Gibb, "Defensive Communication," Journal of Communication, 1961, 141–148; and "Reach Out: Effective Communication," Sunday Business Post, April 14, 2013.

Some steps to achieving nondefensive communication are build relationships first, frame your message into terms that acknowledge the receiver's point of view, free yourself of prejudice and bias, practice full disclosure, and pick a time and place conducive to communicating and listening. Finally, avoid *jargon*.[143]

Given that we want you to learn how to promote nondefensive communication, we encourage you to complete Self-Assessment 15.4. It assesses whether a current or past work environment is supportive of nondefensive communication.

---

connect SELF-ASSESSMENT 15.4

Does Your Organization Have a Supportive or Defensive Communication Climate?

The following survey was designed to assess the supportive and defensive communication climate of your organization. Please be prepared to answer these questions if your instructor has assigned Self-Assessment 15.4 in Connect.

1. Where does the work environment stand in terms of having a supportive or defensive communication climate?

2. Based on your survey scores, what advice would you give to management in order to promote a more supportive communication climate? Be specific.

3. Considering your project teams at school, what can you do to create a more supportive communication climate in these teams?

Using Empathy

Although researchers propose multiple types of empathy, the general consensus is that **empathy** represents the ability to recognize and understand another person's feelings and thoughts.[144] It is a reflective technique that fosters open communication. Empathy works for managers because it is not the same thing as uncritically accepting others' words and behavior; rather, it relies on a conscious effort to understand the emotional impact of our own words and behavior.[145] According to Anand Mahindra, CEO of the Indian multinational organization Mahindra Group, "true empathy is rooted in humility and the understanding that there are many people with as much to contribute in life as you."[146]

Being empathetic requires two key actions. The first is mindfulness. Empathy necessitates that we place our attention on the feelings and emotions being displayed both verbally and nonverbally by others. The second action is to incorporate our understanding of another person's feelings and thoughts into our communications. This will lead us to use language that fits the receiver's perspective.

Using empathy. Does the sales representative on the right appear empathetic toward the customer's complaint about returning an appliance? How might empathy be shown in this context?
© allesalltag/Alamy

Empathy leads to more effective communication and interaction because people feel heard.[147] It also sends the message that we care about others. Although women are often more empathetic, studies show that everyone can learn this skill with training and practice.[148] In fact, medical students in the United States are increasingly being trained to use empathy when talking with patients, and the admissions test for medical school will now include questions designed to test applicants' existing understanding of psychology and human behavior. "Empathy is a cognitive attribute, not a personality trait," says Mohammadreza Hojat, a research professor of psychiatry at Jefferson Medical College.[149]

Being an Effective Listener

"Listening is the single most important and underrated skill in business, in social media, and in life. It's something we can always improve on," says Dave Kerpen, founder and CEO of social media software firm Likeable Local.[150] Richard Branson, entrepreneurial founder and CEO of the Virgin Group, agrees. The lesson he learned from his father was "Listen more than you speak. Nobody learned anything by hearing themselves speak."[151]

Actively listening, truly listening, requires more than just hearing, which is merely the physical component. **Active listening** is the process of actively decoding and interpreting verbal messages. Active listening requires full attention and processing of information, which hearing does not.

Understand me. What's the recipe for effective listening—for really finding out what someone has to say? Probably it is *listen, watch, write, think, question.* What do you do to fight flagging concentration if you're tired or bored? You suppress negative thoughts, ignore distractions about the speaker's style of delivery or body language, and encourage the speaker with eye contact, an interested expression, and an attentive posture. This will make you more involved and interested in the subject matter. © Image Source/PunchStock RF

There is general consensus that listening is a cornerstone skill of communication competence. In studies that support this conclusion, active listening made receivers feel more understood. It also led people to conclude that their conversations were more helpful, sensitive, and supportive.[152] Clearly, active listening yields positive outcomes.

Unfortunately, many of us think we are good listeners when evidence suggests just the opposite. For example, researchers estimate that typical listeners retain only 20%–50% of what they hear.[153]

Why do you think we miss or lose so much of what we hear? One reason is that we have the cognitive capacity to process words at a much higher rate than people speak. This means our cognitive processes are being underutilized, leading to daydreaming and distractions. Noise is another reason. A third reason, and one you can control, is your motivation to listen and your listening style. It takes effort to actively listen. You won't be a better listener unless you are motivated to become one.

Understand Your Listening Style—or Styles   You can improve your communication competence by understanding your typical listening style. There are four styles:[154]

1. **Active—I'm fully invested.** Active listeners are "all in." They are motivated to listen and give full attention when others are talking. They focus on what is being communicated and expend energy by participating in the discussion. They put their phone away, withhold judgment, and listen silently. They also use positive body language, such as leaning in or making direct eye contact, to convey their interest.[155]

2. **Involved—I'm partially invested.** Involved listeners devote only some of their attention and energy to listening. They reflect on what is being said and half-halfheartedly participate in the discussion. Their nonverbal cues can show interest and noninterest in the same conversation. If you tend to check your texts while having a meal with friends, you may be only an involved listener in the real-life interaction. Next time try having everyone put his or her phone in the center of the table until the check arrives.

3. **Passive—It's not my responsibility to listen.** Passive listeners are not equal partners in a speaking–listening exchange. They assume the speaker is responsible for the quality of the interaction and believe their role is to passively take in information. Passive listeners will display attentiveness, but they can fake it at times. Overall, they don't expend much motivation or energy in receiving and decoding messages. Is this your listening style during course lectures?

4. **Detached—I'm uninterested.** Detached listeners tend to withdraw from the interaction. They appear inattentive, bored, distracted, and uninterested. They may start using mobile devices during the speaking–listening exchange. Their body language will reflect lack of interest, such as slumping and avoiding direct eye contact. It is all too easy to tune out an unimaginative PowerPoint presentation during a meeting, for example.

Do you think you are an effective listener? Do you have a sense for what may be your bad listening habits? You can find out by completing Self-Assessment 15.5.

connect SELF-ASSESSMENT 15.5

Assessing Your Listening Style

The following survey was designed to assess the overall strength of your listening skills. Please be prepared to answer these questions if your instructor has assigned Self-Assessment 15.5 in Connect.

1. Is your listening style detached, passive, or involved? Based on your survey scores, what can you do to become more of an involved listener? Be specific.

2. Think of two ways you can practice better listening in your teams at work or school. Be specific.

Concentrate on the Content of the Message   Effective listening is a learned skill, so it takes energy and desire to develop it. Basically, however, it comes down to *paying attention to the content of the message.* Following are some suggestions for increasing your listening skills, which you can practice in your college lectures and seminars. *(See Table 15.10.)*

TABLE 15.10   Tips for Effective Listening

1. **Show respect.** Give everyone the opportunity to explain his or her ideas without interrupting. Actively try to help the sender convey his or her message.

2. **Listen from the first sentence.** Turn off your internal thoughts and whatever you were thinking about prior to the interaction.

3. **Be mindful.** Stay in the moment and focus on the sender. Don't try to figure out what the speaker is *going* to say or mentally compose your response.

4. **Keep quiet.** You have two ears and one mouth; use them accordingly. Try to use the 80/20 rule: Your conversational partner should speak 80% of the time, and you should speak 20%.

5. **Ask good questions.** Asking relevant questions clarifies what is being said and demonstrates that you are listening.

6. **Paraphrase and summarize.** Paraphrasing amounts to repeating back to someone what you just heard that person say. Summarizing is used to integrate or consolidate an entire conversation. Both these techniques enhance communication accuracy because they help ensure you are correctly understanding the messages.

7. **Remember what was said.** Either take notes or make an effort to log critical information into your mental computer.

8. **Involve your body.** Use nonverbal cues to demonstrate interest and involvement.

Sources: Based on J. Keyser, "Active Listening Leads to Business Success," T+D, July 2013, pp. 26–28; and B. Brooks, "The Power of Active Listening," The American Salesman, December 2010, pp. 28–30. T. Bradberry, "7 Most Common Habits of the Best Listeners," Inc., http://www.inc.com/travis-bradberry/7-things-great-listeners-do-differently.html, accessed July 2016.

Being an Effective Writer

Writing is an essential management skill, all the more so because e-mail and texting have replaced the telephone in so much of business communication. Taking a business writing class can be a major advantage. (Indeed, as a manager, you may have to identify employees who need writing training.) Following are some tips for writing business communications more effectively.

Start with Your Purpose   Rather than building up to the point, if you are delivering routine or positive news you should start by telling your purpose and stating what you expect of the reader. Along the same lines, when e-mailing, make sure the subject

TABLE 15.11

Five Rules for Business Writing, Both Online and Offline

DON'T . . .

1. Begin an e-mail with "Hey." "Hi" or "Hello" is more appropriate.

2. Use abbreviations or emojis.

DO . . .

3. Spell words correctly.

4. Use complete sentences.

5. Use proper capitalization and punctuation.

Source: Derived from J. R. Fine, "Enhancing Gen Y Communication Skills," Society for Human Resource Management, March 13, 2009. G. Leibowitz, "6 Tips for Writing Emotionally Intelligent Emails," Inc., http://www.inc.com/glenn -leibowitz/how-to-write-emotionally -intelligent-emails.html, accessed July 2016.

line clearly expresses your reason for writing. For instance, "Who is available Thursday afternoon?" does not inform the reader of your topic as well as "Davis project meeting moved to Thursday 3 p.m." does.

Write Simply, Concisely, and Directly   Short and sweet is the key.[156] Keep your words simple and use short words, sentences, and phrases. Be direct instead of vague, and use active rather than passive voice. (Directness, active voice: "Please call a meeting for Wednesday." Vagueness, passive voice: "It is suggested that a meeting be called for Wednesday.")

Know Your Audience   Send your message to all who need the information it contains, but *only* to those people. Resist the urge to include everyone, and be especially careful, in responding to messages, to think before you click "Reply All." If you are feeling emotional as you write, don't click "Send" at all but instead save your draft, take a break of at least a few hours, and go back to it later. Your feelings may have changed and your communication, and your relationships, will likely be better for it.

Don't Show Ignorance of the Basics   Texting has made many people more relaxed about spelling and grammar rules. Although this is fine among friends, as a manager you'll need to create a more favorable impression in your writing. Besides using spelling and grammar checkers, proofread your writing before sending it on. Check people's names and titles in particular, and be especially aware that auto-correct features can make incorrect assumptions about what you meant to say.

Some other tips are shown at left. *(See Table 15.11.)*

Being an Effective Speaker

We speak in many different circumstances, from one-on-one conversations, to meetings, to formal presentations. In terms of personal oral communication, most of the best advice comes under the heading of listening, since effective listening governs the amount and content of the talking you need to do.[157]

The ability to talk to a room full of people—to make an oral presentation—is one of the greatest skills you can have. And in case you think you don't have this skill, "everyone has public speaking ability," according to one writer for the London Speaker Bureau. It's simply that some people are more practiced because they have the opportunity to use it more than others.[158]

While 20% of working professionals in a recent survey said they take almost any steps to avoid public speaking, 70% agreed that the ability to make a skillful presentation was "critical" to their careers. And even more said they would like to be better at it.[159] In fact, reports of how widespread fear of public speaking is are probably exaggerated; it's likely that about 40%–45% of the population shares this fear.[160] Some people find public speaking a stimulating challenge and an opportunity to burnish their professional skills and reputation.

However you feel or think you feel about public speaking, there is no doubt you'll have to call upon your presentation skills during your career. You can find some good models in the many TED talks available online.[161] And you can do away with a great deal of anxiety about speaking in public by knowing what and how to prepare. For instance, ask ahead of time about who the audience will be, how much time you will be allowed, what technology might be available for incorporating audio or visual material, who else may be speaking, and whether there will be a question-and-answer session afterwards. Arrive early and check the room to be sure promised equipment is in place and working. As for the content of your presentation, Dale Carnegie's classic advice still holds: (1) Tell them what you're going to say. (2) Say it. (3) Tell them what you said.[162]

1. Tell Them What You're Going to Say   The introduction should take 5%–15% of your speaking time, and it should prepare the audience for the rest of the speech. Avoid jokes and such tired phrases as "I'm honored to be with you here today. . . ." Because everything in your speech should be relevant, be bold and go right to the point with a "grabber" such as a personal story or compelling comparison that attracts listeners' attention and prepares them to follow you closely.[163] For example:

> *"Good afternoon. You may not have thought much about identity theft, and neither did I until my identity was stolen—twice. Today I'll describe how our supposedly private credit, health, employment, and other records are vulnerable to theft and how you can protect yourself."*

2. Say It   The main body of the speech takes up 75%–90% of your time. The most important thing to realize is that your audience won't remember more than a few points, anyway. Choose them carefully and cover them as succinctly as possible.

Needless to say, your success rests largely on how well you deliver this part of the speech. Be sure you have done your homework. Speak about what you know best, understand your audience's point of view and preconceptions, and check and recheck your facts. These preparatory steps enhance your confidence and ensure you have credibility with your listeners.

When you practice this part of your presentation, be particularly attentive to transitions during the main body of the speech. Listening differs from reading in that the listener has only one chance to get your meaning. Thus, be sure you constantly provide your listeners with guidelines and transitional phrases so they can see where you're going. Example:

> *"There are five ways the security of your supposedly private files can be compromised. The first way is. . . . The second way takes place when. . . . "*

3. Tell Them What You Said   The end might take 5%–10% of your time. Many professional speakers consider the conclusion to be as important as the introduction, so don't drop the ball here. You need a solid, strong, persuasive wrap-up.

Predictor for success. Enjoying public speaking and being good at it are the top predictors of success and upward mobility. Do you think you could develop these skills? © Hill Street Studios/Blend Images/Alamy RF

Use some sort of signal phrase that cues your listeners that you are heading into your wind-up. Examples:

> *"Let's review the main points. . . ."*
> *"In conclusion, what CAN you do to protect against unauthorized invasion of your private files? I point out five main steps. One. . . ."*

Give some thought to the last thing you will say. It should be strongly upbeat, a call to action, a thought for the day, a little story, a quotation. Examples:

> *"I want to leave you with one last thought. . . ."*
> *"Finally, let me close by sharing something that happened to me. . . ."*
> *"As Albert Einstein said, 'Imagination is more important than knowledge.'"*

Then say, "Thank you," and stop. ●

active listening 535

communication 504

crowdsourcing 525

culture 515

cyberloafing 528

decoding 505

defensive communication 533

downward communication 510

empathy 534

encoding 505

external communication 511

feedback 506

formal communication channels 509

grapevine 511

horizontal communication 510

identity theft 529

informal communication channels 511

jargon 506

linguistic style 519

media richness 508

medium 505

message 505

mindlessness 515

noise 506

nondefensive communication 533

nonverbal communication 516

paraphrasing 506

privacy 529

receiver 505

security 528

sender 505

social media 520

social media policy 531

upward communication 510

Key Points

15.1 The Communication Process: What It Is, How It Works

- Communication is the transfer of information and understanding from one person to another. The process involves sender, message, and receiver; encoding and decoding; the medium; feedback; and dealing with "noise."

- The sender is the person wanting to share information. The information is called a message. The receiver is the person for whom the message is intended. Encoding is translating a message into understandable symbols or language. Decoding is interpreting and trying to make sense of the message. The medium is the pathway by which a message travels. Feedback is the process in which a receiver expresses his or her reaction to the sender's message.

- The entire communication process can be disrupted at any point by noise, defined as any disturbance that interferes with the transmission of a message.

- For effective communication, a manager must select the right medium. Media richness indicates how well a particular medium conveys information and promotes learning. The richer a medium is, the better it is at conveying information. Face-to-face presence is the richest; an advertising flyer would be one of the lowest. A rich medium is best for nonroutine situations and to avoid oversimplification. A lean medium is best for routine situations and to avoid overloading.

15.2 How Managers Fit into the Communication Process

- Communication channels may be formal or informal.

- Formal communication channels follow the chain of command and are recognized as official. Formal communication is of three types: (1) Vertical communication is the flow of messages up and down the organizational hierarchy. (2) Horizontal communication flows within and between work units; its main purpose is coordination. (3) External communication flows between people inside and outside the organization.

- Informal communication channels develop outside the formal structure and do not follow the chain of command. Two aspects of informal channels are the grapevine and face-to-face communication. (1) The grapevine is the unofficial communication system of the informal organization. The grapevine is faster than formal channels, is always operating, but is not always accurate. (2) Face-to-face communication builds trust between managers and employees. Managers should set aside time for such communication and hone their listening skills.

15.3 Barriers to Communication

- Barriers to communication are of five types: (1) Physical barriers are exemplified by walls, background noise, and time-zone differences. (2) Personal barriers are individual attributes that hinder communication. (3) Cross-cultural barriers are more common in view of globalization. (4) Nonverbal barriers often arise in cross-cultural communication and when verbal and nonverbal messages conflict. (5) Gender differences result in part from bias and assumptions that can be overcome.

- Nine personal barriers are (a) variable skills in communicating effectively, (b) variations in frames of reference and experiences that affect how information is interpreted, (c) variations in trustworthiness and credibility, (d) oversized egos, (e) faulty listening skills, (f) tendency to judge others' messages, (g) inability to listen with understanding, (h) stereotypes (oversimplified beliefs about a certain group of people) and prejudices, and (i) nonverbal communication (messages sent outside of the written or spoken word, including body language).

- Six ways in which nonverbal communication is expressed are through (1) eye contact, (2) facial expressions, (3) body movements and gestures, (4) touch, (5) setting, and (6) time.

15.4 Social Media and Management

- Social media contribute heavily to employee and employer productivity. They are widely used in employment recruiting and have applications in organizational innovation (via crowdsourcing), in sales, and in reputation management.
- Social media have costs as well. Cyberloafing—the personal use of computers and digital devices at work—costs organizations time and money. Security issues arise when careless or disgruntled employees put the organization's online environment at risk. Everyone must take responsibility for ensuring the privacy of his or her own and the organization's information and communication. Finally, controlling the flow of e-mail is a challenge for many.
- Texting's organizational applications and use may be growing, but personal texts should be strictly limited during the workday.
- Managers should engage employees in the creation of fair and effective social media policy to ensure

social media tools are consistently put to constructive work purposes.

15.5 Improving Communication Effectiveness

- People tend to favor only a few of five listening styles—appreciative, empathic, comprehensive, discerning, and evaluative. Active listening, the process of actively decoding and interpreting verbal messages, requires full attention and processing of information. To become a good listener, you should concentrate on the content of the message, not delivery; ask questions and summarize the speaker's remarks; listen for ideas; resist distractions and show interest; and give the speaker a fair hearing.
- To become an effective writer, start with your purpose. Write simply, concisely, and directly. Know your audience, and follow basic spelling and grammar rules for appropriately formal communication.
- To become an effective speaker, study successful models, know your subject, and prepare and rehearse ahead of time. For the presentation itself, follow three simple rules. Tell people what you're going to say. Say it. Tell them what you said.

Understanding the Chapter: What Do I Know?

1. Explain the communications process.
2. What are some common sources of noise in communication?
3. Explain the differences between formal and informal communication channels.
4. What are the five types of barriers to communication and examples of each?
5. Explain how social media can contribute to employee productivity.
6. How do social media make employers more productive?
7. What are some of the costs of social media in organizations?
8. Describe the managerial implications of texting at work.
9. What should managers know about creating a social media policy?
10. Explain the five listening styles and how to be a good listener.

Management in Action

Nokia Actively Uses Social Media to Communicate

Nokia is a Finnish multinational communications and information technology company. It was founded in 1865. In 2015, the company had 114,256 employees and four business groups: Nokia Networks, Nokia Technologies, Alcatel-Lucent, and Nokia Bell Labs. Total revenue in 2015 was 23.22 billion euros.[164]

The company's vision is to be an "innovation leader in the technologies that connect people and things." Making this happens involves pursuing a strategy of "creating a new type of network that's intelligent, efficient, and secure, and advancing the technologies that

tap its power through smart devices and sensors."[165] It is not surprising that Nokia would focus on using social media for its internal communications, given the company's history, vision, and strategic focus.

Nokia created a Social Media Communications Team in 2008 to improve communications. The team's goal is to "Encourage the use of social media internally to bring out the company's unique authentic voice and to engage in social media externally on behalf of Nokia, and contributing to product and service announcements by opening up a dialogue and driving online engagement."[166]

Nokia's Communication Strategy

Nokia's communication strategy entails a three-pronged approach using social media: (1) build relationships, (2) improve products and services, and (3) demonstrate corporate values and leadership.[167] The two key tools being used in this pursuit are BlogHub and VideoHub.

BlogHub. Members of the Social Media team believe BlogHub is the most effective internal communication tool used at Nokia. According to Molly Schonthal, former team member in North America, "The BlogHub lowers barriers for employees to find conversations relevant to them." BlogHub gives all employees a voice because communication spreads in all directions—horizontally, upward and downward. This contrasts with the top-down communication approach used in many companies. Schonthal concluded BlogHub provides a "dynamic community that is ruled by members, not executives."[168]

BlogHub enables employees to share ideas and update others on what they are doing. This fosters collaboration and breaks down communication silos. It also provides valuable information to management. One blogger noted that "BlogHub is an effective way to gather employee feedback on various issues and track the conversations that are happening inside the company. One of the primary ways that is accomplished is via a voting mechanism, enabling employees to rate blog posts, with the most popular entries rising to the top."[169]

Nokia Conversations is one specialized internal blog run by Phil Schwarzmann, its editor-in-chief. One feature focuses on telling employee stories about interesting people or interesting aspects of someone's job. For example, one story pertained to a 6'11" employee who played basketball for Notre Dame and now plays for a Finnish league. Other stories involve people who live the Nokia values of

- Respect—treating each other with respect and working hard to earn it from others.
- Achievement—working with others to deliver superior results and win in the marketplace.
- Renewal—develop your skills and grow the business.
- Challenge—avoid complacency and question the status quo.[170]

VideoHub. This collaborative tool allows employees to post and share videos. It contains a combination of professionally produced corporate or marketing videos and employee-generated content. The company provides a network of trained employees who help employees create short videos.

Videos of Nokia's quarterly business reviews represent examples of formal videos. These videos feature "top leaders' insights into the company's performance on a quarterly basis. The video is largely based on professionally conducted recording and editing, but is often complemented by employee-generated video clips."[171]

One example of less formal videos entailed management's requests of clips of employees who exemplify the company's values. Over 100 video clips were created. Johanna Komonen, Nokia's communications manager, commented that "Nokia is a very non-hierarchical company and I don't think you could ask people to make videos that are honest unless they felt confident enough to know that it's their video. We don't tell anyone what to put in their video, they know that it's their video and their views."[172]

All told, this tool "acts as a hub through which Nokia's employees can post, view and discuss work-related videos. Employees are encouraged to keep the clips to only a few minutes or so in length, with even the professional shot Quarterly Business Review lasting only around eight minutes."[173]

Communication Doesn't Stop with BlogHub and VideoHub

Other communication tools include the following:

- *Live Meeting* enables employees to ask questions online during presentations. Employees can also send text messages if they can't be online during the presentation.
- *Road shows* are used to educate employees about new products. "Regionally, mini product launches—aka 'mobility happy hours' are held so employees can ask questions and become familiar with Nokia devices."[174]
- *Video conferencing* is used to communicate across geographical boundaries. Annual communications meetings are also accessible with this medium in order to cut down on travel costs.
- *Electronic newsletters* are used on daily, weekly, or monthly bases to communicate about important topics and Nokia businesses and their initiatives.
- *Corporate intranet* is used to communicate about organizational charts and human resource benefits.
- *Flat Screen Displays* are located around regional offices and provide consistently streamed information about corporate issues, information, and real-time business metrics.[175]

Social Media Certification

Nokia has highly invested in its communication strategy. To facilitate its success, the company developed a six-part social media certification. Employees must complete the process before actively using the social media tools. To be certified, employees must[176]

1. Be prepared
2. Be transparent
3. Be smart
4. Be nice
5. Be yourself
6. Be professional

FOR DISCUSSION

1. To what extent is Nokia's use of social media consistent with recommendations about matching the richness of media to the situation at hand?

2. How does Nokia's use of social media tend to eliminate barriers to communication? Explain.

3. To what extent is Nokia experiencing any of the downsides to social media? Explain.

4. What are the primary benefits of Nokia's communication strategy?

5. What does this case teach you about interpersonal and organizational communication? Explain.

Legal/Ethical Challenge

Was the Firing of Curt Schilling for His Social Media Post Fair?

Curt Shilling was a six-time professional baseball player All-Star. His career record was 216–146 and his performance in the postseason even better at 11–2. This level of performance clearly helped him land a job at ESPN. He started working for the network in 2010, and he was fired after sharing a Facebook post in April 2016.

ESPN was a little lenient in allowing Schilling's political leanings and related comments during his tenure, according to Alex Reimer, a *Forbes* reporter. ESPN did not discipline Schilling for "railing against the theory of evolution on Twitter or for saying in March that Hillary Clinton should be 'buried under a jail' if she shared classified information on her private email server." ESPN did this despite informing all employees that they should avoid making political statements, according to Reimer.[177] Reimer further wrote that "on the occasions Schilling was suspended, such as when he tweeted a meme [a meme is a cultural item presented as an image or a phrase that is spread via the Internet, often in a humorous manner] comparing radical Muslims to Nazis, it was for his crassness rather than his politics."[178]

Schilling's ultimate firing was due to his sharing an anti-transgender image along with some commentary. The image "showed an overweight man wearing a wig and women's clothing with parts of the T-shirt cut out to expose his breasts. It says: "LET HIM IN! to the restroom with your daughter or else you're a narrow-minded, judgmental, unloving racist bigot who needs to die."[179] He added his own comments about the rights of transgenders' bathroom use that ESPN found offensive.

The *New York Daily News* reported that "Schilling's remarks were in support of a North Carolina law that bars people in the state from using a bathroom other than the one for their biological gender."[180] According to The *New York Times*, ESPN issued a statement saying they were an inclusive company and that Schilling's "conduct was unacceptable."[181]

Schilling claims that he isn't "transphobic or homophobic and 'wouldn't care' if his son wanted to be a woman."[182] He also commented, on a personal blog, that "let's make one thing clear right upfront. If you get offended by ANYTHING in this post, that's your fault, all yours."[183] Schilling, in turn, has been very critical of ESPN since his dismissal.

SOLVING THE CHALLENGE

Do you think it was fair for ESPN to fire Curt Schilling for expressing his views on social media?

1. No. ESPN was displaying political correctness rather than supporting one of its employees' rights to express his views about transgender bathroom rights. He should be reinstated.

2. Yes. ESPN told its employees not to make political statements and Schilling clearly ignored this recommendation. One needs to be very careful communicating when employed in the broadcasting industry.

3. Invent other options.

Controlling

16 Control Systems and Quality Management

Techniques for Enhancing Organizational Effectiveness

Major Questions You Should Be Able to Answer

16.1 Control: When Managers Monitor Performance

Major Question: Why is control such an important managerial function?

16.2 Levels and Areas of Control

Major Question: How do successful companies implement controls?

16.3 The Balanced Scorecard and Strategy Maps

Major Question: How can the balanced scorecard and strategy maps help me establish standards and measure performance?

16.4 Some Financial Tools for Control

Major Question: Financial performance is important to most organizations. What are the financial tools I need to know about?

16.5 Total Quality Management

Major Question: How do top companies improve the quality of their products or services?

16.6 Managing Control Effectively

Major Question: What are the keys to successful control, and what are the barriers to control success?

16.7 Managing for Productivity

Major Question: How do managers influence productivity?

Improving Productivity: Going beyond Control Techniques to Get the Best Results

How, as a manager, can you increase work productivity—get better results with what you have to work with? In this chapter we discuss control techniques for achieving better results. What are other ways for improving productivity? Following are some suggestions.[1]

Establish Base Points, Set Goals, and Measure Results

To be able to tell whether your work unit is becoming more productive, you need to establish systems of measurement. You can start by establishing the base point, such as the number of customers served per day, the quantity of products produced per hour, and the like. You can then set goals to establish new levels you wish to attain and institute systems of measurement with which to ascertain progress. Finally, you can measure the results and modify the goals or work processes as necessary.

Use Technology and Social Media

Not only can technology enhance performance; for instance, managers of virtual teams can hire the best-qualified workers no matter where they are. It can also offer new ways to measure and control results.[2] During its "ice bucket" fund-raising challenge, the nonprofit ALS Association could easily track the number of Facebook videos posted (1.2 million) and related Twitter posts (2.2 million). The campaign raised $115 million after going viral.[3] Mobile apps can also serve as control mechanisms.[4]

Improve Match between Employees and Jobs

You can take steps to ensure the best fit between employees and their jobs, including improving employee selection, paying attention to training, redesigning jobs, and providing financial incentives that are tied to performance. Factors to look for in selection include cultural fit and training and experience.[5]

Encourage Employee Involvement and Innovation

Companies improve performance by funding research and development (R&D) departments. Google spends more than 13% of its annual revenue on R&D.[6] As a manager, you can encourage your employees, who are closest to the work process, to come up with suggestions for improving their own operations. And, of course, you can give workers a bigger say in doing their jobs, allow employee flextime, and reward people for learning new skills and taking on additional responsibility.

Encourage Employee Diversity

By hiring people who are diverse in gender, age, race, ethnicity, and ability, you're more likely to have a workforce with different experiences, outlooks, values, and skills. Microsoft recently began a human resources effort specifically to hire people with autism and received hundreds of resumes. "By adjusting our hiring practices, we are able to recruit from a new talent pool—a talent pool that is rich with mad skills," said Jenny Lay-Flurrie, the company's chief accessibility officer. "We're hiring these folks because they're amazingly talented individuals who are going to help us do amazing things at Microsoft."[7]

Redesign the Work Process

Some managers think performance can be enhanced through cost cutting, but this is not always the case. It may be that the work process can be redesigned to eliminate inessential steps or more directly attack a problem. To better select top managers as it grew, Uber changed its interview process to focus less on asking applicants about their past. Instead, its recruiters had them describe, on the spot, how they would solve a realistic challenge the company might face.[8]

For Discussion Some observers think the pressure on managers to perform will be even more intense than before, because the world is undergoing a transformation on the scale of the industrial revolution 200 years ago as we move further into an information-based economy.[9] In what ways do you think you'll have to become a champion of adaptation?

FORECAST What's Ahead in This Chapter

The final management function, control, is monitoring performance, comparing it with goals, and taking corrective action as needed. We define *managing for performance* and explain its importance. We then identify six reasons for the need of management control, explain the steps in the control process, and describe three types of control managers use. Next we cover levels and areas of control and financial tools for control, as well as ways to control the supply chain and special considerations for service organizations. We discuss the balanced scorecard and total quality management (TQM). We describe the four keys to successful control and five barriers to successful control. We conclude by considering how to achieve higher productivity.

16.1   Control: When Managers Monitor Performance

MAJOR QUESTION

Why is control such an important managerial function?

THE BIG PICTURE

Controlling is monitoring performance, comparing it with goals, and taking corrective action. This section describes six reasons control is needed and four steps in the control process.

Control is making something happen the way it was planned to happen. **Controlling is defined as monitoring performance, comparing it with goals, and taking corrective action as needed.** Controlling is the fourth management function, along with planning, organizing, and leading, and its purpose is plain: to make sure that performance meets objectives.

- **Planning** is setting goals and deciding how to achieve them.
- **Organizing** is arranging tasks, people, and other resources to accomplish the work.
- **Leading** is motivating people to work hard to achieve the organization's goals.
- **Controlling** is concerned with seeing that the right things happen at the right time in the right way.

All these functions affect one another and in turn affect an organization's performance and productivity. *(See Figure 16.1.)*

FIGURE 16.1   Controlling for effective performance

What you as a manager do to get things done, with controlling shown in relation to the three other management functions. (These are not lockstep; all four functions happen concurrently.)

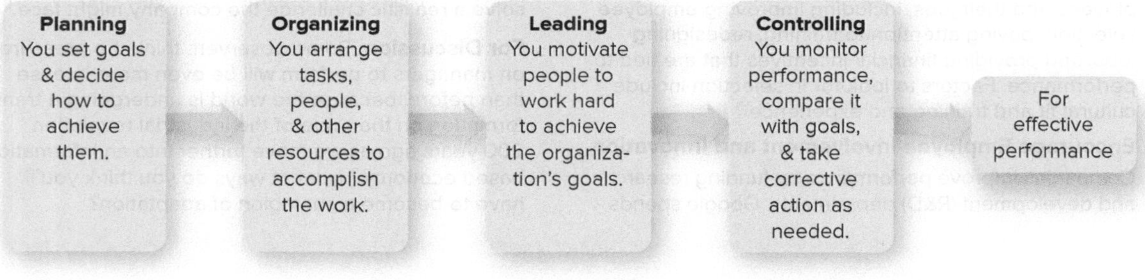

Planning	Organizing	Leading	Controlling	
You set goals & decide how to achieve them.	You arrange tasks, people, & other resources to accomplish the work.	You motivate people to work hard to achieve the organization's goals.	You monitor performance, compare it with goals, & take corrective action as needed.	For effective performance

Why Is Control Needed?

Lack of control mechanisms can lead to problems for both managers and companies. For example, in the wake of 11 reported deaths and dozens of injuries, more than 100 million autos have been recalled in the United States and worldwide due to faulty airbags manufactured by Takata, a Japanese auto parts maker.[10] As the company's CEO resigned and the scope of the ongoing recall grew,[11] *The New York Times* reported that faulty airbags continued to be installed in new U.S. cars, including Fiat Chrysler, Toyota, Volkswagen, and Mitsubishi.[12] Could greater control have helped avoid or reduce the consequences of these situations? Of course. Control can save lives!

Control matters. The National Highway Traffic Safety Administration (NHTSA) concluded that the airbag recall from 14 different automarkers is the largest and most complex in U.S. history. The airbags, which were made by Takata, involved car models from 2002 through 2015. The purpose of management control system is to prevent mistakes, errors, and design flaws from reaching consumers. © Jochen Tack/Alamy

There are six reasons control is needed.

1. To Adapt to Change and Uncertainty

Markets shift. Consumer tastes change. New competitors appear. Technologies are reborn. New materials are invented. Government regulations are altered. All organizations must deal with these kinds of environmental changes and uncertainties. Control systems can help managers anticipate, monitor, and react to these changes.

Example: Self-driving cars are in the testing stage at many companies around the world. Early indications, including the recent death of a driver in a collision on a Florida highway, suggest that autonomous cars are probably years away from becoming a reality.[13] But if successful, they are sure to bring changes in traffic patterns, safety regulations, road use and signage, insurance policies, auto design, and even car ownership patterns and customer expectations. As one writer predicts, "Driving is still going to be about the experience, but not the experience of driving."[14]

2. To Discover Irregularities and Errors

Small problems can mushroom into big ones. Cost overruns, manufacturing defects, employee turnover, bookkeeping errors, and customer dissatisfaction are all matters that may be tolerable in the short run. But in the long run, they can bring about even the downfall of an organization.

Example: The National Highway Traffic Safety Administration (NHTSA) and Tesla Motors are both investigating the causes of the 2016 crash that killed the driver of a self-driving Tesla car on a Florida highway. Tesla says the car's camera, part of its beta-phase Autopilot system, failed to spot the white tractor-trailer crossing the driver's path on a bright day. NHTSA wants to know why. The agency, which is developing standards for self-driving cars, has also asked Tesla to share its reconstruction of the accident and has imposed a deadline to be enforced by the prospect of thousands of dollars in fines. If defects in the Autopilot system are found, a product recall could follow.[15]

3. To Reduce Costs, Increase Productivity, or Add Value

Control systems can reduce labor costs, eliminate waste, increase output, and increase product delivery cycles. In addition, controls can help add value to a product so that customers will be more inclined to choose them over rival products.

Example: Simple changes to an office environment can change employee attitudes and have a positive impact on productivity.[16] The use of color, arrangement of space, type of seating and lighting, and presence or absence of music can all affect productivity, perhaps by as much as 20%. Control mechanisms to monitor the results of such changes can be as simple as periodic employee satisfaction surveys.[17]

4. To Detect Opportunities and Increase Innovation

Hot-selling products. Competitive prices on materials. Changing population trends. New overseas markets. Controls can help alert managers to innovative opportunities that might have otherwise gone unnoticed.[18]

Example: Uniqlo, the big Asian apparel retailer, is locked in competition for global market share with "fast fashion" clothiers Zara (from Spain), H&M (Sweden), and online stores. Like those at most businesses, Uniqlo managers look at a monthly metric called EBIDTA, earnings before interest, depreciation, taxes, and amortization, to gauge their success in each new market they enter.[19]

5. To Provide Performance Feedback

Can you improve without feedback? When a company becomes larger or when it merges with another company, it may find it has several product lines, materials-purchasing policies, customer bases, and worker needs that conflict with each other. Controls help managers coordinate these various elements by providing feedback.[20]

Example: Global companies like Pepsi-Cola must manage broad and diverse arrays of brands and products at locations around the world. To ensure the same high level of quality everywhere despite dealing with a virtual army of suppliers, Pepsi relies on an interlocking set of sustainability and quality control policies covering everything from ingredients to packaging. It must abide by regulations imposed by the U.S. Food and Drug Administration and by agencies around the globe, including the European Food Safety Authority and Health Canada, for instance.[21]

6. To Decentralize Decision Making and Facilitate Teamwork

Controls allow top management to decentralize decision making at lower levels within the organization and to encourage employees to work together in teams. Facing a possible shortage of doctors in some areas of medicine, for instance, health care professionals are anticipating a rise in teamwork, small group practices, and the delegation of some routine patient services to nurse practitioners.[22] Controls, including secure digital patient records, will be important in ensuring high-quality and personalized care.

The six reasons are summarized below. *(See Figure 16.2.)*

FIGURE 16.2

Six reasons control is needed

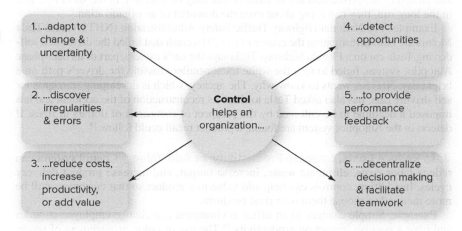

Steps in the Control Process

Control systems may be altered to fit specific situations, but generally they follow the same steps. The four **control process steps** are **(1) establish standards; (2) measure performance; (3) compare performance to standards; and (4) take corrective action, if necessary.** *(See Figure 16.3.)*

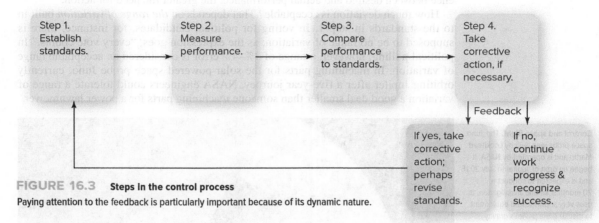

FIGURE 16.3   **Steps in the control process**
Paying attention to the feedback is particularly important because of its dynamic nature.

Let's consider these four steps.

1. Establish Standards: "What Is the Outcome We Want?"   **A control standard,** or *performance standard* or simply *standard,* **is the desired performance level for a given goal.** Standards may be narrow or broad, and they can be set for almost anything, although they are best measured when they can be made quantifiable.

Nonprofit institutions might have standards for level of charitable contributions, number of students or volunteers retained, or degree of legal compliance. For-profit organizations might have standards of financial performance, employee hiring, manufacturing defects, percentage increase in market share, percentage reduction in costs, number of customer complaints, and return on investment. Service organizations may look at number of customers, clients, or patients served; time spent with each; and resulting level of satisfaction. More subjective standards, such as level of employee satisfaction, can also be set, although they may have to be expressed more quantifiably in terms of, say, reduced absenteeism and sick days and increased job applications.

One technique for establishing standards is to use *the balanced scorecard,* as we explain later in this chapter.

2. Measure Performance: "What Is the Actual Outcome We Got?"   The second step in the control process is to measure performance, such as by number of products sold, units produced, or cost per item sold.[23]

Example: Some performance goals may seem difficult to quantify and therefore measure, but the key is to make them concrete. For instance, "Be on time for all meetings" and "Update your team members once a week on the status of your project" are more measurable standards than "Be punctual" and "Keep everyone informed."[24]

Performance data are usually obtained from three sources: (1) employee behavior and deliverables; (2) peer input or observations; and (3) personal observation, as when a manager takes a stroll on the factory floor to see what employees are doing.

As we've hinted, measurement techniques can vary for different industries, such as for manufacturing industries versus service industries. We discuss this further later in the chapter.

3. Compare Performance to Standards: "How Do the Desired and Actual Outcomes Differ?"

The third step in the control process is to compare measured performance against the standards established. Most managers are delighted with performance that exceeds standards, which becomes an occasion for handing out bonuses, promotions, and perhaps offices with a view. For performance that is below standards, they need to ask: Is the deviation from performance significant? The greater the difference between desired and actual performance, the greater the need for action.

How much deviation is acceptable? That depends on *the range of variation* built in to the standards in step 1. In voting for political candidates, for instance, there is supposed to be no range of variation; as the expression goes, "every vote counts." In political polling, however, a range of 3%–4% error is considered an acceptable range of variation. In machining parts for the solar-powered space probe Juno, currently orbiting Jupiter after a five-year journey, NASA engineers could tolerate a range of variation a good deal smaller than someone machining parts for a power lawnmower.

Control and space flight. The Juno space probe was built by Lockheed Martin and is operated by NASA. It began an orbit of Jupiter in July 2016 and is expected to conduct a 20 month scientific investigation. It uses very sophisticated equipment to measure the planet's gravity field, magnetic field, and polar magnestosphere. This type of equipment requires high levels of accuracy. Source: NASA/JPL-Caltech

The range of variation is often incorporated in computer systems into a principle called management by exception. **Management by exception** is a control principle that states that managers should be informed of a situation only if data show a significant deviation from standards.

4. Take Corrective Action, If Necessary: "What Changes Should We Make to Obtain Desirable Outcomes?"

This step concerns *feedback*—modifying, if necessary, the control process according to the results or effects. This might be a dynamic process that will produce different effects every time you put the system to use. There are three possibilities here: (1) Make no changes. (2) Recognize and reinforce positive performance. (3) Take action to correct negative performance.

When performance meets or exceeds the standards set, managers should give rewards, ranging from giving a verbal "Job well done" to more substantial payoffs such as raises, bonuses, and promotions to reinforce good behavior.

When performance falls significantly short of the standard, managers should carefully examine the reasons and take the appropriate action. Sometimes the standards themselves were unrealistic, owing to changing conditions, in which case the standards need to be altered. Sometimes employees haven't been given the resources for achieving the standards. And sometimes the employees may need more attention from management as a way of signaling that their efforts have been insufficient in fulfilling their part of the job bargain.

Steps in the Control Process: What's Expected of UPS Drivers?   EXAMPLE

To help younger drivers train for successful careers, UPS worked with a U.S. Department of Labor financial grant and research gleaned from studying the way people who grew up with video games and smartphones learn. The result was a high-tech training center called Integrad®, which now operates in locations in seven different states. The program has so far trained more than 7,500 drivers and more than 1,500 managers in "safe work methods, safe driving methods, customer service methods, training in using the handheld computer (DIAD—acronym for Delivery Information Acquisition Device) for recording delivery information, proper package selection, and UPS history."[25]

Establishing Standards. UPS establishes standards for its drivers that project the number of miles driven, deliveries, and pickups. A typical day for a driver in Louisville, Kentucky, might include driving 60 miles to make 125 deliveries.[26]

Measuring Performance. UPS managers get a constant stream of feedback about drivers' performance from the DIAD device and from two onboard computer systems. ORION optimizes the drivers' routes, and Telematics relays information about how often drivers back up and whether they are wearing seat belts. "Everything the driver does is being measured," says the company's business manager in Louisville.[27]

Comparing Performance to Standards. UPS managers compare a driver's performance (miles driven and number of pickups and deliveries) with the standards that were set for his or her particular route. A range of variation may be allowed to take into account such matters as winter or summer driving or traffic conditions that slow productivity.

Taking Corrective Action. When a UPS driver fails to perform according to the standards set for him or her, a supervisor then rides along and gives suggestions for improvement. If drivers are unable to improve, they are warned, then suspended, and then dismissed. Sometimes performance problems can be system-wide, and then solutions must be as well. After unexpected volume left the company with 1 million undelivered packages on Christmas Eve in 2013, the company invested $150 million in better preparing for the holiday rush and hired more than 100,000 temporary employees, which proved to be too many and had a negative impact on fourth-quarter earnings.[28]

YOUR CALL

The UPS controls were devised by industrial engineers based on experience. Do you think the same kinds of controls could be established for, say, filling out tax forms for H&R Block?

Types of Controls

There are three types of control: feedforward, concurrent, and feedback. They vary based on the timing of when control takes place.

Feedforward Control   **Feedforward control** focuses on preventing future problems. It does this by collecting performance information about past performance and then planning to avoid pitfalls or roadblocks prior to starting a task or project.[29] Nestle is a global food and nutrition company that uses feedforward control.

Nestle's quality management system "starts on farms." The company works with local farmers to improve "the quality of their produce and adopt environmentally sustainable farming practices." Doing this helps provide Nestle with high-quality raw materials, and it "enables farmers to protect or even increase their income," according to corporate documents.[30]

Concurrent Control   **Concurrent control** entails collecting performance information in real time. This enables managers to determine if employee behavior and organizational processes conform to regulations and standards. Corrective action can then be taken immediately when performance is not meeting expectations. For instance, trucking companies use GPS tracking to monitor "where company vehicles go, when they get there and how fast they move between destinations. It helps managers plan more efficient routes and alerts drivers to adjust routes in the event of an accident ahead. It also encourages employees to stay on task rather than running personal errands."[31]

Technology is typically used for concurrent control. Word-procesing software is a good example. It immediately lets us know when we misspell words or use incorrect grammar. Corporate online monitoring of our e-mail and Internet use is another example of concurrent control.

Feedback Control   This form of control is extensively used by supervisors and managers. **Feedback control amounts to collecting performance information after a task or project is done.** This information then is used to correct or improve future performance. Classic examples include receiving test scores a week after taking the test, receiving customer feedback after purchasing a product, receiving student ratings of a teaching performance weeks after teaching a class, rating the quality of a movie after watching it, and participating in a performance review at work.

The problem with feedback control is that it occurs too late. For instance, if an instructor is doing a bad job in the classroom, he or she needs to make changes right away. Learning 10 weeks later that his or her performance was ineffective does not help current students. The same is true when it comes to customer satisfaction and quality. On the positive side, many people want feedback, and late is better than never.

IBM recognized the limitations of providing feedback in annual performance reviews. The company scrapped its 10-year-old system, called Personal Business Commitments, and replaced it with one called Checkpoint. The new system requires employees to set short-term goals, and managers provide quarterly feedback on their progress.[32] ●

Small business. What type of control is most important for small businesses? Do you think employees in small companies, such as a garden pots store, need less control than employees in large companies?
© Don Mason/Blend Images/Getty Images RF

16.2 Levels and Areas of Control

MAJOR QUESTION **How do successful companies implement controls?**

THE BIG PICTURE

This section describes three levels of control—strategic, tactical, and operational—and six areas of control: physical, human, informational, financial, structural (bureaucratic and decentralized), and cultural. We also look at the supply chain and special considerations for control mechanisms in service firms.

How are you going to apply the steps of control to your own management area? Let's look at this in several ways: First, you need to consider the *level* of management at which you operate—top, middle, or first level. Second, you need to consider the *areas* that you draw on for resources—physical, human, information, and/or financial. Finally, we look at the *type of firm*. If you manage a manufacturing firm, you will have *supply chain* issues that require controls at many points, while if your firm is a service provider, you still require controls, but of a different type.

Levels of Control: Strategic, Tactical, and Operational

There are three levels of control, which correspond to the three principal managerial levels: *strategic* planning by top managers, *tactical* planning by middle managers, and *operational* planning by first-line (supervisory) managers and team leaders.

1. Strategic Control by Top Managers   **Strategic control** is monitoring performance to ensure that strategic plans are being implemented and taking corrective action as needed. Strategic control is mainly performed by top managers, those at the CEO and VP levels, who have an organizationwide perspective.[33]

For example, former Ford Motor Company CEO Alan Mulally (who retired in 2014) brought the company back from the financial brink by instituting a weekly meeting with senior managers. Each manager presented a report on his or her areas, coded in green, yellow, or red to indicate whether business was on target or needed improvement.[34]

2. Tactical Control by Middle Managers   **Tactical control** is monitoring performance to ensure that tactical plans—those at the divisional or departmental level—are being implemented and taking corrective action as needed. Tactical control is done mainly by middle managers, those with such titles as "division head," "plant manager," and "branch sales manager." Reporting is done on a weekly or monthly basis.

3. Operational Control by First-Line Managers   **Operational control** is monitoring performance to ensure that operational plans—day-to-day goals—are being implemented and taking corrective action as needed. Operational control is done mainly by first-line managers, those with titles such as "department head" or "supervisor." It also includes team leaders. Reporting is done on a daily basis.

Considerable interaction occurs among the three levels, with lower-level managers providing information upward and upper-level managers checking on some of the more critical aspects of plan implementation below them.

Six Areas of Control

The six areas of organizational control are *physical, human, informational, financial, structural,* and *cultural.*

1. Physical Area   The physical area includes buildings, equipment, and tangible products.

Examples: Equipment controls monitor the use of computers, cars, HVAC equipment, and other machinery. The speedometer in your car is a physical control. Quality controls ensure that products are being built according to certain acceptable standards. Inventory-management controls keep track of how many products are in stock, how many will be needed, and what their delivery dates are. If you have ever searched for a popular item on Amazon.com, for instance, you may have seen a notification like "Only 5 left in stock (more on the way)." The company's sophisticated inventory controls supply the information that makes these notifications possible. Lowe's, a home improvement retailer, is experimenting with robot inventory checkers that roam the aisles, deftly avoiding shoppers while scanning product bar codes on the shelves.[35]

2. Human Resources Area   The controls used to monitor employees include personality tests and drug testing for hiring, performance tests during training, performance evaluations to measure work productivity, and employee surveys to assess job satisfaction and leadership. Airbnb's human resource function has expanded its role and likely its control functions as well, as the following Example box describes.

EXAMPLE   Airbnb Revolutionizes Human Resources

Mark Levy is the Global Head of Employee Experiences at Airbnb, the online company that brought sharing to the business of finding a place to stay when traveling. Airbnb has more than 1 million listings in 34,000 cities around the world; they range from a fold-out couch in someone's living room to a 17-bedroom private chateau in France. The company's innovation was to use the Internet to put hosts and guests in touch.

When Levy was hired, the company had a human resources department split into several functions reporting to one overall leader. Levy did not like this structure. He preferred a structure organized around "employee experiences," to parallel the company's existing customer experience group. Among the new function's responsibilities are traditional HR concerns like recruiting, development, and compensation benefits, but also "facilities, food, global citizenship," and employee events and recognition. "Every aspect of creating the employee experience is focused on designing an extraordinary physical, emotional, intellectual, virtual, and aspirational experience for Airbnb employees."

One HR innovation is the company's use of storyboarding to map the ideal recruiting experience and ways in which recruiters can serve as "the ideal host." Another is using crowdsourcing to poll employees on what new skills and knowledge they need to develop in their careers, instead of imposing career development from the top down. Airbnb's goal is to refashion the workplace as "an experience."[36]

YOUR CALL

What traditional control functions does Airbnb's Employee Experience Group fulfill? What new responsibilities has the group taken on? How can it measure its own performance in recreating "the workplace as an experience"?

---

3. Informational Area   Production schedules, sales forecasts, environmental impact statements, analyses of competition, and public relations briefings all are controls on an organization's various information resources. Among the factors that will govern a decision about whether a high-speed passenger-rail line is to be built in Oregon, for instance, is an environmental impact statement being prepared by the state's Department of Transportation.[37]

4. Financial Area   Are bills being paid on time? How much money is owed by customers? How much money is owed to suppliers? Is there enough cash on hand to meet payroll obligations? What are the debt-repayment schedules? What is the advertising budget? Clearly, the organization's financial controls are important because they can affect the preceding three areas. If Oregon's high-speed rail line becomes a reality, one of the major tasks for project managers will be controlling the cost of building it, which estimates say could rise as high as $4.5 billion.[38]

5. Structural Area How is the organization arranged from a hierarchical or structural standpoint?[39] Two examples are *bureaucratic control* and *decentralized control*.

- **Bureaucratic control. Bureaucratic control** is an approach to organizational control that is characterized by use of rules, regulations, and formal authority to guide performance. This form of control attempts to elicit employee compliance, using strict rules, a rigid hierarchy, well-defined job descriptions, and administrative mechanisms such as budgets, performance appraisals, and compensation schemes (external rewards to get results). The foremost example of use of bureaucratic control is the traditional military organization.

  Bureaucratic control works well in organizations in which the tasks are explicit and certain. While rigid, it can be an effective means of ensuring that performance standards are being met. However, it may not be effective if people are looking for ways to stay out of trouble by simply following the rules, or if they try to beat the system by manipulating performance reports, or if they try to actively resist bureaucratic constraints.

- **Decentralized control. Decentralized control** is an approach to organizational control that is characterized by informal and organic structural arrangements, the opposite of bureaucratic control. This form of control aims to get increased employee commitment, using the corporate culture, group norms, and workers taking responsibility for their performance. Decentralized control is found in companies with a relatively flat organization.

6. Cultural Area The cultural area is an informal method of control. It influences the work process and levels of performance through the set of norms that develop as a result of the values and beliefs that constitute an organization's culture. If an organization's culture values innovation and collaboration, as at many tech start-ups, for instance, then employees are likely to be evaluated on the basis of how much they engage in collaborative activities and enhance or create new products.

Bureaucratic control. In businesses such as construction of large subdivisions, tasks are explicit and certain, and employees are expected to perform them the same way each time. However, a small contractor, such as one building custom houses, need not be bureaucratic.
© MyLoupe/Universal Images Group/ UIG/Getty Images

Controlling the Supply Chain

The supply chain is the sequence of suppliers that contribute to creating and delivering a product, from raw materials to production to final buyers. Supply chains are a major cost center for most companies, and the way firms structure the distribution of their products can have enormous financial impact. In recognition of this impact, companies are paying closer attention to the sourcing, shipping, and warehousing of their products and of the ingredients and component parts they require. Many organizations are creating specialized supply chain departments that look specifically at cost and quality control in these areas and the way they contribute to the cost and quality of finished products. Managing supply chain functions has become so important that some academic management departments now offer undergraduate and master's degrees in supply chain management, including at Arizona State University, for example.

At Hostess Brands, a dramatic change in the way products are delivered to stores is credited with helping the snack food company recover from bankruptcy. Hostess used to follow the traditional model for perishable items, sending 8,000 of its own drivers out to deliver Twinkies and other products directly to store shelves. After declaring bankruptcy, however, the firm revamped its process and adopted a much less expensive distribution plan. Now it delivers goods only as far as retailers' distribution centers, and retailers take on the job of stocking their own individual stores. After also drastically cutting the size of its workforce, the company recently took in revenues of $650 million under new ownership.[40]

At Target, with annual sales in the $75 billion range,[41] the supply chain has evolved with advances in online shopping. Where the goal was once to deliver goods from suppliers to regional warehouses in a straight line, now, says the company's CIO, Mike McNamara, "All of our inventory is available to all our guests, all the time. We will ship from a point to a guest that makes the most economic sense, or gives the guest the shortest lead time. That means that the thing that was once linear is now a network."[42]

Amazon has been experimenting with using drones as "the delivery truck of the future." The company hopes drones will someday be able to accurately deliver packages weighing up to five pounds ("the vast majority of the things we sell at Amazon") within 30 minutes in both cities and rural areas. It warns that drones won't become a reality anytime soon, however.[43]

Control in Service Firms

Service providers, such as income-tax preparers, hospitals and dental practices, consultants, accountants, hair and nail salons, stockbrokers, hotels, and airlines, differ from manufacturers in several ways. The most obvious is that service companies cannot hold any inventory of their services, which are intangible; instead they provide these services only on demand. Your new haircut does not exist until you sit down in the stylist's chair, for example.

Another difference is that service firms usually develop a personal, if temporary, relationship with their client or customer. Your haircut or flu shot is provided only to you, in other words, and the seat you buy on a plane heading to Amsterdam can be filled only by you. Some services are highly perishable. If you don't show up for your flight to Amsterdam, your ability to occupy that particular seat on that particular plane vanishes forever, along with your chance to sleep in the hotel room you reserved at your destination. The education you acquire in college is another example of the personal nature of service; that education is yours alone.[44]

The U.S. service industry has grown considerably in the last few decades as a great deal of manufacturing activity has moved overseas. Before World War II, there were about two service-industry jobs for every manufacturing job in the United States. Today the ratio of service to manufacturing employment is almost seven to one.[45]

Since services are provided by humans (for the most part), everything we have outlined in this chapter that relates to measuring and controlling employee behavior applies to the role of control in service organizations. Clearly, training and education affect the quality of any service. Health care organizations operate under high control standards, for example, as evidenced by the many years of education and training required to obtain a license to practice medicine or dentistry. The same holds for the practice of law. Ongoing training and certification are a form of control for airline pilots, tax accountants (CPAs), teachers, physical therapists, and personal trainers. •

16.3 The Balanced Scorecard and Strategy Maps

MAJOR QUESTION

How can the balanced scorecard and strategy maps help me establish standards and measure performance?

THE BIG PICTURE

The balanced scorecard helps managers establish goals and measures for four strategic perspectives. A visual representation of the relationships among balanced scorecard perspectives is the strategy map.

Wouldn't you, as a top manager, like to have displayed in easy-to-read graphics all the information on sales, orders, and the like assembled from data pulled in real-time from corporate software? The technology exists and it has a name: a *dashboard*, like the instrument panel in a car.

Bob Parsons, founder of GoDaddy, believed in dashboards. "Measure everything of significance. Anything that is measured and watched improves," he said.[46]

Throughout this book we have stressed the importance of *evidence-based management*—the use of real-world data rather than fads and hunches in making management decisions. When properly done, the dashboard is an example of the important tools that make this kind of management possible. The balanced score-card is another.

The Balanced Scorecard: A Dashboard-like View of the Organization

Robert Kaplan is a professor of accounting at the Harvard Business School and a leading authority on strategic performance measurement. David Norton is co-founder of Balanced Scorecard Collaborative. Kaplan and Norton developed what they call the **balanced scorecard, which gives top managers a fast but comprehensive view of the organization via four indicators: (1) customer satisfaction, (2) internal processes, (3) innovation and improvement activities, and (4) financial measures.**

"Think of the balanced scorecard as the dials and indicators in an airplane cock-pit," write Kaplan and Norton. For a pilot, "reliance on one instrument can be fatal. Similarly, the complexity of managing an organization today requires that managers be able to view performance in several areas simultaneously."[47] It is not enough, say Kaplan and Norton, to simply measure financial performance, such as sales figures and return on investment. Operational matters, such as customer satisfaction, are equally important.[48]

The Balanced Scorecard: Four "Perspectives"   The balanced scorecard establishes (a) *goals* and (b) *performance measures* according to four "perspectives," or areas—*financial, customer, internal business,* and *innovation and learning. (See Figure 16.4, next page.)*

1. Financial Perspective: "How Do We Look to Shareholders?"   Corporate financial strategies and goals generally fall into two buckets: revenue growth and productivity growth. Revenue growth goals might focus on increasing revenue from

FIGURE 16.4   **The balanced scorecard: Four perspectives**

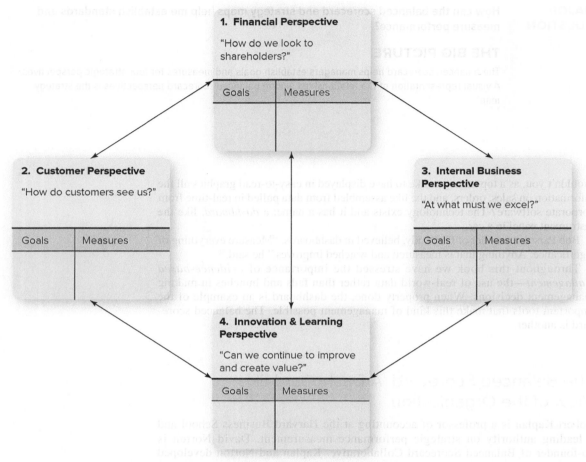

1. Financial Perspective

"How do we look to shareholders?"

Goals	Measures

2. Customer Perspective

"How do customers see us?"

Goals	Measures

3. Internal Business Perspective

"At what must we excel?"

Goals	Measures

4. Innovation & Learning Perspective

"Can we continue to improve and create value?"

Goals	Measures

Source: Adapted from R. S. Kaplan and D. P. Norton, "The Balanced Scorecard—Measures That Drive Performance," Harvard Business Review, *January–February 1992, pp. 71–79.*

both new and existing customers. Equipment manufacturer John Deere, for instance, is pursuing new revenue by developing software services that provide information and guidance to farmers in the field. It is doing this to offset a recent 5% decrease in revenue.[49] Productivity metrics like revenue per employee or total output produced divided by number of employees are common organization-level goals. We can also measure productivity in terms of costs. For example, Bob Evans Farms, Inc., is closing 27 underperforming restaurants in an attempt to decrease costs and improve profitability.[50]

2. Customer Perspective: "How Do Customers See Us?"   Many companies view customers as one of their most important constituents. The balanced scorecard translates this belief into measures such as market share, customer acquisition, customer retention, customer satisfaction/loyalty, product/service quality, response time (the time between order and delivery), and percentage of bids won.

Sunnybrook Health Sciences Centre, part of the University of Toronto Faculty of Medicine, has 1.2 million patient visits a year. The four "quality of care" goals in its balanced scorecard all relate to the ways in which its constituents—patients and partners—experience the organization. The goals are:

- **Goal 1**
  Improve the patient experience and outcomes through inter-professional, high quality care.

- **Goal 2**
  Focus on the highest levels of specialized care in support of our Academic Health Sciences Centre definition.

- **Goal 3**
  Work with system partners and government to build an integrated delivery system in support of our communities and our Academic Health Sciences Centre definition.

- **Goal 4**
  Achieving excellence in clinical care associated with our strategic priorities.[51]

3. Internal Business Perspective: "What Must We Excel At?" The internal business perspective focuses on "what the organization must excel at" to effectively meet its financial objectives and customers' expectations. A team of researchers identified four critical high-level internal processes that managers are encouraged to measure and manage:

1. Innovation.
2. Customer service and satisfaction.
3. Operational excellence, which includes safety and quality.
4. Good corporate citizenship.[52]

These processes influence productivity, efficiency, quality, safety, and a host of other internal metrics. Companies tend to adopt continuous improvement programs in pursuit of upgrades to their internal processes. Consider how Citi modified its workflow processes to reduce costs.

Example: Citi recently worked with commercial vehicle manufacturer Navistar to eliminate the need for thousands of paper checks it was sending its suppliers. The bank used its Citi Payment Exchange system to set up a secure, cloud-based accounts payable function for Navistar. Andrew Bernardi, cash operations director at Navistar, says the effect was to "convert more than 1,100 suppliers to electronic payments and eliminate more than 70,000 check payments handled by our A/P (accounts payable) group." Since it can cost companies anywhere from $30 to $60 to process a single paper check, taking a large company's payment process paperless can save millions of dollars a year.[53]

4. Innovation and Learning Perspective: "Can We Continue to Improve and Create Value?" Learning and growth of employees are the foundation for all other goals in the balanced scorecard. The idea here is that capable and motivated employees, who possess the resources and culture needed to get the job done, will provide higher-quality products and services in a more efficient manner. Making this happen requires a commitment to invest in progressive human resource practices and technology. Typical metrics in this perspective are employee satisfaction/engagement, employee retention, employee productivity, training budget per employee, technology utilization, and organizational climate and culture. Many are tracked with employee surveys to gauge attitudes and opinions.

To what extent is/was your current or past employer committed to the innovation and learning of its employees? You can find out by completing Self-Assessment 16.1.

≡ connect SELF-ASSESSMENT 16.1

Assessing the Innovation and Learning Perspective of the Balanced Scorecard

The following survey was designed to assess the innovation and learning perspective of the balanced scorecard. Please be prepared to answer these questions if your instructor has assigned Self-Assessment 16.1 in Connect.

1. Where does the company stand in terms of commitment to innovation and learning? Are you surprised by the results?

2. Use the three highest and lowest scores to identify the strengths and weaknesses of this company's commitment to innovation and learning.

3. Based on your answer to question 2, provide three suggestions for what management could do to improve its commitment to innovation and learning.

Strategy Mapping: Visual Representation of the Path to Organizational Effectiveness

Have you ever worked for a company that failed to effectively communicate its vision and strategic plan? If yes, then you know how it feels to be disengaged because you don't know how your work contributes to organizational effectiveness. Kaplan and Norton recognized this common problem and developed a tool called a strategy map.

A **strategy map** is a "visual representation of a company's critical objectives and the crucial relationships among them that drive organizational performance." Maps show relationships among a company's strategic goals. This helps employees understand how their work contributes to their employer's overall success.[54] They also provide insight into how an organization creates value to its key constituents. For example, a map informs others about the knowledge, skills, and systems that employees should possess (innovation and learning perspective) to innovate and build internal capabilities (internal business perspective) that deliver value to customers (customer perspective), which eventually creates higher shareholder value (financial perspective).

We created an illustrative strategy map in Figure 16.5. Starting with learning and growth, the arrows in the diagram show the logic that connects goals to internal processes, to customers, to financial goals, and finally to the long-term goal of providing shareholder value. For example, you can see that organizational culture affects the internal process goals related to innovation, operational improvements, and good corporate citizenship. This causal structure provides a strategic road map of how the company plans to achieve organizational effectiveness.

You can also detect which of the four perspectives is most important by counting the number of goals in each perspective. For this sample map, there are four, five, eight, and four goals for the financial, customer, internal processes, and learning and growth perspectives, respectively. You can also see that internal process goals affect eight other goals—count the number of arrows coming from internal process goals. All told, the beauty of a strategy map is that it enables leaders to present a strategic road map to employees on one page. It also provides a clear statement about the criteria used to assess organizational effectiveness.

There is one final benefit to strategy maps. They serve as the starting point for any organization that wants to implement goal cascading or management by objectives. ●

FIGURE 16.5 Sample strategy map for Dr Pepper Snapple Group

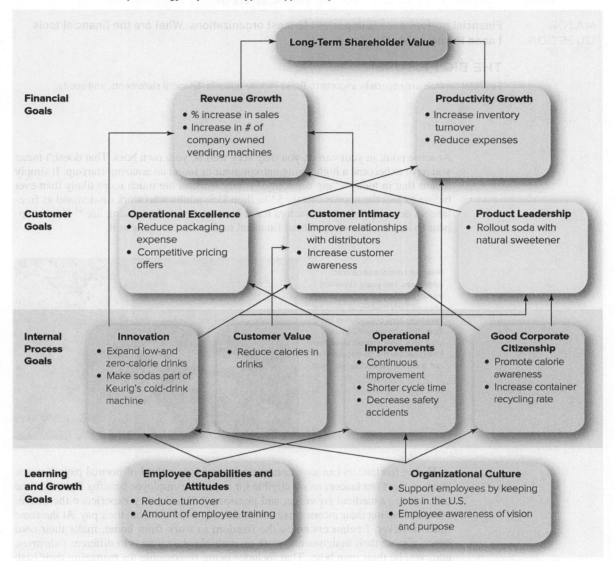

Sources: This map was based on information in "Dr Pepper Snapple Group to Boost Container Recycling, and More. . . ," TheShelbyReport.com, February 12, 2016; C. Choi, "Dr Pepper to Test Naturally Sweetened Sodas," FoodManufacturing.com, February 13, 2014; A. Gasparro and M. Esterl, "Keurig Reels In Dr Pepper for Its Coming Soda Machine," TheWallStreetJournal.com, January 7, 2015; S. Frizell, "Coke and Pepsi Pledge to Cut Calories," Time.com, September 23, 2014; M. Esterl, "How Dr Pepper Cuts Costs. And Then Cuts Costs Some More," The Wall Street Journal, February 16, 2016, p R2; "Vision—Call to Breakthrough ACTION," DrPepperSnappleGroup.com, accessed May 12, 2016.

16.4   Some Financial Tools for Control

Financial performance is important to most organizations. What are the financial tools I need to know about?

THE BIG PICTURE

Financial controls are especially important. These include budgets, financial statements, and audits.

At some point in your career, you may very well be your own boss. That doesn't mean you have to become a high-flying entrepreneur or found an amazing start-up. It simply means that in today's "gig economy," young workers are much more likely than ever before to join the approximately 53 million U.S. adults who work on-demand as freelancers or independent contractors for at least part of their working life.[55] If this happens to be you, knowledge about financial tools will serve you well.

Financial control and contract employees. Five young coworkers meeting to discuss a project. One or more are likely freelancers given the increasing trend of companies hiring them. Hiring freelancers can save labor costs but it also can leave them feeling outside the normal comings and goings of the work environment.
© Ingram Publishing RF

Hiring freelancers can save companies as much as a third of normal payroll costs, because most freelancers aren't eligible for expensive employee benefits like paid time off, company medical coverage, and pensions.[56] Nor do they experience the convenience of having their income taxes automatically withheld from their pay. At the same time, however, freelancers enjoy the freedom to work from home, make their own hours, choose their assignments, work on multiple assignments in different industries, and, yes, be their own boss. That includes being responsible for managing their cash flow and business expenses, as well as for setting money aside to pay their own income taxes, both of which can be a challenge when income is seasonal, variable, or both.

With this in mind, you can probably appreciate how important it is for you to understand the basics of financial controls. Whether as the manager of your own small "gig economy" business or as a manager on staff in an organization, you will need to monitor finances and be sure revenues are covering costs.

There are a great many kinds of financial controls, but here let us look at the following: *budgets, financial statements,* and *audits.* (Necessarily, this is merely an overview of this topic. Financial controls are covered in detail in other business courses.)

Budgets: Formal Financial Projections

A budget is a formal financial projection. It states an organization's planned activities for a given period of time in quantitative terms, such as dollars, hours, or number of products. Budgets are prepared not only for the organization as a whole but also for the divisions and departments within it. The point of a budget is to provide a yardstick against which managers can judge how well they are controlling monetary expenditures.

Various software tools are also available to help you manage personal or freelance budgeting, such as QuickBooks and apps like Mint and Venmo.[57]

Historically, managers have used three budget-planning approaches. Two of them—the Planning Programming Budgeting System and Zero Base Budgeting—are no longer favored and are now infrequently used. The dominant approach today is incremental budgeting.[58]

Incremental Budgeting   **Incremental budgeting** allocates increased or decreased funds to a department by using the last budget period as a reference point; only incremental changes in the budget request are reviewed. One difficulty is that incremental budgets tend to lock departments into stable spending arrangements; they are not flexible in meeting environmental demands. Another difficulty is that a department may engage in many activities—some more important than others—but it's not easy to sort out how well managers performed at the various activities. Thus, the department activities and the yearly budget increases take on lives of their own.

Fixed versus Variable Budgets   In general, we can identify two types of incremental budgets: *fixed* and *variable*.

- **Fixed budgets—where resources are allocated on a single estimate of costs.** Also known as a *static budget,* a **fixed budget** allocates resources on the basis of a single estimate of costs. That is, there is only one set of expenses; the budget does not allow for adjustment over time. For example, you might have a budget of $50,000 for buying equipment in a given year—no matter how much you may need equipment exceeding that amount.

- **Variable budgets—where resources are varied in proportion with various levels of activity.** Also known as a *flexible budget,* a **variable budget** allows the allocation of resources to vary in proportion with various levels of activity. That is, the budget can be adjusted over time to accommodate pertinent changes in the environment. For example, you might have a budget that allows you to hire temporary workers or lease temporary equipment if production exceeds certain levels. As a freelancer, you might set up your budget to allow for the unexpected, like the purchase of a second monitor for your laptop if you accept an assignment that requires it.

Financial Statements: Summarizing the Organization's Financial Status

A financial statement is a summary of some aspect of an organization's financial status. The information contained in such a statement is essential in helping managers maintain financial control over the organization.

There are two basic types of financial statements: the *balance sheet* and the *income statement*.

The Balance Sheet: Picture of Organization's Financial Worth for a Specific Point in Time   A **balance sheet** summarizes an organization's overall financial worth—that is, assets and liabilities—at a specific point in time.

Assets are the resources that an organization controls; they consist of current assets and fixed assets. *Current assets* are cash and other assets that are readily convertible to cash within one year's time. Examples are inventory, sales for which payment has not been received (accounts receivable), and U.S. Treasury bills or money market mutual funds.

Fixed assets are property, buildings, equipment, and the like that have a useful life that exceeds one year but that are usually harder to convert to cash. *Liabilities* are claims, or debts, by suppliers, lenders, and other nonowners of the organization against a company's assets. If you are a member of the gig economy, the quarterly estimated federal and local taxes you will need to pay on your annual income are a financial liability of your business.

The Income Statement: Picture of Organization's Financial Results for a Specified Period of Time

The balance sheet depicts the organization's overall financial worth at a specific point in time. By contrast, the **income statement** summarizes an organization's financial results—revenues and expenses—over a specified period of time, such as a quarter or a year.

You will need to understand an income statement if you end up self-employed or start a business. We created a sample profit and loss statement for a two-person operation consisting of an owner and one employee *(see Table 16.1)*. The company is doing quite well with $204,357 of net income, computed by subtracting total expenses from

TABLE 16.1

Sample Profit and Loss Statements

LACI, THE COMPUTER DOCTOR PROFIT & LOSS JANUARY 1 THROUGH DECEMBER 31, 2016		
Income:		Jan 1–Dec 31, 16
Sales		481,219.00
Services Income		23,050.00
Total Income		504,269.00
Parts and Materials	45,711.60	
Gross Profit		458,557.40
Expenses:		
Bank Service Charges		150.00
Charitable Donations		2,000.00
Dues and Subscriptions		1,520.88
Insurance:		
General Liability Insurance	1,925.00	
Workman's Compensation Insurance	1,016.00	
Total Insurance Expense:		2,941.00
Payroll Taxes:		
Payroll 941	13,992.76	
Federal Unemployment Tax	103.00	
State Unemployment Tax	210.00	
Total Payroll Taxes:		14,305.76
Payroll:		
Officer Wages	150,000.00	
Salary and Wages	49,896.50	
Total Payroll:		199,896.50
Accounting and Legal		1,402.75
Automobile Expenses:		
Maintenance	140.16	
Gas	1,012.92	
License	828.31	
Total Automobile Expenses:		1,981.39
Office Rent		24,000.00
Office supplies		1,775.00
Repairs and Maintenance		285.19
Telephone and Internet		1,856.25
Utilities		2,085.09
TOTAL EXPENSE:		254,199.81
NET INCOME:		204,357.59

Source: Angelo Kinicki

gross profit. You can also see the types of expenses that confront any small business. You have expenses for insurance, payroll and payroll taxes, accounting, auto, rent, supplies, and other expenses.

Audits: External versus Internal

When you think of auditors, do you think of grim-faced accountants looking through a company's books to catch embezzlers and other cheats? That's one function of auditing, but besides verifying the accuracy and fairness of financial statements, the audit also is intended to be a tool for management decision making. **Audits are formal verifications of an organization's financial and operational systems.**

You can imagine that audits of medium and large companies entail collecting, analyzing, and interpreting large amounts of information. Because of this, more and more companies are using data analytics to conduct audits; we discussed data analytics in Chapter 7. Regarding the use of analytics, one expert concluded, "The use of analytics in the audit process results in better audit planning, focus, and recommendations."[59]

Audits are of two types—*external* and *internal.*

External Audits—Financial Appraisals by Outside Financial Experts   An **external audit** is a formal verification of an organization's financial accounts and statements by outside experts. The auditors are certified public accountants (CPAs) who work for an accounting firm (such as PricewaterhouseCoopers) that is independent of the organization being audited. Their task is to verify that the organization, in preparing its financial statements and in determining its assets and liabilities, followed generally accepted accounting principles.[60]

Internal Audits—Financial Appraisals by Inside Financial Experts   An **internal audit** is a verification of an organization's financial accounts and statements by the organization's own professional staff. Their jobs are the same as those of outside experts—to verify the accuracy of the organization's records and operating activities. Internal audits also help uncover inefficiencies and thus help managers evaluate the performance of their control systems.

We would like to end this section on financial tools in a more personal manner by assessing your financial literacy. Self-Assessment 16.2 evaluates your knowledge in matters associated with interest-bearing accounts, investments, inflation, pensions, creditworthiness, and insurance. It's a fun way to find out if your financial literacy is up to speed. ●

Accountants at the Academy Awards? Brie Larson on the left with Leonardo DiCaprio holding their Academy Awards in 2016. Every year since 1929 the secret ballots for Oscar nominees voted on by members of the Academy of Motion Picture Arts and Sciences have been tabulated by accountants from the firm now known as PricewaterhouseCoopers. The accounting firm takes this event very seriously; secrecy is tight, and there is no loose gossip around the office water cooler. Two accountants tally the votes, stuff the winners' names in the envelopes—the ones that will be handed to award presenters during the Academy Awards—and then memorize the winners' names, just in case the envelopes don't make it to the show. Accounting is an important business because investors depend on independent auditors to verify that a company's finances are what they are purported to be. © Helga Esteb/Shutterstock RF

---

connect SELF-ASSESSMENT 16.2

Assessing Your Financial Literacy

The following survey was designed to assess your financial literacy. Please be prepared to answer these questions if your instructor has assigned Self-Assessment 16.2 in Connect.

1. Where do you stand in terms of financial literacy?

2. Look at the statements you got incorrect, and identify the specific aspects of financial knowledge that you may be lacking.

3. What can you do to improve your financial literacy? Be specific.

16.5 Total Quality Management

How do top companies improve the quality of their products or services?

THE BIG PICTURE

Total quality management (TQM) is dedicated to continuous quality improvement, training, and customer satisfaction. Two core principles are people orientation and improvement orientation. Some techniques for improving quality are employee involvement, benchmarking, outsourcing, reduced cycle time, and statistical process control.

In 2015, Midway USA, a fast-growing online retailer of equipment for hunting, shooting, and outdoor sports, became one of the rare two-time winners of the prestigious Baldrige Award. This award is "given by the President of the United States to businesses and to education, health care, and nonprofit organizations that apply and are judged to be outstanding in seven areas of performance excellence." The seven areas are leadership; strategy; customers, analysis, and knowledge management; workforce; operations; and results.[61]

Customer satisfaction is Midway's No. 1 goal. Thus, the company, headquartered in Missouri, has incorporated customer data into its performance improvement system, and results are impressive. With more than 1.2 million active customers visiting its site, Midway has succeeded in earning a consistent customer approval rating of over 90%, beating out its top competitors for two years in a row. At the same time, Midway has boosted its employee satisfaction rating from 76% to 83% over the last 11 years, in part by asking employees to identify and prioritize what they need in order to achieve job satisfaction. Company managers are then able to help meet those requirements. Career development at the company is a given; more than 80 management positions are filled from within, because nearly 40% of its 350 employees participate in a formal leadership training program that includes mentoring and attendance at strategy meetings.[62]

Midway excels in managing its supply chain as well. It ships out inventory more efficiently than 10 years ago (as measured by a statistic known as "inventory turns") yet keeps up an in-stock rate for its products of almost 83%. The company's seven-step strategy development process begins with a performance review and an analysis of its

Quality control at Midway. MidwayUSA is a privately held retailer of hunting and outdoor-related products. It's business requires the accurate application of management control systems. Here we see the outbound shipping lanes of a large system of conveyors the company uses to manage distribution of its products from the receiving docks to the UPS trucks. In order to maintain accuracy and efficiency, the company relies on a variety of tools associated with total quality management. © MidwayUSA

strengths, weaknesses, challenges, and opportunities. Finally, Midway has donated more than $100 million to charity since 2008, enforces waste recovery and recycling practices, helps send local children to conventions where they learn about environmental management, and runs a virtually paperless operation. No mail orders are accepted.[63]

As we saw in Chapter 2, two strategies for ensuring quality are *quality control,* the strategy for minimizing errors by managing each stage of production, and *quality assurance,* focusing on the performance of workers and urging them to strive for "zero defects."

Deming Management: The Contributions of W. Edwards Deming to Improved Quality

Previously, Frederick Taylor's scientific management philosophy, designed to maximize worker productivity, had been widely instituted. But by the 1950s, scientific management had led to organizations that were rigid and unresponsive to both employees and customers. **W. Edwards Deming's** challenge, known as **Deming management, proposed ideas for making organizations more responsive, more democratic, and less wasteful.** These included the following principles.

1. Quality Should Be Aimed at the Needs of the Consumer
"The consumer is the most important part of the production line," Deming wrote.[64] Thus, the efforts of individual workers in providing the product or service should be directed toward meeting the needs and expectations of the ultimate user.

2. Companies Should Aim at Improving the System, Not Blaming Workers
Deming suggested that U.S. managers were more concerned with blaming problems on individual workers rather than on the organization's structure, culture, technology, work rules, and management—that is, "the system." By treating employees well, listening to their views and suggestions, Deming felt, managers could bring about improvements in products and services.

3. Improved Quality Leads to Increased Market Share, Increased Company Prospects, and Increased Employment
When companies work to improve the quality of goods and services, they produce less waste, experience fewer delays, and are more efficient. Lower prices and superior quality lead to greater market share, which in turn leads to improved business prospects and consequently increased employment.

4. Quality Can Be Improved on the Basis of Hard Data, Using the PDCA Cycle
Deming suggested that quality could be improved by acting on the basis of hard data. The process for doing this came to be known as the **PDCA cycle, a Plan-Do-Check-Act cycle using observed data for continuous improvement of operations.** *(See Figure 16.6.)* Like the steps in the control process in Figure 16.3, step 3 ("Check") is a *feedback* step, in which performance is compared to goals. Feedback is instrumental to control.

Core TQM Principles: Deliver Customer Value and Strive for Continuous Improvement

Total quality management (TQM) is defined as a comprehensive approach—led by top management and supported throughout the organization—dedicated to continuous quality improvement, training, and customer satisfaction. In Chapter 2 we said there are four components to TQM:

1. Make continuous improvement a priority.
2. Get every employee involved.
3. Listen to and learn from customers and employees.
4. Use accurate standards to identify and eliminate problems.

FIGURE 16.6

**The PDCA cycle:
Plan-Do-Check-Act**

The four steps continuously
follow each other, resulting in
continuous improvement.

*Source: From W. Edwards Deming.
Out of the Crisis, Plan Do Study
Act Cycle, page 88, © 2000
Massachusetts Institute of
Technology, by permission
of MIT Press.*

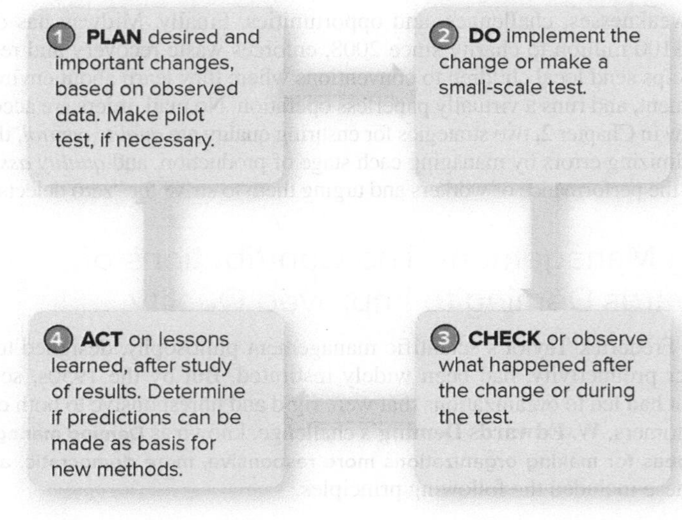

① **PLAN** desired and important changes, based on observed data. Make pilot test, if necessary.

② **DO** implement the change or make a small-scale test.

④ **ACT** on lessons learned, after study of results. Determine if predictions can be made as basis for new methods.

③ **CHECK** or observe what happened after the change or during the test.

These may be summarized as **two core principles of TQM**—namely, (1) people orientation—everyone involved with the organization should focus on delivering value to customers—and (2) improvement orientation—everyone should work on continuously improving the work processes.[65] Let's look at these further.

1. People Orientation—Focusing Everyone on Delivering Customer Value

Organizations adopting TQM value people as their most important resource—both those who create a product or service and those who receive it. Thus, not only are employees given more decision-making power, so are suppliers and customers.

This people orientation operates under the following assumptions.

- **Delivering customer value is most important.** The purpose of TQM is to focus people, resources, and work processes to deliver products or services that create value for customers. Toyota is a long-time practitioner of TQM; its Lexus plant in Georgetown, Kentucky, produces about half a million cars a year. The 750 employees who worked on the first Lexus line to be built in the United States received millions of hours of special sensory training "so they could see, hear, feel and smell what a Lexus should be." Some repeatedly took apart and rebuilt a small fleet of cars to understand thousands of parts, and they studied with master craftsmen in Japan.[66] The Example box on Kia explains how the company focuses on this proposition.

- **People will focus on quality if given empowerment.** TQM assumes that employees (and often suppliers and customers) will concentrate on making quality improvements if given the decision-making power to do so. The reasoning here is that the people actually involved with the product or service are in the best position to detect opportunities for quality improvements. In support of this conclusion, research shows lack of employee involvement as the biggest obstacle to successful TQM implementation.[67]

- **TQM requires training, teamwork, and cross-functional efforts.** Employees and suppliers need to be well trained, and they must work in teams. Teamwork is considered important because many quality problems are spread across functional areas. For example, if cell-phone design specialists conferred with marketing specialists (as well as customers and suppliers), they would find that the challenge of using a cell phone for older people is pushing 11 tiny buttons to call a phone number.

Kia Vaults to Highest Quality Rating

The small Korean automaker Kia Motors recently surprised car buyers and the entire auto industry by taking the No. 1 spot in J.D. Power and Associates's annual Initial Quality Survey, the first time in 27 years that a non-luxury brand came in ahead of past winners like Porsche and Lexus as well as beating out closer competitors like Toyota and Hyundai. "Ranking number one in the entire industry for initial quality is the result of Kia's decade-long focus on craftsmanship and continuous improvement, and reflects the voice of our customers, which is the ultimate affirmation," said Michael Sprague, chief operating officer and executive vice president of Kia Motors America.

Auto industry analysts say Kia's accumulating quality improvements over the last few years have not gone unnoticed. Better interiors and higher-than-expected ride quality were cited, along with "top notch" quality for the price and a low incidence of problems in the first 90 days of ownership (an industry standard in which Porsche has previously excelled).

Despite massive and widely reported airbag recalls that have affected many of the big automakers, Kia is not alone in achieving quality improvements, analysts say. According to Renee Stephens, J.D. Power's vice president of U.S. automotive quality, "Tracking our data over the past several years, it has become clear that automakers are listening to the customer, identifying pain points and are focused on continuous improvement. Even as they add more content, including advanced technologies that have had a reputation for causing problems, overall quality continues to improve."

Kia cites its focus on customers' needs and the challenge to achieve "the highest possible level of customer satisfaction" as the guiding forces behind its "most stringent quality controls." It boasts having "one of the most state-of-the-art, ecologically compatible, and productive auto plants in Europe," with high technology standards and efficient monitoring. Its head designer is an award winner, and many new Kia models have earned international design recognition—more "vivid evidence of our high standards." The company also promises high fuel efficiency and an "EcoDynamics" label on some models that signifies reduced CO_2 emissions.[68]

YOUR CALL

What internal factors do you think account for Kia's reaching the top of the J.D. Power survey? Have any external factors like improving competition played a role?

2. Improvement Orientation—Focusing Everyone on Continuously Improving Work Processes   Although big schemes, grand designs, and crash programs have their place, the lesson of the quality movement from overseas is that the way to success is through continuous, small improvements. **Continuous improvement is defined as ongoing, small, incremental improvements in all parts of an organization**—all products, services, functional areas, and work processes.

This improvement orientation focuses on increasing operational performance and makes the following assumptions.[69]

- **It's less expensive to do it right the first time.** TQM assumes that it's better to do things right the first time than to do costly reworking. To be sure, creating high-quality products and services requires a costly investment in training, equipment, and tools, for example. But it is less expensive than dealing with poor quality and the poor customer relationships that result.

- **It's better to make small improvements all the time.** This is the assumption that continuous improvement must be an everyday matter, that no improvement is too small, that there must be an ongoing effort to make things better a little bit at a time all the time. At Daimler, for instance, finished cars are packed so tightly together in storage yards that it's difficult for workers to read the RFID (radio frequency identification) tags used to control inventory. That's where drones come in, reading the tags quickly and inexpensively and at any hour when humans are not in the lot. The next small improvement? Smaller drones.[70]

- **Accurate standards must be followed to eliminate small variations.** TQM emphasizes the collection of accurate data throughout every stage of the work process. It also stresses the use of accurate standards (such as benchmarking) to evaluate progress and eliminate small variations, which are the source of many quality defects.

- **There must be strong commitment from top management.** Employees and suppliers won't focus on making small, incremental improvements unless managers go beyond lip service to support high-quality work, as do the top managers at Ritz-Carlton, Amazon.com, and Ace Hardware.

Continuous improvement. Instead of making a walkway or street by laying bricks one at a time, how about using something like this? Dave Dyer of Swiss firm ABB Consulting points to this brick-laying machine as a great example of continuous improvement, one of the two core principles of TQM. The operators, he writes, "feed the bricks into the machine via gravity, there are no moving parts, and the path is laid as the machine moves. It's amazing!" What examples of continuous improvement can you think of?
© epa european pressphoto agency b.v./Alamy

Kaizen is a Japanese philosophy of small continuous improvement that seeks to involve everyone at every level of the organization in the process of identifying opportunities and implementing and testing solutions.[71] It offers advantages for large and small companies alike, whether manufacturers or service firms, as the Example box shows.

EXAMPLE Kaizen Principles in Action

Herman Miller, the U.S. manufacturer of office equipment and chairs, has increased productivity 500% and quality 1,000% in the years since adopting Kaizen methods. The company's renowned Aeron chairs are now produced in 17 seconds, compared to 82 before Kaizen.[72]

At Studio 904, a Seattle hair salon, Kaizen principles led to a change in work flow so that everyone on staff can provide all styling services. Thus, customers no longer have to wait for each step during their visit to be performed by a dedicated stylist who may be working with more than one client at a time.[73]

Wagamama, a trendy UK restaurant chain expanding to the United States, saw early adoption of technology as the improvement identified by Kaizen principles. The company was years ahead of its competition in building an iPhone app and

developing the Qkr! app, which allows customers to split the bill with friends by paying for specific menu items on their iOS and Android phones. Wagamama has issued wireless handheld devices to staff for taking diners' orders and accepting payments and is now moving most of its tools to a cloud-based system.[74]

YOUR CALL

Some recommended tips for implementing Kaizen methods include actively looking for unconventional ideas, thinking about how to do something instead of why it can't be done, and avoiding both excuses and perfection.[75] Do you think this is good advice for Herman Miller, Studio 904, and Wagamama? Why or why not?

Applying TQM to Services

Manufacturing industries provide tangible products (think jars of baby food); service industries provide intangible products (think child care services). Manufactured products can be stored (such as dental floss in a warehouse); services generally need to be consumed immediately (such as dental hygiene services). Services tend to require a good deal of people effort (although some services can be provided by machines, such as vending machines and ATMs). Finally, services are generally provided at locations and times convenient for customers; that is, customers are much more involved in the delivery of services than they are in the delivery of manufactured products.

One clear prerequisite for providing excellent service is effective training. Isadore Sharp, founder and chair of Four Seasons Hotels and Resorts, recently experienced outstanding room service while visiting one of the chain's new facilities, in a location where few employees could have been expected to have prior experience of hospitality industry standards. When he asked the server where she had learned to perform so well, she replied, "They let me take everything home for me to practice with my family."[76] It takes more than training, however, to provide high-quality service (see the Practical Action box).[77]

What Makes a Service Company Successful? Four Core Elements | PRACTICAL ACTION

With services now employing more than 75% of U.S. workers, universities are bringing more research attention to what is being called "services science." This is a field that uses management, technology, mathematics, and engineering expertise to improve the performance of service businesses, such as retailing and health care.[78]

Harvard Business School scholar Frances X. Frei has determined that a successful service business must make the right decisions about four core elements and balance them effectively.[79]

The Offering: Which Features Are Given Top-Quality Treatment? Which service attributes, as informed by the needs of customers, does the company target for excellence and which does it target for inferior performance? Does a bank, for example, offer more convenient hours and friendlier tellers (excellence) but pay less attractive interest rates (inferior performance)?

The Funding Mechanism: Who Pays for the Service? How should the company fund its services? Should it have the customer pay for them? This can be done in a palatable way, as when Starbucks funds its stuffed-chair ambience by charging more for coffee. Or it can be done by making savings in service features, as when Progressive Casualty Insurance cuts down on frauds and lawsuits by deploying its own (rather than independent) representatives to the scene of an auto accident.

Or should the company cover the cost of excellence with operational savings, as by spending now to save later or having the customer do the work? Call centers usually charge for customer support, but Intuit offers free support and has product-development people, as well as customer-service people, field calls so that subsequent developments in Intuit software are informed by direct knowledge of customer problems. Other companies, such as most gas stations, save money by having customers pump their own gas.

The Employee Management System: How Are Workers Trained and Motivated? Service companies need to think about what makes their employees *able* to achieve excellence and what makes them reasonably *motivated* to achieve excellence. For instance, bank customers may expect employees to meet a lot of complex needs, but the employees aren't *able* to meet these needs because they haven't been trained. Or they aren't *motivated* to achieve excellence because the bank hasn't figured out how to screen in its hiring, as in hiring people for attitude first and training them later versus paying more to attract highly motivated people.

The Customer Management System: How Are Customers "Trained"? Like employees, customers in a service business must also be "trained" as well, as the airlines have done with check-in. At Zipcar, the popular car-sharing service, the company keeps its costs low by depending on customers to clean, refuel, and return cars in time for the next user. In training customers, service companies need to determine which customers they're focusing on, what behaviors they want, and which techniques will most effectively influence customer behavior.

YOUR CALL

Pick a services company you're familiar with, such as Domino's, Starbucks, Amazon, REI, or the college bookstore. In integrating the four core features just discussed, a service company needs to evaluate itself on the following: Are the decisions it makes in one area supported by those it makes in the other areas? Does the service model create long-term value for customers, employees, and shareholders? Is the company trying to be all things to all people or specific things to specific people? How do you think the company you picked rates?

Perhaps you're beginning to see how judging the quality of services is a different animal from judging the quality of manufactured goods, because it comes down to meeting the customer's *satisfaction*, which may be a matter of *perception*. (After all, some hotel guests, restaurant diners, and supermarket patrons, for example, are more easily satisfied than others.)

Some people view college students as customers. Do you? For those schools that care about the quality of what they offer, it is important to assess student satisfaction with the college or university as a whole. If you are curious about your level of satisfaction with your college or university, then complete Self-Assessment 16.3.

≡connect SELF-ASSESSMENT 16.3

Assessing Your Satisfaction with Your College or University Experience

The following survey was designed to assess the extent to which you are satisfied with your college experience. Please be prepared to answer these questions if your instructor has assigned Self-Assessment 16.3 in Connect.

1. What is your level of satisfaction? Are you surprised by the results?

2. Based on your scores, identify three things that your college or university might do to improve student satisfaction. Be specific.

3. Are students really customers? Explain your rationale.

Some TQM Tools, Techniques, and Standards

Several tools and techniques are available for improving quality. We described benchmarking in Chapter 10. Here we describe *outsourcing, reduced cycle time, statistical process control, Six Sigma, and quality standards ISO 9000 and ISO 14000.*

Outsourcing: Let Outsiders Handle It   **Outsourcing** (discussed in detail in Chapter 4) **is the subcontracting of services and operations to an outside vendor.** Usually, this is done to reduce costs or increase productivity.[80] Outsourcing short-term and project work to freelance or contract workers in the so-called gig economy also saves companies many employee-related expenses.

Outsourcing is also being done by many state and local governments, which, under the banner known as privatization, have subcontracted traditional government services such as fire protection, correctional services, and medical services.

Reduced Cycle Time: Increasing the Speed of Work Processes   Another TQM technique is the emphasis on increasing the speed with which an organization's operations and processes can be performed. This is known as **reduced cycle time, or reduction in steps in a work process,** such as fewer authorization steps required to grant a contract to a supplier. The point is to improve the organization's performance by eliminating wasteful motions, barriers between departments, unnecessary procedural steps, and the like.

At Ralph Lauren, a recent slowdown in sales and an increase in inventory prompted the company to look for ways to reduce production time for its high-fashion products from 15 months to 9, which will help it better match supply to demand, reduce excess inventory, and lower the volume of goods that need to be sold at marked-down prices.[81]

Bar-code scanners, not the type used at checkout counters to track inventory, are increasingly used to decrease the time it takes for employees to select, pack, and ship products. Exel Logistics, for example, found that bar-code scanners decreased the rate of assembling orders by 10%–20%.[82]

Statistical Process Control: Taking Periodic Random Samples   As the pages of this book were being printed, instruments called densitometers and colorimeters were used to measure ink density and trueness of color, taking samples of printed pages at fixed intervals. This is an ongoing check for quality control.

All kinds of products require periodic inspection during their manufacture: hamburger meat, breakfast cereal, flashlight batteries, wine, and so on. The tool often used for this is **statistical process control, a statistical technique that uses periodic random samples from production runs to see if quality is being maintained within a standard range of acceptability.** If quality is not acceptable, production is stopped to allow corrective measures.

Statistical process control is the technique that McDonald's uses, for example, to make sure that the quality of its burgers is always the same, no matter where in the world they are served. Companies such as Intel and Motorola use statistical process control to ensure the reliability and quality of their products.

Six Sigma and Lean Six Sigma: Data-Driven Ways to Eliminate Defects
Sigma is the Greek letter statisticians use to define a standard deviation. In the quality-improvement process known as Six Sigma, the higher the sigma, the fewer the deviations from the norm—that is, the fewer the defects. Developed by Motorola in 1985, Six Sigma has since been embraced by General Electric, Allied Signal, American Express, 3M, and other companies.[83] There are two variations, *Six Sigma* and *Lean, Six Sigma.*

- **Six Sigma. Six Sigma is a rigorous statistical analysis process that reduces defects in manufacturing and service-related processes.** By testing thousands of variables and eliminating guesswork, a company using the technique attempts to improve quality and reduce waste to the point where errors nearly vanish. In everything from product design to manufacturing to billing, the attainment of Six Sigma means there are no more than 3.4 defects per million products or procedures.[84]

  Six Sigma may also be thought of as a philosophy—to reduce variation in your company's business and make customer-focused, data-driven decisions. The method preaches the use of Define, Measure, Analyze, Improve, and Control (DMAIC). Team leaders may be awarded a Six Sigma "black belt" for applying DMAIC.

- **Lean Six Sigma.** More recently, companies are using an approach known as **Lean Six Sigma, which focuses on problem solving and performance improvement—speed with excellence—of a well-defined project.**[85]

  3M Company's latest five-year plan includes improvements to its supply chain and an increased focus on Lean Six Sigma in order to bring about "improved customer service, operational efficiencies, and an increased cash flow."[86]

Six Sigma and Lean Six Sigma may not be perfect, since they cannot compensate for human error or control events outside a company.[87] Still, they let managers approach problems with the assumption that there's a data-oriented, tangible way to approach problem solving.

ISO 9000 and ISO 14000: Meeting Standards of Independent Auditors   If you're a sales representative for Du Pont, a U.S. chemical company, how will your overseas clients know your products have the quality they are expecting? If you're a purchasing agent for an Ohio-based tire company, how can you tell whether the synthetic rubber you're buying overseas is adequate?

At one time, buyers and sellers simply had to rely on a supplier's past reputation or personal assurances. In 1979, the International Organization for Standardization (ISO), based in Geneva, Switzerland, created a set of quality standards known as the 9000 series. There are two such standards:

- **ISO 9000. The ISO 9000 series** consists of quality-control procedures companies must install—from purchasing to manufacturing to inventory to shipping—that can be audited by independent quality-control experts, or "registrars." The goal is to reduce flaws in manufacturing and improve productivity by adopting eight "big picture" Quality Management Principles:

  - Customer focus.
  - Leadership.
  - Involvement of people.
  - Process approach.
  - System approach to management.
  - Continual improvement.
  - Factual approach to decision making.
  - Mutually beneficial supplier relationships.[88]

  Companies must document their ISO 9000 procedures and train their employees to use them. The ISO 9000 series of standards was expanded to include ISO 9001:2008. "ISO 9001 is the only standard within the ISO 9000 family that an organization can become certified against, because it is the standard that defines the requirements of having a Quality Management System."[89] This global management standard is adopted by over 1 million companies in 176 countries worldwide.[90]

- **ISO 14000. The ISO 14000 series** extends the concept, identifying standards for environmental performance. ISO 14000 dictates standards for documenting a company's management of pollution, efficient use of raw materials, and reduction of the firm's impact on the environment.

Takeaways from TQM Research

TQM principles have been used by thousands of organizations through the years. Although companies do not always use the tools, techniques, and processes as suggested by experts, a team of researchers concluded that the far majority of TQM adopters follow its general principles, which in turn fosters improved operational performance.[91] Researchers also identified four key inhibitors to successfully implementing TQM: (1) the failure to provide evidence supporting previous improvement activities, (2) the lack of a champion who is responsible for leading the implementation, (3) the inability to measure or track results of the program, and (4) the failure to develop a culture of quality or continuous learning.[92] Managers need to overcome these roadblocks for TQM to deliver its intended benefits. •

16.6   Managing Control Effectively

MAJOR QUESTION

What are the keys to successful control, and what are the barriers to control success?

THE BIG PICTURE

This section describes four keys to successful control and five barriers to successful control.

How do you as a manager make a control system successful, and how do you identify and deal with barriers to control? We consider these topics next.

The Keys to Successful Control Systems

Successful control systems have a number of common characteristics: (1) They are strategic and results oriented. (2) They are timely, accurate, and objective. (3) They are realistic, positive, and understandable and they encourage self-control. (4) They are flexible.

1. They Are Strategic and Results Oriented   Control systems support strategic plans and are concentrated on significant activities that will make a real difference to the organization. Thus, when managers are developing strategic plans for achieving strategic goals, that is the point at which they should pay attention to developing control standards that will measure how well the plans are being achieved.

Example: Companies whose strategies include a commitment to sustainable methods can be guided by standards set by the Sustainability Accounting Standards Board, which sets reporting guidelines for "[disclosing] sustainability performance information to stakeholders."[93]

Charity control. Laura Arrillaga-Andreessen (shown here with husband Marc Andreessen, left, and Facebook CEO Mark Zuckerberg at a 2012 conference in Sun Valley, Idaho) is a Stanford University professor of philanthropy who aims to make giving not only more effective and wide ranging but also more accessible to people of all ages and income levels, including Millennials. Part of her vision is to enable donations through mobile microfinancing and smartphone money transfers. Do you think philanthropic organizations should use the same type of control mechanisms as for-profit organizations? © Paul Sakuma/AP Photo

2. They Are Timely, Accurate, and Objective   Good control systems—like good information of any kind—should be

- **Timely—meaning when needed.** The information should not necessarily be delivered quickly, but it should be delivered at an appropriate or specific time, such as every week or every month. And it certainly should be often enough to allow employees and managers to take corrective action for any deviations.

- **Accurate—meaning correct.** Accuracy is paramount, if decision mistakes are to be avoided. Inaccurate sales figures may lead managers to mistakenly cut or increase sales promotion budgets. Inaccurate production costs may lead to faulty pricing of a product.

- **Objective—meaning impartial.** Objectivity means control systems are impartial and fair. Although information can be inaccurate for all kinds of reasons (faulty communication, unknown data, and so on), information that is not objective is inaccurate for a special reason: It is biased or prejudiced. Control systems need to be considered unbiased for everyone involved so that they will be respected for their fundamental purpose—enhancing performance.

3. They Are Realistic, Positive, and Understandable and Encourage Self-Control   Control systems have to focus on working for the people who will have to live with them. Thus, they operate best when they are made acceptable to the organization's members who are guided by them.[94] Thus, they should

- **Be realistic.** They should incorporate realistic expectations. If employees feel performance results are too difficult, they are apt to ignore or sabotage the performance system.

- **Be positive.** They should emphasize development and improvement. They should avoid emphasizing punishment and reprimand.

- **Be understandable.** They should fit the people involved, be kept as simple as possible, and present data in understandable terms. They should avoid complicated computer printouts and statistics.

- **Encourage self-control.** They should encourage good communication and mutual participation. They should not be the basis for creating distrust between employees and managers.

4. They Are Flexible   Control systems must leave room for individual judgment, so that they can be modified when necessary to meet new requirements.

Barriers to Control Success

Among the several barriers to a successful control system are the following.

1. Too Much Control   Some organizations, particularly bureaucratic ones, try to exert too much control. They may try to regulate employee behavior in everything from dress code to timing of coffee breaks. This leads to micromanagement, which frustrates employees and may lead them to ignore or try to sabotage the control process.

Among the telltale signs that you (or your boss) might be a micromanager, someone who is unable to delegate tasks and decisions and insists on taking an inappropriately detailed focus on subordinates' work, are

1. Working excessive hours and weekends and skipping vacation.
2. Checking everyone's work because no one else can do things right.
3. Needing to be copied on and approve everything.

4. Requiring others to continually check in and be constantly available.

5. Having to hire new people all the time because turnover is so high.[95]

Micromanagement is a form of overcontrol that is counterproductive for several reasons. Employees are more effective and achieve greater job satisfaction if they feel empowered to use their own judgment as far as possible to get the job done. And micromanagers can become bottlenecks who actually slow the flow of work and decisions, if not stop it altogether. Some solutions, if you recognize yourself in this profile, are to start by delegating small decisions, recognizing that the worst-case scenario you likely imagine if you let go is probably not going to happen, and accepting that some degree of uncertainty is inevitable in management, and in life.[96]

2. Too Little Employee Participation As highlighted by W. Edwards Deming, which was discussed in Chapter 2, employee participation can enhance productivity. Involving employees in both the planning and the execution of control systems can bring legitimacy to the process and heighten employee morale.

3. Overemphasis on Means Instead of Ends We said that control activities should be strategic and results oriented. They are not ends in themselves but the means to eliminating problems. Too much emphasis on accountability for weekly production quotas, for example, can lead production supervisors to push their workers and equipment too hard, resulting in absenteeism and machine breakdowns. Or it can lead to game playing—"beating the system"—as managers and employees manipulate data to seem to fulfill short-run goals instead of the organization's strategic plan.

4. Overemphasis on Paperwork A specific kind of misdirection of effort is management emphasis on getting reports done, to the exclusion of other performance activity. Reports are not the be-all and end-all. Undue emphasis on reports can lead to too much focus on quantification of results and even to falsification of data.

5. Overemphasis on One Instead of Multiple Approaches One type or method of control may not be enough. By having multiple control activities and information systems, an organization can have multiple performance indicators, thereby increasing accuracy and objectivity. A recent study found that control systems affect each other and thus must be integrated.[97] ●

Temptation. Because legal gambling is a heavy cash business, casinos need to institute special controls against employee theft, including extensive human resource controls like a criminal background check and character, reference, and credit checks.[98] An operational control casinos also implement is the "eye in the sky" closed-circuit camera over card and craps tables.
© Stefan Huwiler/Rolf Nussbaumer Photography/Alamy

16.7 Managing for Productivity

How do managers influence productivity?

THE BIG PICTURE

The purpose of a manager is to make decisions about the four management functions—planning, organizing, leading, and controlling—to get people to achieve productivity and realize results. Productivity is defined by the formula of outputs divided by inputs for a specified period of time. Productivity matters because it determines whether the organization will make a profit or even survive.

In Chapter 1, we pointed out that as a manager in the 21st century you will operate in a complex environment in which you will need to deal with seven challenges—managing for (1) competitive advantage, (2) diversity, (3) globalization, (4) information technology, (5) ethical standards, (6) sustainability, and (7) your own happiness and life goals.

Within this dynamic world, you will draw on the practical and theoretical knowledge described in this book to make decisions about the four management functions of planning, organizing, leading, and controlling. The purpose is to get the people reporting to you *to achieve productivity and realize results*. This process is diagrammed below, pulling together the main topics of this book. *(See Figure 16.7.)*

FIGURE 16.7

**Managing for productivity
and results**

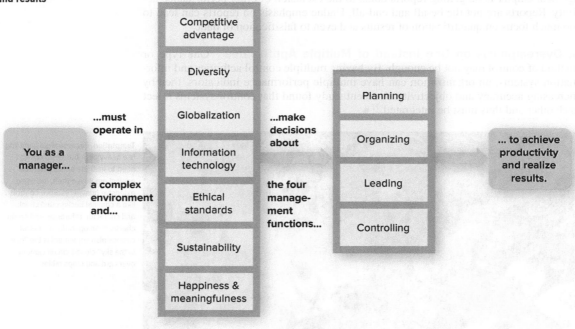

What Is Productivity?

Productivity can be applied at any level, whether for you as an individual, for the work unit you're managing, or for the organization you work for. Productivity is defined by the formula of *outputs divided by inputs* for a specified period of time. Outputs are all the goods and services produced. Inputs are not only labor but also capital, materials, and energy. That is,

$$\text{Productivity} = \frac{\text{Outputs}}{\text{Inputs}} \quad \text{or} \quad \frac{\text{Goods} + \text{Services}}{\text{Labor} + \text{Capital} + \text{Materials} + \text{Energy}}$$

What does this mean to you as a manager? It means that you can increase overall productivity by making substitutions or increasing the efficiency of any one element: labor, capital, materials, energy. For instance, you can increase the efficiency of labor by substituting capital in the form of equipment or machinery, as in employing a backhoe instead of laborers with shovels to dig a hole.[99] Or you can increase the efficiency of materials inputs by expanding their uses, as when lumber mills discovered they could sell not only boards but also sawdust and wood chips for use in gardens. Or you can increase the efficiency of energy by putting solar panels on a factory roof so the organization won't have to buy so much electrical power from utility companies.

Why Increasing Productivity Is Important

The more goods and services that are produced and made easily available to us and for export, the higher our standard of living. Increasing the gross domestic product (GDP)—the total dollar value of all the goods and services produced in the United States—depends on raising productivity, as well as on a growing workforce.

Table 16.2 shows the GDP for the U.S. and 11 other countries in 2005 and 2015. As you might expect, China showed the greatest increase over time, followed by

TABLE 16.2   Global Gross Domestic Product (GDP)

COUNTRY	2005	2015	%CHANGE
Brazil	2208.7	1772.6	−25%
Canada	1613.5	1552.4	−4%
China	6005.2	10,982.8	+45%
Denmark	319.8	295.0	−8%
France	2651.8	2421.6	−10%
Germany	3423.5	3357.6	−2%
India	1708.5	2090.7	+18%
Singapore	236.4	292.7	+19%
Sweden	488.4	492.6	+1%
United Kingdom	2403.0	2849.3	+16%
United States	14,964.4	17,947.0	+17%
Venezuela	294.5	239.6	−23%

Note: All numbers shown in Billion US Dollars.

Source: Knoema, GDP by Country, https://knoema.com/tbocwag/gdp-by-country-1980-2015?country+United%20 States, accessed July 20, 2016.

India and the U.S. Some of this growth is due to increased investments in information technology.[100]

The U.S. Productivity Track Record

During the 1960s, productivity in the United States averaged a hefty 2.9% a year, then sank to a disappointing 1.5% right up until 1995. Because the decline in productivity no longer allowed the improvement in wages and living standards that had benefited so many U.S. workers in the 1960s, millions of people took second jobs or worked longer hours to keep from falling behind. From 1995 to 2000, however, during the longest economic boom in U.S. history, the productivity rate jumped to 2.5% annually, as the total output of goods and services rose faster than the total hours needed to produce them. From the business cycle peak in the first quarter of 2001 to the end of 2007, productivity grew at an annual rate of 2.7%.[101]

Then came the recession year 2008, when it fell to 2%. Then, from the fourth quarter of 2008 to the fourth quarter of 2009, productivity rose 5.4%—"a turnaround unprecedented in modern history," said *Newsweek*—it also rose an impressive 4.1% in 2010.[102] Recently, however, productivity has been declining globally, not only in developed economies such as the United States, Japan, and Europe but also in China, which had been growing rapidly for some time. Productivity has even been zero or negative in some countries. Gains in productivity are expected to remain small for the short term.[103]

Globalization, which has made national economies far more interconnected and dependent on one another, helps increase the ripple effects of any country's economic downturns on its neighbors and trading partners. Climate change is also affecting productivity as extreme weather becomes more common, bringing droughts, floods, and other uncommon events to areas unused to dealing with them.[104]

Wind farms. This aerial view of a wind farm in Altamont Pass, California, is a great illustration of how the energy industry is changing in response to climate change. Wind farms consist of a group of turbines used to generate electricity. They are located on land and offshore. The largest onshore wind farms are located in Germany, and Europe leads the world in creating offshore wind energy.
© Kim Steele/Getty Images RF

The Role of Information Technology

As many industrialized countries continue to struggle with recovery from the 2008–2009 global financial crisis, wages have stagnated for most of their workers, even as productivity gains from information technology—automation and the Internet, shareware, cloud computing, and other communication technologies, for example—have slowed. Financial rewards for tech innovation have concentrated among a very few inventors and entrepreneurs, while wage gains even in the United States and the UK are stalled at about 1% a year, less in Germany, Italy, and Japan.[105]

Some observers say the problem is not a lack of productivity growth but a measurement error. New technologies are difficult to value, and new companies that charge users nothing and try to earn revenue from advertising (that users can sometimes avoid) are entering a new world we may be incorrectly assessing with old tools.[106]

In particular, many companies have implemented **enterprise resource planning (ERP) software systems, information systems for integrating virtually all aspects of a business,** helping managers stay on top of the latest developments.

Managing Individual Productivity

Individual employees, managers, and organizations all share responsibility for increasing individual productivity. Individuals contribute by proactively bringing their skills, energy, talents, and motivation to work on a daily basis. They also can increase productivity by engaging in self-development and organizational citizenship. This is most likely to happen, however, when employees work for supportive and talented managers. This is where managers enter the productivity equation.

Managers need to bring their "best selves" to work just like any other employee. In addition, they can use many of the concepts, tools, and techniques discussed throughout this book to help develop their managerial and leadership skills. Managerial behavior is a key input to individual productivity. We believe it is essential for managers to take a learning orientation toward their jobs. This implies that managers will attempt to continuously improve their leadership skills. This might involve taking courses at a local college or university, enrolling in company sponsored training programs, obtaining advice from an executive coach or mentor, or reading relevant books.

Organizations contribute to individual productivity by providing positive work environments and cultures that promote employee engagement, satisfaction, and flourishing. This ultimately involves investing in training and development for all employees. It also entails investing in resources people need to increase their productivity. Companies can invest in information technology that helps people to reduce distractions and focus on completing tasks. Cloud computing tools, for example, are a way to reduce manual tasks, share responsibility, and eliminate most paperwork.[107] ●

Epilogue: The Keys to Your Managerial Success

What are nine keys to personal managerial success?

THE BIG PICTURE

As we end the book, this section describes some life lessons to take away.

We have come to the end of the book, our last chance to offer some suggestions to take with you that we hope will benefit you in the coming years. Following are some life lessons pulled from various sources that can make you a "keeper" in an organization and help you be successful.

- **Find your passion and follow it.** Jane Chen is the founder and CEO of Embrace Innovations, which markets to developing countries a line of inexpensive, portable incubators for premature babies. Chen's inspiration is the great medieval and Renaissance cathedrals in Europe. Unlikely? Not really. These architectural wonders, which took generations to build, were created by people inspired to contribute to something greater than themselves, even if they would not live to see it.[108] Find something that inspires you, that you love to do, and do it vigorously.

- **Encourage self-discovery, and be realistic.** To stay ahead of the pack, you need to develop self-awareness, have an active mind, and be willing to grow and change. Legendary designer Diane von Furstenberg recalls the lesson she learned from early mistakes that reduced her control over her business and diluted her brand: "Your worst moments are your best souvenirs."[109]

- **Every situation is different, so be flexible.** No principle, no theory will apply under all circumstances. Industries, cultures, supervisors, employees, and customers will vary. It's not a sign of weakness to be willing to change something that isn't working or to try something new.[110] Justin Tobin, founder and president of consultancy firm DDG, credits his mother with teaching him that "experimentation leads to the discovery of a unique identity and that everything in life and work is completely subjective. What one person likes, another might not, and that's not only okay, it's encouraged inside innovative organizations."[111]

- **Fine-tune your soft skills—your people skills.** Today we live and work in a team universe. Try getting feedback on your interpersonal skills from friends, colleagues, and team members and develop a plan for improvement. Even nonverbal communication is a people skill. Dave Kerpen, CEO of Likeable Local, once made an important contact with someone who started a conversation with him at a crowded event because he was wearing distinctive orange shoes. Now Kerpen wears orange shoes every day.[112]

- **Learn how to develop leadership skills.** Every company should invest in the leadership development of its managers if it is to improve the quality of its future leaders. But you can also work to develop your own leadership skills. For instance, offer to help others, take the initiative when action is needed (sometimes called being a self-starter), and don't be afraid to ask for more responsibility to demonstrate what you're capable of.[113] Another life lesson: If you set the bar high, even if you don't reach it, you end up in a pretty good place—that is, achieving a pretty high mark.

- **Treat people as if they matter, because they do.** If you treat employees, colleagues, and customers with dignity, they respond accordingly. Bryce Drew, head coach of the Valparaiso men's basketball team, the Crusaders, says this about his players: "The person is more important than the result. We're going to recruit families. We're going to recruit players that want to be part of our family here. That's how we live our daily life and that's how we treat our team. I think when people sign on to come here, they know they're coming to be more than basketball players. They're coming to be cared for and develop into men."[114]

- **Draw employees and peers into your management process.** The old top-down, command-and-control model of organization is moving toward a flattened, networked kind of structure. Managers now work more often with peers, where lines of authority aren't always clear or don't exist, so that one's persuasive powers become key. Power has devolved to front-line employees who are closest to the customer and to small, focused, self-managed teams that have latitude to pursue new ideas. Ask them what they think are the best ways to get things done.[115]

- **Keep your cool, and take yourself lightly.** The more unflappable you appear in difficult circumstances, the more you'll be admired by your bosses and coworkers. Having a sense of humor helps. There may be no more serious workplace in the United States than the White House, but President Obama brought a gentle streak of wry humor to many informal occasions.[116] At the 2015 White House correspondents' dinner, he quipped, "After the midterm elections, my advisers asked me, 'Mr. President, do you have a bucket list?' And I said, 'I have something that rhymes with bucket.'"[117]

- **Go with the flow, and stay positive.** Life has its ebbs and flows. You'll have good times and bad. During this journey, don't focus too heavily on negative events and thoughts. Negative thoughts rob you of positive energy and your ability to perform at your best. In contrast, a positive approach toward life is more likely to help you flourish.[118]

We wish you the very best of luck. And we mean it!

Angelo Kinicki
Brian K. Williams

Key Points

16.1 Control: When Managers Monitor Performance

- Controlling is defined as monitoring performance, comparing it with goals, and taking corrective action as needed.

- There are six reasons that control is needed: (1) to adapt to change and uncertainty; (2) to discover irregularities and errors; (3) to reduce costs, increase productivity, or add value; (4) to detect opportunities; (5) to deal with complexity; and (6) to decentralize decision making and facilitate teamwork.

- There are four control process steps. (1) The first step is to set standards. A control standard is the desired performance level for a given goal. (2) The second step is to measure performance, based on written reports, oral reports, and personal observation. (3) The third step is to compare measured performance against the standards established. (4) The fourth step is to take corrective action, if necessary, if there is negative performance.

16.2 Levels and Areas of Control

- In applying the steps and types of control, managers need to consider (1) the level of management at which they operate, (2) the areas they can draw on for resources, and (3) the style of control philosophy.

- There are three levels of control, corresponding to the three principal managerial levels. (1) Strategic control, done by top managers, is monitoring performance to ensure that strategic plans are being implemented. (2) Tactical control, done by middle managers, is monitoring performance to ensure that tactical plans are being implemented. (3) Operational

control, done by first-level or supervisory managers, is monitoring performance to ensure that day-to-day goals are being implemented.

- Most organizations have six areas that they can draw on for resources. (1) The physical area includes buildings, equipment, and tangible products; these use equipment control, inventory-management control, and quality controls. (2) The human resources area uses personality tests, drug tests, performance tests, employee surveys, and the like as controls to monitor people. (3) The informational area uses production schedules, sales forecasts, environmental impact statements, and the like to monitor the organization's various resources. (4) The financial area uses various kinds of financial controls, as we discuss in Section 16.4. (5) The structural area uses hierarchical or other arrangements such as bureaucratic control, which is characterized by use of rules, regulations, and formal authority to guide performance, or decentralized control, which is characterized by informal and organic structural arrangements. (6) The cultural area influences the work process and levels of performance through the set of norms that develop as a result of the values and beliefs that constitute an organization's culture.

16.3 The Balanced Scorecard and Strategy Maps

- To establish standards, managers often use the balanced scorecard, which provides a fast but comprehensive view of the organization via four indicators: (1) financial measures, (2) customer satisfaction, (3) internal processes, and (4) innovation and improvement activities.

- The strategy map, a visual representation of the four perspectives of the balanced scorecard—financial, customer, internal business, and innovation and learning—enables managers to communicate their goals so that everyone in the company can understand how their jobs are linked to the overall objectives of the organization.

16.4 Some Financial Tools for Control

- Financial controls include (1) budgets, (2) financial statements, and (3) audits.
- A budget is a formal financial projection. The most important budget-planning approach is incremental budgeting, which allocates increased or decreased funds to a department by using the last budget period as a reference point; only incremental changes in the budget request are reviewed. Budgets are either fixed, which allocate resources on the basis of a single estimate of costs, or variable, which allow resource allocation to vary in proportion with various levels of activity.
- A financial statement is a summary of some aspect of an organization's financial status. One type, the balance sheet, summarizes an organization's overall financial worth—assets and liabilities—at a specific point in time. The other type, the income statement, summarizes an organization's financial results—revenues and expenses—over a specified period of time.
- Audits are formal verifications of an organization's financial and operational systems. Audits are of two types. An external audit is formal verification of an organization's financial accounts and statements by outside experts. An internal audit is a verification of an organization's financial accounts and statements by the organization's own professional staff.

16.5 Total Quality Management

- Much of the impetus for quality improvement came from W. Edwards Deming, whose philosophy, known as Deming management, proposed ideas for making organizations more responsive, more democratic, and less wasteful.
- Among the principles of Deming management are (1) quality should be aimed at the needs of the consumer; (2) companies should aim at improving the system, not blaming workers; (3) improved quality leads to increased market share, increased company prospects, and increased employment; and (4) quality can be improved on the basis of hard data, using the PDCA, or plan-do-check-act, cycle.
- Total quality management (TQM) is defined as a comprehensive approach—led by top management and supported throughout the organization—dedicated to continuous quality improvement (such as through Kaizen), training, and customer satisfaction. The two core principles of TQM are people orientation and improvement orientation.
- In the people orientation, everyone involved with the organization is asked to focus on delivering value to customers, focusing on quality. TQM requires training, teamwork, and cross-functional efforts.
- In the improvement orientation, everyone involved with the organization is supposed to make ongoing, small, incremental improvements in all parts of the organization. This orientation assumes that it's less expensive to do things right the first time, to do small improvements all the time, and to follow accurate standards to eliminate small variations.
- Several techniques are available for improving quality. (1) Outsourcing is the subcontracting of services and operations to an outside vendor. (2) Reduced cycle time consists of reducing the number of steps in a work process. (3) Statistical process control is a statistical technique that uses periodic random samples from production runs to see if quality is being maintained within a standard range of acceptability. (4) Six Sigma is a rigorous statistical analysis process that reduces defects in manufacturing and service-related processes. (5) ISO 9000 consists of quality-control procedures companies must install—from purchasing to manufacturing to inventory to shipping—that can be audited by independent quality-control experts, or "registrars. ISO 14000 extends the concept to environmental performance.

16.6 Managing Control Effectively

- Successful control systems have four common characteristics: (1) They are strategic and results oriented. (2) They are timely, accurate, and objective. (3) They are realistic, positive, and understandable and they encourage self-control. (4) They are flexible.
- Among the barriers to a successful control system are the following: (1) Organizations may exert too much control. (2) There may be too little employee participation. (3) The organization may overemphasize means instead of ends. (4) There may be an overemphasis on paperwork. (5) There may be an overemphasis on one approach instead of multiple approaches.

16.7 Managing for Productivity

- A manager has to deal with six challenges—managing for competitive advantage, diversity, globalization, information technology, ethical standards, sustainability, and his or her own happiness and meaningfulness.
- Managers must make decisions about the four management functions—planning, organizing, leading, and controlling—to get people to achieve productivity and realize results.
- Productivity is defined by the formula "outputs divided by inputs for a specified period of time." Productivity matters because it determines whether the organization will make a profit or even survive.
- Much of productivity growth is thought to result from the implementation of information technology, including enterprise resource planning (ERP) systems, though wages in most industrialized countries have not kept up. Productivity depends on control.

1. What is control, and what are six reasons control is needed?

2. Explain the steps in the control process, and describe the three levels of control.

3. Distinguish among the six areas of organizational control: physical, human, informational, financial, structural, and cultural.

4. Explain the four indicators of the balanced scorecard, and state what a strategy map is.

5. What are four mechanisms of success for measurement-managed firms and four barriers to effective measurement?

6. Define incremental budgeting, and give some examples of types of budgets.

7. Explain the following financial tools used for control: financial statement, balance sheet, income statement, and audits (both external and internal).

8. Discuss total quality management, its two core principles, and the concept of continuous improvement.

9. Explain the following TQM tools and techniques: reduced cycle time, the ISO 9000 series, the ISO 14000 series, statistical process control, and Six Sigma and Lean Six Sigma.

10. What is the formula for defining productivity?

Management in Action

Chipotle's Operational Problems Make People Sick

Steve Ells, Chipotle's co-chief executive officer, founded the company in 1993. It has expanded to more than 1,900 locations and over 59,000 employees.

Chipotle was built on the idea that is possible to deliver a fast-food experience relying on "high-quality raw ingredients, classic cooking techniques, and distinctive interior design." In other words, fast-food service would resemble a fine dining experience. This idea morphed into the marketing slogan "Food with Integrity." Chipotle's commitment reflects the company's "devotion to finding the very best ingredients we can—with respect for animals, farmers, and the environment."[119] Its marketing messages claimed that its fresh ingredients and naturally raised meat were better than those of competitors and better for all humanity. The goal was to position the fast-food chain as a healthy choice.

Healthy Choice?

Chipotle encountered a crisis in 2015. It began when 234 customers and employees were infected with a norovirus at a Chipotle in Simi Valley, California, in August. According to the government's Centers for Disease Control and Prevention (CDC), a "Norovirus is a very contagious virus that can infect anyone. You can get it from an infected person, contaminated food or water, or by touching contaminated surfaces. The

virus causes your stomach or intestines or both to get inflamed. This leads you to have stomach pain, nausea, and diarrhea and to throw up. These symptoms can be serious for some people, especially young children and older adults."[120] The virus is often transmitted when people fail to wash their hands after using the bathroom.

Sixty-four more people became sick in August and September from salmonella-tainted tomatoes eaten at 22 outlets in Minnesota; nine were hospitalized. In November, norovirus was found again, this time in people eating at a Chipotle's in Boston. One hundred forty Boston College students became ill, along with 16 students and three health care professionals who came in contact with infected people. The source of this outbreak was a sick employee who was not sent home after reporting to work.

Then 55 people were infected with the *E. coli* bacteria in 11 states. The majority of cases were found in Oregon and Washington in October 2015, and 21 people were hospitalized. In December, the CDC verified that 5 more people in three states had contacted a different and rare type of *E. coli*. The common factor across the cases was eating a meal at a Chipotle Mexican Grill restaurant.[121] All told, public health officials estimate that about 500 people around the United States became sick after eating at Chipotle.[122]

The inconsistency between the marketing theme of "Food with Integrity" and the food-related illnesses tainted the company's reputation and business results. *Bloomberg Businessweek* reported that Chipotle's stock dropped 30% between August and December 2015, and sales dropped 16% in November.

Did Chipotle's Supply Chain and Work Processes Contribute to the Problem?

Chipotle uses about 100 suppliers for its meals, as well as local farms from which the company prefers to get its fresh produce. Local farms are within 350 miles of a restaurant and contribute about 10% of the produce. Meats come from various sources in the United States and Australia. "Chipotle began importing beef from Australia two years ago because it could not find enough domestically raised grass-fed beef to meet growing demand," said CEO Steve Ells.[123] The company also employs high-end commissaries to prepare some food items. *Bloomberg Businessweek* noted the source(s) of *E. coli* came from somewhere in this supply chain.[124]

According to *CNN Money*, "Neither Chipotle nor the CDC has been able to determine what specific food is the cause of the disease *[E.coli]*. The CDC said that 'a common meal item or ingredient served at Chipotle Mexican Grill restaurants in several states is a likely cause of this outbreak.'"[125] The CDC also said Chipotle had been very cooperative during its investigation, but "when a restaurant serves foods with several ingredients that are mixed or cooked together and then used in multiple food items, it can be more difficult for epidemiologic studies to identify the specific ingredient that is contaminated."[126]

Although the company has standards and protocols in place for handling and processing food, some think Chipotle did not go far enough. A *Forbes* reporter concluded that "Chipotle is a company so out of control and negligent that it repeatedly endangers the public." He based this harsh conclusion partly on a statement the company made in a report to the Securities and Exchange Commission. Chipotle said, "We may be at a higher risk for food-borne illness outbreaks than some competitors." The report also stated that these illnesses were more likely "due to our use of fresh produce and meats rather than frozen, and our reliance on employees cooking with traditional methods rather than automation." The reporter concluded by wondering "whether Chipotle's 'traditional methods' include employees' neglecting to wash their hands before preparing foods, which is how norovirus is usually spread."[127]

The Company Makes Operational Changes

The company closed its stores in Oregon and Washington in November 2015 to determine the cause of the *E. coli* outbreak. CEO Ellis visited the *Today* show in December and "apologized to everyone who'd fallen ill, and announced a comprehensive food-safety program that he said would far excel industry norms." He never explained why the company had not instituted more rigorous safety standards, but he noted that Chipotle "will shift more food preparation out of restaurants and into centralized kitchens."[128]

Before reopening the restaurants in Oregon and Washington, Chipotle took the following actions:[129]

- Confirmed that no employees in these restaurants were sickened.

- Expanded testing of fresh produce, raw meat, and dairy items before restocking restaurants.

- Implemented additional safety procedures and audits in all its 2,000 restaurants to ensure that robust food safety standards were in place.

- Worked closely with federal, state, and local government agencies to ensure that robust food safety standards were in place.

- Conducted additional deep cleaning and sanitization in all its closed restaurants (also to be done at all restaurants nationwide).

Chipotle went one step further by hiring Mansour Samadpour, head of IEH Laboratories & Consulting Group, to develop a broader and more extensive food safety program. *Bloomberg Businessweek* concluded that Samadpur's plan includes "changes at every step of Chipotle's system. More food will be prepared ahead of time, out of sight at commissaries, and transported to 19 distributions centers. . . . Produce will be screened for pathogens in small batches using what Chipotle calls high-resolution DNA-based tests."[130] The company also instituted the following operational changes:[131]

- Cheese will now arrive in restaurants pre-shredded.

- Ingredients like onions will be macerated with lemon or lime juice to kill germs.

- Sixty samples of every 2,000 pounds of steak will be tested before the meat is sent to stores.

- Tomatoes, cilantro, and other ingredients will be chopped in centralized locations rather than in stores, so they can be tested.

What Next?

Chipotle is actively trying to attract former and new customers. The company is offering "burrito giveaways and free chips with guacamole or salsa." It also launched an advertising campaign including direct-mail coupons. Company executives "described the early giveaways as a success and said the gap between free versus paid entrees had narrowed. The company also announced plans for more freebies."[132]

Operationally, the new safety standards will be too expensive for small, local farms to accommodate, leading to less use by Chipotle of local produce. A blogger noted that "the decision to move away from the chain's preference for local produce, when available, for its burritos, salads and rice bowls is a significant shift for the fast-casual chain, which has prided itself on providing fresher ingredients than its competitors."[133]

Time will tell whether the operational changes at Chipotle bring its customers back.

FOR DISCUSSION

1. Which of the six reasons that control is needed are apparent in this case? Explain.

2. What levels and areas of control were ineffectively used by Chipotle? Discuss.

3. If you were charged with creating a balanced scorecard for Steve Ellis, what SMART goals (see Chapter 5), would you use as standards to assess performance in the four categories in your scorecard? Develop one SMART goal for each scorecard category.

4. To what extent does Chipotle use the PDCA process? Explain your rationale.

5. Which of the keys to successful control systems are being used by Chipotle? Explain.

6. What are the most important takeaways from this case? Discuss.

Legal/Ethical Challenge

Is GPS Tracking of Employee Actions an Effective Form of Management Control?

More companies are using GPS apps to track the whereabouts of their employees. Companies claim such devices increase productivity and help locate employees in times of a crisis, such as the 2016 terrorist attack in Paris.[134]

For example, the city of Aurora, Colorado, installed tracking devices inside its sweepers and snowplows "to make sure they're being used as taxpayers intended. Management claims a 15% increase in productivity by having the tracking devices in the vehicles.[135] Driver Maria Coleman said, "It's Big Brother. It's watching you, making sure you do what you're supposed to do, but if you are doing what you're supposed to be doing then you shouldn't have a problem."

Companies also use tracking devices as part of their wellness program. *The Wall Street Journal* reported that 40%–50% of companies with wellness programs use them to provide employees with feedback about their progress. In this application, however, tracking behavior is optional.[136]

The practice of tracking is now heading to the courts. Myrna Arias, a former sales executive for money-transfer company Intermex Wire Transfer, sued the company after she was fired for failing to use a Xora app that "contained a global positioning system function which tracked the exact location of the person possessing the smartphones on which it was installed."

Arias's boss, John Stubits, admitted that she would be tracked both on and off the clock. He "bragged that he knew how fast she was driving at specific moments ever since she had installed the app on her phone."[137] Arias agreed to use the app during work hours but thought it was an invasion of privacy during nonwork hours. Stubits "told Arias she was required to keep her phone on '24/7' to answer client calls." Arias decided to de-install "the app to protect her privacy and was scolded by Stubits. A few weeks later, Intermex fired her."[138]

SOLVING THE CHALLENGE

What would you do if you were the CEO of Intermex and in charge of deciding what do about the Arias case and the use of tracking employees?

1. I appreciate the value of people flourishing at work, but this is a sales context and the company needs to be responsive to customer issues 24/7. I thus would fight the lawsuit and keep using the tracking device. Tracking employees during off hours is not an invasion of privacy.

2. People won't flourish if the company doesn't change its ways. I would settle the lawsuit but continue to monitor employees only during work hours. It's an invasion of privacy to track people when they are not at work.

3. Settle the lawsuit and continue to track employees 24/7. I would also make all current and new employees sign a waiver indicating that it is a job requirement to use the tracking device 24/7. People can leave if they don't want to abide by the policy.

4. Invent other options.

Appendix

The Project Planner's Toolkit
Flowcharts, Gantt Charts, and Break-Even Analysis

Major Question You Should Be Able to Answer

MAJOR QUESTION

How can you use planning tools to enhance your performance and achieve utmost success?

THE BIG PICTURE

Three tools used in project planning, which was covered in Chapter 5, are flowcharts, Gantt charts, and break-even analysis.

Project planning may begin (in the definition stage) as a back-of-the-envelope kind of process, but the client will expect a good deal more for the time and money being invested. Fortunately, there are various planning and monitoring tools that give the planning and execution of projects more precision. Three tools in the planner's toolkit are (1) flowcharts, (2) Gantt charts, and (3) break-even analysis.

Tool #1: Flowcharts—for Showing Event Sequences and Alternate Decision Scenarios

A *flowchart* is a useful graphical tool for representing the sequence of events required to complete a project and for laying out "what-if" scenarios. Flowcharts have been used for decades by computer programmers and systems analysts to make a graphical "road map," as it were, of the flow of tasks required. These professionals use their own special symbols (indicating "input/output," "magnetic disk," and the like), but there is no need for you to make the process complicated. Generally, only three symbols are needed: (1) an oval for the "beginning" and "end," (2) a box for a major activity, and (3) a diamond for a "yes or no" decision. *(See Figure A.1, next page.)*

Computer programs such as iGrafx's ABC FlowCharter are available for constructing flowcharts. You can also use the drawing program in word processing programs such as Microsoft Word.

FIGURE A.1 **Flowchart: website, print, or television?**

Example of a flowchart for improving a company's advertising.

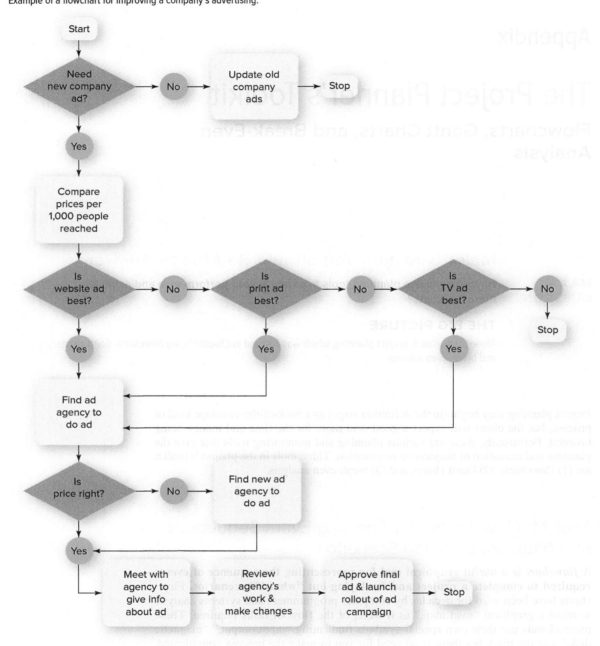

Benefits Flowcharts have two benefits:

- **Planning straightforward activities.** A flowchart can be quite helpful for planning ordinary activities—figuring out the best way to buy textbooks or a car, for example. It is also a straightforward way of indicating the sequence of events in, say, thinking out a new enterprise that you would then turn into a business plan.

- **Depicting alternate scenarios.** A flowchart is also useful for laying out "what-if" scenarios—as in if you answer "yes" to a decision question you should follow Plan A, if you answer "no" you should follow Plan B.

Limitations Flowcharts have two limitations:

- **No time indication.** They don't show the amounts of time required to accomplish the various activities in a project. In building a house, the foundation might take only a couple of days, but the rough carpentry might take weeks. These time differences can't be represented graphically on a flowchart (although you could make a notation).

- **Not good for complex projects.** They aren't useful for showing projects consisting of several activities that must all be worked on at the same time. An example would be getting ready for football season's opening game, by which time the players have to be trained, the field readied, the programs printed, the band rehearsed, the ticket sellers recruited, and so on. These separate activities might each be represented on their own flowcharts, of course. But to try to express them all together all at once would produce a flowchart that would be unwieldy, even unworkable.

Tool #2: Gantt Charts—Visual Time Schedules for Work Tasks

We have mentioned how important deadlines are to making a project happen. Unlike a flowchart, a Gantt chart can graphically indicate deadlines.

The Gantt chart was developed by **Henry L. Gantt,** a member of the school of scientific management (discussed in Chapter 2). **A *Gantt chart* is a kind of time schedule—a specialized bar chart that shows the relationship between the kind of work tasks planned and their scheduled completion dates.** *(See Figure A.2, below.)*

FIGURE A.2 **Gantt chart for designing a website**

This shows the tasks accomplished and the time planned for remaining tasks to build a company website.

Accomplished: ||||||||||
Planned: \\\\\\\\

Stage of development	Week 1	Week 2	Week 3	Week 4	Week 5
1. Examine competitors' websites	|||||||||||||||||| ||||||||||	||||||||||			
2. Get information for your website	|||||||||||||||||| ||||||||||	|||||||||||||||| ||||||||||			
3. Learn Web-authoring software		|||||||||||||||| ||||||||||	|||||||||||||||| ||||||||||		
4. Create (design) your website			\\\\\\\\\\	\\\\\\\\\\\\\\\\ \\	\\\\\
5. "Publish" (put) website online					\\\\\\\\\\\\\\

A number of software packages can help you create and modify Gantt charts on your computer. Examples are CA-SuperProject, Microsoft Project, Primavera Sure-Trak Project Manager, and TurboProject Professional.

Benefits   There are three benefits to using a Gantt chart:

- **Express time lines visually.** Unlike flowcharts, Gantt charts allow you to indicate visually the time to be spent on each activity.
- **Compare proposed and actual progress.** A Gantt chart may be used to compare planned time to complete a task with actual time taken to complete it, so that you can see how far ahead or behind schedule you are for the entire project. This enables you to make adjustments so as to hold to the final target dates.
- **Simplicity.** There is nothing difficult about creating a Gantt chart. You express the time across the top and the tasks down along the left side. As Figure A.2 shows, you can make use of this device while still in college to help schedule and monitor the work you need to do to meet course requirements and deadlines (for papers, projects, tests).

Limitations   Gantt charts have two limitations:

- **Not useful for large, complex projects.** Although a Gantt chart can express the interrelations among the activities of relatively small projects, it becomes cumbersome and unwieldy when used for large, complex projects. More sophisticated management planning tools may be needed, such as PERT networks.
- **Time assumptions are subjective.** The time assumptions expressed may be purely subjective; there is no range between "optimistic" and "pessimistic" of the time needed to accomplish a given task.

Tool #3: Break-Even Analysis—How Many Items Must You Sell to Turn a Profit?

***Break-even analysis* is a way of identifying how much revenue is needed to cover the total costs of developing and selling a product.** Let's walk through the computation of a break-even analysis, referring to the illustration. *(See Figure A.3.)* We assume

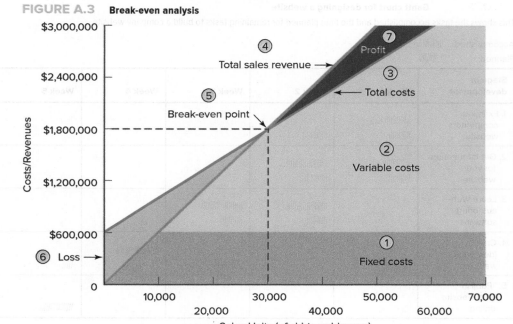

FIGURE A.3   Break-even analysis

you are an apparel manufacturer making shirts or blouses. Start in the lower-right corner of the diagram on the previous page and follow the circled numbers as you read the descriptions below.

① *Fixed costs (green area):* Once you start up a business, whether you sell anything or not, you'll have expenses that won't vary much, such as rent, insurance, taxes, and perhaps salaries. These are called *fixed costs,* **expenses that don't change regardless of your sales or output.** Fixed costs are a function of time—they are expenses you have to pay out on a regular basis, such as weekly, monthly, or yearly. Here the chart shows the fixed costs (green area) are $600,000 per year no matter how many sales units (of shirts or blouses) you sell.

② *Variable costs (blue area):* Now suppose you start producing and selling a product, such as blouses or shirts. At this point you'll be paying for materials, supplies, labor, sales commissions, and delivery expenses. These are called *variable costs,* **expenses that vary directly depending on the numbers of the product that you produce and sell.** (After all, making more shirts will cost you more in cloth, for example.) Variable costs, then, are a function of volume—they go up and down depending on the number of products you make or sell. Here the variable costs (blue area) are relatively small if you sell only a few thousand shirts but they go up tremendously if you sell, say, 70,000 shirts.

③ *Total costs (first right upward-sloping line—green plus blue area added together):* The sum of the fixed costs and the variable costs equals the total costs (the green and blue areas together). This is indicated by the line that slopes upward to the right from $600,000 to $3,000,000.

④ *Total sales revenue (second right upward-sloping line):* This is the total dollars received from the sale of however many units you sell. The sales revenue varies depending on the number of units you sell. Thus, for example, if you sell 30,000 shirts, you'll receive $1,800,000 in revenue. If you sell 40,000 shirts, you'll receive somewhat more than $2,400,000 in revenue.

⑤ *Break-even point (intersection of dashed lines):* Finding this point is the purpose of this whole exercise. **The** *break-even point* **is the amount of sales revenue at which there is no profit but also no loss to your company.** On the graph, this occurs where the "Total sales revenues" line crosses the "Total costs" line, as we've indicated here where the dashed lines meet. This means that you must sell 30,000 shirts and receive $1,800,000 in revenue in order to recoup your total costs (fixed plus variable). Important note: Here is where pricing the shirts becomes important. If you raise the price per shirt, you may be able to make the same amount of money (hit your break-even point) by selling fewer of them—but that may be harder to do because customers may resist buying at the higher price.

⑥ *Loss (red area):* If you fail to sell enough shirts at the right price (the break-even point), you will suffer a loss. *Loss* **means your total costs exceed your total sales revenue.** As the chart shows, here you are literally "in the red"—you've lost money.

⑦ *Profit (black area):* Here you are literally "in the black"—you've made money. All the shirts you sell beyond the break-even point constitute a profit. *Profit* **is the amount by which total revenue exceeds total costs.** The more shirts you sell, of course, the greater the profit.

    The kind of break-even analysis demonstrated here is known as the *graphic method.* The same thing can also be done algebraically.

Benefits   Break-even analysis has two benefits:

- **For doing future "what-if" alternate scenarios of costs, prices, and sales.** This tool allows you to vary the different possible costs, prices, and sales quantities to do rough "what-if" scenarios to determine possible pricing and sales goals. Since the numbers are interrelated, if you change one, the others will change also.

> **EXAMPLE**   **Break-Even Analysis: Why Do Airfares Vary So Much?**
>
> Why do some airlines charge four times more than others for a flight of the same distance?
>
> There are several reasons, but break-even analysis enters into it.
>
> United Airlines's average cost for flying a passenger 1 mile in a recent year was 11.7 cents, whereas Southwest's was 7.7 cents. Those are the break-even costs. What they charged beyond that was their profit.
>
> Why the difference? One reason, according to a study by the U.S. Department of Transportation, is that Southwest's expenses are lower. United flies more long routes than short ones, so its costs are stretched out over more miles,
>
> making its costs for flying shorter routes higher than Southwest's.
>
> Another factor affecting airfares is the type of passengers flying a particular route—whether they are high-fare-paying business travelers or more price-conscious leisure travelers. Business travelers often don't mind paying a lot (they are reimbursed by their companies), and those routes (such as Chicago to Cincinnati) tend to have more first-class seats, which drives up the average price. Flights to vacation spots (such as Las Vegas) usually have more low-price seats because people aren't willing to pay a lot for pleasure travel. Also, nonstop flight fares often cost more than flights with connections.

■ **For analyzing the profitability of past projects.** While break-even analysis is usually used as a tool for future projects, it can also be used retroactively to find out whether the goal of profitability was really achieved, since costs may well have changed during the course of the project. In addition, you can use it to determine the impact of cutting costs once profits flow.

Limitations   Break-even analysis is not a cure-all.

■ **It oversimplifies.** In the real world, things don't happen as neatly as this model implies. For instance, fixed and variable costs are not always so readily distinguishable. Or fixed costs may change as the number of sales units goes up. And not all customers may pay the same price (some may get discounts).

■ **The assumptions may be faulty.** On paper, the formula may work perfectly for identifying a product's profitability. But what if customers find the prices too high? Or what if sales figures are outrageously optimistic? In the marketplace, your price and sales forecasts may really be only good guesses.

CHAPTER 1

1. B. Vlasic, "New GM Chief Is Company Woman, Born to It," *The New York Times,* December 11, 2013, pp. A1, A3.
2. Dave Cole, chairman of Auto Harvest, quoted in C. Woodyard, "Barra Came Up Through Ranks at GM," *USA Today,* December 11, 2013, p. 2B.
3. R. Wright, "Barra to Steer GM on Steady Path," *The Financial Times,* December 11, 2013, p. 18.
4. B. Vlasi, "G.M. Chairwoman Is Named Chairwoman, Affirming Her Leadership," *The New York Times,* January 5, 2016, p. B3.
5. Wright, "Barra to Steer GM on Steady Path."
6. Rometty, quoted in C. Hymowitz and S. Frier, "IBM's Rometty Breaks Ground as 100-Year-Old Company's First Female Leader," *Bloomberg Businessweek,* October 26, 2011, www.bloomberg.com/news/2011-10-25/ibm-names-rometty-to-succeed-palmisano-as-its-first-female-chief-executive.html (accessed February 22, 2016).
7. Rometty, quoted in C. C. Miller, "For Incoming IBM Chief, Self-Confidence Rewarded," *The New York Times,* October 28, 2011, pp. B1, B10; and in J. B. Stewart, "Top Aide to a CEO: Her Husband," *The New York Times,* November 5, 2011, pp. B1, B2.
8. R. Barker, "No, Management Is *Not* a Profession," *Harvard Business Review,* July–August 2010, pp. 52–60.
9. M. P. Follett, quoted in J. F. Stoner and R. E. Freeman, *Management,* 5th ed. (Englewood Cliffs, NJ: Prentice Hall, 1992), p. 6.
10. S. McChrystal, *Team of Teams* (New York: Penguin Publishing Group, 2015).
11. J. Sharkey, "Airline Hits Sour Notes with the Wait Times on Customer Calls," *The New York Times,* January 21, 2014, p. B4; and C. Elliott, "Maybe You Shouldn't Accept Apology," *USA Today,* February 10, 2014, p. 3B.
12. "Customer Service Buying Guide," Consumer Reports, July 2015, www.consumerreports.org/cro/customer-service/buying-guide.htm (accessed February 4, 2016).
13. Quote attributed to Tim Suther, Vice President, Global Multichannel Marketing Services, Acxiom, reported in D. Dodds, "What Is Customer Experience?" *Huffpost Business,* January 8, 2016, www.huffingtonpost.com/don-dodds what-is-customer-experience_b_89362 86.html (accessed February 4, 2016).
14. United Nations report, November 2015, reported in S. Rosenbloom, "How to Deal with Flight Delays and Other Travel Headaches," *The New York Times,* January 10, 2016, p. TR-4.
15. C. Elliott, "Coach Class Continues Downward Spiral," *Reno Gazette-Journal,* December 14, 2015, p. 5B; reprinted from *USA Today.*
16. Associated Press, "Record Number of Flights Canceled in Brutal Winter," *San Francisco Chronicle,* February 16, 2014, p. A12.
17. J. Thomas, quoted in Elliott, "Maybe You Shouldn't Accept Apology." Thomas is co-author, with G. Chapman, of *When Sorry Isn't Enough: Making Things Right with Those You Love* (Chicago: Moody Publishers, 2013).
18. Mitch Robertson, reported in Elliott, "Maybe You Shouldn't Accept Apology."
19. "Get2Human.com (How to Get to a Human Quickly)," *GetHuman.com,* www.get2human.com/Get2Human_list.asp?industry=travel (accessed February 4, 2016).
20. G. Colvin, "Catch a Rising Star," *Fortune,* February 6, 2006, pp. 46–50.
21. Bureau of Labor Statistics, "Usual Weekly Earnings of Wage and Salary Workers, Fourth Quarter 2015," *News Release,* January 22, 2016, www.bls.gov/news.release/pdf/wkyeng.pdf (accessed January 25, 2016).
22. See also *The Rising Cost of* Not *Going to College,* Pew Research Center, February 11, 2014, www.pewsocialtrends.org/2014/02/11/the-rising-cost-of-not-going-to-college/ (accessed January 25, 2016).
23. G. Solomon, "15 Top-Paid CEOs," *Money,* May 16, 2015, http://money.cnn.com/gallery/news/companies/2015/05/16/top-paid-ceos/index.html (accessed January 25, 2016). See also D. Gelles, "For the Highest-Paid CEOs, the Party Goes On," *The New York Times,* May 16, 2015, www.nytimes.com/2015/05/17/business/for-the-highest-paid-ceos-the-party-goes-on.html?_r=0. See also "Equilar 200 Highest Paid CEO Rankings," *The New York Times,* www.equilar.com/reports/18-200-highest-paid-CEO-rankings-2015.html (both accessed January 25, 2016).
24. T. Francis and J. S. Lublin, "CEO Pay Shrank Most Since Financial Crisis," *The Wall Street Journal,* April 7, 2016, www.wsj.com/articles/ceo-pay-shrank-most-since-financial-crisis-1460074559 (accessed July 28, 2016).
25. "Chief Executive Officer Salaries," Salary.com, January 2016, www1.salary.com/Chief-Executive-Officer-salary.html; and Bureau of Labor Statistics, "Top Executives," *Occupational Outlook Handbook,* December 17, 2015 www.bls.gov/ooh/Management/Top-executives.htm (both accessed January 25, 2016).
26. Bureau of Labor Statistics, "Management Occupations," *Occupational Outlook Handbook,* December 17, 2015, www.bls.gov/ooh/management/home.htm (accessed January 25, 2014).
27. Survey by H. Park, J. M. Twenge, P. M. Greenfield, "The Great Recession: Implications for Adolescent Values and Behavior," *Social Psychological and Personality Science,* Vol. 5, No. 3 (2014), pp. 310–318.
28. B. Schwartz, "Rethinking Work," *The New York Times,* August 30, 2015, pp. SR-1, SR-4. Schwartz is author of *Why We Work* (New York: Simon & Schuster, 2015).
29. 2013 CareerBuilder survey, reported in D. Auerbach, "Mentors Helpful at Every Career Stage," *Reno Gazette-Journal,* February 9, 2014, p. 10F. See also S. Burn, "Why You Should Be a Mentor," *Forbes,* May 20, 2015, www.forbes.com/sites/chicceo/2015/05/20/why-you-should-be-a-mentor/#2c7ec51424d0 (accessed February 8, 2016).
30. F. Namin-Hedayati, "Mark Zuckerberg's Leadership Qualities," Center for Work Life, Orlando, FL, www.centerforworklife.com/mark-zuckerbergs-leadership-qualities (accessed February 5, 2016).
31. M. Csikszentmihalyi, *Flow: The Psychology of Optimal Experience* (New York: Harper Collins, 1990); *Beyond Boredom and Anxiety* (San Francisco: Jossey-Bass, 1975); *Creativity: Flow and the Psychology of Discovery and Invention* (New York: Harper Perennial, 1996); *Finding Flow: The Psychology of Engagement with Everyday Life* (New York: Basic Books, 1998); and *Good Business: Leadership, Flow, and the Making of Meaning* (New York: Penguin Books, 2003). See also M. Csikszentmihalyi and J. Nakamura, "Positive Psychology: Where Did It Come From, Where Is It Going?" In K. M. Sheldon, T. B. Kashdan, and M. F. Steger, eds., *Designing Positive Psychology* (New York: Oxford University Press, 2011), pp. 2–9.
32. Interview with Brian Chesky by A. Kessler, "The 'Sharing Economy' and Its Enemies," *The Wall Street Journal,* January 18–19, 2014, p. A11.
33. J. Weed, "Airbnb Grows to a Million Rooms and Hotel Rivals Are Quiet, for Now," *The New York Times,* May 11, 2015, p. B4; M. B. Weiner, "Home Sharing Seems to Be Here to Stay," *San Francisco Chronicle,* August 30, 2015, p. L4; C. Elliott, "Big Hotels' Plan to Win Customers from Airbnb," *Fortune.com,* January 27, 2016, http://fortune.com/2016/01/27/big-hotels-airbnb (accessed February 9, 2016); and M. della Cava, "Beyoncé's 'Super' $10,000-a-Night Airbnb Digs," *USA Today,* February 8, 2016, www.usatoday.com/story/tech/news/2016/02/08/beyonces-super-10000-night-airbnb-digs/80032066 (accessed February 9, 2016).
34. Weiner, "Home Sharing Seems to Be Here to Stay."
35. See "The Sharing Economy: Why Even the Mainstream Wants a Piece of the Pie," *Knowledge@Wharton,* November 27, 2013, https://www.google.com/search?q=The+Sharing+Economy%3A+Why+Even+the+Mainstream+Wants+a+Piece+of+the+Pie&ie=utf-8&oe=utf-8&aq=t&rls=org.mozilla:en-US:official&client=firefox-a&channel=np&source=hp (accessed February 9, 2016); and S. E. Needlema and A. Loten, "Startups Want to Be the Next Airbnb, Uber," *The Wall Street Journal,* May 8, 2014, p. B4; C. Said, "Sharing Comes of Age," *San Francisco Chronicle,* May 14, 2014, pp. C1, C3; and *The Sharing Economy,* Consumer Intelligence Series, Price water house Coopers, 2015, pwc.com/CISsharing (accessed February 9, 2016).
36. Weed, "Airbnb Grows to a Million Rooms, and Hotel Rivals Are Quiet, for Now."
37. Elliott, "Big Hotels' Plan to Win Customers from Airbnb"; C. Jones, "New App Creates Pop-up Social Networks at Hotels," *Reno Gazette-Journal,* January 26, 2015, p. 5B, reprinted from *USA Today;* B. Prunty, "Hotels Make an Extra Effort to Ensure Guests a Good Night's Sleep," *The New York Times,* July 21, 2015, p. B4; M. C. White, "Hotels Remake Rooms for a More Casual Style of Work," *The New York Times,* September 8, 2015, p. B5; N. Trejos, "The Incredible Shrinking Hotel Room," *Reno Gazette-Journal,* September 20, 2015, p. 4U, reprinted from *USA Today;* and J. Kell, "Hilton Debuts New Chain to Win over Millennials," *Fortune.com,* January 25, 2016, http://fortune.com/2016/01/25/hilton-new-chain-millennials (accessed February 9, 2016).
38. See J. W. O'Neill and Y. Ouyang, *From Air Mattresses to Unregulated Business: An Analysis of the Other Side of Airbnb.* Pennsylvania State University, January 2016, https://fortunedotcom.files.wordpress.com/2016/01/pennstate_airbnbreport_.pdf (accessed February 10, 2016). See also C. Elliott, "Airbnb Runs 'Illegal Hotels,' Hotel Industry Study Claims," *Fortune.com,* January 20, 2016, http://fortune.com/2016/01/20/airbnb-illegal-hotels-study (accessed February 10, 2016).
39. P. Coy, M. Conlin, and M. Herbst, "The Disposable Worker," *Business Week,* January 18, 2010, pp. 32–39.
40. Forecast by eMarketer, reported in CloudCommerce, Inc., "CloudCommerce Comments on $3.5 Trillion Global E-Commerce Forecast," *Yahoo! Finance,* December 15, 2015, http://finance.yahoo.com/news/cloudcommerce-comments-3-5-trillion-080000716.html;_ylt=AwrTccuTgbtWM50A2m8nnlIQ;_ylu=X3oDMTBzdmVvZmlwBGNvbG8DZ3ExBHBvcwMxMAR2dGlkAwRzZWMDc3l- (accessed February 10, 2016).
41. See Forrester Research, "112 Results for 'Disruption' in Everything," https://www.forrester.com/search?range=504001&N=20450%200&tmtxt=+disruption&page=1 (accessed February 10, 2016).
42. See J. Temple, "Data Explosion Revolutionizing Online World," *San Francisco Chronicle,* October 19, 2011, pp. D1, D4; N. Singer, "Just Give Me the Right to Be Forgotten," *The New York Times,* August 21, 2011, p. BUS-3; and "Ignore That Smartphone," The Week, December 27, 2013, p. 21.
43. IDC, "Data Growth, Business Opportunities, and the IT Imperative," *EMC Digital Universe,* April 2014, www.emc.com/leadership/digital-universe/2014iview/executive-summary.htm (accessed February 10, 2016).
44. The source of this information is Voucher Cloud, reported in "How Much Data Is Created Daily?" Storage Servers, February 6, 2016, https://storageservers.wordpress.com/2016/02/06/how-much-data-is-created-daily (accessed February 10, 2016).
45. Thomas L. Friedman "If I Had a Hammer," *The New York Times,* January 12, 2014, p. SR-11.
46. See D. Rothman, "How Technology Is Destroying Jobs," *MIT Technology Review,* June 12, 2013, https://www.technologyreview.com/s/515926/how-technology-is-destroying-jobs; and A. Smith and J. Anderson, *AI, Robotics, and the Future of Jobs,* Pew Research Center, August 6, 2014, www.pewinternet.org/2014/08/06/future-of-jobs (both accessed February 10, 2016). Also see J. Markoff, *Machines of Loving Grace: The Quest for Common Ground between Humans and Robots* (New York: Ecco Press, 2015).
47. See R. S. Gajendran, D. A. Harrison, and K. Delaney-Klinger, "Are Telecommuters Remotely Good Citizens? Unpacking Telecommuting's Effects on Performance via I-Deals and Job Resources," *Personnel Psychology,* Summer 2015, pp. 353–393.
48. S. L. Colby and J. M. Ortman, "Projections of the Size and Composition of the U.S. Population: 2014 to 2060," *Current Population Reports,* March 2015, U.S. Census Bureau, Figure 1, https://www.census.gov/content/dam/Census/library/publications/2015/demo/p25-1143.pdf (accessed February 10, 2016).
49. Colby and Ortman, "Projections of the Size and Composition of the U.S. Population: 2014 to 2060," Table 2.
50. Colby and Ortman, "Projections of the Size and Composition of the U.S. Population: 2014 to 2060," Table 1.
51. See, for instance, S. E. Page, *The Difference: How the Power of Diversity Creates Better Groups, Firms, Schools and Societies* (Princeton, NJ: Princeton University Press, 2007); C. Dreifus, "In Professor's Model, Diversity = Productivity," *The New York Times,* January 8, 2008, p. D2; A. Garnero and F. Rycx, "The Heterogeneous Effects of

Workforce Diversity on Productivity, Wages, and Profits," Discussion Paper No. 7350, April 2013, Institute for the Study of Labor (IZA), Bonn, http://ftp.iza.org/dp7350.pdf (accessed February 10, 2016); and "PwC's Robert E. Moritz: 'Diverse Teams Give You the Best Thinking,'" Knowledge@Wharton, December 24, 2013, http://knowledge.wharton.upenn.edu/article/leadership-beyond-bottom-line (accessed February 10, 2016).
52. A. Simone, "The 'How Are You?' Culture Clash," *The New York Times*, January 20, 2014, p. A15.
53. D. Tannen, "Greetings, from Around the World," letter, *The New York Times*, January 24, 2014, p. A24.
54. T. L. Friedman, *The World Is Flat: A Brief History of the Twenty-first Century* (New York: Picador, 2007).
55. See N. Bloom and J. Van Reenan, "Why Do Management Practices Differ across Firms and Countries?" *Journal of Economic Perspectives*, Vol. 24, No. 1 (2010), pp. 203–24.
56. This happened with the Carnival Lines cruise ship *Carnival Triumph* in early 2013, which caught fire at sea after precautions were ignored about the risk of leaks from engine fuel hoses. See K. Stock, "Carnival Launches Radical Money-Back Guarantee," *San Francisco Chronicle*, September 22, 2013, p. D6; and Associated Press, "Filing Shows Carnival Knew of Fire Risk," *San Francisco Chronicle*, December 19, 2013, p. A14.
57. D. Kushner, "The Dead End on Silk Road," *Rolling Stone*, February 13, 2014, pp. 52–59. See also L. Neumeister, "November Federal Trial Set in Silk Road Marketplace Case," *Reno Gazette-Journal*, February 9, 2014, p. 12F.
58. L. Seagall, "Silk Road's Ross Ulbricht Sentenced to Life," *CNN Money*, May 29, 2015, http://money.cnn.com/2015/05/29/technology/silk-road-ross-ulbricht-prison-sentence/index.html (accessed February 13, 2016).
59. M. Kouchaki and I. H. Smith, "The Morning Morality Effect: The Influence of Time of Day on Unethical Behavior," *Psychological Science*, January 2014, pp. 95–102. See also N. L. Mead, R. F. Baumeister, F. Gino, M. E. Schweitzer, D. Ariely, "Too Tired to Tell the Truth: Self-Control Resource Depletion and Dishonesty," *Journal of Experimental Social Psychology*, May 2009, pp. 594–597.
60. J. Roberts and D. Wasieleski, "Moral Reasoning in Computer-Based Task Environments: Exploring the Interplay between Cognitive and Technological Factors on Individuals' Propensity to Break Rules," *Journal of Business Ethics*, October 2012, pp. 355–376.
61. N. E. Ruedy, C. Moore, F. Gino, and M. E. Schweitzer, "The Cheater's High: The Unexpected Affective Benefits of Unethical Behavior," *Journal of Personality and Social Psychology*, October 2013, pp. 531–548.
62. See "Ethics Pays," EthicalSystems.org, http://ethicalsystems.org/content/ethics-pays (accessed February 21, 2016).
63. A. Tugend, "In Life and Business, Learning to Be Ethical," *The New York Times*, January 11, 2014, p. B5.
64. A. E. Tenbrunsel, University of Notre Dame, quoted in Tugend, "In Life and Business, Learning to Be Ethical."
65. T. L. Friedman, *Hot, Flat, and Crowded: Why We Need a Green Revolution—and How It Can Renew America* (New York: Picador, 2009).
66. A. Gore, *An Inconvenient Truth* (Emmaus, PA: Rodale, 2006). See also A. Gore, *The Future: Six Drivers of Global Change* (New York: Random House, 2013). For a more recent climate-change overview, see W. Nordhous, *The Climate Casino: Risk, Uncertainty, and Economics in a Warming World* (New Haven, CT: Yale University Press, 2013).
67. This definition of *sustainability* was developed in 1987 by the World Commission on Environment and Development.
68. See J. Kaeser, "Industry Must Lead on Climate Change," *The New York Times*, September 22, 2015, p. A27.
69. Z. Beauchamp, "The Chamber of Commerce's Surprising Comments on a Carbon Tax and How It Could Change the Game in Congress," *Climate Progress*, September 5, 2013, http://thinkprogress.org/climate/2013/09/05/2500831/chamber-carbon-tax/#; and G. Goldman, "Who Stands with the U.S. Chamber of Commerce on Climate Change? New Data Says Few (Still)," *The Equation*, blog of the Union of Concerned Scientists, January 20, 2015, http://blog.ucsusa.org/gretche goldman/who-stands-with-the-u-s-chamber-of-commerce-on-climate-change-new-data-says-few-still-788 (both accessed February 10, 2016).
70. J. Aaker, Stanford Graduate School of Business, quoted in C. B. Parker, "Stanford Research: The Meaningful Life Is a Road Worth Traveling," *Stanford Report*, January 1, 2014, http://news.stanford.edu/news/2014/january/meaningful-happy-life-010114.html (accessed February 3, 2016). The study is R. F. Baumeister, K. D. Vohs, J. L. Aaker, and E. N. Garbinsky, "Some Key Differences between a Happy Life and a Meaningful Life," *Journal of Positive Psychology*, Vol. 8, No. 6 (2013), pp. 505–516. See also E. E. Smith and J. L. Aaker, "Millennial Searchers," *The New York Times*, December 1, 2013, pp. SR-1, SR-6.
71. See M. Seligman, *Flourish* (New York: Free Press, 2011).
72. S. Armour, "Who Wants to Be a Middle Manager?" *USA Today*, August 13, 2007, pp. 1B, 2B; A. Bryant, "I Never Wanted to Be a Manager. But I've Learned," *The New York Times*, October 23, 2011, Business Section, p. 2; and "Boss's Job Safe: Most Workers Don't Want It," *HR Magazine*, December 2011, p. 14.
73. Indeed, 63% of senior managers in one survey were seriously considering leaving their organizations, almost twice that of nonmanagers, according to a Mercer survey of 3,000 employees, reported in "Senior Managers on Fence," *Reno Gazette-Journal*, November 1, 2015, p. 6B, reprinted from *USA Today*.
74. O. Pollar, "Are You Sure You Want to Be a Manager?" *San Francisco Examiner*, October 4, 1998, p. J-3.
75. P. Drucker, reported in R. L. Knowdell, "A Model for Managers in the Future Workplace: Symphony Conductor," *The Futurist*, June–July 1998, p. 22.
76. "Chief Executive Officer Salaries"; and Bureau of Labor Statistics, "Top Executives."
77. The role of middle managers is discussed by C. R. Ren and C. Guo, "Middle Managers' Strategic Role in the Corporate Entrepreneurial Process: Attention-Based Effects," *Journal of Management*, November 2011, pp. 1586–1610.
78. J. Useem, "Are Bosses Necessary?" *The Atlantic*, October 2015, pp. 28–32; and Tony Hsieh, interviewed by D. K. Berman, "The No-Boss Company," *The Wall Street Journal*, October 27, 2015, p. R3.
79. Susan L. Solomon, interviewed by A. Wolfe, "Susan L. Solomon," *The Wall Street Journal*, February 6–7, 2016, p. C11; and "Susan L. Solomon," New York Stem Cell Foundation, http://nyscf.org/about-us/boards-councils/board-of-directors/item/228-susan-l-solomon-chief-executive-officer (accessed February 8, 2016).
80. P. M. Blau and W. R. Scott, *Formal Organizations* (San Francisco: Chandler, 1962).
81. R. L. Zweigenhaft and G. W. Domhoff, *The New CEOs: Women, African American, Latino, and Asian American Leaders of Fortune 500 Companies* (Lanham, MD: Rowman & Littlefield, 2011).
82. R. L. Katz, "Skills of an Effective Administrator," *Harvard Business Review*, September–October, 1974, p. 94. Also see M. K. De Vries, "Decoding the Team Conundrum: The Eight Roles Executives Play," *Organizational Dynamics*, Vol. 36, No. 1 (2007), pp. 28–44.
83. B. Vlasic, "New GM Chief Is Company Woman, Born to It," *The New York Times*, December 11, 2013, pp. A1, A3.
84. Dan Akerson, quoted in R. Wright and H. Foy, "GM Beats Rivals to Put Woman in Driving Seat," *Financial Times*, December 11, 2013, p. 1.
85. Vlasic, "New GM Chief Is Company Woman, Born to It."
86. M. Vella, "Automakers Want to Sell You Much More Than Just a Car," *Time*, January 25, 2016, p. 14.
87. Gary Cowger, who mentored Barra, quoted in D.-A. Durbin and T. Krishner, "Mary Barra, a Child of GM, Prepares to Lead It," *AP*, December 24, 2013, http://bigstory.ap.org/article/mary-barra-child-gm-prepares-lead-it (accessed February 27, 2016).
88. Barra, quoted in Vlasic, "New GM Chief Is Company Woman, Born to It."
89. J. Bennett and S. Murray, "Longtime Insider Is GM's First Female CEO," *The Wall Street Journal*, December 11, 2013, pp. A1, A10.
90. M. Spector and C. M. Matthews, "GM Admits to Criminal Wrongdoing," *The Wall Street Journal*, September 18, 2015, pp. B1, B2; M. Spector, "GM Does a U-Turn in Ignition-Switch Case Motion," *The New York Times*, October 7, 2015, p. B4; G. Nagesh and J. S. Lublin, "Investors Yet to Value GM Changes," *The Wall Street Journal*, February 1, 2016, www.wsj.com/articles/investors-yet-to-value-gm-changes-1454371679 (accessed February 12, 2016).
91. G. Nagesh, "GM's Long-Haul Plan," *The Wall Street Journal*, October 26, 2015, p. R2; Nagish and Lublin, "Investors Yet to Value GM Changes"; and B. Vlasic, "Buoyed by North America, GM Posts $9.7 Billion Profit for 2015," *The New York Times*, February 4, 2016, p. B2.
92. See M. C. White, "The Real Reason New College Grads Can't Get Hired," *Time*, November 10, 2013, http://business.time.com/2013/11/10/the-real-reason-new-college-grads-cant-get-hired (accessed February 28, 2016).
93. Dan Akerson, quoted in Vlasic, "New GM Chief Is Company Woman, Born to It."
94. Vlasic, "New GM Chief Is Company Woman, Born to It."
95. Durbin and Krishner "Mary Barra, a Child of GM, Prepares to Lead It."
96. A. Kay, "Traits That Can Help You Beat Odds, Get Hired," *USA Today*, January 11, 2014, www.usatoday.com/story/money/columnist/kay/2014/01/11/at-work-beat-odds-get-hired/4387681 (accessed February 10, 2016).
97. For a thorough discussion about the failings of undergraduate education, see R. Arum and J. Roksa, *Aspiring Adults Adrift: Tentative Transitions of College Graduates* (Chicago: University of Chicago Press, 2014).
98. S. Y. Lee, Y. Shin, D. Lee, "The Option Value of Human Capital: Higher Education and Wage Inequality," *NBER Working Paper* No. 21725, November 2015, National Bureau of Economic Research, www.nber.org/papers/w21724.pdf (accessed February 10, 2016).
99. B. Hershbein and M. S. Kearney, *Major Decisions: What Graduates Earn over Their Lifetimes*, September 29, 2014, The Hamilton Project, Brookings Institution, www.hamiltonproject.org/papers/major_decisions_what_graduates_earn_over_their_lifetimes (accessed February 10, 2016). For the decline in high school graduates' earnings, see M. S. Kearney, B. Hershbein, and E. Jácome, *Profiles of Change: Employment, Earnings, and Occupations from 1990–2013*, April 21, 2015. The Hamilton Project, Brookings Institution, www.brookings.edu/blogs/up-front/posts/2015/04/21-employment-earnings-occupations-profiles-from-1990-to-2013-kearney-hershbein (accessed February 10, 2016).
100. See M. McArdle, "College Pays Off, on Average. Your Results May Vary," *Bloomberg View*, November 16, 2015, www.bloombergview.com/articles/2015-11-16/college-pays-off-on-average-your-results-may-vary- (accessed February 10, 2016). Also see K. Carey, "How One's Choice of College Affects Future Earnings," *The New York Times*, September 15, 2015, p. A3.
101. *The Rising Cost of Not Going to College*.
102. *State of St. Louis Workforce 2013*, survey by Workforce Solutions Group, St. Louis Community College, www.stlcc.edu/Workforce-Solutions/St-Louis-Workforce/Reports/State-of-St-Louis-Workforce-Report-2013.pdf (accessed February 10, 2016).
103. *Falling Short? College Learning and Career Success. Selected Findings from Online Surveys of Employers and College Students Conducted on Behalf of the Association of American Colleges & Universities*, January 20, 2015, Hart Research Associates, Washington, DC, https://www.aacu.org/leap/public-opinion-research/2015-survey-results (accessed February 10, 2016).
104. Quoted by Eric Zuckerman, president of Pac Tem Group, posted on Andrea Kay blog, August 5, 2015, http://andreakay.com/blog (accessed February 12, 2016). Andrea Kay is author of *This Is How to Get Your Next Job: An Inside Look at What Employers Really Want* (New York: AMACOM, 2013).
105. See G. Johnson, "The Gradual Extinction of Accepted Truths," *The New York Times*, August 25, 2015, p. D6.
106. See, for example, H. E. Marano, "Crisis U," *Psychology Today*, September/October 2015, pp. 64–71; C. Friedersorf, "The Anti-Free-Speech Movement at UCLA," *The Atlantic*, October 15, 2015, www.theatlantic.com/politics/archive/2015/10/the-anti-free-speech-movement-at-ucla/410638 (accessed February 12, 2016); "College Campuses: Free Speech vs. the Right Not to Be Offended," *The Week*, November 27, 2015, p. 16; and J. H. McWhorter, "Closed Minds on Campus," *The Wall Street Journal*, November 28–29, pp. C1, C2.

107. P. Tetlock and D. Gardner, *Superforecasting: The Art and Science of Prediction* (New York: Crown Publishing, 2015).

108. P. Tetlock and D. Gardner, interviewed in "Why an Open Mind Is Key to Making Better Predictions," *Knowledge@Wharton*, October 2, 2015, http://knowledge.wharton.upenn.edu/article/why-an-open-mind-is-key-to-making-better-predictions (accessed February 12, 2016).

109. K. Cameron and J. McNaughtan, "Positive Organizational Change," *The Journal of Applied Behavioral Science*, Vol. 50 (2014), pp. 445–462. See also E. Sepala, *The Happiness Track: How to Apply the Science of Happiness to Accelerate Your Success* (New York: HarperCollins, 2016).

110. T. Foulk, quoted in R. E. Silverman, "Workplace Rudeness Is as Contagious as a Cold," *The Wall Street Journal*, August 12, 2015, p. B7. See Y. Foulk, A. Woolum, and A. Erez, "Catching Rudeness Is Like Catching a Cold: The Contagion Effects of Low-Intensity Negative Behaviors," *Journal of Applied Psychology*, Vol. 101, No. 1 (2016), pp. 50–67.

111. P. Korkki, "Thwarting the Jerk at Work," *The New York Times*, November 22, 2015, p. BU-4. See also A. Gerbasi, C. L. Porath, A. Parker, G. Spreitzer, and R. Cross, "Destructive De-energizing Relationships: How Thriving Buffers Their Effect on Performance," *Journal of Applied Psychology*, Vol. 100, No. 5 (2015), pp. 1423–1433.

112. CEO recruiter, quoted in Colvin, "Catch a Rising Star."

113. Colvin, "Catch a Rising Star."

114. H. Mintzberg, *The Nature of Managerial Work* (New York: Harper & Row, 1973).

115. Mintzberg, *The Nature of Managerial Work*.

116. Ed Reilly, quoted in W. J. Holstein, "Attention-Juggling in the High-Tech Office," *The New York Times*, June 4, 2006, sec. 3, p. 9.

117. J. P. Kotter, "What Effective General Managers Really Do," *Harvard Business Review*, March–April 1999, pp. 145–159.

118. J. J. Deal, "Always On, Never Done? Don't Blame the Smartphone," Center for Creative Leadership, April 2015, www.ccl.org/leadership/pdf/research/AlwaysOn.pdf (accessed February 28, 2016).

119. S. M. MacDermid, M. D. Lee, and M. L. Buck, "Alternative Work Arrangements among Professionals and Managers: Rethinking Career Development and Success," *Journal of Management Development*, Vol. 20, No. 4 (2001), pp. 305–317.

120. B. Groysberg and R. Abrahams, "Manage Your Work, Manage Your Life," *Harvard Business Review*, March 2014, pp. 58–66.

121. N. Bowles, "Concept of Work/Life Balance on Its Way to Being Obsolete," *San Francisco Chronicle*, November 2, 2013, pp. D1, D3; and H. L. Gray, "7 Tips for Work-Life Balance as an Entrepreneur," *Inc.*, February 11, 2016, www.huffingtonpost.com/haley-lynn-gray/7-tips-for-work-life-balance-as-an-entrepreneur_b_9206250.html (accessed February 13, 2016).

122. J. Cooper-Kahn and L. Dietzel, "What Is Executive Functioning?" *LD Online*, 2008, www.ldonline.org/article/What_Is_Executive_Functioning%3F (accessed February 28, 2016). See also P. P. Zelazo, "Executive Function and Emotion Regulation: A Developmental Perspective," Ph.D. paper presented May 2010 at the Annual International Trauma Conference, Boston, MA.

123. Study by William Becker, cited in S. Shellenbarger, "Which Professions Can Make You Smarter," *The Wall Street Journal*, December 9, 2015, p. D2. The study is M. Butts, W. J. Becker, and W. R. Boswell, "Hot Buttons and Time Sinks: The Effects of Electronic Communication During Nonwork Time on Emotions and Work-Nonwork Conflict," *Academy of Management Journal*, Vol. 58 (2015), pp. 763–788.

124. A. Levit, "Make Way for Generation Z," *The New York Times*, March 29, 2015, p. BU-7; and A. Williams, "Move Over Millennials: Here Comes Generation Z," *The New York Times*, September 29, 2015, pp. ST-1, ST-18.

125. R. Hannaman, "Understanding Generation Z: The Workforce of the Future," *Nevada Appeal*, December 25, 2011, p. C6. See also B. Tulgan and Rainmaker Thinking, *Meet Generation Z: The Second Generation within the Giant "Millennial" Cohort*, Rainmaker Thinking, Whitepaper, October 7, 2013, http://rainmakerthinking.com/assets/uploads/2013/10/Gen-Z-Whitepaper.pdf (accessed February 28, 2016).

126. A. Smith, L. Rainie, and K. Zickhur, "College Students and Technology," Pew Research Internet Project, July 19, 2011, www.pewinternet.org/2011/07/19/college-students-and-technology (accessed February 28, 2016).

127. B. R. McCoy, "Digital Distractions in the Classroom: Student Classroom Use of Digital Devices for Non-class Related Purposes," *Journal of Media Education*, October 2013, pp. 5–13.

128. Psychiatrist Edward M. Hallowell, quoted in A. Tugend, "Multitasking Can Make You Lose . . . Um . . . Focus," *The New York Times*, October 25, 2008, p. B7. Hallowell is the author of *Crazy Busy: Overstretched, Overbooked, and About to Snap!* (New York: Ballantine, 2006).

129. W. Gallagher, quoted in book review, D. G. Myers, "Please Pay Attention," *The Wall Street Journal*, April 20, 2009, p. A13. Gallagher is author of *Rapt* (New York: Penguin Press, 2009).

130. J. Tierney, "Ear Plugs to Lasers: The Science of Concentration," *The New York Times*, May 5, 2009, p. D2.

131. See D. Goleman, "The Focused Leader," *Harvard Business Review*, December 2013, pp. 50–60; and A. Beard, "Spotlight: Interview with Ellen Langer—Mindfulness in the Age of Complexity," *Harvard Business Review*, March 2014, pp. 68–73.

132. P. Steel, "The Nature of Procrastination: A Meta-Analytic and Theoretical Review of Quintessential Self-Regulatory Failure," *Psychological Bulletin*, January 2007, pp. 65–94. For one writer's account of weaning himself off his smartphone, see T. Wayne, "The 7-Day Digital Diet," *The New York Times*, February 8, 2014, pp. ST-1, ST-16.

133. J. White and J. Bennett, "Letter from GM CEO: 'Deeply Regret' Need to Recall 1.6 Million Cars," *The Wall Street Journal*, March 4, 2014, http://blogs.wsj.com/corporate-intelligence/2014/03/04/letter-from-gm-ceo-deeply-regret-ne... (accessed March 5, 2016). Also see J. Bennett, "Recall Is First Big Test for GM Chief Barra," *The Wall Street Journal*, March 5, 2014, http://online.wsj.com/news/articles/SB10001424052702304360704579419494191216588 (accessed March 5, 2016).

134. Definition by Paul Graham, head of business accelerator Y Combinator, cited in N. Robehmed, "What Is a Startup?" *Forbes*, December 16, 2013, www.forbes.com/sites/natalierobehmed/2013/12/16/what-is-a-startup/print (accessed February 14, 2016).

135. M. Corona, "From Truckee to the World Stage," *Reno Gazette-Journal*, February 17, 2014, pp. 1A, 3A.

136. A. Gardella, "An Entrepreneur Who Wouldn't Be Stopped by Anything," *The New York Times*, December 26, 2013, p. B3.

137. J. Wortham, "Search for a Niche, and You Might Find a Crowd," *The New York Times*, February 9, 2014, p. BU-3.

138. V. Meewes, "Steep Progress," Good, March 5, 2015, https://www.good.is/features/fair-trade-tea (accessed February 14, 2016). See also C. Dunn, "Brother-and-Sister Brewer," *Fortune*, November 18, 2013, p. 22.

139. S. Finz, "How Smashburger May Find Its Niche," *San Francisco Chronicle*, September 27, 2013, pp. C1, C5.

140. M. Glassman, "Correlations: Job Creators No More," *Bloomberg Businessweek*, February 10–16, 2014, p. 18.

141. S. A. Shane, "How Start-Ups Really Create Jobs—and What This Means for Employment Growth," *The New York Times*, October 19, 2009, http://boss.blogs.nytimes.com/2009/10/19/how-start-ups-really-create-jobs-and-what-this-means-for-employment-growth (accessed February 14, 2016).

142. A. Vance, "Time for Microsoft to Tap Its Inner Google," *Bloomberg Businessweek*, February 10–16, 2014, pp. 8–9. See also D. Clark, M. Langley, and S. Ovide, "Microsoft's CEO Pick: From India to Insider," *The Wall Street Journal*, February 1–2, 2014, pp. A1, A2.

143. R. Branson, "Richard Branson on Intrapreneurs," *Entrepreneur.com*, January 31, 2011, www.entrepreneur.com/article/218011 (accessed February 28, 2016). See also A. Bruzzese, "Entrepreneurialism at Work," *The Arizona Republic*, January 15, 2014, p. CL-1.

144. N. Singer, "The Watchful Lab of Dr. Bell," *The New York Times*, February 16, 2014, pp. BU-1, BU-4, BU-5.

145. P. F. Drucker, *Innovation and Entrepreneurship* (New York: Harper & Row, 1986), pp. 27–28.

146. A. M. Webber, "Danger: Toxic Company," *Fast Company*, November 1998, pp. 152–161.

147. D. C. McClelland, *The Achieving Society* (New York: Van Nostrand, 1961); D. C. McClelland, *Human Motivation* (Glenview, IL: Scott, Foresman, 1985); D. L. Sexton and N. Bowman, "The Entrepreneur: A Capable Executive and More," *Journal of Business Venturing*, Vol. 1 (1985), pp. 129–140; T. Begley and D. P. Boyd, "Psychological Characteristics Associated with Performance in Entrepreneurial Firms and Smaller Businesses," *Journal of Business Venturing*, Vol. 2 (1987), pp. 79–93; D. Hisrich, "Entrepreneurship/Intrapreneurship," *American Psychologist*, February 1990, p. 218; and C. R. Kuehl and P. A. Lambing, *Small Business: Planning and Management* (Fort Worth, TX: Dryden Press, 1990).

148. "Who Are U.S. Entrepreneurs?" infographic based on *2012 Global Entrepreneurship Monitor (GEM) United States Report*, published by Babson College and Baruch College, www.babson.edu/news-events/babson-news/PublishingImages/babson-gem-info-graphic-692.png (accessed February 28, 2016).

149. For more about measuring entrepreneurial orientation, see V. Taatila and S. Down, "Measuring Entrepreneurial Orientation of University Students," *Education+ Training*, Vol. 54, No. 8/9 (2012), pp. 744–760.

150. This box is adapted from B. K. Williams and S. C. Sawyer, *Using Information Technology: A Practical Introduction*, 11th ed. (New York: McGraw-Hill, 2015).

151. T. Schwartz, "The Personal Energy Crisis," *The New York Times*, July 24, 2011, p. BU8.

152. W. Gallagher, cited in blog by J. Tierney, "Attention Must Be Paid—but How?" *The New York Times–Tierney Lab*, May 4, 2009, http://tierneylab.blogs.nytimes.com/ (accessed February 28, 2016). Gallagher is author of *Rapt* (New York: The Penguin Press, 2009).

153. W. Gallagher, quoted in Tierney, "Attention Must Be Paid—but How?"

154. F. P. Robinson, *Effective Study*, 4th ed. (New York: Harper & Row, 1970).

155. H. C. Lindgren, *The Psychology of College Success: A Dynamic Approach* (New York: Wiley, 1969).

156. R. J. Palkovitz and R. K. Lore, "Note Taking and Note Review: Why Students Fail Questions Based on Lecture Material," *Teaching of Psychology*, Vol. 7 (1980), pp. 159–161.

157. J. Covert, "Marissa Mayer, Yahoo! Fend Off Shareholders' Fiery Attack," http://nypost.com/2016/01/16/marissa-mayer-yahoo-fend-off-shareholders-fiery-attack/ (accessed January 19, 2016).

158. J. Covert, "Marissa Mayer, Yahoo! Fend Off Shareholders' *Fiery Attack*," http://nypost.com/2016/01/16/marissa-mayer-yahoo-fend-off-shareholders-fiery-attack/ (accessed January 19, 2016).

159. M. Yianopoulos, "Marissa Mayer Has Become a Symbol of Silicon Valley's Disastrous Tokenism," http://www.breitbart.com/tech/2016/01/18/marissa-mayer-become-symbol-silicon-valleys-disastrous-tokenism/ (accessed January 19, 2016).

160. J. Covert, "Marissa Mayer, Yahoo! Fend Off Shareholders' Fiery Attack," http://nypost.com/2016/01/16/marissa-mayer-yahoo-fend-off-shareholders-fiery-attack/ (accessed January 19, 2016), pp.162–163.

161. V. Goel, "Yahoo's Brain Drain Shows a Loss of Faith Inside the Company," http://www.cnbc.com/marissa-mayer/ (accessed January 19, 2016).

162. M. Yianopoulos, "Marissa Mayer Has Become a Symbol of Silicon Valley's Disastrous Tokenism," http://www.breitbart.com/tech/2016/01/18/marissa-mayer-become-symbol-silicon-valleys-disastrous-tokenism/ (accessed January 19, 2016).

163. V. Goel, "Yahoo's Brain Drain Shows a Loss of Faith Inside the Company," http://www.cnbc.com/marissa-mayer/ (accessed January 19, 2016).

164. M. Yianopoulos, "Marissa Mayer Has Become a Symbol of Silicon Valley's Disastrous Tokenism," http://www.breitbart.com/tech/2016/01/18/marissa-mayer-become-symbol-silicon-valleys-disastrous-tokenism/ (accessed January 19, 2016).

165. V. Goel, "Yahoo's Brain Drain Shows a Loss of Faith Inside the Company," http://www.cnbc.com/marissa-mayer/ (accessed January 19, 2016).

166. D. Macmillan and D. Mattioli, "Yahoo to Cut 15% of Workforce, Explore Strategic Options" *The Wall Street Journal,* February 2, 2016, http://www.wsj.com/articles/yahoo-plans-to-say-it-is-exploring-strategic-options-1454444977.
167. J. Covert and C. Atkinson, "'No Layoffs...This Week': Marissa Mayer's Twisted Joke Kills Morale," http://nypost.com/2016/01/18/marissa-mayers-job-safety-joke-doesnt-sit-well-with-workers/ (accessed January 19, 2016).
168. M. Yianopoulos, "Marissa Mayer Has Become a Symbol of Silicon Valley's Disastrous Tokenism," http://www.breitbart.com/tech/2016/01/18/marissa-mayer-become-symbol-silicon-valleys-disastrous-tokenism/ (accessed January 19, 2016).

CHAPTER 2

1. H. Ruchlis and S. Oddo, *Clear Thinking: A Practical Introduction* (Amherst, NY: Prometheus Books, 1990), p. 109.
2. Ruchlis and Oddo, *Clear Thinking: A Practical Introduction*, p. 110.
3. C. S. Dweck, *Mindset: The New Psychology of Success* (New York: Ballantine Books, 2006), pp. 12–13.
4. Tom Peters, quoted in J. A. Byrne, "The Man Who Invented Management," *BusinessWeek,* November 28, 2005, www.businessweek.com/stories/2005-11-27/the-man-who-invented-management (accessed January 22, 2016).
5. Byrne, "The Man Who Invented Management." See also R. Karlgaard, "Peter Drucker on Leadership," *Forbes.com,* November 19, 2004, www.forbes.com/2004/11/19/cz_rk_1119drucker.html; B. J. Feder, "Peter F. Drucker, a Pioneer in Social and Management Theory, Is Dead at 95," *The New York Times,* November 12, 2005, www.nytimes.com/2005/11/12/business/peter-f-drucker-a-pioneer-in-social-and-management-theory-is-dead-at-95.html?_r=0; and P. Sullivan, "Management Visionary Peter Drucker Dies," *The Washington Post,* November 12, 2005, www.washingtonpost.com/wp-dyn/content/article/2005/11/11/AR2005111101938.html (all accessed March 5, 2016).
6. C. M. Christensen and M. E. Raynor, "Why Hard-Nosed Executives Should Care about Management Theory," *Harvard Business Review,* September 2003, pp. 67–74.
7. Christensen and Raynor, "Why Hard-Nosed Executives Should Care about Management Theory," p. 68.
8. S. L. Montgomery and D. Chirot, quoted in F. Zakaria, "Something in the Air," The New York Times Book Review, August 23, 2015, pp. 14–15. Montgomery and Chirot are authors of *The Shape of the New: Four Big Ideas and How They Made the Modern World* (Princeton, NJ: Princeton University Press, 2015).
9. R. Sadun and J. V. Reenen, "Does Management Work?" *Harvard Business Review,* November 2012, pp. 76–82. Researchers studied thousands of organizations and found that more successful companies employed the following three management practices: setting stretch goals, basing compensation and promotions on performance, and monitoring results. A one-point increment on a five-point scale management practice scale resulted in improvements of 23% in productivity, 14% in market capitalization, and 1.4 % growth in annual sales.
10. G. Hamel, *The Future of Management* (Boston: Harvard Business School Press, 2007).
11. *ValveHandbook for New Employees* (Bellevue, WA: Valve Press, 2012), p. 4, http://media.steampowered.com/apps/valve/Valve_NewEmployeeHandbook.pdf (accessed March 10, 2016).
12. R. E. Silverman, "Who's the Boss? There Isn't One," *The Wall Street Journal,* June 19, 2012, http://www.wsj.com/articles/SB10001424052702303379204577474953586383604 (accessed January 22, 2016).
13. S. Knight, "Valve's New Employee Handbook Is Chock-Full of Awesome, Read It Now," *TechSpot,* April 23, 2012, www.techspot.com/news/48303-valves-new-employee-handbook-is-chock-full-of-awesome-read-it-now.html (accessed March 10, 2016).
14. T. Kastelle, "Hierarchy Is Overrated," *Harvard Business Review, HBR Blog Network,* November 20, 2013, http://blogs.hbr.org/2013/11/hierarchy-is-overrated (accessed March 10, 2016).
15. For more on the history of management, see W. Kiechel III, "The Management Century," *Harvard Business Review,* November 2012, pp. 62–75.
16. See N. Bloom, R. Sadun, and J. Van Reenen, "Does Management Really Work?" *Harvard Business Review,* November 2012, pp. 76–82. The authors argue that organizations are more likely to succeed if they adopt good management's basic features—targets, incentives, and monitoring—all components of the four principal functions of management: planning, organizing, leading, and controlling.
17. B. Rice, "The Hawthorne Defect: Persistence of a Flawed Theory," *Psychology Today,* February 1982, pp. 70–74. See also S. Highhouse, "Applications of Organizational Psychology: Learning through Failure or Failure to Learn?" pp. 331–348 in L. L. Koppes, *Historical Perspectives in Industrial and Organizational Psychology* (Hillsdale, NJ: Lawrence Erlbaum, 2007).
18. A. Maslow, "A Theory of Human Motivation," *Psychological Review,* July 1943, pp. 370–396.
19. D. McGregor, *The Human Side of Enterprise* (New York: McGraw-Hill, 1960).
20. The history of the office workplace is described in N. Saval, *Cubed: A Secret History of the Workplace* (New York: Doubleday, 2014).
21. M. Konnikova, "The Open Office Trap," *The New Yorker,* January 7, 2014, www.newyorker.com/business/currency/the-open-office-trap (accessed January 23, 2016).
22. Ben Waber, CEO of Sociometric Solutions, Boston, reported in R. Feintzeig, "Bosses Take a Stand on Where Workers Sit," *The Wall Street Journal,* October 9, 2013, p. B8.
23. J. Wajcman and E. Rose, "Constant Connectivity: Rethinking Interruptions at Work," *Organization Studies,* July 2011, pp. 941–961.
24. A. Codrea-Rado, "Open-Plan Offices Make Employees Less Productive, Less Happy, and More Likely to Get Sick," *Bloomberg Businessweek,* May 21, 2013, http://qz.com/85400/moving-to-open-plan-offices-makes-employees-less-productive-less-happy-and-more-likely-to-get-sick (accessed January 23, 2016). See also V. Wong, "Ending the Tyranny of the Open-Plan Office," *Bloomberg.com,* July 1, 2013, www.bloomberg.com/bw/articles/2013-07-01/ending-the-tyranny-of-the-open-plan-office (accessed January 23, 2016). More than a hundred studies about office environments were reviewed by M. C. Davis, D. J. Leach, and C. W. Clegg, "The Physical Environment of the Office: Contemporary and Emerging Issues," *International Review of Industrial and Organization Psychology,* Vol. 26 (2011), pp. 193–237.
25. Among some studies supporting these conclusions: G. W. Evans and D. Johnson, "Stress and Open-Office Noise," *5* Vol. 85, No. 5 (2000), pp. 779–783; A. Brennan and J. S. Chugh, "Traditional versus Open Office Design: A Longitudinal Field Study," Vol. 34, No. 3 (2002), pp. 279–299; A. Maher and C. von Hippel, "Individual Differences in Employee Reactions to Open-Plan Offices," Journal of Environmental Psychology, Vol. 25, Iss. 5, pp. 219–229; T. L. Smith-Jackson and K. W. Klein, "Open-Plan Offices: Task Performance and Mental Workload," *Journal of Environmental Psychology,* Vol. 29, Iss. 2 (2009), pp. 279–289; C. M. Mak and Y. P. Lui, "The Effect of Sound on Office Productivity," Vol. 33, No. 3 (2011), pp. 339–345; J. H. Pejtersen, H. Feveile, K. B. Christensen, and H. Burr, "Sickness Absence Associated with Shared and Open-Plan Offices—A National Cross Sectional Questionnaire Survey," *Scandinavian Journal of Work, Environment, & Health,* Vol. 37, No. 5 (2011), pp. 376–382; and H. Rasila and P. Rothe, "A Problem Is a Problem Is a Benefit? Generation Y Perceptions of Open-Plan Offices," *Property Management,* Vol. 30, Iss. 4, (2012), pp. 362–375; C. Congdon, D. Flynn, and M. Redman, "Balancing 'We' and 'Me': The Best Collaborative Spaces Also Support Solitude," *Harvard Business Review,* October 2014, pp. 50–57; and D. Ward, "Beyond the Open Office," *HRMagazine,* April 2015, https://www.questia.com/read/1P3-3646614171/beyond-the-open-office (accessed January 25, 2016).
26. S. Shellenbarger, "The Biggest Distraction in the Office Is Sitting Next to You," *The Wall Street Journal,* September 11, 2013, pp. D1, D3.
27. Sigal Barsade, quoted in Feintzeig, "Bosses Take a Stand on Where Workers Sit."
28. A. Bruzzese, "Introverts and Extroverts Each Need Tolerance," *Reno Gazette-Journal,* September 14, 2013, p. 11A.
29. Paul English, reported in Feintzeig, "Bosses Take a Stand on Where Workers Sit."
30. B. Sisario, "The Sweet, Streaming Sound of Data," *The New York Times,* March 7, 2014, pp. B1, B6.
31. Tim Westergren, quoted in N. Kaiser, "Interview with Tim Westergren, CEO of Pandora," *nPost,* October 26, 2006, www.npost.com/blog/2006/10/26/interview-with-tim-westergren-ceo-of-pandora (accessed March 10, 2014). See also R. Walker, "The Song Decoders," *The New York Times Magazine,* October 18, 2009, www.nytimes.com/2009/10/18/magazine/18Pandora-t.html?pagewanted=all&_r=0 (accessed March 10, 2016).
32. Reported in J. Hahn, "Pandora Is Losing the Music Streaming War, Throws Shade at Spotify," *DigitalTrends.com,* October 25, 2015, www.digitaltrends.com/apple/pandora-is-losing-ground-in-the-music-streaming-war-thanks-in-part-to-apple-music (accessed August 15, 2016).
33. S. F. Brown, "Wresting New Wealth from the Supply Chain," *Fortune,* November 9, 1998, pp. 204[C]–204[Z]. See also M. Maynard, "Toyota Shows Big Three How It's Done," *The New York Times,* January 13, 2006, pp. C1, C4.
34. See P. Davidson, "Lean Manufacturing Helps Companies Survive," *USA Today,* November 2, 2009, pp. 1B, 2B. See also B. R. Staats and D. M. Upton, "Lean Knowledge Work," *Harvard Business Review,* October 2011; and T. Agan, "The Secret to Lean Innovation Is Making Learning a Priority," *HBR Blog Network,* January 23, 2014, http://blogs.hbr.org/2014/01/the-secret-to-lean-innovation-is-making-learning-a-priority (accessed March 10, 2016).
35. V. Colliver, "Following 'Toyota Way' to Efficiency," *San Francisco Chronicle,* October 9, 2013, pp. E1, E6.
36. J. Wolfers, "Making Government Work More Like Google," *The New York Times,* September 27, 2015, p. BU-6.
37. Social and Behavioral Sciences Team, Annual Report (Washington, DC: Executive Office of the President, National Science and Technology Council, September 2015).
38. Social and Behavioral Sciences Team, Annual Report (Washington, DC: Executive Office of the President, National Science and Technology Council, September 2015).
39. Research report by the Society for Human Resource Management, *2012 Employee Benefits: The Employee Benefits Landscape in a Recovering Economy* (Alexandria, VA: SHRM, 2012), www.shrm.org/research/surveyfindings/articles/documents/2012_empbenefits_report.pdf (accessed March 10, 2016).
40. L. Petrecca, "Quirky Perks for Workers: Pet Insurance, Massages," *USA Today,* December 30, 2011, p. 1A; B. Haislip, "Beer on Fridays. Pets in the Office. Weekly Yoga," *The Wall Street Journal,* August 19 2013, p. R7; A. Bruzzese, "The Little Things, Perks Can Keep Employees Happy," *Reno Gazette-Journal,* September 7, 2013, p. 9A; and A. Gardella, "Debating Which Perks Best Motivate Employees. Free Lunch?" *The New York Times,* April 7, 2014, http://boss.blogs.nytimes.com/2014/04/07/debating-which-perks-best-motivate-employees-free-lunch/?_r=0 (accessed January 23, 2016).
41. P. McCord, "How Netflix Reinvented HR," *Harvard Business Review,* January–February 2014, pp. 70–76.
42. Daniel Pink, reported in L. Maw, "What We Really Want from Work," *Huffington Post,* July 16, 2012, www.huffingtonpost.com/liz-maw/work-culture_b_1676043.html (March 10, 2016).
43. "Happiness at Work" survey results, reported in R. E. Silverman, "Are You Happy at Work?" *The Wall Street Journal,* October 16, 2012, http://blogs.wsj.com/atwork/2012/10/16/are-you-happy-at-work (accessed March 10, 2016). See also *The Happiness at Work Survey,* by Delivering Happiness at Work, www.happinessatworksurvey.com.
44. C. Zukin and M. Szeltner, *Talent Report: What Workers Want in 2012,* Net Impact, May 2012, https://netimpact.org/learning-resources/research/what-workers-want/talent-report-what-workers-want-in-2012 (accessed March 10, 2016).
45. "The Top Gurus," *The Wall Street Journal,* May 5, 2008, p. B6.
46. G. Hamel, with B. Breen, *The Future of Management* (Boston: Harvard Business School Press, 2007), p. 6.

47. G. Hamel, "Break Free!" *Fortune,* September 19, 2007, http://money.cnn.com/magazines/fortune/fortune_archive/2007/10/01/100352608/index.htm (accessed March 14, 2016).

48. J. Pfeffer and R. I. Sutton, "Profiting from Evidence-Based Management," *Strategy & Leadership,* Vol. 34, No. 2 (2006), pp. 35–42. See also J. Pfeffer and R. I. Sutton, "Evidence-Based Management," *Harvard Business Review,* January 2006, pp. 63–74; and J. Pfeffer and R. Sutton, "Trust the Evidence, Not Your Instincts," *The New York Times,* September 4, 2011, p. BU-8. Pfeffer and Sutton are authors of *Hard Facts, Dangerous Half-Truths, and Total Nonsense* (Boston: Harvard Business School Press, 2006).

49. C. Hymowitz, "Executives Must Stop Jumping Fad to Fad and Learn to Manage," *The Wall Street Journal,* May 15, 2006, p. B1. See also M. Miller, *The Tyranny of Dead Ideas: Letting Go of the Old Ways of Thinking to Unleash a New Prosperity* (New York: Times Books, 2009).

50. S. Cummings and T. Bridgman, "The Relevant Past: Why the History of Management Should Be Critical for Our Future," *Academy of Management Learning & Education,* Vol. 10, No. 1 (2011), pp. 77–93.

51. Christensen and Raynor, "Why Hard-Nosed Executives Should Care about Management Theory."

52. D. M. Rosseau, "Is There Such a Thing as 'Evidence-Based Management'?" *Academy of Management Review,* April 2006, pp. 256–269. Other debates about evidence-based management may be found in T. Reay, W. Berta, and M. Kazman Kohn, "Where's the Evidence on Evidence-Based Management?" *Academy of Management Perspectives,* November 2009, pp. 5–18; R. Briner, D. Denyer, and D. M. Rousseau, "Evidence-Based Management: Concept Cleanup Time?" *Academy of Management Perspectives,* November 2009, pp. 19–32; and S. D. Charlier, K. G. Brown, and S. L. Rynes, "Teaching Evidence-Based Management in MBA Programs: What Evidence Is There?" *Academy of Management Learning & Education,* Vol. 10, No. 2 (2011), pp. 222–236.

53. Pfeffer and Sutton, "Profiting from Evidence-Based Management."

54. R. I. Sutton, interviewed in "Asked & Answered: Prove It," *Stanford Magazine,* May/June 2006, www.stanfordalumni.org/news/magazine/2006/mayjun/dept/management.html (accessed March 14, 2016). Discussions about the need for an evidence-based process in medicine may be found in D. Sanghavi, "Plenty of Guidelines, but Where's the Evidence?" *The New York Times,* December 9, 2008, p. D6; and R. Winslow, "Study Questions Evidence behind Heart Therapies," *The Wall Street Journal,* February 25, 2009, p. D1.

55. D. Pound, "2014 Cadillac CTS 3.6 vs. 2014 Audi A6 3.0T, 2014 BMW 535i xDrive, 2014 Mercedes-Benz E350," *Car and Driver,* November 2013, www.caranddriver.com/comparisons/2014-cadillac-cts-36-vs-audi-a6-bmw-535i-mercedes-e350-comparison-test-review (accessed March 15, 2016).

56. A. Garvin, "Building a Learning Organization," *Harvard Business Review,* July/August 1993, pp. 78–91; and R. Hodgetts, F. Luthans, and S. Lee, "New Paradigm Organizations: From Total Quality to Learning to World-Class," *Organizational Dynamics,* Winter 1994, pp. 5–19D. See also T. Kelly, "Measuring Informal Learning: Encourage a Learning Culture and Track It!" *Training Industry,* March 21, 2014, www.trainingindustry.com/professional-education/articles/measuring-informal-learning.aspx (accessed January 23, 2016).

57. R. P. Mai, *Learning Partnerships: How Leading American Companies Implement Organizational Learning* (Chicago: Irwin, 1996); C. Chadwick and J. L. Raver, "Motivating Organizations to Learn: Goal Orientation and Its Influence on Organizational Learning," *Journal of Management,* March 2015, pp. 957–986; and C. Ben-Oz and H. R. Greve, "Short- and Long-Term Performance Feedback and Absorptive Capacity," *Journal of Management,* November 2015, pp. 1827–1853.

58. R. J. Grossman, "A Culture of Learning," *HR Magazine,* May 2015, p. 37.

59. B. Breen, "How EDS Got Its Groove Back," *Fast Company,* September 2001, p. 106.

60. D. Ulrich, T. Jick, and M. Von Glinow, "High-Impact Learning: Building and Diffusing Learning Capability," *Organizational Dynamics,* Autumn 1993, pp. 52–66; S. F. Slater, "Learning to Change," *Business Horizons,* November–December 1995, pp. 13–20; and D. M. Noer, *Breaking Free: A Prescription for Personal and Organizational Change* (San Francisco: Jossey-Bass, 1996).

61. Pfeffer and Sutton, "Profiting from Evidence-Based Management."

62. L. Kwoh, "Memo to Staff: Take More Risks," *The Wall Street Journal,* March 20, 2013, p. B8.

63. R. Jana, "Inspiration from Emerging Economies," *Business Week,* March 23 and 30, 2009, p. 41.

64. J. Wieczner, "The New Geek Squad (That's Fixing Best Buy)," *Fortune Magazine,* November 1, 2015, pp. 142–148.

65. M. Hiltzik, "Is Best Buy's Turnaround a Roadmap for Competing with Amazon?" www.latimes.com/business/hiltzik/la-fi-mh-is-best-buy-s-turnaround-a-roadmap-for-competing-with-amazon-20150902-column.html (accessed January, 19, 2016).

66. J. Wieczner, "The New Geek Squad (That's Fixing Best Buy)," *Fortune,* November 1, 2015, pp. 142–148.

67. J. Vomhof, Jr., "Best Buy CEO Hubert Joly's Four Tips for Turnarounds," www.bizjournals.com/twincities/news/2014/04/15/best-buy-ceo-hubert-joly-turnaround-tips.html (accessed January 19, 2016).

68. J. Wieczner, "The New Geek Squad (That's Fixing Best Buy)," *Fortune,* November 1, 2015, pp. 142–148.

69. Wieczner, "The New Geek Squad (That's Fixing Best Buy)."

70. Hiltzik, "Is Best Buy's Turnaround a Roadmap for Competing with Amazon?"

71. Wieczner, "The New Geek Squad (That's Fixing Best Buy)."

72. Trefis Team, "Disappointing Holiday Sales, Bbt Is Best Buy on a Turnaround Track?" www.forbes.com/sites/greatspeculations/2016/01/19/disappointing-holiday-sales-but-is-best-buy-on-a-turnaround-track/#2715e4857a0b3d3bd168326b (accessed January 19, 2016).

CHAPTER 3

1. Marianne Jennings, professor of legal and ethical studies, W.P. Carey School of Business, Arizona State University, quoted in "College Cheating Is Bad for Business," *Knowledge@W.P. Carey,* September 24, 2008, www.caseplace.org/d.asp?d=3446 (accessed February 16, 2016).

2. B. Carey, "Stumbling Blocks on the Path of Righteousness," *The New York Times,* May 5, 2009, p. D5.

3. M. H. Bazerman and A. E. Tenbrunsel, "Stumbling into Bad Behavior," *The New York Times,* April 20, 2011, p. A2.

4. M. H. Bazerman and A. E. Tenbrunsel, *Blind Spots: Why We Fail to Do What's Right, and What We Can Do about It* (Princeton, NJ: Princeton University Press, 2011); and M. R. Banaji and A. G. Greenwald, *Blindspot: Hidden Biases of Good People* (New York: Delacorte Press, 2013). For more on this subject, see J. P. Gaspar, E. E. Levine, and M. E. Schweitzer, "Why We Should Lie," *Organizational Dynamics,* Vol. 44 (2015), pp. 306–309; and T. Zhang, P. O. Fletcher, F. Gino, and M. H. Bazerman, "Reducing Bounded Ethicality: How to Help Individuals Notice and Avoid Unethical Behavior," *Organizational Dynamics,* Vol. 44 (2015), pp. 310–331.

5. Poll by Beneson Strategy Group for Common Sense Media, "35% of Teenagers Admit to Using Cell Phones to Cheat," reported in *Common Sense Media,* June 18, 2009, https://www.commonsensemedia.org/about-us/news/press-releases/35-of-teens-admit-to-using-cell-phones-to-cheat (accessed February 16, 2016); and J. Tucker, "Tech-Savvy Students Invent New Ways to Cheat," *San Francisco Chronicle,* June 19, 2009, pp. A1, A16.

6. B. Staples, "Cutting and Pasting: A Senior Thesis by (Insert Name)," *The New York Times,* July 13, 2010, p. A24.

7. See N. Angier, "Spite Is Good. Spite Works," *The New York Times,* April 1, 2014, pp. D1, D3.

8. D. J. Palazzzo, Y.-J. Lee, R. Warnakulasooriya, and D. E. Pritchard, "Patterns, Correlates, and Reduction of Homework Copying," *Physical Review Special Topics,* March 2010, http://prst-per.aps.org/abstract/PRSTPER/v6/i1/e010104 (accessed March 31, 2014).

9. J. Wicks, quoted in G. Rifkin, "Making a Profit and a Difference," *The New York Times,* October 5, 2006, p. C5.

10. See for example, G Kaul and T Duggan, "Mindful Diners' Quest for Fair Trade," *San Francisco Chronicle,* September 8, 2015, pp. A1, A8, A9.

11. Jon Miller, interviewed by W. Henisz, "Big Business and the New Norm: Doing Good at the Core, Not the Periphery," *Knowledge@Wharton,* March 21, 2014, http://knowledge.wharton.upenn.edu/article/big-business-can-fix-world (accessed February 16, 2016). Miller is co-author, with Lucy Parker, of *Everybody's Business: The Unlikely Story of How Big Business Can Fix the World* (London: Biteback Publishing, 2013).

12. Rob Michalak, reported in D. Gelles, "Gobble Up, but Still Doing Good for the World," *The New York Times,* August 23, 2015, p. BU-3.

13. J. Garofoli, "Box to Donate Its Product to Nonprofits," *San Francisco Chronicle,* May 28, 2014, pp. C1, C6.

14. J. Hidalgo, "Better World Books Distribution Center Plans to Hire 100 Workers," *Reno Gazette-Journal,* January 15, 2016, pp. 7A, 8A.

15. For various definitions of Generation Y and Generation Z, see W. J. Schroer, "Generations X, Y, Z, and the Others—Cont'd," *The Social Librarian,* www.socialmarketing.org/newsletter/features/generation3.htm (accessed February 14, 2016).

16. J. Wingard, "How Companies Are Managing the Millennial Generation," *Knowledge@Wharton,* March 5, 2015, http://knowledge.wharton.upenn.edu/article/how-companies-should-manage-millennials (accessed February 16, 2016).

17. E. E. Smith and J. L. Aaker, "Millennial Searchers," *The New York Times,* December 1, 2013, pp. SR-1, SR-6.

18. A. Levit and S. Licina, "How the Recession Shaped Millennial and Hiring Manager Attitudes about Millennials' Future Careers," 2011 report commissioned by the Career Advisory Board and conducted by Harris Interactive, www.careeradvisoryboard.org/public/uploads/2011/10/Future-of-Millennial-Careers-Report.pdf (accessed February 14, 2016). See also L. Caraher, *Millennials & Management: The Essential Guide to Making It Work at Work* (Boston: Bibliomotion, 2014); and A. S. Poswolski, "What Millennial Employees Really Want," *Fast Company,* June 4, 2015, www.fastcompany.com/3046989/what-millennial-employees-really-want (accessed February 16, 2016).

19. H. Park, J. M. Twenge, and P. M. Greenfield, "The Great Recession: Implications for Adolescent Values and Behavior," *Social Psychological and Personality Science,* Vol. 5, No. 3. (2014), pp. 310–318. See also R. A. VanMeter, D. B. Grisaffe, L. B. Chonko, and J. A. Roberts, "Generation Y's Ethical Ideology and Its Potential Workplace Implications," *Journal of Business Ethics,* Vol. 117 (2013), pp. 93–109.

20. J. Wingard, "How Companies Are Managing the Millennial Generation," Knowledge@Wharton, March 5, 2015, http://knowledge.wharton.upenn.edu/article/how-companies-should-manage-millennials (accessed February 16, 2016). K. Fagan, "Survivors: New Life Comes with Healing," *San Francisco Chronicle,* September 6, 2015, pp. A1, A12–A13.

21. J. Van Derbeken, "PG&E Lags in Gas Safety," *San Francisco Chronicle,* September 9, 2015, pp. A1, A8; J. Van Derbeken, "Problems Persist in PG&E's Records," *San Francisco Chronicle,* October 9, 2015, pp. A1, A10; J. Van Derbeken, "PG&E Order Records Tossed, Ex-Official Says," *San Francisco Chronicle,* January 14, 2016, pp. A1, A10; J. Van Derbeken, "PG&E Records in Carmel Blast under a Cloud," *San Francisco Chronicle,* January 17, 2016, pp. A1, A17; and J. Van Derbeken, "PG&E Lost South Bay Records on Repairs," *San Francisco Chronicle,* February 1, 2016, pp. A1, A6.

22. "PG&E's Shame," editorial, *San Francisco Chronicle,* January 16, 2012, p. A9.

23. J. Van Derbeken, "PG&E Incentive System Blamed for Leak Oversights," *San Francisco Chronicle,* December 25, 2011, p. A1; and E. Nalder, "PG&E Diverted Safety Money for Profit, Bonuses," *San Francisco Chronicle,* January 13, 2012, p. A1.

24. Audit by Overland Consulting, reported in Nalder, "PG&E Diverted Safety Money for Profit, Bonuses."

25. Nalder, "PG&E Diverted Safety Money for Profit, Bonuses." Overland Consulting proposed that PG&E could sustain penalties totaling $2.45 billion. See arguments by ratepayer advocates T. Long, "PG&E's Fearmongering Tactics," *San Francisco Chronicle*, September 11, 2013, p. A10; and J. P. Como and T. Long, "PG&E Penalties Realistic, Benefit Ratepayers," *San Francisco Chronicle*, February 6, 2014, p. A10.
26. J. Van Derbecken, "PG&E Faces Criminal Indictment in Disaster That Left 8 People Dead," *San Francisco Chronicle*, April 3, 2014, pp. A1, A12. See also M. Gutierrez, "PG&E's Blast-Fine Tax Benefit Remains," *San Francisco Chronicle*, September 5, 2015, pp. C1, C4.
27. J. Van Derbeken, "PG&E Conduct Hindered Probe, Say San Bruno Investigators," *San Francisco Chronicle*, September 13, 2015, pp. A1, A16.
28. J. Van Derbeken, "PG&E Lags in Gas Safety," *San Francisco Chronicle*, September 9, 2015, pp. A1, A8; J. Van Derbeken, "Problems Persist in PG&E's Records," *San Francisco Chronicle*, October 9, 2015, pp. A1, A10; J. Van Derbeken, "PG&E Order Records Tossed, Ex-Official Says," *San Francisco Chronicle*, January 14, 2016, pp. A1, A10; J. Van Derbeken, "PG&E Records in Carmel Blast under a Cloud," *San Francisco Chronicle*, January 17, 2016, pp. A1, A17; and J. Van Derbeken, "PG&E Lost South Bay Records on Repairs," *San Francisco Chronicle*, February 1, 2016, pp. A1, A6.
29. On March 27, 2014, PG&E executives said they anticipated facing a criminal charge in connection with the San Bruno explosion, but denied that its employees willfully violated federal safety rules. See C. Sweet, "PG&E Expects Criminal Charges over Pipeline Explosion," *The Wall Street Journal*, March 27, 2014, http://online.wsj.com/news/articles/SB10001424052702304688104579465780254871444?mg=reno64-wsj&url=http%3A%2F%2Fonline.wsj.com%2Farticle%2FSB10001424052702304688104579465780254871444.html (accessed March 30, 2016); and "Don't Delay on PG&E Filing," editorial, *San Francisco Chronicle*, March 31, 2014, p. A11.
30. J. Goodnight, quoted in D. A. Kaplan, "The Best Company to Work For," *Fortune*, February 8, 2010, pp. 56–64.
31. M. Moskowitz and R. Levering, "The 100 Best Companies to Work For," *Fortune*, March 15, 140–154.
32. "The Employee Ownership 100: America's Largest Majority Employee-Owned Companies," The National Center for Employee Ownership, August 2013, www.nceo.org/articles/employee-ownership-100 (accessed March 22, 2016).
33. See W. Lee, "A Mixed Message from the top at Yahoo," *San Francisco Chronicle*, February 20, 2016, pp. A1, A8; and V. Goel and L. Picker, "Yahoo Takes Formal Step toward a Possible Sale," *The New York Times*, February 20, 2016, p. B2.
34. 24/7 Wall St., "America's Most Hated Companies," *MarketWatch*, January 14, 2016, www.marketwatch.com/%28S%28pvdkqo55zqclup455onso4ug%29%29/story/americas-most-hated-companies-2016-01-14/print?guid=170ad8fb-f412-4619-8eb2-d96dbd5a89d8 (accessed February 18, 2016).
35. Jeff Bezos, quoted in J. Nocera, "Put Buyers First? What a Concept," *The New York Times*, January 5, 2008, pp. B1, B9.
36. Shep Hyken, customer service consultant, quoted in K. Aho, "2013 Customer Service Hall of Fame," *MSN Money*, July 17, 2013, http://money.msn.com/investing/2013-customer-service-hall-of-fame (accessed March 31, 2016).
37. M. B. Sauer, T. C. Frohlich, and S. Stebbins, "Customer Service Hall of Fame," 24/7 Wall Street, July 23, 2015, http://247wallst.com/special-report/2015/07/23/customer-service-hall-of-fame-2/4 (accessed February 18, 2016).
38. C. Smith, "By the Numbers: 110+ Amazing Amazon Statistics (January 2016)," Digital Stats, January 28, 2016, http://expandedramblings.com/index.php/amazon-statistics/ (accessed February 18, 2016).
39. R. Rubin, "States Set Up Fight over Web Sales Tax," *The Wall Street Journal*, February 23, 2016, www.wsj.com/articles/states-seek-new-ways-to-tax-online-sales-1456262265?mod=djem10point (accessed March 7, 2016).
40. For examples of stakeholder complaints, see S. Head, "Worse than Wal-Mart: Amazon's Sick Brutality and Secret History of Ruthlessly Intimidating Workers," *Salon*, February 23, 2014, www.salon.com/2014/02/23/worse_than_wal_mart_amazons_sick_brutality_and_secret_history_of_ruthlessly_intimidating_workers (accessed February 18, 2016); D. Streitfeld, "Complaints as Amazon Raises Cost of Prime," *The New York Times*, March 14, 2014, pp. B1, B4; S. Soper, "Amazon Worker Forces Changes as Labor Board Forces Changes," *BloombergBusiness*, November 18, 2014, www.bloomberg.com/news/articles/2014-11-18/amazon-settles-labor-board-complaint-on-workers-rights (accessed February 18, 2016); S. Perez, "Despite Consumer Complaints, Amazon Prime Day Sales Soar," *TechCrunch.com*, July 15, 2015, http://techcrunch.com/2015/07/15/despite-complaints-consumer-demand-for-amazon-prime-day-was-huge (accessed February 18, 2016); and J. Kantor and D. Streitfield, "Inside Amazon: Wrestling Big Ideas in a Bruising Workplace," *The New York Times*, August 15, 2015, www.nytimes.com/2015/08/16/technology/inside-amazon-wrestling-big-ideas-in-a-bruising-workplace.html?_r=2 (accessed February 18, 2016).
41. J. Roettgers, "Amazon Clocks $197 Billion in Revenue in 2015," *Variety*, January 28, 2016, https://www.yahoo.com/movies/amazon-clocks-107-billion-revenue-2015-210927786.html (accessed February 18, 2016).
42. See, for example, M. Gottfried, "E-Commerce Is behind Pier 1's Dive," *The Wall Street Journal*, December 18, 2015, p. C8; S. Kapner, S. Nassauer, and L. Stevens, "Malls Reel as Web Roars," *The Wall Street Journal*, December 24, 2015, pp. A1, A2; S. Kapner, J. S. Lublin, and D. Mattioli, "Kohl's Weighs Net Steps as Woes Mount," *The Wall Street Journal*, January 11, 2016, p. B3; L. Pleven, "Mall Owners Get Set for Tougher Times," *The Wall Street Journal*, January 27, 2016, p. C6; L. Moyer, "E-Commerce Stutters, and Profit Falls for Walmart," *The New York Times*, February 19, 2016, p. B3; and T. Lee, "Macy's Takes Risk with Closing of 100 Stores," *San Francisco Chronicle*, August 12, 2016, pp. A1, A10.
43. H. Tabuchi, "Stores Suffer from a Shift of Behavior in Buyers," *The New York Times*, August 14, 2015, B1. For more on this subject, see J. Hamblin, "Buy Experiences, Not Things," *The Atlantic*, October 7, 2014, www.theatlantic.com/business/archive/2014/10/buy-experiences/381132 (accessed March 7, 2016); and A. Kumar, M. A. Killingsworth, and T. Gilovich, "Waiting for Merlot: Anticipatory Consumption of Experiential and Material Purchases," *Psychological Science*, Vol. 25, No. 10 (2014), pp. 1924–1931.
44. Bureau of Labor Statistics, U.S. Department of Labor, "Union Members Summary," *Economic News Release*, January 28, 2016, www.bls.gov/news.release/union2.nr0.htm (accessed February 18, 2016).
45. Bureau of Labor Statistics, U.S. Department of Labor, "Union Members Summary."
46. J. Jones, J. Schmitt, and N. Woo, *Women, Working Families, and Unions*, Center for Economic and Policy Research, June 2014, http://cepr.net/documents/women-union-2014-06.pdf (accessed February 18, 2016).
47. "Town Is Reeling after New Factory Shuts Its Doors," *San Francisco Chronicle*, November 8, 2013, p. D4, reprinted from *The New York Times*.
48. "Oakland Plays It Cool with NFL," editorial, *San Francisco Chronicle*, January 4, 2016, p. A11.
49. See J. Longman, "To NFL Owner, It's Business; to St. Louis Fans, It's Personal," *The New York Times*, January 14, 2016, pp. A1, B10; M. Powell, "Hello, They Must Be Going," *The New York Times*, January 14, 2016, p. B1, B10; and K. Belson, "Newer Owners Show Muscle in Tug of War," *The New York Times*, January 14, 2016, p. B1, B11.
50. T. Lee, "Economic Studies of Stadiums Send Wrong Message," *San Francisco Chronicle*, August 16, 2015, pp. D1, D5. See also E. Brown, J. Carlton, and M. Futterman, "Cities Rethink Sports-Team Deals," *The Wall Street Journal*, January 14, 2016, pp. B1, B2.
51. A. Damon, "The Producer," *Reno Gazette-Journal*, January 26, 2014, pp. 1A, 8A; and A. Damon, "Lights! Camera! Incentives!" *USA Today*, January 28, 2014, p. 6B. See also E. Schwartzel, "As Movie Production Scatters, So Do Tinseltown's Hired Hands," *The Wall Street Journal*, January 30, 2014, pp. A1, A10.
52. St. Cowley, "Buffalo Entice Entrepreneurs to Relocate with $5 Million in Rewards," *The New York Times*, November 5, 2015, p. B4.
53. A. Satariano, "How Arizona Town Landed Apple," *San Francisco Chronicle*, February 16, 2014, p. G3.
54. For an account of incentives offered to attract General Electric from Fairfield, Connecticut, to Boston, see T. Mann and J. Kamp, "GE Decamps to Boston," *The Wall Street Journal*, January 14, 2016, pp. B1, B2.
55. L. Story, "As Companies Seek Tax Deals, Governments Pay High Price," *The New York Times*, December 1, 2012, www.nytimes.com/2012/12/02/us/how-local-taxpayers-bankroll-corporations.html?pagewanted=all&_r=0 (accessed March 30, 2016). See also T. Moroney, "Putting a New Name on an Old Idea to Fix Inner Cities," *Bloomberg Businessweek*, January 27–February 2, 2014, pp. 25–26.
56. B. Jansen, "Drones Eclipse Piloted Planes," *Reno Gazette-Journal*, February 9, 2016, p. 1B, reprinted from *USA Today*. See also "Ruling Drones, before They Rule Us," editorial, *The New York Times*, January 10, 2016, p. A24.
57. M. Gay, "Cities Move to Curb Carriages," *The Wall Street Journal*, March 24, 2014, p. A3; and N. N. Grynbaum, "City Announces Deal on Carriage Horses in Central Park," *The New York Times*, January 18, 2016, p. A18.
58. B. Griggs, "Jada Pinkett Smith, Spike Lee to Boycott Oscars Ceremony," *CNN*, January 19, 2016, www.cnn.com/2016/01/18/entertainment/oscars-boycott-spike-lee-jada-pinkett-smith-feat/index.html (accessed February 22, 2016).
59. See M. Vick, "Chris Rock's Oscars Monologue: 'Hollywood Is Sorority Racist,'" *TV Guide*, February 28, 2016, www.tvguide.com/news/chris-rock-oscars-monologue-hollywood-sorority-racist (accessed March 8, 2016).
60. A. Auriemma, "Chiefs at Big Firms Often Last to Know," *The Wall Street Journal*, April 3, 2014, p. B1, B2.
61. C. Jensen, "In GM Recalls, Inaction and a Trail of Fatal Crashes," *The New York Times*, March 3, 2014, pp. B1, B2. See also D. Ivory, R. R. Ruiz, and B. Vlasic, "Sending Alerts, GM Delayed Recall of Cars," *The New York Times*, April 20, 2014, pp. News-1, News-15.
62. S. Hughes and J. Bennett, "Size, Cost of GM's Recalls Mount," *The Wall Street Journal*, April 1, 2014, pp. B1, B2.
63. B. Vlasic and H. Stout, "GM Turns to Hired Crisis Managers," *The New York Times*, April 4, 2014, pp. B1, B4.
64. J. Nocera, "GM's Cobalt Crisis," *The New York Times*, April 8, 2014, p. A21.
65. Wharton professor of legal studies and business ethics Amy Sepinwall, quoted in "The Price of the GM Recalls: Advice for Mary Barra," *Knowledge@Wharton*, April 9, 2014, http://knowledge.wharton.upenn.edu/article/price-gm-recalls-advice-mary-barra (accessed April 9, 2016).
66. Data from U.S. Census Bureau, reported in A. Johnson, "45 Million People Live in Poverty, but You Wouldn't Know It from Watching 2016 Coverage," *AlterNet*, January 5, 2016, www.alternet.org/election-2016/45-million-americans-live-poverty-you-wouldnt-know-it-watching-2016-coverage (accessed February 19, 2016).
67. Bureau of Labor Statistics, *International Comparisons of Manufacturing Productivity and Unit Labor Cost Trends 2008*, October 22, 2009, www.bls.gov/news.release/prod4.nr0.htm (accessed March 31, 2016); Bureau of Labor Statistics, reported in P. Wiseman, "Productivity Leaps at 6.2% Rate as Firms Wait to Hire," *USA Today*, February 5, 2010, p. 3B; Bureau of Labor Statistics, "Productivity and Costs, Fourth Quarter and Annual Averages 2011, Revised," *Economic News Release*, March 7, 2012, www.bls.gov/news.release/archives/prod2_03072012.pdf (accessed March 31, 2014); Bureau of Labor Statistics, "Productivity and Costs, Fourth Quarter and Annual Averages 2013, Revised," *Economic News Release*, March 6, 2014, www.bls.gov/news.release/prod2.nr0.htm (accessed March 31, 2016); Bureau of Labor Statistics, "Productivity and Costs, Fourth Quarter and Annual Averages 2014, Revised," *Economic News Release*, March 5, 2015, www.bls.gov/news.release/archives/prod2_03052015.pdf (accessed February 19, 2016); and Bureau of Labor Statistics, "Productivity and Costs, Fourth Quarter and Annual Averages 2015, Revised," *Economic News Release*, February 4, 2016, www.bls.gov/news.release/prod2.nr0.htm (accessed February 19, 2016).
68. M. Hanlon, "The Golden Quarter," *Aeon Magazine*, December 2014, https://aeon.co/essays/has-progress-in-science-and-technology-come-to-a-halt (accessed March 3, 2016).

69. Robert J. Gordon, reported in A. Davidson, "Do Technological Advances Determine the Health of Our Economy?" *The New York Times Magazine*, February 21, 2016, pp. 16–20. Gordon is author of *The Rise and Fall of American Growth: The U.S. Standard of Living since the Civil War* (Princeton, NJ: Princeton University Press, 2016).
70. M. Hanlon, "The Golden Quarter," *Aeon Magazine*, December 2014, https://aeon.co/essays/has-progress-in-science-and-technology-come-to-a-halt (accessed March 3, 2016).
71. See V. Wadhwa, "2015 Was a Tipping Point for Six Technologies That Will Change the World," *The Washington Post*, December 28, 2015, https://www.washingtonpost.com/news/innovations/wp/2015/12/28/2015-was-a-tipping-point-for-six-technologies-which-will-change-the-world (accessed March 3, 2016).
72. M. Muro and K. Kline, "High-Tech Advances Bring 'Hacker' Ethos to Factories," *San Francisco Chronicle*, February 21, 2016, Insight section, p. E7.
73. Wadhwa, "2015 Was a Tipping Point for Six Technologies That Will Change the World."
74. A. Smith, "U.S. Smartphone Use in 2015," Pew Research Center Report, April 1, 2015, www.pewinternet.org/2015/04/01/us-smartphone-use-in-2015 (accessed March 3, 2016).
75. For a thoughtful discussion of the transformational effects of mobile devices on people's behavior, see J. Weisberg, "We Are Hopelessly Hooked," *The New York Review of Books*, February 25, 2016, pp. 6–9.
76. R. Cohen, "Smartphone Era Politics," *The New York Times*, February 23, 2016, p. A27.
77. D. Bennett, "'Peak Car' and the Beginning of the End of the Commute," *Bloomberg Businessweek*, November 13, 2013, www.bloomberg.com/bw/articles/2013-11-13/peak-car-and-the-beginning-of-the-end-of-the-commute (accessed February 19, 2016). See also D. Schaper, "Like Millennials, More Older Americans Steering Away from Driving," MPR News, February 11, 2016, www.npr.org/2016/02/11/466178523/like-millennials-more-older-americans-steering-away-from-driving (accessed February 19, 2016); and Recent Decreases in the Proportion of Persons with a Driver's License across All Age Groups, Report UMTRI-2016-4, University of Michigan Transportation Research Institute, January 2016, www.umich.edu/~umtriswt/PDF/UMTRI-2016-4_Abstract_English.pdf (accessed February 19, 2016).
78. D. Pitt, Associated Press, "Piano Stores Closing as Fewer Children Taking Up Instrument," *Nevada Appeal*, January 4, 2015, p. C7.
79. Associated Press, "Casinos Woo Coveted Millennials with Tattoos, Mixed Martial Arts," *San Francisco Chronicle*, February 6, 2016, p. A6.
80. F. Newport, "In U.S., 87% Approve of Black-White Marriage, vs. 4% in 1958," *Gallup*, July 25, 2013, www.gallup.com/poll/163697/approve-marriage-blacks-whites.aspx; J. M. Jones, "Same-Sex Marriage Support Solidifies above 50% in U.S.," *Gallup*, May 13, 2013, www.gallup.com/poll/162398/sex-marriage-support-solidifies-above.aspx; and Social Service Survey, reported in C. Ingraham, "A Majority Favors Marijuana Legalization for First Time, According to Nation's Most Authoritative Survey," *The Washington Post*, March 4, 2015, https://www.washingtonpost.com/news/wonk/wp/2015/03/04/majority-of-americans-favor-marijuana-legalization-for-first-time-according-to-the-nations-most-authoritative-survey (all accessed February 19, 2016).
81. Associated Press, "Slumping Soda Sales Eat into Coca-Cola Profit," *San Francisco Chronicle*, February 19, 2014, p. C6; M. Esterl, "The Diet Soda Business Is in Free Fall," *The Wall Street Journal*, April 1, 2014, p. B1; M. Esterl, "New Diet Pepsi Tests Loyalists' Tastes," *The Wall Street Journal*, October 9, 2015, p. B6.
82. Y. Alcindor, "Killer Diseases Creeping Back," *USA Today*, April 7, 2014, p. 1A; and Y. Alcindor, "Diseases Get Second Life," *USA Today*, April 7, 2014, p. 5A.
83. Obesity report from Centers for Disease Control and Prevention, reported in L. Szabo, "Obesity Rate for Young Children Plummets," *USA Today*, February 26, 2014, p. 4B. See also M. Beck and A. Schatz, "American Eating Habits Take a Healthier Turn," *The Wall Street Journal*, January 17, 2014, pp. A1, A4.
84. M. Schweitzer and E. E. Levine, "The Affective and Interpersonal Consequences of Obesity," *Organizational Behavior and Human Decision Processes*, Vol. 127 (2015), pp. 66–84.
85. B. Wolf, "9 Fast Food Trends for 2016," *QSR Magazine*, January 2016, https://www.qsrmagazine.com/reports/9-fast-food-trends-2016 (accessed February 20, 2016).
86. G. Toppo and P. Overberg, "1-Person Households Grow More Common," *USA Today*, August 28, 2013, p. 3A; N. Shah, "'Baby Bust' Starts to Ease," *The Wall Street Journal*, September 5, 2013, p. B3; and Pew Research Center tabulations of U.S. Census data, in "Fewer Putting a Ring on It," *USA Today*, March 25, 2014, p. 1A.
87. R. Kochhar, "10 Projections for the Global Population in 2050," Pew Research Center report, February 3, 2014, www.pewresearch.org/fact-tank/2014/02/03/10-projections-for-the-global-population-in-2050 (accessed February 20, 2016).
88. S. Kent, "Shell Drops Arctic Oil Exploration," *The Wall Street Journal*, September 29, 2015, pp. A1, A10; and K. Johnson, "Exuberance and Disappointment at Shell's About-face in the Arctic," *The New York Times*, September 29, 2015, p. A13.
89. C. Davenport, "In Climate Move, Administration to Halt New Coal Mining Leases on Public Lands," *The New York Times*, January 15, 2016, p. A17.
90. See, for instance, J. Gillis and N. St. Fleur, "Global Companies Joining Climate Change Efforts," *The New York Times*, September 23, 2015, p. B3; P. Fimrite and K. Alexander, "Scientists Alarmed at Ocean Warming," *San Francisco Chronicle*, November 8, 2015, pp. A1, A8; and D. Perlman, "Oceans Heating Up, Both Faster, Deeper," *San Francisco Chronicle*, January 19, 2016, pp. A1, A6.
91. Data from unnamed 2006 study cited in "Guilty as Charged," *The Economist*, February 2, 2013, www.economist.com/news/leaders/21571141-cheaper-legal-education-and-more-liberal-rules-would-benefit-americas-lawyersand-their (accessed March 31, 2014).
92. "Google Pressed on Searches," *San Francisco Chronicle*, April 1, 2014, p. D2.
93. M. Scott, "Google Takes New Steps to Comply with European Privacy Ruling," *The New York Times*, February 12, 2016, p. B3.
94. Data from Secretary of Education Arne Duncan, reported in D. Skorton and G. Altschuler, "America's Foreign Language Deficit," *Forbes*, August 27, 2012, www.forbes.com/sites/collegeprose/2012/08/27/americas-foreign-language-deficit/#51f2b679382f (accessed February 20, 2016).
95. A. Friedman, "America's Lacking Language Skills," *The Atlantic*, May 10, 2015, www.theatlantic.com/education/archive/2015/05/filling-americas-language-education-potholes/392876/ (accessed February 20, 2016).
96. Dooley, "Why Your Next CEO Shouldn't Be American," *Forbes*, September 30, 2012, www.forbes.com/sites/rogerdooley/2012/10/30/foreign-language-effect/#505fafe14d2d (accessed February 20, 2016). Dooley cites B. Keysar, S. L. Hayakawa, and S. G. An, "The Foreign-Language Effect: Thinking in a Foreign Tongue Reduces Decision Biases," *Psychological Science*, April 18, 2012, pp. 661–668.
97. Survey of 764 employees by Stroz Friedberg, *On the Pulse: Information Security Risk in American Business*, January 2014, www.strozfriedberg.com/wp-content/uploads/2014/01/Stroz-Friedberg_On-the-Pulse_Information-Security-in-American-Business.pdf (accessed February 20, 2016).
98. L. T. Hosmer, *The Ethics of Management* (Homewood, IL: Irwin, 1987). See also S. Welch, "The Uh-Oh Feeling," *O Magazine*, November 2007, pp. 117–120. For more on money-and-ethics matters, see J. Fleming and L. Schwartz, *Isn't It Their Turn to Pick Up the Check?* (New York: Free Press, 2008).
99. See, for example, M. Spector and A. Harder, "VW's U.S. Chief Apologizes, Says Engineers at Fault," *The Wall Street Journal*, October 9, 2015, pp. B1, B2; and D. Hakim, "Cars Failed Fumes Test in Europe for Years," *The New York Times*, February 8, 2016, pp. B1, B2.
100. *Falling Short? College Learning and Career Success. Selected Findings from Online Surveys of Employers and College Students Conducted on Behalf of the Association of American Colleges & Universities*, January 20, 2015, Hart Research Associates, Washington, DC, https://www.aacu.org/leap/public-opinion-research/2015-survey-results (accessed March 8, 2016).
101. Study by LRN, consultant on corporate ethics, cited in "Corporate Ethics Affect Employee Productivity," *HR Magazine*, July 2007, p. 16.
102. "Is Your Doctor on a Drug Maker's Payroll?" editorial, *USA Today*, February 21, 2014, p. 6A. See also S. S. Wang, "Doctors, Device Makers: Close Ties," *The Wall Street Journal*, March 14, 2014, p. B7.
103. S. Saul, "Unease on Industry's Role in Hypertension Debate," *The New York Times*, May 20, 2006, pp. A1, B9; C. Arnst, "Hey, You Don't Look So Good," *BusinessWeek*, May 8, 2006, pp. 30–32; and A. Schwarz, "The Selling of Attention Deficit Disorder," *The New York Times*, December 15, 2013, pp. News-1, News-26, News-27.
104. P. Loftus, "Doctors Face New Scrutiny over Gifts," *The Wall Street Journal*, August 23, 2013, pp. A1, A4; and J. Kassirer, "Will Doctors Think Twice in Bright Light of Sunshine?" *San Francisco Chronicle*, January 19, 2014, p. E5.
105. B. Kabanoff, "Equity, Equality, Power, and Conflict," *Academy of Management Review*, April 1991, pp. 416–441. See also S. T. Hannah, B. J. Avolio, D. R. May, "Moral Maturation and Moral Conation: A Capacity Approach to Explaining Moral Thought and Action," *Academy of Management Review*, Vol. 36 (2011), pp. 633–685.
106. Example given by accounting professor D. Jordan Lowe, in "Making Ethical Decisions: Mood Matters," November 13, 2015, W. P. Carey School of Business, Arizona State University, http://research.wpcarey.asu.edu/accounting/making-ethical-decisions-mood-matters (accessed February 20, 2016). The research appeared in E. N. Johnson, D. J. Lowe, and P. M. J. Reckers, "The Influence of Mood on Subordinates' Ability to Resist Coercive Pressure in Public Accounting," Contemporary Accounting Research, May 25, 2015, http://onlinelibrary.wiley.com/doi/10.1111/1911-3846.12141/full.
107. D. Fritzsche and H. Baker, "Linking Management Behavior to Ethical Philosophy: An Empirical Investigation," *Academy of Management Journal*, March 1984, pp. 166–175.
108. J. P. Dietrich, A. L. Van Gaest, S. A. Strickland, and M. R. Arkoosh, "The Impact of Temperature Stress and Pesticide Exposure on Mortality and Disease Susceptibility of Endangered Pacific Salmon," *Chemosphere*, February 19, 2014, www.ncbi.nlm.nih.gov/pubmed/24559935 (accessed March 31, 2016).
109. Privacy Rights Clearinghouse, "Workplace Privacy and Employee Monitoring," revised January 2016, www.privacyrights.org/workplace-privacy-and-employee-monitoring (accessed March 31, 2016).
110. B. Van Voris, "SAC's Mathew Martoma Seeks Freedom in Appeals Court Bid," *Bloomberg Businessweek*, October 28, 2015, www.bloomberg.com/news/articles/2015-10-28/sac-s-mathew-martoma-seeks-freedom-in-appeals-court-bid (accessed February 20, 2016).
111. D. Glovin, "Galleon Co-founder Gets 11-Year Term for Insider Trading," *San Francisco Chronicle*, October 14, 2011, pp. D1, D6.
112. A. Stevenson and M. Goldstein, "Doctor Tells of Leaking Data to a 'Friend' at SAC," *The New York Times*, January 18, 2014, pp. B1, B2; and Van Voris, "SAC's Mathew Martoma Seeks Freedom in Appeals Court Bid."
113. D. R. Baker, "2 Men Accused of Cashing in on Wives' Calls," *San Francisco Chronicle*, April 1, 2014, pp. A1, A9.
114. B. Levisohn, "How to Make a Madoff," *BusinessWeek*, December 16, 2008, www.businessweek.com/investor/content/dec2008/pi20081215_232943.htm?chan=investing_investing+index+page_top+stories (accessed March 31, 2016). See also D. Gross, "Membership Has Its Penalties," *Newsweek*, January 12, 2009, p. 18; and M. Hosenball, "Made Money with Madoff? Don't Count on Keeping It," *Newsweek*, January 12, 2009, p. 9.
115. D. R. Henriques, "Madoff, Apologizing, Is Given 150 Years," *The New York Times*, June 30, 2009, pp. A1, B4. For more on Ponzi schemers and other scam artists, see M. Konnikova, *The Confidence Game: Why We Fall for It . . . Every Time* (New York: Viking, 2016).
116. C. Krauss, "Financier Is Sentenced to 110 Years for Fraud," *The New York Times*, June 15, 2012, p. B1; and S. Cohn, "Five Years after Stanford Scandal, Many Victims Penniless," *CNBC*, February 15, 2014. For more on Ponzi schemers and other scam artists, see M. Konnikova, *The Confidence Game: Why We Fall for It . . . Every Time* (New York: Viking, 2016).

117. F. Norris, "Goodbye to Reforms of 2002," *The New York Times,* November 6, 2009, pp. B1, B6.
118. See "Has Sarbanes-Oxley Failed?" *The New York Times,* July 24, 2012, www.nytimes.com/roomfordebate/2012/07/24/has-sarbanes-oxley-failed?action=click&module=Search&region=searchResults%230&version=&url=http%3A%2F%2Fquery.nytimes.com%2Fsearch%2Fsitesearch%2F%23%2FSarbOx%2F (accessed March 31, 2016).
119. L. Moyer, "Monsanto Will Pay $80 Million to SEC," *The New York Times,* February 10, 2016, p. B3.
120. F. J. Evans, quoted in C. S. Stewart, "A Question of Ethics: How to Teach Them?" *The New York Times,* March 21, 2004, sec. 3, p. 11.
121. D. A. Kaplan, "MBAs Get Schooled in Ethics," *Fortune,* October 26, 2009, p. 27; and M. Wecker, "Business Schools Increasingly Require Students to Study Ethics," *U.S. News & World Report,* September 20, 2011, www.usnews.com/education/best-graduate-schools/top-business-schools/articles/2011/09/20/business-schools-increasingly-require-students-to-study-ethics (accessed February 22, 2016). But see R. Fisman and A. Galinsky, "Can You Train Business School Students to Be Ethical?" *Slate,* September 4, 2012, www.slate.com/articles/business/the_dismal_science/2012/09/business_school_and_ethics_can_we_train_mbas_to_do_the_right_thing_.html (accessed February 22, 2016).
122. "Cheating in College: The Numbers and Research," Best College Reviews, www.bestcollegereviews.org/cheating (accessed March 8, 2016).
123. Josephson Institute Center for Youth Ethics, "2012 Report Card on the Ethics of American Youth," November 20, 2012, and "2010 Report Card on the Ethics of American Youth," February 10, 2011, http://charactercounts.org/programs/reportcard/2012/index.html andhttp://charactercounts.org/programs/reportcard/2010/index.html (both accessed March 8, 2016).
124. S. H. E. Costa and R. David, "Goldman, JPMorgan Said to Fire 30 Analysts for Cheating on Tests," *BloombergBusiness,* October 16, 2015, www.bloomberg.com/news/articles/2015-10-16/goldman-sachs-said-to-dismiss-20-analysts-for-cheating-on-tests (accessed March 8, 2016).
125. L. Kohlberg, "Moral Stages and Moralization: The Cognitive Developmental Approach," in T. Lickona, ed., *Moral Development and Behavior: Theory, Research, and Social Issues* (New York: Holt, Rinehart and Winston, 1976), pp. 31–53; and J. W. Graham, "Leadership, Moral Development and Citizenship Behavior," *Business Ethics Quarterly,* January 1995, pp. 43–54. See also S. J. Reynolds and T. L. Ceranic, "The Effects of Moral Judgment and Moral Identity on Moral Behavior: An Empirical Examination of the Moral Individual," *Journal of Applied Psychology,* November 2007, pp. 1610–1624.
126. Adapted in part from W. E. Stead, D. L. Worrell, and J. Garner Stead, "An Integrative Model for Understanding and Managing Ethical Behavior in Business Organizations," *Journal of Business Ethics,* March 1990, pp. 233–242. Also see D. Lange, "A Multidimensional Conceptualization of Organizational Corruption Control," *Academy of Management Review,* July 2008, pp. 710–729; J. DesJardins, *An Introduction to Business Ethics,* 3rd ed. (New York: McGraw-Hill, 2009); and M. J. Pearsall and A. P. J. Ellis, "Thick as Thieves: The Effects of Ethical Orientation and Psychological Safety on Unethical Team Behavior," *Journal of Applied Psychology,* Vol. 96 (2011), pp. 401–411.
127. Society for Human Resource Management Weekly Survey, 2005, cited in J. Thilmany, *HR Magazine,* September 2007, pp. 105–112.
128. T. R. Mitchell, D. Daniels, H. Hopper, J. George-Falvy, and G. R. Ferris, "Perceived Correlates of Illegal Behavior in Organizations," *Journal of Business Ethics,* April 1996, pp. 439–455. See also M. W., "Ethics Training Works," *Training,* November 2005, p. 15; L. Paine, R. Deshpandé, J. D. Margolis, and K. E. Bettcher, "Up to Code: Does Your Company's Conduct Meet World-Class Standards?" *Harvard Business Review,* December 1, 2005, pp. 122–135; and J. Brockner, "Why It's So Hard to Be Fair," *Harvard Business Review,* March 1, 2006, pp. 122–132.
129. "Whistle-blower Law Protects Outside Consults, Too," *San Francisco Chronicle,* March 5, 2014, p. A6.
130. R. Pear, "Whistleblowers Likely to Get Stronger Federal Protections," *The New York Times,* March 15, 1999, pp. A1, A17.
131. T. Herman, "Tipster Rewards Require Patience," *The Wall Street Journal,* December 26, 2007, p. D3.
132. "The Age of the Whistleblower," *The Economist,* December 5, 2015, www.economist.com/news/business/21679455-life-getting-better-those-who-expose-wrongdoing-companies-continue-fight (accessed February 24, 2016).
133. Ethics Resource Center, *National Business Ethics Survey of the U.S. Workforce,* 2013 (Arlington, VA: Ethics Resource Center, 2014).
134. A. Tugend, "Opting to Blow the Whistle or Choosing to Walk Away," *The New York Times,* September 21, 2013, p. B5.
135. [1] K. Eagan, E. B. Stozenberg, J. J. Ramirez, M. C. Aragon, M. R. Suchard, and S. Hutado, *The American Freshman: National Norms, Fall 2014* (Los Angeles: Higher Education Research Institute, University of California, Los Angeles, 2014).
136. See D. W. Organ, *Organizational Citizenship Behavior: The Good Soldier Syndrome* (Lexington, MA: Lexington Books, 1988).
137. N. F. Taylor, "What Is Corporate Social Responsibility?" *Business News Daily,* June 19, 2015, www.businessnewsdaily.com/4679-corporate-social-responsibility.html (accessed February 23, 2016).
138. A. B. Carroll, "Managing Ethically with Global Stakeholders: A Present and Future Challenge," *Academy of Management Executive,* May 2004, p. 118. Also see B. W. Husted and D. B. Allen, "Corporate Social Responsibility in the Multinational Enterprise: Strategic and Institutional Approaches," *Journal of International Business Studies,* November 2006, pp. 838–849; and A. B. Carroll, "Corporate Social Responsibility: The Centerpiece of Competing and Complementary Frameworks," *Organizational Dynamics,* April–June 2015, pp. 87–96.
139. See "How Emerging Multinationals Are Embracing Social Responsibility," Knowledge @ Wharton, November 12, 2015, http://knowledge.wharton.upenn.edu/article/why-emerging-multinationals-are-embracing-social-responsibility (accessed February 24, 2016).
140. M. Friedman, *Capitalism and Freedom* (Chicago: University of Chicago Press, 1962). See also S. Gallagher, "A Strategic Response to Friedman's Critique of Business Ethics," *Journal of Business Strategy,* January 2005, pp. 55–60.
141. P. Samuelson, "Love That Corporation," *Mountain Bell Magazine,* Spring 1971.
142. *Sustainable Company/Sustainable World: Salesforce.com Sustainability Report FY2012,* Salesforce.com, San Francisco, www.salesforce.com/assets/pdf/misc/SustainabilityReport.pdf (accessed February 24, 2016). See also J. Temple, "Salesforce's Philosophy: Share," *San Francisco Chronicle,* November 18, 2013, pp. A1, A9; and J. Garofoli, "Big Push for Tech to Fight Poverty," *San Francisco Chronicle,* March 7, 2014, pp. A1, A11.
143. J. Tucker, "Benioff's Unique Donations to Schools," *San Francisco Chronicle,* August 24, 2015, pp. A1, A6.
144. D. Gallagher, "Making It Rain at Salesforce.com," *The Wall Street Journal,* February 26, 2015, p. C8.
145. "Public Says Climate Change Is Real," Monmouth University Poll, January 5, 2016, www.monmouth.edu/assets/0/32212254 770/3221 2254991/32212254992/32212254994/32212254995/30064771087/bbab2f4a-3eef-4772-9b82-8fbdd996452a.pdf (accessed February 23, 2016).
146. Intergovernmental Panel on Climate Change, United Nations, *Climate Change 2013: The Physical Science Basis—Summary for Policymakers,* September 28, 2013, www.climatechange2013.org/images/report/WG1AR5_SPM_FINAL.pdf (accessed February 23, 2016).
147. Definitions adapted from U.S. Environmental Protection Agency, "Climate Change: Basic Information," February 23, 2016, https://www3.epa.gov/climatechange/basics/ (accessed February 23, 2016).
148. M. Hume, Why We Disagree about Climate Change: Understanding Controversy, Inaction, and Opportunity (Cambridge: Cambridge University Press, 2010).
149. C. Davenport, "Threat to Bottom Line Spurs Action on Climate," *The New York Times,* January 24, 2014, pp. A1, A21.
150. J. Schwartz, "Coca-Cola Says It's Close to Water Replenishment Goal," *The New York Times,* p. B3.
151. Gillis and St. Fleur, "Global Companies Joining Climate Change Efforts." See also "Green Evolution: How Business Is Joining the Environmental Movement," *Knowledge@Wharton,* December 10, 2015, http://knowledge.wharton.upenn.edu/article/green-evolution-how-business-is-joining-the-environmental-vanguard (accessed February 23, 2016).
152. A. G. Robinson and D. M. Schroeder, "Greener and Cheaper," *The Wall Street Journal,* March 23, 2009, p. R4; and R. Farzad, "The Scrappiest Car Manufacturer in America," *Bloomberg Businessweek,* June 6, 2011, pp. 68–74.
153. D. Palmquist, "Conservancy Science at Dow's Freeport, TX, Site," The Nature Conservancy, www.nature.org/science-in-action/science-features/dow-analyses.xml (accessed March 31, 2016).
154. Gretchen Daily, quoted in C. Lochhead, "Ecologists Try in Quiet Ways to Save the Planet," *San Francisco Chronicle,* January 5, 2014, pp. A1, A8. Also see "What Is Natural Capital?" World Forum on Natural Capital, http://naturalcapitalforum.com/about; and "Natural Capital: Placing Nature at the Core of the Economy," British Ecological Society, June 3, 2015, www.britishecologicalsociety.org/blog/2015/06/03/natural-capital-placing-nature-at-the-core-of-the-economy/ (both accessed February 23, 2016).
155. "StEP Launches Interactive E-Waste Map, December 12, 2013, United Nations University, Tokyo, http://unu.edu/media-relations/releases/step-launches-interactive-world-e-waste-map.html#info (accessed February 23, 2016).
156. Intergovernmental Panel on Climate Change, United Nations, "Climate Change 2014: Impacts, Adaptation, and Vulnerability—Summary for Policymakers," March 31, 2014, http://ipcc-wg2.gov/AR5/images/uploads/IPCC_WG2AR5_SPM_Approved.pdf (accessed February 23, 2016). See account of this report in J. Gillis, "U.N. Says Lag in Confronting Climate Woes Will Be Costly," *The New York Times,* January 17, 2014, p. A8.
157. See also W. Mauldin, "Nations Delay Climate Pledges," *The Wall Street Journal,* August 24, 2015, p. A9; "Proof That a Price on Carbon Works," editorial, *The New York Times,* January 19, 2016, p. A22; and M. Urban and L. Deegan, "T-Shirt Weather in the Arctic," *The New York Times,* February 6, 2016, p. A21.
158. The source of Bill Gates's net worth is Bloomberg as of February 2016, cited in "Bill Gates Net Worth," *The Richest,* www.therichest.com/celebnetworth/celebrity-business/tech-billionaire/bill-gates-net-worth (accessed February 23, 2016). For more on the Gates foundation, see C. Dreifus, "A Partnership Built on Change," *The New York Times,* October 8, 2013, pp. D1, D5.
159. T. Egan, "Billionaires and Boasts," *The New York Times,* January 23, 2014, www.nytimes.com/2014/01/24/opinion/egan-billionaires-and-boasts.html?ref=gatesbillandmelindafoundation&_r=0 (accessed February 23, 2016). See also B. Kowitt, "The Young Buffetts," *Fortune,* October 7, 2013, p. 22; J. Wattles, "10 More Billionaires Join Buffet-Gates Giving Pledge," *CNN Money,* June 3, 2015, http://money.cnn.com/2015/06/02/news/companies/giving-pledge-billionaires-buffett-gates (accessed February 23, 2016); and J. Heilpern, "Out to Lunch with Melinda Gates," *Vanity Fair,* October 2015, p. 161.
160. A.-A. Jarvis, "Pulling Off an Impressive Feet," *Newsweek,* July 3–10, 2006, p. 64. See also shareyoursoles.org, the charity's website.
161. Associated Press, "Apple CEO Says He Will Give Away Most of Fortune," *San Francisco Chronicle,* March 28, 2015, p. D2.
162. See D. Brooks, "How to Leave a Mark," *The New York Times,* January 27, 2015, p. A19; T. Cowen, "For Small Donors, Better Giving through Science," *The New York Times,* August 16, 2015, p. BU-6; J. Surowiecki, "In Defense of Philanthrocapitalism," *The New Yorker,* December 21 & 28, p. 40; and P. Sullivan, "A Philanthropist Drills Down to Discover Why Programs Work." *The New York Times,* February 6, 2016, p. B4.

163. A. Fox, "Corporate Social Responsibility Pays Off," *HR Magazine*, August 2007, pp. 43–47; and A. C. Brooks, "Handsome Is as Handsome Gives," *The Wall Street Journal*, November 26, 2013, p. A13. For an explanation of methodologies for rating corporate social responsibility, see M. A. Delmas, D. Etzion, and N. Nairn-Birch, "Triangulating Environmental Performance: What Do Corporate Responsibility Ratings Really Capture?" *The Academy of Management Perspective*, Vol. 27, No. 3 (2013), pp. 255–267. See also F. P. Morgeson, H. Aguinis, D. A. Waldman, and D. S. Siegel, "Extending Corporate Social Responsibility Research to the Human Resource Management and Organizational Behavior Domains: A Look to the Future," *Personnel Psychology*, Vol. 66 (2013), pp. 805–824.

164. R. Gildea, "Consumer Survey Confirms Corporate Social Action Affects Buying Decisions," *Public Relations Quarterly*, Winter 1994, pp. 20–21.

165. Reported in C. Brooks, "Shoppers Willing to Pay More to Socially Responsible Companies," *Business News Daily*, March 12, 2012, www.businessnewsdaily.com/2273-shoppers-pay-socially-responsible-companies.html (accessed February 24, 2016).

166. O. Demirtas and A. A. Akdogan, "The Effect of Ethical Leadershipl Behavior on Ethical Climate, Turnover Intention, and Affective Commitment," *Journal of Business Ethics*, August 2015, pp. 59–67.

167. See T. W. H. Ng and D. C. Feldman, "Ethical Leadership: Meta-Analytic Evidence of Criterion-Related and Incremental Validity," *Journal of Applied Psychology*, May 2015, pp. 948–965; and D. A. Waldman, M. Z. Carter, and P. W. Hom, "A Multilevel Investigation of Leadership and Turnover Behavior," *Journal of Management*, September 2015, pp. 1724–1744.

168. See Ng and Feldman, "Ethical Leadership: Meta-Analytic Evidence of Criterion-Related and Incremental Validity," and W. Zhu, H. He, L. K. Treviño, M. M. Chao, and W. Wang, "Ethical Leadership and Follower Voice and Performance: The Role of Follower Identifications and Entity Morality Beliefs," *The Leadership Quarterly*, October 2015, pp. 702–718.

169. M. Baucus and D. Baucus, "Paying the Piper: An Empirical Examination of Longer-Term Financial Consequences of Illegal Corporate Behavior," *Academy of Management Journal*, Vol. 40, No. 1 (1997), pp. 129–151.

170. 2003 survey by Wirthlin Worldwide, cited in *The Hidden Costs of Unethical Behavior*, p. 2.

171. 2000 National Business Ethics Survey, cited in *The Hidden Costs of Unethical Behavior*, p. 3.

172. Report to the Nations on Occupational Fraud & Abuse: 2014 Global Fraud Study, Association of Certified Fraud Examiners, www.acfe.com/rttn/docs/2014-report-to-nations.pdf (accessed February 24, 2016).

173. 2003 survey by Wirthlin Worldwide, cited in*The Hidden Costs of Unethical Behavior*, p. 2.

174. J. Chakravarthy, E. deHaan, and S. Rajgopal, "Reputation Repair after a Serious Restatement," *The Accounting Review*, 2013, in press. See also Stanford Graduate School of Business, "How Corporations Can Regain Financial Value after Scandal," *Science Daily*, January 15, 2014, www.sciencedaily.com/releases/2014/01/140115172643.htm (accessed March 31, 2016). But also see M. Orlitzky, "Corporate Social Responsibility, Noise, and Stock Market Volatility," *The Academy of Management Perspectives*, Vol. 27, No. 3 (2013), pp. 238–254.

175. A discussion of ethics and financial performance is provided by R. M. Fulmer, "The Challenge of Ethical Leadership," *Organizational Dynamics*, August 2004, pp. 307–317.

176. H. Syse of the Peace Research Institute, Oslo, Norway, quoted in "Special Report on Business Ethics: Enhancing Corporate Governance," press release, Knowledge@Wharton, February 25, 2016, http://knowledge.wharton.upenn.edu/special-report/special-report-on-business-ethics-enhancing-corporate-governance/?utm_source=kw_newsletter&utm_medium=email&utm_campaign=2016-02-25 (accessed February 26, 2016). The report is Special Report on BusinessEthics: Enhancing Corporate Governance, February 2016, Knowledge@Wharton and AKO Foundation, http://d1c25a6gwz7q5e.cloudfront.net/reports/2016-02-25-Enhancing-Corporate-Governance.pdf (accessed February 26, 2016).

177. For more on this topic, see D. Barton and M. Wiseman, "Where Boards Fall Short," *Harvard Business Review*, January–February 2015, pp. 99–104; and G. Subramanian, "Corporate Governance 2.0," *Harvard Business Review*, March 2015, pp. 97–105. See also S. Schreter, "Tips on Creating a Helpful Board," *San Francisco Chronicle*, January 25, 2014, pp. D1, D2; and T. Lee, "Directors Need Directions," *San Francisco Chronicle*, February 28, 2016, pp. D1, D6.

178. C. Helman, "The Two Sides of Aubrey," *Forbes.com*, October 24, 2011, www.forbes.com/forbes/2011/1024/feature-aubrey-mcclendon-hero-energy-chesapeake-risk-christopher-helman.html (accessed March 31, 2016).

179. See "The Shameful State of Chesapeake's Board," *24/7 Wall Street*, April 19, 2012, http://247wallst.com/energy-business/2012/04/19/the-shameful-state-of-chesapeakes-board-chk-brk-a-unp-nov (accessed February 26, 2016).

180. M. Leder, "For Chesapeake's Chief, Some Big Money in Maps," *New York Times DealBook*, May 1, 2009, http://dealbook.nytimes.com/2009/05/01/for-chesapeakes-chief-some-big-money-in-maps; and M. Leder, "Chesapeake's McClendon Buys Back the Maps," *Footnoted.org*, November 3, 2011, www.footnoted.com/buried-treasure/chesapeakes-mcclendon-buys-back-the-maps (all accessed March 31, 2016).

181. Chesapeake Energy proxy filing notes, reported in Leder, "Chesapeake's McClendon Buys Back the Maps."

182. C. Helman, "In Legal Settlement, Chesapeake's McClendon to Buy Back Antique Maps," *Forbes.com*, November 3, 2011, www.okctalk.com/showthread.php?t=28160&page=1 (accessed March 31, 2016).

183. Helman, "In Legal Settlement, Chesapeake's McClendon to Buy Back Antique Maps"; and P. M. "Shale-Gas Reserves Have Potential to Reignite U.S. Economy," *Bloomberg Business*, November 2, 2011, www.bloomberg.com/news/arti-

cles/2011-11-03/shale-gas-reserves-have-potential-to-reignite-u-s-economy (accessed February 26, 2016).

184. S. Finkelstein, "The Five Worst CEOs of 2012," *The Washington Post*, December 18, 2012, https://www.washingtonpost.com/national/on-leadership/the-five-worst-ceos-of-2012/2012/12/18/0f353f14-4940-11e2-ad54-580638ede391_story.html (accessed February 26, 2016).

185. C. Helman, "Man on Fire: Aubdrey McClendon Raises Billions to Finance His Redemption," *Forbes*, February 27, 2014, www.forbes.com/sites/christopherhelman/2014/02/27/man-on-fire-aubrey-mcclendon-raises-billions-to-finance-his-redemption (accessed 2016 March 31, 2014); and K. Kelly, "Aubrey McClendon Launching 'Blank Check' Company, CNBC," April 24, 2015, www.cnbc.com/2015/04/24/aubrey-mcclendon-launching-blank-check-company.html (accessed February 26, 2016). See also R. Dezember, B. Olson, and E. Ailworth, "McClendon Bet Big on Comeback," *The Wall Street Journal*, March 8, 2016, pp. B1, B2.

186. T. Puko, A. Sider, and E. Ailworth, "Chesapeake Woes Rattle Pipeline Partners," *The Wall Street Journal*, February 9, 2016, pp. B1, B5.

187. A. Harder and B. Kendall, "Former Chesapeake CEO Indicted for Bid Rigging," *The Wall Street Journal*, March 2, 2016, pp. A1, A2; and E. Ailworth and A. B. Olson, "McClendon's Death Casts Cloud over Probe," *The Wall Street Journal*, March 4, 2016, pp. B1, B2.

188. B. Olson, R. Dezember, and L. Cook, "Indicted Oil Titan Killed in Car Crash," *The Wall Street Journal*, March 3, 2016, pp. A1, A8.

189. R. Hurley, "Trust Me," *The Wall Street Journal*, October 24, 2011, p. R4. Hurley is author of *The Decision to Trust: How Leaders Can Create High-Trust Companies* (San Francisco: Jossey-Bass, 2011).

190. P. Elkind, "How Ice Cream Maker Blue Bell Blew It," http://fortune.com/2015/09/25/blue-bell-listeria-recall/ (accessed January 26, 2016).

191. Gerald Bland in P. Elkin, "Ice Cream Melting on the Fctory Floor: Ugly Tales from Blue Bell" *Fortune* October 13, 2015. Copyright © 2015 Time Inc. Used with permission.

192. Gerald Bland in P. Elkin, "Ice Cream Melting on the Fctory Floor: Ugly Tales from Blue Bell" *Fortune* October 13, 2015. Copyright © 2015 Time Inc. Used with permission.

193. P Elkind, "How Ice Cream Maker Blue Bell Blew It," *Fortune*, September 25, 2015. http://fortune.com/2015/09/25/blue-bell-listeria-recall/, (accessed January 26, 2016).

194. J. Newman, "Ice-Cream Recall Sends Chill through Food Industry," http://www.wsj.com/articles/ice-cream-recall-sends-chill-through-food-industry-1438437781 (accessed January 26, 2016).

195. M. Gray, "Blue Bell: Better Testing Finds Potential Listeria Presence," http://www.cnn.com/2016/01/08/us/blue-bell-listeria-recall/ (accessed January 26, 2016).

196. J. Mitchell, "How to Apply for Student-Debt Forgiveness for Victims of School Fraud," January 20, 2016, http://blogs.wsj.com/briefly/2016/01/20/student-debt-for-giveness-for-victims-of-school-fraud-at-a-glance/, accessed January 26, 2016.

197. J. Mitchell, "Thousands Want Student Loans Cancelled," *The Wall Street Journal*, January 21, 2016, p. A3.

CHAPTER 4

1. 17 Reasons Why Around the World Travel Is Good for You," Airtreks, www.airtreks.com/ready/17-reasons-why-trael-is-good-for-you (accessed March 14, 2016).

2. "Hilton Survey Looks at Millennial Business Travel Trends," *International Meetings Review*, July 18, 2013, www.internationalmeetingsreview.com/research-education/hilton-survey-looks-millennial-business-travel-trends-96305 (accessed March 14, 2016).

3. See "Business Meetings: The Case for Face-to-Face," Forbes Insights, 2009, www.forbes.com/forbesinsights/Business_Meetings_FaceToFace (accessed March 27, 2016); C. Duffy and M. B. McEuen, "The Future of Meetings: The Case for Face-to-Face," *Cornell Hospitality Industry*, October 1, 2010, pp. 6–13; and "Managing Across Distance in Today's Economic Climate: The Value of Face-to-Face Communication," A report by Harvard Business Review Analytic Services, April 2011, https://hbr.org/resources/pdfs/comm/british-airways/hbras_ba_report_web.pdf (accessed March 27, 2016).

4. R. Bullock, "Face-to-Face Communication: Why It Still Matters for Leadership," Scontrio-Powell, May 6, 2014, www.scontrino-powell.com/2014/face-to-face-communication-a-critical-leadership-skill (accessed March 27, 2016).

5. Paul Calello of Credit Suisse, quoted T. Lowry and F. Balfour, "It's All about the Face-to-Face," *BusinessWeek*, January 28, 2008, pp. 48, 50.

6. Don G. Lents, chairman of international law firm Bryan Cave, quoted in J. Sharkey, "E-Mail Saves Time, but Being There Says More," *The New York Times*, January 26, 2010, p. B7.

7. A. Ross, "You Will Speak Every Language," *The Wall Street Journal*, January 30–31, 2016, p. C3.

8. S. Jakab, "Drama Becomes Urban Outfitters," *The Wall Street Journal*, August 17, 2015, p. C1.

9. J. Raymond, "To Asia and Back, Sleep Not an Option," *The New York Times*, January 3, 2012, p. B6.

10. L. Bergson, "A Road Scholar's Bag of Tricks," *BusinessWeek*, September 29, 2003, www.bloomberg.com/news/articles/2003-09-28/a-road-scholars-bag-of-tricks (accessed March 14, 2016).

11. R. Yu, "Cultural Training Has Global Appeal," *USA Today*, December 22, 2009, p. 3B.

12. Patrica Rossi, quoted in A. Bruzzese, "Business Traveler? Use Downtime to Make Contacts," *Reno Gazette-Journal*, July 11, 2013, p. 5A.

13. R. Simmermaker, *How Americans Can Buy American: The Power of Consumer Patriotism*, 3rd ed. (Orlando, FL: Rivercross Publications, 2010).

14. Roger Simmermaker, quoted in W. T. Price, "Exploring Financial Viability of Buying American Products," *Reno Gazette-Journal*, September 10, 2011, pp. 6A, 8A.

15. Survey by Consumer Reports National Research Center, reported in G. Karp, "Finding Value in 'Made in the USA," *Chicago Tribune*, November 4, 2013, http://articles.chicagotribune.com/2013-11-04/site/sc-cons-1031-karpspend-20131104_1_ftc-case-products-usa (accessed March 15, 2016).

16. "Made in America," *Consumer Reports*, May 21, 2015, www.consumerreports.org/cro/magazine/2015/05/made-in-america/index.htm (accessed March 27, 2015).

17. International Monetary Fund, reported in B. Arends, "It's Official: America is Now No. 2," *Market Watch*, December 4, 2014, www.marketwatch.com/story/its-official-america-is-now-no-2-2014-12-04 (accessed March 5, 2016).

18. Rankings determined according to gross domestic product based on purchasing-power-parity per capita, according to the International Monetary Fund, reported in V. Pasquali, "Richest Countries in the World," *Global Finance Magazine*, March 5, 2016, https://www.gfmag.com/global-data/economic-data/richest-countries-in-the-world?page=12 (accessed March 5, 2016).

19. "2016 Index of Economic Freedom," The Heritage Foundation in partnership with *The Wall Street Journal*, www.heritage.org/index/ranking (accessed March 5, 2016).

20. See the related discussion in J. McGregor and S. Hamm, "Managing the Global Workforce," *BusinessWeek*, January 28, 2008, p. 34; C. Boles, "Last Call? Gates Pushes Globalism in Remarks," *The Wall Street Journal*, March 13, 2008, p. B3; and M. Herbst, "Guess Who's Getting the Most Work Visas," *BusinessWeek*, March 17, 2008, pp. 62, 64.

21. Cellular Telecommunications Industry Association, cited in A. Dunkin, "Smart, Useful—and They Won't Put a Sag in Your Suit," *BusinessWeek*, May 30, 1994, p. 141.

22. *The World in 2015:* ICT Facts and Figures, International Telecommunications Union, Geneva, www.itu.int/en/ITU-D/Statistics/Pages/facts/default.aspx www.itu.int/en/ITU-D/Statistics/Documents/facts/ICTFactsFigures2013-e.pdf (accessed March 5, 2016).

23. *The World in 2015: ICT Facts and Figures.*

24. See J. Quittner, "Tim Berners-Lee," *Time*, March 29, 1999, pp. 193–194.

25. "Quarterly Retail E-Commerce Sales 4th Quarter 2015," *U.S. Census Bureau News*, February 7, 2016, www.census.gov/retail/mrts/www/data/pdf/ec_current.pdf (accessed March 5, 2016).

26. Hardy, "Amazon Building a Tech Business for the Long Haul," *The New York Times*, October 12, 2015, p. B4.

27. T. Lee, "E-Commerce is Booming—Can Someone Tell Gap?" *San Francisco Chronicle*, March 9, 2016, pp. C1, C5.

28. M. Anderson, "Technology Device Ownership: 2015," Pew Research Center, October 29, 2015, www.pewinternet.org/2015/10/29/technology-device-ownership-2015 (accessed March 27, 2016).

29. A. Smith, "U.S. Smartphone Use in 2015," Pew Research Center, April 1, 2015, www.pewinternet.org/2015/04/01/us-smartphone-use-in-2015 (accessed March 27, 2016).

30. L. Cosseboom, "10 of the Most Mobile Shopping Apps in Indonesia," *Tech in Asia*, February 12, 2015, https://www.techinasia.com/indonesia-10-ecommerce-mobile-shopping-sites-2015 (accessed March 27, 2016).

31. N. Purnell and J. Osawa, "Peer-to-Peer E-Commerce Apps by Startups Flourish in Asia," *The Wall Street Journal*, March 28, 2016, p. B3.

32. R. M. Kantor, quoted in K. Maney, "Economy Embraces Truly Global Workplace," *USA Today*, December 31, 1998, pp. 1B, 2B.

33. M. Collins, "The Pros and Cons of Globalization," *Forbes*, May 6, 2015, www.forbes.com/sites/mikecollins/2015/05/06/the-pros-and-cons-of-globalization (accessed March 7, 2016). Collins is the author of *Saving American Manufacturing* (Chicago: Vantage Press, 2006).

34. R. Carr, "What's Behind the Recent Rise in Auto Plant Develoment," *National Real Estate in Investor*, December 31, 2015, http://nreionline.com/industrial/whats-behind-recent-rise-auto-plant-development (accessed March 5, 2016).

35. Foreign Direct Investment in the United States: 2014 Report, Organization for International Investment, Washington, D.C., www.ofii.org/sites/default/files/FDIUS2014.pdf (accessed March 6, 2016).

36. G. Easterbrook, "The Boom Is Nigh," *Newsweek*, February 22, 2010, pp. 48–49. Easterbrook is the author of *Sonic Boom: Globalization at Mach Speed* (New York: Random House, 2009). See also P. Ghemawat, *World 3.0: Global Prosperity and How to Achieve It* (Boston: Harvard Business Review Press, 2011), who argues that globalization, when finally realized, will offer more benefits than threats.

37. Collins, "The Pros and Cons of Globalization."

38. L. Uchitelle, "Another Shifting Industry," *The New York Times*, January 19, 2010, pp. B1, B5.

39. J. Brustein, "App Economy Jobs Appear Destined to Go Overseas," *San Francisco Chronicle*, September 15, 2013, p. D2.

40. See D. H. Autor, D. Dorn, and G. H. Hanson, "The China Syndrome: Local Labor Market Effects of Import Competition in the United States," *American Economic Review*, Vol. 103, No. 2 (2013), pp. 2121–2168; D. Acemoglu, D. Autor, D. Dorn, G. H. Hanson, and B. Price, "The Rise of China and the Future of U.S. Manufacturing," *Vox*, September 2014, www.voxeu.org/article/rise-china-and-future-us-manufacturing (accessed March 15, 2016).

41. See S. Rattner, "The Myth of Industrial Rebound," *The New York Times*, January 26, 2014, pp. SR-1, SR-8; C. Kenney, "Factory Jobs Are Gone. Get Over It," *Bloomberg Businessweek*, January 27–February 2, 2014, pp. 12–13; A. Semuels, "Ghost Towns of the 21st Century," *The Atlantic*, October 20, 2015, www.theatlantic.com/business/archive/2015/10/ghost-towns-of-the-21st-century/411343/ (accessed March 7, 2016); and A. Semuels, " 'Good' Jobs Aren't Coming Back to the U.S.," *The Atlantic City Lab*, October 26, 2015, www.theatlantic.com/business/archive/2015/10/onshoring-jobs/412201 (accessed March 7, 2016).

42. M. Collins, "The Pros and Cons of Globalization," *Forbes*, May 6, 2015, www.forbes.com/sites/mikecollins/2015/05/06/the-pros-and-cons-of-globalization (accessed March 7, 2016). Collins is the author of *Saving American Manufacturing* (Chicago: Vantage Press, 2006).

43. N. Negroponte, quoted in Maney, "Economy Embraces Truly Global Workplace." See also S. Fidler, "Globalization: Battered but Not Beaten," *The Wall Street Journal*, January 21, 2015, p. A6.

44. See D. Cimilluca, "Mergers Set a Record as Firms Bulk Up," *The Wall Street Journal*, December 21, 2015, p. A10.

45. L. Hoffman, R. Rubin, and J. D. Rockoff, "Taxes Drive Drug Merger," *The Wall Street Journal*, October 30, 2015, pp. A1, A2.

46. T. Lee, "Blockbuster Drug Deals," *San Francisco Chronicle*, November 1, 2015, pp. D1, D5.

47. A. Massa, "Yelp Purchases Food-Ordering Service Eat24," *San Francisco Chronicle*, February 11, 2015, p. C3; and J. A. Trachtenberg, "Time Inc. Buys Hello Giggles, Aiming for Young Female Audience," *The Wall Street Journal*, October 19, 2015, p. B6.

48. "How Mergers Damage the Economy," editorial, *The New York Times*, November 1, 2015, p. SR-10.

49. See editorial, "Beer Industry Harmed by Purchase of Distributors," *Reno Gazette-Journal*, October 30, 2015, p. 6A, reprinted from *USA Today*.

50. *Consumer Intelligence Series: The Sharing Economy*, Pricewaterhouse Coopers, April 2015, www.pwc.com/us/en/industry/entertainment-media/publications/consumer-intelligence-series/assets/pwc-cis-sharing-economy.pdf (accessed March 27, 2016).

51. C. Said, "Poshmark Apparel App Adds Indie Designers," *San Francisco Chronicle*, October 28, 2015, pp. C1, C3.

52. G. Rifkin, "A Start-Up Helps Homeless Artists," *The New York Times*, February 18, 2016, p. B5.

53. P. McDonald, quoted in M. L. Levin, "Global Experience Makes Candidates More Marketable," *The Wall Street Journal*, September 11, 2007, p. B6.

54. C. Johannsen, "Unemployed, Educated, and Indebted: More Millennials Seeking Work Outside U.S.," *College USA Today*, May 17, 2011, http://college.usatoday.com/2011/05/17/unemployed-educated-and-indebted-more-millennials-seeking-work-beyond-u-s; R. Florida, "Why Americans Emigrate," *The New York Times*, July 22, 2013, www.nytimes.com/roomfordebate/2012/01/08/is-the-us-still-a-land-of-opportunity/why-americans-seek-opportunity-abroad; and A. Lam, "Go Far East, Young Man: Americans Abroad," *Huffington Post*, January 7, 2014, www.huffingtonpost.com/andrew-lam/go-far-east-young-man-ame_b_4556047.html (all accessed April 15, 2016). See also P. Caligiuri, "Developing Culturally Agile Global Business Leaders," *Organizational Dynamics*, July–September 2013, pp. 175–182.

55. R. C. Carter, senior vice president for human resources at A&E Television Networks, quoted in H. Chura, "A Year Abroad (or 3) as a Career Move," *The New York Times*, February 26, 2006, www.nytimes.com/2006/02/25/business/worldbusiness/25abroad.html?pagewanted=all&_r=0 (accessed March 9, 2016).

56. This definition was adapted from A. K. Gupta, V. Govindarajan, and H. Wang, *The Quest for Global Dominance: Transforming Global Presence into Global Competitive Advantage*, 2nd ed. (San Francisco: Jossey-Bass, 2008). See "Definition of Global Mindset," *Financial Times*, http://lexicon.ft.com/Term?term=global-mindset (accessed March 14, 2016).

57. "Definition of Global Mindset."

58. K. Reinhard, quoted in S. McCartney, "Teaching Americans How to Behave Abroad," *The Wall Street Journal*, April 11, 2006, pp. D1, D4. See also Yu, "Cultural Training Has Global Appeal."

59. *The World Citizens Guide* is available at www.worldcitizensguide.org/pressDownloads/WorldCitizensGuide.pdf.

60. DDB Worldwide survey, cited in J. Clark, "That 'Ugly American' Image is Getting a Makeover Guide," *USA Today*, April 28, 2006, p. 9D.

61. K. Reinhardt, interviewed in "Business for Diplomatic Action," *PBS.org*, May 22, 2006, www.pbs.org/pov/borders/2006/talk/keith_reinhard/000239.html (accessed March 14, 2016).

62. Lowry and Balfour, "It's All about the Face-to-Face."

63. E. Schmitt, "A Man Does Not Ask a Man about His Wife," *The New York Times*, January 8, 2006, sec. 4, p. 7.

64. D. K. Tatlow, "Cautious Chinese Gain Comfort with Hugs," *The New York Times*, May 9, 2014, p. A6.

65. For examples of correct business card etiquette in China, see G. Stoller, "Cultural Studies Pay in China," *USA Today*, December 30, 2013, p. 4B.

66. T. Rivas, "Name Game Hits a Global Roadblock," *The Wall Street Journal*, May 30, 2006, p. B5.

67. B. Morris, "The Pepsi Challenge: Can This Snack and Soda Giant Go Healthy?" *Fortune*, March 3, 2008, pp. 55–56.

68. L. Nardon and R. M. Steers, "The New Global Manager: Learning Cultures on the Fly," *Organizational Dynamics*, January–March 2008, pp. 47–59.

69. "The Biggest Companies in the World in 2015," *The Telegraph*, July 22, 2015, www.telegraph.co.uk/business/2015/02/11/the-biggest-companies-in-the-world-in-2015/toyota-car (accessed March 10, 2016).

70. E. Matchar, "Can't Find a Job? Move Overseas," *The Washington Post*, November 23, 2012, https://www.washingtonpost.com/opinions/cant-find-a-job-move-overseas/2012/11/23/b7322ef4-3273-11e2-9cfa-e41bac906cc9_story.html (accessed March 9, 2016).

71. Study by The Boston Consulting Group and The Network, reported in E. Martin, "59% of Millennials in the U.S. Would Move to Another Country for a Job," *Business Insider*, October 7, 2014, www.businessinsider.com/millennials-moving-abroad-for-jobs-2014-10; and online poll by Transferwise, reported in S. Whitten, "Survey Says: 35 Percent of Americans Would Expatriate," *CNBC*, July 1, 2015, www.cnbc.

com/2015/06/30/survey-says-35-percent-of-americans-would-expatriate.html (both accessed March 9, 2016).

72. R. Florida, "Why Americans Seek Opportunity Abroad," *The New York Times*, July 22, 2013, www.nytimes.com/roomfordebate/2012/01/08/is-the-us-still-a-land-of-opportunity/why-americans-seek-opportunity-abroad (accessed March 9, 2016).

73. J. Haltiwanger, "Working Abroad Makes You More Versatile, Creative, and Successful," *Elite Daily*, June 12, 2015, http://elitedaily.com/life/culture/working-abroad-versatile-creative-successful/1062445 (accessed March 9, 2016).

74. C. M. Gray, "The Smart Career Move You Haven't Considered: Working Abroad," *Forbes*, October 11, 2013, www.forbes.com/sites/dailymuse/2013/10/11/the-smart-career-move-you-havent-considered-working-abroad (accessed March 9, 2016).

75. J. Iman, "Studying Abroad Could Give You an Edge in the Job Market," *CNN*, April 4, 2014, www.cnn.com/2014/03/25/travel/irpt-study-abroad (accessed March 9, 2016).

76. Data from J. Costanzo and A. K. von Koppenfels, "Counting the Uncountable: Overseas Americans," *Migration Information Source*, May 17, 2013, Migration Policy Institute, www.migrationpolicy.org/article/counting-uncountable-overseas-americans (March 9, 2016).

77. N. Bloom and J. Van Reenen, "Why Do Management Practices Differ across Firms and Countries?" *Journal of Economic Perspectives*, Winter 2010, pp. 203–224.

78. G. Stoller, "Doing Business Abroad? Simple Faux Pas Can Sink You," *USA Today*, August 24, 2007, pp. 1B, 2B.

79. G. Stoller, "Doing Business Abroad? Simple Faux Pas Can Sink You," *USA Today*, August 24, 2007, pp. 1B, 2B.

80. M. R. Haas and J. N. Cummings, "Barriers to Knowledge Seeking within MNC Teams: Which Differences Matter Most?" *Journal of International Business Studies*, Vol. 46, Issue 1 (2015), pp. 36–62.

81. See S. Cerocke, "Some Business Functions Are Worth Outsourcing," *Reno Gazette-Journal*, December 12, 2013, p. 5A.

82. J. Rae-Dupree, "U.S. Scientists Are Leaving the Country and Taking the Innovation Economy with Them," *Forbes*, September 25, 2013, www.forbes.com/sites/janetraedupree/2013/09/25/us-scientists-are-leaving-the-country-and-taking-the-innovation-economy-with-them/#7d58dd6a67af (accessed March 10, 2016).

83. See, for example, J. Edelson, "The True Cost of Offshoring Your App Development," *Forbes*, May 29, 2014, www.forbes.com/sites/theyec/2014/05/29/the-true-cost-of-offshoring-your-app-development/#24fdcfd91c73 (accessed March 10, 2016).

84. T. C. Frohlich and M. B. Sauter, "Ten Classic American Brands That Are Foreign-Owned," *24/7 Wall St.*, November 26, 2013, http://247wallst.com/special-report/2013/11/26/ten-classic-american-brands-that-are-foreign-owned; and M. Mabe, "Famous American Brands in Non-American Hands," *Bloomberg Business*, www.bloomberg.com/ss/08/07/0709_icons/1.htm (accessed March 9, 2016).

85. D. A. Heenan and H. V. Perlmutter, *Multinational Organization Development* (Reading, MA: Addison-Wesley, 1979). See also M. Javidan and D. Bowen, "The 'Global Mindset' of Managers," *Organizational Dynamics*, April 1, 2013, pp. 145–155.

86. D. Jones, "Do Foreign Executives Balk at Sports Jargon?" *USA Today*, March 30, 2007, pp. 1B, 2B.

87. R. Kopp, "International Human Resource Policies and Practices in Japanese, European, and United States Multinationals," *Human Resource Management*, Winter 1994, pp. 581–599. For more on ethnocentrism, see C. Storti, "The Argument for Ethnocentrism," *Profiles in Diversity Journal*, June 5, 2012, www.diversityjournal.com/9336-the-argument-for-ethnocentrism (accessed August 10, 2016); and D. Weinstein, "Exploring Ethnocentrism in Business Courses and Business," *Business and Management Research*, September 10, 2013, Vol. 2, No. 3 (2013), pp. 120–136.

88. C. Duhigg and K. Bradsher, "How U.S. Lost Out on iPhone Work," *The New York Times*, January 22, 2012, News section, pp. 1, 22, 23; "How iPhone Is Made: The Global Assembly Line," *FinancesOnline.com*, http://financesonline.com/hello-world-the-economics-of-iphone (accessed March 9, 2016); and C. Minasians, "Where Are the iPhone, iPad, and Mac Designed, Made, and Assembled: A Comprehensive Breakdown of Apple's Product Supply Chain," *Macworld*, January 27, 2016, www.macworld.co.uk/feature/apple/are-apple-products-truly-designed-in-california-made-in-china-3633832 (accessed March 9, 2016).

89. W. J. Holstein, "Colonial Roots Have Spread Worldwide," *The New York Times*, June 16, 2007, p. B3; and J. R. Hagerty, "Ethan Allen Turns the Tables in China," *The Wall Street Journal*, January 2, 2013, http://online.wsj.com/news/articles/SB10001424127887323635504578213620282829396 (accessed April 15, 2016).

90. S. Ramachandran and M. Armental, "Netflix Adds More Overseas Subscribers," *The Wall Street Journal*, January 20, 2016; and E. Steel, "Netflix Accelerates Ambitious Global Expansion as U.S. Growth Slows," *The New York Times*, January 21, 2016, p. B3.

91. K. Yovino, "6 American Movies That Saw More Success Overseas," *Movies Cheat-Sheet*, January 18, 2016, www.cheatsheet.com/entertainment/6-u-s-films-that-had-more-success-overseas.html/?a=viewall (accessed March 14, 2016).

92. N. Purnell, "Apple Makes iPhone Push in India," *The Wall Street Journal*, January 21, 2016, p. B4.

93. P. Rana, "Ikea's India Bet Hits Thicket of Rules," *The Wall Street Journal*, February 24, 2016, pp. A1, A14.

94. C. Rogers and J. D. Stoll, "Ford to Shift Work Abroad," *The Wall Street Journal*, July 9, 2015, www.wsj.com/articles/ford-to-move-current-small-car-production-outside-u-s-1436463445 (accessed March 14, 2016). See also C. Rogers, "Ford to More Than Double Mexico Production Capacity in 2018," *The Wall Street Journal*, February 8, 2016, www.wsj.com/articles/ford-to-more-than-double-mexico-production-capacity-in-2018-1454857923 (accessed March 14, 2016).

95. B. Elbiri, "With a Following Abroad, Woody Allen Banks His Laughs in Euros," *Bloomberg Businessweek*, July 31, 2013, www.businessweek.com/articles/2013-07-31/woody-allens-blue-jasmine-banks-its-laughs-in-euros (accessed April 15, 2016). See also N. Kulish and M. Cieply, "Around World in One Movie: Film Financing's Global Future," *The New York Times*, December 6, 2011, pp. A1, A3.

96. R. Hagerty and M. Magnier, "Companies Tiptoe Back toward 'Made in the U.S.A.,'" *The Wall Street Journal*, January 13, 2015, www.wsj.com/articles/companies-tiptoe-back-toward-made-in-the-u-s-a-1421206289; M. Woolhouse, "Some Offshored Manufacturing Jobs Return to U.S.," *Boston Globe*, July 26, 2015, https://www.bostonglobe.com/business/2015/07/26/some-companies-bringing-manufacturing-back-mass-from-overseas/GdJ3H5CGA9d8QFaFI6BAUN/story.html; and "In the Changing Global Supply Chain, There's No 'Shore' Thing," *Knowledge@Wharton*, March 3, 2016, http://knowledge.wharton.upenn.edu/article/rebalancing-the-global-supply-chain (all accessed March 14, 2016).

97. D. Cave, "As Ties with China Unravel, U.S. Companies Head to Mexico," *The New York Times*, June 1, 2014, p. A6.

98. A. Hersch and and E. Gurwitz, "Offshoring Work Is Taking a Toll on the American Economy," Center for American Progress, July 30, 2014, www.americanprogress.org/issues/economy/news/2014/07/30/94864/offshoring-work-is-taking-a-toll-on-the-u-s-economy; and A. Hersch, "Why Wages Are Not Returning as Job Growth Increases," Center for American Progress, January 12, 2015, https://www.americanprogress.org/issues/economy/news/2015/01/12/104179/why-wages-are-not-returning-as-job-growth-increases (accessed March 14, 2016).

99. *The Low-Wage Recovery and Growing Inequality*, National Employment Law Project, August 2012, www.nelp.org/content/uploads/2015/03/LowWageRecovery2012.pdf; and *Tracking the Low-Wage Recovery*, National Employment Law Project, April 27, 2014, www.nelp.org/publication/tracking-the-low-wage-recovery-industry-employment-wages (accessed March 14, 2016).

100. "Jobs Overseas Outsourcing Statistics," Statistic Brain Research Institute, www.statisticbrain.com/outsourcing-statistics-by-country (accessed March 14, 2016).

101. B. Schlender, "Peter Drucker Sets Us Straight," *Fortune*, January 12, 2004, pp. 115–118.

102. J. Thottam, "Is Your Job Going Abroad?" *Time*, March 1, 2004, pp. 26–34.

103. F. Levy, quoted in D. Wessel, "The Future of Jobs: New Ones Arise, Wage Gap Widens," *The Wall Street Journal*, April 2, 2004, pp. A1, A5.

104. A. M. Chaker, "Where the Jobs Are," *The Wall Street Journal*, March 18, 2004, pp. D1, D3; J. Shinal, "Which Types of Jobs Will Be in Demand?" *San Francisco Chronicle*, March 25, 2004, pp. C1, C4; and D. Wessel, "The Future of Jobs: New Ones Arise, Wage Gap Widens," *The Wall Street Journal*, April 2, 2004, pp. A1, A5. For some caveats about offshoring, see M. Bolch, "Going Global," *Training*, January 2008, pp. 28–29; M. Weinstein, "On Target Offshore," *Training*, January 2008, pp. 34–36; and M. Bandyk, "Now Even Small Firms Can Go Global," *U.S. News & World Report*, March 10, 2008, p. 52. See also A. Kiersz, "The 20 Best Jobs of the Future," *Business Insider*, January 22, 2014, www.businessinsider.com/best-jobs-of-the-future-2014-1; M. Grothaus, "The Top Jobs in 10 Years Might Not Be What You Expect," *Fast Company*, May 18, 2015, www.fastcompany.com/3046277/the-new-rules-of-work/the-top-jobs-in-10-years-might-not-be-what-you-expect; and *The Future of Jobs: Employment, Skills, and Workforce Strategy for the Fourth Industrial Revolution*, World Economic Forum, January 2016, www3.weforum.org/docs/WEF_FOJ_Executive_Summary_Jobs.pdf (all accessed March 14, 2016).

105. E. A. Spiegel, "America Can 'Insource' Jobs through Innovation," *USA Today*, January 25, 2012, p. 11A.

106. J. Spohrer, quoted in Shinal, "Which Types of Jobs Will Be in Demand?"

107. J. Shinal, "Which Types of Jobs Will Be in Demand?" *San Francisco Chronicle*, March 25, 2004, pp. C1, C4.

108. B. Schlender, "Peter Drucker Sets Us Straight," *Fortune*, January 12, 2004, pp. 115–118.

109. P. Drucker, quoted in Schlender, "Peter Drucker Sets Us Straight."

110. Analysis of Labor Department statistics by Economic Policy Institute, Washington, D.C., reported in D. Leonhardt, "Is College Worth It? Clearly, New Data Say," *The New York Times*, May 27, 2014, www.nytimes.com/2014/05/27/upshot/is-college-worth-it-clearly-new-data-say.html?_r=0 (accessed March 14, 2015). See also S. Y. Lee, Y. Shin, and D. Lee, "The Option Value of Human Capital: Higher Education and Wage Inequality," *NBER Working Paper No. 21724*, November 2015, National Bureau of Economic Research. They write, "In the early 1980s, American men with at least four years of college education earned about 40% more on average than those whose education ended with high school. By 2005, the college wage premium rose to above 90%."

111. "Annual Earnings of Young Adults," *Current Population Survey*, updated May 2015, National Center for Education Statistics, https://nces.ed.gov/programs/coe/indicator_cba.asp (accessed March 27, 2016).

112. M. Bartiromo, "Toys R Us Makes Play for Global Sales," *USA Today*, December 19, 2011, p. 4B; "Toys 'R' Us Launches E-Commerce Site in Poland," *Ecommerce News*, October 17, 2014, http://ecommercenews.eu/toysrus-launches-ecommerce-site-in-poland (accessed March 14, 2016); S. Finz, "Gap Turning to Foreign Market," *San Francisco Chronicle*, October 14, 2011, pp. D1, D6; P. Rana, "A Sneak-Peek Inside Gap's First India Store," *The Wall Street Journal*, May 29, 2015, http://blogs.wsj.com/indiarealtime/2015/05/29/a-sneak-peek-inside-gaps-first-india-store (accessed March 14, 2016); "Tiffany Opens First Store in Russia," *Zacks*, June 4, 2013, www.zacks.com/stock/news/100746/Tiffany-Opens-First-Store-in-Russia, and "Tiffany Opens Its First Store in Bangkok, Thailand," Tiffany & Co. press release, July 1, 2015, http://press.tiffany.com/News/NewsItem.aspx?id=266 (both accessed March 14, 2016); J. Jargon and D. Molinski, "Can Starbucks Sell Its Coffee in Colombia?" *The Wall Street Journal*, August 27, 2013, p. B3; and D. White, "Starbucks to Open First Store in Italy," *Time*, February 29, 2016, http://time.com/4241023/starbucks-to-open-first-store-in-italy (accessed March 14, 2016).

113. J. Newcomer, "Guess Who Save the Buick? China," *Consumer Warning Network*, August 24, 2010, www.consumerwarningnetwork.com/2010/08/24/guess-who-saved-the-buick-china/; and M. Oberman, "GM Bests Americans Will Buy Cars Made in China," *Yahoo! News*, January 10, 2016, http://news.yahoo.com/gm-bets-americans-buy-cars-made-china-052846718.html;_ylt=A86.J72TiONWehwAD0OnnIIQ;_ylu=X3o DMTEyM243czlhBGNvbG8DZ3ExBHBvcwM5BHZ0aWQDQjE3MThfMQRzZWMDc3l- (both accessed March 11, 2016).

114. K. Bradsher, "China's Embrace of Foreign Cars," *The New York Times*, April 9, 2014, pp. B1, B6.

115. K. Bradsher, "7 U.S. Solar Panel Makers File Case Accusing China of Violating Trade Rules," *The New York Times*, October 20, 2011, pp. B1, B10. See also E. Wesoff, "Reports: Hint of a Settlement in the U.S.-China Solar Panel Trade Case," *Greentech Solar*, March 18, 2014, www.greentechmedia.com/articles/read/Reports-Hints-of-a-Settlement-in-the-US-China-Solar-Panel-Trade-Case (accessed April 15, 2016).

116. M. L. Wald and K. Bradsher, "4 U.S. Makers of Towers for Wind Turbines File Complaint over China's Steel Subsidies," *The New York Times*, December 30, 2011, p. B2.

117. S. Terlep, "Auto Makers Face Changes in China," *The Wall Street Journal*, January 6, 2012, p. B4.

118. A. Young, "$724,000 for a Ferrari? China's Rich Are Getting Shafted Buying Luxury Cars, but Who's Ripping Them Off?" *International Business Times*, July 31, 2013, www.ibtimes.com/724000-ferrari-chinas-rich-are-getting-shafted-buying-luxury-cars-whos-ripping-them-1365037 (accessed March 12, 2016).

119. "China to Cancel Car Import Quota in 2005," *China Daily*, February 13, 2004, www.chinadaily.com.cn/english/doc/2004-02/13/content_305954.htm (accessed January 31, 2012).

120. M. Levi and E. Economy, "China Runs into Natural Resources Pushback," *The Wall Street Journal*, April 4, 2014, p. A11.

121. K. Maher and H. J. Pulizzi, "Chinese Slapped in Steel Dispute," *The Wall Street Journal*, December 31, 2009, p. A3; and R. G. Matthews, "U.S. Levies Antidumping Duty on Chinese Pipes," *The Wall Street Journal*, January 5, 2011, http://online.wsj.com/news/articles/SB10001424052748704723104576062093718977006 (accessed April 15, 2016).

122. P. Baker, "U.S. Will Restore Full Relations with Cuba, Erasing a Last Trace of Cold War Hostility," *The New York Times*, December 18, 2014, p. A1; and A. Mallin, "President Obama and the First Family Arrive in Cuba for Historic Visit," *ABC News*, March 20, 2016, http://abcnews.go.com/US/president-obama-family-arrive-cuba-historic-visit/story?id=37791583 (accessed March 31, 2016).

123. See A. Gomez, "U.S. Approves More Business Trade with Cuba," *Reno Gazette-Journal*, January 27, 2016, p. 5B, reprinted from *USA Today*; F. Schwartz and C. E. Lee, "Deals in Offing for U.S. Firms in Cuba," *The Wall Street Journal*, March 12–13, 2016, pp. A1, A8; and Associated Press, "U.S. Punches New Holes in Trade Embargo," *San Francisco Chronicle*, March 16, 2016, p. A4.

124. These definitions are found in "What Are Embargoes and Sanctions?" New York District Export Council, www.newyorkdec.org/what-are-embargoes-and-sanctions.html (accessed March 13, 2016).

125. P. Mozur, "U.S. Restricts Sales to the Chinese Phone Maker ZTE, Saying It Breached Sanctions," *The New York Times*, March 8, 2016, p. B3.

126. J. Bhagwati, *Protectionism* (Cambridge, MA: MIT Press, 1988).

127. See "Global Trade After Doha's Failure," editorial, *The New York Times*, January 1, 2016, p. A18.

128. C. H. Lin, "Role of Foreign Direct Investment in Telecommunication Industries: A Developing Countries' Perspective," *Contemporary Management Research*, March 2008, pp. 29–42; and M. A. Yusuf and K. Coghill, "Unilateral Liberalisation and WTO GATS Commitments: The Telecommunications Sector in Selected Countries," *Asian-Pacific Economic Literature*, January 2010, pp. 43–64.

129. N. Lakhani, "World Bank's Ethics under Scrutiny after Honduras Loan Investigation," *The Guardian*, January 13, 2014, www.theguardian.com/global-development/poverty-matters/2014/jan/13/world-bank-ethics-scrutiny-honduras-loan-investigation (accessed April 15, 2016).

130. J. Northam, "The World Bank Gets an Overhaul—and Not Everyone's Happy," *Parallels*, National Public Radio, March 13, 2014, www.npr.org/blogs/parallels/2014/03/13/289819931/the-world-bank-gets-an-overhaul-and-not-everyones-happy (accessed April 15, 2016).

131. A. Lowrey, "World Bank to Lift Lending to Developing Countries," *The New York Times*, April 2, 2014, p. A3.

132. A. Lowrey, "International Monetary Fund Offers Short-Term Credit as Insurance for Nations," *The New York Times*, November 23, 2011, p. B4.

133. Associated Press, "IMF Says Wealth Gaps Can Hurt Economic Growth," *San Francisco Chronicle*, March 14, 2014, p. C3; E. Porter, "In New Tack, IMF Aims at Income Inequality," *The New York Times*, April 9, 2014, pp. B1, B2; and A. Lowrey, "After Slide, Rich Nations Now Lifting Growth, IMF Reports," *The New York Times*, April 9, 2014, p. B2. See also I. Talley, "IMF Chief Urges Bigger Global Financial Safety Net," *The Wall Street Journal*, February 4, 2016, www.wsj.com/articles/imf-chief-urges-bigger-global-financial-safety-net-1454602504 (accessed March 11, 2016).

134. "Congress Gets Out of the IMF's Way," editorial, *The New York Times*, December 22, 2015, p. A24; and J. Calmes, "Deal to Overhaul IMF May Give U.S. a Vital Lift," *The New York Times*, January 7, 2016, pp. B1, B4.

135. M. A. Villarreal and I. F. Fergusson, *The North American Free Trade Agreement*, Congressional Research Service, April 16, 2015, www.fas.org/sgp/crs/row/R42965.pdf (accessed March 14, 2016).

136. M. Stevenson, Associated Press, "NAFTA Alters Mexico in 20 Years, but Fails Many Economic Goals," *Reno Gazette-Journal*, January 2, 2014, pp. 6A, 5A. This view is echoed in M. A. Sergie, "NAFTA's Economic Impact," Council on Foreign Relations,

February 14, 2014, www.cfr.org/trade/naftas-economic-impact/p15790 (accessed March 11, 2016).

137. "NAFTA's 20-Year Legacy and the Fate of the Trans-Pacific Partnership," Public Citizen's Global Trade Watch, February 2014, www.citizen.org/documents/NAFTA-at-20.pdf (accessed April 15, 2016).

138. Wharton management professor Mauro Guillen, reported in "NAFTA, 20 Years Later: Do the Benefits Outweigh the Costs?" *Knowledge@Wharton*, February 19, 2014, https://knowledge.wharton.upenn.edu/article/nafta-20-years-later-benefits-outweigh-costs (accessed April 15, 2016).

139. R. E. Scott, "Fast Track to Lost Jobs and Lower Wages," *Huffington Post*, April 12, 2015, www.huffingtonpost.com/robert-e-scott/fast-track-to-lost-jobs-a_b_7042270.html (accessed August 10, 2016).

140. Howard Dean, quoted as guest on "The Last Word With Lawrence O'Donnell," MSNBC, transcript, April 21, 2915, www.msnbc.com/transcripts/the-last-word/2015-04-21 (accessed March 14, 2016).

141. K. Amadeo, "GDP per Capita," *About.com*, January 20, 2016 http://useconomy.about.com/od/glossary/g/Gdp-Per-Capita.htm (accessed March 11, 2016).

142. See, for example, "Euro Could Replace Dollar as Top Currency—Greenspan," Reuters, September 17, 2007, www.reuters.com/article/greenspan-euro-idUSL1771147920070917 (accessed March 11, 2016).

143. V. Pop, "Europe Seeks to Restore Its Open Borders," *The Wall Street Journal*, March 5–6, 2016, p. A7.

144. W. Mauldin, "Trade Pact's Gains Seen as Uneven," *The Wall Street Journal*, January 7, 2016, p. A7.

145. World Bank, *Global Economic Prospects: Potential Macroeconomic Implications of the Trans-Pacific Partnership Agreement*, January 2016, www.worldbank.org/content/dam/Worldbank/GEP/GEP2016a/Global-Economic-Prospects-January-2016-Implications-Trans-Pacific-Partnership-Agreement.pdf (accessed March 12, 2016).

146. J. Papier, "The Incredible Shrinking Dollar," PWJohnson Wealth Management, www.pwjohnson.com/resources/articles/falling_dollar.pdf (accessed April 15, 2016).

147. Cost of Living Comparison between Chicago (United States) and London (United Kingdom), Expatistan, August 10, 2016, www.expatistan.com/cost-of-living/comparison/chicago/london (accessed August 10, 2016).

148. The financial analyst was Jim O'Neill of Goldman Sachs, who coined the term BRIC in 2001; it became BRICS in 2010 after the inclusion of South Africa. See W. Bello, "The BRICS: Challengers to the Global Status Quo," *Foreign Policy in Focus*, August 29, 2014, http://fpif.org/brics-challengers-global-status-quo (accessed March 11, 2016).

149. See P. Gillespie, "Russia and China Have Had Enough of Western Banking," *CNN Money*, May 4, 2015, http://money.cnn.com/2015/05/04/news/economy/russia-approves-brics-reserve-bank-imf (accessed March 11, 2016).

150. C. A. Kupchan, "The World in 2050: When the 5 Largest Economies Are the BRICs and Us," *The Atlantic*, February 17, 2012, www.theatlantic.com/business/archive/2012/02/the-world-in-2050-when-the-5-largest-economies-are-the-brics-and-us/253160 (accessed March 11, 2016).

151. A. Riley, "No, the BRICS Aren't Overtaking America," *The Daily Beast*, December 12, 2015, www.thedailybeast.com/articles/2015/12/13/no-the-brics-aren-t-overtaking-america.html (accessed March 12, 2016).

152. See R. Chidambaram, interviewed in Knowledge@Wharton radio show, "Investing in Asia: Why Challenging Does Not Mean Impossible," *Knowledge@Wharton*, February 17, 2016, http://knowledge.wharton.upenn.edu/article/investing-in-challenging-markets-like-asia (accessed March 12, 2016).

153. D. Levin, "China Entices, but Doing Business Proves Hard," *The New York Times*, November 4, 2015, pp. B1, B8.

154. See L. Elliott, "World Bank Issues 'Perfect Storm' Warning for 2016," *The Guardian*, January 5, 2016, www.theguardian.com/business/2016/jan/06/world-bank-perfect-storm-warning-2016-slowdown-brics-economies (accessed March 12, 2016); R. Foroohar, "Made in China: The Next Global Recession," *Time*, January 25, 2016, pp. 35–38; and M. Zhao and B. Naughton, "Trouble Ahead: What's Next for the Chinese Economy?" *Knowledge@Wharton*, March 9, 2016, http://knowledge.wharton.upenn.edu/article/naughton-zhao-chinese-economy (accessed March 12, 2016).

155. P. Eavis, "Worth Trillions, Bad Loans Haunt Global Economy," *The New York Times*, February 4, 2016, pp. A1, B4.

156. A. Shell, "China Angst Shows Fragility of Global Markets," *Reno Gazette-Journal*, January 5, 2016, p. 4B, reprinted from *USA Today*. See also R. Barley, "China Could Redraw the Markets' Map," *The Wall Street Journal*, March 10, 2016, p. C10.

157. E. Wong and N. Gough, "China Boldly Tries to Steer Economic Narrative," *The New York Times*, February 26, 2016, pp. A1, B5.

158. Riley, "No, the BRICS Aren't Overtaking America."

159. "Will India Overcome Challenges to Build Smart Cities?" *Knowledge@Wharton*, February 26, 2016, http://knowledge.wharton.upenn.edu/article/will-india-build-its-smart-cities (accessed March 12, 2016).

160. S. McClain, "India to Become World's Second-Largest Internet User Base," *The Wall Street Journal*, November 17, 2015, www.wsj.com/articles/india-to-become-worlds-second-largest-internet-user-base-1447776612 (accessed March 13, 2016).

161. *Global Trends 2030: Alternative Worlds*, National Intelligence Council, December 2012, https://globaltrends2030.files.wordpress.com/2012/11/global-trends-2030-november2012.pdf (accessed March 13, 2016).

162. "Brazil: Country at a Glance," The World Bank, www.worldbank.org/en/country/brazil (accessed March 13, 2016).

163. K. Allen, "Brazil's Economy Slumps to 25-Year Low," *The Guardian*, March 3, 2016, www.theguardian.com/business/2016/mar/03/brazil-economy-low-oil-prices-inflation (accessed March 13, 2016).

164. M. Dickerson and L. Magalhaes, "Brazil's Seniors Are Fine When They Cut the Line," *The Wall Street Journal*, February 24, 2016, pp. A1, A14.

165. Dean Foster, president of Dean Foster Associates, an intercultural consulting firm, quoted in T. Mohn, "Going Global, Going Stateside," *The New York Times*, March 9, 2010, p. B8.

166. C. Sang-Hun, "In Korea, Spam Is the Stuff Gifts Are Made Of," *The New York Times*, January 27, 2014, pp. A1, A7.

167. "How Cultures Collide," *Psychology Today*, July 1976, p. 69.

168. See P. R. Harris and R. T. Moran, *Managing Cultural Differences*, 4th ed. (Houston: Gulf Publishing, 1996), pp. 223–228; and M. Hilling, "Avoid Expatriate Culture Shock," *HR Magazine*, July 1993, pp. 58–63. See also R. J. Reichard, S. A. Serrano, M. Condren, N. Wilder, M. Dollwet, and W. Wang, "Engagement in Cultural Trigger Events in the Development of Cultural Competence," *Academy of Management Learning & Education*, Vol. 14, No. 4 (2015), pp. 461–481; and S. Ciffe, "Companies Don't Go Global, People Do," *Harvard Business Review*, October 2015, pp. 82–88.

169. For complete details, see G. Hofstede, *Culture's Consequences: International Differences in Work-Related Values*, abridged ed. (Newbury Park, CA: Sage, 1984); "The Interaction between National and Organizational Value Systems," *Journal of Management Studies*, July 1985, pp. 347–357; and "Management Scientists Are Human," *Management Science*, January 1994, pp. 4–13.

170. M. Javidan and R. J. House, "Cultural Acumen for the Global Manager: Lessons from Project GLOBE," *Organizational Dynamics*, Spring 2001, pp. 289–305; R. J. House, P. J. Hanges, M. Javidan, P. W. Dorfman, and V. Gupta, eds., *Culture, Leadership, and Organizations: The GLOBE Study of 62 Societies* (Thousand Oaks, CA: Sage, 2004); and M. Javidan, P. W. Dorfman, M. S. de Luque, and R. J. House, "In the Eye of the Beholder: Cross Cultural Lessons in Leadership from Project GLOBE," *Academy of Management Perspectives*, February 2006, pp. 67–90.

171. See J. Marcus and H. Le, "Interactive Effects of Levels of Individualism–Collectivism on Cooperation: A Meta-Analysis," *Journal of Organizational Behavior*, August 2013, pp. 813–834.

172. On this note, see B. S. Reiche, P. Cardona, Y.-T. Lee et al., "Why Do Managers Engage in Trustworthy Behavior? A Multilevel Cross-Cultural Study in 18 Countries," *Personnel Psychology*, Vol. 67, No. 1 (2014), pp. 61–98.

173. See S. Davis, "The State of Global Leadership Development," Training, July/August 2015, pp. 52–55.

174. A discussion of Japanese stereotypes in America can be found in L. Smith, "Fear and Loathing of Japan," *Fortune*, February 26, 1990, pp. 50–57. See also V. Taras, P. Steel, and B. L. Kirkman, "Three Decades of Research on National Culture in the Workplace: Do the Differences Still Make a Difference?" *Organizational Dynamics*, Vol. 40 (2001), pp. 189–198.

175. T. Neeley, "Global Business Speaks English," *Harvard Business Review*, May 2012, pp. 116–124.

176. G. A. Michaelson, "Global Gold," *Success*, March 1996, p. 16. English is increasingly becoming the language of business and more and more is being taught in foreign business universities. See D. Carvajal, "English as Language of Global Education," *The New York Times*, April 11, 2007, p. A21.

177. M. Dingemanse, F. Torreira, and N. J. Enfield, "Is 'Huh?' a Universal Word? Conversational Infrastructure and the Convergent Evolution of Linguistic Items," *PLOS ONE*, November 8, 2013. doi:10.1371/journal.pone.0078273.

178. Harris Poll, National Foreign Language Center, reported in "Lingua Franca?" *USA Today*, February 23, 1999, p. 1A; and "How Many People in the World Speak English 2013?" *Exploredia*, February 25, 2011, http://exploredia.com/how-many-people-in-the-world-speak-english-2013 (accessed April 15, 2016).

179. D. Einstein, "Free Translation Apps Can Turn Smart Phone into Interpreter," *San Francisco Chronicle*, August 8, 2011, p. D1. See also A. Ross, "You Will Speak Every Language," *The Wall Street Journal*, January 30–31, 2016, p. C3.

180. December 2011 Gallup poll, reported in C. Aylott, "Chinese Is Third Most-Offered Foreign Language in U.S. Schools," *Emerging Money*, February 14, 2012, www.nasdaq.com/article/chinese-is-third-mostoffered-foreign-language-in-us-schools-cm120643 (accessed March 14, 2016).

181. Samir Khalaf, quoted in H.M. Fattah, "Why Arab Men Hold Hands," *The New York Times*, May 1, 2005, sec. 34, p. 2.

182. "How Cultures Collide."

183. Kari Heistad, CEO of Culture Coach International, quoted in E. Maltby, "Expanding Abroad? Avoid Cultural Gaffes," *The Wall Street Journal*, January 19, 2010, p. B5. See also L. Nardon, R. M. Steers, and C. J. Sanchez-Runde, "Seeking Common Ground: Strategies for Enhancing Multicultural Communication, *Organizational Dynamics*, Vol. 40 (2011), pp. 85–95.

184. Neil Currie, quoted in K. Tyler, "Global Ease," *HR Magazine*, May 2011, pp. 41–48. For more about negotiating across cultures, see E. Meyer, "Getting to *si, Ja, Oui, Hai*, and *Da*," *Harvard Business Review*, December 2015, pp. 74–80.

185. Michael Norman, senior vice president at Sibson Consulting, quoted in H. Seligson, "For American Workers in China, a Culture Clash," *The New York Times*, December 24, 2009, pp. B1, B2.

186. K. Seong-Kon, writing in *The Korea Herald*, summarized in "A Society That Needs No Appointment," *The Week*, May 29, 2009, p. 14.

187. E. T. Hall, *The Hidden Dimension* (New York: Doubleday, 1966).

188. Miguel Carbayo, quoted in J. Yardley, "Spain, Land of 10 P.M. Dinner, Ponders a More Standard Time," *The New York Times*, February 18, 2014, pp. A1, A12.

189. D. Roman, "In Spain, It Can Be a Pain to Keep Up with the Clock," *The Wall Street Journal*, October 25, 2013, pp. A1, A12.

190. D. Roman, "In Spain, It Can Be a Pain to Keep Up with the Clock," *The Wall Street Journal*, October 25, 2013, pp. A1, A12.

191. Ignacio Buqueras, quoted in Yardley, "Spain, Land of 10 P.M. Dinner, Ponders a More Standard Time."

192. D. Roman, "In Spain, It Can Be a Pain to Keep Up with the Clock," *The Wall Street Journal*, October 25, 2013, pp. A1, A12.

193. See S. Ricker, CareerBuilder.com, "Workplace Behaviors around the World," *Reno Gazette-Journal*, November 10, 2013, p. 10D.

194. A. R. Sorkin, "A Financial Mirage in the Desert," *The New York Times*, December 1, 2009, pp. B1, B5.

195. Results adapted from and value definitions quoted from S. R. Safranski and I.-W. Kwon, "Religious Groups and Management Value Systems," in R. N. Farner and E. G. McGoun, eds., *Advances in International Comparative Management*, Vol. 3 (Greenwich, CT: JAI Press, 1988), pp. 171–183.

196. J. Forero and M. Armas, "Venezuela Data Show World's Top Inflation," *The Wall Street Journal*, February 19, 2016, p. A6.

197. See "Corruption Worsens in Conflict Areas," *San Francisco Chronicle*, December 4, 2013, p. A4, reprinted from *Los Angeles Times*.

198. Adapted from Adherents.com, "Major Religions of the World Ranked by Major Adherents," last modified August 9, 2007, www.adherents.com/Religions_By_Adherents.html (accessed March 14, 2016).

199. P. Mozur, "Fight at Foxconn Highlights Unrest at Chinese Factories," *The Wall Street Journal*, September 24, 2013, p. B5; E. Dou and P. Mozur, "iPhone Factory Deaths Dog Apple and Supplier Pegatron," *The Wall Street Journal*, December 12, 2013, p. B6; and K. O'Keeffe, "Underage Garment Workers Dodge Rules in Cambodia," *The Wall Street Journal*, December 30, 2013, pp. B1, B5.

200. B. Egelko, "Costco Sells Slave-Labor Seafood, Lawsuit Says," *San Francisco Chronicle*, August 20, 2015, pp. D1, D2.

201. Estimate by the International Labor Organization, reported in T. Lee, "Tech Joins Slavery Fight," *San Francisco Chronicle*, January 31, 2016, pp. D1, D3.

202. J. Costanzo and A. von Koppenfels, "Counting the Uncountable: Overseas Americans," *Migration Information Source*, May 17, 2013, www.migrationpolicy.org/article/counting-uncountable-overseas-americans (accessed April 15, 2016).

203. R. Feintzeig, "After Stints Abroad, Re-Entry Can Be Hard," *The Wall Street Journal*, September 18, 2013, p. B6.

204. J. S. Black and H. B. Gregersen, "The Way to Manage Expats," *Harvard Business Review*, March–April 1999, p. 53.

205. I. Urbina, "In Buying Cheap Clothes, U.S. Flouts Own Counsel," *The New York Times*, December 23, 2013, pp. A1, A6.

206. See A. Maingault, L. Albright, and V. Neal, "Policy Tips, Repatriation, Safe Harbor Rules," *HRMagazine*, March 2008, pp. 34–35.

207. S. Dallas, "Rule No. 1: Don't Diss the Locals," *BusinessWeek*, May 15, 1995, p. 8. Also see M. A. Shaffer, D. A. Harrison, H. Gregersen, J. S. Black, and L. A. Ferzandi, "You Can Take It with You: Individual Differences and Expatriate Effectiveness," *Journal of Applied Psychology*, January 2006, pp. 109–125.

208. Costco, *Wikipedia*, January 19, 2016.

209. R. Feintzeig, "After Stints Abroad, Re-Entry Can Be Hard," *The Wall Street Journal*, September 18, 2013, p. B6.

210. P. Soni, "An Investor's Guide to Costco Wholesale: A Growing Retailer," January 19, 2016, http://marketrealist.com/2016/01/analyzing-investment-fundamentals-costco-wholesale-corp/, (accessed January 21, 2016).

211. Trefis Team, "Costco Beats On Profits and Shows Significant Revenue Growth Potential," March 16, 2015, http://www.nasdaq.com/article/costco-beats-on-profits-and-shows-significant-revenue-growth-potential-cm455263, accessed January 19, 2016.

212. "Costco in Australia: Cultural Success," http://www.kwintessential.co.uk/resources/costco-australia-cultural-success.html, accessed January 27, 2016.

213. M. Dalton and S. Meichtry, "Rouhani Visit Ends on Note of Discord," *The Wall Street Journal*, January 29, 2016, p. A12.

214. M. Dalton and S. Meichtry, "Rouhani Visit Ends on Note of Discord," *The Wall Street Journal*, January 29, 2016, p. A12.

CHAPTER 5

1. D. H. Autor, "Skills, Education, and the Rise of Earnings Inequality among the 'Other 99 Percent,'" *Science*, May 23, 2014, pp. 843–851.

2. "Earnings and Unemployment Rates by Educational Attainment, 2015," *Current Population Survey*, U.S. Bureau of Labor Statistics, March 15, 2016, www.bls.gov/emp/ep_chart_001.htm (accessed March 28, 2016).

3. "The Rising Cost of Not Going to College," Pew Research Center, Social & Demographic Trends, February 11, 2014, www.pewsocialtrends.org/2014/02/11/the-rising-cost-of-not-going-to-college (accessed March 23, 2016).

4. K. Buckles, A. Hagemann, O Malamud, M. S. Morrill, and A. K. Wozniak, "The Effect of College Education on Health," *NBER Working Paper No. 19222*, July 2013, National Bureau of Economic Research, www.nber.org/papers/w19222 (accessed March 28, 2016).

5. "College Grads Happier," Pew Research Center, November 3, 2010, www.pewsocialtrends.org/2006/02/13/are-we-happy-yet/29-3 (accessed March 28, 2016).

6. See E. A. Locke and G. P. Latham, "Building a Practically Useful Theory of Goal Setting and Task Motivation," *American Psychologist*, September 2002, pp. 705–717.

7. B. Gleeson, "Setting Stretch Goals: All In, All the Time," *Inc.*, December 28, 2012, www.inc.com/brent-gleeson/setting-stretch-goals.html (accessed May 27, 2016).

8. C. Fussman, "Richard Branson: What I've Learned," *Esquire*, January 29, 2007, www.esquire.com/news-politics/interviews/a2037esq0102-jan-branson (accessed March 28, 2016).

9. S. B. Sitkin, K. E. See, C.C. Miller, M. W. Lawless, and A. M. Carton, "The Paradox of Stretch Goals: Organizations in Pursuit of the Seemingly Impossible," *Academy of Management Review*, Vol. 36, No. 3 (2011), pp. 544–566; and D. T. Welsh and L. D.

Ordóñez, "The Dark Side of Consecutive High Performance Goals: Linking Goal Setting, Depletion, and Unethical Behavior," *Organizational Behavior and Human Decision Processes,* Vol. 123, Issue 2 (2014), pp. 79–89.

10. See K. Unsworth, G. Yeo, and J. Beck, "Multiple Goals: A Review and Derivation of General Principles," *Journal of Organizational Behavior,* November 2014, pp. 1064–1078; and S. S. Wang, "Never Procrastinate Again," *The Wall Street Journal,* September 1, 2015, pp. D1, D2.

11. See C. Bentley, "'I'm Going to Do It!' versus Honoring Intention: How to Set Goals and Really Keep Them," *Business Strategy Series,* Vol. 15, No. 4 (2012), pp. 193–195; and K. L. Milkman and K. G. Volpp, "How to Keep Your Resolutions," *The New York Times,* January 5, 2014, p. SR-14.

12. C. Bentley, "'I'm Going to Do It!' versus Honoring Intention: How to Set Goals and Really Keep Them," p. 195.

13. Mark Zuckerberg, quoted in S. Murphy Kelly, "Facebook Changes Its 'Move Fast and Break Things' Motto," *Mashable,* April 30, 2014, http://mashable.com/2014/04/30/facebooks-new-mantra-move-fast-with-stability/#.4Lfl3bl7sqW (accessed March 19, 2016). See also S. Fiergerman, "Are Facebook's 'Move Fast and Break Things' Days Over?" *Mashable,* March 13, 2013, http://mashable.com/2014/03/13/facebook-move-fast-break-things/#XUbMhtL5H8qJ (accessed March 19, 2016).

14. R. Kreitner, *Management,* 11th ed. (Boston: Houghton Mifflin, 2008), p. 147.

15. Lucinda Cross, quoted in L. Furgison, "Lessons Learned: Without a Business Plan, I Had No Direction," Bplans, http://articles.bplans.com/lessons-learned-without-a-business-plan-i-had-no-direction (accessed March 23, 2016).

16. B. Honig and T. Karlsson, "Institutional Forces and the Written Business Plan," *Journal of Management,* Vol. 30, No. 1 (2004), pp. 29–48. See also F. Delmar and S. Shane, "Does Business Planning Facilitate the Development of New Ventures?" *Strategic Management Journal,* December 2003, pp. 1165–1185.

17. T. Berry, "Why Plan Your Business? Look at This Data," Bplans, http://timberry.bplans.com/real-data-on-the-success-of-business-planning.html (accessed March 24, 2016). See also R. Lesonsky, "A Business Plan Doubles Your Chances for Success, Says a New Survey," *Small Business Trends,* June 20, 2010, http://smallbiztrends.com/2010/06/business-plan-success-twice-as-likely.html (accessed March 24, 2016).

18. S. A. Shane, "Why Don't All Entrepreneurs Write Business Plans?" *The New York Times,* November 9, 2009, http://boss.blogs.nytimes.com/2009/11/09/why-dont-all-entrepreneurs-write-business-plans/comment-page-3/?_r=0 (accessed November 23, 2016).

19. Study by William Bygrave and others of Babson College graduates, reported in M. Henricks, "Do You Really Need a Business Plan?" *Entrepreneur,* December 2008, www.entrepreneur.com/article/198618 (accessed March 24, 2016).

20. W. D. Bygrave, J. E. Lange, A. Mollov, M. Pearlmutter, and S. Singh, "Pre-Startup Formal Business Plans and Post-Startup Performance: A Study of 116 New Ventures," *Venture Capital Journal,* October 2007, http://papers.ssrn.com/sol3/papers.cfm?abstract_id=1269484 (accessed March 24, 2016).

21. See also K. K. Spors, "Do Start-Ups Really Need Formal Business Plans?" *The Wall Street Journal,* January 9, 2007, p. B9.

22. Statistic from Amar Bhidé *Origin and Evolution of New Business,* reported in R. Finkelstein, "What Successful Companies Have in Common," *Entrepreneur,* February 24, 2006, www.entrepreneur.com/article/83764 (accessed March 24, 2016).

23. T. Kastelle, "Why Your Business Model Must Evolve," *The Discipline of Innovation,* May 26, 2012, http://timkastelle.org/blog/2012/05/why-your-business-model-must-evolve (accessed March 24, 2016).

24. D. Shah, "Fall in Love with Your Business, Not Your Business Plan," *OnStartups.com,* March 30, 2012, http://onstartups.com/tabid/3339/bid/80497/Fall-In-Love-With-Your-Business-Not-Your-Business-Plan.aspx (accessed March 24, 2016).

25. A. A. Thompson Jr. and A. J. Strickland III, *Strategic Management: Concepts and Cases,* 13th ed. (New York: McGraw-Hill/Irwin, 2003).

26. D. J. Collis and M. G. Rukstad, "Can You Say What Your Strategy Is?" *Harvard Business Review,* April 2008, pp. 82–90.

27. See G. Hamel, with B. Breen, *The Future of Management* (Boston: Harvard Business School Press, 2007), p. 191; and C. Rampell, "How Industries Survive Change, If They Do," *The New York Times,* November 16, 2008, Week in Review section, p. 3. For a discussion of the effect of the web on newspapers, see E. Alterman, "Out of Print," *The New Yorker,* March 31, 2008, pp. 48–59; P. R. Kann, "Quality Reporting Doesn't Come Cheap," *The Wall Street Journal,* September 26, 2009, p. A15; and B. Evangelista, "Internet Seen as Shaping Delivery, Sharing of News," *San Francisco Chronicle,* March 1, 2010, pp. D1, D2.

28. A. Busch III, quoted in interview with G. Hamel, "Turning Your Business Upside Down," *Fortune,* June 23, 1997, pp. 87–88.

29. L. G. Hrebiniak, "Obstacles to Effective Strategy Implementation," *Organizational Dynamics,* February 2006, pp. 12–31.

30. See R. L. Martin, "The Big Lie of Strategic Planning," *Harvard Business Review,* January–February 2014, pp. 79–84.

31. H. Mintzberg, "The Strategy Concept II: Another Look at Why Organizations Need Strategies," *California Management Review,* Vol. 30, No. 1 (1987), pp. 25–32.

32. G. Hamel, with B. Breen, *The Future of Management* (Boston: Harvard Business School Press, 2007), p. 191.

33. P. Cohan, "Five Commandments for Faster Growth," *Knowledge@Wharton,* March 9, 2016, http://knowledge.wharton.upenn.edu/article/five-commandments-for-faster-growth (accessed March 27, 2016).

34. V. Yee, "Where Did You Want That Pizza? In the Park, between the Trees," *The New York Times,* October 6, 2013, p. News-21; and J. Brustein, "People Want More Takeout, Ordered Online," *San Francisco Chronicle,* February 24, 2014, pp. D1, D3.

35. S. Berfield, "New Vending Machines Offer Fresher Items," *San Francisco Chronicle,* February 16, 2014, p. C3; and O. Kharif, "Personalized Prices May Become the Norm," *San Francisco Chronicle,* November 24, 2013, p. D3.

36. See R. G. McGrath, "Transient Advantage," *Harvard Business Review,* June 2013, pp. 61–70.

37. D. Clark and R. McMillan, "Giants Tighten Grip on Internet Economy," *The Wall Street Journal,* November 6, 2011, pp. B1, B4; and F. Manjoo, "'Frightful 5' to Dominate Digital Life a Long Time," *The New York Times,* January 21, 2016, pp. B1, B7. See also J. Graham, "Top Stories of 2015," *Reno Gazette-Journal,* January 2, 2016, p. 5B, reprinted from *USA Today;* the article reports that the companies dominating the 2015 tech headlines were Amazon, Apple, Facebook, and Google.

38. Clark and McMillan, "Giants Tighten Grip on Internet Economy."

39. Manjoo, "'Frightful 5' to Dominate Digital Life a Long Time."

40. See M. Anderson, "As Amazon Turns 20, a Look at Its Biggest Bets," *Reno Gazette-Journal,* July 19, 2015, pp. 1D, 5D.

41. Manjoo, "'Frightful 5' to Dominate Digital Life a Long Time."

42. M. Wolff, "The End of Yahoo Is Justly Near," *Reno Gazette-Journal,* December 21, 2016, p. 4B, reprinted from *USA Today;* J. Swartz, "The Inescapable Truth about Yahoo," *Reno Gazette-Journal,* January 2, 2016, p. 5B, reprinted from *USA Today;* W. Lee, "A Mixed Message from the Top at Yahoo," *San Francisco Chronicle,* February 20, 2016, pp. A1, A8; and V. Goel and L. Picker, "Yahoo Takes Formal Step toward a Possible Sale," *The New York Times,* February 20, 2016, p. B2.

43. Anshu Sharma, quoted in C. Mims, "Why Companies Are Being Disrupted," *The Wall Street Journal,* January 25, 2016, p. B4.

44. See C. Said, "Shuddle 'Uber for Kids' Service Reaches End of Road," *San Francisco Chronicle,* April 14, 2016, www.sfchronicle.com/business/article/Shuddle-Uber-for-kids-service-reaches-end-7249450.php. See also D. Martin, "A Verizon Vet Is Launching an 'Uber for Kids," *BostInno,* February 10, 2016, http://bostinno.streetwise.co/2016/02/10/transportation-for-children-zemcar-is-like-uber-for-kids (both accessed April 16, 2016). Also see E. Zimmerman, "Ride-Hailing Start-Ups Find Demand in 'Uber for Children' Niche," *The New York Times,* April 14, 2016, p. B4.

45. See J. B. Barney, "Firm Resources and Sustained Competitive Advantage," *Journal of Management,* Vol. 19 (1991), pp. 99–120.

46. E. Bernstein, "An Emotion We Need More of," *The Wall Street Journal,* March 22, 2016, pp. D1, D4.

47. P. F. Drucker, *The Practice of Management* (New York: Harper & Row, 1954), p. 122.

48. T. A. Stewart, "A Refreshing Change: Vision Statements That Make Sense," *Fortune,* September 30, 1996, pp. 195–196.

49. For application of vision to nonprofits, see A. Kilpatrick and L. Silverman, "The Power of Vision," *Strategy & Leadership,* February 2005, pp. 24–26. Also see J. Michalski, "BNSF's Leadership Engine," *Organizational Dynamics,* Vol. 42, No. 1 (2013), pp. 35–45.

50. See C. Christensen, "How Will You Measure Your Life?" *Harvard Business Review,* July–August 2010, pp. 46–51.

51. Adapted from H. L. Rossi, "7 Core Values Statements That Inspire," *Fortune.com,* March 13, 2015, http://fortune.com/2015/03/13/company-slogans/ (accessed March 21, 2016).

52. Eric Johnson, quoted in Rossi, "7 Core Values Statements That Inspire."

53. "Discover Our Vision, Mission, and Values," Hilton Worldwide, http://hiltonworldwide.com/about/mission (accessed March 21, 2016).

54. Zuckerberg outlined five core values for Facebook in a letter to potential investors, which appeared in regulatory filings that Facebook Inc. first submitted in February 2012 for its initial public offering of stock. A portion of the letter appeared in Associated Press, "CEO Zuckerberg: Facebook's 5 Core Values," *CBS Money Watch,* May 17, 2012, www.cbsnews.com/news/ceo-zuckerberg-facebooks-5-core-values (accessed March 21 2016).

55. "Patagonia: Aligning Values and Workforce," *In a Future Age,* October 21, 2010, https://inafutureage.wordpress.com/2010/10/21/patagonia-aligning-values-and-workforce (accessed March 21, 2016).

56. P. J. Below, G. L. Morrisey, and B. L. Acomb, *The Executive Guide to Strategic Planning* (San Francisco: Jossey-Bass, 1987), p. 2.

57. Laurence D. Fink, quoted in A. R. Sorkin, "Some Heresy on Wall St.: Look Past the Quarter," *The New York Times,* February 2, 2016, pp. B1, B4.

58. S. Silverthorne, "The High Risks of Short-Term Management," *Working Knowledge,* April 11, 2012, http://hbswk.hbs.edu/item/the-high-risks-of-short-term-management (accessed March 25, 2016); interview of F. Brochet, M. Loumioti, and G. Serafeim. In a study of 280 CEOs by research firm Oxford Economics, 7 in 10 CEOs investors' emphasis on short-term rewards present an obstacle to long-term planning; see L. Kwoh, "More Revealing CEOs," *The Wall Street Journal,* January 31, 2012, p. B6. See also F. Broche, M. Loumioti, and G. Serafeim, "Short-Termism, Clientele, and Firm Risk," *HBS Working Paper,* August 2012, Harvard Business School Working Knowledge, http://hbswk.hbs.edu/item/short-termism-investor-clientele-and-firm-risk (accessed March 25, 2015).

59. Tim Cook, quoted in D. Hsu and M. Campello, "Will Slowing Growth Take a Bite Out of Apple?" *Knowledge@Wharton,* February 1, 2016, http://knowledge.wharton.upenn.edu/article/how-apple-can-combat-slowing-growth (accessed April 1, 2016).

60. A. Lashinsky, "Bezos Prime," *Fortune,* April 1, 2016, pp. 70–79.

61. S. Soper, "Jeff Bezos Sells More Than $500 Million in Amazon Shares," *Bloomberg Business,* August 6, 2015, www.bloomberg.com/news/articles/2015-08-06/jeff-bezos-sells-more-than-500-million-in-amazon-shares (accessed March 25, 2016).

62. Bezos, quoted in J. B. Stewart, "At Amazon, Talking Long Term," *The New York Times,* December 17, 2011, pp. B1, B7. See also M. Gottfried, "Amazon: It's Not Just for Christmas," *The Wall Street Journal,* February 1–2, 2014, p. B14.

63. Stewart, "At Amazon, Talking Long Term."

64. Bezos, quoted in Stewart, "At Amazon, Talking Long Term."

65. S. Woo and J. Letzing, "Amazon's Spending Habit Hurts Profit," *The Wall Street Journal,* February 1, 2012, pp. B1, B2.

66. H. Tabuchi, "In Online Race, It's Amazon and Also-Rans," *The New York Times,* December 31, 2016, pp. B1, B4; T. Lee, "Amazon: Now It's Disrupting a Heck of a Lot More Than Just Bookstores," *San Francisco Chronicle,* March 13, 2016, pp. D1, D3.
67. F. Manjoo, "Long Game at Amazon Produces Juggernaut," *The New York Times,* November 19, 2015, pp. B1, B11.
68. Q. Hardy, "Amazon Building a Tech Business for the Long Haul," *The New York Times,* October 12, 2015, p. B4.
69. G. Bensinger, "Amazon Dashes High Expectations," *The Wall Street Journal,* January 20, 2016, pp. B1, B4. See also M. Gottfried, "Amazon: Why Wall Street Is Still Expecting Too Much," *The Wall Street Journal,* March 26–27, 2016, p. B10.
70. L. Bossidy and R. Charan, *Execution: The Discipline of Getting Things Done* (New York: Crown Business, 2002), p. 227.
71. C. Shine, "Southwest Announces Record $620 Million Profit Share for Employees," *The Dallas Morning News,* February 11, 2016, http://aviationblog.dallasnews.com/2016/02/southwest-announces-record-620-million-profit-share-for-employees.html (accessed March 24, 2016).
72. "Southwest Airlines Careers," Southwest Airlines website, www.southwest.com. https://www.southwest.com/html/about-southwest/careers/index.html?clk=GFOOTER-ABOUT-CAREERS (accessed April 19, 2016).
73. "Southwest Corporate Fact Sheet," Southwest Airlines website, http://swamedia.com/channels/Corporate-Fact-Sheet/pages/corporate-fact-sheet#fleet (accessed March 25, 2016).
74. James Parker, quoted in W. J. Holstein, "At Southwest, the Culture Drives Success," *BusinessWeek.com,* February 21, 2008, www.bloomberg.com/news/articles/2008-02-21/at-southwest-the-culture-drives-successbusinessweek-business-news-stock-market-and-financial-advice (accessed March 25, 2016). Parker is author of *Do the Right Thing: How Dedicated Employees Create Loyal Customers and Large Profits* (Philadelphia: Wharton School Publishing, 2008). See also interview with founder and former CEO Herb Kelleher in J. Reingold, "*Still* Crazy after All These Years," *Fortune,* January 14, 2013, pp. 92–97.
75. S. Tully, "Southwest Bets Big on Business Travelers," *Fortune.com,* September 23, 2015, http://fortune.com/2015/09/23/southwest-airlines-business-travel; and A. Levine-Weinberg, "Southwest Airlines' Business Travel Appeal Has Limits," *The Motley Fool,* September 28, 2016, www.fool.com/investing/general/2015/09/28/southwest-airlines-business-travel-appeal-has-limi.aspx (both accessed March 25, 2016).
76. Abigail Johnson, co-founder of public relations firm Roeder-Johnson, quoted in Tully, "Southwest Bets Big on Business Travelers."
77. Report by former CEO Herb Kelleher, in S. Rose, "How Herb Keeps Southwest Hopping," *Money,* June 1999, pp. 61–62.
78. Willie Wilson, quoted in J. Bailey, "On Some Flights, Millionaires Serve the Drinks," *The New York Times,* May 15, 2006, pp. A1, A16.
79. J. Nicas and S. Carey, "Southwest Air Faces Grown-Up Woes," *The Wall Street Journal,* April 2, 2014, pp. A1, A14.
80. S. McCartney, "Rating U.S. Airlines: The Best and Worst of 2015," *The Wall Street Journal,* January 16, 2016, pp. D1, D2.
81. C. Jones, "Southwest Announces First International Flights," *USA Today,* January 27, 2014, www.usatoday.com/story/travel/flights/2014/01/27/southwest-launches-international-services/4938011 (accessed March 25, 2016).
82. R. Jones and R. Wall, "Budget Airlines Now Take on Long Hauls," *The Wall Street Journal,* May 30, 2014, p. B3.
83. Nicas and Carey, "Southwest Air Faces Grown-Up Woes."
84. B. Kesling and D. Nissenbaum, "Goal to Slash Wait Times Was 'Unrealistic,' Aide Said," *The Wall Street Journal,* May 24–25, 2014, p. A4. See also B. Hollingsworth, "Inspector General: VA Schedulers 'Zeroed Out' Wait Times for Texas Veterans Seeking Health Care," *CNS News.com,* March 23, 2016, http://cnsnews.com/news/article/barbara-hollingsworth/inspector-general-va-schedulers-zeroed-out-wait-times-texas (accessed April 1, 2016); and D. Slack, "VA Bosses Falsified Veterans' Wait Times," *Reno Gazette-Journal,* April 8, 2016, pp. 1B, 2B, reprinted from *USA Today.*
85. K. Fehrenbacher, "Apple, Walmart, Coca-Cola, Others Commit to White House Climate Change Pledge," *Fortune,* July 27, 2015, http://fortune.com/2015/07/27/apple-walmart-coca-cola-others-commit-to-white-house-climate-change-pledge (accessed March 25, 2016).
86. J. Worland, "Why Big Business Is Taking Climate Change Seriously," *Time,* September 23, 2015, http://time.com/4045572/big-business-climate-change (accessed March 25, 2016).
87. "The Power of Partnerships: How a Tenacious NGO and the World's Largest Retailer Found Environmental Success," Environmental Defense Fund, February 2016, http://business.edf.org/files/2016/02/EDF-Walmart-10-Year-Journey-Case-Study.FINAL_.pdf (accessed March 25, 2016). Also see E. Sturcken, "How 10 Years in the Trenches with Walmart Built an On-Ramp for the Future," *EDF+Business,* February 16, 2016, http://business.edf.org/blog/2016/02/16/how-10-years-in-the-trenches-with-walmart-built-an-on-ramp-for-the-future; and F. Krupp, "Walmart: The Awakening of an Environmental Giant," *Huffington Post,* February 17, 2016, www.huffingtonpost.com/fred-krupp/walmart-the-awakening-of_b_9253920.html (both accessed March 25, 2016).
88. M. Barbaro, "Wal-Mart Sets Agenda of Change," *The New York Times,* January 24, 2008, p. C3; and K. Ohannessian, "CEO Lee Scott Speaks about Wal-Mart's New Strategies," *FastCompany.com,* January 24, 2008, www.fastcompany.com/680015/ceo-lee-scott-speaks-about-wal-marts-new-strategies (accessed March 24, 2016).
89. A. S. Ross, "Wal-Mart's Grand Green Alternative," *San Francisco Chronicle,* February 28, 2010, pp. D1, D2.
90. L. Hardesty, "Walmart Will Increase Use of Renewables 600% over 2010 Levels," *Energy Manager Today,* April 16, 2013, www.energymanagertoday.com/walmart-will-increase-use-of-renewables-600-over-2010-levels-091022/ (accessed March 25, 2016). See also CEO Michael Duke interviewed by G. Baker, "Wal-Mart's Green Initiative: Status Report," *The Wall Street Journal,* April 9, 2014, p. R3.
91. L. Walker, "Walmart Beats Emissions Goal a Year Early," *Environmental Leader,* March 6, 2013; U.S. Environmental Protection Agency, www.environmentalleader.com/2013/03/06/walmart-beats-emissions-goal-a-year-early (accessed March 25, 2016).
92. Gwen Ruta, Environmental Defense Fund, reported in M. Gunther, "Wal-Mart's BIG Problem: Climate Change," *Organic Consumers Association,* June 23, 2009, https://www.organicconsumers.org/news/wal-marts-big-problem-climate-change (accessed March 25, 2016).
93. S. Mitchel, "Walmart's Assault on the Climate," Institute for Local Self-Reliance, November 2013, www.ilsr.org/wp-content/uploads/2013/10/ILSR-_Report_Walmart-ClimateChange.pdf (accessed March 25, 2016).
94. See M. Gunther, "Walmart Is Slapping Itself on the Back for Sustainability, but It Still Has a Way to Go," *The Guardian,* November 18, 2015, www.theguardian.com/sustainable-business/2015/nov/18/walmart-climate-change-carbon-emissions-re-newabe-energy-environment (accessed March 25, 2016).
95. U.S. Environmental Protection Agency, "National Top 100, Green Power Partnership," January 25, 2016, https://www3.epa.gov/greenpower/toplists/top100.htm (accessed March 25, 2016).
96. Drucker, *The Practice of Management.*
97. See R. Liddell, "Employee-Crafted Goals Pay Off," *HR Magazine,* July 2013, p. 63.
98. E. A. Lock and G. P. Latham, "Building a Practically Useful Theory of Goal Setting and Task Motivation," *American Psychologist,* September 2002, pp. 705–717.
99. The performance management process is discussed by H. Aguinis and C. Pierce, "Enhancing the Relevance of Organizational Behavior by Embracing Performance Management Research," *Journal of Organizational Behavior,* January 2008, pp. 139–145.
100. R. Rodgers and J. E. Hunter, "Impact of Management by Objectives on Organizational Productivity," *Journal of Applied Psychology,* April 1991, pp. 322–336.
101. This example was taken from a graphic illustration by A. Kinicki that came from a client and is used for training managers in cascading; copyright ©2016 by Kinicki and Associates, Inc. For more on goal cascading, see A. J. Kinicki, K. J. L. Jacobson, B. M. Galvin, and G. E. Prussia, "A Multilevel Systems Model of Leadership," *Journal of Leadership & Organizational Studies,* May 2011, pp. 133–149.
102. P. Trunk, "Leaving Your Options Open Sets You Back," Penelope Trunk blog, July 11, 2014, http://blog.penelopetrunk.com/2014/07/11/leaving-your-options-open-sets-you-back (accessed April 1, 2016).
103. H. G. Halvorson, "Why Keeping Your Options Open Is a Really, Really Bad Idea," *Fast Company,* May 27, 2011, www.fastcompany.com/1755546/why-keeping-your-options-open-really-really-bad-idea (accessed April 1, 2016).
104. D. Ariely, *Predictably Irrational: The Hidden Forces That Shape Our Decisions,* revised and expanded edition (New York: Harper Collins, 2010).
105. D. Ariely, quoted in J. Tierney, "The Advantages of Closing a Few Doors," *The New York Times,* February 26, 2008, pp. D1, D6.
106. "Interbrand Releases 2015 Best Global Brands Report," Reuters, October 5, 2015, http://uk.reuters.com/article/idUKnMKWmhPNya+1cc+MKW20151005?type=companyNews (accessed April 1, 2016). See also Interbrand, "2015 Best Global Brands," 2016, http://interbrand.com/best-brands/best-global-brands/2015/ranking (accessed April 1, 2016).
107. D. Pierce, "iPhone Killer: The Secret History of the Apple Watch," *Wired,* May 2015, www.wired.com/1205/04/the-apple-watch (accessed April 8, 2016).
108. Hsu, quoted in Hsu and Campello, "Will Slowing Growth Take a Bite Out of Apple?"
109. A. Tonner, "How Successful Was the Apple Watch Last Quarter?" *The Motley Fool,* February 4, 2016, www.fool.com/investing/general/2016/02/04/how-successful-was-the-apple-watch-last-quarter.aspx (accessed April 8, 2016).
110. See M. D. Shear, "With Taps on the Wrist, a Watch Points to the Future," *The New York Times,* December 31, 2015, p. B6.
111. Pierce, "iPhone Killer: The Secret History of the Apple Watch."
112. Shear, "With Taps on the Wrist, a Watch Points to the Future."
113. IDC, reported in M. Grothaus, "Apple Shipped 11.6 Million Apple Watches in 2015, Says IDC," *Fast Company,* February 25, 2016, www.fastcompany.com/3057139/fast-feed/apple-sold-116-million-apple-watches-in-2015-says-idc (accessed April 8, 2016).
114. "Apple Watch Claims over 50% of 2015 Smartwatch Market in Less Than a Year of Sales," Juniper Research, January 12, 2016, www.juniperresearch.com/press/press-releases/apple-watch-claims-over-50-of-2015-smartwatch (accessed April 8, 2016).
115. N. Lomas, "Why the Apple Watch Price Cut Is Smart Thinking," TechCrunch, March 22, 2016, http://techcrunch.com/2016/03/22/why-the-apple-watch-price-cut-is-smart-thinking (accessed April 8, 2016).
116. See C. Passariello, "Apple's Foray into Luxury," *The Wall Street Journal,* September 12–13, 2015, pp. B1, B4.
117. See M. Hamblen, "Apple Watch's $50 Price Drop Shows Reaction to Slow 2015 Sales," *ComputerWorld,* March 22, 2016, www.computerworld.com/article/3047192/wearables/apple-watchs-50-price-drop-shows-reaction-to-slow-2015-sales.html (accessed April 8, 2016).
118. B. Kowitt, "Big Agriculture Gets Its Sh*t Together," *Fortune Magazine,* February 1, 2016, pp. 86–92.
119. "Our Story," http://fofarms.com/about-us, accessed February 2, 2016.
120. B. Kowitt, "Big Agriculture Gets Its Sh*t Together," *Fortune Magazine,* February 1, 2016, pp. 86–92.
121. D. Carden, "Logistics Keeps Fair Oaks Farms Moo-ving," September 23, 2015, http://www.nwitimes.com/business/local/logistics-keeps-fair-oaks-farms-moo-ving/article_312607af-d011-5f00-89d4-92e190c1fde0.html, accessed February 2, 2016.
122. E. Quinlan, "New Milk Set to Shake Up Dairy Industry," February 9, 2015, http://agrinews-pubs.com/Content/Auction-Calendar/Livestock/Article/New-milk-set-to-shake-up-dairy-industry-/15/7/12031, accessed February 2, 2016.

123. J. Drucker and Z. R. Mider, "Tax Inversion: How U.S. Companies Buy Tax Breaks," November 23, 2015, http://bloombergview.com/quicktake/tax inversion.

124. L. Picker, "Tyco Merger Will Shift Tax Liability Overseas," *The New York Times*, January 26, 2016, p. B1.

CHAPTER 6

1. G. Hamel, "What Is Management's Moonshot?" *Management 2.0*, December 7, 2007, https://hbr.org/2007/12/what-is-managements-moonshot (accessed April 13, 2016). See also G. Hamel, "Moon Shots for Management," *Harvard Business Review*, February 2009, pp. 91–98.

2. D. Rigby and B. Bilodeau, "Management Tools and Trends 2015," Bain & Company, June 10, 2015, www.bain.com/publications/articles/management-tools-and-trends-2015.aspx (accessed April 13, 2016). See also D. K. Rigby, "Management Tools 2015: An Executive's Guide," Bain & Company, www.bain.com/Images/BAIN_GUIDE_Management_Tools_2015_executives_guide.pdf (accessed April 13, 2016).

3. J. Best, *Flavor of the Month: Why Smart People Fall for Fads* (Berkeley: University of California Press, 2006).

4. J. Best, interviewed by A. Manser, "Flavor of the Month," *UDaily*, University of Delaware website, May 22, 2006, www.udel.edu/PR/UDaily/2006/may/jbest052206.html (accessed May 24, 2016).

5. G. James, "World's Worst Management Fads," *Inc.com*, May 10, 2013, www.inc.com/geoffrey-james/worlds-worst-management-fads.html (accessed April 13, 2016).

6. K. Daum, "Define Your Core Values: 5 Steps," *Inc.com*, April 26, 2013, www.inc.com/kevin-daum/define-your-personal-core-values-5-steps.html (accessed April 26, 2016).

7. J. Pfeffer and R. I. Sutton, "Profiting from Evidence-Based Management," *Strategy & Leadership*, Vol. 34, No. 2 (2006), pp. 35–42.

8. Kevin Coyne, quoted in J. Surowiecki, "The Return of Michael Porter," *Fortune*, February 1, 1999, pp. 135–138.

9. G. Colvin, "There's No Quit in Michael Porter," *Fortune*, October 29, 2012, pp. 162–166.

10. M. E. Porter, "What Is Strategy?" *Harvard Business Review*, November–December 1996, pp. 61–78. Porter has updated his 1979 paper on competitive forces in M. E. Porter, "The Five Competitive Forces That Shape Strategy," *Harvard Business Review*, January 2008, pp. 79–93.

11. Porter, "What Is Strategy?"

12. J. A. Byrne, "Going Where the Money Is," *BusinessWeek*, January 26, 1998, p. 14, review of A. J. Slywotzky and D. J. Morrison, with B. Andelman, *The Profit Zone* (New York: Times Business, 1998).

13. D. Streitfeld, "Seeking the Captive Consumer," *The New York Times*, February 13, 2012, pp. B1, B7.

14. M. Gartenberg, Gartner analyst, quoted in Streitfeld, "Seeking the Captive Consumer."

15. F. Manjoo, "Paranoia Feeds Amazon's Growth," *The Wall Street Journal*, November 14, 2013, pp. B1, B7. See also "Network Revolution: Creating Value through Platforms, People, and Technology," *Knowledge@Wharton*, April 14, 2016, http://knowledge.wharton.upenn.edu/article/the-network-revolution-creating-value-through-platforms-people-and-digital-technology (accessed April 27, 2016).

16. See L. Stevens, "'Free' Shipping Crowds Out Small Retailers," *The Wall Street Journal*, April 28, 2016, pp. B1, B2.

17. Harold Pollack, quoted in S. Clifford and C. C. Miller, "Rooting for the Little Guy," *The New York Times*, January 16, 2012, pp. B1, B2.

18. N. Shirouzu, "Toyoda Rues Excessive Profit Focus," *The Wall Street Journal*, March 2, 2010, p. B3. Also see K. Linebaugh, D. Searcey, and N. Shirouzu, "Secretive Culture Led Toyota Astray," *The Wall Street Journal*, February 10, 2010, pp. A1, A6; N. Bunkley, "1.1 Million Toyotas Recalled to Correct Engine Problems," *The New York Times*, August 27, 2010, p. B2; M. Ramsey, "Toyota Fixes Five Million Recalled Cars," *The Wall Street Journal*, October 5, 2010, p. B4; D. Leinwand and C. Woodyard, "No Flaws Found in Toyota Electronics," *USA Today*, February 9, 2011, p. 1B; and M. Ramsey, J. Mitchell, and C. Dawson, "U.S. Absolves Toyota Electronics," *The Wall Street Journal*, February 9, 2011, pp. B1, B2.

19. R. Farzad and M. Arndt, "Stuck with Sears," *Bloomberg Businessweek*, April 5, 2010, pp. 41–48; and A. Ahmed, "Sales Down, Sears to Shut 120 Stores," *The New York Times*, December 28, 2011, pp. B1, B5.

20. B. Dobbin, "Snapshot of an Icon's Fall," *Reno Gazette-Journal*, October 6, 2011, pp. 5A, 6A; M. Spector and A. D. Mattioli, "Kodak: Tech Firms Hastened Slide," *The Wall Street Journal*, January 20, 2012, pp. B1, B5; and M. Daneman, "Can Kodak Reinvent Itself After Bankruptcy?" *Rochester Democrat and Chronicle*, September 1, 2013, www.usatoday.com/story/money/business/2013/09/01/can-kodak-reinvent-itself/2752173 (accessed April 18, 2016).

21. Leo J. Thomas, quoted in "What's Wrong with This Picture: Kodak's 30-Year Slide into Bankruptcy," *Knowedge@Wharton*, February 1, 2012, http://knowledge.wharton.upenn.edu/article/whats-wrong-with-this-picture-kodaks-30-year-slide-into-bankruptcy (accessed April 18, 2016).

22. David A. Glocker, in "What's Wrong with This Picture: Kodak's 30-Year Slide into Bankruptcy."

23. C. Burritt, "Kodak Trying to Bring Its Digital Revival into Focus," *San Francisco Chronicle*, September 6, 2011, pp. D1, D3. See also N. McAlone, "This Man Invented the Digital Camera in 1975—and His Bosses at Kodak Never Let It See the Light of Day," *Business Insider*, August 17, 2015, www.businessinsider.com/this-man-invented-the-digital-camera-in-1975-and-his-bosses-at-kodak-never-let-it-see-the-light-of-day-2015-8 (accessed April 18, 2016).

24. R. Adner, "Many Companies Still Don't Know How to Compete in the Digital Age," *Harvard Business Review*, March 28, 2016, https://hbr.org/2016/03/many-companies-still-dont-know-how-to-compete-in-the-digital-age (accessed April 18, 2016).

25. See A. Kinicki, K. Jacobson, B. Galvin, and G. Prussia, "A Multilevel Systems Model of Leadership," *Journal of Leadership & Organizational Studies*, May 2011, pp. 133–149.

26. G. Toppo, "Libraries' Choice: Change or Die," *Reno Gazette-Journal*, June 7, 2014, pp. 1B, 2B, reprinted from *USA Today*.

27. Walt Disney, quoted in B. Nanus, *Visionary Leadership: Creating a Compelling Sense of Direction for Your Organization* (San Francisco: Jossey-Bass, 1992), p. 28.

28. Google vision statement quoted in A. Thompson, "Google's Vision Statement & Mission Statement," Panmore Institute, September 20, 2015, http://panmore.com/google-vision-statement-mission-statement (accessed April 13, 2016).

29. Smithsonian home page, https://www.si.edu/About/Mission (accessed April 13, 2016).

30. P. M. Lancioni, "Make Your Values Mean Something," *Harvard Business Review*, July 2002, pp. 113–117.

31. HEART Principles, reported in H. L. Rossi, "7 Core Values Statements That Inspire," *Fortune*, March 13, 2015, http://fortune.com/2015/03/13/company-slogans (accessed April 23, 2016).

32. Whole Foods Market, "Our Core Values," www.wholefoodsmarket.com/mission-values/core-values (accessed April 23, 2016).

33. Nanus, *Visionary Leadership: Creating a Compelling Sense of Direction for Your Organization*, pp. 28–29.

34. C. Moody, "Startup Culture: Values vs. Vibe," Chrismoody.com, February 15, 2011, http://chrismoody.com/startup-culture (accessed April 23, 2016).

35. The Forbes Funds, "Organizational Assessment," http://forbesfunds.org/tools/building-management-capacity/organizational-assessment (accessed May 21, 2014).

36. A. Newcomb, "CES 2016: The Biggest Takeaways on the Future of Tech," *ABC News*, January 11, 2016, http://abcnews.go.com/Technology/ces-2016-biggest-take-aways-future-tech/story?id=36216616 (accessed April 14, 2016).

37. Toyota Motor president Akio Toyoda, quoted in A. Ohnsman, J. Green, and K. Inoue, "The Humbling of Toyota," *Bloomberg Businessweek*, March 22 & 29, 2010, pp. 32–36.

38. M. Ramsey and C. Dawson, "Toyota, Honda Lose U.S. Edge," *The Wall Street Journal*, November 15, 2010, pp. B1, B2.

39. A. Taylor III, "Toyota's Comeback Kid," *Fortune*, February 27, 2012, pp. 72–79; and C. Dawson, "Toyota Chief Grabs the Wheel to Turn Around Humbled Auto Giant," *The Wall Street Journal*, July 13, 2014, pp. A1, A8.

40. H. Tabuchi, "Toyota Bounces Back with Help from Eager American Buyers and a Weak Yen," *The New York Times*, May 9, 2013, p. B3; H. Tabuci, "Profit Is Up 70% at Toyota, Close to Its Old Milestone," *The New York Times*, November 7, 2013, p. B3; and Y. Takahashi, "Toyota Predicts Record Net," *The Wall Street Journal*, February 5, 2014, p. B7.

41. Y. Kubota, "Toyota Profit Edges Up as Weak Yen's Benefits Wear Off," *The Wall Street Journal*, February 2, 2016, www.wsj.com/articles/toyota-raises-outlook-slightly-cost-cuts-boost-quarterly-profit-1454653966; and K. Inagaki, "Toyota Suffers First Profit Fall in Two Years," *Financial Times*, February 5, 2016, www.ft.com/cms/s/0/0b462a2a-cbe3-11e5-be0b-b7ece4e953a0.html (both accessed April 25, 2016).

42. D. Wakabayashi, "'Toyota Way' Retains Management Followers," *The Wall Street Journal*, February 26, 2010, p. B4.

43. Ohnsman, Green, and Inoue, "The Humbling of Toyota."

44. Toyota top engineer Takeshi Uchiyamada, quoted in Taylor, "Toyota's Comeback Kid."

45. D. Miller, "Winners and Losers in J.D. Power's 2016 Vehicle Dependability Study," *The Motley Fool*, March 5, 2016, www.fool.com/investing/general/2016/03/05/winners-and-losers-in-jd-powers-2016-vehicle-depen.aspx (accessed April 25, 2016).

46. Y. Takahashi, "Toyota Accelerates Its Cost-Cutting Efforts," *The Wall Street Journal*, December 23, 2009, p. B4; C. Woodyard, "Toyota's Reputation Needs Some TLC," *USA Today*, December 31, 2009, pp. 1B, 2B; M. Maynard and H. Tabuchi, "Rapid Growth Has Its Perils, Toyota Learns," *The New York Times*, January 28, 2010, pp. A1, B4; K. Linebaugh and N. Shirouzu, "Toyota Heir Faces Crisis at the Wheel," *The Wall Street Journal*, January 28, 2010, pp. A1, A8; and M. Dolan, "Supplier Perplexed by Toyota's Action," *The Wall Street Journal*, January 28, 2010, p. A9.

47. Taylor, "Toyota's Comeback Kid," p. 75.

48. J. R. Healey and A. DeBarros, "Toyota Tops Speed Control Complaints," *USA Today*, March 26, 2010, pp. 1B, 2B.

49. N. Bunkley, "Toyota Halts Production of 8 Models," *The New York Times*, January 27, 2010, pp. B1, B2; J. R. Healey, "Toyota Halts U.S. Sales of 8 Models," *USA Today*, January 27, 2010, p. 1A; and C. Said, "Reports on Priuses Add to Toyota's Woes," *San Francisco Chronicle*, February 4, 2010, pp. D1, D2.

50. Leinwand and Woodyard, "No Flaws Found in Toyota Electronics"; and Ramsey, Mitchell, and Dawson, "U.S. Absolves Toyota Electronics."

51. D. Q. Weber, "Toyota Agrees to $1.2 Billion Penalty Ending U.S. Probe," *Bloomberg.com*, March 19, 2014, www.bloomberg.com/news/2014-03-19/u-s-says-toyota-agrees-to-1-2-billion-settlement-ending-probe.html (accessed May 24, 2016).

52. Reuters, "Toyota Admits It Misled the Public about Multiple Safety Issues," *Huffington Post*, March 19, 2014, www.huffingtonpost.com/2014/03/19/toyota-fine-misleading-public_n_4992609.html (accessed April 25, 2016).

53. C. Trudell and Y. Hagiwara, "Toyota Recalls More Than 6 Million Vehicles Worldwide," *Bloomberg.com*, April 9, 2014, www.bloomberg.com/news/articles/2014-04-09/toyota-recalls-6-76-million-vehicles-worldwide-including-rav4 (accessed April 25, 2016).

54. Associated Press, "Nearly 1.4 Million Vehicles Added to Toyota Airbag Recall," *The New York Times*, June 17, 2015, p. B2.

55. "Toyota Recalls 320,000 Vehicles for Safety Issues," *CNBC.com*, February 2, 2016, www.cnbc.com/2016/02/02/toyota-recalls-320000-vehicles-for-safety-issue.html;

and A. Krok, "Alert Your Grandma: Toyota Recalls 2016 Avalon, Camry for Airbag Issue," *CNET.com*, April 14, 2016, www.cnet.com/roadshow/news/toyota-recalls-2016-avalon-camry-for-airbag-issue (both accessed April 25, 2016).

56. James P. Womack, quoted in Maynard and Tabuchi, "Rapid Growth Has Its Perils, Toyota Learns."

57. C. Dawson, "Toyota Overhauls Vehicle R&D Efforts," *The Wall Street Journal*, April 10, 2012, p. B6.

58. See, for example, B. Vlasic, "Toyota Moves to Revamp Its Lexus Luxury Line," *The New York Times*, September 27, 2012, p. B2; C. Woodyard and J. R. Healey, "Toyota Beefs Up Tundra for a Fight," *USA Today*, February 8, 2013, pp. 1B, 2B; and B. Vlasic, "Toyota Fashions a Bolder Image for the Practical Prius," *The New York Times*, September 10, 2015, p. B3.

59. N. Bunkley, "Ford and Toyota to Work Together on Hybrid System for Trucks," *The New York Times*, August 23, 2011, p. B3; J. Bennett and M. Ramsey, "Putting Egos Aside, Ford, Toyota Pair Up for Hybrids," *The Wall Street Journal*, August 23, 2011, pp. B1, B2; and E. Pfanner, "Toyota Shows Off a Sedan Powered by Hydrogen Fuel Cells," *The New York Times*, November 21, 2013, pp. B1, B4.

60. J. Markoff, "Toyota Aims to Make Car a Co-Pilot for Drivers," *The New York Times*, September 5, 2015, pp. B1, B3.

61. A. Shah, "Toyota Looks to Daihatsu to Crack Indian Small Car Market," Reuters, February 3, 2016, www.reuters.com/article/us-autoshow-india-toyota-idUSKCN0VC28Q (accessed April 27, 2016).

62. H. Tabuchi, "Files Show That Takata Was Worried about Costs," *The New York Times*, April 14, 2016, pp. B1, B6.

63. See, e.g., Z. Tufekci, "VW's Cheating Software," *The New York Times*, September 24, 2015, p. A33; Associated Press, "Multistate Probe of VW Could Take Years," *San Francisco Chronicle*, October 21, 2015, p. C4; K. Pender, "Resale Prices of Diesel VWs Plunge," *San Francisco Chronicle*, November 12, 2015, pp. C1, C5; W. Boston and S. Sloat, "VW's Global Sales Fall Amid Emissions Woes," *The Wall Street Journal*, November 14, 2016, p. B3; C. Woodyard, "Justice Dept. Alleges VW Violated Clean Air Act," *Reno Gazette-Journal*, January 5, 2016, p. 4B, reprinted from *USA Today*; D. Hakim, "VW's Crisis Response: Driving in Circles," *The New York Times*, February 28, 2016, pp. BU-1, BU-5; J. Ewing, "VW Scandal Clouds Prospects for Diesel," *The New York Times*, March 4, 2016, p. B3; and "Can Volkswagen Move beyond Its Diesel Emissions Scandal?," *Knowledge @ Wharton*, April 26, 2016, http://knowledge.wharton.upenn.edu/article/can-volkswagen-move-beyond-its-diesel-emissions-scandal (accessed April 27, 2016).

64. J. R. Healey and F. Meier, "At General Motors, a History of Failures," *USA Today*, June 6–8, 2014, p. 1A; B. Vlasic, "GM Inquiry Cites Years of Neglect over Fatal Defect," *The New York Times*, June 6, 2014, pp. A1, B6; and C. Isadore, "GM's Total Recall Cost: $4.1 Billion," *CNN Money*, February 4, 2015, http://money.cnn.com/2015/02/04/news/companies/gm-earnings-recall-costs (accessed April 26, 2016).

65. D. Welch, K. Naughton, and B. Helm, "Detroit's Big Chance," *Bloomberg Businessweek*, February 22, 2010, pp. 38–44.

66. Y. Kageyama, "Toyota Lifts Profit Forecast as Disaster Woes Fade," HighBeam Research, February 7, 2012, www.highbeam.com/doc/1A1-4ce3ead63a83407e8edd5037ad103572.html (accessed April 27, 2016).

67. Y. Kubota, "Quakes Expose Supply-Chain Frailty," *The Wall Street Journal*, April 19, 2016, p. B5.

68. Kubota, "Toyota Profit Edges Up as Weak Yen's Benefits Wear Off."

69. C. Rogers, "Japanese Car Makers Lose Their Midsize Edge," *The Wall Street Journal*, May 6, 2013, pp. B1, B4.

70. "Selected Automakers' U.S. Market Share in March 2016, by Manufacturer," *Statista*, March 2016, www.statista.com/statistics/343162/market-share-of-major-car-manufacturers-in-the-united-states (accessed April 27, 2016).

71. M. DeBord, "Toyota's Blind Spot," *The New York Times*, February 6, 2010, p. A17.

72. For forecasting related to public policy and political polling, see "Why Even the Best Forecasters Sometimes Miss the Mark," Knowledge@Wharton, April 19, 2016, http://knowledge.wharton.upenn.edu/article/why-even-the-best-forecasters-sometimes-miss-the-mark (accessed April 24, 2016).

73. E. Porter, "For Insurers, No Doubts on Climate Change," *The New York Times*, May 15, 2013, pp. B1, B2.

74. "Hurricanes," Insurance Information Institute, 2014, www.iii.org/fact-statistic/hurricanes (accessed April 25, 2016). See also A. C. Kaufman, B. Walsh, and S. Nasiripour, "Warren Buffet Is Wrong about Climate Change," *Huffington Post*, February 29, 2016, www.huffingtonpost.com/entry/warren-buffett-climate-change_us_56d36cade4b03260bf773563 (accessed April 25, 2016).

75. W. B. Gail, "A New Dark Age Looms," *The New York Times*, April 19, 2016, p. A25. Gail is author of *Climate Conundrums: What the Climate Debate Reveals about Us* (Chicago: University of Chicago Press, 2014).

76. C. Paris and J. Chiu, "Cosco Maps Artic Route for Asia-to-Europe Trade," *The Wall Street Journal*, October 30, 2015, p. B6.

77. P. J. Gleckler, P. J. Durack, R. J. Stouffer, G. C. Johnson, and C. E. Forest, "Industrial-Era Global Ocean Heat Uptake Doubles in Recent Decades," *Nature Climate Change*, Vol. 6 (2016), pp. 394–398; and R. M. DeContol and D. Pollard, "Contribution of Antarctica to Past and Future Sea-Level Rise," *Nature*, Vol. 531 (2016), pp. 591–597. See also D. Perlman, "Oceans Heating Up Both Faster, Deeper," *San Francisco Chronicle*, January 19, 2016, pp. A1, A6; and J. Gillis, "Ice-Sheet Melt Seen Harming Cities by 2100," *The New York Times*, March 31, 2016, pp. A1, A10.

78. See description of these governmental efforts in "5 Global Warming Contingency Plans Being Made Now," The Geneva Association, Toronto, March 7, 2014, https://www.genevaassociation.org/media/869448/07032014_listosaur_ocean-warming.pdf (accessed April 24, 2016). Also see J. Gillis, "Greenhouse Gas Linked to Floods Along U.S. Coasts," *The New York Times*, February 23, 2016, pp. A1, A10; and J. Schwartz, "Climate Change Countdown," *The New York Times*, April 5, 2016, pp. D1, D3.

79. E. Kolbert, "The Seige of Miami," *The New Yorker*, December 21 & 28, pp. 42–50.

80. C. McHale and S. Leurig, "Stormy Future for U.S. Property/Casualty Insurers: The Growing Costs and Risks of Extreme Weather Events," Ceres, Boston, September 2012, www.ceres.org/resources/reports/stormy-future/view (accessed April 25, 2016).

81. W. Koch, "Insurers Not So Hot on Climate Change," *USA Today*, March 8, 2013, p. 3B.

82. E. Mills, "Insurers as Partners in Inclusive Green Growth," Laurence Berkeley National Laboratory, University of California, Berkeley, prepared for the World Bank Group's International Finance Corporation as input to the G20, Washington, D.C., 2013, http://evanmills.lbl.gov/pubs/pdf/Insurers-as-partners-in-inclusive-green-growth.pdf (accessed April 25, 2016).

83. Carl Hedde, head of risk accumulation for Munich Re America, quoted in M. Jones, "The Insurance Industry Responds to Climate Change Risk," *Risk Management Monitor*, February 2, 2015, www.rmmagazine.com/2015/02/02/threat-level-rising-the-insurance-industry-responds-to-climate-change-risk/ (accessed April 25, 2016).

84. C. Goldwasser, "Benchmarking: People Make the Process," *Management Review*, June 1995, p. 40.

85. H. Rothman, "You Need Not Be Big to Benchmark," *Nation's Business*, December 1992, pp. 64–65.

86. M. E. Porter, *Competitive Strategy* (New York: The Free Press, 1980). See also Porter, "The Five Competitive Forces That Shape Strategy," 2008.

87. P. L. Brown, "Surfers in Turmoil with the Loss of a Major Supplier," *The New York Times*, December 30, 2006, p. A12; and M. Overfelt, "Rough Surf," *USA Today*, February 17, 2006, http://money.cnn.com/magazines/fsb/fsb_archive/2006/02/01/8368201/index.htm (accessed May 24, 2016).

88. R. Coelho, "Energy Self-Sufficiency in Brazil," Advanced Biofuels USA, December 9, 2013, http://advancedbiofuelsusa.info/energy-self-sufficiency-in-brazil (accessed May 24, 2016).

89. J. Beckerman, "Etsy Posts Big Gains in Revenue, Users," *The Wall Street Journal*, February 24, 2016, p. B1.

90. H. Tabuchi, "Etsy Welcomes Manufacturers to Artisanal Fold," *The New York Times*, September 14, 2015, pp. B1, B2. See also A. Larocca, "Etsy Wants to Crochet Its Cake and Eat It Too," *New York Magazine*, April 4–17, 2016, pp. 39–45.

91. S. Elliott, "Still Ticking, Timex Nods to Heritage in a Fast World," *The New York Times*, January 22, 2014, p. B6.

92. B. Sisario and K. Russell, "Sales Hold Steady for a Radically Changed Music Industry," *The New York Times*, March 25, 2016, pp. B1, B7.

93. H. Karp, "Streaming Gives Music Industry a Lift," *The Wall Street Journal*, April 13, 2016, p. B4.

94. C. Rogers and G. Nagesh, "Ford to Audition Supercar Buyers," *The Wall Street Journal*, April 14, 2016, p. B7.

95. N. D. Schwartz, "In Age of Broad Wealth Gap, Not Everyone Is in the Same Boat," *The New York Times*, April 24, 2016, pp. News-1, News-22.

96. D. Gannon, "Green Toys," *Inc.*, April 11, 2011, www.inc.com/best-industries-2011/green-toys.html; and B. Yerak, "From Frozen Food to Green Toys," *Chicago Tribune*, November 10, 2013, http://articles.chicagotribune.com/2013-11-10/business/ct-biz-1110-green-toys--20131110_1_toy-industry-osi-playthings/2 (both accessed May 24, 2016).

97. J. Bennett, "Delphi Wins Tax Battle, Offers Bullish Sales View," *The Wall Street Journal*, April 14, 2016, p. B3.

98. K. Stock, "Indian Motorcycles Finally Rev Up to Speed for Polaris," *Bloomberg Businessweek*, January 28, 2014, www.justcarnews.com/indian-motorcycles-finally-rev-up-to-speed-for-polaris.html (accessed May 24, 2016).

99. F. A. Hanssen, "Vertical Integration During the Hollywood Studio Era," *The Journal of Law & Economics*, August 2010, pp. 519–43.

100. K. Favaro, "Vertical Integration 2.0: An Old Strategy Makes a Comeback," *Strategy+Business*, May 6, 2015, www.strategy-business.com/blog/Vertical-Integration-2-0-An-Old-Strategy-Makes-a-Comeback?gko=41fe1 (accessed April 26, 2016).

101. W. C. Kim and R. Mauborgne, *Blue Ocean Strategy: How to Create Uncontested Market Space and Make the Competition Irrelevant*, expanded edition (Boston: Harvard Business School Press, 2015).

102. B. W. Barry, "A Beginner's Guide to Strategic Planning," *The Futurist*, April 1998, pp. 33–36; from B. W. Barry, *Strategic Planning Workbook for Nonprofit Organizations*, revised and updated (St. Paul, MN: Amherst H. Wilder Foundation, 1997).

103. L. Bossidy and Ram Charan, with C. Burck, *Execution: The Discipline of Getting Things Done* (New York: Crown Business, 2002).

104. Results can be found in "Wanted: Employees Who Get Things Done," *HR Magazine*, January 2008, p. 10.

105. Also see R. Kaplan and D. Norton, "Mastering the Management System," *Harvard Business Review*, January 2008, pp. 66–77.

106. Execution is also discussed by C. Montgomery, "Putting Leadership Back into Strategy," *Harvard Business Review*, January 2008, pp. 54–60; and J. Lorsch and R. Clark, "Leading from the Boardroom," *Harvard Business Review*, April 2008, pp. 105–111.

107. "About the IKEA Group, Welcome Inside Our Company," http://www.ikea.com/ms/en_US/this-is-ikea/company-information/index.html, accessed March 22, 2016.

108. B. Kowitt, "It's IKEA's World," *Fortune Magazine*, March 15, 2015, pp. 166–175.

109. O. Jurevicius, "SWOT Analysis of IKEA," *Strategic Management Insight*, February 15, 2013, https://www.strategicmanagementinsight.com/swot-analyses/ikea-swot-analysis.html, accessed March 22, 2016.

110. B. Kowitt, "It's IKEA's World," *Fortune Magazine*, March 15, 2015, pp. 166–175.

111. B. Kowitt, "It's IKEA's World," *Fortune Magazine*, March 15, 2015, pp. 166–175.
112. A. Lutz, "IKEA's Strategy for Becoming the World's Most Successful Retailer," *Business Insider*, January 15, 2015, http://www.businessinsider.com/ikeas-strategy-for-success-2015-1, accessed March 22, 2016.
113. "It's Official: Companies with Women on the Board Perform Better," December 8, 2015, http://www.weform.org/agenca/2015/12/its-official-women-on-boards-boost-business/, accessed March 21, 2016.
114. J. Lublin, "Female Directors: Why So Few?" *The Wall Street Journal*, December 27, 2011, B5.

CHAPTER 7

1. M. H. Bazerman, *Judgment in Managerial Decision Making*, 7th ed. (New York: Wiley, 2008). See also D. E. Bell, H. Raiffa, and A. Tversky, eds., *Decision Making: Descriptive, Normative, and Prescriptive Interactions* (Cambridge: Cambridge University Press, 1988).
2. M. Easterby-Smith and M. A. Lyles, *The Blackwell Handbook of Organizational Learning and Knowledge Management* (Oxford: Blackwell Publishing, 2003).
3. B. Fischoff, "Hindsight ± Foresight: The Effect of Outcome Knowledge on Judgment under Uncertainty," *Journal of Experimental Psychology: Human Perception and Performance*, Vol. 1 (1975), pp. 288–299.
4. D. Kaplan, "Starbucks: The Art of Endless Transformation," *Inc.*, June 2014, pp. 82–86, 128.
5. "Starbucks Company Statistics," *Statistics Brain*, August 12, 2013, www.statisticbrain.com/starbucks-company-statistics (accessed June 13, 2014).
6. C. C. Miller, "A Changed Starbucks; A Changed CEO," *The New York Times*, March 13, 2011, p. BU-1.
7. H. Schultz, quoted in J. H. Ostdick, "Rekindling the Heart & Soul of Starbucks," *Success*, www.success.com/article/rekindling-the-heart-soul-of-starbucks (accessed May 2, 2016).
8. J. Jargon, "Starbucks CEO to Focus on Digital," *The Wall Street Journal*, January 30, 2014, p. B6; B. Gruley and L. Patton, "The Arabica Project," *Bloomberg Businessweek*, February 17–23, 2014, pp. 64–69; B. Horovitz, "Starbucks Serving Alcohol at More Locations," *USA Today*, March 21, 2014, p. 5B; S. Rubenstein, "Starbucks to Bid Au Revoir to Its La Boulange Cafes," *San Francisco Chronicle*, June 17, 2015, p. C2; J. Jargon, "Starbucks Expands Push into Mobile," *The Wall Street Journal*, October 7, 2015, p. B8; J. Jargon, "Starbucks Gets Boost from Christmas Sales, Mobile-Payment App," *The Wall Street Journal*, January 22, 2016, p. B3; Associated Press, "Starbucks Will Close Its Teavana 'Tea Bars,'" *San Francisco Chronicle*, January 23, 2016, p. D2; and Associated Press, "Boutique Coffee Shops Jolt Chains to Step Up Game," *San Francisco Chronicle*, March 26, 2016, p. D2.
9. B. Horovitz, "Starbucks Climbs to No. 2 in Sales," *Reno Gazette-Journal*, March 21, 2015, p. 4B, reprinted from *USA Today*; C. Fraley, "Starbucks Corporation: Will the Caramelized Honey Latte Sweeten SBUX Stock?" *Investor Place*, March 23, 2016, http://investorplace.com/2016/03/starbucks-stock-sbux-caramelized-honey-latte (accessed May 2, 2016); and H. Malcolm, "Starbucks Sales Up as New Stores, Customer Loyalty Grow in Q2," *USA Today*, April 21, 2016, http://www.usatoday.com/story/money/2016/04/21/starbucks-sales-up-new-stores-customer-loyalty-grow-q2/83280066 (accessed May 2, 2016).
10. A. Ripley, "Starbucks the Benevolent?" *The Atlantic*, February 3, 2016, www.theatlantic.com/business/archive/2016/02/starbucks-benevolence-rent-college/459732 (accessed May 2, 2016). See also A. Madhani, "From the Ground Up: Starbucks in Ferguson," *Reno Gazette-Journal*, April 30, 2016, pp. 2B, 2B, reprinted from *USA Today*.
11. B. Horovitz, "Why People Love to Love-Hate Starbucks," *USA Today*, February 12, 2014, p. 2A.
12. D. Kahneman, *Thinking, Fast and Slow* (New York: Farrar, Straus and Giroux, 2011), pp. 20–22.
13. Book review of Kahneman, *Thinking, Fast and Slow*, by J. Holt, "Two Brains Running," *The New York Times*, November 25, 2011, www.nytimes.com/2011/11/27/books/review/thinking-fast-and-slow-by-daniel-kahneman-book-review.html?_r=0 (accessed May 3, 2016).
14. "Wean Wall Street Off Its Gambling Addictions," editorial, *USA Today*, March 1, 2010, p. 15A.
15. Chip Heath, quoted in J. Rae-Dupree, "Innovative Minds Don't Think Alike," *The New York Times*, December 30, 2007, business section, p. 3. C. Heath and D. Heath are coauthors of *Made to Stick: Why Some Ideas Survive and Others Die* (New York: Random House, 2007).
16. G. Tett, *The Silo Effect: The Peril of Expertise and the Promise of Breaking Down Barriers* (Boston: Little, Brown, 2015).
17. K. A. Dolan and L. Kroll, "Forbes 2016 World Billionaires: Meet the Richest People on the Planet," *Yahoo! News*, March 1, 2016, https://www.yahoo.com/news/forbes-2016-world-s-billionaires—meet-the-richest-people-on-the-planet-152937843.html?ref=gs (accessed May 3, 2016).
18. A. Dvorkin, "The Real Secret behind Warren Buffet's Success Is Finally Revealed," *Invest with Alex*, March 20, 2014, www.investwithalex.com/the-real-secret-behind-warren-buffetts-success-is-finally-revealed (accessed May 3, 2016).
19. J. Nocera, "How Buffett Does It," *The New York Times*, March 3, 2015, p. A27.
20. L. Lofton, *Warren Buffett Invests Like a Girl* (New York: HarperBusiness, 2011). See also K. Kristof, "The Secrets of Women Investors," *Kiplinger's Personal Finance*, April 2016, http://m.kiplinger.com/article/investing/T031-C000-S002-the-secrets-of-women-investors.html (accessed May 3, 2016).
21. A. Markels, "Built to Make Billions?" *U.S. News & World Report*, August 6, 2007, pp. 51–52.
22. For more on Buffett's investment strategy, see L. Haris, "Advice from Warren Buffett That Could Make You Rich," *CNN.com*, February 28, 2016, http://money.cnn.com/

2015/02/28/investing/warren-buffett-advice/index.html (accessed May 3, 2016); M. Levine, "Warren Buffett Explains His Cozy Embrace," *BloombergView.com*, February 28, 2015, www.bloombergview.com/articles/2015-02-28/warren-buffett-explains-his-cozy-embrace (accessed May 3, 2016); Nocera, "How Buffett Does It"; and J. Sommer, "Buffett's Awesome Feat, Revisited," *The New York Times*, March 8, 2015, p. BU-3.
23. A. Lusardi and O. S. Mitchell, "Financial Literacy around the World: An Overview," *Journal of Pension Economics and Finance*, October 2011, pp. 497–508.
24. Annamaria Lusardi, quoted in A. Tugend, "Women Know More about Finances Than They Get Credit For," *The New York Times*, May 18, 2013, p. B5.
25. S. Constable, "In the Battle over Financial Literacy, Neither Men or Women Are Winners," *The Wall Street Journal*, June 15, 2015, p. R8. The research is found in T. Bucher-Koenen, A. Lusardi, R. J. M. Alessie, and M. van Rooij, "How Financially Literate Are Women? An Overview and New Insights," *Global Financial Literacy Excellence Center Working Paper No. 2014-5*, December 15, 2014, http://papers.ssrn.com/sol3/papers.cfm?abstract_id=2585187; and A. S. Mitchell and A. Lusardi, "Financial Literacy and Economic Outcomes: Evidence and Policy Implications," *Global Financial Literacy Excellence Center Working Paper No. 2015-1*, January 7, 2015, http://gflec.org/wp-content/uploads/2015/03/WP-2015-1-Financial-Literacy-and-Economic-Outcomes.pdf (both accessed May 3, 2016).
26. B. M. Barber and T. Odean, "Boys Will Be Boys: Gender, Overconfidence, and Common Stock Investment," *Quarterly Journal of Economics*, February 2001, pp. 261–292.
27. D. Mitchell, "At Last, Buffett's Key to Success," *The New York Times*, April 5, 2008, p. B5. See also J. Clements, "He Invests, She Invests: Who Gets the Better Returns?" *The Wall Street Journal*, February 6, 2008, p. D1; C. Benko and B. Pelstar, "How Women Decide," *Harvard Business Review*, September 2013, pp. 78–84; and M. P. Dunleavey, "Mars, Venus, and the Handling of Money," *The New York Times*, February 23, 2014, p. BU-5.
28. R. Carden, "Behavioral Economics Show That Women Tend to Make Better Investments Than Men," *The Washington Post*, October 11, 2013, www.washingtonpost.com/business/behavioral-economics-show-that-women-tend-to-make-better-investments-than-men/2013/10/10/5347f40e-2d50-11e3-97a3-ff2758228523_story.html (accessed June 9, 2016).
29. T. Huston, "Are Women Better Decisions Makers?" *The New York Times*, October 19, 2014, p. SR-9.
30. M. Mather and N. R. Lighthall, "Risk and Reward Are Processed Differently in Decisions Made Under Stress," *Current Directions in Psychological Science*, Vol. 21, No. 1 (2012), pp. 36–41.
31. Julie Nelson, reported in S. Constable, "Everybody Knows Men Take More Investing Risks Than Women. Is It True?" *The Wall Street Journal*, September 21, 2015, p. R7. See J. A. Nelson, "Are Women Really More Risk-Averse Than Men? A Re-Analysis of the Literature Using Expanded Methods," *Journal of Economic Surveys*, Vol. 29, Iss. 3 (2015), pp. 566–585.
32. A. Farnham, "Teaching Creativity Tricks to Buttoned-Down Executives," *Fortune*, January 10, 1994, pp. 94–100.
33. S. Holmes, "The 787 Encounters Turbulence," *BusinessWeek*, June 19, 2006, pp. 38–40.
34. For a discussion of the strategy behind the Dreamliner, see C. Masters, "How Boeing Got Going," *Time*, September 10, 2007, pp. Global 1–Global 6.
35. E J. Langer, "Minding Matters: The Consequences of Mindlessness-Mindfulness," *Advances in Experimental Social Psychology*, 1989, 138.
36. R. Yu, "Boeing Again Delays Dreamliner's Debut," *USA Today*, January 17, 2008, p. 3B; and J. L. Lunsford, "Boeing Delays Dreamliner Delivery Again," *The Wall Street Journal*, April 10, 2008, p. B3.
37. C. Drew, "Another Flight Delay for Troubled Dreamliner," *The New York Times*, June 24, 2009, p. B3; P. Sanders, D. Michaels, and A. Cole, "Boeing Delays New Jet Again," *The Wall Street Journal*, June 24, 2009, pp. A1, A6; D. Reed, "Problems Pile Up on Boeing," *USA Today*, June 24, 2009, pp. 1B, 2B; P. Sanders, "Boeing Settles in for a Bumpy Ride," *The Wall Street Journal*, October 7, 2009, p. B1; D. Michaels and P. Sanders, "Dreamliner Production Gets Closer Monitoring," *The Wall Street Journal*, October 7, 2009, pp. B1, B2; and P. Sanders, "At Boeing, Dreamliner Fix Turns Up New Issue," *The Wall Street Journal*, November 13, 2009, pp. B1, B2.
38. P. Sanders and D. Michaels, "Boeing Looks Beyond Dreamliner's First Flight," *The Wall Street Journal*, June 29, 2009, pp. B1, B2.
39. C. Jones, "New Era in Aircraft Arrives," *USA Today*, October 21, 2011, pp. 1B, 3B; and B. Mutzabaugh, "First Dreamliner Fliers Sing Its Praises," *USA Today*, October 28, 2011, pp.1B, 2B.
40. M. I. Wald and J. Mouawad, "Boeing Acknowledges Tests Underestimated Battery Risks in 787," *The New York Times*, April 24, 2013, p. B3; B. Jansen, "NTSB Urges More Tests on Boeing 787 Dreamliners," *USA Today*, May 23, 2014, p. 3B; C. Drew, "787 Fire Inquiry Focuses on Transmitter," *The New York Times*, July 16, 2013, pp. B1, B8; and B. Jansen, "Investigators Trace 787 Fire to Battery-Powered Device," *USA Today*, July 19, 2013, p. 2B.
41. J. Ostrower, "New Boeing Woe: 787 Wing Defect," *The Wall Street Journal*, March 8–9, 2014, pp. B1, B4.
42. L Lorenzetti, "FAA Says Boeing 787 Dreamliners Have 'Urgent Safety Issue,'" *Fortune.com*, April 25, 2016, http://fortune.com/2016/04/25/boeing-dreamliner-safety-issue/ (accessed May 8, 2016).
43. A. Pasztor, "Boeing Takes Passing Grade on Dreamliner," *The Wall Street Journal*, March 20, 2014, p. B10.
44. J. Ostrower, "Steady Demand for New Jets Lifts Boeing," *The Wall Street Journal*, April 24, 2014, p. B3.
45. See, e.g., G. Hobica, "In Appreciation of the Boeing 787 Dreamliner," *Huffington Post*, April 6, 2016, www.huffingtonpost.com/george-hobica/in-appreciation-of-the-

bo_b_9625832.html; and "3 Incredible Features of the Boeing 787 Dreamliner," *Aviation Gossip,* April 30, 2016, www.aviationgossip.com/3-incredible-features-of-the-boeing-787-dreamliner (both accessed May 8, 2016).

46. Hobica, "In Appreciation of the Boeing 787 Dreamliner."

47. J. Ostrower, "Boeing Earnings Fall as Jet Charges Mount," *The Wall Street Journal,* April 28, 2016, p. B3.

48. Estimates by Barclays Capital, reported in J. Ostrower, "Critical Mission for Boeing: Slashing Dreamliner Costs," *The Wall Street Journal,* January 8, 2014, pp. B1, B2.

49. A. Levine-Weinberg, "Why Boeing's 787-10 Is Critical for Dreamliner Profitability," *The Motley Fool,* www.fool.com/investing/general/2016/02/22/why-boeings-787-10-is-critical-for-dreamliner-prof.aspx (accessed May 8, 2016).

50. P. Ausick, "Is the 787 Over-Hyped for Boeing?" *24/7 Wall Street,* March 18, 2016, http://247wallst.com/aerospace-defense/2016/03/18/is-the-787-over-hyped-for-boeing (accessed May 8, 2016).

51. H. A. Simon, *Administrative Behavior,* 3rd ed. (New York: Free Press, 1996); and H. A. Simon, "Making Management Decisions: The Role of Intuition and Emotion," *The Academy of Management Executive,* February 1987, pp. 57–63.

52. D. Farrell and F. Grieg, *How Falling Gas Prices Fuel the Consumer: Evidence from 25 Million People,* JPMorgan Chase & Co. Institute, October 2015, https://www.jpmorganchase.com/content/dam/jpmorganchase/en/legacy/corporate/institute/document/jpmc-institute-gas-report.pdf (accessed May 7, 2016). See also B. Appelbaum, "When Gas Prices Drop, People Buy Fancier Gas," *The New York Times,* October 20, 2015, p. A3.

53. J. Brustein and S. Soper, "Who's Alexa?" *Bloomberg Businessweek,* May 2–May 8, 2016, pp. 31–33.

54. J. Wortham, "Once Just a Site with Funny Cat Pictures, and Now a Web Empire," *The New York Times,* June 14, 2010, pp. B1, B8.

55. See also D. Kahneman and G. Klein, "Conditions for Intuitive Expertise: A Failure to Disagree," *American Psychologist,* September 2009, pp. 515–526. For an analysis on training human intuition to perceive patterns among massive data overload, see B. Carey, "Learning to See Data," *The New York Times,* March 29, 2015, pp. SR-1, SR-4.

56. See C. C. Miller and R. D. Ireland, "Intuition in Strategic Decision Making: Friend or Foe in the Fast-Paced 21st Century?" *Academy of Management Executive,* February 2005, p. 20.

57. These suggestions were based in part on E. Sadler-Smith and E. Shefy, "The Intuitive Executive: Understanding and Applying 'Gut Feel' in Decision Making," *Academy of Management Executive,* November 2004, p. 88.

58. See E. Dane and M. G. Pratt, "Exploring Intuition and Its Role in Managerial Decision Making," *Academy of Management Review,* January 2007, pp. 33–54.

59. See D. Begley, "You Might Help a Teen Avoid Dumb Behavior by Nurturing Intuition," *The Wall Street Journal,* November 3, 2006, p. B1.

60. Advice attributed to Sunny Vanderbeck of Satori Capital, Dallas, in V. Harnish, "Finding the Route to Growth," *Fortune,* May 18, 2014, p. 45.

61. Courage and intuition are discussed by K. K. Reardon, "Courage as a Skill," *Harvard Business Review,* March 2007, pp. 51–56.

62. M. B. Zuckerman, "Policing the Corporate Suites," *U.S. News & World Report,* January 19, 2004, p. 72.

63. See, for example, A. Blinder, "Mine Chief Is Sentenced in Conspiracy over Safety," *The New York Times,* April 7, 2016, pp. A12, A17; and B. McLean, "Poison Pill," *Vanity Fair,* February 2016, pp. 106–109, 142–144.

64. Bill Gates, quoted in R. A. Guth, "Bill Gates Issues Call for Kinder Capitalism," *The Wall Street Journal,* January 24, 2008, pp. A1, A15. See also C. Boles, "Last Call? Gates Pushes Globalism in Remarks," *The Wall Street Journal,* March 13, 2008, p. B3; and M. J. Sandel, "What Isn't for Sale?" *The Atlantic,* April 2012, pp. 62–66. Sandel is author of *What Money Can't Buy: The Moral Limits of Markets* (London: Penguin Books, 2012).

65. C. McNamara, "Complete Guide to Ethics Management: An Ethics Toolkit for Managers," www.mapnp.org/library/ethics/ethxgde.htm (accessed June 14, 2014).

66. See D. Meinert, "Creating an Ethical Culture," *HR Magazine,* April 2014, pp. 23–27.

67. Warby Parker cofounder Neil Blumenthal, quoted in L. Philip, "Warby Parker's Philanthropic Vision," *Philadelphia Style,* August 29, 2012, http://phillystylemag.com/warby-parker-philanthropy-visionspring (accessed May 9, 2016).

68. C. E. Bagley, "The Ethical Leader's Decision Tree," *Harvard Business Review,* February 2003, pp. 18–19.

69. Bagley, p. 19.

70. Bagley, p. 19.

71. The website YourMorals.org studies morality and values, offering questionnaires for readers to fill out. Some of the results are described in J. Haidt, *The Righteous Mind: Why Good People Are Divided by Politics and Religion* (New York: Random House, 2012).

72. B. Hall, "Google's Project Oxygen Pumps Fresh Air into Management," *TheStreet,* February 11, 2014, https://www.thestreet.com/story/12328981/1/googles-project-oxygen-pumps-fresh-air-into-management.html (accessed May 20, 2016). See also A. Bryant, "The Quest to Build a Better Boss," *The New York Times,* March 13, 2011, p. BU-1; and D. A. Garvin, "How Google Sold Its Engineers on Management," *Harvard Business Review,* December 2013, pp. 74–82; and L. Bock, *Work Rules! Insights from Inside Google That Will Transform How Live and Lead* (New York: Hatchette, 2015).

73. J. Pfeffer and R. I. Sutton, "Profiting from Evidence-Based Management," *Strategy & Leadership,* Vol. 34, No. 2 (2006), pp. 35–42; and J. Pfeffer and R. I. Sutton, "Evidence-Based Management," *Harvard Business Review,* January 2006, pp. 63–74. See also J. Pfeffer and R. Sutton, "Trust the Evidence, Not Your Instincts," *The New York Times,* September 4, 2011, p. BU-8. Pfeffer and Sutton have also produced a book, *Hard Facts, Dangerous Half-Truths, and Total Nonsense: Profiting from Evidence-Based Management* (Cambridge, MA: Harvard Business School Press, 2006). For a discussion of the book, see C. Hymowitz, "Executives Must Stop Jumping Fad to Fad and Learn to Manage," *The Wall Street Journal,* May 15, 2006, p. B1.

74. See also Pfeffer's recent book, *Leadership BS: Fixing Workplaces and Careers One Truth at a Time* (New York: HarperCollins, 2015). Additional discussion of this topic may be found in T. Reay, W. Berta, and M. Kazman Kohn, "What's the Evidence on Evidence-Based Management?" *Academy of Management Perspectives,* November 2009, pp. 5–18; and R. B. Briner, D. Denyer, and D. M. Rousseau, "Evidence-Based Management" Concept Cleanup Time?" *Academy of Management Perspectives,* November 2009, pp. 19–32.

75. Pfeffer and Sutton, "Profiting from Evidence-Based Management."

76. J. Wortham, "In Tech, Starting Up by Failing," *The New York Times,* January 18, 2012, pp. B1, B6.

77. Reported in A. Shontell, "The Tech 'Titanic': How Red-Hot Startup Fab raised $330 Million and Then Went Bust," *Business Insider,* February 6, 2015, www.businessinsider.com/how-billion-dollar-startup-fab-died-2015-2 (accessed May 9, 2016).

78. C. Garling, "Excessive Hype Does Promising Products No Favors," *San Francisco Chronicle,* September 27, 2013, p. C5.

79. Bryant, "Google's Quest to Build a Better Boss."

80. Pfeffer and Sutton, "Profiting from Evidence-Based Management."

81. S. Kapner, "Macy's Reignites Retail Worries," *The Wall Street Journal,* May 12, 2016, pp. A1, A2.

82. Pfeffer and Sutton, "Evidence-Based Management," pp. 66–67.

83. J. Pfeffer, "Lay Off the Layoffs," *Newsweek,* February 15, 2010, pp. 32–37.

84. "U.S. Men & Women Agree Southwest Airlines, Google and Dove Are Most Desired Brands in 2012," *PR Newswire,* February 17, 2012, www.prnewswire.com/news-releases/us-men—women-agree-southwest-airlines-google-and-dove-are-most-desired-brands-in-2012-139506748.html (accessed June 14, 2014).

85. "Southwest Airlines," *Rankings per Brand,* www.rankingthebrands.com/Brand-detail.aspx?brandID=2107 (accessed May 12, 2016).

86. G. Loveman, "Diamonds in the Data Mine," *Harvard Business Review,* May 2003, pp. 109–113. See also T. Davenport, L. Prusak, and B. Strong, "Putting Ideas to Work," *The Wall Street Journal,* March 10, 2008, p. R11.

87. T. H. Davenport, "Competing on Analytics," *Harvard Business Review,* January 2006, pp. 99–107.

88. S. Baker, "How Much Is That Worker Worth?" *BusinessWeek,* March 23 & 30, 2009, pp. 46–48.

89. D. Robson, "Considered a Data Dinosaur, a Sport Is Trying an Analytic Approach," *The New York Times,* August 14, 2015, p. B8.

90. M. Lewis, *Moneyball: The Art of Winning an Unfair Game* (New York: W.W. Norton, 2004). For comment on the Oakland A's and *Moneyball,* see J. Manuel, "Majoring in Moneyball," *Baseball America Features,* December 23, 2003, www.baseballamerica.com/today/features/031223collegemoneyball.html; J. Zasky, "Pay for Performance, Stupid," *Failure Magazine,* June 2003, http://failuremag.com/archives_business_sports_money-ball.html; R. Van Zandt, "Billy Beane's Perfect Draft: A Baseball Revolution?" *BaseballEvolution.com,* April 13, 2006, http://baseballevolution.com/guest/richard/rvz-beanel.html; and "Moneyball: The Art of Winning an Unfair Game," *Wikipedia,* July 12, 2006, http://en.wikipedia.org/wiki/Moneyball (all accessed June 14, 2016).

91. For more on the use of technology and software in baseball, see A. Schwarz, "Digital Eyes Will Chart Baseball's Unseen Skills," *The New York Times,* July 10, 2009, pp. A1, A3; and R. Sandomir, "Bloomberg Technology Embraces Baseball," *The New York Times,* December 6, 2009, Sports section, pp. 1, 6; J. Swartz, "Batting Cleanup for Giants: Technology," *USA Today,* April 1, 2013, p. 3B; M. Futterman, "Deee-fense: Baseball's Big Shift," *The Wall Street Journal,* March 2, 2014, pp. D1, D2; J. Shea, "Second to None," *San Francisco Chronicle,* April 23, 2014, pp. N2, N6; P. White, "Batters Getting Battered," *USA Today,* May 13, 2014, pp. 1C, 4C; and S. Kroner, "A Shift in Thinking," *San Francisco Chronicle,* May 31, 2014, pp. B1, B8. For a discussion of the analytics of the Super Bowl–winning NFL team the New England Patriots, see C. Price, *The Blueprint: How the New England Patriots Beat the System to Create the Last Great NFL Superpower* (New York: Thomas Dunne/St. Martin's Press, 2007). For uses of analytics in the National Hockey League, see P. Pickens, "Devils Go All In on Analytics (Ex-Poker Pro Helps)," *The New York Times,* September 18, 2015, p. B11.

92. D. Barbarisi, "Building Royals from Baseball's Scrap Heap," *The Wall Street Journal,* November 2, 2015, p. B9.

93. B. Cohen, "Remaking Basketball the Warriors' Way," *The Wall Street Journal,* April 7, 2016, pp. A1, A12. See also M. Johnson, "Now NBA Defenses Got Turned Inside Out," *The Wall Street Journal,* March 2, 2015, p. B8; and B. Schoenfeld, "Team Building," *The New York Times Magazine,* April 3, 2016, pp. 33–37, 56–59.

94. ESPN study, cited in R. Kroichick, "Guided by Tech—but Where?" *San Francisco Chronicle,* March 27, 2016, pp. B1, B7.

95. Lacob, quoted in Schoenfeld, "Team Building."

96. T. H. Davenport, "Competing on Analytics," *Harvard Business Review,* January 2006, pp. 99–107.

97. G. Bensinger and L. Stevens, "Delivery Startup to Get Funding from UPS," *The Wall Street Journal,* February 24, 2016, p. B6.

98. "UPS Explores Drone Deliveries of Life-Saving Medicines," *Phys Org,* May 9, 2016, http://phys.org/news/2016-05-ups-explores-drone-deliveries-life-saving.html (accessed May 13, 2016).

99. Davenport, "Competing on Analytics."

100. H. Weinzierl, "New Digital Universe Study Reveals Big Data Gap: Less Than 1% of World's Data Is Analyzed, Less Than 20% Is Protected," *EMC Newsroom,* December 11, 2012, www.emc.com/about/news/press/2012/20121211-01.htm (accessed May 13, 2016).

101. J. Thomas, "Where Is the World Supposed to Put All of Its Data?" *Forbes.com,* February 17, 2015, www.forbes.com/sites/ibm/2015/02/17/where-is-the-world-supposed-to-put-all-of-its-data/#33e2a986112c (accessed May 13, 2016).

102. A. Brust, "Big Data: Defining Its Definition," *ZDNet,* March 1, 2012, www.zdnet.com/article/big-data-defining-its-definition/ (accessed May 13, 2016).

103. S. Lohr, "Amid the Flood, a Catchphrase Is Born," *The New York Times,* August 12, 2012, p. BU-3.
104. M. S. Malone, "The Big-Data Future Has Arrived," *The Wall Street Journal,* February 23, 2016, p. A17.
105. McKinsey Global Institute report, May 2011, quoted in J. Temple, "Big Data Can Lead to Big Breakthroughs in Research," *San Francisco Chronicle,* December 9, 2011, www.sfgate.com/cgi-bin/article.cgi?f=/c/a/2011/12/08/BUDC1M9I8A.DTL (accessed June 14, 2014). See also T. H. Davenport, "Keep Up with the Quants," *Harvard Business Review,* July–August 2013, pp. 120–123; B. Roberts, "The Benefits of Big Data," *HR Magazine,* October 2013, pp. 21–30; and G. Dutton, "What's the Big Deal about Big Data?" *Training,* March/April 2014, pp. 16–19.
106. NewVantage Partners, *Big Data Executive Survey 2016: An Update on the Adoption of Big Data in the Fortune 1000,* http://newvantage.com/wp-content/uploads/2016/01/Big-Data-Executive-Survey-2016-Findings-FINAL.pdf (accessed May 13, 2016).
107. See T. H. Davenport, "Analytics 3.0," *Harvard Business Review,* December 2013, pp. 65–72.
108. Temple, "Big Data Can Lead to Big Breakthroughs in Research."
109. A. Stuart, "Metrics Sell Doughnuts and More," *The Wall Street Journal,* December 22, 2015, p. B6.
110. S. Ovide and E. Dwoskin, "The Data-Driven Rebirth of a Salesman," *The Wall Street Journal,* September 15, 2015, pp. B1, B4.
111. J. Hidalgo, "Is Whole Foods or Trader Joe's Better?" *Reno Gazette-Journal,* August 15, 2015, pp. 7A, 8A.
112. "Should Hiring Be Based on Gut—or Data?" *Knowledge@Wharton,* August 24, 2015, http://knowledge.wharton.upenn.edu/article/should-hiring-be-based-on-gut-or-data (accessed May 13, 2016). See also M. Luca, J. Kleinberg, and S. Mullainathan, "Algorithms Need Managers, Too," *Harvard Business Review,* January–February 2016, pp. 97–101.
113. M. Anderson, "Data-Driven Approach Becoming Common," *Reno Gazette-Journal,* August 18, 2015, p. 6A.
114. R. E. Silverman, "Bosses Tap Big Data to Flag Workers' Ills," The Wall Street Journal, February 17, 2016, pp. B1, B7.
115. J. Markoff, "Government Aims to Build a 'Data Eye in the Sky,'" *The New York Times,* October 11, 2011, p. D1. See also A. Vance, "Data Analytics: Crunching the Future," *Bloomberg Businessweek,* September 8, 2011, www.bloomberg.com/news/articles/2011-09-08/data-analytics-crunching-the-future (accessed May 13, 2016); and Q. Hardy, "Bigger Patterns in Big Data," *The New York Times,* February 20, 2012, p. B4.
116. B. Sisario, "Discography Site Charms Album Fans," *The New York Times,* December 30, 2015, pp. B1, B4; and B. Sisario, "Going to the Ends of the Earth to Get the Most Out of Music," *The New York Times,* June 8, 2015, pp. B1, B4.
117. S. Ember, "As Digital Upends TV Viewing, Data Reigns," *The New York Times,* May 12, 2015, pp. B1, B6; and "How Data Analytics Is Shaping What You Watch," *Knowledge@Wharton,* September 3, 2015, http://knowledge.wharton.upenn.edu/article/how-data-analytics-is-shaping-what-you-watch/ (accessed May 13, 2016).
118. A. Alter and K. Russell, "Moneyball for Book Publishers, Tracking the Way We Read," *The New York Times,* March 15, 2016, pp. B1, B6.
119. J. Bunge, "On the Farm: A Bountiful Harvest of Data," *The Wall Street Journal,* September 2, 2015, p. B1.
120. Malone, "The Big-Data Future Has Arrived."
121. Malone, "The Big-Data Future Has Arrived"; and L. Landro, "Mining Malpractice Data to Make Health Care Safer," *The Wall Street Journal,* May 10, 2016, p. D3.
122. See C. Mims, "Easy-to-Use Yelp and Google Hold Pointers to Fix Balky Governments," *The Wall Street Journal,* May 9, 2016, pp. B1, B5; C. Dougherty, "Alphabet Unit to Help Cities Untangle Their Traffic Snarls," *The New York Times,* March 18, 2016, p. D4; and "Startup Helps Make Sense of Transit Data," *San Francisco Chronicle,* March 20, 2016, pp. D1, D2, reprinted from *Los Angeles Times.*
123. J. Zweig, "The Anti-Poverty Experiment," *The Wall Street Journal,* June 6–7, 2015, pp. C1, C2; and A. Duglo, "What Data Can Do to Fight Poverty," *The New York Times,* January 31, 2016, p. SR-12.
124. See, e.g., J. D. Goodman, "Program Fails to Reduce Youth Crime, Report Finds," *The New York Times,* January 5, 2016, pp. A17, A19.
125. M. Madden and L. Rainee, "Americans' Attitudes about Privacy, Security, and Surveillance," Pew Research Center, May 20, 2015, www.pewinternet.org/2015/05/20/americans-attitudes-about-privacy-security-and-surveillance (accessed May 15, 2016).
126. E. Lichtblau, "Hackers Get Employee Records at Justice and Homeland Security Departments," *The New York Times,* February 9, 2016, p. A11.
127. S. Sposito, "Nasty Virus Can Hold Your Computer Hostage," *San Francisco Chronicle,* February 20, 2016, pp. D1, D4; S. Sposito, "Hospital Hacking Reveals Digital Dangers," *San Francisco Chronicle,* February 17, 2016, pp. C1, C5; and S. Cowley and L. Stack, "A Web Crime on the Rise: Hackers Lock Out Users and Demand a Ransom," *The New York Times,* February 19, 2016, p. B3.
128. J. Knoll, "Target Readies $10 Million Settlement over Data Breach," *USA Today,* March 19, 2015, p. 1B.
129. Associated Press, "Cyberthieves Fleece Mattel for $3 Million in Growing Scam," *San Francisco Chronicle,* March 30, 2016, p. A4.
130. N. Perlroth, "Hackers Get Inside a Jeep, and Fiat Chrysler Is Dismayed," *The New York Times,* July 22, 2015, p. B4; and M. Spector, "Car-Safety Debate: Is a Hacked Vehicle Also Defective?" *The Wall Street Journal,* August 25, 2015, pp. B1, B4.
131. Estimate by the Federal Reserve Bank of Boston, reported in K. Burne, "Cybercrime Prevention Effort Draws Interest," *The Wall Street Journal,* April 19, 2016, p. C7.
132. "Companies Put Cybersecurity Pros in the Boardroom to Help Counter Hacks," *San Francisco Chronicle,* August 30, 2015, p. D5, reprinted from *Los Angeles Times.*
133. See Silverman, "Bosses Tap Big Data to Flag Workers' Ills"; and P. Hagin, "As Wearables in the Workplace Spread, So Do Legal Concerns," *The Wall Street Journal,* March 14, 2016, p. R7. See also K. Eaton, "Ways to Track Personal Habits and Identify Patterns," *The New York Times,* January 21, 2016, p. B6.
134. The discussion of styles was based on material contained in A. J. Rowe and R. O. Mason, *Managing with Style: A Guide to Understanding, Assessing and Improving Decision Making* (San Francisco: Jossey-Bass, 1987), pp. 1–17.
135. A. M. Carton and A. S. Rosette, "Explaining Bias against Black Leaders: Integrating Theory on Information Processing and Goal-Based Stereotyping," *Academy of Management Journal,* December 1, 2011, pp. 1141–1158.
136. See Rowe and Mason, *Managing with Style*; M. J. Dollinger and W. Danis, "Preferred Decision-Making Styles: A Cross-Cultural Comparison," *Psychological Reports,* 1998, pp. 755–761; and K. R. Brousseau, M. J. Driver, G. Hourihan, and R. Larsson, "The Seasoned Executive's Decision-Making Style," *Harvard Business Review,* February 2006, pp. 111–112.
137. C. E. Cryder, J. S. Lerner, J. J. Gross, and R. E. Dahl, "Misery Is Not Miserly: Sad and Self-Focused Individuals Spend More," *Psychological Science,* June 1, 2008, pp. 525–530. See also S. Finkelstein, J. Whitehead, and A. Campbell, "How Inappropriate Attachments Can Drive Good Leaders to Make Bad Decisions," *Organizational Dynamics,* Vol. 38 (2009), pp. 83–92.
138. D. Gilbert, *Stumbling on Happiness* (New York: Vintage, 2007).
139. D. D. Wheeler and I. L. Janis, *A Practical Guide for Making Decisions* (New York: Free Press, 1980), pp. 34–35; and I. L. Janis and L. Mann, *Decision Making: A Psychological Analysis of Conflict, Choice, and Commitment* (New York: The Free Press, 1977).
140. R. Beck, "The Difference a Year Made in Mortgage Mess," *San Francisco Chronicle,* December 26, 2007, p. D2. See also S. Lohr, "Wall Street's Math Wizards Forgot a Few Variables," *The New York Times,* September 13, 2009, business section, p. 3; D. Leonhardt, "If Fed Missed Bubble, How Will It See the Next One?" *The New York Times,* January 6, 2010, pp. A1, A4; and J. Pressley, "They Did the Math—and Lost Billions," *Bloomberg Businessweek,* March 1, 2010, p. 70.
141. Decision Research study, reported in J. Zweig, "This Is Your Brain on a Hot Streak," *The Wall Street Journal,* February 11, 2012, pp. B1, B2.
142. S. S. Iyengar and M. Lepper, "When Choice Is Demotivating: Can One Desire Too Much of a Good Thing?" *Journal of Personality and Social Psychology,* Vol. 79 (2000), pp. 995–1006. Sheena Iyengar is author of *The Art of Choosing* (New York: Hachette Book Group, 2010).
143. P. Steel, "The Nature of Procrastination: A Meta-Analytic and Theoretical Review of Quintessential Self-Regulatory Failure," *Psychological Bulletin,* Vol. 133 (2007), pp. 65–94.
144. "Don't Mention It: How 'Undiscussables' Can Undermine an Organization," Knowledge@Wharton, December 20, 2011, http://knowledge.wharton.upenn.edu/article.cfm?articleid=2921 (accessed June 14, 2016).
145. Gurnek Bains, CEO of YSC, London, quoted in C. Hymowitz, "Best Way to Save: Analyze Why Talent Is Going Out the Door," *The Wall Street Journal,* September 24, 2007, p. B1.
146. K. Thornton, "Trying to Outrun the Fire," *The New York Times,* May 7, 2016, p. A19.
147. Wheeler and Janis, *A Practical Guide for Making Decisions.*
148. J. Wooden, quoted in M. D. White, "The Reinvention Imperative," *Harvard Business Review,* November 2013, p. 42.
149. T. D. O'Connor Jr., quoted in K. Rosman, "In Digital Era, Paper Makers Manage to Fight, Not Fold," *The Wall Street Journal,* March 8–9, 2014, pp. A1, A10.
150. Rosman, "In Digital Era, Paper Makers Manage to Fight, Not Fold."
151. "Mohawk and Arjowiggins Creative Papers Announce Strategic Alliance," Brand Packaging, May 12, 2015, www.brandpackaging.com/articles/85034-mohawk-and-arjowiggins-creative-papers-announce-strategic-alliance (accessed May 16, 2016).
152. D. Kahnemann and A. Tversky, "Judgment under Uncertainty: Heuristics and Biases," *Science,* Vol. 185 (1974), pp. 1124–1131; A. Tversky and D. Kahneman, "Availability: A Heuristic for Judging Frequency and Probability," *Cognitive Psychology,* Vol. 5 (1975), pp. 207–232; A. Tversky and D. Kahneman, "The Belief in the Law of Numbers," *Psychological Bulletin,* Vol. 76 (1971), pp. 105–110; D. R. Bobocel and J. P. Meyer, "Escalating Commitment to a Failing Course of Action: Separating the Roles of Choice and Justification," *Journal of Applied Psychology,* June 1994, pp. 360–363; B. M. Shaw, "The Escalation of Commitment to a Course of Action," *Academy of Management Review,* October 1981, pp. 577–587; K. Sengupta, T. Abdel-Hamid, and L. Van Wassenhove, "The Experience Trap," *Harvard Business Review,* February 2008, pp. 94–101; M. Heilman and T. Okimoto, "Motherhood: A Potential Source of Bias in Employment Decisions," *Journal of Applied Psychology,* January 2008, pp. 189–198; M. C. Mankins, "The Five Traps of High-Stakes Decision Making," *Harvard Business Review,* November 14, 2013, https://hbr.org/2013/11/the-five-traps-of-high-stakes-decision-making (accessed May 16, 2016); J. B. Soll, K. L. Milkman, and J. W. Payne, "Outsmart Your Own Biases," *Harvard Business Review,* May 2015, pp. 64–71; and Tett, *The Silo Effect: The Peril of Expertise and the Promise of Breaking Down Barriers.*
153. D. Stanglin and J. Estepa, "Winners in 3 States to Split Record $1.6B Powerball Jackpot," Janury 14, 2016, www.usatoday.com/story/money/nation-now/2016/01/14/powerball-thursday/78779006/ (accessed May 16, 2016).
154. N. Hertz, "Why We Make Bad Decisions," *The New York Times,* October 20, 2013, p. SR-6.
155. See S. Borenstein, "Disasters Often Stem from Hubris," *The Arizona Republic,* July 10, 2010, p. A4.
156. D. Kahneman, "The Surety of Fools," *The New York Times Magazine,* October 19, 2011, pp. 30–33, 62.
157. S. Li, Y. Sun, and Y. Wang, "50% Off or Buy One, Get One Free? Frame Preference as a Function of Consumable Nature in Dairy Products," *Journal of Social Psychology,* Vol. 147 (2007), pp. 413–421.

158. See S. Benartzi, "How People Err in Estimating Their Spending in Retirement," *The Wall Street Journal*, March 28, 2016, p. R4.

159. K. Johnson, "$86M Aircraft Has Never Left the Ground," *USA Today*, March 31, 2016, p. 2B.

160. See J. Ross and B. M. Staw, "Organizational Escalation and Exit: Lessons from the Shoreham Nuclear Power Plant," *Academy of Management Journal*, August 1993, pp. 701–732.

161. G. W. Hill, "Group versus Individual Performance: Are $n + 1$ Heads Better Than 1?" *Psychological Bulletin*, May 1982, pp. 517–539. Also see W. T. H. Koh, "Heterogeneous Expertise and Collective Decision-Making," *Social Choice and Welfare*, April 2008, pp. 457–473.

162. N. F. R. Maier, "Assets and Liabilities in Group Problem Solving: The Need for Integrative Function," *Psychological Review*, Vol. 74 (1967), pp. 239–249.

163. Maier, "Assets and Liabilities in Group Problem Solving: The Need for Integrative Function."

164. For more about groupthink, see R. J. Shiller, "Challenging the Crowd in Whispers, Not Shouts," *The New York Times*, November 2, 2008, Business section, p. 5; J. Zweig, "How Group Decisions End Up Wrong-Footed," *The Wall Street Journal*, April 25–26, 2009, p. B1; S. Cain, "The Rise of the New Groupthink," *The New York Times*, January 15, 2012, pp. WR1, WR6; and J. Lehrer, "Groupthink," *The New Yorker*, January 30, 2012, pp. 22–27.

165. Methods for increasing group consensus were investigated by R. L. Priem, D. A. Harrison, and N. K. Muir, "Structured Conflict and Consensus Outcomes in Group Decision Making," *Journal of Management*, December 22, 1995, pp. 691–710.

166. I. Janis, *Groupthink*, 2nd ed. (Boston: Houghton Mifflin, 1982), p. 9. See also K. D. Lassila, "A Brief History of Groupthink," *Yale Alumni Magazine*, January–February 2008, pp. 59–61, www.philosophy-religion.org/handouts/pdfs/BRIEF-HISTORY_GROUPTHINK.pdf (accessed August 10, 2016).

167. J. Sonnenfeld, "Another Suicidal Board? How DuPont's Directors Failed Ellen Kullman," *Fortune*, October 15, 2015, http://fortune.com/2015/10/13/dupont-board-ellen-kullman/?iid=sr-link7#160 (accessed September 14, 2016).

168. See A. Bruzzese, "Keep Remote Workers in the Loop," *Arizona Republic*, March 2, 2011.

169. Janis, *Groupthink*, pp. 174–175.

170. Surowiecki, quoted in Kemper, "Senate Intelligence Report: Groupthink Viewed as Culprit in Move to War." See also J. A. LePine, "Adaptation of Teams in Response to Unforeseen Change: Effects of Goal Difficulty and Team Composition in Terms of Cognitive Ability and Goal Orientation," *Journal of Applied Psychology*, Vol. 90 (2005), pp. 1153–1167.

171. C. R. Sunstein and R. Hastie, "How to Defeat Groupthink: Five solutions," *Fortune*, January 13, 2015, http://fortune.com/2015/01/13/groupthink-solutions-information-failure/?iid=sr-link2#160 (accessed September 14, 2016).

172. See D. L. Gladstein and N. P. Reilly, "Group Decision Making under Threat: The Tycoon Game," *Academy of Management Journal*, September 1985, pp. 613–627.

173. These conclusions were based on the following studies: J. H. Davis, "Some Compelling Intuitions about Group Consensus Decisions, Theoretical and Empirical Research, and Interpersonal Aggregation Phenomena: Selected Examples, 1950–1990," *Organizational Behavior and Human Decision Processes*, June 1992, pp. 3–38; and J. A. Sniezek, "Groups under Uncertainty: An Examination of Confidence in Group Decision Making," *Organizational Behavior and Human Decision Processes*, June 1992, pp. 124–155.

174. M. W. Blenko, M. C. Mankins, and P. Rogers, "The Decision-Driven Organization," *Harvard Business Review*, June 2010, pp. 55–62.

175. T. Rogers, "How to Design Small Decision Groups," *Amazing Applications of Probability and Statistics*, www.intuitor.com/statistics/SmallGroups.html (accessed June 12, 2016).

176. Supporting results can be found in J. R. Hollenbeck, D. R. Ilgen, D. J. Sego, J. Hedlund, D. A. Major, and J. Phillips, "Multilevel Theory of Team Decision Making: Decision Performance in Teams Incorporating Distributed Expertise," *Journal of Applied Psychology*, April 1995, pp. 292–316.

177. See D. H. Gruenfeld, E. A. Mannix, K. Y. Williams, and M. A. Neale, "Group Composition and Decision Making: How Member Familiarity and Information Distribution Affect Process and Performance," *Organizational Behavior and Human Decision Processes*, July 1996, pp. 1–15.

178. P. L. McLeod, R. S. Baron, M. W. Marti, and K. Yoon, "The Eyes Have It: Minority Influence in Face-to-Face and Computer-Mediated Group Discussions," *Journal of Applied Psychology*, Vol. 82 (1997), pp. 706–718.

179. Results can be found in C. K. W. De Dreu and M. A. West, "Minority Dissent and Team Innovation: The Importance of Participation in Decision Making," *Journal of Applied Psychology*, December 2001, pp. 1191–1201.

180. G. M. Parker, *Team Players and Teamwork: The New Competitive Business Strategy* (San Francisco: Jossey-Bass, 1990).

181. These recommendations were obtained from Parker, *Team Players and Teamwork: The New Competitive Business Strategy*.

182. A. F. Osborn, *Applied Imagination: Principles and Procedures of Creative Thinking*, 3rd ed. (New York: Scribner's, 1979). For an example of how brainstorming works, see P. Croce, "Think Brighter," *FSB*, January 2006, p. 35.

183. M. Oppezzo and D. L. Schwartz, "Give Your Ideas Some Legs: The Positive Effect of Walking on Creative Thinking," *Journal of Experimental Psychology: Learning, Memory, and Cognition*, Vol. 40, No. 4 (2014), pp. 1142–1152.

184. W. H. Cooper, R. Brent Gallupe, S. Pallard, and J. Cadsby, "Some Liberating Effects of Anonymous Electronic Brainstorming," *Small Group Research*, April 1998, pp. 147–178.

185. See K. Eaton, "Finding the Right App to Unblock Those Creative Juices," *The New York Times*, February 27, 2014, p. B9.

186. For more on brainstorming and sparking creativity, see also Kon Leong, interviewed by A. Bryant, "The First Rule of Brainstorming: Suspend Disbelief," *The New York Times*, January 20, 2013, p. BU-2; "How Seemingly Irrelevant Ideas Lead to Breakthrough Innovation," *Knowledge@Wharton*, January 30, 2013, https://knowledge.wharton.upenn.edu/article/how-seemingly-irrelevant-ideas-lead-to-breakthrough-innovation (accessed June 12, 2016); S. Shellenbarger, "Tactics to Spark Creativity," *The Wall Street Journal*, April 3, 2013, pp. D1, D2; A. Gopnik, "For Innovation, Dodge the Prefrontal Police," *The Wall Street Journal*, April 6–7, 2013, p. C4; G. Lindsay, "Engineering Serendipity," *The New York Times*, April 7, 2013, p. SR-12; "How to Come Up with a Great Idea," *The Wall Street Journal*, April 29, 2013, pp. R1, R2; D. Boyd and J. Goldenberg, "Think Inside the Box," *The Wall Street Journal*, June 15–16, 2013, pp. C1, C2; T. Parker-Pope, "Do Brain Workouts Do Work? Science Isn't Sure," *The New York Times*, March 11, 2014, p. D2; and S. Lewis, *The Rise: Creativity, the Gift of Failure, and the Search for Mastery* (New York: Simon & Schuster, 2014).

187. See N. C. Dalkey, D. L. Rourke, R. Lewis, and D. Snyder, *Studies in the Quality of Life: Delphi and Decision Making* (Lexington, MA: Lexington Books, 1972). An application of the Delphi technique can be found in T. Grisham, "The Delphi Technique: A Method for Testing Complex and Multifaceted Topics," *International Journal of Managing Projects in Business*, Vol. 2, No. 1 (2009), pp. 112–130.

188. B. K. Williams and S. C. Sawyer, *Using Information Technology: A Practical Introduction to Computers & Communications*, 11th ed. (New York: McGraw-Hill, 2015), pp. 435–436.

189. David Dorfman, quoted in H. Lancaster, "How Life Lessons Have Helped a Successful Manager," *San Francisco Sunday Examiner & Chronicle*, August 15, 1999, p. CL–33.

190. J. S. Hammond, R. L. Keeney, and H. Raiffa, *Smart Choices: A Practical Guide to Making Better Decisions* (Boston: Harvard Business School Press, 1999).

191. O. Pollar, "Six Steps for Making Tough Choices," *San Francisco Examiner & Chronicle*, April 4, 1999, p. J-3.

192. Lorien Pratt and Mark Zangari, reported in "Making Good Decisions," *The Straits Times*, August 6, 2009, p. C26.

193. "Leading Motor Vehicle Manufacturers Worldwide in 2014 and 2015, Based on Global Sales (in million units)," *Statista 2016*, http://www.statista.com/statistics/275520/ranking-of-car-manufacturers-based-on-global-sales/, accessed March 29, 2016.

194. N. Bomey, "Deception at Heart of VW Emissions Scandal," *USA Today*, September 23, 2015, p. B4.

195. C. Atiyeh, "Everything You Need to Know About the VW Diesel Emissions Scandal," *Car and Driver*, January 7, 2016, http://blog.caranddriver.com/everything-you-need-to-know-about-the-vw-diesel-emissions-scandal/, accessed January 19, 2016.

196. W. Boston, M. Spector, and A. Harder, "VW Scandal Threatens to Upend CEO," *The Wall Street Journal*, September 23, 2015, pp. A1, A2.

197. D. Lawrence, B. Elgin, and V. Silver, "Fraudvergnügen, How Could Volkswagen's Top Engineers Not Have Known?," *Bloomberg Businessweek*, October 26–November 1, 2015, pp. 50–55.

198. D. Lawrence, B. Elgin, and V. Silver, "Fraudvergnügen, How Could Volkswagen's Top Engineers Not Have Known?," *Bloomberg Businessweek*, October 26–November 1, 2015, pp. 50–55.

199. C. Atiyeh, "VW CEO: We Won't Be World's No. 1 Automaker by 2018, Every Single Model under Review," *Car and Driver*, October 29, 2015, http://blog.caranddriver.com/vw-ceo-we-wont-be-worlds-no-1-automaker-by-2018-every-single-model-under-review/, accessed March 30, 2016.

200. See E. Curwen, "VW Engineers Blame Targets for Scandal," *The Times*, November 9, 2015, p. 46.

201. W. Boston, "VW Seeks Whistleblowers," *The Wall Street Journal*, November 11, 2015, p. B3.

202. W. Boston, "VW Still a Work in Process," *The Wall Street Journal*, February 24, 2016, p. B7.

203. W. Boston, "VW Still a Work in Process," *The Wall Street Journal*, February 24, 2016, p. B7.

204. M. Thompson, "Volkswagen Suspends 9 Managers Over Diesel Scandal," *CNN Money*, December 10, 2015, http://money.cnn.com/2015/12/10/news/companies/volkswagen-scandal-investigation/index.html, accessed March 30, 2016.

205. D. Lawrence, B. Elgin, and V. Silver, "Fraudvergnügen, How Could Volkswagen's Top Engineers Not Have Known?," *Bloomberg Businessweek*, October 26–November 1, 2015, pp. 50–55.

206. S. J. Ewing, "Michael Horn Resigns as Volkswagen of America President and CEO," *Autoblog*, March 9, 2016, http://www.autoblog.com/2016/03/09/michael-horn-resigns-volkswagen-america-official/, accessed March 30, 2016.

207. D. Lawrence, B. Elgin, and V. Silver, "Fraudvergnügen, How Could Volkswagen's Top Engineers Not Have Known?," *Bloomberg Businessweek*, October 26–November 1, 2015, pp. 50–55.

208. G. Ruddick, "VW Gets Go-Ahead to Repair Diesel Cars Affected by Emissions Scandal," *The Guardian*, December 16, 2015, http://www.theguardian.com/business/2015/dec/16/vw-gets-go-ahead-to-repair-diesel-cars-affected-by-emissions-scandal, accessed, January 19, 2016.

209. C. Fleming, "California Regulators Reject VW Repair Plan for Diesel Vehicles Linked to Scandal," *Los Angeles Times*, January 12, 2016, http://www.latimes.com/business/autos/la-fi-hy-carb-rejects-vw-diesel-plan-20160112-story.html, accessed March 30, 2016.

210. See W. Boston, A. Viswanatha, and S. Sloat, "VW Shares Fall in Wake of U.S. Claims," *The Wall Street Journal*, January 6, 2016, p. B3; W. Boston, "VW Appoints Manager for North America," *The Wall Street Journal*, January 20, 2016, p. B4; and N. Bomey, "Feds Seek $15B for VW Diesel Claims," *USA Today*, March 30, 2016, p. B1.

211. Z. Whittaker, "Apple vs. FBI: Here's Everything You Need to Know (FAQ)," February 19, 2016, http://www.zdnet.com/article/apple-iphone-fbi-backdoor-what-you-need-to-know-faq/ accessed March 31, 2016.

212. R. Robb, "Robb: Apple Is Right About Terrorist's iPhone," February 21, 2016, http://www.azcentral.com/staff/16975/robert-robb/, accessed March 31, 2016.

213. J. Wattles, "Apple CEO Tim Cook: Unlocking Terrorist's iPhone Is 'Bad for America'," February 25, 2016, http://money.cnn.com/2016/02/24/news/companies/apple-tim-cook-abc-interview/index.html, accessed March 31, 2016.

214. J. Wattles, "Apple CEO Tim Cook: Unlocking Terrorist's iPhone Is 'Bad for America'," February 25, 2016, http://money.cnn.com/2016/02/24/news/companies/apple-tim-cook-abc-interview/index.html, accessed March 31, 2016.

215. R. McMillan, "Apple Fight Sets Off Race Among Hackers," *The Wall Street Journal*, March 24, 2016, B1, B5.

216. D. Barrett and D. Wakabayashi, "FBI Says It Cracked Terrorist's iPhone," *The Wall Street Journal*, March 29, 2016, A1, A5.

217. K. Johnson and E. Weise, "iPhone Case Leaves 1,000 Locked Devices in Limbo," *USA Today*, March 30, 2016, B1.

218. D. Barrett, "U.S. Renews Apple Fight," *The Wall Street Journal*, April 9–10, 2016, A1, A5.

219. D. Wakabayashi, "U.S. Eyes New Way to Unlock iPhone," *The Wall Street Journal*, March 22, 2016, A1, A2.

CHAPTER 8

1. J. Welch and S. Welch, "Dear Graduate . . . ," *BusinessWeek*, June 19, 2006, p. 100.

2. Bonnie Scherry, director of corporate HR at G&A Partners, quoted in M. Tarpey, "How to Get Noticed by Your Boss," *Reno Gazette-Journal*, September 6, 2015, p. 4D.

3. E. Holton, S. Naquin, and E. Holton, *So You're New Again: How to Succeed When You Change Jobs* (San Francisco: Berrett-Koehler Publishers, 2001); M. Watkins, *The First 90 Days: Critical Success Strategies for New Leaders at All Levels* (Boston: Harvard Business School Press, 2003); J. S. Lublin, "How to Win Support from Colleagues at Your New Job," *The Wall Street Journal*, November 25, 2003, p. B1; L. Wolgemuth, "Breaking Out of the First-Job Trap," *U.S. News & World Report*, March 24/March 31, 2008, pp. 56, 58; L. Buhl, "7 Deadly Sins for New Hires," *San Francisco Chronicle*, April 4, 2010, p. E14; S. S. Wang, "The Science of Standing Out," *The Wall Street Journal*, March 18, 2014, pp. D1, D4; P. Korkki, "Be Inquisitive at the Office, and Impress," *The New York Times*, September 6, 2015, p. BU-6; and Tarpey, "How to Get Noticed by Your Boss."

4. M. Sunnafrank and A. Ramirez Jr., "At First Sight: Persistent Relational Effects of Get-Acquainted Conversations," *Journal of Social and Personal Relationships*, June 1, 2004, pp. 361–379. See also J. Zaslow, "First Impressions Get Faster," *The Wall Street Journal*, February 16, 2006, p. D4.

5. Roger Ailes, then CEO of Fox News, in "Your First Seven Seconds," *Fast Company*, June–July 1998, p. 184.

6. Thom Singer, quoted in A. Bruzzese, "You Must Keep Networking Even after You Get in the Door," *Reno Gazette-Journal*, February 25, 2010, p. 5A.

7. K. Madden, "Start New Job on the Right Foot," *Reno Gazette-Journal*, March 18, 2012, p. 1-J.

8. A. W. Brooks, F. Gino, and M. E. Schweitzer, "Smart People Ask for (My) Advice: Seeking Advice Boosts Perceptions of Competence," *Management Science*, June 2015, pp. 1421–1435. See also F. Gino, A. W. Brooks, and M. E. Schweitzer, "Anxiety, Advice, and the Ability to Discern: Feeling Anxious Motivates Individuals to Seek and Use Advice," *Journal of Personality and Social Psychology*, March 2012, pp. 497–512.

9. L. P. Frankel, in "Your First Impression," *Fast Company*, June–July 1998, p. 188.

10. Brett Wilson, interviewed by A. Bryant, "It's All in the Follow-Through," *The New York Times*, May 25, 2014, p. BU-2.

11. C. R. Mainardi, "How CEOs Get Strategy Wrong, and How They Can Get It Right," *The Wall Street Journal*, May 23, 2016, p. R8.

12. See C. A. Hartnell, A. J. Kinicki, L. S. Lambert, M. Fugate, and P. D. Corner, "Do Similarities or Differences between CEO Leadership and Organizational Culture Have a More Positive Effect on Firm Performance? A Test of Competing Predictions," *Journal of Applied Psychology*, June 2016, pp. 846–861. See also "Why CEO Style Should Contrast with Culture," *W.P. Carey Research & Ideas*, April 5, 2016, http://research.wpcarey.asu.edu/management-entrepreneurship/why-ceo-style-should-contrast-with-culture (accessed May 27, 2016).

13. E. H. Schein, "Culture: The Missing Concept in Organization Studies," *Administrative Science Quarterly*, June 1996, p. 236.

14. E. H. Schein, "The Role of the Founder in Creating Organizational Culture," *Organizational Dynamics*, Summer 1983, pp. 13–28; E. H. Schein, *Organizational Culture and Leadership* (San Francisco: Jossey-Bass, 1985); and E. H. Schein, "Organizational Culture," *American Psychologist*, Vol. 45 (1990), pp. 109–119.

15. P. Miller, interviewed by A. Bryant, "To Work Here, Win the 'Nice' Vote," *The New York Times*, July 19, 2015, p. BU-2.

16. G. Schott, interviewed by A. Bryant, "The Threats to a Positive Workplace," *The New York Times*, August 30, 2015, p. BU-2.

17. Wilson, quoted in Bryant, "It's All in the Follow-Through."

18. B. Widdicombe, "Staff's Young. So's the Boss. Problem?" *The New York Times*, March 20, 2016, pp. ST-1, ST-13.

19. R. Winkler, "Zenefits Warned Employees on Risqué Behavior," *The Wall Street Journal*, February 23, 2016, p. B4.

20. R. Feintzeig, "When 'Nice' Is a Four-Letter Word," *The Wall Street Journal*, December 31, 2015, pp. D1, D3.

21. See J. Ewing, "VW Investigation Focus to Include Managers Who Turned a Blind Eye," *The New York Times*, October 26, 2016, p. B3; W. Boston, "VW Still a Work in Progress," *The Wall Street Journal*, February 24, 2016, p. B7; J. Soble, "Mitsubishi Discloses It Cheated on Fuel Test," *The New York Times*, April 21, 2016, pp. B1, B2; and "Mitsubishi Cheating Scandal Expands to More Models," *San Francisco Chronicle*, May 12, 2016, p. C6, reprinted from *The New York Times*.

22. T. L. Friedman, "Just Doing It," *The New York Times*, April 18, 2010, Week in Review section, p. 10.

23. "EndoStim Names New CEO," *St. Louis Post-Dispatch*, May 17, 2016, www.stltoday.com/business/local/endostim-names-new-ceo/article_991da0e4-6156-50c3-8e8b-c60cf79ca113.html (accessed May 17, 2016).

24. K. K. Reardon, *The Secret Handshake: Mastering the Politics of the Business Inner Circle* (New York: Doubleday, 2002).

25. K. K. Reardon, interviewed by J. Vishnevsky, "Ask the Expert: Kathleen Kelley Reardon," *U.S. News & World Report*, July 25, 2005, p. EE10. See also T. Bradberry, "6 Powerful Ways to Win at Office Politics," *Huffington Post*, December 31, 2015, www.huffingtonpost.com/dr-travis-bradberry/6-powerful-ways-to-win-at_b_8870506.html (accessed May 17, 2016).

26. E. H. Schein, *Organizational Culture and Leadership*, 2nd ed. (San Francisco: Jossey-Bass, 1992).

27. C. Suddath, "Inside the Elephant Room," *Bloomberg Businessweek*, December 16, 2012, pp. 84–85.

28. M. C. Imd, J. S. Harrison, R. E. Hoskisson, and K. J. Imd, "Walking the Talk: A Multistakeholder Exploration of Organizational Authenticity, Employee Productivity, and Post-Merger Performance," *Academy of Management Perspectives*, Vol. 28, No. 1 (2014), pp. 38–56.

29. P. Wahba, "She Thanks You for Not Smoking," *Fortune*, September 15, 2015, p. 126.

30. Anastasia Kelly, former chief lawyer for AIG, quoted in interview with C. Loomis, "Inside the Crisis at AIG," *Fortune*, March 1, 2010, pp. 47–54.

31. Nick Friedman, quoted in B. Haislip, "When Entrepreneurs Realize 'Anything Goes' Has to Go," *The Wall Street Journal*, June 12, 2014, p. R4.

32. A thorough description of the competing values framework is provided in K. S. Cameron, R. E. Quinn, J. Degraff, and A. V. Thakor, *Creating Values Leadership* (Northampton, MA: Edward Elgar, 2006); and K. S. Cameron and R. E. Quinn, *Diagnosing and Changing Organizational Culture* (New York: Addison-Wesley, 1999). See also C. A. Hartnell, A. Y. Ou, and A. Kinicki, "Organizational Culture and Organizational Effectiveness: A Meta-Analytic Investigation of the Competing Values Framework's Theoretical Suppositions," *Journal of Applied Psychology*, Vol. 96, No. 4 (2011), pp. 677–694.

33. B. Salzman, quoted in "Acuity: Job Requirement: Have Fun at Work," *Fortune*, March 15, 2016, p. 30.

34. K. V. Brown, "Failures Helps Google Succeed," *San Francisco Chronicle*, January 22, 2015, pp. A1, A10. See also T. Lee, "Google Redoes Rules to Keep Its 'Googliness,'" *San Francisco Chronicle*, June 21, 2014, pp. A1, A8; and C. Dougherty, "Google Moves to Keep Lead as Innovator," *The New York Times*, August 11, 2015, pp. A1, B4.

35. J. B. Stewart, "A Fearless Culture Fuels Tech," *The New York Times*, June 19, 2015, pp. B1, B7.

36. Travis Kalanick, quoted in R. Blumenstein, "The Mind-Set at Uber," *The Wall Street Journal*, October 27, 2015, p. R5.

37. D. MacMillan and L. Fleisher, "Hard-Driving Uber Gives Compromise a Try," *The Wall Street Journal*, January 30, 2015, pp. A1, A10.

38. S. Fiegerman, "Driven: Uber's Campaign to Run Over Competitors and Win the World," *Mashable*, August 22, 2014, http://mashable.com/2014/08/21/uber-strategy/#zEZD693Z0qqP (accessed May 18, 2016).

39. D. McGinn, "The Numbers in Jeff Bezos's Head," *Harvard Business Review*, November 2014, p. 58.

40. C. Read, "Shape Your Culture, Shape Your Company's Future," *LinkedIn Influencer*, April 2, 2014, www.linkedin.com/today/post/article/20140402135914-322581966-shape-your-culture-shape-your-company-s-future?trk=mp-reader-card (accessed June 26, 2014).

41. "Pfizer: A Sudden Change at the Helm," *PharmExec.com*, December 6, 2010, http://blog.pharmexec.com/2010/12/06/pfizer-a-sudden-change-at-the-helm; P. Elkind and J. Reingold, with D. Burke, "Inside Pfizer's Palace Coup," *Fortune*, July 28, 2011, http://fortune.com/2011/07/28/inside-pfizers-palace-coup; and L. Timmerman, "The Fall of Pfizer: How Big Is Too Big for Pharma Innovation?" *Xconomy*, August 29, 2011, www.xconomy.com/national/2011/08/29/the-fall-of-pfizer-how-big-is-too-big-for-pharma-innovation (all accessed June 26, 2016).

42. G. Harris, "Pfizer Pays $2.3 Billion to Settle Marketing Case," *The New York Times*, September 3, 2009, www.nytimes.com/2009/09/03/business/03health.html?_r=1&scp=1&sq=Pfizer%20Fraud%20September%202009&st=cse (accessed June 20, 2016).

43. J. Kindler, quoted in R. M. Murphy, "Why Doing Good Is Good for Business," *Fortune*, February 8, 2010, pp. 90–95.

44. B. Breen, "The Thrill of Defeat," *Fast Company*, June 2004, pp. 76–81. A comprehensive article about companies that cultivate cultures that embrace failure and learn from it is J. McGregor, "How Failure Breeds Success," *BusinessWeek*, July 10, 2006, pp. 42–52.

45. J. McGregor, "The Chore Goes Offshore," *BusinessWeek*, March 23 & 30, 2009, pp. 50–51.

46. M. J. de la Merced and L. Picker, "Chief of Pfizer Defends Merger as Good for U.S.," *The New York Times*, November 24, 2015, pp. A1, B9.

47. Editorial, "A Sickly Deal," *San Francisco Chronicle*, November 24, 2015, p. A11.

48. R. Merle and C. Y. Johnson, "Pfizer, Allergan Call Off $160 Billion Merger after U.S. Moves to Block Inversions," *The Washington Post*, April 6, 2016, https://www.washingtonpost.com/business/economy/pfizer-allergan-call-off-160-billion-merger-after-us-moves-to-block-inversions/2016/04/06/4fd55446-fc11-11e5-80e4-c381214de1a3_story.html (accessed May 25, 2016).

49. T. E. Deal and A. A. Kennedy, *Corporate Cultures: The Rites and Rituals of Corporate Life* (Reading, MA: Addison-Wesley, 1982), p. 22. See also T. E. Deal and A.A. Kennedy, *The New Corporate Cultures: Revitalizing the Workplace after Downsizing,*

Mergers, and Reengineering (Cambridge, MA: Perseus, 2000). The section on organizational socialization was adapted from A. Kinicki and M. Fugate, *Organizational Behavior: A Practical, Problem-Solving Approach* (New York: McGraw-Hill Education, 2016), pp. 502–507.

50. L. Collins, "House Perfect," *The New Yorker,* October 3, 2011, pp. 54–65.

51. M. Moskowitz and R. Levering, "The 100 Best Companies to Work For," *Fortune,* February 3, 2014, pp. 108–120.

52. Marc Benioff, interviewed by C. Rose, "Charlie Rose Talks to Marc Benioff," *Bloomberg Businessweek,* December 5–December 11, 2011, p. 52. See also D. A. Kaplan, "Salesforce's Happy Workforce," *Fortune,* January 19, 2012, http://fortune.com/2012/01/19/salesforces-happy-workforce; and A. Greenberg, "Salesforce.com Offers 5 Keys to Engagement," *BenefitsPro.com,* April 10, 2014, www.benefitspro.com/2014/04/10/salesforcecom-offers-5-keys-to-engagement (both accessed May 19, 2016).

53. Ingvar Kamprad, quoted in L. Collins, "House Perfect," p. 60.

54. S. Bailey, "Benefits on Tap," *Bloomberg Businessweek,* March 21–March 27, 2011, pp. 96–97; and L. Buchman, "It's All about Ownership," *Inc.,* April 18, 2013, www.inc.com/audacious-companies/leigh-buchanan/new-belgium-brewing.html (accessed May 17, 2016).

55. J. Van Maanen, "Breaking In: Socialization to Work," in R. Dubin, ed., *Handbook of Work, Organization, and Society* (Chicago: Rand-McNally, 1976), p. 67.

56. D. C. Feldman, "The Multiple Socialization of Organization Members," *Academy of Management Review,* April 1981, pp. 309–381.

57. M. Weinstein, "Miami Children's Hospital Puts People First," *Training,* January/February 2012, pp. 43–48.

58. A. Y. Ou, C. Hartnell, A. Kinicki, E. Karam, and D. Choi, "Culture in Context: A Meta-Analysis of the Nomological Network of Organizational Culture." Presentation as part of symposium Connecting Culture and Context: Insights from Organizational Culture Theory and Research at the 2016 National Academy of Management meeting in Anaheim, California.

59. Survey by employment website Glassdoor, reported in L. Hill, "Only BFFs Need Apply," *Bloomberg Businessweek,* January 7–13, 2013, pp. 63–65.

60. See L. Hill, "Job Applicants' Cultural Fit Can Trump Qualifications," *Bloomberg Businessweek,* January 3, 2013, www.businessweek.com/articles/2013-01-03/job-applicants-cultural-fit-can-trump-qualifications (accessed May 16, 2016).

61. A. L. Kristof-Brown, R. D. Zimmerman, and E. C. Johnson, "Consequences of Individuals' Fit at Work: A Meta-Analysis of Person-Job, Person-Organization, Person-Group, and Person-Supervisor Fit," *Personnel Psychology,* Summer 2005, pp. 281–342; and A. L. Kristoff-Brown, J. Y. Seong, D. S. Degeest, W-W. Park, and D-S. Hong, "Collective Fit Perceptions: A Multilevel Investigation of Person-Group Fit with Individual-Level and Team-Level Outcomes," *Journal of Organizational Behavior,* October 2014, pp. 969–989.

62. See L. Rivera, "Hiring as Cultural Matching: The Case of Elite Professional Service Firms," *American Sociological Review,* December 2012, pp. 999–1022.

63. See A. Kinicki, "'Fitting in' Important at Workplace," *Arizona Republic,* June 8, 2015, www.azcentral.com/story/money/business/career/2015/06/07/fitting-important-workplace/28592961/ (accessed May 18, 2016); C. Boho, "How to Find the Right Cultural Fit," *Arizona Republic,* November 15, 2015, p. 4E; and Robert Half International, "Are You a Good Fit to Work for Small Company?" *Arizona Republic,* November 15, 2015, p. 6E.

64. A. S. Boyce, L. R. G. Nieminen, M. A. Gillespie, A. M. Ryan, and D. R. Denison, "Which Comes First, Organizational Culture or Performance? A Longitudinal Study of Causal Priority with Automobile Dealerships," *Journal of Organizational Behavior,* April 2015, pp. 339–359.

65. The mechanisms are based on material contained in E. H. Schein, "The Role of the Founder in Creating Organizational Culture," *Organizational Dynamics,* Summer 1983, pp. 13–28.

66. Jess Lee, interviewed by A. Bryant, "In a Corporate Culture, It's a Gift to Be Simple," *The New York Times,* November 22, 2013, p. B2.

67. Walmart's values are stated on its corporate website, "Working at Walmart," http://corporate.walmart.com/our-story/working-at-walmart (accessed May 25, 2016).

68. David Cote, interviewed by A. Bryant, "Decisiveness Is a Double-Edged Sword," *The New York Times,* November 3, 2013, p. BU-2.

69. R. E. Silverman, "Bringing Happy Hour to the Office," *The Wall Street Journal,* June 26, 2013, p. B8.

70. See E. Silverman, "Glaxco Widening Access to Its Medicines in Poor Countries," Stat, March 31, 2016, https://www.statnews.com/pharmalot/2016/03/31/glaxosmithkline-patents; and "Ranking," Access to Medicine Index 2014, Access to Medicine Foundation, Haarlem, The Netherlands, www.accesstomedicineindex.org/ranking (both accessed May 27, 2016). See also D. G. McNeil Jr., "Ally for the Poor in an Unlikely Corner," *The New York Times,* February 9, 2010, pp. D1, D6.

71. L. Feisher, "Booker Faces Storm, Critics," *The Wall Street Journal,* December 30, 2010, http://online.wsj.com/news/articles/SB10001424052970203525404576050242601770616 (accessed June 26, 2016).

72. D. Moss, "Triage: Methodically Developing Its Employees," *HR Magazine,* July 2007, p. 45.

73. J. S. Lublin, "This CEO Used to Have an Office," *The Wall Street Journal,* March 13, 2013, pp. B1, B8.

74. "Cost-Efficient, Open-Space Office Designs: Ditching Desks—and Privacy," *Knowledge @Wharton,* June 19, 2013, https://knowledge.wharton.upenn.edu/article/cost-efficient-open-space-office-designs-ditching-desks-and-privacy (accessed June 20, 2016).

75. Moss, "Triage: Methodically Developing Its Employees."

76. Rebecca Ratner, quoted in J. Larrere, "Develop Great Leaders," *Leadership Excellence,* April 2010, p. 12.

77. Adam Nash, interviewed by A. Bryant, "Teaching All Employees to Keep Score," *The New York Times,* June 13, 2014, p. B2.

78. J. Useem, "Are Bosses Necessary?" *The Atlantic,* October 2015, pp. 28–32; D. K. Berman, "The No-Boss Company," *The Wall Street Journal,* October 27, 2015, p. R3; and B. Lam, "Why Are So Many Zappos Employees Leaving?" *The Atlantic,* January 15, 2016, www.theatlantic.com/business/archive/2016/01/zappos-holacracy-hierarchy/424173 (accessed May 25, 2016).

79. D. MacMillan, "Survivor: CEO Edition," *Bloomberg Businessweek,* March 1, 2010, pp. 33–38.

80. See B. W. Swider, R. D. Zimmerman, and M. R. Barrick, "Searching for the Right Fit: Development of Applicant Person-Organization Fit Perceptions During the Recruitment Process," *Journal of Applied Psychology,* May 2015, pp. 880–893; and A. L. Kristof-Brown, J. Y. Seong, D. S. Degeest, W-W. Park, and D-S. Hong, "Collective Fit Perceptions: A Multilevel Investigation of Person-Group Fit with Individual-Level and Team-Level Outcomes," *Journal of Organizational Behavior,* October 2014, pp. 969–989.

81. C. I. Barnard, *The Functions of the Executive* (Cambridge, MA: Harvard University Press, 1938), p. 73.

82. P. M. Blau and W. R. Scott, *Formal Organizations* (San Francisco: Chandler, 1962).

83. University of Pittsburgh professor James Craft, quoted in "Avoiding 'Pink Slips of the Tongue,'" *San Francisco Chronicle,* April 8, 2016, p. C2, reprinted from *Pittsburgh Post-Gazette.*

84. See B. Kellerman, "What Every Leader Needs to Know about Followers," *Harvard Business Review,* December 2007, pp. 84–91; M. Gottfredson, S. Schaubert, and H. Saenz, "The New Leader's Guide to Diagnosing the Business," *Harvard Business Review,* February 2008, pp. 63–73; S. D. Friedman, "Be a Better Leader, Have a Richer Life," *Harvard Business Review,* April 2008, pp. 112–118; and B. Reeves, T. W. Malone, and T. O'Driscoll, "Leadership's Online Labs," *Harvard Business Review,* May 2008, pp. 58–66; F. Vincent, "Ten Tips for New Executives," *The Wall Street Journal,* February 4, 2014, p. A9; and M. Ipe, "Building Strong Relationships Is Key for Workplace Leaders," *W.P. Carey Research & Ideas,* March 21, 2016, http://research.wpcarey.asu.edu/management-entrepreneurship/building-strong-relationships-is-key-for-workplace-leaders (accessed May 25, 2016).

85. Harvard Business School professor Linda Hill, reported in Ipe, "Building Strong Relationships Is Key for Workplace Leaders."

86. Vincent, "Ten Tips for New Executives."

87. E. H. Schein, *Organizational Psychology,* 3rd ed. (Englewood Cliffs, NJ: Prentice-Hall, 1980).

88. See J. P. Friesen, A. C. Kay, R. P. Eibach, and A. D. Galinsky, "Seeking Structure in Social Organization: Compensatory Control and the Psychological Advantages of Hierarchy," *Journal of Personality and Social Psychology,* Vol. 106 (2014), pp. 590–609. This work on hierarchies existing within flat organizations is also described in M. Hutson, "Espousing Equality, but Embracing a Hierarchy," *The New York Times,* June 22, 2014, p. BU-3.

89. For an overview of the span of control concept, see D. D. Van Fleet and A. G. Bedeian, "A History of the Span of Management," *Academy of Management Review,* July 1977, pp. 356–372.

90. Research by V. Smeets and F. Warzynski, "Too Many Theories, Too Few Facts? What the Data Tell Us about the Link between Span of Control, Compensation, and Career Dynamics," *Labour Economics, Special Issue on Firms and Employees,* Vol. 15 (2008). The study was reported in G. Anders, "Overseeing More Employees—With Fewer Managers," *The Wall Street Journal,* March 24, 2008, p. B6.

91. T. A. Stewart, "CEOs See Clout Shifting," *Fortune,* November 6, 1989, p. 66.

92. J. Schleckser, "When to Delegate? Try the 70 Percent Rule," *Inc.* August 14, 2014, www.inc.com/jim-schleckser/the-70-rule-when-to-delegate.html (accessed May 25, 2016).

93. J. Welch, quoted in "Former GE CEO Jack Welch Offers 'Winning' Advice on How to Succeed in Business," Kellogg School of Management, Northwestern University, April 22, 2005, www.kellogg.northwestern.edu/news_articles/2005/welch_winning.aspx (accessed June 2, 2016).

94. O. Pollar, "Don't Overlook the Importance of Delegating," *San Francisco Examiner,* August 9, 1999, p. J-3.

95. C. M. Avery, M. A. Walker, and E. O'Toole, *Teamwork Is an Individual Skill: Getting Your Work Done When Sharing Responsibility* (San Francisco: Berrett-Koehler, 2001); S. Gazda, "The Art of Delegating: Effective Delegation Enhances Employee Morale, Manager Productivity, and Organizational Success," *HR Magazine,* January 2002, pp. 75–79; R. Burns, *Making Delegation Happen: A Simple and Effective Guide to Implementing Successful Delegation* (St. Leonards, Australia: Allen & Unwin, 2002); D. M. Genett, *If You Want It Done Right, You Don't Have to Do It Yourself! The Power of Effective Delegation* (Sanger, CA: Quill Driver Books, 2003); R. Charan, "People Acumen," *Fast Company,* December 2007, www.theleadershiphub.com/vault/files/People%20Acumen%20%20%20Ram%20Charan_0.pdf (accessed May 25, 2016).

96. E. Raudsepp, "Why Supervisors Don't Delegate," *Supervision,* May 1979, pp. 12–15; D. Anderson, "Supervisors and the Hesitate to Delegate Syndrome," *Supervision,* November 1992, pp. 9–11; Pollar, "Don't Overlook the Importance of Delegating"; Avery et al., *Teamwork Is an Individual Skill;* Burns, *Making Delegation Happen;* and Genett, *If You Want It Done Right, You Don't Have to Do It Yourself!*

97. C. C. Miller, "Google's Chief Works to Trim a Bloated Ship," *The New York Times,* November 10, 2011, pp. A1, A3. See also Lee, "Google Redoes Rules to Keep Its 'Googliness.'"

98. L. Hoffman, "The Conglomerate Is Embraced by Google," *The Wall Street Journal,* August 12, 2015, p. C4.

99. Editorial, "A Is for Alphabet," *San Francisco Chronicle,* August 12, 2015, p. A11.

100. F. Manjoo, "Google Seeks New Horizons: A Reorganization Gives the Founders Room to Dream Big beyond Search," *The New York Times,* August 11, 2015, pp. B1,

B4; T. Lee, "Alphabet: When Innovation Becomes a Corporate Concept," *San Francisco Chronicle,* August 12, 2015, pp. C1, C5; and "What's Behind Google's Alphabet Restructuring?" *Knowledge@Wharton,* August 14, 2015, http://knowledge.wharton.upenn.edu/article/googles-alphabet-reorg-can-the-whole-live-up-to-one-of-its-parts (accessed May 25, 2016).

101. This section was adapted from R. Kreitner and A. Kinicki, *Organizational Behavior,* 10th ed. (New York: McGraw-Hill/Irwin, 2013), pp. 503–508.

102. "Company Info," Whole Foods Market website, www.wholefoodsmarket.com/company-info (accessed May 25, 2016).

103. "The World's Most Admired Companies," *Fortune,* March 1, 2016, pp. 109–116.

104. R. Levering, "The 100 Best Companies to Work For," *Fortune,* March 15, 2016, pp. 141–166.

105. C. Fishman, "Whole Foods Is All Teams," *Fast Company,* Greatest Hits, Vol. 1 (1997), pp. 103–113. See also A. Bruce, S. M. Montanez, and S. Montanez, *Leaders Start to Finish: A Road Map for Developing Top Performers* (Alexandria, VA: ASTD Press, 2012), p. 143; and D. Gray and T. V. Wal, *The Connected Company* (New York: Norton, 2014), pp. 130–131.

106. G. Hamel, "Break Free," *Fortune,* September 19, 2007, http://archive.fortune.com/magazines/fortune/fortune_archive/2007/10/01/100352608/index.htm (accessed May 26, 2016).

107. A. Gasparro, "Natural Grocers Lose Vigor," *The Wall Street Journal,* April 10, 2014, pp. B1, B2; and B. Kowitt, "Whole Foods Takes Over America," *Fortune,* April 28, 2014, pp. 70–77.

108. Adapted from "Boundaryless," *Encyclopedia of Small Business,* ed. K. Hillstrom and L. C. Hillstrom (Farmington Hills, MI: Thomson Gale, 2002); and Seattle, WA: eNotes.com, 2006), http://business.enotes.com/small-business-encyclopedia/boundaryless (accessed June 20, 2014). Regarding the impact of web services on organizational boundaries, see R. D. Hof, "Web 2.0: The New Guy at Work," *BusinessWeek,* June 19, 2006, pp. 58–59.

109. N. Anand and R. L. Daft, "What Is the Right Organization Design?" *Organizational Dynamics,* Vol. 36 (2007), pp. 329–344.

110. S. Siekman, "The Snap-Together Business Jet," *Fortune,* January 21, 2002, http://archive.fortune.com/magazines/fortune/fortune_archive/2002/01/21/316585/index.htm (accessed May 25, 2016); and Anand and Daft, "What Is the Right Organization Design?" p. 336.

111. M. J. Mandel and R. D. Hof, "Rethinking the Internet," *BusinessWeek,* March 26, 2001, p. 118.

112. Adapted from "Virtual Organization," Whatis.com, http://whatis.techtarget.com/definition/virtual-organization (accessed May 25, 2016).

113. R. E. Silverman, "Step into the Office-Less Company," *The Wall Street Journal,* September 4, 2012, p. B6.

114. M. Sappington, "When to Go Unvirtual," *Inc.,* April 2010, p. 73.

115. S. Monson, "Maid to Order," *Seattle Times,* April 16, 2006, http://old.seattletimes.com/html/businesstechnology/2002932996_hospitality16.html (accessed June 23, 2016).

116. H. Touryalai, "Ready, Set, Clean! Secrets to Cleaning a Marriott Hotel Room," *Forbes,* June 26, 2013, www.forbes.com/sites/halahtouryalai/2013/06/26/ready-set-clean-secrets-to-cleaning-a-marriott-hotel-room/#36bc03aa7d0f (accessed May 25, 2016).

117. T. Burns and G. M. Stalker, *The Management of Innovation* (London: Tavistock, 1961). See also W. D. Sine, H. Mitsuhashi, and D. A. Kirsch, "Revisiting Burns and Stalker: Formal Structure and New Venture Performance in Emerging Economic Sectors," *Academy of Management Journal,* February 2006, pp. 121–132.

118. T. J. Peters and R. H. Waterman, *In Search of Excellence* (New York: Harper & Row, 1982).

119. A. Westervelt, "Creative Ways to Live under the Same Roof," *The Wall Street Journal,* June 12, 2014, p. R4.

120. P. R. Lawrence and J. W. Lorsch, *Organization and Environment* (Homewood, IL: Irwin, 1967).

121. A. D. Chandler Jr., *Strategy and Structure: Chapters in the History of the Industrial Enterprise* (Cambridge, MA: MIT Press, 1962).

122. "Gore at a Glance: Overview Fast Facts," http://www.gore.com/en_xx/aboutus/fastfacts/index.html?isAjax=true, accessed April 4, 2016.

123. D. Roberts, "A Latticework of Workers," *Fortune,* March 5, 2015, 130–134.

124. D. Roberts, "A Latticework of Workers," *Fortune,* March 5, 2015, 130–134.

125. "Our Culture: A Team-Based, Flat Lattice Organization," http://www.gore.com/en_xx/aboutus/culture/index.html, accessed April 4, 2016.

126. D. Roberts, "A Latticework of Workers," *Fortune,* March 5, 2015, p. 134.

127. "Working in Our Unique Culture," http://www.gore.com/en_xx/careers/whoweare/ourculture/gore-company-culture.html, accessed April 4, 2016.

128. Excerpted from "What We Believe," https://www.gore.com/en_xx/careers/whoweare/whatwebelieve/gore-culture.html, accessed April 4, 2016.

129. "Our Culture: A Team-Based, Flat Lattice Organization," http://www.gore.com/en_xx/aboutus/culture/index.html, accessed April 4, 2016.

130. Excerpted from E. Van Der Koogh, "Profile: WL Gore & Associates," February 11, 2014, http://21stcenturymba.com/pioneers/profile-gore/, accessed April 4, 2016.

131. D. Roberts, "A Latticework of Workers," *Fortune,* March 5, 2015, pp. 130–134.

132. See S. Marks, "Should Company Outings Be Mandatory?" November 5, 2012, https://www.recruiter.com/i/should-company-outings-be-mandatory/, accessed April 4, 2016.

133. M. Kendall, "What's So Bad About Mandatory Workplace Socializing?" February 24, 2016, http://qz.com/623260/whats-so-bad-about-mandatory-workplace-socializing/, accessed April 4, 2016.

CHAPTER 9

1. See K. Tyler, "Generation Gaps," *HR Magazine,* January 2008, pp. 69–72; and M. C. White, "The Real Reason New College Grads Can't Get Hired," *Time,* November 10, 2013, http://business.time.com/2013/11/10/the-real-reason-new-college-grads-cant-get-hired (accessed May 31, 2016); S. Ricker, "Soft Skills Factor into a Job Search," *Reno Gazette-Journal,* September 29, 2013, p. 9F; and A. Bruzzese, "Digital Natives Require 'Soft Skills' to Secure a Job," *Reno Gazette-Journal,* January 11, 2014, p. 7A.

2. Annie Shanklin Jones of I.B.M., quoted in P. Korkki, "Please, No Board Shorts in the Boardroom," *The New York Times,* May 24, 2009, p. BU-9.

3. A. Bruzzese, "Learn the Customs, Dress Code of Your New Corporate Culture," *Reno Gazette-Journal,* April 17, 2009, p. 7A.

4. See M. W. Kraus and W. B. Berry, "Sartorial Symbols of Social Class Elicit Class-Consistent Behavioral and Physiological Responses: A Dyadic Approach," *Journal of Experimental Psychology,* December 2014, pp. 2330–2340; and M. L. Stepian, S. N. Ferber, J. M. Gold, and A. M. Rutchick, "The Cognitive Consequences of Formal Clothing," *Social Psychological and Personality Science,* August 2015, pp. 661–668.

5. C. Larson, "The Chinese Take Their Etiquette Seriously," *Bloomberg Business week,* June 3–June 9, 2013, pp. 15–16.

6. D. Robinson, "Business Meal Manners," *San Francisco Chronicle,* November 23, 2008, p. H2; D. Robinson, "Manners Matter at Work, Too," *San Francisco Chronicle,* April 5, 2009, p. D7; J. Thompson, "How to Put Success on the Menu," *Reno Gazette-Journal,* March 10, 2013, p. 7F; and S. Ricker, "Manners Make for Good Business," *Reno Gazette-Journal,* April 13, 2014, p. 8D.

7. Online survey by Harris Interactive in the United States for Lookout, May 8–10, 2012, among 2,097 adults ages 18 and older, reported in "Mobile Mindset Study," https://www.lookout.com/img/images/lookout-mobile-mindset-2012.pdf (accessed May 31, 2016).

8. Robert Half survey of 659 human resource managers, reported in "Do Breaches in Tech Etiquette Hurt Work Life?" *USA Today,* February 19, 2014, p. 1B.

9. Jive/Harris survey of 1,098 employees, reported in "Most Annoying Smartphone Behaviors at Work," *USA Today,* January 17, 2014, p. 1B.

10. B. Feiler, "Should You Google at Dinner?" *The New York Times,* December 12, 2010, p. ST-2; A. Bruzzese, "Put Down That Smartphone in Meetings, at Lunch," *Reno Gazette-Journal,* March 24, 2011, p. 8A; K. Komando, "Mind Your Tech Manners in the New Year Ahead," *Reno Gazette-Journal,* December 29, 2013, p. 6F; and K. Komando, "Bad Tech Habits and How to Stop Them," *Reno Gazette-Journal,* June 28, 2014, p. 8A.

11. *The 2015 Jobvite Recruiter Nation Survey,* https://www.jobvite.com/wp-content/uploads/2015/09/jobvite_recruiter_nation_2015.pdf (accessed May 31, 2016). See also B. Evangelisa, "Good Online Manners Key in Job Search," *San Francisco Chronicle,* September 6, 2013, pp. C1, C4.

12. R. Levering, "The 100 Best Companies to Work For," *Fortune,* March 15, 2016, pp. 142–165.

13. A. Fisher, "How to Get Hired by a 'Best' Company," *Fortune,* February 4, 2008, p. 96.

14. See A. Lashinsky, "Google Is No. 1: Search and Enjoy," *Fortune,* January 10, 2007, http://archive.fortune.com/2007/01/05/magazines/fortune/Search_and_enjoy.fortune/index.htm (accessed June 1, 2016); and Levering, "The 100 Best Companies to Work For," p. 145.

15. E. Schmidt, quoted in interview by A. Lashinsky, "Back2Back Champs," *Fortune,* February 4, 2008, p. 70.

16. A. Barr, "Alphabet Reports Rising Profits at Core Google Businesses," *The Wall Street Journal,* February 1, 2016, www.wsj.com/articles/alphabet-reports-rising-profits-at-core-google-businesses-1454361634 (accessed June 1, 2016).

17. J. Welch, quoted in N. M. Tichy and S. Herman, *Control Your Destiny or Someone Else Will: How Jack Welch Is Making General Electric the World's Most Competitive Corporation* (New York: Doubleday, 1993), p. 251.

18. See Levering, "The 100 Best Companies to Work For."

19. L. Weber and R. Feintzeig, "Is It a Dream or a Drag? Companies without HR," *The Wall Street Journal,* April 9, 2014, pp. B1, B7.

20. See J. Slocum, D. Lei, and P. Butler, "Executing Business Strategies through Human Resource Management Practices," *Organizational Dynamics,* April–June 2014, pp. 73–87; and S. Aryee, F. O. Walumbwa, E. Y. M. Seidu, and L. E. Otaye, "Impact of High-Performance Work Systems on Individual- and Branch-Level Performance: Test of a Multilevel Model of Intermediate Linkages," *Journal of Applied Psychology,* March 2012, pp. 287–300; and C. Chadwick, J. F. Super, and K. Kwon, "Resource Orchestration in Practice: CEO Emphasis on SHRM, Commitment-Based HR Systems, and Firm Performance," *Strategic Management Journal,* Vol. 36 (2015), pp. 360–376.

21. P. Capelli and A. Crocker-Hefter, "Distinctive Human Resources Are Firms' Core Competencies," *Organizational Dynamics,* Winter 1996, pp. 7–22. See also R. R. Kehoe and P. M. Wright, "The Impact of High-Performance Human Resource Practices on Employees' Attitudes and Behaviors," *Journal of Management,* February 2013, pp. 366–391; P. Cappelli, "Why We Love to Hate HR . . . and What HR Can Do about It," *Harvard Business Review,* July–August 2015, pp. 54–61; "Has Human Resources Lost Its Edge in a Tech-Driven World?" *Knowledge@Wharton,* May 19, 2015, http://knowledge.wharton.upenn.edu/article/has-human-resources-lost-its-edge-in-a-tech-driven-world (accessed June 1, 2016); R. Charan, D. Barton, and D. Carey, "People before Strategy: A New Role for the CHRO," *Harvard Business Review,* July–August 2015, pp. 63–71; and J. Schramm, "On the Same Page," *HR Magazine,* October 15, 2015, p. 69.

22. B. E. Becker, M. A. Huselid, and D. Ulrich, *The HR Scorecard: Linking People, Strategy, and Performance* (Boston: Harvard Business School Press, 2001), p. 4.

23. Becker, Huselid, and Ulrich, *The HR Scorecard,* p. 4. See also D. Stamps, "Measuring Minds," *Training,* May 2000, pp. 76–85; C. A. Bartlett and S. Ghoshal, "Building Competitive Advantage through People," *MIT Sloan Management Review,* Winter

2002, pp. 34–41; G. Gohlander, S. Snell, and A. Sherman, *Managing Human Resources*, 13th ed. (Mason, OH: South-Western Publishing, 2004); and R. Rodriguez, "Meet the New Learning Executive," *HR Magazine*, April 2005, pp. 64–69.

24. Levering, "The 100 Best Places to Work For."

25. See M. Feffer, "New Connections," *HR Magazine*, April 2015, pp. 46–52.

26. See L. Rainie, "Incentives—and Pressures—for U.S. Workers in a 'Knowledge Economy,'" Pew Research Center, March 23, 2016, www.pewresearch.org/fact-tank/2016/03/23/incentives-and-pressures-for-u-s-workers-in-a-knowledge-economy (accessed June 1, 2016).

27. C. M. Barnes, K. Jiang, and D. P. Lepak, "Sabotaging the Benefits of Our Own Human Capital: Work Unit Characteristics and Sleep," *Journal of Applied Psychology*, February 2016, pp. 209–221.

28. T. Casciaro, F. Gino, and M. Kouchake, "Managing Yourself: Learn to Love Networking," *Harvard Business Review*, May 2016, pp. 104–107.

29. R. J. Mirabile, "The Power of Job Analysis," *Training*, April 1990, pp. 70–74; and S. F. Mona, "The Job Description," *Association Management*, February 1991, pp. 33–37. See also C. Lagorio-Chafkin, "How to Write a Job Description," *Inc.*, April 1, 2010, www.inc.com/guides/2010/04/writing-job-description.html; and L. Weber, "Help Wanted—on Writing Job Descriptions," *The Wall Street Journal*, October 2, 2013, http://online.wsj.com/news/articles/SB10001424052702303643304579107793132 873508 (both accessed June 29, 2014).

30. T. S. Bernard, "Job Hunting in the Digital Age," *The New York Times*, April 10, 2016, Education Life section, p. 19.

31. J. Sullivan, interviewed by N. Waller, "The Key to Making Sure You Hire the Best Performers," *The Wall Street Journal*, June 2, 2016, p. B6.

32. Dave Lefkow, CEO of TalentSpark, quoted in C. Winkler, "Quality Check," *HR Magazine*, May 2007, pp. 93–98.

33. R. Zeidner, "People Promoted to the Top Jobs Measure Up," *HR Magazine*, April 2010, p. 20. The article reports on a study by Y. Zhang and N. Rajagopalan, "Once an Outsider, Always an Outsider? CEO Origin, Strategic Change, and Firm Performance," *Strategic Management Journal*, Vol. 31 (2010), pp. 969–989. See also M. Bidwell, "Paying More to Get Less: The Effects of External Hiring versus Internal Mobility," *Administrative Science Quarterly*, Vol. 56 (201)), pp. 369–407; "Why External Hires Get Paid More, and Perform Worse, Than Internal Staff," *Knowledge@Wharton*, March 28, 2012, http://knowledge.wharton.upenn.edu/article.cfm?articleid=2961 (accessed July 5, 2016); and P. Cappelli, M. Hamori, and R. Bonet, "Who's Got Those Top Jobs?" *Harvard Business Review*, March 2014, pp. 75–79.

34. "More Firms Rehiring Workers Who Left," *San Francisco Chronicle*, April 1, 2016, p. C3, reprinted from S *Pittsburgh Post-Gazette*. See also L. Gellman, "Ex-Employees: Gone, Not Forgotten," *The Wall Street Journal*, February 22, 2016, p. R8.

35. B. Tedeschi, "Searching for a Job? Try Looking at Your Hand-Held First," *The New York Times*, May 19, 2011, p. B8; B. Evangelista, "More Job Seekers Turning to Online Social Networks," *San Francisco Chronicle*, November 17, 2011, p. D5; and R. S. Chauhan, M. Buckley, and M. Harvey, "Facebook and Personnel Selection: What's the Big Deal?" *Organizational Dynamics*, Vol. 42 (2013), pp. 126–134.

36. See J. Schramm, "Are You on #SocialMedia?" *HR Magazine*, January 2016, p. 57.

37. Survey conducted by Potential Park Communications, Stockholm, reported in J. Walker, "Young Job Seekers Turn to Smartphones," *The Wall Street Journal*, March 7, 2012, p. B9. See also L. Weber, "Job Hunt Moves to Mobile Devices," *The Wall Street Journal*, April 24, 2013, p. B8.

38. B. Thorley, "How to Recruit Top Talent Employees through Social Networking," *The Kinesis Blog*, March 3, 2014, www.kinesisinc.com/social-media/how-to-recruit-top-talent-employees-through-social-networking (accessed June 2, 2016). See also E. Holcomb, "Job Hunting in the Age of LinkedIn," *The Wall Street Journal*, January 29, 2014, p. A17; and K. Eaton, "Remember Want Ads for Jobs? Now You Find Them on a Phone," *The New York Times*, January 30, 2014, p. B11.

39. See B. Evangelista, "New LinkedIn App Focuses on Helping Graduating Collegians," *San Francisco Chronicle*, April 18, 2016, pp. D1, D4.

40. See D. Monaghan, "Global and Cultural Effectiveness: Recruiting Is Social and Talent Is Local," *HR Magazine*, December 2015/January 2016, p. 38.

41. See E. Krell, "Look Outside or Seek Within?" *HR Magazine*, January/February 2016, pp. 61–64.

42. Respondents to the Society for Human Resource Management's *2007 E-Recruiting Survey* reported that employee referrals generated the highest quality of job candidates and best return on investment for their organization. See T. Minton-Eversole, "E-Recruitment Comes of Age, Survey Says," *HR Magazine*, August 2007, p. 34. Also see D. G. Allen and R. V. Mahto, "Web-Based Recruitment: Effects of Information, Organizational Brand, and Attitudes Toward a Web Site on Applicant Attraction," *Journal of Applied Psychology*, November 2007, pp. 1696–1708.

43. Sullivan, interviewed by N. Waller, "The Key to Making Sure You Hire the Best Performers."

44. Tedeschi, "Searching for a Job? Try Looking at Your Hand-Held First"; Evangelista, "More Job Seekers Turning to Online Social Networks"; Walker, "Young Job Seekers Turn to Smartphones"; Reid Hoffman, interviewed by A. Kessler, "Job Hunting in the Network Age," *The Wall Street Journal*, July 19–20, 2014, p. A9; and T. S. Bernard, "Job Hunting in the Digital Age," *The New York Times*, April 10, 2016, Education Life, p. 19.

45. C. Said, "BlueCrew Applies Tech to Fill Blue-Collar Jobs, *San Francisco Chronicle*, March 2, 2016, pp. C1, C6.

46. S. E. Needleman, "Play This Game and Win a Job!" *The Wall Street Journal*, March 14, 2016, www.wsj.com/articles/play-this-game-and-win-a-job-1457921553 (accessed June 4, 2016).

47. R. Feintzeig, "With 'Blind Hiring,' It's Not Who You Are, It's What You Know," *The Wall Street Journal*, January 6, 2016, pp. B1, B4; and W. Lee, "Woo Sets Up Blind Dates for Workers, Employers," *San Francisco Chronicle*, March 4, 2016, pp. C1, C3.

48. L. M. Katz, "Cool and Competent," *HR Magazine*, March 2015, pp. 57–60.

49. P. McCord, "How Netflix Reinvented HR," *Harvard Business Review*, January–February 2014, pp. 71–76. See also S. M. Gully, J. M. Phillips, W. G. Castellano, K. Han, and A. Kim, "A Mediated Moderation Model of Recruiting Socially and Environmentally Responsible Job Applicants," *Personnel Psychology*, Vol. 66, No. 4 (2013), pp. 935–974; A. C. Klotz, S. P. Da Motta Veiga, M. R. Buckley, and M. B. Gavin, "The Role of Trustworthiness in Recruitment and Selection: A Review and Guide for Future Research," *Journal of Organizational Behavior*, Vol. 34, No. S1 (2013), pp. S104–S119; K. Tyler, "New Kids on the Block," *HR Magazine*, October 2013, pp. 35–40; and R. J. Thomas, "Building a Game-Changing Talent Strategy," *Harvard Business Review*, January–February 2014, pp. 63–68.

50. See J. M. Phillips, "Effects of Realistic Job Previews on Multiple Organizational Outcomes: A Meta-Analysis," *Academy of Management Journal*, December 1998, pp. 673–690.

51. M. A. Tucker, "Show and Tell," *HR Magazine*, January 2012, pp. 51–53.

52. F. Chideya, interviewed by D. Graham, "'The Episodic Career': Navigating Today's Job Market," *Knowledge@Wharton*, February 3, 2016, http://knowledge.wharton.upenn.edu/article/episodic-career-navigating-todays-job-market (accessed June 15, 2016).

53. L. F. Katz and A. B. Krueger, "The Rise and Nature of Alternative Work Arrangements in the United States, 1995–2015," Working paper, March 29, 2015, http://krueger.princeton.edu/sites/default/files/akrueger/files/katz_krueger_cws_-_march_29_20165.pdf (accessed June 15, 2016).

54. N. Irwin, "Job Growth in Past Decade Was in Temp and Contract," *The New York Times*, March 31, 2015, p. A3. See also K. Pender, "How Contractors and Employees Differ," *San Francisco Chronicle*, September 20, 2015, pp. D1, D3; and S. Westly, "A Third Definition of Contractors and Employees," *San Francisco Chronicle*, February 21, 2016, p. E6.

55. See D. Farrell and F. Greig, "Paychecks, Paydays, and the Online Platform Economy: Big Data on Income Volatility," J.P. Morgan Chase Institute, February 2016, https://www.jpmorganchase.com/corporate/institute/document/jpmc-institute-volatility-2-report.pdf (accessed June 15, 2016). See also E. Morath, "Top Earners Gain in Gig Economy," *The Wall Street Journal*, May 4, 2016, p. A21.

56. "Intuit 2020 Report: Twenty Trends That Will Shape the Next Decade," Intuit, October 2010, http://http-download.intuit.com/http.intuit/CMO/intuit/futureofsmallbusiness/intuit_2020_report.pdf (accessed June 15, 2016).

57. F. Chideya, *The Episodic Career: How to Thrive at Work in the Age of Disruption* (New York: Atria, 2016).

58. F. Chideya, interviewed by D. Graham, "'The Episodic Career': Navigating Today's Job Market," *Knowledge@Wharton*, February 3, 2016, http://knowledge.wharton.upenn.edu/article/episodic-career-navigating-todays-job-market (accessed June 15, 2016).

59. A. Bruzzese, "Lying on Resume Is Treading on Dangerous Ground," *Reno Gazette-Journal*, March 8, 2012, p. 5A.

60. CareerBuilder 2015 survey, reported in "Liar, Liar, Resume on Fire," *HR Magazine*, October 2015, p. 18.

61. R. Feintzeig and R. E. Silverman, "Background Checks Are Booming," *The Wall Street Journal*, May 11, 2016, p. B7.

62. For examples, see P. Anand, "5 Big Shots Who Lied on Their Resumes," MarketWatch, September 20, 2014, www.marketwatch.com/story/5-big-shots-who-lied-on-their-resumes-2014-09-18 (accessed June 4, 2016).

63. C. W. Nevius, "If You Like Fiction, Read the Job Resumes," *San Francisco Chronicle*, February 28, 2006, pp. B1, B2. See also D. Koeppel, "That Padded Résumé Won't Help Break Your Fall," *San Francisco Chronicle*, April 23, 2006, p. F5; reprinted from *The New York Times*.

64. A. Efrati and J. S. Lublin, "Resume Trips Up Yahoo Chief," *The Wall Street Journal*, May 5–6, 2012, pp. A1, A12.

65. Report by Automatic Data Processing, Roseland, NJ, cited in J. L. Seglin, "Lies Can Have a (Long) Life of Their Own," *The New York Times*, June 16, 2002, sec. 3, p. 4. See also S. Armour, "Security Checks Worry Workers," *USA Today*, June 19, 2004, p. 1B.

66. J. S. Lublin, "Job Hunters with Gaps in Their Resumes Need to Write Around Them," *The Wall Street Journal*, May 6, 2003, p. B1.

67. P. Cohen, "Perils of a Gap in the Resume," *The New York Times*, May 20, 2016, pp. B1, B6.

68. M. Conlin, "Don't Hedge Your Age," *BusinessWeek*, October 6, 2003, p. 14. See also C. Dahle, "A Nip and Tuck for the Resume," *The New York Times*, April 17, 2005, sec. 3, p. 10.

69. B. Bergstein, "Ex-Wiki Exec's Criminal History," *San Francisco Chronicle*, December 27, 2007, pp. C1, C2.

70. D. Belkin, "More Job Seekers Scramble to Erase Their Criminal Past," *The Wall Street Journal*, November 11, 2009, pp. A1, A16.

71. See the website of The National Reentry Resource Center, a project of the Council of State Governments Justice Center, https://csgjusticecenter.org/reentry (accessed June 4, 2016). Also see Associated Press, "Public Face of Re-entry Effort Speaks from Experience," *San Francisco Chronicle*, April 27, 2016, p. A6.

72. See E. Krell, "Unmasking Illegal Workers," *HR Magazine*, December 2007, pp. 49–52; and S. Berfield, "Illegals and Business: A Glimpse of the Future?" *Business Week*, January 14, 2008, pp. 52–54.

73. W. M. Welch, "Employee Screenings See Growth," *USA Today*, June 24, 2009, p. 3A. The adverse effect of E-Verify on agricultural hiring is described in N. Leiber, "A Verification System for New Hires Backfires," *Bloomberg Businessweek*, October 24–October 30, 2011, p. 60.

74. L. Radnofsky and M. Jordan, "Illegal Workers Slip by System," *The Wall Street Journal*, February 25, 2010, p. A6.

75. B. Braccio Hering, "Words to Use, Lose on Resume," *Reno Gazette-Journal*, June 26, 2011, p. 1F; K. Madden, "Increase Job Search Success," *Reno Gazette-Journal*,

August 14, 2011, p. 1F; D. Auerbach, "Error-Free Resumes, Cover Letters a Must," *Reno Gazette-Journal,* October 23, 2011, p. 1F; and R. E. Silverman, "No More Resumes, Say Some Firms," *The Wall Street Journal,* January 24, 2012, p. B6.

76. D. Paletta, "Security Clearance to Probe Social Media," *The Wall Street Journal,* May 14–15, 2016, p. A3.

77. L. Weber, "Your Resume vs. Oblivion," *The Wall Street Journal,* January 24, 2012, pp. B1, B6.

78. L. Weber, "When the Going Gets Tough, Job Hunters Call in the Stunt Resume," *The Wall Street Journal,* January 24, 2014, pp. A1, A6.

79. M. Korn, "Giant Resumes Fail to Impress," *The Wall Street Journal,* February 6, 2014, p. B7.

80. References are even a problem in faculty hiring in universities. See D. M. Barden, "The Unreliability of References," *The Chronicle of Higher Education,* January 11, 2008, pp. C1, C4.

81. A. Bruzzese, "Don't Let References Torpedo Your Job Chances," *Reno Gazette-Journal,* January 26, 2012, pp. 5A, 6A.

82. A. Martin, "As a Hiring Filter, Credit Checks Draw Questions," *The New York Times,* April 10, 2010, pp. B1, B4.

83. C. Choi, "Credit Reports: Who's Looking at Yours, and Why?" *Reno Gazette-Journal,* April 12, 2010, p. 8A.

84. Based on P. Bathurst, "How to Avoid Those Fatal Interview Mistakes," *The Arizona Republic,* March 9, 2008, p. EC1; "Preparation Key to Snaring Job," *The Arizona Republic,* April 15, 2009, p. EC1; T. Musbach, "Common Interview Surprise: Inappropriate Questions," *San Francisco Chronicle,* January 3, 2010, p. D1; J. S. Lublin, "The New Job Is in the Details," *The Wall Street Journal,* January 5, 2010, p. D5; "4 Keys to Interview Success," *The Arizona Republic,* April 4, 2010, p. EC1; A. Bruzzese, "Market Yourself Like a Product to Get Employers' Attention," *USA Today,* December 2, 2011, www.usatoday.com/money/jobcenter/workplace/bruzzese/story/2011-11-30/learn-to-market-yourself-to-get-job/51482754/1 (accessed March 15, 2012); and K. Madden, "Proper Preparation Enhances Job Interviews," *Reno Gazette-Journal,* February 25, 2012, p. 1F. For a discussion of standard interview questions, see survey by jobs website Glassdoor.com, reported in "Job Interviews Touch on Weak Economy," *The Wall Street Journal,* January 3, 2012, p. B7.

85. For some interview preparation tips, see A. Bruzzese, "Tips to Prepare Well for Job Interview via Video," *Reno Gazette-Journal,* January 24, 2013, p. 6A; C. Wang, "Interview Anxiety Is Common," *The Arizona Republic,* October 19, 2013, www.azcentral.com/business/jobs/articles/20131014interview-anxiety-common.html (accessed July 5, 2016); "Interview Pointers for Body Language," *The Arizona Republic,* October 30, 2013, p. CL1; R. Walker, "How to Explain That Lost Job," *The New York Times,* November 17, 2013, p. BU-7; D. Auerbach, "Negotiate for a Better Starting Salary," *Reno Gazette-Journal,* December 8, 2013, p. 8F; and E. Bernstein, "What Verbal Tics May Be Saying about Us," *The Wall Street Journal,* January 21, 2014, p. D3; "Job Interview Process Is Taking Much Longer," *San Francisco Chronicle,* June 19, 2015, p. C2, reprinted from *The Washington Post;* E. Gray, "Top 10 Things Not to Do in an Interview," *Arizona Republic,* August 19, 2015, p. 1CL; S. Ricker, "Be Prepared for the 3 Toughest Interview Questions," *Reno Gazette-Journal,* August 30, 2015, p. 4F; and "Take Stress Out of Job Interview," *San Francisco Chronicle,* October 16, 2015, p. C2, reprinted from *Pittsburgh Post-Gazette.*

86. N. P. Podsakoff, S. W. Whiting, P. M. Podsakoff, and P. Mishra, "Effects of Organizational Citizenship Behaviors on Selection Decisions in Employment Interviews," *Journal of Applied Psychology,* Vol. 96 (2011), pp. 310–326.

87. V. Oliver, "Blew the Job Interview? There's Still Hope," *San Francisco Chronicle,* July 11, 2014, p. C2.

88. See "Carefully Chosen References Can Give You an Edge," *Arizona Republic,* October 26, 2011, p. CL1.

89. *Background Checking—The Use of Criminal Background Checks in Hiring Decisions,* survey by Society for Human Resource Management, July 19, 2012, https://www.shrm.org/research/surveyfindings/articles/pages/criminalbackgroundcheck.aspx (accessed June 5, 2016).

90. M. Korn, "Job Hunt? Dig Up Those SAT Scores," *The Wall Street Journal,* February 26, 2014, pp. B1, B8.

91. J. Silver-Greenberg and M. Corkery, "Bank Account Screening Tool Is Scrutinized as Excessive," *The New York Times,* June 16, 2014, pp. B1, B2.

92. A. Finder, "When a Risqué Online Persona Undermines a Chance for a Job," *The New York Times,* June 11, 2006, pp. A1, A24; and S. E. Needleman, "Job Hunters, Beware," *The Wall Street Journal,* February 2, 2010, p. D4.

93. A. Acquisti and C. Fong, "An Experiment in Hiring Discrimination via Online Social Networks," *Social Science Research Network,* November 21, 2013, http://papers.ssrn.com/sol3/papers.cfm?abstract_id=2031979 (accessed July 5, 2016).

94. Associated Press, "Job Seekers Asked for Facebook Keys," *San Francisco Chronicle,* March 21, 2012, pp. D1, D2. For more about the effects of social media on hiring, see S. Hananel, "Facebook Tricky for Employers, Workers," *Reno Gazette-Journal,* October 2, 2011, p. 5E; K. Weise, "Who Does Google Think You Are?" *Bloomberg Businessweek,* February 6–February 12, 2012, pp. 39–40; A. Townsend, "This Is Your Life," *Time,* February 13, 2012, pp. 34–39; L. Kwoh, "Workplace Crystal Ball, Courtesy of Facebook," *The Wall Street Journal,* February 21, 2012, p. B8; K. Pender, "Behavior on Social Networks Could Cost Students," *San Francisco Chronicle,* March 6, 2012, pp. D1, D5; K. Trinko, "Keep Your Hands Off of My Facebook Password," *USA Today,* March 14, 2012, p. 9A; and L. Andrews, *I Know Who You Are and I Saw What You Did: Social Networks and the Death of Privacy* (New York: Free Press, 2012).

95. M. Madden, *Privacy Management on Social Media Sites,* Pew Research Center, Pew Internet & American Life Project, February 24, 2012, www.pewinternet.org/~/media/Files/Reports/2012/PIP_Privacy_management_on_social_media_sites_022412.pdf (accessed July 5, 2016). See also J. Angwin, "Sites Are Accused of Privacy Failings," *The Wall Street Journal,* February 13, 2012, pp. B1, B8: B. Evangelista, "Is It Time to Unfriend?" *San Francisco Chronicle,* February 25, 2012, pp. D1, D3; and B. Ortutay, "Profile Pruning," *Reno Gazette-Journal,* February 28, 2012, p. 6A.

96. R. Feintzeig, "Hiring on the Fast Track," *The Wall Street Journal,* September 17, 2015, pp. B1, B2.

97. S. Shellenbarger, "The Six-Month Job Interview," *The Wall Street Journal,* January 20, 2016, pp. D1, D4.

98. S. E. Needleman, "The New Trouble on the Line," *The Wall Street Journal,* June 2, 2009, pp. B7, B10; and K. Tyler, "Who You Gonna Call?" *HR Magazine,* April 2014, pp. 65–67.

99. D. S. Chapman, K. L. Uggerslev, and J. Webster, "Applicant Reactions Face-to-Face and Technology-Mediated Interviews: A Field Investigation," *Journal of Applied Psychology,* Vol. 88 (2003), pp. 944–953.

100. See J. Levashina and M. A. Campion, "Measuring Faking in the Employment Interview: Development and Validation of an Interview Faking Behavior Scale," *Journal of Applied Psychology,* November 2007, pp. 1638–1656.

101. E. D. Pursell, M. A. Campion, and S. R. Gaylord, "Structured Interviewing: Avoiding Selection Problems," *Personnel Journal,* November 1980; and J. Levashina, C. J. Hartwell, F. P. Morgeson, and M. A. Campion, "The Structured Employment Interview: Narrative and Quantitative Review of the Research Literature," *Personnel Psychology,* Vol. 67, No. 1 (2014), pp. 241–293.

102. M. C. Blackman, "Personality Judgment and the Utility of the Unstructured Employment Interview," *Basic and Applied Social Psychology,* Vol. 24 (2002), pp. 241–250. See also B. W. Swider, M. R. Barrick, T. B. Harris, and A. C. Stoverink, "Managing and Creating an Image in the Interview: The Role of Interviewee Initial Impressions," *Journal of Applied Psychology,* Vol. 96 (2011), pp. 1275–1288.

103. A. Arredondo, "Prepare Yourself for the Behavioral Interview," *The Arizona Republic,* March 2, 2008, p. EC1; K. Weirick, "The Perfect Interview," *HR Magazine,* April 2008, pp. 85–88; and AllBusiness.com, "Interviewing Skills Will Help Land the Right Employee for Your Firm," *San Francisco Chronicle,* April 9, 2008, p. C4; M. Weinstein, "You're Hired!" *Training,* July/August 2011, pp. 34–37; A. Bryant, "A Deal-Breaker Question for Job Interviews," *The New York Times,* August 28, 2011, p. BU-2; Y. Gonzalez, "Prepare for the Tough Questions," *The Arizona Republic,* November 13, 2011, p. EC1; V. Kaskey, "5 Tips to Make a Great First Impression," *The Arizona Republic,* November 6, 2011, p. EC1; A. Bruzzese, "Your First 'Hello' Can Make or Break a Job Search," *Reno Gazette-Journal,* February 23, 2012, p. 6A.

104. L. G. Otting, "Don't Rush to Judgment," *HR Magazine,* January 2004, pp. 95–98.

105. M. P. Cronin, "This Is a Test," *Inc.,* August 1993, pp. 64–68. See also A. Fox, "Upon Further Assessment . . . ," *HR Magazine,* August 2013, pp. 39–45; and B. Roberts, "Most Likely to Succeed," *HR Magazine,* April 2014, pp. 69–71. For information on how blanket screening policies can cause a firm problems, see L. M. Sixel, "Flexibility Rules," *San Francisco Chronicle,* January 25, 2014, pp. D1, D2.

106. J. S. Lublin, "What Won't You Do for a Job?" *The Wall Street Journal,* June 2, 2009, pp. B7, B11.

107. M. J. Frase, "Smart Selections," *HR Magazine,* December 2007, pp. 63–67.

108. M. Jordan, "Uncle Sam Wants You—Unless You're 71% of Youths," *The Wall Street Journal,* June 28–29, 2014, pp. A1, A5.

109. T. Gutner, "Applicants' Personalities Put to the Test," *The Wall Street Journal,* August 26, 2008, p. D4.

110. On the subject of job tryouts, see M. Mullenweb, "The CEO of Automattic on Holding 'Auditions' to Build a Strong Team," *Harvard Business Review,* April 2014, pp. 39–42.

111. For more about skills testing, see J. T. Arnold, "Getting Facts Fast," *HR Magazine,* February 2008, pp. 57–62.

112. J. Hodges, "a) Doctor b) Builder c) Cop d) HELP!" *The Wall Street Journal,* April 22, 2010, p. D2.

113. D. P. Shuit, "At 60, Myers-Briggs Is Still Sorting Out and Identifying People's Types," *Workforce Management,* December 2003, pp. 72–74.

114. See, for instance, "Are Resumes Passé? Enter the EQ Test," *Knowledge@Wharton,* June 18, 2014, http://knowledge.wharton.upenn.edu/article/resumes-passe-enter-eq-test (accessed June 5, 2016); and D. Meinert, "Heads Up!" *HR Magazine,* June 2015, pp. 88–98.

115. Scott Erker, Development Dimensions International, reported in Gutner, "Applicants' Personalities Put to the Test."

116. "Personality Assessment Soars at Southwest," *Training,* January 2008, p. 14.

117. "Out of Sight, Yes. Out of Mind, No," *BusinessWeek,* February 18, 2008, p. 60.

118. Senior vice president of human resources Linda Matzigkeit, quoted in M. Bolch, "Nice Work," *HR Magazine,* February 2008, pp. 78–81.

119. B. Rose, "Critics Wary as More Jobs Hinge on Personality Tests," *Chicago Tribune,* October 31, 2004, p. 15.

120. S. Clifford, "The Science of Hiring," *Inc.,* August 2006, pp. 90–98.

121. V. Knight, "More Employers Are Using Personality Tests as Hiring Tools," *CareerJournal.com,* March 21, 2006, www.careerjournal.com/jobhunting/interviewing/20060321-knight.html (accessed July 5, 2014).

122. "Types of Employment Tests," Society for Industrial & Organizational Psychology, www.siop.org/workplace/employment%20testing/testtypes.aspx (accessed July 5, 2016).

123. B. Roberts, "Your Cheating Heart," *HR Magazine,* June 2011, pp. 55–60.

124. For a discussion of some of these tests, see P. Bathurst, "Pre-Job Tests Weed Out Imperfect Fits," *The Arizona Republic,* January 28, 2007, p. EC1.

125. D. Cadrain, "Are Your Employee Drug Tests *Accurate?*" *HR Magazine,* January 2003, pp. 41–45.

126. P. Korkki, "Workers May Lie about Drug Use, but Hair Doesn't," *The New York Times,* December 13, 2009, Business section, p. 2.

127. Quest Diagnostics, reported in J. Calmes, "One Step Short of Hired," *The New York Times,* May 18, 2016, pp. B1, B3.

128. K. Glazebrook, interviewed by C. Massey, in "Chuck That CV: Using Behavioral Science to Recruit the Best Hires," Knowledge@Wharton, May 19, 2016, http://knowledge.wharton.upenn.edu/article/chuck-cv-using-behavioral-science-recruit-best-hires (accessed June 12, 2016).

129. See J. Bersin, "The Geeks Arrive in HR: People Analytics Is Here," *Forbes,* February 1, 2015, www.forbes.com/sites/joshbersin/2015/02/o1/geeks-arrive-in-hr-people-analytics-is-here (accessed June 14, 2016).

130. See L. Adler, "Boost Quality of Hire with Real-Time Feedback," *HR Magazine,* March 1, 2016, www.shrm.org/publications/hrmagazine/editorialcontent/2016/0316/pages/0316-hiring-metrics.aspx (accessed June 12, 2016).

131. M. Hoffman, L. B.Kahn, and D. Li, "Discretion in Hiring," *NBER Working Paper* No. 21709, National Bureau of Economic Research, November 2015, www.nber.org/papers/w21709 (accessed June 12, 2016).

132. S. Miller, "Satisfaction with Pay, Benefits Falling," *HR Magazine,* January 2007, pp. 38–39. See also C. Palmeri, "Workers Say: 'We Want an Upgrade,'" *BusinessWeek,* April 16, 2007, p. 11.

133. "How Effective Is Incentive Pay?" *HR Magazine,* January 2008, p. 12.

134. A. Colquitt. "A Pleasant Death of Performance-Based Pay," Administration, August 31, 2015, www.hrps.org/blogpost/1297410/225487/A-Pleasant-Death-of-Performance-Based-Pay (accessed June 15, 2016).

135. D. L. McClain, "Tricks for Motivating the Pay to Motivate the Ranks," *The New York Times,* November 15, 1998, sec. 3, p. 5; S. Thurm, "'Pay for Performance' No Longer a Punchline," *The Wall Street Journal,* March 21, 2013, pp. B1, B6; S. Harris, "Retaining and Motivating Skilled Labor," *Training,* July/August 2013, pp. 22–23; and A. R. Sorkin, "A Question of What's a Reasonable Reward," *The New York Times,* March 25, 2014, pp. B1, B5.

136. Bureau of Labor Statistics, "Employer Costs for Employee Compensation—December 2015," *Economic News Release,* March 10, 2016, www.bls.gov/news.release/ecec.nr0.htm (accessed June 6, 2016).

137. Onboarding is discussed by T. Arnold, "Ramping Up Onboarding," *HR Magazine,* May 2010, pp. 75–76.

138. R. Rigby, "Balloons and Buddies That Help New Recruits Fit In," *Financial Times,* March 17, 2008, www.ft.com/cms/s/0/203f63b6-f44a-11dc-aaad-0000779fd2ac.html; and M. Hogan, "How to Get Employee Onboarding Right," *Forbes,* May 29, 2015, www.forbes.com/sites/theyec/2015/05/29/how-to-get-employee-onboarding-right/#32d5ace21efa (both accessed June 5, 2016).

139. Brookings Institution, cited in Shellenbarger, "Companies Are Finding It Really Pays to Be Nice to Employees," *The Wall Street Journal,* July 22, 1998, p. B1.

140. K. Oakes, "How Long Does It Take to Get Fully Productive?" *Training Industry Quarterly,* Winter 2012, pp. 40–41.

141. G. R. Jones, "Organizational Socialization as Information Processing Activity: A Life History Analysis," *Human Organization,* Vol. 42, No. 4 (1983), pp. 314–320.

142. J. Bersin, "The New Best Practices of a High-Impact Learning Organization," Bersin by Deloitte, September 4, 2012, www.bersin.com/blog/post/The-New-Best-Practices-of-a-High-Impact-Learning-Organization.aspx (accessed June 5, 2016). The study is D. Mallon, J. Clarey, and M. Vickers, *The High-Impact Learning Maturity Model,* Bersin & Associates, September 4, 2012.

143. Business advisory firm CEB, reported in A. Elejalde-Ruiz, "Career Development Is Top Priority for Employers Seeking to Retain Talent," *Chicago Tribune,* March 29, 2016, www.chicagotribune.com/business/careers/ct-career-development-perk-0330-biz-20160329-story.html (accessed June 5, 2016). For a different view, see J. Chatterjee, interviewed in "Can Employee Training Lead to Higher Profits" *Knowledge@Wharton,* December 16, 2015, http://knowledge.wharton.upenn.edu/article/can-employee-training-lead-higher-profits (accessed June 5, 2016).

144. *2015 Manpower Talent Shortage Survey,* reported in E. E. Gordon, "Training and the Bottom Line," *Training,* November/December 2015, pp. 38–39.

145. See R. Saunderson, "Learning Technology Paves the Way for Change," *Training,* September/October 2015, pp. 62–63; M. Weinstein, "It's Not All Fun and Games," *Training,* September/October 2015, pp. 36–41.

146. See Saunderson, "Learning Technology Paves the Way for Change"; L. Kolodny, "A New Way to Train Workers, One Small Bite at a Time," *The Wall Street Journal,* March 14, 2016, p. R6; and A. M. Paul, "How to Make Microlearning Matter," SHRM, May 1, 2016, https://www.shrm.org/publications/hrmagazine/editorialcontent/2016/0516/pages/0516-microlearning.aspx (accessed June 5, 2016).

147. Kolodny, "A New Way to Train Workers, One Small Bite at a Time."

148. See "2015 Training Industry Report," *Training,* November/December 2015, https://trainingmag.com/trgmag-article/2o15-training-industry-report (accessed June 6, 2016).

149. S. Boller, "The Myth of 'Micro-Learning,'" Bottom-Line Performance, May 13, 2015, www.bottomlineperformance.com/the-myth-of-micro-learning (accessed June 6, 2016).

150. P. Rajasethupathy, reported in Kolodny, "A New Way to Train Workers, One Small Bite at a Time."

151. For a discussion from a training standpoint of how the brain learns, see A. Fox, "The Brain at Work," *HR Magazine,* March 2008, pp. 37–42.

152. "What If You Held a Training Session and No One Showed Up?" *Training,* January 2006, p. 10.

153. Study by consulting firm Watson Wyatt Worldwide (now Towers Watson), reported in M. Ipe, "Feedback Essential for Employee Growth," *Arizona Republic,* October 2, 2015, www.azcentral.com/story/money/business/jobs/2015/10/02/feedback-essential-employee-growth/73044324 (accessed June 6, 2016).

154. C. Groscurth. "Great Managers Can Fix Broken Performance Management Systems," *Gallup Business Journal,* June 14, 2015, www.gallup.com/businessjournal/183770/great-managers-fix-broken-performance-management-systems.aspx (accessed June 13, 2016).

155. Adapted from A. J. Kinicki, K. J. L. Jacobson, S. J. Peterson, and G. E. Prussia, "Development and Validation of the Performance Management Behavior Questionnaire," *Personnel Psychology,* Vol. 66 (2013), pp. 1–45.

156. J. Gruss, "Burger Hustle," *Business Observer,* November 2, 2012, www.businessobserverfl.com/section/detail/burger-hustle (accessed June 6, 2016). See also T. Monaghan and R. Anderson, *Pizza Tiger* (New York: Random House, 1996).

157. H. Aguinis, H. Joo, and R. K. Gottfredson, "What Monetary Rewards Can and Cannot Do: How to Show Employees the Money," *BusinessHorizons,* Vol. 56 (2013), pp. 241–249. See also E. McClean and C. J. Collins, "High-Commitment HR Practices, Employee Effort, and Firm Performance: Investigating the Effects of HR Practices Across Employee Groups within Professional Services Firms," *Human Resource Management,* May–June 2011, pp. 341–363; E. Marescaux and S. De Winne, "HR Practices and HRM Outcomes: The Role of Basic Need Satisfaction," *Personnel Review,* Vol. 42, No. 1 (2013), pp. 4–27; and J. Slocum, D. Lei, and P. Buller, "Executing Business Strategies through Human Resource Management Practices," *Organizational Dynamics,* Vol. 43 (2014), pp. 73–87.

158. S. A. Culbert, "Yes, Everyone Really Does Hate Performance Reviews," *The Wall Street Journal,* April 11, 2010, www.wsj.com/articles/SB127093422486175363 (accessed June 6, 2016).

159. S. A. Culbert and L. Rout, *Get Rid of Performance Reviews! How Companies Can Stop Intimidating, Start Managing—and Focus on What Really Matters* (New York: Business Plus, 2010).

160. See L. Kwoh, "Difficult Bosses Hurt Workers' Motivation," *The Wall Street Journal,* February 29, 2012, p. B8.

161. W. E. Deming, reported by D. S. Perrin, in P. Downs, "Bringing Back Employee Reviews," *The New York Times,* June 26, 2014, p. B5.

162. CEB Global, reported in D. Wilkie, "Is the Annual Performance Review Dead?" *HR Magazine,* October 2015, pp. 11–12. See also R. Feintzeig, "The Trouble with Grading Employees," *The Wall Street Journal,* April 22, 2015, pp. B1, B7; and P. Cappelli, interviewed in "An Imperfect Test: The Problem with Job Performance Appraisals," *Knowledge@Wharton,* May 23, 2016, http://knowledge.wharton.upenn.edu/article/the-problem-with-job-performance-appraisals (accessed June 6, 2016).

163. Aubrey Daniels, quoted in C. Suddath, "You Get a D+ in Teamwork," *Bloomberg Businessweek,* November 11–November 17, 2013, p. 91.

164. Statistic from CEB Global, reported in D. Meinert, "Reinventing Reviews," *HR Magazine,* April 2015, pp. 37–42. See also R. E. Silverman, "Work Reviews Losing Steam," *The Wall Street Journal,* December 19, 2011, p. B7.

165. D. J. Cohen, "HR Metrics: A Must," *HR Magazine,* February 2003, p. 136. On the subject of quantifying performance appraisals, see also K. Tyler, "Evaluating Values," *HR Magazine,* April 2011, pp. 57–61.

166. The term "Munchausen at work" was created by Georgia Institute of Technology business professor Nathan Bennett. See N. Bennett, "Munchausen at Work," *Harvard Business Review,* November 16, 2007, pp. 24–25.

167. J. McGregor, "Job Review in 140 Keystrokes," *BusinessWeek,* March 23 and 30, 2009, p. 58.

168. L. Kwoh, "'Rank and Yank' Retains Vocal Fans," *The Wall Street Journal,* January 31, 2012, p. B6.

169. Statistic from CEB, reported in J. McGregor, "Why Performance Reviews Like Yahoo's Are Out of Favor," *The Washington Post,* February 2, 2016, https://www.washingtonpost.com/news/on-leadership/wp/2016/02/02/why-performance-reviews-like-yahoos-are-out-of-favor (accessed June 6, 2016).

170. Statistic from Brandon Hall Group, reported in McGregor, "Why Performance Reviews Like Yahoo's Are Out of Favor."

171. See Meinert, "Reinventing Reviews."

172. S. Scherreik, "Your Performance Review: Make It Perform," *BusinessWeek Online,* December 17, 2001, www.businessweek.com/magazine/content/01_51/b3762136.htm?chan=search (accessed July 5, 2014); and J. McGregor, "The Struggle to Measure Performance," *BusinessWeek Online,* January 9, 2006, www.businessweek.com/magazine/content/06_02/b3966060.htm?chan=search (accessed July 5, 2014). See also criticism of forced ranking in J. Pfeffer and R. I. Sutton, *Hard Facts, Dangerous Half-Truths & Total Nonsense: Profiting from Evidence-Based Management* (Boston: Harvard Business School Press, 2006).

173. See D. Rock and B. Jones, "Why More and More Companies Are Ditching Performance Ratings," *Harvard Business Review,* September 8, 2015, https://hbr.org/2015/09/why-more-and-more-companies-are-ditching-performance-ratings (accessed June 6, 2016). Also see R. Feintzeig, "The Trouble with Grading Employees," *The Wall Street Journal,* April 22, 2015, pp. B1, B7.

174. L. Barry, quoted in "It's Official: Forced Ranking Is Dead," *Deloitte CIO Journal,* June 10, 2014, http://deloitte.wsj.com/cio/2014/06/10/its-official-forced-ranking-is-dead (accessed June 6, 2016).

175. Wilkie, "Is the Annual Performance Review Dead?"; and R. E. Silverman, "GE Tries to Reinvent the Employee Review, Encouraging Risks," *The Wall Street Journal,* June 8, 2014, pp. B1, B6.

176. L. A. Bossidy, "What Your Leader Expects of You," *Harvard Business Review,* April 3, 2007, pp. 58–65.

177. See Meinert, "Reinventing Reviews"; Wilkie, "Is the Annual Performance Review Dead?"; J. Bersin, "Prediction 2: Performance Management Will Continue to Be Redesigned," *SHRM,* January 7, 2015, https://www.shrm.org/publications/hrmagazine/editorialcontent/2015/010215/pages/010215-hr-prediction-two.aspx (accessed June 6, 2016); and S. Miller, "Prediction: Redesign of Performance Management," *SHRM,* January 20, 2015 https://www.shrm.org/hrdisciplines/compensation/articles/pages/performance-management-redesigned.aspx (accessed June 6, 2016).

178. W. Kirn, "More Than a Numbers Game," *The New York Times Magazine*, May 10, 2009, pp. 13–14.

179. Definitions adapted from R. Mayhew, "Employee Turnover vs. Attrition," *Chron*, http://smallbusiness.chron.com/employee-turnover-vs-attrition-15846.html (accessed June 7, 2016).

180. For a discussion of workplace discipline, see L. E. Atwater, J. F. Brett, and A. C. Charles, "The Delivery of Workplace Discipline: Lessons Learned," *Organizational Dynamics*, Vol. 36 (2007), pp. 392–403.

181. A. Sherman, "Do You Feel like You've Hit a Brick Wall at Work?" *The Arizona Republic*, March 21, 2010, p. C1. See also B. B. Hagerty, "Quit Your Job," *The Atlantic*, April 2016, pp. 22–23.

182. W. Boston, "Auto Maker Weighs Rotating Executives," *The Wall Street Journal*, December 21, 2015, p. B3.

183. See "How Layoffs Hurt Companies," *Knowledge@Wharton*, April 12, 2016, http://knowledge.wharton.upenn.edu/article/how-layoffs-cost-companies (accessed June 7, 2016).

184. T. Lee, "Fired CEOs 'Pursue Other Opportunities,'" *San Francisco Chronicle*, May 30, 2016, pp. A1, A6.

185. M. Conlin, "When the Laid-Off Are Better Off," *BusinessWeek*, November 2, 2009, p. 65.

186. D. Mattioli, "Layoff Sign: Boss's Cold Shoulder," *The Wall Street Journal*, October 23, 2008, p. D6.

187. D. Lyons, "Congratulations! You've Been Fired," *The New York Times*, April 10, 2016, p. SR-7.

188. S. Gleason and R. Feintzeig, "Startups Are Quick to Fire," *The Wall Street Journal*, December 12, 2013, www.wsj.com/articles/SB10001424052702304202204579254540454121188 (accessed June 6, 2016).

189. U.S. Equal Employment Opportunity Commission, "Federal Laws Prohibiting Job Discrimination Questions and Answers," November 21, 2009, https://www.eeoc.gov/facts/qanda.html (accessed June 6, 2016).

190. C. Hymowitz, "Why Managers Take Too Long to Fire Employees," *San Francisco Examiner*, February 21, 1999, p. J-2; reprinted from *The Wall Street Journal*.

191. For a discussion of the threat of litigation attending dismissals, see M. Orey, "Fear of Firing," *BusinessWeek*, April 23, 2007, pp. 52–62.

192. R. Moss Kanter, "Show Humanity When You Show Employees the Door," *The Wall Street Journal*, September 21, 1997, p. A22. See also J. Goudreau, "Survivor Employees: What You Need to Know," *Forbes*, December 9, 2009, www.forbes.com/2009/12/09/layoff-survivor-stress-guilt-forbes-woman-well-being-employees.html (accessed June 6, 2016).

193. Kanter, "Show Humanity When You Show Employees the Door."

194. W. Lee, "Best Time to Drop the Hatchet at Work," *San Francisco Chronicle*, April 6, 2016, pp. C1, C3.

195. D. Auerbach, "Bouncing Back from a Job Loss," *Reno Gazette-Journal*, November 16, 2014, p. 6E.

196. E. Spain and B. Groysberg, "Making Exit Interviews Count," *Harvard Business Review*, April 2016, pp. 88–95.

197. S. Shellenbarger, "Bye, Boss, Let's Stay Friends Forever," *The Wall Street Journal*, August 19, 2015, pp. D1, D3.

198. J. Preston, "Laid-Off Americans, Required to Zip Lips on Way Out, Are Growing Bolder," *The New York Times*, June 12, 2016, pp. News-11, News-19.

199. R. Huppke, "The Argument for Increasing Minimum Wage," *Chicago Tribune*, March 3, 2014, http://articles.chicagotribune.com/2014-03-03/business/ct-biz-0303-work-advice-huppke-20140303_1_minimum-wage-arindrajit-dube-future-increases; and "Four Reasons Not to Raise the Minimum Raise," Cato Institute, http://object.cato.org/sites/cato.org/files/four_reasons_not_to_raise_the_minimum_wage.pdf (both accessed June 13, 2016).

200. For more about legislation updating the Toxic Substances Control Act of 1976, see C. Davenport and E. Huetteman, "Deal Is Reached to Expand Rules on Toxic Chemicals," *The New York Times*, May 20, 2016, p. A3; and F. Krupp, "When Red and Blue in Congress Makes Green," *The Wall Street Journal*, June 10, 2016, p. A13.

201. S. G. Stolberg and R. Pear, "A Stroke of a Pen, Make That 20, and Its Official," *The New York Times*, March 24, 2010, p. A19; C. Martin, "In the Health Law, an Open Door for Entrepreneurs," *The New York Times*, November 24, 2013, p. BU-3; H. Knight, "Health Efforts Work—Experts," *San Francisco Chronicle*, November 30, 2013, pp. A1, A9; and Associated Press, "Uninsured Rate Decreases as Law Takes Effect," *San Francisco Chronicle*, January 24, 2014, p. A13.

202. See Commonwealth Fund, "Affordable Care Act Tracking Survey February–April 2016," May 26, 2016, www.commonwealthfund.org/interactives-and-data/surveys/2016/aca-tracking-feb-apr-2016 (accessed June 6, 2016).

203. See S. E. Needleman, "More Programs to Halt Bias against Gays," *The Wall Street Journal*, November 26, 2007, p. B3. A countertrend to age discrimination may be the result of baby boomers retiring, bringing an overall shortfall in workers; see M. Sedensky, "Oldies but Goodies," *Reno Gazette-Journal*, September 14, 2013, pp. 11A, 12A.

204. J. Coffman, O. Gadiesh, and W. Miller, *The Great Disappearing Act: Gender Parity Up the Corporate Ladder*, World Economic Forum White Paper, survey by Bain & Co. and *Harvard Business Review*, January 30, 2010, www.bain.com/bainweb/publications/publications_detail.asp?id=27564&menu_url=publications%5Fresults%2Easp (accessed July 5, 2016).

205. "Women CEOs of the S&P 500," Catalyst, June 6, 2016, www.catalyst.org/knowledge/women-ceos-sp-500 (accessed June 6, 2016).

206. K. Bellstrom, "Why 2015 Was a Terrible Year to Be a Female Fortune 500 CEO," *Fortune*, December 15, 2015, http://fortune.com/2015/12/23/2015-women-fortune-500-ceos (accessed June 6, 2016).

207. U.S. Equal Employment Opportunity Commission, "EEOC Releases FY 2015 Enforcement and Litigation Data," press release, February 11, 2016, https://www.eeoc.gov/eeoc/newsroom/release/2-11-16.cfm (accessed June 6, 2016).

208. See J. Adamy and P. Overberg, "Pay Gap Widest for Elite Jobs," *The Wall Street Journal*, May 18, 2016, pp. A1, A10; and U.S. Bureau of Labor Statistics, Department of Labor, *Highlights of Women's Earnings in 2014*, Report 1058, November 2015, Table 2, www.bls.gov/opub/reports/womens-earnings/archive/highlights-of-womens-earnings-in-2014.pdf (accessed June 6, 2016).

209. Adamy and Overberg, "Pay Gap Widest for Elite Jobs."

210. See J. Platt, S. Prins, and K. Keyes, "Unequal Depression for Equal Work? How the Wage Gap Explains Gendered Disparities in Mood Disorders," *Social Science & Medicine*, Vol. 149 (2016), pp. 1–8.

211. Womenable and American Express OPEN, *The 2015 State of Women-Owned Businesses Report*, www.womenable.com/content/userfiles/Amex_OPEN_State_of_WOBs_2015_Executive_Report_finalsm.pdf (accessed June 6, 2016).

212. JMG Consulting LLC and Wyckoff Consulting LLC, "Venture Capital, Social Capital, and the Funding of Women-Led Businesses," for SBA Office of Advocacy, April 2013, https://www.sba.gov/sites/default/files/files/rs406tot%284%29.pdf (accessed June 6, 2016). See also J. Tozzi, "Female-Led Companies Paid Off Well for VC Firms," *San Francisco Chronicle*, April 22, 2013, pp. D1, D4.

213. C. G. Brush, P. G. Greene, L. Balachandra, and A. E. Davis, *Diana Report—Women Entrepreneurs 2014: Bridging the Gender Gap in Venture Capital*, Arthur M. Blank Center for Entrepreneurship, Babson College, September 2014, www.babson.edu/Academics/centers/blank-center/global-research/diana/Documents/diana-project-executive-summary-2014.pdf (accessed June 6, 2016).

214. See L. Petrecca, "And Now, a Word about Diversity," *USA Today*, June 19, 2014, p. 3B; J. Guynn and E. Weise, "Danger of Digital Divide," *USA Today*, June 27, 2014, pp. 5B, 6B; K. V. Brown, "Think Pink? That's No Way to Get Women into Tech Jobs," *San Francisco Chronicle*, July 6, 2014, pp. A1, A12; and F. Manjoo, "Exposing Hidden Bias at Google," *The New York Times*, September 25, 2014, pp. B1, B9.

215. See E. Pollack, "What Really Keeps Women Out of Tech," *The New York Times*, October 11, 2015, p. SR-3. See also S. Cheryan, A. Master, and A. N. Meltzoff, "Cultural Stereotypes as Gatekeepers: Increasing Girls' Interest in Male-Dominated STEM Fields by Diversifying Stereotypes," *Frontiers in Psychology*, February 11, 2015, pp. 1–8; and A. Master, S. Cheryan, and A. N. Meltzoff, "Computing Whether She Belongs: Stereotypes Undermine Girls' Interest and Sense of Belonging in Computer Science," *Journal of Educational Psychology*, Vol. 108, No. 3 (2016), pp. 424–437.

216. J. Guynn, "Sexism in Tech Buzz Gets Louder," *USA Today*, July 2, 2014, pp. 1B, 2B.

217. J. Garofoli, "'Bro Culture' Locks Many Minorities Out," *San Francisco Chronicle*, February 7, 2014, pp. C1, C2.

218. See J. Palamino, "Tech Fueling Gender Gap in Earnings," *San Francisco Chronicle*, February 21, 2016, pp. A1, A15; G. Wells, "Tech Firms Help Women on Track," *The Wall Street Journal*, April 11, 2016, p. B5; C. Passariello, "Silicon Valley Gets Agitated," *The Wall Street Journal*, April 23–24, 2016, pp. A1, A8; M. Isaac, "Women in Tech Join Forces to Campaign for Diversity," *The New York Times*, May 4, 2016, pp. B1, B4; and M. Lang, "Regulators Tackle Tech Diversity," *San Francisco Chronicle*, May 19, 2016, pp. C1, C3.

219. For a discussion of how to implement affirmative action, see J. Mendez, "The Four Key Components of a Successful Affirmative Action Plan," *PeopleFluent*, January 21, 2016, www.peoplefluent.com/blog/the-four-key-components-of-a-successful-affirmative-action-program (accessed June 6, 2016).

220. See J. A. Kovacs, D. M. Truxillo, T. N. Bauer, and T. Bodner, "Perceptions of Affirmative Action Based on Socioeconomic Status: A Comparison with Traditional Affirmative Action," *Employee Responsibilities Rights Journal*, Vol. 26 (2014), pp. 35–57.

221. E. H. James, A. P. Brief, J. Dietz, and R. R. Cohen, "Prejudice Matters: Understanding the Reactions of Whites to Affirmative Action Programs Targeted to Benefit Blacks," *Journal of Applied Psychology*, December 2001, pp. 1120–1128.

222. For a review of related research, see L. M. Leslie, D. M. Mayer, and D. A. Kravitz, "The Stigma of Affirmative Action: A Stereotyping-Based Theory and Meta-Analytic Test of the Consequences for Performance," *Academy of Management Journal*, August 2014, pp. 964–989.

223. M. Rotundo, D.-H. Nguyen, and P. R. Sackett, "A Meta-Analytic Review of Gender Differences in Perceptions of Sexual Harassment," *Journal of Applied Psychology*, October 2001, pp. 914–922.

224. Most research on sexual harassment has focused on harassment inside organizations. For a discussion of harassment beyond the boundaries of the organization, see H. J. Gettman and J. J. Gelfand, "When the Customer Shouldn't Be King: Antecedents and Consequences of Sexual Harassment by Clients and Customers," *Journal of Applied Psychology*, May 2007, pp. 757–770.

225. S. Armour, "More Men Say They Are Sexually Harassed at Work," *USA Today*, September 17, 2004, p. 1B; C. A. Pierce and H. Aguinis, "Legal Standards, Ethical Standards, and Responses to Social–Sexual Conduct at Work," *Journal of Organizational Behavior*, Vol. 26 (2005), pp. 727–732; L. A. Baar, "Harassment Case Proceeds Despite Failure to Report," *HR Magazine*, June 2005, p. 159; and S. Shellenbarger, "Supreme Court Takes on How Employers Handle Worker Harassment Complaints," *The Wall Street Journal*, April 13, 2006, p. D1.

226. Survey in 2007 by Novations Group, Boston, reported in D. Stead, "Is the Workplace Getting Raunchier?" *BusinessWeek*, March 17, 2008, p. 19.

227. J. Macur, "On Social Media, Misogyny Runs Amok," *The New York Times*, April 29, 2016, pp. B9, B13.

228. Bill Lepowsky, quoted in K. V. Brown, "Far beyond School Playground, Bullying Common in Workplace," *San Francisco Chronicle*, November 6, 2011, pp. A1, A10.

229. Jill Brooke, quoted in K. V. Brown, "Far beyond School Playground, Bullying Common in Workplace," *San Francisco Chronicle*, November 6, 2011, pp. A1, A10. Brooke is

author of *The Need to Say No: The Importance of Setting Boundaries in Love, Life, & Your World—How to Be Bullish and Not Bullied* (New York: Random House, 2013).

230. The 27% figure appeared in the Workplace Bullying Institute, "The 2014 WBI U.S. Workplace Bullying Institute," February 2014, www.workplacebullying.org/wbiresearch/wbi-2014-us-survey (accessed June 6, 2016). The 37% figure appeared in a 2007 survey by Zogby International, reported in T. Parker-Pope, "When the Bully Sits in the Next Cubicle," *The New York Times*, March 25, 2008, p. D5. The 51% figure appeared in Society for Human Resource Management, "SHRM Survey Findings: Workplace Bullying," February 28, 2012, https://www.shrm.org/research/surveyfindings/articles/pages/workplacebullying.aspx (accessed June 6, 2016).

231. D. T. Eesley and P. A. Meglich, "Empirical Evidence of Abusive Supervision in Entrepreneurial and Small Firms," *Journal of Ethics and Entrepreneurship*, Spring 2013, pp. 39–60.

232. Society for Human Resource Management, "SHRM Survey Findings: Workplace Bullying." See also E. Bernstein, "Lessons for Shutting Down a Grownup Cyberbully," *The Wall Street Journal*, May 17, 2016, p. D2.

233. D. C. Treadway, B. A. Shaughnessy, J. W. Breland, J. Yang, and M. Reeves, "Political Skill and the Job Performance of Bullies," *Journal of Managerial Psychology*, Vol. 28, No. 3 (2013), pp. 273–289.

234. Darren C. Treadway, quoted in R. E. Silverman, "Bullies Don't Finish Last, Study Indicates," *The Wall Street Journal*, July 3, 2013, p. B6.

235. See R. Feintzeig, "When Co-Workers Don't Play Nice," *The Wall Street Journal*, August 28, 2013, p. B6. Also see interview with psychiatrist J. Foster, head of the Professionalism Program at Penn Medicine at Pennsylvania Hospital, Philadelphia, in "How Disruptive Behavior by Employees Can Devastate a Workplace," *Knowledge@Wharton*, March 27, 2013, http://knowledge.wharton.upenn.edu/article/how-disruptive-behavior-by-employees-can-devastate-a-workplace (accessed June 6, 2016).

236. Gary Namie, quoted in Brown, "Far Beyond School Playground, Bullying Common in Workplace."

237. A. Piore, "Kick Me or Don't," *Bloomberg Businessweek*, November 26–December 2, 2012, pp. 94–95.

238. "Results of the 2007 WBI U.S. Workplace Bullying Survey," Workplace Bullying Institute, www.workplacebullying.org/wbiresearch/wbi-2007 (accessed July 3, 2016).

239. H. Benson, "Porters Found Road to Success Aboard Nation's 'Rolling Hotels,'" *San Francisco Chronicle*, February 11, 2009, pp. A1, A12.

240. "Mixed View of Impact of Long-Term Decline in Union Membership," Pew Research Center, April 27, 2015, www.people-press.org/2015/04/27/mixed-views-of-impact-of-long-term-decline-in-union-membership (accessed June 7, 2016).

241. L. Uchitelle, "Unions Yield on Wage Scales to Preserve Jobs," *The New York Times*, November 20, 2010, p. A1; M. Maynard, "By Helping Detroit, Did the UAW Lose Its Future?" *Forbes*, February 17, 2014, www.forbes.com/sites/michelinemaynard/2014/02/17/by-helping-detroit-did-the-uaw-lose-its-future/#83a8e7b6e2b9 (accessed June 7, 2016); F. V. Vernuccio and T. Bowman, "Right to Work Buffs Up the Rust Belt," *The Wall Street Journal*, September 17, 2015, p. A15; and M. Hiltzik, "Are Those Detested Two-Tiered UAW Contracts Finally on the Way Out?" *Los Angeles Times*, October 13, 2015, www.latimes.com/business/hiltzik/la-fi-mh-is-the-two-tiered-union-contract-20151013-column.html (accessed June 7, 2016).

242. J. L. Brown, P. R. Martin, D. V. Moser, and R. A. Weber, "The Consequences of Hiring Lower-Wage Workers in an Incomplete-Contract Environment," *The Accounting Review*, May 2015, pp. 941–966.

243. See, for example, J. Silver-Greenberg and M. Corkery, "Bank Customers Likely to Regain Access to Courts," *The New York Times*, May 5, 2016, pp. A1, B3; J. Silver-Greenberg and M. Corkery, "Start-Ups Turn to Arbitration in the Workplace," *The New York Times*, May 15, 2016, pp. News-1, News-4; and "Don't Force Students to Sign Away Their Rights," editorial, *The New York Times*, June 10, 2016, p. A26.

244. See, for example, J. Silver-Greenberg and R. Gebeloff, "Arbitration Everywhere, Stacking Deck of Justice," *The New York Times*, November 1, 2015, pp. News-1, News-22, News-23; J. Silver-Greenberg and M. Corkery, "A 'Privatization of the Justice System,'" *The New York Times*, November 2, 2015, pp. A1, B4, B5; and M. Corkery and J. Silver-Greenberg, "When Scripture Is the Rule of Law," *The New York Times*, November 3, 2015, pp. A1, B6, B7. See also A. Prior, "Which Is Better? Arbitration or Class Action?" *The Wall Street Journal*, November 14, 2015, p. B7.

245. G. Zoroya and C. MacLeod, "A World Apart, Meat Workers Share a Bond," *USA Today*, June 26, 2013, pp. 1B, 2B. See also J. Randle, "Little Change at Virginia's China-Owned Smithfield Foods," Voice of America, September 21, 2015, www.voanews.com/content/china-owned-smithfield-foods-growing-little-change/2972885.html (accessed June 10, 2016).

246. M. Trottman, "Ruling Clears Way for Unions," *The Wall Street Journal*, August 28, 2015, pp. A1, A4.

247. S. Greenhouse, "Workers Organize, but Don't Unionize, to Get Protection under Labor Law," *The New York Times*, September 7, 2015, pp. B1, B5.

248. K. Cao and E. Newcomer, "Uber Pledges to Back Drivers Guild in N.Y.," *San Francisco Chronicle*, May 11, 2016, pp. C1, C3; and N. Scheiber and M. Isaac, "A Guild, Short of a Union, for New York Uber Drivers," *The New York Times*, May 11, 2016, pp. B1, B6.

249. See R. E. Silverman, "Workplace Democracy Catches On," *The Wall Street Journal*, March 28, 2016, p. B5. See also L. Weber and R. E. Silverman, "Workers Get New Tools for Airing Their Gripes," *The Wall Street Journal*, August 26, 2015, pp. B1, B4.

250. See V. Luckerson, "Google Overtakes Apple as the World's Most Valuable Public Company," *Time.com*, February 1, 2016, http://time.com/4203279/google-earnings-goog-apple-appl-market-cap/, accessed May 2, 2016; *Google.com*, https://www.google.com/about/company/facts/locations/, accessed May 3, 2016; and "Alphabet Inc," *CnnMoney.com*, May 3, 2016, http://money.cnn.com/quote/profile.html?symb=GOOG, accessed May 3, 2016.

251. F. Manjoo, "How Google Became Such a Great Place to Work," Slate.com, January 21, 2013, http://www.slate.com/articles/technology/technology/2013/01/google_people_operations_the_secrets_of_the_world_s_most_scientific_human.html, accessed May 3, 2016.

252. F. Manjoo, "How Google Became Such a Great Place to Work," Slate.com, January 21, 2013, http://www.slate.com/articles/technology/technology/2013/01/google_people_operations_the_secrets_of_the_world_s_most_scientific_human.html; accessed May 3, 2016.

253. R. Gillett, "The 19 Toughest Interview Questions You May Have to Answer If You Want to Work at Google, the Best Company in America," BusinessInsider.com, April 30, 2016, http://www.businessinsider.com/best-company-in-america-interview-questions-2016-4, accessed May 3, 2016.

254. "Why Does Google Recruiting Take So Long?" *Forbes.com*, January 9, 2015, http://www.forbes.com/sites/quora/2015/01/09/why-does-google-recruiting-take-so-long/#795521e51291, accessed May 3, 2016.

255. L. Bock, "Here's Google's Secret to Hiring the Best People," Wired.com, April 7, 2015, http://www.wired.com/2015/04/hire-like-google/, accessed May 3, 2016.

256. S. Kessler, "Here's a Google Perk Any Company Can Imitate: Employee-to-Employee Learning," FastCompany.com, March 26, 2013, http://www.fastcompany.com/3007369/heres-google-perk-any-company-can-imitate-employee-employee-learning accessed May 3, 2016.

257. E. B. Boyd, "Training Secrets from inside the Googleplex," FastCompany.com, June 6, 2011, http://www.fastcompany.com/1761778/training-secrets-inside-googleplex, accessed May 3, 2016.

258. E. B. Boyd, "Training Secrets from inside the Googleplex," *FastCompany.com*, June 6, 2011, http://www.fastcompany.com/1761778/training-secrets-inside-googleplex, accessed May 3, 2016.

259. E. B. Boyd, "Training Secrets from inside the Googleplex," *FastCompany.com*, June 6, 2011, http://www.fastcompany.com/1761778/training-secrets-inside-googleplex, accessed May 3, 2016.

260. S. Lebowitz, "Here's How Performance Reviews Work at Google," *Business Insider.com*, June 15, 2015, http://www.businessinsider.com/how-google-performance-reviews-work-2015-6, accessed May 3, 2016.

261. "Non-Compete Clause," Wikipedia, March 19, 2016, https://en.wikipedia.org/wiki/Non-compete_clause.

262. G. Bensinger, "Amazon Sues New Target Executive," *The Wall Street Journal*, March 23, 2016, B1.

263. A. Viswanatha, "Noncompete Pacts Hobble Rookies," *The Wall Street Journal*, February 3, 2016, B1, B5.

264. A. Viswanatha, "Noncompete Pacts Hobble Rookies," *The Wall Street Journal*, February 3, 2016, B1, B5.

265. A. Viswanatha, "Noncompete Pacts Hobble Rookies," *The Wall Street Journal*, February 3, 2016, B1, B5.

CHAPTER 10

1. T. Peters, interviewed by S. Heywood, A. De Smet, and A. Webb, "Tom Peters on Leading the 21st Century Organization," *McKinsey Quarterly*, September 2014, www.mckinsey.com/business-functions/organization/our-insights/tom-peters-on-leading-the-21st-century-organization (accessed June 30, 2016).

2. M. McGuinn, quoted in C. Hymowitz, "Task of Managing in Workplace Takes a Careful Hand," *The Wall Street Journal*, July 1, 1997, p. B1.

3. See "Fear of Failure Hampers Innovation," *Training*, May/June 2016, p. 6. See also *Innovation: The New Competitive Equation*, Brightidea and BPI Network, April 2015, www.bpinetwork.org/thought-leadership/studies/52 (accessed June 22, 2016).

4. Hymowitz, "Task of Managing in Workplace Takes a Careful Hand."

5. M. Weinstein, "Innovate or Die Trying," *Training Magazine*, May 2006, pp. 38–44; D. Hall, "The Customer Is Clueless," *BusinessWeek SmallBiz*, Spring 2006, p. 20; D. Brady, "Ideas That Bloom," *Business Week Small Biz*, Spring 2006, pp. 46–53; P. Loewe and J. Dominiquini, "Overcoming the Barriers to Effective Innovation," *Strategy & Leadership*, Vol. 34, No. 1 (2006), pp. 24–31; B. Pike, "Change and Growth," *Training*, September/October 2015, pp. 60–61; D. Petersen, "Brian Helmick: Tips for Creating a Profitable Startup," *Insights by Stanford Business*, September 1, 2015, https://www.gsb.stanford.edu/insights/brian-helmick-tips-creating-profitable-startup (accessed June 22, 2016).

6. A. Grant, interviewed in "'Originals': How Anyone Can Become a Trailblazer," Knowledge@Wharton, February 2, 2016, http://knowledge.wharton.upenn.edu/article/how-non-conformists-move-the-world (accessed June 22, 2016). Grant is author of *Originals: How Non-Conformists Move the World* (New York: Penguin Random House, 2016).

7. Anthony Creed, quoted in D. Kirkpatrick, "Throw It at the Wall and See If It Sticks," *Fortune*, December 12, 2005, pp. 142–150.

8. Bruce Judson, quoted in J. M. Pethokoukis, "Bootstrapping Your Way into Business," *U.S. News & World Report*, March 27, 2006, p. 58. See also M. Bandyk, "Launching a Start-Up? Here's What Really Works," *U.S. News & World Report*, February 18, 2008, p. 58.

9. T. Williams, C. G. Worley, and E. E. Lawler III, "The Agility Factor," *Strategy & Business*, April 15, 2013, www.strategy-business.com/article/00188?gko=6a0ba (accessed June 30, 2016).

10. "Jake Gyllenhaal Quotes and Sayings," inspiringquotes.us, www.inspiringquotes.us/author/4741-jake-gyllenhaal (accessed June 16, 2016).

11. AT&T CEO Randall Stephenson, quoted in Q. Hardy, "AT&T's New Line: Adapt, or Else," *The New York Times*, February 14, 2016, pp. BU-1, BU-5.

12. P. Drucker, "The Future That Has Already Happened," *The Futurist*, November 1998, pp. 16–18.

13. "Intuit 2020 Report: Twenty Trends That Will Shape the Next Decade," Intuit, October 2010, http://http-download.intuit.com/http.intuit/CMO/intuit/futureofsmallbusiness/intuit_2020_report.pdf (accessed June 15, 2016).

14. K. Albrecht, "Eight Supertrends Shaping the Future of Business," *The Futurist*, September–October 2006, pp. 25–29; J. C. Glenn, "Scanning the Global Situation and Prospects for the Future," *The Futurist*, January–February 2008, pp. 41–46; M. J. Cetron and O. Davies, "Trends Shaping Tomorrow's World: Forecasts and Implications for Business, Government, and Consumers (Part One)," *The Futurist*, March–April 2008, pp. 35–52; M. J. Cetron and O. Davies, "Trends Shaping Tomorrow's World: Forecasts and Implications for Business, Government, and Consumers (Part Two)," *The Futurist*, May–June 2008, pp. 35–50; M. Richarme, "Ten Forces Driving Business Futures," *The Futurist*, July–August 2009, pp. 40–43; N. Easton, "*Fortune*'s Guide to the Future," *Fortune*, January 16, 2012, pp. 45–57; J. Morgan, "Five Trends Shaping the Future of Work," *Forbes*, June 20, 2013, www.forbes.com/sites/jacobmorgan/2013/06/20/five-trends-shaping-the-future-of-work/#4082ca392161 (accessed June 15, 2016); "The Future Issue," *Fortune*, January 13, 2014; and "The Future of Everything," *The Wall Street Journal*, July 8, 2014, pp. R1–R24.

15. C. Anderson, quoted in A. T. Saracevic, "Economic Theories in 'The Long Tail' Don't Deserve Short Shrift," *San Francisco Chronicle*, July 16, 2006, pp. F1, F5.

16. R. O. Bagley, "Speed to Market: An Entrepreneur's View," *Forbes*, May 1, 2013, www.forbes.com/sites/rebeccabagley/2013/05/01/speed-to-market-an-entrepreneurs-view/#6ea412712b3c (accessed June 17, 2016).

17. C. M. Christensen, *The Innovator's Dilemma: When New Technologies Cause Great Firms to Fail* (Boston, MA: Harvard Business School Press, 1997). See also J. Howe, "The Disruptor," *Wired*, March 2013, pp. 74–78; J. Lepore, "The Disruption Machine," *The New Yorker*, June 23, 2014, pp. 30–36; and "Has 'Disruptive Innovation' Run Its Course? Not Yet . . . ," *Knowledge@Wharton*, July 9, 2014, http://knowledge.wharton.upenn.edu/article/disruptive-innovation-run-course-yet (accessed July 10, 2016).

18. See C. Mims, "Why Companies Are Being Disrupted," *The Wall Street Journal*, January 25, 2016, p. B4.

19. R. G. McGrath, "Transient Advantage," *Harvard Business Review*, June 2013, pp. 62–70.

20. A. Picchi, "5 Mistakes That Doomed RadioShack," *CBS News Moneywatch*, February 3, 2015, www.cbsnews.com/news/5-mistakes-that-doomed-radioshack/ (accessed June 17, 2016); C. Mims, "RadioShack Suffered as Free Time Evaporated," *The Wall Street Journal*, February 9, 2015, pp. B1, B6; and P. Brickley, "RadioShack's Survival Prospects Dim," *The Wall Street Journal*, March 20, 2015, p. B2.

21. Scott Galloway, New York University's Stern Business School, quoted in Picchi, "5 Mistakes That Doomed RadioShack."

22. J. Bois, "A Eulogy for RadioShack, the Panicked and Half-Dead Empire," SB*Nation, December 2, 2015, www.sbnation.com/2014/11/26/7281129/radioshack-eulogy-stories (accessed June 17, 2016).

23. See M. Ramsey, "Self-Driving Cars Imperil Body Shops," *The Wall Street Journal*, March 6, 2015, p. B3.

24. T. Johnson, "Mexico Takes Flight as Hub for Aerospace Industry," McClatchy Newspapers, July 18, 2012, www.mcclatchydc.com/2012/07/18/156657/mexico-takes-flight-as-hub-for.html (accessed June 17, 2016); F. Saliba, "Mexico Aims High with Investment in Burgeoning Aviation Industry," *The Guardian*, June 25, 2013, www.theguardian.com/world/2013/jun/25/mexico-aviation-supply-industry-growth (accessed June 17, 2016); P. Gallant, "How Bombardier's Experiment Became Ground Zero for Mexico's Economic Revolution," *Canadian Business*, April 15, 2014, www.canadianbusiness.com/global-report/how-bombardiers-experiment-became-ground-zero-for-mexicos-economic-revolution (accessed June 17, 2016); and "Aerospace Industry in Mexico," PwC, May 2015, https://www.pwc.com/mx/es/knowledge-center/archivo/20150604-gx-publication-aerospace-industry.pdf (accessed June 17, 2016).

25. P. Davidson, "Foreign Manufacturers Bringing Jobs to U.S.," *USA Today*, May 15, 2013, www.usatoday.com/story/money/business/2013/05/15/foreign-manufacturers-bringing-jobs-to-us/2070327 (accessed July 8, 2016).

26. M. B. Sauter and S. Stebbins, "Manufacturers Bringing Most Jobs Back to America," *USA Today*, April 23, 2016, www.usatoday.com/story/money/business/2016/04/23/24-7-wallst-economy-manufacturers-jobs-outsourcing/83406518 (accessed June 17, 2016).

27. K. Bradsher, "China Drawing High-Tech Research from U.S.," *The New York Times*, March 18, 2010, pp. A1, A14.

28. Albrecht, "Eight Supertrends Shaping the Future of Business."

29. See analysis by J. Zumbrun, "The Rise of Knowledge Workers Is Accelerating Despite the Threat of Automation," *The Wall Street Journal*, May 4, 2016, http://blogs.wsj.com/economics/2016/05/04/the-rise-of-knowledge-workers-is-accelerating-despite-the-threat-of-automation (accessed June 17, 2016).

30. D. Autor, reported in T. Aeppel, "Be Calm, Robots Aren't About to Take Your Job, MIT Economist Says," *The Wall Street Journal*, February 25, 2015, http://blogs.wsj.com/economics/2015/02/25/be-calm-robots-arent-about-to-take-your-job-mit-economist-says (accessed June 17, 2016).

31. See *Capitalizing on Complexity: Insights from the Global Chief Executive Officer Study*, International Business Machines, Somers, New York, 2010, www-01.ibm.com/common/ssi/cgi-bin/ssialias?htmlfid=GBE03301USEN&appname=wwwsearch; *Leading Through Connections: Insights from the IBM Global CEO Study*, International Business Machines, Somers, New York, 2012, www-935.ibm.com/services/us/en/c-suite/ceostudy2012; and *PwC's Annual Global CEO Survey*, PricewaterhouseCoopers, 2016, www.pwc.com/gx/en/ceo-agenda/ceosurvey/2016.html (all accessed June 17, 2016).

32. E. Allday, "Vaccine Avoiders Put State at Risk," *San Francisco Chronicle*, February 8, 2015, pp. A1, A14; and E. Allday, "Measles Outbreak Unusual for State," *San Francisco Chronicle*, March 8, 2015, pp. A1, A14.

33. T. S. S. Rao and C. Andrade, "The MMR Vaccine and Autism: Sensation, Refutation, Retraction, and Fraud," *Indian Journal of Psychiatry*, Vol. 53, No. 2 (2011), pp. 95–96.

34. P. Offit, "The Anti-vaccination Epidemic," *The Wall Street Journal*, September 15, 2014, p. A21.

35. G. Bellafante, "Vaccine Fear Goes Viral," *The New York Times*, October 12, 2014, p. MB-1.

36. R. Gold, B. Casselman, and G. Chazan, "Oil Well Lacked Safeguard Device," *The Wall Street Journal*, April 29, 2010, pp. A1, A8; S. Power and J. R. Emshwiller, "Investigators Focus on Failed Device," *The Wall Street Journal*, May 6, 2010, p. A5; and D. Vergano, "New Equipment Headed to Battle Oil Spill," *USA Today*, May 6, 2010, p. 5A.

37. J. Scheck and S. Williams, "BP: The Makeover," *The Wall Street Journal*, October 25, 2013, pp. B1, B2.

38. C. Robertson and J. Schwartz, "How a Gulf Settlement That BP Once Hailed Became Its Target," *The New York Times*, April 27, 2014, News-1, News 20.

39. A. Neuhauser, "Judge Approves $20B Settlement in 2010 BP Oil Spill," *U.S. News & World Report*, April 4, 2016, www.usnews.com/news/articles/2016-04-04/judge-approves-20b-settlement-in-2010-bp-deepwater-horizon-oil-spill (accessed June 30, 2016).

40. P. Robertson, D. Roberts, and J. Porras, "Dynamics of Planned Organizational Change: Assessing Empirical Support for a Theoretical Model," *Academy of Management Journal*, Vol. 36, No. 3 (1993), pp. 619–634.

41. M. Whitman, quoted in Q. Hardy, "Shifting Tech Scene Unsettles Big Players," *The New York Times*, August 22, 2013, pp. B1, B8.

42. A. Carr, "The Messy Business of Reinventing Happiness," *FastCompany*, April 15, 2015, www.fastcompany.com/3044283/the-messy-business-of-reinventing-happiness (accessed June 17, 2016). See also C. Kuang, "Disney's $1 Billion Bet on a Magical Wristband," *Wired*, March 10, 2015, www.wired.com/2015/03/Disney-magicband (accessed June 17, 2016).

43. Duncan Dickson, University of Central Florida, quoted in S. Sekusa, "Disney Gets Personal with New MyMagic+ System," *USA Today*, January 27, 2014, www.usatoday.com/story/dispatches/2014/01/27/disney-mymagic-vacation-planning/4582957 (accessed July 8, 2016).

44. B. Barnes, "A Billion-Dollar Bracelet Is the Key to a Disney Park," *The New York Times*, April 1, 2014, www.nytimes.com/2014/04/02/business/billion-dollar-bracelet-is-key-to-magical-kingdom.html?_r=1 (accessed June 17, 2016). See also C. J. Barker, "DisneyWorld 2014: More Magical than Ever," *New York Amsterdam News*, May 15, 2014, http://amsterdamnews.com/news/2014/may/15/disney-world-2014-more-magical-ever (accessed June 17, 2016).

45. S. Pedicini, "Phones, Not Magic Bands, Will Be the Future of Disney's MyMagic+," *Orlando Sentinel*, April 9, 2016, www.orlandosentinel.com/travel/attractions/the-daily-disney/os-disney-magicbands-phones-20160408-story.html (accessed June 17, 2016).

46. R. Fry, "For the First Time in Modern Era, Living with Parents Edges Out Other Living Arrangements for 18- to 34-Year-Olds," Pew Research Center, May 24, 2016, www.pewsocialtrends.org/2016/05/24/for-first-time-in-modern-era-living-with-parents-edges-out-other-living-arrangements-for-18-to-34-year-olds (accessed June 17, 2016).

47. K. Schwab, "The Fourth Industrial Revolution: What It Means, How to Respond," World Economic Forum, January 14, 2016, https://www.weforum.org/agenda/2016/01/the-fourth-industrial-revolution-what-it-means-and-how-to-respond (accessed June 17, 2016).

48. M. Isaac, "G.M., Expecting Rapid Change, Invests $500 Million in Lyft," *The New York Times*, January 5, 2016, p. B1.

49. B. Libert, M. Beck, and J. Wind, "How Automakers Can Think Like a Disruptor," *Knowledge@Wharton*, June 17, 2016, http://knowledge.wharton.upenn.edu/article/headline-automakers-can-think-like-disruptor (accessed June 22, 2016); M. Vella, "Automakers Want to Sell You Much More Than Just a Car," *Time*, January 25, 2016, p. 14; and K. Naughton and D. Welch, "Detroit Has Valley Envy," *Bloomberg Businessweek*, May 2–8, 2016, pp. 21–22.

50. Associated Press, "Town Glimpses Transit Future—Driverless Buses," *San Francisco Chronicle*, October 9, 2015, p. A5; Associated Press, "Driverless Taxi a Glimpse of the Future," *San Francisco Chronicle*, January 6, 2016, p. A4; M. Ramsey and G. Nagesh, "GM, Lyft to Test Self-Driving Taxes," *The Wall Street Journal*, May 6, 2016, pp. A1, A9; and J. Markoff, "Want to Buy a Self-Driving Car? Big-Rig Trucks May Come First," *The New York Times*, May 17, 2016, pp. B1, B6.

51. B. Snavely and N. Bomey, "White House Proposes $4B for Self-Driving Cars," *Reno Gazette-Journal*, January 15, 2016, p. 1B, reprinted from *USA Today*.

52. L. Kaye, "Brazil's Natural Cosmetics Now the World's Largest B Corp," *TriplePundit*, December 29, 2014, www.triplepundit.com/2014/12/brazils-natura-cosmetics-now-worlds-largest-b-corp (accessed June 17, 2016).

53. D. Dahlhoff and A. Mantis of research group NPD, interviewed in "How Millennials, Gen Xers, and Baby Boomers Shop Differently," *Knowledge@Wharton*, May 31, 2016, http://knowledge.wharton.upenn.edu/article/new-tools-answer-age-old-question-of-what-do-customers-want (accessed June 18, 2016).

54. See E. Fragouli and B. Ibidapo, "Leading in Crisis: Leading Organizational Change & Business Development," *International Journal of Information, Business and Management*, Vol. 7, No. 3 (2015), pp. 71–90.

55. See J. Onyang-Omara and K. Hjelmgaard, " 'Brexit' Is Here: What Happens Next," *Reno Gazette-Journal*, June 25, 2016, p. 2B, reprinted from *USA Today*; S. Fidler, V. Pop, and J. Gross, "U.K. Vote Sets Off Shockwaves," *The Wall Street Journal*, June 25–26, 2016, pp. A1, A6; G. Baker, "Britain Fires a Shot Heard Round the World," *The Wall Street Journal*, June 25–26, 2016, pp. A1, A7; and S. Wilmot, "Why the U.K.'s 'Brexit' Move Will Raise Trade Barriers," *The Wall Street Journal*, June 25–26, 2016, p. B10.

56. E. Dou and D. Wakabayashi, "Apples Hits New Hurdle in China," *The Wall Street Journal*, June 18–19, 2016, pp. A1, A9; and A. Back, "Yet Another Chinese Setback for Apple," *The Wall Street Journal*, June 18–19, 2016, p. B12.

57. D. Cuellar, "Philadelphia City Council Passes Beverage Tax with 13-4 Vote," 6abc. com, June 19, 2016, http://6abc.com/news/philadelphia-city-council-passes-beverage-tax-/1388228/ (accessed June 19, 2016).

58. S. Oster, "Inside One of the World's Most Secretive iPhone Factories," *Bloomberg*, April 25, 2016, http://www.bloomberg.com/news/features/2016-04-24/inside-one-of-the-world-s-most-secretive-iphone-factories (accessed June 15, 2016).

59. D. Seetharaman and N. Andrews, "Facebook to Train against Bias," *The Wall Street Journal*, June 24, 2016, p. B3.

60. This three-way typology of change was adapted from discussion in P. C. Nutt, "Tactics of Implementation," *Academy of Management Journal*, June 1986, pp. 230–261.

61. Radical organizational change is discussed by T. E. Vollmann, *The Transformational Imperative* (Boston: Harvard Business School Press, 1996).

62. See J. Vanian, "Amazon's Drone Testing Takes Flight in Yet Another Country," *Fortune*, February 1, 2016, http://fortune.com/2016/02/01/amazon-testing-drones-netherlands, accessed June 27, 2016; and "Amazon Prime Air," Amazon website, https://www.amazon.com/b?node=8037720011 (both accessed June 27, 2016).

63. K. Lewin, *Field Theory in Social Science* (New York: Harper & Row, 1951).

64. T. T. Lee, "Adopting a Personal Digital Assistant System: Application of Lewin's Change Theory," *Journal of Advanced Nursing*, August 2006, pp. 487–496; B. Garrett and G. Klein, "Value of Wireless Personal Digital Assistants for Practice: Perceptions of Advanced Practice Nurses," *Journal of Clinical Nursing*, August 2008, pp. 2146–2154; S. Bassendowski, P. Petrucka, L. Breitkreuz, J. Partyka, L. MacDougall, B. Hanson, and K. Ayers, "Integration of Technology to Support Nursing Practice: A Saskatchewan Initiative," *Online Journal of Nursing Informatics*, June 2011, http://ojni.org/issues/?p=635 (accessed June 17, 2016); P. Divall, J. Camosso-Stefinovic, and R. Baker, "The Use of Personal Digital Assistants in Clinical Decision Making by Health Care Professionals: A Systematic Review," *Health Informatics Journal*, Vol. 19, No. 1 (2013), pp.16–18; S. Mickan, H. Atherton, N. W. Roberts, C. Heneghan, and J. K. Tilson, "Use of Handheld Computers in Clinical Practice: A Systematic Review," *BMC Medical Informatics and Decision Making*, Vol. 14 (2014), p. 56; and P. Guo, K. Watts, and H. Wharrad, "An Integrative Review of the Impact of Mobile Technologies used by Healthcare Professionals to Support Education and Practice," *Nursing Open*, April 2016, pp. 66–78.

65. The role of learning within organizational change is discussed by C. Hendry, "Understanding and Creating Whole Organizational Change through Learning Theory," *Human Relations*, May 1996, pp. 621–641; and D. Ready, "Mastering Leverage, Leading Change," *Executive Excellence*, March 1995, pp. 18–19.

66. L. R. Hearld and J. A. Alexander, "Governance Processes and Change within Organizational Participants of Multi-Sectoral Community Health Care Alliances: The Mediating Role of Vision, Mission, Strategy Agreement, and Perceived Alliance Value," *American Journal of Community Psychology*, March 2014, pp. 185–197.

67. A. E. Rafferty, N. L. Jimmieson, and A. A. Armenakis, "Change Readiness: A Multi-level Review," *Journal of Management*, January 2013, pp. 110–135.

68. See S. Ng and C. Dulaney, "P&G's Sales Shrink as It Remakes Itself," *The Wall Street Journal*, October 24–25, 2015, p. B3; and S. Terlep, "P&G Posts Higher Profit, but Sales Volume Declines Across Most Businesses," *The Wall Street Journal*, April 26, 2016, hwww.wsj.com/articles/p-g-earnings-top-expectations-but-volumes-fall-1461670557 (accessed June 19, 2016).

69. See S. Nguyen, "The Link between Industrial/Organizational Psychology, Organization Development, and Change Management," *Workplace Psychology*, May 9, 2016, https://workplacepsychology.net/2016/05/09/the-link-between-industrial-organizational-psychology-organization-development-and-change-management (accessed June 14, 2016). See also D. Aguyirre, A. Brown, and A. Harshak, "Making Change Happen, and Making It Stick: Delivering Sustainable Organizational Change," *Strategy &*, October 5, 2010, www.strategyand.pwc.com/reports/making-change-happen-making-stick-2 (accessed June 14, 2016).

70. C. Spreitzer, reported in P. Korkki, "Thwarting the Jerk at Work," *The New York Times*, November 22, 2015, p. BU-4. See also A. Gerbasi, C. L. Porath, A. Parker, G. Spreitzer, and R. Cross, "Destructive De-energizing Relationships: How Thriving Buffers Their Effect on Performance," *Journal of Applied Psychology*, Vol. 100, No. 5 (2015), pp. 1423–1433.

71. See Steve Lohr, "Setting Free the Squares," *The New York Times*, November 15, 2015, pp. BU-1, BU-5. See also T. Brown and R. Martin, "Design for Action," *Harvard Business Review*, September 2015, pp. 56–64.

72. M. Fugate, A. Kinicki, and C. L. Scheck, "Coping with an Organizational Merger over Four Stages," *Personnel Psychology*, Winter 2002, pp. 905–928.

73. Eli Chait, quoted in S. Finz, "Crunching Dining Data," *San Francisco Chronicle*, March 7, 2013, pp. C1, C5.

74. E. Chait, "Daily Deals vs. Happy Hours: The Impact of Internal Marketing Promos," *Street Fight*, November 16, 2012, http://streetfightmag.com/2012/11/16/daily-deals-vs-happy-hours-the-impact-of-internal-marketing-promos (accessed July 8, 2016).

75. "The Feedback Loop: More Data Doesn't Always Mean Better Customer Service," *Knowledge@Wharton*, April 23, 2014, http://knowledge.wharton.upenn.edu/article/feedback-loop-data-doesnt-always-mean-better-customer-service (accessed July 8, 2016).

76. E. Chait, "The Best and Worst Days of 2012 for Restaurant Business," *Inside Scoop SF*, December 18, 2014, http://insidescoopsf.sfgate.com/blog/2012/12/18/the-best-and-worst-days-of-2012-for-restaurant-business (accessed July 8, 2016).

77. See Q. Hardy, "Big Data's Little Brother," *The New York Times*, November 11, 2014, pp. B1, B4.

78. See "Change Management: The HR Strategic Imperative as a Business Partner," *Research Quarterly*, Fourth Quarter 2007, pp. 1–9; and D. A. Garvin, A. C. Edmondson, and F. Gino, "Is Yours a Learning Organization?" *Harvard Business Review*, March 2008, pp. 109–116.

79. W. G. Dyer, *Team Building: Current Issues and New Alternatives*, 3rd ed. (Reading, MA: Addison-Wesley, 1995).

80. See M. Bennett, "The Role of OD," *Training Journal*, March 2014, www.trainingjournal.com (accessed June 30, 2016).

81. See P. Atkinson, "OD Strategies: Installing a Lean and Continuous Improvement Culture," *Management Services*, Winter 2014, pp. 12–17.

82. P. J. Robertson, D. R. Roberts, and J. I. Porras, "Dynamics of Planned Organizational Change: Assess Empirical Support for a Theoretical Model," *Academy of Management Journal*, June 1993, pp. 619–634.

83. C.-M. Lau and H.-Y. Ngo, "Organization Development and Firm Performance: A Comparison of Multinational and Local Firms," *Journal of International Business Studies*, First Quarter 2001, pp. 95–114.

84. A. G. Lafley, interviewed by R. O. Crockett in "How P&G Plans to Clean Up," *BusinessWeek*, April 13, 2009, p. 44.

85. Lafley, quoted in Crockett, "How P&G Plans to Clean Up."

86. A. G. Lafley, interviewed by K. Dillon, "'I Think of My Failures as a Gift,'" *Harvard Business Review*, April 2011, pp. 68–74.

87. J. Welch and S. Welch, "Finding Innovation Where It Lives," *BusinessWeek*, April 21, 2008, p. 84.

88. This discussion is adapted from R. Kreitner and A. Kinicki, *Organizational Behavior*, 10th ed. (McGraw-Hill/Irwin, 2013), p. 526, which is based on S. Berkun, *The Myths of Innovation* (Sebastapol, CA: O'Reilly Media, Inc., 2007).

89. R. Pannett, "An End to Laundry? The Promise of Self-Cleaning Fabric," *The Wall Street Journal*, April 26, 2016, p. D3.

90. A. Filev, "What Every Entrepreneur Should Learn from GoPro Founder Nick Woodman," *Fortune*, March 23, 2016, http://fortune.com/2016/03/23/gopro-founder-nick-woodman-good-business-ideas (accessed June 21, 2016).

91. See D. Kiley and C. Matlack, "Fiat: On the Road Back to America," *BusinessWeek*, April 20, 2009, p. 28.

92. S. Frier and A. Satariano, "Microsoft Pays $26 Billion for LinkedIn in Biggest Deal Yet," Bloomberg.com, June 13, 2016, www.bloomberg.com/news/articles/2016-06-13/microsoft-to-buy-linkedin-in-deal-valued-at-26-2-billion-ipe079k9 (accessed June 29, 2016).

93. T. Rawlins, senior quality manager for business excellence at Microsoft, interviewed in "How Microsoft's 'Garage' Keeps Its Innovative Spark Burning," *Knowledge@Wharton*, March 4, 2016, http://knowledge.wharton.upenn.edu/article/how-microsofts-garage-keeps-its-innovative-spark-burning (accessed June 14, 2016). For more on motivating employee ideas at a large technology company, see M. Gibbs, S. Neckermann, and C. Siemroth, "A Field Experiment in Motivating Employee Ideas," *SSRN*, December 16, 2015, http://papers.ssrn.com/sol3/papers.cfm?abstract_id=2420965 (accessed June 22, 2016).

94. T. Lee, "Adobe Workers Fuel Innovation," *San Francisco Chronicle*, June 21, 2015, pp. D1, D3.

95. See U. Jayasinghe and J. Nicas, "'Project Loon' Is Aloft in Sri Lanka," *The Wall Street Journal*, February 17, 2016, p. B6.

96. C. Jackson, "Snowflake Entrepreneurs," *Growthology*, January 16, 2015, Kauffman Foundation, www.kauffman.org/blogs/growthology/2015/01/snowflake-entrepreneurs (accessed June 30, 2016).

97. A. V. Bhidé, reported in G. Gendron, "The Origin of the Entrepreneurial Species," *Inc.*, February 2000, pp. 105–114.

98. S. Bhattacharya, "Indian Drugmakers Target Niche Markets," *The Wall Street Journal*, April 19, 2016, p. B6.

99. Maxine Clark, quoted in D. Eng, "Who Built Build-a-Bear?" *Fortune*, March 19, 2012, pp. 49–52.

100. A. Schrager, "Failed Entrepreneurs Find More Success the Second Time," Bloomberg.com, July 28, 2014, www.bloomberg.com/news/articles/2014-07-28/study-failed-entrepreneurs-find-success-the-second-time-around (accessed June 29, 2016).

101. S. A. Shane, *The Illusions of Entrepreneurship: The Costly Myths That Entrepreneurs, Investors, and Policy Makers Live By* (New Haven, CT: Yale University Press, 2008).

102. Scott Shane, interviewed by J. Tozzi, "The Entrepreneurship Myth," *Business Week*, January 23, 2008, www.bloomberg.com/news/articles/2008-01-23/the-entrepreneurship-mythbusinessweek-business-news-stock-market-and-financial-advice (accessed June 22, 2016).

103. G. P. Pisano, "You Need an Innovation Strategy," *Harvard Business Review*, June 2015, p. 46.

104. See N. Anderson, K. Potocnik, and J. Zhou, "Innovation and Creativity in Organizations: A State-of-the-Science Review, Prospective Commentary, and Guiding Framework," *Journal of Management*, July 2014, pp. 1297–1333.

105. Pisano, "You Need an Innovation Strategy," pp. 44–54.

106. Pisano, "You Need an Innovation Strategy," p. 48.

107. A. Ignatius, "How Indra Nooyi Turned Design Thinking into Strategy," *Harvard Business Review*, September 2015, pp. 81–85.

108. Risk-averse culture is the key obstacle to innovation, according to a survey by the Boston Consulting Group, as reported in J. Birkinshaw and M. Haas, "Increase Your Return on Failure," *Harvard Business Review*, May 2016, pp. 88–93. An innovative culture and climate are also associated with the creation of new ideas and products, as supported by A. S-Y. Chen and Y-H. Hou, "The Effects of Ethical Leadership, Voice Behavior, and Climates for Innovation on Creativity: A Moderated Mediation Examination," *The Leadership Quarterly*, 2016, pp. 1–13; and A. Oh, C. A. Hartnell, A. J. Kinicki, and D. Choi, "Culture in Context: A Meta-Analysis of the Nomological Network of Organizational Culture," paper presented at the 2016 National Academy of Management Meeting, Anaheim, CA.

109. Ed Catmull, quoted in J. Birkinshaw and M. Haas, "Increase Your Return on Failure," *Harvard Business Review*, May 2016, pp. 88–93.

110. See L. Kwoh, "Memo to Staff: Take More Risks," *The Wall Street Journal*, March 20, 2013, p. B8.

111. R. Cross, C. Ernst, D. Assimakopoulos, and D. Ranta, "Investing in Boundary-Spanning Collaboration to Drive Efficiency and Innovation," *Organizational Dynamics*, July-September 2015, pp. 206–207.

112. See N. Anderson, K. Potocnik, and J. Zhou, "Innovation and Creativity in Organizations: A State-of-the-Science Review, Prospective Commentary, and Guiding Framework," *Journal of Management*, July 2014, pp. 1297–1333; X.-H. Wang, Y. Fang, I. Qureshi, and O. Janssen, "Understanding Employee Innovative Behavior: Integrating the Social Network and Leader-Member Exchange Perspectives," *Journal of Organizational Behavior*, April 2015, pp. 403–420; and F. C. Godart, W. W. Maddux, A. V. Shipilov, and A. D. Galinsky, "Fashion with a Foreign Flair: Professional Experiences Abroad Facilitate the Creative Innovations of Organizations," *Academy of Management Journal*, February 2015, pp. 195–122.

113. See X. Huang, J. P-A. Hsieh, and W. He, "Expertise Dissimilarity and Creativity: The Contingent Roles of Tacit and Explicit Knowledge," *Journal of Applied Psychology*, September 2014, pp. 816–830.

114. D. Leonard and R. Clough, "Move Fast and Break Things," *Bloomberg Businessweek*, March 21–27, 2016, pp. 58–59.

115. See J. Chowhan, "Unpacking the Black Box: Understanding the Relationship between Strategy, HRM Practices, Innovation, and Organizational Performance," *Human Resource Management Journal*, April 2016, pp. 112–133; and M. Diaz-Fernandez, M. Bornay-Barrachina, and A. Lopez-Cabrales, "Innovation and Firm Performance: The Role of Human Resource Management Practices," *Evidence-Based HRM: A Global Forum for Empirical Scholarship*, April 2015, pp. 64–80.

116. G. Dutton, "A Eureka! Moment," *Training*, January/February 2016, pp. 114–115.

117. D. Meinert, "Wings of Change," *HR Magazine*, November 2012, pp. 30–36.

118. B. Jaruzelski, K. Schwartz, and V. Staak, "The Top Innovators and Spenders," *Global Innovation 1000 Study*, 2015, Booz & Company, www.strategyand.pwc.com/global/home/what-we-think/innovation1000/top-innovators-spenders (accessed June 22, 2016).

119. "Forbes Announces Fifth Annual List of the World's Most Innovative Companies," *Forbes*, August 19, 2015, www.forbes.com/sites/forbespr/2015/08/19/forbes-announces-fifth-annual-list-of-the-worlds-most-innovative-companies/#7d1547c3fcfe; "50 Smartest Companies 2016," *MIT Technology Review*, https://www.technologyreview.com/lists/companies/2016; and M. Quincy, "The Best Cars of 2015," *Consumer Reports*, December 28, 2015, www.consumerreports.org/cars/the-best-cars-of-2015 (all accessed June 22, 2016).

120. P. McKinney, "Leaders in Innovation: How They're Creating Cultures of Creativity," Phil McKinney blog, June 2, 2016, http://philmckinney.com/leaders-innovation-theyre-creating-cultures-creativity (accessed June 22, 2016).

121. M. Boyadjis, A. Rassweiler, and S. Brinley, "Tesla Motors: A Case Study in Disruptive Innovation," *IHS Automotive Blog*, October 8, 2014, http://blog.ihs.com/q14-tesla-motors-a-case-study-in-disruptive-innovation (accessed June 22, 2016).

122. Tesla executive George Ell, quoted in D. Nicholson, "Inside Tesla—a Rare Glimpse of Electric Carmaker's Culture," *Forbes*, November 9, 2014, www.forbes.com/sites/davidnicholson/2014/11/09/inside-tesla-a-rare-glimpse-of-electric-carmakers-culture/#c34762137fea (accessed June 22, 2016).

123. Boyadjis, Rassweiler, and Brinley, "Tesla Motors: A Case Study in Disruptive Innovation."

124. Nicholson, "Inside Tesla—A Rare Glimpse of Electric Carmaker's Culture."

125. C. Sandström, "How Disruptive Is Tesla, Really?" *MIT Technology Review*, July 7, 2015, https://www.technologyreview.com/s/539081/how-disruptive-is-tesla-really (accessed June 22, 2016).

126. B. L. Karafiath and J. Brewer, "Tesla Motors: How to Contain the Fires?" *Culture 2*, December 1, 2013, www.culture2inc.com/2013/12/01/elon-musk-tesla-fires (accessed June 22, 2016).

127. J. Zhou, "Four Tips for 'Going Tesla' to Create an Open and Innovative Culture," *Soapbox Innovations*, July 10, 2014, https://soapboxhq.com/blog/four-tips-going-tesla-create-open-innovative-culture (accessed June 22, 2016).

128. L. Bossidy and Ram Charan, with C. Burck, *Execution: The Discipline of Getting Things Done* (New York: Crown Business, 2002).

129. B. Burnes, "Understanding Resistance to Change—Building on Coch and French," *Journal of Change Management*, Vol. 15, No. 2 (2015), pp. 92–116.

130. See L. Brimm, "Managing Yourself: How to Embrace Complex Change," *Harvard Business Review*, September 2015, pp. 108–112.

131. D. A. Tucker, J. Hendy, and J. Barlow, "The Importance of Role Sending in the Sensemaking of Change Agent Roles," *Journal of Health Organization and Management*, Vol 29 (2015), pp. 1047–1064.

132. See S. H. Appelbaum, M. C. Degbe, O. MacDonald, and T.-S. Nguyen-Quang, "Organizational Outcomes of Leadership Style and Resistance to Change (Part One)," *Industrial and Commercial Times*, Vol. 47 (2015), pp. 73–80.

133. Adapted in part from J. D. Ford, L. W. Ford, and A. D'Amelio, "Resistance to Change: The Rest of the Story," *Academy of Management Review*, April 2008, pp. 362–377.

134. See S. Oreg, M. Bayazit, M. Vakola, L. Arciniega, et al., "Dispositional Resistance to Change: Measurement Equivalence and the Link to Personal Values across 17 Nations," *Journal of Applied Psychology*, Vol. 23 (2008), pp. 935–944.

135. See J. B. Riley, "What to Do When Employees Are Gaming the System: Overcoming Resistance to Change," *Global Business and Organizational Excellence*, January/February 2016, pp. 31–37.

136. J. Georgalis, R. Samaratunge, and N. Kimberley, "Change Process Characteristics and Resistance to Organisational Change: The Role of Employee Perceptions of Justice," *Australian Journal of Management*, Vol. 40 (2015), pp. 89–113.

137. Details of this example are provided by B. Schlender, "Inside the Shakeup at Sony," *Fortune*, April 4, 2005, pp. 94–104.

138. R. Best, "Why JC Penney's Most Important Asset Is Its Management Team," March 8, 2016, http://www.investopedia.com/articles/markets/030816/why-jcpenneys-most-important-asset-its-management-team-jcp-aapl.asp.

139. R. Best, "Why JC Penney's Most Important Asset Is Its Management Team," March 8, 2016, http://www.investopedia.com/articles/markets/030816/why-jcpenneys-most-important-asset-its-management-team-jcp-aapl.asp.

140. P. Wahba, "The Man Who's Re-[Re-Re-] Inventing J.C. Penney, *Fortune*, March 1, 2016, 77–86.

141. R. Best, "Why JC Penney's Most Important Asset Is Its Management Team," March 8, 2016, http://www.investopedia.com/articles/markets/030816/why-jcpenneys-most-important-asset-its-management-team-jcp-aapl.asp.

142. P. Wahba, "The Man Who's Re-[Re-Re-] Inventing J.C. Penney," *Fortune*, March 1, 2016, pp. 77–86.

143. See "CNBC Exclusive: CNBC Transcript: J.C. Penney CEO Marvin Ellison Speaks with CNBC's Courtney Reagan on 'Power Lunch' Today," February 29, 2016, http://www.cnbc.com/2016/02/29/cnbc-exclusive-cnbc-transcript-jc-penney-ceo-marvin-ellison-speaks-with-cnbcs-courtney-reagan-on-power-lunch-today.html; K. Gustafson, "Guess What? JC Penney Is Now Ahead of the Curve," May 13, 2016, http://www.cnbc.com/2016/05/13/guess-what-jc-penney-is-now-ahead-of-the-curve.html; and C. Kern, "JC Penney Focuses on Ecommerce to Continue Turnaround," August 19, 2015, http://www.innovativeretailtechnologies.com/doc/jcpenney-focuses-on-ecommerce-to-continue-turnaround-0001.

144. R. Best, "Why JC Penney's Most Important Asset Is Its Management Team," March 8, 2016, http://www.investopedia.com/articles/markets/030816/why-jcpenneys-most-important-asset-its-management-team-jcp-aapl.asp.

145. "CNBC Exclusive: CNBC Transcript: J.C. Penney CEO Marvin Ellison Speaks with CNBC's Courtney Reagan on 'Power Lunch' Today," February 29, 2016, http://www.cnbc.com/2016/02/29/cnbc-exclusive-cnbc-transcript-jc-penney-ceo-marvin-ellison-speaks-with-cnbcs-courtney-reagan-on-power-lunch-today.html.

146. "CNBC Exclusive: CNBC Transcript: J.C. Penney CEO Marvin Ellison Speaks with CNBC's Courtney Reagan on 'Power Lunch' Today," February 29, 2016, http://www.cnbc.com/2016/02/29/cnbc-exclusive-cnbc-transcript-jc-penney-ceo-marvin-ellison-speaks-with-cnbcs-courtney-reagan-on-power-lunch-today.html.

147. https://en.wikipedia.org/wiki/List_of_top_United_States_patent_recipients#2015, last modified January 19, 2016, accessed May 25, 2016.

148. T. C. Frhlich, "The World's Most Innovative Companies," January 13, 2015, http://247wallst.com/special-report/2015/01/13/the-worlds-most-innovative-companies, accessed May 25, 2016.

149. S. Decker and D. Voreaos, "Fired L'Oreal Lawyer Says Patent Push Was Only Cosmetic," April 21, 2015, http://www.bloomberg.com/news/articles/2015-04-21/fired-l-oreal-lawyer-says-company-patent-push-was-only-cosmetic. accessed May 25, 2016.

150. S. Decker and D. Voreaos, "Fired L'Oreal Lawyer Says Patent Push Was Only Cosmetic," April 21, 2015, http://www.bloomberg.com/news/articles/2015-04-21/fired-l-oreal-lawyer-says-company-patent-push-was-only-cosmetic. accessed May 25, 2016.

CHAPTER 11

1. J. Kriegel, interviewed in "'Y' Generational Stereotypes Are Bad for Business," Knowledge@Wharton, June 22, 2016, http://knowledge.wharton.upenn.edu/article/why-generational-stereotypes-are-bad-for-business (accessed July 1, 2016). Kriegel is author of *Unfairly Labeled: How Your Workplace Can Benefit from Ditching Generational Stereotypes* (Hoboken, NJ: John Wiley & Sons, 2016).

2. F. Manjoo, "Companies in Pursuit of a Mythical Millennial," *The New York Times*, May 26, 2016, pp. B1, B7.

3. Kriegel, interviewed in "'Y' Generational Stereotypes Are Bad for Business."

4. Millennial expert Lindsey Pollak, reported in L. Gellman, "Helping Bosses Decode Millennials," *The Wall Street Journal*, May 18, 2016, pp. B1, B7.

5. L. McCleod, reported in Gellman, "Helping Bosses Decode Millennials."

6. See J. Wingard, interviewed in "How Companies Are Managing the Millennial Generation," *Knowledge@Wharton*, March 5, 2015, https://www.google.com/search?q=How+Companies+Are+Managing+the+Millennial+Generation&ie=utf-8&oe=utf-8 (accessed July 1, 2016); L. Evans, "This Is How Millennials Will Change Management," *Fast Company*, October 29, 2015, www.fastcompany.com/3052617/the-future-of-work/this-how-millennials-will-change-management (accessed July 1, 2016); C. Groden, "Five Things You Can Do to Attract Millennial Talent," *Fortune.com*, March 4, 2016, http://fortune.com/2016/03/04/attracting-millennial-talent/ (accessed July 1, 2016); and D. Huang and L. Gellman, "Millennial Employees Confound Wall Street," *The Wall Street Journal*, April 9–10, 2016, pp. A1, A8.

7. See D. Wilkie, "Millennials: They're Just Like Us," *HR Magazine*, April 2015, p. 16.

8. *Myths, Exaggerations, and Uncomfortable Truths: The Real Story Behind Millennials in the Workplace*, IBM Institute for Business Value, January 2015, IBM Corporation, Somers, NY, https://public.dhe.ibm.com/common/ssi/ecm/gb/en/gbe03637usen/GBE03637USEN.PDF (accessed July 1, 2016).

9. B. Drake, "6 New Findings about Millennials," Pew Research Center, March 7, 2014, www.pewresearch.org/fact-tank/2014/03/07/6-new-findings-about-millennials; and R. Fry, "For First Time in Modern Era, Living with Parents Edges Out Other Living Arrangements for 18- to 34-Year-Olds," Pew Research Center, May 24, 2016, www.pewsocialtrends.org/2016/05/24/for-first-time-in-modern-era-living-with-parents-edges-out-other-living-arrangements-for-18-to-34-year-olds (both accessed July 1, 2016).

10. For a thorough discussion of personality psychology, see D. P. McAdams and J. L. Pals, "A New Big Five: Fundamental Principles for an Integrative Science of Personality," *American Psychologist*, April 2006, pp. 204–217.

11. See S. A. Woods, F. Lievens, F. De Fruyt, and B. Wille, "Personality Across Working Life: The Longitudinal and Reciprocal Influences of Personality on Work," *Journal of Organizational Behavior*, Vol. 34, No. S1 (2013), pp. S7–S25.
12. The landmark report is J. M. Digman, "Personality Structure: Emergence of the Five-Factor Model," *Annual Review of Psychology*, Vol. 41 (1990), pp. 417–440.
13. T. Chamorro-Premuzic, "Managing Yourself: Ace the Assessment," *Harvard Business Review*, July-August, 2015, pp. 118–121.
14. D. Meinert, "Heads Up: Personality Assessments Are Being Used More Often in the Hiring Process. But What Do They Really Tell You?" *HR Magazine*, June 2015, pp. 88–98.
15. See M. R. Barrick and M. K. Mount, "The Big Five Personality Dimensions and Job Performance: A Meta-Analysis," *Personnel Psychology*, Spring 1991, p. 21; J. M Beus, L. Y. Dhanani, and M. A. McCord, "A Meta-Analysis of Personality and Workplace Safety: Addressing Unanswered Questions," *Journal of Applied Psychology*, Vol. 100, No. 2 (2015), pp. 481–498.
16. See F. P. Morgeson, M. A. Campion, R. L. Dipboye, J. R. Hollenbeck, K. Murphy, and N. Schmitt, "Reconsidering the Use of Personality Tests in Personnel Selection," *Personnel Psychology*, Autumn 2007, pp. 683–729; and D. Armstrong, "Malingerer Test Roils Personal-Injury Law," *The Wall Street Journal*, March 5, 2008, pp. A1, A13.
17. Chamorro-Premuzic, "Managing Yourself: Ace the Assessment."
18. See Chamorro-Premuzic, "Managing Yourself: Ace the Assessment"; D. Meinert, "Heads Up: Personality Assessments Are Being Used More Often in the Hiring Process. But What Do They Really Tell You?" *HR Magazine*, June 2015, pp. 88–98; and H. Aguinis, S. A. Carpenter, and C. A. Pierce, "Revival of Test Bias Research in Pre-Employment Testing," *Journal of Applied Psychology*, Vol. 94, No. 10 (2010), pp. 648–680.
19. R. Silverman, "Genetic Testing May Be Coming to An Office Near You," *The Wall Street Journal*, December 16, 2015, pp. B1, B6.
20. See F. P. Morgeson, M. A. Campion, R. L. Dipboye, J. R. Hollenbeck, K. Murphy, and N. Schmitt, "Reconsidering the Use of Personality Tests in Personnel Selection," *Personnel Psychology*, Autumn 2007, pp. 683–729; and D. Armstrong, "Malingerer Test Roils Personal-Injury Law," *The Wall Street Journal*, March 5, 2008, pp. A1, A13.
21. See, for example, V. Gecas, "The Social Psychology of Self-Efficacy," in W. R. Scott and J. Blake, eds., *Annual Review of Sociology*, Vol. 15 (Palo Alto, CA: Annual Reviews, 1989), pp. 291–316; C. K. Stevens, A. G. Bavetta, and M. E. Gist, "Gender Differences in the Acquisition of Salary Negotiation Skills: The Role of Goals, Self-Efficacy, and Perceived Control," *Journal of Applied Psychology*, October 1993, pp. 723–735; and D. Eden and Y. Zuk, "Seasickness as a Self Fulfilling Prophecy: Raising Self-Efficacy to Boost Performance at Sea," *Journal of Applied Psychology*, October 1995, pp. 628–635.
22. J. Barling and R. Beattie, "Self-Efficacy Beliefs and Sales Performance," *Journal of Organizational Behavior Management*, Spring 1983, pp. 41–51.
23. A. D. Stajkovic and F. Luthans, "Self-Efficacy and Work-Related Performance: A Meta-Analysis," *Psychological Bulletin*, September 1998, pp. 240–261.
24. For more on learned helplessness, see M. J. Martinko and W. L. Gardner, "Learned Helplessness: An Alternative Explanation for Performance Deficits," *Academy of Management Review*, April 1982, pp. 195–204; and C. R. Campbell and M. J. Martinko, "An Integrative Attributional Perspective of Employment and Learned Helplessness: A Multimethod Field Study," *Journal of Management*, No. 2, 1998, pp. 173–200.
25. W. S. Silver, T. R. Mitchell, and M. E. Gist, "Response to Successful and Unsuccessful Performance: The Moderating Effect of Self-Efficacy on the Relationship between Training and Newcomer Adjustment," *Journal of Applied Psychology*, April 1995, pp. 211–225.
26. See J. V. Vancouver, K. M. More, and R. J. Yoder, "Self-Efficacy and Resource Allocation: Support for a Nonmonotonic, Discontinuous Model," *Journal of Applied Psychology*, January 2008, pp. 35–47.
27. The positive relationship between self-efficacy and readiness for retraining is documented in L. A. Hill and J. Elias, "Retraining Midcareer Managers: Career History and Self-Efficacy Beliefs," *Human Resource Management*, Summer 1990, pp. 197–217.
28. V. Gecas, "The Self-Concept," in R. H. Turner and J. F. Short Jr., eds., *Annual Review of Sociology*, Vol. 8 (Palo Alto, CA: Annual Reviews, 1982); also see N. Branden, *Self-Esteem at Work: How Confident People Make Powerful Companies* (San Francisco: Jossey-Bass, 1998).
29. P. G. Dodgson and J. V. Wood, "Self-Esteem and the Cognitive Accessibility of Strengths and Weaknesses after Failure," *Journal of Personality and Social Psychology*, July 1998, pp. 178–197; and D. B. Fedor, J. M. Maslyn, W. D. Davis, and K. Mathieseon, "Performance Improvement Efforts in Response to Negative Feedback: The Roles of Source Power and Recipient Self-Esteem," *Journal of Management*, January–February 2001, pp. 79–97.
30. B. R. Schlenker, M. F. Weigold, and J. R. Hallam, "Self-Serving Attributions in Social Context: Effects of Self-Esteem and Social Pressure," *Journal of Personality and Social Psychology*, May 1990, pp. 855–863; and P. Sellers, "Get Over Yourself," *Fortune*, April 2001, pp. 76–88.
31. D. A. Stinson, C. Logel, M. P. Zanna, J. G. Holmes, J. V. Wood, and S. J. Spencer, "The Cost of Lower Self-Esteem: Testing a Self- and Social-Bonds Model of Health," *Journal of Personality and Social Psychology*, March 2008, pp. 412–428.
32. E. Diener and M. Diener, "Cross-Cultural Correlates of Life Satisfaction and Self-Esteem," *Journal of Personality and Social Psychology*, April 1995, p. 662.
33. J. W. McGuire and C. V. McGuire, "Enhancing Self-Esteem by Directed-Thinking Tasks: Cognitive and Affective Positivity Asymmetries," *Journal of Personality and Social Psychology*, June 1996, p. 1124.
34. For an overall view of research on locus of control, see P. E. Spector, "Behavior in Organizations as a Function of Employee's Locus of Control," *Psychological Bulletin*, May 1982, pp. 482–497; and R. E. Johnson, C. C. Rosen, C.-H. Chang, and S.-H. Lin, "Getting to the Core of Locus of Control: Is It an Evaluation of the Self or the Environment?" *Journal of Applied Psychology*, Vol. 100, No. 5 (2015), pp. 1568–1578.
35. C. Wu, M. Griffin, and S. Parker, "Developing Agency Through Good Work: Longitudinal Effects of Job Autonomy and Skill Utilization on Locus of Control," *Journal of Vocational Behavior*, Vol. 89 (2015), pp. 102–108.
36. J. D. Mayer, R. D. Roberts, and S. G. Barsade, "Human Abilities: Emotional Intelligence," *Annual Review of Psychology*, January 2008, http://papers.ssrn.com/sol3/papers.cfm?abstract_id=1082096 (accessed July 1, 2016).
37. Results are based on N. Sánchez-Álvarez, N. Extremera, and P. Fernández-Berrocal, "The Relation between Emotional Intelligence and Subjective Well-Being: A Meta-Analytic Investigation," *The Journal of Positive Psychology*, May 2016, pp. 276–285; D. Joseph, J. Jin, D. A. Newman, and E. H. O'Boyle, "Why Does Self-Reported Emotional Intelligence Predict Job Performance? A Meta-Analytic Investigation of Mixed EI," *Journal of Applied Psychology*, March 2015, pp. 298–342; and M. R. Parke, M-G. Seo, and E. N. Sherf, "Regulating and Facilitating: The Role of Emotional Intelligence in Maintaining and Using Positive Affect for Creativity," *Journal of Applied Psychology*, 2015, pp. 917–934.
38. D. Goleman, "What Makes a Leader," *Harvard Business Review*, November–December 1998, pp. 93–102.
39. See J. E. Stellar, V. M. Manzo, M. W. Kraus, and D. Keltner, "Class and Compassion: Socioeconomic Factors Predict Responses to Suffering," *Emotion*, June 2012, pp. 449–459; K. Rollag, "Succeed in New Situations," *Harvard Business Review*, December 2015, pp. 112–115; and E. Bernstein, "It's Worth Learning to Be More Empathetic," *The Wall Street Journal*, May 3, 2016, pp. D1, D2.
40. The Personal Profile Analysis (PPA), by Thomas International, is described in M. Weinstein, "Emotional Evaluation," *Training*, July/August 2009, pp. 20–23.
41. See A. Chapman, "Empathy, Trust, Diffusing Conflict and Handling Complaints," *Businessballs.com*, www.businessballs.com/empathy.htm (accessed July 19, 2016).
42. Andrew Biga and Ryan Dullagan of Jet Blue, in "Should Hiring Be Based on Gut—or Data?" Knowledge at Wharton, August 24, 2015, http://knowledge.wharton.upenn.edu/article/should-hiring-be-based-on-gut-or-data/ (accessed July 11, 2016).
43. "Why Compassion Serves You Better Than Self-interest," *Knowledge@Wharton*, January 25, 2016, http://knowledge.wharton.upenn.edu/article/compassion-serves-better-self-interest (accessed July 11, 2016). Adapted from E. Seppala, *The Happiness Track: How to Apply the Science of Happiness to Accelerate Your Success* (New York: HarperOne, 2014).
44. See K. Cameron and J. McNaughtan, "Positive Organizational Change," *Journal of Applied Behavioral Science*, December 2014, pp. 445–462.
45. See M. Rokeach, *Beliefs, Attitudes, and Values* (San Francisco: Jossey-Bass, 1968), p. 168.
46. See S. H. Schwartz, "An Overview of the Schwartz Theory of Basic Values," *Online Readings in Psychology and Culture*, December 1, 2012, http://dx.doi.org/10.9707/2307-0919.1116 (accessed July 11, 2016).
47. For an application see D. Iliescu, D. Ispas, C. Sulea, and A. Ilie, "Vocational Fit and Counterproductive Work Behaviors: A Self-Regulation Perspective," *Journal of Applied Psychology*, January 2015, pp. 21–39.
48. M. Fishbein and I. Ajzen, *Belief, Attitude, Intention and Behavior: An Introduction to Theory and Research* (Reading, MA: Addison-Wesley Publishing, 1975), p. 6.
49. See M. Reid and A. Wood, "An Investigation into Blood Donation Intentions Among Non-Donors," *International Journal of Nonprofit and Voluntary Sector Marketing*, February 2008, pp. 31–43; and J. Ramsey, B. J. Punnett, and D. Greenidge, "A Social Psychological Account of Absenteeism in Barbados," *Human Resource Management Journal*, April 2008, pp. 97–117.
50. See T. A. Judge, C. J. Thoresen, J. E. Bono, and G. K. Patton, "The Job Satisfaction–Job Performance Relationship: A Qualitative and Quantitative Review," *Psychological Bulletin*, May 2001, pp. 376–407.
51. C. Mims, "Apps Tell Boss What Workers Really Think," *The Wall Street Journal*, June 22, 2015, pp. B1, B2.
52. J. S. Becker, "Empirical Validation of Affect, Behavior, and Cognition as Distinct Components of Attitude," *Journal of Personality and Social Psychology*, May 1984, pp. 1191–1205; the components or structure of attitudes is thoroughly discussed by A. P. Brief, *Attitudes in and around Organizations* (Thousand Oaks, CA: Sage, 1998), pp. 49–84.
53. L. Festinger, *A Theory of Cognitive Dissonance* (Stanford, CA: Stanford University Press, 1957).
54. R. Moss Kanter, "How Great Companies Think Differently," *Harvard Business Review*, November 2011, pp. 66–78.
55. "How Emerging Multinationals Are Embracing Social Responsibility," *Knowledge@Wharton*, November 12, 2015, http://knowledge.wharton.upenn.edu/article/why-emerging-multinationals-are-embracing-social-responsibility (accessed July 3, 2016).
56. A. H. Tangari, J. Kees, J. C. Andrews, and S. Burton, "Can Corrective Ad Statements Based on *U.S. v. Philip Morris USA Inc.* Impact Consumer Beliefs about Smoking?" *Journal of Public Policy & Marketing*, Vol. 29, No. 2 (2010), pp. 153–169; and H. Blanton, L. B. Snyder, E. Strauts, and J. G. Larson, "Effect of Graphic Cigarette Warnings on Smoking Intentions in Young Adults," *PLOS One*, May 7, 2014, http://journals.plos.org/plosone/article/asset?id=10.1371%2Fjournal.pone.0096315.PDF (accessed June 27, 2016).
57. Adapted from R. Kreitner and A. Kinicki, *Organizational Behavior*, 10th ed. (New York: McGraw-Hill/Irwin, 2013), Figure 7–1, p. 181.
58. Definition adapted from C. M. Judd and B. Park, "Definition and Assessment of Accuracy in Social Stereotypes," *Psychological Review*, January 1993, p. 110. See also D. T. Wegener, J. K. Clark, and R. E. Petty, "Not All Stereotyping Is Created Equal: Differential Consequences of Thoughtful versus Nonthoughtful Stereotyping," *Journal of Personality and Social Psychology*, January 2006, pp. 42–59.
59. R. Riffkin, "Americans Still Prefer a Male Boss to a Female Boss," Gallup.com, October 14, 2014, www.gallup.com/poll/178484/americans-prefer-male-boss-female-boss.aspx; and "Women and Leadership," Pew Research Center, January 14, 2015, www.pewsocialtrends.org/2015/01/14/women-and-leadership (both accessed June 27, 2016). See also S. C. Paustian-Underdahl, L. S. Walker, and D. J. Woehr, "Gender and Perceptions of Leadership Effectiveness: A Meta-Analysis of Contextual Moderators," *Journal of Applied Behavior*, Vol. 99, No. 6 (2014), pp. 1129–1145.

60. See J. A. Segal, "How Gender Bias Hurts Men," *HR Magazine*, October 2015, pp. 74–75.
61. See A. J. Koch, S. D. D'Mello, and P. R. Sackett, "A Meta-Analysis of Gender Stereotypes and Bias in Experimental Simulations of Employment Decision Making," *Journal of Applied Psychology*, January 2015, pp. 128–161; and J. V. Sanchez-Hucles and D. D. Davis, "Women and Women of Color in Leadership," *American Psychologist*, April 2010, pp. 171–181.
62. T. W. H. Ng and D. C. Feldman, "Evaluating Six Common Stereotypes about Older Workers with Meta-Analytical Data," *Personnel Psychology*, Vol. 65, No. 4 (2012), pp. 821–858.
63. *Staying Ahead of the Curve 2013: The AARP Work and Career Study—Older Workers in an Uneasy Job Market*, AARP, January 2014, www.aarp.org/content/dam/aarp/research/surveys_statistics/general/2014/Staying-Ahead-of-the-Curve-2013-The-Work-and-Career-Study-AARP-res-gen.pdf (accessed June 27, 2016).
64. See T. DeAngelis, "Unmasking 'Racial Micro Aggressions,'" *Harvard Business Review*, February 2009, pp. 42–46.
65. See M. D. C. Triana, M. Jayasinghe, and J. R. Pieper, "Perceived Workplace Racial Discrimination and Its Correlates: A Meta-Analysis," *Journal of Organizational Behavior*, May 2015, pp. 491–513.
66. H. R. Roberts, "Implicit Bias and Social Justice," *Open Society Foundations*, December 18, 2011, https://www.opensocietyfoundations.org/voices/implicit-bias-and-social-justice (accessed July 13, 2016).
67. "Helping Courts Address Implicit Bias: Frequently Asked Questions," National Center for State Courts, www.ncsc.org/~/media/Files/PDF/Topics/Gender%20and%20Racial%20Fairness/Implicit%20Bias%20FAQs%20rev.ashx (accessed July 13, 2016).
68. S. Mullainathan, "The Measuring Sticks of Racial Bias," *The New York Times*, January 4, 2015, p. BU-6.
69. M. Bertrand and S. Mullainathan, "Are Emily and Greg More Employable Than Lakisha and Jamal? A Field Experiment on Labor Market Discrimination," *American Economic Review*, September 2004, pp. 991–1013. For more on the subject of implicit bias, see J. Holroyd, "Implicit Bias, Awareness, and Imperfect Cognitions," *Consciousness and Cognition*, Vol. 33 (2015), pp. 511–523; and T. Vierkant and R. Hardt, "Explicit Reasons, Implicit Stereotypes, and the Effortful Control of the Mind," *Ethical Theory and Moral Practice*, Vol. 18 (2015), pp. 251–265.
70. R. D. Godsil, "Breaking the Cycle: Implicit Bias, Racial Anxiety, and Stereotype Threat," *Poverty & Race*, January/February 2015, www.prrac.org/newsletters/janfeb2015.pdf (accessed July 13, 2016).
71. See C. N. Macrae and S. Quadflieg, "Perceiving People," in S. T. Fiske, D. T. Gilbert, and G. Lindzey (Eds.), *Handbook of Social Psychology* (New York: John Wiley & Sons, 2010), pp. 428–463; and M. Snyder and A. A. Stukas, Jr., "Interpersonal Processes: The Interplay of Cognitive, Motivational, and Behavioral Activities in Social Interaction," in J. T. Spence, J. M. Darley, and D. J. Foss (Eds.), *Annual Review of Psychology* (Palo Alto, CA: Annual Review, 1999), pp. 273–303.
72. I. Waismel-Manor and Y. Tsfati, "Do Attractive Congresspersons Get More Media Coverage?" *Political Communication*, Vol. 28 (2011), pp. 440–463; and A. E. White, D. T. Kenrick, and S. L. Neuberg, "Beauty at the Ballot Box: Disease Threats Predict Preference for Physically Attractive Leaders," *Psychological Science*, December 2013, pp. 2429–2436.
73. M. M. Clifford and E. H. Walster, "The Effect of Physical Attractiveness on Teacher Expectation," *Sociology of Education*, Vol. 46 (1973), pp. 248–258; and P. Kenealy, N. Frude, and W. Shaw, "Influence of Children's Physical Attractiveness on Teacher Expectation," *The Journal of Social Psychology*, Vol. 128, No. 3 (2001), pp. 373–383.
74. M. M. Mobius and T. S. Rosenblat, "Why Beauty Matters," *American Economic Review*, Vol. 96, No. 1 (2006), pp. 222–235; and J. T. Halford and S. H. C. Hsu, "Beauty Is Wealth: CEO Appearance and Shareholder Value," *Social Science Research Network*, December 19, 2014, http://papers.ssrn.com/sol3/papers.cfm?abstract_id=2357756 (accessed June 27, 2016). See also A. R. Sorkin, "Never Mind the Résumé: How Hot Is the CEO?" *The New York Times*, January 7, 2014, pp. B1, B4.
75. R. Adams, M. Keloharju, and S. Knüpfer, "Are CEOs Born Leaders? Lesson from Traits of a Million Individuals," *Social Science Research Network*, June 24, 2016, http://papers.ssrn.com/sol3/papers.cfm?abstract_id=2436765 (accessed June 27, 2016).
76. D. S. Hamermesh and J. Abrevaya, "Beauty Is the Promise of Happiness?" *European Economic Review*, Vol. 64 (2013), pp. 351–368.
77. D. S. Hamermesh, "Ugly? You May Have a Case," *The New York Times*, August 27, 2011, www.nytimes.com/2011/08/28/opinion/sunday/ugly-you-may-have-a-case.html (accessed July 19, 2016).
78. D. S. Hamermesh, *Beauty Pays: Why Attractive People Are More Successful* (Princeton, NJ: Princeton University Press, 2011).
79. Hamermesh, *Beauty Pays: Why Attractive People Are More Successful*.
80. Hamermesh, quoted in S. Jayson, "The Ugly Truth: Good Looks Make You Richer, Happier," *USA Today*, March 30, 2011, p. 2B.
81. M. M. Mobius and T. S. Rosenblat, "Why Beauty Matters," *American Economic Review*, March 2006, pp. 222–235.
82. H. R. Varian, "Beauty and the Fattened Wallet," *The New York Times*, April 6, 2006, www.nytimes.com/2006/04/06/business/06scene.html?ref=halrvarian (accessed June 27, 2016).
83. Varian, "Beauty and the Fattened Wallet."
84. M. W. Howard and M. J. Kahana, "A Distributed Representation of Temporal Context," *Journal of Mathematical Psychology*, Vol. 46 (2002), pp. 269–299.
85. T. Odean and B. M. Barber, "All That Glitters: The Effect of Attention and News on the Buying Behavior of Individual and Institutional Investors," *The Review of Financial Studies*, Vol. 21, No. 2 (2008), pp. 785–818. See also P. Sullivan, "Want an Active Investment Manager? Here's What to Look For," *The New York Times*, March 30, 2012, p. B8.
86. E. Jackson, "Ten Biggest Mistakes Bosses Make in Performance Reviews," *Forbes*, January 9, 2012, www.forbes.com/sites/ericjackson/2012/01/09/ten-reasons-performance-reviews-are-done-terribly/#74aeeb2e59c3 (accessed June 27, 2016).
87. See D. Dickey and C. Pearson, "Recency Effect in College Student Course Evaluations," *Practical Assessment, Research & Evaluation*, June 2005, http://pareonline.net/pdf/v10n6.pdf (accessed June 27, 2016).
88. Josh Brown, chief executive of Ritholz Wealth Management, quoted in S. Constable, "The 'Recency Effect' Can Trip Up Investors," *The Wall Street Journal*, April 6, 2014, www.wsj.com/articles/SB10001424052702304709904579409042190896498 (accessed June 27, 2016).
89. C. Richards, "Tomorrow's Market Probably Won't Look Anything Like Today," *The New York Times*, February 13, 2012, http://bucks.blogs.nytimes.com/2012/02/13/tomorrows-market-probably-wont-look-anything-like-today/?_r=0 (accessed June 27, 2016).
90. S. J. Linton and L. E. Warg, "Attributions (Beliefs) and Job Satisfaction Associated with Back Pain in an Industrial Setting," *Perceptual and Motor Skills*, February 1993, pp. 51–62.
91. C. Forelle and S. Fidler, "Europe's Original Sin," *The Wall Street Journal*, March 3, 2010, p. A1.
92. See J. Weaver, J. F. Moses, and M. Snyder, "Self-Fulfilling Prophecies in Ability Settings," *Journal of Social Psychology*, Vol. 156, No 2 (2016), pp. 179–189.
93. D. B. McNatt, "Ancient Pygmalion Joins Contemporary Management: A Meta-Analysis of the Result," *Journal of Applied Psychology*, April 2000, pp. 314–322. See also T. Inamori and F. Analoui, "Beyond Pygmalion Effect: The Role of Managerial Perception," *Journal of Management Development*, Vol. 29 (2010), pp. 306–321.
94. These recommendations were adapted from J. Keller, "Have Faith—in You," *Selling Power*, June 1996, pp. 84, 86; R. W. Goddard, "The Pygmalion Effect," *Personnel Journal*, June 1985, p. 10; J. S. Livingston, "Pygmalion in Management," *Harvard Business Review*, January 2003, https://hbr.org/2003/01/pygmalion-in-management (accessed June 27, 2016); R. E. Riggio, "Pygmalion Leadership: The Power of Positive Expectations," *Psychology Today*, April 18, 2009, https://www.psychologytoday.com/blog/cutting-edge-leadership/200904/pygmalion-leadership-the-power-positive-expectations (accessed June 27, 2016); and G. Swanson, "The Pygmalion Effect: How It Drives Employee Performance," LinkedIn, September 24, 2014, https://www.linkedin.com/pulse/20140924142003-9878138-the-pygmalion-effect-how-it-drives-employees-performance (accessed June 27, 2016).
95. See J. K. Harter, F. L. Schmidt, and T. L. Hayes, "Business-Unit-Level Relationship between Employee Satisfaction, Employee Engagement, and Business Outcomes: A Meta-Analysis," *Journal of Applied Psychology*, April 2002, pp. 268–279.
96. W. H. Macey, B. Schneider, K. M. Barbera, and S. A. Young, *Employee Engagement: Tools for Analysis, Practice, and Competitive Advantage* (West Sussex, United Kingdom: Wiley-Blackwell, 2009), p. 20.
97. See J. Robison, "Building Engagement in This Economic Crisis," *Gallup Management Journal*, February 19, 2009, http://gmj.gallup.com/content/115213/Building-Engagement-Economic-Crisis.aspx (accessed July 11, 2016).
98. See J. Harter and A. Adkins, "Engaged Employees Less Likely to Have Health Problems," December 18, 2015, www.gallup.com/poll/187865/engaged-employees-less-likely-health-problems.aspx (accessed July 11, 2016); M. S. Christian, A. S. Garza, and J. E. Slaughter, "Work Engagement: A Quantitative Review and Test of Its Relations with Task and Contextual Performance," *Personnel Psychology*, Vol. 64 (2011), pp. 89–136; and M. S. Cole, F. Walter, A. G. Bedeian, and E. H. O'Boyle, "Job Burnout and Employee Engagement: A Meta- Analytic Examination of Construct Proliferation," *Journal of Management*, September 2012, pp. 1550–1581.
99. See Christian, Garza, and Slaughter, "Work Engagement: A Quantitative Review and Test of Its Relations with Task and Contextual Performance." See also R. Saunderson, "Is There Something Wrong with Employee Engagement?" *Training*, July/August 2015, pp. 70–71.
100. See W. A. Kahn, "Psychological Conditions of Personal Engagement and Disengagement at Work," *Academy of Management Journal*, December 1990, p. 75.
101. These five job dimensions are developed by researchers at Cornell University as part of the Job Descriptive Index. For a review of the development of the JDI, see P. C. Smith, L. M. Kendall, and C. L. Hulin, *The Measurement of Satisfaction in Work and Retirement* (Skokie, IL: Rand McNally, 1969).
102. See A. J. Kinicki, F. M. McKee-Ryan, C. A. Schriesheim, and K. P. Carson, "Assessing the Construct Validity of the Job Descriptive Index: A Review and Meta-Analysis," *Journal of Applied Psychology*, February 2002, pp. 14–32.
103. B. Cheng, M. Kan, G. Levanon, and R. L. Ray, "Job Satisfaction: 2015 Edition: A Lot More Jobs—A Little More Satisfaction," The Conference Board, September 9, 2015, www.conferenceboard.ca/e-library/abstract.aspx?did=7401 (accessed June 27, 2016).
104. Society for Human Resource Management, "Employee Job Satisfaction 2005–2015," 2016, https://www.shrm.org/Research/SurveyFindings/Articles/Documents/2016-Employee-Job-Satisfaction-and-Engagement-Report-Executive-Summary.pdf (accessed June 27, 2016).
105. P. Davidson, "Overworked and Underpaid?" *USA Today*, April 16, 2012, pp. 1A, 2A.
106. The various models are discussed in T. A. Judge, C. J. Thoresen, J. E. Bono, and G. K. Patton, "The Job Satisfaction–Job Performance Relationship: A Qualitative and Quantitative Review," *Psychological Bulletin*, May 2001, pp. 376–407. See also Kreitner and Kinicki, *Organizational Behavior*, pp. 168–170.
107. Judge, Thoresen, Bono, and Patton, "The Job Satisfaction–Job Performance Relationship: A Qualitative and Quantitative Review." Also see M. Riketta, "The Causal Relation between Job Attitudes and Performance: A Meta-Analysis of Panel Studies," *Journal of Applied Psychology*, March 2008, pp. 472–481.
108. Survey of adults conducted for Adecco Staffing North America, reported in K. Gurchiek, "Good News for Moms Reconsidering Work," *HR Magazine*, July 2006, p. 30.
109. See A. H. Kabins, X. Xu, M. E. Bergman, C. M. Berry, and V. L Wilson, "A Profile of Profiles: A Meta-Analysis of the Nomological Net of Commitment Profiles," *Journal of Applied Psychology*, June 2016, pp. 881–904.

110. For a review of commitment research, see the entire May 2016 issue in the *Journal of Organizational Behavior*, May 2016, pp. 489–632.

111. M. C. Kocakulah, A. G. Kelley, K. M. Mitchell, and M. P. Ruggieri, "Absenteeism Problems and Costs: Causes, Effects, and Cures," *International Business & Economics Research Journal*, May/June 2016, pp. 81–88.

112. Results can be found in M. R. Barrick and R. D. Zimmerman, "Reducing Voluntary Turnover through Selection," *Journal of Applied Psychology*, January 2005, pp. 159–166.

113. Costs of turnover are discussed by R. W. Griffeth and P. W. Hom, *Retaining Valued Employees* (Thousand Oaks, CA: Sage, 2001).

114. H. Boushey and S. J. Glynn, "There Are Significant Business Costs to Replacing Employees," Center for American Progress, November 16, 2012, https://www.americanprogress.org/wp-content/uploads/2012/11/CostofTurnover.pdf (accessed June 27, 2016).

115. Onboarding is discussed by T. Arnold, "Ramping Up Onboarding," *HR Magazine*, May 2010, pp. 75–76; and D. Robb, "New-Hire Onboarding Portals Provide a Warmer Welcome," *HR Magazine*, December 2015/January 2016, pp. 58–60.

116. Techniques for reducing turnover are discussed by M. A. Tucker, "Show and Tell," *HR Magazine*, January 2012, pp. 51–53; E. Krell, "5 Ways to Manage High Turnover," *HR Magazine*, April 2012, pp. 63–65; A. Quirk, "The Business Case for Flex," *HR Magazine*, April 2012, pp. 44–46; K.-H. Oehler, "Should Companies Have Free Rein to Use Predictive Analytics?" *HR Magazine*, June 2015, p. 26; and C. C. Manz, M. Fugate, P. W. Hom, and J. P. Millikin, "When Having to Leave Is a 'Good Thing': A Case for Positive Involuntary Turnover," *Organizational Dynamics*, Vol. 44 (2015), pp. 57–64.

117. D. W. Organ, "The Motivational Basis of Organizational Citizenship Behavior," in B. M. Staw and L. L. Cummings, eds., *Research in Organizational Behavior* (Greenwich, CT: JAI Press, 1990), p. 46.

118. See N. P. Podsakoff, S. W. Whiting, P. M. Podsakoff, and B. D. Blume, "Individual- and Organizational-Level Consequences of Organizational Citizenship Behaviors: A Meta-Analysis," *Journal of Applied Psychology*, January 2009, pp. 122–141; D. S. Whitman, D. L. Van Rooy, and C. Viswesvaran, "Satisfaction, Citizenship Behaviors, and Performance in Work Units: A Meta-Analysis of Collective Relations," *Personnel Psychology*, Spring 2010, pp. 41–81; and J. P. Trougakos, D.J. Beal. B. H. Cheng, I. Hideg, and D. Zweig, "Too Drained to Help: A Resource Depletion Perspective on Daily Interpersonal Citizenship Behaviors," *Journal of Applied Psychology*, Vol. 100, No. 1 (2015), pp. 227–236.

119. See P. E. Spector and S. Fox, "Theorizing about the Deviant Citizen: An Attributional Explanation of the Interplay of Organizational Citizenship and Counterproductive Work Behavior," *Human Resource Management Review*, June 2010, pp. 132–143; K. Tyler, "Helping Employees Cool It," *HR Magazine*, April 2010, pp. 53–55; M. S. Hershcovis, "'Incivility, Social Undermining, Bullying . . . Oh My!': A Call to Reconcile Constructs within Workplace Aggression Research," *Journal of Organizational Behavior*, Vol. 32 (2010), pp. 499–519; J. Wu and J. M. Lebreton, "Reconsidering the Dispositional Basis of Counterproductive Work Behavior: The Role of Aberrant Personality," *Personnel Psychology*, Vol. 64 (2011), pp. 593–626; and L. L. Meier and P. E. Spector, "Reciprocal Effects of Work Stressors and Counterproductive Work Behavior: A Five-Wave Longitudinal Study," *Journal of Applied Psychology*, May 2013, pp. 529–539.

120. Study by Georgetown University and Thunderbird School of Global Management, cited in R. Feintzeig, "When Co-workers Don't Play Nice," *The Wall Street Journal*, August 28, 2013, p. B6.

121. J. Janove, "Jerks at Work," *HR Magazine*, May 2007, pp. 111–117.

122. S. Dilchert, D. S. Ones, R. D. Davis, and C. D. Rostow, "Cognitive Ability Predicts Objectively Measured Counterproductive Work Behaviors," *Journal of Applied Psychology*, May 2007, pp. 616–627; and B. Iliescu, D. Ispas, C. Sulea, and A. Ilie, "Vocational Fit and Counterproductive Work Behaviors: A Self-Regulation Perspective," *Journal of Applied Psychology*, Vol. 100, No. 1 (2015), pp. 21–39.

123. J. R. Detert, L. K. Treviño, E. R. Burris, and M. Andiappan, "Managerial Modes of Influence and Counterproductivity in Organizations: A Longitudinal Business-Unit-Level Investigation," *Journal of Applied Psychology*, July 2007, pp. 993–1005.

124. C. Porath, "How to Avoid Hiring a Toxic Employee," *Harvard Business Review*, February 3, 2016, https://hbr.org/2016/02/how-to-avoid-hiring-a-toxic-employee (accessed July 3, 2016).

125. T. Foulk, quoted in R. E. Silverman, "Workplace Rudeness Is as Contagious as a Cold," *The Wall Street Journal*, August 12, 2015, p. B7. See also T. Foulk, A. Woolum, and A. Erez, "Catching Rudeness Is Like Catching a Cold: The Contagion Effects of Low-Intensity Negative Behaviors," *Journal of Applied Psychology*, Vol. 101, No. 1 (2016), pp. 50–67.

126. G. Spreizer, quoted in B. Hyslop, "Bad Attitudes Can Sap Workers' Energy and Productivity," *Providence Journal*, July 4, 2015, reprinted from *Pittsburgh Post-Gazette*, www.providencejournal.com/article/20150704/NEWS/150709967 (accessed July 3, 2016). See also P. Korkki, "Thwarting the Jerk at Work," *The New York Times*, November 22, 2015, p. BU-4.

127. See C. L. Porath and A. Erez, "Does Rudeness Really Matter? The Effects of Rudeness on Task Performance and Helpfulness," *Academy of Management Journal*, Vol. 50, No. 5 (2007), pp. 1181–1197; A. Gerbasi, C. L. Porath, A. Parker, G. Spreitzer, and R. Cross, "Destructive De-energizing Relationships: How Thriving Buffers Their Effect on Performance," *Journal of Applied Psychology*, Vol. 100, No. 5 (2015), pp. 1423–1433; and C. L. Porath, A. Gerbasi, and S. L. Schorch, "The Effects of Civility on Advice, Leadership, and Performance," *Journal of Applied Psychology*, Vol. 100, No. 5 (2015), pp. 1527–1541.

128. C. Porath, "No Time to Be Nice," *The New York Times*, June 21, 2015, p. SR–1.

129. M. Housman and D. Minor, "Toxic Workers," Harvard Business School, Working Paper 16-057, November 2015, www.hbs.edu/faculty/Publication%20Files/16-057_d45c0b4f-fa19-49de-8f1b-4b12fe054fea.pdf (accessed July 3, 2016).

130. N. Torres, "It's Better to Avoid a Toxic Employee Than Hire a Superstar," *Harvard Business Review*, December 9, 2015, https://hbr.org/2015/12/its-better-to-avoid-a-toxic-employee-than-hire-a-superstar (accessed July 3, 2016).

131. C. Porath and C. Pearson, "The Price of Incivility," *Harvard Business Review*, January–February 2013, https://hbr.org/2013/01/the-price-of-incivility (accessed July 3, 2016).

132. M. Schwantes, "5 Sure Signs That You Work in a Toxic Office," *Inc.*, February 18, 2016, www.inc.com/marcel-schwantes/5-sure-signs-that-you-work-in-a-toxic-office.html (accessed July 3, 2016).

133. J. S. Passel and D. Cohn, "Chapter 2: Industries of Unauthorized Immigrant Workers," Pew Research Center, March 26, 2015, www.pewhispanic.org/2015/03/26/chapter-2-industries-of-unauthorized-immigrant-workers (accessed June 27, 2016).

134. D. R. Hekman, K. Aquino, B. P. Owens, T. R. Mitchell, P. Schilpzand, and K. Leavitt, "An Examination of Whether and How Racial and Gender Biases Influence Customer Satisfaction," *Academy of Management Journal*, Vol. 55 (2010), pp. 643–666.

135. A. Davis, W. Kimball, and E. Gould, *The Class of 2015*, Economic Policy Institute, May 27, 2015, www.epi.org/publication/the-class-of-2015 (accessed June 27, 2016).

136. S. E. Page, *The Difference: How the Power of Diversity Creates Better Groups, Firms, Schools, and Societies*, new edition (Princeton, NJ: Princeton University Press, 2008). Page is also the author of *Diversity and Complexity* (Princeton, NJ: Princeton University Press, 2011).

137. S. E. Page, quoted in C. Dreifus, "In Professor's Model, Diversity = Productivity," *The New York Times*, January 8, 2008, p. D2. See also G. A. Van Kleef and C. K. W. De Dreu, "Bridging Faultlines by Valuing Diversity: Diversity Beliefs, Information-Elaboration, and Performance in Diverse Work Groups," *Journal of Applied Psychology*, September 2007, pp. 1189–1199; S. A. Hewlett, M. Marshall, and L. Sherbin, "How Diversity Can Drive Innovation," *Harvard Business Review*, December 2013, p. 30; and M. P. Gregoire, interviewed by A. Bryant, "A Diverse Team Is a Creative Team," *The New York Times*, January 12, 2014, p. BU-2.

138. M. Loden, *Implementing Diversity* (Chicago: Irwin, 1996), pp. 14–15.

139. L. Boyle, "'Even WE'VE Been the Victims of Racism': Obamas Reveal How President Was Mistaken for a Valet and Michelle Was Confused for a Target Worker—When She Was Already First Lady," *Daily Mail*, December 17, 2014, www.dailymail.co.uk/news/article-2877456/The-Obamas-open-racism-President-mistaken-valet-secret-White-House-dance-parties.html (accessed June 27, 2016).

140. S. Ghumman and A. M. Ryan, "Not Welcome Here: Discrimination Towards Women Who Wear the Muslim Headscarf," *Human Relations*, May 2013, pp. 671–698.

141. B. Schlender, "Peter Drucker Takes the Long View," *Fortune*, September 28, 1998, pp. 162–173.

142. B. Stokes, "The Countries That Will Be Most Impacted by Aging Population," Pew Research Center, February 4, 2014, www.pewresearch.org/fact-tank/2014/02/04/the-countries-that-will-be-most-impacted-by-aging-population (accessed June 27, 2016).

143. Central Intelligence Agency, *The World Factbook, 2016*, https://www.cia.gov/library/publications/the-world-factbook/fields/2177.html (accessed June 27, 2016); and "38% of People Are Older Than Their Boss," *Southwest*, April 2015, p. 47.

144. J. M. Ortman, V. A. Velkoff, and H. Hogan, "An Aging Nation: The Older Population in the United States," *Current Population Reports*, May 2014, P25-1140, U.S. Census Bureau.

145. S. Greenfield, "Hagerstown McDonald's Honors Its Oldest Worker in the Nation," *The Baltimore Sun*, December 28, 2015, www.baltimoresun.com/business/bs-bz-mcdonalds-employee-20151228-story.html (accessed June 27, 2016).

146. "Labor Force Projections to 2024: The Labor Force Is Growing, but Slowly," *Monthly Labor Review*, December 2015, www.bls.gov/opub/mlr/2015/article/labor-force-projections-to-2024-1.htm (accessed June 27, 2016).

147. "Labor Force Projections to 2024: The Labor Force Is Growing, but Slowly."

148. *The 2016 State of Women-Owned Businesses Report: A Summary of Important Trends, 2007–2016*, American Express OPEN and Womenable, April 2016, http://about.americanexpress.com/news/docs/2016x/2016SWOB.pdf (accessed June 26, 2016).

149. "Women CEOs of the S&P 500," Catalyst, June 6, 2016, www.catalyst.org/knowledge/women-ceos-sp-500; and V. Zarya, "The Percentage of Female CEOs in the Fortune 500 Drops to 4%," *Fortune*, June 6, 2016, http://fortune.com/2016/06/06/women-ceos-fortune-500-2016 (both accessed June 27, 2016).

150. See J. Adamy and P. Overberg, "Pay Gap Widest for Elite Jobs," *The Wall Street Journal*, May 18, 2016, pp. A1, A10; and U.S. Bureau of Labor Statistics, Department of Labor, *Highlights of Women's Earnings in 2014*, Report 1058, November 2015, Table 2, www.bls.gov/opub/reports/womens-earnings/archive/highlights-of-womens-earnings-in-2014.pdf (accessed June 27, 2016).

151. U.S. Bureau of Labor Statistics, Department of Labor, *Highlights of Women's Earnings in 2014*.

152. *2013 Catalyst Census: Fortune 500 Executive Officers and Top Earners*. December 10, 2013, www.catalyst.org/knowledge/2013-catalyst-census-fortune-500-women-executive-officers-and-top-earners (accessed July 19, 2016).

153. For further discussion of various aspects of the glass ceiling, see A. H. Eagly and L. L. Carli, *Through the Labyrinth* (Boston: Harvard Business School Press, 2007).

154. J. A. Segal, "Everyone, Lean In," *HR Magazine*, January/February 2015, pp. 74–76; C. C. Miller, "What We Can Do to Close the Pay Gap," *The New York Times*, January 17, 2016, p. BU-6; and T. Cowen, "More Time to Unwind, Unless You're a Woman," *The New York Times*, June 5, 2016, p. BU-3.

155. See S. C. Paustain-Underdahl, L. S. Walker, and D. J. Woehr, "Gender and Perceptions of Leadership Effectiveness: A Meta-Analysis of Contextual Moderators," *Journal of Applied Psychology*, November 2014, pp. 1129–1145.

156. K. Wisul, "The Bottom Line on Women at the Top," *Bloomberg.com*, January 25, 2004, www.bloomberg.com/news/articles/2004-01-25/the-bottom-line-on-women-at-the-top (accessed June 26, 2016); D. Kirka, "For Business, More Women at Top Means Bigger Profits," *Arizona Republic*, March 24, 2015, pp. 10A, 11A; and "Exploring the Leadership Gender Gap," *Training*, May/June 2016, p. 6.

157. JMG Consulting LLC and Wyckoff Consulting LLC, "Venture Capital, Social Capital, and the Funding of Women-Led Businesses," for SBA Office of Advocacy, April

2013, https://www.sba.gov/sites/default/files/files/rs406tot%284%29.pdf (accessed June 27, 2016). See also J. Tozzi, "Female-Led Companies Paid Off Well for VC Firms," *San Francisco Chronicle*, April 22, 2013, pp. D1, D4.

158. S. L. Colby and J. M. Ortman, "Projections of the Size and Composition of the U.S. Population: 2014 to 2060," *Current Population Reports*, March 2015, U.S. Census Bureau, https://www.census.gov/content/dam/Census/library/publications/2015/demo/p25-1143.pdf (accessed June 27, 2016).

159. C. DeNavas-Walt and B. D. Proctor, "Income and Poverty in the United States: 2014," *Current Population Reports*, September 2015, U. S. Census Bureau, https://www.census.gov/content/dam/Census/library/publications/2015/demo/p60-252.pdf (accessed June 27, 2016).

160. See U.S. Equal Employment Opportunity Commission, "Race-Based Charges FY 1997–FY 2015," www.eeoc.gov/eeoc/statistics/enforcement/race.cfm (accessed June 27, 2016); B. Leonard, "Web, Call Center Fuel Rise in EEOC Claims," *HR Magazine*, June 2008, p. 30; and M. Luo, "In Job Hunt, Even a College Degree Can't Close the Racial Gap," *The New York Times*, December 1, 2009, pp. A1, A4.

161. F. Newport, "Americans Greatly Overestimate Percent Gay, Lesbian in U.S.," *Gallup Social Issues*, May 21, 2015, www.gallup.com/poll/183383/americans-greatly-overestimate-percent-gay-lesbian.aspx (accessed June 26, 2016).

162. J. M. Jones, "Majority in U.S. Now Say Gays and Lesbians Born, Not Made," *Gallup Social Issues*, May 20, 2015, www.gallup.com/poll/183332/majority-say-gays-lesbians-born-not-made.aspx?utm_source=Social%20Issues&utm_medium=newsfeed&utm_campaign=tiles (accessed June 26, 2016).

163. Human Rights Campaign, "The Cost of the Closet and the Rewards of Inclusion," May 2014, http://hrc-assets.s3-website-us-east-1.amazonaws.com//files/assets/resources/Cost_of_the_Closet_May2014.pdf#__utma=149406063.1657137034.1405894648.1405894648.1405894648.1&__utmb=149406063.3.9.1405894715072&__utmc=149406063&__utmx=-&__utmz=149406063. 1405894648.1.1. utmcsr=google|utmccn=%28organic%29|utmcmd=organic|utmctr=%28not%20provided%29&__utmv=-&__utmk=3520176 (accessed June 27, 2016). See also B. R. Ragins, R. Singh, and J. M. Cornwell, "Making the Invisible Visible: Fear and Disclosure of Sexual Orientation at Work," *Journal of Applied Psychology*, July 2007, pp. 1103–1118; and "A Broken Bargain: Unchecked Discrimination Against LGBT Workers," Movement Advancement Project, May 2014, www.lgbtmap.org/file/unchecked-discrimination-against-lgbt-workers.pdf (accessed June 27, 2016).

164. M. V. L. Badgett, L. E. Durso, A. Kastanis, and C. Mallory, "The Business Impact of LGBT-Supportive Workplace Policies," Williams Institute on Sexual Orientation and Gender Identity Law and Public Policy, UCLA School of Law, May 2013, http://williamsinstitute.law.ucla.edu/wp-content/uploads/Business-Impact-of-LGBT-Policies-May-2013.pdf (accessed June 27, 2016). See also S. Milligan, "A Remarkable Transformation," *HR Magazine*, September 2015, pp. 28–33.

165. M. V. Badgett and H. Lau, "Bias in the Workplace: Consistent Evidence of Sexual Orientation and Gender Identity Discrimination," Williams Institute on Sexual Orientation and Gender Identity Law and Public Policy, UCLA School of Law, June 2007, http://williamsinstitute.law.ucla.edu/wp-content/uploads/Badgett-Sears-Lau-Ho-Bias-in-the-Workplace-Jun-2007.pdf (accessed July 19, 2016).

166. M. Huston, "None of the Above," *Psychology Today*, March/April, 2015, pp. 28–30.

167. G. J. Gates, *UCLA Study Estimates Approximately 700,000 Transgender People in the U.S.A.*, June 4, 2011, Williams Institute, UCLA School of Law, https://helenhill.wordpress.com/2011/06/04/ucla-study-estimates-approximate-700000-transgender-people-in-the-usa (accessed July 9, 2016)

168. M. Schulman, "Generation LGBTQIA," *The New York Times*, January 10, 2013, pp. E1, E8.

169. A. L. Ball, "The Symbols of Change," *The New York Times*, November 8, 2015, pp. ST-1, ST14; and J. Bosman and M. Rich, "As Transgender Students Make Gains, Schools Hesitate at Bathrooms," *The New York Times*, November 4, 2015, pp. A14, A16.

170. Human Rights Campaign survey, cited in "Top U.S. Firms Support Gays, Pressure States over Same-Sex Marriage," *South China Morning Post*, July 6, 2013, www.scmp.com/business/companies/article/1276364/top-us-firms-support-gays-pressure-states-over-same-sex-marriage (accessed July 19, 2016).

171. Kennedy, quoted in W. Richey, "Supreme Court Declares Same-Sex Couples' 'Fundamental Right' to Marry," *The Christian Science Monitor*, June 26, 2015, www.csmonitor.com/USA/Justice/2015/0626/Supreme-Court-declares-same-sex-couples-fundamental-right-to-marry (accessed June 27, 2016).

172. M. W. Brault, "Americans with Disabilities: 2010," *Current Population Reports*, July 2012, U.S. Census Bureau, www.census.gov/prod/2012pubs/p70-131.pdf (accessed July 19, 2016). M. Ramsey, "Ready, Willing and Disabled," *HR Magazine*, October 2015, pp. 8–54.

173. See D. C. Baldridge and M. L. Swift, "Withholding Requests for Disability Accommodation: The Role of Individual Differences and Disability Attributes," *Journal of Management*, March 2013, pp. 743–762.

174. Brault, "Americans with Disabilities: 2010."

175. See M. Korn, "Disability Studies Become a Hot Subject on Campus," *The Wall Street Journal*, March 6, 2014, p. B7.

176. A. Pyke, "Half a Million People with College Degrees Are Working for Minimum Wage," *ThinkProgress*, March 31, 2014, http://thinkprogress.org/economy/2014/03/31/3420987/college-degree-minimum-wage (accessed July 1, 2016). On the matter of the promise of upward mobility often not being fulfilled, see also Q. Bui, "Hidden Side of the College Dream: Mediocre Graduation Rates," *The New York Times*, June 2, 2016, p. A11.

177. M. Steinbaum and A. Clemens, "The Cruel Game of Musical Chairs in the U.S. Labor Market," Washington Center for Equitable Growth, September 2, 2015, http://equitablegrowth.org/research-analysis/cruel-game-musical-chairs-u-s-labor-market (accessed July 1, 2016).

178. "High School Dropout Rates: Indicators on Children and Youth," *Child Trends Databank*, November 2015, www.childtrends.org/wp-content/uploads/2014/10/01_Dropout_Rates.pdf (accessed July 1, 2016).

179. A. Bernstein, "The Time Bomb in the Workforce: Illiteracy," *BusinessWeek*, February 25, 2002, p. 122. See also M. Kutner, M. Greenberg, and J. Baer, *National Assessment of Adult Literacy (NAAL): A First Look at the Literacy of America's Adults in the 21st Century* (Washington, DC: National Center for Educational Statistics, 2005); and D. F. Mellard, E. Fall, and K. L. Woods, "A Path Analysis of Reading Comprehension for Adults with Low Literacy," *Journal of Learning Disabilities*, March–April 2010, pp. 154–165.

180. M. Loden, *Implementing Diversity*; E. E. Spragins, "Benchmark: The Diverse Work Force," *Inc.*, January 1993, p. 33; and A. M. Morrison, *The New Leaders: Guidelines on Leadership Diversity in America* (San Francisco: Jossey-Bass, 1992).

181. N. Silver, "Jeremy Lin Is No Fluke," *The New York Times*, February 11, 2012, http://fivethirtyeight.blogs.nytimes.com/2012/02/11/jeremy-lin-is-no-fluke (accessed July19, 2016).

182. P. Zho and D. D. Park, "Which Organizations Are Best in Class in Managing Diversity and Inclusion, and What Does Their Path of Success Look Like?" Cornell University, ILR School, April 1, 2013, http://digitalcommons.ilr.cornell.edu/cgi/viewcontent.cgi?article=1045&context=student (accessed July 19, 2016).

183. J. A. Gonzalez and A. DeNisi, "Cross-Level Effects of Demography and Diversity Climate on Organizational Attachment and Firm Effectiveness," *Journal of Organizational Behavior*, January 2009, p. 24.

184. Y. Chung, H. Liao, S. E. Jackson, M. Subramony, S. Colakoglu, and Y. Jiang, "Cracking but Not Breaking: Joint Effects of Faultline Strength and Diversity Climate on Loyal Behavior," *Academy of Management Journal*, October 2015, pp. 1495–1515; and S. A. Boehm, F. Kunze, and H. Bruch, "Spotlight on Age-Diversity Climate: The Impact of Age-Inclusive HR Practices on Firm-Level Outcomes," *Personnel Psychology*, 2014, pp. 667–704.

185. Y. Chung, H. Liao, S. E. Jackson, M. Subramony, S. Colakoglu, and Y. Jiang, "Cracking but Not Breaking: Joint Effects of Faultline Strength and Diversity Climate on Loyal Behavior," *Academy of Management Journal*, October 2015, pp. 1495–1515; and S. A. Boehm, F. Kunze, and H. Bruch, "Spotlight on Age-Diversity Climate: The Impact of Age-Inclusive HR Practices on Firm-Level Outcomes," *Personnel Psychology*, 2014, pp. 667–704.

186. Bureau of Labor Statistics, "Table 4, Families with Own Children: Employment Status of Parents by Age of Youngest Child and Family Type, 2014–2015 Annual Averages," *Economic News Release*, April 22, 2016, www.bls.gov/news.release/famee.t04.htm (accessed July 19, 2016).

187. C. Benko, "Up the Ladder? How Dated, How Linear," *The New York Times*, November 9, 2008, Business section, p. 2; K. Evans, "In Downturn's Wake, Women Hold Half of U.S. Jobs," *The Wall Street Journal*, November 12, 2009, http://online.wsj.com/article/SB125797318108844061.html (accessed July 14, 2014); and M. P. McQueen, "Better Education Shields Women from Worst Job Cuts," *The Wall Street Journal*, February 12, 2010, http://online.wsj.com/news/articles/SB10001424052748703389004575033762482114190 (accessed July 19, 2014).

188. See L. Peppard, "Hostile Environment for Female Firefighter Upheld," *HR Magazine*, March 2015, p. 70.

189. See C. Jones, "Still Thriving in the Workplace: Sex Harassment," *USA Today*, July 8, 2016, p. 4B.

190. R. S. Lazarus, *Psychological Stress and Coping Processes* (New York: McGraw-Hill, 1966); and R. S. Schuler, "Definition and Conceptualization of Stress in Organizations," *Organizational Behavior and Human Performance*, April 1980, p. 1980.

191. American Psychological Association, *Stress in America: Paying with Our Health*, February 4, 2015, https://www.apa.org/news/press/releases/stress/2014/stress-report.pdf (accessed July 1, 2016).

192. Harris Interactive survey for American Psychological Association, "2013 Work and Well-Being Survey," APA Center for Organizational Excellence, March 2013, www.apaexcellence.org/assets/general/2013-work-and-wellbeing-survey-results.pdf (accessed July 1, 2016).

193. American Institute of Stress, cited in J. W. Upson, D. J. Ketchen Jr., and R. D. Ireland, "Managing Employee Stress: A Key to the Effectiveness of Strategic Supply Chain Management," *Organizational Dynamics*, Vol. 36 (2007), pp. 78–92.

194. See E. Zimmerman, "When Stress Flirts with Burnout," *The New York Times*, January 17, 2010, Business section, p. 7.

195. S. Shellenbarger, "'Desk Rage': To Vent or Not to Vent," *The Wall Street Journal*, January 26, 2010, p. D3.

196. Supportive results can be found in F. M. McKee-Ryan, Z. Song, C. R. Wanberg, and A. J. Kinicki, "Psychological and Physical Well-Being during Unemployment: A Meta-Analytic Study," *Journal of Applied Psychology*, January 2005, pp. 53–76; and F. M. McKee-Ryan, M. Virick, G. E. Prussia, J. Harvey, and J. D. Lilly, "Life after the Layoff: Getting a Job Worth Keeping," *Journal of Organizational Behavior*, May 2009, pp. 561–580.

197. M. Luo, "For Workers at Closing Plant, Ordeal Included Heart Attacks," *The New York Times*, February 25, 2010, pp. A1, A17.

198. M. R. Frone, "Are Work Stressors Related to Employee Substance Use? The Importance of Temporal Context in Assessments of Alcohol and Illicit Drug Use," *Journal of Applied Psychology*, January 2008, pp. 199–206; and "Lee Hecht Harrison Poll Finds Most Workers Losing Sleep Due to Work-Related Stress," Lee Hecht Harrison, April 27, 2015, www.lhh.com/press-room/news/survey-finds-most-workers-losing-sleep-due-to-work-related-stress (accessed July 1, 2016). See also R. A. Clay, "The Changing Workplace," *Monitor on Psychology*, September 2015, pp. 37–41.

199. H. Selye, *Stress without Distress* (New York: Lippincott, 1974), p. 27.

200. R. S. Lazarus and S. Folkman, "Coping and Adaptation," in W. D. Gentry, ed., *Handbook of Behavioral Medicine* (New York: Guilford, 1982).

201. Selye, *Stress without Distress*, pp. 28–29.

202. See M. B. Hargrove, D. L. Nelson, and C. L. Cooper, "Generating Eustress by Challenging Employees: Helping People Savor Their Work," *Organizational Dynamics*, Vol. 42 (2013), pp. 61–69.
203. J. Hoffman, "Don't Worry about Fretting," *The New York Times*, November 3, 2015, p. D3. The study described is K. Sweeny, C. A. Reynolds, A. Falkenstein, S. E. Andrews, and M. D. Dooley, "Two Definitions of Waiting Well," *Emotion*, Vol. 15, No. 6 (2015), pp. 129–143. See also K. Sweeny and A. Falkenstein, "Is Waiting the Hardest Part? Comparing the Emotional Experiences of Awaiting and Receiving Bad News," *Personality and Social Psychology Bulletin*, Vol. 41, No. 11 (2015), pp. 1551–1559.
204. See J. K. Norem and N. Cantor, "Defensive Pessimism: Harnessing Anxiety as Motivation," *Journal of Personality and Social Psychology*, Vol. 51, No. 6 (1986), pp. 1208–1217.
205. G. Steinberg, quoted in S. Shellenbarger, "The Unexpected Benefits of Being a Worrywart at Work," *The Wall Street Journal*, April 1, 2015, pp. D1, D2. Steinberg is author of *Full Throttle: 122 Strategies to Supercharge Your Performance at Work* (Hoboken, NJ: John Wiley & Sons, 2009), about building emotional strength at work.
206. Shellenbarger, "The Unexpected Benefits of Being a Worrywart at Work."
207. M. Beck, "When Fretting Is in Your DNA: Overcoming the Worry Gene," *The Wall Street Journal*, January 15, 2008, p. D1. See also L. M. Hilt, L. C. Sander, S. Nolen-Hoeksema, and A. A. Simen, "The BDNF Val66Met Polymorphism Predicts Rumination and Depression Differently in Young Adolescent Girls and Their Mothers," *Neuroscience Letters*, December 2007, pp. 12–16.
208. M. Friedman and R. H. Rosenman, *Type A Behavior and Your Heart* (Greenwich, CT: Fawcett Publications, 1974), p. 84.
209. See M. S. Taylor, E. A. Locke, C. Lee, and M. E. Gist, "Type A Behavior and Faculty Research Productivity: What Are the Mechanisms?" *Organizational Behavior and Human Performance*, December 1984, pp. 402–418; S. D. Bluen, J. Barling, and W. Burns, "Predicting Sales Performance, Job Satisfaction, and Depression by Using the Achievement Strivings and Impatience–Irritability Dimensions of Type A Behavior," *Journal of Applied Psychology*, April 1990, pp. 212–216.
210. S. Booth-Kewley and H. S. Friedman, "Psychological Predictors of Heart Disease: A Quantitative Review," *Psychological Bulletin*, May 1987, pp. 343–362; S. A. Lyness, "Predictors of Differences between Type A and B Individuals in Heart Rate and Blood Pressure Reactivity," *Psychological Bulletin*, September 1993, pp. 266–295; and T. Q. Miller, T. W. Smith, C. W. Turner, M. L. Guijarro, and A. J. Hallet, "A Meta-Analytic Review of Research on Hostility and Physical Health," *Psychological Bulletin*, March 1996, pp. 322–348.
211. See 2016 study by CareerCast, reported in C. Brooks, "Most (and Least) Stressful Jobs for 2016," *Business News Daily*, January 7, 2016, www.businessnewsdaily.com/1875-stressful-careers.html (accessed July 11, 2016).
212. J. O'Donnell, "Wanted: Retail Managers," *USA Today*, December 24, 2007, pp. 1B, 3B; and A. Salario, "Retail Manager Stressed by 'Never Enough' Sales Strategy," *Womensenews*, July 15, 2013, http://womensenews.org/2013/07/retail-manager-stressed-never-enough-sales-strategy/ (accessed July 1, 2016).
213. M. Richtel, "In Web World of 24/7 Stress, Writers Blog Till They Drop," *The New York Times*, April 6, 2008, news section, pp. 1, 23.
214. See S. Diestel, W. Rivkin, and K.-H. Schmidt, "Sleep Quality and Self-Control Capacity as Protective Resources in the Daily Emotional Labor Process: Results from Two Diary Studies," *Journal of Applied Psychology*, Vol. 100, No. 3 (2015), pp. 809–827.
215. "Stressful Jobs That Pay Badly," *CNN Money*, March 7, 2014, http://money.cnn.com/gallery/pf/jobs/2013/03/07/jobs-stress-pay (accessed July 19, 2016).
216. E. Bernstein, "When a Co-Worker Is Stressed Out," *The Wall Street Journal*, August 26, 2008, http://online.wsj.com/news/articles/SB121970425860670819 (accessed July 19, 2014); and S. Shellenbarger, "The Problem with Busy Colleagues: Secondhand Stress," *The Wall Street Journal*, December 11, 2014, pp. D1, D4.
217. R. B. Williams, "How Bad Bosses Can Make You Sick," *Psychology Today*, February 13, 2011, https://www.psychologytoday.com/blog/wired-success/201102/how-bad-bosses-can-make-you-sick (accessed July 1, 2016).
218. J. Schaubroeck and D. C. Ganster, "Chronic Demands and Responsivity to Challenge," *Journal of Applied Psychology*, February 1993, pp. 73–85; E. Demerouti, A. B. Bakker, F. Nachreiner, and W. B. Schaufeli, "The Job Demands Resources Model of Burnout," *Journal of Applied Psychology*, June 2001, pp. 499–512.
219. J. M. Plas, *Person-Centered Leadership: An American Approach to Participatory Management* (Thousand Oaks, CA: Sage, 1996). See also "Stressed Out by Work? You're Not Alone," *Knowledge@Wharton*, October 30, 2014, http://knowledge.wharton.upenn.edu/article/stressed-work-youre-alone; and J. Bruce, "Are You Too Stressed to Work? You're Not Alone," *Forbes*, October 20, 2014, www.forbes.com/sites/janbruce/2015/10/20/are-you-too-stressed-to-work/#48fdbc07515e (both accessed July 3, 2016).
220. M. Patsalos-Fox, quoted in W. J. Holstein, "Tension Headaches in the Corner Office," *The New York Times*, March 12, 2006, sec. 3, p. 1.
221. See H. Mitchell, "Does Being Stressed Out Make You Forgetful?" *The Wall Street Journal*, March 17, 2015, p. D1; E. Bernstein, "Venting Isn't Good for Us," *The Wall Street Journal*, August 11, 2015, pp. D1, D4; and "Stress, Fatigue Lead to Lashing Out," *San Francisco Chronicle*, March 18, 2016, p. C2, reprinted from *Pittsburgh Post-Gazette*.
222. M. Staver, quoted in C. H. Deutsch, "Winning the Battle against Burnout," *The New York Times*, August 27, 2006, sec. 3, p. 5.
223. See A. Tugend, "Dealing with Burnout, Which Doesn't Always Stem from Overwork," *The New York Times*, November 30, 2013, p. B6.
224. See M. P. Leiter, J. J. Hakanen, K. Ahola, S. Toppinen-Tanner, A. Koskinen, and A. Väänänen, "Organizational Predictors and Health Consequences in Burnout: A 12-Year Cohort Study," *Journal of Organizational Behavior*, October 2013, pp. 959–973; and D. M. Owens, "Stressed Out," *HR Magazine*, March 2014, pp. 44–45. See also A. R. Sorkin, "Reflections on Stress and Hours on Wall St.," *The New York Times*, June 2, 2015, pp. B1, B4.
225. S. Sabia, A. Elbaz, A. Britton, S. Bell, A. Dugravot, M. Shipley, M. Kivimaki, and A. Singh-Manoux, "Alcohol Consumption and Cognitive Decline in Early Old Age," *Neurology*, January 15, 2014, www.neurology.org/content/early/2014/01/15/WNL.0000000000000063.short (accessed July 19, 2016).
226. See H. Park and M. Bloch, "Epidemic of Drug Overdose Deaths Ripples Across America," *The New York Times*, January 20, 2016, p. A13; G. Glaser, "Rehab Rooted in Science," *The New York Times*, February 23, 2016, pp. D1, D4; and A. Petersen, "A Mental Health Quandary," *The Wall Street Journal*, March 8, 2016, pp. D1, D2.
227. M. Ferri, L. Amato, and M. Davoli, "Alcoholics Anonymous and Other 12-Step Programmes for Alcohol Dependence (Review)," *Cochrane Library*, Issue 3 (2009), pp. 1–26. See also J. Rockoff, "Go Cold Turkey? Science Seeks Better Way to Beat Addiction," *The Wall Street Journal*, December 24, 2013, pp. D1, D4; G. Glaser, "Cold Turkey Isn't the Only Route," *The New York Times*, January 2, 2014, p. A15; S. G. Freedman, "Alcoholics Anonymous without the Religion," *The New York Times*, February 22, 2014, p. A14; and L. Dodes, *The Sober Truth: Debunking the Bad Science Behind 12-Step Programs and the Rehab Industry* (Boston: Beacon Press, 2014).
228. See D. Wilkie, "Help Keep Employees' Stress in Check," *HR Magazine*, May 2015, p. 16.
229. See S. Price, "Ante Up for Wellness," *HR Magazine*, February 2012, pp. 40–42; S. J. Wells, "Wellness Rewards," *HR Magazine*, February 2012, pp. 67–69; and J. Marchant, interviewed in "Chronic Stress: A Case of Mind Over Matter?" *Knowledge@Wharton*, March 4, 2016, http://knowledge.wharton.upenn.edu/article/chronic-stress-a-case-of-mind-over-matter (accessed July 3, 2016).
230. See K. Pho, "Do Corporate Wellness Programs Really Work?" *USA Today*, September 12, 2013, p. 10A; S. Hananel, "A Workout During Work," *Reno Gazette-Journal*, September 12, 2013, p. 7F; N. Hellmich, "Healthy, Wellness, and Wise about Costs," *USA Today*, December 13, 2013, p. 8B; A. Lukits, "Take Your Bike to Your Desk to Improve Health," *The Wall Street Journal*, May 27, 2014, p. D2; and A. Bruzzese, "Mindful Eating, Exercise Boost Work Performance," *Reno Gazette-Journal*, January 18, 2014, p. 9A.
231. A. Ferguson, "Too Stressed to Exercise? Try Some Meditation," *Reno Gazette-Journal*, July 12, 2016, p. 1C.
232. "Chanting Alleviates Urban Stress," *San Francisco Chronicle*, April 27, 2016, p. A4.
233. "Mentors Help Reduce Stress, Burnout," *San Francisco Chronicle*, February 26, 2016, p. C2, reprinted from *Pittsburgh Post-Gazette*.
234. J. Brown, "Marck Zuckerberg: The Introvert Who Revolutionized Social ... Life & Lessons," http://www.onelifesuccess.net/mark-zuckerberg-the-introvert-who-revolutionised-social-life-lessons, accessed June 2, 2016.
235. See "The Top 20 Valuable Facebook Statistics-Updated May 2016," http://zephoria.com/top-15-valuable-facebook-statistics, accessed June 3, 2016; and "Facebook's Revenue and Net Income from 2007 to 2015 (in Million Dollars)," http://www.statista.com/statistics/277229/facebooks-annual-revenue-and-net-income, accessed June 3, 2016.
236. J. A. Vargas, "The Face of Facebook," September 20, 2010, http://www.newyorker.com/magazine/2010/09/20/the-face-of-facebook, accessed June 2, 2016.
237. A. Wasson, "5 Personality Traits of Mark Zuckerberg," April 9, 2016, http://www.businessalligators.com/5-personality-traits-mark-zuckerberg.
238. J. Brown, "Marck Zuckerberg: The Introvert Who Revolutionized Social ... Life & Lessons," http://www.onelifesuccess.net/mark-zuckerberg-the-introvert-who-revolutionised-social-life-lessons, accessed June 2, 2016.
239. J. Brown, "Marck Zuckerberg: The Introvert Who Revolutionized Social ... Life & Lessons," http://www.onelifesuccess.net/mark-zuckerberg-the-introvert-who-revolutionised-social-life-lessons, accessed June 2, 2016.
240. "Mark Zukerberg's IPO Letter Describing Facebook's Purpose, Values, & Social Mission," February 5, 2012, http://prosperosworld.com/mark-zukerbergs-ipo-letter-describing-facebooks-purpose-values-social-mission/2012.
241. "The 5 Values Mark Zuckerberg Built Facebook On," http://under30ceo.com/the-5-values-mark-zuckerberg-built-facebook-on, accessed June 2, 2016.
242. "Mark Zukerberg's IPO Letter Describing Facebook's Purpose, Values, & Social Mission," February 5, 2012, http://prosperosworld.com/mark-zukerbergs-ipo-letter-describing-facebooks-purpose-values-social-mission/2012.
243. E. Peck, "Facebook Employees Are Insanely Happy with Their Jobs," March 2, 2016, http://www.huffingtonpost.com/entry/facebook-employees-happy_us_56d7049ae4b0871f60ed564f.
244. See M. Williams, "Driving Diversity at Facebook," June 25, 2015, http://newsroom.fb.com/news; and C. Forrest, "Diversity Stats: 10 Tech Companies That Have Come Clean," *Tech Republic*, August 28, 2014, http://www.techrepublic.com/article/diversity-stats-10-tech-companies-that-have-come-clean/, accessed March 3, 2016.
245. See M. Williams, "Driving Diversity at Facebook," June 25, 2015, http://newsroom.fb.com/news.
246. See M. Williams, "Driving Diversity at Facebook," June 25, 2015, http://newsroom.fb.com/news.
247. P. Greenberg, "Airline Seats Are Now 1.5 Inches Narrower Than They Used to Be," February 14, 2014, http://qz.com/177043/airline-seats-are-now-1-5-inches-narrower-than-they-used-to-be.
248. Excerpted from K. Mayo, "Economy Plus Size," *Bloomberg Businessweek*, May 6–May 12, 2013, p. 81.
249. A. Schmertz, "Senator Schumer's Silly Idea About Airline Seat Sizes," March 7, 2016, http://www.huffingtonpost.com/andrew-schmertz/senator-schumers-silly-id_b_9400796.html.
250. See "Airline Seat," *Wikipedia*, http://en.wikipedia.org/wiki/Airline_seat, last modified September 21, 2016, accessed September 27, 2016.
251. A. Spaeth, "Swiss Flies First Passenger Flight with New Bombardier Jetliner," June 7, 2016, http://www.cnn.com/2016/06/06/aviation/bombardier-cseries-cs100-swiss-first-passenger-flight/index.html.

CHAPTER 12

1. Associated Press, "9-to-5 Becoming Less Popular Way to Make Living," *San Francisco Chronicle*, June 7, 2015, p. D3.

2. N. Irwin, "Job Growth in Past Decade Was in Temp and Contract," *The New York Times*, March 31, 2016, p. A3; and A. Louie Sussman and J. Zumbrun, "'Gig' Economy Spreads Broadly," *The Wall Street Journal*, March 26–27, 2016, pp. A1, A2.

3. "Millennials Want Flexible Schedules," *San Francisco Chronicle*, June 5, 2015, p. C2. See also Maynard Webb, interviewed by E. Chhabra, "Reinventing Work," *San Francisco Chronicle*, February 16, 2013, pp. D1, D4. Webb is author, with Carlye Adler, of *Rebooting Work: Transform How You Work in the Age of Entrepreneurship* (San Francisco: Jossey-Bass, 2013). See also S. Westly, "A Third Definition of Contractors and Employees," *San Francisco Chronicle*, February 21, 2016, p. E6.

4. See *The 2015 Workplace Flexibility Study*, CareerArc and Workplace Trends.com, February 3, 2015, https://workplacetrends.com/the-2015-workplace-flexibility-study (accessed July 11, 2016).

5. P. Moen, E. L. Kelly, E. Tranby, and Q. Huang, "Can Real Work-Time Flexibility Promote Health Behaviors and Well-Being?" *Journal of Health and Social Behavior*, December 2011, pp. 404–429; E. Kelly, P. Moen, M. Oakes, W. Fan et al., "Changing Work and Work-Family Conflict: Evidence from the Work, Family, and Health Network," *American Sociological Review*, June 1, 2014, pp. 485–516; S. White, "Working from Home Can Benefit Employers as Much as Employees," *Monster.com*, November 3, 2014, www.monster.com/technology/a/The-Benefits-of-Working-From-Home (accessed July 11, 2016); and A. North, "Flexible Work: Nice If You Can Get It," *The New York Times*, February 17, 2015, http://op-talk.blogs.nytimes.com/2015/02/17/flexible-work-nice-if-you-can-get-it/?_r=0 (accessed July 11, 2016).

6. See F. Witsil, "Is Part-Time Work the New Normal?" *Reno Gazette-Journal*, September 3, 2013, p. 5A; reprinted from *Detroit Free Press*.

7. V. L. Brescoll, J. Glass, and A. Sedlovskaya, "Ask and Ye Shall Receive? The Dynamics of Employer-Provided Flexible Work Options and the Need for Public Policy," *Journal of Social Issues*, June 2013, pp. 367–388.

8. K. Matos and E. Galinsky, *2014 National Study of Employers*, Families and Work Institute and Society for Human Resource Management, http://familiesandwork.org/downloads/2014NationalStudyOfEmployers.pdf (accessed July 11, 2016).

9. "When Working at Home Is Productive, and When It's Not," *Knowledge@Wharton*, March 13, 2013, http://knowledge.wharton.upenn.edu/article/when-working-at-home-is-productive-and-when-its-not (accessed July 11, 2016); N. Bloom and J. Liang, "To Raise Productivity, Let More Employees Work from Home," *Harvard Business Review*, January–February 2014, pp. 28–29; and N. Bilton, "Staying Connected While Staying at Home," *The New York Times*, March 17, 2014, p. B7.

10. J. M. Jones, "In U.S. Telecommuting for Work Climbs to 37%," Gallup, August 19, 2015, https://www.google.com/search?q=in+U.S.+Telecommuting+for+Work+Climbs+to+37%25&ie=utf-8&oe=utf-8 (accessed July 4, 2016).

11. P. Korkki, "Yes, Flexible Hours Ease Stress. but Is Everyone on Board?" *The New York Times*, August 24, 2014, p. BU-4.

12. *2015 Employee Benefits: An Overview of Employee Benefits Offerings in the U.S.*, a research report by the Society for Human Resource Management, https://www.shrm.org/Research/SurveyFindings/Articles/Documents/2015-Employee-Benefits.pdf (accessed July 4, 2016).

13. R. Feintzeig, "Getting Paid to Live Near Your Job," *The Wall Street Journal*, February 24, 2016, pp. B1, B7.

14. Adapted from definition in T. R. Mitchell, "Motivation: New Directions for Theory, Research, and Practice," *Academy of Management Review*, January 1982, p. 81.

15. See R. M. Ryan and E. L. Deci, "Intrinsic and Extrinsic Motivations: Classic Definitions and New Directions," *Contemporary Educational Psychology*, January 2000, pp. 54–67.

16. G. Lubold, "To Lure Drone Pilots, Air Force Plans Incentives," *The Wall Street Journal*, July 15, 2015, p. A4.

17. M. S. Patel, D. A. Asch, R. Rosin, D. S. Small, et al. "Framing Financial Incentives to Increase Physical Activity among Overweight and Obese Adults," *Annals of Internal Medicine*, March 15, 2016, pp. 385–394. See also M. S. Patel, D. A. Asch, and K. G. Volpp, "Paying Employees to Lose Weight," *The New York Times*, March 6, 2016, p. SR-10.

18. Patel, Asch, and Volpp, "Paying Employees to Lose Weight." See also *High Performance Health Care: Best Practices in Health Care*, 2015 20th Annual Willis Towers Watson/National Business Group on Health Best Practices in Health Care Employer, https://www.towerswatson.com/en-US/Insights/IC-Types/Survey-Research-Results/2015/11/full-report-2015-towers-watson-nbgh-best-practices-in-health-care-employer-survey (accessed July 4, 2016).

19. S. Vozza, "Why Every Company Should Pay Employees to Volunteer," *Fast Company*, March 11, 2014, www.fastcompany.com/3027465/dialed/why-every-company-should-pay-employees-to-volunteer (accessed July 4, 2016).

20. M. C. Kocakulah, A. G. Kelley, K. M. Mitchell, and M. P. Ruggieri, "Absenteeism Problems and Costs: Causes, Effects and Cures," *International Business & Economics Research Journal*, May/June 2016, pp. 81–88; and C. White, "The Impact of Motivation on Customer Satisfaction Formation: A Self-Determination Perspective," *European Journal of Marketing*, Vol. 49 (2015), pp. 1923–1940.

21. A. Maslow, "A Theory of Human Motivation," *Psychological Review*, July 1943, pp. 370–396. See also H. J. Venter, "Maslow's Self-Transcendence: How It Can Enrich Organization Culture and Leadership," *International Journal of Business, Humanities, and Technology*, December 2012, pp. 64–71; B. Libert, J. Wind, and M. B. Fenley, "Why Businesses Should Serve Consumers' 'Higher Needs,'" *Knowledge@Wharton*, August 29, 2014, http://knowledge.wharton.upenn.edu/article/why-businesses-should-serve-consumers-higher-needs/ (accessed July 9, 2016); and D. White and P. White, "Entrepreneurs Turn the Classic Theory of Maslow's Hierarchy of Needs on Its Head," *Entrepreneur*, November 3, 2015, https://www.entrepreneur.com/article/252362 (accessed July 9, 2016).

22. C. Conley, *Peak: How Great Companies Get Their Mojo from Maslow* (San Francisco: Jossey-Bass, 2007).

23. C. Conley, interviewed by D. Schawbel, "How Emotional Equations Can Change Your Life," *Forbes*, January 12, 2012, www.forbes.com/sites/danschawbel/2012/01/12/how-emotional-equations-can-change-your-life/#7cc3b8b92e19 (accessed July 9, 2016). Conley is the author of *Emotional Equations: Simple Truths for Creating Happiness + Success* (New York: Free Press, 2012).

24. C. Conley, interviewed in E. Schurenberg, "Chip Conley: The 5 Things Everyone Wants from You," *Inc.*, December 12, 2011, www.inc.com/eric-schurenberg/Chip-Conley-5-Things-Everyone-Wants.html (accessed July 9, 2016). See also C. Webb, interviewed in "How to Have a Good Day at Work," *Knowledge@Wharton*, July 7, 2016, http://knowledge.wharton.upenn.edu/article/160523b_kwradio_webb-caroline-webb (accessed July 9, 2016). Caroline Webb is the author of *How to Have a Good Day: Harness the Power of Behavioral Science to Transform Your Working Life* (New York: Crown Business, 2016).

25. Chip Conley, interviewed by M. Hofman, "The Idea That Saved My Company," *Inc.*, October 11, 2007, www.inc.com/magazine/20071001/the-idea-that-saved-my-company.html (accessed July 9, 2016).

26. C. Conley, interviewed in K. Pattison, "Chip Conley Took the Maslow Pyramid, Made It an Employee Pyramid, and Saved His Company," *Fast Company*, August 26, 2010, www.fastcompany.com/1685009/chip-conley-wants-your-employees-to-hit-their-peak (accessed July 9, 2016).

27. Conley, interviewed in Schurenberg, "Chip Conley: The 5 Things Everyone Wants from You."

28. "Hotel Rex," review by Tablet Hotels, July 9, 2016, https://www.tablethotels.com/en/san-francisco-bay-area-hotels/hotel-rex?arrDate=2016-07-09&depDate=2016-07-10&nA=1&nC=0&nR=1&hotelId=72&pid=392&language=en (accessed July 7, 2016).

29. Conley, in Schurenberg, "Chip Conley: The 5 Things Everyone Wants from You."

30. Hofman, "The Idea That Saved My Company."

31. D. Kenrick, quoted in W. Kremer and C. Hammond, "Abraham Maslow and the Pyramid That Beguiled Business," *BBC World Service*, September 1, 2013, www.bbc.com/news/magazine-23902918 (accessed July 9, 2016).

32. See W. B. Swann Jr., C. Chang-Schneider, and K. I. McClarty, "Do People's Self-Views Matter?" *American Psychologist*, February–March 2007, pp. 84–94.

33. D. C. McClelland, *Human Motivation* (Glenview, IL: Scott, Foresman, 1985).

34. D. McClelland and H. Burnham, "Power Is the Great Motivator," *Harvard Business Review*, March–April 1976, pp. 100–110.

35. Some of these recommendations are based on "McClelland's Human Motivation Theory," *Mind Tools*, www.mindtools.com/pages/article/human-motivation-theory.htm (accessed May 22, 2013).

36. S. W. Spreier, M. H. Fontaine, and R. L. Malloy, "Leadership Run Amok," *Harvard Business Review*, June 2006, pp. 72–82.

37. R. M. Ryan and E. L. Deci, "Self-Determination Theory and the Facilitation of Intrinsic Motivation, Social Development, and Well-Being," *American Psychologist*, January 2000, pp. 68–78.

38. See C. M. Moran, J. M. Diefendorff, T.-Y. Kim, and Z.-Q. Liu, "A Profile Approach to Self-Determination Theory Motivations at Work," *Journal of Vocational Behavior*, December 2012, pp. 354–363; and R. A. Kusurkar, T. J. Ten Cate, C. M. P. Vos, P. Westers, and G. Croisset, "How Motivation Affects Academic Performance: A Structural Equation Modelling Analysis," *Advances in Health Science Education*, March 2013, pp. 57–69.

39. See M. Chiniara and K. Bentein, "Linking Servant Leadership to Individual Performance: Differentiating the Mediating Role of Autonomy, Competence, and Relatedness Need Satisfaction," *The Leadership Quarterly*, February 2016, pp. 124–141.

40. Reported in J. McCarthy, "Stop Trying to Motivate Your Employees! (Self-Determination Theory at Work)," *Positive Psychology Wellbeing in the World of Work*, May 15, 2012, http://psychologyofwellbeing.com/201205/stop-trying-to-motivate-your-employees-self-determination-theory-at-work.html (accessed July 9, 2015).

41. McCarthy, "Stop Trying to Motivate Your Employees! (Self-Determination Theory at Work)."

42. McCarthy, "Stop Trying to Motivate Your Employees! (Self-Determination Theory at Work)."

43. F. Herzberg, B. Mausner, and B. B. Snyderman, *The Motivation to Work* (New York: Wiley, 1959); and F. Herzberg, "One More Time: How Do You Motivate Employees?" *Harvard Business Review*, January–February 1968, pp. 53–62. For a modern look at the application of Herzberg's theory, see C. Christensen, "Clayton Christensen on How to Find Work That You Love," *Fast Company*, May 14, 2012, www.fastcompany.com/1836982/clayton-christensen-how-find-work-you-love (accessed July 9, 2016).

44. A. Taube, "Why the Container Store Pays Its Retail Employees $50,000 a Year," *Business Insider*, October 16, 2014, www.businessinsider.com/the-container-store-pays-employees-50000-a-year-2014-10 (accessed July 16, 2016).

45. S. Shellenbarger, "How Many Team-Building Hiking Trips Can a Marriage Take?" *The Wall Street Journal*, June 24, 2015, www.wsj.com/articles/how-many-team-building-raft-trips-can-your-marriage-take-1435078725 (accessed July 16, 2016).

46. Anecdote recounted by Chip Conley of Joie de Vivre Hotels, reported in Schurenberg," Chip Conley: The 5 Things Everyone Wants from You."

47. Survey by the Conference Board, reported in P. Korkki, "With Jobs Few, Most Workers Aren't Satisfied," *The New York Times*, January 10, 2009, Business section, p. 2. See also P. Coy, "Are Your Employees Just Biding Their Time?" *BusinessWeek*, November 16, 2009, p. 27.

48. See L. Weber, "Roughly Half of U.S. Workers Are Satisfied," *The Wall Street Journal*, July 20, 2016, p. B8.

49. Society for Human Resource Management, *Employee Satisfaction and Engagement: Revitalizing a Changing Workforce*, 2016, https://www.shrm.org/Research/

SurveyFindings/Articles/Documents/2016-Employee-Job-Satisfaction-and-Engage-ment-Report.pdf (accessed July 5, 2016).

50. See J. Flint, "How to Be a Player," *Bloomberg Businessweek*, January 24–January 30, 2011, pp. 108–109.

51. J. B. Stewart, "A Place to Play for Google Staff," *The New York Times*, March 16, 2013, pp. B1, B6; and J. D'Onfro and L. England, "An Inside Look at Google's Best Employee Perks," *Inc./Business Insider*, September 21, 2015, www.inc.com/business-insider/best-google-benefits.html (accessed July 5, 2016).

52. J. S. Adams, "Toward an Understanding of Inequity," *Journal of Abnormal and Social Psychology*, November 1963, pp. 422–436; and J. S. Adams, "Injustice in Social Exchange," in L. Berkowitz, ed., *Advances in Experimental Social Psychology*, 2nd ed. (New York: Academic Press, 1965), pp. 267–300.

53. D. F. Larcker, N. E. Donatiello, and B. Tavan, "Americans and CEO Pay: 2016 Public Perception Survey on CEO Compensation," CGRI Survey Series. Corporate Governance Research Initiative, Stanford Rock Center for Corporate Governance, February 2016, https://www.gsb.stanford.edu/faculty-research/publications/americans-ceo-pay-2016-public-perception-survey-ceo-compensation; and D. Choe, "CEO Pay in 2015: When a $468,449 Raise is Typical," Associated Press, May 25, 2016, http://bigstory.ap.org/article/3ecc98d4f30b41818d8e8ae032095f42/ceo-pay-climbs-again-even-their-stock-prices-dont (both accessed July 5, 2016).

54. Larcker, Donatiello, and Tavan, "Americans and CEO Pay: 2016 Public Perception Survey on CEO Compensation."

55. "Thievery in Workplaces—Trillion-Dollar Industry: Honesty in Deep Decline—Business Theft Becoming Epidemic," *BizShifts—Trends*, July 25, 2015, http://bizshifts-trends.com/2015/07/29/thievery-in-workplaces-trillion-dollar-industry-honesty-in-deep-decline-business-theft-becoming-epidemic (accessed July 9, 2016).

56. The comparison process was discussed by S. T. Fiske, "Envy Up, Scorn Down: How Comparison Divides Us," *American Psychologist*, November 2010, pp. 698–706.

57. For a thorough review of organizational justice theory and research, see R. Cropanzano, D. E. Rupp, C. J. Mohler, and M. Schminke, "Three Roads to Organizational Justice," in G. R. Ferris, ed., *Research in Personnel and Human Resources Management*, Vol. 20 (New York: JAI Press, 2001), pp. 269–329.

58. J. A. Colquitt, D. E. Conlon, M. J. Wesson, C. O. L. H. Porter, and K. Y. Ng, "Justice at the Millennium: A Meta-Analytic Review of 25 Years of Organizational Justice Research," *Journal of Applied Psychology*, June 2001, p. 426.

59. D. Jacobe, "Half of Americans Say They Are Underpaid," Gallup Organization, August 18, 2008, www.gallup.com/poll/109618/half-americans-say-they-underpaid.aspx (accessed July 18, 2016).

60. A. Lucchetti and B. Philbin, "Bankers Get IOUs Instead of Bonus Cash," *The Wall Street Journal*, January 16, 2013, p. A1.

61. S. Tangirala and R. Ramanujam, "Ask and You Shall Hear (but Not Always): Examining the Relationship between Manager Consultation and Employee Voice," *Personnel Psychology*, Vol. 65, No. 2 (2012), pp. 251–252.

62. E. R. Burris, "The Risks and Rewards of Speaking Up: Managerial Responses to Employee Voice," *Academy of Management Journal*, August 2012, pp. 851–875.

63. D. Cote, "Honeywell's CEO on How He Avoided Layoffs," *Harvard Business Review*, June 2013, pp. 43–46.

64. D. S. Whitman, S. Caleo, N. C. Carpenter, M. T. Horner, and J. B. Bernerth, "Fairness at the Collective Level: A Meta-Analytic Examination of the Consequences and Boundary Conditions of Organizational Justice Climate," *Journal of Applied Psychology*, July 2012, pp. 776–791.

65. V. H. Vroom, *Work and Motivation* (New York: Wiley, 1964).

66. C. Wallis, "How to Make Great Teachers," *Time*, February 25, 2008, pp. 28–34; "Teacher Bonus Systems Tested," *Reno Gazette-Journal*, October 22, 2008, p. 1D; S. Dillon, "Incentives for Advanced Work Let Pupils and Teachers Cash In," *The New York Times*, October 3, 2011, pp. A1, A13; S. Dillon, "In Washington, Large Rewards in Teacher Pay," *The New York Times*, January 1, 2012, News section, pp. 1, 18; and W. Kopp, "The Trouble with Humiliating Teachers," *The Wall Street Journal*, March 7, 2012, p. A15.

67. A Hudson survey of 10,000 employees March 20–26, 2006, found that 48% of managers but only 31% of nonmanagers agreed with the statement "Employees who do a better job get paid more"; 46% of managers but only 29% of nonmanagers agreed with the statement "My last raise was based on performance." Information cited in "Reasons for Raises," *BusinessWeek*, May 29, 2006, p. 11.

68. See M. J. Pearsall, M. S. Christian, and A. P. J. Ellis, "Motivating Interdependent Teams: Individual Rewards, Shared Rewards, or Something in Between?" *Journal of Applied Psychology*, January 2010, pp. 183–191.

69. B. Silverman, "CEOs and the Pay-for-Performance Puzzle," *Bloomberg Businessweek*, September 23, 2009, www.bloomberg.com/news/articles/2009-09-23/ceos-and-the-pay-for-performance-puzzle (accessed August 7, 2016).

70. D. FitzGerald, "Staples Managers Fail to Meet Goals, but Get a Bonus," *The Wall Street Journal*, May 27, 2014, p. B3.

71. For more about the problem of linking executive compensation to performance, see J. Anderson, "Tying One's Pay to Performance: What a Concept," *The New York Times*, July 15, 2005, p. C7; G. Farrell and B. Hansen, "Stocks May Fall, but Pay Doesn't," *USA Today*, April 10, 2008, pp. 1B, 2B; M. J. Canyon, "Executive Compensation and Incentives," *Academy of Management Perspectives*, February 2006, pp. 25–44; J. B. Stewart, "Rewarding CEOs Who Fail," *The New York Times*, October 1, 2011, p. B1; J. S. Lublin, "Longstanding Pay Practices under Attack by Activists," *The Wall Street Journal*, March 21, 2013, pp. B1, B2; "CEO Compensation: Do Performance Incentives Pay Off?" *Knowwpcarey*, June 27, 2013, http://knowwpcarey.com/article.cfm?cid=10&aid=1420 (accessed August 7, 2016); A. R. Sorkin, "A Question of What's a Reasonable Reward," *The New York Times*, March 25, 2014, pp. B1, B5; P. Eavis, "Invasion of the Supersalaries," *The New York Times*, April 13, 2014, pp. BU-1, BU4; J. Nocera, "CEO Pay Goes Up, Up, and Away," *The New York Times*, April 15, 2014,

p. A2; and "Using Incentives to Calibrate a CEO's 'Risk Appetite,'" *Knowledge@Wharton*, May 10, 2014, http://knowledge.wharton.upenn.edu/article/using-incentives-calibrate-ceos-risk-appetite (accessed August 7, 2016).

72. Tim Richard, quoted in D. Dullum, "Principal Nominated for Rodel Honor," *Florence Reminder Blade-Tribune*, October 31, 2013, www.trivalleycentral.com/florence_reminder_blade_tribune/education/principal-nominated-for-rodel-honor/article_00078a42-41a6-11e3-a29b-0019bb2963f4.html (accessed August 7, 2016).

73. Richard, quoted in C. Creno, "Program Helps Students Succeed," *The Arizona Republic*, November 27, 2012, p. B2.

74. See J. Schroeder and A. Fishbach, "How to Motivate Yourself and Others? Intended and Unintended Consequences," *Research in Organizational Behavior*, Vol. 35 (2015), pp. 123–141; and E. A. Locke and G. P. Latham, "Building a Practically Useful Theory of Goal Setting and Task Motivation," *American Psychologist*, September 2002, pp. 705–717.

75. See G. P. Latham and E. A. Locke, "Enhancing the Benefits and Overcoming the Pitfalls of Goal Setting," *Organizational Dynamics*, November 2006, pp. 332–340.

76. See D. Morisano, J. B. Hirsh, J. B. Peterson, R. O. Phil, and B. M. Shore, "Setting, Elaborating, and Reflecting on Personal Goals Improves Academic Performance," *Journal of Applied Psychology*, March 2010, pp. 255–264.

77. A. Fox, "Put Plans into Action," *HRMagazine*, April 2013, pp. 27–31.

78. D. Meinert, "An Open Book," *HR Magazine*, April 2013, p. 46.

79. DDI Pulse of the Workforce Survey of 1,000 employees, reported in "Stagnating on the Job," *USA Today*, September 21, 2009, p. 1B.

80. See G. R. Oldham and J. R. Hackman, "Not What It Was and Not What It Will Be: The Future of Job Design," *Journal of Organizational Behavior*, February 2010, pp. 463–479.

81. See the related discussion in S. Wagner-Tsukamoto, "An Institutional Economic Reconstruction of Scientific Management: On the Lost Theoretical Logic of Taylorism," *Academy of Management Review*, January 2007, pp. 105–117; and P. R. Lawrence, "The Key Job Design Problem Is Still Taylorism," *Journal of Organizational Behavior*, February 2010, pp. 412–421.

82. M. A. Campion and C. L. McClelland, "Follow-Up and Extension of the Interdisciplinary Costs and Benefits of Enlarged Jobs," *Journal of Applied Psychology*, June 1993, pp. 339–351.

83. Herzberg et al., *The Motivation to Work*.

84. R. Levering, "The 100 Best Companies to Work For 2016," *Fortune*, March 15, 2016, p. 152.

85. J. R. Hackman and G. R. Oldham, *Work Redesign* (Reading, MA: Addison-Wesley, 1980).

86. See B. Reagan, "Perks with a Payoff," *The Wall Street Journal*, October 24, 2011, p. R3. Some employees have resisted such employer efforts, as when PepsiCo tried to charge its employees $50 a month if they smoke or have obesity-related medical problems; see H. Rosenkrantz and D. Stanford, "PepsiCo Workers Balk at 'Sin Tax,'" *San Francisco Chronicle*, March 18, 2012, p. D5.

87. Dr. Paul H. Grundy, I.B.M.'s director of Health Care Technology and Strategic Initiatives, quoted in M. Freudenheim, "A Model for Health Care That Pays for Quality," *The New York Times*, November 7, 2007, p. C3. See also C. Lochhead, "Lessons on Health Care from Europe," *San Francisco Chronicle*, January 29, 2009, pp. A1, A18.

88. S. Frier, "Wellpoint to Tie Payouts to Quality," *San Francisco Chronicle*, January 28, 2012, p. D3.

89. See M. Evans, "How Much Doctors Are Paid for Quality May Not Matter Much," *Modern Healthcare*, April 6, 2015, www.modernhealthcare.com/article/20150406/NEWS/150409927; and S. Rice, "Physician Quality Pay Not Paying Off," *Modern Healthcare*, May 30, 2015, www.modernhealthcare.com/article/20150406/NEWS/150409927 (accessed July 5, 2016).

90. See E. L. Thorndike, *Educational Psychology: The Psychology of Learning*, Vol. II (New York: Columbia University Teachers College, 1913); B. F. Skinner, *Walden Two* (New York: Macmillan, 1948); B. F. Skinner, *Science and Human Behavior* (New York: Macmillan, 1953); and D. Mozingo, "Contingencies of Reinforcement," in F. R. Volker, Ed. *Encyclopedia of Autism Spectrum Disorders* (New York: Appleton-Century-Crofts, 1969), p. 799.

91. Thorndike, *Educational Psychology: The Psychology of Learning*, Vol. II.

92. W. Neuman, "Flights at JFK Sit on Tarmac for Hours," *The New York Times*, December 29, 2010, p. A23.

93. J. Jargon, "Chipotle Ties Pay to Share Price," *The Wall Street Journal*, March 14, 2016, p. B3.

94. L. Fedow, "Why Chipotle Shouldn't Tie CEO Pay to Stock Price," *CNBC*, March 15, 2016, www.cnbc.com/2016/03/15/why-chipotle-shouldnt-tie-ceo-pay-to-stock-price.html (accessed July 9, 2016).

95. M. Meehan, "Tying Executive Pay to Sustainability Performance," *Forbes*, October 25, 2010, www.forbes.com/2010/10/25/executive-compensation-linkage-technology-sustainability-goals.html (accessed July 14, 2016).

96. Bennett Freeman, former senior vice president for social research and policy of the Calvert Group, quoted in K. Larsen, "Why Tying CEO Pay to Sustainability Still Isn't a Slam Dunk," *GreenBiz*, May 26, 2015, https://www.greenbiz.com/article/why-tying-ceo-pay-sustainability-still-isnt-slam-dunk (accessed July 14, 2016).

97. A. J. Wowak, M. J. Mannor, and K. D. Wowak, "Throwing Caution to the Wind: The Effect of CEO Stock Option Pay on the Incidence of Product Safety Problems," *Strategic Management Journal*, July 2015, pp. 1082–1092.

98. *Fidelity Investments®Evaluate a Job Offer Study*, reported in J. Chew, "Why Millennials Would Take a $7,600 Pay Cut for a New Job," *Fortune*, April 8, 2016, http://fortune.com/2016/04/08/fidelity-millennial-study-career (accessed July 7, 2016).

99. J. Hofherr, "Millennials Would Take a $7,600 Pay Cut for a Better Work Life," *Boston.com*, April 8, 2016, https://www.boston.com/jobs/jobs-news/2016/04/08/millennials-work-life-balance-over-salary (accessed July 7, 2016).

100. See Gallup Organization study, reported in A. Mann and N. Dvorack, "Employee Recognition: Low Cost, High Impact," Gallup, June 28, 2016, www.gallup.com/businessjournal/193238/employee-recognition-low-cost-high-impact.aspx?g_source=ELEMENT_4_RECOGNITION_AND_PRAISE&g_medium=topic&g_campaign=tiles (accessed July 7, 2016). See also J. Yang and A. Gonzalez, "Most Preferred Forms of Recognition at Workplace," *USA Today,* May 4, 2009, p. 1B; and N. Lublin, "Two Little Words," *Fast Company,* November 2010, p. 56; L. Freifeld, "Why Cash *Doesn't* Motivate," *Training,* July–August 2011, pp. 17–22. These results are also in line with a survey by the Society for Human Resource Management, *2011 Job Satisfaction Survey Report,* in which employees said the top five "very important" aspects of job satisfaction were job security, opportunity to use skills and abilities, organization's financial stability, compensation pay, and benefits. See Society for Human Resource Management, "Employee Job Satisfaction: The External Forces Influencing Employee Attitudes," *Workplace Visions,* issue 4, 2011, www.shrm.org/Research/FutureWorkplaceTrends/Documents/11-0697%20Workplace_Visions_Issue4%20FINAL.pdf (accessed July 7, 2016).
101. K. Peters and S. Lewis-Kulin, "How to Create a Culture That Works for All Ages," *Fortune.com,* June 28, 2016, http://fortune.com/tag/100-best-companies-to-work-for/ (accessed July 7, 2016). See also Great Place to Work Institute, Trust Index Employee Survey, described in L. Petrecca, "Tech Companies Top List of 'Great Workplaces,'" *USA Today,* October 31, 2011, p. 7B.
102. See T. Francis and J. S. Lublin, "Divide Persists between Pay, Performance," *The Wall Street Journal,* June 3, 2016, pp. B1, B5.
103. E. White, "The Best vs. the Rest," *The Wall Street Journal,* January 30, 2006, pp. B1, B3; and J. Pfeffer, "Stopping the Talent Drain," *Business 2.0,* July 2006, p. 80.
104. For an alternative approach to paying salespeople, see S. Perman, "For Some, Paying Sales Commissions No Longer Makes Sense," *The New York Times,* November 21, 2013, p. B4.
105. P. Hodson, *2008 Proxy Season Foresights #2—Performance Targets Targeted,* February 15, 2008, Corporate Library, www.thecorporatelibrary.com/info.php?id=88 (accessed August 7, 2016). This study by Corporate Library, an independent governance research organization for the Securities and Exchange Commission, is reported in E. Simon, "How Execs Get Bonus Not Clear," *San Francisco Chronicle,* February 21, 2008, p. C3.
106. M. Atih, "Using 'Gainsharing' to Achieve Sustainability Goals," *HDT Truckinginfo,* April 2, 2014, www.truckinginfo.com/blog/market-trends/story/2014/04/using-gainsharing-to-achieve-sustainability-goals.aspx (accessed July 5, 2016).
107. K. K. Spors, "Top Small Workplaces 2009: Mike's Carwash," *The Wall Street Journal,* September 28, 2009, p. R5.
108. Atih, "Using 'Gainsharing' to Achieve Sustainability Goals."
109. National Center for Employee Ownership, reported in S. Sharf, "Why Starbucks Pays Its Baristas with Stock: A Beginner's Guide to Company Stock," *Forbes,* May 18, 2015, www.forbes.com/sites/samanthasharf/2015/03/18/why-starbucks-pays-its-baristas-with-stock-a-beginners-guide-to-company-stock/#2f5b88d05039 (accessed July 6, 2016).
110. A. Verasai, "A Starbucks Turnaround Success Story," *The HR Digest,* December 25, 2014, www.thehrdigest.com/starbucks-turn-around-success-story (accessed July 7, 2016). See also J. A. Michelli, *The Starbucks Experience: 5 Principles for Turning Ordinary into Extraordinary* (New York: McGraw-Hill Press, 2007).
111. See J. Whitcomb, "Culture of Learning Supports High Employee Satisfaction," *Training,* July/August 2015, pp. 60–61.
112. J. Kauffman, "Pizza Performance Spun Off a Full-Scale Culinary Empire," *San Francisco Chronicle,* March 22, 2015, pp. A1, A4.
113. Accenture, "Defining Success: 2013 Global Research Results," www.accenture.com/SiteCollectionDocuments/PDF/Accenture-IWD-2013-Research-Deck-022013.pdf (accessed August 8, 2016). See also C. Brooks, "Career Success Means Work-Life Balance, Study Finds," *Huffington Post,* March 5, 2013, www.huffingtonpost.com/2013/03/05/career-success-means-work-life-balance_n_2812707.html (accessed August 8, 2016).
114. *The Millennials: Confident. Connected. Open to Change,* Pew Research Center Publications, February 2010, www.pewsocialtrends.org/2010/02/24/millennials-confident-connected-open-to-change (accessed July 8, 2016).
115. *Fidelity Investments® Evaluate a Job Offer Study,* reported in Chew, "Why Millennials Would Take a $7,600 Pay Cut for a New Job."
116. A. Adkins, "What Millennials Want from Work and Life," Gallup Organization, May 11, 2016, www.gallup.com/businessjournal/191435/millennials-work-life.aspx (accessed July 12, 2016).
117. Definition from I. E. Tatara, *Work-Life Benefits: Everything You Need to Know to Determine Your Work-Life Program* (Chicago: CCH KnowledgePoint, 2002), p. 2.
118. J. Sahadi, "No. 1 Cause of Bad Work-Life Balance? Bad Bosses," *CNNMoney,* April 21, 2015, http://money.cnn.com/2015/04/21/pf/work-life-balance (accessed August 1, 2016).
119. A. B. Groysberg and R. Abrahams, "Manage Your Work, Manage Your Life," *Harvard Business Review,* March 2014, pp. 58–66; S. Wojcicki, "Paid Maternity Leave Is Good for Business," *The Wall Street Journal,* December 17, 2014, p. A17; X. X. Miller, "The Economic Benefits of Paid Parental Leave," *The New York Times,* February 1, 2015, p. BU-3; "Benefits of Shared Child Care," *The New York Times,* September 1, 2015, p. D4; and R. Feintzeig, "More Pay for New Parents," *The Wall Street Journal,* August 11, 2015, p. D4.
120. See C. C. Miller, "Leaps in Leave, If Only Parents Would Take It," *The New York Times,* September 2, 2015, pp. A1, A3; and R. Lieber, "Paid Leave for Fathers. Any Takers?" *The New York Times,* August 8, 2015, pp. B1, B5; and R. E. Silverman, "Challenges of the 'Daddy Track,'" *The Wall Street Journal,* September 2, 2015, pp. B1, B5.
121. K. Doerer, "U.S. Has a Lousy Work-Life Balance," PBS NewsHour, July 3, 2015, www.pbs.org/newshour/updates/u-s-lousy-work-life-balance (accessed July 7, 2016).
122. *The 2015 Workplace Flexibility Study.* Also see L. Dishman, "Why Managers and Employees Have Wildly Different Ideas about Work-Life Balance," *Fast Company,* February 5, 2015, www.fastcompany.com/3041908/the-future-of-work/the-surprising-gap-between-work-life-balance-beliefs-and-reality (both accessed July 7, 2016).
123. See N. Scheiber, "When Shifting Work Schedules Hurt Children's Well-Being," *The New York Times,* August 13, 2015, pp. B1, B6; and "Schedules That Don't Work," *The New York Times,* September 1, 2015, p. A20.
124. P. Moen, E. L. Kelly, W. Fanc, S.-R.Leea, D. Almeidad, et al. "Does a Flexibility/Support Organizational Initiative Improve High-Tech Employees' Well-Being? Evidence from the Work, Family, and Health Network," *American Sociological Review,* February 2016, pp. 134–164.
125. See C. Rexrode, "Citi to Millennials: Take a Year Off," *The Wall Street Journal,* March 17, 2016, pp. C1, C2.
126. C. Kane, "These 21 Companies Will Pay You to Take Time Off," *Fortune.com,* March 16, 2015, http://fortune.com/2015/03/16/paid-sabbaticals (accessed July 8, 2016).
127. M. Lang, "Unlimited Vacation Can Have Limited Benefits," *San Francisco Chronicle,* July 11, 2016, pp. D1, D2.
128. K. Tyler, "Sabbaticals Pay Off," *HR Magazine,* December 1, 2011, https://www.shrm.org/hr-today/news/hr-magazine/pages/1211tyler.aspx (accessed July 8, 2016).
129. Business advisory firm CEB, reported in A. Elejalde-Ruiz, "Career Development Is Top Priority for Employers Seeking to Retain Talent," *Chicago Tribune,* March 29, 2016, www.chicagotribune.com/business/careers/ct-career-development-perk-0330-biz-20160329-story.html (accessed June 5, 2016). For a different view, see J. Chatterjee, interviewed in "Can Employee Training Lead to Higher Profits?" *Knowledge@Wharton,* December 16, 2015, http://knowledge.wharton.upenn.edu/article/can-employee-training-lead-higher-profits (accessed June 5, 2016).
130. J. Sturges, N. Conway, D. Guest, and A. Liefooghe, "Managing the Career Deal: The Psychological Contract as a Framework for Understanding Career Management, Organizational Commitment, and Work Behavior," *Journal of Organizational Behavior,* November 2005, pp. 821–38; J. Badal, "'Career Path' Programs Help Retain Workers," *The Wall Street Journal,* July 24, 2006, pp. B1, B4; and M. Zhang, "15 Companies That Will Help Pay Your College Tuition," *Business Insider,* June 16, 2014, www.businessinsider.com/companies-that-will-pay-for-your-tuition-2014-6 (accessed July 8, 2016).
131. See "2015 Training Industry Report," *Training,* November/December 2015, https://trainingmag.com/trgmag-article/2o15-training-industry-report (accessed June 6, 2016).
132. "2015 Training Industry Report."
133. M. E. Seligman, *Flourish* (New York: Free Press, 2011).
134. B. L. Fredrickson and M. F. Losada, "Positive Affect in the Complex Dynamics of Human Flourishing," *American Psychologist,* 2005, pp. 678–86.
135. C. D. Ryff, B. H. Singer, and G. D. Love, "Positive Health: Connecting Well-Being with Biology," *Philosophical Transactions of the Royal Society of London, Biological Sciences,* September 29, 2004, pp. 1383–1394; C. L. M. Keyes and E. J. Simoes, "To Flourish or Not: Positive Mental Health and All-Cause Mortality," *American Journal of Public Health,* November 2012, p. 2164–2172; and Seligman, *Flourish.*
136. D. Wilkie, "Help Keep Employees' Stress in Check," *HR Magazine,* May 2015, p. 16.
137. "Lee Hecht Harrison Poll Finds Most Workers Losing Sleep Due to Work-Related Stress," *Yahoo! Finance,* April 27, 2015, http://finance.yahoo.com/news/lee-hecht-harrison-poll-finds-100000997.html (accessed August 8, 2015); and D. Meinert, "A Hidden Epidemic," *HR Magazine,* March 2016, pp. 31–36.
138. S. Barsade and O. A. O'Neill, "Manage Your Emotional Culture," *Harvard Business Review,* January-February 2016, p. 65.
139. J. Vatner, "Changing a Culture by Removing Walls," *The New York Times,* February 10, 2010, p. B7.
140. C. Congdon, D. Flynn, and M. Redman, "Balancing 'We' and 'Me,'" *Harvard Business Review,* October 2014, p. 57.
141. D. Ward, "Beyond the Open Office," *HR Magazine,* April 2015, pp. 31–35.
142. N. M. Ashkanasy, O. B. Ayoko, and K. A. Jehn, "Understanding the Physical Environment of Work and Employee Behavior: An Affective Events Perspective," *Journal of Organizational Behavior,* November 2014, pp. 1169–1184.
143. A. Hedge, quoted in P. Wen, "Drab Cubicles Can Block Workers' Creativity, Productivity," *San Francisco Chronicle,* March 10, 2000, pp. B1, B3; reprinted from *Boston Globe.*
144. See A. Johnson, "It's True: A Nicer Office Can Boost Morale," *The Arizona Republic,* September 3, 2007, www.azcentral.com/arizonarepublic/business/articles/0903biz-workenvironment0903.html (accessed August 7, 2014), which describes a study by Harvard Medical School psychologist Nancy Etcoff that reinforces the idea that a person's physical environment has a big impact on his or her mood at work. Also see I. DeBare, "Shared Work Spaces a Sign of the Times," *San Francisco Chronicle,* February 19, 2008, pp. A1, A7.
145. T. Hill, "Tear Down Those Walls?" *Training,* January/February 2016, pp. 118–119.
146. Ward, "Beyond the Open Office."
147. Survey by B2B marketplace Approved Index, reported in K. Higgenbottom, "Bad Bosses at the Heart of Employee Turnover," *Forbes,* September 8, 2015, www.forbes.com/sites/karenhigginbottom/2015/09/08/bad-bosses-at-the-heart-of-employee-turnover/#35cfb2344075 (accessed July 6, 2016).
148. Gallup survey, reported in B. Snyer, "Half of Us Have Quit Our Job Because of a Bad Boss" *Fortune.com,* April 2, 2015, http://fortune.com/2015/04/02/quit-reasons/ (accessed July 6, 2016).
149. T. Schwartz and C. Porath, "Why You Hate Work," *The New York Times,* June 1, 2014, p. SR-1, reporting on Towers Watson 2012 global workforce study of 32,000 employees.
150. See M. Dewhurst, M. Guthridge, and E. Mohr, "Motivating People Getting Beyond Money," *McKinsey Quarterly,* November 2009, www.mckinsey.com/business-functions/organization/our-insights/motivating-people-getting-beyond-money (accessed July 6, 2016).
151. J. Lintern, "How to Turn Disgruntled Staff into Your Most Valuable Employees," LinkedIn.com, April 7, 2016, https://www.linkedin.com/pulse/how-turn-disgruntled-staff-your-most-valuable-james-lintern (accessed July 7, 2016).

152. See J. Scorza, "2, 4, 6, 8! How Do You Appreciate?" *HR Magazine,* November 2015, pp. 53–57.

153. J. W. Giulioni, "Ruining Recognition," *Training,* May/June 2015, pp. 12–13.

154. See D. H. Pink, *Drive: The Surprising Truth about What Motivates Us* (New York: Riverhead, 2010). The book proposes that workers are more efficient, loyal, and creative when they feel that their work has meaning.

155. Dale Carnegie Training survey, reported in G. Dutton, "What Motivates Workers at Small Firms?" *Training,* July/August 2015, pp. 24–25.

156. V. E. Frankl, *Man's Search for Meaning* (New York: Pocket Books, 1959).

157. Seligman, *Flourish.*

158. R. Levering, "The 100 Best Companies to Work for 2016," *Fortune,* March 15, 2016, pp. 143–165.

159. Seligman, *Flourish.*

160. Levering, "The 100 Best Companies to Work For 2016," pp. 143–165.

161. "Acuity Insurance," https://en.wikipedia.org/wiki/Acuity_Insurance, last modified January 12, 2016.

162. See "Acuity Insurance: Great Place to Work 2016," http://reviews.greatplacetowork.com/acuity, accessed June 8, 2016.

163. "Acuity Insurance: Great Place to Work 2016," http://reviews.greatplacetowork.com/acuity, accessed June 8, 2016.

164. "Acuity Insurance: Great Place to Work 2016," http://reviews.greatplacetowork.com/acuity, accessed June 8, 2016.

165. "The Container Store: Great Place to Work 2016," http://reviews.greatplacetowork.com/the-container-store?utm_source=fortune&utm_medium=list-page&utm_content=reviews-link&utm_campaign=2016-100-best, accessed June 8, 2016.

166. R. Feintzeig, "Container Store Bests on $50,000 Retail Worker," *The Wall Street Journal,* http://www.wsj.com/container-store-bets-on-50-000-retail-worker-1413340639, accessed June 8, 2016.

167. R. Feintzeig, "Container Store Bests on $50,000 Retail Worker," *The Wall Street Journal,* http://www.wsj.com/container-store-bets-on-50-000-retail-worker-1413340639, accessed June 8, 2016.

168. L. Shelley, "The Container Store: A Culture Organized for Inspired Employees," February 12, 2015, https://www.linkedin.com/pulse/container-store-culture-organized-inspired-employees-lisa-shelley.

169. "The Container Store: Great Place to Work 2016," http://reviews.greatplacetowork.com/the-container-store?utm_source=fortune&utm_medium=list-page&utm_content=reviews-link&utm_campaign=2016-100-best, accessed June 8, 2016.

170. M. Schnurman, "Secret to Container Store's Success: Invest in People First," *The Dallas Morning News,* November 4, 2013, http://www.dallasnews.com/business/columnists/mitchell-schnurman/20131104-secret-to-container-stores-success-invest-in-people-first.ece.

171. V. Kopytoff, "In Major Blow to NCAA, Judge Rules That Colleges Can Pay Athletes," *Fortune,* August 8, 2014, http://fortune.com/2014/08/08/judge-deals-major-blow-to-ncaa-by-ruling-athletes-can-be-paid (accessed August 12, 2014).

172. J. Nocera, "A Way to Start Paying College Athletes," *The New York Times,* January 8, 2016, http://nyti.ms/1Rz9Xzz.

173. C. Isidore, "Wildly Profitable College Football About to Get More Profitable," *CNN Money,* January 13, 2015.

174. M. Strachan, "NCAA Schools Can Absolutely Afford to Pay College Athletes, Economists Say," March 27, 2015, http://www.huffingtonpost.com/2015/03/27/ncaa-pay-student-athletes_n_6940836.html.

CHAPTER 13

1. Steimle J., "6 Tips For Managing A Distributed Team." http://www.forbes.com/sites/joshsteimle/2015/12/11/6-tips-for-managing-a-distributed-team/#5a7c0ec55f58, accessed October 10, 2016.

2. Steimle, J. "6 Tips for Managing A Distributed Team," http://www.forbes.com/sites/joshsteimle/2015/12/11/6-tips-for-managing-a-distributed-team, accessed October 10, 2016; Biz 3.0 "20 Tips from Virtual Companies on Building Remote Teams," https://biz30.timedoctor.com/20-responses-from-the-top-companies-who-have-virtual-teams/, accessed October 10, 2016.

3. Biz 3.0 "20 Tips from Virtual Companies on Building Remote Teams," https://biz30.timedoctor.com/20-responses-from-the-top-companies-who-have-virtual-teams/, accessed October 10, 2016.

4. Biz 3.0 "20 Tips from Virtual Companies on Building Remote Teams," https://biz30.timedoctor.com/20-responses-from-the-top-companies-who-have-virtual-teams/, accessed October 10, 2016.

5. Biz 3.0 "20 Tips from Virtual Companies on Building Remote Teams," https://biz30.timedoctor.com/20-responses-from-the-top-companies-who-have-virtual-teams/, accessed October 10, 2016.

6. P. F. Drucker, "The Coming of the New Organization," *Harvard Business Review,* January–February 1988, pp. 45–53.

7. See K. Caprino, "How Companies Like Uber, Facebook and Salesforce Engage in Team-Building (It's Not What You Think)," http://www.forbes.com/sites/kathycaprino/2016/01/14/how-companies-like-uber-facebook-and-salesforce-engage-in-team-building-its-not-what-you-think/#6a95018e6157, accessed July 2016.

8. S. E. Page, quoted in C. Dreifus, "In Professor's Model, Diversity = Productivity," *The New York Times,* January 8, 2008, p. D2. On the subject of diversity in teams, see also A. N. Pieterse, D. van Knippenberg, and D. van Dierendonck, "Cultural Diversity and Team Performance: The Role of Team Member Goal Orientation," *Academy of Management Journal,* June 2013, pp. 782–804; interview with Robert E. Moritz, chairman and senior partner of Pricewaterhouse Coopers LLP, in "PwC's Robert E. Moritz: 'Diverse Teams Give You the Best Thinking,'" *Knowledge@Wharton,* December 24, 2013,

http://knowledge.wharton.upenn.edu/article/leadership-beyond-bottom-line (accessed August 10, 2014); and Michael P. Gregoire, CEO of CA Technologies, interviewed by A. Bryant, "A Diverse Team Is a Creative Team," *The New York Times,* January 12, 2014, p. BU-2.

9. This definition is based in part on one found in D. Horton Smith, "A Parsimonious Definition of 'Group': Toward Conceptual Clarity and Scientific Utility," *Sociological Inquiry,* Spring 1967, pp. 141–167.

10. J. R. Katzenbach and D. K. Smith, *The Wisdom of Teams: Creating the High-Performance Organization* (Boston: Harvard Business School Press, 1993), p. 45.

11. J. R. Katzenbach and D. K. Smith, "The Discipline of Teams," *Harvard Business Review,* March–April 1995, p. 112.

12. CEO Rod Drury, quoted in http://fortune.com/2016/05/03/leaders-motivate-teams/?iid=sr-link2.

13. See R. Cross, N. Nohria, and A. Parker, "Six Myths about Informal Networks—and How to Overcome Them," *MIT Sloan Management Review,* Spring 2002, pp. 67–75; and C. Shriky, "Watching the Patterns Emerge," *Harvard Business Review,* February 2004, pp. 34–35.

14. D. Krackhardt and J. R. Hanson, "Informal Networks: The Company behind the Chart," *Harvard Business Review,* July-August 1993, p. 104. See also R. Cross and L. Prusack, "The People Who Make Organizations Go—or Stop," *Harvard Business Review,* June 3003, pp. 104–112; and R. McDermott and D. Archibald, "Harnessing Your Staff's Informal Networks," *Harvard Business Review,* March 2010, pp. 82–89.

15. Study by Center for Workforce Development, Newton, MA, reported in M. Jackson, "It's Not Chitchat, It's Training," *San Francisco Chronicle,* January 7, 1998, p. D2.

16. K. Kim, H. M. Collins, J. Williamson, and J. Chapman, *Participation in Adult Education and Lifetime Learning: 2000–01,* NCES 2004-050, U.S. Department of Education, National Center for Education Statistics (Washington, DC: U.S. Government Printing Office, 2008). For more on informal learning, see L. Dublin, "Formalizing Informal Learning," *Chief Learning Officer,* March 2010, www.clomedia.com/features/2010/March/2870/index.php (accessed August 10, 2014).

17. T. Lytle, "Catering to an Hourly Workforce," *HR Magazine,* April 2016, 49.

18. K. K. Spors, "Getting Workers to Share Their Know-How with Peers," *The Wall Street Journal,* April 3, 2008, p. B6.

19. Forrester Research, reported in R. Reitsma, "The Data Digest: How Democratization of Technology Empowers Employees," *Forrester Blogs,* February 11, 2011, http://blogs.forrester.com/reineke_reitsma/11-02-11-the_data_digest_how_democratization_of_technology_empowers_employees (accessed August 10, 2014).

20. For more on social networks and employee collaboration, see R. Shah, "A New Organizational Learning Goal: The Accrual of Awareness," *Forbes,* May 1, 2012, www.forbes.com/sites/rawnshah/2012/05/01/a-new-organizational-learning-goal-the-accrual-of-awareness; M. Benioff, "Welcome to the Social Media Revolution," *BBC News,* May 10, 2012, www.bbc.co.uk/news/business-18013662; and S. Aral, C. Dellarocas, and D. Godes, "Introduction to the Special Issues—Social Media and Business Transformation: A Framework for Research," *Information Systems Research,* March 2013, pp. 3–13. Also see Cisco study that found that allowing employees to bring their own handheld device to work could help encourage workplace collaboration, reported in "Cisco Study: IT Saying Yes to BYOD," *Market Watch,* May 16, 2012, www.marketwatch.com/story/cisco-study-it-saying-yes-to-byod-2012-05-16 (all accessed August 10, 2014).

21. From "How Herman Miller Has Designed Employee Loyalty" http://www.fastcompany.com/1689839/how-herman-miller-has-designed-employee-loyalty.

22. L. MacDonald, "What is a Self-Managed Team," *Houston Chronicle,* 2016, http://smallbusiness.chron.com/selfmanaged-team-18236.html, accessed June 29, 2016.

23. See D. W. Parker, M. Holesgrove, and R. Pathak, "Improving Productivity with Self-Organized Teams and Agile Leadership," *International Journal of Productivity and Performance Management,* 2015, 112–128; and C. Post, "When Is Female Leadership an Advantage? Coordination Requirements, Team Cohesion, and Team Interaction Norms," *Journal of Organizational Behavior,* 2015, pp. 1153–1175.

24. Based on three meta-analyses covering 70 studies. See P. S. Goodman, R. Devadas, and T. L. Griffith Hughson, "Groups and Productivity: Analyzing the Effectiveness of Self-Managed Teams," in *Productivity in Organizations,* ed. J. P. Campbell, R. J. Campbell, and Associates (San Francisco: Jossey-Bass, 1998), pp. 295–327. Also see S. Kauffeld, "Self-Directed Work Groups and Team Competence," *Journal of Occupational and Organizational Psychology,* March 2006, pp. 1–21; and K. A. Smith-Jentsch, J. A. Cannon-Bowers, S. L. Tannenbaum, and E. Salas, "Guided Team Self-Correction: Impacts on Team Mental Models, Processes, and Effectiveness," *Small Group Research,* June 2008, pp. 303–327.

25. N. Collins, Y.-M. Chou, and M. Warner, "Member Satisfaction, Communication and Role of Leader in Virtual Self-Managed Teamwork: Case Studies in Asia-Pacific Region," *Human Systems Management,* 2014, 155–170.

26. J. E. Hoch and S. W. Kozlowski, "Leading Virtual Teams: Hierarchical Leadership, Structural Supports, and Shared Team Leadership," *Journal of Applied Psychology,* 2012, 1–13.

27. L. Gilson, M. Maynard, N. Young, M. Varianien, and M. Hakonen, "Virtual Teams Research: 10 Years, 10 Themes, and 10 Opportunities," *Journal of Management,* July 2015, 1313–1337.

28. Adapted from F. Siebdrat, M. Hoegl, and J. Ernst, "How to Manage Virtual Teams," *MIT Sloan Management Review,* Summer 2009, 63–68; see Also B. L. Kirkman, B. Rosen, C. B. Gibson, P.E. Tesluk, and S.O. McPherson, "Five Challenges to Virtual Team Success: Lessons from Sabre, Inc.," *Academy of Management Executive,* August 2002, 67–79.

29. J.E. Hoch and S. W. Kozlowski, "Leading Virtual Teams: Hierarchical Leadership, Structural Supports, and Shared Team Leadership," *Journal of Applied Psychology,* 2012, 1–13.

30. "The Challenges of Working in Virtual Teams," RW3 Culture Wizard, http://rw-3.com/VTSReportv7.pdf.

31. "Virtual Teams," *Society for Human Resource Management*, July 13, 2012, https://www.shrm.org/hr-today/trends-and-forecasting/research-and-surveys/pages/virtualteams.aspx.

32. Adapted from A. Bruzzese, "Keep Remote Workers in the Loop," *The Arizona Republic*, March 2, 2011; and D. Clemons and M. Kroth, *Managing the Mobile Workforce* (New York: McGraw-Hill, 2010).

33. See A. Bruzzese, "Keep Remote Workers in the Loop," *Arizona Republic*, March 2, 2011.

34. See A. Bruzzese, "Keep Remote Workers in the Loop," *The Arizona Republic*, March 2, 2011.

35. B. Leonard, "Managing Virtual Teams," *HR Magazine*, June 1, 2011. See also N. Lockwood, "Successfully Transitioning to a Virtual Organization: Challenges, Impact, and Technology," *Society of Human Resource Management—Research Quarterly*, First Quarter 2010.

36. E. Martinez-Mareno, A. Zornoza, P. Gonzalez-Navarro, and L. F. Thompson, "Investigating Face-to-Face and Virtual Teamwork over Time: When Does Early Task Conflict Trigger Relationship Conflict?" *Group Dynamics: Theory, Research, and Practice*, 2012, 159–171; and, T. D. Golden, J. F. Veiga, and R. N. Dino. "The Impact of Professional Isolation on Teleworker Job Performance in Turnover Intentions: Does Time Spent Teleworking, Interacting Face to Face, or Having Access to Communication-Enhancing Technology Matter?" *Journal of Applied Psychology*, 2008, 1412–1421.

37. E. Martinez-Mareno, A. Zornoza, P. Gonzalez-Navarro, and L. F. Thompson, "Investigating Face-to-Face and Virtual Teamwork over Time: When Does Early Task Conflict Trigger Relationship Conflict?" Group Dynamics: Theory, Research, and Practice, 2012, 159–171; and, T. D. Golden, J. F. Veiga, and R. N. Dino, "The Impact of Professional Isolation on Teleworker Job Performance in Turnover Intentions: Does Time Spent Teleworking, Interacting Face to Face, or Having Access to Communication-Enhancing Technology Matter?" *Journal of Applied Psychology*, 2008, 1412–1421.

38. E. Meyer, "The Four Keys to Success with Virtual Teams," *Forbes.com*, August 19, 2010, http://www.forbes.com/2010/08/19/virtual-teams-meetings-leadership-managing-cooperation_print.html; see also R. F. Maruca, "How Do You Manage an Off-Site Team?" *BusinessWeek*, September 30, 2007, http://www.businessweek.com.

39. See B. W. Tuckman, "Developmental Sequence in Small Groups," *Psychological Bulletin*, June 1965, pp. 384–399; and B. W. Tuckman and M.A.C. Jensen, "Stages of Small-Group Development Revisited," *Group & Organization Studies*, December 1977, pp. 419–427.

40. See F. P. Morgeson, M. H. Reider, and M. A. Campion, "Selecting Individuals in Team Settings: The Importance of Social Skills, Personality Characteristics, and Teamwork Knowledge," *Personnel Psychology*, Autumn 2005, pp. 583–611.

41. See J.-L. Farh, C. Lee, and C. I. C. Farh, "Task Conflict and Team Creativity: A Question of How Much and When," *Journal of Applied Psychology*, Vol. 95, No. 6 (2010), pp. 1173–1180.

42. For related research, see M. Van Vugt and C. M. Hart, "Social Identity as Social Glue: The Origins of Group Loyalty," *Journal of Personality and Social Psychology*, April 2004, pp. 585–598.

43. T. Hall, "Does Cohesion Positively Correlate to Performance in All Stages of a Group's Life Cycle," *Journal of Organizational Culture, Communications and Conflict*, January 2015, pp. 58–69.

44. See M. S. Cole, H. Bruch, and B. Vogel, "Energy at Work: A Measurement Validation and Linkage to Unit Effectiveness," *Journal of Organizational Behavior*, May, 2012, pp. 445–467.

45. Adapted from D. D. Warrick, "What Leaders Can Learn about Teamwork and Developing High Performance Teams from Organizations Development Practitioners," *Performance Improvement*, March 2016, 13–21; and T. Daniel, "Developing and Sustaining High-Performing Work Teams," SHRM, July 23, 2015, https://www.shrm.org/templatestools/toolkits/pages/developingandsustaininghigh-performanceworkteams.aspx; see also S. Buchold and T. Roth, *Creating the High-Performance Team* (New York: John Wiley & Sons, 1987).

46. F. P. Morgeson, D. S. DeRue, and E. P. Karam, "Leadership in Teams: A Functional Approach to Understanding Leadership Structures and Processes," *Journal of Management*, January 2010, pp. 5–39.

47. J. Hildreth and C. Anderson, "Failure at the Top: How Power Undermines Collaborative Performance," *Journal of Personality and Social Psychology*, February 2016, 261–286.

48. J. Hu and R. Liden, "Making a Difference in the Teamwork: Linking Team Prosocial Motivation to Team Processes and Effectiveness," *Academy of Management Journal*, August 2015, vol. 1102–1127.

49. See K. Goldstein, "Fostering Team Collaboration," Leadership Excellence Essentials, January, 2016, http://web.a.ebscohost.com.access.library.unisa.edu.au/ehost/pdfviewer/pdfviewer?vid=46&sid=d82496f2-0036-407c-8177-a25b4767d243%40sessionmgr4005&hid=4209; and M. Haas and M. Mortensen, "The Secrets of Great Teamwork," *Harvard Business Review*, June 2016, 71–76.

50. David Burkus, "Why Whole Foods Builds Its Entire Business On Teams," http://www.courant.com/business/top-workplaces/hc-tw14-whole-foods-20140921-story.html, June 8, 2016.

51. See C. Duhigg, "What Google Learned from Its Quest to Build the Perfect Team," http://www.nytimes.com/2016/02/28/magazine/what-google-learned-from-its-quest-to-build-the-perfect-team.html?_r=0, accessed July 2016.

52. See J. O'Toole and W. Bennis, "What's Needed Next: A Culture of Candor," *Harvard Business Review*, June 2009, pp. 54–61; M. Yakovleva, R. R. Reilly, and R. Werko, "Why Do We Trust? Moving Beyond Individual to Dyadic Perceptions," *Journal of Applied Psychology*, January 2010, pp. 79–91; and J. P. MacDuffie, "Inter-Organizational Trust and the Dynamics of Distrust," *Journal of International Business Studies*, January 2011, pp. 35–47.

53. M. A. Drescher, M. A. Korsgaard, I. M. Welpe, A. Picot, and R. T. Wigand, "The Dynamics of Shared Leadership: Building Trust and Enhancing Performance," *Journal of Applied Psychology*, September 2014, 771–783.

54. See K. Caprino, "How Companies Like Uber, Facebook and Salesforce Engage In Team-Building (It's Not What You Think)," http://www.forbes.com/sites/kathycaprino/2016/01/14/how-companies-like-uber-facebook-and-salesforce-engage-in-team-building-its-not-what-you-think/#7c9c52316157, accessed July 2016.

55. Goal monitoring for teams was examined by T. L. Rapp, D. G. Bachrach, A. A. Rapp, and R. Mullins, "The Role of Team Goal Monitoring in the Curvilinear Relationship between Team Efficacy and Team Performance," *Journal of Applied Psychology*, September 2014, 976–987.

56. J. Schaubroeck, S. S. K. Lam, and S. E. Cha, "Embracing Transformational Leadership: Team Values and the Impact of Leader Behavior on Team Performance," *Journal of Applied Psychology*, July 2007, pp. 1020–1030.

57. E. Bernstein, J. Bunch, N. Canner, and M. Lee, "Beyond the Holacracy Hype," *Harvard Business Review*, July-August 2016, p. 43.

58. S. H. Courtright, G. R. Thurgood, G. L. Stewart, and A. J. Pierotti, "Structural Interdependence in Teams: An Integrative Framework and Meta-Analysis," *Journal of Applied Psychology*, November 2015, 1825–1846.

59. S. H. Courtright, G. R. Thurgood, G. L. Stewart, and A. J. Pierotti, "Structural Interdependence in Teams: An Integrative Framework and Meta-Analysis," *Journal of Applied Psychology*, November 2015, 1825–1846.

60. M. D. Watkins, "Leading the Team You Inherit," *Harvard Business Review*, June 2016, pp. 61–67.

61. See J. Morgan, "The Chief People Officer of Cisco Shares Her Top Three Tips for Building High-Performing Teams," http://www.forbes.com/sites/jacobmorgan/2016/04/06/the-chief-people-officer-of-cisco-shares-her-top-three-tips-for-building-high-preforming-teams/#3c3d3b1051ce, accessed July 2016.

62. See J. Y. Seong, W-W. Park, D-S. Hong, and Y. Shin, "Person-Group Fit: Diversity Antecedents, Proximal Outcomes, and Performance at the Group Level," *Journal of Management*, July 2015, p. 43.

63. See L. L. Gilson, M. T. Maynard, N. C. J. Young, M. Vartiainen, and M. Hakonen, "Virtual Team Research: 10 Years, 10 Themes, and 10 Opportunities," *Journal of Management*, July 2015, pp. 1313–1337; and C. Cheng, R. Y. J. Chua, M. W. Morris, and L. Lee, "Finding the Right Mix: How the Composition of Self-Managing Multicultural Teams' Cultural Value Orientation Influences Performance over Time," *Journal of Organizational Behavior*, 2012, 389–411.

64. B. H. Bradley, A. C. Klotz, B. E. Postlethwaite, and K. G. Brown, "Ready to Rumble: How Team Personality Composition and Task Conflict Interact to Improve Performance," *Journal of Applied Psychology*, May 2015, 385–392.

65. F. Hattke and S. Blaschke, "Striving for Excellence: The Role of Top Management Team Diversity in Universities," *Team Performance Management*, 2015, 121–138.

66. See D. M. Fisher, "Distinguishing between Taskwork and Teamwork Planning in Teams: Relations with Coordination and Interpersonal Processes," *Journal of Applied Psychology*, Vol. 99, No. 3 (2014), pp. 423–436.

67. D. C. Feldman, "The Development and Enforcement of Group Norms," *Academy of Management Review*, January 1984, pp. 47–53.

68. D. C. Feldman, "The Development and Enforcement of Group Norms," *Academy of Management Review*, January 1984, pp. 47–53.

69. J. Morgan, "The Chief People Officer Of Cisco Shares Her Top Three Tips For Building High-Performing Teams," http://www.forbes.com/sites/jacobmorgan/2016/04/06/the-chief-people-officer-of-cisco-shares-her-top-three-tips-for-building-high-preforming-teams/#32a8632751ce, accessed October 10, 2016.

70. D. Sager, "Steelers work on team building at Dave and Buster's," http://steelerswire.usatoday.com/2015/06/08/steelers-work-on-team-building-at-dave-and-busters/, accessed October 10, 2016.

71. J. Motivalli, "5 Inspiring Companies That Rely on Teamwork to Be Successful," http://www.success.com/article/5-inspiring-companies-that-rely-on-teamwork-to-be-successful, accessed October 10, 2016.

72. Some discussions of sources of conflict appear in E. Bernstein, "When a Coworker Is Stressed Out," *The Wall Street Journal*, August 26, 2008, pp. D1, D2.

73. J. A. Wall Jr. and R. Robert Callister, "Conflict and Its Management," *Journal of Management*, No. 3 (1995), p. 517.

74. Cooperative conflict is discussed in D. Tjosvold, *Learning to Manage Conflict: Getting People to Work Together Productively* (New York: Lexington, 1993); and D. Tjosvold and D. W. Johnson, *Productive Conflict Management Perspectives for Organizations* (New York: Irvington, 1983). See also A. C. Amason, K. R. Thompson, W. A. Hochwarter, and A. W. Harrison, "Conflict: An Important Dimension in Successful Management Teams," *Organizational Dynamics*, Autumn 1995, pp. 20–35; and A. C. Amason, "Distinguishing the Effects of Functional and Dysfunctional Conflict on Strategic Decision Making: Resolving a Paradox for Top Management Teams," *Academy of Management Journal*, February 1996, pp. 123–148.

75. See J. Russel, "How to Recognize and Deal with Bullying at Work," April 3, 2016, http://www.latimes.com/business/la-fi-0403-career-coach-bullies-20160402-story.html, accessed July 2016.

76. See S. Branch and J. Murray, "Workplace Bullying: Is Lack of Understanding the Reason for Inaction?" *Organizational Dynamics*, October-December 2015, 287–295.

77. K. L. Zellars, B. J. Tepper, and M. K. Duffy, "Abusive Supervision and Subordinates' Organizational Citizenship Behavior," *Journal of Applied Psychology*, December 2002, pp. 1068–1076. For more on this kind of abusive behavior, see M. Korn and R. Feintzeig, "Is the Old-School, Hard-Nosed Boss Obsolete?" *The Wall Street Journal*, May 23, 2014, pp. B1, B2; and E. Schwitzgebel, "The Essence of Jerkitude," *The Week*, July 4, 2014, pp. 36–37.

78. See S. J. Motowidlo and H. J. Kell, "Job Performance," in *Handbook of Psychology* (Vol. 12), ed. N. W. Schmitt and S. Highhouse (Hoboken, NJ: John Wiley & Sons, Inc., 2012).

79. R. I. Sutton in "Breakthrough Ideas for 2004: The HBR List," *Harvard Business Review*, February 2004, pp. 13–24, 32–37. Sutton's topic was headed "More Trouble Than They Are Worth." His book based on these ideas is *The No Asshole Rule: Building a Civilized Workplace and Surviving One That Isn't* (New York: Random House, 2007).

80. See J. Russel, "How to Recognize and Deal with Bullying at Work," April 3, 2016, http://www.latimes.com/business/la-fi-0403-career-coach-bullies-20160402-story.html, accessed July 2016.

81. A. M. O'Leary-Kelly, R. W. Griffin, and D. J. Glew, "Organization-Motivated Aggression: A Research Framework," *Academy of Management Review*, January 1996, pp. 225–253. See also G. A. Van Kleef and S. Côté, "Expressing Anger in Conflict: When It Helps and When It Hurts," *Journal of Applied Psychology*, November 2007, pp. 1557–1569.

82. See D. Hansen, "7 Tips for Turning Conflict into Creativity," April 14, 2016, http://www.forbes.com/sites/drewhansen/2016/04/14/conflict-and-creativity/2/#2b90160920e6, accessed July 2016.

83. K. Duncum, "Turning Conflict into Cooperation," *Bloomberg Businessweek*, October 15, 2010, www.businessweek.com/managing/content/oct2010/ca20101014_882756.htm (accessed August 10, 2014).

84. See P. L. Costa, A. M. Passos, and A. B. Bakker, "Direct and Contextual Influence of Team Conflict on Team Resources, Team Work Engagement, and Team Performance," *Negotiation and Conflict Management Research*, 2015, pp. 211–227; and C. Porath, T. Foulk, and A. Erez, "How Incivility Hijacks Performance: It Robs Cognitive Resources, Increases Dysfunctional Behavior, and Infects Team Dynamics and Functioning," *Organizational Dynamics*, 2015, 258–265.

85. K. T. Kishida, D. Yang, K. H. Quartz, S. R. Quartz, and P. R. Montague, "Implicit Signals in Small Group Settings and Their Impact on the Expression of Cognitive Capacity and Associated Brain Responses," *Philosophical Transactions of the Royal Society B*, March 5, 2012, pp. 704–716.

86. E. Bernstein, "Speaking Up Is Hard to Do: Researchers Explain Why," *The Wall Street Journal*, February 7, 2012, pp. D1, D4.

87. "Help for the Tongue-Tied," sidebar to Bernstein, p. D4.

88. See K. A. Crowne, "What Leads to Cultural Intelligence?" *Business Horizons*, September–October 2008, pp. 391–399; and N. Goodman, "Cultivating Cultural Intelligence," *Training*, March–April 2011, p. 38. On the subject of listening, see Bob Farrell, CEO of Kewill, interviewed by A. Bryant, "Always Take the Time to Listen," *The New York Times*, June 27, 2014, p. B2.

89. See E. Reid and L. Ramarajan, "Managing the High Intensity Workplace," *Harvard Business Review*, June 2016, 85–90.

90. C. Nohe and L. Meier, "The Chicken or the Egg? A Meta-Analysis of Panel Studies of the Relationship between Work-Family Conflict and Strain," *Journal of Applied Psychology*, 2015, 522–536.

91. T. Allen, R. Johnson, K. Kiburz, and K. Shockley, "Work-Family Conflict and Flexible Work Arrangements: Deconstructing Flexibility," *Personnel Psychology*, 2013, 345–376.

92. N. Mccarthy, "Millennials Place Work/Life Balance Before Career Progression [Infographic]," May 11, 2016, http://www.forbes.com/sites/niallmccarthy/2016/05/11/millennials-place-worklife-balance-before-career-progression-infographic/#54c1c1ed1aa1, accessed October 10, 2016.

93. Forbes.Com, "The 25 Big Companies with the Best Work Life Balance," http://www.forbes.com/pictures/efkk45ejigd/the-25-big-companies-with-the-best-work-life-balance/#3e2c216f5af1, accessed October 10, 2016.

94. T.C. Frohlich, M.B. Sauter, and S. Stebbins, "The 12 Worst Companies to Work For," August, 19, 2015, http://www.msn.com/en-us/money/inside-the-ticker/the-12-worst-companies-to-work-for/ar-AAcIMbT, accessed October 10, 2016.

95. T. Loose, "10 Best and Worst Jobs for Work-Life Balance," January 6, 2016, http://www.huffingtonpost.com/gobankingrates/10-best-and-worst-jobs-fo_b_8924278.html, accessed October 10, 2016.

96. The Muse, "How To Stealthily Figure Out If A Company Really Does Believe In Work-Life Balance," May 17, 2016, http://www.forbes.com/sites/dailymuse/2016/05/17/how-to-stealthily-figure-out-if-a-company-really-does-believe-in-work-life-balance/#78ae350c4d55, accessed October 10, 2016.

97. S. G. Katzenstein, "The Debate on Structured Debate: Toward a Unified Theory," *Organizational Behavior and Human Decision Processes*, June 1996, pp. 316–332.

98. Adapted from T. Allessandra and P. Hunsaker, *Communicating at Work* (New York: Fireside, 1993), p. 107. See also the core emotional elements of negotiation (appreciation, affiliation, autonomy, status, and role) in R. Kreitner and A. Kinicki, *Organizational Behavior*, 10th ed. (New York: McGraw-Hill, 2013), p. 389.

99. M. A. Rahim, "A Strategy for Managing Conflict in Complex Organizations," *Human Relations*, January 1985, p. 84; and M. A. Rahim and N. R. Magner, "Confirmatory Factor Analysis of the Styles of Handling Interpersonal Conflict: First-Order Factor Model and Its Invariance across Groups," *Journal of Applied Psychology*, February 1995, pp. 122–132. See also N. M. Atteya, "The Conflict Management Grid: A Selection and Development Tool to Resolve the Conflict between the Marketing and Sales Organizations," *International Journal of Business and Management*, Vol. 7, No. 13 (2012), pp. 28–37.

100. M. A. Rahim, "A Strategy for Managing Conflict in Complex Organizations," *Human Relations*, January 1985, p. 84.

101. J. Camp, "Schools' Negotiating Lessons Just Don't Work," *San Francisco Chronicle*, August 10, 2014, p. D7.

102. D. Hansen, "7 Tips For Turning Conflict Into Creativity," April 14, 2016, http://www.forbes.com/sites/drewhansen/2016/04/14/conflict-and-creativity/2/#26d0edf720e6, accessed October 10, 2016; S. Lee, "Conflict Is Good for Creativity," June 18, 2015, http://knowledge.insead.edu/leadership-organisations/conflict-is-good-for-creativity-4105, accessed October 10, 2016; S. Venkatesh, June 15, 2015,

http://www.fastcocreate.com/1682575/how-to-use-conflict-to-unlock-creativity, accessed October 10, 2016.

103. http://www.brainyquote.com/quotes/quotes/l/leonardber140536.html.

104. Robinson K. and Aronica L. *The Element: How Finding Your Passion Changes Everything*, New York: Penguin, 2009.

105. "Whole Foods Market," https://en.wikipedia.org/wiki/Whole_Foods_Market, last modified June 17, 2016.

106. R. Levering, "The 100 Best Companies to Work for 2016," *Fortune*, March 15, 2016, 143–165.

107. "Whole Foods Market: Our Core Values," http://www.wholefoodsmarket.com/mission-values/core-values, accessed June 24, 2016.

108. "Whole Foods Market: Our Core Values," http://www.wholefoodsmarket.com/mission-values/core-values, accessed June 24, 2016.

109. Christine Rowland, "Whole Foods Market's Organizational Culture Analysis," http://panmore.com/whole-foods-market-organizational-culture-analysis, September 17, 2015.

110. Matthew Sturdevant, "Top Large Employer: Whole Foods Teamwork Is a Natural," http://www.courant.com/business/top-workplaces/hc-tw14-whole-foods-20140921-story.html, September 21, 2014.

111. David Burkus, "Why Whole Foods Builds Its Entire Business on Teams," http://www.courant.com/business/top-workplaces/hc-tw14-whole-foods-20140921-story.html, June 8, 2016.

112. David Burkus, "Why Whole Foods Builds Its Entire Business On Teams," http://www.courant.com/business/top-workplaces/hc-tw14-whole-foods-20140921-story.html, June 8, 2016.

113. David Burkus, "Why Whole Foods Builds Its Entire Business on Teams," http://www.courant.com/business/top-workplaces/hc-tw14-whole-foods-20140921-story.html, June 8, 2016.

CHAPTER 14

1. R. L. Knowdell, "The 10 New Rules for Strategizing Your Career," *The Futurist*, June–July 1998, pp. 19–24. See also K. Madden, "Plan a Successful Career Change," *Reno Gazette-Journal*, March 11, 2012, p. 1F; B. Marcus, "10 Tips to Get Unstuck and Move Your Career Forward in 2016" January 4, 2016, http://www.forbes.com/sites/bonniemarcus/2016/01/04/10-tips-to-get-unstuck-and-move-your-career-forward-in-2016/#11e4a9ad21f2 accessed July 2016; A. Wicker, "The New Way to Advance Your Career: Hire a Strengths Coach," June 19, 2015, http://www.forbes.com/sites/learnvest/2015/06/19/the-new-way-to-advance-your-career-hire-a-strengths-coach/#4ba6eb96d28f, accessed July 2016; L. Celestino, "The Skills Most Companies Look For in Employees," May 15, 2016, http://fortune.com/2016/05/15/leadership-skills-for-success/?iid=sr-link8, accessed July 2016.

2. M. S. Rao, "Myths and Truths about Skills," *T&D*, May 7, 2012.

3. F. Levy and J. Rodkin, "The Bloomberg Recruiter Report: Job Skills Companies Want but Can't Get," *Bloomberg Business*, February 9, 2016, http://www.bloomberg.com/graphics/2016-job-skills-report.

4. P. G. Northouse, *Leadership: Theory and Practice*, 6th ed. (Thousand Oaks, CA: Sage, 2012), 3.

5. "2014 Training Industry Report," *Training*, November/December 2014, 16–17; and "2015 Training Industry Report," *Training*, November/December 2015, 20–21.

6. See T. J. Quigley and D. C. Hambrick, "Has the 'CEO Effect' Increased in Recent Decades? A New Explanation for the Great Rise in America's Attention to Corporate Leaders," *Strategic Management Journal*, 2015, pp. 21–830.

7. A review of power research can be found in R. E. Sturm and J. Antonakis, "Interpersonal Power: A Review, Critique, and Research Agenda," *Journal of Management*, January 2015, 136–163.

8. See L. Sutton, "5 Employee Incentives That Actually Work" September 9, 2015, http://www.fastcompany.com/3050833/know-it-all/five-employee-incentives-that-actually-work, accessed July 2016.

9. See B. George, "The Massive Difference between Negative and Positive Leadership," March 21, 2016, http://fortune.com/2016/03/21/negative-positive-leadership-politics-ford-alan-mulally/?iid=sr-link2, accessed July 2016.

10. See L. Reston, "Jeb Bush's Leadership Style: Tough, Methodical, Sometimes Rigid," June 16, 2015, http://www.forbes.com/sites/laurareston/2015/06/16/jeb-bushs-leadership-style-tough-methodical-sometimes-rigid/#238ad7ffbf8a, accessed July 2016.

11. See C. Gallo, "40 Years Later, Steve Jobs' Success Secrets Still Apply to Aspiring Leaders," March 21, 2016, http://www.forbes.com/sites/carminegallo/2016/03/31/40-years-later-steve-jobs-success-secrets-still-apply-to-aspiring-leaders/#57fc24319b75, accessed July 2016.

12. See K. Blazek, "A Participatory Leadership Style: Nike's CEO Mark Parker," January 19, 2016, http://www.boothco.com/360-feedback-resources/leadership-style-nikes-ceo-mark-parker/, accessed July 2016.

13. See J. Henderson, "5 Ways To Exert Your Influence At Work—Without Making Office Enemies," February 27, 2015, http://www.forbes.com/sites/learnvest/2015/02/27/5-ways-to-exert-your-influence-at-work-without-making-office-enemies/#480f3f176e9b, accessed July 2016.

14. See "Tips for Writing Effective Personal Fundraising Emails," February 1, 2016, http://support.causevox.com/article/123-tips-for-writing-effective-personal-fundraising-appeals, accessed July 2016.

15. See A. Goldman, "Lust, Favors and Nepotism: Leadership Promotions Turn Toxic," January 2, 2015, https://www.psychologytoday.com/blog/transforming-toxic-leaders/201501/lust-favors-and-nepotism-leadership-promotions-turn-toxic, accessed July 2016.

16. See D. Schawbel, "Cory Booker: Leading through Uniting People and Communities," February 16, 2016, http://www.forbes.com/sites/danschawbel/2016/02/16/cory-booker-leading-through-uniting-people-and-communities/#5fb2f4c9444b, accessed July 2016.
17. See C. Myers, "Why Bullies Make Bad Leaders," *Forbes,* April 2, 2016, http://www.forbes.com/sites/chrismyers/2016/04/01/why-bullies-make-bad-leaders/2/#4184b2d03b49, accessed July 2016.
18. See L. Reston, "Jeb Bush's Leadership Style: Tough, Methodical, Sometimes Rigid," June 16, 2015, http://www.forbes.com/sites/laurareston/2015/06/16/jeb-bushs-leadership-style-tough-methodical-sometimes-rigid/#1245ed8ebf8a, accessed July 2016.
19. B. M. Bass and R. Bass, *The Bass Handbook of Leadership: Theory, Research, and Managerial Applications,* 4th ed. (New York: Free Press, 2008), 654.
20. See R. Cross, N. Nohria, and A. Parker, "Six Myths about Informal Networks—and How to Overcome Them," *MIT Sloan Management Review,* Spring 2002, pp. 67–75; and C. Shriky, "Watching the Patterns Emerge," *Harvard Business Review,* February 2004, pp. 34–35.
21. D. Krackhardt and J. R. Hanson, "Informal Networks: The Company behind the Chart," *Harvard Business Review,* July-August 1993, p. 104. See also R. Cross and L. Prusack, "The People Who Make Organizations Go—or Stop," *Harvard Business Review,* June 3003, pp. 104–112; and R. McDermott and D. Archibald, "Harnessing Your Staff's Informal Networks," *Harvard Business Review,* March 2010, pp. 82–89.
22. A. Lashinsky, "The Decade of Steve," *Fortune,* November 5, 2009, http://tech.fortune.cnn.com/2009/11/05/the-decade-of-steve (accessed August 14, 2014).
23. R. M. Stogdill, *Handbook of Leadership* (New York: Free Press, 1974). See also B. M. Bass and R. Bass, *The Bass Handbook of Leadership: Theory, Research, and Managerial Applications,* 4th ed. (New York: Free Press, 2008). An udpate on the role of intelligence can be found in M. Daly, M. Egan, and F. O'Reilly, "Childhood General Cognitive Ability Predicts Leadership Role Occupancy across Life: Evidence from 17,000 Cohort Study Participants," *The Leadership Quarterly,* 2015, pp. 323–341.
24. B. M. Bass and R. Bass, *The Bass Handbook of Leadership: Theory, Research, and Managerial Applications,* 4th ed. (New York: Free Press, 2008).
25. But see D. S. DeRue, J. D. Nahrgang, N. Wellman, and S. E. Humphrey, "Trait and Behavioral Theories of Leadership: An Integration and Meta-Analytic Test of Their Relative Validity," *Personnel Psychology,* Vol. 64 (2011), pp. 7–52.
26. These results are based on D. S. DeRue, J. D. Nahrgang, N. Wellman, S. E. Humphrey, "Trait and Behavioral Theories of Leadership: An Integration and Meta-Analytic Test of Their Relative Validity," *Personnel Psychology,* Vol. 64 (2011), pp. 7–52; D. L. Joseph, L Y. Dhanani, W. Shen, B. C. McHugh, and M. A. McCord, "Is a Happy Leader a Good Leader? A Meta-Analytic Investigation of Leader Trait Affect and Leadership," *The Leadership Quarterly,* 2015, pp. 558–577; and E. H. O'Boyle Jr., D. F. Forsyth, G. C. Banks, and M. A. McDaniel, "A Meta-Analysis of the Dark Triad and Work Behavior: A Social Exchange Perspective," *Journal of Applied Psychology,* May 2012, 557–579.
27. See S. M. Spain, P. Harms, and J. M. Lebreton, "The Dark Side of Personality at Work," *Journal of Organizational Behavior,* February 2014, pp. S41–S60.
28. B. M. Galvin, D. A. Waldman, and P. Balthazard, "Visionary Communication Qualities as Mediators of the Relationship between Narcissism and Attributions of Leader Charisma," *Personnel Psychology,* Autumn 2010, p. 510.
29. Ibid., pp. 509–537; and O'Boyle et al., "A Meta-Analysis of the Dark Triad and Work Behavior," *Journal of Applied Psychology,* Vol 97(3), May 2012, 557–579.
30. See J. Hogan, R. Hogan, and R. B. Kaiser, "Management Derailment," in S. Zedeck, ed., *APA Handbook of Industrial and Organizational Psychology* (Washington, DC: American Psychological Association, 2011), pp. 555–575. Also see M F. R. Kets de Vries, "Coaching the Toxic Leader," *Harvard Business Review,* April 2014, pp. 101–109.
31. See "Blakes Bio," http://www.toms.com/blakes-bio, accessed July 2016.
32. See "The World's 19 Most Disappointing Leaders," *Fortune,* March 30, 2016, http://fortune.com/2016/03/30/most-disappointing-leaders/, accessed July 2016.
33. Gender and the emergence of leaders was examined by A. H. Eagly and S. J. Karau, "Gender and the Emergence of Leaders: A Meta-Analysis," *Journal of Personality and Social Psychology,* May 1991, 685–710; and R. Ayman and K. Korabik, "Leadership: Why Gender and Culture Matter," *American Psychologist,* April 2010, 157–170.
34. See A. H. Eagly, S. J. Karau, and B. T. Johnson, "Gender and Leadership Style among School Principals: A Meta-Analysis," *Educational Administration Quarterly,* February 1992, 76–102.
35. See D. W. Parker, M. Holesgrove, and R. Pathak, "Improving Productivity with Self-Organized Teams and Agile Leadership," *International Journal of Productivity and Performance Management,* 2015, 112–128; and C. Post, "When Is Female Leadership an Advantage? Coordination Requirements, Team Cohesion, and Team Interaction Norms," *Journal of Organizational Behavior,* 2015, pp. 1153–1175.
36. See S. C. Paustian-Underdahl, L. S. Walker, and D. J. Woehr, "Gender and Perceptions of Leadership Effectiveness: A Meta-Analysis of Contextual Moderators," *Journal of Applied Psychology,* November 2014, pp. 1129–1145.
37. See S. Reva, "5 Leadership Lessons from Canadian Prime Minister Justin Trudeau," *Fast Company,* June 29, 2016, http://www.fastcompany.com/3061046/lessons-learned/5-leadership-lessons-from-canadian-prime-minister-justin-trudeau accessed July 2016.
38. See K. Vick, "Person of the Year 2015: Chancellor of the Free World," *Time,* http://time.com/time-person-of-the-year-2015-angela-merkel/, accessed July 2016.
39. See R. Reiss, "Leaders Share How the Cognitive Era Is Transforming Business," *Forbes,* January 6, 2016, http://www.forbes.com/sites/robertreiss/2016/01/06/leaders-share-how-the-cognitive-era-is-transforming-business/#701183b125f7, accessed July 2016.
40. See A. Colberg, "Fortune 500 CEO: The One Quality Every Leader Must Have," *Fortune,* May 9, 2016 http://fortune.com/2016/05/09/fortune-500-assurant-ceo-success-quality/, accessed July 2016.
41. See L. Shaw, "Top Three Leadership Skills Often Overlooked," *Forbes,* November 7, 2015, http://www.forbes.com/sites/lyndashaw/2015/11/07/top-three-leadership-skills-often-overlooked/#177653f6775f, accessed July 2016.
42. See S. Krupp, "Growing Your Business: Strategic Leadership Skills for the Long Game," April 23, 2015, https://www.entrepreneur.com/article/245354, accessed July 2016.
43. See A. and J. Bornstein, March 22, 2016, "22 Qualities That Make a Great Leader," https://www.entrepreneur.com/article/270486, accessed July 2016.
44. M. Buck and M. Martin, "Leaders Teaching Leaders," *HR Magazine,* September 2012, 60–62.
45. See R. Wartzman, "Admire Elon Musk All You Want, but Please Don't Manage Like Him," *Fortune,* January 21, 2015, http://fortune.com/2015/01/21/elon-musk-micro-management-control/?iid=sr-link4, accessed July 2016.
46. See J. Alsever, "Is Software Better at Managing People Than You Are?" *Fortune,* March 21, 2016, http://fortune.com/2016/03/21/software-algorithms-hiring/?iid=sr-link9, accessed July 2016.
47. M. Javidan, A. Bullough, and R. Dibble, "Mind the Gap: Gender Differences in Global Leadership Self-Efficacies," *Academy of Management Perspectives,* February 2016, 59–73.
48. See H. Friend, "Leading a multicultural team is about respect and understanding," *The Guardian,* April 3, 2014, https://www.theguardian.com/careers/careers-blog/management-leadership-cultural-differences, accessed October 17, 2016.
49. See: Ten Tips for Leading a Multicultural Team, *Internations,* https://www.internations.org/magazine/ten-tips-for-leading-a-multicultural-team-17056, accessed July 2016.
50. G. Yukl, "Effective Leadership Behavior: What We Know and What Questions Need More Attention," *Academy of Management Perspectives,* November 2012, p. 69.
51. DeRue et al., "Trait and Behavioral Theories of Leadership," *Personnel Psychology,* Vol. 64 (2011), pp. 7–52.
52. See The Bill and Melinda Gates Foundation, "Who We Are," http://www.gatesfoundation.org/Who-We-Are, accessed July 2016.
53. A definition and description of transactional leadership is provided by Bass and Bass, *The Bass Handbook of Leadership,* pp. 618–648. See also D. S. DeRue, J. D. Nahrgang, N. Wellman, S. E. Humphrey, "Trait and Behavioral Theories of Leadership: An Integration and Meta-Analytic Test of Their Relative Validity," *Personnel Psychology,* Vol. 64 (2011), pp. 7–52.
54. S. Perman, "For Some Paying Sales Commissions No Longer Makes Sense," The New York Times, November 21, 2013, p. B4.
55. T. A. Judge, R. F. Piccolo, and R. Ilies, "The Forgotten Ones? The Validity of Consideration and Initiating Structure in Leadership Research," *Journal of Applied Psychology,* February 2004, pp. 36–51.
56. DeRue et al., "Trait and Behavioral Theories of Leadership," *Personnel Psychology,* Vol. 64 (2011), pp. 7–52,
57. G. Yukl, "Effective Leadership Behavior: What We Know and What Questions Need More Attention," *Academy of Management Perspectives,* November 2012, pp. 66–85.
58. T. A. Judge, R. F Piccolo, and R. Ilies, "The Forgotten Ones? The Validity of Consideration and Initiating Structure in Leadership Research," *Journal of Applied Psychology,* February 2004, pp. 36–51.
59. See C. K Lam, X. Huang, and S. C. H. Chan, "The Threshold Effect of Participative Leadership and the Role of Leader Information Sharing," *Academy of Management Journal,* 2015, pp. 836–855; Y. Dong, H. Liao, A. Chuang, J. Zhou, and E. M. Campbell, "Fostering Employee Service Creativity: Joint Effects of Customer Empowering Behaviors and Supervisory Empowering Leadership," *Journal of Applied Psychology,* September 2015, pp. 1364–1380; and M. T. Maynard, L. L. Gilson, and J. E. Mathieu, "Empowerment—Fad or Fab? A Multilevel Review of the Past Two Decades of Research," *Journal of Management,* July 2012, pp. 1231–1281.
60. M. Moskowitz and R. Levering, "The 100 Best Companies to Work For," *Fortune,* February 4, 2013, p. 88.
61. M. Littman, "Best Bosses Tell All," Working Woman, October 2000, p. 55.
62. See T. Biemann, E. Kearney, and K. Margraf, "Empowering Leadership and Managers' Career Perceptions: Examining Effects at Both the Individual and the Team Level," *The Leadership Quarterly,* 2015, pp. 775–789.
63. T. W. H. Ng and D. C. Feldman, "Ethical Leadership: Meta-Analytic Evidence of Criterion-Related and Incremental Validity," *Journal of Applied Psychology,* May 2015, 948–965.
64. See W. Zhu, H. He, L. K. Trevino, M. M. Chao, and W. Wang, "Ethical Leadership and Follower Voice and Performance: The Role of Follower Identifications and Entity Morality Beliefs," *The Leadership Quarterly,* 2015, pp. 702–718.
65. See T. W. H. Ng and D. C. Feldman, "Ethical Leadership: Meta-Analtyic Evidence of Criterion-Related and Incremental Validity," *Journal of Applied Psychology,* May 2015, pp. 948–965.
66. See K. Daum, "How This Founder of a $150 Million Company Empowers His Employees," *Inc.,* October 2, 2015, http://www.inc.com/kevin-daum/7-ways-of-empowering-employees-that-earned-builddirect-over-50-million-in-fundin.html, accessed July 2016.
67. An overall summary of servant leadership is provided by L. C. Spears, *Reflections on Leadership: How Robert K. Greenleaf's Theory of Servant-Leadership Influenced Today's Top Management Thinkers* (New York: Wiley, 1995). See also D. Van Dierendonck, "Servant Management: A Review and Synthesis," *Journal of Management,* Vol. 37 (2011), pp. 1228–1261.
68. See V. Giang, "The Pros and Cons of New Unconventional Leadership Styles," *Fast Company,* June 3, 2016, http://www.fastcompany.com/3060371/how-to-be-a-success-at-everything/the-pros-and-cons-of-new-unconventional-leadership-styles, accessed July 2016.
69. See J. McGregor, "Howard Schultz Wants You to Try Some Civility with Your Coffee, *The Washington Post,* March 23, 2016, https://www.washingtonpost.com/news/

on-leadership/wp/2016/03/23/howard-schultz-wants-you-to-try-some-civility-with-your-coffee/, accessed July 2016.

70. See *Forbes*, Howard Shultz's Net Worth as of October 17, 2016, http://www.forbes.com/profile/howard-schultz/, accessed July 2016; T. Loudenback, *Business Insider,* October 21, 2015, "The incredible rags-to-riches story of Starbucks billionaire Howard Schultz," http://www.businessinsider.com/howard-schultz-profile-2015-10, accessed July 2016.

71. See Z. Chen, J. Zhu, and M. Zhou, "How Does a Servant Leader Fuel the Service Firm? A Multilevel Model of Servant Leadership, Individual Self Identity, Group Competition Climate, and Customer Service Performance," *Journal of Applied Psychology,* March 2015, pp. 511–521; and S. J. Peterson, B. M. Galvin, and D. Lange, "CEO Servant Leadership: Exploring Executive Characteristics and Firm Performance," *Personnel Psychology,* August 2, 2012, pp. 565–596.

72. B. M. Bass, "From Transactional to Transformational Leadership: Learning to Share the Vision," *Organizational Dynamics,* Vol. 18 (1990), pp. 19–31.

73. Results can be found in A. H. Eagly, M. C. Johannesen-Schmidt, and M. L. van Engen, "Transformational, Transactional, and Laissez-Faire Leadership Styles: A Meta-Analysis Comparing Women and Men," *Psychological Bulletin,* June 2003, pp. 569–591.

74. See DeRue et al., "Trait and Behavioral Theories of Leadership."

75. F. E. Fiedler, "Assumed Similarity Measures as Predictors of Team Effectiveness," *Journal of Abnormal and Social Psychology,* Vol. 49 (1954), pp. 381–388; F. E. Fiedler, *Leader Attitudes and Group Effectiveness* (Urbana, IL: University of Illinois Press, 1958); and F. E. Fiedler, *A Theory of Leadership Effectiveness* (New York: McGraw-Hill, 1967).

76. See M. V. Vugt, R. Hogan, and R. B. Kaiser, "Leadership, Followership, and Evolution," *American Psychologist*, April 2008, pp. 182–196.

77. R. J. House, "A Path-Goal Theory of Leader Effectiveness," *Administrative Science Quarterly,* September 1971, pp. 321–338.

78. See P. M. Podsakoff, S. B. MacKenzie, M. Ahearne, and W. H. Bommer, "Searching for a Needle in a Haystack: Trying to Identify the Illusive Moderators of Leadership Behaviors," *Journal of Management,* 1995, 422–470; and S. H. Malik, "Leadership Behavior and Acceptance of Leaders by Subordinates: Application of Path Goal Theory in Telecom Sector," *International Journal of Trade, Economics and Finance,* April 2014, 170–175.

79. See G. Wang, I-S. Oh, S. H. Courtright, and A. E. Colbert, "Transformational Leadership and Performance Across Criteria and Levels: A Meta-Analytic Review of 25 Years of Research," *Group & Organization Management,* Vol. 36, No. 2 (2011), pp. 223–270.

80. Results can be found in P. M. Podsakoff, S. B. MacKenzie, M. Ahearne, and W. H. Bommer, "Searching for a Needle in a Haystack: Trying to Identify the Illusive Moderators of Leadership Behaviors," *Journal of Management,* Vol. 21, No. 3 (1995), pp. 423–470.

81. The steps were developed by H. P. Sims Jr., S. Faraj, and S. Yun, "When Should a Leader Be Directive or Empowering? How to Develop Your Own Situational Theory of Leadership," *Business Horizons,* March–April 2009, 149–158.

82. For a complete description of the full-range leadership theory, see B. J. Bass and B. J. Avolio, *Revised Manual for the Multi-Factor Leadership Questionnaire* (Palo Alto, CA: Mindgarden, 1997).

83. See Wang et al., "Transformational Leadership and Performance Across Criteria and Levels." *Organizational Management,* Volume 36, No. 2 (April 2011), pp. 223–270.

84. U. R. Dundum, K. B. Lowe, and B. J. Avolio, "A Meta-Analysis of Transformational and Transactional Leadership Correlates of Effectiveness and Satisfaction: An Update and Extension," in B. J. Avolio and F. J. Yammarino, eds., *Transformational and Charismatic Leadership: The Road Ahead* (New York: JAI Press, 2002), p. 38.

85. Supportive results can be found in T. A. Judge and J. E. Bono, "Five-Factor Model of Personality and Transformational Leadership," *Journal of Applied Psychology,* October 2000, pp. 751–765; and S. Oreg and Y. Berson, "Leadership and Employees' Reactions to Change: The Role of Leaders' Personal Attributes and Transformational Leadership," *Personnel Psychology,* Vol. 64 (2011), pp. 627–659.

86. Supportive research is summarized by Antonakis and House, "The Full-Range Leadership Theory: The Way Forward." See also W. Zhu, R. E. Riggio, B. J. Avolio, and J. J. Sosik, "The Effect of Leadership on Follower Moral Identity: Does Transformational/Transactional Style Make a Difference?" *Journal of Leadership & Organizational Studies,* Vol. 18 (2011), pp. 150–163.

87. These definitions are derived from R. Kark, B. Shamir, and C. Chen, "The Two Faces of Transformational Leadership: Empowerment and Dependency," *Journal of Applied Psychology,* April 2003, pp. 246–255. See A. E. Colbert, A. L. Kristof-Brown, B. H. Bradley, and M. R. Barrick, "CEO Transformational Leadership: The Role of Goal Importance Congruence in Top Management Teams," *Academy of Management Journal,* February 2008, pp. 81–96.

88. A historical review of transformational leadership is provided by D. V. Knippenberg and S. B. Sitkin, "A Critical Assessment of Charismatic–Transformational Leadership Research: Back to the Drawing Board?" *The Academy of Management Annals,* 2013, 1–60.

89. B. Nanus, *Visionary Leadership* (San Francisco: Jossey-Bass, 1992), p. 8.

90. See Y. Berson, N. Halevy, B. Shamir, and M. Erez, "Leading from Different Psychological Distances: A Construal-Level Perspective on Vision Communication, Goal Setting, and Follower Motivation," *The Leadership Quarterly,* 2015, pp. 143–155.

91. See D. Hoffeld, "7 Scientifically Proven Habits of Charismatic Leaders," *Fast Company,* February 3, 2016, http://www.fastcompany.com/3056232/how-to-be-a-success-at-everything/7-scientifically-proven-habits-of-charismatic-leaders, accessed July 2016.

92. See H. Innam, "Lead Like the Pope: Six Lessons on Transformational Leadership," *Forbes,* October 1, 2015 http://www.forbes.com/sites/hennainam/2015/10/01/lead-like-the-pope-6-lessons-on-transformational-leadership/#2794ce3d5fd2, accessed July 2016.

93. See J. Stillman, "The Incredibly Boring Trait That All Great Leaders Need," *Inc,* July 18, 2014 http://www.inc.com/jessica-stillman/the-incredibly-boring-trait-that-all-great-leaders-need.html, accessed July 2016.

94. B. Kowitt, *Fortune,* August 20, 2015, "John Mackey, The Conscious Capitalist," http://fortune.com/2015/08/20/whole-foods-john-mackey/, accessed July 2016.

95. *Forbes 100,* "The World's Most Powerful Women," 2016 ranking, http://www.forbes.com/profile/indra-nooyi/, accessed July 2016.

96. See R. Feloni, "Pepsi CEO Indra Nooyi Explains How an Unusual Daily Ritual Her Mom Made Her Practice as a Child Changed Her Life," *Business Insider,* September 9, 2015, http://www.businessinsider.com/pepsico-indra-nooyi-life-changing-habit-2015-9, accessed July 2016.

97. H. Schultz, "Indra Nooyi," *Time,* April 30, 2008, www.time.com/time/specials/2007/article/0,28804,1733748_1733758,00.html (accessed August 17, 2014). See also D. Brady, "Keeping Cool in Hot Water," *BusinessWeek*, June 11, 2007, p. 49.

98. See L. Gensler, "Pepsi's Quarterly Profit Rises 31% Despite Challenges Abroad," *Forbes,* February 11, 2016, http://www.forbes.com/sites/laurengensler/2016/02/11/pepsi-fourth-quarter-earnings/#10f2c3606e23, accessed July 2016.

99. See H. Lui, and A. Chuang, "Transforming Service Employees and Climate: A Multilevel, Multisource Examination of Transformational Leadership in Building Long-Term Service Relationships," *Journal of Applied Psychology,* July 2007, pp. 1006–1019.

100. Results can be found in U. R. Dundum, K. B. Lowe, and B. J. Avolio, "A Meta-Analysis of Transformational and Transactional Leadership Correlates of Effectiveness and Satisfaction: An Update and Extension," in B. J. Avolio and F. J. Yammarino, eds., *Transformational and Charismatic Leadership: The Road Ahead* (New York: JAI Press, 2002), pp. 39–70; and A. Erez, V. F. Misangyi, D. E. Johnson, M. A. LePine, and K. C. Halverson, "Stirring the Hearts of Followers: Charismatic Leadership as the Transferal of Affect," *Journal of Applied Psychology,* May 2008, pp. 602–615.

101. See R. Kark, B. Shamir, and C. Chen, "The Two Faces of Transformational Leadership: Empowerment and Dependency," *Journal of Applied Psychology,* April 2003, pp. 246–255.

102. D. N. Den Hartog and F. D. Belschak, "When Does Transformational Leadership Enhance Employee Proactive Behavior? The Role of Autonomy and Role Breadth Self-Efficacy," *Journal of Applied Psychology,* January 2012, pp. 194–202.

103. Supportive results can be found in B. M. Bass, B. J. Avolio, D. I. Jung, and Y. Berson, "Predicting Unit Performance by Assessing Transformational and Transactional Leadership," *Journal of Applied Psychology,* April 2003, pp. 207–218; and D. N. Den Hartog and F. D. Belschak, "When Does Transformational Leadership Enhance Employee Proactive Behavior? The Role of Autonomy and Role Breadth Self-Efficacy," *Journal of Applied Psychology,* January 2012, pp. 194–202.

104. D. A. Waldman, M. Z. Carter, and P. W. Hom, "A Multilevel Investigation of Leadership and Turnover Behavior," *Journal of Management,* September 2015, pp. 1724–1744.

105. B. J. Avolio, R. J. Reichard, S. T. Hannah, F. O Walumbwa, and A. Chan, "A Meta-Analytic Review of Leadership Impact Research: Experimental and Quasi-Experimental Studies," *Leadership Quarterly,* Vol. 20 (2009), pp. 764–784; J. Kanengieter and A. Rajagopal-Durbin, "Wilderness Leadership—On the Job," *Harvard Business Review,* April 2012, pp. 127–131.

106. G. Graen and J. F. Cashman, "A Role-Making Model of Leadership in Formal Organizations: A Developmental Approach," in J. G. Hunt and L. L. Larson, eds., *Leadership Frontiers* (Kent, OH: Kent State University Press, 1975), pp. 143–165; F. Dansereau Jr., G. Graen, and W. J. Haga, "A Vertical Dyad Linkage Approach to Leadership within Formal Organizations: A Longitudinal Investigation of the Role-Making Process," *Organizational Behavior and Human Performance,* February 1975, pp. 46–78; and K. S. Wilson, H.-P. Sin, and D. E. Conlon, "What About the Leader in Leader–Member Exchange? The Impact of Resource Exchanges and Substitutability in the Leader," *Academy of Management Review,* July 2010, pp. 358–372.

107. See D. Duchon, S. G. Green, and T. D. Taber, "Vertical Dyad Linkage: A Longitudinal Assessment of Antecedents, Measures, and Consequences," *Journal of Applied Psychology,* February 1986, pp. 56–60.

108. See R. Martin, Y. Guillaume, G. Thomas, A. Lee, and O. Epitropaki, "Leader-Member Exchange (LMX) and Performance: A Meta-Analytic Review," *Personnel Psychology,* 2016, 67–121; and J. H. Dulebohn, W. H. Bommer, R. C. Liden, R. L. Brouer, and G. R. Ferris, "A Meta-Analysis of Antecedents and Consequences of Leader-Member Exchange: Integrating the Past with an Eye toward the Future," *Journal of Management,* November 2012, 1715–1759.

109. See X-A. Zhang, N. Li, J. Ullrich, and R. V. Dick, "Getting Everyone on Board: The Effect of Differentiated Leadership by CEOs on Top Management Team Effectiveness and Leader-Rated Firm Performance," *Journal of Management,* November 2015, pp. 1898–1933; and A. N. Li and H. Liao, "How Do Leader-Member Exchange Quality and Differentiation Affect Performance in Teams: An Integrated Multilevel Dual Process Model," *Journal of Applied Psychology,* September 2014, pp. 847–866.

110. Cooperative conflict is discussed in D. Tjosvold, *Learning to Manage Conflict: Getting People to Work Together Productively* (New York: Lexington, 1993); and D. Tjosvold and D. W. Johnson, *Productive Conflict Management Perspectives for Organizations* (New York: Irvington, 1983). See also A. C. Amason, K. R. Thompson, W. A. Hochwarter, and A. W. Harrison, "Conflict: An Important Dimension in Successful Management Teams," *Organizational Dynamics,* Autumn 1995, pp. 20–35; and A. C. Amason, "Distinguishing the Effects of Functional and Dysfunctional Conflict on Strategic Decision Making: Resolving a Paradox for Top Management Teams," *Academy of Management Journal,* February 1996, pp. 123–148.

111. A. Y. Ou, A. S. Tsui, A. J. Kinicki, D. A. Waldman, Z. Xiao, and L. J. Song, "Humble Chief Executive Officers' Connections to Top Management Team Integration and Middle Managers' Responses," *Administrative Science Quarterly,* March 2014, 34–72.

112. See L. Merrill, "Study: Humble Bosses Are Best," *The Arizona Republic,* July 30, 2014, A14, A18; and A. Y. Ou, A. S. Tsui, A. J. Kinicki, D. A. Waldman, Z. Xiao, and L. J. Song, "Humble Chief Executive Officers' Connections to Top Management Team Integration and Middle Managers' Responses," *Administrative Science Quarterly,* 2014, 34–72.

113. J. Prime and E. Salib, "The Best Leaders Are Humble Leaders," *Harvard Business Review*, May 12, 2014, https://hbr.org/2014/05/the-best-leaders-are-humble-leaders, accessed April 25, 2016.

114. See J. Prime and E. Salib, "The Best Leaders Are Humble Leaders," *Harvard Business Review*, May 12, 2014, https://hbr.org/2014/05/the-best-leaders-are-humble-leaders, accessed April 25, 2016.

115. See A. Y. Ou, A. S. Tsui, A. J. Kinicki, D. A. Waldman, Z. Xiao, and L. J. Song, "Humble Chief Executive Officers' Connections to Top Management Team Integration and Middle Managers' Responses," *Administrative Science Quarterly*, 2014, 34–72.

116. Authentic leadership is discussed by H. Leroy, F. Anseel, W. L. Gardner, and L. Sels, "Authentic Leadership, Authentic Followership, Basic Need Satisfaction, and Work Role Performance: A Cross-Level Study," *Journal of Management*, September 2015, pp. 1677–1697.

117. J. Zenger and J. Folkman, "We Like Leaders Who Underrate Themselves," *Harvard Business Review*, November 2015, https://hbr.org/2015/11/we-like-leaders-who-underrate-themselves, accessed April 25, 2016.

118. R. Levering, "The 100 Best Companies to Work for 2016," *Fortune*, March 15, 2016, 160.

119. The role of followers is discussed by D. S. DeRue and S. J. Ashford, "Who Will Lead and Who Will Follow? A Social Process of Leadership Identity Construction in Organizations," *Academy of Management Review*, October 2010, pp. 627–647.

120. See R. Goffee and G. Jones, "Followership: It's Personal, Too," *Harvard Business Review*, December 2001, p. 148.

121. See B. M. Bass and R. Bass, *The Bass Handbook of Leadership: Theory, Research, and Managerial Applications*, 4th ed. (New York: Free Press), 2008.

122. See L. Bossidy, "What Your Leader Expects of You and What You Should Expect in Return," *Harvard Business Review*, April 2007, pp. 58–65.

123. See G. Moran, "5 Ways Being a Good Follower Makes You a Better Leader," *Fast Company*, April 30, 2014, http://www.fastcompany.com/3029840/bottom-line/5-ways-being-a-good-follower-makes-you-a-better-leader, accessed July 2016; L. Mcleod, "7 Ways to Become Your Boss' Dream Employee," https://www.themuse.com/advice/7-ways-to-become-your-boss-dream-employee, accessed July 2016.

124. Alisa Priddle, "Mary Barra Assumes Combined Chairman and CEO Role at GM," *Detroit Free Press*, January 4, 2016, http://www.freep.com/story/money/cars/general-motors/2016/01/04/mary-barra-gm-chairman-ceo/78267000/.

125. General Motors Co GM," *Morningstar*, http://financials.morningstar.com/ratios/r.html?t=GM, accessed July 6, 2016.

126. B. Rosen, "Leadership Journeys—Mary Barra," May 31, 2016, http://www.iedp.com/articles/leadership-journeys-mary-barra.

127. D. J. Chew, "What Volkswagen's Next CEO Can Learn from GM's Mary Barra," September 23, 2015, http://fortune.com/2015/09/23/volkswagen-ceo-mary-barra-GM.

128. G. Gardner, "Barra Named Crisis Manager of the Year By Fortune," December 29, 2014, http://www.freep.com/story/money/cars/general-motors/2014/12/29/barra-crisis-manager-fortune/21007491.

129. G. Colvin, "How CEO Mary Barra Is Using the Ignition-Switch Scandal to Change GM's Culture," Fortune.com, September 18, 2015, http://fortune.com/2015/09/18/mary-barra-gm-culture.

130. G. Colvin, "How CEO Mary Barra Is Using the Ignition-Switch Scandal to Change GM's Culture," Fortune.com, September 18, 2015, http://fortune.com/2015/09/18/mary-barra-gm-culture.

131. J. Chew, "What Volkswagen's Next CEO Can Learn from GM's Mary Barra," September 23, 2015, http://fortune.com/2015/09/23/volkswagen-ceo-mary-barra-GM.

132. J. Chew, "What Volkswagen's Next CEO Can Learn from GM's Mary Barra," September 23, 2015, http://fortune.com/2015/09/23/volkswagen-ceo-mary-barra-GM.

133. M. Burden, "GM CEO: Behavior Change Will Improve Company," *The Detroit News*, October 8, 2014, http://www.detroitnews.com/story/business/autos/general-motors/2014/10/08/gm-ceo-behavior-change-improve-company/16926111.

134. K. J. Jusko, "CEO Mary Barra Is Driving Culture Change at General Motors," *Industry Week*, November 14, 2014, http://www.industryweek.com/quality/ceo-mary-barra-driving-culture-change-general-motors.

135. S. Engelmeier, "Did Mary Barra's Inclusive Leadership Style Propel Her to the Top?" *Industry Week*, January 22, 2014, http://www.industryweek.com/companies-amp-executives/did-mary-barra-s-inclusive-leadership-style-propel-her-to-top.

136. S. Engelmeier, "Did Mary Barra's Inclusive Leadership Style Propel Her to the Top?" *Industry Week*, January 22, 2014, http://www.industryweek.com/companies-amp-executives/did-mary-barra-s-inclusive-leadership-style-propel-her-to-top.

137. S. Snyder, "Five Leadership Lessons from General Motors CEO, Mary Barra," January 15, 2014, http://snyderleadership.com/2014/01/15/five-leadership-lessons-from-general-motors-ceo-mary-barra.

138. R. Feloni, "Why GM CEO Mary Barra Will End an Important Meeting to Go to Her Daughter's Soccer Game," *Business Insider*, April 1, 2015, http://www.businessinsider.com/gm-ceo-mary-barra-on-work-life-balance-2015-4.

139. P. M. Burden, "GM CEO: Behavior Change Will Improve Company," *The Detroit News*, October 8, 2014, http://www.detroitnews.com/story/business/autos/general-motors/2014/10/08/gm-ceo-behavior-change-improve-company/16926111/.

140. R. Ruiz, "4 Cancer Charities Are Accused of Fraud," *The New York Times*, May 19, 2015, http://www.nytimes.com/2015/05/20/business/4-cancer-charities-accused-in-ftc-fraud-case.html?_r=0.

141. K. B. Grant, "Cancer Charities Scammed Millions from Donors, Feds Say," May 19, 2015, http://www.nbcnews.com/business/business-news/cancer-charities-scammed-millions-consumers-feds-say-n361341.

142. R. Ruiz, "4 Cancer Charities Are Accused of Fraud," *The New York Times*, May 19, 2015, http://www.nytimes.com/2015/05/20/business/4-cancer-charities-accused-in-ftc-fraud-case.html?_r=0.

143. K. B. Grant, "Cancer Charities Scammed Millions from Donors, Feds Say," May 19, 2015, http://www.nbcnews.com/business/business-news/cancer-charities-scammed-millions-consumers-feds-say-n361341.

144. K. B. Grant, "Cancer Charities Scammed Millions from Donors, Feds Say," May 19, 2015, http://www.nbcnews.com/business/business-news/cancer-charities-scammed-millions-consumers-feds-say-n361341.

CHAPTER 15

1. Adapted from M. Civiello, "Communication Counts in Landing a Job," *Training & Development*, February 2009, 82–83; M. Hogan, "4 Tips for Better Interpersonal Communication During Interviews," February 6, 2015, https://www.recruiter.com/i/4-steps-for-better-interpersonal-communication-during-interviews/, accessed July 2016.

2. See Hart Research Associates, "Falling Short? College Learning and Career Success," Association of American Colleges and Universities, January 20, 2015, http://www.aacu.org/sites/default/files/files/LEAP/2015employerstudentsurvey.pdf.

3. See R. S. Wyer, Jr., and L. J. Shrum, "The Role of Comprehension Processes in Communication and Persuasion," *Media Psychology*, April 2015, 163–195.

4. J. Kotter, "Power, Dependence, and Effective Management," *Harvard Business Review*, Vol. 55 (1977), pp. 125–136.

5. T. Musbach, "The Most Annoying, Overused Words in the Workplace," *San Francisco Chronicle*, October 11, 2009, p. A1.

6. R. Bogosian "Volkswagen's New CEO Must Tackle This Other Problem," *Fortune*, September 26, 2015, http://fortune.com/2015/09/26/volkswagen-scandal-matthias-mueller/?iid=sr-link8, accessed July 2016; G. Gates, J. Ewing, K. Russell, D. Watkins, "Explaining Volkswagen's Emissions Scandal," *New York Times*, September 12, 2016, http://www.nytimes.com/interactive/2015/business/international/vw-diesel-emissions-scandal-explained.html?_r=1, accessed July 2016; J. Ewing, "VW Says Old Memo Told Winterkorn of Emissions Irregularities," *New York Times*, March 2, 2016, http://www.nytimes.com/2016/03/03/business/vw-says-old-memo-told-winterkorn-of-emissions-irregularities.html, accessed July 2016.

7. See J. Carreyrou, "Under Fire, Theranos CEO Stifled Bad News," *Wall Street Journal*, July 10, 2016, http://www.wsj.com/articles/under-fire-theranos-ceo-stifled-bad-news-1468195377, accessed July 2016; and R Winkler, "Tech Investors Look for Lessons in Theranos," *The Wall Street Journal*, July 14, 2016, pp. B1, B4.

8. J. Demers, "Communication in 2015: Text, Voice, Video or In-Person?," *Inc*, January 29, 2015, http://www.inc.com/jayson-demers/communication-in-2015-text-voice-video-or-in-person.html, accessed July 2016; P. Simon, "When Email and Texting Are Insufficient: An Interview with the Phone Lady," *The Huffington Post*, August 24, 2015, http://www.huffingtonpost.com/phil-simon/when-email-and-texting-is_b_8034216.html, accessed July 2016.

9. See V. Peltokorpi, "Corporate Language Proficiency and Reverse Knowledge Transfer in Multinational Corporations: Interactive Effects of Communication Media Richness and Commitment to Headquaters," *Journal of International Management*, 2015, pp. 49–62.

10. R. L. Daft and R. H. Lengel, "Information Richness: A New Approach to Managerial Behavior and Organizational Design," in B. M. Staw and L. L. Cummings, eds., *Research in Organizational Behavior* (Greenwich, CT: JAI Press, 1984), p. 196; and R. H. Lengel and R. L. Daft, "The Selection of Communication Media as an Executive Skill," *Academy of Management Executive*, August 1988, pp. 225–232.

11. D. R. Dunaetz, T. C. Lisk, and M. M. Shin, "Personality, Gender, and Age As Predictors of Media Richness Preference," *Advantages in Multimedia*, 2015, pp. 1–9.

12. See B. Barry and I. S. Fulmer, "The Medium and the Message: The Adaptive Use of Communication Media in Dyadic Influence," *Academy of Management Review*, April 2004, pp. 272–292; and A. F. Simon, "Computer-Mediated Communication: Task Performance and Satisfaction," *The Journal of Social Psychology*, June 2006, pp. 349–379.

13. For discussion of uses of social media, see A. M. Kaplan and M. Haenlein, "Users of the World, Unite! The Challenges and Opportunities of Social Media," *Business Horizons*, January–February 2010, pp. 59–68; G. A. Fowler, "Are You Talking to Me?" *The Wall Street Journal*, April 25, 2011, p. R5; T. L. Griffith, "Tapping into Social Media Smarts," *The Wall Street Journal*, April 25, 2011, p. R6; and A. Samuel, "Better Leadership through Social Media," *The Wall Street Journal*, April 2, 2012, p. R4.

14. K. Kuhn, T. Galloway, and M. Collins-Williams, "Near, Far, and Online: Small Business Owners' Advice-Seeking from Peers," *Journal of Small Business and Enterprise Development*, 2016, pp. 189–206.

15. C. K. Goman, "What Leaders Don't Know about the Rumor Mill," *Forbes*, November 30, 2013, http://www.forbes.com/sites/carolkinseygoman/2013/11/30/what-leaders-dont-know-about-the-rumor-mill/#3dea041b3165, accessed July 2016; L. Ryan, "The Truth about the Company Grapevine," *Forbes*, December 30, 2014, http://www.forbes.com/sites/lizryan/2014/12/30/the-truth-about-the-company-grapevine/#5339d0f42632, accessed July 2016.

16. C. K. Goman, "What Leaders Don't Know about the Rumor Mill," *Forbes*, November 30, 2013, http://www.forbes.com/sites/carolkinseygoman/2013/11/30/what-leaders-dont-know-about-the-rumor-mill/2/#2ab53c07487d, accessed July 2016.

17. J. Humphrey "Why You Need To Master In-Person Conversations In Your Slack-Driven Office," *Fast Company*, July 1, 2016, http://www.fastcompany.com/3061470/how-to-be-a-success-at-everything/why-you-need-to-master-in-person-conversations-in-your-sla, accessed July 2016.

18. A. Davis, "Leaders: 6 Reasons Face-to-Face Communication Is Best," *Inc.*, November 30, 2015, http://www.inc.com/alison-davis/leaders-6-reasons-face-to-face-communication-is-best.html, accessed July 2016.

19. J. Sharlach, "Communicating: Making Your Case to Employees," *Huffington Post*, February 9, 2016, http://www.huffingtonpost.com/jeffrey-sharlach/communicating-making-your-case-to-employees_b_9169946.html; A. Davis, "5 Simple Changes That

Will Dramatically Improve Employee Communication," March 18, 2016, http://www.inc.com/alison-davis/make-1-simple-change-to-dramatically-improve-employee-communication.html, accessed July 2016; R. Yekutiel, "A CEO's New Year's resolutions to improve employee satisfaction," *Fortune*, January 7, 2015, http://fortune.com/2015/01/07/a-ceos-new-years-resolutions-to-improve-employee-satisfaction/?iid=sr-link1, accessed July 2016; Panopto, "Best Practices for Holding and Recording Town Hall Meetings," February 10, 2015, https://www.panopto.com/blog/best-practices-for-holding-and-recording-town-hall-meetings/, accessed July 2016; E. G. Goldman, "Everybody's Talking But Is Anyone Listening?," *Huffington Post*, October 2, 2014, http://www.huffingtonpost.com/ellen-g-goldman/everybodys-talking-but-is_b_5913706.html, accessed July 2016.

20. See W. Minozzi, M. A. Neblo, K. M. Esterling, and D. M. J. Lazer, "Field Experiment Evidence of Substantive, Attributional, and Behavioral Persuasion by Member of Congress in Online Town Halls," March 31, 2015, http:www.pnas.org/cgi/doi/10.1073/pnas.1418188112.

21. L. Montini, "How to Streamline Your Meetings (Infographic)," *Inc.*, August 22, 2014, http://www.inc.com/laura-montini/infographic/maximizing-your-meetings.html, accessed July 2016.

22. A. Bruzzese, "Tame the Meeting Beast with These 8 Tips," *Reno Gazette-Journal*, March 1, 2012, p. 8A.

23. N. Hartman, "Seven Steps to Running the Most Effective Meeting Possible," *Forbes*, February 5, 2014, http://www.forbes.com/sites/forbesleadershipforum/2014/02/05/seven-steps-to-running-the-most-effective-meeting-possible/#2db4326c1054, accessed July 2016; E. McKelvey, "Why Daily Meetings Aren't a Complete Waste of Time," *Fortune*, June 15, 2015, http://fortune.com/2015/06/15/erin-mckelvey-productivity-at-work/, accessed July 2016.

24. N. Wingfield, "Forget Beanbag Chairs. Amazon Is Giving Its Workers Treehouses," *New York Times*, July 10, 2016, http://www.nytimes.com/2016/07/11/technology/forget-beanbag-chairs-amazon-is-giving-its-workers-treehouses.html, accessed July 2016.

25. See J. Katz, M. DuBois, and S. Wigderson, "Learning by Helping? Undergraduate Communication Outcomes Associated with Training or Service-Learning Experiences," *Teaching of Psychology*, 2014, pp. 251–255.

26. M. Levin, "The 1 Thing That Will Make You a Great Communicator," *Inc.*, June 24, 2016, http://www.inc.com/marissa-levin/the-1-thing-that-will-get-people-to-listen-to-you-instantly.html, accessed July 2016.

27. The role of trust in communication was studied by O. Temby, J. Sandall, R. Cooksey, and G. M. Hickey, "Examining the Role of Trust and Informal Communication on Mutual Learning in Government: The Case of Climate Change Policy in New York," *Organization and Environment*, 2016, pp. 1–27; and K. Boies, J. Fiset, and H. Gill, "Communication and Trust Are Key: Unlocking the Relationship Between Leadership and Team Performance and Creativity," *The Leadership Quarterly*, 2015, pp. 1080–1094.

28. M. Zwilling, "Entrepreneurs Face Serious Communication Barriers," *Forbes*, July 7, 2013, http://www.forbes.com/sites/martinzwilling/2013/07/07/entrepreneurs-face-serious-communication-barriers/#177b3d385398, accessed July 2016.

29. R. Riggio, "Are All Leaders Narcissists?" *Psychology Today*, December 13, 2012, https://www.psychologytoday.com/blog/cutting-edge-leadership/201212/are-all-leaders-narcissists?collection=62261, accessed July 2016.

30. S. Moore, "Why It's Not about You (and Why That's Awesome)," *Huffington Post*, September 6, 2014, http://www.huffingtonpost.com/susie-moore/why-its-not-about-you-and_b_5744522.html, accessed July 2016.

31. E J. Langer, "Minding Matters: The Consequences of Mindlessness-Mindfulness," *Advances in Experimental Social Psychology*, 1989, 138.

32. "Neuroscience: The Next Competitive Advantage," *360 Magazine*, June 14, 2015, http://www.steelcase.com/insights/articles/think-better/. Accessed October 2016.

33. I. Pozin, "Think You're a Good Communicator? Better Think Again," *Inc.*, April 28, 2016, http://www.inc.com/ilya-pozin/think-youre-a-good-communicator-better-think-again.html, accessed July 2016.

34. C. R. Rogers and F. J. Roethlisberger, "Barriers and Gateways to Communication," *Harvard Business Review*, July–August 1952, pp. 46–52.

35. Reuters, "Meet the Man Running Bernie Sanders' Twitter Account," *Forbes*, April 4, 2016, http://fortune.com/2016/04/04/bernie-sanders-social-media/, accessed October 2016.

36. A. Hofschneider, "That Thing with the Buttons and Receiver? Pick It Up," *The Wall Street Journal*, August 28, 2013, D1, D2.

37. I. Pozin, "Think You're a Good Communicator? Better Think Again," *Inc.*, April 28, 2016, http://www.inc.com/ilya-pozin/think-youre-a-good-communicator-better-think-again.html, accessed July 2016.

38. George Ritzer, *Introduction to Sociology*, SAGE Publications, Inc., 2013, p. 116.

39. C. Béal and K. Mullan, "Issues in Conversational Humour from a Cross-Cultural Perspective: Comparing French and Australian Corpora," in B. Peeters, K. Mullan, and C. Béal (Eds.), *Cross-Cultural Speaking, Speaking Cross-Culturally*, United Kingdom: Cambridge Scholars Publishing, 2013, pp. 107–140.

40. Businesstopia, "Cultural Barriers to Communication," https://www.businesstopia.net/communication/cultural-barriers-communication, accessed July 2016.

41. B. Patel, "Communicating across Cultures: Proceedings of a Workshop to Assess Health Literacy and Cross-Cultural Communication Skills," *Journal of Pharmacy Practice and Research*, 2015, pp. 49–56.

42. S. Maslin, "A Brooklyn Ambulance Service Speaks Chinese, Like Its Patients," *The New York Times*, May 23, 2016, http://www.nytimes.com/2016/05/24/nyregion/a-brooklyn-ambulance-service-speaks-chinese-like-its-patients.html?_r=2, accessed July 2016.

43. M. Carteret, "Cross-Cultural Communication for EMS," *The American Ambulance Association*, June 25, 2015, https://the-aaa.org/2015/06/25/cross-cultural-communication-for-ems/, accessed July 2016.

44. On the Move and M. Sandlin, "Intercultural Training Important to Expats' Success," April 26, 2013, *Houston Chronicle*, http://www.chron.com/jobs/article/Intercultural-training-important-to-expats-4467195.php#, accessed July 2016.

45. Research on nonverbal communication can be found in M. Nesic and V. Nesic, "Neuroscience of Nonverbal Communication," in A. Kostic and D. Chadee (Eds.), *The Social Psychology of Nonverbal Communication*, New York, Palgrave Macmillan, 2015, pp. 30–64.

46. C. Bank, "Barriers to Nonverbal Communication," October 6, 2015, http://www.livestrong.com/article/189396-barriers-to-nonverbal-communication/, accessed July 2016.

47. Related research was conducted by Y. Sato, "Retrospective Verbal Reports As a Way to Investigate Cross-Cultural Pragmatic Problems in Oral Interaction," in B. Peeters, K. Mullan, and C. Béal (Eds.), *Cross-Cultural Speaking, Speaking Cross-Culturally*, United Kingdom: Cambridge Scholars Publishing, 2013, pp. 11–46.

48. C. Banks, "Barriers to Nonverbal Communication," October 6, 2015, http://www.livestrong.com/article/189396-barriers-to-nonverbal-communication/, accessed July 2016.

49. See R. Buck and M. Miller, "Beyond Facial Expression: Spatial Distance as a Factor in the Communication of Discrete Emotions," in A. Kostic and D. Chadee (Eds.), *The Social Psychology of Nonverbal Communication*, New York, Palgrave Macmillan, 2015, pp. 172–196.

50. *Translate Media*, "The Meaning of a Smile In Different Cultures," June 25, 2015, https://www.translatemedia.com/us/blog-us/the-meaning-of-a-smile-in-different-cultures/, accessed July 2016.

51. P. Economy, "9 Body Language Habits That Make You Look Really Unprofessional," *Inc.*, May 13, 2016, http://www.inc.com/peter-economy/9-body-language-habits-that-make-you-look-really-unprofessional.html, accessed July 2016.

52. See L. Talley and S. Temple, "How Leaders Influence Followers through the Use of Nonverbal Communication," *Leadership & Organization Development Journal*, 2015, pp. 69–80. Also see A. Mcconnon, "To Be a Leader, Watch Your Body Language," *The Wall Street Journal*, October 3, 2016, p. R8.

53. C. Blank, "Barriers to Nonverbal Communication," October 6, 2015, http://www.livestrong.com/article/189396-barriers-to-nonverbal-communication/, accessed July 2016.

54. See A. Stoy, "Project Communication Tips: Nonverbal Communication in Different Cultures," *Bright Hub Project Management*, 2012, http://www.brighthubpm.com/monitoring-projects/85141-project-communication-tips-nonverbal-communication-in-different-cultures.

55. D. Carnes, "Do Men & Women Use Nonverbal Communication Differently?," May 17, 2015, http://www.livestrong.com/article/172581-do-men-women-use-nonverbal-communication-differently/, accessed July 2016.

56. S. Johnson, "How a Woman Can Improve Gender Workplace Communication," *The Houston Chronicle*, http://work.chron.com/woman-can-improve-gender-workplace-communication-6587.html, accessed July 2016.

57. L. Evans, "Are We Speaking a Different Language? Men and Women's Communication Blind Spots," *Fast Company*, June 11, 2014, http://www.fastcompany.com/3031631/strong-female-lead/are-we-speaking-a-different-language-men-and-womens-communication-blind-s, accessed July 2016.

58. L. Evans, "Are We Speaking a Different Language? Men and Women's Communication Blind Spots," *Fast Company*, June 11, 2014, http://www.fastcompany.com/3031631/strong-female-lead/are-we-speaking-a-different-language-men-and-womens-communication-blind-s, accessed July 2016.

59. L. Evans, "Are We Speaking A Different Language? Men And Women's Communication Blind Spots," *Fast Company*, June 11, 2014, http://www.fastcompany.com/3031631/strong-female-lead/are-we-speaking-a-different-language-men-and-womens-communication-blind-s, accessed July 2016.

60. D. Tannen, "The Power of Talk: Who Gets Heard and Why," in *Negotiation: Readings, Exercises, and Cases*, 3rd ed., R. J. Lewicki and D. M. Saunders, eds. (Burr Ridge, IL: Irwin/McGraw-Hill, 1999), pp. 147–148.

61. Forbes Coaches Council, "11 Ways to Develop a More Inclusive Communication Style at Work," *Forbes*, June 7, 2016, http://www.forbes.com/sites/forbescoachescouncil/2016/06/07/11-ways-male-leaders-can-adjust-communication-in-order-to-be-more-inclusive-to-women/, accessed July 2016; L. Evans, "Are We Speaking a Different Language? Men and Women's Communication Blind Spots," *Fast Company*, June 11, 2014, https://www.fastcompany.com/3031631/strong-female-lead/are-we-speaking-a-different-language-men-and-womens-communication-blind-s; J. Humphrey, "The Communication Style You Need To Break Into The Boys' Club," *Fast Company*, March 12, 2015, http://www.fastcompany.com/3043463/strong-female-lead/when-men-wont-listen-how-to-speak-up-and-hold-your-own, accessed July 2016.

62. "Me or the Device?," *USA Today*, July 15, 2016, p. B1.

63. A. Pilon, "Business Users Trial New Facebook Live Streaming Video—We Have Examples," *Small Business Trends*, February 1, 2016, http://smallbiztrends.com/2016/02/facebook-live-examples-streaming-video.html, accessed July 2016.

64. See B. Nguyen, X. Yu, T. C. Melewar, and J. Chen, "Brand Innovation and Social Media: Knowledge Acquisition from Social Media, Market Orientation, and the Moderating Role of Social Media Strategic Capability," *Industrial Marketing Management*, 2015, pp. 11–25; and N. Jones, R. Borgma, and E. Ulusoy, "Impact of Social Media on Small Businesses," *Journal of Small Business and Enterprise Development*, 2015, pp. 611–632.

65. D. M. Herszenhorn and E. Huetteman, "House Democrats' Gun-Control Sit-In Turns into Chaotic Showdown with Republicans," *New York Times*, June 22, 2016, http://www.nytimes.com/2016/06/23/us/politics/house-democrats-stage-sit-in-to-push-for-action-on-gun-control.html, accessed July 2016.

66. C.K. Johnson, S. Karnowski, "Stopped 52 times by police: Was it racial profiling?," *The Washington Post*, July 9, 2016, https://www.washingtonpost.com/national/

stopped-52-times-by-police-was-it-racial-profiling/2016/07/09/81fe882a-4595-11e6-a76d-3550dba926ac_story.html, accessed July 2016; B. Stelter, "Philando Castile and the power of Facebook Live," July 7, 2016, http://money.cnn.com/2016/07/07/media/facebook-live-streaming-police-shooting/, accessed July 2016; R. Iyenger, "Read Mark Zuckerberg's Response to the Video of Philando Castile's Shooting," *Time,* July 7, 2016, http://time.com/4397677/philando-castile-shooting-facebook-live-zuckerberg-statement/, accessed July 2016.

67. K. Ashford, "Employees Feel Guilty for Texting at Work (Do You?)," *Forbes,* April 27, 2015, http://www.forbes.com/sites/kateashford/2015/04/27/guilty-for-texting/#1b4494318397, accessed July 2016.

68. S. Olenski, "How FlightHub Infiltrates Emerging Markets Using Social Media," *Forbes,* November 7, 2015, http://www.forbes.com/sites/steveolenski/2015/11/07/how-flighthub-infiltrates-emerging-markets-using-social-media/#572658d1535e, accessed July 2016.

69. R. Maurer, "Survey: Employers Using Social Media to Find Passive Candidates," *Society for Human Resource Management,* January 7, 2016, https://www.shrm.org/ResourcesAndTools/hr-topics/talent-acquisition/Pages/Using-Social-Media-Find-Passive-Candidates.aspx, accessed July 2016.

70. J. Budzienski, "3 Ways to Be Constantly Recruiting Star Talent through Social Media," *Entrepreneur,* April 23, 2015, https://www.entrepreneur.com/article/245295, accessed July 2016.

71. M. Deutsch, "Are Recruiters Texting Candidates and Hiring Managers?," February 7, 2016, https://www.topechelon.com/blog/recruiter-training/do-you-send-text-messages-to-candidates-or-hiring-managers/, accessed July 2016.

72. R. Maurer, "Survey: Employers Using Social Media to Find Passive Candidates," *Society for Human Resource Management,* January 7, 2016, https://www.shrm.org/ResourcesAndTools/hr-topics/talent-acquisition/Pages/Using-Social-Media-Find-Passive-Candidates.aspx, accessed July 2016.

73. R. Maurer, "Survey: Employers Using Social Media to Find Passive Candidates," *Society for Human Resource Management,* January 7, 2016, https://www.shrm.org/ResourcesAndTools/hr-topics/talent-acquisition/Pages/Using-Social-Media-Find-Passive-Candidates.aspx, accessed July 2016.

74. J. Budzienski, "3 Ways to Be Constantly Recruiting Star Talent through Social Media," *Entrepreneur,* April 23, 2015, https://www.entrepreneur.com/article/245295, accessed July 2016.

75. J. Budzienski, "3 Ways to Be Constantly Recruiting Star Talent Through Social Media," *Entrepreneur,* April 23, 2015, https://www.entrepreneur.com/article/245295, accessed July 2016.

76. S. Kumar, "Why Monitoring Employees' Social Media Is a Bad Idea," *Time,* May 22, 2015, http://time.com/3894276/social-media-monitoring-work/, accessed July 2016.

77. M. Biro, "4 Reasons Social Media Is A Critical Recruiting Tool," *Forbes,* November 25, 2015, http://www.forbes.com/sites/meghanbiro/2015/11/25/4-reasons-social-media-is-a-critical-recruiting-tool/#a62911e7f021, accessed July 2016.

78. S. Kumar, "Why Monitoring Employees' Social Media Is a Bad Idea," *Time,* May 22, 2015, http://time.com/3894276/social-media-monitoring-work/, accessed July 2016.

79. C. Matyszczkyk, "Why HR Professionals Are Wrong about Social Media," *Inc.,* March 21, 2016, http://www.inc.com/chris-matyszczyk/why-hr-professionals-are-wrong-about-social-media.html, accessed July 2016.

80. J. T. O'Donnell, "3 Tips to Make Employers Come to You," *Inc.,* April 11, 2016, http://www.inc.com/jt-odonnell/3-tips-to-make-for-making-employers-come-to-you.html, accessed July 2016.

81. A.J. Agrawal, "The Risks of Posting Impulsively On Social Media," *Inc.,* May 3, 2016, http://www.inc.com/aj-agrawal/the-risks-of-posting-impulsively-on-social-media.html, accessed July 2016.

82. R. Maurer, "Survey: Employers Using Social Media to Find Passive Candidates," *Society for Human Resource Management,* January 7, 2016, https://www.shrm.org/ResourcesAndTools/hr-topics/talent-acquisition/Pages/Using-Social-Media-Find-Passive-Candidates.aspx, accessed July 2016.

83. D. Meinert, "Social Media Screening Leads to Hiring Discrimination," *HR Magazine,* January 2014, p. 14; A. E. Marwick, *Status Update:Celebrity, Publicity and Branding in the Social Media Age* (New Haven: Yale University Press, 2013); and J. Shinal, "Social Media Can Bring Politics to the Corner Office," *USA Today,* April 11, 2014, p. 7B. See also "When Worlds Collide: Navigating the Minefield of Social Media," *Knowledge@Wharton,* June 9, 2014, http://knowledge.wharton.upenn.edu/article/social-media-social-minefield (accessed August 18, 2014); B. Adams, "How Richard Branson Plans to Make Over $7 Million a Year From . . . Recruiting?," *Inc.,* June 20, 2016, http://www.inc.com/bryan-adams/how-virgin-media-plans-to-make-over-7-million-a-year-from-recruiting.html, accessed July 2016.

84. S. Vozza, "What Happened When I Gave Up Social Media For A Month," *Fast Company,* July 6, 2016, http://www.fastcompany.com/3061454/your-most-productive-self/what-happened-when-i-gave-up-social-media-for-a-month, accessed July 2016.

85. B. A. Lautsch and E. E. Kossek, "Managing a Blended Workforce: Telecommuters and Non-Telecommuters," *Organizational Dynamics,* 2011, 10–17; J. Meister, "Want to Be a More Productive Employee? Get on Social Networks," *Forbes,* April 18, 2013, http://www.forbes.com/sites/jeannemeister/2013/04/18/want-to-be-a-more-productive-employee-get-on-social-networks/, accessed October 3, 2013.

86. S. Patel, "How To Boost Productivity As A Remote Employee," *Forbes,* March 2, 2016, http://www.forbes.com/sites/sujanpatel/2016/03/02/how-to-boost-productivity-as-a-remote-employee/5/#1adc908752d9, accessed July 2016.

87. N. Burton, "14 Habits of the Most Productive Remote Workers," *Fast Company,* June 8, 2015, http://www.fastcompany.com/3060650/your-most-productive-self/14-habits-of-the-most-productive-remote-workers accessed July 2016; D. Aamoth, *Fast Company,* June 15, 2016, http://www.fastcompany.com/3060764/app-economy/25-free-chrome-extensions-to-make-you-an-incredibly-productive-person, accessed July 2016.

88. Inc. Video, D. Brown, http://www.inc.com/damon-brown/why-every-entrepreneur-should-take-a-social-media-break.html, accessed July 2016.

89. A. Peters, "One Trick to Make Employees Happy: Ban Emails on Nights and Weekends," *Fast Company,* June 1, 2016, http://www.fastcoexist.com/3060349/one-trick-to-make-employees-happy-ban-emails-on-nights-and-weekends, accessed July 2016.

90. A. Dan, "Why P&G Is Quickly Shifting to a Digital-First Approach to Building Brands," *Forbes,* March 12, 2015, http://www.forbes.com/sites/avidan/2015/03/12/why-pg-is-quickly-shifting-to-a-digital-first-approach-to-building-brands/#373514272753.

91. R.E. Ployhart, "Social Media in the Workplace: Issues and Strategic Questions," *SHRM Executive Briefing,* November 2011. www.shrm.org/about/foundation/products/documents/social%20media%20briefing-%20final.pdf (accessed August 18, 2014). See also "Should Companies Monitor Their Employees' Social Media?" *The Wall Street Journal,* May 12, 2014, pp. R1, R2.

92. A. Schneider, "Fantasy Football Expected to Cost $8 Billion in Lost Work Time This NFL Season," KUHF Public Radio, September 3, 2013, http://app1.kuhf.org/articles/1377884091-Fantasy-Football-Expected-To-Cost-$8-Billion-In-Lost-Work-Time-This-NFL-Season.html (accessed August 18, 2014).

93. Challenger, Gray, & Christmas, Inc., "Fantasy Football to Cost Employers $16B in 2015," August 18, 2015, https://www.challengergray.com/press/press-releases/fantasy-football-cost-employers-16b-2015.

94. M. Mansfield, "What Is Slack and How Do I Use It for My Team?" December 22, 2015, http://smallbiztrends.com/2015/12/slack-use-team.html, accessed July 2016.

95. "A Slack customer story: LUSH Fresh Handmade Cosmetics: Reducing email while growing globally." https://slack.com/customers/lush, accessed July 2016.

96. G. Fleishman, "10 Ways to Make Slack Simpler, Safer, and Less Annoying," *Fast Company,* June 22, 2016, http://www.fastcompany.com/3060718/10-ways-to-make-slack-simpler-safer-and-less-annoying, accessed July 2016.

97. J. Boitnott, "Why a Kitchen Knife Shows What You Need to Know About Crowdsourcing," *Inc.,* October 19, 2015, http://www.inc.com/john-boitnott/how-a-kitchen-knife-demonstrates-the-power-of-crowdsourcing.html, accessed July 2016.

98. S. Lohr, "Netflix Awards $1 Million Prize and Starts a New Contest," *New York Times,* September 21, 2009, http://bits.blogs.nytimes.com/2009/09/21/netflix-awards-1-million-prize-and-starts-a-new-contest/, accessed July 2016.

99. C. Desmarais, "Need Help? Crowdsource Your Work," *Inc.,* July 27, 2015, http://www.inc.com/christina-desmarais/need-help-crowdsource-your-work.html, accessed July 2016.

100. J. Degraff, "Why Crowdsourcing Has Ruined the Art of Innovation," *Inc.,* December 21, 2015, http://www.inc.com/jeff-degraff/why-crowdsourcing-has-ruined-the-art-of-innovation.html, accessed July 2016.

101. D. L. Roberts and F. T. Piller, "Finding the Right Role for Social Media in Innovation," *MIT Sloan Management Review,* Spring 2016, pp. 41–42.

102. These four conclusions were based on N. Jones, R. Borgman, and E. Ulusoy, "Impact of Social Media on Small Businesses," *Journal of Small Business and Enterprise Development,* 2015, Vol 22, pp. 611–632.

103. See Y. Liu and R. A. Lopez, "The Impact of Social Media Conversations on Consumer Brand Choices," *Marketing Letters,* 2016, pp. 1–13.

104. See R. Guesalaga, "The Use of Social Media in Sales: Individual and Organizational Antecedents, and the Role of Customer Engagement in Social Media," *Industrial Marketing Management,* 2016, pp. 71–79; and L. Collier, "Should You Let Your Employees Shop Online at Work?" *OfficeDepot Solutions Center,* October 26, 2015, http://solutions.officedepot.com/leadership/article/should-you-let-your-employees-shop-online-at-work.

105. See R. Guesalaga, "The Use of Social Media in Sales: Individual and Organizational Antecedents, and the Role of Customer Engagement in Social Media," *Industrial Marketing Management,* 2016, pp. 71–79; and L. Collier, "Should You Let Your Employees Shop Online at Work?" *OfficeDepot Solutions Center,* October 26, 2015, http://solutions.officedepot.com/leadership/article/should-you-let-your-employees-shop-online-at-work.

106. J. Martin, "12 standout social media success stories," March 25, 2015, http://www.cio.com/article/2901047/social-media/12-standout-social-media-success-stories.html#slide12, accessed July 2016.

107. J. Martin, "11 most memorable social media marketing successes of 2015," *CIO,* October 1, 2015, http://www.cio.com/article/2988313/social-networking/11-most-memorable-social-media-marketing-successes-of-2015, accessed July 2016.

108. Guest, "10 Brands Doing an Amazing Job on Social Media," *Ad Week,* July 30, 2015, http://www.adweek.com/socialtimes/michael-patterson-10-brands-amazing-social-media/624169, accessed July 2016.

109. See V. Dutot, E. L. Galvez, and D. W. Versailles, "CSR Communications Strategies through Social Media and Influence on E-Reputation," *Management Decision,* 2016, pp. 363–389; and C. Dijkmans, P. Kerkhof, and C. J. Beukeboom, "A Stage to Engage: Social Media Use and Corporate Reputation," *Tourism Management,* 2015, pp. 58–67.

110. S. E. Bohr, "The Link Between Social Media Activity And Corporate Reputation," *Forbes,* July 14, 2014, http://www.forbes.com/sites/onmarketing/2014/07/14/the-link-between-social-media-activity-and-corporate-reputation/#2fe7397e6d45, accessed July 2016.

111. J. LeBret, "Company Reputation Management With Social Media," *Forbes,* November 4, 2014, http://www.forbes.com/sites/jabezlebret/2014/11/04/company-reputation-management-with-social-media/2/#76682d1d125a, accessed July 2016; P. Cohen, "4 Ways Social Media Can Ruin Your Reputation," *Social Media Today,* February 14, 2014, http://www.socialmediatoday.com/content/4-ways-social-media-can-ruin-your-reputation, accessed July 2016.

112. J. LeBret, "Company Reputation Management with Social Media," *Forbes,* November 4, 2014, http://www.forbes.com/sites/jabezlebret/2014/11/04/company-

reputation-management-with-social-media/2/#a336992125ac, accessed July 2016.

113. S. Lucas, "Social Media Means Everything You Do Is Public," *Inc.*, June 30, 2016, http://www.inc.com/suzanne-lucas/social-media-means-everything-you-do-is-public.html, accessed July 2016.

114. J. Budzienski, "3 Ways to Be Constantly Recruiting Star Talent through Social Media," April 23, 2015, *Entrepreneur*, https://www.entrepreneur.com/article/245295, accessed July 2016.

115. J. Meister, "Want to Be a More Productive Employee? Get on Social Networks," *Forbes*, April 18, 2013, http://www.forbes.com/sites/jeannemeister/2013/04/18/want-to-be-a-more-productive-employee-get-on-social-networks/, accessed October 3, 2013; C. Zakrzewski, *Wall Street Journal*, March 13, 2016, "The Key to Getting Workers to Stop Fooling Around Online," http://www.wsj.com/articles/the-key-to-getting-workers-to-stop-wasting-time-online-1457921545, accessed October 2016.

116. C. Conner, "Wasting Time at Work: The Epidemic Continues," *Forbes*, July 31, 2015, http://www.forbes.com/sites/cherylsnappconner/2015/07/31/wasting-time-at-work-the-epidemic-continues/#4050cab03ac1.

117. L. Collier, "Should You Let Your Employees Shop Online at Work?," *OfficeDepot Solutions Center*, October 26, 2015, http://solutions.officedepot.com/leadership/article/should-you-let-your-employees-shop-online-at-work; C. Zakrzewski, "The Key to Getting Workers to Stop Wasting Time Online," *Wall Street Journal*, March 13, 2016, http://www.wsj.com/articles/the-key-to-getting-workers-to-stop-wasting-time-online-1457921545, accessed July 2016.

118. C. Zakrzewski, "The Key to Getting Workers to Stop Wasting Time Online," *Wall Street Journal*, March 13, 2016, http://www.wsj.com/articles/the-key-to-getting-workers-to-stop-wasting-time-online-1457921545, accessed July 2016.

119. D. Lavenda, "Loafing Online Can Be a Valuable Part of a Productive Workday," *Fast Company*, April 10, 2013, http://www.fastcompany.com/3008031/loafing-online-can-be-valuable-part-productive-work-day, accessed July 2016.

120. For accounts of security problems, see J. Angwin, *Dragnet Nation: A Quest for Privacy, Security, and Freedom in a World of Relentless Surveillance* (New York: Henry Holt, 2014). See also "Internet Security: The Problem with Passwords," *The Week*, June 6, 2014, p. 20; N. Perlroth and D. Gelles, "Russian Hackers Steal Passwords of Billion Users," *The New York Times*, August 6, 2014, pp. A1, A3; M. Snider, "Net Breach an Opportunity to Improve Password Practices," *USA Today*, August 7, 2014, p. 3A; E. Weise, "The Internet of (Unsafe) Things," *USA Today*, August 8, 2014, pp. 1B, 2B; and G. Fields and J. R. Emshwiller, "As Arrest Records Mount, Consequences Last a Lifetime," *The Wall Street Journal*, August 119, 2014, pp. A1, A12.

121. Norton *Cyber Crime Report for 2013*, reported in P. Paganini, "2013 Norton Report, the Impact of Cybercrime According to Symantec," *Security Affairs*, October 9, 2013, http://securityaffairs.co/wordpress/18475/cyber-crime/2013-norton-report.html (accessed August 18, 2014).

122. J. Keller, "How Businesses Stay Safe and Secure Using Social Media," http://www.webroot.com/us/en/business/resources/articles/social-media/how-businesses-stay-safe-and-secure-using-social-media, accessed July 2016; J. L. Schiff, "6 Biggest Business Security Risks and How You Can Fight Back," January 20, 2015, http://www.cio.com/article/2872517/data-breach/6-biggest-business-security-risks-and-how-you-can-fight-back.html?page=2, accessed July 2016.

123. J. Menn, "A particularly destructive type of hacking is far more widespread than previously believed," *Business Insider*, April 2015, http://www.businessinsider.com/r-exclusive-destructive-hacking-attempts-target-critical-infrastructure-in-americas-survey-2015-4, accessed July 2016.

124. J. L. Schiff, "6 Biggest Business Security Risks and How You Can Fight Back," January 20, 2015, http://www.cio.com/article/2872517/data-breach/6-biggest-business-security-risks-and-how-you-can-fight-back.html, accessed July 2016.

125. Federal Communications Commission, "Cyber Security Planning Guide," https://transition.fcc.gov/cyber/cyberplanner.pdf. accessed July 2016.

126. S. Lucas, "Social Media Means Everything You Do Is Public," *Inc.*, June 30, 2016, http://www.inc.com/suzanne-lucas/social-media-means-everything-you-do-is-public.html, accessed July 2016.

127. K. Ashford, "Employees Feel Guilty for Texting at Work (Do You?)," *Forbes*, April 27, 2015, http://www.forbes.com/sites/kateashford/2015/04/27/guilty-for-texting/2/#7e64f28b6e99, accessed July 2016.

128. K. Ashford, "Employees Feel Guilty For Texting At Work (Do You?)," *Forbes*, April 27, 2015, http://www.forbes.com/sites/kateashford/2015/04/27/guilty-for-texting/2/#1594aa326e99, accessed July 2016.

129. Privacy Rights Clearinghouse, "Workplace Privacy and Employee Monitoring," April 1, 2016, https://www.privacyrights.org/workplace-privacy-and-employee-monitoring, accessed July 2016.

130. S. Kumar, "Why Monitoring Employees' Social Media is a Bad Idea," *Time*, May 22, 2015, http://time.com/3894276/social-media-monitoring-work/, accessed July 2016.

131. The Radicati Group, Inc., "Email Statistics Report, 2015-2019," February 2015, http://www.radicati.com/wp/wp-content/uploads/2015/02/Email-Statistics-Report-2015-2019-Executive-Summary.pdf, accessed July 2016.

132. R. Mazin, "It's Time to Tame Workplace Texting," https://www.allbusiness.com/its-time-to-tame-workplace-texting-16706751-1.html, accessed July 2016.

133. K. Ashford, "Employees Feel Guilty for Texting at Work (Do You?)," *Forbes*, April 27, 2015, http://www.forbes.com/sites/kateashford/2015/04/27/guilty-for-texting/2/#172ce0a96e99, accessed July 2016.

134. R. Weborg, "Why Texting Needs to be a Part of Your Workforce Optimization Strategy," March 30, 2016, http://www.icmi.com/Resources/Workforce-Management/2016/03/Why-Texting-Needs-to-be-a-Part-of-Your-Workforce-Optimization-Strategy, accessed July 2016.

135. M. Lepore, "Should You Text Your Boss? 5 Tips for Texting Professionally," July 10, 2014, http://skillcrush.com/2014/07/10/5-tips-texting-professionally/, accessed July 2016; H. Crawford, "6 Rules for Texting at Work," February 26, 2015, http://money.usnews.com/money/blogs/outside-voices-careers/2015/02/26/6-rules-for-texting-at-work, accessed July 2016.

136. K. Ashford, "Employees Feel Guilty for Texting at Work (Do You?)," *Forbes*, April 27, 2015, http://www.forbes.com/sites/kateashford/2015/04/27/guilty-for-texting/#72616c678397, accessed July 2016.

137. D. Kline, "Here's What People Are Using Social Media for at Work," June 27, 2016, http://www.fool.com/investing/2016/06/27/heres-what-people-are-using-social-media-for-at-wo.aspx, accessed July 2016.

138. Intel.com "Intel Social Media Guidelines," http://www.intel.com/content/www/us/en/legal/intel-social-media-guidelines.html, accessed July 2016.

139. K. D'Angelo, "5 Terrific Examples of Company Social Media Policies," http://blog.hirerabbit.com/5-terrific-examples-of-company-social-media-policies/, accessed July 2016.

140. W. Vanderbloemen, "How to Safeguard Your Business against a Social Media Nightmare," *Forbes*, June 17, 2016, http://www.forbes.com/sites/williamvanderbloemen/2016/06/17/how-to-safeguard-your-business-against-a-social-media-nightmare/#352271b448ac, accessed July 2016.

141. P. Economy, "10 Secret Communication Skills of the Best Leaders," *Inc.*, November 5, 2015, http://www.inc.com/peter-economy/10-secret-communication-skills-of-top-leaders.html, accessed July 2016.

142. National Association of Colleges and Employers, "Job Outlook 2016: Attributes Employers Want to See on New College Graduates' Resumes," November 18, 2015, http://www.naceweb.org/s11182015/employers-look-for-in-new-hires.aspx, accessed July 2016.

143. M. Zwilling, "Entrepreneurs Face Serious Communication Barriers," *Forbes*, July 7, 2013, http://www.forbes.com/sites/martinzwilling/2013/07/07/entrepreneurs-face-serious-communication-barriers/#15cde9605398, accessed July 2016.

144. See D. Goleman, *Focus: The Hidden Driver of Excellence* (New York: HarperCollins Publishers, 2013).

145. J. Linkner, "Empathy Is the New Killer App," *Inc.*, June 7, 2016 http://www.inc.com/josh-linkner/empathy-is-the-new-killer-app.html, accessed July 2016.

146. Ashoka, *(Contributor)*, "Empathy, Not Bureaucracy, Makes Organizations Great—Leadership Lessons from Anand Mahindra," *Forbes*, July 6, 2016, http://www.forbes.com/sites/ashoka/2016/07/06/empathy-not-bureaucracy-makes-organizations-great-leadership-lessons-from-anand-mahindra/#14602846493f, accessed July 2016.

147. O. S. Itani and A. E. Inyang, "The Effects of Empathy and Listening of Salespeople on Relationship Quality in the Retail Banking Industry," *International Journal of Bank Marketing*, 2015, pp. 692–716.

148. See E. Bernstein, "It's Worth Learning to Be More Empathetic," *The Wall Street Journal*, May 3, 2016, D1, D2; and G. Colvin, "Humans Are Underrated," *Fortune*, August 1, 2015, 101–113.

149. S.G. Boodman, "How to Teach Doctors Empathy," *The Atlantic*, March 15, 2015, http://www.theatlantic.com/health/archive/2015/03/how-to-teach-doctors-empathy/387784/, accessed July 2016.

150. S. Lebowitz, "A CEO Says This is the Single Most Important and Underrated Skill in Business—and in Life," *Business Insider*, February 24, 2016, http://www.businessinsider.com/ceo-listening-is-the-key-to-success-in-business-2016-2, accessed July 2016.

151. Linkedin "Virgin Founder Richard Branson: Why You Should Listen More Than You Talk," *Fortune*, February 3, 2015, http://fortune.com/2015/02/03/virgin-founder-richard-branson-why-you-should-listen-more-than-you-talk/?iid=sr-link4, accessed July 2016.

152. See K. J. Lloyd, D. Boer, J. W. Keller, and S. Voelpel, "Is My Boss Really Listening to Me? The Impact of Perceived Supervisor Listening on Emotional Exhaustion, Turnover Intention, and Organizational Citizenship Behavior," *Journal of Business Ethics*, 2015, pp. 509–524.

153. See J. Keyser, "Active Listening Leads to Business Success," *T+D*, July 2013, 26–28.

154. This discussion is based on C. G. Pearce, I. W. Johnson, and R. T. Barker, "Assessment of the Listening Styles Inventory: Progress in Establishing Reliability and Validity," *Journal of Business and Technical Communication*, January 2003, 84–113.

155. T. Bradberry, "7 Most Common Habits of the Best Listeners," *Inc.*, April 13, 2016, http://www.inc.com/travis-bradberry/7-things-great-listeners-do-differently.html, accessed July 2016.

156. J. Haden, "6 Ways to Write Irresistibly Effective Emails," *Inc.*, November 9, 2015, http://www.inc.com/jeff-haden/6-ways-to-write-irresistibly-effective-emails.html, accessed July 2016.

157. J. Samton, "How to Speak—and Listen—Like an Executive," *Inc.*, July 5, 2016, http://www.inc.com/julia-samton/learn-to-speakem-and-/emlisten-like-an-executive-.html, accessed July 2016.

158. W. Taylor, "The Role of Public Speaking in Career Growth," April 6, 2016, http://www.hrcsuite.com/public-speaking-career-growth/, accessed July 2016.

159. C. Gallo, "New Survey: 70% Say Presentation Skills Are Critical For Career Success," *Forbes*, September 25, 2014, http://www.forbes.com/sites/carminegallo/2014/09/25/new-survey-70-percent-say-presentation-skills-critical-for-career-success/#15ab6f3710c9, accessed July 2016.

160. Public Speaking Power, "What Percentage of People Are Afraid of Public Speaking," January 16, 2014, http://publicspeakingpower.com/percentage-of-people-afraid-of-public-speaking/, accessed July 2016.

161. T. Hixon, "What Entrepreneurs Can Learn About Public Speaking From TED Talks," *Forbes*, March 1, 2016, http://www.forbes.com/sites/toddhixon/2016/03/01/entrepreneurs-time-to-tune-up-your-public-speaking/#6f0d49172e69, accessed July 2016.

162. G. Genard, "How to Open a Presentation: Tell 'Em What You're Going to Say," November 22, 2015, http://www.genardmethod.com/blog/bid/192061/How-to-Open-a-Presentation-Tell-Em-What-You-re-Going-to-Say, accessed July 2016.

163. IESE Business School, "12 Tips For Public Speaking," *Forbes,* April 18, 2016, http://www.forbes.com/sites/iese/2016/04/18/12-tips-for-public-speaking/#3fae354d5af3, accessed July 2016.

164. "Nokia: Our Vision," http://company.nokia.com/en/about-us/our-company/our-vision, accessed July 11, 2016.

165. "Nokia–Internal Communications via Social Media," Social Media for Business Performance, May 29, 2013, https://smbp.uwaterloo.ca/2013/05/nokia-internal-communication-via-social-media, accessed July 11, 2016.

166. "Nokia–Internal Communications via Social Media," *Social Media for Business Performance,* May 29, 2013, https://smbp.uwaterloo.ca/2013/05/nokia-internal-communication-via-social-media, accessed July 11, 2016.

167. C. Mehallow, "Employees Get Involved in Social Media at Nokia," *Triple Pundit,* November 15, 2010, http://www.triplepundit.com/2010/11/involving-employees-in-social-media-at-nokia, accessed July 11, 2016.

168. "Nokia's Internal Communication Driven by Social Media," Simply Communicate, http://www.simply-communicate.com/case-studies/company-profile/nokia's-internal-communication-driven-social-media, accessed July 11, 2016.

169. V. Barve, "Social Media for Organizational Communication," November 28, 2015, https://www.linkedin.com/pulse/social-media-organizational-communication-vikas-barve, accessed July 11, 2016.

170. "Nokia: Our Values," http://company.nokia.com/en/about-us/our-company/our-values, accessed July 11, 2016.

171. "Maximizing the Business Value of Video at Nokia Using Formal Training and Channel Integration," https://www.melcrum.com/research/harness-digital-technologies/maximizing-business-value-video-nokia-using-formal-training, accessed July 11, 2016.

172. "Maximizing the Business Value of Video at Nokia Using Formal Training and Channel Integration," https://www.melcrum.com/research/harness-digital-technologies/maximizing-business-value-video-nokia-using-formal-training, accessed July 11, 2016.

173. "Maximizing the Business Value of Video at Nokia Using Formal Training and Channel Integration," https://www.melcrum.com/research/harness-digital-technologies/maximizing-business-value-video-nokia-using-formal-training, accessed July 11, 2016.

174. "Nokia's Internal Communication Driven by Social Media," Simply Communicate, http://www.simply-communicate.com/case-studies/company-profile/nokia's-internal-communication-driven-social-media, accessed July 11, 2016.

175. "Nokia's Internal Communication Driven by Social Media," *Simply Communicate,* http://www.simply-communicate.com/case-studies/company-profile/nokia's-internal-communication-driven-social-media, accessed July 11, 2016.

176. C. Mehallow, "Employees Get Involved in Social Media at Nokia," Triple Pundit, November 15, 2010, http://www.triplepundit.com/2010/11/involving-employees-in-social-media-at-nokia, accessed July 11, 2016.

177. A. Reimer, "After His ESPN Firing, Curt Schilling Is Now a Martyr for the Right-Wing," *Forbes,* May 17, 2016, http://www.forbes.com/sites/alexreimer/2016/05/17/after-his-espn-firing-curt-schilling-is-now-a-martyr-for-the-right-wing/#64c3dcfa3821.

178. A. Reimer, "After His ESPN Firing, Curt Schilling Is Now a Martyr for the Right-Wing," *Forbes,* May 17, 2016, http://www.forbes.com/sites/alexreimer/2016/05/17/after-his-espn-firing-curt-schilling-is-now-a-martyr-for-the-right-wing/#64c3dcfa3821.

179. R. Sandomir, "Curt Schilling, ESPN Analyst, Is Fired over Offensive Social Media Post," *The New York Times,* April 20, 2016, http://www.nytimes.com/2016/04/21/sports/baseball/curt-schilling-is-fired-by-espn.html?_r=0.

180. A. Grautski, "Curt Schilling Goes on Social Media Bender after Firing," *New York Daily News,* April 22, 2016, http://www.nydailynews.com/sports/baseball/curt-schilling-social-media-bender-espn-firing-article-1.2611099.

181. R. Sandomir, "Curt Schilling, ESPN Analyst, Is Fired over Offensive Social Media Post," *The New York Times,* April 20, 2016, http://www.nytimes.com/2016/04/21/sports/baseball/curt-schilling-is-fired-by-espn.html?_r=0.

182. A. Grautski, "Curt Schilling Goes on Social Media Bender After Firing," *New York Daily News,* April 22, 2016, http://www.nydailynews.com/sports/baseball/curt-schilling-social-media-bender-espn-firing-article-1.2611099.

183. R. Sandomir, "Curt Schilling, ESPN Analyst, Is Fired over Offensive Social Media Post," *The New York Times,* April 20, 2016, http://www.nytimes.com/2016/04/21/sports/baseball/curt-schilling-is-fired-by-espn.html?_r=0.

CHAPTER 16

1. Some new ideas are found in M. Lam, M. O'Donnell, and D. Robertson, "Achieving Employee Commitment for Continuous Improvement Initiatives," *International Journal of Operations & Production Management,* 2015, pp. 201–215; and L. L. Bernardino, F. Teixeira, A. R. de Jesus, A. Barbosa, M. Lordelo, and H. A. Lepikson, "After 20 Years, What Has Remained of TQM?" *International Journal of Productivity and Performance Management,* 2016, pp. 378–400.

2. H. Chun, J.-W. Kim, and J. Lee, "How Does Information Technology Improve Aggregate Productivity? A New Channel of Productivity Dispersion and Reallocation," *Research Policy,* 2015, pp. 999–1016.

3. J. Martin, "12 Standout Social Media Success Stories," *CIO,* March 25, 2015, http://www.cio.com/article/2901047/social-media/12-standout-social-media-success-stories.html#slide2, accessed July 2016.

4. D. Williams, "10 Mobile Apps To Organize Your Business," *Forbes,* February 7, 2013, http://www.forbes.com/sites/davidkwilliams/2013/02/07/10-mobile-apps-to-organize-your-business/#bf6974e5411e, accessed July 2016.

5. S. Heathfield, "Assess Job Fit When You Select Employees," *The Balance,* August 29, 2016, http://humanresources.about.com/od/glossaryj/g/job-fit.htm, accessed July 2016.

6. R. Hackett, "The 10 Biggest R&D Spenders Worldwide," *Fortune,* November 17, 2014, http://fortune.com/2014/11/17/top-10-research-development/, accessed July 2016.

7. J. Warnick, "Unique Microsoft Hiring Program Opens More Doors to People with Autism," *Microsoft,* 2016, http://news.microsoft.com/stories/people/kyle-schwaneke.html, accessed July 2016.

8. F. Fatemi, "Progress versus Process: How to Get the Best of Both Worlds," *Forbes,* July 5, 2016, http://www.forbes.com/sites/falonfatemi/2016/07/05/get-it-done-or-do-it-right-how-to-get-the-best-of-both-worlds/#2f402d9143b4, accessed July 2016.

9. See, for example, G. Colvin, "Who Wants to Be the Boss?" *Fortune,* February 20, 2006, pp. 76–78.

10. See H. Ueno, "Japan Recalls 7 Million More Cars with Takata Airbags," *New York Times,* May 28, 2016, http://www.nytimes.com/2016/05/28/business/international/japan-takata-airbag-recall.html, accessed July 2016; The Editorial Board, *New York Times,* June 3, 2016, "Why Are Cars with Killer Airbags Still Being Sold?" http://www.nytimes.com/2016/06/03/opinion/why-are-they-still-selling-cars-with-killer-airbags.html, accessed July 2016.

11. J. Snoble, *New York Times,* June 29, 2016, "Takata Chief Executive to Resign as Financial Pressure Mounts," http://www.nytimes.com/2016/06/29/business/international/japan-takata-ceo.html, accessed July 2016.

12. "Why Are Cars with Killer Airbags Still Being Sold?" *New York Times,* June 3, 2016, http://www.nytimes.com/2016/06/03/opinion/why-are-they-still-selling-cars-with-killer-airbags.html, accessed July 2016.

13. N. Boudette and J. Markoff, "The Fully Self-Driving Car Is Still Years Away," *New York Times,* July 2, 2016, http://www.nytimes.com/2016/07/02/business/international/bmw-tesla-self-driving-car-mobileye-intel.html, accessed July 2016.

14. C. Silver, "As Self-Driving Cars Change Transportation, How Will Infrastructure Adapt?" *Forbes,* June 28, 2016, http://www.forbes.com/sites/curtissilver/2016/06/28/as-self-driving-cars-change-transportation-infrastructure/#4bd150c93f2b, accessed July 2016.

15. N. Boudette and J. Markoff, "The Fully Self-Driving Car Is Still Years Away," *New York Times,* July 2, 2016, http://www.nytimes.com/2016/07/02/business/international/bmw-tesla-self-driving-car-mobileye-intel.html?_r=0, accessed July 2016; B. Vlasic and N. Boudette, "As U.S. Investigates Fatal Tesla Crash, Company Defends Autopilot System," *New York Times,* July 13, 2016, http://www.nytimes.com/2016/07/13/business/tesla-autopilot-fatal-crash-investigation.html, accessed July 2016.

16. See N. M. Ashkanasy, O. B. Ayoko, and K. A. Jehn, "Understanding the Physical Environment of Work and Employee Behavior: An Affective Events Perspective," *Journal of Organizational Behavior,* November 2014, 1169–1184.

17. A. Johnson, "6 Small Office Changes That Create Big Productivity Increases," *Inc.,* March 24, 2016, http://www.inc.com/anna-johansson/6-simple-office-improvements-that-actually-increase-productivity.html, accessed July 2016.

18. N. Vitezic, and V. Vitezic, "A Conceptual Model of Linkage Between Innovation Management and Controlling in the Sustainable Environment," *The Journal of Applied Business Research,* January/February 2015, pp. 175–184.

19. L. Miller, "Uniqlo Faces Margin Squeeze from Zara, New-Store Costs: Chart," *Bloomberg,* July 2016, http://www.bloomberg.com/news/articles/2016-07-12/uniqlo-faces-margin-squeeze-from-zara-new-store-costs-chart, accessed July 2016.

20. See M. Schröder, S. Schmitt, and R. Schmitt, "Design and Implementation of Quality Control Loops," *The TQM Journal,* 2015, pp. 294–302.

21. Pepsico, "What We Believe," http://www.pepsico.com/Purpose/Performance-with-Purpose/policies, accessed July 2016.

22. L. Silverman, "The Cure for a Doctor Shortage: Primary Care and Teamwork," *Marketplace,* January 20, 2016, http://www.marketplace.org/2016/01/20/education/cure-doctor-shortage-primary-care-and-teamwork, accessed July 2016.

23. See L. Katz, "Monitoring Employee Productivity: Proceed with Caution," *SHRM,* June 1, 2015, https://www.shrm.org/publications/hrmagazine/editorialcontent/2015/0615/pages/0615-employee-monitoring.aspx Accessed July 2016.

24. The HR Specialist (Contributor), "How to Write Performance Goals: 10 Sample Phrases," *Business Management Daily,* September 2, 2015, http://www.businessmanagementdaily.com/44391/how-to-write-performance-goals-10-sample-phrases#_, accessed July 2016.

25. Ups.com, "UPS Pressroom," https://www.pressroom.ups.com/pressroom/ContentDetailsViewer.page?ConceptType=FactSheets&id=1460489309501-709, accessed July 2016.

26. "UPS Sets Efficiency Standards by Monitoring Drivers' Every Move," WDRB, March 24, 2015, http://www.wdrb.com/story/28604605/ups-sets-efficiency-standards-by-monitoring-drivers-every-move, accessed July 2016.

27. "UPS Sets Efficiency Standards by Monitoring Drivers' Every Move," WDRB, March 24, 2015, http://www.wdrb.com/story/28604605/ups-sets-efficiency-standards-by-monitoring-drivers-every-move, accessed July 2016.

28. Reuters, "UPS to Hire Up to 95,000 Workers for Holiday Season," September 15, 2015, http://www.businessinsider.com/r-ups-to-hire-up-to-95000-workers-for-holiday-season-2015-9, accessed July 2016.

29. See M. Goldsmith, "10 Surefire Reasons to Try Feedforward," *Huffington Post,* October 26, 2014, http://www.huffingtonpost.com/marshall-goldsmith/10-surefire-reasons-to-tr_b_5718907.html, accessed July 2016.

30. Nestle, "Quality and Safety," 2016, http://nestle.com/aboutus/quality-and-safety, accessed July 19, 2016.

31. E. Dontigney, "Examples of Concurrent Control in Management," *Houston Chronicle, 2016,* http://smallbusiness.chron.com/examples-concurrent-control-management-80471.html, accessed July 2016.

32. C. Zillman, "IBM Is Blowing Up Its Annual Performance Review," *Fortune,* February 1, 2016, http://fortune.com/2016/02/01/ibm-employee-performance-reviews, accessed July 2016.

33. J. Kerr, "Welcome to Strategic Planning 2.0," *Inc.*, June 13, 2016, http://www.inc.com/james-kerr/welcome-to-strategic-planning-2-0.html, accessed July 2016.

34. B. G. Hoffman, "Inside Ford's Fight to Avoid Disaster," *The Wall Street Journal*, March 9, 2012, pp. B1, B7; and N. E. Boudette, C. Rogers, and J. S. Lublin, "Mulally's Legacy: Setting Ford on a Stronger Course," *The Wall Street Journal*, April 21, 2014, http://online.wsj.com/news/articles/SB10001424052702304049904579515852823291232 (accessed August 31, 2014).

35. J. Markoff, "Artificial Intelligence Swarms Silicon Valley on Wings and Wheels," *New York Times*, July 18, 2016, http://www.nytimes.com/2016/07/18/technology/on-wheels-and-wings-artificial-intelligence-swarms-silicon-valley.html, accessed July 2016.

36. J. Meister, "AirBnB Chief Human Resource Officer Becomes Chief Employee Experience Officer," *Forbes*, July 21, 2015, http://www.forbes.com/sites/jeannemeister/2015/07/21/airbnbs-chief-human-resource-officer-becomes-chief-employee-experience-officer/#69ff25c77b64, accessed July 2016; J. Morgan, "The Globe Head of Employee Experience at Airbnb on Why They Got Rid of Human Resources," *Forbes*, February 1, 2016, http://www.forbes.com/sites/jacobmorgan/2016/02/01/global-head-employee-experience-airbnb-rid-of-human-resources/#3f189e515274, accessed July 2016; B. Pemberton, "The Most Expensive Airbnb Properties in the World: Listings So Flash That Starts Such as Beyonce and Justin Bieber Are Splashing over £7,000 A NIGHT to Stay in Them," *Daily Mail*, March 21, 2016, http://www.dailymail.co.uk/travel/travel_news/article-3502670/The-expensive-Airbnb-listings-world-Listings-flash-stars-Beyonce-Justin-Bieber-splashing-7-000-NIGHT-stay-them.html, accessed July 2016.

37. D. Dietz, "Oregon Rail Officials Look to Push High-Speed Passenger Rail Service into Distant Future," *The Register Guard*, July 17, 2016, http://registerguard.com/rg/news/local/34570094-75/oregon-rail-officials-look-to-push-high-speed-passenger-rail-service-into-distant-future.html.csp, accessed July 2016.

38. D. Dietz, "Oregon Rail Officials Look to Push High-Speed Passenger Rail Service into Distant Future," *The Register Guard*, July 17, 2016, http://registerguard.com/rg/news/local/34570094-75/oregon-rail-officials-look-to-push-high-speed-passenger-rail-service-into-distant-future.html.csp, accessed July 2016.

39. R. E. Walton, "From Control to Commitment in the Workplace," *Harvard Business Review*, March–April 1985, pp. 76–84.

40. S. Banker, "A Supply Chain Transformation Saves an Iconic Brand," *Forbes*, July 9, 2016, http://www.forbes.com/sites/stevebanker/2016/07/09/a-supply-chain-transformation-saves-an-iconic-brand/#4cf305d8111b, accessed July 2016.

41. Marketwatch, "Annual Finanicals for Target Corp.," 2016, http://www.marketwatch.com/investing/stock/tgt/financials, accessed July 2016.

42. P. High, "Target CIO Mike McNamara's Priorities: Digital And Supply Chain Innovation," *Forbes*, July 5, 2016, http://www.forbes.com/sites/peterhigh/2016/07/05/target-cio-mike-mcnamaras-priorities-digital-and-supply-chain-innovation/3/#3fb5b78872d1, accessed July 2016.

43. L. Eadicicco, "Amazon Reveals New Details about Drone Deliveries," *Time*, January 19, 2016, http://time.com/4185117/amazon-prime-air-drone-delivery/, accessed July 2016.

44. I. Linton, "Five Differences Between Service and Manufacturing Organizations," *Houston Chronicle*, http://smallbusiness.chron.com/five-differences-between-service-manufacturing-organizations-19073.html, accessed July 2016.

45. Bureau of Labor Statistics, "Employment by Major Industry Sector," December 2015, http://www.bls.gov/emp/ep_table_201.htm, accessed July 2016; D. Short, "The Epic Rise of America's Services Industry [CHARTS]," *Business Insider*, September 1, 2014, http://www.businessinsider.com/growth-of-us-services-economy-2014-9, accessed July 2016.

46. "6 Benefits to Building Your Dashboard Today," *Guiding Metrics*, http://guiding-metrics.com/benefits-of-metrics/6-benefits-to-building-your-dashboard-today/, accessed May 14, 2016.

47. R. S. Kaplan and D. P. Norton, "The Balanced Scorecard—Measures That Drive Performance," *Harvard Business Review*, January–February 1992, pp. 71–79.

48. For more on the uses of the balanced scorecard, see K. R. Thompson and N. J. Mathys, "The Aligned Balanced Scorecard: An Improved Tool for Building High Performance Organizations," *Organizational Dynamics*, October–December 2008, pp. 378–393; S. C. Voelpel and C. K. Streb, "A Balanced Scorecard for Managing the Aging Workforce," *Organizational Dynamics*, Vol. 39 (2009), pp. 84–90; R. S. Kaplan, D. P. Norton, and B. Rugelsjoen, "Managing Alliances with the Balanced Scorecard," *Harvard Business Review*, January–February 2010, pp. 114–120; E. Tapinos, R. G. Dyson, and M. Meadows, "Does the Balanced Scorecard Make a Difference to the Strategy Development Process?" *Journal of the Operational Research Society*, Vol. 62 (2011), pp. 888–899; M. L. Werner and F. Xu, "Executing Strategy with the Balanced Scorecard," *International Journal of Financial Research*, January 2012, pp. 88–94; K. R. Thompson and N. J. Mathys, "It's Time to Add the Employee Dimension to the Balanced Scorecard," *Organizational Dynamics*, January 2013, pp. 135–144; and A. Janes, "Empirical Verification of the Balanced Scorecard," *Industrial Management & Data Systems*, Vol. 114, No. 2 (2014), pp. 203–219.

49. M. Lev-Ram, "John Deere, Modern Farmer," *Fortune*, December 1, 2015, 67–70.

50. A. Hufford, "Bob Evans to Close Some Locations," *The Wall Street Journal*, April 26, 2016, B3.

51. Sunnybrook Hospital, "Strategic Balanced Scorecard," June 2016, http://sunnybrook.ca/scorecard/, accessed July 2016.

52. See R. S. Kaplan and D. P. Norton, "Having Trouble with Your Strategy? Then Map It," *Harvard Business Review*, September–October 2000, 167–176.

53. T. Groenfeldt, "Citi Helps Clients on the Long Road to a Paperless Office in Treasury," *Forbes*, October 19, 2015, http://www.forbes.com/sites/tomgroenfeldt/2015/10/19/citi-helps-clients-on-the-long-road-to-a-paperless-office-in-treasury/=#5ab0436172e4, accessed July 2016.

54. A sample map for a university can be found in S. Han and Z. Zhong, "Strategy Maps in University Management: A Comparative Study," *Educational Management Administration & Leadership*, 2015, pp. 939–953.

55. "The Gig Economy by the Numbers," *Time*, June 7, 2016, http://time.com/money/4358945/gig-economy-numbers-statistics/, accessed July 2016; S. Hill, "How Big Is the Gig Economy?" *Huffington Post*, September 16, 2015, http://www.huffingtonpost.com/steven-hill/how-big-is-the-gig-econom_b_8147740.html, accessed July 2016.

56. "The Gig Economy by The Numbers," *Time*, June 7, 2016, http://time.com/money/4358945/gig-economy-numbers-statistics/, accessed July 2016.

57. T. Barrabi, "Best Budgeting Apps for Millennials: 3 Money-Saving Options for Young Adults," *International Business Times*, October 1, 2015, http://www.ibtimes.com/best-budgeting-apps-millennials-3-money-saving-options-young-adults-2118739, accessed July 2016.

58. A history of budgeting is provided by M. M. Ibrahim, "A Budget for All Seasons," *International Review of Management and Business Research*, December 2015, pp. 963–972.

59. J. Soileau, L. Soileau, and G. Sumners, "The Evolution of Analytics and Internal Audit," *The EDP Audit, Control, and Security Newsletter*, 2015, p. 13.

60. External auditing is discussed by R. Kral, "Ensuring a High Quality Audit: Who Is Responsible? Five Ideas for Audit Committees to Maximize Value from the External Audit Process," *The EDP Audit, Control, and Security Newsletter*, 2016, pp. 5–12.

61. The Foundation for the Malcolm Baldrige National Quality Award, http://www.baldrigepe.org/, accessed July 2016; "From Baldrige Performance Excellence Program. 2015. 2015–2016 Baldrige Excellence Framework: A Systems Approach to Improving Your Organization's Performance. Gaithersburg, MD: U.S. Department of Commerce, National Institute of Standards and Technology," http://www.nist.gov/baldrige/publications/upload/2015_2016_Baldrige_Framework_BNP_Free_Sample.pdf, accessed July 2016.

62. "Malcolm Baldrige National Quality Award 2015 Award Recipient, Small Business MidwayUSA," http://www.nist.gov/baldrige/award_recipients/midwayusa.cfm, accessed July 2016.

63. "Malcolm Baldrige National Quality Award 2015 Award Recipient, Small Business MidwayUSA," http://www.nist.gov/baldrige/award_recipients/midwayusa.cfm, accessed July 2016.

64. W. E. Deming, *Out of the Crisis* (Cambridge, MA: MIT Press, 1986), p. 5.

65. R. N. Lussier, *Management: Concepts, Applications, Skill Development* (Cincinnati, OH: South-Western College Publishing, 1997), p. 260.

66. J. Muller, "Toyota Workers in Kentucky Elevate Their Senses to Properly Build a Lexus," *Forbes*, April 19, 2016, http://www.forbes.com/sites/joannmuller/2016/04/19/toyota-workers-in-kentucky-elevate-their-senses-to-properly-build-a-lexus/#38ec09167554, accessed July 2016.

67. See M. Jaeger and D. Adair, "Perception of TQM Benefits, Practices and Obstacles," *The TQM Journal*, 2016, pp. 317–336.

68. D. Kiley, "Shocker: Kia Tops Porsche and Lexus for Highest Rating on Initial Quality from J.D. Power," *Forbes*, June 22, 2016, http://www.forbes.com/sites/davidkiley5/2016/06/22/man-bites-dog-kia-tops-porsche-and-lexus-for-quality/#c1f75ed5ced3, accessed July 2016; Kia, "Quality by Kia," http://www.kia.com/eu/quality/quality-by-kia/, accessed July 2016.

69. See J. Garcia-Bernal and M. Ramirez-Aleson, "Why and How TQM Leads to Performance Improvements," *The Quality Management Journal*, 2015, pp. 23–37.

70. S. Banker, "Drones and Robots in the Warehouse," *Forbes*, June 24, 2016, http://www.forbes.com/sites/stevebanker/2016/06/24/drones-and-robots-in-the-warehouse/#4a1e692d6ed7, accessed July 2016.

71. A. Choudhury, "Kaizen with Six Sigma Ensures Continuous Improvement," https://www.isixsigma.com/methodology/kaizen/kaizen-six-sigma-ensures-continuous-improvement/, accessed July 2016.

72. L. Flory, "How 5 Companies Used Kaizen Effectively," October 7, 2014, http://blog.effexms.com/how-5-companies-used-kaizen-effectively, accessed July 2016.

73. N. Wagner, "The Advantages of the Kaizen Philosophy," *Houston Chronicle*, http://smallbusiness.chron.com/advantages-kaizen-philosophy-61502.html, accessed July 2016.

74. R. Preston, "Trendy Restaurant Wagamama Puts Cloud on the Menu," *Forbes*, June 2, 2016, http://www.forbes.com/sites/oracle/2016/06/02/trendy-restaurant-wagamama-puts-cloud-on-the-menu/#3eb3805254b0, accessed July 2016.

75. A. Choudhury, "Kaizen with Six Sigma Ensures Continuous Improvement," https://www.isixsigma.com/methodology/kaizen/kaizen-six-sigma-ensures-continuous-improvement/, accessed July 2016.

76. M. Solomon, "Secrets of Consistent Customer Service: How to Be Great Again and Again," *Forbes*, March 31, 2014, http://www.forbes.com/sites/micahsolomon/2014/03/31/customer-service-experience-standards-lessons-from-four-seasons-hotels-and-elsewhere/#7b2564e93f9a, accessed July 2016.

77. See J. Garcia-Bernal and M. Ramirez-Aleson, "Why and How TQM Leads to Performance Improvements," *The Quality Management Journal*, 2015, pp. 23–37.

78. S. Lohr, "Academia Dissects the Service Sector, but Is It a Science?" *The New York Times*, April 18, 2008, www.nytimes.com/2006/04/18/business/18services.html (accessed September 3, 2014).

79. F. X. Frei, "The Four Things a Service Business Must Get Right," *Harvard Business Review*, April 2008, pp. 70–80.

80. S. Bakhtiari, "Productivity, Outsourcing and Exit: The Case of Australian Manufacturing," *Small Business Economics*, 2015, pp. 425–447.

81. Trefles Team, "What Are The Challenges Facing Ralph Lauren?," *Forbes*, June 14, 2016, http://www.forbes.com/sites/greatspeculations/2016/06/14/what-are-the-challenges-facing-ralph-lauren/#5c567c2c3214, accessed July 2016.

82. L. Chao, "Bar-Code Scanners Pick Up Speed," *The Wall Street Journal*, January 8, 2016, p. B6.

83. See B. Burnseed and E. Thornton, "Six Sigma Makes a Comeback," *Bloomberg Businessweek*, September 10, 2009, www.businessweek.com/magazine/content/09_38/b4147064137002.htm (accessed September 3, 2014).

84. An application is provided by B. W. Jacobs, M. Swink, and K. Linderman, "Performance Effects of Early and Late Six Sigma Adoptions," *Journal of Operations Management*, 2015, pp. 244–257.

85. See M. Poppendieck, "Why the Lean in Lean Six Sigma?" *The Project Management Best Practices Report*, June 2004, www.poppendieck.com/pdfs/Lean_Six_Sigma.pdf (accessed September 3, 2014).

86. Trefis Team, "Why Has 3M's Stock Risen over 20% since the Beginning of the Year?" *Forbes*, July 18, 2016, http://www.forbes.com/sites/greatspeculations/2016/07/18/why-has-3ms-stock-risen-over-20-since-the-beginning-of-the-year/#6c0aea29436a, accessed July 2016.

87. A. Rongala, "Top 10 Reasons Why Organizations Do Not Use Lean Six Sigma," *Invensis*, November 19, 2015, http://www.invensislearning.com/blog/top-10-reasons-why-organizations-do-not-use-lean-six-sigma/, accessed July 2016.

88. The British Assessment Bureau, "ISO 9000 & ISO 9001 DIFFERENCES," May 8, 2011, http://www.british-assessment.co.uk/guides/whats-the-difference-between-iso-9000-9001/, accessed July 2016.

89. B. Kumar, "What's the Differences between ISO 9000 & ISO 9001?" May 25, 2015, https://www.quora.com/What%E2%80%99s-the-difference-between-ISO-9000-9001, accessed July 2016.

90. "ISO 9000," *Wikipedia*, en.wikipedia.org/wiki/ISO_9000, accessed October 28, 2016.

91. L. L. Bernardino, F. Teixeira, A. R. de Jesus, A. Barbosa, M. Lordelo, and H. A. Lepikson, "After 20 Years, What Has Remained of TQM?" *International Journal of Productivity and Performance*, 2016, pp. 378–400.

92. See D. Jurburg, E. Viles, C. Jaca, and M. Tanco, "Why Are Companies Still Struggling to Reach Higher Continuous Improvement Maturity Levels? Empirical Evidence from High Performance Companies," *The TQM Journal*, 2015, pp. 316–327; and R. V. D. Gonzalez and M. F. Martins, "Capability for Continuous Improvement: Analysis of Companies from Automotive and Capital Goods Industries," *The TQM Journal*, 2016, pp. 250–274.

93. J. Thomson, "Why CFOs Should Embrace Sustainability For Strategic Growth," *Forbes*, December 3, 2015, http://www.forbes.com/sites/jeffthomson/2015/12/03/why-cfos-should-embrace-sustainability-for-strategic-growth/#1fed30ed5047, accessed July 2016.

94. See S. Su, K. Baird, and H. Schoch, "Management Control System Effectiveness," *Pacific Accounting Review*, 2015, pp. 28–50.

95. L. Daskal, "17 Signs You're Actually a Micromanager," *Inc.*, May 27, 2016, http://www.inc.com/lolly-daskal/17-signs-you-re-actually-a-micromanager.html, accessed July 2016.

96. K. Boogaard, "4 Ways to Stop Yourself from Micromanaging," *Inc.*, March 14, 2016, http://www.inc.com/the-muse/how-to-stop-micromanaging.html, accessed July 2016.

97. A. K. Srivastava, "Modeling Organizational and Information Systems for Effective Strategy Execution," *Journal of Enterprise Information Management*, 2015, pp. 556–578.

98. K. Zheng, "What Kind of Background Checks Do Casino Dealers Have to Pass?," http://yourbusiness.azcentral.com/kind-background-checks-casino-dealers-pass-6567.html, accessed July 2016; "Background Checks—Casino Employment," http://www.jobmonkey.com/casino/background_checks/, accessed July 2016.

99. When labor costs rise, productivity slows down, unless other variables are changed. When companies are able to get more output from fewer workers, productivity rises. See C. Dougherty, "Workforce Productivity Falls," *The Wall Street Journal*, May 4, 2012, p. A5.

100. M. Hajli, J. M. Sims, and V. Ibragimov, "Information Technology (IT) Productivity Paradox in the 21st Century," *International Journal of Productivity and Performance Management*, 2015, pp. 457–478.

101. Office of Macroeconomic Analysis, U.S. Treasury, "Profile of the Economy," February 16, 2012, www.docstoc.com/docs/117787321/Profile-of-the-Economy (accessed September 3, 2014).

102. D. Gross, "Listen, the U.S. Is Better, Stronger, and Faster Than Anywhere Else in the World," *Newsweek*, May 7, 2012, pp. 22–30.

103. B. Eichengreen, D. Park, and K. Shin, "The Global Productivity Lump: Common and Country-Specific Factors," September 17, 2015, http://voxeu.org/article/global-productivity-slump, accessed July 2016; Total Economy Database: Key Findings, 2016, https://www.conference-board.org/data/economydatabase/, accessed July 2016.

104. B. Hays, "Effects of Warmer Weather on Productivity Being Felt Worldwide, Scientists Say," *UPI*, June 10, 2016, http://www.upi.com/Science_News/2016/06/10/Effects-of-warmer-weather-on-productivity-being-felt-worldwide-scientists-say/2061465584525/, accessed July 2016.

105. The Economist, "Technology Isn't Working," October 4, 2014, http://www.economist.com/news/special-report/21621237-digital-revolution-has-yet-fulfil-its-promise-higher-productivity-and-better, accessed July 2016.

106. T. Worstall, "As Delong Says, Brookings Is Wrong on the Productivity Slowdown," *Forbes*, March 5, 2016, http://www.forbes.com/sites/timworstall/2016/03/05/as-delong-says-brookings-is-wrong-on-the-productivity-slowdown/#69d4e7716c82, accessed July 2016.

107. R. Fujioka, "3 Ways Cloud Technology Is Boosting Productivity," *Inc.*, July 12, 2016, http://www.inc.com/russ-fujioka/3-ways-cloud-technology-is-boosting-productivity.html, accessed July 2016.

108. S. Sharf, "What's Your Passion? How Following Your Gut Can Lead to Huge Success," http://www.forbes.com/sites/samanthasharf/2016/05/12/whats-your-passion-how-following-your-gut-can-lead-to-huge-success/#af88b5d4935d, accessed July 2016.

109. B. Scott, "Diane Von Furstenberg on Self-Discovery, Acceptance, and the American Dream," http://www.inc.com/bartie-scott/diane-von-furstenberg-and-seth-meyers-on-becoming-the-woman-you-want-to-be.html, accessed July 2016.

110. V. Lipman, "The Hardest Thing for New Managers," http://www.forbes.com/sites/victorlipman/2016/06/01/the-hardest-thing-for-new-managers/#2d3a7bca218f, accessed July 2016.

111. S. Vozza, "12 Lessons from Business Leaders' Moms," http://www.fastcompany.com/3045952/hit-the-ground-running/12-lessons-from-business-leaders-moms, accessed July 2016.

112. J. Hall, "10 Simple Ways to Improve Your People Skills and Build Relationships," http://www.forbes.com/sites/johnhall/2016/03/20/10-simple-ways-to-improve-your-people-skills-and-build-relationships/#20bc20e62174, accessed July 2016.

113. C. Liu, "4 Easy Ways to Become a Better Leader at Work," http://www.inc.com/the-muse/develop-leadership-skills-4-easy-steps.html, accessed July 2016.

114. J. Benjamin, "For Bryce Drew, People Matter More Than Results," http://www.forbes.com/sites/joshbenjamin/2016/03/29/for-bryce-drew-people-matter-more-than-results/#205789764887, accessed July 2016.

115. J. Benjamin, "For Bryce Drew, People Matter More Than Results," http://www.forbes.com/sites/joshbenjamin/2016/03/29/for-bryce-drew-people-matter-more-than-results/#1eddcba07648, accessed July 2016.

116. E. Heil, "Barack Obama, the First Alt-Comeday President," https://www.washingtonpost.com/news/reliable-source/wp/2016/04/25/barack-obama-the-first-alt-comedy-president/, accessed July 2016.

117. E. Heil, "President Obama's 10 Most Hilarious Lines from the White House Correspondents' Dinners," https://www.washingtonpost.com/news/reliable-source/wp/2016/04/25/president-obamas-10-most-hilarious-lines-from-the-white-house-correspondents-dinners/?tid=a_inl, accessed July 2016.

118. See M. P. Seligman, *Flourish* (New York: Free Press, 2011).

119. "Our Company," https://chipotle.com/company, accessed July 18, 2016.

120. "Norovirus," Centers for Disease Control and Prevention, http://www.cdc.gov/norovirus, last updated April 26, 2016.

121. "FDA Invesigates Multistate Outbreak of E. coli 026 Infections Linked to Chipotle Mexican Grill Restaurants," February 1, 2016, http://www.fda.gov/Food/RecallsOutbreaksEmergencies/Outbreaks/ucm470410.htm.

122. S. Berfield, "The Sustainable Locally Sourced Free-Range Humanely Raised Made-To-Order Toxic Burrito," *Bloomberg Businessweek*, December 28, 2015—January 10, 2016, pp. 44–49.

123. H. Peterson, "There's a New Theory About the Source of the Chipotle E.coli Outbreak," *Business Insider*, February 5, 2016, http://www.businessinsider.com/chipotle-source-of-e-coli-outbreaks-2016-2.

124. S. Berfield, "The Sustainable Locally Sourced Free-Range Humanely Raised Made-to-Order Toxic Burrito," *Bloomberg Businessweek*, December 28, 2015—January 10, 2016, pp. 44–49.

125. P. R. La Monica, "Can Chipotle Recover From E.coli Outbreak?" December 8, 2015, http://money.cnn.com/2015/12/07/investing/chipotle-stock-e-coli/index.html.

126. P. R. La Monica, "Chipotle E. coli Outbreak 'Appears to Be Over,' Says CDC," *CNN Money*, February 1, 2016, http://money.cnn.com/2016/02/01/investing/chipotle-cdc-e-coli/index.html.

127. H. I. Miller, "Chipotle: The Long Defeat of Doing Well," *Forbes*, December 14, 2015, http://www.forbes.com/sites/henrymiller/2015/12/14/chipotle-the-long-defeat-of-doing-nothing-well/#5e8c12b36cc9.

128. S. Berfield, "The Sustainable Locally Sourced Free-Range Humanely Raised Made-To-Order Toxic Burrito," *Bloomberg Businessweek*, December 28, 2015—January 10, 2016, pp. 44–49.

129. "FDA Invesigates Multistate Outbreak of E. coli 026 Infections Linked to Chipotle Mexican Grill Restaurants," February 1, 2016, http://www.fda.gov/Food/RecallsOutbreaksEmergencies/Outbreaks/ucm470410.htm.

130. S. Berfield, "The Sustainable Locally Sourced Free-Range Humanely Raised Made-to-Order Toxic Burrito," *Bloomberg Businessweek*, December 28, 2015—January 10, 2016, pp. 44–49.

131. "Chipotle Tweaks Recipes, Ingredient Preparation after E. Coli Scare," Fox News, December 20, 2015, http://www.foxnews.com/leisure/2015/12/30/chipotle-tweaks-recipes-ingredient-preparation-after-e-coli-scare/.

132. J. Jargon, "Chipotle Counters Frightful Results," *The Wall Street Journal*, April 23, 2016, http://www.wsj.com/articles/chipotle-counters-frightful-results-1461403834.

133. A. Madhani, "Chipotle to Tighten Produce Supplier Rules after E. coli Outbreak," *USA Today*, December 2, 2015, http://www.usatoday.com/story/money/2015/12/02/chipotle-tightens-produce-supplier-guidelines-after-ecoli-outbreak/76681228/.

134. J. L. Levere, "In Emergencies, Companies Are Turning to Employee-Tracking Services," *The New York Times*, January 26, 2015, http://nyti.ms/1ynBeqY.

135. "Companies Tracking Employees' Every Move," January 4, 2016, http://abcnews.go.com/WNT/story?id=131333&page=1, accessed March 28, 2016.

136. P. Haggin, "As Wearables in the Workplace Spread, So Do Legal Concerns," *The Wall Street Journal*, March 14, 2016, p. R7.

137. "Companies Tracking Employees' Every Move," January 4, 2016, http://abcnews.go.com/WNT/story?id=131333&page=1, accessed March 28, 2016.

138. A. Gardella, "Employer Sued for GPS-Tracking Salesperson 24/7," June 5, 2015, http://www.forbes.com/sites/adrianagardella/2015/06/05/employer-sued-for-gps-tracking-salesperson-247/#784f833336d4.

Brainwriting, 231

Brand recognition, 526

Brazil, 127–128

Break-even analysis *A way of identifying how much revenue is needed to cover the total costs of developing and selling a product,* A4–A6

Brexit (Britain exit of EU), 125

Bribes, 136

BRICS countries, 127, *127*

Budgets *A formal financial projection,* **562**–563

Buffers *Administrative changes that managers can make to reduce the stressors that lead to employee burnout,* **388**

Bullying *Repeated mistreatment of one or more persons by one or more perpetrators. It's abusive, physical, psychological, verbal, or nonverbal behavior that is threatening, humiliating, or intimidating,* **312**–313, *313*

Bureaucracy, 48

Bureaucratic control *The use of rules, regulations, and formal authority to guide performance,* **555**, *555*

Burnout *State of emotional, mental, and even physical exhaustion,* **387**

Business analytics, 215–216

Business model *Outline of need the firm will fill, the operations of the business, its components and functions, as well as the expected revenues and expenses,* **144**

Business plan *A document that outlines a proposed firm's goals, the strategy for achieving them, and the standards for measuring success,* **144**

Business skills, *475*

Buzzwords, 506

CAFTA-DR. *See* Central America Free Trade Agreement (CAFTA-DR)

Canada, 124

Career counseling, 388

Cascading goals *Objectives are structured in a unified hierarchy, becoming more specific at lower levels of the organization,* **162**

Causal attribution *The activity of inferring causes for observed behavior,* **371**–372

Cell phones, 515, 530–531. *See also* Smartphones

Central America Free Trade Agreement (CAFTA-DR) *Trade agreement involving the United States and Costa Rica, the Dominican Republic, El Salvador, Guatemala, Honduras, and Nicaragua and which is intended to reduce tariffs and other barriers to free trade,* **125**

Centralized authority *Organizational structure in which important decisions are made by upper managers—power is concentrated at the top,* **263**

Chain of command, 260–261

Change. *See* Organizational change

Change agent *A person inside or outside the organization who can be a catalyst in helping deal with old problems in new ways,* **339**, 350

Changing stage of organizational change, 335

Charisma *Form of interpersonal attraction that inspires acceptance and support,* **490**

Charismatic leadership *Once assumed to be an individual inspirational and motivational characteristic of particular leaders, now considered part of transformational leadership,* **490**

Cheating, 17, 71, 235–237

China, 127–128

Civil Rights Act (1991), *309*

Civil Rights Act, Title VII (1964), *309,* 312

Clan culture *Type of organizational culture that has an internal focus and values flexibility rather than stability and control,* 246, **247**

Classical model of decision making. *See* Rational model of decision making

Classical viewpoint *In the historical perspective, the viewpoint that emphasizes finding ways to manage work more efficiently; it has two branches—scientific and administrative,* **45**–48, *46*

Clawbacks *Rescinding the tax breaks when firms don't deliver promised jobs,* 79

Climate change *Refers to major changes in temperature, precipitation, wind patterns, and similar matters occurring over several decades,* 94–95, 159–160, 168, *184,* 184–185

Closed shop, *315*

Closed system *A system that has little interaction with its environment,* **57**

Cloud computing *The storing of software and data on gigantic collections of computers located away from a company's principal site,* **14**

Coalition tactics, 469

Code of ethics *A formal, written set of ethical standards that guide an organization's actions,* **90**

Coercive power *One of five sources of a leader's power that results from the authority to punish subordinates,* **467**

Cognitive abilities, *475*

Cognitive component of an attitude *The beliefs and knowledge one has about a situation,* **365**

Cognitive dissonance *Psychological discomfort a person experiences between his or her cognitive attitude and incomparable behavior,* 365, **365**–**366**, 406

COLA. *See* Cost-of-living adjustment (COLA) clause

Collaborating, conflict and, 458

Collaborative computing *Using state-of-the-art computer software and hardware, to help people work better together,* **15**

Collective bargaining *Negotiations between management and employees regarding disputes over compensation, benefits, working conditions, and job security,* **308**

College graduates, underemployed, 382

Commitment bias, 226

Common purpose *A goal that unifies employees or members and gives everyone an understanding of the organization's reason for being,* **260**

Commonweal organizations, 22

Communication barriers

cross-cultural, 515–516

explanation of, **513**

gender, 517–519, *518*

nonverbal, 516–517, *517*

personal, 514–515

physical, 513–514

Communication *The transfer of information and understanding from one person to another,* **504**. *See also* Social media

barriers to, 513–519

conflict due to failures in, 454

cultural differences in, 134, 515–516

effectiveness of, 533–539

formal channels of, 509–511, *510*

gender differences in, 517–519, *518*

hiring process and, 503

informal channels of, 511–512

medium for, 507–508

in meetings, 512

nonverbal, 516–517, *517*

process of, 504–506, *505*

social media and, 520–532

verbal vs. written, 26

Communities, as stakeholders, 79–80

Compensation *Payment comprising three parts: wages or salaries, incentives, and benefits,* **293**

of chief executives, 7

issues related to, 308, *309,* 315–316

types of, 293–294

Competence needs, 402

Competing values framework (CVF), 246–247, *247*

Competition

conflict and, 456, *456*

international, *106*

organizational change and, 327

Competitive advantage *The ability of an organization to produce goods or services more effectively than competitors do, thereby outperforming them,* **11**

cultural differences and, 132–133

strategic management and, 147–148

struggle for, 11–12

Competitive intelligence *Gaining information about one's competitors' activities so that one can anticipate their moves and react appropriately,* 179, **179**–180

Competitive pressure, 66–68

Competitors *People or organizations that compete for customers or resources,* **78,** 186

Complexity, controls to deal with, *547*

Complexity theory *The study of how order and pattern arise from very complicated, apparently chaotic systems,* **57**

Compromising, conflict and, 458

Computer-aided decision making, 231–232

Conceptual decision-making style, 221

Conceptual skills *Skills that consist of the ability to think analytically, to visualize an organization as a whole and understand how the parts work together,* **23**–24

Concurrent control *Entails collecting performance information in real time,* **552**

Confirmation bias *Biased way of thinking in which people seek information to support their point of view and discount data that does not,* **225**

Conflict *Process in which one party perceives that its interests are being opposed or negatively affected by another party,* **451**

constructive, 456–457

functional vs. dysfunctional, 451–452

intergroup, 454

management of, 339, 452

methods to handle, 457–459

multicultural, 454

nature of, 451

performance and, 453, *453*

personality, 453

programmed, 456–457

resistance to change and, 351

role, 386

work–family, 454–455, *455*

Conglomerate, 264

Conscientiousness, 358

Consensus *General agreement; group solidarity,* **230**

Consideration *A leadership behavior that is concerned with group members' needs and desires and that is directed at creating mutual respect or trust,* **479**

Consolidated Omnibus Budget Reconciliation Act (COBRA) (1985), *309*

Consultation, 469

Contemporary perspective *In contrast to the historical perspective, the business approach that includes the systems,*

GLOSSARY/SUBJECT INDEX

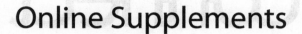

Online Supplements

Connect Online Access for Management, Eighth Edition

McGraw-Hill Connect is a digital teaching and learning environment that improves performance over a variety of critical outcomes. With Connect, instructors can deliver assignments, quizzes and tests easily online. Students can practice important skills at their own pace and on their own schedule.

HOW TO REGISTER

Using a <u>Print Book</u>?
To register and activate your Connect account, simply follow these easy steps:
1. **Go to the Connect course web address provided by your instructor or visit the Connect link set up on your instructor's course within your campus learning management system.**
2. **Click on the link to register.**
3. **When prompted, enter the Connect code found on the inside back cover of your book and click Submit. Complete the brief registration form that follows to begin using Connect.**

Using an <u>eBook</u>?
To register and activate your Connect account, simply follow these easy steps:
1. **Upon purchase of your eBook, you will be granted automatic access to Connect.**
2. **Go to the Connect course web address provided by your instructor or visit the Connect link set up on your instructor's course within your campus learning management system.**
3. **Sign in using the same email address and password you used to register on the eBookstore. Complete your registration and begin using Connect.**

*Note: Access Code is for one use only. If you did not purchase this book new, the access code included in this book is no longer valid.

Need help? Visit mhhe.com/support